IBM 11940

DATE DUE

INDEX TO COLLECTIVE BIOGRAPHIES FOR YOUNG READERS

Fourth Edition

INDEX TO
Collective Biographies
FOR
Young Readers

◆◆◆

Fourth Edition

Karen Breen
Consultant, Children's Services, Queens Borough Public Library
Queens, New York

R.R. BOWKER COMPANY
New York & London, 1988

To my husband who did everything
else so I could do this

Published by R. R. Bowker Company,
a division of Reed Publishing (U.S.A.) Inc.
Copyright © 1988 by Reed Publishing (U.S.A.) Inc.
All rights reserved
Printed and bound in the United States of America

Library of Congress Cataloging-in-Publication Data

Breen, Karen, 1943–
    Index to collective biographies for young readers / Karen Breen.
        p. cm.
    Rev. ed. of: Index to collective biographies for young readers /
Judith Silverman. 3rd ed., 1979
        ISBN 0-8352-2348-5
        1. Biography—Juvenile literature—Indexes. 2. Biography—
Juvenile literature—Bibliography. 3. Publishers and publishing—
United States—Directories. I. Silverman, Judith, 1933– Index to collective
biographies for young readers. II. Title. III. Title: Collective
biographies for young readers.
Z5301.B77 1988
[CT104]
016.92—dc19
                                                        88-19410
                                                        CIP

Contents

Preface

The first edition of this book originated in 1970 as a personal file by Judith Silverman, then a children's librarian in a public library and later a librarian in a junior high school. It grew out of the constant need that faces all librarians working with students to provide short biographical material about historic and contemporary figures of note. That first edition indexed 471 volumes and was titled *Index to Young Readers' Collective Biographies*. In 1975, the Indexed Books by Title section was added to the second edition and 249 more volumes were indexed. In 1979, 222 new books were indexed and the title was changed. The present fourth edition of *Index to Collective Biographies for Young Readers* is being published in response to the continuing demand for another update.

There are approximately 9,773 people listed in this new edition, representing the contents of 1,129 collective biographies. New to the fourth edition are 2,528 people from 187 indexed volumes including such diverse titles as *Modern Soccer Superstars* and *Women Who Work with Animals*. Although most of the books are considered most suitable for elementary and junior high school reading levels, many of them appear on the shelves of high schools as well. If the collective biography could be read and understood by a sixth grade student, it was included here even though it might have been intended for a high school or adult audience.

Most of the titles indexed in the first three editions have been retained, since many titles on library shelves remain useful long after publication. Out-of-print books have been noted by an "o.p." after the title listing in two sections: Key to Symbols and Indexed Books by Title. It is a sad commentary on the state of children's and young adult publishing to note how many of these very useful works are, in fact, out of print.

The *Index* aims to be inclusive rather than selective; the inclusion of a title does not imply that it is a recommended work. Covering a large selection of titles, the fourth edition supplies librarians with a guide to many of the titles they already own or would like to purchase. The Indexed Books by Title section is useful as a purchasing aid, since it lists all of the biographees included in each title.

Titles included in this volume were selected from the following sources: the shelf list holdings of the Queens Borough Public Library, the Brooklyn Public Library, the New York Public Library, and the Nassau Library System, Long Island, New York; ordering guides of the Board of Education of New York City; *The Elementary School Library Collection* (Bro-Dart); and *Books in Print* (R. R. Bowker). Finally, publishers were queried as to the titles in their backlists that were appropriate.

The book has two main sections. The first, Alphabetical Listing of Biographees, contains pertinent data about birth, death, nationality, and field of activity, followed by symbols indicating in which titles the person's biography appears.

The second section, Subject Listing of Biographees, lists these persons under fields of activity and nationalities. Twenty-five new subject areas have been added in this edition including Libyans, Martial Arts Figures, and Eccentrics, among others. The following sources were used to ascribe nationalities and to place individuals under appropriate subject headings: *Biography and Genealogy Master Index, Webster's Biographical Dictionary, The Columbia Encyclopedia, Who's Who in America, Who Was Who in America, International Who's Who, Current Biography, World Book Encyclopedia,* and *Encyclopedia Americana.* For people who were more difficult to locate, various biographical sources in specific subjects (science, law, blacks, women) were consulted.

About 90 percent of all subject headings have been determined by consulting Sears or Library of Congress List of Subject Headings. Current usage accounts for the remainder. For example, DISABLED has been substituted for HANDICAPPED and NATIVE AMERICANS for INDIANS, AMERICAN.

I would like to acknowledge the support of the Interlibrary Loan Division of the Queens Borough Public Library and its Head, Phyllis Poses, who tirelessly tracked down the books I could not find in local libraries. A special word of thanks to Ramona Koch, whose research assistance was invaluable in establishing the accuracy of the information contained in these pages. Thank you to Nancy Bucenec who calmly fixed my mistakes and encouraged my progress. And most of all, thank you to Judith Silverman, without whose original work this one would have been simply impossible.

How to Use This Book

ALPHABETICAL LISTING OF BIOGRAPHEES

In this section each person found in a collective biography is listed alphabetically by last name with birth and death dates, nationality, and field or activity for which he or she is best known. The symbols following this information denote the titles of the books in which the biographical material appears. A Key to Symbols follows this How to Use section. Each symbol consists of either letters or letter-and-number combinations. Example:

> Campbell, Donald Malcolm (1921–1967). English
> automobile and speedboat racer. ALBA; ST-1

If no nationality is noted, the person is usually American. In a few instances, however, nationality could not be determined. Since World War II there has been much emigration and immigration and in these cases an attempt has been made to show both the country of nationality and of birth. Example:

> Chain, Ernst Boris (1906–1979). English bio-
> chemist, born Germany. BEK†; COLA†; GRB-1;
> LAE; LET; POB; RIF

In the following entry the absence of nationality denotes an American:

> Horney, Karen (1885–1952). Psychiatrist, born
> Germany. FLA; LEG; RAAG†

Generally, the given name noted in the usual biographical sources is used. However, for sports figures, entertainers, and some others, the common nickname is used to aid in identification and the given name follows in parentheses. Example:

> Reiser, Pete (Harold Patrick) (1920–). Baseball
> player. GEB; RIGA†; ROC; VAE

SUBJECT LISTING OF BIOGRAPHEES

This is an alphabetical list of fields of activity and nationalities. Individuals noted in the first section can be located here under subject headings that describe them, with the exception of those with only minor (daggered) listings.

Subject headings are as specific as possible. Thus, Enrico Fermi appears under PHYSICISTS rather than under the term SCIENTISTS; Alexandre Eiffel is under ENGINEERS, CIVIL rather than ENGINEERS; and Robert C. Weaver is under CABINET MEMBERS, U.S. rather than GOVERNMENT WORKERS. Many cross-references are included leading from general categories to specific ones. An Index of Subject Headings precedes the Subject Listing of Biographees.

The order of information in the entries in this section is the same as in the Alphabetical Listing of Biographees regarding names, dates, nationality, and book title symbols.

DAGGERS (†)

A dagger next to a book symbol denotes that there is either less than a full page of biographical information about that person in that particular title, or that the person is merely noted in passing. The dagger symbol is used only if the biographee is listed in either the book's table of contents or index, enabling the reader to locate the information easily.

Key to Indexed Books

BEA Beard, Annie E. S. *Our Foreign-Born Citizens*. T Y Crowell, 6th rev. ed., 1968

BEB Beard, Charles A. & Beard, William. *The Presidents in American History*. Messner, rev. ed., 1985

BEBA Bearden, Romare & Henderson, Harry. *Six Black Masters of American Art*. Doubleday, 1972 (o.p.)

BEC Beckwith, Yvonne, ed. *People and Great Deeds*. Standard Ed., 1966 (o.p.)

BED Bell, Joseph N. *World Series Thrills: Ten Top Thrills from 1912 to 1960*. Messner, 1962 (o.p.)

BEE Benét, Laura. *Famous American Humorists*. Dodd, 1959 (o.p.)

BEF ———. *Famous American Poets*. Dodd, 1950 (o.p.)

BEG ———. *Famous English and American Essayists*. Dodd, 1966 (o.p.)

BEGA ———. *Famous New England Authors*. Dodd, 1970 (o.p.)

BEH ———. *Famous Poets for Young People*. Dodd, 1964 (o.p.)

BEI ———. *Famous Storytellers for Young People*. Dodd, 1968 (o.p.)

BEJ Bennett, Lerone, Jr. *Pioneers in Protest*. Johnson Chi, 1968 (o.p.)

BEK Berger, Melvin. *Famous Men of Modern Biology*. T Y Crowell, 1968

BEKA ———. *Masters of Modern Music*. Lothrop, 1970 (o.p.)

BEKB Berger, Phil. *Great Running Backs in Pro Football*. Messner, 1970 (o.p.)

BEL ———. *Heroes of Pro Basketball*. Random, 1968 (o.p.)

BELA Berke, Art. *Unsung Heroes of the Major Leagues*. Random, 1976 (o.p.)

BELB Berkow, Ira. *Beyond the Dream: Occasional Heroes of Sports*. Atheneum, 1975 (o.p.)

BEM Berkowitz, Freda P. *On Lutes, Recorders and Harpsichords: Men and Music of the Baroque*. Atheneum, 1967 (o.p.)

BEN ———. *Unfinished Symphony*. Atheneum, 1963 (o.p.)

BENA Bernard, Jacqueline. *Voices from the Southwest*. Scholastic, 1972 (o.p.)

BEO Berry, Erick & Best, Herbert. *Men Who Changed the Map, vol. 1, A.D. 400–1914*. Funk & W, 1967 (o.p.)

BEOA Berry, James R. *Kids on the Run*. Four Winds, 1978 (o.p.)

BEP Bethell, Jean. *The How and Why Wonder Book of Famous Scientists*. G&D, 1964 (o.p.)

BI Biddle, Marcia McKenna. *Contributions of Women: Labor*. Dillon, 1979

BIA Bixby, William. *Great Experimenters*. McKay, 1964 (o.p.)

BLA Blassingame, Wyatt. *The Look-It-Up Book of Presidents*. Random, rev. ed., 1984

BLB ———. *Naturalists-Explorers*. Watts, 1964 (o.p.)

BLC Blassingame, Wyatt & Glendinning, Richard. *The Frontier Doctors*. Watts, 1963 (o.p.)

BLD ———. *Men Who Opened the West*. Putnam, 1966 (o.p.)

BLE Bliven, Bruce. *A Mirror for Greatness: Six Americans*. McGraw, 1975 (o.p.)

BLF Bloom, Naomi. *Contributions of Women: Religion*. Dillon, 1978 (o.p.)

BLG Blumberg, Rhoda. *First Ladies: A First Book*. Watts, updated ed., 1981 (o.p.)

BLW Boardman, Fon W., Jr. *Tyrants and Conquerors*. Walck, 1977 (o.p.)

BOA Bolton, Sarah K. *Famous American Authors*. T Y Crowell, 1954 (o.p.)

BOB ———. *Famous Men of Science*. T Y Crowell, 1960 (o.p.)

BOC ———. *Lives of Girls Who Became Famous*. T Y Crowell, 1949 (o.p.)

BOD ———. *Lives of Poor Boys Who Became Famous*. T Y Crowell, rev. ed., 1962 (o.p.)

BOE Bonner, M. G. *Baseball Rookies Who Made Good*. Knopf, 1954 (o.p.)

BOF Bontemps, Arna. *Famous Negro Athletes*. Dodd, 1964 (o.p.)

BOG ———. *We Have Tomorrow*. HM, 1945 (o.p.)

BOH Borer, Mary C. *Women Who Made History*. Warne, 1963 (o.p.)

BOHA Borstein, Larry. *After Olympic Glory: The Lives of Ten Outstanding Medalists*. Warne, 1978 (o.p.)

BOHA-1 Bowe, Frank. *Comeback: Six Remarkable People Who Triumphed over Disability*. Har-Row, 1981

BOHB Bowman, Kathleen. *New Women in Art and Dance*. Creative Ed, 1976

BOHC ———. *New Women in Entertainment*. Creative Ed, 1976

BOHD ———. *New Women in Media*. Creative Ed, 1976

BOHE ———. *New Women in Medicine*. Creative Ed, 1976 (o.p.)

BOHF ———. *New Women in Politics*. Creative Ed, 1976

BOHG ———. *New Women in Social Sciences*. Creative Ed, 1976

BOI Boyd, Mildred. *Rulers in Petticoats*. Criterion Bks., 1966 (o.p.)

BOJ   Boynick, David K. *Women Who Led the Way: Eight Pioneers for Equal Rights* (Original title: *Pioneers in Petticoats*). T Y Crowell, 1959

BOK   Boys Life Editors. *Ahead of Their Time.* Putnam, 1968 (o.p.)

BR   Braider, Donald. *Five Early American Painters.* Hawthorn, 1969 (o.p.)

BRA   Braun, Saul. *Seven Heroes: Medal of Honor Stories of the War in the Pacific.* Putnam, 1965 (o.p.)

BRAA   Braun, Thomas. *The Hitters* (Stars of the NL & AL). Creative Ed, 1976 (o.p.)

BRB   Brawley, Benjamin. *Negro Builders and Heroes.* Univ. of North Carolina Pr., 1937

BRBA   Brennan, Dennis. *Adventures in Courage: The Skymasters.* Reilly & Lee, 1968 (o.p.)

BRBB   Brenner, Rica. *Poets of Our Time.* HarBraceJ, 1941 (o.p.)

BRBB-1 Breslin, Herbert H., ed. *The Tenors.* Macmillan, 1974 (o.p.)

BRBC   Briggs, Peter. *Men in the Sea.* S&S, 1968 (o.p.)

BRBD   Brimberg, Stanlee. *Black Stars.* Dodd, 1974 (o.p.)

BRBE   Brin, Ruth F. *Contributions of Women: Social Reform.* Dillon, 1977 (o.p.)

BRBF   Brooks, Janice. *Kings and Queens: The Plantagenets of England.* Nelson, 1975 (o.p.)

BRC   Brosnan, Jim. *Great Baseball Pitchers.* Random, 1965 (o.p.)

BRD   ———. *Great Rookies of the Major Leagues.* Random, 1966 (o.p.)

BRE   ———. *Little League to Big League.* Random, 1968 (o.p.)

BRF   Brower, Harriette. *Story-Lives of Master Musicians.* Ayer repr. of 1922 facsimile ed.

BRF-1   Brower, Millicent. *Young Performers: On the Stage, in Film, and on TV.* Messner, 1985

BRG   Brown, Vashti & Brown, Jack. *Proudly We Hail.* HM, 1968 (o.p.)

BRGA   Bruner, Richard. *Black Politicians.* McKay, 1971 (o.p.)

BU   Buckmaster, Henrietta. *The Fighting Congressmen.* Scholastic, 1971 (o.p.)

BUA   ———. *Women Who Shaped History.* Macmillan, 1966 (o.p.)

BUB   Buehr, Walter. *Westward—With American Explorers.* Putnam, 1963 (o.p.)

BUC   Burch, Gladys. *Modern Composers for Young People.* Dodd, 1941 (o.p.)

BUD   Burch, Gladys & Wolcott, John. *Famous Composers for Young People.* Dodd, 1939 (o.p.)

BUD-1   Burchard, S. H. *Book of Baseball Greats.* HarBraceJ, 1983 (o.p.)

BUDA   Burgess, Mary W. *Contributions of Women: Education.* Dillon, 1975 (o.p.)

BUE   Burlingame, Roger. *Inventors behind the Inventor.* HarBraceJ, 1947 (o.p.)

BUF   ———. *Scientists behind the Inventors.* HarBraceJ, 1960 (o.p.)

BUFA   Burt, Olive W. *Black Women of Valor.* Messner, 1974 (o.p.)

BUG   ———. *Mountain Men of the Early West.* Hawthorn, 1967 (o.p.)

BUH   ———. *Negroes in the Early West.* Messner, 1969 (o.p.)

BUI   ———. *Young Wayfarers of the Early West.* Hawthorn, 1968 (o.p.)

BUIA   Buske, Morris, ed. *Presidents of the United States.* Childrens, 1975 (o.p.)

BUIB   ———, ed. *Significant American Colonial Leaders.* Childrens, 1975 (o.p.)

BUIB-01 Busnar, Gene. *Superstars of Country Music.* Messner, 1984

BUIB-1 ———. *Superstars of Rock: Their Lives and Music.* Messner, 1980

BUIB-2 ———. *Superstars of Rock Two.* Messner, 1984

BUIC   Butcher, Grace. *Women in Sports: Motorcycling.* Harvey, 1976 (o.p.)

BUJ   Butler, Hal. *Baseball All-Star Game Thrills.* Messner, 1968 (o.p.)

BUJA   ———. *Sports Heroes Who Wouldn't Quit.* Messner, 1973 (o.p.)

BUJB   ———. *Baseball's Champion Pitchers: The Cy Young Award Winners.* Messner, 1974 (o.p.)

BUJC   ———. *Baseball's Most Valuable Players.* Messner, 1977 (o.p.)

BUR-1   Burr, Lonnie. *Two for the Show: Great Comedy Teams.* Messner, 1979 (o.p.)

CAA   Cane, Philip. *Giants of Science.* G&D, 1959 (o.p.)

CAAA   Canning, John, ed. *One Hundred Great Kings, Queens and Rulers of the World.* Taplinger, 1978, pap.

CAB   Cannon, Grant G. *Great Men of Modern Agriculture.* Macmillan, 1963 (o.p.)

CAC   Cantwell, Robert. *Famous American Men of Letters.* Dodd, 1956 (o.p.)

CAD   Carmer, Carl, ed. *A Cavalcade of Young Americans.* Lothrop, 1958 (o.p.)

CAE   Carr, Albert. *Men of Power: A Book of Dictators.* Viking, rev. ed., 1956 (o.p.)

CAF   Carse, Robert. *The Young Colonials.* Norton, 1963 (o.p.)

CAF-1 Carwell, Hattie. *Blacks in Science: Astrophysicist to Zoologist.* Exposition, 1977 (o.p.)

CAG Cary, Sturges P. *Arrow Book of Presidents.* Scholastic, 1969 (o.p.)

CAGA Cathon, Laura E. & Schmidt, Thusnelda. *For Patriot Dream.* Abingdon, 1970 (o.p.)

CAH Cavanah, Frances. *Meet the Presidents.* Macrae, rev. ed., 1965 (o.p.)

CAHA ———, ed. *We Wanted to Be Free: The Refugees' Own Stories.* Macrae, 1971 (o.p.)

CHA Chaffin, Lillie & Butwin, Miriam. *America's First Ladies 1789 to 1865.* Lerner, 1969

CHB ———. *America's First Ladies 1865 to Present Day.* Lerner, 1969

CHC Chandler, Anna C. *Story-Lives of Master Artists.* Lippincott, rev. ed., 1953 (o.p.)

CHD Chandler, Caroline A. *Famous Men of Medicine.* Dodd, 1950 (o.p.)

CHE ———. *Famous Modern Men of Medicine.* Dodd, 1965 (o.p.)

CHF Chapin, Victor. *Giants of the Keyboard.* Lippincott, 1967

CHFA ———. *The Violin and Its Masters.* Lippincott, 1969 (o.p.)

CHFB Chittenden, Elizabeth F. *Profiles in Black and White: Stories of Men and Women Who Fought Against Slavery.* Scribner, 1973 (o.p.)

CHG Churchill, Winston. *Heroes of History: A Selection of Churchill's Favorite Historical Characters.* Dodd, 1968 (o.p.)

CL Clark, Margaret G. *Their Eyes Are on the Stars: Four Black Writers.* Garrard, 1973

CL-01 Clark, Philip. *In Profile: Tyrants of the Twentieth Century.* Silver Burdett, 1981

CL-04 Clark, Steven. *Fight Against Time: Five Athletes—A Legacy of Courage.* Atheneum, 1979 (o.p.)

CL-06 Clary, Jack. *The Captains.* Atheneum, 1978 (o.p.)

CL-1 ———. *Main Men of the Seventies: The Quarterbacks.* National Football League, 1975 (o.p.)

CLA Clymer, Eleanor & Erlich, Lillian. *Modern American Career Women.* Dodd, 1959 (o.p.)

CLC Clyne, Patricia Edwards. *Patriots in Petticoats.* Dodd, 1976

CO Coan, Howard. *Great Pass Catchers in Pro Football.* Messner, 1971 (o.p.)

CO-1 Coates, Ruth Allison. *Great American Naturalists.* Lerner, 1974 (o.p.)

COA Coffman, Ramon P. *Famous Kings and Queens for Young People.* Dodd, 1974 (o.p.)

COB Coffman, Ramon P. & Goodman, Nathan. *Famous Authors for Young People.* Dodd, 1943 (o.p.)

COC ———. *Famous Explorers for Young People.* Dodd, 1945 (o.p.)

COD ———. *Famous Generals and Admirals for Young People.* Dodd, 1945 (o.p.)

COE ———. *Famous Pioneers for Young People.* Dodd, 1945 (o.p.)

COE-1 Cohen, Daniel & Cohen, Susan. *Heroes of the Challenger.* Archway, 1986, pap.

COE-2 Cohen, Daniel. *Masters of Horror.* Clarion, 1984

COEA ———. *Masters of the Occult.* Dodd, 1971 (o.p.)

COF Cohen, Tom. *Three Who Dared.* Doubleday, 1969 (o.p.)

COF-1 Collier, James Lincoln. *The Great Jazz Artists.* Four Winds, 1977 (o.p.)

COFA Collins, David. *Great American Nurses.* Messner, 1971 (o.p.)

COFB Collins, David R. *Football Running Backs: Three Ground Gainers.* Garrard, 1976

COG Commager, Henry Steele. *Crusaders for Freedom.* Doubleday, 1962 (o.p.)

COG-1 Conta, Marcia Maher. *Women for Human Rights.* Raintree, 1979

COGA Cook, Fred J. *The Demagogues.* Macmillan, 1972 (o.p.)

COGB ———. *The Muckrakers: Crusading Journalists Who Changed America.* Doubleday, 1972 (o.p.)

COGC ———. *American Political Bosses and Machines.* Watts, 1973 (o.p.)

COH Cook, Roy. *Leaders of Labor.* Lippincott, 1966 (o.p.)

COI Cooke, Donald E. *Atlas of the Presidents.* Hammond, rev. ed., 1985

COJ ———. *Fathers of America's Freedom: The Story of the Signers of the Declaration of Independence.* Hammond, 1969 (o.p.)

COJA ———. *Presidents in Uniform.* Hastings, 1969 (o.p.)

COJB Coolidge, Olivia. *Makers of the Red Revolution.* HM, 1963 (o.p.)

COK ———. *Lives of Famous Romans.* HM, 1965 (o.p.)

COKA Cooper, Alice C. & Palmer, Charles A., eds. *Twenty Modern Americans.* HarBraceJ, 1942 (o.p.)

COKB Corn, Kahane & Moline, Jacki. *Madcap Men and Wacky Women from History.* Messner, 1987

and the United Kingdom. Watts, 1971 (o.p.)

GRAB-01 Green, Richard L. *A Salute to Black Civil Rights Leaders.* Empak, 1987, pap.

GRAB-02 ———. *A Salute to Black Pioneers.* Empak, 1986, pap.

GRAB-03 ———. *A Salute to Black Scientists and Inventors.* Empak, 1985, pap.

GRAB-04 ———, ed. *A Salute to Historic African Kings and Queens.* Empak, 1988, pap.

GRAB-05 ———. *A Salute to Historic Black Abolitionists.* Empak, 1988, pap.

GRAB-1 Greenbaum, Louise G. *Contributions of Women: Politics and Government.* Dillon, 1977 (o.p.)

GRAB-3 Greene, Laura. *Computer Pioneers.* Watts, 1985

GRAC Gridley, Marion E. *Contemporary American Indian Leaders.* Dodd, 1972 (o.p.)

GRAD ———. *American Indian Women.* Hawthorn, 1974 (o.p.)

GRB Grierson, John. *Heroes of the Polar Skies.* Meredith, 1967 (o.p.)

GRB-1 Gross, David C. *Pride of Our People: The Stories of One Hundred Outstanding Jewish Men and Women.* Doubleday, 1979 (o.p.)

GRBA Gross, Marthe. *The Possible Dream: Ten Who Dared.* Chilton, 1970 (o.p.)

GRC Grosseck, Joyce & Attwood, Elizabeth. *Great Explorers.* Fideler, 1967 (o.p.)

GUA Gumbiner, Joseph H. *Leaders of Our People, Book 1.* UAHC, 1963 (o.p.)

GUB ———. *Leaders of Our People, Book 2.* UAHC, 1965 (o.p.)

GUB-1 Gunther, Marc. *Basepaths: From the Minor Leagues to the Majors and Beyond.* Scribner, 1984

GUBA Gurko, Miriam. *The Ladies of Seneca Falls: The Birth of the Women's Rights Movement.* Schocken, 1976, pap.

GUC Gutman, Bill. *Famous Baseball Stars.* Dodd, 1973 (o.p.)

GUCA ———. *Football Superstars of the '70's.* Messner, 1977 (o.p.)

GUD ———. *Gamebreakers of the N.F.L.* Random, 1973 (o.p.)

GUDA ———. *Great Baseball Stories Today and Yesterday.* Messner, 1978 (o.p.)

GUE ———. *Modern Baseball Superstars.* Dodd, 1973 (o.p.)

GUEA ———. *Modern Basketball Superstars.* Dodd, 1975 (o.p.)

GUEB ———. *Modern Football Superstars.* Dodd, 1974 (o.p.)

GUEC ———. *Modern Hockey Superstars.* Dodd, 1976 (o.p.)

GUEC-1 ———. *Modern Soccer Superstars.* Dodd, 1979

GUED ———. *Modern Women Superstars.* Dodd, 1977

GUED-01 ———. *More Modern Baseball Superstars.* Dodd, 1978 (o.p.)

GUED-1 ———. *More Modern Women Superstars.* Dodd, 1979

GUEE ———. *Munson*Garvey*Brock*Carew.* G&D, 1976 (o.p.)

GUF ———. *New Breed Heroes of Pro Football.* Messner, 1973 (o.p.)

GUG ———. *New Breed Heroes in Pro Baseball.* Messner, 1974 (o.p.)

GUH ———. *Superstars of the Sports World.* Messner, 1978 (o.p.)

GUJ ———. *Women Who Work with Animals.* Dodd, 1982

HA Haber, Louis. *Black Pioneers of Science and Invention.* HarBraceJ, 1970

HA-1 ———. *Women Pioneers of Science.* HarBraceJ, 1979

HAA Hagedorn, Hermann. *Eleven Who Dared.* Scholastic, 1967 (o.p.)

HAB Halacy, Dan. *The Master Spy.* McGraw, 1968 (o.p.)

HAC Halacy, Daniel S., Jr. *They Gave Their Names to Science.* Putnam, 1967 (o.p.)

HACA Hall, Moss. *Go Indians! Stories of the Great Indian Athletes of the Carlisle School.* Ritchie, 1971 (o.p.)

HACB Hancock, Carla. *Seven Founders of American Literature.* Blair, 1976 (o.p.)

HAD Hand, Jack. *Great Running Backs of the N.F.L.* Random, 1966 (o.p.)

HAE ———. *Heroes of the N.F.L.* Random, 1965 (o.p.)

HAF Hano, Arnold. *Greatest Giants of Them All.* Putnam, 1967 (o.p.)

HAFA Harries, Joan. *They Triumphed over Their Handicaps.* Watts, 1981 (o.p.)

HAG Harris, John Norman. *Knights of the Air: Canadian Aces of World War I.* St. Martin, 1958 (o.p.)

HAG-1 Harris, Stacy. *Comedians of Country Music.* Lerner, 1978

HAGA Hasegawa, Sam. *The Coaches* (Stars of the NFL). Creative Ed, 1975 (o.p.)

HAGB ———. *The Linebackers* (Stars of the NFL). Creative Ed, 1975 (o.p.)

HAGC ———. *The Quarterbacks* (Stars of the NFL). Creative Ed, 1975 (o.p.)

HAGD Haskins, James. *Leaders of the Middle East.* Enslow, 1985

HAH ———. *A Piece of the Power: Four Black Mayors.* Dial, 1972 (o.p.)

KEE 1964 young readers memorial ed., abridged. (o.p.)

KEE Kenworthy, Leonard S. *Twelve Citizens of the World.* Doubleday, 1953 (o.p.)

KEF Kenworthy, Leonard S. & Ferrari, Erma. *Leaders of New Nations.* Doubleday, 1968 (o.p.)

KEG Kerby, Elizabeth Poe. *The Conquistadors.* Putnam, 1969 (o.p.)

KEH Kerr, Colman. *Great Adventurers.* Follett, 1967 (o.p.)

KIA King-Hall, Stephen. *Three Dictators: Mussolini, Hitler, Stalin.* Transatlantic, 1964 (o.p.)

KIB Kirk, Rhina. *Circus Heroes and Heroines.* Hammond, 1972 (o.p.)

KL Klapthor, Margaret Brown. *The First Ladies.* White House Historical Assn., 1981

KLA Klein, Aaron E. *The Hidden Contributors: Black Scientists and Inventors in America.* Doubleday, 1971 (o.p.)

KLB Klein, Dave. *Great Infielders of the Major Leagues.* Random, 1972 (o.p.)

KLBA ———. *Pro Basketball's Big Men.* Random, 1973 (o.p.)

KLBB ———. *On the Way Up: What It's Like in the Minor Leagues.* Messner, 1977 (o.p.)

KLC ———. *Rookie: The World of the N.B.A.* Regnery, 1971 (o.p.)

KLCA ———. *Stars of the Major Leagues.* Random, 1974

KLD Klinger, Gene. *The Spectaculars.* Reilly & Lee, 1971 (o.p.)

KN Knight, David C. *The Spy Who Never Was and Other True Spy Stories.* Doubleday, 1978 (o.p.)

KNA Knight, Frank. *Stories of Famous Explorers by Land.* Westminster, 1965 (o.p.)

KNB ———. *Stories of Famous Explorers by Sea.* Westminster, 1964 (o.p.)

KOA Kostman, Samuel. *Twentieth Century Women of Achievement.* Rosen, 1976 (o.p.)

KR Krishef, Robert K. & Harris, Stacy. *The Carter Family: Country Music's First Family.* Lerner, 1978

KRI Krishef, Robert K. *More New Breed Stars.* Lerner, 1980

KRI-1 ———. *The New Breed.* Lerner, 1978

KUA Kubiak, Daniel James. *Ten Tall Texans.* Naylor, rev. ed., 1970 (o.p.)

LA Lake, Bonnie & Krishef, Robert K. *Western Stars of Country Music.* Lerner, 1978 (o.p.)

LA-1 Land, Barbara. *The New Explorers: Women in Antarctica.* Dodd, 1981

LAA ———. *The Telescope Makers: From Galileo to the Space Age.* T Y Crowell, 1968 (o.p.)

LAA-1 Langley, Andrew. *In Profile: Explorers on the Nile.* Silver Burdett, 1981

LAA-2 ———. *In Profile: The First Men around the World.* Silver Burdett, 1983 (o.p.)

LAB Lansing, Marion. *Liberators and Heroes of South America.* Ayer repr. of 1940 facsimile ed.

LABA Lardner, Rex. *The Great Golfers.* Putnam, 1970 (o.p.)

LAC ———. *Ten Heroes of the Twenties.* Putnam, 1966 (o.p.)

LACA Larranaga, Robert D. *Famous Crimefighters.* Lerner, 1970 (o.p.)

LACB ———. *Pirates and Buccaneers.* Lerner, 1970

LAD Larsen, Egon. *Men Who Fought for Freedom.* Roy, 1958 (o.p.)

LAE ———. *Men Who Shaped the Future: Stories of Invention and Discovery.* Roy, 1954 (o.p.)

LAF Lavine, Sigmund A. *Famous American Architects.* Dodd, 1967 (o.p.)

LAG ———. *Famous Industrialists.* Dodd, 1961 (o.p.)

LAH ———. *Famous Merchants.* Dodd, 1965 (o.p.)

LAHA Lawrence, Andrew. *Tennis: Great Stars, Great Moments.* Putnam, 1976 (o.p.)

LAI Lawson, Don. *Famous American Political Families.* Abelard, 1965 (o.p.)

LEA Legum, Colin & Legum, Margaret. *The Bitter Choice: Eight South Africans' Resistance to Tyranny.* World Pub., 1968 (o.p.)

LEAA Leipold, L. Edmond. *America Becomes Free.* T. S. Denison, 1972 (o.p.)

LEAB ———. *Americans Born Abroad.* T. S. Denison, 1973 (o.p.)

LEB ———. *Citizens Born Abroad.* T. S. Denison, 1967 (o.p.)

LEC ———. *Crusaders for a Cause.* T. S. Denison, 1967 (o.p.)

LED ———. *Explorers of Our Land.* T. S. Denison, 1967 (o.p.)

LEDA ———. *Famous American Architects.* T. S. Denison, 1972 (o.p.)

LEE ———. *Famous American Artists.* T. S. Denison, 1969 (o.p.)

LEF ———. *Famous American Athletes.* T. S. Denison, 1969 (o.p.)

LEG ———. *Famous American Doctors.* T. S. Denison, 1969 (o.p.)

LEGA ———. *Famous American Engineers.* T. S. Denison, 1972 (o.p.)

LEGB ———. *Famous American Fiction Writers.* T. S. Denison, 1972 (o.p.)

LEH ———. *Famous American Indians.* T. S. Denison, 1967 (o.p.)

LEHA ———. *Famous American Labor Leaders.* T. S. Denison, 1972 (o.p.)

LEHB ———. *Famous American Musicians.* T. S. Denison, 1972 (o.p.)

LEI ———. *Famous American Negroes.* T. S. Denison, 1967 (o.p.)

LEJ ———. *Famous American Poets.* T. S. Denison, 1969 (o.p.)

LEJA ———. *Famous American Teachers.* T. S. Denison, 1972 (o.p.)

LEK ———. *Famous American Women.* T. S. Denison, 1967 (o.p.)

LEL ———. *Famous Scientists and Astronauts.* T. S. Denison, 1967 (o.p.)

LEM ———. *Founders of Fortunes,* Book 1. T. S. Denison, 1967 (o.p.)

LEN ———. *Founders of Fortunes,* Book 2. T. S. Denison, 1967 (o.p.)

LEO ———. *Founders of Our Cities.* T. S. Denison, 1967 (o.p.)

LEOA ———. *Great American Artists.* T. S. Denison, 1973 (o.p.)

LEOB ———. *Great American Poets.* T. S. Denison, 1973 (o.p.)

LEP ———. *Heroes in Time of War.* T. S. Denison, 1967 (o.p.)

LEPA ———. *Heroes of a Different Kind.* T. S. Denison, 1973 (o.p.)

LEPB ———. *Heroes of Today—The Astronauts.* T. S. Denison, 1973 (o.p.)

LEPC ———. *Makers of a Better America.* T. S. Denison, 1972 (o.p.)

LEPD ———. *Our Country Grows Up.* T. S. Denison, 1972 (o.p.)

LEPE ———. *They Gave Their Lives.* T. S. Denison, 1972 (o.p.)

LEPF ———. *When Our Country Was Very Young.* T. S. Denison, 1972 (o.p.)

LEQ Lengyel, Cornel. *Presidents of the United States.* Western Pub., rev. ed., 1969 (o.p.)

LEQA ———. *Presidents of the United States.* Western Pub., rev. ed., 1977 (o.p.)

LEQB Lerner, Peter Morris. *Famous Chess Players.* Lerner, 1973 (o.p.)

LER Levinger, Elma Ehrlich. *Great Jewish Women.* Behrman, 1940 (o.p.)

LERA ———. *Great Jews Since Bible Times.* Behrman, 1926

LES ———. *They Fought for Freedom and Other Stories: Heroes of Jewish History.* UAHC, 1953 (o.p.)

LES-1 Levinson, Nancy Smiler. *Contributions of Women: Business.* Dillon, 1981

LES-2 ———. *The First Women Who Spoke Out.* Dillon, 1983

LET Levitan, Tina. *The Laureates: Jewish Winners of the Nobel Prize.* Twayne, 1960 (o.p.)

LETA ———. *Jews in American Life.* Hebrew Pub., 1969

LETB Levy, Elizabeth. *By-lines: Profiles in Investigative Journalism.* Four Winds, 1975 (o.p.)

LETC ———. *Doctors for the People: Profiles of Six Who Serve.* Knopf, 1977 (o.p.)

LETD ———. *Lawyers for the People: A New Breed of Defenders and Their Work.* Knopf, 1974 (o.p.)

LEU Lewis, Mildred & Lewis, Milton. *Famous Modern Newspaper Writers.* Dodd, 1962 (o.p.)

LEV Libby, Bill. *Baseball's Greatest Sluggers.* Random, 1973

LEVA ———. *Champions of the Indianapolis 500: The Men Who Have Won More Than Once.* Dodd, 1976 (o.p.)

LEW ———. *The Coaches.* Regnery, 1972 (o.p.)

LEX ———. *Great American Race Drivers.* Regnery, 1970 (o.p.)

LEXA ———. *Heroes of Stock Car Racing.* Random, 1975 (o.p.)

LEY ———. *Heroes of the Hot Corner: Great Third Basemen of the Major Leagues.* Watts, 1972 (o.p.)

LEYA ———. *Pro Hockey Heroes of Today.* Random, 1974 (o.p.)

LEYB ———. *Stars of the Olympics.* Hawthorn, 1975 (o.p.)

LEYC ———. *Superdrivers: Three Auto Racing Champions.* Garrard, 1977

LEZ ———. *Star Pitchers of the Major Leagues.* Random, 1971 (o.p.)

LEZA ———. *Star Quarterbacks of the N.F.L.* Random, 1970 (o.p.)

LEZB ———. *Star Running Backs of the N.F.L.* Random, 1971

LEZC Lieberman, Mark. *The Pacifists: Soldiers without Guns.* Praeger, 1972 (o.p.)

LIA Life International. *Nine Who Chose America.* Dutton, 1959 (o.p.)

LIAA Liss, Howard. *Baseball's Zaniest Stars.* Random, 1971 (o.p.)

LIAB ———. *Hockey's Greatest All-Stars.* Hawthorn, 1972 (o.p.)

LIB ———. *The Making of a Rookie.* Random, 1968

LIBA ———. *AFL Dream Backfield.* Cowles Bk. Co., 1969 (o.p.)

MEB ——. *Champions of the Four Freedoms*. Little, 1966 (o.p.)

MEC ——. *In Search of Peace: The Winners of the Nobel Peace Prize, 1901–1975*. Abingdon, 1978 (o.p.)

MIA Miers, Earl Schenck. *America and Its Presidents*. G&D, 1966 (o.p.)

MIB Milne, Lorus J. & Milne, Margery J. *Famous Naturalists*. Dodd, 1952 (o.p.)

MIC Mitchison, Naomi. *African Heroes*. FS&G, 1968 (o.p.)

MO Mondey, David. *In Profile: Women of the Air*. Silver Burdett, 1981 (o.p.)

MOA Montgomery, Elizabeth Rider. *The Story behind Popular Songs*. Dodd, 1958 (o.p.)

MOB Moore, Patrick. *Exploring the World*. Watts, 1966 (o.p.)

MOBA Moore, William. *The Atomic Pioneers: From Irish Castle to Manhattan Project*. Putnam, 1970 (o.p.)

MOC Morriss, Frank. *Saints for the Small*. Bruce Wis, 1964 (o.p.)

MOCA Morse, Charles & Morse, Ann. *The Running Backs* (Stars of the NFL). Creative Ed, 1975 (o.p.)

MOCB Motz, Lloyd. *On the Path of Venus*. Pantheon, 1976

MOD Moyer, John W. *Famous Indian Chiefs*. Hubbard Pr., 1957 (o.p.)

MUA Muir, Jane. *Famous Modern American Women Writers*. Dodd, 1959 (o.p.)

MUB ——. *Of Men and Numbers: The Story of the Great Mathematicians*. Dodd, 1961 (o.p.)

MUB-1 Murphy, Jim. *Baseball's All-Time All-Stars*. Clarion, 1984

MUC Murray, Tom, ed. *Sport Magazine's All-Time Stars*. Atheneum, 1977 (o.p.)

NAA Nason, Thelma Campbell. *Under the Wide Sky: Tales of New Mexico and the Spanish Southwest*. Follett, 1965 (o.p.)

NAB Nathan, Dorothy. *Women of Courage*. Random, 1964 (o.p.)

NAC Navy Times Editors. *Great American Naval Heroes*. Dodd, 1965 (o.p.)

NE Neilson, Winthrop & Neilson, Frances. *Seven Women: Great Painters*. Chilton, 1969 (o.p.)

NEA Newcombe, Jack. *The Fireballers: Baseball's Fastest Pitchers*. Putnam, 1964 (o.p.)

NEAA Newlon, Clarke. *Famous Mexican-Americans*. Dodd, 1972 (o.p.)

NEB ——. *Famous Pioneers in Space*. Dodd, 1963 (o.p.)

NEBA ——. *The Men Who Made Mexico*. Dodd, 1973 (o.p.)

NEBB ——. *Famous Puerto Ricans*. Dodd, 1975 (o.p.)

NEBB-1 Newman, Fred. *In Profile: Leaders of the Russian Revolution*. Silver Burdett, 1981 (o.p.)

NEC Newton, Douglas. *The First Book of Kings*. Watts, 1961 (o.p.)

NIA Nies, Judith. *Seven Women: Portraits from the American Radical Tradition*. Penguin, 1978, pap.

NOA Northcroft, Dora. *Famous Girls of the Past*. Verry, 1966 (o.p.)

OBA O'Brien, Andy. *Young Hockey Champions*. Norton, 1969 (o.p.)

OBB ——. *Superstars: Hockey's Greatest Players*. McGraw, 1973 (o.p.)

OCA O'Connor, Dick. *American Olympic Stars*. Putnam, 1976 (o.p.)

OCB O'Connor, Karen. *Contributions of Women: Literature*. Dillon, 1984

OJA Ojigbo, A. Okion, comp. *Young and Black in Africa*. Random, 1971 (o.p.)

OLA Olcott, Frances Jenkins. *Good Stories for Great Birthdays*. HM, 1922 (o.p.)

OLAA Olney, Ross. *Great Auto Racing Champions*. Garrard, 1973

OLAB ——. *Kings of Motor Speed*. Putnam, 1970 (o.p.)

OLB ——. *Kings of the Drag Strip*. Putnam, 1968 (o.p.)

OLC ——. *Men Against the Sea*. G&D, 1969 (o.p.)

OLCA ——. *Auto Racing's Young Lions*. Putnam, 1977 (o.p.)

OLCB ——. *Superstars of Auto Racing*. Putnam, 1975 (o.p.)

OLCC ——. *Modern Auto Racing Superstars*. Dodd, 1978 (o.p.)

OLD Olney, Ross & Graham, Richard W. *Kings of the Surf*. Putnam, 1969 (o.p.)

OLDA Olney, Ross R. *Modern Drag Racing Superstars*. Dodd, 1981

OLDB ——. *Modern Motorcycle Superstars*. Dodd, 1980

OLDC ——. *Modern Speed Record Superstars*. Dodd, 1982

OLDD ——. *Super Champions of Auto Racing*. Clarion, 1984

OLDE ——. *Super Champions of Ice Hockey*. Clarion, 1982

ONA O'Neill, Mary. *Saints: Adventures in Courage*. Doubleday, 1963 (o.p.)

ORA Orr, Frank. *Great Goalies of Pro Hockey*. Random, 1973

ORB ——. *Hockey Stars of the 70s*. Putnam, 1973 (o.p.)

SUK   Sutcliff, Rosemary. *Heroes and History.* Putnam, 1965 (o.p.)

SUKA   Sutton, Felix. *Indian Chiefs of the West.* Messner, 1970 (o.p.)

SUL   ———. *Sons of Liberty.* Messner, 1969 (o.p.)

SWE   Sweeney, James B. *Famous Aviators of World War II.* Watts, 1987

SWE-1 ———. *Army Leaders of World War II.* Watts, 1984

SWI   Swiger, Elinor Porter. *Women Lawyers at Work.* Messner, 1978 (o.p.)

TA   Tassin, Raymond J. *Double Winners of the Medal of Honor.* Daring, 1986

TAC   Taylor, A. J. P. *The War Lords.* Penguin, pap., 1979

TEA   Terkel, Studs. *Giants of Jazz.* T Y Crowell, 1957 (o.p.)

TEB   ———. *Giants of Jazz.* T Y Crowell, rev. ed., 1975

THA   Tharp, Edgar. *Giants of Invention.* G&D, 1971 (o.p.)

THC   ———. *Giants of Space.* G&D, rev. ed., 1970 (o.p.)

THD   Thorne, Ian. *The Great Centers* (Stars of the NHL). Creative Ed, 1976 (o.p.)

THE   ———. *The Great Defensemen* (Stars of the NHL). Creative Ed, 1976 (o.p.)

THF   ———. *The Great Goalies* (Stars of the NHL). Creative Ed, 1976 (o.p.)

THG   ———. *The Great Wingmen* (Stars of the NHL). Creative Ed, 1976 (o.p.)

TRA   Trease, Geoffrey. *Seven Kings of England.* Vanguard, 1955

TRB   ———. *Seven Queens of England.* Vanguard, 1953

TRBA   ———. *Seven Sovereign Queens.* Vanguard, 1968 (o.p.)

TRC   ———. *Seven Stages.* Vanguard, 1964

TRC-1 Triggs, Tony D. *In Profile: Founders of Religions.* Silver Burdett, 1981 (o.p.)

TRD   Truman, Margaret. *Women of Courage.* Morrow, 1976 (o.p.)

TU   Tuck, Jay Nelson & Vergara, Norma C. *Heroes of Puerto Rico.* Fleet, 1971

TUA   Turnbull, E. Lucia. *Legends of the Saints.* Lippincott, 1959 (o.p.)

TUB   Tuttle, Anthony. *The Catchers* (Stars of the NL & AL). Creative Ed, 1976 (o.p.)

UN   Ullman, Michael. *Jazz Lives: Portraits in Words and Pictures.* New Republic, 1980 (o.p.)

UNA   Unstead, Robert J. *Royal Adventurers.* Follett, 1963 (o.p.)

UNB   ———. *Some Kings and Queens.* Follett, 1962 (o.p.)

VAA   Vance, Marguerite. *Hear the Distant Applause! Six Great Ladies of the American Theatre.* Dutton, 1963 (o.p.)

VAB   ———. *The Lamp Lighters: Women in the Hall of Fame.* Dutton, 1960 (o.p.)

VAC   ———. *Six Queens: The Wives of Henry VIII.* Dutton, 1965 (o.p.)

VACA   Van Riper, Guernsey, Jr. *Behind the Plate: Three Great Catchers.* Garrard, 1973 (o.p.)

VACB   ———. *The Mighty Macs: Three Famous Baseball Managers.* Garrard, 1972 (o.p.)

VAD   ———. *Yea Coach! Three Great Football Coaches.* Garrard, 1966 (o.p.)

VAD-6 Van Steenwyk, Elizabeth. *Stars on Ice.* Dodd, 1980

VADA   ———. *Women in Sports: Figure Skating.* Harvey, 1976 (o.p.)

VADB   ———. *Women in Sports: Rodeo.* Harvey, 1978 (o.p.)

VAE   Vass, George. *Champions of Sports: Adventures in Courage.* Reilly & Lee, 1970 (o.p.)

VEA   Vecsey, George. *Baseball's Most Valuable Players.* Random, 1966 (o.p.)

VIA   Vinton, Iris. *Our Nation's Builders.* Merrill, 1968 (o.p.)

WA   Walker, Greta. *Women Today: Ten Profiles.* Hawthorn, 1975 (o.p.)

WA-1   Walter, Claire. *Women in Sports: Skiing.* Harvey, 1977 (o.p.)

WAA   Waltrip, Lela & Waltrip, Rufus. *Cowboys and Cattlemen.* McKay, 1967 (o.p.)

WAB   ———. *Indian Women: Thirteen Who Played a Part in the History of America from Earliest Days to Now.* McKay, 1964 (o.p.)

WABC   Warren, Ruth. *A Pictorial History of Women in America.* Crown, 1975 (o.p.)

WAC   Wayne, Bennett, ed. *Heroes of the Home Run.* Garrard, 1973

WAD   ———, ed. *Three Jazz Greats.* Garrard, 1973 (o.p.)

WAE   ———, ed. *Women Who Dared to Be Different.* Garrard, 1973

WAF   ———. *Adventurers in Buckskin.* Garrard, 1973

WAG   ———. *Big League Pitchers and Catchers.* Garrard, 1974

WAH   ———. *Black Crusaders for Freedom.* Garrard, 1974

WAI   ———, ed. *The Founding Fathers.* Garrard, 1975

WAJ   ———, ed. *Four Women of Courage.* Garrard, 1975

WAK   ———, ed. *Hockey Hotshots.* Garrard, 1977

YOE ——. *Modern Americans in Science and Technology.* Dodd, 1962 (o.p.)

YOF ——. *Women of Modern Science.* Greenwood repr. of 1959 ed., 1984

YOFA Young, Bob & Young, Jan. *Liberators of Latin America.* Lothrop, 1970 (o.p.)

YOG ——. *Seven Faces West.* Messner, 1969 (o.p.)

YOH Young, Patricia. *Great Performers.* Walck, 1967 (o.p.)

YOI Young, Margaret B. *Black American Leaders.* Watts, 1969 (o.p.)

YOJ Young, Percy M. *More Music Makers.* Roy, 1962 (o.p.)

YOK ——. *Music Makers.* Roy, 1968 (o.p.)

YOL ——. *Music Makers of Today.* Roy, 1958 (o.p.)

YOM ——. *World Conductors.* Abelard, 1965 (o.p.)

ZAA Zanger, Jack. *Great Catchers of the Major Leagues.* Random, 1970

Biographees

Alphabetical Listing of Biographees

A

Aaron of Tulchin. Polish rabbi. GEF

Aaron, Chloe (1938–). Television programming executive. SMBB-2

Aaron, Hank (1934–). Baseball player. ASBA; BELB; BRAA; BUD-1; DA; DAFD; DOF-1; FRC-1†; FRD; GAB; GEC; GR; GUC; GUDA; GUE; KADA; LEV; MUB-1; MUC; PEC; PRA; RAAA; RIGA†; SA-3; SH; SHB; SHH

Aaron, Henry (1914–). Conductor. STM†

Abad Queipo, Manuel (1751–1825). Spanish bishop. WOB

Abarbanel, Isaac, see Abravanel, Isaac.

Abas, Mathys (1924–). Conductor, born the Netherlands. STM†

Abba Arika, see Rav.

Abbé Pierre, see Pierre, Abbé.

Abbey, Edwin Austin (1852–1911). Painter. CHC

Abbott, Berenice (1898–). Photographer. SUAA

Abbott, Bud (William) (1895–1974). Comedian. BUR-1; ED-1†

Abbott, Robert Sengstacke (1870–1940). Journalist, founded *Chicago Defender*. ADA; ADB; HUA; ROG; STO

Abd-al-Rahman, see Abd-er-Rahman I.

Abd-er-Rahman I (731–788). Muslim Ommiad emir. CAAA

Abdul-Jabbar, Kareem (1947–). Basketball player. AAS-35; ARB-1; ASBA; FRD; GAB; GUEA; KADA; KLBA; KLC; RAAB; SA; SA-1; SA-2

Abdur Rahman Sadi el Timbuctoo (1596–1660). African historian. ADA

Abel, John Jacob (1857–1938). Pharmacologist, physiological chemist. POB

Abel, Rudolf Ivanovich (1902–1971). Russian spy. HAB; KN

Abernathy, Ralph David (1926–). Clergyman, civil rights leader. YOI

Aboab, Isaac de Fonseca (1605–1693). Dutch Sephardic rabbi. LETA

Abrabanel, Isaac, see Abravanel, Isaac.

Abraham. Hebrew patriarch. GEF

Abraham. Saint. DAD-2

Abraham (c. 1790–c. 1870). Interpreter for Seminoles. GRAB-02; WIBA

Abrahams, Harold (1899–1978). English track athlete. SLA

Abrahams, Peter (1919–). South African author. OJA

Abramowicz, Daniel. Football player. DEHA

Abravanel, Isaac (1437–1508). Portuguese statesman, theologian. GUA; KAB; KAC; LERA; LES

Abravanel, Maurice (1903–). Conductor, born Turkey. STM

Abzug, Bella (1920–). Congresswoman. GIB-1; GRAB-1†

Ace, Jane (1905–1974). Comedienne. MASB

Acheson, Dean Gooderham (1893–1971). Secretary of state. HEEA

Achilleus. Saint. DAD-2†

Adair, Bethenia, see Owens-Adair, Bethenia.

Adair, James (1709?–1783). Pioneer trader. STA

Adam, Marianne. German track athlete. HOBAA†

Adams, Abigail (1744–1818). Wife of John Adams. ARAB; BAG; BAG-1; BLG†; CHA; DAD; HIBD; JOCA; KL; MAA; MAU; PRB; ROH; ROHA; WABC†; WAQ

Adams, Adrienne (1906–). Illustrator. SMAB

Adams, Ansel E. (1902–1984). Photographer. FOD

Adams, Babe (Charles Benjamin) (b. 1883). Baseball player. GIB

Adams, Charles Francis (1807–1886). Diplomat. LAI

Adams, Diana (1927?–). Dancer. ATA

Adams, Eugene (1907–). Conductor. STM†

Adams, Eugene W. (1920–). Veterinarian. HAMA

Adams, Franklin Pierce (1881–1960). Humorist, columnist. ALA

Adams, Henry (b. 1843). Pioneer. KADB

Adams, Henry (Hank) (1944–). American Indian leader. GRAC

Adams, Henry Brooks (1838–1918). Historian. HIB

Adams, John (1735–1826). President of U.S. ARAB; BAEA; BAEB; BAG; BAG-1; BEB; BLA; BLE; BUIA; BUIB; CAG; CAH; COI; COJ; COS; DAFA; DUB; DUC; DUCA; FEA; FEAB; FEB; FRBA; HAN; HAOA; HIH; HOEA; KEC†; LAI; LEQ; LEQA; MAB; MABA; MAC; MIA; OLA; PED; ROH; ROHA; ROK†; SUBB; WHD

Adams, John Capen (also known as James Capen Adams) (1812?–1860). Frontiersman. COE

Adams, John Couch (1819–1892). English astronomer. SOB; SUE

Adams, John Quincy (1767–1848). President of U.S. BAEB; BAG; BAG-1; BEB; BLA; BUIA; CAG; CAH; COG; COI; COS; DAE; DUB; DUC; DUCA; FOR; FRBA; HEEA; HIH; KEC; KED; LAI; LEQ; LEQA; MAB; MABA; MAL; MIA; PED; RED; ROH; ROHA; ROK†; SUBB; WHD

Adams, Louisa Catherine (1775–1852). Wife of John Quincy Adams. BAG; BAG-1; BLG†; CHA; KL; MAA; MAU; PRB; ROH; ROHA

Adams, Maude (1872–1953). Actress. GIBA†; VAA

Adams, Neal. Cartoonist. GOB-1

Adams, Samuel (1722–1803). American Revolutionary patriot. ARAA; ARAB; BAEA; BUIB; COJ; DAC; DIA; FEAB; HAN; HIBD; LAI; MAC; SUL

Addams, Jane (1860–1935). Social worker. AAS-34; BOC; BRBE; CAGA; COG; COKA; CUC; DEDA; DOD; FEC; FOH; FOJ; GIBA; LEZC; MAN; MASA; MAT; MEA; MEC; NAB; PA; PACA; SHFE†; STJ; STLA; WABC†; WECB; WIC

Adderley, Herb. Football player. JOA

Addison, Thomas (1793–1860). English physician. POB

Ade, George (1866–1944). Humorist, playwright. BEE

Adelaide of Turin (c. 1020–1091). Saint. DAD-3

Adelman, Susan. Surgeon. FOC-1

Adenauer, Konrad (1876–1967). German chancellor. WEA

Adh-Dhîb, Muhammed (1931?–). Discoverer of Dead Sea Scrolls at 15. FOR

Adler, Felix (1851–1933). Educator, ethical reformer, born Germany. BEA

Adler, Felix (d. 1960). Clown. KIB

Adler, Kurt Herbert (1905–1988). Conductor, chorus master, born Austria. STM†

Adler, Peter (1899–). Conductor, born Czechoslovakia. STM†

Adrian, Edgar Douglas (1889–1977). English physiologist. RIF

Aelred (1110–1167). Saint. DAD-2

Affonso I (1506–1545). King of Kongo. DOA; GRAB-04; MIC

Agassiz, Alexander (1835–1910). Oceanographer, zoologist, born Switzerland. COR

Agassiz, Louis (1807–1873). Naturalist, born Switzerland. HYB; MIB

Agatha (d. 250?). Saint. DAD-2; QUA

Ager, Milton (1893–1979). Songwriter. MOA

Agganis, Harry (1930–1955). Football player. CL-04; HIE

Agnes (291–304). Saint. DAD-1; DAD-2; ONA; QUA; WIB

Agnes of Montepulciano (c. 1268–1317). Saint. DAD-2

Agnesi, Maria Gaetana (1718–1799). Italian mathematician. SC†

Agnew, Spiro Theodore (1918–). Vice president of U.S. FEA; HAOA; HOEA

Agnodice (fl. 300 b.c.). Greek physician. SC

Agnon, Shmuel Yosef (1888–1970). Israeli author. GRB-1; ROGA

Agricola, Georgius (1494–1555). German mineralogist. FE; SHFB

Agricola, Gnaeus Julius (37–93). Roman general. COM

Agrippa, Cornelius Heinrich (1486?–1535). German philosopher. COEA; ED-5

Agrippa von Nettesheim, see Agrippa, Cornelius Heinrich.

Aguilar, Grace (1816–1847). English author. LER; PEB

Aguirre, Lope de (c. 1510–1561). Spanish adventurer. KNA

Ahab (d. 853? b.c.). King of Israel. JOBB

Aidan (d. 651). Saint. DAD-3

Ailey, Alvin (1931–). Dancer, choreographer. AB; DOF-1

Akbar the Great (1542–1605). Emperor of Hindustan. CAAA

Akeley, Carl Ethan (1864–1926). Explorer, naturalist. BAB

Akeley, Delia J. Denning (1870?–1933?). Explorer. RIG

Akeman, David "Stringbean" (1915–1973). Comedian. HAG-1

Akhnaton (fl. 1379–1362 b.c.). King of Egypt. CAAA; GRAB-04; JOBB; NEC; UNA

Akiba ben Joseph (c. 50–132). Palestinian rabbi. GEF; GRB-1; GUA; KAB; KAC; LERA

Akihito, Togusama (1933–). Crown prince of Japan. NEC†

Alban (3d or 4th century). Saint. DAD-2; ONA

Albéniz, Isaac (1860–1909). Spanish composer, pianist. KAE; SAA

Albert (d. 997). Saint. WIB

Albert I (1875–1934). King of the Belgians. CAAA

Albert the Great (1206–1280). Saint, German scientist, theologian. CUA; DAD-3; MOC; ONA; QUA

Albert, Marv (1943–). Sports announcer. SLA†

Albertus Magnus, see Albert the Great.

Albright, Tenley (1935–). Skater, physician. BOHA; HOBA; HOBAA; HOBB; LEYB†; PIBA

Alcibiades (c. 450–404 B.C.). Athenian general, statesman. PLA

Alcindor, Lewis, see Abdul-Jabbar, Kareem.

Alcock, Sir John (1892–1919). English aviator. COC†; HAMY

Alcott, Bronson (1799–1888). Educator. ASB; COG; DEDA; WOAA

Alcott, Louisa May (1832–1888). Author. ASB; BEGA; BOA; BOC; COB; DEI; DEJ; STJ; STLA; WOAA

Alcuin (735–804). English educator. FRC

Alderson, Nannie (1860–1947). Ranch owner. JOB

Alderwick, Edgar J. (1890–). Conductor. STM†

Aldridge, Ira (1805?–1867). Actor. ADA; ADB; BRB†; HODA; HUA; PECA; ROF; ROG

Aldridge, Lionel. Football player. JOA†

Aldrin, Edwin E., Jr. (1930–). Astronaut. HOBB; LEPB; THC

Alegria, Ciro (1909–1967). Peruvian author. WO

Aleijadhino (Antônio Francisco Lisboa) (1738–1841). Brazilian architect, sculptor. BACA

Alekhine, Alexander (1892–1946). Russian chess player. LEQB

Alexander. Saint. DAD-3

Alexander I (1777–1825). Tsar of Russia. RIA

Alexander II (1818–1881). Tsar of Russia. RIA

Alexander III (1845–1894). Tsar of Russia. RIA

Alexander III, the Great (356–323 B.C.). King of Macedon. CAAA; COD; DEI; DEJ; FRE; JOBB; KEH; KNA; MOB; NEC; PLA; UNB

Alexander the Coalman (d. 275). Saint. DAD-3

Alexander, Archie A. (1888–1958). Engineer. BRB†

Alexander, Grover Cleveland (1887–1950). Baseball player. ALB; DAFC; DAFD; DAG; DAGA; DEG†; GIB; MUB-1; NEA; RIGA†; SHA

Alexander, Harold Rupert Leofric George, 1st earl (1891–1969). British field marshal. COD†

Alexander, Joe (1898–1975). Football player. SLA†

Alexander, Moses (1853–1932). Governor. LETA

Alexander, William (1726–1783). American Revolutionary patriot. BUIB†

Alexander Nevski (1220?–1263). Russian saint and hero. MAJ

Alexis. Saint. DAD-3

Alfred the Great (849–899). King of the West Saxons. CAAA; CHG; COA; DEC; DEI; DEJ; HEA; JOBB; MAJ; NEC; SUK; TRA; UNB

Ali, Muhammad (Cassius Clay) (1942–). Boxer. ASB-1; ASBA; BELB; BOHA; DAGA; FOR; GED; HOBC; HOCG; KADA; LEYB†; PAW; RAAC; RICA

Alice de Bourgotte (d. 1466). Saint. QUA

Al-Khwarizmi, see Khwarizmi, al-.

Allard, Martine. Actress. BRF-1

Allen, Arthur A. (1885–1964). Ornithologist. MIB†

Allen, Dede (1923–). Film editor. GIB-1†

Allen, Ethan (1738–1789). American Revolutionary soldier. BUIB†; RAD; SOA

Allen, Florence Ellinwood (1884–1966). Jurist. WHE

Allen, Fred (1894–1956). Comedian. ALC

Allen, George (1922–). Football coach. AAS-12; HAGA; LEW

Allen, Gracie (Grace Ethel Cecile Rosalie) (1906–1964). Comedienne. BUR-1; MASB

Allen, Hervey (1889–1949). Author. CON

Allen, Lisa-Marie (1960–). Skater. VAD-6

Allen, Macon B. (fl. 1845). Lawyer. BRB†

Allen, Maria (fl. 1776). American Revolutionary patriot. CAD

Allen, Mel (1913–). Sports announcer. SLA†

Allen, Richard (1760–1831). Bishop. A founder of African Methodist Episcopal Church. ADA; ADB; BEJ; BRB; DADA; DOG; GRAB-05; HUA; PECA; ROG; WIBA

Allen, Richie (Richard Anthony) (1942?–). Baseball player. BRD; GUE; GUG; LEY

Allen, Woody (1935–). Actor, motion picture director. ED-1†; SMBB-3

Allenby, Edmund Henry Hynman, 1st viscount (1861–1936). British field marshal. ARD

Allers, Franz (1905–). Conductor, born Czechoslovakia. STM†

Allesandro, Victor (1915–). Conductor. STM

Alligood, Douglass L. Advertising executive. STAA

Allingham, William (1824–1889). Irish poet. BEH

Allison, Bob (1934–). Baseball player. BRD

Allison, Bobby (Robert Arthur) (1937–). Automobile racer; aviator. LEXA; OLCC

Allon, Yigal (1918–1980). Israeli general. GRB-1; ROGA

Alloo, Modeste. Conductor, educator, born Belgium. STM†

Allston, Washington (1779–1843). Painter. FRA

Allucio. Saint. DAD-3

Almagro, Diego de (1475?–1538). Spanish soldier. ROL

Almeida, Antonio de (1928–). Conductor, born France. STM†

Almon, Bill (1952–). Baseball player. GUB-1

Alonso, Alicia (1921–). Cuban dancer. ATA; WO

Alou, Felipe (1935–). Dominican baseball coach. DEHA-1

Aloysius Gonzaga (1568–1591). Saint. DAD-1; DAD-2; MOC

Alphege of Canterbury (954–1012). Saint. DAD-2

Alphonsus Liguori (1696–1787). Saint. DAD-3

Alphonsus Rodriguez (1531–1617). Saint. DAD-3; MOC

Alston, Charles H. (1907–). Painter. ADB

Alston, Walter E. (1911–1984). Baseball manager. AAS-1; FRC-01; FRC-1†; LEW; SMG

Altgeld, John Peter (1847–1902). Governor, born Germany. KEC†; WECB

Altman, Robert (1925–). Motion picture director. SMBB-3

Altoha, Wallace (1870?–1937). Ranch owner. WAA

Alvarado, Pedro de (1495?–1541). Spanish soldier. ROL

Alvord, Burt (d. 1923). Outlaw. WIAA-1

Alworth, Lance (1940–). Football player. CO; DEHA; FRD; KADA; LIBA

Amadeus IX, Blessed (1435–1472). DAD-2

Ambrose (340–397). Saint. DAD-3; ONA

Amenhotep IV, see Akhnaton.

American Friends Service Committee. MEA; MEC

American Library Association. Founded 1876. MEB

Ames, Julie. Aviator. HIFD

Amevor, Charlotte (1932–). Painter. FAH

Amfiteatrof, Daniele (1901–). Conductor, born Russia. STM†

Amherst, Jeffrey (1717–1797). British field marshal. SOA

Amin, Idi (1925?–). Ex-president of Uganda. CL-01

Amini bin Saidi (1904?–). African tribesman. PEA

Amon, Chris (1943–). New Zealand automobile racer. JA

Amos, John. Football player. BELB

Ampère, André Marie (1775–1836). French mathematician, physicist. CAA; DUA; FE; SHFB; SIA

Amundsen, Roald (1872–1928). Norwegian polar explorer. BAB; COC†; COL; DOBB; DOC; GRB; GRC; KEH; KNA†; KNB†; MOB; PRC; ROL; WIA-1

Amurath, see Murad I and II.

Anaximander (611–547 B.C.). Greek astronomer, philosopher. SIB†

Ancerl, Karel (1908–1973). Czechoslovakian conductor. YOM†

Ancker-Johnson, Betsy (1927–). Physicist, automotive executive. GL; LES-1†

Anders, William Alison (1933–). Astronaut. LEPB

Andersen, Hans Christian (1805–1875). Danish author. BEI; COB; COG; DEI; DEJ; RAC

Anderson, Adrienne Adams, see Adams, Adrienne.

Anderson, Clifford (1904–). Conductor. STM†

Anderson, Donny (1943–). Football player. JOA†; LEZB

Anderson, Douglas Dorland (1936–). Archaeologist. POC

Anderson, Elizabeth Garrett (1836–1917). English physician. HUE; MAJ; MASA

Anderson, Evelyn M. (1899–). Physiologist. HOG

Anderson, Jo. Slave, inventor. HAL†

Anderson, John Henry (Professor) (1814–1874). Scottish magician. FOGA; GIA

Anderson, Kenneth Allan (1943–). Football player. AAS-20; CL-1

Anderson, Lonzo (1905–). Author. SMAB

Anderson, Marian (1902–). Singer. ADA; ADB; BOC; BRG; DOBA; DOF-1; FAA; FLD; GIBA; HUA; HUC; JOC; KE; KOA; LEHB; LEI; MAM; PACA; RIC; RICA; ROF; SC-02; SMBA; STF; STLA; STO; TRD

Anderson, Mary A. (1859–1940). Actress. VAA

Anderson, Osborne Perry (1830–1871). Abolitionist. GRAB-05

Anderson, Paul (1932–). Weightlifter. OCA

Anderson, Robert B. (1917–). Conductor. STM†

Anderson, Sherwood (1876–1941). Author. CON

Anderson, Sparky (George Lee) (1934–). Baseball manager. SMG

Anderson, William Robert (1921–). Naval officer. COR; SCBA

Anderton, Carol. Bowler. HOBAA†

Andrada e Silva, José Bonifácio de, see Bonifácio, José.

André, John (1751–1780). British spy. LOA; SOA

Andrée, Salomon A. (1854–1897). Swedish polar explorer. DOC†; GRB

Andretti, Mario (1940–). Automobile racer, born Italy. ABB; FOI; JA; LEX; OLAB; OLCC; ORD; YAA

Andrew (1st century). Saint, apostle. DAD-3; ONA; QUA

Andrews, Benny (1930–). Painter. FAH

Andrews, Roy Chapman (1884–1960). Naturalist, explorer. BAB

Andriamanjato, Rahantavololona. Malagasy engineer. CRA

Andrianov, Nikolai (1952–). Russian gymnast. LIE

Andrie, Eugene (1914–). Conductor. STM†

Anello, John (1909–). Conductor. STM†

Angela dei Merici (1474?–1540). Saint. Founded Order of Brescia. DAD-2; QUA

Angelico, Fra (1400–1455). Italian painter. MAI

Angell, Sir Norman (1874–1967). English author. MEA; MEC; WIC

Angelo. Runaway. BEOA

Angelou, Maya (1928–). Author. DADB; OCB

Anglund, Joan Walsh (1926–). Author, illustrator. SM

Anguiano, Lupe (1929–). Social worker, educator. NEAA

Anilewicz, Mordecai (1919–1943). Polish resistance worker. GRB-1

Ankhesnamun (fl. 1358 B.C.). Queen of Egypt. COLB

Anne. Saint, mother of Virgin Mary. DAD-1; DAD-3; ONA; QUA; WIB

Anne (1665–1714). Queen of Great Britain and Ireland. DEC; GRAB†; LIDA; SCC; TRB

Anne (1950–). Princess of Great Britain. HOBAA

Anne of Cleves (1515–1557). Consort of Henry VIII, king of England. MAOA; VAC

Annie. Runaway. BEOA

Anning, Mary (1799–1847). English fossil finder at 11. FOR

Anselm of Canterbury (1033–1109). Saint. DAD-2

Ansermet, Ernest (1883–). Swiss conductor. STM†

Anson, Cap (Adrian Constantine) (1851–1922). Baseball player, manager. ALB; DAFC; DAFD; DAH; FRC-01

Antar (525?–615). Arabian hero and poet. ADA; ADB

Antek, Samuel. Conductor. STM†

Anthony of Egypt (250–356). Saint. DAD-2

Anthony of Padua (1195–1231). Saint. DAD-1; DAD-2; MOC; ONA; QUA

Anthony, Mary. Feminist. GUBA

Anthony, Sister (Mary Ellen O'Connell) (1814–1897). Nun, nurse, born Ireland. COFA

Anthony, Susan Brownell (1820–1906). Feminist. ASB-1; BOC; BOJ; COG; CUC; DABB; DAD; DEDA; DOD; ELA; GIBA†; GUBA; LEK; LES-2; NAB; PA; SMC; STJ; STLA; TRD; VAB; WABC; WAR

Antigua. Spy. DAF-1†

Antin, Mary (1881–1949). Author, born Russia. CAHA

Antoine, Albert C. Rocket propulsion researcher. CAF-1

Antonini, Alfredo (1901–). Conductor, musical director, born Italy. STM†

Antonino. Saint. DAD-2

Antonius, Marcus, see Antony, Mark.

Antony (251–356). Saint, first Christian monk. ONA

Antony, Mark (83–30 B.C.). Roman soldier, politician. PLA

Anysia. Saint. DAD-3

Anza, Juan Bautista de (1735–1788). Spanish explorer. YOG

Apache Kid (fl. 1880–1890). Outlaw. SUJ

Aparicio, Luis (1934–). Baseball player, born Venezuela. FRC-1†; KLB; RIGA†; ROC

Apgar, Virginia (1909–1974). Physician. RAAG

Apollo (c. 316–395). Saint. ONA

Apollonia of Alexandria. Saint. DAD-2

Apollonius of Perga (fl. 247–205 B.C.). Greek mathematician. SIB†

Apollonius of Tyana (c. 3 B.C.–c. 100 A.D.). Greek magician. ED-5

Appert, Nicolas (c. 1750–1841). French inventor. FE

Applebee, Constance (b. 1874). Field hockey coach, born England. HOBAA

Appleseed, Johnny, see Chapman, John.

Appling, Luke. Baseball player. ALB; BOE; DAFC; DAFD; HIF; RIGA†

Apps, Syl (1915–). Canadian hockey player. MANA

Apps, Syl, II (1947–). Canadian hockey player. FICA-1

Aquinas, Thomas, Saint, see Thomas Aquinas.

Arafat, Yasir (1929–). Palestinian guerrilla leader, born Egypt. HAGD

Arboleya, Carlos (1929–). Banker, born Cuba. FOW

Arcaro, Eddie (1916–). Jockey. ASBA; DAG; DAGA; LYD

Archibald (d. 675). Saint. WIB

Archibald, Nate "Tiny" (1948–). Basketball player. AAS-6; ARB-4; HIBAA

Archimedes (287?–212 B.C.). Greek mathematician, inventor. ASA; BEP; CAA; DOE; EVC; FE; MAQ; MUB; SHFB; SIA; STN; THA

Arden, Elizabeth (1884–1966). Cosmetician. LAH; LES-1

Arden, Eve (1912–). Actress. MASB

Arentsen, Harold W. (1897–). Conductor. STM†

Arfons, Art (1926–). Automobile racer. LEX

Ariadne (2500 B.C.). Legendary Cretian princess. PA

Aristarchus of Samos (3d century B.C.). Greek astronomer. MOCB; SIB†

Aristotle (384–322 B.C.). Greek philosopher. CAA; DEI; DEJ; FE; FRC; LO; OZA; PIA; SIA; SIB†

Arizin, Paul (1929–). Basketball player. PE

Arkwright, Sir Richard (1732–1792). English inventor, manufacturer. FAB; FE

Armas, Jay J. (1933?–). Private investigator. HAFA

Armistead, James (fl. 1781–1824). American Revolutionary patriot. DAF-1; STQ†; WIBA

Armour, Philip Danforth (1832–1901). Industrialist. LAG; WED

Armour, Richard Willard (1906–). Poet. ALA

Armstrong, Charles (1886–1967). Physician. CHE†

Armstrong, Edwin Howard (1890–1954). Electrical engineer. MAPA

Armstrong, Harry George (1899–). Physician. ED

Armstrong, Henry (1912–). Boxer. BUJA; DAG; DAGA; FOI

Armstrong, Leslie H. (1909–). Conductor. STM†

Armstrong, Louis "Satchmo" (1900–1971). Trumpeter. ADA; ADB; COF-1; FLD; HUC; LEHB; RIC; RICA; ROF; TEA; TEB; WAD

Armstrong, Neil A. (1930–). Astronaut. DEJ; FRE; LEPB†; THC

Arnaz, Desi (1917–1986). Entertainer, born Cuba. FOW

Arne, Thomas Augustine (1710–1778). English composer. YOJ

Arnett, Hannah. American Revolutionary patriot. CLC†

Arnold, Benedict (1741–1801). General, traitor. HAN; LOA; SOA

Arnold, Henry Harley (1886–1950). General. ARC; SWE-1

Arnold, Matthew (1822–1888). English poet, critic. COP

Arnoldson, Klas Pontus (1844–1916). Swedish pacifist. MEC; WIC

Arnovich, Morrie (Morris) (1910–1959). Baseball player. RI; SLA†

Aronson, Henry M. (1935?–). Civil rights worker. COF

Arrhenius, Svante August (1859–1927). Swedish chemist. FE

Arroyo, Luis (1927–). Baseball player. SHE

Arroyo, Martina (1936?–). Singer. AB

Arthur (6th century). King of the Britons. JOBB; NEC; SUK

Arthur, Chester Alan (1830–1886). President of U.S. ALE; BAEB; BAG; BAG-1; BEB; BLA; BUIA; CAG; CAH; COI; COS; DAE; DUC; DUCA; FEA; FRBA; HAOA; HIH; HOEA; KEA; LEQ; LEQA; MAB; MABA; MIA; PED; ROH; ROHA; ROK†; SUBB; WHD

Arthur, Ellen Lewis (1837–1880). Wife of Chester Alan Arthur. BAG; BAG-1; BLG†; CHB; KL; MAA; MAU; PRB; ROH; ROHA

Artigas, José Gervasio (1764–1850). Uruguayan general. LAB; WOB

Aryabhatta (c. 475–550). Indian mathematician, astronomer. STN

Asbjörnsen, Peter Christen (1812–1885). Norwegian author. SMAB

Asbury, Francis (1745–1816). Bishop, born England. BUIB†; CAGA

Ascari, Alberto (1919–1955). Italian automobile racer. YAA

Asclepios, see Asklepios.

Asen, Simon (1911–). Conductor. STM†

Ashburn, Richie (1927–). Baseball player. BOE; BRD

Ashe, Arthur (1943–). Tennis player. AAS-28; FOX; GLC; GRBA; HI; HOBC; HOD-1; KADA; LAHA; LYC

Asher, Barry (1946–). Bowler. SLA

Ashford, Bailey Kelly (1873–1934). Surgeon. ED

Ashford, Emmett Littleton (1915?–1980). Baseball umpire. HOBC

Ashford, Evelyn (1957–). Track athlete. SUDB

Ashi (352–427). Babylonian rabbi. GEF; GUA

Ashkenasi, Shmuel (1941–). Israeli violinist. EWC

Ashley, Lord, see Shaftesbury, Anthony Ashley Cooper, 7th earl of.

Ashmun, Jehudi (1794–1828). Clergyman, agent to Liberia. WOA

Ashurbanipal (fl. 669–626 B.C.). King of Assyria. CAAA

Askia Muhammad (1494–1529). Emperor of Timbuktu. ADA; ADB; BRB†; DOA; GRAB-04

Askin, Rosemary. Geologist, polar researcher. LA-1

Asklepios (c. 1300 B.C.). Greek physician. SHG

Asoka the Great (d. 232 B.C.). Indian king of Magadha. CAAA; NEC

Aspasia (fl. 2d century). Roman physician. SC

Asper, Frank W. (1892–). Conductor. STM†

Assad, Hafez el- (1928?–). President of Syria. HAGD

Asser, Tobias M. C. (1838–1913). Dutch statesman. LET; MEC†; WIC

Astell, Mary (1668–1731). English author. BOH

Aston, Francis William (1877–1945). English chemist, physicist. RID; SHFB†

Astor, John Jacob (1763–1848). Pioneer fur trader, financier, born Germany. CUB; CUC; HOF; LEM; LEPC; LOB

Asturias, Miguel Angel (1899–1974). Guatemalan author. WO

Atahualpa (1500?–1533). Incan king. CAAA

Atanasoff, John Vincent (1903–). Computer pioneer. GRAB-3†

Ataturk, Mustafa Kemal (1881–1938). President of Turkish Republic. ARA; CAAA; HAK

Athanasia. Saint. DAD-3

Athanasius (4th century). Saint. DAD-2

Atkinson, Brooks (1894–1984). Drama critic. LEU

Attell, Abe (1884–1969). Boxer. SLA

Attila the Hun (406?–453). King of the Huns. BEO; BLW; CAAA; DEI; JOBB

Attles, Alvin (1936–). Basketball player, coach. ARB-2

Attucks, Crispus (1723?–1770). American Revolutionary patriot. ADA; ADB; BEJ; BRB; BRG; BUIB†; DAF-1; EMA; GRAB-02; HUB; JOC; LEI; PECA; ROG; STQ†; WIBA

Atwood, Genevieve (1946–). State legislator, state geologist. WIAA-02

Auden, Wystan Hugh (1907–1973). Poet, born England. BEA; BRBB; COP

Audrey (c. 630–679). Saint. DAD-2

Audubon, John James (1785–1851). Ornithologist, painter, born Haiti. BEA; BEC; BOK; CO-1; CORA; CUC; DEI; DEJ; FOH; HEB; HYB; LEAB; LEB; LOB; MAL; MIB; SIE; WAP

Auenbrugger, Leopold (1722–1809). Austrian physician. FAF; SHG

Auerbach, Red (Arnold) (1917–). Baseball coach. HEH; HID; LEW†; SLA

Augustine (354–430). Saint. DAD-3; LO; MOC; ONA; QUA

Augustine of Canterbury (d. 604). Saint. DAD-2

Augustus (63 B.C.–14 A.D.). Emperor of Rome. CAAA; COK; NEC

Aulaire, Edgar Parin d' (1898–). Author, illustrator, born Switzerland. SMAB

Aulaire, Ingri d' (1904–1980). Author, illustrator, born Norway. SMAB

Auld, Sophia (fl. 1825). Teacher of Frederick Douglass. STG

Austen, Jane (1775–1817). English author. BOH; COO; SMA; STK

Austin, Andy (Ann Collier) (1935–). Television artist. SMBB-2

Austin, Beth. Martial artist. AT

Austin, Moses (1761–1821). Pioneer. AKC; LYF; VIA

Austin, Stephen Fuller (1793–1836). Pioneer, colonizer of Texas. AKC; KUA; LYF; MAO; VIA

Austin, Tracy (1962–). Tennis player. AAS-23; AAS-29; FOR; GUED-1; HOCG

Autori, Franco. Conductor, born Italy. STM†

Autry, Gene (1907–). Actor, singer. LA

Aveling, Thomas (1824–1881). English inventor, engineer. LAE

Avellino, Andrew (1521–1608). Saint. DAD-3

Avery, John "Long Ben" (b. 1665). English pirate. LACB

Avicenna (980–1037). Arabian physician. CHD†; SHG†

Avogadro, Amedeo (1776–1856). Italian chemist, physicist. CAA; MOBA; SHFB

Avshalomov, Jacob (1919–). Conductor, born China. STM†

Awendes (fl. 1823). Seneca Indian boy. CAD

Ayub Khan, Mohammad (1907–1974). Ex-president of Pakistan. WEC

Azikiwe, Nnamdi (1904–). Governor-general of Nigeria. ADA

B

Baade, Walter (1893–1960). Astronomer, born Germany. SUE

Baal Shem Tov, see Israel ben Eliezer.

Babashoff, Shirley (1957–). Swimmer. GLA; JABA

Babbage, Charles (1792–1871). English mathematician. COLA; FE; FRE; GRAB-3; WEF

Babbitt, Milton (1916–). Composer. EWAA

Babcock, Stephen Moulton (1843–1931). Chemist. DEA

Babilee, Jean (1923–). French dancer. ATA

Babilonia, Tai (1960–). Skater. VAD-6

Baca, Elfego (1865–1945). Lawyer, sheriff. BENA

Bach, Carl Philipp Emanuel (1714–1788). German composer. KAE; SAA†; YOM†

Bach, Johann Christian (1735–1782). German composer, organist. CHF; SAA†; YOM†

Bach, Johann Sebastian (1685–1750). German composer, organist. BEN; BRF; BUD; DEI; DEJ; FIE; GOB; KAE; SAA; WIA; YOK; YOM†

Bach, Wilhelm Friedemann (1710–1784). German composer, organist. SAA†

Bache, Alexander Dallas (1806–1867). Physicist. SIA

Bache, Sarah (Sally) Franklin (1743–1808). Benjamin Franklin's daughter. WABC†

Bacher, Aron "Ali" (1942–). South African cricket player. SLA†

Backer, Steve. Jazz producer. UN

Backus, John W. (1924–). Computer pioneer. GRAB-3†

Bacon, Francis (1561–1626). English author, philosopher. BEG; LO; STI†

Bacon, Gertrude (1874–1949). Aviator. HIFD†

Bacon, Mary (1950?–). Jockey. HOBAA

Bacon, Roger (1214?–1294). English scientist, philosopher. MAQ

Bademus. Saint. DAD-2

Baden-Powell, Robert Stephenson Smyth, 1st baron (1857–1941). English soldier, founder of English Boy Scouts. EVA; SEB

Bader, Douglas (1911–1982). English aviator. HAMY

Badillo, Herman (1929–). Lawyer, government official. FOW; NEBB; WO

Baeck, Leo (1873–1956). German rabbi. GEF; GRB-1; GUB; KAB

Baekeland, Leo Hendrik (1863–1944). Chemist, inventor, born Belgium. FE; THA; YOE

Baeta, Henrietta Louise (1881–1971). Mother of Annie Jiagge. CRA

Baeyer, Adolf von (1835–1917). German chemist. LET

Baffin, William (1584–1622). English navigator. ROL†

Bagley, Sarah G. (fl. 1835–1847). Union leader. WABC

Bailey, Ann "Mad Ann" (1742–1825). Frontier heroine. CLC; DOD; STJ

Bailey, Bob (Robert Sherwood) (1942–). Baseball player. LEY†

Bailey, Mollie Arline (1841–1918). Circus owner. KIB

Bailey, William H. Conductor. STM†

Bailie, Ann Eckels. Mathematician. HOG

Bailie, Sally (1937–). Horse trainer, born England. GUJ

Baines, Harold (1959–). Baseball player. HEFB†

Baird, John Logie (1888–1946). Scottish inventor. EVC; FE; PRC; SHFB; THA

Bajazet or Bajazid, see Bayezid I.

Bajer, Frederik (1839–1922). Danish statesman. MEC†; WIC

Baker, Al "Bubba" (1956–). Football player. AAS-16

Baker, Augusta (1911–). Librarian. FLD

Baker, Buck (Elzie Wylie) (1919–). Automobile racer. LEX†; OLCA

Baker, Buddy (Elzie Wylie, Jr.) (1941–). Automobile racer. OLCA

Baker, Lady Florence von Sass (fl. 1863–1893). English explorer, born Hungary. RIG

Baker, Home Run (John Franklin) (1886?–1963). Baseball player. ALB; DAFD; LEY; RIGA†

Baker, Israel (1919–). Conductor. STM†

Baker, John. Manager, Buffalo Bill's Wild West Show. JOD

Baker, John. Soldier, WW I. BRB†

Baker, Josephine (1906–1975). Singer. ROF

Baker, Lafayette Curry (1826–1868). Spy. SUG

Baker, Mary "Caraboo" (c. 1826). English imposter. COKB

Baker, Matt. Cartoonist. GOB-1

Baker, Sir Samuel White (1821–1893). English explorer. LAA-1; ROL

Baker, Sara Josephine (1873–1945). Physician, reformer. PACB

Bakewell, Robert (1725–1795). English agriculturist. CAB

Balaban, Emanuel (1895–). Conductor. STM†

Balakireff, Mili Alekseyevich (1837–1910). Russian composer. POG; SAA†

Balanchine, George (1904–1983). Choreographer, born Russia. ASB-1; DU-1

Balazs, Frederic. Conductor, born Hungary. STM†

Balboa, Vasco Núñez de (1475–1517). Spanish explorer. COC; KNA; ROL

Balch, Emily Green (1867–1961). Economist, sociologist. MEC; SHFE†; WIC

Baldorioty de Castro, Román (1822–1889). Puerto Rican political leader. TU

Baldwin, Abraham (1754–1807). Senator. BUIB†; FEAA

Baldwin, Frank (1842–1923). Soldier. TA

Baldwin, James (1924–1987). Author. DADB; KE; LEGB; RICA

Baldwin, Maria L. (1856–1922). Educator. BRB

Bales, Richard (1915–). Conductor. STM†

Balewa, Sir Abubakar Tafawa (1912–1966). Prime minister of Nigeria. KEF

Ball, Albert (1897–1917). English aviator, WWI. HAMY

Ball, Ernest (1878–1927). Songwriter. MOA

Ball, Lucille (1911–). Comedienne. MASB

Ballard, Audreen. Journalist. STAA

Ballard, Ernesta Drinker (1920–). Horticulturist. GIB-1

Ballard, Kaye (1926–). Comedienne, singer. MASB

Ballard, Louis W. (1931–). Composer. GRAC

Ballinger, James S. (1925–). Conductor. STM†

Balsamo, Joseph (Cagliostro) (1743–c. 1800). Italian magician, charlatan. ED-5

Baltimore, Lords, see Calvert family members.

Balzac, Honoré de (1799–1850). French author. DEI; DEJ

Bam, Brigalia (1933–). South African social worker. CRA

Bamberger, Carl (1902–). Conductor, born Austria. STM†

Bamboschek, Giuseppe (1890–). Conductor, born Italy. STM†

Bancroft, Anne (1931–). Actress. DI-1†

Bancroft, George (1800–1891). Historian, diplomat. HIB

Banda (1900–1950). Indonesian spy. SUG

Bandaranaike, Sirimavo (1916–). Sri Lankan ex-prime minister. GI

Bando, Salvatore Leonard (1944–). Baseball player. CL-06; KLBB; LEY

Banfill, B. J. Australian nurse. WRA

Banks, Ernie (1931–). Baseball player. DA; DAFD; DRA; FRC-1†; RIGA†; SHB; VEA

Banks, Sir Joseph (1743–1820). English naturalist. BLB

Banneker, Benjamin (1731–1806). Mathematician. ADA; ADB; BEJ; BRB; BRG; DOB; EMA; GRAB-03; HA; HAM; HODA; JOC; KLA; PECA; ROG; STQ; WIAB; WIBA

Bannister, Edward M. (1833–1901). Painter, born Canada. ADA; ADB

Bannister, Roger Gilbert (1929–). English track athlete. AAS-26; ALBA; ASB-1; ASBA; DAFB; DAG; DAGA; DAJ; PRC

Banting, Sir Frederick Grant (1891–1941). Canadian physician. AAS-31; BEK; DOE; HUD; POB; RIF; ROA

Banuelos, Romana Acosta (1925–). Ex-treasurer of U.S. FOW

Bar Cochba, Simon (d. 135). Hebrew leader. LERA

Bar-Ilian, David (1930–). Israeli pianist. EWC

Barachisius. Saint. DAD-2†

Bárány, Robert (1876–1936). Austrian physician. LET

Barati, George (1913–). Conductor, born Hungary. STM†

Barbara (d. 235?). Saint. QUA

Barbatus (d. 682). Saint. DAD-2

Barber, Linda Elaine. FAA inspector. SMBC-2

Barber, Samuel (1910–1981). Composer. BAD; KAE; MAF; POF

Barbirolli, John (1899–1970). English conductor. STM†; YOM

Barbosa, José Celso (1857–1921). Puerto Rican political leader. STC; TU

Barbour, Thomas (1884–1946). Naturalist. MIB

Barcelo, Gertrudis (La Doña Tules) (d. 1852). Frontierswoman. RAB; WIAA-2

Bard, Samuel (1742–1821). Physician. MAR

Bardeen, John (1908–). Physicist. AAS-33†; GRAB-3; MAPA

Barenboim, Daniel (1942–). Israeli pianist. EWC

Barents, Willem (d. 1597). Dutch explorer. DOC; KNB; MOB; ROL†

Barera, Orlando (1907–). Conductor, born Italy. STM†

Barker, Penelope (fl. 1774). American Revolutionary patriot. CLC

Barker, Sarah (b. 1803). Colonial girl. CAD

Barker, William George (d. 1930). Canadian aviator, WW I. HAG

Barkley, Alben William (1877–1956). Vice president of U.S. FEA; HAOA; HOEA

Barkley, Doug (Norman Douglas) (1937–). Canadian hockey player, coach. FICB

Barks, Carl (1901–). Cartoonist. GOB-1

Barlass, Kate (15th century). Scottish heroine. MAJ

Barlow, Howard (1892–1972). Conductor. STM†

Barlow, Joel (1754–1812). Poet, diplomat. DOG

Barna, Gyozo Victor (1911–1972). English table tennis player, born Hungary. SLA

Barnabas (1st century). Saint. DAD-2

Barnard, Christiaan N. (1922–). South African surgeon. DEJ; DU-1; FE

Barnard, Henry (1811–1900). Educator. FRC†

Barnard, Kate (1875–1930). Journalist, social reformer. PACB; TRD; VIA

Barnardo, Thomas John (1845–1905). Irish physician, social reformer. EVA

Barnett, Claude Albert (1889–1967). Journalist. ADB

Barnett, Ida Wells (1862–1931). Journalist, reformer. ADB; BRBE†; BUFA; HUB; LOAV; PACB; PECA; ROG; STAB-1; TRD

Barnett, John M. (1917–). Conductor. STM†

Barney, Joshua (1759–1818). Naval officer. BUIB†; MAE

Barney, Lemuel J. Football player. FRD; ST

Barney, Rex (1924–). Baseball player. NEA

Barnum, Phineas Taylor (1810–1891). Circus showman. DEI; DEJ; KIB; KLD

Barone, Joseph (1910–). Conductor. STM†

Barrie, Sir James M. (1860–1937). Scottish author, playwright. COB

Barringer, Emily Dunning (1876–1961). Physician. FLA; MASA

Barron, Gayle (1945–). Track athlete. HIA-01

Barron, Herman (1909–1976). Golfer. SLA

Barron, Robert Louis (1897–). Conductor. STM†

Barrow, Ed (1868–1953). Baseball business manager. ALB

Barry, Dan (1923–). Cartoonist. GOB-1

Barry, James, pseud. (1795–1865). English army physician. MASA

Barry, John (1745–1803). Naval officer, born Ireland. RAD

Barry, Rick (1944–). Basketball player. ARB-3; DEHA-1; FRD; HOCA; RAAB; SA-1; SA-2

Barrymore, Ethel (1879–1959). Actress. DI-1; GIBA†; STLA

Barsimson, Jacob (fl. 1654). Colonial settler. LETA†

Bart, Jean (1651–1702). French privateer. KEH

Barth, Belle (1911–1971). Comedienne. MASB

Barth, George W. (1907). Conductor. STM†

Barthé, Richmond (1901–). Sculptor. ADA; ADB; BRB†; RIC; RICA

Bartholdi, Frédéric Auguste (1834–1904). French sculptor. DIA

Bartholomea (1807–1833). Saint. DAD-1

Bartholomew. Saint, apostle. DAD-3

Bartholomew (d. 1193). Saint. TUA

Bartlett, Josiah (1729–1795). American Revolu

tionary patriot, physician. BAEA; BUIB†; COJ†; FEAB; MAC

Bartlett, Robert Abram (1875–1946). Arctic explorer. DOC†

Bartók, Béla (1881–1945). Hungarian composer. ASB-1; BEKA; BUC; FIE†; KAE; SAA; YOL

Bartolomey the Portuguese. Buccaneer. LACB

Barton, Clara (1821–1912). Nurse, founder of American Red Cross. BEC; BOC; CUC; DED; DEI; DEJ; DOD; FOH; GIBA; JOCA; LEK; LEPC; MAK; MAT; PA; SMC; STJ; STLA; WABC†

Bartram, John (1699–1777). Botanist. CO-1; JEA

Bartram, William (1739–1823). Naturalist. BLB; CO-1; JEA

Bartz, Jennifer (1955–). Swimmer. RYX

Baruch, Bernard M. (1870–1965). Financier, statesman. GRB-1; LETA

Barzin, Leon (1900–). Conductor, born Belgium. STM†

Bascom, Willard (1917–). Mining and ocean engineer. COR

Basie, Count (William) (1904–1984). Band leader. TEA; TEB; WAD†

Basil III Ivanovich (1479–1533). Grand duke of Moscow. RIA

Basil the Great (329–379). Saint. DAD-2

Basilissa. Saint. DAD-2†

Bason, Caesar. American Revolutionary patriot. WIBA

Bass, Dick (Richard Lee) (1937–). Football player. BEKB; LEZB

Bass, George (1763–1812). English explorer. KNB†; ROL†

Bass, George F. (1932–). Underwater archaeologist. POC

Bass, Sam (1851–1878). Outlaw. JOBA; REE; SUJ

Bassett, Ebenezer D. (1833–1908). Diplomat. ADA; ADB

Bassett, Richard (1745–1815). Senator. BUIB†; FEAA

Bastian, Adolf (1826–1905). German ethnologist. HAO

Bastie, Maryse. French aviator. HIFD

Bates, Abigail (fl. 1814). Heroine, War of 1812. CLC

Bates, Ann (fl. 1778). Spy. AND

Bates, Daisy Gaston (1922–). Civil rights leader. AKB; DOF-1; GRAB-01; STF

Bates, Katherine Lee (1859–1929). Poet. CAGA

Bates, Laverne (1934–). Martial artist. AT

Bates, Mercedes (1915–). Food industry executive. FRBD

Bates, Rebecca (fl. 1814). Heroine, War of 1812. CLC

Bathgate, Andy (Andrew James) (1932–). Canadian hockey player. ORC

Bathildis (d. 680). Saint, queen of France. DAD-2

Batista, Fulgencio (1901–1973). President of Cuba. ARA

Batlle y Ordóñez, José (1865–1929). President of Uruguay. WOB

Batten, Jean (1909–1982). New Zealand aviator. HIFD; MO

Battles, Cliff (d. 1981). Football player, coach. DAFG; SUD

Bauer, Georg, see Agricola, Georgius.

Bauer, Hank (Henry Albert) (1922–). Baseball player, manager. GIB

Bauer, Henry (1895–). Banker. PAA

Bauer, Leroy. Conductor. STM†

Baugh, Laura Z. (1955–). Golfer. HOBAA

Baugh, Sammy (Samuel Adrian) (1914–). Football player, coach. ANC; ASBA; DAB; DAFB; DAFG; DAG; DAGA; DAI; DEH; DUD; DUE; HEI; HOC; RAAD; SUC; SUD

Baughan, Maxie. Football player. KABA

Baum, Lyman Frank (1856–1919). Author. BEI

Baumgartner, Leona (1902–). Physician. FLA

Bayes, Nora (1880–1928). Singer, comedienne. MASB

Bayezid I (1347–1403). Sultan of Ottoman Empire. BEO

Bayi, Filbert (1954–). Tanzanian track athlete. AAS-26; LEYB†

Baylor, Ed (Elgin) (1935?–). Basketball player. BEL; HEHA; HID; PE; RAAB

Bazna, Elyesa (1904–). Turkish spy. HAB

Beach, Mrs. H. H. A. (Amy Marcy Cheney) (1867–1944). Composer. SC-02†

Beach, Sylvia (fl. 1919). Bookstore owner. WABC†

Beachey, Lincoln (1887–1915). Aviator. HAMY

Beadle, George Wells (1903–). Geneticist. RIF

Beamon, Bob (1946?–). Track athlete. OCA

Bean, "Judge" Roy (1825–1904). Frontier justice of the peace. SUI

Beard, Andrew J. Inventor. GRAB-03; STQ†

Beard, Charles Austin (1874–1948). Historian. HIB

Beard, Frank (1939–). Golfer. BELB

Bearden, Gene (Henry) (1920–). Baseball player. BUJA

Bearden, Romare (1914–1988). Painter. FAH

Beasely, Julie. Psychologist. HOG†

Beaton, Cecil W. (1904–1980). Photographer, born England. FOD

Beatty, Clyde (1905–1965). Animal trainer. KIB

Beatty, David, 1st earl (1871–1936). British admiral. ARD

Beauchamp, Bobby. Skater. VAD-6

Beaumont, William (1785–1853). Surgeon. BLC; ED

Beaux, Cecilia (1863–1942). Painter. NE

Bechet, Sidney (1897–1959). Saxophonist. WAD†

Beck, Charles Clarence (1910–). Cartoonist. GOB-1

Beck, Gary. Automobile racer. OLDA

Beck, Trudy (1960?–). Motorcyclist. BUIC

Beckenbauer, Franz (1945–). German soccer player. ADL

Beckert, Glenn Alfred (1940–). Baseball player. KLB

Becket, Thomas à, see Thomas à Becket.

Beckh, Herbert. Red Cross delegate. DED

Beckwith, Henry. Cowboy. STQ

Beckwourth, James P. (1798–1866). Frontiersman. ADB; BUH; GRAB-02; HAP; HUB; JO; KADB; LEI; PECA; ROG; SCB; STQ; WIBA

Becquerel, Antoine Henri (1852–1908). French physicist. ASA; FE; MOBA; SHFB; SOB

Bede the Venerable (672–735). Saint. DAD-2

Bedell, Grace (b. 1849). CAD

Bedford, Gunning (1747–1812). Judge. BUIB†; FEAA

Bednarik, Chuck (Charles Phillip) (1925–). Football player. ANA; DAFG; DAI; SUD

Beebe, William (1877–1962). Naturalist. BAB; COKA; COLA; COR; MIB†

Beech, Olive Ann (1903–). Aviation executive. LES-1; PAA

Beecham, Sir Thomas (1879–1961). English conductor. EWB; STM†; YOM

Beecher, Catharine Esther (1800–1878). Educator. BUDA†; FRC; WABC

Beecher, Lyman (1775–1863). Clergyman. COGA

Beernaert, Auguste Marie François (1829–1912). Belgian statesman. MEC†; WIC

Beethoven, Ludwig van (1770–1827). German composer. BEN; BRF; BUD; DEI; DEJ; FIE; FRE; GOB; KAE; MAJ; SAA; WIA; YOK; YOM†

Beeton, Isabella Mary (1836–1865). Author. BOH

Begin, Menachem (1913–). Israeli ex-prime minister, born Poland. ASB-1; GRB-1; HAGD

Behaim, Martin (1459?–1507). German geographer. VIA

Behr, Jan (1911–). Conductor, born Czechoslovakia. STM†

Behring, Emil von (1854–1917). German bacteriologist. AAS-31; BEK†; DEB; RIE; RIF; ROA

Beiderbecke, Bix (Leon Bismarck) (1903–1931). Cornetist. COF-1; TEA; TEB; WAD†

Beijerinck, Martinus Willem (1851–1931). Dutch botanist. SUF

Beinum, Eduard van (1901–1959). Dutch conductor. STM; YOM†

Belafonte, Harry (1927–). Singer. LOB; ROF

Belasco, David (1854–1931). Playwright, theater producer. LETA

Belfield, Wendell. Veterinarian. CAF-1

Belgrano, Manuel (1770–1820). Argentine general. LAB

Beliveau, Jean (1931–). Canadian hockey player. FICA; FR; LIAB; OBA; OBB; ORC; RAAF

Bell, Alexander Graham (1847–1922). Inventor, born Scotland. ASB-1; BEA; COL; CUC; DEI; DEJ; DOE; EBA; EVC; FAB; FE; FRE; HYA; LEAB; LEB; MAL; MAT; SHFB; SIA; THA

Bell, Bert (de Benneville) (1895–1959). Football commissioner. DAB; SUD

Bell, Buddy (David Gus) (1951–). Baseball player. KLBB

Bell, Caroline D. (1928–). English refugee, WW II. CAHA

Bell, Sir Charles (1774–1842). Scottish surgeon. RIB

Bell, Edward A. (1930–). English refugee, WW II. CAHA

Bell, Marion Shaw (1786–1876). Wife of Dr. Charles Bell. RIB

Bell, Tom, pseud. (d. 1856). Outlaw. WIAA-1

Bellamy, Charles (fl. 1726). Pirate. WHA†

Bellamy, Walt (1939–). Basketball player. HOCA

Bellarmine, Robert (1542–1621). Saint. DAD-2; QUA

Bellingshausen, Fabian von (1778–1852). Russian explorer. DOC†; MOB; ROL†

Bello, Andrés (1781–1865). Chilean statesman, born Venezuela. WOB

Belloc, Hilaire (1870–1953). English author. BEH

Bellows, Carole Kamin (1935–). Lawyer. SWI

Bellows, George Wesley (1882–1925). Painter. MAG; SIE

Belmont, Joe. Basketball coach. LEW

Belote, Melissa (1956–). Swimmer. RYA; ST-2

Beloved Woman, see Ward, Nancy.

Beltoise, Jean-Pierre (1937–). French automobile racer. JA

Belyayev, Pavel (1925–1970). Russian astronaut. THC

Beman, Nathan (b. 1766). Colonial boy. CAD

Bemelmans, Ludwig (1898–1962). Author, illustrator, born Austria. SM

Ben Eliezer, Israel, see Israel ben Eliezer.

Ben-Gurion, David (1886–1973). Israeli prime minister. GRB-1; GUB; KE; KEF; ROGA; WEA

Ben-Porat, Miriam (1918–). Israeli Supreme Court justice, born Lithuania. GRB-1

Ben Yehudah, Eliezer (1858–1922). Lithuanian Hebraist. GRB-1; GUB; PEB; ROGA

Ben-Zvi, Yitzhak (1884–1963). President of Israel, born Russia. GRB-1

Bench, Johnny Lee (1947–). Baseball player. BELB; FRD; GUDA; GUE; GUG; HOCM; KLCA; MUB-1; RIGA†; SHH; TUB

Benchley, Robert (1889–1945). Humorist. BEE

Bender, Chief (Charles Albert) (1883–1954). Baseball player. ALB; DAFD; HACA

Benedict (480–543). Saint. CHD†; DAD-1; DAD-2; ONA

Benedict the Moor (1526–1589). Saint. DAD-1; DAD-2

Benét, Rosemary Carr (1898–1962). Poet. BEH

Benét, Stephen Vincent (1898–1943). Author, poet. BEF; BEH; BOA; BRBB; SIF

Benét, William Rose (1886–1950). Poet, editor. BEF

Bénézet (1165–1184). Saint. ONA

Bengston, Phil (1913?–). Football coach. JOA†

Benirschke, Rolf (1955–). Football player. AAS-17

Benítez, Jaime (1908–). Educator. NEBB

Benjamin of Tudela (d. 1173). Spanish traveler. LES

Benjamin, Bennie (1907–). Songwriter. HUC

Benjamin, Judah Philip (1811–1884). Senator. LETA

Bennett, Hugh Hammond (1881–1960). Agricultural chemist. MAL

Bennett, Lerone, Jr. (1928–). Author, editor. STAA†

Bennett, Robert LaFollette (1912–). Lawyer. GRAC

Benny, Jack (1894–1974). Comedian. ALC

Bent, William (1809–1869). Pioneer trader. FOC

Benton, Thomas Hart (1782–1858). Senator, congressman. KEC; KED

Benz, Karl (1844–1929). German engineer, automobile manufacturer. FAB; FE

Berens, Fritz (1907–). Conductor, born Austria. STM†

Berenson, Gordon (1941?–). Hockey player. FICA

Berg, Alban (1885–1935). Austrian composer. KAE

Berg, Gertrude (1899–1966). Actress, playwright. MASB

Berg, Moe (Morris) (1902–1972). Baseball player, spy. BELB; RI; SLA†

Berg, Patty (Patricia Jane) (1918?–). Golfer. HOBA; HOBAA

Berg, Sharon (1955–). Swimmer. RYX

Bergeman, Gerald (1940?–). Winner, Young American Medal for Bravery. ANCA

Berger, Isaac (Ike) (1936–). Weightlifter, born Israel. SLA

Berger, Karl (1935–). Vibraphonist, born Germany. UN

Berger, Meyer (1898–1959). Journalist. LEU

Bergey, Bill L. (1945–). Football player. RUA; SMJ

Bergmann, Carl (1821–1876). Conductor, born Germany. YOM

Bergmann, Gretel (Margarethe) (1914–). Track athlete, born Germany. SLA

Bergmann, Richard (1919–1970). Table tennis player. SLA†

Bergson, Henri (1859–1941). French philosopher. LET

Bering, Vitus J. (1680–1741). Danish explorer. KNB; ROL

Berkowitz, Mickey (1954–). Israeli basketball player. SLA†

Berle, Milton (1908–). Comedian. ALC

Berlenbach, Paul. Boxer. PIB; PIBA

Berlin, Irving (1888–). Composer, born Russia. ASB-1; BAD; EWA; LEHB; LETA; LIA; MOA

Berliner, Emile (1851–1929). Inventor, born Germany. HYA; LETA

Berlioz, Hector (1803–1869). French composer. BRF; FIE; KAE; SAA; YOM†

Berman, Harry. Conductor, born Russia. STM†

Berman, Sara Mae. Track athlete. HOBAA†

Bernadette of Lourdes (1844–1879). Saint. DAD-1; DAD-2

Bernard of Clairvaux (1090–1153). Saint. DAD-3; QUA

Bernard of Menthon (996?–1081?). Saint. MOC; ONA

Bernardine of Siena (1380–1444). Saint. DAD-1; DAD-2

Bernhard, Sandra (1955–). Actress. MASB

Bernhardt, Sarah (1844–1923). French actress. MAT-1; PA

Bernstein, Carl (1944–). Journalist. LETB

Bernstein, Leonard (1918–). Composer, conductor. EWA; EWD; KAE; LEHB; LETA; MAF; POF; SAA†; STM; YOM†

Berra, Yogi (Lawrence Peter) (1925–). Baseball player, manager. BOE; DA; DAA; DAFB; DAFC; DAFD; DAH; FRC-1†; GIB; GUDA; HIC; HOCM; RIGA†; ROB; SHD; SHF; VEA; ZAA

Berrigan, Daniel (1921–). Priest, pacifist. LEZC

Berrigan, Philip (1923–). Priest, pacifist. LEZC

Berry, Charles A. (1923–). Physician. POE

Berry, Leonidas Harris. Physician. CAF-1

Berry, Martha McChesney (1866–1942). Educator. BUDA; FLB; FOG; LEJA; MAO

Berry, Raymond (1933–). Football player. CO; DAFG; DEHA; HAE

Bertha (d. 725). Saint. DAD-3; QUA

Bertillon, Alphonse (1853–1914). French criminologist. FE; LACA; LID

Bertrand, Louis (1526–1581). Saint. DAD-3

Beruria (2d century). Wife of Rabbi Meir of Palestine. LER

Berzelius, Jöns Jakob, baron (1779–1848). Swedish chemist. MOBA; SHFB

Beshar, Christine (1929–). Lawyer, born Germany. SMBB

Besse, Martial. American Revolutionary soldier. DAF-1†

Bessel, Friedrich Wilhelm (1784–1846). German astronomer. SUE

Bessemer, Sir Henry (1813–1898). English engineer, inventor. ASA; EBA; FAB; FE; LAE; THA

Best, Charles H. (1899–1978). Canadian physiologist. BEK†; RIF†

Betances y Alarcón, Ramón Emeterio (1827–1898). Puerto Rican physician. TU; WO

Bethune, Mary McLeod (1875–1955). Educator. ADA; ADB; BRB; BUDA; CAGA; DOF-1; FLB; FLD; GEE; GIBA; JOC; KOA; LEJA; LOAV; NAB; PECA; RIC; RICA; ROG; STLA; STO; WABC†; WIAA-8; YOI

Bethune, Thomas Green (1849–1908). Pianist. ROF†

Bettenhausen, Gary (1941?–). Automobile racer. OLCA

Bettenhausen, Merle. Automobile racer. OLCA

Bettenhausen, Tony (Melvin Eugene) (1916–1961). Automobile racer. LEX; OLCA

Bettenhausen, Tony Lee. Automobile racer. OLCA†

Bettignies, Louise de (1888?–1918). French spy. SEB; SUG

Bevens, Bill (Floyd C.) (1917–). Baseball player. BED; BOE

Beveridge, Albert Jeremiah (1862–1927). Senator. KEC†

Bhave, Vinoba (1895–1982). Indian mystic, reformer. BAF; RODA

Bialik, Chaim Nachman (1873–1934). Russian Hebrew poet. GEF; GRB-1; GUB; KAD; PEB

Bibb, Henry (1815–1854). Abolitionist. GRAB-05

Bibb, William Wyatt (1781–1820). Senator, congressman. SEC

Bibiana. Saint. DAD-3

Bibo, Franz. Conductor, educator, born Germany. STM†

Bichier Des Agnes, Jeanne Elisabeth. Saint. DAD-3

Bickerdyke, Mary Ann Ball (1817–1901). Nurse. MAK; WABC†; WRA

Bidwill, Charles E. (1895?–1947). Football team owner. SUD

Bierstadt, Albert (1830–1902). Painter, born Germany. HEDA

Big Eyes (fl. 1535). Wichita Indian woman. WAB

Biggers, John (1924–). Painter. FAH

Bigler, Steve. Surf rider. OLD

Bikila, Abebe (1932–1973). Ethiopian track athlete. AAS-30; DAJ; HIA-01†; LEYB

Biletnikoff, Frederick. Football player. DEHA; SMI

Bill, Buffalo, see Cody, William Frederick.

Billiart, Marie Rose, Blessed (1751–1816). DAD-2

Billick, George (1910–). Bowler. ALBA

Billings, John Shaw (1838–1913). Physician, librarian. ED

Billings, William (1746–1800). Composer. YOJ

Billy the Kid (1859–1881). Outlaw. JOBA; REE; SUJ

Bing, Dave (1943–). Basketball player. ARB-4; BEL; PAW

Binga, Jesse (1865–1950). Banker. ADA; ADB

Bingaman, Les (1926–). Football player. AAS-32

Bingay, Roberta Gibb. Track athlete. HOBAA†

Bingham, George Caleb (1811–1879). Painter. FRA; HEDA; LEE; SIE

Binkley, Lee. Canadian hockey player. FICB

Bird, Isabella Lucy (1831–1904). English traveler. JOB; RIG

Bird, Larry (1956–). Basketball player. AAS-8

Birdseye, Clarence (1886–1956). Inventor, food executive. LAG

Birdsong, Otis (1955–). Basketball player. AAS-8

Biro, Charles (1911–1972). Cartoonist. GOB-1

Biscoe, John (1794–1843). British sailor. ROL†

Bishop, Claire Huchet. Author, born France. SMB

Bishop, Isabella Lucy Bird, see Bird, Isabella Lucy.

Bishop, William Avery (1894–1956). Canadian aviator, WW I. HAG; HAMY

Bismarck, Otto von (1815–1898). German statesman. CAE

Bitter, John. Conductor. STM†

Bizet, Georges (1838–1875). French composer. BAE; KAE; SAA

Bjarni, see Herjolfsson, Bjarni.

Bjerknes, Vilhelm (1862–1951). Norwegian physicist. FE

Bjorklund, Garry (1951–). Track athlete. HIA-01

Bjurstedt, Molla (1892?–1959). Tennis player, born Norway. HOBAA

Black, Joe (1924–). Baseball player. BOE; SHE

Black, Joseph (1728–1799). Scottish chemist. BUF

Black, Norman. Conductor. STM†

Black, Winifred (1863–1936). Journalist. JAE

Black Bart (fl. 1875). Outlaw. JOBA; REE; SUJ; WIAA-1

Black Hawk (1767–1838). Sac and Fox Indian chief. DEDB; HEC; MOD; STAB; WAL

Black Jack, see Ketchum, Thomas Edward.

Black Mary, *see* Fields, Mary.

Black Patti, *see* Jones, Sisseretta.

Black Swan, The, *see* Greenfield, Elizabeth Taylor.

Blackbeard (d. 1718). English pirate. LACB; PABB; SC-1; WHA

Blackbourn, Liz (Lisle W.). Football coach. JOA†

Blackmore, Richard Doddridge (1825–1900). English author. COO†

Blackstone, Harry (1885–1965). Magician. KEB

Blackton, Jay (1909–). Conductor. STM†

Blackwell, Antoinette Brown, *see* Brown, Antoinette Blackwell.

Blackwell, Elizabeth (1821–1910). Physician, born England. BOC; BUA; CHD; COG; CUC; DOD; GEE; GIBA; HUE; JOCA; LOB; MASA; RAAG†; SC†; SMC; TRD; WABC; YOC

Blackwell, Ewell (1922–). Baseball player. NEA

Blackwell, Lucy Stone, *see* Stone, Lucy.

Blaik, Earl Henry (1892–). Army football coach. RAE

Blaine, James Gillespie (1830–1893). Statesman. HEEA; WHD†

Blair, Henry (fl. 1834). Inventor. HAL†

Blair, John (1732–1800). Supreme Court justice. BUIB†; FEAA

Blair, Matt (1950–). Football player. AAS-15

Blair, Wren. Hockey coach. LEW

Blaise (d. 316). Saint. DAD-2; PEE; WIB

Blake, Florence G. (1907–). Nurse. YOB

Blake, Ran (1935–). Composer, pianist. UN

Blake, Toe (Hector) (1912–). Canadian hockey coach. LEW; ORC

Blake, William (1757–1827). English poet, illustrator, engraver. BEH; COP

Blalock, Alfred (1899–1964). Surgeon. CHE

Blanchard, Doc (Felix) (1924–). Football player. DAFB; DAFG; DAI; DEHB; HIE; HOC

Blanchard, Sophie (d. 1817). Balloonist. HIFD†

Blanchard, Theresa Weld, *see* Weld, Theresa.

Bland, James A. (1854–1911). Composer. ADA; ADB; HUC; LEHB; MOA

Blanda, George (1927–). Football player. AAS-17; DAFG; GUD; LIBA; LIBB

Blankers-Koen, Fanny (Francina) (1918–). Dutch track athlete. DAJ; HOBAA

Blatch, Harriot Stanton (1856–1940). Feminist. LES-2; WABC†

Blavatsky, Elena Petrovna (1831–1891). Russian theosophist. COEA; MAT-1

Blazejowski, Carol (1956–). Basketball player. GUED-1

Blegvad, Erik (1923–). Danish illustrator. SMAB

Blegvad, Lenore (1926–). Author. SMAB

Bleier, Rocky (1946–). Football player. AAS-27

Blériot, Louis (1872–1936). French aviator. BRBA; COC†; EDA; KEH

Bley, Carla (1939–). Composer. SC-02†

Bligh, William (1754–1817). English naval officer. SCBA

Bloch, Alexander (1881–). Conductor. STM†

Bloch, Ernest (1880–1959). Composer, born Switzerland. GRB-1; KAE

Bloch, Felix (1905–1983). Physicist, born Switzerland. LET

Block, Herbert Lawrence (1909–). Cartoonist. DEDC

Blomberg, Ron (1948–). Baseball player. SLA

Blood, Johnny, sobriquet (1903–1985). Football player. DAB; DAFG; DAI; JOA†; SUD

Bloomer, Amelia Jenks (1818–1894). Social reformer. ARB; DEDA; GUBA; LES-2

Bloomfield, Theodore (1923–). Conductor. STM†

Blount, Mel (1948–). Football player. AAS-13

Blount, Mildred E. Hat designer. BOG

Blount, William (1749–1800). Congressman, senator. BUIB†; FEAA; MAO

Blow, Susan Elizabeth (1843–1916). Educator. BUDA†

B. L. T., *see* Taylor, Bert Leston.

Blue, Vida (1949–). Baseball player. AAS-2; BUJB; FRD; GUG

Blue Spruce, George (1931–). Dentist. GRAC

Blum, Léon (1872–1950). French statesman. ARAA

Blum, Walter (1934–). Jockey. SLA†

Blumberg, Judy. Skater. VAD-6

Blume, Judy (1938–). Author. GL-1

Blumenthal, David (1917–). Conductor. STM†

Blunt, Roger R. (1930–). Army officer. RAE

Bly, Nellie, pseud., *see* Cochrane, Elizabeth.

Blyleven, Bert (1951–). Baseball player, born the Netherlands. HEFB†

Blyth, Chay (fl. 1966). English adventurer. OLC

Blythe, Jarrett (1886–). Cherokee Indian leader. GRAC

Boadicea, *see* Boudicca.

Bobola, Andrew (1591–1657). Saint. DAD-2

Boccherini, Luigi (1743–1805). Italian composer. KAE

Boccioni, Umberto (1882–1916). Italian painter. WIAA

Bock, Jerry (1928–). Composer. EWA

Bodian, David (1910–). Anatomist. CHE†

Bodmer, Karl (1809–1893). Swiss painter. HEDA; HOD

Boggs, Wade (1958–). Baseball player. HEFB†

Böhm, Karl (1894–1981). Austrian conductor. STM†

Bohr, Niels H. D. (1885–1962). Danish physicist. CAA; COLA; FE; LET; MOBA; RID; SIA

Boivin, Leo (1932–). Canadian hockey player. OBA

Bok, Edward William (1863–1930). Author, editor, born the Netherlands. BOD; CAGA; CUC; FLBA; LOB

Boles, Charles E., *see* Black Bart.

Boleyn, Anne (1507–1536). Second wife of Henry VIII, king of England. MAOA; VAC

Bolívar, Simón (1783–1830). South American statesman. BAA; BACA; CAE; LAB; LAD; OLA; STP; WO; YOFA

Bolland, Adrienne. French aviator. HIFD†

Bombard, Alain Louis (1924?–). French physician and adventurer. ELA; HAQ

Bombeck, Erma (1927–). Author. GL-1

Bomhard, Moritz (1912–). Conductor, born Germany. STM†

Bonaparte, Napoléon, *see* Napoleon I.

Bonaventure (1217–1274). Saint. DAD-3

Bond, Carrie Jacobs, *see* Jacobs-Bond, Carrie.

Bond, George F. (1915–). Physician. BRBC; COR

Bond, Julian (1940–). State legislator, civil rights leader. BRGA; DU

Bonds, Bobby Lee (1946–). Baseball player. KLCA

Bonga, George (b. 1802). Fur trader. KADB; WIBA

Bonheur, Rosa (1822–1899). French painter. BOC

Boniface (672–754). Saint. DAD-2

Boniface of Tarsus. Saint. DAD-2

Bonifácio, José (1763–1838). Brazilian statesman. LAB; WOB

Bonnet, Stede (d. 1718). English pirate. WHA

Bonney, Maurice (1923–). Conductor. STM†

Bonnin, Gertrude Simmons (1875–1936?). Sioux Indian educator. GRAD

Bonny, Anne (1700–1720). English pirate. PABB; SC-1; WHA†

Bontemps, Arna (1902–1973). Author. ADB; ROE

Boone, Daniel (1734–1820). Frontiersman. BUB; COE; CUC; DEI; DEJ; EVD; FIA; FOC; HEB; LED; LEPD; MAO; MAT; VIA; WAN

Boone, Jemima (b. 1762). Indian captive. CAD

Boosler, Elayne (1953–). Comedienne. MASB

Booth, Albie (1908–). Football player. FOI; HIE

Booth, Edwin Thomas (1833–1893). Actor. SHFA

Booth, Evangeline Cory (1865–1950). English Salvation Army commander. STP

Booth, Hubert Cecil (1871–1955). English inventor. LAE

Booth, John Wilkes (1838–1865). Actor. RABA; SHFA

Booth, Junius Brutus (1796–1852). Actor, born England. SHFA

Booth, William (1829–1912). English religious leader, founder Salvation Army. EVA

Borden, Gail (1801–1874). Inventor. FAB; MAL

Bordet, Jules (1870–1961). Belgian bacteriologist. RIF

Borg, Björn (1956–). Swedish tennis player. AAS-28; FOX; GLC

Borgen, Chris (1933?–). Television newscaster. STAA

Borgenicht, Louis (fl. 1889). Businessman. LETA

Borges, Jorge Luis (1899–1986). Argentine author. WO

Borgia, Francis (1510–1572). Saint. DAD-3

Boris. Saint. DAD-3

Boris, Ruthanna (1918–). Dancer, choreographer. ATA

Borlaug, Norman Ernest (1914–). Microbiologist. MEC

Borman, Frank (1928–). Astronaut. LEPB; RAE; THC

Born, Max (1882–1970). German physicist. LET

Borodin, Alexander P. (1833–1887). Russian composer. BAE; KAE; POG; SAA

Borotra, Jean (1898?–). French tennis player. FOX†

Borromeo, Charles (1538–1584). Saint. DAD-3; QUA

Bosco, John (1815–1888). Saint. DAD-1; DAD-2

Bosomworth, Mary Musgrove Matthews (1700–1762?). Creek Indian princess. GRAD

Bossy, Mike (1957–). Canadian hockey player. AAS-22; OLDE

Bostock, Lyman (1950–1978). Baseball player. AAS-24

Boston, Ralph (1939–). Track athlete. DAJ

Botticelli, Sandro (1444?–1510). Italian painter. JAA; KAA; MAI

Bottomley, Jim (1900–). Baseball player. DEG†; FRC-1†

Botvid (d. 1120). Saint. DAD-3

Botvinnik, Mikhail M. (1911–). Russian chess player. LEQB

Boucher, François (1703–1770). French painter. MAH†

Boucher, Helene (1908–1934). French aviator. HIFD

Boudicca (d. 62 A.D.). Queen of the Iceni. BOI; CAAA; TRBA

Boudreau, Lou (1917–). Baseball player. VEA

Boulez, Pierre (1925–). French composer, conductor. EWAA

Boult, Adrian (1889?–1983). English conductor. STM†; YOM†

Bourgeois, Léon Victor Auguste (1851–1925). French statesman. MEC†; WIC

Bourgeois, Louyse (1563–1636). French midwife. MASA

Bourguiba, Habib ben Ali (1904–). President of Tunisia. KEF

Bourke-White, Margaret (1904–1971). Photographer. FAA; FOE; GEE; GIBA; HOE; ROJ; SQB; SUAA

Bousfield, Maudelle Brown (fl. 1906). Educator. BRB

Boussingault, Jean Baptiste (1802–1887). French agricultural chemist. CAB

Boutnikoff, Ivan (1893–). Russian conductor. STM†

Bouton, James Alan (1939–). Baseball player, sportscaster. HOBB

Bovet, Daniele (1907–). Italian pharmacologist, born Switzerland. RIF

Bowditch, Nathaniel (1773–1838). Astronomer, mathematician. MAL

Bowen, J. W. E. (1855–1933). Clergyman. BRB†

Bower, Johnny (1924?–). Canadian hockey player. ORA

Bowers, Eilley Orrum (fl. 1858). Mine owner, born Scotland. WIAA-2

Bowie, David (1947–). English singer, actor. BUIB-2

Bowie, James (1799–1836). Soldier. AKC; HEB; KUA; LYF; VIA

Bowie, Walter (1837?–1864). Spy. FOA

Bowles, Michael (1909–). Irish conductor. STM†

Bowser, Mary Elizabeth (fl. 1861–1865). Spy. LOAV

Boyd, Belle (1844–1900). Spy. FOA; MAO; SEB; SUG; WABC†

Boyd, Louise Arner (1887–1972). Arctic explorer. RIG

Boyd, Oil Can (Dennis) (1959–). Baseball player. GUB-1

Boyer, Clete (Cletis LeRoy) (1937–). Baseball player. KLB

Boyer, Ken (1931–1982). Baseball player. DEG; KLB; LEY†; VEA

Boyington, Pappy (Gregory) (1913–1988). Aviator. HAMY

Boyle, Robert (1627–1691). English physicist, chemist. CAA; FE; MOBA; SIA

Brabham, Jack (1926–). Australian automobile racer. ABB; JA; YAA

Brace, Charles Loring (1826–1890). Social worker. COG

Bradbury, Ray (1920–). Author. DU-1

Braden, Anne (1924–). Civil rights worker. STG

Bradford, Alex (1926?–1978). Singer, composer. AB

Bradford, William (1590–1657). Pilgrim father. DAC; DIA; MAT; OLA; VIA

Bradley, Bill. Football player. GUCA; ST

Bradley, Bill (William Warren) (1943–). Basketball player, senator. BOHA; BRE; HOC; PAW

Bradley, Guy (1870–1905). Game warden. CORA

Bradley, Isaac (b. 1680). Indian captive. CAD

Bradley, Lucretia. Balloonist. HIFD†

Bradley, Omar Nelson (1893–1981). General. ARC; RAE

Bradshaw, Terry (1948–). Football player, sportscaster. AAS-20; CL-1; GUCA; RUA; ST

Bradstreet, Anne Dudley (1612?–1672). Poet. JOCA; OCB; VIA; WABC†

Brady, James Buchanan ("Diamond Jim") (1856–1917). Financier. COKB; LAH

Brady, Matthew B. (1823–1896). Photographer. HOE; SUAA

Bragg, Don (1935–). Pole vaulter. LEYB†

Brahe, Sophia (16th century). Danish astronomer. SC†

Brahe, Tycho (1546–1601). Danish astronomer. MOCB; PIA; SIB

Brahms, Johannes (1833–1897). German composer. BEN; BRF; BUD; DEI; DEJ; FIE; KAE; SAA; WIA; YOK

Braille, Louis (1809–1852). French teacher of the blind. EVA; FE; FOR; FRB; FRE

Braithwaite, William Stanley (1878–1962). Poet, critic. BRB†; DOF-1; ROE

Bramah, Joseph (1748–1814). English inventor. FE

Brandeis, Louis Dembitz (1856–1941). Supreme Court justice. ALD; EIA; FLC; GEF; GRB-1; GUB; LETA

Brandt, Willy (1913–). German ex-chancellor. MEC; WECA

Branover, Herman (1931–). Israeli physicist, educator, born Russia. GRB-1

Branson, Herman (1914–). Biophysicist. CAF-1

Brant, Joseph (1742–1807). Mohawk Indian war chief. DEDB; HEC; HEGA

Brant, Molly (Degonwadonti) (1736–1796). American Revolutionary patriot. AND

Branting, Karl Hjalmar (1860–1925). Swedish statesman. MEC†; WIC

Braque, Georges (1882–1963). French painter. MAH

Brasiliano, Roc (fl. 1660). Brazilian pirate. LACB

Bratkowski, Zeke. Football player. JOA†

Brattain, Walter Houser (1902–1987). Physicist. AAS-33†; GRAB-3; MAPA

Braun, Wernher von, see Von Braun, Wernher.

Brawley, Edward M. (1851–1923). Clergyman. BRB†

Brawner, Clint. Racing car mechanic. LEW†

Braxton, Anthony (1945–). Saxophonist. UN

Braxton, Carter (1736–1797). American Revolutionary patriot. BAEA; BUIB†; COJ†; FEAB

Brayton, Matthew (1818–1862). Indian captive. HEE

Brazile, Robert (1953–). Football player. AAS-15; SMJ

Brazza, Pierre Paul François Camille Savorgnan de (1852–1905). French explorer. ROL

Bream, Julian (1933–). English classical guitarist, lutist. EWC

Brearly, David (1745–1790). Jurist. BUIB†; FEAA

Brecheen, Harry (1914–). Baseball player. GIB

Breckenridge, William (1906–1959). Canadian soldier, born Scotland. RADA

Breckinridge, John Cabell (1821–1875). Vice president of U.S. FEA; HAOA; HOEA

Breckinridge, Mary (1877–1965). Nurse. COFA; MAK; WRA

Breedlove, Craig (1938–). Automobile racer. LEX; OLAB; OLDC; YAA

Bregman, James Steven (1941–). Judo champion. SLA†

Breisach, Paul (1896–). Conductor, born Austria. STM†

Brendan of Clonfert (484–577). Saint. REC

Brenner, Victor David (1871–1924). Sculptor, born Russia. LETA

Brent, Margaret (1600?–1671?). Feminist. GUBA†; VIA; WABC

Bresnahan, Roger (1880–1944). Baseball player. ALB; DAFD; HAF; HIC; SHD

Brett, George Howard (1953–). Baseball player. AAS-3; HEFB†; KLBB; RIGA†

Breuer, Marcel Lajos (1902–1981). Architect, born Hungary. LAF

Brews, Sidney (1899–1972). South African golfer. SLA†

Brezhnev, Leonid Ilyich (1906–1982). Russian communist leader. WEC

Brian Boru (926–1014). King of Ireland. CAAA

Briand, Aristide (1862–1932). French statesman. MEC†; WIC

Brice, Fanny (1891–1951). Singer, comedienne. DI-1†; MASB; PHA

Bricken, Carl (1898–). Conductor. STM†

Brickley, Charley (1898–1949). Football player. DAFG

Brico, Antonia (1902–). Conductor, born the Netherlands. SC-02; STM†

Bridgeman, Junior (Ulysses) (1953–). Basketball player. AAS-25

Bridger, James (1804–1881). Pioneer, scout. BUG; BUI; COE; FOC; HEB; LED; LEPD; WAF

Bridges, Calvin Blackman (1889–1938). Geneticist. BEK†

Bridget of Kildare, Saint, see Brigid of Kildare.

Bridget of Sweden (1303–1373). Saint. DAD-3; ONA; QUA

Bridgetower, George Augustus (1780–1860). Polish violinist. ADA; ADB

Bridgman, Laura Dewey (1829–1889). Blind, deaf teacher of the deaf and blind. LYA

Briefer, Dick. Cartoonist. GOB-1

Brieff, Frank (1912–). Conductor. STM†

Brigid of Kildare (453–523). Saint. DAD-1; DAD-2; FAD; MAK†; ONA; REC; TUA

Brill, Abraham Arden (1874–1948). Psychiatrist, born Austria. LETA

Brimmer, Andrew J. (1926–). Economist. YOI

Brindley, James (1716–1772). English engineer. EVB

Brine, James (1812–1902). English trade unionist. LAD

Brini, Beltrando M. (1907–). Conductor. STM†

Brink, Carol Ryrie (1895–1981). Author. SMB

Brissie, Lou (Leland V.). Baseball player. SCA

British Friends Service Council. MEA

Britten, Benjamin (1913–1976). English composer. BEKA; KAE; YOJ

Britton, Elizabeth Gertrude (1858–1934). Botanist. EMB†

Broadwick, Tiny. Parachutist. HIFD†

Brock, Louis Clark (1939–). Baseball player. BRAA; GUDA; GUEE; RIGA†; SA-3

Brockington, John (1948–). Football player. GUF; MOCA; ST

Brockman, Shimson (1958–). Israeli boat racer. SLA

Broderick, Matthew (1962–). Actor. BRF-1

Brodeur, Richard (1952–). Canadian hockey player. AAS-21

Brodie, John (1935?–). Football player. DUD

Brody, Gyorgy (1908–1967). Hungarian water polo player. SLA†

Brody, Tal (1943–). Israeli basketball player, born U.S. SLA

Broege, Carl. Lawyer. LETD

Broekman, David. Composer, conductor, born the Netherlands. STM†

Broglie, Louis-Victor de (1892–1987). French physicist. FE

Bromfield, Louis (1896–1956). Author. CON

Broneer, Oscar (1894–). Archaeologist, born Sweden. POC

Bronowski, Jacob (1908–1974). English mathematician, author, born Poland. GRB-1

Brontë, Anne (1820–1849). English author. COO; SMA; STK

Brontë, Charlotte (1816–1855). English author. COO; SMA; STK

Brontë, Emily Jane (1818–1848). English author. COO; SMA; STK

Brooke, Edward William (1919–). Ex-senator. ADB; DOF-1; DU†; FAG; FLD; LEI; YOI

Brooke, Rupert (1887–1915). English poet. COP

Brooks, Angie Elizabeth (1928–). Liberian U.N. official. CRA

Brooks, Gwendolyn (1917–). Poet. ADA; ADB; DRA; ROE

Brooks, Mel (Melvin Kaminsky) (1926–). Actor, comedian, motion picture director. BUR-1; SMBB-3

Brooks, Van Wyck (1886–1963). Author, critic. CAC

Broom, Jacob (1752–1810). Businessman. FEAA

Broonzy, Big Bill (1893–1959). Singer. SUH

Brorsen, Metha (1964?–). Rodeo rider. VADB

Brosnan, Jim (1929–). Baseball player. SHE

Brothers, Joyce (1927–). Psychologist, TV personality. BOHG

Broun, Heywood Campbell (1888–1939). Journalist. LEU

Brounoff, Zelman. Conductor. STM†

Brourman, Jacques (1931–). Conductor. STM†

Brouthers, Dan (Dennis) (1858–1932). Baseball player. ALB

Brower, David Ross (1912–). Conservationist. SQA

Brown, Antoinette Blackwell (1825–1921). Ordained minister. BLF†; BOJ; LES-2

Brown, Arthur Whitten (1886–1948). Scottish aviator. COC†; HAMY

Brown, Bill (William Dorsey). Football player. BEKB

Brown, Bobbie E. (fl. 1945). Soldier, WW II. REA

Brown, Bobby (Robert William) (1924–). Baseball player. BOE

Brown, Charlotte Hawkins (1883–1961). Educator. BRB

Brown, Clara (1803–1885). Businesswoman. GRAB-02; KADB

Brown, Claude (1937–). Author. DADB

Brown, Dorothy (1919–). Surgeon. LETC

Brown, Earlene (1935–). Track athlete. HOBAA†

Brown, Fred (1948–). Basketball player. AAS-8

Brown, H. Arthur (1907–). Conductor. STM†

Brown, H. Rap (1943–). Black leader. HAI

Brown, Harold (1927–). Ex-Secretary of Defense. GRB-1

Brown, Harry John. Conductor. STM†

Brown, Henry "Box" (b. 1816). Abolitionist. BRG; JOC

Brown, James (1928–). Singer. DRA

Brown, Jill Elaine. Aviator. SMBC-2

Brown, Jim (James Nathaniel) (1936–). Football player, actor. AAS-35; AKB; ALBA; BEKB; BOF; DAFB; DAFG; DAI; DUF; HAD; HEI; HIE; HOBC; HOC; KADA; RAAE; SID

Brown, John (1736–1803). Businessman. SEC

Brown, John (1800–1859). Abolitionist. BEJ; DEI; DEJ; STJA

Brown, Joseph (b. 1773). Indian captive. HEE

Brown, Kay (1932?–). Painter. FAI

Brown, Larry (1940–). Basketball coach. SLA†

Brown, Larry (1947–). Football player. AAS-27; DUF; GUEB; GUF; LEZB; ST

Brown, Louise (1943–). Lawyer. SMBB

Brown, Marcia (1918–). Author, illustrator. SM

Brown, Melvin L. (d. 1950). Soldier. REA

Brown, Molly (Maggie Tobin) (1873?–1932). Eccentric. RAB

Brown, Nacio Herb (1896–1964). Songwriter. MOA

Brown, Paul (1908–). Football coach. AAS-12; DAFG; SUD

Brown, Pete Earlie (1935–). Golfer. HOBC

Brown, Rabbit (Richard) (1880–1937). Singer, guitarist. SUH

Brown, Rachel Fuller (1898–). Biochemist. HA-1; YOF

Brown, Robert Stanford. Football player. ST

Brown, Roger. Basketball player. HIBA

Brown, Roger (1937–). Football player. AAS-32

Brown, Thomas (b. 1740). Indian captive. HEE

Brown, Three-Fingered (Mordecai) (1876–1948). Baseball player. ALB; DAFC; DAFD; DAH; FRC-1†; RIGA†; SCA

Brown, Warren (1948?–). Journalist. STAA

Brown, William Wells (1815–1884). Author. CL; DADA; GRAB-05

Browne, Frances (1816–1879). Irish author. BEI

Browne, Michael (1967?–). Winner, Young American Medal for Bravery. ANCA

Browning, Elizabeth Barrett (1809–1861). English poet. BOC

Browning, John Moses (1855–1926). Inventor, gunmaker. HYA†

Browning, Pete (Louis Rogers) (1861–1905). Baseball player. SMK

Browning, Robert (1812–1889). English poet. COP

Bruce, Blanche K. (1841–1898). Senator. ADA; ADB; BRB; BU; PECA; STD; YOI

Bruce, Sir David (1855–1931). Australian bacteriologist. DEB; ROA

Bruce, Louis R. (1906–). Government official. GRAC

Bruce, Robert the (1274–1329). King of Scotland. CAAA; HEA; MAJ; SUK

Bruch, Max (1838–1920). German composer. KAE

Bruckner, Anton (1824–1896). Austrian composer. KAE; SAA

Bruegel, Pieter, the Elder (1520?–1569). Flemish painter. KAA; MAI

Brugnon, Jacques (1895–1978). French tennis player. FOX†

Bruhns, Karen Olsen (1941–). Archaeologist. WIAA-01

Brumel, Valeri (1942–). Russian track athlete. DAFB; DAJ; GED

Brumidi, Constantino (1805–1880). Painter, born Italy. MAS

Brunel, Isambard Kingdom (1806–1869). English civil engineer. EVB; FE

Brunhoff, Jean de (1899–1937). French author, illustrator. SMAB

Brunhoff, Laurent de (1925–). French author, illustrator. SMAB

Bruno (b. 1101). Saint. DAD-3

Brunson, Dorothy (1938–). Radio and advertising executive. GLO

Brutus, Dennis (1924–). South African poet. LEA

Bruun, Anton Frederick (1901–1961). Danish oceanographer. BRBC

Bryan, Blackshear Morrison (1900–). General. RAE

Bryan, Dorothy (1896?–1984). Author. SMAB

Bryan, Jimmy (James Ernest) (1927–1960). Automobile racer. LEX

Bryan, Marguerite. Illustrator. SMAB

Bryan, William Jennings (1860–1925). Political leader. GO; WHD

Bryant, Paul "Bear" (1913–1983). Football player, coach. LEW

Bryant, William Cullen (1794–1878). Poet. BEF; BEGA; BOA; HACB; SIF

Buchanan, Franklin (1800–1874). Naval officer. ICA

Buchanan, James (1791–1868). President of U.S. BAEB; BAG; BAG-1; BEB; BLA; BUIA; CAG; CAH; COI; COS; DUC; DUCA; FRBA; HEEA; HIH; LEQ; LEQA; MAB; MABA; MIA; PED; ROH; ROHA; ROK†; SUBB; WHD

Buchwald, Art (1925–). Author, columnist. LEU

Buck, Pearl S. (1892–1973). Author. COKA; CON; GIBA†; HEF; KOA; LEGB; MUA; OCB; SHFE

Buckley, Emerson (1916–). Conductor. STM†

Buckner, Aylett C. (fl. 1822). Pioneer. VIA

Buckner, Quinn (1954–). Basketball player. AAS-6

Buckpasser. Racehorse. PAW

Bucyk, John Paul (1935–). Canadian hockey player. OBB

Buddha (Gautama Buddha) (563?–483 B.C.). Indian philosopher, founder of Buddhism. FRE; TRC-1

Budge, Don (John Donald) (1915–). Tennis player. DAG; DAGA; FOX; HI; LAHA

Buff, Conrad (1886–1975). Author, illustrator, born Switzerland. SMAB

Buff, Mary Marsh (1890–1970). Author, illustrator. SMAB

Buffalo Bill, *see* Cody, William Frederick.

Buisson, Ferdinand (1841–1932). French educator. MEC†; WIC

Buketoff, Igor (1915–). Conductor. STM†

Bulette, Julia (1832?–1867). Frontierswoman. RAB†; WIAA-2

Bulfinch, Charles (1763–1844). Architect. LAF; LEDA

Bulkeley, Morgan (1837–1922). Baseball executive. ALB

Bulkeley, Peter (1583–1659). Founder of Concord, Massachusetts. WOAA

Bull, Dixey (fl. 1632). English pirate. WHA†

Bull, Ole (1810–1880). Norwegian violinist. BOD; CHFA

Bulloch, Archibald (1730–1777). American Revolutionary patriot. SEC

Bultema, John. Adventurer. WIAA-5

Bulwer-Lytton, Edward George Earle Lytton, baron Lytton, *see* Lytton, Edward George Earle Lytton Bulwer, 1st baron.

Bunche, Ralph Johnson (1904–1971). Statesman. ADA; ADB; BRG; DOF-1; FEC; FLD; HUA; JOC; KEE; LEI; MEA; MEC; RIC; RICA; STO; WIC; YOI

Bunning, Jim (James Paul David) (1931–). Baseball player. LEZ; PRA

Bunsen, Robert Wilhelm (1811–1899). German chemist. SHFB

Buonarroti, Michelangelo, *see* Michelangelo Buonarroti.

Buoniconti, Nick (1940–). Football player. DEHA-1

Burbank, Luther (1849–1926). Horticulturist. BOB; CO-1; CUC; DEI; DEJ; DOCA; DOE; FOH; HYB; WAP

Burdan, Molly (1853–1888). Frontierswoman. RAB

Burdette, Lew (1926–). Baseball player. DEHA-1; GIB

Burgess, Smoky (Forrest H.) (1927?–). Baseball player. DAFD; DAH

Burgin, Richard (1892–). Conductor, born Poland. STM†

Burgos, Julia de (1914–1953). Puerto Rican poet. WO

Burgoyne, John (1722–1792). British Army officer. AKA; RAD; SOA

Burke, Johnny (1908–1964). Songwriter. MOA

Burke, Robert O'Hara (1820–1861). Irish explorer. ROL; WIA-1

Burke, Yvonne Brathwaite (1932–). Congresswoman, lawyer. BOHF; FOC-1; WIAA-02

Burkett, Jesse (1870–1953). Baseball player. ALB

Burleigh, Henry Thacker (1866–1949). Singer.
 ADA; ADB; BRB†; DOF-1

Burnet, Sir Macfarlane (1899–1985). Australian
 virologist. RIF

Burnett, Carol (1933–). Actress. MASB

Burnett, Frances Hodgson (1849–1924). Author,
 born England. BEI

Burney, Fanny (1752–1840). English author.
 NOA; SMA

Burnham, Daniel Hudson (1846–1912). Architect.
 LAF

Burningham, Charlene. Weaver, sculptor. BOHB

Burns, George (1896–). Comedian. BUR-1

Burns, John Francis (1933–). Comedian, television writer, producer. BUR-1

Burns, Kenneth Charles "Jethro." Comedian,
 singer. HAG-1

Burns, Maurice (1935?–). Painter. FAI

Burns, Robert (1759–1796). Scottish poet. COB

Burr, Aaron (1756–1836). Vice president of U.S.
 BUIB; FEA; GO; HAOA; HOEA

Burr, Seymour (fl. 1775). American Revolutionary patriot. WIBA

Burroughs, Jeff (1951–). Baseball player. BUJC

Burroughs, John (1837–1921). Naturalist. CO-1;
 CORA; MIB

Burroughs, Nannie Helen (1883–1961). Educator.
 LOAV

Burroughs, William S. (1855–). Computer pioneer. GRAB-3†

Burrows, Rube (1854–1890). Outlaw. REE

Burton, Marie. Painter. BOHB

Burton, Sir Richard Francis (1821–1890). English
 explorer. COL; MOB; ROL

Buscema, John (1927–). Cartoonist. GOB-1

Busch, Mary. School board commissioner. WHE†

Bush, George (1924–). Vice president of U.S.
 HAOA; HOEA

Bush, George W. (1791–1867). Pioneer. BUH;
 GRAB-02; KADB; PECA; SCB; STQ†

Bush, Robert Eugene (fl. 1945). Naval medical
 corpsman. REA

Bush, Vannevar (1890–1974). Electrical engineer.
 LEGA; YOD

Bushnell, David (1742?–1824). Inventor. HYA†

Busoni, Ferruccio (1866–1924). Italian pianist,
 composer. CHF

Bussey, Sheila (1950?–). Rodeo rider. VADB

Butkus, Dick (Richard Marvin) (1942–). Football
 player. ANA; ASBA; DAFG; FRD; GUF;
 HAGB; KABA; KADA; ST

Butler, Matthew Calbraith (1836–1909). Confederate Army soldier. MAD

Butler, Nicholas Murray (1862–1947). Educator.
 MEA; MEC; WIC

Butler, Norman. Assassin. RABA†

Butler, Pierce (1744–1822). Senator. BUIB†;
 FEAA

Butler, Smedley Darlington (1881–1940). Marine
 officer. TA

Butler, Walter (1752–1781). British soldier. SOA

Button, Dick (1929–). Skater. DAG; DAGA; HEG;
 HOC; LEYB; LIEA

Buttons, Red (1919–). Actor. ALC

Butz, Dave (1950–). Football player. AAS-32

Buxtehude, Dietrich (1637–1707). Swedish composer, organist. BEM

Buxton, Angela (1934–). English tennis player.
 SLA

Buys-Ballot, Christoph Hendrik (1817–1890).
 Dutch meteorologist. HAC†

Buzonas, Gail Johnson. Swimmer. GLA

Buzzi, Ruth (1937–). Comedienne. MASB

Bwembya (b. 1886?). African tribesman. PEA

Byard, Carole Marie (1941–). Painter. FAI

Byers, William Newton (1831–1903). Pioneer.
 YOG

Bykovsky, Valeri (1934–). Russian astronaut.
 THC

Byler, Kenneth. Conductor. STM†

Byrd, Harry (1925–). Baseball player. BOE

Byrd, Manford, Jr. (1928–). School administrator.
 DRA

Byrd, Richard Evelyn (1888–1957). Polar ex-
 plorer, admiral. BAB; COC; COKA; CUC;
 DOC; ELA; FAA; FOH; GRB; ICA; LAC; NAC;
 ROL

Byrd, William (1543–1623). English composer, organist. KAE

Byrne, Jane (1934–). Mayor. WHE

Byrne, John (1950–). Cartoonist, born England.
 GOB-1

Byron, Lady Augusta Ada, see Lovelace, Lady Ada
 (Byron).

Byron, George Gordon Noel, 6th baron (1788–
 1824). English poet. COP; DEI

C

Cabeza de Vaca, Álvar Núñez (1490–1557). Spanish explorer. BLD†; KEG; LYF; NAA; ROL

Cable, George Washington (1844–1925). Author.
 STJC

Cabot, John (1450–1498). Italian explorer. GRAA;
 GRC; KNB; MOB; ROL

Cabot, Sebastian (1476–1557). Italian explorer.
 MOB; ROL†

Cabral, Pedro Álvares (1460?–1526). Portuguese
 navigator. ROL†

Cabrini, Frances Xavier (1850–1917). Saint, born
 Italy. ASB; BLF†; DAD-1; DAD-3; MAS; STLA

Caesar, Gaius Julius (100–44 B.C.). Roman general, statesman. CAAA; COD; COK; COM; DEI; DEJ; KEH; PLA; UNA

Caesar, Irving (1895–). Songwriter. MOA†

Caesar, Sid (1922–). Comedian. ALC

Caffey, Leo Roy. Football player. JOA

Caffie, Barbara J. (1936?–). Television newscaster. STAA

Cage, John (1912–). Composer. BEKA; EWAA

Cagle, Red (Christian Keener) (d. 1942). Football player. HIE

Cagliostro, Comte de, *see* Balsamo, Joseph.

Caillé, René Auguste (1799–1838). French explorer. ROL

Cain, Richard H. (1825–1887). Congressman. ADA; ADB

Caius. Saint. DAD-2

Cajetan (1480–1547). Saint. DAD-3

Calamity Jane (1852?–1903). Frontier character, markswoman. RAB; SUI

Calas, Jean (1688–1762). French merchant. COG

Calderone, Mary Steichen (1904–). Physician, public health educator. BOHE; GIB-1

Caldwell, Earl (1938?–). Journalist. STAA

Caldwell, Erskine (1903–1987). Author. CAC†

Caldwell, Sarah (1924–). Conductor. GIB-1; SC-02†

Calhoun, John Caldwell (1782–1850). Statesman. FEA; HAOA; HOEA; KEC†; STH

Call, Richard Keith (1791–1862). Governor. SEC

Callaway, Liz. Actress, singer. BRF-1

Callison, Johnny (1939–). Baseball player. BUJ

Callistus I (fl. 217). Saint, pope. DAD-3

Callow, Russell S. (1890–1961). Rowing coach. HEH

Calvert, Cecilius, 2nd baron Baltimore (1605–1675). First proprietor of colony of Maryland. LEO; MEB

Calvert, Charles, 3rd baron Baltimore (1637–1715). Second proprietor of Maryland. LEO; MEB

Calvert, George, 1st baron Baltimore (1580?–1632). English proprietor in America. MEB; VIA

Calvin, Mack (1948–). Basketball player. HIBAA

Calvin, Melvin (1911–). Chemist. BEK

Cambourakis, Nicos (1910–). Conductor, born Greece. STM†

Camero, Manuel (b. 1751). Settler. WIBA

Camillus de Lellis (1550–1614). Saint. DAD-1; DAD-3

Camp, Walter Chauncey (1859–1925). Football coach. DAFG; DAG; DAGA; DAI

Campanella, Roy (1921–). Baseball player. BOE; BUD-1; DADB; DAFC; DAFD; DAG; DAGA; FRC-1†; GEB; GUDA; HIC; HOCM; LYA; MUC; RIGA†; SCA; SHD; SHF; VACA; WAG; ZAA

Campaneris, Bert (Dagoberto Blanco) (1942–). Cuban baseball player. SMF

Campbell, Archie (1914–1987). Comedian. HAG-1

Campbell, Barbara. Reporter. STAA†

Campbell, Billie L. Structural engineer. GL

Campbell, Donald Malcolm (1921–1967). English automobile and speedboat racer. ALBA; ST-1

Campbell, Earl (1955–). Football player. AAS-10; DEHB

Campbell, Elmer Simms (1906–1971). Cartoonist. ADA; ADB; BOG

Campbell, Glen (1936–). Singer. KRI-1

Campbell, Sir Malcolm (1885–1949). English automobile and speedboat racer. YAA

Campbell, Robert L. Soldier, WW I. BRB†

Campbell, Robin (1958?–). Track athlete. GLB

Campion, Edmund (1540–1581). English Jesuit martyr. DAD-3; MAJ

Canadeo, Tony. Football player. JOA†

Candelaria, Andrea Castanon (1785–1899). Texas patriot. KUA

Canessa, Roberto (1953?–). Uruguayan rugby player. WIAA-5

Canisius, Peter (1521–1597). Saint. DAD-2

Cannizzaro, Stanislao (1826–1910). Italian chemist. MOBA

Cannon, Annie Jump (1863–1941). Astronomer. EMB

Cannon, Jimmy (1909–1973). Sportswriter. BELB

Cano, Juan Sebastian del (d. 1526). Spanish navigator. ROL†

Cañonero. Racehorse. IZA

Canova, Judy (1916–1983). Singer, comedienne. MASB

Cantinflas (Mario Moreno) (1911–). Mexican actor. NEBA; WO

Cantor, Eddie (1892–1964). Comedian. ALC; LETA; PHA

Cantor, Georg (1845–1918). German mathematician. MUB

Cantrick, Robert (1917–). Conductor. STM†

Canute II, the Great (944?–1035). King of the Danes. CAAA; JOBB

Canute IV (d. 1086). Saint, king of Denmark. DAD-2

Capa, Robert (1913–1954). Photographer, born Hungary. HOE

Capablanca, José R. (1888–1942). Cuban chess player. LEQB

Capodanno, Vincent R. (d. 1967). Chaplain. ARBA

Capp, Al (Alfred G. Caplin) (1909–1979). Cartoonist. GEA

Capra, Frank (1897–). Motion picture director, born Italy. ED-1†; FLBC; SMBC

Captain Jack (d. 1873). Modoc warrior subchief.
HED

Captein, Jacques E. J. (b. 1745). Dutch clergyman, born Africa. ADA; ADB

Caracciola, Rudolf (1901–1959). German automobile racer. COKC; YAA

Caracciolo, Francis (1563–1608). Saint. DAD-2

Caractacus (fl. 50 A.D.). British chieftain. MAJ;
SUK

Caradoc, see Caractacus.

Carano, Ugo (1909–). Conductor, born Italy.
STM†

Caravaggio, Michelangelo da (1565–1609). Italian painter. KAA

Cardano, Girolamo (1501–1576). Italian mathematician, physician, astrologer. MUB

Cárdenas, Lázaro (1895–1970). Mexican soldier, statesman. ARAA; NEBA; ROGB

Cardozo, Benjamin Nathan (1870–1938). Supreme Court justice. FLC

Cardozo, Francis Louis (1837–1903). State official. BRB†

Carew, Rod (Rodney Cline) (1945–). Baseball player, born Panama. AAS-3; BRAA; GUDA; GUED-01; GUEE; IZA; MUC; RIGA†

Carewe, John (1933–). English conductor. YOM†

Carey, Max (1890–). Baseball player. ALB; ROC

Carleton, Sir Guy, 1st baron Dorchester, see Dorchester, Sir Guy Carleton, 1st baron.

Carleton, Mark Alfred (1866–1925). Botanist.
DEA

Carl-Gustav (1946–). Crown prince of Sweden.
NEC†

Carlisle, Bill (b. 1890). Train robber. REE

Carlos, John (1945?–). Track athlete. BELB

Carlsen, Henrik K. (1915–). Sea captain, born Denmark. SUA

Carlson, Chester F. (1906–1968). Inventor. FE;
MAPA

Carlson, Earl (1897–). Physician, victim of cerebral palsy. LEG

Carlson, Evans Fordyce (1896–1947). General.
ARC

Carlson, George (1887–1962). Cartoonist. GOB-1

Carlton, Steven Norman (1944–). Baseball player. BUJB; GUG; RIGA†; SA-3; SHH

Carlyle, Thomas (1795–1881). Scottish author, historian. COB

Carmel, Zephania (1940–1980). Israeli boat racer, born Iraq. SLA†

Carmichael, Berthel. Mathematician. CAF-1

Carmichael, Harold (1949–). Football player.
AAS-18

Carmichael, Hoagy (1899–1981). Songwriter.
MOA

Carmichael, Stokely (1941–). Black leader. HAI

Carnegie, Andrew (1835–1919). Industrialist, born Scotland. BEA; CUC; DEI; DEJ; EVA; LAG; LEM; LOB; MAL; WED

Carney, William H. (b. 1840?). Soldier. STQ†

Carnot, Nicholas Léonard Sadi (1796–1832). French physicist. HAC; SHFB

Caro, Joseph (1488–1575). Spanish Talmudist.
KAC

Caron, Leslie (1933–). French dancer, actress.
ATA

Carothers, Wallace Hume (1896–1937). Inventor.
FE

Carpenter, Howard (1944?–1967). Soldier. ARBA

Carpenter, John Alden (1876–1951). Composer.
BAD; BUC

Carpenter, Malcolm Scott (1925–). Astronaut, aquanaut. COR; NEB; THC

Carpenter, William (1937–). Football player. DIA;
RAE

Carpentier, Alejo (1904–). Cuban author. WO

Carpini, Giovanni de Piano (c. 1180–1252). Italian traveler. KNA

Carr, Frederick. Football player. SMJ

Carr, Harold Noflet (1921–). Airline executive.
PAA

Carr, Joseph (1880–1939). Football executive.
DAB; SUD

Carr, Leroy (1899–1935). Singer. SUH

Carr, Vikki. Singer. NEAA; WH

Carrel, Alexis (1873–1944). Surgeon, biologist, born France. POB; RIF

Carreño, Teresa (1853–1917). Venezuelan pianist.
CHF

Carrier, Willis Haviland (1876–1950). Electrical engineer, inventor. FAB; YOE

Carroll, Charles (1737–1832). American Revolutionary patriot. BAEA; BUIB†; COJ; FEAB†;
MAC

Carroll, Charles Curtis "Corky" (1947?–). Surf rider. OLD

Carroll, Daniel (1730–1796). Congressman.
BUIB†; FEAA

Carroll, Jean (c. 1915–). Comedienne. MASB

Carroll, John (1735–1815). Archbishop. BUIB†

Carroll, Lewis, pseud. (1832–1898). English author. BEH; COB; COO

Carroll, Pat (1927–). Actress. MASB

Carruthers, George (c. 1940–). Physicist. CAF-1

Carson, Kit (Christopher) (1809–1868). Scout, Indian agent. BUG; BUI; CAD; COE; DEI; DEJ; FIA; FOC; NAA; WAF

Carson, Rachel (1907–1964). Author, marine biologist. CO-1; COR; CORA; ELA; EMB; FRE; GIBA; HIBB; PACA; SC; SQA; WAP

Carter, Alan (1904–). Conductor. STM†

Carter, Alvin Pleasant (1891–1960). Singer. KR

Carter, Betty (1930–). Singer. UN

Carter, Charles J. (Carter the Great) (1874–1936). Magician. KEB

Carter, Don (1930–). Bowler. DEHA-1

Carter, Duane, Sr. (1913?–). Automobile racer. OLCA

Carter, Gary (1954–). Baseball player. HEFB†

Carter, Howard (1873–1939). English archaeologist. WOA

Carter, Jimmy (James Earl) (1924–). President of U.S. BAG-1; BEB; BLA; COI; COS; DUCA; FRBA; LEQA; SUBB; WHD

Carter, Maybelle (1909–1978). Singer. KR

Carter, Ovie (1946?–). Photographer. STAA

Carter, Pancho (Duane, Jr.). Automobile racer. OLCA

Carter, Rosalynn Smith (1927–). Wife of Jimmy Carter. BAG-1; BLG; KL; MAU; SMBD

Carter, Sara (1899–). Singer. KR

Cartier, Jacques (1491–1557). French explorer. ABA; GRC; KEH; MOB; ROL

Cartier-Bresson, Henri (1908–). French photographer. HOE

Cartouche, Dominique (Louis Dominique Bourguignon) (1693–1721). French criminal. SUG

Cartwright, Alexander (1820–1892). Baseball pioneer. ALB; DAFD; DAG; DAGA; SMK

Cartwright, Edmund (1743–1823). English inventor. EBA

Caruso, Enrico (1873–1921). Italian singer. ASB-1; COKB; DEI; DEJ; YOH

Carvalho, Eleazar de (1915–). Conductor, born Brazil. STM†

Carvaljal, Felix (b. 1873?). Cuban track athlete. DAJ; FIC

Carver, George Washington (1864–1943). Botanist. ADA; ADB; ASA; ASB; ASB-1; BEC; BOD; BRB†; BRBD; CAF-1; CAGA; CO-1; COKA; CORA; CUC; DOE; DOF-1; EVD; FID; FRE; GRAB-03; HA; HAM; HODA; HUA; JOC; KE; KLA; LEI; LEPC; MAN; MAT; MEB; RIC; RICA; ROG; YOE

Cary, Lott (1780–1828). Missionary. BRB†

Cary, Mary Ann Shadd (1823–1893). Abolitionist. LOAV; WABC†

Casals, Pablo (1876–1973). Spanish cellist. CAHA

Casals, Rosemary (1948–). Tennis player. MATA; SUDA

Casanova de Seingalt, Giovanni Giacomo (1725–1798). Italian adventurer. DEI; DEJ; JAC

Case, Sandra Williams. Aviator. SMBC-2

Casey, Hugh (1913–1951). Baseball player. SHE

Cash, Johnny (1932–). Singer. BUIB-01

Cashman, Katharine. Geologist, polar researcher. LA-1

Cashman, Wayne (1945–). Canadian hockey player. THG

Casimir (1458–1484). Saint. DAD-2; ONA

Casper, Billy (William Earl) (1931–). Golfer. KADA; LABA

Casper, Dave (1951–). Football player. AAS-19

Cass, Lewis (1782–1866). Statesman. WHD†

Cassatt, Mary (1845–1926). Painter. CUC; FOGB; FRA; LEE; MAG; NE; STJ; STLA; WABC†

Cassidy, Butch (George Leroy Parker) (1867–1912). Outlaw. JOBA; REE; SUJ†

Cassin, René (1887–1976). French statesman. MEC†; WIC

Castillo, Rosa. Migrant worker. WECC

Castle, Frederick W. (d. 1944). Aviator, WW II. REA

Caston, Saul (1901–). Conductor. STM

Castro, Fidel (1926–). Cuban premier. ARA; BAGA; DU-1; HAK; WEA

Castro, Raúl Héctor (1916–). Governor, born Mexico. WH

Cather, Willa (1873–1947). Author. BOA; CON; CUC; HEF; LEK; MUA; OCB; STLA

Catherine II, the Great (1729–1796). Empress of Russia. BEO; BOI; CAAA; COKB; DAK; DEI; DEJ; FAE; LIDA; RIA; TRBA

Catherine of Alexandria (4th century). Saint. DAD-3; PEE; QUA

Catherine of Aragon (1485–1536). Consort of Henry VIII, king of England. MAOA; VAC

Catherine of Genoa (1447–1510). Saint. MOC

Catherine of Ricci (1522–1590). Saint. DAD-2

Catherine of Siena (1347–1380). Saint. DAD-1; DAD-2; ONA; TUA

Catherine of Sweden (1331–1381). Saint. DAD-2

Catherine de Medici (1519–1589). Queen of France. BOI; CAAA; FAE; LIDA

Catlett, Elizabeth (1915–). Sculptor. FAH

Catlin, George (1796–1872). Painter. FOC; HEB; HEDA; HOD

Cato, Marcus Porcius (234–149 B.C.). Roman statesman. PLA

Catt, Carrie Chapman (1859–1947). Feminist. COG; FAA; JOCA; WABC†

Cauthen, Steve (1960–). Jockey. HOCG

Cavell, Edith (1865–1915). English nurse. HAA; MAJ; MAK; RADA; WRA

Cavendish, Henry (1731–1810). English chemist, physicist. CAA; FE; SHFB

Cavendish, Margaret (1623–1674). English author. SC†

Cawley, Evonne Goolagong (1951–). Australian tennis player. AAS-29; FR-1; GLC; HOBAA; LAHA; MATA; SUDA

Caxton, William (1422?–1491). English printer. DEI; DEJ

Cayting, Stanley (1898–). Conductor. STM†

Cayton, Horace R. (1903–1970). Sociologist. BOG; DADB

Cecil of Chelwood, Edgar Algernon Robert Gascoyne-Cecil, 1st viscount (1864–1958). British statesman. MEC†; WIC

Cecilia. Saint. DAD-1; DAD-3

Cecilia, Sister. Nun, born Czechoslovakia. CAHA

Cedeño, Cesar (1951–). Dominican baseball player. GUG; KLCA

Celeste N. Reformed drug addict. SIAA

Celestine V (1215–1296). Saint, pope. DAD-2

Celibidache, Sergio (1912–). Rumanian conductor. YOM†

Cellier, Elizabeth (fl. 1680). English midwife. MASA†

Cellini, Benvenuto (1500–1571). Italian goldsmith, sculptor. DEI; DEJ; JAC; RAC

Cepeda, Orlando (1937–). Baseball player. BRD; FOW; PRA

Cerdan, Marcel, Jr. (1916–1949). French boxer. BELB

Ceresole, Pierre (1879–1945). Swiss humanitarian. KEE

Cerioli, Constanza, Blessed (1816–1865). DAD-3

Cernan, Eugene A. (1934–). Astronaut. THC

Cerny, Harold Earl (1907–). Conductor. STM†

Cerny, Robert George (1908–). Architect. LEDA

Cervantes Saavedra, Miguel de (1547–1616). Spanish author. KEH; WO

Cesnola, Luigi Palma di (1832–1904). Archaeologist, born Italy. MAS

Cetewayo (c. 1836–1884). Zulu chief. BRB†; CAAA; MIC

Cézanne, Paul (1839–1906). French painter. ASB-1; KAA; MAH; WIAA

Chacon, Augustin (d. 1902). Mexican outlaw. JOBA

Chadwick, Florence May (1918–). Swimmer. DAG; DAGA; HOBA; HOBAA

Chadwick, Henry (1824–1908). Baseball pioneer. ALB

Chadwick, Sir James (1891–1974). English physicist. FE; RID

Chaffee, Roger Bruce (1935–1967). Astronaut. LEPB†

Chaffee, Suzy (1947–). Skier. FRCA; HOBAA

Chagall, Marc (1887–1985). Russian painter. GRB-1; WIAA

Chain, Ernst Boris (1906–1979). English biochemist, born Germany. BEK†; COLA†; GRB-1; LAE; LET; POB; RIF

Chait, Donna. Basketball player. HOBAA†

Chaka (1787–1829). Zulu chief. ADA; ADB; BRB†; GRAB-04; MIC

Chalmers, Willie (b. 1765). Colonial boy. CAD

Chamberlain, Sir Austen (1863–1937). English statesman. MEC†; WIC

Chamberlain, Wilt (Wilton Norman) (1936–). Basketball player. AAS-35; ALBA; ASBA; BEL; BOF; DEHA-1; ETA; GUEA; HEHA; HID; HOC; KADA; KLBA; PE; RAAB

Chamberlin, Guy (1894–1967). Football player, coach. DAFG†; SUD

Chambers, Annette. Engineer. HOG†

Champe, Elizabeth (fl. 1780). Wife of American Revolutionary patriot. CLC

Champlain, Samuel de (1567–1635). French explorer. ABA; COC; HIBC; KNA; ROL

Chance, Dean (1941–). Baseball player. DEE

Chance, Frank (1877–1924). Baseball player, manager. ALB; DAFD; FRC-01

Chancellor, Richard (d. 1556). English explorer. KNB; ROL†

Chandler, Dana C. (1941–). Painter. FAI

Chandler, Don. Football player. JOA

Chandragupta Maurya (c. 321–c. 298 B.C.). King of Magadha. CAAA

Chanel, Coco (1883–1971). French fashion designer. FRBD

Chanel, Peter (1803–1841). Saint. DAD-2

Chaney, James Earl (1943–1964). Civil rights worker. STJB†

Chang Ch'ien (d. 114?). Chinese minister. ROL†

Channing, Carol (1921–). Actress. MASB

Chantal, Jane Frances de (1572–1641). Saint. DAD-1; DAD-3

Chapin, Jane. Travel industry executive. LES-1†

Chaplin, Sir Charles Spencer (1889–1977). English actor. ASB-1; COKB; ED-1; SMBC

Chapman, Carrie, see Catt, Carrie Chapman.

Chapman, Frank Michler (1864–1945). Ornithologist. MIB

Chapman, John (Johnny Appleseed) (1774–1847). Pioneer. BAC; BEC; CAGA; CO-1; HEB; LEC; LEPD; SQA

Chapman, Maria Weston (1806–1885). Abolitionist. LES-2†

Chapple, Stanley (1900–). Conductor, born England. STM†

Charboneau, Baptiste (1805–1885). Pioneer fur trader. JOD

Chardin, Jean Baptiste Siméon (1699–1779). French painter. MAH†

Chardin, Pierre Teilhard de, see Teilhard de Chardin, Pierre.

Chardon, Yves. Cellist, born France. STM†

Charlemagne (742–814). King of the Franks. BEO; CAAA; COA; DEI; DEJ; HEA; JOBB; NEC; UNA

Charles (1948–). Prince of Wales. NEC†

Charles I (1600–1649). King of England, Scotland, and Ireland. CAAA; DEC; GRAB; SCC; TRA

Charles II (1630–1685). King of England, Scotland, and Ireland. CAAA; DEC; GRAB; JAC; SCC; TRA; UNA

Charles V (1500–1558). Holy Roman Emperor and king of Spain as Charles I. CAAA; COA

Charles XII (1682–1718). King of Sweden. CAAA

Charles of Blois, Blessed (1319–1364). DAD-3

Charles, Ray (1930–). Singer, pianist. HAFA

Charles, Walter. Conductor. STM†

Charlton, Cornelius (1930?–1951). Soldier. ARBA; DIA

Charlton, Samuel (1760–1843). American Revolutionary patriot. WIBA†

Chartz, Marcelline. Computer expert. HOG†

Chase, Harold (1883–1947). Baseball player. SMK

Chase, Lucia (1907–1986). Co-founder American Ballet Theatre. FOGC†

Chase, Mary Ellen (1887–1973). Author. CON

Chase, Salmon Portland (1808–1873). Supreme Court justice. FLC

Chase, Samuel (1741–1811). American Revolutionary patriot, jurist. BAEA; BUIB†; COJ; FEAB; MAC

Chateaubriand, François René (1768–1848). French author, statesman. RAC

Chatelet, Marquise du. Gabrielle Émilie Le Tonnelier du Breteuil (1706–1749). French author, physicist. SC

Chatham, Alice King. Sculptor. HOG

Chato, El. Bandit. WIAA-1

Chaucer, Geoffrey (1340?–1400). English poet. COP

Chausson, Ernest Amédée (1855–1899). French composer. KAE

Chauviré, Yvette (1917–). French dancer. ATA

Chávez, Carlos (1899–1978). Mexican composer. KAE; NEBA; ROGB; STM†; WO

Chavez, Cesar Estrada (1927–). Labor leader. DU-1; FOW; HAJ; NEAA; WO

Chavis, John (1763?–1838). Clergyman, educator. BRB; DOB

Chavoor, Sherm. Swimming coach. LEW

Chaykin, Howard. Cartoonist. GOB-1

Cheatham, Doc (1905–). Trumpeter. UN

Cheech (Richard Marin) (1946–). Comedian. BUR-1

Cheevers, Gerry (1940–). Canadian hockey player. LEYA; ORA

Chekhov, Anton Pavlovich (1860–1904). Russian author. ASB-1; POFA

Cheng, Chi (1944–). Chinese track athlete. AAS-24; HOBAA; ST-1

Chenkin, George B. (1897?–1962). Detective. LACA

Chennault, Claire Lee (1890–1958). General. SWE

Cheops (fl. 2900 B.C.). King of Egypt. CAAA

Cherkassky, Paul. Conductor, born Russia. STM†

Cherniavsky, Josef. Conductor, born Russia. STM†

Cherokee Bill (b. 1876). Outlaw. KADB; SUJ

Cherubini, Luigi (1760–1842). Italian composer. KAE

Chesbro, Happy Jack (John Dwight) (1874–1931). Baseball player. ALB

Chesnutt, Charles Waddell (1858–1932). Author. ADA; ADB; BRB†; CL; DOF-1

Chester, Raymond (1948–). Football player. AAS-19

Chesterton, Gilbert Keith (1874–1936). English author. BEG

Chestnut, Mary Boykin Miller (1823–1886). Diarist. WABC†

Chevalier, Ann. Television photographer. BOHD

Chew, Ng Poon, see Ng Poon Chew.

Chiang Kai-shek (1886–1975). Chinese nationalist leader. ARA; ASB-1; DOF; SPA

Chiang Mei-ling (1897–). Wife of Chiang Kai-shek. EUA; PA

Chicago, Judy. Painter. FOGB†

Chichester, Sir Francis (1901–1972). English cartographer, yachtsman. OLC

Child, Julia (1912–). Chef. GIB-1

Child, Lydia Maria (1802–1880). Abolitionist. LES-2†

Chim, see Seymour, David.

Chin, Tiffany. Skater. VAD-6†

Chinaglia, Giorgio (1947–). Soccer player, born Italy. ADL

Chisholm, Shirley (1924–). Congresswoman. BRGA; COG-1; DRA; DU; FLD; GIBA; ROJ; WHE; YOI

Chisum, John Simpson (1824–1884). Cattleman. NAA; WAA

Chittenden, Thomas (1730–1797). Governor. SEC

Chizhova, Nadyezhda. Russian track athlete. HOBAA†

Chizick, Sarah. Israeli settler. LER

Chodorov, Ya'acov (1927–). Israeli soccer player, born Palestine. SLA†

Chong, Tommy (1939–). Comedian. BUR-1

Chopin, Frédéric François (1810–1849). Polish composer. BEN; BRF; BUD; DEI; DEJ; FIE; GOB; KAE; MANB; SAA; WIA; YOJ

Chou En-lai (1898–1976). Chinese communist leader. SPA

Chouteau, René Auguste (1749–1829). Pioneer fur trader. BUI

Chouteau, Yvonne (1929–). Dancer. ATA

Christian IV (1577–1648). King of Denmark and Norway. HEA

Christian, Charles (1919–1942). Guitarist. WAD†

Christian, Minas (1921–). Conductor. STM†

Christie, Agatha (1891–1976). English author. SMA

Christie, David (1960?–). Winner, Young American Medal for Bravery. ANCA

Christie, Robert (1961?–). Winner, Young American Medal for Bravery. ANCA

Christina. Saint. QUA

Christina (1626–1689). Queen of Sweden. BOI; COKB; TRBA; UNA

Christmann, Arthur (1908–). Conductor. STM†

Christmas, Walter. Public relations director. STAA

Christophe, Henri (1767–1820). King of Haiti. ADA; ADB; DAF-1†; JO; STQ†; WIBA

Christopher (3d century). Saint. FAD; ONA; PEE

Chrysler, Walter Percy (1875–1940). Automobile manufacturer. COKA

Chulalongkorn, see Rama V.

Chung Ling Soo, see Robinson, William Ellsworth.

Churchill, John, see Marlborough, John Churchill, 1st duke of.

Churchill, Sir Winston Leonard Spencer (1874–1965). English statesman, author. ASB-1; CHG; CUC; DEI; DEJ; DOF; ELA; EVA; FLBB; FRE; HIB†; JAC; JAD; KE; RADA; TAC; YOA

Chute, Marchette (1909–). Author. MUA

Ciaran (516–549). Saint. TUA

Ciccarelli, Dino (1960–). Canadian hockey player. AAS-22

Cicero, Marcus Tullius (106–43 b.c.). Roman statesman. COK; PLA

Cid Campeador, El (1040?–1099). Spanish soldier, hero. HEA

Cierpinski, Waldemar (1950–). German track athlete. AAS-30

Cimara, Pietro (1887–). Conductor, born Italy. STM†

Cinque, Joseph (1811–1852). African insurrectionist. ADA; ADB; BRB†; ROG; WOA

Cisneros, Henry (1947–). Mayor. HOD-1

Citation. Racehorse. BELB

Claiborne, William Charles (1775–1817). Governor. MAO; SEC

Clair, Dick (Richard Clair Jones) (1931?–). Comedian, television writer. BUR-1

Clancy, King (Francis Michael) (1903–1986). Canadian hockey player. OBA; OBB

Clapperton, Hugh (1788–1827). Scottish explorer. ROL†

Clapton, Eric (1945–). English singer, guitarist. BUIB-1

Clare (1193?–1253). Saint, founded Poor Clares. DAD-1; DAD-3; MAK†; ONA; QUA

Clark, Abraham (1726–1794). American Revolutionary patriot. BAEA; BUIB†; COJ†; FEAB; MAC†

Clark, Beverly. Lawyer. FOC-1

Clark, Dutch (Earl Harry) (1906–1978). Football player. DAB; DAFG; HEI; SUD

Clark, Eugenie (1922–). Ichthyologist, oceanographer. EMB; HAKA

Clark, George Rogers (1752–1818). Colonial soldier. BUIB; DAFA; HEB; RAD; SOA; VIA

Clark, James (1936–1968). Scottish automobile racer. ALBA; COKC; JA; ORD; YAA

Clark, Kenneth Bancroft (1914–). Educator. DOF-1; FAG; YOI

Clark, Mark Wayne (1896–1984). General. RAE

Clark, Roy. Singer, guitarist. HAG-1

Clark, Ruth (1942–). Personnel service executive. GLO

Clark, Septima Poinsette (1898–1987). Educator. BUFA

Clark, William (1770–1838). Explorer. BLC; BUB; COC; CUC; DOBB; FIA; FOB; FOC; GRC; HEB; HIBC; JEA; LED; MAO; ROL†

Clarke, Bobby (Robert Earle) (1949–). Canadian hockey player. AAS-27; CL-06; FICA-1; GUEC; GUH; LEYA; MANA; ORB; THD

Clarke, Bruce Cooper (1901–). General. RAE

Clarke, Fred (1872–1960). Baseball player, manager. ALB; FRC-01

Clarke, Nancy Talbot (1825–1901). Physician. MASA

Clarke, Ron. Australian track athlete. DAJ

Clarkson, John (1862?–1909). Baseball player. ALB

Claudius Ptolemy, see Ptolemy.

Clausen, Alden Winship (1923–). Banker. DU-1

Clauss, Carin (1939–). Labor lawyer. BI†

Claver, Peter (1580–1654). Saint. DAD-3

Clay, Ann. American Revolutionary patriot. CLC†

Clay, Cassius, see Ali, Muhammad.

Clay, Henry (1777–1852). Statesman. GO; HEEA; STH; WHD

Clay, Lucius DuBignon (1897–1978). General. RAE

Claybourne, Braxton Daniel (1877–1935). Cowboy. JO

Cleage, Albert B. (1912–). Clergyman. HAI

Cleave, Mary (1947–). Astronaut. FOJ-1

Cleaver, Eldridge (1935–). Black leader. DADA; HAI

Clemenceau, Georges (1841–1929). French statesman. ASB-1; COKB

Clemens, Samuel Langhorne, see Twain, Mark, pseud.

Clemente, Roberto (1934–1972). Baseball player. BUD-1; BUJ; DAFC; DAFD; FOW; FRC-1†; FRD; GUE; IZA; KADA; NEBB; PEC; PRA; RIGA†; SHH; WH-2; WO

Clementi, Muzio (1752–1832). Italian composer, pianist. CHF

Cleopatra. Saint. DAD-3

Cleopatra (69–30 B.C.). Queen of Egypt. BOI; CAAA; COA; DEI; DEJ; FAE; LIDA; PA; TRBA

Cleva, Fausto (1902–1972). Conductor, born Italy. STM†

Cleveland, Frances Folsom (1864–1947). Wife of Grover Cleveland. BAG; BAG-1; BLG; CHB; KL; MAA; MAU; PRB; ROH; ROHA

Cleveland, Grover (1837–1908). President of U.S. BAEB; BAG; BAG-1; BEB; BLA; BUIA; CAG; CAH; COI; COS; DUB; DUC; DUCA; FRBA; HIH; LEQ; LEQA; MAB; MABA; MIA; PED; ROH; ROHA; ROK†; SUBB; WHD

Clevenger, Johanna. Psychiatrist. FOC-1

Cliburn, Van (1934–). Pianist. EWC; LEHB

Clinton, DeWitt (1769–1828). Statesman. MAL; WHD†

Clinton, George (1739–1812). Vice president of U.S. BUIB†; FEA; HAOA; HOEA

Clinton, Sir Henry (1738–1795). English general. AKA; SOA

Clotilda (470–545). Saint. DAD-2

Clouet, François (1510?–1572). French painter. MAH†

Clouet, Jean (c. 1485–1540). French painter. MAH†

Clower, Jerry (1926–). Comedian. HAG-1

Cluytens, André. Belgian conductor. STM†

Clymer, George (1739–1813). American Revolutionary patriot. BAEA; BUIB†; COJ†; FEAA; FEAB

Clyne, Bernie (1931?–). Lawyer. LETD

Coatsworth, Elizabeth (1893–). Author. SMB

Cobb, Geraldyn M. (1931–). Aviator. GEDB; HIFD

Cobb, James. Son of Ty Cobb. BELB

Cobb, John (1899–1952). English automobile racer. YAA

Cobb, Ty (Tyrus Raymond) (1886–1961). Baseball player. AAS-35; ALB; ASBA; BELB†; COKB; DAFB; DAFC; DAFD; DAG; DAGA; DAH; EPA; FRC-1†; GEC; GR; GUC; GUDA; HEG; HIF; HOC; MUB-1; MUC; RIGA†; ROC; SH; SHH; SID; WAC

Cobb, Will (1876–1930). Songwriter. MOA†

Cobb, William Montague (1904–). Anatomist. CHE; HAMA

Cobham, Captain. English pirate. WHA†

Coca, Imogene (1908–). Comedienne. MASB

Cochet, Henri (1901–1987). French tennis player. FOX

Cochise (1815?–1874). Apache Indian chief. DEDB; HEC; MAEA

Cochran, Barbara Ann (1951–). Skier. FRCA; HOBAA†; LEYB†; RYX; ST-2; WA-1

Cochran, Jacqueline (1906–1980). Cosmetician, aviator. CLA; GEDB; HAMY; HIFD; MO; WAJ

Cochran, Linda (1954–). Skier. HOBAA†; RYX

Cochran, Marilyn (1950–). Skier. HOBAA†; RYX

Cochrane, Elizabeth (1867–1922). Journalist. JAE; JOCA; SQB; WAE

Cochrane, Mickey (Gordon S.) (1903–1962). Baseball player. ALB; DAFD; GUDA; HIC; HIF; HOCM; RIGA†; SHD; SHH; VACA; WAG; ZAA

Cockcroft, Sir John Douglas (1897–1967). English physicist. FE

Cockerell, Sir Christopher (1910–). English inventor. FE; MAPA

Cockerell, Lila (1922–). Mayor. GRAB-1†

Codgen, Claude. Surf rider. OLD

Codona, Alfredo (1894–1937). Italian circus aerialist. SUA

Cody, William Frederick (Buffalo Bill) (1846–1917). Scout, showman. BUI; COE; DEI; DEJ; KEH; KIB; WAF

Coe, Sebastian (1956–). English track athlete. AAS-26

Coe, Urling C. (fl. 1905). Physician. WAA

Coffin, Levi (1798–1877). Abolitionist. COG

Cohan, George Michael (1878–1942). Actor, composer. EWA; MOA

Cohen, Andy (Andrew) (1904–). Baseball player. RI; SLA

Cohen, Eli (1924–1965). Israeli spy, born Egypt. GRB-1

Cohen, Maxwell (1908–). Lawyer. UN

Cohen, Robert (1930–). Boxer, born Algeria. SLA†

Cohen-Mintz, Tanhum (1939–). Israeli basketball player, born Latvia. SLA†

Cohn, Arthur (1910–). Conductor. STM†

Cohn, Waldo (1910–). Conductor. STM†

Coictier, Jacques (1482–1506). French physician. MAR

Coka, Gilbert (1910–). African educator. PEA

Colan, Gene (1926–). Cartoonist. GOB-1

Colavito, Rocky (Rocco Domenico) (1933–). Baseball player. DA

Colbert, Lester (1905–). Automobile industry executive. PAA

Colbert, Nathan (1946–). Baseball player. KLCA

Colburn, Zerah (1804–1839). Mathematical prodigy. FOR

Colden, Cadwallader (1688–1776). Botanist, born Ireland. PAC

Colden, Jane, *see* Farquhar, Jane Colden.

Cole, Jack (1914–1958). Cartoonist. GOB-1

Cole, Nat "King" (1919–1965). Pianist, singer. ROF

Cole, Thomas (1801–1848). Painter, born England. HEDA; LEB

Coleman, Albert (1910–). French conductor. STM†

Coleman, Bessie (1893–1926). Aviator. HIFD; LOAV

Coleman, Mary Stallings. Judge. SWI

Coleman, Ornette (1930–). Saxophonist. COF-1; WAD†

Coleman, Valerie D. Television reporter. STAA

Coleridge, Samuel Taylor (1772–1834). English poet. COP; RAC

Coleridge-Taylor, Samuel (1875–1912). English composer. ADA; ADB; BRB†

Colfax, Schuyler (1823–1885). Vice president of U.S. FEA; HAOA; HOEA

Collazo, Oscar (1914–). Revolutionist. RABA

Collett, Glenna (1903–). Golfer. HOBA; HOBAA; JAB

Collins, Daniel A. (1916–). Dentist. HAMA

Collins, Doug (1951–). Basketball player. ARB-4

Collins, Eddie (1887–1951). Baseball player. ALB; DAFD; DAG; DAGA; HIF; MUB-1; RIGA†; ROC

Collins, Gary. Football player. CO

Collins, Jimmy (1870?–1943). Baseball player. ALB; LEY†

Collins, Joanne. City councilwoman. WHE†

Collins, Judy (1939–). Singer, guitarist. BOHC; SC-02

Collins, Martha Layne (1936–). Governor. WHE†

Collins, Michael (1930–). Astronaut. COQ; LEPB†; THC†

Collishaw, Raymond (1893–). Canadian aviator, WW I. HAG

Colman of Kilmacduagh (d. 632). Saint. ONA

Colón, Miriam. Actress. NEBB

Colonne, Edouard (1838–1910). French conductor. YOM

Colt, Samuel (1814–1862). Inventor. FRB; HEB; HOF; HYA†

Colter, John (1775–1813). Trapper, explorer. BUB; BUG; FOC; JAC; LED

Coltrane, John William (1926–1967). Saxophonist. COF-1; TEB; WAD†

Colum, Padraic (1881–1972). Author, born Ireland. BEI

Columba, Saint, *see* Columcille, Saint.

Columban (543?–615). Saint. DAD-1; DAD-3; REC

Columbus, Christopher (1451–1506). Italian explorer. ASB; COC; DAF; DEI; DEJ; DOBB; DYA; EVD; GRC; KEH; KNB; MAT; MOB; OLA; PRC; ROL; VIA; WIA-1

Columcille (521–597). Saint. CHD†; DAD-2; REC

Comaneci, Nadia (1961–). Romanian gymnast. FOR; GUED; LIE

Combs, Bob. Little League coach. LEW

Comenius, John Amos (1592–1670). Czechoslovakian theologian, educator. FRC

Comiskey, Charles Albert (1859–1931). Baseball player, manager. ALB; SMK

Commoner, Barry (1917–). Biologist. SQA

Comparetti, Ermanno F. (1909–). Conductor, born Italy. STM†

Compton, Arthur Holly (1892–1962). Physicist. BAF; BOB; RID

Compton, Karl Taylor (1887–1954). Physicist. BOB

Compton, Wilson Martindale (1890–1967). Economist. BOB

Comstock, Anna Botsford (1854–1930). Naturalist, wood engraver. EMB†; PAC; YOC

Comstock, Anthony (1844–1915). Reformer. DEDA

Comstock, John Henry (1849–1931). Entomologist. PAC

Conant, James Bryant (1893–1978). Educator. LEJA

Conaway, James Bennett. Journalist. STAA

Concello, Antoinette. Aerialist. KIB

Concello, Arthur Vas. Aerialist. KIB

Concklin, Seth (fl. 1851). Abolitionist. STJA

Conde, Carlos. Civil rights leader. NEAA

Cone, Cynthia. Anthropologist. BOHG

Conerly, Charley (1922–). Football player. DUD; DUE

Confucius (551–479 B.C.). Chinese philosopher. DEI; DEJ; LO; SPA

Congreve, Sir William (1772–1828). English inventor. STMA

Conkling, Hilda (1910–1986). Child poet. FOR

Conner, Bart (1958–). Gymnast. LIE

Connibear, Hiram (d. 1917). Rowing coach. DAG; DAGA

Connolly, Harold (1931–). Track athlete. HIA

Connolly, James B. (1868–1957). Track athlete. DAG; DAGA; DAJ; DEF

Connolly, Maureen (1934–1969). Tennis player. ALBA; DAG; DAGA; FR-1; HI; HOBA; HOBAA†; SUDA†

Connolly, Olga Fikotova (1933–). Track athlete, born Czechoslovakia. HOBA; HOBAA

Connolly, Thomas Henry (1870–1961). Baseball umpire. ALB

Connor, Patrick Edward (1820–1891). Journalist, born Ireland. SEC

Connors, Chuck (1924–). Actor. HOBB

Connors, Jimmy (James Scott) (1952–). Tennis player. AAS-28; FOX; GLC; LAHA

Conrad of Piacenza (d. 1351). Saint. MOC

Conrad, Charles, Jr. (1930–). Astronaut. THC

Conrad, Con (Conrad Dober) (1891–1938). Songwriter. MOA

Conrad, Joseph (1857–1924). English author, born Poland. COO; MANB; STL

Constantine (1940–). Prince of Greece. NEC†

Constantine I, the Great (280–337). Emperor of Rome. CAAA; COK; NEC

Contardo Ferrini, Blessed. DAD-3

Conte, Joseph (1914–). Conductor. STM†

Conway, James Sevier (1798–1855). Governor. SEC

Conyers, John, Jr. (1929–). Congressman. BRGA; DU†; YOI

Conzelman, Jimmy (James Gleason) (1898?–). Football coach. SUD

Cook, Bill (b. 1873). Outlaw. SUJ

Cook, Greg (Gregory Lynn) (1947?–). Football player. LEZA

Cook, James (1728–1779). English explorer. COC; COL; DAF; DOBB; DOC; DYA; FAF; GRC; KEH; KNB; LAA-2; MOB; ROL; WIA-1

Cook, Judy, see Souter, Judy Cook.

Cook, Leon F. (1939–). American Indian leader. GRAC

Coolbaugh, Blaine. Conductor. STM†

Coolidge, Calvin (1872–1933). President of U.S. ALE; BAEB; BAG; BAG-1; BEB; BLA; BOD; BUIA; CAG; CAH; COI; COS; DUB; DUC; DUCA; FEA; FRBA; HAOA; HIH; HOEA; LEQ; LEQA; MAB; MABA; MIA; PED; ROH; ROHA; ROK†; SUBB; WHD

Coolidge, Grace Anna (1879–1957). Wife of Calvin Coolidge. BAG; BAG-1; BLG; CHB; KL; MAA; MAAA; MAU; PRB; ROH; ROHA

Cooney, Joan Ganz (1929–). Television producer. GIB-1; LES-1

Cooper, Anthony Ashley, see Shaftesbury, Anthony Ashley Cooper, 7th earl of.

Cooper, Arvazine Angeline (1845–1929). Pioneer. MAV

Cooper, Dan B. (fl. 1971). Hijacker. WIAA-1

Cooper, Earl (1886–1965). Automobile racer. LEX

Cooper, Emil (1880–1960). Conductor, born Russia. STM†

Cooper, Irving Spencer (1922–1985). Surgeon. HEFA

Cooper, James Fenimore (1789–1851). Author. BOA; CAC; CUC; DEI; DEJ; HACB; HEF; LEGB

Cooper, John (1832–1891). Sailor, born Ireland. TA

Cooper, Leroy Gordon, Jr. (1927–). Astronaut. THC

Cooper, Mort (1913–). Baseball player. DEG†

Cooper, Peter (1791–1883). Manufacturer. HOF

Cooper, Polly. American Revolutionary patriot. CLC†

Cooper, Walker (1914–1958). Baseball player. DEG†; HIC

Coosaponakeesa, see Bosomworth, Mary Musgrove Matthews.

Cope, Edward Drinker (1840–1897). Paleontologist. HYB

Copeland, Lillian (1904–1964). Track athlete. SLA

Copernicus, Nicolaus (1473–1543). Polish astronomer. ASA; BEP; BOB; CAA; COL; DOE; FE; MANB; MOCB; PIA; POD; SHFB; SIA; SIB; STI; SUE

Copland, Aaron (1900–). Composer. BAD; BEKA; BEN; KAE; KE; MAF; POF; SAA†; YOL

Copley, John Singleton (1738–1815). Painter. BR; MAG; SIE

Coppin, Fanny Jackson (1836–1913). Educator. BRB

Coppola, Anton (1918–). Conductor. STM†

Coppola, Francis (1939–). Motion picture director. SMBB-3

Corbett, Jim (James John) (1866–1933). Boxer. RAAC

Corbett, William (1763–1835). Journalist. SQB†

Corbin, Margaret (1751–1800). American Revolutionary patriot. AND; CLC; RAD

Cordero y Molina, Rafael (1790–1868). Puerto Rican educator. TU

Cordiner, Ralph (1900–1973). Corporation executive. PAA

Corelli, Arcangelo (1653–1713). Italian composer. BEM; CHFA; KAE; YOM†

Corelli, Franco (1924?–). Italian singer. BRBB-1

Cori, Carl Ferdinand (1896–1984). Biochemist, born Czechoslovakia. RIF

Cori, Gerty Theresa (1896–1957). Biochemist, born Czechoslovakia. RIF; SC†; SHFE†; YOF

Coriolis, Gaspard Gustave de (1792–1843). French mathematician. HAC

Corkle, Francesca (1952–). Dancer. FOGC†

Corliss, George Henry (1817–1888). Inventor. HYA†

Cornell, Ezra (1807–1874). Financier. BOD

Cornell, Katharine (1898–1974). Actress. BOC; DI-1†; GIBA†

Cornick, Wade (1965?–). Winner, Young American Medal for Bravery. ANCA

Cornish, Samuel E. (19th century). Clergyman, journalist. BEJ

Cornwallis, Charles Cornwallis, 1st marquis (1738–1805). English general. AKA; SOA

Coronado, Francisco Vásquez de (1510–1554). Spanish explorer. ASB; BLD; COC; GAA; KEG; NAA; ROL

Corot, Jean Baptiste (1796–1875). French painter. CHC; DEI; DEJ; MAH

Corregidora, La, see Dominguez, (Maria) Josefa Ortiz de.

Correll, Charles J. (1890–1972). Comedian. BUR-1

Corrigan, Mairead (1944–). Irish social reformer. AAS-34; COG-1; SHFE†

Cortes, Hernando (1485–1547). Spanish explorer. BEO; COC; GAA; KEG; KNA; MOB; ROL

Cortez, Mario (1902–). Cellist, born Italy. STM†

Cortor, Eldzier (1916–). Painter. FAH

Cosby, Bill (1937–). Actor, entertainer. HOBB

Cosell, Howard (1920–). Sports announcer. SLA†

Cosmas (3d century). Saint. CHD†; DAD-3

Costain, Thomas B. (1885–1965). Author. CON

Costanza, Margaret (Midge) (1928?–). Ex-presidential aide. GRAB-1†

Costello, Larry (1932–). Basketball player, coach. DEHA-1

Costello, Lou (Louis Francis) (1908–1959). Comedian. BUR-1; ED-1†

Costello, Patty. Bowler. HOBAA†

Cottam, Clarence (1899–). Biologist, conservationist. MIB†

Cotter, Jim (b. 1834). Stowaway. CAD

Cottolengo, Joseph Benedict. Saint. DAD-1

Cottrell, Frederick Gardner (1877–1948). Chemist. MAPA; YOE

Coughlin, Charles Edward (1891–1979). Clergyman, born Canada. COGA

Coulomb, Charles Augustin de (1736–1806). French physicist. SHFB

Couperin, François (1668–1733). French composer, harpsichordist. BEM; KAE

Cournand, André Frédéric (1895–1988). Physiologist, born France. RIF

Cournoyer, Ivan Serge (1943–). Canadian hockey player. CL-06; LEYA; THG

Court, Margaret (1942–). Australian tennis player. AAS-29; FR-1; HOBAA†; MATA; SUDA

Courtney, Clint (1927–). Baseball player. BOE

Courtright, T. I. (1848–1887). Law officer. SUI

Courvoisier, Jean. Swiss Red Cross delegate. DED

Cousineau, Tom (1957–). Football player. AAS-15

Cousins, Jane "Casey" (1924–). Real estate executive. LES-1

Cousteau, Jacques Yves (1910–). French underwater explorer. COR; DU-1; ELA; FE; OLC; PRC; SCBA; SQA

Cousy, Bob (Robert) (1928–). Basketball player. ASBA; BEL; BUJA; DAG; DAGA; DEHA-1; FOI; HEG; HEHA; HID; HOC; PE; SID

Covilham, Peter de (1450?–1545). Portuguese explorer. KNA

Coward, Noel (1889–1973). English composer, playwright. ASB-1

Cowell, Henry Dixon (1897–1965). Composer. POF

Cowens, Dave (1948–). Basketball player. AAS-5; ARB-1; BELB; GUEA; KLC; RUB

Cowley, Abraham (1618–1667). English poet. COP

Cox, Diane (1958?–). Motorcyclist. BUIC

Cox, Fred (1938–). Football player. AAS-17

Cox, Herald Rea (1907–). Virologist. PAB

Cox, James Middleton (1870–1957). Politician. WHD†

Cox, Lynne (1958–). Swimmer. HOBAA†

Cox, Wally (1924–1973). Actor. ALC

Crabbe, Buster (1908–1983). Swimmer. LEYB†

Crabtree, Lotta (1847–1924). Comedienne. MASB

Craft, Ellen (c. 1826–1897). Runaway slave. CHFB; LOAV; STAB-1

Craft, Robert (1923–). Conductor. STM†; YOM†

Craft, William (fl. 1860). Runaway slave. CHFB

Craig, Daniel (1814–1895). Journalist. SQB

Craig, Jim (1957–). Hockey player. OLDE

Craik, Dinah Mulock (1826–1887). English author. BEI

Cramer, Johann Baptist (1771–1858). German pianist, composer. CHF

Cramer, Scott. Skater. VAD-6

Crandall, Delmar Wesley (1930–). Baseball player. HIC

Crandall, Prudence (1803–1889). Educator, abolitionist. BUA; CHFB; TRD; WABC†

Crandall, Reed (d. 1982). Cartoonist. GOB-1

Crane, Jocelyn (1909–). Zoologist. YOF

Crane, Stephen (1871–1900). Author. CAC; HEF; JAD; STL

Cranmer, Thomas (1489–1556). Archbishop of Canterbury. MAJ

Crawford, Jane Todd (1763–1842). Pioneer. RIB

Crawford, Marianne. Basketball player. HOBAA†

Crawford, Wahoo Sam (Samuel Earl) (b. 1880). Baseball player. ALB; RIGA†

Crawford, Wilford B. (1911–). Conductor. STM†

Crazy Horse (1849?–1877). Sioux chief. DEDB; HEC; HEGA; STAB; SUKA; WAM

Creelman, James (1859–1915). Journalist. FLBB

Cremer, Sir William Randal (1838–1908). English pacifist. MEA; MEC; WIC

Crémieux, Isaac-Adolphe (1796–1880). French statesman. KAD

Crescenti, Pasquale (1895–). Conductor, born Italy. STM†

Cresques Lo Juheu (fl. 1375). Spanish mapmaker. GEF

Creston, Paul (1906–). Composer. POF

Crick, Francis H. C. (1916–). English biologist. BEK; FE; FRE†; RIF

Crocker, Charles (1822–1888). Financier. BLD†

Crocker, Hannah Mather (1752–1829). Feminist, author. WABC†

Crockett, Davy (1786–1836). Frontiersman. AKC; COE; FOC; KUA; LYF; MAO; WAN

Crockett, George (1909–). Jurist. DU†

Crockett, Ivory (1950?–). Track athlete. LEYB†

Croesus (d. 547 B.C.). King of Lydia. COA; JOBB

Croghan, George (d. 1782). Pioneer trader. VIA

Cromwell, Dean Bartlett (1879–1962). Track coach. HEH

Cromwell, John P. (1901–1943). Naval officer, WW II. REA

Cromwell, Nolan (1955–). Football player. AAS-13

Cromwell, Oliver (1599–1658). Lord Protector of England. CAAA; CAE; DEC; DEI; DEJ; GRAB

Cromwell, Oliver (1753?–1853?). American Revolutionary soldier. ADB; DAF-1†; WIBA

Cromwell, Richard (1626–1712). Lord Protector of England. GRAB†

Cromwell, Townsend (1922–1958). Oceanographer. BRBC

Cronin, Joe (1906–1984). Baseball player, manager. ALB; DAFD; FRC-01; HIF; MUB-1; MUC

Cronkite, Walter (1916–). Radio and television commentator. JAD

Cronquist, Robert (1929–). Conductor. STM†

Crookes, Sir William (1832–1919). English physicist, chemist. FE; SIA

Crosby, Bob. Rodeo cowboy. WAA

Crosby, Enoch (b. 1750). Spy. FOA

Crowley, Aleister (1875–1947). English magician. ED-5

Crowley, James (1902?–1986). Football player. DAG; DAGA; DAI; HIE

Crowther, Samuel Ajayi (1808–1891). Nigerian bishop. POA

Crumbine, Samuel Jay (1862–1954). Physician. BLC; LEG

Crummell, Alexander (1819–1898). Missionary. ADA; ADB; BRB†; GRAB-05

Crump, Diane. Jockey. HOBA†; HOBAA†

Cruyff, Johan (1947–). Dutch soccer player. ADL

Csonka, Larry (1946–). Football player. AAS-10; BELB; DUF; GUEB; GUF; LEZB; MOCA; ST

Cuauhtémoc (1495–1525). Aztec emperor. ROGB

Cueller, Mike (Miguel) (1937–). Baseball player. BELA

Cuffe, Paul (1759–1817). Seaman, colonizer. ADA; ADB; BRB; DOB; GRAB-02; HUB; PECA; WIBA

Cui, César Antonovich (1835–1918). Russian composer. POG; SAA†

Cukela, Louis (1888–1956). Marine officer, born Serbia. TA

Cukor, George (1899–1983). Motion picture director. SMBC

Cullen, Countee (1903–1946). Poet. ADA; ADB; ROE

Culver, Carmen (1939–). Television screenwriter. SMBB-2

Cummings, Candy (William Arthur) (1848–1924). Baseball player. ALB

Cummings, Terry (1961–). Basketball player. AAS-7

Cunegundes. Saint. DAD-2

Cuneo, Ann Curtis, see Curtis, Ann.

Cunitz, Maria (17th century). Silesian astronomer. SC†

Cunningham, Billy (1943–). Basketball player. SA

Cunningham, Glenn (1909–1988). Track athlete. AAS-26; BUJA; DAG; DAGA; DAJ; GEA; HOC; LYA; LYC; PIB; PIBA; SCA

Cure d'Ars, see Vianney, Jean Baptiste Marie.

Curie, Marie Sklodowska (1867–1934). French chemist, physicist, born Poland. ASA; ASB-1; BEC; BEP; BOB; BOC; BOH; BUF; CAA; COL; DEI; DEJ; DOE; EVD; FE; FRE; HUE; KOA; MAJ; MANB; MASA; PA; PAC; POD; RID; SC; SHFB; SHFE†; SIA; STI

Curie, Pierre (1859–1906). French chemist. ASA; BOB; BUF; DOE; PAC; RID; STI

Curlee-Salisbury, Joan (1930–). Psychologist. BRBE†

Currie, Dan. Football player. JOA†

Curry, George (1863–1947). Governor. SEC

Curry, George E. Journalist. STAA

Curry, John (1949–). English skater. LIEA; VAD-6

Curtice, Harlow H. (1893–1962). Automobile industry executive. PAA

Curtis, Ann (1926–). Swimmer. HOBA†; HOBAA; JAB

Curtis, Charles (1860–1936). Vice president of U.S. FEA; HAOA; HOEA; LEH

Curtis, Edgar (1914–). Conductor, born Scotland. STM†

Curtis, Edward Sheriff (1868–1952). Photographer. SUAA

Curtis, Isaac (1950–). Football player. RUA

Curtis, Mike (1943–). Football player. KABA; ST

Curtiss, Glenn Hammond (1878–1930). Inventor, aviator. BOK; HAMY; HOF

Cushing, Harvey Williams (1869–1939). Surgeon. CHD; CHE†; SIC

Cushing, William Barker (1842–1874). Naval officer. ICA

Cushman, Charlotte Saunders (1816–1876). Actress. STJ; VAA; VAB

Cushman, Cliff. Track athlete. LYD

Cushman, Pauline (1833–1893). Civil War spy. RAB

Custer, Elizabeth Bacon (1842–1933). Wife of General Custer. JOB

Custer, George Armstrong (1839–1876). General. ARE; LEP; LEPE

Custer, Thomas Ward (1845–1876). Soldier. TA

Cuthbert (635?–687). Saint. CHD†; DAD-2

Cuvier, Georges (1769–1832). French zoologist. FE

Cuyler, Hazen Shirley "Kiki" (1899–1950). Baseball player. RIGA†

Cyprian. Saint. DAD-3

Cyril (827–869). Saint. DAD-3

Cyril of Jerusalem (d. 387). Saint. DAD-2

Cyrus (600?–529 B.C.). King of Persia. CAAA; COA

Czerny, Karl (1791–1857). Austrian composer, pianist. CHF

Czolgosz, Leon F. (1873–1901). Assassin. RABA

D

Dabney, Austin (fl. 1779–1821). American Revolutionary soldier. DAF-1; WIBA†

Dabney, Mrs. Civil War spy. STQ

Dacanay, Pattie. Martial artist. AT

Da Gama, Vasco, see Gama, Vasco da.

Daggett, Polly. Colonial girl. CAD

Daguerre, Louis Jacques (1787–1851). French inventor. FE; FRE; THA

Dahia al-Kahina (fl. 667–702). African queen. GRAB-04

Dailey, Ulysses Grant (1885–1961). Surgeon. ADA; ADB

Daimler, Gottlieb (1834–1900). German engineer, inventor. EBA; FE; THA

Dale, Carroll. Football player. JOA†

Dale, Sir Henry Hallett (1875–1968). English physiologist. RIF

Dale, Jerome (1964?–). Winner, Young American Medal for Bravery. ANCA

Daley, Buddy Leo (1932–). Baseball player. GEA

Daley, Cass (1915–1975). Comedienne. MASB

Dali, Salvador (1904–). Spanish painter. WIAA

Dallas, George Mifflin (1792–1864). Vice president of U.S. FEA; HAOA; HOEA

Dalstrom, Ingeborg. Student nurse. WRA

Dalton, John (1766–1844). English chemist, physicist. CAA; FE; MOBA; SHFB; SIA; STI

Dalton brothers (fl. 1890). Outlaw gang. JOBA; REE; SUJ

Daltrey, Roger (1945–). English singer. BUIB-2

Dalvit, Lewis (1925–). Conductor. STM†

Daly, Daniel Joseph (1873–1937). Marine. TA

Daly, Moe (Maurice Francis) (d. 1944). Army officer. RAE

Daly, Thomas Augustine (1871–1948). Columnist, poet. BEH

Dam, Henrik (1895–1976). Danish biochemist. RIF

Damian (d. 303). Saint. CHD†

Damiani, Leo (1912–). Conductor. STM†

Damien. Saint. DAD-3

Damien de Veuster, Joseph (Father Damien) (1840–1889). Belgian missionary. EVD; HAA; HEA; MAJ; MAN; STP; WRA

Dampier, Louis (1944–). Basketball player. HIBAA

Dampier, William (1652–1715). English pirate, explorer. KNB; MOB

Damrosch, Walter (1862–1950). Conductor, born Germany. CUC

Dana, James Dwight (1813–1895). Geologist. HYB

Dana, Richard Henry, Jr. (1815–1882). Author, sailor. BEGA; SUFA

D'Andrea, Frank (1914–). Conductor. STM†

Daniel, Captain. Pirate. WHA†

Daniel, Erno (1918–). Conductor, born Hungary. STM†

Danielian, Leon (1920–). Dancer. ATA

Daniels, David. Conductor, born Poland. STM†

Daniels, Mel. Basketball player. HIBA

Daniels, Susan (1948–). Psychologist. BOHA-1

Danilova, Alexandra. Russian dancer. ATA

Danilowitz, Abraham Phineas (1908–). South African bowls champion. SLA†

Danning, Harry (1911–). Baseball player. RI; SLA

Dante, Alighieri (1265–1321). Italian poet. DEI; DEJ

Dantley, Adrian (1956–). Basketball player. AAS-7

Darby, Abraham (c. 1678–1717). English manufacturer. FE

D'Arc, Jeanne, see Joan of Arc.

Darcy, Tom (Thomas Francis). Cartoonist. DEDC

Darden, Christine (1942–). Aerospace engineer. FOC-1

Dario, Rubén (Felix Rubén Garcia Sarmiento) (1867–1916). Nicaraguan poet. WO

Darius (558?–486? B.C.). King of Persia. CAAA; COA

Dark, Alvin (1923–). Baseball player, manager. BOE

Darken, Lawrence Stamper (1909–). Chemist. PAB

Darling, Grace Horsley (1815–1842). English heroine. MAJ; STP

Darling, Jay Norwood (1876–1962). Cartoonist. DEDC

Darling, Ron (1960–). Baseball player. GUB-1

Darmon, Pierre (1934–). French tennis player, born Tunisia. SLA†

Darragh, Lydia B. (1728?–1789). Spy. AND; CLC; KN

Darrow, Clarence Seward (1857–1938). Lawyer. LAC; WECB

Dart, Isom, pseud. (1849–1900). Outlaw. KADB

D'Artega, Alfonso (1907–). Mexican conductor. STM†

Darwin, Charles Robert (1809–1882). English naturalist. ASA; BEK; BEP; BLB; CAA; CAB; COL; DEI; DEJ; DOE; FE; FRE; MIB; MOB; POD; SIA; SOB; STI

Dash, James Allan. Conductor. STM†

Dat-So-La-Lee (1830–1925). Washoe Indian basket maker. WAB

D'Aulaire, Edgar Parin, see Aulaire, Edgar Parin d'.

D'Aulaire, Ingri, see Aulaire, Ingri d'.

Daumier, Honoré (1808–1879). French painter. KAA

D'Autremont brothers (fl. 1904–1958). Train robbers. WIAA-1

Davenport, Homer Calvin (1867–1912). Cartoonist. DEDC

Davenport, Thomas (1802–1851). Inventor. HYA†; MAP

David. Israeli pilgrim, born Yemen. GRB-1

David (c. 1012–972 B.C.). King of Israel. BEC; CAAA; GEF; JOBB; STP

David (500?–589). Saint. ONA

David I of Scotland (b. 1080). Saint. DAD-2

David, François-Eugène. Swiss journalist, Red Cross delegate. DED

David, Jacques Louis (1748–1825). French painter. KAA; MAH†

Davidman, Elazar (1936–). Israeli tennis player. SLA†

Davidson, J. Brownlee (1880–1957). Agricultural engineer. LEGA; YOD

Davie, William Richardson (1756–1820). Lawyer, governor, born England. FEAA

Davies, Arthur B. (1862–1928). Painter. LEE; SIE

Davies, Mary Carolyn. Poet. BEF

Davis, Al (1929–). Football coach, owner. SLA

Davis, Belva. Television newscaster. STAA

Davis, Benjamin Jefferson (1903–1964). Communist leader. DADA

Davis, Benjamin O. (1877–1970). General. ADA; ADB; FLD

Davis, Benjamin O., Jr. (1912–). General. ADA; ADB; BOG; BRG; FLD; HUB; RIC; STO; STQ

Davis, Ernie (1939–1963). Football player. CL-04

Davis, Glenn (1924–). Football player. DAFB; DAFG; DAI; DEHB; HIE; HOC

Davis, Jack (1926–). Cartoonist. GOB-1

Davis, Jefferson (1808–1889). Confederate president. MAO

Davis, Joan (1907–1961). Actress. MASB

Davis, John (1550?–1605). English explorer. ROL†

Davis, John William (1873–1955). Political leader. WHD†

Davis, Johnny (1955–). Basketball player. AAS-6

Davis, Mac (1942–). Singer. KRI

Davis, Miles Dewey, Jr. (1926–). Trumpeter. WAD†

Davis, Muriel. Gymnast. HOBAA†

Davis, Pauline Wright (1813–1876). Feminist. GUBA†; LES-2

Davis, Richard Harding (1864–1916). Journalist. FLBB; JAD

Davis, Sam (1842–1863). Confederate scout. MAO

Davis, Sammy, Jr. (1925–). Entertainer. DOBA; DOF-1; ROF

Davis, Stuart (1894–). Painter. FRA

Davis, Walt (1930?–). Track athlete. DAG; DAGA

Davis, Willie (1934–). Football player. ANA; JOA

Davis, Willie (1940–). Baseball player. LYE

Davison, Ann (fl. 1952). English adventurer. HAQ

Davison, Frederic Ellis (1917–). General. DRA

Davy, Sir Humphry (1778–1829). English chemist. CAA; COL; DUA; FE; SHFB; SOB; STI; THA

Dawes, Charles Gates (1865–1951). Vice president of U.S. FEA; HAOA; HOEA; MEC†; WIC

Dawkins, Peter (1938?–). Army officer. RAE

Dawson, Lenny (1935–). Football player. DEH; DUD; DUE; LEZA; LIBA; RAAD; SHEA

Dawson, Merna. Chemist. HOG

Dawson, William L. (1886–1970). Congressman. DU†

Dawson, William Levi (1898–). Composer. ADA; ADB

Day, Clarence S., Jr. (1874–1935). Author. BEE

Day, Dorothy (1897–1980). Journalist. BLF; COG-1; NIA; ROJ

Day, Enid. Nurse's aide. WRA

Day, James E. (1905–1980). Stock exchange executive. PAA

Day, Ned (Edward Gately) (1911?–1971). Bowler. DAG; DAGA

Dayan, Moshe (1915–1981). Israeli foreign minister. ROGA; GRB-1; WECA

Dayton, Jonathan (1760–1824). Senator. BUIB†; FEAA

Dean, Al. Racing car manager. LEW

Dean, Dizzy (Jay Hanna) (1911–1974). Baseball player, sportscaster. ALB; BED; BOE; BRC; BUD-1; DAFB; DAFD; DEG; FRC-1†; GIB; GRA; HOC; LIAA; NEA; RIGA†; SHH; SMK

Dean, Fred (1952–). Football player. AAS-16

Dean, Laura. Dancer, choreographer. GLO

Dean, Paul (1913–1981). Baseball player. GRA; NEA

Dean, Silas (1737–1789). Diplomat. BUIB†

Dean, Stewart (fl. 1785). Sea captain. CAD

Dean, William Frishe (1899–1981). General. REA

De Angeli, Marguerite (1889–1987). Author, illustrator. SMB

Dearborn, Henry (1751–1829). Secretary of War. BUIB†

DeBakey, Michael Ellis (1908–). Surgeon. CHE†

Debbie P. (1960–). Physically disabled. SIAA

De Beausoliel, Martine (17th century). French mineralogist. SC†

DeBerry, William Nelson (b. 1870). Clergyman. BRB†

Deborah. Biblical prophetess, judge. GEF; LER

De Broglie, Louis-Victor, see Broglie, Louis-Victor de.

Debs, Eugene Victor (1855–1926). Socialist leader. ARB; SEA; WECB

de Burgos, Julia, see Burgos, Julia de.

DeBusschere, Dave (1940–). Basketball player. DEHA-1; HIBA

Debussy, Claude Achille (1862–1918). French composer. BRF; BUD; FIE; KAE; SAA

De Carava, Roy R. (1919–). Photographer. FAH

Decatur, Stephen (1779–1820). Naval officer. COD; CUC; ICA; NAC

Decker, Mary (1958–). Track athlete. AAS-26; HOBAA†; LEYB†; ST-2; SUDB

Dee, John (1527–1608). English mathematician, astrologer. COEA; CUA; ED-5

Dee, Ruby (1924?–). Actress. FAG

Deere, John (1804–1886). Manufacturer. HOF

De Falla, Manuel, see Falla, Manuel de.

Defauw, Désiré (1885–). Belgian conductor. STM†

Defoe, Daniel (1660–1731). English author. COO; SEB

De Forest, Lee (1873–1961). Inventor. COLA; CUC; FAB; HYA; LEL; MAP; THA

De Frank, Vincent. Conductor. STM†

Degas, Edgar (1834–1917). French painter. KAA; MAH

De Gaulle, Charles, see Gaulle, Charles de.

Degonwadonti, see Brant, Molly.

de Grasse, François Joseph, see Grasse, François Joseph de.

DeJong, Meindert (1910–). Author, born the Netherlands. SMB

DeKalb, Baron, see Kalb, Johann.

De Kooning, Willem (1904–). Painter, born the Netherlands. WIAA

Delacroix, Eugène (1798–1863). French painter. KAA; MAH

DeLamielleure, Joe (1951–). Football player. AAS-11

Delanoue, Jeanne, Blessed (1666–1736). DAD-3

Delany, Martin R. (1812–1885). Ethnologist. ADA; ADB; BRB; GRAB-05

Deledda, Grazia (1875–1936). Italian author. SHFE†

deLeeuw, Adele (1899–). Author. SMAB

deLeeuw, Cateau (1903–). Author, illustrator. SMAB

deLeeuw, Diane (1956–). Skater, born the Netherlands. VAD-6; VADA

de Leon, David (1813–1872). Physician. GRB-1

Delgado, Estrella (1958?–). Migrant worker. WECC

Delilah. Biblical character. SUG

Delius, Frederick (1862–1934). English composer. BUC; KAE; SAA†

della Francesca, Piero, see Francesca, Piero della.

Dello Joio, Norman (1913–). Composer. MAF; POF

De Long, George Washington (1844–1881). Naval officer, explorer. DOC†

Deloria, Vine, Jr. (1934?–). American Indian leader, author. GRAC

Delvecchio, Alex (Fats) (1931–). Canadian hockey player, coach. DEHA-1

DeMar, Clarence (1888?–1958). Track athlete. DAG; DAGA; DAJ; HIA-01†; PIB

De Mille, Agnes (1908–). Dancer, choreographer. CLA; FOGC; GIB-1; STLA

DeMille, Cecil Blount (1881–1959). Motion picture producer. ASB-1; FLBC

Demmert, Archie W. (1909–). Educator. GRAC

Democritos, Bolos (fl. 200 B.C.). Greek alchemist. CUA; FE

DeMont, Rick (Richard) (1956?–). Swimmer. LEYB†

Demosthenes (384–322 B.C.). Athenian orator, statesman. PLA

Dempsey, Jack (1895–1983). Boxer. ASBA; BELB†; DAG; DAGA; HEG; HOC; LAC; LEF; RAAC; SID

Dempsey, Tom (1941–). Football player. AAS-17; AAS-27; BELB; LIBB

Denecke, Henry (1914–). Conductor. STM†

Dengler, Dieter (1938?–). Aviator, born Germany. ARBA

Denham, Dixon (1786–1828). English traveler. ROL†

Dennis, John (1922–). Conductor. STM†

Densen-Gerber, Judianne (1934–). Psychiatrist. GIB-1

Denver, John (1943–). Singer. KRI-1

DePalma, Brian (1940–). Motion picture director. SMBB-3

De Palma, Ralph (1883?–1956). Automobile racer, born Italy. LEX; OLAA; YAA

De Paolo, Peter (b. 1887). Automobile racer. YAA

DePriest, James (1936–). Conductor. AB

De Priest, Oscar (1871–1951). Congressman. ADA; ADB; YOI

De Quincey, Thomas (1785–1859). English author. BEG

Derby, Elias H. (1739–1799). Merchant. BUIB†

Derby, Richard W. (1712–1783). Merchant. BUIB†

Derham, James (b. 1762). Physician. BRB†; WIBA

Dern, Bruce (1936–). Actor, track athlete. BELB

De Rochambeau, see Rochambeau, comte de.

Derricotte, Juliette (1897–1931). Social worker. BUFA

De Sable, Jean Baptiste Pointe, see Pointe de Sable, Jean Baptiste.

de Sautuola, Maria (1870–1946). Spanish discoverer of prehistoric cave paintings at 8. FOR

Descartes, René (1596–1650). French philosopher, mathematician. LO; MUB; OZA; SHFB; SIA; STN

De Seversky, Alexander P. (1894–1974). Aeronautical engineer, born Russia. GEA

De Smet, Pierre Jean (1801–1873). Belgian missionary. ASB

De Soto, Hernando (1500–1542). Spanish explorer. DEI; DEJ; GRC; LED; LEPF; ROL

Dessalines, Jean Jacques (1758–1806). Emperor of Haiti. ADA; ADB

Dett, Robert Nathaniel (1882–1943). Composer. ADA; ADB; BRB†

Deutsch, Albert (1905–1961). Public health pioneer. CHE†

De Varona, Donna (1947–). Swimmer, TV broadcaster. BOHA

Devereux, Henry Kelsey. Colonial boy. CAD

Devlin, Harry (1918–). Author, illustrator. SMAB

Devlin, Wende (1918–). Author, illustrator. SMAB

Devore, Joshua (1887–1954). Baseball player. BED

DeVries, Yuan Lin. Biochemist, polar researcher. LA-1

Dewar, Sir James (1842–1923). Scottish chemist, physicist. SHFB

Dewey, George (1837–1917). Admiral. COD; CUC; ICA; NAC

Dewey, John (1859–1952). Educator, philosopher. CUC; FRC†; LEJA; OZA

Dewey, Thomas Edmund (1902–1971). Governor. GO; WHD†

Dewhurst, Colleen (1924?–). Actress, born Canada. DI-1†

Dianous, Jacques (d. 1881). French soldier. WOA

Dias, Bartholomeu (1450?–1500). Portuguese navigator. ROL

Diaz, Bartholomeu, see Dias, Bartholomeu.

Díaz, Bernal (b. 1492). Spanish soldier, author. BACA

Díaz, Justino (1940–). Singer. NEBB

Díaz, Porfirio (1830–1915). President of Mexico. BAGA; NEBA; WOB

Di Blasi, Francesco. Conductor. STM†

Di Cecco, Mario. Conductor, born Italy. STM†

Dick, George Frederick (1881–1967). Physician. RIE

Dick, Gladys H. (1881–1963). Physician. RIE

Dickens, Charles (1812–1870). English author. BOD; COB; COO; DEI; DEJ; HOA; STK

Dickerson, Eric (1960–). Football player. AAS-35

Dickey, Bill (William Malcolm) (1907–). Baseball player. ALB; DAFD; GUDA; HIC; HIF; MUB-1; MUC; RIGA†; ROB; SHD; VACA; WAG; ZAA

Dickey, Sarah (1838–1904). Educator. CHFB

Dickieson, George W. (1912–). Conductor. STM†

Dickinson, Eleanor Creekmore (1931–). Artist. FOGB†

Dickinson, Emily (1830–1886). Poet. BEF; BEGA; EOB; HIG; LEK; MUA; OCB; SIF; STLA; WABC†; WHB

Dickinson, John (1732–1808). Statesman. BUIB†; FEAA

Dickinson, Velvalee. Spy. KN

Dickson, Harry Ellis (1908–). Conductor. STM†

Didrikson, Babe (Mildred) (1914–1956). Track athlete, golfer. ASB-1; ASBA; CLA; DAG; DAGA; DAJ; DEF; FRB; GED; GEDA; GEE; GIBA; HIA; HOBA; HOBAA; JAB; LEYB; LYB; PACA; PIB; PIBA; RYA; SCA; SID; ST-2; STLA; VAE

Diego, José de (1866–1918). Puerto Rican poet. STC; TU

Dierdorf, Dan (1949–). Football player. AAS-11

Diesel, Rudolf C. (1858–1913). German inventor. FAB; FE; LAE; MAP; THA

Dietz, Howard (1896–1983). Songwriter. MOA†

Dietz, Johann (1665–1738). German barber-surgeon. RAC

Diggs, Charles Cole (1922–). Congressman. DU†

Dill, Robert F. (1927–). Marine geologist. OLC

Dillard, Harrison (1924?–). Track athlete. DAG; DAGA; DAJ; LEYB; PAW

Diller, Phyllis (1917–). Comedienne. MASB

Dillon, Will (1877–1966). Songwriter. MOA†

Dilworth, Mary Jane (1831–1877). Educator. BUI

Di Maggio, Joseph Paul (1914–). Baseball player. ALB; ALBA; ASBA; BELB; BOE; BUD-1; BUJ; DA; DAA; DAFB; DAFC; DAFD; DAG; DAGA; DAH; DEE; FIAA; GEC; GR; GUC; HIF; HOC; MUC; PAW; RIGA†; ROB; SH; SHB; SHC; SHF; SHH; VEA; WAC

Dimock, Susan. Physician. COFA†

D'Indy, Vincent, see Indy, Vincent d'.

Ding, see Darling, Jay Norwood.

Diocletian (245–313). Emperor of Rome. COK

Dionne, Marcel (1951–). Canadian hockey player. AAS-22; AAS-23; FICA-1; FICC; MANA; OLDE; ORB

Dischinger, Terry (1942?–). Baseball player. HOCA

Dismas (1st century). Saint. MOC

Disney, Walt (Walter Elias) (1901–1966). Producer of animated cartoons. ASB-1; COKA; FLBC; LAG; LEN; LEPA; PABA; WAO

Disraeli, Benjamin, 1st earl of Beaconsfield (1804–1881). Prime minister of Great Britain. DEI; DEJ; PEB

Ditka, Michael (1939–). Football player, coach. ANB; BRE

Ditko, Steve (1927–). Cartoonist. GOB-1

Ditmars, Raymond Lee (1876–1942). Naturalist. MIB†

Dix, Dorothea Lynde (1802–1887). Reformer. BRBE†; BUA; DAD; DEDA; DOD; FID; MASA; STLA; WABC†; WAJ; YOC

Dix, Henry (1850?–1938). Manufacturer, born Russia. LETA

Dixon, Dean (1915–1976). Conductor. ADA; ADB; BOG; HUC; RIC; RICA; STM†

Dixon, Hewritt (1940–). Football player. LEZB

Dixon, Jeremiah (fl. 1763–1767). English surveyor. HIBC†

Dixon, Mort (1892–1956). Songwriter. MOA†

Doctor J., see Erving, Julius.

Dodge, Grace (1856–1914). Reformer. WABC†

Dodge, Grenville Mellen (1831–1916). General, civil engineer. MAT

Dodge, Henry (1782–1867). Governor, senator. SEC

Dodge, Mary Mapes (1831–1905). Author, editor. BEI; COB; STJ; YOC

Dodgson, Charles, see Carroll, Lewis, pseud.

Dodson, Jacob (b. 1825). Explorer. BUH; SCB; STQ

Doherty, Robert Ernest (1885–1950). Engineering educator. YOD

Doisy, Edward Adelbert (1893–1986). Biochemist. RIF

Dolan, Harry (1927–). Author. DADA

Dole, Elizabeth (1936–). Ex-Secretary of Transportation. WHE

Dolin, Anton (1904–1983). English dancer, choreographer. ATA

Domagk, Gerhard (1895–1964). German chemist. AAS-31; RIF; ROA

Domingo, Placido (1941–). Spanish singer. BRBB-1

Dominguez, (Maria) Josefa Ortiz de (1768–1824). Mexican patriot. NEBA; ROGB

Dominic (1170–1221). Saint. DAD-3; ONA

Dominic of Silos (d. 1076). Saint. DAD-3

Domitilla. Saint. DAD-2†

Donaldson, Walter (1893–1947). Songwriter. MOA

Donizetti, Gaetano (1797–1848). Italian composer. KAE

Donlon, Mary Honor. Jurist. CLA

Donne, Maria Dalle (1778–1842). Italian physician. SC†

Donnelly, Ignatius (1831–1901). Author, congressman. LEO

Donner party, see Reed, Virginia, member of group.

Donohue, Mark (1937–1975). Automobile racer. DI-2; JA; OLCB; ORD

Donovan, Art (1933–). Football player. SUD

Donovan, William Joseph (1883–1959). General. ARD; FAA

Dooley, Thomas Anthony (1927–1961). Physician. ASB

Doolin, Bill (d. 1896). Outlaw. JOBA; SUJ

Doolittle, James Harold (1896–). General. ARC; HAMY; SUA; SWE

Door, Rheta Childe (1872–1948). Journalist. JAE

Doppler, Christian Johann (1803–1853). Austrian physicist, mathematician. FE; HAC; SHFB

Dorati, Antal (1906–). Conductor, born Hungary. STM; YOM

Dorchester, Sir Guy Carleton, 1st baron (1724–1808). British governor. AKA

Dorion, Marie (fl. 1812). Indian woman. GRAD†

Dorothea (d. 303). Saint. DAD-2; FAD; ONA; QUA

Dorset, Marion (1872–1935). Chemist. DEA

Dorsett, Tony Drew (1954–). Football player. AAS-10; DEHB

Dositheus. Saint. DAD-2

Dos Passos, John Roderigo (1896–1970). Author. CAC†

Dostoevski, Fëdor Mikhailovich (1821–1881). Russian novelist. POFA

Dotson, John L., Jr. Journalist. STAA

Doughty, Charles Montagu (1843–1926). English poet, traveler. MOB; ROL†; WIA-1

Douglas, Catherine, see Barlass, Kate.

Douglas, David (1798–1834). Scottish botanist. JEA

Douglas, Emory (1943–). Graphic artist. FAI

Douglas, Helen Gahagan (1900–1980). Congresswoman. GRAB-1†

Douglas, Lloyd C. (1877–1951). Clergyman, author. CON

Douglas, Stephen Arnold (1813–1861). Political leader. WHD†

Douglass, Frederick (1817–1895). Abolitionist. ADA; ADB; AKB; BEJ; BRB; BRBD; BRG; DEDA; GRAB-05; HUA; HUB; JO; JOC; MAT; PECA; ROG; SPB; SQB; STD; STO; WAH; WIAB; YOI

Dow, Neal (1804–1897). Temperance advocate. DEDA

Dowler, Boyd. Football player. JOA†

Down, Linda (1956–). University counselor. GLO

Downie, William (fl. 1850). Gold prospector. FOC

Downing, George Thomas (1819–1903). Civil rights leader, restauranteur. GRAB-01

Doyle, Sir Arthur Conan (1859–1930). Scottish author. COO

Doyle, Edward J. (d. 1942). Army officer. RAE

Doyle, Mike. Surf rider. OLD

Drake, Edwin Laurentine (1819–1880). Oil industry pioneer. FAB

Drake, Sir Francis (1540–1596). English explorer, privateer. DYA; GRAA; KEH; LAA-2; LACB; MOB; ROL

Drake, Frank Donald (1930–). Radio astronomer. COQ

Draper, Joanna (b. 1854). Author, former slave. DADB

Draper, Ruth (1884–1956). Actress, comedienne. MASB

Draughon, Roland (1947–). Journalist. STAA

Dreiser, Theodore (1871–1945). Author. CAC†; CON†

Dreschkoff, Gisela. Physicist, polar researcher, born Germany. LA-1

Dressen, Charlie (1898–1966). Baseball player, manager. FRC-01

Dressler, Marie (1869–1934). Comedienne, born Canada. MASB

Drew, Charles Richard (1904–1950). Surgeon. ADA; ADB; DOF-1; FRE; GRAB-03; HA; HAM; HODA; KLA; PECA; RIC; RICA; ROG; STE; STO; STQ†; WEF

Drew, Louisa Lane (1820–1897). Actress, born England. WABC†

Dreyfus, Alfred (1859–1935). French soldier. PEB

Dreyfus, René (1905–). French automobile racer. SLA

Dreyfuss, Barney (1865–1932). Baseball executive, born Germany. SLA

Driscoll, John Leo. Football player, coach. SUD

Dropo, Walt (1924–). Baseball player. BOE†

Drummond, William J. (1945?–). Journalist. STAA

Dryden, John (1631–1700). English poet. COP

Dryden, Ken (Kenneth Wayne) (1947?–). Canadian hockey player. FICA-1; FICC; GUEC; LEYA; ORA; ORB; THF

Drysdale, Don (Donald Scott) (1936–). Baseball player. GEB; GEC; LEZ; NEA; PRA; SA-3; SHA

Duane, William (1760–1835). Journalist. SQB†

Duarte, Juan Pablo (1813–1876). Dominican revolutionist. WO

Dubin, Al (1891–1945). Songwriter, born Switzerland. MOA

Dubinsky, David (1892–1982). Labor leader, born Poland. BEA; COH; DABA; LEHA; LIA; SEA

DuBois, Alice, pseud., see Bettignies, Louise de.

Dubois, Eugène (1858–1940). Dutch paleontologist. SOB

Du Bois, William Edward Burghardt (1868–1963). Sociologist, editor, author. ADA; ADB; BEJ; BRB; BRBD; DABB; DOF-1; GRAB-01; PECA; RICA; ROG; STB; STJB; STO; YOI

Dubuffet, Jean (1901–1985). French painter. WIAA

Duchamp, Marcel (1887–1968). Painter, born France. WIAA

Duchesne, Rose Philippine, Blessed (1769–1852). DAD-3

Ducloux, Walter (1913–). Conductor, educator, born Switzerland. STM†

Ducommun, Élie (1833–1906). Swiss journalist. MEC†; WIC

Du Coudray, Angélique Marguérite le Boursier (1712–1789). French midwife. MASA†

Dudley, William (1922?–). Football player. DAFG; SUD

Duer, William (1747–1799). American Revolutionary patriot. BUIB†

Duffy, Hugh (1866–1954). Baseball player. ALB

Dukas, Paul (1865–1935). French composer. KAE

Duke, James Buchanan (1856–1925). Industrialist. WED

Dulce, Sister (Dulce Lopes Pontes) (1913–). Brazilian nun. MAK

Dull Knife (1828?–1879). Cheyenne Indian war chief. MOD

Dulles, John Foster (1888–1959). Secretary of State. HEEA

Duluth, Daniel Greysolon, sieur (1636–1710). French explorer. ABA

Dumas, Alexandre (Dumas père) (1802–1870). French author. ADA; ADB; DEI; DEJ; JO

Dumont, Eleanore (Madame Moustache) (d. 1879). Frontierswoman. RAB†

Dumont d'Urville, Jules Sébastian César (1790–1842). French explorer. ROL†

Dunant, Jean Henri (1828–1910). Swiss founder of Red Cross. DED; EVA; MEA; MEC; WIC; WRA

Dunbar, Bonnie (1949–). Astronaut. FOJ-1

Dunbar, Ernest. Journalist. STAA

Dunbar, Paul Laurence (1872–1906). Poet. ADA; ADB; BEF; BRB; HUA; LEI; ROE; ROG

Duncan, David Douglas (1916–). Photographer. FOD; HOE

Duncan, Isadora (1878–1927). Dancer. EOB; FOGC; MAT-1; STLA; WABC†

Duncan, Jim (1946?–). Football player. BELB

Duncan, Marilyn I. (1945?–). Journalist. STAA

Duncan, Richard (1913–). Conductor. STM†

Duncan, Rosetta (1900–1959). Comedienne. MASB

Duncan, Vivien (1902–). Comedienne. MASB

Duncanson, Robert S. (1817–1872). Painter. ADA; ADB; BEBA

Dunham, Katherine (1910–). Dancer. ADA; ADB; FOGC; RIC; RICA

Duniway, Abigail Scott (1834–1915). Feminist. GEE; ROI; WABC

Dunlop, Florence (1896–1963). Canadian educator. FLB

Dunlop, John Boyd (1840–1921). Irish inventor, born Scotland. FE

Dunn, Mary Eubanks (1947–). Archaeologist. WIAA-01

Dunne, Finley Peter (1867–1936). Humorist. BEE

Du Pont, Eleuthère Irénée (1771–1834). Industrialist, born France. LEM; LOB

Duren, Ryne (Rinold George) (1929–). Baseball player. SHE

Dürer, Albrecht (1471–1528). German painter, engraver. CHC; KAA; MAI

Durnan, Bill (William Ronald) (1915–). Canadian hockey player. ORA; ORC

Durocher, Leo (1906–). Baseball manager. DEG; FRC-01; LEW; ROAA

DuSable, Jean Baptiste, see Pointe de Sable, Jean Baptiste.

Dussek, Jan Ladislav (1760–1812). Czech pianist, composer. CHF

Duval, William Pope (1784–1854). Governor. MAO

Duvalier, François (1907–1971). President of Haiti. ARA; BAGA

Duvoisin, Roger (1904–1980). Author, illustrator, born Switzerland. SM

Dvořak, Antonin (1841–1904). Czech composer. BAE; BEN; BUC; DEI; DEJ; FIE†; KAE; SAA; YOJ

Dyck, Anthony van, see Van Dyck, Sir Anthony.

Dyer, Mary (1591?–1660). Quaker martyr. CRB; WABC†

Dymphna, see Dympna.

Dympna (7th century). Saint. DAD-1

E

Eads, Valerie. Martial artist. AT

Eakins, Thomas (1844–1916). Painter. FRA; MAG; SIE

Earhart, Amelia (1898–1937). Aviator. BOC; BOJ; COC†; COKA; DOD; ELA; EVD; FAA; GEDB; GIBA; HAMY; HAQ; LAC; LEK; MAT-1; MO; NAB; PA; SMC; STLA; WABC†; WAE; YOC

Earle, Sylvia, see Mead, Sylvia Earle.

Early, Peggy Ann. Jockey. HOBAA†

Earp, Wyatt Berry Stapp (1848–1929). Law officer. COE; SUI

East, Edward Murray (1879–1938). Geneticist. CAB

Eastman, George (1854–1932). Inventor, industrialist. CUC; FE; LAG; LEM; MAL; RIBA

Eaton, Ralph (1899?–). General. RADA

Eaton, Roy (1930–). Advertising executive. STAA

Eccles, Sir John Carew (1903–). Australian physiologist. RIF†

Echániz, José (1905–). Pianist, born Cuba. STM†

Echeverría, Luís (1922–). Ex-president of Mexico. NEBA

Eckert, J. Presper (1919–). Computer pioneer. GRAB-3

Eddy, Mary Baker (1821–1910). Christian Science leader. BLF; BUA; KOA; STLA; WABC†

Ederle, Gertrude C. (1906–). Swimmer. BUJA; DAG; DAGA; HOBA; HOBAA; RYA†

Edes, Benjamin (1732–1803). Journalist. SQB†

Edgren, Edith Svensson (1899?–). Housekeeper, born Sweden. BAEA-1

Edison, Thomas Alva (1847–1931). Inventor. ASA; ASB-1; BEC; BIA; BOB; BOD; BUE; CAD; COKB; COL; CUC; DEI; DEJ; DOE; EBA; EVC; FAB; FE; FOH; FRE; HYA; LEN; LEPA; MAT; PRC; RAA; RIBA; SHFB; SIA; THA

Edith of Wilton. Saint. DAD-3

Edmonds, Sarah Emma (1841–1898). Nurse, spy. FOA; KN; SUG; WABC†

Edmonds, Walter Dumaux (1903–). Author. CON

Edmund the Martyr (841–869). Saint. DAD-3; MOC

Edmund Rich (1170?–1240). Saint. QUA

Edward I (1239–1307). King of England. BRBF; CAAA; DEC; GRAB; SCC

Edward II (1284–1327). King of England. BRBF; DEC; GRAB†; SCC

Edward III (1312–1377). King of England. BRBF; CAAA; DEC; GRAB; SCC

Edward IV (1442–1483). King of England. BRBF; DEC; GRAB; SCC

Edward V (1470–1483). King of England. BRBF; DEC; GRAB†; SCC

Edward VI (1537–1553). King of England and Ireland. DEC; GRAB†; SCC

Edward VII (1841–1910). King of Great Britain and Ireland. CAAA; DEC; GRAB†; SCC

Edward VIII (1894–1972). King of Great Britain and Ireland. DEC; GRAB†; SCC

Edward the Confessor (1002?–1066). Saint, king of the English. DAD-3; GRAB†; QUA; SCC

Edwards, Gus (1879–1945). Songwriter, born Germany. MOA

Edwards, Harry (1942–). Athlete. AKB

Edwards, William J. (b. 1869). Educator. DADB

Egan, Raymond B. (1890–1952). Songwriter, born Canada. MOA†

Egan, Sister Jogues (Joan) (1918–). Nun, educator, born Ireland. SMBB-1

Eglevsky, André (1917–1977). Dancer, born Russia. ATA

Ehmke, Howard John (1894–1959). Baseball player. REB; WAG

Ehrenburg, Ilya Grigoryevich (1891–1967). Russian author. KE

Ehricke, Krafft Arnold (1917–1984). Aeronautical engineer, born Germany. NEB

Ehrlich, Julius (1894–). German conductor. STM†

Ehrlich, Paul (1854–1915). German bacteriologist. AAS-31; ASA; BEK; DEB; FE; LET; POB; RIE; RIF; ROA; SUF

Ehrlich, Paul Ralph (1932–). Biologist, entomologist. CORA

Eichelberger, Robert Lawrence (1886–1961). General. RAE

Eiffel, Alexandre Gustave (1832–1923). French engineer. EVB

Eijkman, Christian (1858–1930). Dutch bacteriologist. RIF

Einhorn, David (1809–1879). Rabbi, born Germany. GUB

Einstein, Albert (1879–1955). Theoretical physicist, born Germany. ASA; ASB-1; BEA; BEP; BOB; BUF; CAA; COL; CUC; DEI; DEJ; DOE; FE; FRE; GEF; GRB-1; GUB; KE; LEL; LES; LET; LETA; MAM; MOBA; POD; RID; SHFB; SIA; YOA

Einthoven, Willem (1860–1927). Dutch physiologist. AAS-33; FE; RIF

Eisenberg, Shaul (1921–). Israeli businessman, born Germany. GRB-1

Eisenberg, Walter (1914–). Conductor. STM†

Eisenhower, Dwight David (1890–1969). President of U.S. ARC; ASB-1; BAEB; BAG; BAG-1; BEB; BLA; BUIA; CAG; CAH; COD†; COI; COJA; COS; DEI; DEJ; DUB; DUC; DUCA; FAA; FRBA; HIH; KE; LEP; LEQ; LEQA; MAB; MABA; MIA; PED; RAE; ROH; ROHA; ROK†; SCA; SUBB; SWE-1; WEE; WHD

Eisenhower, Mamie Geneva (1896–1979). Wife of Dwight David Eisenhower. BAG; BAG-1; BLG; CHB; KL; MAA; MAU; PRB; ROH; ROHA

Eisner, Will (1917–). Cartoonist. GOB-1

El Chato, see Chato, El.

Elder, Leigh. Conductor. STM†

Eleanor of Aquitaine (1122?–1204). Consort of Henry II, king of England. BOI; DAK

Elgar, Sir Edward William (1857–1934). English composer. BAE; BEN; BUC; GOA; KAE; SAA†; YOK

Elias, Lee (1920–). Cartoonist, born England. GOB-1

Eliav, Aryeh Lyova (1921–). Israeli political figure, born Russia. GRB-1

Elijah. Hebrew prophet. GEF

Elijah ben Solomon (Elijah Gaon) (1720–1797). Lithuanian Hebrew scholar. KAC; LERA; PEB

Eliot, George, pseud. (1819–1880). English author. COO; SMA; STL

Eliot, Martha May (1891–1978). Physician. CHE

Eliot, Thomas Stearns (1888–1965). English poet, born U.S. ASB-1; BRBB; COP

Elizabeth I (1533–1603). Queen of England and Ireland. BOI; CAAA; CHG; COA; DAK; DEC; DEI; DEJ; FAE; FRE; GRAB; HAA; LIDA; PA; SCC; TRB; UNB

Elizabeth II (1926–). Queen of Great Britain and Northern Ireland. BOI; DEC; DU-1; FAE; GRAB; LIDA; SCC; TRB; WEB

Elizabeth of Hungary (1207–1231). Saint. DAD-1; DAD-3; HEA; MAK†; MOC; ONA; QUA; TUA

Elizabeth of Portugal (1271–1336). Saint. DAD-3; MOC

Elizabeth Petrovna (1709–1762). Empress of Russia. LIDA; RIA

Eller, Carl (1942–). Football player. GUF; SMD

Ellery, William (1727–1820). American Revolutionary patriot. BAEA; BUIB†; COJ†; FEAB; MAC

Ellington, Anna. Neurologist. BOHE

Ellington, Duke (Edward Kennedy) (1899–1974). Band leader, composer. ADA; ADB; ASB-1; COF-1; DOF-1; HODA; HUC; MOA; RIC; RICA; ROF; TEA; TEB; WAD

Elliott, Bob (Robert Bracket) (1923–). Comedian. BUR-1

Elliott, Herb (1938–). Australian track athlete. AAS-26

Elliott, Robert B. (1842–1884). Congressman. ADA; ADB; BRB; PECA

Ellman, Annie (1950–). Martial artist. AT

Ellsberg, Edward (1891–). Admiral. OLC

Ellsworth, Lincoln (1880–1951). Polar explorer. GRB

Ellsworth, Oliver (1745–1807). Supreme Court justice. FEAA

Elrod, Henry Talmage (1905–1941). Marine aviator. BRA; REA

Emberley, Barbara (1932–). Author. SMAB

Emberley, Edward Randolph (1931–). Illustrator. SMAB

Embery, Joan (1949–). Zoo promoter. GUJ

Emerson, Gladys Anderson (1903–). Biochemist. EMB†; HA-1; YOF

Emerson, Ralph Waldo (1803–1882). Poet, philosopher. BEF; BEG; BEGA; BLE; BOA; CAC; CUC; DEI; DEJ; HEF; RED; SIF; SUFA; WHB; WOAA

Emerson, William. Minister. WOAA†

Emerson, William, Jr. (b. 1770). Minister. WOAA†

Emiliani, Jerome (1486–1537). Saint. DAD-3

Emily de Rodat. Saint. DAD-3

Emin Pasha, Mehmed (alias Eduard Schnitzer) (1840–1892). German traveler. ROL†

Emmons, Lucretia. American Revolutionary patriot. CLC†

Empedocles (c. 490–430 B.C.). Greek philosopher. FE

Encarnacion, Rosario de Jesus. Philippine teacher, civic leader. RODA

Encarnacion, Silvino (1913–). Philippine civic leader. RODA

Ender, Kornelia (1958–). German swimmer. SUBB-1

Enders, John Franklin (1897–1985). Bacteriologist. CHE†; COLA†; RIF; SUF

Enesco, Georges (1881–1955). Romanian composer, violinist. KAE; YOM†

Engel, Lehman (1910–1982). Conductor, composer. STM†

Engstrom, Elmer William (1901–1984). Electronics executive. PAB

Ennis, Del (1925–). Baseball player. BOE

Enright, Elizabeth (1909–1968). Author. SMB

Entwistle, John (1944–). English musician. BUIB-2

Ephrem (306–373). Saint. DAD-2

Eppes, Maria Jefferson (1778–1804). Daughter of Thomas Jefferson. PRB

Epstein, Charlotte (1884–1938). Swimming administrator. SLA

Epstein, Michael (1943–). Baseball player. SLA†

Equiano, Olaudah (Gustavus Vassa) (1745–1801). English adventurer. ADA; ADB; OJA

Erasmus, Desiderius (1466–1536). Dutch scholar. DEI; DEJ

Eratosthenes (c. 275–195 B.C.). Greek astronomer, geographer. PIA; SHFB

Erhard, Ludwig (1897–1977). German chancellor. WEB

Eric IX (Eric the Saint) (d. 1160). King of Sweden. QUA

Eric the Red (fl. 10th century). Norse navigator. DYA; KEH; KNB; MOB; ROL†

Ericsson, John (1803–1889). Inventor, born Sweden. HYA

Ericsson, Leif (fl. 1000). Norse explorer. COC; HEA; MOB; ROL†; VIA†

Erlanger, Joseph (1874–1965). Physiologist. LET; RIF

Errol, Leon (1881–1951). Comedian. ED-1†

Erskine, Thomas (1750–1823). English jurist. COG

Erte (Romain de Tirtoff) (1892–). French artist, costume designer, born Russia. ASB-1

Erving, Julius (Dr. J.) (1950–). Basketball player. AAS-5; ARB-3; GUEA; GUH; SA-1; SA-2

Escalante, Silvestre Vélez de (fl. 1768–1779). Spanish explorer, missionary. FOC

Escobar, Marisol (1930–). Venezuelan sculptor. FOGB†

Eshkol, Levi (1895–1969). Israeli prime minister, born Russia. GRB-1

Esnault-Pelteri, Robert (1881–1957). French engineer. STMA

Esposito, Phil (1942–). Canadian hockey player. AAS-21; DEHA-1; FICA; FR; FRD; GUEC; LEYA; OBB; OLDE; ORC; RAAF; THD

Esposito, Tony (Anthony James) (1943–). Canadian hockey player. LEYA; ORA; ORB; THF

Esposito, Vince. Physician. LETC

Essegian, Chuck (Charles Abraham) (1931–). Baseball player. DEHA-1

Esteban or Estevanico (d. 1539). Spanish explorer. ADB; BLD†; BUH; GRAB-02; HAP; HUB; JO†; KADB; LEI; PECA; SCB; STQ; VIA; WIBA

Esther. Biblical character. LER; STP

Estournelles de Constant, Paul Henri Benjamin,

baron d' (1852–1924). French statesman. MEC†; WIC

Estrada, Isabel. Physician. FOC-1

Estrada, Miguel (1938–). Migrant worker. WECC

Esty, Jane (1943–). Manufacturer. LES-1†

Ethelreda, Saint, *see* Audrey.

Ets, Marie Hall (1895–). Author, illustrator. SM

Eucherius of Orléans (7th century). Saint. DAD-2

Euclid (fl. 300 B.C.). Greek mathematician. CAA; MUB; SHFB; STN

Eudes, John (1601–1680). Saint. DAD-3

Eudocia. Saint. DAD-2

Eudoxus (408–355 B.C.). Greek astronomer, mathematician. SIB†

Eugenie (1826–1910). Wife of Napoleon III. COKB

Euler, Leonhard (1707–1783). Swiss mathematician, physicist. MUB

Eulogius (580–607). Saint, bishop. DAD-3

Eulogius of Spain (810–859). Saint. DAD-2

Euphrasia (380–410). Saint. DAD-2

Eustis, William (1753–1825). Diplomat. BUIB†

Evans, Clifford (1920–). Archaeologist. PAC

Evans, Dale (1912–). Actress, singer. LA

Evans, Sir Edward Ratcliffe Garth Russell (1881–1957). British explorer. ROL

Evans, George (1920–). Cartoonist. GOB-1

Evans, Jane (1944–). Mail-order executive. FRBD

Evans, John (1814–1897). Physician, educator. SEC

Evans, Merle (1894–1987). Circus bandmaster. KIB

Evans, Oliver (1755–1819). Inventor. HYA

Evans, Walker (1903–1975). Photographer. SUAA

Evaristus (fl. 97–105). Saint, pope. DAD-3

Everard Hanse, Blessed. DAD-3

Everett, Ronald McKinley, *see* Karenga.

Everett, William Blake (1917–1973). Cartoonist. GOB-1

Evers, Charles (1922–). Mayor. DU; FAG; HAH

Evers, John Joseph (1883–1947). Baseball player. ALB; DAFD

Evers, Medgar Wiley (1925–1963). Civil rights leader. DADA†; DOF-1; FLD

Evers, Myrlie (1932?–). Wife of Medgar Evers. DU†

Evert, Chris (Christine Marie) (1954–). Tennis player. AAS-29; BELB; FR-1; GLC; GUED; GUH; HOBAA; LAHA; MATA; SUDA

Every, Henry. English pirate. WHA†

Ewing, Buck (William) (1859–1906). Baseball player. ALB; HAF

Ewing, Juliana H. Gatty (1841–1885). English author. BEI

Ewing, W. Maurice (1906–1974). Geologist, oceanographer. BRBC; COR

Ewry, Ray C. (b. 1873). Track athlete. DAG; DAGA; DAJ; FIC; LEYB†

Eyck, Hubert van (1366–1426). Flemish painter. MAI

Eyck, Jan van (1370?–1440?). Flemish painter. KAA; MAI

Eyre, Edward John (1815–1901). English explorer. ROL†

Ezekiel, Sir Moses Jacob (1844–1917). Sculptor. LETA

Ezra (5th century B.C.). Hebrew priest. GEF

F

Faas, Horst (1933–). German photographer. HOE

Faber, Red (Urban Charles) (b. 1888). Baseball player. ALB

Fabian, Robert (1901–1978). English detective. LID

Fabiola (fl. 380). Roman matron. MAK†

Fabius (Quintus Fabius Maximus Verrucosus) (d. 203). Roman soldier, statesman. PLA

Fabre, Jean Henri (1823–1915). French entomologist. MIB

Fabricius ab Aquapendente, Hieronymus (1537–1619). Italian anatomist. POB

Facey, Thomas. Conductor. STM†

Factor, Pompey (d. 1928). Soldier. KADB

Fader, Daniel. Educator. EOA

Fafunwa, Babs. Nigerian educator. OJA

Faget, Maxime A. Aeronautical engineer. POE

Fahd ibn Abdul Aziz al Saud (1922–). Saudi king. HAGD

Fahrenheit, Gabriel Daniel (1686–1736). German physicist. SHFB

Fain, Ferris (1922–). Baseball player. BOE

Fain, Samuel S. (1909–). Conductor. STM†

Fairbanks, Charles Warren (1852–1918). Vice president of U.S. FEA; HAOA; HOEA

Fairchild, David Grandison (1869–1954). Botanist. MIB

Fairchild, Sherman Mills (1896–1971). Inventor. MAPA

Fairfield, John (1830?–1860). Abolitionist. STG

Fairgrave, Phoebe (1903–). Aviator, government official. HIFD

Fairly, Ron (1938–). Baseball player. BELA

Falconieri, Juliana (1270–1341). Saint. DAD-2

Falla, Manuel de (1876–1946). Spanish composer. BUC; KAE; SAA†; YOL

Fallaci, Oriana (1930–). Italian journalist. LETB

Fangio, Juan Manuel (1912–). Argentine automobile racer. ABB; COKC; JA; YAA

Fantozzi, William (1896–). Conductor. STM†

Faraday, Michael (1791–1867). English chemist,

physicist. ASA; BEP; BIA; BOB; BOD; CAA; COLA; DEI; DEJ; DOE; DUA; FE; MAQ; SHFB; SIA; STI; THA

Farber, Bea. Harness racing driver. FOC-1

Farbman, Harry. Conductor. STM†

Fargo, William G. (1818–1881). Freight and banking executive. DOCA

Farjeon, Eleanor (1881–1965). English author. BEH; SMB

Farmer, James (1920–). Civil rights leader. DRA; GRAB-01; STF

Farmer, Moses G. (1820–1893). Inventor. HYA†

Farquhar, Jane Colden (1724–1766). Botanist. EMB†; PAC

Farr, Mel (1943–). Football player. LEZB

Farragut, David Glasgow (1801–1870). Admiral. BOD; CUC; FIA; FID; ICA; NAC

Farrar, Geraldine (1882–1967). Singer. WABC†

Farrell, Eileen (1920–). Singer. SAB

Farrell, James Thomas (1904–1979). Author. CAC†

Farrelly, Bernard. Australian surf rider. OLD

Farrington, Wallace (1871–1933). Governor. SEC

Fatio, Louis, *see* Pacheco, Luis.

Faulkner, William (1897–1962). Author. ASB-1; CAC; CON; FLBA; HEF

Fauré, Gabriel Urbain (1845–1924). French composer. KAE

Faurot, Joseph A. (1872–1942). Criminologist. LACA

Fauset, Crystal Bird (1893–1965). State legislator. LOAV

Faust, Johann (fl. 1530). German magician, fortune-teller. ED-5†

Faustinus. Saint. DAD-2

Fawcett, Percy Harrison (1867–1925?). English explorer. KNA; ROL†

Fazenda, Louise (1895–1962). Comedienne. MASB

Federspiel, Joe. Football player. SMJ

Feelings, Muriel (1938–). Author. SMAB

Feelings, Tom (1933–). Illustrator. SMAB

Felber, Herman. Conductor. STM†

Feliciano, José (1945–). Singer. FOW; LYA; WH-2

Felicie, Jacoba (fl. 1322). French medical practitioner. MASA†; SC

Felicitas. Saint. DAD-2

Felicity. Saint. DAD-3

Felix. Saint. DAD-3

Felix of Cantalice (1515–1587). Saint. DAD-2

Félix, Elisa Rachel (1821–1858). French actress, born Switzerland. LER; PEB

Felix, Ray (1930–). Basketball player. HOCA

Feller, Bob (Robert William) (1918–). Baseball player. ALB; BOE; BRC; DAFD; DAG; DAGA; DEE; FRC-1†; GEC; GRA; HIF; HOC; LEF; NEA; REB; SHH; WAG

Felt, Dorr E. Computer pioneer. GRAB-3†

Felton, John, Blessed (d. 1570). DAD-3

Fencik, Gary (1954–). Football player. AAS-13

Fender, Freddy (1937–). Singer. KRI

Fendler, Edvard (1902–). Conductor, born Germany. STM†

Fennell, Frederick (1914–). Conductor. STM†

Fenton, Carroll Lane (1900–1969). Author, illustrator. SMAB

Fenton, Mildred Adams. Author. SMAB

Fenton, Roger (1819–1869). English photographer. HOE

Fenwick, Millicent (1910–). Congresswoman. WIAA-02

Feoktistov, Konstantin (1926–). Russian astronaut. THC

Ferber, Edna (1887–1968). Author. CON; LETA; ROJ

Ferdinand V (1452–1516). King of Castile and León. CAAA; NEC

Ferguson, Angella D. (1925–). Pediatrician. HAMA

Ferguson, Harry George (1884–1960). Irish manufacturer. LAE

Ferguson, Joe. Football player. CL-1

Ferguson, John. Canadian hockey player. FICB

Ferkauf, Eugene (1921–). Merchant. GRB-1; LAH

Fermi, Enrico (1901–1954). Physicist, born Italy. BEA; BIA; BOB; CAA; COLA; CUC; FE; FRE; LEL; LET; MAS; RID; SHFB; SIA; YOE

Fermi, Laura (1907–1977). Author, wife of Enrico Fermi, born Italy. CAHA

Ferraro, Geraldine (1935–). Congresswoman. GLO; WHE

Ferrell, Wes (1908–1976). Baseball player. RIGA†

Ferrer, José (1912–). Actor, director. FOW

Ferrera, Don. Conductor. STM†

Ferrier, David (1843–1928). Scottish neurologist. POB

Fetter, Everett (1908–). Conductor. STM†

Feuerbach, Allan (1948–). Track athlete. LEYB†

Few, William (1748–1828). Banker, senator. BUIB†; FEAA

Fibingerova, Helena. Czech track athlete. HOBAA†

Fidelis of Sigmaringen (1578–1622). Saint. DAD-2

Fiedler, Arthur (1894–1979). Conductor. STM†

Field, Cyrus West (1819–1892). Financier. MAL

Field, Eugene (1850–1895). Poet, journalist. BEE; BEF; BEH; LEJ; LEOB

Field, John (1782–1837). Irish pianist, composer. CHF

Field, Rachel (1894–1942). Author. BEH

Field, Stephen D. (1846–1913). Inventor. HYA†

Field, Stephen Johnson (1816–1899). Supreme Court justice. FLC

Fields, Dorothy (1905–1974). Librettist. MOA†

Fields, Gracie (1898–1979). English singer, comedienne. MASB

Fields, Jackie (1908–). Boxer. SLA

Fields, Mary (1832–1914). Pioneer. BUH; GRAB-02; KADB

Fields, Totie (1931–1978). Comedienne. MASB

Fields, W. C. (William Claude) (1880–1946). Actor. COKB; ED-1; KLD; MAOB; PHA

Fiesole, Giovanni, *see* Angelico, Fra.

Fifield, Elaine (1931–). Australian dancer. ATA

Figueroa, Carmen Sanabria de (1882–1954). Pianist. NEBB

Figueroa, Ed. Baseball player. KLBB

Figueroa, Jesús (1878–1971). Band leader. NEBB

Figueroa, José (1905–). Violinist. NEBB

Figueroa Family. Musicians. NEBB

Filippo, Lippi, *see* Lippi, Fra Filippo.

Fillmore, Abigail Powers (1798–1853). First wife of Millard Fillmore. BAG; BAG-1; BLG†; CHA; KL; MAA; MAU; PRB; ROH; ROHA

Fillmore, Caroline Carmichael (d. 1881). Second wife of Millard Fillmore. BAG†; BAG-1†; ROH†

Fillmore, Millard (1800–1874). President of U.S. ALE; BAEB; BAG; BAG-1; BEB; BLA; BUIA; CAG; CAH; COI; COS; DUC; DUCA; FEA; FRBA; HAOA; HIH; HOEA; LEQ; LEQA; MAB; MABA; MIA; PED; ROH; ROHA; ROK†; SUBB; WHD

Findlay, Francis M. (1894–). Conductor. STM†

Fine, Larry (1911–1975). Comedian. BUR-1; ED-1†

Fine, Lou (1915–1971). Cartoonist. GOB-1

Fine, Vivian (1913–). Composer, educator. SC-02†

Fingers, Rollie (1946–). Baseball player. AAS; RIGA†

Fink, Mike (1770?–1823?). Frontiersman. VIA†

Finkelstein, Beatrice. Nutritionist. HOG

Finlay, Carlos Juan (1833–1915). Cuban physician. FOW; SHG; SIC†; WO

Finnian (b. 549). Saint. DAD-3

Fiorato, Hugo (1914–). Conductor. STM†

Fiore, Roland (1923–). Conductor. STM†

Fiorito, Eunice (1930–). Advocate for the disabled. BOHA-1

Firestone, Harvey Samuel (1868–1938). Industrialist. LAG

Fischel, Arnold (fl. 1862). LETA†

Fischer, Bobby (Robert James) (1943–). Chess player. BELB; FOR; LEQB; RHA

Fischer, Irwin (1903–). Conductor. STM†

Fischer, Martin. Conductor. STM†

Fischer, Pat (1940–). Football player. RUC

Fischer, Richard (1923–). Conductor. STM†

Fish, Jennifer. Skater. HOBAA†

Fishback, Margaret (1904–1985). Poet. ALA

Fisher, Anna (1949–). Astronaut, physician. FOI-1; HIFD†; RAAG†

Fisher, Frank E. (1917–). Conductor. STM†

Fisher, Harry (1882–1967). Basketball player, coach. SLA

Fisk, Carlton (1947–). Baseball player. GUG; HEFB†; HOCM; KLCA; TUB

Fisk Jubilee Singers. Choral group. HUC

Fiske, Minnie Maddern (1865–1932). Actress. DI-1; GIBA†; VAA; WABC†

Fitch, Bill (1936?–). Basketball coach. ARB-2

Fitch, John (1743–1798). Inventor. BUE; BUIB†; HYA

Fittipaldi, Emerson (1946–). Brazilian automobile racer. ABB; OLCB

Fitzgerald, Ella (1918–). Singer. ASB-1

Fitzgerald, Francis Scott Key (1896–1940). Author. ASB-1; CON

Fitzpatrick, Daniel Robert (1891–). Cartoonist. DEDC

Fitzpatrick, Thomas (1799–1854). Pioneer trapper. BUG

Fitzsimmons, Robert P. (1863–1918). English boxer. DAG; DAGA; RAAC

Fitzsimons, Thomas (1741–1811). Businessman, born Ireland. FEAA

Fizdale, Robert (1920–). Pianist. EWC

Flaherty, Robert Joseph (1884–1951). Motion picture producer. FLBC

Flam, Herbert (1928–). Tennis player. SLA

Flamel, Nicholas (1330–1418). French alchemist. CUA

Flamsteed, John (1646–1719). English astronomer. SHFB

Flanagan, Tommy (1930–). Pianist. UN

Flanders, Ralph Edward (1880–1970). Mechanical engineer. YOD

Flannan. Saint. DAD-3

Flatow, Alfred (b. 1869). German gymnast. SLA

Flaubert, Gustave (1821–1880). French author. HOA

Fleischer, Nat (1887–1972). Boxing promoter, editor. SLA

Fleisher, Leon (1928–). Pianist. EWC

Fleming, Sir Alexander (1881–1955). Scottish bacteriologist. AAS-31; ASB-1; BEK; BEP; BOB; CAA; COLA; FE; HUD; LAE; POB; RIF; ROA; SHG; SUF

Fleming, Sir John Ambrose (1849–1945). English electrical engineer. BUF†; SHFB

Fleming, Peggy (1948–). Skater. GRBA; HOBA; HOBAA; LEYB; LIEA; LYC; RYA; VADA

Fleming, Reggie (1936–). Hockey player, born Canada. FICB

Fleming, Williamina (1857–1911). Astronomer, born Scotland. PACB

Fletcher, Alice Cunningham (1838–1923). Ethnologist. WABC†

Fletcher, Grant (1913–). Conductor. STM†

Fletcher, John Gould (1886–1950). Poet, critic. SIF

Fletcher, Lizzie (b. 1863). Indian captive. JOD

Fletcher, Mary (b. 1851?). Indian captive. JOD

Flexner, Abraham (1866–1959). Educator. LETA

Flick, Elmer (1876–1971). Baseball player. ALB

Flinders, Matthew (1774–1814). English explorer. KNB; ROL

Flipper, Henry Ossian (1856–1940). Army officer. HAP; HODA; KADB

Flock, Tim. Automobile racer. LEX

Flood, Curtis Charles (1938–). Baseball player. HOBC

Flood, James (fl. early 18th century). Jamaican pirate. WHA

Flora of Beaulieu. Saint. DAD-3

Flora, William (d. 1820). Soldier. DAF-1†; WIBA

Florey, Sir Howard Walter (1898–1968). Australian pathologist. BEK†; COLA†; LAE; POB; RIF; SHG

Floyd, Theodora A. (1896–). Nurse. YOB

Floyd, William (1734–1821). American Revolutionary patriot. BAEA; BUIB†; COJ†; FEAB; MAC

Fluckey, Eugene Bennett (1913–). Naval officer. BRA

Flume, Jimmie. Scientist. HOG

Flutie, Doug (1962–). Football player. DEHB

Fly, William. Pirate. WHA†

Flynn, Elizabeth Gurley (1890–1964). Communist leader. ARAA

Flynt, Josiah, see Willard, Josiah Flynt.

Foch, Ferdinand (1851–1929). French soldier. ARD; COD

Foillan. Saint. DAD-3

Fokker, Anthony (1890–1939). Dutch aviator, inventor. HAMY

Foley, Robert F. (1941–). Army officer. RAE

Follen, Charles Theodore (1795–1840). Abolitionist, born Germany. CUB

Follmer, George (1934–). Automobile racer. OLCB

Fonck, René (1894–1953). French aviator, WWI. HAMY

Fontaine, Madeleine, Blessed. DAD-2

Fonteyn, Margot (1919–). English dancer. ATA

Foote, Alexander (1905–). English spy. SEB

Ford, Barney (fl. 1860). Businessman. GRAB-02; KADB

Ford, Elizabeth Bloomer (1918–). Wife of Gerald R. Ford. BAG-1; BLG; KL; MAU; SMBD

Ford, Gerald R. (1913–). President of U.S. BAG-1; BEB; BEB-1; BLA; BUIA; COI; COS; DUCA; FEA; FRBA; HAOA; HOEA; LEQA; SUBB; WHD

Ford, Henry (1863–1947). Industrialist. ASB-1; BOD; BUE; COKB; CUC; DEI; DEJ; EVB; FAC; FE; FOH; FRE; LAG; LEM; MAL; MAT; WED

Ford, John (1895–1973). Motion picture director. FLBC; SMBC

Ford, Phil (1956–). Basketball player. AAS-6

Ford, Whitey "Duke of Paducah" (1901–). Comedian. HAG-1

Ford, Whitey (Edward Charles) (1928–). Baseball player. BOE; BRC; DAFC; GIB; FRC-1†; HIF; MUB-1; MUC; RIGA†; ROB; SHA

Foreman, Chuck (Walter Eugene) (1950–). Football player. AAS-10; MOCA

Forester, Bill. Football player. JOA†

Forester, David. Conductor. STM†

Forman, James (1928–). Black leader. HAI

Forrest, Edwin (1806–1872). Actor. SHFA

Forrest, Nathan Bedford (1821–1877). General. ARE; MAD

Forssmann, Werner (1904–1979). German surgeon. RIF

Forstat, Milton (1910–). Conductor. STM†

Forsyth, Jane (1929–). Animal trainer. GUJ

Forten, Charlotte (1838–1904). Abolitionist. CHFB

Forten, James (1766–1842). Abolitionist. ADA; ADB; BUIB†; DAF-1; EMA; GRAB-03; HAL†; JOC; STQ†; WIBA

Fortmann, Daniel John (1916–). Football player. DAFG†; SUD

Fortune, Amos (c. 1710–1801). Ex-slave. WIBA

Foss, Lukas (1922–). Composer, born Germany. MAF; POF; STM†

Foster, Abigail Kelley (1810–1887). Abolitionist. LES-2; WABC†

Foster, George (1948–). Baseball player. AAS-4; GUED-01

Foster, Gloria (1936–). Actress. AB

Foster, Stephen Collins (1826–1864). Songwriter. BAD; BUD; CUC; DEI; DEJ; KAE; MOA; POF; SMBA; WIA

Fothergill, Dorothy. Bowler. HOBAA†

Foucault, Jean Bernard Léon (1819–1868). French physicist. CAA; FE; SHFB

Fouquet, Jean (1416?–1480). French painter. MAH†

Four Chaplains (d. 1943). FIA

Four Horsemen of Notre Dame. Football players. DAFG; DAG; DAGA; DAI; HIE

Fourier, Peter (1565–1640). Saint. DAD-3

Fournier, Pierre (1906–1986). French cellist. EWC

Fouts, Dan (1951–). Football player. AAS-20

Fowler, Lydia Folger (1822–1879). Physician. MASA

Fox, Carol (1926–1981). Opera company executive. SC-02†

Fox, George (1624–1691). English Quaker leader. FOJ

Fox, George Lansing (1900–1943). Chaplain. FIA

Foxx, James Emory (1907–1967). Baseball player. ALB; DA; DAA; DAFD; FRC-1†; LEV; RAAA; RIGA†; SHB; SHF

Foyt, Anthony Joseph (1935–). Automobile racer. ABB; ASBA; DI-2; KADA; LEVA; LEX; LEXA; OLAA; OLCB; OLCC; ORD; YAA

F. P. A., see Adams, Franklin Pierce.

Fracastoro, Girolamo (1483–1553). Italian physician. POB

Fracht, J. Albert (1904–). Conductor, born Poland. STM†

Fragonard, Jean-Honoré (1732–1806). French painter. MAH†

Frances of Rome (1384–1440). Saint. DAD-1

Francesca, Piero della (1420?–1492). Italian painter. JAA; MAI

Francia, José Gaspar Rodríguez (1766–1840). Paraguayan chief of state. WOB

Francis de Posadas. Saint. DAD-3

Francis de Sales (1567–1622). Saint. DAD-2

Francis of Assisi (1182–1226). Saint. BEC; DAD-1; DAD-3; FAD; HEA; MOC; ONA; PEE; QUA; TUA

Francis of Paola (1416–1507). Saint. DAD-2

Francis, Edward (1872–1957). Bacteriologist. DEA

Francis, Milly Hadjo (b. 1802). Creek Indian. GRAD

Francis, Miriam B. (1930–). Artist. FAI

Francis, Russ (1953–). Football player. AAS-19

Francis, Thomas, Jr. (1900–1969). Virologist. BEK†; CHE†

Francis Joseph I (1830–1916). Emperor of Austria. CAAA

Francis Xavier (1506–1552). Saint. DAD-1; DAD-3; KNA

Francisco, Peter (1760?–1831). Colonial boy. CAD

Franck, César Auguste (1822–1890). French composer, organist, born Belgium. BRF; KAE

Franck, James (1882–1964). Physicist, born Germany. LET

Franco, Francisco (1892–1975). Spanish chief of state. ARA; CAE

Franco, Grotti, Blessed, see Franco, Lippi, Blessed.

Franco, Lippi, Blessed (1211–1291). DAD-3

Frank, Anne (1919–1945). German Nazi victim, author. ELA; FOR; GRB-1

Frank, Johann Peter (1745–1821). German physician. MAR

Frankel, Zecharias (1801–1875). German rabbi. KAD

Frankenthaler, Helen (1928–). Painter. FOGB

Frankfurter, Felix (1882–1965). Supreme Court justice, born Austria. LIA; LOB

Frankl, Viktor. Concentration camp survivor, born Germany. WIAA-5

Franklin, Ann Smith (1696–1763). Printer. WABC†

Franklin, Aretha (1942–). Singer. AB; BUIB-1; JOE

Franklin, Benjamin (1706–1790). Statesman, scientist. ALCA; ARAB; ASB; BAEA; BLE; BOD; BUE; BUIB; CAA; COJ; COR; CUC; DAC; DAFA; DEDC; DEI; DEJ; DUA; FE; FEAA; FEAB; FEB; FIA; FID; FOB; FOH; HAN; HYA; HYB; LEAA; LEC; MAC; MAQ; MAT; OLA; SHFB; SIA; SQB; STH; STI; VIA; WAI

Franklin, Frederic (1914–). English dancer. ATA

Franklin, Irene (1876–1941). Singer, comedienne. MASB

Franklin, Sir John (1786–1847). English explorer. DOC; KNB; MOB; ROL

Franklin, John Hope (1915–). Historian, educator. ADB; FLD

Franklin, Sidney (1903–1976). Bullfighter. SLA

Franklin, Tony (1956–). Football player. AAS-17

Franks, David Salisbury (d. 1793). American Revolutionary patriot. LETA

Franz, Josef, see Francis Joseph I.

Fraser, Dawn (1937–). Australian swimmer. HOBAA†

Fraser, Gretchen Kunigk (1919–). Skier. HOBA; HOBAA; JAB; LEYB

Fraser, Harvey Reed (1916–). General, educator. RAE

Fratianne, Linda (1960–). Skater. VAD-6

Fraunhofer, Joseph von (1787–1826). German physicist. FE; LAA; SHFB; SUE

Frazetta, Frank (1928–). Cartoonist. GOB-1

Frazier, Joe (1944–). Boxer. ASBA; BELB; GEDA

Frazier, Walt (1945–). Basketball player. ARB-4; DEHA-1; GUEA; SA; SA-1; SA-2

Freccia, Massimo (1906–). Conductor, born Italy. STM

Frederick (d. 838). Saint. QUA

Frederick I, called Frederick Barbarossa (1123?–1190). Holy Roman Emperor. CAAA

Frederick II (1194–1250). King of Sicily and Holy Roman Emperor. BEO; CAAA

Frederick II, the Great (1712–1786). King of Prussia. CAAA; CAE; COA; COD; COKB; DEI; DEJ; NEC; UNA

Frederick, Jane (1952–). Track athlete. GLB

Frederick, Pauline (1908–). Radio commentator. CLA

Frederick William I (1688–1740). King of Prussia. COA

Free, "World B" (Lloyd) (1953–). Basketball player. AAS-8

Freehan, Bill (1941–). Baseball player. BRE; ZAA

Freeman, Jordian (d. 1781). American Revolutionary patriot. STQ†

Freeman, Mary Eleanor Wilkins (1852–1930). Author. BEGA

Fregosi, James Louis (1942–). Baseball player. LEY

Freiburghaus, George E. Conductor. STM†

Freier, Recha (1892–). Israeli resistance leader, born Germany. GRB-1

Frémont, John Charles (1813–1890). Army officer, explorer. BUB; CUC; DOCA; FOC; HEB; HIBC; HOB; LED; ROL; WHD

Fremstad, Anna Olivia (1872–1951). Singer, born Sweden. WABC†

French, Daniel Chester (1850–1931). Sculptor. WOAA†

Freneau, Philip Morin (1752–1832). Poet, journalist. BUIB†

Frescobaldi, Girolamo (1583–1643). Italian composer, organist. BEM

Freud, Anna (1895–1982). English psychiatrist, born Austria. CHE

Freud, Martha Bernays (1861–1951). Wife of Sigmund Freud. RIB

Freud, Sigmund (1856–1939). Austrian psychiatrist. ASB-1; CHD; FRE; KE; POD; RIB; ROA; WEF

Frey, Charles N. (b. 1885). Chemist. PAB

Fricsay, Ferenc (1914–1963). Hungarian conductor. STM†; YOM

Fried, Alfred Hermann (1864–1921). Austrian pacifist. LET; MEC†; WIC

Friedan, Betty (1921–). Author, feminist. GIB-1; WA

Friedlander, Ethan (1957–). Israeli boat racer. SLA

Friedman, Benny (1905–1982). Football player. DAFG; SLA

Friedman, Herbert (1916–). Physicist. LAA

Friedman, Max (b. 1889). Basketball player. SLA

Friedmann, Roseli Ocampo (1937–). Microbiologist, polar researcher. LA-1

Frietchie, Barbara (1766–1862). Civil War heroine. DOD

Friganza, Trixie (1870–1955). Comedienne. MASB

Friml, Rudolf (1879–1972). Composer, born Czechoslovakia. EWA; MOA

Frisch, Frank (1898–1973). Baseball player, manager. ALB; DAFD; DEG; HAF; RIGA†; SHF; VEA

Frobisher, Sir Martin (1535?–1594). English explorer. DOC; GRAA; KNB; ROL†

Froebel, Friedrich Wilhelm (1782–1852). German educator. COG; FRC

Froissart, Jean (1337–1407). French historian. HIB

Frost, Robert (1874–1963). Poet. ASB-1; BEF; BEGA; BEH; HEF; KE; LEJ; LEOB; SIF; WHB

Fry, Elizabeth Gurney (1780–1845). English reformer. BOH; NOA; STP

Fry, Johnny (c. 1953–). Sky diver. HAFA

Frye, Harry Richard. Surf rider. OLD

Fuchs, Becky (1955?–). Rodeo rider. VADB

Fuchs, Jeno (1882–1954). Hungarian fencer. SLA†

Fuchs, Sir Vivian Ernest (1908–). English geologist. DOC†; KNA†; MOB; ROL

Fulbright, James William (1905–). Ex-senator. ARB

Fulgentius. Saint. DAD-2

Fulks, Joe (1922?–). Basketball player. PE

Fuller, Alfred Carl (1885–1973). Manufacturer. LAG

Fuller, Loie (1862–1928). Dancer. WABC†

Fuller, Margaret (1810–1850). Author, feminist. BOC; GUBA; STLA; WABC

Fuller, Peggy (1955?–). Motorcyclist. BUIC

Fuller, Richard Buckminster (1895–1983). Architect. LAF

Fuller, Samuel Carter. Neurologist. BRB†

Fuller, Sarah (1836–1927). Educator. BUDA†

Fuller, Solomon Carter (1872–1953). Psychiatrist, pathologist. HAMA

Fulton, Robert (1765–1815). Engineer, inventor. COL; CUC; DEI; DEJ; EBA; EVC; FAB; FE; HYA; LAE; LEL; MAL; THA

Funk, Casimir (1884–1967). Biochemist, born Poland. PIAA

Funston, George Keith (1910–). Business executive. PAA

Fuqua, Frenchy. Football player. BELB

Furtwaengler, Wilhelm (1886–1954). German conductor. EWB; YOM†

G

Gabelich, Gary (1940–). Automobile racer. OLDC; ST-1

Gable, Dan (1949?–). Wrestler. BELB; LEYB†

Gabriel of Our Lady of Sorrows. Saint. DAD-2

Gabriel, Archangel. DAD-2; QUA

Gabriel, Roman (1940–). Football player. DUD; DUE; LEZA; SHEA

Gabrieli, Giovanni (c. 1555–1612). Italian composer. BEM

Gaedel, Eddie. Midget. LIAA†

Gaffaney, Mary (1925–). Aviator. GEDB†

Gág, Wanda (1893–1946). Author, illustrator. SM

Gagarin, Yuri Alekseyevich (1934–1968). Russian astronaut. KEH; MOB; NEB; PRC; THC

Gage, Thomas (1721–1787). English general. AKA; BUIB†; SOA

Gahadiyas. Seneca Indian boy. CAD

Gahan, Edward J. Conductor. STM†

Gainsborough, Thomas (1727–1788). English painter. CHC; DEI; DEJ

Galard, Geneviève de (1925–). French nurse. MAK

Galbraith, John Kenneth (1908–). Economist, diplomat. KE

Galen (130–200). Greek physician. CAA; CHD; POD; ROA; SHG; SIA; SIC

Galilei, Galileo (1564–1642). Italian astronomer, physicist. ASA; BEC; BEP; BOB; CAA; COL; DEI; DEJ; DOE; EVC; FE; FRB; FRE; LAA; MAQ; MOCB; PIA; SHFB; SIA; SIB; STI; SUE; THA

Gall (d. 646). Saint. MOC

Gall (1840?–1894). Sioux Indian chief. DEDB

Galla Placidia (388–450). Roman empress of the West. TRBA

Gallagher, Alan Mitchell (1945–). Baseball player. LEY

Gallatin, Albert (1761–1849). Statesman, born Switzerland. DOG

Gallitzin, Demetrius Augustine (1770–1840). Missionary, born Russia. ASB

Galois, Evariste (1811–1832). French mathematician. MUB; STN

Galvani, Luigi (1737–1798). Italian physicist, physician. DUA; MAQ

Galvin, Edward J. (1882–1956). Irish bishop. REC

Galvin, James F. (1856–1902). Baseball player. ALB

Gama, Vasco da (c. 1469–1524). Portuguese explorer. COC; COL; DAF; GRC; KEH; MOB; ROL

Gamaliel (d. 50?). Palestinian rabbi. GUA

Gamberg, Abe (1893–). Businessman, born Russia. BAEA-1

Gandhi, Indira Nehru (1917–1984). Indian prime minister. ASB-1; DU-1; GI; LIDA; WECA

Gandhi, Mohandas Karamchand (1869–1948). Indian nationalist leader. ASB-1; BEC; DEI; DEJ; DOF; FOJ; FRE; HAA; HAJ; KE; KEE; LAD; MAN; STP; YOA

Gannet, Deborah Sampson (fl. 1776). American Revolutionary patriot. AND; CLC; HODA; RAD; ROG; STQ†; WIBA

Gansz, George (1924–). Conductor. STM†

Gaon of Vilna, see Elijah ben Solomon.

Garbo, Greta (1905–). Actress, born Sweden. ASB-1

Garcia (fl. 1813). Runaway slave, Indian leader. KADB

Garcia, Forresto (1954?–). Migrant worker. WECC

Garcia, Hector (1914–). Physician, born Mexico. FOW

Garcilaso de la Vega (called el Inca) (1539?–1616). Peruvian historian. BACA

Garden, Mary (1874–1967). Singer. WABC†

Gardiner, David (b. 1636). Colonist. CAF

Gardiner, Lion (1599–1663). Colonist. CAF

Gardiner, Tenley Albright, see Albright, Tenley.

Gardner, Randy (1958–). Skater. VAD-6

Gardner, Samuel (1896–). Violinist, conductor, born Russia. STM†

Garfield, James Abram (1831–1881). President of U.S. BAEB; BAG; BAG-1; BEB; BLA; BUIA; CAG; CAH; COI; COJA; COS; DUC; DUCA; FRBA; HIH; KEA; LEQ; LEQA; MAB; MABA; MIA; PED; ROH; ROHA; ROK†; SUBB; WHD

Garfield, Lucretia Rudolph (1832–1918). Wife of James Garfield. BAG; BAG-1; BLG†; CHB; KL; MAA; MAU; PRB; ROH; ROHA

Garibaldi, Giuseppe (1807–1882). Italian patriot. BOD; MAJ

Garland, Hamlin (1860–1940). Author. CAC†

Garland, Judy (1922–1969). Actress, singer. FOR

Garlits, Don (1932?–). Automobile racer. LEX; LEYC; OLB; OLCB; OLDA; ORD; ST-1; YAA

Garms, Shirley Rudolph (1924–). Bowler. JAB; LEF

Garner, John Nance (1868–1967). Vice president of U.S. FEA; HAOA; HOEA

Garner, "Kati" (Nancy) (1953–). Diver. HAKA

Garnet, Henry Highland (1815–1882). Abolitionist. ADA; ADB; BEJ; BRB†; GRAB-05; ROG

Garrett, Eileen J. (1893–1970). Irish medium. COEA

Garrett, Elizabeth, see Anderson, Elizabeth Garrett.

Garrett, Michael Lockett (1944–). Football player. BEKB; LEZB

Garrett, Patrick Floyd (1850–1908). Law officer. SUI

Garrett, Robert. Track athlete. DEF; FIC

Garrison, William Lloyd (1805–1879). Abolitionist. BEJ; BOD; COG; COGA; ELA; LEC; LEZC; RED; SPB; STJA

Garros, Roland (d. 1918). French aviator, WW I. HAMY

Garvey, Marcus A. (1887–1940). Jamaican Black leader. ADA; ADB; ARAA; BEJ; BRBD; GRAB-01; JO

Garvey, Steven Patrick (1948–). Baseball player. AAS-3; BUJC; GUED-01; RIGA†; GUEE; SMF

Gary, Elbert Henry (1846–1927). Business executive. HOF

Gaska, Zigmont (1908–). Conductor. STM†

Gasser, Herbert Spencer (1888–1963). Physiologist. RIF

Gaston, Arthur George (1892–). Insurance executive. ADA; ADB

Gates, Everett (1914–). Conductor. STM†

Gates, Horatio (1728?–1806). American Revolutionary soldier. BUIB†

Gatheru, R. Mugo. African college professor. OJA

Gatling, Richard Jordan (1818–1903). Inventor. HYA†

Gauguin, Paul (1848–1903). French painter. KAA; MAH; WIAA

Gaulle, Charles de (1890–1970). French president. ASB-1; CAAA; KE; WEA

Gauss, Karl Friedrich (1777–1855). German mathematician. COLA; DUA; MUB; SIA; STN

Gautama Buddha, see Buddha.

Gautier, Felisa Rincón de, see Rincón de Gautier, Felisa.

Gay, Mary Ann Harris (fl. 1864). Author. WABC†

Gayle, Crystal (1951–). Singer. KRI

Gay-Lussac, Joseph Louis (1778–1850). French chemist, physicist. SHFB

Gebert, Ernst (1901–1961). Conductor, born Germany. STM†

Geddes, Sir Patrick (1854–1932). Scottish botanist. COLA

Gehrig, Lou (1903–1941). Baseball player. ALB; BEC; BOE; BUD-1; DA; DAA; DAFB; DAFC; DAFD; DAG; DAGA; DAH; FRC-1†; GIB; GR; GUC; HIF; HOC; LIC; LYB; MUB-1; MUC; RAAA; RIGA†; ROB; SCA; SHB; SHC; SHH; WAC

Gehringer, Charles Leonard (1903–). Baseball player. ALB; HIF; RIGA†

Geiger, Abraham (1810–1874). German theologian. KAD

Geiger, Johannes Wilhelm (1882–1945). German physicist. HAC

Geisel, Theodore, see Seuss, Dr.

Geisler, Lloyd (1913–). Conductor. STM†

Gejvall, Nils-Gustaf (1915–). Swedish osteologist. POC

Gellée, Claude, see Lorrain, Claude.

Gemma (1878–1903). Saint. DAD-1

Genesius. Saint. MOC; PEE

Genesko, Lynn (1955–). Swimmer. RYX

Genet, Arthur Samuel (1909–). Transportation executive. PAA

Geneviève (420?–500?). Saint. DAD-2; MOC; ONA

Genghis Khan (1162–1227). Mongol conqueror. BEO; BLW; CAAA; COD; KEH; NEC; UNA

Geoffrion, Bernard "Boom-Boom" (1931–). Canadian hockey player. OBA; ORC; RAAF

George (d. 303?). Saint. DAD-2; ONA; PEE; QUA

George I (1660–1727). King of Great Britain and Ireland. DEC; GRAB; SCC

George II (1683–1760). King of Great Britain and Ireland. DEC; GRAB; SCC

George III (1738–1820). King of Great Britain and Ireland. DEC; GRAB; SCC; SOA

George IV (1762–1830). King of Great Britain and Ireland. DEC; GRAB; SCC

George V (1865–1936). King of Great Britain and Northern Ireland. CAAA; DEC; GRAB; SCC

George VI (1895–1952). King of Great Britain and Northern Ireland. CAAA; DEC; GRAB; NEC; SCC; TRA

George, Graham (1912–). English conductor. STM†

George G. (1953–). Immigrant, born Cuba. SIAA

Gerard Sagredo (980–1046). Saint. QUA

Gerhart, Russell (1904–). Conductor. STM†

Gerkowski, Raymond (1906–). Conductor. STM†

Germain, George Sackville, 1st viscount Sackville (1716–1785). English colonial administrator. SOA

Germaine. Saint. DAD-1; DAD-2

German sisters (Addie, Catherine, Julia, Sophia) (fl. 1870). Indian captives. JOB; JOD

Germanus of Auxerre. Saint. DAD-3

Geronimo (c. 1829–1909). Apache Indian war chief. DEDB; HEC; LEH; MOD; STAB†; SUKA

Gerry, Elbridge (1744–1814). Vice president of U.S. BAEA; BUIB†; COJ†; FEA; FEAA; FEAB; HAOA; HOEA; MAC

Gershwin, George (1898–1937). Composer. ALD; BAD; BEKA; BUC; CUC; DEI; DEJ; EWA; FIE; KAE; LAC; LETA; MAF; MOA; POF; SAA†; WIA; YOJ

Gershwin, Ira (1896–1983). Lyricist. MOA†

Gertrude the Great (1256–1302). Saint. DAD-1; DAD-3; QUA

Gervin, George (1952–). Basketball player. AAS-8

Gesualdo, Carlo (1560–1613). Italian composer. BEM

Getty, J. Paul (1892–1976). Oil executive. COKB; DU-1

Giacomin, Edward (1939–). Hockey player. FICA

Giammona, Louie (1953–). Football player. AAS-25

Giannini, Amadeo Peter (1870–1949). Banker. MAS

Gibb, Barry (1946–). English singer. BUIB-1

Gibb, Maurice (1949–). English singer. BUIB-1

Gibb, Robin (1949–). English singer. BUIB-1

Gibbon, Edward (1737–1794). English historian. HIB

Gibbons, Floyd Phillips (1887–1939). Journalist. FLBB

Gibbs, Charles (1794–1831). Pirate. WHA†

Gibbs, Josiah Willard (1839–1903). Physicist. SIA

Gibbs, Mifflin W. (1828–1903). Jurist. KADB

Gibson, Althea (1927–). Tennis player. AAS-29; BOF; BRG; FOG; FR-1; HOBA; HOBAA; HOBC; LOAA; PIB; PIBA; RICA; ROJ; RYA†; SMC; SUDA†; VAE

Gibson, Bob (Robert) (1935–). Baseball player. BUJ†; DEG; FRC-1†; FRD; KADA; LEZ; MUB-1; PAW; PRA; RIGA†; SA-3; SHA

Gibson, Guy Penrose (1919–1944). English aviator, WWII. HAMY

Gibson, Josh (1911–1947). Baseball player. AAS-24; DAFD

Gibson, Kenneth Allen (1932–). Mayor. BRGA; DU; HAH

Giffen, Isaac Newton (b. 1848). Confederate soldier. CAD

Gifford, Frank (1930–). Football player, TV sportscaster. HAE

Gigante, Charles (1911–). Conductor. STM†

Giggans, Jim. Television newscaster. STAA

Gilbert, Edwina (1931–). Airline executive. GEDB†

Gilbert, Gilles (1949–). Canadian hockey player. THF

Gilbert, Sir Humphrey (1539?–1583). English navigator. ROL†

Gilbert, Sir Joseph Henry (1817–1901). English agricultural chemist. CAB

Gilbert, Rod (Rodrique Gabriel) (1941–). Canadian hockey player. DEHA-1; LEYA; OBB

Gilbert, William (1540–1603). English physician, physicist. SHFB; SIA

Gilbert, William Schwenk (1836–1911). English composer. ASB-1

Gilbreth, Lillian M. (1878–1972). Engineer. BOJ; EMB; CLA; LEGA; STLA

Gilchrist, Cookie (Carlton C.) (1935–). Football player. LIBA

Gildersleeve, Virginia Crocheron (1877–1965). Educator. CLA; FLB

Gilels, Emil G. (1916–1985). Russian pianist. EWC

Giles (7th century). Saint. DAD-3; FAD

Giliani, Alessandra (c. 1307–1326). Italian anatomist. SC†

Gill, Jocelyn Ruth (1916–). Astronomer. POE

Gill, John (1732–1785). Journalist. SQB†

Gillain, Marie Anne Victoire (1783–1847). French midwife. MASA†

Gillespie, Dizzy (John Birks) (1917–). Trumpeter. TEA; TEB; UN; WAD†

Gillespie, Frank L. (1867–1925). Insurance executive. ADB

Gillett, Joshua (fl. 1813). Pioneer boy. BAC

Gilliam, John Rally (1945–). Football player. SMI

Gilliam, Junior (James) (1928–1978). Baseball player, coach. BOE†

Gillian (d. 1340). Saint. WIB

Gillman, Sidney (1911–). Football player, coach. SLA

Gilman, Charlotte Perkins (1860–1935). Feminist. NIA

Gilman, Nicholas (1755–1814). Senator. BUIB†; FEAA

Gilmore, Artis (1948–). Basketball player. AAS-5; SA-1

Gilpin, Charles Sidney (1878–1930). Actor. ADA; ADB; DOF-1

Gilruth, Robert Rowe (1913–). Aeronautical engineer. POE

Gimbel, Adam (1817–1896). Merchant, born Germany. LETA

Ginsburg, Henry T. (1892–). Conductor. STM†

Ginsburg, Ruth Bader (1933–). Jurist. GIB-1; SWI

Ginther, Paul Richard (1930–). Automobile racer. LEX

Giorgione, Il (c. 1478–1510). Italian painter. JAA

Giotto di Bondone (c. 1266–1337). Italian painter. CHC; JAA; KAA; MAI

Gipp, George (1895–1920). Football player. DAFB; DAFG; DAG; DAGA; DAI; HIE

Glackens, William James (1870–1938). Painter. DEDC

Gladstone, James (b. 1887). Canadian politician. GRAC

Glaser, Pamela (1957–). Karate champion. SLA†

Glasgow, Ellen (1873–1945). Author. CON†

Glasgow, Nancy Payne (1955?–). Motorcyclist. BUIC

Glazunov, Aleksandr Konstantinovich (1865–1936). Russian composer. POG

Gleason, Jackie (1916–1987). Comedian. ALC

Gleb. Saint. DAD-3

Glendower, Owen (1359?–1416). Welsh rebel. SUK

Glenn, John Herschel, Jr. (1921–). Astronaut, senator. BAB; COQ; DIA; LEL; LEPB; NEB; THC

Glennon, Nan. Mechanical engineer. HOG

Glickman, Marty (1917–). Sportscaster. SLA†

Glickstein, Shlomo (1958–). Israeli tennis player. SLA

Glidden, Bob. Automobile racer. OLDA

Glière, Reinhold Moritzovich (1875–1956). Russian composer. POG

Glinka, Mikhail Ivanovich (1804–1857). Russian composer. KAE; POG; SAA

Glover, John (1732–1797). General. MAE; SOA

Gluck, Christoph Willibald (1714–1787). German composer. BRF; BUD; KAE; SAA

Glueck, Nelson (1900–1971). Archaeologist. GRB-1

Gobat, Charles Albert (1843–1914). Swiss statesman. MEC†; WIC

Gobel, George (1919–). Comedian. ALC; HAG-1

Goddard, Mary Katherine (1736–1816). Journalist. YOC

Goddard, Robert Hutchings (1882–1945). Physicist. ASA; BOK; COLA; COQ; FAA; FE; LEGA; NAA; NEB; RIBA; SIA; STMA; THA; THC; YOE

Godden, Rumer (1907–). English author. SMA; SMB

Godfrey, Arthur (1903–1983). Entertainer. ALC

Godiva, Lady (c. 1040–1080). English legendary horseback rider. COKB

Godolphin, Margaret (1652–1678). Wife of Sidney Godolphin. NOA

Godric (1065?–1170). Saint. MOC

Godunov, Boris Fëdorovich (1551?–1605). Tsar of Russia. RIA†

Godwin, Mary Wollstonecraft (1759–1797). English author. BOH; GUBA

Goeppert-Mayer, Maria (1906–1972). Theoretical physicist, born Germany. HA-1; SC†; SHFE

Goethals, George Washington (1858–1928). Army officer, engineer. LEGA; RAE

Goethe, Johann Wolfgang von (1749–1832). German poet. DEI; DEJ

Gogh, Vincent van (1853–1890). Dutch painter. DEI; DEJ; KAA; MAH; WIAA

Gogol, Nikolai Vasilievich (1809–1852). Russian author. POFA

Go-Hung (254–334). Chinese alchemist. CUA

Goings, William (fl. 1821). Rancher. KADB

Gold, Arthur (1919–). Canadian pianist. EWC

Gold, Shirley (1925–). State legislator. WHE†

Goldberg, Arthur J. (1908–). Statesman. LETA; WEC

Goldberg, Marshall (1917–). Football player. HIE; SLA

Goldberg, Whoopi (1950–). Actress. MASB

Goldberger, Joseph (1874–1929). Physician, born Austria. ALD; DEA; GEF

Golden, Bill (1933–). Automobile racer. OLAB

Goldfadden, Abraham (1840–1908). Founder of Yiddish theater. LETA

Goldhaber, Gertrude Scharff, see Scharff-Goldhaber, Gertrude.

Goldhaber, Maurice (1911–). Physicist, born Austria. PAC

Goldman, Connie. Broadcaster. BOHD

Goldman, Emma (1869–1940). Anarchist, born Russia. WABC†

Goldovsky, Boris (1908–). Conductor, born Russia. STM†

Goldsworthy, Bill (William Alfred) (1944–). Canadian hockey player. LEYA; ORB

Goldwater, Barry (1909–). Senator. WHD†

Goldwyn, Samuel (1882–1974). Motion picture producer. LETA

Golgi, Camillo (1844–1926). Italian neurologist. RIF

Golschmann, Vladimir (1893–1972). Conductor, born France. STM

Gomelsky, Alexander "Sascha" (1926–). Russian basketball coach. SLA†

Gomez, Benjamin (fl. 1791). Businessman. LETA

Gomez, Lefty (1909–). Baseball player. BOE; LIAA; ROB

Gomez, Manuel (1949–). Artist. FAI

Gompers, Samuel (1850–1924). Labor leader, born England. ARAA; BEA; COH; CUC; DABA; FAC; FOB; GRB-1; LEHA; LETA; LOB; MAL; MEB; SEA

Gonzales, Pancho (Richard Alonzo) (1928–). Tennis player. AAS-28; ASBA; BELB; DEHA-1; FOW; FOX; HI; HOC; LAHA; LYE; NEAA

Gonzales, Rodolfo (1929–). Social welfare leader. NEAA

Gonzalez, Henry Barbosa (1916–). Congressman. NEAA; WH-1

Gonzalez, Natividad Martinez (1907–). Housewife, born Mexico. BAEA-1

González Prada, Manuel (1848–1918). Peruvian reformer. WOB

Goodall, Jane (1934–). English anthropologist. BOHG; DU-1; SC

Goode, Alexander David (1911–1943). Chaplain. FIA; GEF; GRB-1

Gooden, Dwight (1964–). Baseball player. HEFB†

Goodman, Andrew (1943–1964). Civil rights worker. STJB†

Goodman, Benny (1909–1986). Clarinetist, band leader. COF-1; TEA; TEB; WAD†

Goodnight, Charles (1836–1929). Cattleman. BLD; WAA

Goodpasture, Ernest William (1886–1960). Virologist. SUF

Goodrich, Annie Warburton (1866–1954). Nurse. YOB

Goodrich, Gail (1943–). Basketball player. HIBAA

Goodwill, Linda. Jockey. HOBAA†

Goodwin, Ruby Berkley (1903–). Poet. DADB

Goodyear, Charles (1800–1860). Inventor. DOE; FAB; HOF; HYA; LAE; MAL; MAP; RAA; RIBA

Goolagong, Evonne, see Cawley, Evonne Goolagong.

Goossens, Eugene (1893–1962). English conductor, composer. STM†

Gordon, Dexter (1923–). Saxophonist. UN

Gordon, Morris (1895–). Tailor, born Russia. BAEA-1

Gordon, Richard F., Jr. (1929–). Astronaut. THC

Gordon, Ruth (1896–1985). Actress. DI-1†

Gordon, Sid (1918–1975). Baseball player. RI; SLA

Goreleigh, Rex (1903–). Painter. FAH

Goretti, Mary (1890–1902). Saint. DAD-1; DAD-3

Gorgas, William Crawford (1854–1920). Physician. COL

Gorham, Nathaniel (1738–1796). Statesman. BUIB†; FEAA

Gorki, Maksim (1868–1936). Russian author. POFA

Goron, Marie-François (1847–1933). French detective. LID

Gosden, Freeman (1899–1982). Comedian. BUR-1

Goslin, "Goose" (Leon) (1900–1971). Baseball player. RIGA†

Gosney, Mary Louise. Public relations executive. HOG†

Gossage, "Goose" (Richard) (1951–). Baseball player. AAS

Gotch, Frank (b. 1878). Wrestler. DAG; DAGA

Gottfried, Brian (1952–). Tennis player. SLA

Gottlieb, Eddie (1898–1979). Basketball coach, administrator, born Russia. SLA

Gottschalk, Louis Moreau (1829–1869). Pianist, composer. CHF; LEHB

Gould, Glenn (1932–1982). Canadian pianist. EWC

Gould, Morton (1913–). Composer. POF; STM†

Gould, Shane Elizabeth (1956–). Australian swimmer. HOBAA†; ST-1

Goulding, Denis (1893–). (Born Ireland). BAEA-1

Goulding, Ray (Raymond Walter) (1922–). Comedian. BUR-1

Gounod, Charles François (1818–1893). French composer. BAE; KAE

Gourdine, Meredith (1929–). Physicist. CAF-1

Gouzenko, Igor S. (1915–). Russian ex-government official. CAHA

Gowan, M. Olivia, Sister (1888–). Nurse. YOB

Gowdy, Hank (b. 1889). Baseball player, coach. GIB; HIC

Goya y Lucientes, Francisco José de (1746–1828). Spanish painter. KAA; MAI

Grabarkewitz, Bill (William Cordell) (1946–). Baseball player. LEY

Grabowski, Jim. Football player. JOA†

Gradishar, Randy (1952–). Football player. AAS-15; SMJ

Grady, Henry Woodfin (1850–1889). Journalist. SQB

Graf, Willi (d. 1943). German resistance worker. LAD

Graff, Sunny. Lawyer, martial artist. AT

Graffman, Gary (1918–). Pianist. EWC

Graham, Ennis, pseud., see Molesworth, Mary Louisa.

Graham, James, see Montrose, James Graham, 5th earl and 1st marquis of.

Graham, Katharine Meyer (1917–). Publisher. BOHD

Graham, Martha (1893–). Dancer. BOHB; FOGC; STLA

Graham, Otto (1921–). Football player. ANC; DAFB; DAFG; DAI; DEH; DEHA-1; DUD; DUE; HEI; HOC; RAAD; SUC; SUD

Graham, Robin Lee (1949?–). Mariner. SCBA

Grahame, Kenneth (1859–1932). Scottish author. BEI

Granados, Enrique (1867–1916). Spanish composer. KAE; SAA†

Grandma Moses, see Moses, Anna Mary Robertson.

Grange, Red (Harold Edward) (1903–). Football player. ASBA; COFB; DAB; DAFB; DAFG; DAG; DAGA; DAI; DUF; HAD; HEG; HEI; HIE; HOC; RAAE; SID; SUD

Granger, Hoyle. Football player. BEKB

Grant, Bud (Harold P.) (1927–). Football coach. AAS-12; HAGA

Grant, Danny (1946–). Canadian hockey player. FICC

Grant, David N. W. (1891–1964). Surgeon. ED

Grant, George Barnard (1849–). Computer pioneer. GRAB-3†

Grant, James Augustus (1827–1892). Scottish explorer. ROL†

Grant, Julia Dent (1826–1902). Wife of Ulysses S. Grant. BAG; BAG-1; BLG†; CHB; KL; MAA; MAU; PRB; ROH; ROHA

Grant, M. Earl (1891?–). Financier. DRA

Grant, Micki. Actress, composer, singer. AB

Grant, Ulysses Simpson (1822–1885). President of U.S. BAEB; BAG; BAG-1; BEB; BLA; BUIA; CAG; CAH; COD; COI; COJA; COS; CUC; DEI; DEJ; DUB; DUC; DUCA; FID; FRBA; HIH;

LEP; LEQ; LEQA; MAB; MABA; MIA; PED; RAE; ROH; ROHA; ROK†; SUBB; WHD

Granville, Christine (d. 1952). Polish spy. SEB

Grasse, François Joseph de (1722–1788). French naval officer. SOA

Grassi, Giovanni Battista (1854–1925). Italian zoologist. DEB; ROA

Grasso, Ella (1919–1981). Governor. BOHF; GRAB-1; WHE

Gratz, Rebecca (1781–1869). Philanthropist. GRB-1; LER; LETA; PEB

Gray, Asa (1810–1888). Botanist. HYB

Gray, Elisha (1835–1901). Inventor. HYA†

Gray, Ida (1867–1953). Dentist. LOAV

Gray, Leon (1951–). Football player. AAS-11

Gray, Pete (1917–). Baseball player. BELB; BUJA; DAFD; PIB; PIBA

Gray, Robert (1755–1806). Sea captain, explorer. BUB

Gray, Thomas (1716–1771). English poet. COP

Graziano, Rocky (1922–). Boxer, actor. DEHA-1

Greaves, Clifton (b. 1858?). Buffalo soldier. BUH

Greaves, Red Legs (fl. mid-1600s). Scottish pirate. WHA†

Greco, El (1548?–1614?). Spanish painter, born Greece. CHC; KAA; MAI

Greeley, Horace (1811–1872). Journalist. ARB; FLBA; LEC; MAL; SQB; WHD

Greeley-Smith, Nixola (1880–1919). Journalist. JAE

Green, Abel (1900–1973). Editor. LEU

Green, Anna Catherine (c. 1720–1775). Publisher. WABC†

Green, Charlie. Track athlete. LYE

Green, Dick (fl. 1847). Pioneer. SCB

Green, Ernestene (1939–). Archaeologist. WIAA-01

Green, Hetty (1835–1916). Financier. COKB

Green, Nancy (c. 1834–1923). Posed as "Aunt Jemima." GRAB-02

Green, Patricia (1952–). A.M.E. Zion minister. SMBB-1

Green, Ted (Edward Joseph) (1940–). Canadian hockey player. LOAA

Green, William (1873–1952). Labor leader. COH; DABA; LEHA; SEA

Greenaway, Kate (1846–1901). English illustrator. SM

Greenberg, Hank (Henry Benjamin) (1911–1986). Baseball player. ALB; BOE; DAA; FRC-1†; GR; RI; RIGA†; SLA

Greene, Allen. Conductor. STM†

Greene, Catherine (1755–1814). Inventor. SC†

Greene, Joe (1946–). Football player. RUA

Greene, Nancy (1943–). Canadian skier. FRCA

Greene, Nathanael (1742–1786). General. BUIB†; DAFA; MAE; SOA

Greenfield, Elizabeth Taylor (1809–1876). Singer. LOAV; ROF†

Greenhow, Rose O'Neal (1817–1864). Spy. FOA; HAB; SUG; WABC†

Greenleaf, Ralph (1899?–1950). Billiards player. DAG; DAGA

Greenwood, Charlotte (1893–1978). Actress. MASB

Greer, Hal. Basketball player. HIBA

Gregg, Forrest. Football player. JOA†

Gregg, Josiah (1806–1850). Pioneer. HEB; NAA

Gregg, Maxine. Jazz agent. UN

Gregory I, the Great (c. 540–604). Saint, pope. DAD-2

Gregory VII (b. 1020). Saint, pope. DAD-2

Gregory of Nazianzus (330–390). Saint. DAD-2

Gregory, Cynthia (1946–). Dancer. BOHB; FOGC

Gregory, Darryl (1962?–). Winner, Young American Medal for Bravery. ANCA

Gregory, Dick (1932–). Entertainer. DADB; EOB; RICA

Gregory, Masten (1932–). Automobile racer. LEX†

Grenfell, Sir Wilfred Thomason (1865–1940). English physician. MAN

Gretzky, Wayne (1961–). Canadian hockey player. AAS-22; AAS-35; ASB-1; HOCG; OLDE

Grey, Beryl (1927–). English dancer. ATA

Grey, Lady Jane (1537–1554). Candidate for the throne of England. DEC; SCC†

Grey, Lady Katherine (1540–1568). Sister of Lady Jane Grey. NOA

Grey, Lady Mary (1545–1578). Sister of Lady Jane Grey. NOA

Grich, Bobby (1949–). Baseball player. KLBB

Griebling, Otto (1896–1972). Clown, born Germany. KIB

Grieg, Edvard Hagerup (1843–1907). Norwegian composer. BRF; BUD; DEI; DEJ; FIE†; GOA; KAE; SAA

Grier, Rosie (Roosevelt) (1932–). Football player. AAS-32

Griese, Bob (Robert Allen) (1945–). Football player. AAS-20; CL-1; DUE; FRD; GUF; HAGC; LEZA; ST

Griffes, Charles Tomlinson (1884–1920). Composer. BAD; BUC; KAE; MAF; POF

Griffin, Archie (1954–). Football player. DEHB

Griffin, John (d. 1898). Surgeon. BLC

Griffith, Clark (1869–1955). Baseball manager. ALB

Griffith, David Wark (1875–1948). Motion picture producer. FLBC; SMBC

Griffith, Emile (1938–). Boxer, trainer. DEHA-1

Griffiths, Martha W. (1912–). Congresswoman. GRAB-1

Grigg, Rick (1938?–). Surf rider, oceanographer. OLD

Griggs, Sutton E. (1873–1930). Clergyman. KADB

Grimes, Burleigh (1894–1985). Baseball player, manager. ALB; GEB; RIGA†

Grimké, Angelina Emily (1805–1879). Abolitionist, feminist. CHFB; GUBA; LES-2; STG; WABC†

Grimké, Archibald Henry (1849–1930). Lawyer. DOF-1; ROG

Grimké, Francis James (1850–1937). Clergyman, civil rights leader. BRB†; GRAB-01

Grimké, Sarah Moore (1792–1873). Abolitionist, feminist. CHFB; GUBA; LES-2; NIA; WABC†

Grimm, Jakob (1785–1863). German author. BEI; SMAB

Grimm, Wilhelm Karl (1786–1859). German author. BEI; SMAB

Grissom, Gus (Virgil Ivan) (1926–1967). Astronaut. COQ; LEPB†; NEB†; THC

Groat, Dick (1930–). Baseball player. DEHA-1

Grock, pseud. (1880–1959). German clown. KLD

Grofé, Ferde (1892–1972). Composer. POF

Grogan, Ewart Scott (1874–1967). English zoologist. WOA

Gromyko, Andrei (1909–). Russian Communist leader. DU-1

Gronouski, John Austin (1919–). Diplomat. PIAA

Gropius, Walter Adolf (1883–1969). Architect, born Germany. BEA; FOF; HIFA; LAF

Gropper, William (1897–1977). Painter, illustrator. DEDC

Gros, Antoine Jean (1771–1835). French painter. MAH†

Grosman, Tatyana (1904–). Lithographer, born Russia. GIB-1

Grossfeld, Muriel Davis, see Davis, Muriel.

Grossinger, Jennie (1892–1972). Hotel executive. PAA

Grossman, Noam (1927–). Israeli soldier. GEF

Grossman, Randy (1952–). Football player. SLA

Grote, Jerry (Gerald Wayne) (1942–). Baseball player. TUB

Grouès, Henri, see Pierre, Abbé.

Grove, Lefty (Robert Moses) (1900–1975). Baseball player. ALB; DAFD; HIF; MUB-1; NEA; RIGA†; SHF

Grover, Paul (1908–). Conductor. STM†

Groves, Leslie Richard (1896–1970). General. RAE

Groza, Lou (1924–). Football player. AAS-17; DAFG; DAI; HAE

Gruening, Ernest Henry (1887–1974). Governor. SEC

Grundtvig, Nikolai F. S. (1783–1872). Danish educator. COG

Grunfeld, Ernie (1955–). Basketball player, born Romania. SLA

Guardineer, Fred (1913–). Cartoonist. GOB-1

Guatemoc, see Cuauhtémoc.

Guatemotzin, see Cuauhtémoc.

Gubner, Gary Jay (1942–). Shot putter, weight lifter. SLA†

Guderyahn, Richard (1904–). Conductor. STM†

Gudit (fl. 937–997). Ethiopian queen. GRAB-04

Guericke, Otto von (1602–1686). German physicist. MAQ; SHFB

Guerrero, Pedro (1956–). Dominican baseball player. HEFB†

Guerrero, Vicente (1783?–1831). Mexican statesman. ROGB

Guevara, Ché (Ernesto) (1928–1967). Cuban revolutionary. HAK

Guevremont, Jocelyn (1951–). Canadian hockey player. FICC

Guggenheim, Meyer (1828–1905). Industrialist, born Switzerland. LETA; WED

Guggenheim, Peggy (Marguerite) (1898–1979). Art patron. FOGB†

Guidi, Scipione. Conductor, born Italy. STM†

Guidry, Ron (1950–). Baseball player. AAS-2; HEFB†

Guild, Elizabeth. Psychologist. HOG

Guillen, Nicolás (1902–). Cuban poet. WO

Guinness, Sir Alec (1914–). English actor. ED-1†

Guion, Connie Meyers (1882–1971). Physician. FLA

Guitarman, Arthur (1871–1943). Poet. ALA

Guiteau, Charles Julius (1840?–1882). Assassin. RABA

Gurevitsch, Boris (1931–). Russian wrestler. SLA†

Gurney, Dan (Daniel Saxon) (1931?–). Automobile racer. JA; LEX; YAA

Gustavson, Paul (1917–). Cartoonist, born Finland. GOB-1

Gustavus II (Gustavas Adolphus) (1594–1632). King of Sweden. CAAA; HEA

Gutenberg, Johann (c. 1397–1468). German printer. ASA; COL; DEI; DEJ; EBA; FE; FRE; THA

Guthrie, Alfred Bertram, Jr. (1901–). Author. CON

Guthrie, Janet (1938–). Automobile racer. GUED-1

Gutierrez, Cesar "Coco" (1943–). Baseball player. SA-3

Gutierrez, José Angel. Mexican-American political leader. NEAA

Guttmann, Bela (1900–1981). Hungarian soccer player and coach. SLA†

Guy, Ray (1949–). Football player. RUA

Guynemer, Georges (1894–1917). French aviator, WWI. ARD; HAMY

Guyon, Joe (1892–1971). Football player. DAFG; SUD

Guzmán Blanco, Antonio (1829–1899). Venezuelan president. WOB

Guzmán, Martín Luis (b. 1887). Mexican author. NEBA

Guzman, Virginia Quintana (1940?–). Policewoman. SMBC-3

Gwinnett, Button (1735–1777). American Revolutionary patriot. BAEA; BUIB†; COJ†; FEAB; MAC

Gwyn, Richard, Blessed (d. 1584). DAD-3

Gwynn, Tony (1959–). Baseball player. HEFB†

Gyarmati, Andrea (1954–). Hungarian swimmer. SLA†

Gyles, John (b. 1742?). Indian captive. CAF

H

Haaker, William (1917–). Conductor. STM†

Haber, Fritz (1868–1934). German chemist. FE; LET

Haddon, Elizabeth (fl. 1689). Colonist. WABC†

Hader, Berta (1890?–1976). Author, illustrator. SMAB

Hader, Elmer (1889–1973). Author, illustrator. SMAB

Hadrian (76–138). Emperor of Rome. CAAA; COA; COK

Haesle, Leo M. Conductor. STM†

Hafetz Hayyim, The, see Kagan, Israel Meir.

Hafey, Charles "Chick" (1903–1973). Baseball player. RIGA†

Haffkine, Waldemar Mordecai (1860–1930). Russian bacteriologist. GEF; GRB-1

Hafstad, Lawrence Randolph (1904–). Physicist. PAB

Hagen, Ernest (1913–). Conductor. STM†

Hagen, John P. (1908–). Astronomer. YOE

Hagen, Walter (1892–1969). Golfer. DAG; DAGA; LABA

Hagerman, James J. (fl. 1870). Pioneer. NAA

Hague, Frank (1876–1956). Mayor. COGC

Hahn, Emily (1905–). Mining engineer, traveler. ROJ

Hahn, Otto (1879–1968). German chemist, physicist. FE

Haig, Douglas Haig, 1st earl (1861–1928). British soldier. ARD

Haile Selassie I (1891–1975). Emperor of Ethiopia. ADA; DU-1; GRAB-04

Haile Selassie, Tsahai (1919–1942). Princess of Ethiopia. MAK

Haines, Jesse (1893–1978). Baseball player. DEG†

Haise, Fred W. (1933–). Astronaut. WIAA-5

Haizlip, Ellis. Television producer. AB

Hajos-Guttman, Alfred (1878–1955). Hungarian swimmer. SLA

Halas, George (1895–1983). Football coach. AAS-12; DAB; DAFG; DAI; SUD

Halasz, Laszlo (1905–). Hungarian conductor. STM†

Hale, George Ellery (1868–1938). Astronomer. LAA

Hale, Lucretia Peabody (1820–1900). Author. BEE; BEI

Hale, Nathan (1755–1776). American Revolutionary patriot. BUIB†; DEI; DEJ; EVD; FIA; FID; FOA; HAB; HIBD; KN; LEAA; LEP; LOA; SUG

Hales, Stephen (1677–1761). English physiologist. CAB

Halevi, Judah, see Judah ha-Levi.

Haley, Alex (1921–). Author. DOF-1; STAA

Haley, Margaret (1861–1939). Labor leader. BI†

Hall, Charles Martin (1863–1914). Chemist. FAB; FE; LEN

Hall, Glenn (1931?–). Canadian hockey player. ETB; ORA; ORC; WAK

Hall, Helen (1892–). Social worker. BRBE†

Hall, Horathel (1928?–). Weaver. FAI

Hall, Jim (1935?–). Automobile racer and manufacturer. JA; LEX; YAA

Hall, Karen. Television producer. HOD-1

Hall, Lloyd Augustus (1894–1971). Food chemist. CAF-1; GRAB-03; HA

Hall, Lyman (1724–1790). American Revolutionary patriot. BAEA; BUIB†; COJ†; FEAB; MAC

Hall, Primus (1756–1855). Soldier. PECA†

Hall, Prince (1735?–1807). Abolitionist. ADA; ADB; BEJ; GRAB-05; PECA

Hall, Tom T. (1936–). Singer. KRI-1

Halley, Edmund (1656–1742). English astronomer. MOB; SHFB; SIA

Hallvard (d. 1043). Saint. MOC

Halpern, Charlie. Lawyer. LETD

Hals, Frans (1580–1666). Dutch painter. CHC; MAI

Halsey, William Frederick (1882–1959). Admiral. ARC; ICA; NAC

Halsted, William Stewart (1852–1922). Surgeon. CHE†; LEG; SIC

Ham, Jack (1948–). Football player. AAS-15

Hamer, Fannie Lou (1917–). Civil rights leader. BRBE†; DU; FAG; GRAB-01

Hames, Edwyn H. (1902–). Conductor, born Australia. STM†

Hamill, Dorothy (1956–). Skater. GUED; HOBAA; LIEA; VADA

Hamilton, Alexander (1755–1804). Statesman. BUIB; CUC; DEI; DEJ; FAC; FEAA; FOB; LEB; LOA; MAL; OLA; SEC; SQB†; STH

Hamilton, Alice (1869–1970). Physician. BOJ; BRBE; CHD; FLA; HA-1; MASA; PACA; RAAG†; SC†

Hamilton, Billy (William Robert) (1866–1940). Baseball player. ALB

Hamilton, Edith (1867–1963). Classicist. STLA

Hamilton, Scott (1958–). Skater. VAD-6

Hamlin, Hannibal (1809–1891). Vice president of U.S. FEA; HAOA; HOEA

Hammarskjöld, Dag (1905–1961). Swedish statesman. FOJ; KE; MEC; WIC; YOA

Hammerstein, Oscar, II (1895–1960). Librettist. BEKA†; MOA

Hammett, James (fl. 1830). English trade unionist. LAD

Hammon, Briton (fl. 1747–1759). Indian captive. HAP

Hammon, Jupiter (1720?–1800). Poet. CL; ROE

Hammurabi (c. 1955–1913 B.C.). King of Babylonia. CAAA; JOBB; NEC

Hampton, Wade (1818–1902). General. MAD

Hanaoka, Seishu (1760–1835). Japanese surgeon. RIB

Hanasi, Judah, *see* Judah ha-Nasi.

Hancock, John (1737–1793). American Revolutionary patriot. ARAB; BAEA; BUIB; COJ; FEAB; LOA; MAC; SOA; SUL

Hancock, Winfield Scott (1824–1886). General. WHD†

Handel, George Frederick (1685–1759). English composer, born Germany. BEN; BRF; BUD; FIE; GOA; KAE; SAA; YOK; YOM†

Handy, William Christopher (1873–1958). Composer. ADA; ADB; BAD; HUA; MOA; ROG; WAD

Hanks, Nancy (1927–1983). Chair of National Endowment for the Arts. GIB-1

Hanna, Mark (Marcus Alonzo) (1837–1904). Senator. COGC

Hannah. Biblical character, mother of Samuel. LER

Hannah. Biblical character, mother of the 7 martyrs. LER

Hannah, Bob (1956?–). Motorcyclist. OLDB

Hannah, John (1951–). Football player. AAS-11

Hanner, Dave. Football player. JOA†

Hannibal (247–183 B.C.). Carthaginian general. CAAA; COD; DEI; DEJ; HAA; MAJ

Hannibal, Abram (1697–1782). Russian general. ADA; ADB

Hannikainen, Tauno (1896–). Finnish conductor. STM†

Hanno (fl. 450 B.C.). Carthaginian navigator. DYA

Hansberry, Lorraine (1930–1965). Playwright. FLBA

Hanson, Howard (1896–1981). Composer. MAF; POF; STM†

Hanson, Robert (1920–1944). Marine aviator. BRA

Hanway, Howard. Insurance executive. PAA

Harbach, Otto (1873–1963). Librettist. MOA

Hardeen (Theo Weiss) (1876–1945). Magician. GIA

Hardin, John Welsey (1853–1895). Outlaw. JOBA; REE; SUJ

Harding, Florence Kling (1860–1924). Wife of Warren Gamaliel Harding. BAG; BAG-1; BLG; CHB; KL; MAA; MAU; PRB; ROH; ROHA

Harding, Warren Gamaliel (1865–1923). President of U.S. BAEB; BAG; BAG-1; BEB; BLA; BUIA; CAG; CAH; COI; COS; DUB; DUC; DUCA; FRBA; HIH; LEQ; LEQA; MAB; MABA; MIA; PED; ROH; ROHA; ROK†; SUBB; WHD

Hardy, Oliver (Norvell) (1892–1957). Comedian. BUR-1; ED-1; MAOB; PABA

Hardy, Thomas (1840–1928). English author. COO; STL

Hare, Clayton. Conductor, born Canada. STM†

Hare, James Henry (1856–1946). Photographer, born England. HOE

Hargreaves, James (c. 1722–1778). English inventor, manufacturer. FE

Harkness, Georgia (1891–1974). Theologian. BLF†

Harlan, John Marshall (1833–1911). Supreme Court justice. STJC

Harmon, Ernest Nason (1894–1979). General. RAE

Harmon, Thomas D. (1919–). Football player. HIE

Harold I, the Fairhaired (850?–933). King of Norway. JOBB

Harold II (1022?–1066). King of England. CHG; GRAB†; SCC; UNB

Harpe, Micajah (Big Harpe) (fl. 1790). Outlaw. JOBA

Harpe, Wiley (Little Harpe) (fl. 1790). Outlaw. JOBA

Harper, Beverly (1942–). Management consultant. LES-1†

Harper, Frances Ellen Watkins (1825–1911). Poet. LOAV; ROE; ROG; WABC†

Harper, Terry (Terrance Victor) (1940–). Canadian hockey player. LEYA

Harper, Tommy (1940–). Baseball player. LEY

Harper, Valerie (1940–). Television actress. BOHC

Harrelson, Bud (Derrel McKinley) (1944–). Baseball player. KLBB

Harrelson, Ken (1941–). Baseball player, sportscaster. DEHA-1

Harriman, Edward Henry (1848–1909). Railroad executive. CUC

Harriman, Mercy (b. 1758). Colonial girl. BAC

Harris, Bucky (Stanley Raymond) (1896–1977). Baseball manager. FRC-01

Harris, Emmylou (1947–). Singer. KRI-1

Harris, Franco (1950–). Football player. AAS-10; GUCA; GUH; LIBB

Harris, James. Football player. CL-1

Harris, James. Nuclear chemist. CAF-1†

Harris, Joel Chandler (1848–1908). Author. COB

Harris, Julie (1925–). Actress. DI-1

Harris, LaDonna (1931–). Comanche Indian leader. GRAC

Harris, Patricia R. (1924–1985). Ambassador, educator. YOI

Harris, Roy Ellsworth (1898–1979). Composer. BAD; KAE; MAF; POF

Harris, Sigmund (1883–1964). Football player. SLA

Harris, Tonie (1947–). Martial artist. AT

Harrison, Anna Symmes (1775–1864). Wife of William Henry Harrison. BAG; BAG-1; BLG†; CHA; KL; MAA; MAU; PRB; ROH; ROHA

Harrison, Benjamin (1726–1791). American Revolutionary patriot. BAEA; BUIB†; COJ†; LAI; MAC

Harrison, Benjamin (1833–1901). President of U.S. BAEB; BAG; BAG-1; BEB; BLA; BUIA; CAG; CAH; COI; COJA; COS; DUC; DUCA; FRBA; HIH; LAI; LEQ; LEQA; MAB; MABA; MIA; PED; ROH; ROHA; ROK†; SUBB; WHD

Harrison, Caroline (1832–1892). First wife of President Benjamin Harrison. BAG; BAG-1; BLG†; CHB; KL; MAA; MAU; PRB; ROH; ROHA

Harrison, George (1943–). English singer. BUIB-1; SC-01

Harrison, Guy Fraser (1894–). Conductor, born England. STM

Harrison, John (1693–1776). English horologist, inventor. FEAB; MOB

Harrison, Mary Lord (1858–1948). Second wife of President Benjamin Harrison. BAG†; BAG-1†; ROH†

Harrison, Richard Berry (1864–1935). Actor. ADA; ADB; DOF-1

Harrison, William Henry (1773–1841). President of U.S. BAEB; BAG; BAG-1; BEB; BLA; BUIA; CAG; CAH; COI; COJA; COS; DUC; DUCA; FRBA; HIH; LAI; LEQ; LEQA; MAB; MABA; MIA; PED; ROH; ROHA; ROK†; SEC; SUBB; WHD

Harroun, Ray (1879–1968). Automobile racer. LEX†

Harsanyi, Nicholas. Conductor, educator, born Hungary. STM†

Hart, Ann Morgan, see Hart, Nancy.

Hart, Eddie (1948–). Track athlete. AAS-24

Hart, Ephraim (1747–1825). Financier, born Bavaria. LETA

Hart, Jim (James Warren) (1944–). Football player. CL-1; LIB

Hart, John (1711?–1779). American Revolutionary patriot. BAEA; BUIB†; COJ†; FEAB; MAC†

Hart, Nancy (1735–1830). American Revolutionary patriot. AND; CLC

Hart, Pearl (fl. 1903). Criminal. WIAA-2

Hart, William Sebastian (1920–). Conductor. STM†

Hartack, Bill (1932–). Jockey, sportscaster. DEHA-1

Hartford, George Ludlum (1865–1957). Merchant. LAH

Harth, Sidney (1925–). Conductor. STM†

Hartigan, Grace (1922–). Painter. FOGB†

Hartnett, Gabby (Charles Leo) (1900–1972). Baseball player. ALB; GUDA; HIC; HOCM; RIGA†; SHD; ZAA

Harun al-Rashid (764?–809). Caliph of Baghdad. CAAA

Harvey, Douglas (1924–). Canadian hockey player. LIAB; OBB; ORC

Harvey, William (1578–1657). English physician. ASA; BEP; CAA; CHD; COL; DEI; DEJ; DOE; FE; FRE; POD; ROA; SHG; SIA; SIC; STE

Hashepsowe, see Hatshepsut.

Haskell, Charles Nathaniel (1860–1933). Governor. SEC

Hastie, William Henry (1904–1976). Jurist. ADA†; ADB†; DOF-1

Hata, Sahachiro (1872–1938). Japanese bacteriologist. BEK†

Hatathli, Ned (1923–). College president. GRAC

Hatcher, Orie Latham (1868–1946). Educator, reformer. PACB

Hatcher, Richard Gordon (1933–). Mayor. BRGA; DRA; DU†; FAG; HAH; YOI

Hatshepsut (1578–1457 B.C.). Queen of Egypt. BOI; COLB; GRAB-04

Haury, Emil W. (1905–). Archaeologist. POC

Havlicek, John (1940–). Basketball player. ARB-3; CL-06; DEHA-1; GUEA; PAW; PE; SA; SA-2

Hawkes, Daphne (1938–). Episcopal priest. SMBB-1

Hawking, Stephen (1942–). English physicist. BOHA-1

Hawkins, Coleman (1904–). Saxophonist. COF-1; WAD†

Hawkins, Connie (1942–). Basketball player. AAS-24; DEHA-1; SA

Hawks, Howard (1896–1977). Motion picture producer, director. ED-1†; SMBC

Hawn, Goldie (1945–). Actress, motion picture producer. MASB

Hawthorne, Joseph. Conductor. STM†

Hawthorne, Nathaniel (1804–1864). Author. BEGA; BOA; CAC; COB; HEF; LEGB; STK; SUFA; WHB; WOAA

Hawthorne, Rose, see Lathrop, Rose Hawthorne.

Hay, John Milton (1838–1905). Statesman. HEEA

Haydn, Franz Joseph (1732–1809). Austrian composer. BEN; BRF; BUD; FIE; KAE; SAA; YOK; YOM†

Hayer, Talmadge. Assassin. RABA†

Hayes, Bob (Robert Lee) (1942–). Football player, track athlete. ANB; CO; DAFB; DAJ; DEHA; KADA; OCA; ST-1

Hayes, Denis Allen (1944–). Conservationist. SQA†

Hayes, Elvin (1945–). Basketball player. AAS-5; PE; SA

Hayes, Helen (1900–). Actress. CLA; DI-1; GIBA†

Hayes, Janet Gray Frazee (1926–). Ex-mayor. WIAA-02

Hayes, Johnny (1886?–1965). Track athlete. DAJ; DEF

Hayes, Lester (1955–). Football player. AAS-13

Hayes, Lucy Ware (1831–1889). Wife of Rutherford Birchard Hayes. BAG; BAG-1; BLG†; CHB; KL; MAA; MAU; PRB; ROH; ROHA

Hayes, Roland (1887–1976). Singer. ADA; ADB; BRB†; DOF-1; HUC

Hayes, Rutherford Birchard (1822–1893). President of U.S. BAEB; BAG; BAG-1; BEB; BLA; BUIA; CAG; CAH; COI; COJA; COS; DUC; DUCA; FRBA; HIH; LEQ; LEQA; MAB; MABA; MIA; PED; ROH; ROHA; ROK†; SUBB; WHD

Haymond, Alvin Henry (1942–). Football player. LEZB

Haynes, Abner (1937–). Football player. LIBA

Haynes, George Edmund (1880–1960). Sociologist. GRAB-01

Haynes, Henry Doyle "Homer" (1918?–1970). Comedian, singer. HAG-1

Haynes, Lemuel (1753–1833). Clergyman. ADA; BRB†; BUIB†; DAF-1†; STQ†; WIBA

Haynes, Mike (1953–). Football player. AAS-13

Hays, Isaac (1796–1879). Ophthalmologist. LETA

Hays, Mary, see McCauley, Mary.

Hays, Moses Michael (1739–1805). Businessman. LETA

Haywood, Spencer (1949–). Basketball player. LOAA; SA; SA-1

Haywood, William Dudley (1869–1928). Labor leader. COH; DABA; LEHA; SEA

Hazlitt, William (1778–1830). English author. BEG

Head, Edith (1907–1981). Costume designer. FOG

Healey, Ed (1895?–1978). Football player. SUD

Healy, James Augustine (1830–1900). Bishop. ADA; ADB

Hearne, Samuel (1745–1792). English explorer. ARF

Hearnes, Warren Eastman (1923–). Governor. RAE

Hearst, Phoebe Apperson (1842–1919). Philanthropist. CUC

Hearst, William Randolph (1863–1951). Journalist. ARAA; COKB; CUC

Heath, Allen. Automobile racer, born Canada. LEX

Hebner, Richard Joseph (1947–). Baseball player. LEY

Heck, George A. J. (1905–). Conductor. STM†

Heckler, Margaret (1931–). Ex-Secretary of Health and Human Services. WHE

Hector, Edward (d. 1834). American Revolutionary soldier. DAF-1†; WIBA

Heddy, Kathy (1959?–). Swimmer. GLA

Hedgepeth, Mary. Mathematician. HOG†

Hedin, Sven Anders (1865–1952). Swedish geographer, explorer. BAB; HOB; ROL†

Hedwig (1174–1243). Saint. ONA

Heermann, Walter (1890–). Conductor, born Germany. STM†

Heffelfinger, Pudge (William Walter) (1867–1954). Football player. DAFG; DAG; DAGA; DAI

Hefti, Neal (1922–). Composer, arranger. UN

Hegan, Jim (1920–1984). Baseball player. HIC

Hegel, Georg Wilhelm Friedrich (1770–1831). German philosopher. LO; OZA

Hegyi, Julius (1923–). Conductor. STM†

Heide, Dirk van der, pseud. (1928?–). Author, refugee from Nazis, born the Netherlands. CAHA

Heiden, Beth (1959–). Skater. HOCG

Heiden, Eric (1958–). Skater. HOCG; LIEA

Height, Dorothy (1912–). Civil rights leader. GIB-1†

Heilmann, Harry (1895–1951). Baseball player. ALB; RIGA†

Hein, Mel (Melvin John) (1909–). Football player. DAB; DAFG; DAI; HEI; KABA; SUD

Heine, Heinrich (1797–1856). German poet. PEB

Heine, Jacob von (1800–1879). German physician. CHE†

Heinsohn, Tommy (Thomas William) (1934–). Basketball player. HID; HOCA

Heisman, John William (1869–1936). Football coach. DAFG; VAD

Heiss, Carol (1940–). Skater. DEF; DEHA-1; HOBA; HOBAA; JAB; LEF; PIBA

Held, Anna (1873–1918). Comedienne, born France. PHA

Heldman, Julie (1945–). Tennis player. SLA

Helena. Mesopotamian queen, convert to Judaism. LER

Helena (c. 248–328). Saint. DAD-1; DAD-3; ONA; QUA

Heliodorus. Saint. DAD-3

Hellman, Lillian (1905–1984). Playwright, author. DI-1; GIB-1†

Helme, Johnny. Colonial boy. BAC

Helmholtz, Hermann Ludwig von (1821–1894). German physicist, biologist. SIA

Helpmann, Robert (1909–1986). Australian dancer, choreographer. ATA

Hemingway, Ernest (1899–1961). Author. ASB-1; CAC; CON; HEF; LAC; LEGB

Hemmings, Fred, Jr. Surf rider. OLD

Hench, Philip Showalter (1896–1965). Physician. RIF

Henday, Anthony (fl. 1754). English explorer. ARF

Hendee, Hannah (fl. 1780). American Revolutionary heroine. CLC

Henderson, Arthur (1863–1935). British statesman. MEC†; WIC

Henderson, Fletcher (1898–1952). Band leader. COF-1; WAD†

Henderson, Paul Garnet (1943–). Canadian hockey player. LEYA

Henderson, Ray (1896–1970). Songwriter. MOA

Henderson, Richard (1735–1785). Colonizer. STA

Henderson, Rickey (1958–). Baseball player. HEFB†

Hendl, Walter (1917–). Conductor. STM

Hendricks, Harmon (fl. 1812). Merchant. LETA

Hendricks, Ted (1947–). Football player. AAS-15

Hendricks, Thomas Andrews (1819–1885). Vice president of U.S. FEA; HAOA; HOEA

Hendrix, Jimi (1942–1970). Guitarist. BUIB-1

Henie, Sonja (1913–1969). Norwegian skater, actress. ASBA; DAG; DAGA; GED; GEDA; HOBAA; LEYB†; RYA†

Henkel, Joseph (1890–). Conductor. STM†

Henning, Anne (1956?–). Skater. HOBAA†; LEYB†; ST-2

Henning, Doug (1947–). Canadian magician. FOGA

Henri (1933–). Pretender to the throne of France. NEC†

Henri, Robert (1865–1929). Painter. MAG

Henrich, Tommy (1916–). Baseball player. BOE

Henry (973–1024). Saint. DAD-3; QUA

Henry (Henry the Navigator) (1394–1460). Prince of Portugal. GRC; KNB; MOB

Henry I (1068–1135). King of England. BRBF; DEC; GRAB†; SCC

Henry II (1133–1189). King of England. BRBF; CAAA; CHG; DEC; GRAB; SCC

Henry III (1207–1272). King of England. BRBF; DEC; GRAB; SCC

Henry IV (1367–1413). King of England. BRBF; DEC; GRAB†; SCC

Henry IV, of Navarre (1553–1610). King of France. CAAA; JOBB

Henry V (1387–1422). King of England. BRBF; CAAA; CHG; DEC; GRAB†; SCC

Henry VI (1421–1471). King of England. BRBF; DEC; GRAB; SCC

Henry VII (1457–1509). King of England. CAAA; DEC; GRAB; SCC

Henry VIII (1491–1547). King of England. CAAA; CHG; DEC; DEI; DEJ; GRAB; JOBB; NEC; SCC

Henry, Algernon P. Radio engineer. BOG

Henry, "Big Mouth." Cowboy. STQ†

Henry, Sir Edward Richart, bart (1850–1931). British government official. LACA

Henry, Joseph (1797–1878). Physicist. ASA; BUE; BUF; CAA; DUA; FE; HYB; SHFB; SIA; SOB

Henry, Marguerite (1902–). Author. SMB

Henry, O., pseud. (1862–1910). Author. CAC; CUC; DEI; DEJ

Henry, Patrick (1736–1799). American Revolutionary patriot. ARAB; BUIB; CUC; DAC; DAF-2; DEI; DEJ; FIA; FID; HAK; HAN; OLA; SUL; VIA†

Henry, Pete (Wilbur) (1897–1952). Football player. DAB; DAFG; SUD

Henson, Josiah (1789–1883). Abolitionist. CAHA; GRAB-05

Henson, Matthew Alexander (1866–1955). Arctic explorer. ADA; ADB; BRB; BRG; COLA†; DOC†; GRAB-02; HAM; HAQ; HODA; HUB; JOC; LEI; PECA; ROG; STQ

Henze, Cynthia. Aviator. FOC-1

Hepburn, Audrey (1929–). English actress. FOG

Heracleides (4th century B.C.). Greek philosopher. SIB†

Herber, Arnie (1910–1969). Football player. JOA†; SUD

Herbert (970–1021). Saint. QUA

Herbert, Victor (1859–1924). Composer, born Ireland. BAD; CUC; DEI; DEJ; EWA; KAE; MOA

Herbert, Walter. Conductor. STM†

Herbert, Walter William (1934–). British surveyor. ROL

Herblock, see Block, Herbert Lawrence.

Hereward (fl. 1070–1071). English patriot. SUK

Herford, Beatrice (1868–1952). Comedienne, born England. MASB

Herford, Oliver (1863–1935). Poet. ALA

Herjolfsson, Bjarni (fl. 985). Norse explorer. DYA; MOB†; VIA†

Herman, Babe (Floyd Caves) (1903?–1987). Baseball player. GEB; LIAA

Herman, Woody (1914–1987). Clarinetist, band leader. TEA; TEB

Herman Joseph. Saint. DAD-2

Hermann, Bernard (1911–). Conductor. STM†

Hermenegild (d. 585). Saint. DAD-2

Hernandez, Keith (1953–). Baseball player. AAS-3

Hernandez, Raphael (1893–). Composer. FOW

Herod the Great (73?–4 B.C.). King of Judea. CAAA; LERA

Herodotus (484?–425 B.C.). Greek historian. HIB; ROL†

Herr, Tom (1956–). Baseball player. HEFB†

Herrera, Efren (1951–). Football player. AAS-17

Herrmann, Alexander (Herrmann the Great) (1843–1896). Magician, born Germany. FOGA; GIA; KEB

Herschel, Caroline (1750–1848). English astronomer, born Germany. COLA†; NOA; PAC; SC†

Herschel, Sir William (1738–1822). English astronomer, born Germany. BOB; COLA; FE; LAA; PAC; PIA; SIA; SUE

Herscovici, Henry (1927–). Israeli marksman, born Romania. SLA†

Hershkowitz, Victor (1918–). Handball player. SLA

Herst, Richard, Blessed. DAD-3

Herty, Charles Holmes (1867–1938). Chemist. MAL

Hertz, Gustav (1887–1975). German physicist. LET

Hertz, Heinrich Rudolf (1857–1894). German physicist. CAA; COLA; FE; SHFB; SIA; SOB

Hertzsprung, Ejnar (1873–1967). Danish astronomer. SUE

Herz, Henriette (1764–1847). German society leader. LER

Herz, Hermann (1908–). German conductor. STM†

Herzl, Theodor (1860–1904). Hungarian author, Zionist. GRB-1; GUB; KAB; KAD; LERA; LES; PEB; ROGA

Herzog, Maurice (1919–). French mountaineer. HAQ; HOB; KEH

Herzog, Whitey (1931–). Baseball player, manager. FRC-01

Hesse, Hermann (1877–1962). German author. KE

Heston, William (b. 1878). Football player. DAFG†

Hevesy, George de (1885–1966). Hungarian chemist. LET

Hewes, Joseph (1730–1779). American Revolutionary patriot. BAEA; BUIB†; COJ†; FEAB; MAC

Hewitt, Margaret. Nurse-midwife. BOHE

Heyerdahl, Thor (1914–). Norwegian anthropologist. BAB; OLC; SCBA

Heyison, Marc. Baseball player. GUB-1

Heyman, Art (1942–). Basketball player. SLA

Heyse, Paul Johann (1830–1914). German author. LET

Heyward, Thomas, Jr. (1746–1809). American Revolutionary patriot. BAEA; BUIB†; COJ†; FEAB; MAC†

Hiawatha (fl. 1550). Onondaga Indian chief. ROD

Hickman, Robert T. (b. 1831). Escaped slave. KADB

Hickok, Wild Bill (James Butler) (1837–1876). Law officer, scout. COE; SUI

Hicks, Alfred (1898–). Conductor. STM†

Hicks, Beatrice Alice (1919–). Engineering executive. PAA

Hicks, Elias (1748–1830). Quaker minister. BUIB†

Hicks, Nancy. Journalist. STAA

Hidalgo y Costilla, Miguel (1753–1811). Mexican revolutionist. BAA; BACA; NEBA; ROGB; WO; YOFA

Higgins, Marguerite (1920–1966). Journalist. ARBA; FLBB; JAD; JAE

Higgins, Maureen Anne. F.B.I. agent. SMBC-3

Hightower, Rosella (1920–). Dancer. ATA

Hilarion (4th century). Saint. DAD-3

Hilary of Poitiers (315–367). Saint. DAD-2

Hildegard of Bingen (1098–1179). Saint. DAD-3; MAK†; MASA; SC

Hill, Archibald Vivian (1886–1977). English physiologist. RIF

Hill, Calvin (1947–). Football player. AAS-25; LEZB

Hill, Graham (1929–1975). English automobile racer. COKC; JA

Hill, James Jerome (1838–1916). Railroad builder. LEM; WED

Hill, L. Rosa Minoka (fl. 1935). Mohawk physician. GRAD†

Hill, Pamela (1938–). Television producer. SMBB-2

Hill, Patty Smith (1868–1946). Educator. BUDA

Hill, Phil (1927–). Automobile racer. ABB; COKC; JA; LEX; OLAB

Hill, Sir Rowland (1795–1879). English postal reformer. EVA

Hillary, Sir Edmund (1919–). Mountaineer. ASB-1; BAB; COLA; DU-1; KEH; MOB; PRC; ROL†

Hillegas, Michael (1729–1804). Merchant. BUIB†

Hillel (fl. 30 B.C.–10 A.D.). Babylonian rabbi. GEF; GRB-1; GUA; KAB; KAC; LERA; LES

Hiller, John (1943–). Baseball player. AAS-27; PAW

Hilliard, William Arthur (1927?–). Journalist. STAA†

Hillman, Sidney (1887–1946). Labor leader, born Lithuania. COH; DABA; SEA

Hills, Carla Anderson (1934–). Lawyer, ex-cabinet member. SWI

Hilsberg, Alexander (1900–1961). Conductor, born Russia. STM

Hilton, Conrad Nicholson (1887–1979). Hotel executive. LAG; LEN; PAA

Hilton, Henry (d. 1899). Heir to Alexander Stewart fortune. HOF†

Hindemith, Paul (1895–1963). Composer, born Germany. BEKA; KAE; SAA; YOL

Hindenburg, Paul von (1847–1934). German president. ARD

Hine, Lewis (1874–1940). Photographer. SUAA

Hines, Earl Kenneth (1905–1983). Pianist. COF-1; UN; WAD†

Hinkey, Frank (1871–1925). Football player. DAFG

Hinkle, Clarke (1912–). Football player. DAFG†; JOA†; SUD

Hinton, Alfred (1940–). Painter. FAI

Hinton, William A. (1883–1959). Pathologist. BRB†; HAMA

Hipparchus (2d century B.C.). Greek astronomer. PIA; SIB†

Hippocrates (460–377 B.C.). Greek physician. CAA; CHD; DEI; DEJ; DOE; FE; POD; ROA; SHG; SIC

Hirohito (1901–). Japanese emperor. ASB-1; DU-1; WEB

Hirsch, Clara de (1833–1899). Belgian philanthropist. LER

Hirsch, Elroy "Crazylegs" (1924–). Football player. CO; DAFG; HAE; SUD

Hirsch, Samson Raphael (1808–1888). German theologian. KAD

Hitchcock, Alfred Joseph (1899–1980). Motion picture director, born England. ASB-1; BEA; FLBC; PABA; SMBC

Hitchcock, Thomas, Jr. (1900–1944). Polo player. DAG; DAGA

Hitler, Adolf (1889–1945). German chief of state. ARA; ASB-1; BLW; CAE; CL-01; DOF; KIA; TAC

Hlavaty, Jana (1941–). Skier, born Czechoslovakia. WA-1

Ho Chi Minh (1890–1969). Vietnamese communist leader. ASB-1; HAK; WECA

Hoad, Lew (1934–). Australian tennis player. HI

Hobart, Garret A. (1844–1899). Vice president of U.S. FEA; HAOA; HOEA

Hobby, Oveta Culp (1905–). Ex-cabinet member. STLA

Hobday, Geoffrey (1912–). English conductor. STM†

Hodge, Leslie. Australian conductor. STM†

Hodges, Ben (d. 1929). Cattle thief. KADB

Hodges, Gil (1924–1972). Baseball player. DA; DAA; GEB; KLB

Hodges, Thomas J., see Bell, Tom, pseud.

Hodgkin, Alan Lloyd (1914–). English biophysicist. RIF†

Hodgkin, Dorothy Crowfoot (1910–). English crystallographer. HA-1; SHFE

Hoe, Richard March (1812–1886). Inventor. HYA†

Hoffenstein, Samuel Goodman (1890–1947). Poet, born Lithuania. ALA

Hoffer, George Nissley (1887–1963). Botanist. DEA

Hoffman, Irwin (1924–). Conductor. STM†

Hoffman, Malvina (1887–1966). Sculptor. CLA; COKA; STLA; WABC†

Hofmann, Adele (1926–). Physician. RAAG

Hofmann, Hans (1880–1966). Painter, born Germany. BEA; WIAA

Hogan, Ben (1912–). Golfer. ASBA; BUJA; DAG; DAGA; DEHA-1; FOI; HOC; LABA; PAW; PIB; PIBA; SCA; SICA; VAE

Hogan, Henry (fl. 1875). Soldier, born Ireland. TA

Hogan, Shanty (James Francis) (1906–1967). Baseball player. LIAA†

Hogarth, William (1697–1794). English painter. KAA

Hogg, Helen Sawyer, see Sawyer, Helen.

Hoist the Flag. Racehorse. BELB

Holbein, Hans (the Younger) (1497–1543). German painter. KAA

Holiday, Billie (1915–1959). Singer. BRBD; COF-1; JOE; SUH; TEA; TEB; WAD†

Holland, Jerome H. (1916–). Diplomat, football player. HOBB

Holland, John Philip (1842–1914). Inventor, born Ireland. COR; HYA; THA

Hollard, Michel Louis. French spy. HAB

Hollerith, Herman (1860–). Computer pioneer. GRAB-3†

Holli, Matti (1916–). Finnish conductor. STM†

Holliday, Doc (John Henry) (1852–1887). Outlaw. JOBA

Holliday, Judy (1921–1965). Actress. MASB

Hollingworth, Leta Stetter (1886–1939). Psychologist. HA-1; PACB

Holloman, Alva (1926–). Baseball player. GRA

Holly, James Theodore (1829–1911). Clergyman. BRB†

Holm, Eleanor (1914–). Swimmer. HOBAA†; LEYB†

Holman, Eugene (1895–1962). Petroleum executive. PAA

Holman, Marshall (1954–). Bowler. SLA

Holman, Nat (1896–). Basketball coach. BEL; HEHA; HID; SLA

Holmes, David (1770–1832). Governor. SEC

Holmes, John Haynes (1879–1964). Clergyman. LEZC

Holmes, Oliver Wendell (1809–1894). Author. BEF; BEGA; BOA; HEF; SUFA

Holmes, Oliver Wendell, Jr. (1841–1935). Supreme Court justice. COKA; CUC; FLC; MEB; RED

Holovak, Mike (1919–). Football coach. LEW†

Holsendolph, Ernest. Journalist. STAA†

Holsey, Lucius Henry (1845–1920). Clergyman. BRB†

Holter, Ralph B. Conductor. STM†

Holtzman, Elizabeth (1941–). Congresswoman. BOHF

Holtzman, Ken (1945–). Baseball player. RI; SLA

Holum, Dianne (1952?–). Skater. HOBAA†; LEYB†

Holzman, Red (William) (1920–). Basketball coach. ARB-2; SLA

Home, Daniel Dunglas (1833–1886). Scottish spiritualist. COEA

Homer (9th century B.C.?). Greek poet. DEI; DEJ

Homer, Winslow (1836–1910). Painter. CHC; DEI; DEJ; FRA; HEDA; KAA; LEE; LEOA; MAG; SIE; SMBA

Honegger, Arthur (1892–1955). French composer. KAE

Honoratus (d. 430). Saint. DAD-2

Hood, James Walker (1831–1918). Clergyman. BRB†

Hooke, Robert (1635–1703). English physicist. CAA

Hooks, Earl (1927–). Sculptor, ceramist. FAH

Hooper, William (1742–1790). American Revolutionary patriot. BAEA; BUIB†; COJ†; FEAB; MAC†

Hoover, Herbert Clark (1874–1964). President of U.S. BAEB; BAG; BAG-1; BEB; BLA; BUIA; CAG; CAH; COI; COS; CUC; DUB; DUC; DUCA; FRBA; HIH; LEN; LEQ; LEQA; MAB; MABA; MAL; MIA; PED; ROH; ROHA; ROK†; SUBB; WHD

Hoover, J. Edgar (1895–1972). Director of F.B.I. COKA; COKB; LAC; LACA; LID

Hoover, Lou Henry (1875–1944). Wife of Herbert Hoover. BAG; BAG-1; BLG; CHB; KL; MAA; MAU; PRB; ROH; ROHA

Hope, Bob (1903–). Comedian. ALC; ED-1†

Hope, John (1868–1936). Educator. ADA; ADB; BRB; DOF-1

Hopkins, Esek (1718–1802). Naval officer. SOA

Hopkins, Sir Frederick Gowland (1861–1947). English biochemist. RIF

Hopkins, Johns (1795–1873). Financier. CUC

Hopkins, Lightnin' (Sam) (1912–1982). Singer. SUH

Hopkins, Stephen (1707–1785). American Revolutionary patriot. BAEA; BUIB†; COJ†; FEAB; MAC

Hopkinson, Francis (1737–1791). American Revolutionary patriot. BAEA; BUIB†; COJ†; FEAB; MAC

Hoppe, Willie (1887–1959). Billiards player. DAG; DAGA

Hopper, Grace Murray (1906–). Computer pioneer. GIB-1; GRAB-3

Horace (65–8 B.C.). Roman poet. COK

Horatius Cocles (6th century B.C.). Roman soldier. COM; STP

Horn, Ted (1910–1948). Automobile racer. LEX

Horn, Tom (1860–1903). Outlaw. JOBA; KAW; SUI

Horne, Esther Burnett (fl. 1955). Educator. GRAD

Horne, Lena (1917–). Singer. DADB; DOBA; DOF-1; HUC; LEHB; ROF

Horne, Marilyn (1934–). Singer. SAB

Horney, Karen (1885–1952). Psychiatrist, born Germany. FLA; LEG; RAAG†

Hornsby, Rogers (1896–1963). Baseball player. ALB; DAA; DAFB; DAFC; DAFD; DAG; DAGA; DAH; DEG; FIAA; FRC-1†; GR; GUC; GUDA†; MUB-1; MUC; RIGA†; SHH; WAC

Hornung, Paul Vernon (1935–). Football player. BEKB; DEHB; DUF; HAD; HIE; JOA; KADA

Horstmann, Dorothy Millicent (1911–). Physician. CHE†

Horton, George Moses (1798?–1880). Poet. CL

Horton, Myles (1905–). Civil rights worker. STG

Hostos, Eugenio Maríe de (1839–1903). Puerto Rican educator. TU

Hotchkiss, Benjamin B. (1826–1885). Inventor. HYA†

Hotchkiss, Hazel (1886–1974). Tennis player. HOBAA; SUDA†

Houdin, Jean Eugène Robert (1805–1871). French magician. EDA; FOGA; GIA; KEB; KLD

Houdini, Harry (1874–1926). Magician. FOGA; GIA; KEB; KLD; WAO

Hounsfield, Godfrey (1919–). English inventor. AAS-33

Houser, Allan (1914–). Painter, sculptor. GRAC

Houssay, Bernardo Alberto (1887–1971). Argentine physiologist. RIF

Houston, Charles Hamilton (1895–1950). Lawyer. ADA†; ADB†; DOF-1

Houston, Ken (1944–). Football player. RUA

Houston, Samuel (1793–1863). Political leader of Texas. AKC; ARE; BOK; COE; FIA; HEB; KEC; KED; KUA; LYF; MAL; MAO; MAT; SEC; WAN

Houston, Temple. Lawyer. SUI

Houston, William C. (c. 1746–1788). Lawyer. FEAA†

Houstoun, William (1755–1813). Statesman. FEAA†

Hovhaness, Alan (1911–). Composer. POF

Howard, Catherine (1520?–1542). Consort of Henry VIII, king of England. MAOA; VAC

Howard, Cordelia (1848–1941). Actress. CAD

Howard, Elston (1930–1980). Baseball player. HIC; HOCM; PRA; SHD; SHF; ZAA

Howard, Frank (Hondo) (1936–). Baseball player. DA

Howard, Jerry (Curly) (1911–1952). Comedian. BUR-1; ED-1†

Howard, Moe (1905–1975). Comedian. BUR-1; ED-1†

Howard, Samuel (Shemp) (1901–1956). Comedian. BUR-1; ED-1†

Howe, Elias (1819–1867). Inventor. FE; HYA; LAE; RAA; THA

Howe, Gordie (1928–). Hockey player, born Canada. ALBA; ASBA; BUJA; FICA; FR; FRD; HEG; LIAB; OBA; OBB; ORC; PAW; PIBA; RAAF; SICA

Howe, Howard A. Scientist. CHE†

Howe, Julia Ward (1819–1910). Feminist. BOC; DAD; DEDA; DEI; DEJ; GIBA†; WABC†

Howe, Mark Steven (1955–). Canadian hockey player. MANA

Howe, Oscar (1915–). Painter. LEH; LEOA

Howe, Samuel Gridley (1801–1876). Humanitarian. DEDA

Howe, William Howe, 5th viscount (1729–1814). British general. AKA; SOA

Howell, Emily (1939–). Aviator. GEDB

Howell, Henry Vernon (1932–). Canadian hockey player. OBA

Howell, Martin Damon (1926–). Army officer. RAE

Howells, William Dean (1837–1920). Author, critic. CAC†

Howley, Chuck (Charles Louis). Football player. KABA

Howton, Bill (1930–). Football player. ANB

Hoy, Bill (William Ellsworth) (1865–1961). Baseball player. DAFD

Hsuan-Tsang (600?–664). Chinese traveler. ROL

Hsüan Tsung (685–762). Chinese emperor. SPA

Hubbard, Cal (Robert Calvin) (1900–1977). Football player. DAB; DAFG; DAI; HEI; SUD

Hubbard, L. Ron (1911–1986). Scientologist. COEA

Hubbell, Carl Owen (1903–). Baseball player. ALB; BRC; DAFD; DEHA-1; FRC-1†; HAF; REB; RIGA†; SHH; WAG

Hubble, Edwin Powell (1889–1953). Astronomer. SUE

Hubbs, Kenneth Douglas (1941–1964). Baseball player. KLB

Huber, Alice (fl. 1898). Nurse. MAK†

Huber, Kurt (1890?–1943). German resistance worker. LAD

Huber, Linda. Lawyer. LETD

Hubert (7th century). Saint. FAD; QUA

Huddleston, Ned, see Dart, Isom, pseud.

Hudson, Henry (1575?–1611). English explorer. COC; DEI; DEJ; DOC; GRAA; GRC; KNB; MAT; MOB; ROL

Hudson, Lou (1944–). Basketball player. SA

Hudson, William Henry (1841–1922). English author, naturalist. COO

Huerta, Dolores (1930–). Labor leader. BI; BOHF; DI; NEAA

Huff, Sam (Robert Lee) (1934–). Football player. ANA

Hufstedler, Shirley (1925–). Lawyer, jurist. GIB-1

Huggins, Edith. Television newscaster. STAA

Huggins, Miller (1879–1929). Baseball manager. ALB; FRC-01; ROAA

Huggins, Sir William (1824–1910). English astronomer. SUE

Hugh of Grenoble (1053–1131). Saint. DAD-2; QUA

Hugh of Lincoln (1135–1200). Saint. ONA

Hughes, Charles Evans (1862–1948). Supreme Court justice. FLC; HEEA; KEC†; WHD†

Hughes, Howard, Jr. (1905–1976). Aviation, motion picture executive. COKB; DU-1

Hughes, Langston (1902–1967). Author. ADA; ADB; BRBD; CAGA; DADB; DOF-1; JO; LEJ; RIC; RICA; ROE

Hugo, Victor (1802–1885). French author. COKB; DEI; DEJ

Huldah (638–608 B.C.). Biblical prophet. LER

Hull, Agrippa (1759?–1848?). American Revolutionary soldier. DAF-1

Hull, Bobby (Robert Marvin) (1939–). Canadian hockey player. ASBA; DEHA-1; FICA; FR; FRD; KADA; LEYA; LIAB; LYB; OBA; OBB; ORC; RAAF; SUB; WAK

Hull, Cordell (1871–1955). Statesman. HEEA; MEC†; WIC

Hull, Dennis William (1944–). Canadian hockey player. FICB; LEYA

Hulme, Dennis Clive (1936–). New Zealand automobile racer. ABB; JA

Humboldt, Alexander von (1769–1859). German naturalist. BLB; HOB; KNA; MOB; ROL; WIA-1

Hume, David (1711–1776). Scottish philosopher. HIB†

Hume, Jo Ann (1955–). Stock exchange executive. LES-1†

Hummel, Johann Nepomuk (1778–1837). German composer. CHF

Humperdinck, Engelbert (1854–1921). German composer. BAE; BUC

Humphrey, Hubert Horatio (1911–1978). Vice president of U.S., senator. FEA; HADA; HOEA; WEC; WHD

Hunayn. Arabian physician. SHG†

Hundhammer, Paul. Baseball player. GUB-1

Hung Hsiu-ch'üan (1812–1864). Chinese revolutionist. SPA

Hunna (d. 679). Saint. MOC

Hunnicutt, James (fl. 1865). Abolitionist. STG

Hunt, Alexander Henry (1866–1938). Educator. DOF-1

Hunt, George Wylie (1859–1934). Governor. SEC

Hunt, Harriot Kenzia (1805–1875). Physician, feminist. MASA†

Hunt, James (1947–). English automobile racer. ABB; OLCC

Hunt, Nathan (fl. 1840). Colonial basket maker. BAC

Hunt, Richard H. (1935–). Sculptor. ADB

Hunt, Ron (Ronald Kenneth) (1941–). Baseball player. SA-3

Hunter, Alberta (1895–1984). Singer. GIB-1

Hunter, Anne Home (1742–1821). Wife of John Hunter. RIB

Hunter, Catfish (James Augustus) (1946–). Baseball player. GUB-1; KLCA; SMH

Hunter, John (1728–1793). Scottish surgeon, anatomist. FE; MAR; RIB; SIC

Hunter, William (1718–1783). Scottish anatomist. MAR

Hunter-Gault, Charlayne (1942?–). Broadcast journalist. GLO; STAA

Huntington, Samuel (1731–1796). American Revolutionary patriot. BAEA; BUIB†; COJ; FEAB

Huntley, Joni. Track athlete. GLB

Hurst, George (1926–). Scottish conductor. STM†

Hurtubise, Jim (1931?–). Automobile racer. LEX; OLAB; PIBA

Hussein, Taha (1889–1973). Egyptian author, educator. BAF

Hussein Ibn Talal (1935–). King of Jordan. HAGD; KEF

Huston, John (1906–1987). Motion picture director, screenwriter, actor. SMBC

Hutchins, Guy (1905–). Conductor. STM†

Hutchinson, Abigail (b. 1829?). Singer. CAD

Hutchinson, Anne Marbury (1591–1643). Religious liberal colonist. BLF; CRB; DAD; DOD; JOCA; SMC; VIA; WABC; WAR; YOC

Hutchinson, Thomas (1711–1780). Colonial administrator. BUIB†

Hutson, Don (Donald Montgomery) (1913–). Football player. ANB; CO; DAB; DAFB; DAFG; DAG; DAGA; DAI; HEI; JOA; SUC; SUD

Hutton, Barbara (1912–1979). Millionaire heiress. COKB

Hutton, William (1723–1815). English author. RAC

Huxley, Andrew Fielding (1917–). English physiologist. RIF†

Huxtable, Ada Louise (1921–). Architecture critic, author. GIB-1

Huygens, Christiaan (1629–1695). Dutch mathematician, physicist, astronomer. CAA; COL; FE; SHFB; SIA

Hyacintha (d. 1640). Saint. MOC

Hypatia (370–415). Greek philosopher. SC

I

ibn-Batuta (1304–1377). Mohammedan traveler. ROL

ibn-Ezra, Abraham (1089–1164). Spanish traveler. LERA

ibn-Jubayr (1145–1217). Arabian geographer. ROL†

Ickx, Jacky (Jacques-Bernard) (1945–). Belgian automobile racer. JA

Ide, Simeon (b. 1794?). Colonial boy. BAC

Idris Alaoma (1580–1617). Sultan of Bornu. DOA; MIC

Ighodaro, Irene Elizabeth. Nigerian physician. CRA

Ignatius of Laconi (1701–1781). Saint. DAD-2

Ignatius of Loyola (1491–1556). Saint. DAD-3; FRC; MOC

Ikard, Bose (b. 1847). Cowboy. BUH; HODA; KADB; SCB; STQ

Ikhnaton, *see* Akhnaton.

Ileana. Romanian princess, nurse. WRA

Ima Shalom. Member of Hillel family. LER

Imhotep (fl. 2980–2950 B.C.). Egyptian physician. JO

Imlach, Punch (George) (1918–1987). Canadian hockey coach. LEW

Indian Emily (d. 1873). Apache Indian girl. WAB

Indy, Vincent d' (1851–1931). French composer. KAE

Ingersoll, Jared (1749–1822). Jurist. BUIB†; FEAA

Ingersoll, Robert Green (1833–1899). Lawyer, agnostic. WECB

Ingles, Mary (fl. 1755). Indian captive. STA

Ingolf (10th century). Norse explorer. MOB

Ingres, Jean Auguste Dominique (1780–1867). French painter. MAH†

Inness, George (1825–1894). Painter. FRA; HEDA; MAG; SIE

Insana, Silvio. Italian conductor. STM†

International Red Cross of Geneva. MEA

Iredell, James (1751–1799). Supreme Court justice. SEC

Irenaeus (140–202). Saint. DAD-2

Irene (d. 653). Saint. QUA

Irey, Elmer Lincoln (1888–1948). Government official. LID

Irigoyen, Hipólito (1850–1933). President of Argentina. WOB

Irvin, Monte (1919–). Baseball player. FRC-1†

Irving, Sir Henry (1838–1905). English actor. TRC

Irving, Washington (1783–1859). Author. BEG; BOA; CAC; COB; HACB; HEF; LEGB; MAL

Irwin, George (1921–). Conductor. STM†

Irwin, May (1862–1938). Comedienne, born Canada. MASB

Irwin-Williams, Cynthia (1936–). Archaeologist. WIAA-01

Isaac, Levi (1740–1809). Polish rabbi. KAD

Isabel (1225–1270). Saint. WIB

Isabella I (1451–1504). Queen of Castile and Leon. BOI; CAAA; DAK; FAE; LIDA; PA; TRBA

Isaiah. Biblical prophet. KAB

Isbell, Cecil. Football player. JOA†

Iselin, Columbus O'Donnell (1904–1971). Oceanographer. BRBC

Isidore (1070–1130). Saint. MOC; ONA

Israel ben Eliezer (Baal Shem Tov) (1700–1760).

Polish Hasidic leader. GEF; GUB; KAC; LERA; LES; PEB

Issel, Dan (1948–). Basketball player. HIBA

Istomin, Eugene (1925–). Pianist. EWC

Iturbi, José (1895–1980). Spanish pianist. STM†

Iturbide, Augustín de (1783–1824). Mexican emperor. NEBA; YOFA

Iula, Robert P. Conductor. STM†

Ivan III, the Great (1440–1505). Grand duke of Moscow. CAAA; RIA

Ivan IV, the Terrible (1530–1584). Tsar of Russia. BLW; JOBB; RIA

Ives, Charles (1874–1954). Composer. BAD; EWAA; FIE; KAE; MAF; POF; SAA†

Ivo, Tommy. Automobile racer. OLB

Iwamatsu, Jun Atsushi, *see* Yashima, Taro.

Izac, Edouard Victor M. (fl. 1918). Naval officer. REA

J

Jabara, James A. (1923–1966). Air Force aviator. ARBA

Jabbar, Kareem Abdul, *see* Abdul-Jabbar, Kareem.

Jabir ibn-Hayyan (721–815). Arabian alchemist. CUA

Jabotinsky, Vladimir (1880–1940). Russian Zionist. GRB-1

Jackson, Andrew (1767–1845). President of U.S. ARE; BAEB; BAG; BAG-1; BEB; BLA; BUIA; CAG; CAH; COD; COI; COJA; COS; DAC; DEI; DEJ; DUB; DUC; DUCA; FRBA; HIH; LEP; LEQ; LEQA; LOA; MAB; MABA; MAO; MIA; OLA; PED; ROH; ROHA; ROK; STH; SUBB; WAN; WHD

Jackson, Charles Thomas (1805–1880). Chemist. LEG†; SHG†

Jackson, David L. (1940?–). Journalist. STAA

Jackson, Harold (1946–). Football player. RUC

Jackson, Jesse Louis (1941–). Clergyman, civil rights leader. DRA; GRAB-01

Jackson, Joe "Shoeless" (1888–1951). Baseball player. RIGA†

Jackson, Mahalia (1911–1972). Singer. HUC; JOE

Jackson, Margaret. Physiologist. HOG

Jackson, Michael (1958–). Singer. BUIB-2

Jackson, Nell (1929–). Track athlete, educator. BOHA

Jackson, Rachel (1767–1828). Wife of Andrew Jackson. BAG; BAG-1; BLG†; CHA; KL; MAA; MAU; PRB; ROH; ROHA

Jackson, Reggie (1946–). Baseball player. AAS-4; BRAA; GUG

Jackson, Saunders (fl. 1849). Pioneer. HODA; SCB

Jackson, Shirley. Theoretical physicist. CAF-1

Jackson, Solomon Henry (d. 1847). Publisher, born England. LETA

Jackson, Suzanne (1944–). Painter. FOGB

Jackson, Thomas Jonathan (Stonewall Jackson) (1824–1863). General. ARE; MAO

Jackson, Travis (1903–1987). Baseball player. HAF

Jackson, William Henry (1843–1942). Photographer. SUAA

Jacobi, Abraham (1830–1919). Pediatrician, born Germany. LETA

Jacobi, Mary Putnam (1842–1906). Physician. FLA; HUE; MASA; RAAG†; WABC†

Jacobs, Helen (1908–). Tennis player. FR-1; SUDA†

Jacobs, Hirsch (1904–1970). Horse trainer. SLA

Jacobs, James (1931–). Handball player. SLA

Jacobs, Lou (1903?–). Clown, born Germany. KIB

Jacobs-Bond, Carrie (1862–1946). Songwriter. MOA; STJ

Jacquard, Joseph-Marie (1752–1834). French inventor. FE

Jadwiga (1373–1399). Queen of Poland. MANB

Jaffe, Charles. Conductor. STM†

Jaffee, Irving (1906–1981). Skater. SLA

Jagger, Mick (1944–). English singer. BUIB-1

Jaissle, Louise. Nurse. WRA

Jalal-ud-Din Muhammad, see Akbar the Great.

James I (1566–1625). King of Great Britain. DEC; GRAB; SCC

James II (1633–1701). King of England, Scotland and Ireland. DEC; GRAB†; SCC

James the Greater. Saint, apostle. DAD-3; QUA

James the Less. Saint, apostle. DAD-2; QUA

James, Don. Surf rider. OLD

James, Edwin (1797–1861). Explorer. FOC

James, Frank (1844–1915). Outlaw. JOBA; REE

James, Henry (1843–1916). Author. ASB-1; CON†; STL

James, Jesse (1847–1882). Outlaw. JOBA; REE; SUJ

James, William (1842–1910). Philosopher, psychologist. LO

James Intercisus. Saint. DAD-3

Jamison, Judith (1944–). Dancer. BOHB; FOGC

Janáček, Leoš (1854–1928). Czech composer. YOL

Jane Frances de Chantal, Saint, see Chantal, Jane Frances de. Saint.

Janiec, Henry (1929–). Conductor. STM†

Janis, Byron (1928–). Pianist. EWC

Janis, Elsie (1889–1956). Mimic. MASB

Jansen, George. Conductor. STM†

Jansky, Karl Guthe (1905–1949). Radio engineer. BUF†; SUE

Janson, Ernest August (1878–1930). Marine. TA

Janssen, Werner (1899–). Conductor. STM†

Jansz, Willem (b. 1570?). Dutch navigator. ROL†

Jarrett, Ned (1932–). Automobile racer. LEX

Jarrett, Vernon D. (1921–). Educator. STAA

Jarvis, Gregory (1944–1986). Astronaut. COE-1

Jarvis, Lucy (1919–). Television producer. GIB-1

Jasper, John (1812–1901). Clergyman. ADA; ADB; BRB

Jay, Allen (1831–1910). Quaker boy. CAD

Jay, John (1745–1829). Supreme Court justice. FLC

Jay, Joseph Richard (1935–). Baseball player. BRE

J. B. (1946?–). Hemophiliac. SIAA

Jeanmaire, Renée (1924–). French dancer. ATA

Jeanne d'Arc, see Joan of Arc, Saint.

Jeff. Runaway. BEOA

Jefferson, John (1956–). Football player. AAS-18

Jefferson, Joseph (1829–1905). Actor. CAD

Jefferson, Lemon (1897–1930). Singer. ADB; COF-1; SUH; WAD†

Jefferson, Martha Wayles Skelton (1748–1782). Wife of Thomas Jefferson. BAG; BAG-1; BLG†; CHA; KL; MAA; MAU; ROH; ROHA

Jefferson, Thomas (1743–1826). President of U.S. ALCA; ARAB; ASB; BAEA; BAEB; BAG; BAG-1; BEB; BEC; BLA; BLE; BUIA; BUIB; CAG; CAH; COG; COI; COJ; COS; CUC; DAC; DAF-2; DAFA; DEI; DEJ; DIA; DUB; DUC; DUCA; FEA; FEAB; FEB; FIA; FID; FOB; FOH; FRBA; FRE; HAN; HAOA; HEEA; HIBC†; HIH; HOEA; LEQ; LEQA; MAB; MABA; MAC; MAT; MEB; MIA; OLA; PED; ROH; ROHA; ROK; STH; SUBB; VIA; WAI; WHD

Jeffrey, Major (fl. 1776). American Revolutionary soldier. WIBA

Jeffries, Jim (James Jackson) (1875–1952). Boxer. RAAC

Jeffries, Rosalind (1930?–). Painter. FAI

Jelesnik, Eugene. Conductor, born Russia. STM†

Jelinek, Otto (1910–). Conductor. STM†

Jellicoe, John Rushworth Jellicoe, 1st earl (1859–1935). British admiral. ARD

Jemison, Mary (1743–1833). Indian captive. DI; HEE

Jenifer, Daniel of St. Thomas (1723–1790). Statesman. BUIB†; FEAA

Jenkins, Carol (1944–). Television newscaster. STAA

Jenkins, Carol Heiss, see Heiss, Carol.

Jenkins, Charles Francis (1867–1934). Inventor. HYA

Jenkins, Ferguson Arthur (1943–). Baseball player. BUJB; GUB-1; GUG; KLCA; RIGA†

Jenkins, Newell (1915–). Conductor. STM†

Jenner, Bruce (1949–). Track athlete. SUBB-1

Jenner, Edward (1749–1823). English physician. ASA; CAA; CHD; COL; FAF†; FE; HUD; POD; RIE; ROA; SHG; SIC; SUF

Jennings, Al (1863–1962). Outlaw. JOBA

Jennings, Hugh Ambrose (1871–1928). Baseball player, manager. ALB; FRC-01

Jennings, Waylon (1937–). Singer. KRI-1

Jensen, Allen (1923–). Conductor. STM†

Jensen, Jackie (1927–1982). Football player. HIE

Jenson, Dylana (1961–). Violinist. SC-02

Jeremiah (650–585 B.C.). Hebrew prophet. GEF

Jerome (342–420). Saint. DAD-3; TUA

Jesus Christ. DEI; DEJ; FRE; HAJ; TRC-1

Jeter, Bob. Football player. JOA

Jethroe, Sam (1922–). Baseball player. BOE

Jewett, Sarah Orne (1849–1909). Author. BEGA

Jewitt, John R. (1783–1821). Indian captive. DI

Jex-Blake, Sophia (1840–1912). English physician. HUE; MASA†; SC†

Jiagge, Annie. Ghanaian jurist. CRA

Jimenez de Quesada, Gonzalo (1500?–1579). Spanish conquistador. ROL†

Jinnah, Mohammed Ali (1876–1948). Governor-general of Pakistan. KEF

Joachim, Joseph (1831–1907). Hungarian violinist, composer. CHFA

Joan (1st century). Saint. QUA

Joan of Arc (1412–1431). Saint. CHG; DAD-1; DAD-2; DEI; DEJ; ELA; EVD; HAA; HEA; MAJ; MOC; ONA; PA; PEE; STP

Joan of Valois (1464–1505). Saint. DAD-2; MOC

Jochanan ben Zakkai, see Johanan ben Zakkai.

Jochebed. Biblical character. LER

Joersz, Eldon. Aviator. OLDC†

Joffre, Joseph Jacques (1852–1931). French field marshal. ARD; RADA

Jogues, Isaac (1607–1646). Saint. DAD-1

Johanan ben Zakkai (d. 80 A.D.?). Palestinian rabbi. GEF; GUA; LERA; LES

Johanos, Donald (1928–). Conductor. STM†

John (1167?–1216). King of England. BRBF; DEC; GRAB†; SCC

John III Sobieski (1624–1696). King of Poland. MAJ

John XXIII (1881–1963). Pope. ASB-1; KE; YOA

John of God (1495–1550). Saint. DAD-2

John of Matha (1160–1213). Saint. DAD-2

John of Pian del Carpine (c. 1180–1252). Franciscan friar. ROL†

John of Sahagun. Saint. DAD-2

John of the Cross (1542–1591). Saint. DAD-3

John the Baptist. Saint. DAD-2; QUA

John the Dwarf (5th century). Saint. MOC; ONA

John, the Evangelist. Saint, apostle. DAD-2; DAD-3; ONA

John, Elton (1947–). English singer, composer. BUIB-1

John, Tommy (1943–). Baseball player. AAS-27; BRE

John Baptiste de la Salle. Saint. DAD-1; DAD-2

John Berchmans (1599–1621). Saint. DAD-1; DAD-3; MOC

John Bosco, Saint, see Bosco, John. Saint.

John Cantius (1390–1473). Saint. DAD-3

John Capistrano (1386–1456). Saint. DAD-2

John Chrysostom (349–407). Saint. DAD-2

John Climacus (579–649). Saint. DAD-2

John Damascene (645–750). Saint. DAD-2

John Gualbert (d. 1073). Saint. DAD-3; MOC

John Joseph of the Cross (1654–1734). Saint. DAD-2

John Kanti, Saint, see John Cantius. Saint.

John Kolobos, Saint, see John the Dwarf. Saint.

John Paul II (1920–). Pope. DU-1; MANB

Johncock, Gordon (1936?–). Automobile racer. OLCB

Johns, Constantine. Conductor, educator. STM†

Johnson, Albert C. (1926–). Conductor. STM†

Johnson, Amy (1903–1941). English aviator. HIFD; MO

Johnson, Andrew (1808–1875). President of U.S. ALE; BAEB; BAG; BAG-1; BEB; BLA; BUIA; CAG; CAH; COI; COS; DAE; DUC; DUCA; FEA; FRBA; HAOA; HIH; HOEA; KEA; KEC†; LEQ; LEQA; MAB; MABA; MIA; PED; ROH; ROHA; ROK†; SUBB; WHD

Johnson, Ban (Byron Bancroft) (1864–1931). Baseball executive. ALB

Johnson, Bob (1946–). Football player. CL-06

Johnson, Britton (fl. 1864). Rancher. HAP†

Johnson, Campbell C. (1921–). Chemical engineer. CAF-1

Johnson, Charles Spurgeon (1893–1956). Sociologist. ADA; ADB

Johnson, Charley (1938–). Football player. ANC; DEH; DEHA-1

Johnson, Claudia Alta (Lady Bird) (1912–). Wife of Lyndon Baines Johnson. BAG; BAG-1; BLG; CHB; KL; MAA; MAU; ROHA; SMBD

Johnson, Dammy Williams. Rodeo rider. VADB

Johnson, E. Pauline (1862–1913). Canadian poet. GRAD

Johnson, Earvin "Magic" (1959–). Basketball player. AAS-6

Johnson, Eliza McCardle (1810–1876). Wife of Andrew Johnson. BAG; BAG-1; BLG†; CHB; KL; MAA; MAU; PRB; ROH; ROHA

Johnson, Gail, see Buzonas, Gail Johnson.

Johnson, Gary "Big Hands" (1952–). Football player. AAS-16

Johnson, Gus. Basketball player. HIBA

Johnson, Henry (b. 1859). Soldier. BUH

Johnson, Henry (1897–1929). Soldier, WWI. BRB†; HUB; STQ†

Johnson, Howard Deering (1897–1972). Restaurant executive. LAH

Johnson, Jack (John Arthur) (1878–1946?). Boxer. BRBD; RAAC

Johnson, James Weldon (1871–1938). Author. ADA; ADB; BRB†; DOF-1; GRAB-02; JO; RIC; RICA; ROE; ROG; STB

Johnson, Jemima. American Revolutionary patriot. CLC†

Johnson, John, Jr. Television producer-director. STAA

Johnson, John H. (1918–). Publisher. ADA; ADB; DOF-1; DRA; PAA; STAA†

Johnson, Junior (Robert Glenn) (1931–). Automobile racer. LEX†; LEXA

Johnson, Lonnie (1889–1970). Singer. SUH

Johnson, Lyndon Baines (1908–1973). President of U.S. ALE; BAEB; BAG; BAG-1; BEB; BLA; BUIA; CAG; CAH; COI; COS; DUB; DUC; DUCA; FEA; FRBA; HAOA; HIH; HOEA; KEA; LEQ; LEQA; MAB; MABA; MIA; PED; ROHA; ROK†; SUBB; WEB; WEE; WHD

Johnson, Malvin Gray (1896–1934). Painter. ADA; ADB

Johnson, Marques (1956–). Basketball player. AAS-5

Johnson, Martin Elmer (1884–1937). Photographer. COKA

Johnson, Mordecai Wyatt (1890–1976). Educator. ADA; ADB; BRB; DOF-1; RIC

Johnson, Osa Helen (1894–1953). Photographer. COKA

Johnson, Pete (1954–). Football player. AAS-32

Johnson, Rafer (1934–). Track athlete. DAJ; FIB; HOBC; HOC; LEYB

Johnson, Richard Mentor (1780–1850). Vice president of U.S. FEA; HAOA; HOEA

Johnson, Ronald Adolphus (1947–). Football player. GUCA; LEZB; ST

Johnson, Samuel (1696–1772). Clergyman. BUIB†

Johnson, Samuel (1709–1784). English lexicographer. BEG; BOD

Johnson, Thomas. Assassin. RABA†

Johnson, Thomas (1732–1819). Supreme Court justice. SEC

Johnson, Thomas A. (1928–). Journalist. STAA

Johnson, Thor (1913–1975). Conductor. STM

Johnson, Trudy (1965?–). Rodeo rider. VADB

Johnson, Walter Perry (1887–1946). Baseball player. AAS-35; ALB; ASBA; BED; BRC; DAFB; DAFC; DAFD; DAG; DAGA; DAH; EPA; FRC-1†; GRA; GUC; GUDA; HIF; MUB-1; MUC; NEA; RIG†; SHA; SICA; WAG

Johnson, Wendell (1906–). Speech therapist. GEA

Johnson, Sir William (1715–1774). British official in American colonies. VIA

Johnson, William Samuel (1727–1819). Senator. BUIB†; FEAA

Johnson, Willie (1902–1949). Singer. SUH

Johnston, Eddie (1935–). Canadian hockey player, manager. DEHA-1

Johnston, Ernest, Jr. (1939?–). Journalist. STAA

Johnston, Harriet Lane, see Lane, Harriet.

Johnston, Joshua (1770–1830). Painter. BEBA; WIBA

Johnston, Richard S. (1926–). Chemist. POE

Joio, Norman dello, see Dello Joio, Norman.

Joliet, Louis (1645–1700). French explorer. ABA; GRC; HIBC; ROL†

Joliot-Curie, Frédéric (1900–1958). French physicist. FE; RID

Joliot-Curie, Irène (1897–1956). French physicist. FE; RID; SC†; SHFE†

Jolson, Al (1886–1950). Actor, singer. LETA

Jonas. Saint. DAD-2

Jonasson, Olga (1934–). Transplant surgeon. RAAG

Jones, Absalom (b. 1747). Clergyman. BRB

Jones, Alan. Automobile racer. OLDD

Jones, Bert (1951–). Football player. AAS-20; CL-1; LIBB

Jones, Bobby (Robert Tyre) (1902–1971). Golfer. ALBA; ASBA; DAG; DAGA; HEG; HOC; LABA; LEF; SICA

Jones, Bobby (1951–). Basketball player. AAS-25

Jones, Dave "Deacon" (1938–). Football player. ANA; KADA

Jones, Donald Forsha (1890–1963). Botanist. CAB

Jones, Frederick McKinley (1892–1961). Inventor. GRAB-03; HAL

Jones, George (1811–1891). Journalist. SQB†

Jones, George Wallace (1804–1896). Senator. SEC

Jones, Grandpa (Louis) (1913–). Comedian. HAG-1

Jones, Harold S. (1909–). Clergyman. GRAC

Jones, Henry (fl. 1843). Founder of B'nai B'rith. LETA

Jones, Horatio (1762–1836). Indian captive. HEE

Jones, Ifor (1900–). Conductor, born Wales. STM†

Jones, J. Randolph (1910–). Conductor. STM†

Jones, James Earl (1931–). Actor. AB

Jones, John (1816–1879). Business executive. ADA; ADB; GRAB-05; KADB

Jones, John Paul (1747–1792). Naval officer. BUIB; COD; CUC; DAC; DAFA; DEI; DEJ;

DYA; FIA; FID; HIBD; ICA; LOA; NAC; OLA; SOA

Jones, K. C. (1932–). Basketball player, coach. ARB-2

Jones, L. Bruce (1905–). Conductor. STM†

Jones, Lauris L. (1917–). Conductor. STM†

Jones, Lawrence. Painter. FAH

Jones, Lois. Geologist, polar researcher. LA-1

Jones, Mary Harris (1830–1930). Labor leader, born Ireland. BI; BRBE†; GEE; MAV; NIA; PACA; TRD; WABC†

Jones, Parnelli (Rufus Parnell) (1933–). Automobile racer. DI-2; LEX; ORD; YAA

Jones, Sisseretta (1863–1933). Singer. ROF†

Jong, Erica (1942–). Author, poet. GL-1

Jonson, Ben (1573?–1637). English playwright, poet. DEI; DEJ

Joplin, Janis (1943–1970). Singer. BUIB-1

Joplin, Scott (1868–1917). Pianist, composer. COF-1

Jorda, Enrique (1911–). Conductor, born Spain. STM

Jordan, Barbara C. (1936–). Congresswoman. BOHF; GRAB-1; YOI

Jordan, David Starr (1851–1931). Zoologist. HYB

Jordan, Henry (1935–). Football player. ANA; JOA

Jordan, James Edward (1897–1988). Comedian. BUR-1

Jordan, Lee Roy. Football player. HAGB

Jordan, Marian Driscoll (1898–1961). Comedienne. BUR-1

Jordan, Sara (1884–1959). Physician. FLA

Joseph. Saint, biblical character, husband of Virgin Mary. DAD-1; DAD-2; ONA; QUA

Joseph (Chief Joseph) (1840?–1904). Nez Percé Indian leader. DEDB; ELA; FRAB; HED; HEGA; MOD; STAB; SUKA; WAM

Joseph of Arimathea. Saint. ONA

Joseph of Cupertino (1603–1663). Saint. DAD-3

Joseph, Jacob (1848–1902). Rabbi, born Russia. LETA

Joseph Calasanctius. Saint. DAD-3

Josephine (1763–1814). Empress of the French. FAE

Josephus Flavius (37–100). Palestinian general, historian. LERA; LES

Joshua ben Chananiah (c. 35–130). Palestinian rabbi. GUA

Joshua ben Levi (3d century). Palestinian rabbi. GUA

Joss, Addie (Adrian) (1880–1911). Baseball player. RIGA†

Josselman of Rosheim (1478?–1554). German knight. GEF

Jouett, Jack (John) (1754–1822). American Revolutionary soldier. CAGA

Jouhaux, Léon (1879–1954). French labor leader, politician. MEC; WIC

Joule, James Prescott (1818–1889). English physicist. FE; SHFB

Jovita. Saint. DAD-2

Joyce, James (1882–1941). Irish author. ASB-1

Joyce, Joan (1940–). Softball player. GUED-1; HOBAA

Juana Inés de la Cruz, Sister (1651–1695). Mexican nun, poet. BACA; ROGB

Juana Maria. Indian princess. WIAA-2

Juantorena, Alberto (1951?–). Cuban track athlete. SUBB-1

Juárez, Benito Pablo (1806–1872). President of Mexico. BAA; BACA; NEBA; ROGB; WO; WOB; YOFA

Jubo Jubogha (fl. 1880). King of Opobo. MIC

Judah, Theodore Dehone (1826–1863). Railroad builder. BLD†

Judah ben Babba (fl. 135). Palestinian rabbi. GEF

Judah ha-Levi (c. 1085–1140). Spanish Hebrew poet, rabbi, physician. GEF; GRB-1; GUA; KAC; LERA; LES

Judah ha-Nasi (Judah the Prince) (135–220). Palestinian rabbi. GUA; KAC; LERA

Judah Maccabaeus, see Maccabaeus, Judah.

Jude. Saint, apostle. DAD-3

Judith. Biblical character. LER

Jugurtha (fl. 188–106 B.C.). African king. GRAB-04

Julia. Saint. DAD-2

Julian. Saint. DAD-2; QUA

Julian (c. 331–363). Roman emperor. ED-5

Julian, Percy Lavon (1899–1975). Chemist. ADA; ADB; DOF-1; FLD; GRAB-03; HA; KLA; STO

Juliana (1909–). Queen of the Netherlands. BOI; FAE

Julio P. (1958?–). Blind boy. SIAA

Julitta (d. 305?). Saint. MOC

Jullien, Louis Antoine (1812–1860). French conductor. YOM

Jung, Carl Gustav (1875–1961). Swiss psychologist, psychiatrist. KE

Junod, Marcel (1904?–1961). Swiss physician, Red Cross delegate. DED

Jupille, Jean Baptiste. French boy inoculated against rabies. FAF

Jurgensen, Sonny (Christian Adolph) (1934–). Football player. DUD; DUE; LEZA; SHEA

Just, Ernest Everett (1883–1941). Biologist. ADA; ADB; BRB†; CAF-1; DOF-1; GRAB-03; HA; HAM; KLA

Justice, Charlie. Football player. HIE

Justin (100–165). Saint. DAD-2; ONA

Justinian I, the Great (483–565). Emperor of the Eastern Roman Empire. BEO; CAAA

K

Kabakoff, Harry. Boxing manager. LEW

Kabalevsky, Dmitri Borisovich (1904–). Russian composer. POG

Kagan, Israel Meir (1838–1933). Polish rabbi. KAD

Kagawa, Toyohiko (1888–1960). Japanese evangelist. BAF; KEE

Kahanamoku, Duke Paoa (1890–1968). Swimmer. FIC; LEYB†; OLD

Kahn, Anthony (1961–). Mechanical engineer. HOD-1

Kahn, Madeline (1942–). Actress, singer. MASB

Kalb, Johann (1721–1780). German soldier of fortune in the American Revolution. SCB-1

Kaline, Albert William (1934–). Baseball player. BELB; BUJ; DA; HOCG; PEC; PRA; SA-3

Kalmar, Bert (1884–1947). Vaudevillean. MOA

Kaman, Charles Huron (1919–). Aviation executive. PAB

Kamehameha I, the Great (1737?–1819). King of Hawaii. NEC

Kandinsky, Wassily (1866–1944). Russian painter. KAA

Kandler, Elizabeth Aytes. Superintendent of corrections. SMBC-3

Kane, Bob (1916–). Cartoonist. GOB-1

Kane, Gil (1926–). Cartoonist, born Russia. GOB-1

Kane, Helen (1904–1966). Singer, comedienne. MASB

Kanell, Billie Gene (d. 1951). Soldier. REA

K'ang-hsi (1654–1722). Emperor of China. NEC

Kanokogi, Rusty (1935–). Martial artist. AT

Kant, Immanuel (1724–1804). German philosopher. LO; OZA

Kaplan, Louis "Kid" (1902–1970). Boxer, born Russia. SLA

Kapp, Joe (1938–). Football player. LEZA; LIBB; LYD; NEAA

Kappel, Frederick Russell (1902–). Utilities executive. PAA

Karajan, Herbert von (1908–). Austrian conductor. EWD; STM†; YOM†

Karamesines, Chris. Automobile racer. OLB

Karamzin, Nikolai Mikhailovich (1766–1826). Russian author. POFA†

Karansky, Priscilla Pepper. Mounted police officer. SMBC-3

Karenga (Ronald McKinley Everett) (1941–). Black Muslim leader. HAI

Karloff, Boris (1887–1969). Actor, born England. COE-2

Kármán, Theodor von (1881–1963). Aeronautical engineer, born Hungary. COQ; NEB

Karsh, Yousuf (1908–). Canadian photographer, born Armenia. FOD

Karski, Jan, pseud. Author, born Poland. CAHA

Kash, Eugene. Canadian conductor. STM†

Kassebaum, Nancy Landon (1932–). Senator. WIAA-02

Kate, Mammy. American Revolutionary patriot. CLC†

Katims, Milton (1909–). Conductor. STM†

Katz, Chaim Moshe. Businessman, born Russia. GRB-1

Katz, David (1924–). Conductor. STM†

Katz, Elias (1901–1947). Finnish track athlete. SLA

Katz, Paul (1907–). Conductor. STM†

Katz, Vera. State legislator. WHE†

Kauff, Benny (1891–1961). Baseball player. SLA

Kauffmann, Angelica (1741–1807). English painter, born Switzerland. BOH; NE

Kaufman, Micha (1946–). Israeli marksman, born Palestine. SLA†

Kaufmann, Walter (1907–). Czech conductor. STM†

Kay, Ulysses (1917–). Composer. ADB; POF

Kayamba, Mdumi Martin (b. 1891). African teacher. PEA

Kaye, Danny (1913–1987). Actor. ED-1†

Kaye, Nora (1920–1987). Dancer. ATA

Kaye-Smith, Sheila (1887–1956). English author. SMA

Kayira, Legson Didimu. Malawian author. OJA

Kazin, Alfred (1915–). Author, critic. RAC

Kazmaier, Dick (1930–). Football player. HIE

Kearny, Stephen Watts (1794–1848). General. BLD

Kearse, Amalya (1937–). Jurist. GLO

Keaton, Buster (1895–1977). Motion picture director, comedian. ED-1; SMBC

Keats, John (1795–1821). English poet. COP

Keefe, Timothy J. (1856–1933). Baseball player. ALB

Keeler, Wee Willie (William Henry) (1872–1923). Baseball player. ALB; DAFD; DAH; FRC-1†

Keeler, William Wayne (1908–). Cherokee Indian chief. GRAC

Keino, Kipchoge (1940–). Kenyan track athlete. AAS-26; LEYB†

Keith, Damon Jerome (1922–). Jurist. DOF-1

Kekule, Friedrich (1829–1896). German chemist. FE

Keleti, Agnes (1921–). Israeli gymnast, born Hungary. SLA

Kell, George Clyde (1922–). Baseball player. BOE; HIF

Kellar, Harry (1849–1922). Magician. GIA; KEB

Kellen, James (1932–). Librarian. GEA

Keller, Billy. Basketball player. HIBAA

Keller, Hannes (1934–). Swiss sea diver. OLC

Keller, Helen Adams (1880–1968). Author. BEC; BOC; CAD; DOD; EVA; EVD; FAA; FOR; FRE; GIBA; MAJ; STLA; WAJ

Keller, Leonard (1909–). Conductor. STM†

Kelley, Chauncey (1915–). Conductor. STM†

Kelley, Florence (1859–1932). Social worker. BRBE; WABC†

Kelley, Jane Holden (1928–). Archaeologist. WIAA-01

Kelley, John A. (1911?–). Track athlete. HIA-01†

Kelley, John J. Track athlete. HIA-01†

Kelley, Larry (Lawrence Morgan) (1915–). Football player. DAFG; DAI

Kellogg, Frank Billings (1856–1937). Statesman. HEEA; MEC†; WIC

Kelly, Alvin "Shipwreck" (1885–1952). Flagpole sitter. COKB

Kelly, Colin (1915–1941). Aviator, WWII. FIA

Kelly, Emmett (1898–1979). Clown. KIB

Kelly, Fanny (1845–1904). Indian captive. DI; JOB

Kelly, John B. (1889–1960). Oarsman. DAG; DAGA

Kelly, John Joseph (1898–1957). Marine. TA

Kelly, King (Michael Joseph) (1857–1894). Baseball player. ALB; DAFD; SMK

Kelly, Leonard Patrick (1927–). Canadian hockey player. FR; LIAB

Kelly, Leroy (1942–). Football player. BEKB; DUF; FRD; LEZB

Kelly, Patsy (1910–1981). Actress. MASB

Kelly, Walter Crawford (1913–1973). Cartoonist. GOB-1

Kelly, William (1811–1888). Inventor. BUE

Kelsey, Frances Oldham (1914–). Physician, born Canada. EOA; TRD

Kelsey, Henry (1670–1729). English explorer. ARF

Kelvin, William Thomson, 1st baron (1824–1907). British mathematician, physicist. BOB; DUA; FE; LAE; SIA

Kemp, Steve (1954–). Baseball player. GUB-1

Kempe, Rudolf (1910–). German conductor. STM†

Kempner, Mary Jean. Navy nurse, WW II. WRA

Kendall, Edward Calvin (1886–1972). Biochemist. RIF

Kennedy, Captain. Pirate. WHA†

Kennedy, Edgar (1890–1948). Comedian. ED-1†

Kennedy, Edward M., Jr. (1961?–). Son of Senator Edward M. Kennedy. HAFA

Kennedy, Edward Moore (1932–). Senator. LAI†

Kennedy, Jacqueline Lee Bouvier, see Onassis, Jacqueline Lee Bouvier Kennedy.

Kennedy, John Fitzgerald (1917–1963). President of U.S. ASB; BAEB; BAG; BAG-1; BEB; BEC; BLA; BUIA; CAAA; CAG; CAH; COI; COJA; COS; CUC; DEI; DEJ; DIA; DUB; DUC; DUCA; FAA; FIA; FRBA; HIH; KE; KEA; LAI; LEPE; LEQ; LEQA; MAB; MABA; MIA; PED; ROH; ROHA; ROK; SCA; SCBA; SUBB; WEA; WEE; WHD; YOA

Kennedy, Joseph Patrick, Sr. (1888–1969). Financier, diplomat. LAI†

Kennedy, Joseph Patrick, Jr. (1915–1944). Aviator, WW II. EDA; LAI†; SUA

Kennedy, Robert Francis (1925–1968). Senator. LAI†; WEC

Kenneth (515–599). Saint. DAD-3; MOC

Kenny, Elizabeth (1886–1952). Australian nurse. BOC; MAK; WRA

Kenton, Simon (1755–1836). Frontiersman. COE

Kenton, Stan (1912–1979). Band leader. TEA

Kenyatta, Jomo (1893?–1978). Prime minister of Kenya. ADA; KEF

Kenyatta, Margaret Wambui (1928–). Kenyan mayor. CRA

Kenyon, Kathleen M. (1906–). English archaeologist. RIG

Keokuk (fl. 1790–1848). Sac Indian chief. DEDB

Keon, David Michael (1940–). Canadian hockey player. FICA; LEYA

Keough, Matt (1955–). Baseball player. AAS-9

Kepler, Johannes (1571–1630). German astronomer. CAA; DOE; FE; LAA; MOCB; PIA; SHFB; SIA; SIB; STI; SUE

Keppler, Joseph (1838–1894). Cartoonist, born Austria. DEDC

Kerensky, Alexander Feodorovitch (1881–1970). Russian political leader. NEBB-1

Keres, Paul (1916–1975). Estonian chess player. LEQB

Kern, Jerome (1885–1945). Composer. BAD; CUC; EWA; MOA; WIA

Kerr, John (1932–). Basketball coach. LEW

Kertesz, André (1894–1985). Photographer, born Hungary. HOE

Kesnar, Maurits (1900–). Conductor, born the Netherlands. STM†

Kessel, Mary Hickman. Social worker. GEA

Ketchel, Stanley (1886–1910). Boxer. DAG; DAGA

Ketchum, Thomas Edward (1865?–1901). Outlaw. WIAA-1

Kettering, Charles F. (1876–1958). Electrical engineer. HYA†; YOE

Kevin. Saint. DAD-1

Keynes, John Maynard (1883–1946). English economist. ASB-1

Kgamanyane (fl. 1820). Chief of the Bakgatla. MIC

Khachaturian, Aram (1903–1978). Russian composer. KAE; POG

Khama III (d. 1980). King of the Bamangwato. MIC

Khomeini, Ruhollah (1900?–). Iranian religious and political leader. HAGD

Khrushchev, Nikita S. (1894–1971). Russian communist leader. ARA; COJB; DOF; KE; WEA

Khufu, *see* Cheops.

Khwarizmi, al- (780–850). Arabian mathematician. STN

Kidd, William (Captain) (1645?–1701). Scottish pirate. LACB; PABB; SC-1

Kieff, Elaine (1948?–). Winner, Young American Medal for Bravery. ANCA

Kieran, John Francis (1892–1981). Journalist. FOE

Kierkegaard, Sören Aabye (1813–1855). Danish philosopher. LO

Kies, Mary (late 19th–early 20th century). Inventor. SC†

Kiesinger, Kurt Georg (1904–). German ex-chancellor. WECA

Kiesling, Walt (1903–1962). Football player, coach. DAFG†; SUD

Kiick, Jim (1946–). Football player. LEZB

Kilgallen, Dorothy (1913–1965). Journalist. JAE

Killebrew, Harmon (1936–). Baseball player. DA; KADA; LEY; PEC; PRA; RAAA; RIGA†; SA-3

Killy, Jean-Claude (1943–). French skier. FRCA; LEYB†

Kilmer, Billy (1939–). Football player. GUF

Kilmer, Gordon (1946–). Winner, Young American Medal for Bravery. ANCA

Kilpatrick, Hugh Judson (1836–1881). General. ARE

Kim, Nelli (1957–). Russian gymnast. LIE; SUBB-1

Kim Yong-gi. Korean agriculturist. RODA

Kimbrell, Marketa (1928–). Actress, born Czechoslovakia. WA

Kiner, Ralph M. (1922–). Baseball player, sportscaster. DA; DAA; RAAA

King, Alan (1927–). Comedian. GRB-1

King, Bernard (1956–). Basketball player. AAS-8

King, Billie Jean (1943–). Tennis player. AAS-29; FR-1; GIB-1; GLC; HI; HOBA; HOBAA; JABA; KOA; LAHA; MATA; RYA; RYX; ST-2; SUDA

King, Clarence (1842–1901). Geologist. YOG

King, Coretta Scott (1927–). Civil rights leader. FAG; GIBA

King, Dana M. Conductor. STM†

King, Ernest Joseph (1878–1956). Admiral. ARC; COD†; NAC

King, John (1865–1938). Sailor, born Ireland. TA

King, John B. (1908–). Educator. FLD

King, John I. (b. 1848). Pioneer, physician. JOD

King, Martin Luther, Jr. (1929–1968). Clergyman, civil rights leader. AAS-34; ADA; ADB; ASB-1; BAF; BRBD; BRG; DEJ; DOF-1; DU-1; ELA; FAA; FEC; FLD; GRAB-01; HAJ; HODA; JO; JOC; KE; LEPE; MEB; MEC; RICA; STO; WEB; WIAA-8; WIC; YOA; YOI

King, Micki (Maxine Joyce) (1944–). Diver. BOHA; HOBAA; JABA; LEYB†; RYA†; RYX; ST-2

King, Richard (1824–1885). Cattleman. KAW; WAA

King, Rufus (1755–1827). Senator, diplomat. BUIB†; FEAA; WHD†

King, William (1768–1852). Governor. SEC

King, William Rufus Devane (1786–1853). Vice president of U.S. FEA; HAOA; HOEA

Kingman, Dave (1948–). Baseball player. AAS-4; LEY†

Kingsford-Smith, Charles (1897–1935). English aviator. HAMY

Kingsley, Charles (1819–1875). English author. BEH; COO

Kingsley, Mary Henrietta (1862–1900). English ethnologist. BOH; DAF; KNA; ROL†; WIA-1

Kinmont, Jill (1938–). Skier. LEYB†

Kinnick, Nile (1919–1943). Football player. HIE

Kiphuth, Robert John Herman (1890–1967). Swimming coach. HEH

Kipling, Rudyard (1865–1936). English author. BEI; COB; COO; COP; STK

Kirby, Jack (1917–). Cartoonist. GOB-1

Kirby, Rollin (1875–1952). Cartoonist. DEDC

Kirchhoff, Gustav Robert (1824–1887). German physicist. FE; SHFB; SUE

Kirchner, Ernst Ludwig (1880–1938). German painter. WIAA

Kirk, Roland (1936–1976). Multi-instrumentalist. UN

Kirk, Tammy Jo (1964–). Motorcyclist. BUIC

Kirkland, Gelsey (1952–). Dancer. FOGC

Kirsh, Maria (18th century). German astronomer. SC†

Kirszenstein-Szewinska, Irena (1946–). Polish track athlete, born Russia. SLA

Kissinger, Henry Alfred (1923–). Ex-Secretary of State, born Germany. MEC

Kitasato, Shibasaburo (1852–1931). Japanese bacteriologist. RIE

Kitchener, Horatio Herbert, 1st earl Kitchener of

Khartoum (1850–1916). British field marshall. ARD

Kitt, Eartha (1928–). Singer. DADB; ROF

Kitt, Howard. Baseball player. BELB

Kittle, Ron (1958–). Baseball player. GUB-1

Kitzinger, G. Chester (1894–). Conductor. STM†

Klecko, Joe (1953–). Football player. AAS-16

Klee, Paul (1879–1940). Swiss painter. KAA; WIAA

Klein, Chuck (1905–1958). Baseball player. DAA

Klein, Ralph (1931–). Israeli basketball player, born Germany. SLA†

Klem, Bill (William Joseph) (1874–1951). Baseball umpire. ALB; DAFD; DAG; DAGA; DAH; FRC-1†

Klemperer, Otto (1885–1973). Conductor, born Germany. EWD; STM†; YOM

Kletzki, Paul (1900–). Polish conductor. STM†

Kline, Nathan Schellenberg (1916–). Psychiatrist. HEFA

Kline, Tony. Lawyer. LETD

Kling, Johnny (1875–1947). Baseball player. HIC; RI; SHD†; SLA

Kloss, Ilana (1956–). South African tennis player. SLA†

Kluger, Ruth. Israeli rescue worker, born Rumania. GRB-1

Knapp, Seaman Asahel (1833–1911). Agriculturist. MAL

Knappertsbusch, Hans (1888–1965). German conductor. STM†

Knefler, Frederick (fl. 1864). Soldier, born Hungary. LETA

Knight, William "Pete." Aviator. ST-1

Knox, Henry (1750–1806). General. BUIB†; DAFA; MAE; SOA

Kocak, Matej (1882–1918). Marine, born Hungary. TA

Koch, Bill (1955?–). Skier. FRCA

Koch, Robert (1843–1910). German bacteriologist. AAS-31; BEK; COL; DEB; DEI; DEJ; FAF; FE; HUD; RIE; RIF; ROA; SUF

Kocher, Emil Theodor (1841–1917). Swiss surgeon. POB; RIF

Kodály, Zoltán (1882–1967). Hungarian composer. KAE

Kodijat, Raden (1890–). Indonesian physician. RODA

Koenig, Friedrich, see König, Friedrich.

Kolar, Victor (1888–1957). Conductor, educator, born Hungary. STM†

Kolberg, Hugo. Conductor, born Poland. STM†

Kold, Christen Mikkelsen (1816–1870). Danish educator. COG

Kolehmainen, Hannes. Finnish track athlete. HIA-01†

Kolff, Willem (1911–). Physician, born the Netherlands. CHE†

Komarov, Vladimir M. (1927–1967). Russian astronaut. THC

Konie, Gwendoline Chomba (1938–). Zambian U.N. delegate. CRA

König, Friedrich (1774–1833). German printer. FE; LAE

Konnerth, Frank J. Conductor, born Rumania. STM†

Konstanty, Jim (Casimer James) (1917–1976). Baseball player. SHE; VEA

Kook, Abraham Isaac (1865–1935). Israeli rabbi. GRB-1

Koontz, Elizabeth (1919–). Educator, civil rights activist. GIB-1

Koontz, Roscoe L. (1922–). Health physicist. CAF-1

Koosman, Jerry (1943–). Baseball player. KLBB

Kopp, Leo (1906–). Conductor, educator, born Hungary. STM†

Korbut, Olga (1956–). Russian gymnast. HOBAA; LIE

Korczak, Janus (1878–1942). Polish physician. GRB-1

Korn, Peter Jona (1922–). Conductor, born Germany. STM†

Korn, Richard (1908–). Conductor. STM†

Kornberg, Arthur (1918–). Biochemist. GRB-1; LET; RIF

Kornilov, Lavr Georgiyevich (1870–1918). Russian general. NEBB-1

Korris, Risa (1946–). Television camera woman. SMBB-2

Kosciusko, Tadeusz (1746–1817). Polish general in American Revolution. HEA; LOB; MANB; PIAA; RAD; SCB-1; STP

Kossel, Albrecht (1853–1927). German physiologist. RIF

Kostka, Stanislaus (1550–1568). Saint. DAD-1; DAD-3

Kosygin, Aleksei N. (1904–1980). Russian communist leader. WEC

Koufax, Sandy (Sanford) (1935–). Baseball player. ALBA; BRC; BUD-1; DAFC; DAFD; DAH; DEHA-1; FRC-1†; GEB; GIB; GRA; GRB-1; GUC; GUDA; HOC; KADA; LYC; MUB-1; MUC; NEA; PAW; PEC; PRA; RI; RIGA†; SHA; SHC; SLA

Kountz, Samuel. Surgeon. CAF-1

Koussevitzky, Serge (1874–1951). Conductor, born Russia. EWB; YOM

Kovago, Jozsef. Mechanical engineer, born Hungary. CAHA

Kozma, Tibor. Conductor, born Hungary. STM†

Kraenzlein, Alvin (1876–1928). Track athlete. DAJ; LEYB†

Kraft, Christopher Columbus, Jr. (1924–). Aeronautical engineer. COQ; POE

Kramer, Barry (1942–). Basketball player. SLA†

Kramer, Jack (John Albert) (1921–). Tennis player. FOX; HI; HOC

Kramer, Jerry (1936–). Football player. DAFG; JOA; PIB; PIBA

Kramer, Joel (1955–). Basketball player. SLA†

Kramer, Ron (1935–). Football player. AAS-19; JOA†

Krasner, Lee (1908–1984). Painter. FOGB†

Kraus, Mary Ellen. Air traffic controller. SMBC-2

Krausz, Laszlo. Violinist, conductor, born Hungary. STM†

Krebs, Sir Hans Adolf (1900–1981). English biochemist, born Germany. LET

Kreisler, Fritz (1875–1962). Violinist, born Austria. CHFA; RADA

Kreutzer, Rodolphe (1766–1831). French violinist. CHFA

Krigstein, Bernard (1919–). Cartoonist. GOB-1

Krips, Josef (1902–1974). Conductor, born Austria. EWD; STM

Kristofferson, Kris (1937–). Actor, singer. KRI

Kritz, Karl (1906–1969). Conductor, born Austria. STM†

Kriza, John (1919–). Dancer. ATA

Kroc, Ray (1902–1984). Restaurant executive. DU-1

Krogh, August (1874–1949). Danish physiologist. RIF

Kroll, Alex. Football player, advertising executive. HOBB

Kronberger, Lily (b. 1885). Hungarian figure skater. SLA†

Kropotkin, Pëtr Alekseevich (1842–1921). Russian philosopher. RAC

Krotoshinsky, Abraham. Soldier, born Poland. GEF; GRB-1

Krueger, John H. (1922–). Conductor. STM†

Krueger, Karl (1894–). Conductor. STM†

Kruger, Harry (1929–). Conductor. STM†

Kruger, Rudolf (1917–). Conductor, born Germany. STM†

Kruger, Stephanus Johannes Paulus (1825–1904). South African statesman. WOA

Krumgold, Joseph (1908–1980). Author. SMB

Krupsak, Mary Anne (1932–). State official. GRAB-1

Krutch, Joseph Wood (1893–1970). Author, critic. CORA

Krylor, Ivan Andreevich (1768–1844). Russian fabulist. POFA†

Kubelik, Rafael (1914–). Czech conductor. STM†; YOM†

Kubert, Joe. Cartoonist. GOB-1

Kubica, Terry. Skater. LEYB†

Kublai Khan (1216–1294). Mongol emperor. CAAA; UNA

Kübler-Ross, Elisabeth (1926–). Psychiatrist, born Switzerland. BOHE; GIB-1

Kubrick, Stanley (1928–). Motion picture director. FLBC

Kuchler, Lena. Israeli child psychologist, born Poland. GRB-1

Kucinski, Leo (1904–). Conductor, born Poland. STM†

Kuenn, Harvey (1930–1988). Baseball player, coach. BOE†; BRD

Kuhl, Benjamin (d. 1944). Outlaw. WIAA-1

Kuhn, Irene Corbally (1900–). Journalist. JAE

Kuhn, Margaret (1905–). Social reformer. COG-1; GIB-1

Kung, Ai-ling Sung (1888–1973). Wife of H. H. Kung. EUA

Kunin, Madeline (1933–). Governor. WHE†

Kunz, George (1947–). Football player. CL-06

Kupper, Sandy. Fire fighter. FOC-1

Kurinsky, Arpad (1898–). Conductor, born Hungary. STM†

Kurkewicz, Walter (1901–). Conductor. STM†

Kurosawa, Akira (1910–). Japanese motion picture director. RODA

Kurtz, Efrem (1900–). Russian conductor. STM†

Kurtzman, Harvey (1924–). Cartoonist. GOB-1

Kurzweil, Fredric (1912–). Conductor, born Austria. STM†

Kuscsik, Nina (1939?–). Track athlete. HOBAA†

Kushnir, David (1931–). Israeli track athlete, born Palestine. SLA†

Kusner, Kathy (1940?–). Jockey. GUED; HOBA; HOBAA; RYA

Kwalick, Ted (Thaddeus John, Jr.) (1947–). Football player. GUCA

Ky, Nguyen Cao (1930–). Ex-president of South Vietnam. WECA

L

Labella, Peter (1921–). Conductor. STM†

Laboulaye, Édouard René Lefebvre de (1811–1883). French journalist, politician. DIA†

Labouré, Catherine (1806–1876). Saint. DAD-3

Labre, Benedict (1748–1783). Saint. DAD-2; MOC

Lachapelle, Marie-Louise (1769–1821). French midwife. MASA†

Lachenal, Louis. French mountaineer. HAQ

La Conte, Emma (fl. 1860s). Letter writer. WABC†

La Corregidora, see Dominguez, (Maria) Josefa Ortiz de.

Lacoste, René (1904?–). French tennis player. FOX

Ladany, Shaul (1936–). Israeli track athlete, born Yugoslavia. SLA†

Ladd, Ernie (1938–). Football player. AAS-32

Ladewig, Marion (1914?–). Bowler. HOBA; HOBAA

Laënnec, René Théophile (1781–1826). French physician. FAF; HUD; SHG

Lafayette, Marie Joseph Paul Yves Roch Gilbert du Motier, marquis de (1757–1834). French statesman and officer. CUC; DEI; FRB; HAN; LAD; LOA; OLA; SCB-1; SOA; STP

Lafitte, Jean (1780?–1826?). French pirate. LACB; SC-1; VIA

La Fleur, Guy Damien (1951–). Canadian hockey player. AAS-22; FICA-1; MANA; OLDE; ORB

La Follette, Philip Fox (1897–1965). Governor. LAI†

La Follette, Robert Marion, Jr. (1895–1953). Senator. LAI

La Follette, Robert Marion, Sr. (1855–1925). Governor, senator. ARAA; LAI

Lafontaine, Henri (1854–1943). Belgian statesman. MEC†; WIC

LaFontant, Jewel Stradford (1922–). Lawyer. SWI

Lagerlof, Selma (1858–1940). Swedish author. PA; SHFE†

Lagrange, Joseph Louis (1736–1813). French mathematician, astronomer. STN

La Guardia, Fiorello Henry (1882–1947). Mayor. MAS

Laing, Hugh (1911–). English dancer. ATA

Lajoie, Napoleon (1875–1959). Baseball player. ALB; DAFC; DAFD; DAH; EP; RIGA†; WAC

Lake, Simon (1866–1945). Mechanical engineer. HYA†; MAP; OLC

Lally, Grace. Nurse. WRA

Lamar, Lucius Quintus Cincinnatus (1825–1893). Senator, congressman. KEC; KED

Lamar, Mirabeau Buonparte (1798–1859). Texas statesman. AKC

La Marchina, Robert (1928–). Conductor. STM†

Lamarck, Jean Baptiste Pierre Antoine de (1744–1829). French naturalist. STI

Lamb, Charles (1775–1834). English author. BEG

Lambeau, Curly (Earl Louis) (1898–1965). Football executive. DAB; DAFG; JOA; SUD

Lambert, Jack (1952–). Football player. AAS-15; SMJ

Lamonica, Daryle Pat (1941–). Football player. LEZA

LaMotta, Jake (1921–). Boxer. BELB

Lamoureux, Charles (1834–1899). French conductor. YOM

Lamson, David (fl. 1775). American Revolutionary patriot. WIBA

Land, Edwin Herbert (1909–). Inventor. FE; MAPA; PAB

Landau, Siegfried (1921–). Conductor, born Germany. STM†

Lander, Richard Lemon (1804–1834). English explorer. ROL†

Landis, Kenesaw Mountain (1866–1944). Baseball commissioner. ALB

Landon, Alfred Mossman (1887–1987). Governor. GO; WHD†

Landowska, Wanda (1877–1959). Polish harpsichordist. FOG

Landry, Greg (Gregory Paul) (1946–). Football player. GUCA; ST

Landry, Tom (Thomas Wade) (1924–). Football coach. AAS-12; HAGA

Landsteiner, Karl (1868–1943). Pathologist, born Austria. CHE†; COLA†; FE; LET; RIF; STE

Landy, Dick. Automobile racer. OLB

Lane, Anna Maria. American Revolutionary patriot. CLC†

Lane, Dick (1928–). Football player. ANA

Lane, Harriet (1830–1903). Niece of President Buchanan. BLG†; CHA; KL; MAA†; PRB; ROH; ROHA; STJ

Lane, Louis (1923–). Conductor. STM†

Lane, Lunsford (b. 1803). Abolitionist. DADA

Lane, Lydia (fl. 1863). Pioneer. NAA

Lane, MacArthur (1942–). Football player. LEZB

Lane, Ralph Norman Angell, see Angell, Sir Norman.

Laney, Lucy (1854–1933). Educator. BRB; BUDA†

Lang, Andrew (1844–1912). Scottish author. BEG

Langdon, Harry (1884–1944). Actor. ED-1

Langdon, John (1741–1819). American Revolutionary statesman. BUIB†; FEAA; SEC

Lange, Arthur (1889–1956). Conductor. STM†

Lange, Christian Louis (1869–1938). Norwegian pacifist, statesman. MEC†; WIC

Lange, Dorothea (1895–1965). Photographer. STLA; SUAA

Lange, Hans (1884–1960). Conductor, born Turkey. STM†

Langer, Jim (1948–). Football player. AAS-11

Langer, Susanne Katherine (1895–1985). Philosopher. STLA

Langford, Anna Riggs (1917–). Lawyer. DRA; DU

Langley, Samuel Pierpont (1834–1906). Astronomer, aviation pioneer. CUC; HYA†; SOB

Langmuir, Irving (1881–1957). Chemist. ASA

Langston, Dicey. American Revolutionary patriot. CAGA

Langston, John Mercer (1829–1897). Educator, diplomat. ADA; ADB; BRB

Lanier, Bob (1948–). Basketball player. CL-06; KLC; RUB

Lanier, Sidney (1842–1881). Poet. SIF

Lanier, Willie Edward (1945–). Football player. GUD; SMJ

Lanning, Van Lier (1912–). Conductor. STM†

Lansing, John, Jr. (1754–1829). Jurist, state legislator. FEAA

Lansing, Robert (1864–1928). Statesman. HEEA

Lansing, Sherry (1944–). Motion picture executive. LES-1†

Lao-tse, *see* Lao-tzu.

Lao-tzu (c. 604–531 B.C.). Chinese philosopher. LO

Lapchick, Joseph Bohomiel (1900–1970). Basketball coach. HEH; HID; LEW†

La Pérouse, Jean François de Galaup, comte de (1741–1788). French explorer. KNB†; MOB

Larcom, Lucy (1824–1893). Poet. WABC†

Lardner, Ring (Ringgold Wilmer) (1885–1933). Humorist. BEE

Laredo, Jaime (1941–). Bolivian violinist. EWC

Largent, Steve (1954–). Football player. AAS-18

Larrey, Dominique Jean (1766–1842). French surgeon. MAR

Larrieu, Francie (1952–). Track athlete. HOBAA; JABA; LEYB†

Larry. Runaway. BEOA

Larsen, Don (1929–). Baseball player. BED; GIB; GRA; SHC

La Salle, Robert Cavelier, sieur de (1643–1687). French explorer. ABA; GRC; KNA; LED; LYF; MAT; ROL

Laskau, Henry Helmut (1916–). Track athlete, born Germany. SLA†

Lasker, Albert (1880–1952). Advertising executive, born Germany. CUC; LETA

Lasker, Emanuel (1868–1941). German chess player. LEQB; RHA

Lasso, Orlando di (1532?–1594). Belgian composer. KAE

Latchom, George. American Revolutionary soldier. DAF-1†

Latham, Lambert. American Revolutionary patriot. DAF-1

Lathrop, Julia Clifford (1858–1932). Social worker. BRBE†; MEB

Lathrop, Rose Hawthorne (Mother Mary Alphonsa) (1851–1926). Philanthropist, nun. MAK; WRA; YOC

Latimer, Lewis Howard (1848–1928). Inventor. GRAB-03; HA; HAL; HODA; KLA; STQ

La Tour, Georges de (1593–1652). French painter. MAH†

Latrobe, Benjamin Henry (1764–1820). Architect, born England. LAF

Latude, Henri Maseres de (1725–1805). French soldier. JAC

Latude, Jean Henry, *see* Latude, Henri Maseres de.

Laubach, Frank (1884–1970). Missionary. COG

Lauda, Niki (Andreas Nikilaus) (1949–). Austrian automobile racer. AAS-9; ABB; OLCC

Laue, Max von (1879–1960). German physicist. FE

Laurel, Stan (Arthur Stanley Jefferson) (1890–1965). Comedian, born England. BUR-1; ED-1; MAOB; PABA

Laurence O'Toole (1128–1180). Saint. DAD-3; REC

Laurencin, Marie (1885–1956). French painter. NE

Laurens, Henry (1724–1792). American Revolutionary patriot. BUIB†

Laurens, John (1754–1782). American Revolutionary officer. MAO; STG

Lavelli, Dante (1923–). Football player. ANB

Laver, Rodney George (1938–). Australian tennis player. AAS-28; ASB-1; ASBA; BELB; FOX; LAHA

Laveran, Charles Louis (1845–1922). French bacteriologist. RIF; SHG

La Vérendrye, Pierre Gaultier de Varennes, sieur de (1685–1749). Canadian explorer. ARF

Lavoisier, Antoine Laurent (1743–1794). French chemist. ASA; CAA; CAB; COL; DOE; MOBA; POD; SHFB; STI

Law, George (1806–1881). Transportation promoter. HOF

Law, Ruth (1887–). Aviator. GEDB†; HIFD

Lawes, Sir John Bennett (1814–1900). English agriculturist. CAB

Lawless, Theodore Kenneth (1892–1971). Dermatologist. ADA; ADB; BRB†; CAF-1; DOF-1

Lawrence (d. 258). Saint. DAD-3; QUA

Lawrence of Arabia, *see* Lawrence, Thomas Edward.

Lawrence of Brindisi (1559–1619). Saint. DAD-3

Lawrence, Andrea Mead (1932–). Skier. HOBA; HOBAA; LEYB

Lawrence, Ernest Orlando (1901–1958). Physicist. ASA; CUC; RID; SIA

Lawrence, Geraldine Anderson. Border Patrol agent. SMBC-3

Lawrence, Jacob (1917–). Painter. ADA; ADB; BEBA; DOF-1; FAH; RIC; RICA

Lawrence, James (1781–1813). Naval officer. ICA; LEAA; LEP; NAC

Lawrence, Mary Wells, *see* Wells, Mary Georgene.

Lawrence, Thomas Edward (1888–1935). British archaeologist, soldier. ARD

Lawrence Justinian (1381–1456). Saint. DAD-3

Lawson, Robert (1892–1957). Author, illustrator. SM

Lawson, Roberta Campbell (1878–1940). Community leader. GRAD

Lay, Benjamin. Abolitionist. STJA

Layden, Elmer (1902?–1973). Football player. DAG; DAGA; DAI; HIE

Layne, Bobby (Robert Lawrence) (1926–1986). Football player. DAFG; DEH; DUD; DUE; SUD

Lazarove, Lydia (1946–). Israeli boat racer, born Bulgaria. SLA†

Lazarus, Emma (1849–1887). Poet. DOD; GRB-1; GUB; LEK; LER; LETA; PEB

Lazzeri, Tony (1904?–). Baseball player. ROB

Leach, Reggie (1950–). Canadian hockey player. AAS-9

Leacock, Stephen Butler (1869–1944). Canadian author. BEE

Leadbelly (Huddie Ledbetter) (1888–1949). Singer. COF-1; HUC; SUH; WAD†

Leah. Biblical character. LER

Leahy, Frank (1908–1973). Football coach. DAFG

Leakey, Louis S. B. (1903–1972). English anthropologist. DU-1

Leand, Andrea (1964–). Tennis player. SLA†

Lear, Edward (1812–1888). English author, illustrator. BEH; SM

Lease, Mary (1853–1933). Politician. WABC†

LeBaron, Eddie (Edward W., Jr.) (1930?–). Football player. DAFG; DAI; FOI; HAE

Le Brun, Charles (1619–1690). French painter. MAH†

Leclair, Jean Marie (1697–1764). French violinist. CHFA

LeClair, Jim. Football player. SMJ

LeClerq, Tanaquil (1929–). French dancer. ATA

Le Corbusier (Charles-Edouard Jeanneret) (1887–1965). French architect, born Switzerland. HIFA

Ledbetter, Huddie, *see* Leadbelly.

Lederberg, Joshua (1925–). Geneticist. GRB-1; LET; RIF

Ledón, Amalia. Mexican diplomat. NEBA

Le-duc-Tho (1941–). Vietnamese government official. MEC†

Ledyard, John (1751–1789). Explorer. BLD; BUB; FOC

Lee, Ann (1736–1784). Religious mystic. AND; BLF; WABC

Lee, Arthur (1740–1792). Diplomat. BUIB†

Lee, Canada (1907–1951). Boxer, actor. ADA; ADB; SCA

Lee, Charles (1731–1782). General. BUIB†; RAD; SOA

Lee, Christopher (1922–). English actor. COE-2

Lee, Francis L. (1734–1797). American Revolutionary patriot. BAEA; BUIB†; COJ†; FEAB

Lee, George (b. 1774). Colonial boy. BAC

Lee, Henry (Light-Horse Harry) (1756–1818). BUIB†; LOA; MAE; SOA

Lee, Jason (1803–1845). Canadian missionary. YOG

Lee, Joseph (1849–1905?). Inventor. GRAB-03

Lee, Judy Ann. Aviator. SMBC-2

Lee, Richard Henry (1732–1794). American Revolutionary patriot. BAEA; BUIB†; COJ; FEAB; MAC

Lee, Robert Edward (1807–1870). General. ASB; CHG; COD; CUC; DEI; DEJ; FIA; FID; HAA; LEP; MAO; MAT; RAE†

Lee, Sammy (1920–). Diver. FOI; PIBA

Lee, Tsung-Dao (1926–). Physicist, born China. BOB

Lee, William. Slave. DAF-1†

Leeghwater, Jan Adriaasz (1575–1650). Dutch engineer. FE

Leeuwenhoek, Anton van (1632–1723). Dutch naturalist. ASA; BEP; CAA; COL; DEB; DOE; FE; MIB; SHFB; SUF; THA

Lefferts, Rebecca (b. 1829?). Colonial girl. BAC

LeFlore, Ron (1948–). Baseball player. AAS-27

Leger. Saint. DAD-3

Léger, Fernand (1881–1955). French painter. WIAA

Le Grand, Pierre. Pirate. WHA†

Lehman, Herbert H. (1878–1963). Governor. GRB-1; LETA

Lehmann, Otto (1908–). German conductor. STM†

Leibniz, Gottfried Wilhelm freiherr von (1646–1716). German mathematician, philosopher. GRAB-3†; SHFB

Leibovitz, Annie (1949–). Photojournalist. BOHD

Leibowitz, Barry (1945–). Israeli basketball player, born United States. SLA†

Leichhardt, Friedrich Wilhelm (1813–1848). German explorer. KNA; ROL†

Leide, Enrico (1897–). Italian conductor. STM†

Leidesdorff, William Alexander (1810–1848). Merchant. ADA; ADB; BUH; GRAB-02; KADB

Leidy, Joseph (1823–1891). Paleontologist. HYB

Leif Ericsson, *see* Ericsson, Leif.

Leining, Regina (b. 1745). Indian captive. HEE

Leinsdorf, Erich (1912–). Conductor, born Austria. BEA; EWD; STM; YOM

Leitzel, Lillian (1882–1931). Aerialist, born Germany. KIB

Le Jeune, Frank F. (1932–). Canadian cellist, conductor. STM†

LeMay, Curtis Emerson (1906–). General. ARC; SWE

Lemkin, Raphael (1900–). Polish lawyer. BAF

Lemm, Wally (1919–). Football coach. LEW

Le Nain, Louis (1593–1648). French painter. MAH†

L'Enfant, Pierre Charles (1754–1825). Engineer, born France. LEO

Lenglen, Suzanne (1899–1938). French tennis player. DAG; DAGA; FR-1; HI; HOBAA; LAHA; SUDA†

Lenin, Nikolai (Vladimir Illich Ulyanov) (1870–1924). Russian communist leader. ARA; ASB-1; CAAA; COJB; DEI; DEJ; DOF; NEBB-1

Lennon, John (1940–1980). English singer. BUIB-1; SC-01

Lenoir, Etienne (1822–1900). French engineer. FE

Lenroot, Katharine F. (1891–). Social worker. CLA

Lenski, Lois (1893–1974). Author, illustrator. SM

Leo I, the Great (390–461). Saint, pope. DAD-2; QUA

Leonard (1677–1751). Saint. WIB

Leonard, Benny (1896–1947). Boxer. DAG; DAGA; SLA

Leonard, Patrick (fl. 1870). Soldier, born Ireland. TA

Leonard, "Sugar" Ray Charles (1946?–). Boxer. LEYB†

Leonardo da Vinci (1452–1519). Italian artist, inventor. CAA; CHC; DEI; DEJ; EVC; FE; JAA; KAA; MAI; SHFB; SIA

Leoncavallo, Ruggiero (1858–1919). Italian composer. KAE

Leone, Lucile Petry (1902–). Nurse. YOB

Leonidas I (d. 480 B.C.). King of Sparta. CAAA; COM; MAJ

Leonov, Alexei A. (1934–). Russian astronaut. THC

Leopold, Aldo (1886–1948). Naturalist. HIBB; MIB†; SQA

Le Prince, Louis Aime Augustin. French inventor. BUE

Lermontov, Mikhail Yurievich (1814–1841). Russian author. POFA†

Lert, Richard. Conductor, born Germany. STM†

Lesseps, Ferdinand de (1805–1894). French engineer. EVB; WOA

Le Sueur, Eustache (1616–1655). French painter. MAH†

Leucippus (5th century B.C.). Greek philosopher. SHFB

Leutze, Emanuel (1816–1868). Painter, born Germany. HEDA

Levenson, Harry (1905–). Conductor. STM†

Levenson, Sam (1911–1980). Humorist. ALC

Leverrier, Urbain Jean Joseph (1811–1877). French astronomer. SUE

Levi, Eliphas (Constant, Alphonse Louis) (1810–1875). French cabalist. ED-5

Levi, Yitzhok (fl. 1789). Ukrainian rabbi. GEF

Lévi-Strauss, Claude (1908–). French anthropologist. HAO

Levin, Aryeh (b. 1885). Israeli rabbi, born Russia. GRB-1

Levin, Sylvan (1903–). Conductor. STM†

Levine, Joseph (1910–). Conductor. STM†

Levine, Maurice (1918–). Conductor. STM†

Levine, Samuel Albert (1891–1966). Cardiologist. LETA

Levinsky, Battling (Barney Lebrowitz) (1891–1949). Boxer. SLA

Levite, Myron (1914–). Conductor, born Russia. STM†

Levitt, William Jaird (1907–). Builder. PAA

Levy, Aaron (1742–1815). Merchant, born the Netherlands. LETA

Levy, Asser (d. 1681?). Pioneer, born the Netherlands. LETA

Levy, Hayman (1721–1789). Fur trader. LETA

Levy, Marv (1928–). Football coach. SLA

Levy, Moses (1757–1826). Jurist. LETA

Levy, Uriah Phillips (1792–1862). Naval officer. ALD; EIA; GEF; GRB-1; LERA; LETA

Lew, Brazillai (b. 1743). American Revolutionary soldier. WIBA

Lewis, Edmonia (1845–1890). Sculptor. ADA; ADB; KADB; ROG

Lewis, Francis (1713–1802). American Revolutionary patriot. BAEA; BUIB†; COJ†; FEAB; MAC

Lewis, Fritz (Fred) (1944–). Basketball player. HIBAA

Lewis, Furry (Walter) (1900–). Singer. SUH

Lewis, Idawally (1814–1910). Lighthouse keeper. CAD; DOD

Lewis, James (1832–1897?). Government official. ADA; ADB

Lewis, James E. (1923–). Sculptor. FAH

Lewis, Jerry (Joseph Levitch) (1926–). Comedian. ALC; BUR-1; ED-1†

Lewis, Jerry Lee (1935–). Singer, pianist. BUIB-01

Lewis, John (1940?–). Civil rights leader. STF

Lewis, John Llewellyn (1880–1969). Labor leader. COH; DABA; FAC; LEHA; SEA

Lewis, Margaret. Pioneer. STJ

Lewis, Mary Edmonia (1846–1890). Sculptor. LOAV

Lewis, Meriwether (1774–1809). Explorer. BLC; BUB; COC; CUC; DOBB; FIA; FOB; FOC; GRC; HEB; HIBC; JEA; LED; MAL; MAO; ROL

Lewis, Pryce (fl. 1861–1864). English spy. FOA

Lewis, Sinclair (1885–1951). Author. BOA; CON; HEF; LEGB

Lewis, Ted "Kid" (1894–1970). English boxer. SLA

Lewis, Tillie (1901–1977). Food packing executive. LES-1

Libby, Willard Frank (1908–1980). Chemist. AAS-33; POC

Libow, Carol. Lawyer. LETD

Lichine, David (1910–). Dancer, choreographer, born Russia. ATA

Lichtenstein, Roy (1923–). Painter. WIAA

Liebenow, Robert C. (1922–). Business executive. PAA

Lieberman, Nancy (1958–). Basketball player. SLA

Liebig, Justus von (1803–1873). German chemist. CAB

Lieu, Winston Hong (1963–). Electrical engineer, born Vietnam. HOD-1

Lifar, Serge (1905–1986). Ballet master of Paris Opera, born Russia. ATA

Light, Allen B. (fl. 1836). Pioneer. SCB; WIBA

Lilienthal, Otto (1848–1896). German aeronautical engineer. BRBA

Lillehei, Clarence Walton (1918–). Surgeon. HEFA; LEG; SIC

Lillie, Beatrice (1898–). English actress, born Canada. MASB

Lilly, Robert Lewis (1939–). Football player. ANA; SMD; ST

Lim, Kim San (1916–). Singapore government official. RODA

Limón, José (1908–1972). Dancer, born Mexico. FOW; WO

Lin Yutang (1895–1976). Author, philologist, born China. KE; LOB

Linacre, Thomas (1460?–1524). English physician. MAR

Lincoln, Abraham (1809–1865). President of U.S. ASB; BAEB; BAG; BAG-1; BEB; BEC; BLA; BOD; BUIA; CAAA; CAG; CAH; CHG; COG; COI; COS; CUC; DAC; DAE; DEI; DEJ; DIA; DUB; DUC; DUCA; EVD; FIA; FOB; FOH; FRBA; HIH; KEA; LEPE; LEQ; LEQA; MAB; MABA; MAT; MIA; OLA; PED; ROH; ROHA; ROK; STH; STJA; SUBB; WHD

Lincoln, Mary Todd (1818–1882). Wife of Abraham Lincoln. BAG; BAG-1; BLG; CHA; KL; MAA; MAU; PRB; ROH; ROHA; WAQ

Lind, Jenny (1820–1887). Swedish singer. BOC; TRC

Lindbergh, Anne Morrow (1906–). Aviator, author. GEDB

Lindbergh, Charles Augustus (1902–1974). Aviator. ASB-1; BRBA; COC†; EVD; FAA; HAA; HAMY; HAQ; LAC; SQA; SUA

Linderman, Bill (1920–1965). Rodeo champion. KAW

Lindgren, Astrid (1907–). Swedish author. SMB

Lindgren, Gerry (1946?–). Track athlete. FOI

Lindo, Moses (d. 1774). Merchant. LETA

Lindsay, John Vliet (1921–). Mayor. WEC

Lindsay, Ted (Robert Blake Theodore) (1925–). Canadian hockey player. FR; LIAB; OBB; ORC; RAAF

Lindsay, Vachel (1879–1931). Poet. BEF; BEH; BRBB; HEF; LEJ; SIF

Lindsey, Mortimer (1888–1959). Bowler. SLA

Lindstrom, Fred (1905–1981). Baseball player. HAF

Link, Edwin Albert (1904–1981). Inventor, aviation executive. BRBC; COR

Linnaeus, Carl (1707–1778). Swedish botanist. BLB; CAB; COLA; FE; MIB; STI

Lionni, Leo (1910–). Author, illustrator, born the Netherlands. SM

Lipkin, Arthur Bennett (1907–). Conductor, born England. STM†

Lipmann, Fritz Albert (1899–1986). Biochemist, born Germany. LET

Lippershey, Hans (1570–1619). Dutch spectacle maker. FE; LAA†

Lippert, Arnold Leroy (1910–). Chemist. PAB

Lippi, Fra Filippo (1406?–1469). Italian painter. CHC

Lippmann, Gabriel (1845–1921). French physicist. LET

Lippmann, Walter (1889–1974). Journalist. FOE

Lipscomb, Gene "Big Daddy" (1931–). Football player. AAS-32

Liquori, Marty (1949–). Track athlete. LEYB†

Lisa, Manuel (1772–1820). Pioneer trader. BUG

Lisboa, Antônio Francisco, see Aleijadinho.

Lister, Joseph, 1st baron Lister of Lyme Regis (1827–1912). English surgeon. ASB-1; BIA; CHD; COL; DOE; FAF; FE; HUD; POD; ROA; SHG; SIC

Liszt, Franz (1811–1886). Hungarian composer, pianist. BRF; BUD; CHF; FIE; KAE; SAA; YOH

Little, Floyd Douglas (1942–). Football player. DUF; LEZB; RUC

Little, Larry (1945–). Football player. GUD; RUA

Little, Malcolm, *see* Malcolm X.

Little Crow (1803?–1863). Sioux Indian leader. HED

Little Stephen, *see* Esteban.

Little Turtle (1752–1812). Miami Indian chief. HED

Litwack, Harry (1907–). Basketball coach, born Austria. SLA

Liut, Mike (1956–). Canadian hockey player. AAS-21

Livingston, Homer J. (1903–1970). Banker. PAA

Livingston, Philip (1716–1778). American Revolutionary patriot. BAEA; BUIB†; COJ†; FEAB; MAC

Livingston, Robert R. (1746–1813). Diplomat. BUE; FEB; HOF; VIA

Livingston, Susan (fl. 1779). American Revolutionary patriot. TRD

Livingston, William (1723–1790). Governor. BUIB†; FEAA; SEC

Livingstone, David (1813–1873). Scottish missionary, explorer. COC; COL; DAF; DOBB; HOB; KNA; LAA-1; MOB; RIB; ROL; STP; WOA

Livingstone, Mary Moffatt (1821–1862). Wife of David Livingstone. RIB

Llewelyn ab Gruffydd (d. 1282). Prince of North Wales. SUK

Lloyd, Chris Evert, *see* Evert, Chris.

Lloyd, Harold (1893–1971). Comedian. ED-1

Lloyd George, David (1863–1945). English statesman. ASB-1

Lobachevsky, Nikolai (1793–1856). Russian mathematician. MUB

Lobengula (c. 1833–1893). King of the Matabele. MIC

Locke, Alain Leroy (1886–1954). Educator. ADA; ADB

Locke, John (1632–1704). English philosopher. LO; OZA

Lockhart, Frank (1902–1928). Automobile racer. LEX†

Lockwood, Belva Ann (1830–1917). Lawyer, feminist. BOJ; WABC

Lockwood, Normand (1906–). Composer. POF

Lody, Karl Hans (d. 1914). German spy. HAB

Loeb, Sophie Irene (1876–1929). Journalist, reformer, born Russia. LER

Loeffler, Friedrich, *see* Löffler, Friedrich.

Loesser, Frank (1910–1969). Composer. EWA; MOA

Loewe, Frederick (1904–1988). Composer, born Austria. EWA

Loewi, Otto (1873–1961). Pharmacologist, born Germany. LET; RIF

Loewy, Raymond (1893–1986). Industrial designer, born France. BEA

Löffler, Friedrich (1852–1915). German bacteriologist. DEA; RIE†; ROA

Lofting, Hugh (1886–1947). Author, born England. SMB

Logan, Arthur Courtney (1909–1973). Surgeon. HAMA

Logan, Greenbury (fl. 1831). Rancher. KADB

Logan, Karen. Basketball player. HOBAA†

Logan, Myra Adele (1908–1977). Surgeon. HA-1; RAAG†

Logan, Rayford Whittingham (1897–1982). Historian. DOF-1

L'Olonnois (1630?–1671). French pirate. LACB

Lomax, Almena. Journalist. STAA

Lombardi, Ernie (1908–). Baseball player. HIC; RIGA†; SHD†; ZAA

Lombardi, Vincent (1913–1970). Football coach. AAS-12; DAFG; DAI; HEH; JOA

Lombardi, Vincent, II (1942–). Son of Vincent Lombardi. BELB

Lomonosov, Mikhail Vasilievich (1711–1765). Russian author. POFA†

London, Jack (1876–1916). Author. CAC; COB; JAD; LEGB

Long, Crawford Williamson (1815–1878). Surgeon. BLC; LEG†; SHG; SIC†

Long, Denise (1951?–). Basketball player. HOBAA†

Long, Earl Kemp (1895–1960). Governor. LAI

Long, Huey Pierce (1893–1935). Governor. COGA; LAI

Long, James (1793?–1822). Adventurer. VIA

Long, Jane W. (1798–1880). Pioneer. MAO

Long, Jefferson Franklin (1836–1900). Congressman. ADA; ADB

Long, Loretta. Actress. BOHD

Long, Russell B. (1918–). Senator. LAI

Longacre, Jay. Adventure runner. BAEC

Longboat, Tom (1888?–). Track athlete. HIA-01†

Longfellow, Henry Wadsworth (1807–1882). Poet. BEF; BEGA; BEH; BOA; COB; DEI; DEJ; HEF; HIG; LEJ; LEOB; MAL; SIF; SMBA; SUFA

Lonsdale, Gordon Arnold (1924?–1970). Russian spy. SEB

Loock, Christine. Diver. GLA

Lope de Vega, Félix (1562–1635). Spanish playwright. WO

Lopez, Aaron (1731–1782). Merchant. LETA

Lopez, Al (1908–). Baseball player, manager. FRC-01; HIC

Lopez, Antonio (1897–). Migrant worker. WECC

Lopez, Nancy (1957–). Golfer. GUED-1

Lopez, Roderigo (1525–1594). Portuguese physician. MAR

Lopez, Trini (1937–). Singer. NEAA; WH-1

Lorenzen, Fred (1933?–). Automobile racer. LEX; LEXA; OLAB

Lorrain, Claude (Claude Gellée) (1600–1682). French painter. MAH†

Losier, Roger. Climbed Mt. Ararat. WIAA-5

Lothrop, Harriet M., *see* Sidney, Margaret, pseud.

Lott, Ronnie (1959–). Football player. AAS-13

Loues, Spiridon (19th century). Greek track athlete. HIA; HIA-01†; LEYB†

Loughborough, Mary Ann Webster (1836–1887). Diarist. MAV

Louis IX (1214–1270). Saint, king of France. CAAA; DAD-3; NEC; ONA; QUA

Louis XI (1423–1483). King of France. CAAA

Louis XIV (1638–1715). King of France. CAAA; COA; JOBB; NEC; UNB

Louis XVI (1754–1793). King of France. CAAA

Louis of Thuringia, Blessed. DAD-3

Louis, Joe (1914–1981). Boxer. ASB-1; ASBA; BELB; BOF; DAG; DAGA; HEG; HOC; LEF; LYE; PAW; RAAC; RIC; RICA; SICA

Louis, Pierre Charles Alexandre (1787–1872). French physician. POB

Louis Napoleon, emperor of the French, *see* Napoleon III.

Loura, Philip (1967?–). Winner, Young American Medal for Bravery. ANCA

Louvestre, Mary (fl. 1861). Slave. HAB

Love, Bob. Basketball player. HIBA

Love, Nancy. Aviator. HIFD

Love, Nat (1854–1921). Cowboy. BRBD; KADB

Lovejoy, Elijah Parish (1802–1837). Abolitionist. CHFB; COG; LEC; LEPE; MAM; MEB

Lovelace, Lady Ada (Byron) (1815–1852). English mathematician. GRAB-3; WEF

Lovelace, William Randolph, II. Surgeon. ED

Loveless, George (fl. 1830). English trade unionist. LAD

Loveless, James (fl. 1830). English trade unionist. LAD

Lovell, James A., Jr. (1928–). Astronaut. LEPB; THC; WIAA-5

Lovellette, Clyde (1929–). Basketball player. DEHA-1

Loving, Oliver (fl. 1886). Cattleman. BLD†

Low, Archibald Montgomery (1888–1956). English engineer. LAE

Low, Juliette (1860–1927). Founder of Girl Scouts. DOD; PACA

Lowe, Jack (1917–). Pianist. EWC

Lowe, Paul (1936–). Football player. LIBA

Lowe, Robert L. Baseball player. DAH

Lowell, Amy (1874–1925). Poet. BEGA; MUA; SIF

Lowell, James Russell (1819–1891). Poet. BEF; BEGA; SUFA

Lowell, Josephine Shaw (1843–1905). Philanthropist. WABC†

Lubetkin, Tzivia (1914–1978). Israeli resistance leader, born Poland. GRB-1

Lubin, David (1849–1919). Agriculturist, born Poland. LETA

Lubis, Mochtar (1922–). Indonesian journalist. RODA

Lubitsch, Ernst (1892–1947). Motion picture director, born Germany. FLBC

Lucas, George (1944–). Motion picture director. SMBB-3

Lucas, Jerry (1940–). Basketball player. GED; GEDA; HEHA; HID; HOCA; RAAB

Lucas, John (1953–). Basketball player. AAS-6

Lucas, Maurice (1952–). Basketball player. AAS-7

Luce, Clare Boothe (1903–1987). Playwright, ambassadoor. CLA; GRAB-1

Lucera, Francis Anthony, Blessed. DAD-3

Lucian (d. 312). Saint. DAD-2

Lucid, Shannon (1943–). Astronaut. FOJ-1

Lucieto, Charles (fl. 1918). French spy. SEB

Luckman, Sidney (1916–). Football player. ANC; DAFG; DAI; DEH; DUD; DUE; HEI; HOC; RAAD; SLA; SUD

Luckner, Felix von (1881–1966). German naval figure. ARD

Lucretius (Titus Lucretius Carus) (96?–55 B.C.). Roman philosophical poet. LO

Lucy (d. 304). Saint. DAD-1; DAD-3; QUA; WIB

Ludendorff, Erich Friedrich (1865–1937). German general. ARD; RADA

Ludger (742–809). Saint. DAD-2

Ludington, Sybil (1761–1839). American Revolutionary patriot. CAD; CLC

Ludwig II (1845–1886). King of Germany. COKB

Lufberg, Raoul Gervais (d. 1918). Aviator, WW I, born France. HAMY

Lugosi, Bela (1886–1956). Actor, born Hungary. COE-2

Luisetti, Hank (Angelo Enrico) (1916–). Basketball player. HID

Luke. Saint. DAD-3; QUA

Luke, Frank, Jr. (d. 1918). Aviator, WW I. HAMY; REA

Lully, Jean Baptiste (1632–1687). French composer, born Italy. BEM; CHFA; KAE; SAA; YOM†

Lumière, Auguste (1862–1954). French inventor. FE

Lumière, Louis (1864–1948). French inventor. FE

Lumley, Harry (1926–). Canadian hockey player. OBA†

Lupicinus. Saint. DAD-2

Lurtsema, Bob (1942–). Football player. AAS-25

Luther, Martin (1483–1546). German religious reformer. DEI; DEJ; FRC; FRE; HAA

Luthuli, Albert John (1899–1967). South African political leader. ADA; FOJ; LEA; MEC; WIC

LuValle, James E. Chemist. BOG

Luzinski, Greg (1950–). Baseball player. GUED-01

Lydwina. Saint. DAD-2

Lyell, Sir Charles (1797–1875). Scottish geologist. BEP; STI

Lyle, Sparky (Albert) (1944–). Baseball player. AAS

Lyman, Roy (1898–). Football player. DAFG; SUD

Lynch, John Roy (1847–1939). Congressman. ADA; ADB

Lynch, Thomas, Jr. (1749–1779). American Revolutionary patriot. BAEA; BUIB†; COJ†; FEAB; MAC†

Lynn, Frederic Michael (1952–). Baseball player. AAS-3; BUJC

Lynn, Janet (1953–). Skater. HOBAA; JABA; RYX; VAD-6; VADA

Lynn, Judy (1936–). Singer. LA

Lynn, Loretta (1935–). Singer. BUIB-01

Lyon, Mary (1797–1849). Educator. BOC; BOJ; BUDA; COG; CUC; DAD; DOD; FLB; FRC; LEJA; STLA; VAB; WABC†

Lyons, Theodore Amar (1900–1986). Baseball player. ALB; RIGA†

Lysenko, Trofim Denisovich (1898–1976). Russian biologist. BEK†

Lytton, Edward George Earle Lytton Bulwer, 1st baron (1803–1873). English author. COO; ED-5

M

Maazel, Lorin (1930–). Conductor. EWD

Mabley, Jackie "Moms" (1897–1975). Comedienne. MASB

McAdam, John Loudon (1756–1836). Scottish engineer. FAB; FE

McAdoo, Bob (1951–). Basketball player. AAS-5; ARB-1; RUB; SA-2

McAfee, George (1918?–). Football player. DAFG†; SUD

McAlister, Jim (1957–). Soccer player. ADL; GUEC-1

MacArthur, Arthur, Jr. (1845–1912). Army officer. EDA

MacArthur, Douglas (1880–1964). General. ARC; ASB-1; COD†; CUC; DEI; DEJ; FAA; LEP; RAE; SWE-1

McArthur, Edwin (1907–). Conductor. STM†

McArthur, Lachlan (1915–). Sales representative, born Scotland. BAEA-1

Macaulay, Thomas Babington Macaulay, 1st baron (1800–1859). English author. BEG; COP

Macauley, Ed (1927?–). Basketball coach. HID

McAuley, Mary Catherine, Mother (1787–1841). Irish. REC

McAuliffe, Christa (1948–1986). Astronaut, teacher. COE-1

MacBride, Sean (1904–1988). Irish statesman. MEC

Maccabaeus, Judah (d. 160 B.C.). Hebrew military leader. GUA; KAB

McCabe, Edwin P. (b. 1850). Politician. KADB

Maccabees (2d–1st century B.C.). Hebrew patriots. LES; STP

McCandless, Bruce (1911–). Naval officer. BRA

McCann, Terry. Wrestler. FOI

McCarey, Leo (1898–1969). Motion picture director. ED-1†

McCarthy, Eugene Joseph (1916–). Senator. WECA

McCarthy, Joseph R. (1908–1957). Senator. COGA

McCarthy, Joseph Vincent (1887–1978). Baseball manager. ALB; FRC-01; HEH; VACB

McCarthy, Mary (1912–). Author. OCB†

McCarthy, Tommy (1864–1922). Baseball player. ALB

McCartney, Paul (1942–). English singer. BUIB-1; SC-01

McCarver, Tim (James Timothy) (1941–). Baseball player. ZAA

McCauley, Mary (Molly Pitcher) (1754–1832). American Revolutionary patriot. AND; CLC; DOD; LEAA; LEK; LOA†; PA; STJ

McClellan, George Brinton (1826–1885). Army officer, governor. GO; WHD†

McClendon, Dorothy. Microbiologist. CAF-1†

McClennan, Tommy (1908–1958?). Singer. SUH

McClintock, Barbara (1902–). Geneticist. SHFE

McClintock, Sir Francis Leopold (1819–1907). British admiral, explorer. DOC

McClintock, Harry (1882–1957). Singer. LA

McCloskey, Robert (1914–). Author, illustrator. SM

McCloy, John (1876–1945). Sailor. TA

McClurg, James (1746–1823). Physician. FEAA

McCluskey, Robert (1930?–). Automobile racer. OLCB

McCormick, Anne O'Hare (1881–1954). Journalist. CLA; WABC†

McCormick, Cyrus Hall (1809–1884). Inventor. CAB; EBA; FAB; FE; HYA; LAG; LEN; MAL; MAT; RAA; WED

McCormick, Patricia Keller (1930–). Diver. HOBA; HOBAA

McCormick, Ricky. Water skier. LYD

McCovey, Willie Lee (1938–). Baseball player. DA; KLB; RIGA†

McCoy, Al (1894–). Boxer. SLA†

McCoy, Elijah (1843–1929). Inventor. ADB; BRB†; GRAB-03; HA; HAL; KLA; STQ†

McCreary, Conn. Jockey. BUJA

McCullers, Carson (1917–1967). Author. OCB†

McCullough, Geraldine (1922–). Sculptor. ADB

McCutcheon, Floretta Doty (1888–1967). Bowler. HOBA; HOBAA; JAB

McDermott, William (1906–). Chilean conductor. STM†

McDivitt, James A. (1929–). Astronaut. THC

MacDonald, Flora (1721–1790). Scottish heroine. MAJ

MacDonald, George (1824–1905). Scottish author. BEI

MacDonald, Peter (1928–). Navajo Indian leader. GRAC

McDonald, Tommy. Football player. CO; FOI; HAE

Macdonough, Thomas (1783–1825). Naval officer. ICA

McDougald, Gil (1928–). Baseball player. BOE

McDoulet, Annie (Cattle Annie) (fl. 1894). RAB†

MacDowell, Edward Alexander (1861–1908). Composer. BAD; BRF; BUD; KAE; MAF; POF

McDowell, Ephraim (1771–1830). Surgeon. BLC; LEG; RIB; SHG; SIC

McDowell, Mary E. (1854–1936). Social reformer. PACB; WABC†

McDowell, Sam (1943–). Baseball player. BRE; LEZ; PRA; SA-3

McDowell, Sarah Shelby (1785–1840). Wife of Dr. Ephraim McDowell. RIB

McElhenny, Hugh (1928–). Football player. BEKB; DUF; HAD; RAAE

McEnroe, John (1959–). Tennis player. AAS-28; HOCG

McEwen, Tom. Automobile racer. LEX†; OLB; OLDA

McFadden, Bernarr (1868–1955). Journalist, founded *Physical Culture*. COKB

MacGahan, Januarius Aloysius (1844–1878). Journalist. FLBB

McGee, Henry W. (1910–). Government employee. YOI

McGee, William Max. Football player. JOA

McGee, Willie (1958–). Baseball player. HEFB†

McGhee, Brownie (Walter Brown) (1915–). Singer. SUH

McGill, Ralph Emerson (1898–1969). Editor. FLBA

McGillicuddy, Cornelius Alexander, *see* Mack, Connie.

McGinley, Phyllis (1905–1978). Author, poet. ALA

McGinnis, George (1950–). Basketball player. ARB-3; SA-1

McGinnis, Terri (1947–). Veterinarian. GUJ

McGinnity, Joseph Jerome (1871–1929). Baseball player. ALB; DAFD; FRC-1†; HAF; RIGA†

McGraw, John Joseph (1875–1934). Baseball manager. AAS-1; ALB; DAFC; DAFD; DAG; DAGA; DAH; FRC-01; FRC-1†; HAF; HEH; LEY†; ROAA; VACB

McGraw, Tug (Frank) (1944–). Baseball player. AAS

McGuffey, William Holmes (1800–1873). Educator. CAGA; CUC; HEB; LEJA; MAL

Mach, Ernst (1838–1916). Austrian physicist. FE; HAC

McHarg, Ian L. (1921–). Scottish architect. CORA

McHenry, James (1753–1816). American Revolutionary patriot, born Ireland. BUIB†; FEAA

McHugh, Jimmy (1894–). Songwriter. MOA

MacInnis, Nina (1954–). Swimmer. RYX

McIntyre, Ken (1931–). Multi-instrumentalist. UN

McIver, Charles Duncan (1860–1906). Educator. MAO

McJunkin, George (1851–1922). Cowboy. KAW

Mack, Connie (Cornelius Alexander McGillicuddy) (1862–1956). Baseball player, manager. AAS-1; ALB; DAFD; DAG; DAGA; FRC-01; FRC-1†; GIB; HEH; ROAA; SMK; VACB

MacKay, Angus (1840–1931). Canadian agriculturist. DEA

McKay, Claude (1890–1948). Author, poet. ADA; ADB; BRB†

McKay, John (1923?–). Football coach. LEW

McKean, Thomas (1734–1817). American Revolutionary patriot. BAEA; BUIB†; COJ†; FEAB; MAC

McKechnie, Bill (1886–1965). Baseball manager. ALB; FRC-01

McKeever, Andrew Edward (d. 1919). Canadian aviator, WWI. HAG

McKenley, Herb. Jamaican track athlete. HIA

MacKenzie, Sir Alexander (1764–1820). Scottish explorer. COC; KNA; MOB; ROL

McKenzie, John Albert (1937–). Canadian hockey player. OBB

MacKenzie, Sir Morell (1837–1892). English laryngologist. MAR

Mackey, John (1942–). Football player. AAS-19; CO; HOBC

McKim, Charles Follen (1847–1909). Architect. LAF

McKinley, Ida Saxton (1847–1907). Wife of William McKinley. BAG; BAG-1; BLG†; CHB; KL; MAA; MAU; PRB; ROH; ROHA

McKinley, William (1843–1901). President of U.S. BAEB; BAG; BAG-1; BEB; BLA; BUIA; CAG; CAH; COI; COJA; COS; DUC; DUCA; FRBA; HIH; KEA; LEQ; LEQA; MAB; MABA; MIA; PED; ROH; ROHA; ROK†; SUBB; WHD

McKinney, Bones (Horace). Basketball player. HID

McKinney, Nina Mae (1913–1967). Actress. LOAV

McKinney, Sally Zumaris (1915–). Nurse. COFA

McKinney, Steve. Skier. FRCA

McKissick, Floyd B. (1922–). Civil rights leader. FAG; HAI; YOI

McKusick, Victor. Geneticist. LETC

McLain, Dennis (1944–). Baseball player. KADA; LEZ; PRA; SHA

MacLaine, Shirley (1934–). Actress. FOGC; ROJ

McLaren, Bruce Leslie (1937–1970). New Zealand automobile racer. JA; ORD

McLean, Ray "Scooter" (d. 1964). Football coach. JOA†

MacLeish, Archibald (1892–1982). Poet, librarian. BRBB

Macleod, John James R. (1876–1935). Scottish physiologist. BEK†; RIF

McLuhan, (Herbert) Marshall (1911–1980). Canadian educator. KE†

McMahon, Jenna (Mary Virginia Skinner) (1933–). Comedienne, television writer. BUR-1

McMaster, John Bach (1852–1932). Historian. HIB

MacMillan, Donald Baxter (1874–1970). Arctic explorer. ROL†

MacMillan, Sir Ernest (1893–). Canadian conductor. STM†

Macmillan, Harold (1894–1986). British statesman. WEA

McMillin, Bo (1895?–1952). Football player. HIE

McMorris, C. H. Admiral. HAQ†

McNair, Alexander (1775–1826). Governor. SEC

McNair, Ronald (1950–1986). Astronaut, physicist. COE-1

McNally, John V., see Blood, Johnny.

McNamara, Rae Hassell. State director of prisons. SMBC-3

McNamara, Robert Strange (1916–). Statesman. WEC

Macnaughton, Robert. Actor. BRF-1

McNeer, May (1902–). Author. SMAB

Macon, Uncle Dave (David Harrison) (1870–1952). Comedian. HAG-1

McPartland, Marian (1920–). Pianist, born England. UN

McPherson, Aimee Semple (1890–1944). Evangelist. WIAA-2

McRae, Thomas Chipman (1851–1929). Governor. MAO

McWhinnie, Mary Alice (d. 1980). Biologist, polar researcher. LA-1

Macy, Anne Sullivan (1866–1936). Teacher of Helen Keller. FAA†; LEJA; SMC; STJ; STLA

Macy, Rowland Hussey (1822–1877). Merchant. LAH

Macy, William K. (1916–). Conductor. STM†

Madeira, Francis (1917–). Conductor. STM†

Madeline of Canossa, Blessed. DAD-3

Madero, Francisco Indalecio (1873–1913). Mexican statesman. NEBA

Madison, Dolley Payne Todd (1768–1849). Wife of James Madison. BAG; BAG-1; BLG; CHA; DAD; DOD; KL; LEK; MAA; MAU; PRB; ROH; ROHA; SMC; STJ; TRD; WABC; WAQ

Madison, Helene (1914–1970). Swimmer. HOBAA†

Madison, James (1751–1836). President of U.S. BAEB; BAG; BAG-1; BEB; BLA; BUIA; BUIB; CAG; CAH; COI; COS; DUB†; DUC; DUCA; FEAA; FRBA; HEEA; HIH; LEQ; LEQA; LOA; MAB; MABA; MEB; MIA; PED; ROH; ROHA; ROK†; STH; SUBB; WHD

Madsen, Chris (1852–1944). Law officer, born Denmark. SUI

Maffitt, John Newland (1819–1886). Naval officer. CAD

Maganini, Quinto (1897–). Conductor. STM†

Magellan, Ferdinand (1480–1521). Portuguese explorer. COC; COL; DYA; EVD; GRC; HEA; KEH; KNB; LAA-2; MOB; PRC; ROL

Maglie, Sal (1917–). Baseball player. BRC; GRA

Magnes, Judah Leon (1877–1948). Rabbi. GUB

Magnuson, Keith Arien (1947–). Canadian hockey player. FICC; ORB

Magnussen, Karen (1952–). Canadian skater. VADA

Magritte, René (1898–1967). Belgian painter. WIAA

Magsaysay, Ramón (1907–1957). President of Philippines. KEF; RODA

Mahan, Eddie (1892?–). Football player. HIE

Mahler, Fritz (1902–). Conductor, born Austria. STM†

Mahler, Gustav (1860–1911). Austrian composer. KAE; SAA; YOM†

Mahoney, Mary Eliza (1845–1926). Nurse. LOAV

Mahovlich, Frank (1938–). Canadian hockey player. LEYA; OBA; OBB; ORC; RAAF

Maimonides (Moses ben Maimon) (1135–1204). Spanish Hebrew philosopher. GEF; GRB-1; GUA; KAB; KAC; LERA; LES; MAR

Mairs, G. Donald (1911–). Conductor. STM†

Majella, Gerard (1726–1755). Saint. DAD-2; DAD-3

Majors, Alexander. Pioneer. EDA

Makeba, Miriam (1932–). South African singer. CRA

Makeda (fl. 960–930 B.C.). Queen of Sheba. GRAB-04

Malachy (1094?–1148). Saint. DAD-3; REC

Malcolm X (1925–1965). Black leader. ADB; AKB; BRBD; DABB; DADB; FAG; GRAB-01; HAI; HAK; HODA; JO; RICA

Malinowski, Bronislaw Kasper (1884–1942). Polish anthropologist. HAO

Malko, Nicolai. Russian conductor. STM†

Mallory, Molla Bjurstedt, *see* Bjurstedt, Molla.

Mallowan, Max E. L. (1904–1978). English archaeologist. POC

Malone, Art. Automobile racer. OLB

Malone, Moses (1955–). Basketball player. AAS-5; AAS-7; HOCG

Maloney, Arnold H. Pharmacologist. BRB†

Maloney, Jim (James William) (1940–). Baseball player. LEZ

Malpighi, Marcello (1628–1694). Italian anatomist. STE

Maltby, Margaret (1860–1944). Physicist. SC†

Malzone, Frank (1930?–). Baseball player. PIB

Man Ray (1890–1976). Painter, photographer. ASB-1

Manasseh ben Israel, *see* Menasseh ben Israel.

Mance, Jeanne (1606–1673). French missionary nurse. MAK

Manco Capac (11th century). Legendary founder of Incas. LAB†

Mandela, Nelson (1918–). South African lawyer. DU-1; LEA

Mandela, Winnie. South African civil rights worker. CRA†

Mandy, Gyula (1899–1969). Hungarian soccer player. SLA†

Maneely, Joe (1926–1958). Cartoonist. GOB-1

Manet, Édouard (1832–1883). French painter. KAA; MAH

Mangrulkar, Latika. Social worker, born India. FOC-1

Mann, Carol (1941–). Golfer. HOBA†; HOBAA†

Mann, Helen. Mathematician. HOG

Mann, Horace (1796–1859). Educator. COG; CUC; FOH; FRC; LEC; LEJA; LEPC; MAT; RED

Mannerheim, Baron Carl Gustaf Emil von (1867–1951). Finnish soldier, statesman. RADA

Manning, Archie (Elisha Archibald) (1949–). Football player. AAS-20; GUCA

Manning, Madeline (1948–). Track athlete. SUDB

Mannock, Edward (1885–1918). English aviator, WWI. SUA

Manns, August (1825–1907). English conductor, born Germany. YOM

Manolete (1917–1947). Spanish bullfighter. PIB

Manry, Robert Neal (1918–1971). Adventurer. OLC

Mansa Musa I (1312–1337). Ruler of Mali. DOA; GRAB-04; PECA; POA

Mantani, Walter (1918–). Conductor. STM†

Manter, Parnel. Colonial girl. CAD

Mantilla, Ray (1934–). Percussionist. UN

Mantle, Elvin C. Father of Mickey Mantle, baseball player. EDA

Mantle, Mickey Charles (1931–). Baseball player. BOE; BUD-1; BUJA; DA; DAA; DAFB; DAFC; DAFD; DAG; DAGA; DAH; DEHA-1; FRC-1†; GEC; GR; GUC; HIF; HOC; LIC; LOAA; LYD; PAW; RAAA; RIGA†; ROB; SA-3; SH; SHB; SHF; SHH; VAE; VEA

Manusevitch, Victor E. (1906–). Conductor, born Russia. STM†

Manush, Heinie (Henry Emmet) (1901–1971). Baseball player. ALB

Manzolini, Anne Morandi (1716–1774). Italian anatomist. RIB

Manzolini, Giovanni (1712–1760). Italian physician. RIB†

Mao Tse-tung (1893–1976). Chinese communist leader. ARA; ASB-1; CAAA; CAE; COJB; DOF; DU-1; HAK; KE; SPA; WEA

Maqdisi, *see* Muqaddasi-al, Muhammad ibn-Ahmad.

Maquinna (fl. 1800). Nootka Indian chief. ROD

Mara, Timothy James (1887–1959). Football executive. DAB; SUD

Maranville, Rabbit (Walter James) (1892?–1954). Baseball player. ALB; DAFC; DAFD; LIAA

Maravich, Pete (1947–1988). Basketball player. ARB-4; FRD; KADA; KLC; SA-1; SA-2

Marble, Alice (1913–). Tennis player. FR-1; JAB; SUDA†

Marceau, Marcel (1923–). French mime. BELB†

Marchand, Colette (1925–). French dancer. ATA

Marchetti, Gino (1927–). Football player. ANA

Marcian (4th century). Saint. DAD-3

Marciano, Rocky (1923–1969). Boxer. ASBA; HOC; RAAC

Marcol, Chester (1949–). Football player, born Poland. GUCA

Marconi, Guglielmo (1874–1937). Italian inventor. AAS-33; BOB; COL; EBA; EVC; FAB; FE; FRE; PRC; SHFB; SIA; THA

Marcos, Father (fl. 1540). Spanish missionary. BLD†

Marcus, Debra Turner (1941–). Israeli track athlete, born England. SLA†

Marcus, Mickey (David Daniel) (1901–1948). Army officer. LETA; RAE; ROGA

Marcus Aurelius (121–180). Emperor of Rome. CAAA; COA; COK

Mardikian, George M. (1903–). Restaurateur, born Armenia. CAHA

Margaret (255–275). Saint. QUA

Margaret (1353–1412). Queen of Norway, Denmark, and Sweden. BOI

Margaret of Cortona (1247–1297). Saint. DAD-2; MOC

Margaret of Scotland (1045–1093). Saint. DAD-1; DAD-2; ONA; TUA

Margaret Mary. Saint. DAD-1; DAD-3

Maria Theresa (1717–1780). Archduchess of Austria. BOI; CAAA; FAE; LIDA; PA; TRBA

Mariamne (d. 29 B.C.). Wife of Herod the Great. LER

Marichal, Juan (1937–). Dominican baseball player. HAF; KADA; LEZ; PEC; PRA; RIGA†

Marie Antoinette (1755–1793). Queen of France. COA; DAK; DEI; DEJ; FAE; UNA

Marillac, Louise de (1591–1660). French nurse. MAK

Marilyn H. (1959?–). Arthritis sufferer. SIAA

Marín Solá, Ramón (1832–1902). Puerto Rican publisher. TU

Marin, John (1870–1953). Painter. FRA

Marion. Runaway. BEOA

Marion, Francis (1732–1795). American Revolutionary commander. ARE; HIBD; MAE; RAD; SOA

Marion, Marty (1917–). Baseball player. DEG†

Maris, Roger Eugene (1934–1985). Baseball player. ALBA; BELB; BRE; DAA; GUDA; KADA; RAAA; ROB; SHB; SHC

Marisol, see Escobar, Marisol.

Mark the Evangelist. Saint. DAD-2

Mark, Herman Francis (1895–). Chemist, born Austria. BOB

Markevitch, Igor (1912–). Russian conductor. STM†

Markham, Edwin (1852–1940). Poet. MAM

Markova, Alicia (1910–). English dancer, ballet mistress. ATA

Marks, Charlie (1881–1971). Comedian. BUR-1

Marlborough, John Churchill, 1st duke of (1650–1722). English military commander. EDA

Marlowe, Christopher (1564–1593). English playwright. TRC

Marlowe, Julia (1866–1950). Actress. VAA; WABC†

Marquand, John Phillips (1893–1960). Author. BEGA; CON

Marquard, Rube (Richard) (1889–1980). Baseball player. DAFD; DAH; FRC-1†; LOAA

Marquette, Jacques (1637–1675). French missionary, explorer. ABA; ASB; GRC; ROL†

Marquette, Turner (1829–1894). Lawyer. SEC

Marquis, Don (1878–1937). Humorist. ALA; BEE

Marrant, John (fl. 1755). Missionary. HAP; WIBA

Marsh, George Perkins (1801–1882). Ecologist, diplomat. CORA; HIBB; SQA

Marsh, Jesse (d. 1966). Cartoonist. GOB-1

Marsh, John (1799–1856). Physician. COE

Marsh, Othniel Charles (1831–1899). Paleontologist. HYB

Marshall, Ellen Church (1905–1965). Stewardess. GEDB†

Marshall, Frank James (1877–1944). Chess player. LEQB

Marshall, George Catlett (1880–1959). General. ARC; COD†; HEEA; MEC†; RADA; SWE-1; WIC

Marshall, George Preston (1896–). Football executive. DAB; SUD

Marshall, Humphrey (1760–1841). Senator. KEC†

Marshall, Jim (James Lawrence) (1937–). Football player. SMD

Marshall, John (1755–1835). Supreme Court justice. BUIB; CUC; DEI; DEJ; FLC; FOB; LOA; MAL; OLA; STH

Marshall, Louis (1856–1929). Lawyer. LETA

Marshall, Michael Grant (1943–). Baseball player. AAS-2; SMH

Marshall, Paule (1929–). Author. GLO

Marshall, Thomas Riley (1854–1925). Vice president of U.S. FEA; HAOA; HOEA

Marshall, Thurgood (1908–). Supreme Court justice. ADA; ADB; BRG; DOF-1; FAG; FLC; FLD; STF; WEC; YOI

Martha. Saint. DAD-3; QUA

Martí, José Julian (1853–1895). Cuban patriot. BAA; WO; YOFA

Martin of Tours (316?–397). Saint. DAD-1; DAD-3; FAD; ONA; QUA

Martin, Alexander (b. 1740). Governor, senator. FEAA

Martin, Andrea. Comedienne. MASB

Martin, Billy (Alfred M.) (1928–). Baseball player, manager. AAS-1; FRC-01; GIB†; SMG

Martin, Dean (Dino Paul Crocetti) (1917–). Comedian, singer. BUR-1

Martin, Dick (1922–). Comedian. BUR-1

Martin, Harvey (1950–). Football player. AAS-16

Martin, Joseph Plumb (b. 1760?). Soldier. HIBD

Martin, Luther (1748–1792). Lawyer. FEAA

Martin, Mary (1904–). Actress. DI-1†

Martin, Pepper (John Leonard) (1904–). Baseball player. BED; BOE; DEG; GIB; ROC

Martin, Richard Lionel (1951–). Canadian hockey player. LEYA; MANA; ORB; THG

Martin, Slater (1925–). Basketball player. HEHA; HID

Martin, Sylvia Wene (1930–). Bowler. HOBA; SLA

Martinez, Antonio José (1793–1865). Mexican priest. BENA

Martinez, Maria Montoya (b. 1881). Pueblo Indian pottery maker. GRAC; GRAD; LEH; WAB

Marvin, Ursula (1921–). Geologist, polar researcher. LA-1

Marx, Chico (Leonard) (1887–1961). Comedian. BUR-1; COKB; ED-1; MAOB

Marx, Groucho (1890–1977). Comedian. ALC; BUR-1; ED-1; MAOB

Marx, Gummo (Milton) (1892–1977). Comedian. BUR-1; MAOB†

Marx, Harpo (Arthur) (1888–1964). Comedian. BUR-1; ED-1; MAOB

Marx, Karl Heinrich (1818–1883). German political philosopher. COJB; FRE; HAK; LO

Marx, Zeppo (Herbert) (1901–1979). Comedian. BUR-1; ED-1; MAOB†

Mary I (1516–1558). Queen of England and Ireland. BOI; DEC; GRAB†; LIDA; SCC; TRB

Mary II (1662–1694). Queen of England, Scotland, and Ireland. DEC†; GRAB†; LIDA†; SCC; TRB

Mary of the Incarnation, Blessed. DAD-2

Mary the Martyr. Saint. DAD-3

Mary, Queen of Scots (1542–1587). BOI; DEI; DEJ; FAE; UNA

Mary, Virgin. DAD-2; QUA

Mary Alphonsa, Mother, see Lathrop, Rose Hawthorne.

Mary Loyola, Sister. Missionary. ROI

Mary Magdalen. Saint. DAD-3; ONA

Mary Magdelen dei Pazzi. Saint. DAD-2

Mary Magdelen Postel (1756–1846). Saint. MOC

Masaccio (1401–1428). Italian painter. JAA; KAA; MAI

Masaryk, Thomas Garrigue (1850–1937). Czech statesman, philosopher. LAD

Mascagni, Pietro (1863–1945). Italian composer. KAE

Masefield, John (1878–1967). English author, poet. COP

Maskelyne, Jasper Nevil (1839–1917). English magician. KEB

Mason, Biddy (1818–1891). Businesswoman. BUH; GRAB-02; KADB; STQ†

Mason, Charles (1730–1787). English astronomer. HIBC†

Mason, Debby. Basketball player. HOBAA†

Mason, George (1725–1792). American Revolutionary patriot. BUIB†; FEAA; MEB

Mason, Stevens Thomson (1811–1843). Governor. SEC

Massasoit (d. 1661). Wampanoag chief. WAL

Massenet, Jules (1842–1912). French composer. BAE; KAE

Massiah, Frederick McDonald (b. 1884). Civil engineer, born West Indies. CAF-1

Massinissa (c. 238–148 B.C.). African king. GRAB-04

Master of the Name, see Israel ben Eliezer.

Masters, Edgar Lee (1869–1950). Poet. SIF

Masters, Sibella (d. 1720). Inventor. SC†

Masterson, Bat (William Barclay) (1853–1921). Law officer. SUI

Mata Hari (Gertrud Margarete Zelle) (1876–1917). Dutch dancer, spy. HAB; KN; SUG

Matesky, Ralph (1913–). Conductor. STM†

Mather, Cotton (1663–1728). Clergyman. BUIB†

Mather, Increase (1639–1723). Clergyman. BUIB†

Mathew, Theobald (1790–1856). Irish priest. REC

Mathews, Edwin Lee (1931–). Baseball player. DA; DAA; DAFD; LEY†; RIGA†; SHB

Mathewson, Christy (1880–1925). Baseball player. ALB; BRC; DAFC; DAFD; DAG; DAGA; DAH; EPA; FRC-1†; GIB; GUC; HAF; MUB-1; MUC; NEA; RIGA†; SHA; WAG

Mathias, Bob (Robert Bruce) (1930–). Track athlete. BOHA; DAFB; DAG; DAGA; DAJ; DEF; FIB; GED; GEDA; HEG; HIA; HOBB; HOC; HOCG; LEF; LEYB; OCA; SICA

Matilda (895–968). Saint. DAD-2; QUA

Matilda, Queen of England, see Maud.

Matisse, Henri (1869–1954). French painter. KAA; MAH; WIAA

Matlack, Jonathan T. (1950?–). Baseball player. KLBB

Matney, William C., Jr. Television newscaster. STAA

Matson, Ollie (1930–). Football player. HAD; RAAE

Matson, Randy (1945–). Track athlete. DAFB; DAJ; HOC

Mattathias (d. 166 B.C.). Hebrew patriot. GEF; GUA

Mattern, David (1890–). Conductor. STM†

Matthew. Saint, apostle. DAD-3

Matthews, Saul (fl. 1776). American Revolutionary patriot. DAF-1†; STQ†; WIBA†

Matthews, Vincent Edward (1947–). Track athlete, wood sculptor. BOHA

Matthias. Saint, apostle. DAD-2; QUA

Mattingly, Don (1961–). Baseball player. HEFB†

Matzeliger, Jan Ernst (1852–1889). Inventor. ADA; ADB; BRB†; BRG; GRAB-03; HA; HAL; KLA; PECA; ROG; STQ†

Mauchly, John W. (1907–1980). Meteorologist, computer pioneer. GRAB-3

Maud (1102–1167). Queen of England. BRBF; TRB

Mauermayer, Gisela (1914?–). German discus thrower. BELB

Mauldin, Bill (William Henry) (1921–). Cartoonist. DEDC

Maury, Matthew Fontaine (1806–1873). Naval officer, oceanographer. COLA; COR; MAL; STI

Mawson, Sir Douglas (1882–1958). Australian explorer, born England. ROL

Maxim, Hiram Percy (1869–1936). Inventor. MAP†

Maxim, Sir Hiram Stevens (1840–1916). English inventor, born U.S. MAP

Maxim, Hudson (1853–1927). Inventor. MAP

Maxwell, James Clerk (1831–1879). Scottish physicist. CAA; DUA; FE; SHFB; SIA

Maxwell, Otis G. (1900–). Conductor. STM†

May, Elaine (1932–). Actress, comedienne, motion picture director. BUR-1; MASB

May, Emmett M. Labor organizer. BOG

Mayberry, John Claiborn (1950–). Baseball player. KLCA

Mayer, Erskine (1891–1957). Baseball player. RI; SLA

Mayer, Maria Goeppert, see Goeppert-Mayer, Maria.

Mayer, Sheldon. Cartoonist. GOB-1

Maymi, Carmen Rosa (1938–). Government official. NEBB; WH-2

Maynard, Don (1937–). Football player. CO; DEHA; LIBA; LIBB

Maynard, Harold Bright (1902–). Industrial engineer. YOD

Maynard, Valerie (1937–). Sculptor. FAI

Mayo, Charles Horace (1865–1939). Surgeon. BOD; CHE; COKA; CUC

Mayo, William James (1861–1939). Surgeon. BOD; CHE; COKA; CUC

Mayo, William Worrall (1819–1911). Surgeon, born England. BOD; CHE; HEB; LEAB; LEB

Mays, Benjamin E. (1895–1984). Educator. ADB; DOF-1

Mays, Carl (1893–1971). Baseball player. DAFD

Mays, Rex (1913?–1949). Automobile racer. LEX

Mays, Willie Howard (1931–). Baseball player. ASBA; BOE; BOF; BRG; BUD-1; BUJ; DA; DAA; DAFB; DAFD; DAGA; DAH; DEE; DEHA-1; FRC-1†; FRD; GEC; GIB; GR; GUC; GUE; HAF; HOC; KADA; LEV; MUB-1; MUC; PRA; RAAA; RIC; RICA; RIGA†; ROC; SA-3; SH; SHB; SHF; SHH; SID; VEA

Mazer, Henry (1919–). Conductor. STM†

Mazeroski, Bill (William Stanley) (1936–). Baseball player. BED; GIB; PRA

Mazursky, Paul (1930–). Motion picture director. SMBB-3

Mazzei, Philip (1730–1816). Italian physician. MAS

Mboya, Thomas Joseph (1930–1969). Kenyan minister of justice. ADA; KE; POA

Mead, Elwood (1858–1936). Engineer. LEGA

Mead, Margaret (1901–1978). Anthropologist. BOHG; CLA; COLA; DU-1; EMB; GIB-1†; HAO; KE†; KOA; NAB; PACA; STLA

Mead, Sylvia Earle (1935–). Aquanaut, oceanographer. GL; HA-1; HAKA

Mead, William Rutherford (1846–1928). Architect. LAF

Meany, George (1894–1980). Labor leader. DABA; DU-1; LEHA; SEA

Meara, Anne (1933–). Actress, comedienne. BUR-1; MASB

Mears, Rick. Automobile racer. OLDD

Mears, Roger. Automobile racer. OLDD

Mechnikov, Ilya Ilich, see Metchnikoff, Élie.

Mecom, Jane Franklin (1712–1794). Sister of Benjamin Franklin. WABC†

Medawar, Peter Brian (1915–1987). British zoologist. CHE†; RIF

Medin, Oskar (1847–1927). Swedish pediatrician. CHE†

Medina, José Toribio (1852–1930). Chilean scholar. WOB

Medwick, Ducky (Joe) (1911–). Baseball player. DEG; LIC; RIGA†

Meek, Joseph L. (1810–1875). Pioneer trapper. BUG; FOC; SEC

Meeker, Ezra (1830–1928). Pioneer. HEB

Meggers, Betty J. (1921–). Anthropologist. PAC

Meggyesy, Dave (1941–). Football player. LOAA

Mehta, Zubin (1936–). Indian conductor. EWD

Meiffret, Jose (1911–). French bicyclist. ST-1

Meiji, see Mutsuhito.

Meineke, Donald Edward. Basketball player. HOCA

Meir (2d century). Palestinian rabbi. GUA

Meir, Golda (1898–1978). Israeli prime minister. GI; GRB-1; KE†; KOA; LIDA; ROGA

Meir ben Baruch of Rothenburg (1220–1293). German rabbi. GEF; GUA; KAC

Meisl, Hugo (1881–1937). Czech soccer administrator. SLA†

Meitner, Lise (1878–1968). Swedish physicist, born Austria. HA-1; RID†; SC†; YOF

Melamed, Avraham (1944–). Israeli swimmer, born Palestine. SLA†

Melania (383–439). Saint. DAD-3

Meléndez, Cóncha (1904–). Puerto Rican poet, educator. NEBB

Melendrez, Antonio (fl. 1860). Mexican outlaw. WIAA-1

Mellette, Arthur (1842–1896). Governor. SEC

Melnick, Bob. Fight manager. LEW†

Melnick, Joseph Louis (1914–). Virologist. CHE†

Melnik, Faina (1945–). Russian track athlete. SLA†

Melnik, Yona (1949–). Israeli judo wrestler, born Germany. SLA†

Meloche, Gilles. Canadian hockey player. FICC

Melton, Bill (William Edwin) (1945–). Baseball player. BELA; LEY

Melville, Herman (1819–1891). Author. CAC; CUC; HACB; HEF; STL; SUFA

Meminger, Dean (1948–). Basketball player. HIBAA

Menasseh ben Israel (1604–1657). Dutch rabbi. GUB; KAB; LERA; LES; PEB

Menchik, Vera (1906–1944). Russian chess player. LEQB

Mencken, Henry Louis (1880–1956). Journalist. BEG

Mendana de Neyra, Álvaro de (1541–1595). Spanish explorer. KNB

Mendel, Gregor Johann (1822–1884). Austrian geneticist. ASA; BEK; BEP; CAA; CAB; COL; FE; HAC; SIA; STI; WEF

Mendele Mocher Sefarim (Shalom Abramovich) (1835–1917). Russian author. GRB-1

Mendeleev, Dmitri I. (1834–1907). Russian chemist. CAA; COLA; FE; MOBA; SHFB

Mendelsohn, Eric (1887–1953). English architect, born Germany. FOF; LEDA

Mendelssohn, Felix (1809–1847). German composer. BEN; BRF; BUD; DEI; DEJ; FIE; GOA; KAE; SAA; YOK; YOM†

Mendelssohn, Moses (1729–1786). German philosopher. GUB; KAB; KAC; LEF; LERA; PEB

Mendesia, Gracia (1510–1568). Portuguese philanthropist. LER; LES

Mendoza, Antonio de (1490–1552). Spanish colonial governor. WOB

Mendoza, Daniel (1764–1836). English boxer. SLA

Menelik II (1844–1913). Emperor of Abyssinia. ADA; ADB; GRAB-03

Menes (fl. 3100–3038 B.C.). King of Egypt. GRAB-04

Menken, Adah Isaacs (1835?–1868). Actress. RAB

Mennin, Peter (1923–1983). Composer. POF

Menninger, Karl Augustus (1893–1966). Psychiatrist. CHE

Menninger, William Claire (1899–1966). Psychiatrist. CHE

Menotti, Gian-Carlo (1911–). Composer, born Italy. BEKA; KAE; LIA; MAF; POF

Mentschikoff, Soia (1915–). Lawyer. SMBB; SWI

Menuhin, Yehudi (1916–). Violinist. COKA

Menzies, Sir Robert Gordon (1894–1978). Australian prime minister. WEB

Mercator, Gerardus (1512–1594). German geographer. FE

Mercer, Asa Shinn (1829–1917). Pioneer. JOB

Mercer, John Francis (1759–1821). Governor, congressman. FEAA

Mercury, Freddie (1946–). English singer. BUIB-2

Meredith, Don (1938–). Football player. DEH

Meredith, James E. (1893?–1957). Track athlete. HIA

Meredith, James Howard (1933–). Civil rights leader. DADA†; FLD; STJB

Mergenthaler, Ottmar (1854–1899). Inventor, born Germany. BEA; CUB; FE; HYA†; LAE; LEB; MAL; THA

Merman, Ethel (1909–1984). Singer. DI-1†

Meron, Rami (1957–). Israeli wrestler, born Russia. SLA†

Merrick, John (1859–1919). Insurance executive. ADB; BRB

Merrimon, Clifton. Soldier, WW I. BRB†

Merton, Thomas (Father M. Louis) (1915–1968). Trappist poet, born France. EOB

Mesa, Antonio. Pioneer. SCB

Meskin, Mort (1916–). Cartoonist. GOB-1

Mesmer, Franz Anton (1734–1815). Austrian physician. COEA

Messing, Shep (1949–). Soccer player. ADL; GUEC-1

Metcalf, Betsy (b. 1787). Colonial girl. BAC

Metchnikoff, Élie (1845–1916). Russian bacteriologist. COL; DEB; LET; RIF; ROA; SOB

Metheny, Linda. Gymnast. HOBAA†

Methodius (826–885). Saint. DAD-3

Meyer, Billy (1954?–). Automobile racer. OLDD

Meyer, Deborah (1952–). Swimmer. HOBAA†; LEYB

Meyer, Louis (1904–). Automobile racer. LEVA; LEX†

Meyerhof, Otto Fritz (1884–1951). Physiologist, born Germany. LET; RIF

Meyers, Mary. Skater. HOBAA†

Meyers, Roger (1948–). Busboy. BOHA-1

Miakovsky, Nikolai Yakovlevich (1891–1950). Russian composer. POG

Michael. Archangel. DAD-1; QUA

Michael. Runaway. BEOA

Michael. Saint. MOC

Michael (1950?–). Leukemia victim. SIAA

Michaelis, John Hersey (1912–). General. ARBA

Michalske, August. Football player, coach. SUD

Michaux, André (1746–1802). French botanist. JEA

Michaux, François André (1770–1855). French botanist. JEA

Michelangelo Buonarroti (1475–1564). Italian artist. CHC; DEI; DEJ; JAA; KAA; MAI

Michelson, Albert Abraham (1852–1931). Physicist, born Germany. CAA; FE; GRB-1; LET; LETA; SIA; STI

Mickiewicz, Adam (1798–1855). Polish poet. MANB

Midas. Legendary king of Phrygia. JOBB

Middleton, Arthur (1742–1787). American Revolutionary patriot. BAEA; BUIB†; COJ†; FEAB; MAC

Middleton, Powell (1904–). Conductor. STM†

Midler, Bette (c. 1945–). Singer, actress. MASB

Midler, Mark (1931–). Russian fencer. SLA†

Mies van der Rohe, Ludwig (1886–1969). Architect, born Germany. FOF; HIFA; LEDA

Mifflin, Thomas (1744–1800). American Revolutionary officer, statesman. BUIB†; FEAB; SEC

Mikan, George L. (1924–). Basketball player. ASBA; BEL; DAG; DAGA; HEHA; HID; HOC; LYE; PE; RAAB; SICA

Mikita, Stan (1940–). Hockey player, born Czechoslovakia. GUEC; LEYA; LIAB; OBA; OBB; ORC; RAAF; THD

Milam, Ben (1788–1835). Soldier. KUA

Miles, Kenneth Henry (1918–1966). Automobile racer, born England. OLAB

Milhaud, Darius (1892–1974). French composer. KAE

Millar, Onnie (1918–). Painter, sculptor. FAI

Millay, Edna St. Vincent (1892–1950). Poet. BEGA; FRB; GIBA†; LEJ; LEOB; MUA; OCB; SIF; STLA; WHB

Milledge, John (1721–1781). Colonist. CAF

Miller, Alfred Jacob (1810–1874). Painter. HEDA; HOD

Miller, Don (1902–1979). Football player. DAG; DAGA; DAI; HIE

Miller, Dorie (1919–1943). Naval hero. HODA; HUB; RIC; STQ†

Miller, Dorothy Canning (1904–). Museum curator. GIB-1

Miller, Frank (1912–). Conductor. STM†

Miller, Frank (1957–). Cartoonist. GOB-1

Miller, Hugh Barr. Sailor, WW II. HAQ

Miller, Karl (1922–). Conductor. STM†

Miller, Kathy (1964?–). Track athlete. HAFA

Miller, Marilyn (1898–1936). Actress. PHA

Miller, Russell C. Surf rider. OLD

Miller, Walter (1890–). Jockey. SLA

Millet, Jean François (1814–1875). French painter. CHC

Milley, Levi (fl. 1958). Coal miner. WIAA-5

Millikan, Robert Andrews (1868–1953). Physicist. CUC

Millner, Wayne (1913–). Football player. SUD

Mills, Alvin (1922–). Conductor. STM†

Mills, Billy (1938–). Track athlete. DEF; GRAC; HIA; LEYB; LYC; OCA

Milne, Alan Alexander (1882–1956). English author. BEH; SMB

Milne, John (1850–1913). English mining engineer. COLA

Milsap, Ronnie (1944–). Singer. KRI-1

Milton, John (1608–1674). English poet. COP

Milton, Thomas Willard (1894?–1962). Automobile racer. LEVA; LEX; YAA

Mimoun, Alain (1921–). Algerian track athlete. LEYB†

Mina, Francisco Javier (1789–1817). Mexican revolutionist. ROGB

Miner, Bill (1847–1913). Outlaw. JOBA

Mingus, Charles (1922–1979). Bassist. UN

Mink, Patsy Takemoto (1927–). Congresswoman. BOHF

Minos. Legendary king of Crete. JOBB

Minoso, Minnie (Saturnino Orestes) (1922–). Cuban baseball player. BOE

Minot, Bryant. Conductor. STM†

Minot, George Richards (1885–1950). Physician. RIF

Minton, Greg (1951–). Baseball player. AAS

Minuit, Peter (1580–1638). Dutch colonial official. LEO; VIA

Miranda, Francisco de (1750?–1816). Venezuelan patriot. BAA; LAB; OLA

Miriam. Biblical character. LER

Miron, Charles. Basketball player. BELB

Mission, Captain. French pirate. WHA†

Mistral, Gabriela (1889–1957). Chilean poet, educator. BACA; SHFE†; WO

Mitchell, Arthur (1934–). Dancer, choreographer. AB

Mitchell, Arthur Wergs (1883–1968). Congressman. ADA; ADB

Mitchell, Bobby (1935–). Football player. ANB; DEHA-1

Mitchell, Clarence, Jr. (1911–1984). Civil rights leader. DOF-1

Mitchell, Clarence, III (1939?–). State legislator. DU

Mitchell, Howard (1911–). Conductor. STM

Mitchell, Joan (1926–). Painter. FOGB†

Mitchell, John R., Jr. (1863–1929). Journalist, reformer. GRAB-01

Mitchell, Margaret (1900–1949). Author. CON; OCB

Mitchell, Maria (1818–1889). Astronomer. CAD;

DOD; EMB†; GEE; GIBA; MAV; SC; STJ;
STLA; VAB; WABC; WAE; YOC

Mitchell, Mildred. Bionicist. HOG

Mitchell, Sir Thomas Livingstone (1792–1855).
Scottish explorer. ROL†

Mitchell, William (1879–1936). General. ARD;
LAC

Mithridates VI (c. 131–63 B.C.). Parthian king of
Pontus. JOBB; SUG

Mitre, Bartolomé (1821–1906). President of Argentina. WOB

Mitropoulos, Dimitri (1896–1960). Conductor,
born Greece. EWB; STM; YOM

Mitscher, Marc A. (1887–1947). Admiral. NAC

Mitterand, François (1916–). French president.
DU-1

Mix, Ronald (1938–). Football player. SLA

Mize, Johnny (1913–). Baseball player. DA; DAA;
DEG; RIGA†

Mizell, Vinegar Bend (Wilmer) (1930–). Baseball
player. DEHA-1

Mizerak, Steve. Pocket billiards player. BELB

Mock, Jerrie (Geraldine) (1925–). Aviator. GEDB

Mockerie, Parmenas (1900–). Kenyan teacher.
PEA

Modern Jazz Quartet. WAD†

Modigliani, Amedeo (1884–1920). Italian painter.
KAA

Modjeska, Helena (1840–1909). Actress, born Poland. MANB; PIAA

Modupe (1901–). Guinean prince. OJA

Moe, Jörgen Ingebretsen (1813–1882). Norwegian
folklorist. SMAB

Moeck, Walter. Conductor. STM†

Moessbauer, Rudolf Ludwig, see Mössbauer, Rudolf Ludwig.

Moffatt, Chester B. Conductor. STM†

Mohammed (570–632). Founder of Islam. BEO;
CAAA; DEI; DEJ; FRE; TRC-1

Mohammed I (1387–1421). Sultan of Turkey.
BEO†

Mohammed II (The Conqueror) (1430–1481). Sultan of Turkey. BEO; BLW; CAAA

Mohammed V (1910–1961). King of Morocco.
KEF

Mohler, John Robbins (1875–1952). Pathologist.
DEA

Mohorovicic, Andrija (1857–1936). Czech geologist. HAC

Moisant, Mathilde. Aviator. HIFD†

Moise, Penina (1797–1880). Hebrew religious educator. LER; LETA

Moissan, Henri (1852–1907). French chemist.
LET

Mo-Keen (1849–1934). Indian medicine man.
JOD

Molesworth, Mary Louisa (1839–1921). Scottish
author. BEI

Molière (Jean Baptiste Poquelin) (1622–1673).
French playwright. TRC

Momaday, N. Scott (1934–). Author. GRAC

Mommsen, Theodor (1817–1903). German historian. HIB

Momsen, Charles Bowers (1896–1967). Admiral,
inventor. OLC

Monbouquette, Bill (1936–). Baseball pitcher.
GRA

Mondale, Walter F. (1928–). Vice president of
U.S. FEA; HAOA; HOEA

Monet, Claude (1840–1926). French painter. KAA

Moneta, Ernesto Teodoro (1833–1918). Italian
journalist, pacifist. MEC†; WIC

Monica (332–387). Saint. DAD-1; DAD-2; MOC;
QUA

Monis, Judah (1683–1764). Rabbi, born Italy.
LETA

Monk, Theolonius (1920–1982). Pianist. COF-1;
WAD†

Monroe, Earl (1946?–). Basketball player. HOCA;
PE; SA-2

Monroe, Elizabeth (1768–1830). Wife of James
Monroe. BAG; BAG-1; BLG†; CHA; KL; MAA;
MAU; PRB; ROH; ROHA

Monroe, Harriet (1861–1936). Poet. STLA

Monroe, James (1758–1831). President of U.S.
BAEB; BAG; BAG-1; BEB; BLA; BUIA; CAG;
CAH; COI; COJA; COS; DEI; DEJ; DUB†;
DUC; DUCA; FRBA; HEEA; HIH; LEQ; LEQA;
LOA; MAB; MABA; MIA; PED; ROH; ROHA;
ROK†; STH; SUBB; WHD

Montagu, Lady Mary Wortley (1689–1762). English author. BOH; RIE†

Montaigne, Michel de (1533–1592). French essayist. RAC

Montalban, Ricardo (1920–). Actor, born Mexico.
FOW; NEAA

Montana, Bob (1920–1975). Cartoonist. GOB-1

Montana, Patsy (1914–). Singer. LA

Montefiore, Judith (1784–1862). Wife of Sir Moses Montefiore. LER

Montefiore, Sir Moses (1784–1885). English philanthropist. GRB-1; KAB; KAD; LERA; LES;
PEB

Montessori, Maria (1870–1952). Italian physician,
educator. STP

Monteux, Pierre (1875–1964). Conductor, born
France. EWB; STM; YOM

Monteverdi, Claudio (1567–1643). Italian composer. BEM; FIE; KAE; SAA

Montez, Lola (1818?–1861). British dancer. RAB;
WABC†

Montezuma II (1480?–1520). Aztec emperor.
CAAA; NEC; ROGB; UNB

Montgolfier, Jacques Étienne (1745–1799).
French inventor. BRBA; EVC; FE

Montgolfier, Joseph Michel (1740–1810). French
inventor. BRBA; EVC; FE

Montgomery, Bernard Law, 1st viscount Montgomery of Alamein (1887–1976). British field
marshal. COD†

Montgomery, Richard (1736–1775). General.
BUIB†

Montgomery, Wilbert (1954–). Football player.
AAS-10

Montoya, Joseph Manuel (1915–1978). Senator.
FOW; NEAA

Montrose, James Graham, 5th earl and 1st marquis of (1612–1650). Scottish soldier. MAJ;
SUK

Moody, Anne (1940–). Civil rights worker. AKB;
DADB

Moody, Lady Deborah (1600–1669?). Landowner,
builder. CRB; JOCA; WABC†

Moody, Dwight Lyman (1837–1899). Evangelist.
LEC

Moody, Helen Wills, see Wills, Helen.

Moog, Andy (1960–). Canadian hockey player.
AAS-21

Moon, Keith (1946–1978). English singer. BUIB-2

Moore, Anne Carroll (1871–1961). Librarian. FOG

Moore, Beverly. Lawyer. LETD

Moore, Carman (1936–). Music critic, composer.
AB

Moore, Clement Clarke (1779–1863). Poet. BEF;
BEH

Moore, Douglas Stuart (1893–1969). Composer.
MAF; POF

Moore, Harry Tyson (1905–1951). Civil rights
leader. DOF-1

Moore, Kofoworola Aina (1913–). Nigerian
tribeswoman. PEA

Moore, Lenny (1933–). Football player. BEKB;
HAE; RAAE

Moore, Marianne Craig (1887–1972). Poet.
BELB†; KE†

Moore, Terry (1912–). Baseball player. DEG†

Moran, Gussie (Gertrude Augusta) (1923–). Tennis player. SUDA†

Moran, Polly (1883–1952). Comedienne. MASB

Morcom, Richard "Boo." Pole vaulter. BELB

More, Hannah (1745–1833). English author. NOA

More, Sir Thomas (Saint Thomas More) (1478–
1535). English statesman, author. DAD-3;
MAJ; MOC; PEE

Morel, Jean. Conductor, born France. STM†

Morelos y Pavon, José Mariá (1765–1815). Mexican patriot. BAA; NEBA; ROGB; WOB; YOFA

Moreno, Mariano (1778–1811). Argentine political leader. LAB

Moreno, Rita (1931–). Actress. DI-1†; WO

Morenz, Howie (1902–1937). Canadian hockey
player. FR; OBB; ORC; SUB; WAK

Moresco, Carlo (1905–). Italian conductor. STM†

Morgan, Arthur Ernest (1878–1975). Engineering
educator. YOD

Morgan, Barbara (1900–). Photographer. BOHB

Morgan, Daniel (1736–1802). General. BUIB†;
HIBD; MAE; SOA

Morgan, Garrett A. (1875–1963). Manufacturer.
ADA; ADB; GRAB-03; HA; HAL; KLA; STQ†

Morgan, Sir Henry (1635?–1688). British buccaneer. LACB; PABB; SC-1

Morgan, Isabel. Scientist. CHE†

Morgan, Joe (1943–). Baseball player. AAS-23;
BUJC; RIGA†; SMF

Morgan, John (1735–1789). Physician. BUIB†

Morgan, John Hunt (1825–1864). Cavalry commander. MAD

Morgan, John Pierpont (1837–1913). Financier.
CUC; FAC; WED

Morgan, Norma (1928–). Painter. FAH

Morgan, Thomas Hunt (1866–1945). Zoologist.
BEK; COLA; RIF

Morgenstern, Sam (1907–). Conductor. STM†

Morisey, A. Alexander. Public relations executive.
STAA

Morison, Samuel Eliot (1887–1976). Historian.
HIB†

Morisot, Berthe (1841–1895). French painter. NE

Morita, Akio (1921–). Japanese electronics executive. DU-1

Morland, Samuel (1625–). Inventor, mathematician. GRAB-3†

Morley, Christopher (1890–1957). Author. ALA;
BEF

Morris, Clara (1848–1925). Actress. STJ

Morris, Dorothy (1916?–). Librarian. HOG†

Morris, Ed (fl. 1861). Pioneer. SCB

Morris, Elias C. (1855–1922). Clergyman. BRB†

Morris, Esther McQuigg Slack (1814–1902). Feminist. WABC†

Morris, Gouverneur (1752–1816). Senator.
BUIB†; FEAA

Morris, John. Climbed Mt. Ararat. WIAA-5

Morris, Kathryn Harper. Airport security agent.
SMBC-3

Morris, Lewis (1726–1798). American Revolutionary patriot. BAEA; BUIB†; COJ†; FEAB; MAC

Morris, Mercury (Eugene) (1947–). Football
player. MOCA

Morris, Robert (1734–1806). American Revolutionary patriot. BAEA; BUIB†; COJ†; FEAA;
FEAB; HAN; MAC

Morrison, Jim (1943–1971). Singer. BUIB-2

Morrissey, Gibson (1918–). Conductor. STM†

Morse, Samuel F. B. (1791–1872). Inventor, painter. BUE; COL; EBA; EVC; FE; HYA; LAE; LEL; MAL; SHFB; THA

Morton, Craig (1943–). Football player. LEZA

Morton, Elizabeth, pseud., see Stern, Elizabeth Gertrude.

Morton, "Jelly Roll" (Ferdinand Joseph) (1885–1941). Pianist. COF-1; HUC; WAD†

Morton, John (1724–1777). American Revolutionary patriot. BAEA; BUIB†; COJ†; FEAB

Morton, Levi Parsons (1824–1920). Vice president of U.S. FEA; HAOA; HOEA

Morton, William (1819–1868). Dentist. DOE; HUD; LEG; MAL; POD; PRC; ROA; SHG; SIC

Mosbacher, Emil, Jr. (1922–). Yachtsman. HOC

Mosby, John Singleton (1833–1916). Confederate officer. MAD

Moscheles, Ignaz (1794–1870). Czech composer. CHF

Moscoso, Teodoro (1910–). Puerto Rican diplomat. NEBB

Moser-Proell, Annemarie. Austrian skier. WA-1

Moses. Hebrew prophet. CAAA; DEI; DEJ; FRE; GEF; KAB

Moses the Black (330–405). Saint. ONA

Moses, Anna Mary Robertson (Grandma Moses) (1860–1961). Painter. CUC; FOGB; PA

Moses, Grandma, see Moses, Anna Mary Robertson.

Moses ben Enoch (d. 965). Spanish rabbi. GUA; LERA

Moses ben Maimon, see Maimonides.

Moshesh, see Moshoeshoe.

Moshoeshoe (1790–1870). Chief of the Basothos. GRAB-04; MIC; POA

Moss, Stirling (1929–). English automobile racer. ABB; COKC; JA; YAA

Mössbauer, Rudolf Ludwig (1929–). German physicist. HAC

Mossman, Burton C. (1867–1956). Cattleman. WAA

Mota, Manny (1938–). Dominican baseball player. AAS-25

Mother Theresa (1910–). Indian humanitarian, born Yugoslavia. ASB-1; DU-1; SHFE

Motley, Constance Baker (1921–). Jurist. DU; FLD; GIB-1; STLA; YOI

Motley, John Lothrop (1814–1877). Historian, diplomat. HIB†

Motley, Marion (1920–). Football player. DAFG; SUD

Moton, Robert Russa (1867–1940). Educator. BRB; DOF-1

Mott, John Raleigh (1865–1955). Social worker. MEC†; WIC

Mott, Lucretia Coffin (1793–1880). Feminist, abolitionist. COG; GIBA†; GUBA; LES-2; STJ; STLA; WABC; WAR; YOC

Motta, Richard (1931–). Basketball coach. LEW

Mountain Wolf Woman (1884–1960). Winnebago Indian. MAV

Moussorgsky, Modest Petrovich, see Mussorgsky, Modest Petrovich.

Moyer, Daniel (b. 1787). Wagon maker. BAC

Moyers, William D. (1934–). Newspaper publisher. GRBA

Moylan, Mary Ellen (1926–). Dancer. ATA

Mozart, Wolfgang Amadeus (1756–1791). Austrian composer. BEC; BEN; BOD; BRF; BUD; DEI; DEJ; FIE; FOR; GOA; KAE; SAA; WIA; YOK; YOM†

Mubarak, Mohamed Hosni (1928–). Egyptian president. HAGD

Muccini, Corrado (1899–1959). Italian conductor. STM†

Mueller, Heinie (Clarence Francis) (1899–). Baseball player. LIAA†

Mueller, Paul Hermann, see Müller, Paul Hermann.

Muhammad ibn'Abdullah (ibn Batutah), see ibn-Batuta.

Muir, John (1838–1914). Naturalist, born Scotland. BEA; BLB; CO-1; CORA; CUC; DOCA; HEB; HIBB; MAL; MIB; SQA; WAP

Muldowney, Shirley. Automobile racer. OLDA; ST-2

Mulford, Ralph (1885–). Automobile racer. LEX†

Mullaney, Joe. Basketball coach. LEW†

Mullen, Patrick (b. 1838). Sailor. TA

Muller, Hermann Joseph (1890–1967). Geneticist. BEK; LET; RIF

Müller, Paul Hermann (1899–1965). Swiss chemist. AAS-31†; RIF

Muller-Schwarze, Christine. Psychologist, polar researcher, born Germany. LA-1

Mulligan, John. Automobile racer. LEX

Mulzac, Hugh Nathaniel (1886–1971). Sea captain, born West Indies. HUB; ROG; STF

Munch, Charles (1891–1968). French conductor. EWD; STM; YOM

Munch, Edward (1863–1944). Norwegian painter. WIAA

Munoz, Michael French (1937–). Surf rider. OLD

Muñoz Marín, Luis (1898–1980). Ex-governor of Puerto Rico. NEBB; STC; TU; WO

Muñoz Rivera, Luis (1859–1916). Puerto Rican political leader. NEBB; STC; TU

Munson, Thurman Lee (1947–1979). Baseball

player. BELA; BUJC; GUDA; GUED-01;
GUEE; HOCM

Muqaddasi-al, Muhammad ibn-Ahmad (c. 950).
Moslem geographer. ROL†

Murad I (1319–1389). Sultan of Turkey. BEO

Murad II (1403?–1451). Sultan of Turkey. BEO

Murcer, Bobby (1945–). Baseball player. GUG;
KLCA

Murdock, William (1754–1839). Scottish inventor. FE; LAE

Murphy, Audie (1925–1971). Soldier, WW II, and
actor. FAA; REA

Murphy, Betty Southard (1929?–). Lawyer. SWI

Murphy, Calvin (1948–). Basketball player. AAS-
23; HIBAA; KLC

Murphy, Carl James (1889–1967). Journalist,
civil rights leader. DOF-1

Murphy, Dale (1956–). Baseball player. HEFB†

Murphy, Isaac (1856–1896). Jockey. HOBC

Murphy, Jeannette Plamondon (1867–1921). Wife
of Dr. John Benjamin Murphy. RIB

Murphy, Jimmy (1894?–1924). Irish automobile
racer. LEX

Murphy, John Benjamin (1857–1916). Surgeon.
RIB

Murphy, John Michael (1926–). Congressman.
RAE

Murphy, Robert Cushman (b. 1887). Naturalist.
MIB†

Murphy, Stanley (1875–1910). Songwriter, born
Ireland. MOA†

Murphy, Thomas R. (1943?–1966). Army officer.
ARBA

Murphy, William Parry (1892–). Physician. RIF

Murray, Anne (1945–). Canadian singer. KRI

Murray, Earl (1926–). Conductor. STM†

Murray, Eddie (1956–). Baseball player. HEFB†

Murray, Harold (1942?–). Winner, Young American Medal for Bravery. ANCA

Murray, John Wilson (b. 1840). Scottish detective. LID

Murray, Judith Sargent (1751–1820). Feminist,
author. WABC†

Murray, Mary Lindley (fl. 1776). American Revolutionary patriot. CLC

Murray, Philip (1886–1952). Labor leader, born
Scotland. BEA; COH; DABA; SEA

Murrell, Christine (1874–1933). Physician.
MASA†

Murrieta, Joaquin (1832?–1853). Mexican outlaw.
JOBA; SUJ; WIAA-1

Murrow, Edward Roscoe (1908–1965). Radio and
television commentator. FAA; FOE; LETB;
SQB

Murtaugh, Danny (1917–1976). Baseball player,
manager. SMG

Musial, Stanley Frank (1920–). Baseball player.
BOE; BUD-1; BUJ; DA; DAA; DAFB; DAFC;
DAFD; DAFG; DAG; DAGA; DAH; DEG;
DEHA-1; FRC-1†; GR; GUC; HOC; MUB-1;
MUC; PIAA; RIGA†; SH; SHB; SHF; SHH;
SICA; VEA

Muskie, Edmund S. (1914–). Senator. PIAA

Mussolini, Benito (1883–1945). Italian chief of
state. ARA; ARAA; ASB-1; CAE; DOF; KIA;
TAC

Mussorgsky, Modest Petrovich (1839–1881). Russian composer. BAE; BUC; FIE†; KAE; POG;
SAA

Muste, Abraham Johannes (1885–1967). Clergyman, pacifist, born the Netherlands. FOJ;
LEZC

Mutsuhito (1852–1912). Emperor of Japan. CAAA

Mydans, Carl (1907–). Photographer. HOE

Myer, Buddy (1904–1974). Baseball player. SLA;
RI

Myers, Isaac (1835–1891). Labor leader. ADB;
GRAB-01

Myers, Joyce Carpenter. Aeronautical engineer.
SMBC-2

Myers, Laurence E. "Lon" (1858–1899). Track athlete. DAJ; SLA

Myers, Myer (1723–1795). Silversmith. LETA

Myerson, Bess (1924–). Municipal official. BOHF;
GRB-1

Myrdal, Alva (1902–1986). Swedish sociologist.
DU-1; SHFE

N

Nabokov, Vladimir (1899–1977). Author, born
Russia. ASB-1

Nabuco, Joaquim (1849–1910). Brazilian diplomat, reformer. WOB

Nachmanides. Spanish philosopher. LERA

Nachtigal, Gustav (1834–1885). German traveler.
ROL†

Nader, Ralph (1934–). Lawyer, reformer. DU-1;
EOA; GRBA

Nagler, Kenneth M. (1920–). Meteorologist. POE

Nagurski, Bronko (1908–). Football player.
ASBA; COFB; COKB; DAB; DAFB; DAFG;
DAG; DAGA; DAI; DUF; HAD; HEI; HIE;
HOC; SUD

Naismith, James A. (1861–1939). Originated
game of basketball. DAG; DAGA

Nalon, Duke. Automobile racer. YAA

Namath, Joe Willie (1943–). Football player.
ASBA; BELB; DAFG; DEHA-1; DUD; DUE;
FRD; GUEB; HAGC; KADA; LEZA; PAW;
RAAD; SHEA; ST

Nance, Jim (1942–). Football player. LEZB; LIBA

Nancy, Tony. Automobile racer. OLB

Nansen, Fridtjof (1861–1930). Norwegian explorer, statesman. COC†; COG; DOC; HEA; KEE; KNB†; MEA; MEC; MOB; ROL; WIC

Nansen, Odd (1901–). Norwegian architect, humanitarian. BAF

Napier, John (1550–1617). Scottish mathematician. SHFB

Napoleon I (Napoleon Bonaparte) (1769–1821). Emperor of the French. BEO; CAAA; CAE; COD; DEI; DEJ; FRE; NEC; UNB

Napoleon III (Louis Napoleon) (1808–1873). Emperor of the French. JAC

Narcissus. Saint. DAD-3

Narváez, Pánfilo de (1480–1528). Spanish soldier. BLD†; KEG

Nascimento, Edson Arantes do, see Pelé.

Nash, Alice Morrison (1879?–1966). Educator. FLB

Nash, Charlie. Irish boxer. BELB

Nash, Ogden (1902–1971). Poet. ALA; BEE

Nasi, Joseph (1510–1579). Portuguese statesman. GUB; KAB; PEB

Nasmyth, James (1808–1890). Scottish engineer. EVB; FE

Nasser, Gamal Abdel (1918–1970). President of United Arab Republic. ARA; KE; KEF; WEA

Nast, Thomas (1840–1902). Cartoonist, born Germany. CUB; DEDC

Nastase, Ilie (1946–). Romanian tennis player. FOX

Nater, Swen (1949?–). Basketball player, born the Netherlands. RUB

National Conference of Christians and Jews. Founded 1928. MEB

Nau, Jean-David, see L'Olonnois.

Naudé, C. F. Beyers (1915–). South African clergyman. LEA

Nava, Julian (1927–). Educator. FOW

Navarro, José Antonio (1795–1870). Army officer. KUA

Navon, Yitzhak (1921–). President of Israel. GRB-1

Navratilova, Martina (1956–). Tennis player, born Czechoslovakia. AAS-29; ASB-1; FR-1

Ndansi Kumalo (b. 1870?). Chief of Mantabele Tribe. PEA

Neals, Otto (1931?–). Sculptor. FAI

Nebuchadnezzar II (d. 562 B.C.). King of Babylon. JOBB

Necker, Oliver (1440?–1484). French barber-surgeon. MAR

Nee, Thomas (1920–). Conductor. STM†

Neel, Alice (1900–1984). Painter. FOGB†

Neel, Boyd (1905–). English conductor. STM†

Nefertari (13th century B.C.). Queen of Egypt. COLB

Nefertiti (fl. 1372–1350 B.C.). Queen of Egypt. COLB; FAE; GRAB-04; JO†; PA

Nehemiah (5th century B.C.). Hebrew leader. GEF

Nehru, Jawaharlal (1889–1964). Prime minister of India. ARAA; ASB-1; KEF; WEA

Neil, Arthur Fowler. English detective. LID

Neilson, Jim (James Anthony) (1940–). Canadian hockey player. LEYA

Nell, William Cooper (1816–1874). Author. CHFB; GRAB-05

Nelson, Bill (William Keith) (1941–). Football player. LEZA

Nelson, Cindy (1955–). Skier. GUED; JABA; WA-1

Nelson, Horatio, viscount (1758–1805). British naval hero. CHG; COD; MAJ; SCBA

Nelson, Thomas (1738–1789). American Revolutionary patriot. BAEA; BUIB†; COJ†; FEAB; MAC

Nelson, Van. Track athlete. LYE

Nelson, Willie (1933–). Singer. BUIB-01; KRI

Neosho (b. 1846). Creek Indian patriot. WAB

Nereus. Saint. DAD-2†

Neri, Philip (1515–1595). Saint. DAD-1; DAD-2; MOC; QUA

Nero (37–68). Emperor of Rome. BLW; COK; DEI; DEJ; JOBB

Neruda, Pablo (1904–1973). Chilean poet, statesman. WO

Nesbit, Edith (1858–1924). English author. BEI

Nestor, Agnes (1880–1948). Labor leader. BI†

Nestorius (d. 451?). Patriarch of Constantinople. SHG

Netanyahu, Yonatan (1946–1976). Israeli army officer. GRB-1

Nettles, Graig (1944–). Baseball player. LEY†

Neumann, John Von, see Von Neumann, John.

Neutra, Richard Joseph (1892–1970). Architect, born Austria. FOF; LAF

Nevelson, Louise (1900–1988). Sculptor, born Russia. BOHB; FOGB; GIB-1

Neverez, Pedro, see Chato, El.

Nevers, Ernie (1903–1976). Football player. DAB; DAFB; DAFG; DAI; HAD; HEI; RAAE; SUD

Nevin, Ethelbert W. (1862–1901). Composer. BAD

Nevins, Allan (1890–1971). Historian. HIB†

Nevski, Alexander, see Alexander Nevski.

Newburger, Nathan (1903–). Conductor. STM†

Newcastle, Margaret Cavendish, duchess of, see Cavendish, Margaret.

Newcomb, Simon (1835–1909). Astronomer, born Nova Scotia. HYB

Newcombe, Donald (1926–). Baseball player. BOE; NEA

Newcomen, Thomas (1663–1729). English inventor, manufacturer. FE

Newell, Homer Edward (1915–). Physicist, mathematician. POE

Newlin, Mike (1949–). Basketball player. AAS-8

Newman, Harry (1909–). Football player. SLA

Newman, John Henry (1801–1890). English theologian. DEI; DEJ

Newsom, Bobo (Louis Norman) (1907–1962). Baseball player. LIAA

Newsome, Effie Lee (b. 1885). Poet. ROE

Newsome, Ozzie (1956–). Football player. AAS-19

Newton, Harold (1906–). Conductor. STM†

Newton, Huey P. (1942–). Black leader. HAI

Newton, Sir Isaac (1642–1727). English mathematician, physicist. ASA; BEP; BIA; BOB; CAA; COL; DEI; DEJ; DOE; FE; FRE; LAA; MAQ; MOCB; MUB; PIA; POD; SHFB; SIA; SIB†; STI; STN; SUE

Newton-John, Olivia (1948–). Australian singer, born England. KRI

Ng Poon Chew (1866–1931). Clergyman, editor, born China. CUC

Nichol, Kathryn (1937–). Pediatrician. BOHE

Nicholas (d. 343). Saint. DAD-3; FAD; ONA; PEE; QUA

Nicholas I (1796–1855). Tsar of Russia. RIA

Nicholas II (1868–1918). Tsar of Russia. RIA

Nichols, Kid (Charles Augustus) (1870–1953). Baseball player. ALB

Nichols, Mary Grove (1810–1884). Reformer. WABC†

Nichols, Mike (Igor Peshowsky) (1931–). Comedian, motion picture and theater producer, director, born Germany. BUR-1

Nichols, Ruth (1901–1960). Aviator. GEDB†; HIFD

Nicklaus, Jack (1940–). Golfer. ASB-1; ASBA; HOC; KADA; LABA

Nicola, William Mozart (The Great Nicola) (1880–1946). Magician. KEB

Nicolle, Charles Jules Henri (1866–1936). French bacteriologist. AAS-31; RIF

Nicollet, Joseph Nicolas (1786–1843). Mathematician, explorer, born France. HIBC†

Niebuhr, Carsten (1733–1815). German explorer. ROL†

Niebuhr, Reinhold (1892–1971). Clergyman. KE†

Niekro, Phil (1939–). Baseball player. AAS-2; BELA

Nielsen, Carl A. (1865–1931). Danish composer. YOL

Niemeyer, Oscar (1907–). Brazilian architect. BACA

Niemi, Allan L. (1918–). Conductor. STM†

Nienhuys, Janna. Dutch nurse. MAK

Niepce, Joseph-Nicephore (1765–1833). French inventor. FE

Nies-Berger, Edouard. Conductor, born France. STM†

Nietzsche, Friedrich Wilhelm (1844–1900). German philosopher. LO

Nightingale, Florence (1820–1910). English nurse. ASB-1; BOC; BOH; COKB; DEI; DEJ; EVD; FAF; FRE; HUE; MAK; MAN; MASA; PA; SC; STP; WRA

Nikisch, Arthur (1855–1922). Hungarian conductor. YOM

Nikolayev, Andrian G. (1929–). Russian astronaut. NEB†; THC

Niland, John Hugh (1944–). Football player. GUF; ST

Nilsson, Birgit (1918–). Swedish singer. SAB

Nilus the Elder (d. 430). Saint. DAD-3

Nimitz, Chester William (1885–1966). Admiral. ARC; ICA; NAC

Nino. Saint. DAD-3

Nino, Pedro Alonso (1468?–1505). Spanish navigator. HODA

Nipkow, Paul (1860–1940). German inventor. FE

Nitschelm, Ade. Hotel owner. PAA

Nitschelm, Terry. Hotel owner. PAA

Nitschke, Ray. Football player. JOA; KABA

Nixon, Gary (1941–). Motorcyclist. OLDB

Nixon, Norm (1955–). Basketball player. AAS-6

Nixon, Richard Milhous (1913–). President of U.S. BAEB; BAG; BAG-1; BEB; BLA; BUIA; CAG; COI; COJA; COS; DUC; DUCA; FEA; FRBA; HAOA; HIH; HOEA; LEQ; LEQA; MABA; ROHA; ROK†; SUBB; WECA; WHD

Nixon, Thelma (Pat) (1912–). Wife of Richard Milhous Nixon. BAG; BAG-1; BLG; CHB; KL; MAU; ROHA; SMBD

Nkrumah, Kwame (1909–1972). Ghanaian president. ADA; JO; KEF; WEA

Noah, Mordecai Manuel (1785–1851). Journalist. LERA; LETA; PEB

Nobel, Alfred Bernhard (1833–1896). Swedish manufacturer, philanthropist. EVA; HAC; LAE; MAP; MEC; RIF

Nobile, Umberto (b. 1885). Italian explorer. GRB; ROL†

Nobis, Tommy (1943–). Football player. ANA; HAGB; KABA

Noble, Edward J. (1882–1958). Manufacturer. LEN

Noble, Gil. Television newscaster. STAA

Noel-Baker, Philip John (1889–1982). English pacifist. MEC†; WIC

Noether, Emmy Amalie (1882–1935). German mathematician. SC†

Nogales, Louis (1943–). College administrator. NEAA

Noguchi, Hideyo (1876–1928). Bacteriologist, born Japan. BEA; SHG†

Noll, Chuck (1932–). Football coach. AAS-12

Noll, Greg (1937–). Surf rider. OLD

Nones, Benjamin (1757–1826). American Revolutionary patriot, born France. GEF; LERA

Nonhelema (fl. 1778). Indian heroine. CLC†

Norbert (d. 1134). Saint. DAD-2

Nordenskjöld, Nils Adolf (1832–1901). Swedish geologist, explorer. COC†; KNB; ROL

Nordling, Klaus (1915–). Cartoonist, born Finland. GOB-1

Norman, Victor (1905–). Norwegian conductor. STM†

Normand, Mabel (1892–1930). Actress. MASB

Norris, George William (1861–1944). Senator. HIBB; KEC; KED; SQA

North, Frederick, 2d earl Guilford and 8th baron North (1732–1792). English statesman. SOA

North, Warren J. Aeronautical engineer. POE

Norton, Eleanor Holmes (1937–). Lawyer. GIB-1; LETD; WA

Norton, Mary (1903–). English author. SMB

Norwood, Virginia. Physicist. HOG

Nosente (b. 1865?). South African tribeswoman. PEA

Notburga (1265–1313). Saint. DAD-3; MOC

Novak, Nina. Polish dancer. ATA

Novara, Sue (1955?–). Bicyclist. HOBAA†

Nowicki, Janet Lynn, see Lynn, Janet.

Nowicki, Matthew (1910–1950). Architect, born Poland. PIAA

Noyes, Alfred (1880–1958). English poet. BEH; COP

Noyes, Frank (1901–). Conductor. STM†

Noyes, John Humphrey (1811–1886). Social reformer. DEDA

Nu (1907–). Burmese statesman. KEF

Nuñez, Tommy (1938–). Basketball referee. WH

Nungesser, Charles (1892–1927). French aviator, WWI. ARD†; SUA

Nunoz, Maria (fl. 1590). Portuguese émigré. LER

Nurmi, Paavo (1897–1973). Finnish track athlete. ASBA; DAFB; DAG; DAGA; DAJ; DEF; FIC; HIA; LEYB; SICA

Nuttall, Thomas (1786–1859). Botanist, ornithologist, born England. JEA

Nutting, Mary Adelaide (1858–1948). Nursing educator, born Canada. YOB

Nuuhiwa, David (1951?–). Surf rider. OLD

Nuvolari, Tazio (1892–1953). Italian automobile racer. COKC; SUA; YAA

Nuxhall, Joe (Joseph Henry) (1928–). Baseball player. BELB

Nyad, Diana (1950–). Swimmer. GLA; GUED-1; HOBAA†

Nye, James Warren (1814–1876). Governor, senator. SEC

Nye, Rich (1944–). Baseball player. BRE

Nyerere, Julius Kambarage (1921–). President of Tanzanian republic. ADA; DU-1; KE; KEF

Nzinga (1582–1663). African queen. GRAB-04; JO; POA

O

Oakley, Annie (1860–1926). Markswoman. DAG; DAGA; KIB; WAE

Oastler, Richard (1789–1861). English reformer. COG

Oatman, Lorenzo (1837–1900?). Pioneer. BUI

Oatman, Mary Ann (1842?–1853?). Indian captive. JOD

Oatman, Olive (1838?–1903). Indian captive. JOD

Oberlander, Fred (1911–). Austrian wrestler. SLA†

Oberth, Hermann Julius (1894–). Romanian physicist. NEB; STMA; THC

Obey, Trudel Mimms. Painter. FAI

Obregón, Álvaro (1880–1928). Mexican politician. NEBA†

O'Brien, Eddie (1930–). Baseball and basketball player. FOI

O'Brien, Johnny (1930–). Baseball and basketball player. FOI

O'Brien, Parry (1932–). Track athlete. DAG; DAGA; GED; GEDA

O'Callahan, Joseph T. (1905–). Chaplain. BRA; REA

Ochoa, Severo (1905–). Biochemist, born Spain. RIF

Ochs, Adolph Simon (1858–1935). Journalist. CUC; LETA

O'Connell, Mary Ellen, see Anthony, Sister.

O'Connor, Basil (1892–1972). Lawyer. CHE†

O'Connor, Flannery (1925–1964). Author. OCB†

O'Connor, Sandra Day (1930–). Supreme Court justice. DU-1; SMBB; WHE

O'Crohan, Tomás (1856–1937). Irish scholar. RAC

O'Dea, Pat (1873–1962). Football player, born Australia. DAFG; DAI

Odo of Cluny (d. 942). Saint. DAD-3

Odoms, Riley (1950–). Football player. AAS-19

O'Donnell, Emmett, Jr. (1906–1971). General. SWE

Oersted, Hans Christian (1777–1851). Danish physicist. DUA

Oerter, Al (1936–). Track athlete. DAJ; LEYB†; OCA

O'Feeney, Sean, *see* Ford, John.

Offenbach, Jacques (1819–1880). French composer. KAE

Ogden, Dunbar (1903–). Clergyman, civil rights worker. STG

Oglethorpe, James Edward (1696–1785). English colonizer of Georgia. LEO; MAO; VIA

O'Hara, Dee. Nurse. COFA; HOG†

O'Hare, Edward "Butch" (1914–). Naval aviator. REA

O'Higgins, Bernardo (1778–1842). Chilean soldier, statesman. BAA; LAB; OLA; STP

Ohm, Georg Simon (1787–1854). German physicist. CAA; DUA; FE

Oistrakh, David (1908–1974). Russian violinist. EWC

O'Keeffe, Georgia (1887–1986). Painter. CLA; FOGB; GIBA; NE

Okker, Tom (1944–). Dutch tennis player. SLA

Old Coyote, Barney (1923–). Educator and government official. GRAC

Oldfield, Barney (Berna Eli) (1878–1946). Automobile racer. DAG; DAGA; LEX†; YAA

Olds, Ransom E. (1864–1950). Manufacturer. HOF†

Olds, Robin (1922?–). Aviator. ARBA

Olga (d. 969). Saint. WIB

Oliva, Tony (Pedro) (1940–). Cuban baseball player. PEC; PRA

Oliver, Al (1946–). Baseball player. AAS-3

Oliver, Donna. Psychologist, polar researcher. LA-1

Oliver, Joe (1885–1938). Cornetist. TEA; TEB; WAD†

Oliver, Kermit (1943–). Painter. FAI

Olivet, Georges (1927?–1960). Red Cross delegate. DED

Olivier, Laurence (1907–). English actor. ASB-1

Olmsted, Frederick Law (1822–1903). Architect. HIBB

Olsen, Merlin (1940–). Football player. FRD

Olson, Edith. Chemist. HOG

Olympias (d. 408). Saint. DAD-3

Omlie, Phoebe Fairgrave (1903?–). Aviation executive. GEDB†

Onassis, Jacqueline Lee Bouvier Kennedy (1929–). Wife of John Fitzgerald Kennedy. BAG; BAG-1; BLG; CHB; KL; MAA; MAU; PRB; ROH; ROHA

Oñate, Cristóbal de (fl. 1598). Son of conqueror of New Mexico. NAA

O'Neal, John. Civil rights worker. COF

O'Neal, Regina. Television producer. FOC-1

O'Neal, Ron. Actor. AB

O'Neil, Kitty (1946–). Stuntwoman, automobile racer. AAS-27; HAFA

O'Neill, Eugene Gladstone (1888–1953). Playwright. ASB-1; BOA; DEI; DEJ; SHFA

O'Neill, James (1847–1920). Actor, born Ireland. SHFA

O'Neill, Stephen Francis (1892–1962). Baseball player, manager. HIC

Onesimus (d. 90?). Saint. DAD-2; MOC

Ongais, Danny (1940–). Automobile racer. LEX

Onizuka, Ellison (1946–1986). Astronaut. COE-1

Onoda, Hiroo (1922–). Japanese soldier. WIAA-5

Oppenheimer, Julius Robert (1904–1967). Physicist. ARB; ASB-1; FE; RID

Opper, Frederick Burr (1857–1937). Illustrator, cartoonist. DEDC

Orchard, Sadie (1863?–1943). Frontierswoman. RAB

Orellana, Francisco de (1500–1549). Spanish explorer. MOB; ROL

Orkhan (1288?–1362). Sultan of Turkey. BEO

Orlean, Judah Leib. Polish educator. GEF

Ormandy, Eugene (1899–1985). Conductor, born Hungary. EWD; STM; YOM

Orner, George. Conductor. STM†

O'Rourke, James Henry (1853–1919). Baseball player. ALB

Orozco, José Clemente (1883–1949). Mexican painter. BACA; KE; ROGB; WO

Orr, Bobby (1948–). Canadian hockey player. ASBA; FICA; FR; FRD; GAB; GUEC; KADA; LEYA; LIAB; OBA; OBB; ORB; ORC; RAAF; THE; WAK

Orr, Jimmy (1935–). Football player. ANB

Orr, John Boyd, 1st baron (1880–1971). Scottish agriculturist. KEE; MEC; WIC

Ortega, Gaspar (1935–). Mexican boxer. IZA

Ortiz, Peter J. Spy. KN

Ortiz Mena, Antonio (1908–). Mexican government official. NEBA

Orwell, George (1903–1950). English author. ASB-1

Osanna of Mantua, Blessed. DAD-2

Osborne, Estelle Massey (1903–). Nurse. YOB

Osceola (c. 1800–1838). Seminole Indian leader. DEDB; HEC; HEGA; JO†; LEH; MAEA; MOD; STAB; WAL

Osei Tutu (1636–1712). King of Ashanti. GRAB-04; MIC

Osgood, Samuel (1748–1813). American Revolutionary patriot. BUIB†

Osler, Grace Revere (1854–1928). Wife of Sir William Osler. RIB

Osler, Sir William (1849–1919). Canadian physician. CHD; RIB

Osman I (1259–1326). Founder of Ottoman Empire. BEO†

Osrin, Raymond Harold (1928–). Cartoonist.
  DEDC
Ossietzky, Carl von (1889–1938). German paci-
  fist. AAS-34; MEA; MEC; WIC
Ossoli, Margaret Fuller, *see* Fuller, Margaret.
Ostermeyer, Micheline (1923–). French track ath-
  lete. HOBAA†
Oswald, Lee Harvey (1939–1963). Assassin. RABA
Othman, *see* Osman I.
Otis, Elisha Graves (1811–1861). Inventor. HOF
Otis, James (1725–1783). American Revolution-
  ary patriot. BUIB†; HAN
Otsugu. Mother of Dr. Seishu Hanaoka. RIB†
Ott, Mel (Melvin Thomas) (1909–1958). Baseball
  player, manager. ALB; BOE; DA; DAA;DDAFB;
  DAFC; DAFD; DAH; FRC-1†; GEC; HAF;
  MUC; RIGA†; SH; SHB
Otto I, the Great (912–973). Holy Roman Em-
  peror. CAAA
Otto, Nikolaus August (1832–1891). German in-
  ventor. FAB; FE; THA
Ouimet, Francis (1894–1967). Golfer. DAG;
  DAGA; LABA
Our Gang. Comedians. ED-1†
Outerbridge, Mary Ewing. Tennis player. SUDA†
Outterbridge, John W. (1933–). Painter, sculptor.
  FAI
Overton, Anthony (1865–1946). Banker. ADA;
  ADB; DOF-1; FLD
Ovett, Steve (1955–). English track athlete. AAS-
  26
Owen, Laurence (1944–1961). Skater. HOBA†;
  HOBAA†
Owen, Mickey (Arnold Malcolm) (1917–). Base-
  ball player. BED; HIC
Owen, Robert (1771–1858). Welsh philanthropist.
  DEDA; EVA
Owen, Steve (1898–1964). Football player, coach.
  SUD
Owen, Wilfred (1893–1918). English poet. COP
Owens, Elisabeth. Lawyer. SWI
Owens, Jesse (1913–1980). Track athlete. ASB-1;
  ASBA; BOF; BOHA; BRB†; DAFB; DAG;
  DAGA; DAJ; DEF; HEG; HIA; HOC; HODA;
  LEYB; LYB; OCA; RIC; RICA; SID; VAE
Owens-Adair, Bethenia (1840–1926). Physician.
  ARB; BLC; JOB

P

Paca, William (1740–1799). American Revolutionary patriot. BAEA; BUIB†; COJ†; FEAB; MAC
Pacheco, Luis (1800–1895). Guide and interpreter. HAP

Pacificus of San Severino (1653–1721). Saint.
  DAD-3
Pacini, Renato (1912–). Conductor. STM†
Paddock, Charles (1900–1943). Track athlete.
  DAG; DAGA; DAJ
Paderewski, Ignace Jan (1860–1941). Polish pia-
  nist, statesman. CHF; MANB; PIAA
Páez, José Antonio (1790–1873). Venezuelan presi-
  dent. LAB
Páez Xaramillo, Pedro (1564–1622). Spanish mis-
  sionary. ROL†
Paganini, Nicolò (1782–1840). Italian violinist.
  CHFA; YOH
Page, Alan (1945–). Football player. GUD; SMD;
  ST
Page, Joseph Francis (1917–1980). Baseball
  player. SHE
Page, Willis (1918–). Conductor. STM†
Paige, Mitchell (b. 1918). Marine, WW II. BRA
Paige, Satchel (Leroy) (1906–1982). Baseball
  player. ASBA; BOF; BRC; BUD-1; DAFC;
  DAFD; DAH; FRC-1†; LIAA†; SMK
Paine, Robert Treat (1731–1814). Jurist. BAEA;
  COJ†; FEAB
Paine, Thomas (1737–1809). Political philoso-
  pher. ALCA; ARAB; ARB; BUIB†; COG; CUC;
  DAFA; FIA; FLBA; HAN; HIBD; MAM; VIA†
Pales, Marx J. (1923–). Conductor. STM†
Palés Matos, Luis (1898–1959). Puerto Rican
  poet. NEBB
Palestrina, Giovanni Pierluigi da (1526?–1594).
  Italian composer. BRF; BUD; KAE; YOJ
Palgrave, William Gifford (1826–1888). Jesuit
  missionary. ROL
Pallotta, Maria Assunta, Blessed (1878–1905).
  DAD-3
Palmateer, Mike (1954–). Canadian hockey
  player. AAS-21
Palmer, Alice Freeman (1855–1902). Educator.
  BUDA†; FLB; VAB
Palmer, Arnold (1929–). Golfer. ASBA; BELB;
  HOC; KADA; LABA
Palmer, Bruce (1908–). Insurance executive. PAA
Palmer, Edward (1831–1911). Botanist, born En-
  gland. CO-1
Palmer, Jim (James Alvin) (1945–). Baseball
  player. AAS-2; BUJB; MUB-1; RIGA†
Palmer, Joseph (1788?–1875). Individualist. ARB
Palmer, L. F., Jr. (1923?–). Journalist. STAA
Palmer, Sandra. Golfer. HOBAA†
Pamphilus (d. 310). Saint. DAD-2
Pancoast, Charles Edward (1818–1906). Pioneer.
  COE
Pancras. Saint. DAD-2†
Pandit, Vijaya Lakshmi (1900–). Indian diplomat.
  KE

Pankhurst, Emmeline Goulden (1858–1928). English feminist. BOH

Pantaleon. Saint. DAD-3

Pantillat, Yair (1939–). Israeli track athlete, born Palestine. SLA†

Papp, Joseph (1921–). Theatrical producer, director. EOA

Paracelsus (Theophrastus Bombastus von Hohenheim) (1493–1541). Swiss physician, alchemist. CUA; ED-5; FE; POB; ROA; SHG

Paranov, Moshe (1895–). Conductor. STM†

Paray, Paul (b. 1886). French conductor. STM

Paré, Ambroise (1510?–1590). French surgeon. CHD; HUD; ROA; SHG; SIC

Parent, Bernard Marcel (1945–). Canadian hockey player. LEYA; THF

Park, Brad (Douglas Bradford) (1948–). Canadian hockey player. FICA-1; FICC; LEYA; OBB; ORB; THE

Park, Mungo (1771–1806). Scottish explorer. KNA; MOB; ROL†

Parker, Alton Brooks (1852–1926). Jurist. WHD†

Parker, Angela Claire (1948?–). Journalist. STAA†

Parker, Charlie (1920–1955). Saxophonist. COF-1; TEB; RICA; WAD†

Parker, Cynthia Ann (1827–1864). Indian captive. HEE; JOB; JOD; WAB

Parker, Dave (1951–). Baseball player. AAS-3

Parker, Dorothy (1893–1967). Author. ALA; OCB

Parker, Ely (1828–1905). Iroquois Indian sachem. HED

Parker, Francis Wayland (1837–1902). Educator. FRC†

Parker, Isaac Charles (1838–1896). Frontier figure. SUI

Parker, Jim (1934–). Football player. BELB

Parker, Quanah (1845?–1911). Comanche Indian chief. FRAB; HED; MOD; WAM

Parker, Sarah Jessica. Actress. BRE-1

Parker, Theodore (1810–1860). Clergyman, abolitionist. CHFB; COG

Parkes, Roger. Conductor. STM†

Parkman, Francis (1823–1893). Historian. CAC; HEB; HIB; SUFA

Parks, David (1944–). Soldier. AKB

Parks, David Wayne (1941–). Football player. ANB

Parks, Gordon Alexander Buchanan (1912–). Photographer. ADA; ADB; DOF-1

Parks, Robert J. (1922–). Electrical engineer. COQ

Parks, Rosa Lee (1913–). Civil rights leader. COG-1; DOF-1; STF

Parr, Catherine (1512–1548). Consort of Henry VIII, king of England. MAOA; VAC

Parrado, Nando (1950?–). Uruguayan rugby player. WIAA-5

Parrington, Vernon Louis (1871–1929). Historian. HIB

Parris, Samuel (1653–1720). Clergyman. COGA

Parry, Sir William Edward (1790–1855). English arctic explorer. KNB†; ROL†

Parry, Zale (1933–). Underwater diving actress. HAKA

Parsons, Sir Charles Algernon (1854–1931). English engineer. EVB; FE; SHFB

Parsons, James A. Chemist. BRB†

Parsons, Johnnie (1918–). Automobile racer. OLAA; OLCA

Parsons, Johnny (1945?–). Automobile racer. OLCA

Parsons, Theophilus (1750–1813). Jurist. SEC

Parsons, William, 3d earl of Rosse (1800–1867). English astronomer. LAA

Partch, Harry (1901–1974). Composer. EWAA

Parton, Dolly (1946–). Singer. BUIB-01; KRI-1

Pascal, Blaise (1623–1662). French philosopher, mathematician. GRAB-3; MUB; SOB

Paschal Baylon (1540–1592). Saint. DAD-2; MOC

Pasquala (1809?–1824). Tulare Indian girl. HED

Pasquel, Jorge (1907–1955). Mexican baseball executive. NEBA

Passy, Frédéric (1822–1912). French economist, statesman. MEA; MEC; WIC

Pasternak, Boris Leonidovich (1890–1960). Russian author. LET; POFA

Pasteur, Louis (1822–1895). French chemist. ASA; BEK; BEP; BUF; CAA; CAB; CHD; COL; DEB; DEI; DEJ; DOE; EVD; FAF; FE; FRE; HUD; POD; RIE; ROA; SHG; SUF

Paston, Margery (mid-15th century). English letter writer. NOA

Pastorini, Dan (1941–). Football player. CL-1

Patek, Fred (1944–). Baseball player. AAS-23

Paterson, William (1745–1806). Supreme Court justice. BUIB†; FEAA

Paton, Alan (1903–1988). South African author. BAF; LEA

Patricia (d. 665?). Saint. ONA

Patrick (389?–461). Saint. DAD-1; DAD-2; FAD; HEA; MOC; ONA; QUA; REC; TUA

Patrick, Lester (1883–1960). Canadian hockey player, coach. DAG; DAGA; HEH; PAW

Patrick, Ruth (1907–). Ecologist. EMB

Patterson, Floyd (1935–). Boxer. DADB; DEF; DEHA-1; LEYB; OCA

Patterson, John (fl. 1898). English engineer. WOA

Patterson, Lawrence Patrick. Editor. STAA

Patton, George Smith, Jr. (1885–1945). General. ARC; ARE; RAE; SWE-1

Paul (d. 67? A.D.). Saint. DAD-1; DAD-2; ONA; QUA

Paul I (1754–1801). Tsar of Russia. RIA

Paul VI (1897–1978). Pope. WEB

Paul, the Egyptian Hermit. Saint, hermit. DAD-2

Paul, John R. (1893–). Virologist. CHE†

Paul, Thomas (1773–1831). Clergyman. ADA; ADB

Paula Cerioli, Blessed, see Cerioli, Constanza, Blessed.

Pauling, Linus Carl (1901–). Chemist. AAS-34; MEB; MEC; WIC

Pavarotti, Luciano (1935–). Italian singer. BRBB-1

Pavlov, Ivan Petrovich (1849–1936). Russian physiologist. ASB-1; CAA; FE; RIF; SIA

Pavlova, Anna (1881–1931). Russian dancer. TRC; YOH

Payer, Julius von (1842–1915). Austrian explorer. COC†

Payne, Daniel Alexander (1811–1893). Bishop. ADA; ADB; BRB

Payne-Gaposhkin, Cecelia Helena (1900–1979). Astronomer, born England. GIB-1†

Payton, Walter (1954–). Football player. AAS-10; AAS-35

Paz, Octavio (1914–). Mexican poet, essayist. WO

Peabody, Elizabeth Palmer (1804–1894). Educator. BUDA†; FLB; LEK; WABC†

Peabody, George (1795–1869). Merchant. LEM

Peace Corps. Founded 1961. MEB

Peale, Charles Willson (1741–1827). Painter. BR; LEE; SIE

Pearce, Louise (1885–1959). Physician. FLA

Pearl, Minnie (Sarah Ophelia Colley) (1912–). Comedienne. HAG-1; MASB

Pearson, Albie (1935–). Baseball player. BRD; FOI

Pearson, David (1934–). Automobile racer. LEX; LEXA; OLAB

Pearson, Drew (1951–). Football player. AAS-18

Pearson, Flora (1851–1925). Pioneer. BUI

Pearson, Lester Bowles (1897–1972). Canadian statesman. MEA; MEC; WEC; WIC

Peary, Robert Edwin (1856–1920). Explorer. BAB; COC†; COLA; CUC; DOBB; DOC; EDA; FIA; GRC; HAQ; ICA; KNB†; NAC; ROL†

Peattie, Donald Culross (1898–1964). Botanist. MIB†

Peck, Annie Smith (1850–1935). Mountaineer. PACB

Peden, Irene. Electrical engineer, polar researcher. LA-1

Pedro I (1798–1834). Emperor of Brazil. LAB; YOFA

Pedro II (1825–1891). Emperor of Brazil. BACA; LAB; OLA

Peel, Sir Robert (1788–1850). English statesman. LACA

Peerce, Jan (1904–1984). Singer. GRB-1

Peeters, Pete (1957–). Canadian hockey player. AAS-21

Peg-Leg Annie (1860?–1933). Frontierswoman. RAB

Pelagius. Saint. DAD-2

Pelé (1940–). Brazilian soccer player. AAS-23; ASB-1; ASBA; FOR; GUEC-1

Peled, Paulina Peisachov (1950–). Israeli tennis player, born Lithuania. SLA†

Pelletier, Wilfrid (1896–1982). Canadian conductor. STM†

Pelty, Barney (1880–1939). Baseball player. SLA

Pence, Donna Marie. Narcotics agent. SMBC-3

Penelope (d. 67? A.D.). Saint. WIB

Penn, John (1740–1788). American Revolutionary patriot. BAEA; BUIB†; COJ†; FEAB; MAC

Penn, William (1644–1718). Founder of Pennsylvania. ASB; COG; DEI; DEJ; FOB; FOJ; HAJ; LAD; LEO; LEPF; LEZC; MAM; MAT; MEB; OLA; VIA

Pennel, John (1940–). Track athlete. DAJ

Penney, James Cash (1875–1971). Merchant. LAH; LEN

Pennington, James W. C. (c. 1809–1870). Civil rights leader, clergyman. GRAB-02

Pennington, John. English conductor. STM†

Pennock, Herbert Jefferis (1894–1948). Baseball player. ALB; RIGA†; ROB

Peoples, Woody (1943–). Football player. AAS-9

Pep, Willie (Guiglermo Papaleo) (1922–). Boxer. DEHA-1

Peppler, Mary Jo (1945?–). Bicyclist. HOBAA

Pepys, Elizabeth (1640–1669). Wife of Samuel Pepys. NOA

Peregrine (13th century). Saint. DAD-1

Peretz, Isaac Leib (1852–1915). Polish Yiddish author. GEF

Perez, George. Cartoonist. GOB-1

Perez, Tony (Atanasio Rigal) (1942–). Cuban baseball player. BELA; LEY; WH-3

Perez de Cuéllar, Javier (1920–). Peruvian United Nations official. DU-1

Pérez Esquivel, Adolfo (1931–). Argentine humanitarian. DU-1

Pergolesi, Giovanni Battista (1710–1746). Italian composer. KAE

Pericles (d. 429 B.C.). Athenian statesman. CAAA; COM; HEA; PLA

Perkin, Sir William Henry (1838–1907). English chemist. ASA; FE; SHFB

Perkins, Don. Football player. BEKB

Perkins, Frances (1882–1965). Social worker, cabinet member. BI; BOC; CLA; SMC; WABC; WHE

Perkins, George (1923–). Conductor. STM†

Perkins, Marion (1908–1961). Sculptor. ADA; ADB

Perlea, Jonel (1901–). Conductor, educator, born Romania. STM†

Perón, Eva Duarte (1919–1952). Wife of Juan Domingo Perón. BAGA; LIDA; PA; WOB

Perón, Isabel (Maria Estela) (1931–). Ex-president of Argentina. LIDA

Perón, Juan Domingo (1895–1974). President of Argentina. ARA; BAGA; CAE; CL-01; WOB

Perpetua (d. 202). Saint. DAD-2

Perranoski, Ronald Peter (1937–). Baseball player. SHE

Perreault, Gilbert (1950–). Canadian hockey player. AAS-22; FICC; LEYA; MANA; ORB; THD

Perrine, Henry (1797–1840). Botanist, physician. BLC; JEA

Perry, Aulcie (1950–). Israeli basketball player, born United States. SLA†

Perry, Fred (1909–). English tennis player. FOX

Perry, Gaylord Jackson (1938–). Baseball player. AAS-2; BUJB; PRA; SMH

Perry, Jean. Journalist. STAA

Perry, Joe (Fletcher) (1927–). Football player. HAD; RAAE

Perry, Matthew Calbraith (1794–1858). Naval officer. COD; ICA; MOB

Perry, Oliver Hazard (1785–1819). Naval officer. ICA; LEP; NAC

Perry, William (1962–). Football player. AAS-32

Pershing, John Joseph (1860–1948). General. ARD; ARE; COD; DEI; DEJ; RAE

Persky, Daniel (1887–1962). Hebraist, educator, born Russia. GRB-1

Pestalozzi, Johann Heinrich (1746–1827). Swiss educational reformer. FRC

Pétain, Henri Philippe (1856–1951). French marshall. ARD; RADA

Pete M. (1955–). Handicapped. SIAA

Peter (d. 67? A.D.). Saint, apostle. DAD-1; DAD-2; DAD-3; MAJ; ONA; QUA

Peter I, the Great (1672–1725). Tsar of Russia. CAAA; COA; COKB; HEA; NEC; RIA; UNB

Peter of Tarentaise (1102–1174). Saint. DAD-2

Peter of Verona. Saint. DAD-2

Peter Chrysologus (400–450). Saint. DAD-3

Peter Nolasco (c. 1182–1249?). Saint. DAD-2

Petersham, Maud (1889–1971). Author, illustrator. SMAB

Petersham, Miska (1888–1960). Author, illustrator, born Hungary. SMAB

Peterson, Esther Eggertsen (1906–). Ex-Director of Consumer Affairs. WIAA-02

Peterson, Helen L. (1915–). Indian leader, government official. GRAC

Peterson, Joel (1968?–). Winner, Young American Medal for Bravery. ANCA

Peterson, LaVerne Ray (1903–). Conductor. STM†

Peterson, Preston. Surf rider. OLD

Petigru, James Louis (1789–1863). Lawyer, state legislator. STH

Petit, Roland (1924–). French dancer, choreographer. ATA

Petrie, Geoff (1948–). Basketball player. KLC; SA-1

Petroc (6th century). Saint. MOC

Petrocelli, Rico (America P.) (1943–). Baseball player. LEY

Petry, Ann (1911–). Author. RIC; RICA

Pettit, Robert (1932–). Basketball player. BEL; HEHA; HID; HOBB; PE; RAAB

Petty, Lee (1915–). Automobile racer. LEX†; LEXA; LEYC; OLCA

Petty, Richard (1937?–). Automobile racer. DI-2; LEX; LEXA; OLCA; OLCB; ORD; YAA

Pfohl, James Christian (1912–). Conductor. STM†

Pheidippides (fl. 490 B.C.). Greek runner. HIA-01†

Phelps, Don G. (1929?–). Radio and television commentator. STAA

Philby, Harry St. John Bridger (1885–1960). British explorer. ROL

Philip. Saint, apostle. DAD-2

Philip (King Philip) (1637–1676). Wampanoag Indian chief. DEDB; HED; HEGA; ROD; STAB†; VIA

Philip (1921–). Consort of Elizabeth II, queen of Great Britain. DEC; SQA

Philip II (1527–1598). King of Spain. CAAA

Philip of Thrace. Saint. DAD-3

Philip of Zell. Saint. DAD-2

Philip, John Woodward (1840–1900). Naval officer. FID

Philip Benizi (1223–1285). Saint. DAD-3

Philippine Duchesne, Blessed, see Duchesne, Rose Philippine, Blessed.

Phillips, Bertrand (1938–). Painter, photographer. FAI

Phillips, Claude (1888–). Conductor. STM†

Phillips, David Graham (1867–1911). Author. COGB

Phillips, John (1719–1795). Merchant. BUIB†

Phillips, John (1832?–1883). Pioneer trapper. SUA

Phillips, Lefty (Harold) (1919–1972). Baseball manager. LEW

Phillips, Samuel (1752–1802). Industrialist. BUIB†

Phillips, Vel (1924–). Government official. YOI

Phillips, Wendell (1811–1884). Abolitionist. BEJ; COG

Philo Judaeus (c. 20 B.C.–50 A.D.). Philosopher. GEF; LERA

Philolaus (5th century B.C.). Greek philosopher. SIB†

Phipps, James (b. 1788). First child vaccinated against smallpox. FAF

Phyfe, Duncan (1768–1854). Cabinetmaker, born Scotland. BAC

Piankhi (fl. 741–721 B.C.). King of Ethiopia. ADA; ADB; GRAB-04

Piasecki, Walter (1916–). Conductor. STM†

Piastro, Mishel. Conductor, born Russia. STM†

Picasso, Pablo (1881–1973). Spanish painter. ASB-1; DABB; DEI; DEJ; DU-1; FOR; FRE; KAA; KE†; MAH; WIAA; WO

Piccard, Auguste (1884–1962). Swiss physicist. BAB; COR; OLC; PRC

Piccard, Jacques (1922–). Swiss oceanographer. BAB; COLA; COR; OLC

Piccard, Jeannette R. (1895–1981). First woman Episcopal priest. BLF†; SMBB-1

Pickens, William (1881–1954). Government official. DADA; DADB

Pickering, Timothy (1745–1829). Statesman. BUIB†

Pickering, William H. (1910–). Physicist, born New Zealand. COQ

Pickersgill, Caroline (b. 1800). Colonial girl. BAC; CAD

Pickersgill, Mary (fl. 1814). Flagmaker. CLC

Pickett, Bill (1861–1932). Cowboy. GRAB-02; HODA; KADB; STQ†; WAA

Picon, Molly (1898–). Actress. MASB

Picotte, Susan LaFlesche (1865–1915). Physician. GRAD; RAAG†

Pierce, Clinton A. (1894–). General. ARE

Pierce, Franklin (1804–1869). President of U.S. BAEB; BAG; BAG-1; BEB; BLA; BUIA; CAG; CAH; COI; COS; DUC; DUCA; FRBA; HIH; LEQ; LEQA; MAB; MABA; MIA; PED; ROH; ROHA; ROK†; SUBB; WHD

Pierce, Jane Appleton (1806–1863). Wife of Franklin Pierce. BAG; BAG-1; BLG†; CHA; KL; MAA; MAU; PRB; ROH; ROHA

Pierce, John Robinson (1910–). Radio and television engineer. COQ

Pierce, William Leigh (c. 1740–1789). Businessman. FEAA†

Pierpont, Francis Harrison (1814–1899). Governor. SEC

Pierpont, James (1660–1714). Clergyman. BUIB†

Pierre, Abbé (Henri Groués) (1910–). French priest, resistance worker. BAF

Piersall, Jim (1929–). Baseball player. VAE

Pietri, Dorando. Italian track athlete. LEYB†

Pike, Lipman (1845–1893). Baseball player, manager. SLA

Pike, Zebulon Montgomery (1779–1813). Explorer. BUB; CUC; FOC; HEB; LED; NAA; ROL†

Pillsbury, Harry Nelson (1872–1906). Chess player. LEQB

Pilote, Pierre Paul (1931–). Canadian hockey player. ORC

Pilpel, Harriet Fleischl (1911–). Lawyer. SWI

Pilsudski, Józef (1867–1935). Polish general, statesman. CAAA

Pinchback, Pinckney Benton Stewart (1837–1921). Political leader. ADA; ADB; BRB†; CHFB

Pinchot, Gifford (1865–1946). Forester. CORA; HIBB; SQA

Pinckney, Charles (1757–1824). Statesman. BUIB†; FEAA; SEC

Pinckney, Charles Cotesworth (1746–1825). Lawyer, military leader. BUIB†; FEAA; WHD†

Pinckney, Eliza Lucas (1723–1793). Agronomist. GUBA†; SC†; WABC

Pinckney, Thomas (1750–1828). Statesman. BUIB†

Pincus, Jacob (1838–1918). Jockey. SLA

Pini, Wendy. Cartoonist. GOB-1

Pinkerton, Allan (1819–1884). Detective, born Scotland. FOA; LACA; LID; SUI

Pinkston, Carmonelle. Personnel administrator. HOG†

Pintong, Nilawan (1916–). Thai editor and publisher. RODA

Pious, Minerva (1909–1979). Comedienne, born Russia. MASB

Pippin, Horace (1888–1946). Painter. ADA; ADB; BEBA

Pire, Georges Henri (1910–1969). Belgian clergyman. MEC; WIC

Pirtle, Sue. Rodeo rider. VADB

Piston, Walter (1894–1976). Composer. BAD; MAF; POF

Pitcher, Molly, see McCauley, Mary.

Pitman, Sir Isaac (1813–1897). English educator, inventor. FE

Pitou, Penny. Skier. HOBA

Pitt, William, 1st earl of Chatham (1708–1778). English statesman. OLA; SOA

Pittman, Dorothy Hughes (1938–). Educator. WA

Pitts, Elijah. Football player. JOA†

Pitts, Zasu (1894?–1963). Actress. MASB

Pius V (1504–1572). Saint, pope. DAD-2

Pius X (1835–1914). Saint, pope. DAD-3

Pius XI (1857–1939). Pope. BOD

Pizarro, Francisco (1471?–1541). Spanish conqueror. GAA; KEG; KNA; MOB; ROL†; WIA-1

Pizarro, Gonzalo (1506?–1548). Spanish soldier. ROL†

Place, Etta (fl. 1900). Outlaw. RAB†

Planck, Max Karl (1858–1947). German physicist. CAA; FE; SHFB

Plank, Eddie (1875–1926). Baseball player. ALB; MUB-1; RIGA†

Plante, Jacques (1929–1986). Canadian hockey player. ETB; FRD; LIAB; OBB; ORA; ORC; WAK

Plato (427–347 B.C.). Greek philosopher. DEI; DEJ; FRC; LO; OZA; SIB†

Pleasant, Mary Ellen (Mammy) (1814?–1904). Businesswoman. BUH; LOAV; STQ†; WIAA-2

Plimsoll, Samuel (1824–1898). English reformer. EVA

Pluhar, Ivan. Escapee from Soviet labor camp, born Czechoslovakia. JAC

Plummer, Electa (b. 1842). Wife of Henry Plummer. JOB

Plummer, Henry (d. 1864). Outlaw. JOBA; WIAA-1

Plunkett, Jim (1947–). Football player. AAS-9; CL-1; DEHB; GUD; NEAA; ST; WH-3

Plunkett, Oliver, Blessed (1629–1681). DAD-3; REC

Plunkett, Sherman (1933–). Football player. AAS-32

Plutarch (46?–120). Greek biographer. HIB

Pocahontas (1595?–1617). Indian princess. CAD; DOD; GRAD; HEC; LEH; LEPF; PA; STJ; VIA; WAB; WABC

Podoloff, Maurice (1890–1985). Basketball administrator. SLA

Poe, Edgar Allan (1809–1849). Author, poet. BEF; BEG; BOA; CAC; COKB; HACB; HEF; HIG; LEGB; SIF; STK

Poindexter, Hildrus A. (1901–). Bacteriologist. BRB†

Pointe de Sable, Jean Baptiste (1745–1818). Founder of Chicago, born Haiti. ADA; ADB; BUH; DOB; GRAB-02; HUB; KADB; LEI; LEPD; PECA; ROG; STQ; WIBA

Pointer, Dick (d. 1827). American Revolutionary patriot. WIBA

Poitier, Sidney (1924–). Actor. ADB; BRG; ROF

Polier, Justine Wise (1903–). Jurist. GIB-1

Poling, Clark (d. 1943). Chaplain. FIA

Polis, Greg (1950–). Canadian hockey player. FICC

Polk, James Knox (1795–1849). President of U.S. BAEB; BAG; BAG-1; BEB; BLA; BUIA; CAG; CAH; COI; COS; DUC; DUCA; FRBA; HIH; LEQ; LEQA; MAB; MABA; MAL; MIA; PED; ROH; ROHA; ROK†; SUBB; WHD

Polk, Sarah Childress (1803–1891). Wife of James Knox Polk. BAG; BAG-1; BLG†; CHA; KL; MAA; MAU; PRB; ROH; ROHA

Pollard, Frederick (1894–1986). Football player. DAFB; DAFG; DAI; HOBC

Pollock, Jackson (1912–1956). Painter. FRA; WIAA

Polo, Marco (1254–1324). Italian traveler. COC; COL; DAF; DEI; DEJ; DYA; FRE; GRC; KEH; KNA; MOB; ROL

Polybius (205?–125? B.C.). Greek historian. HIB

Polycarp (2d century). Saint. DAD-2

Pompey. Slave, American Revolutionary patriot. ROG; WIBA†

Pompey (d. 1788). Indian captive and interpreter. HAP

Ponce de León, Juan (1460–1521). Spanish explorer. COKB; KEG; ROL†

Ponselle, Rosa (1897–1981). Singer. STLA

Pont, John (1928?–). Football coach. LEW

Pontiac (1720?–1769). Ottawa Indian chief. DEDB; HEC; HEGA; LEH; ROD; STAB

Poole, Elizabeth (fl. 1652). Manufacturer. WABC†

Poole, Valter (1903–). Conductor. STM†

Poor, Salem. American Revolutionary patriot. DAF-1†; STQ†; WIBA

Popé (d. 1690). Pueblo Indian medicine man. HED; ROD; STAB†

Pope, Alexander (1688–1744). English poet. COP

Popovich, Marina. Russian test pilot. HIFD

Popovich, Pavel Romanovich (1930–). Russian astronaut. NEB†; THC†

Porphyry (d. 420). Saint. DAD-2

Porres, Martin de (1579–1639). Saint. ADA; ADB; DAD-1; DAD-3; PEE

Porter, Cole (1893–1964). Composer. EWA; MOA

Porter, David (1780–1843). Naval officer. ICA

Porter, David Dixon (1813–1891). Admiral. ICA; NAC

Porter, Edwin Stanton (1870–1941). Inventor. FLBC

Porter, Katherine Anne (1890–1980). Author. OCB†

Porter, Kevin (1950–). Basketball player. AAS-6

Porter, Quincy (1897–1966). Composer. POF

Porter, Sylvia (1913–). Columnist. BOHG; GIB-1; LEU

Porter, William Sydney, see Henry, O., pseud.

Post, Dick (1945–). Football player. LEZB

Post, Wiley (1900–1935). Aviator. COC†; HAMY

Poston, Ersa Hines (1921–). State official. YOI

Poston, Ted (1906–). Journalist. STAA

Pothinus. Saint. DAD-2

Potter, Beatrix (1866–1943). English author, illustrator. SC; SM

Potvin, Denis Charles (1953–). Canadian hockey player. FICA-1; GUEC; MANA; OLDE; THE

Pouissant, Renee (1944–). Television newscaster. SMBB-2

Pound, Ezra (1885–1972). Poet. ASB-1

Poussin, Nicolas (1594–1665). French painter. KAA; MAH†

Powderly, Terence Vincent (1849–1924). Labor leader. COH; DABA; LEHA; SEA

Powell, Adam Clayton, Sr. (1865–1953). Clergyman. ADA; ADB; BRB†; RIC

Powell, Adam Clayton, Jr. (1908–1972). Congressman, clergyman. DU†; HAI; YOI

Powell, Bob (d. 1967). Cartoonist. GOB-1

Powell, Boog (John Wesley) (1941–). Baseball player. DEHA-1; KLB

Powell, Bud (Earl) (1924–1966). Pianist. COF-1; WAD†

Powell, Clilian (1894–). Physician, insurance executive. CAF-1

Powell, John Wesley (1834–1902). Geologist. CORA; FOC; HIBC; LYA

Powell, Marvin (1955–). Football player. AAS-11

Powell, Maude (1869–1920). Violinist. SC-02†

Power Giralt, Ramón (1775–1813). Puerto Rican patriot. TU

Powers, Francis Gary (1929–1977). Spy. KN

Powhatan (1550–1618). Indian chief. ROD

Praxedes. Saint. DAD-3

Prefontaine, Steve R. (1951?–1975). Track athlete. LEYB†

Preisand, Sally (1947–). Rabbi. BLF†

Prendergast, Maurice Brazil (1861–1924). Painter. MAG

Prescott, William Hickling (1796–1859). Historian. CAC; HIB†; SUFA

Presley, Elvis (1935–1977). Singer. BUIB-1

Press, Tamara (1937–). Russian shot-putter. HOBAA†

Pressly, Eleanor C. (1918–). Aeronautical engineer. HOG

Preston, Arthur Murray (1914–). Naval officer. BRA

Preves, Milton (1909–). Conductor. STM†

Previtali, Fernando (1907–). Italian conductor. STM†

Price, Florence Beatrice Smith (1888–1933). Composer. LOAV

Price, James (1752–1785). English chemist. CUA

Price, Joseph C. (1854–1893). Clergyman. BRB†

Price, Leontyne (1927–). Singer. ADB; DOF-1; ROF; SAB; SC-02

Price, Vincent (1911–). Actor. COE-2

Pride, Charley (1938–). Singer. BUIB-01; KRI

Priest, Ivy Baker (1905–1975). Federal government official. FOG

Priestley, Joseph (1733–1804). English chemist. CAA; DABB; FE; SHFB; STI

Prince, Lucy Terry (1731–1821). Poet. KADB

Prinstein, Myer (1880–1928). Track athlete. SLA†

Probst, Christoph (1919?–1943). German resistance worker. LAD

Prochazka, Anne (1897–). Nurse, born Czechoslovakia. YOB

Proctor, Barbara Gardner (1932–). Advertising executive. FRBD

Prokofiev, Sergei Sergeevich (1891–1953). Russian composer. BEKA; BUC; KAE; POG; SAA; YOL

Propper, Gary. Surf rider. OLD

Prosser, Gabriel (1775–1800). Insurrectionist. BRB†; EMA; HUB; ROG

Prothro, Tom (James Thompson) (1920?–). Football coach. LEW

Prowse, Juliet (1937–). Dancer, actress. FOGC†

Prudhomme, Don. Automobile racer. OLB; OLDA

Prudom, Benjie Bell Elizabeth. Rodeo clown. VADB

Pruitt, Greg (1951–). Football player. AAS-10; AAS-23

Pruitt, John Henry (1896–1918). Marine. TA

Pryor, Taylor (1931–). Marine biologist, state legislator. BRBC

Przhevalski, Nikolai M. (1839–1888). Russian explorer. ROL†

Ptolemy (2d century). Greek scientist of Alexandria. MOB; MOCB; PIA; SIA; SIB†

Ptolemy I (Ptolemy Soter) (367?–283 b.c.). King of Egypt. NEC

Publick Universal Friend, see Wilkinson, Jemima.

Puccini, Giacomo (1858–1924). Italian composer. BAE; KAE; SAA

Pulaski, Casimir (1748–1779). Polish nobleman in American Revolution. ARE; LOB; MANB; PIAA; SCB-1; SOA

Pulitzer, Joseph (1847–1911). Journalist, born Hungary. ASB; BEA; CUC; LEM; LOB; LYA; SQB

Pullman, George Mortimer (1831–1897). Inventor. HOF

Pupin, Michael Idvorsky (1858–1935). Physicist, inventor, born Yugoslavia. BUF; LEB; LOB

Purcell, Henry (1659–1695). English composer. BAE; BEM; KAE; SAA; YOK

Purvis, Robert (1810–1898). Abolitionist. GRAB-05

Pushkin, Aleksandr Sergeevich (1799–1837). Russian poet. ADA; ADB; JO; POFA

Putnam, Israel (1718–1790). General. BUIB†; FIA; OLA; SOA

Putnam, Rufus (1738–1824). Soldier. BUIB†

Puttemans, Emiel. Belgian track athlete. LEYB†

Pyle, Ernest Taylor (1900–1945). Journalist. FAA; FIA; FLBB; FOE; JAD; LEU; SQB

Pyle, Howard (1853–1911). Author, illustrator. BEI

Pythagoras (6th century B.C.). Greek philosopher, mathematician. CAA; MUB; SHFB; SIB†

Pytheas (4th century B.C.). Greek navigator. DYA; KNB; MOB; ROL†

Q

Qaddafi, Muammar el- (1942–). Libyan military leader. HAGD

Quaco. Spy. DAF-1†

Quarles, Benjamin (1904–). Author, educator. HODA†

Quarsie, Tetteh (fl. 1879). African laborer. JO

Queler, Eve (1936–). Conductor. WA

Quetzalcoatl. Aztec god. BACA; ROGB

Quick, Flora (Tom King). Rustler. RAB†

Quidde, Ludwig (1858–1941). German historian. MEC†; WIC

Quimby, Edith Hinkley (1891–1982). Biophysicist. EMB†; YOF

Quimby, Harriet (1884–1912). Aviator. GEDB†; HIFD

Quincy, Josiah, Jr. (1772–1864). Educator. BOK

Quinlan, Bill. Football player. JOA†

Quinn, Anthony (1916–). Actor, born Mexico. LOAA; NEAA

Quintilian (Marcus Fabius Quintilianus) (35?–95?). Roman rhetorician. FRC

Quinton, Amelia Stone (1833–1926). Reformer. WABC†

Quinton, Stockwell (fl. 1677). Indian captive. WIAA-5

Quisenberry, Dan (1953–). Baseball player. AAS; HEFB

R

Raab, Emil. Conductor. STM†

Raab, Selwyn (1934?–). Journalist. LETB

Rabb, Maurice. Ophthalmologist. CAF-1†

Rabi, Isidor Isaac (1898–1988). Physicist, born Austria. GRB-1; LET

Raboy, Mac (1916–1967). Cartoonist. GOB-1

Rachel. Biblical character. LER

Rachel (fl. 100). Wife of Akiba ben Joseph, Palestinian rabbi. LER

Rachel, stage name, see Félix, Elisa Rachel.

Rachlin, Ezra (1916–). Conductor. STM†

Rachmaninoff, Sergei (1873–1943). Russian composer, pianist. BAE; BEN; KAE; POG; SAA

Rackam, Jack. Pirate. WHA†

Radatz, Richard Raymond (1937–). Baseball player. SHE

Radbourn, Old Hoss (Charles Gardner) (1853–1897). Baseball player. ALB

Radegonda (fl. 540). German princess. MAK†

Radegund. Saint. DAD-3

Rader, Douglas Lee (1944–). Baseball player. BELA; LEY†

Rader, Peta (1952–). GUJ

Radisson, Pierre Esprit (1636?–1710). French explorer, trader. ARF

Radner, Gilda (1946–). Actress. MASB

Raggio, Louise Ballerstedt (1919–). Lawyer. SWI

Rahman, Tunku Abdul (1903–). Malaysian ex-prime minister. KEF

Raiche, Bessica. Aviator. HIFD†

Rainey, Ma (Gertrude Malissa Nix Pridgett) (1886–1939). Singer. JOE; SUH; WAD†

Raisis, Anthony (1915–). Conductor. STM†

Raleigh, Sir Walter (1552–1618). English statesman, explorer. DEI; DEJ; KNA†; ROL

Ralph. Runaway. BEOA

Rama V (1853–1910). King of Siam. CAAA

Ramcharan, Savitri (1923–). Physician, researcher, born Trinidad. RAAG

Rameau, Jean Philippe (1683–1764). French composer. BEM; KAE

Ramey, Estelle (1917–). Endocrinologist, physiologist. BOHE

Ramírez, Armando Socarras (1963?–). Cuban escapee. CAHA

Ramirez, Doria (1952?–). Migrant worker. WECC

Ramirez, Henry M. (1929–). Government official. NEAA

Ramón y Cajal, Santiago (1852–1934). Spanish histologist. RIF

Ramos, Elaine Abraham. Educator. GRAD

Ramsay, Sir William (1852–1916). British chemist. COLA†; SHFB

Rand, Suzanne (1950–). Comedienne. MASB

Randolph, Asa Philip (1889–1979). Labor leader. ADA; ADB; BRG; COH; DABA; DADA; DOF-1; FLD; GRAB-01; HUA; LEHA; RIC; RICA; SEA; STF; WIAA-8; YOI

Randolph, Edmund Jennings (1753–1813). Governor, cabinet member. BUIB; FEAA; SEC

Randolph, John (1773–1833). Congressman. COKB

Randolph, Martha Jefferson (1772–1836). Daughter of Thomas Jefferson. PRB

Randolph, Peyton (1721–1775). American Revolutionary patriot. BUIB†

Ranger, Joseph (fl. 1776). American Revolutionary patriot. DAF-1†; WIBA†

Ranke, Leopold von (1795–1886). German historian. HIB

Rankin, Jeannette (1880–1973). Congresswoman. FOJ; GRAB-1; WABC†; WHE

Rankin, Judy (Judith Torleumke) (1945–). Golfer. GUED

Raphael. Saint, archangel. DAD-3

Raphael (Raffaello Santi) (1483–1520). Italian painter. CHC; JAA; KAA; MAI

Rapier, James T. (1839–1884). Congressman. ADA; ADB; BU

Rashad, Ahmad (Bobby Moore) (1949–). Football player, sportscaster. AAS-18

Rashi (Solomon ben Isaac) (1040–1105). French Hebraist. GEF; GRB-1; GUA; KAC; LERA; LES

Rashid bin Hassani (1855?). African tribesman. PEA

Rasmussen, Zora. Comedienne. MASB

Raspberry, William J. (1935?–). Columnist. STAA

Rasputin, Grigori (1872–1916). Advisor to the czar of Russia. COKB

Ratelle, Jean (1940–). Canadian hockey player. FICB

Rattlesnake Jake (d. 1884). Outlaw. JOBA

Rav (Abba Arika) (d. 247). Babylonian rabbi. GUA; KAC

Ravel, Maurice (1875–1937). French composer. BUC; KAE; SAA; YOL

Rawlings, Marjorie Kinnan (1896–1953). Author. CON

Rawlinson, Sir Henry Creswicke (1810–1895). English orientalist. COL

Rawls, Betsy (Elizabeth Earle) (1928–). Golfer. HOBAA†

Rawls, Katherine (1918–1982). Swimmer. HOBAA†

Ray, Dixy Lee (1914–). Ex-governor, marine biologist. EMB†; GRAB-1†; WIAA-02

Ray, Hugh (1883–1956). Football executive. SUD

Ray, James Earl (1928–). Assassin. RABA

Rayborn, Calvin (1940–). Motorcyclist. ST-1

Raye, Martha (1916–). Singer, comedienne. MASB

Raymond of Pennafort. Saint. DAD-2

Raymond, Arthur. State legislator and journalist. GRAC

Raymond Nonnatus (1200–1240). Saint. MOC

Razak bin Hussain, Tun Abdul (1922–). Malaysian political leader. RODA

Read, Deborah (c. 1707–1774). Common-law wife of Benjamin Franklin. WABC†

Read, George (1733–1798). American Revolutionary patriot. BAEA; BUIB†; COJ†; FEAA; FEAB; MAC†

Read, Mary (1680–1721). English pirate. PABB; SC-1; WHA†

Reagan, Anne Robbins (Nancy) (1921–). Wife of Ronald Reagan. BLG; KL; MAU; SMBD

Reagan, Ronald Wilson (1911–). President of U.S. BEB; BLA; COI; COS; FRBA; SUBB; WHD

Rebecca. Biblical character. LER

Reber, Grote (1911–). Radio astronomer. LAA; SUE

Rechnitzer, Andreas B. Oceanographer. OLC

Red Cloud (1822–1909). Sioux Indian chief. FRAB; HED; MOD

Red Cross, see International Red Cross of Geneva.

Red Jacket (1758?–1830). Seneca Indian chief. MOD

Redford, Lola (1938–). Ecologist. WA

Redmond, Mary. Colonial girl. CAD

Redmond, Mickey (Michael Edward) (1947–). Hockey player. LEYA; ORB

Reed, Betty Lou (1927–). Assemblywoman. GRAB-1†

Reed, Janet (1916–). Dancer, ballet mistress. ATA

Reed, Virginia (b. 1833). Pioneer with Donner party. FOC

Reed, Walter (1851–1902). Physician. BOB; CHD; CUC; DEB; DOE; ED; EVD; FOH; LEC; LEPC; MAL; ROA; SHG; SIC

Reed, Willis (1942–). Basketball player. BEL; FRD; PAW; PE; RAAB

Reel, Vince (1914–). Track coach. LEW

Reese, Pee Wee (Harold Henry) (1919–). Baseball player. BOE; GEB; KLB

Reeves, Bass (1840–1910). Lawman. KADB

Reeves, Dan (1912–). Football executive. SUD

Reeves, Goebel (1899–1959). Singer. LA

Regis, John Francis (1597–1640). Saint. DAD-2

Rehan, Ada (1860–1916). Actress, born Ireland. VAA

Reich, Haviva (1914–1944). Czech resistance worker. LAD

Reichenfeld, Eugene (1911–). Conductor, born Hungary. STM†

Reichstein, Tadeus (1897–). Swiss organic chemist, born Poland. LET; RIF

Reid, James L. (1844–1910). Agriculturist. DEA†

Reid, Michael B. (1948–). Football player. GUCA

Reifel, Ben (1906–). Congressman. GRAC

Reiner, Carl (1922–). Comedian, motion picture producer. BUR-1

Reiner, Fritz (1888–1963). Conductor, born Hungary. EWB; STM

Reiners, Rudolph (1901–). Conductor. STM†

Reinhardt, Django (1910–1951). French guitarist. COF-1

Reiser, Pete (Harold Patrick) (1920–). Baseball player. GEB; RIGA†; ROC; VAE

Reitsch, Hanna (1912–1979). German aviator. HAMY; HIFD

Rembrandt Hermanszoon van Rijn (1606–1669). Dutch painter. CHC; DEI; DEJ; KAA; MAI

Remigius (c. 437–c. 533). Saint. DAD-3

Remington, Frederic (1861–1909). Painter, sculptor. HEDA; HOD; KAW

Remond, Charles Lenox (1810–1873). Abolitionist. GRAB-05

Remond, Sarah Parker (1826–1894). Abolitionist. GRAB-05

Renault, Louis (1843–1918). French jurist. MEC†; WIC

Rennie, John (1761–1821). Scottish engineer. EVB

Reno brothers (fl. 1860). Outlaws. JOBA; SUJ

Renoir, Auguste (1841–1919). French painter. ASB-1; KAA; MAH

Rentzel, Lance (1943?–). Football player. BELB

Resch, Glenn "Chico" (1948–). Canadian hockey player. AAS-21

Rescigno, Nicola. Conductor. STM†

Resh Lakish, *see* Simeon ben Lakish.

Reshevsky, Samuel (1911–). Chess player, born Poland. LEQB; RHA

Resnik, Judith (1949–1986). Astronaut. COE-1; FOJ-1

Respighi, Ottorino (1879–1936). Italian composer. BUC; KAE

Reston, James Barrett (1909–). Journalist, born Scotland. LEU

Retzlaff, Pete (Palmer Edward) (1932–). Football player. ANB

Reulbach, Edward (1882–1961). Baseball player. SLA

Reuther, Walter Philip (1907–1970). Labor leader. COH; DABA; LEHA; SEA; WEC

Revel, Bernard (1885–1940). Rabbi, educator, born Russia. KAD; LETA

Revelle, Roger (1909–). Oceanographer. BRBC; COR

Revels, Hiram Rhoades (1822–1901). Senator. ADA; ADB; BRB†; BU; YOI

Revere, Paul. Rock singer, pianist. LEHB

Revere, Paul (1735–1818). American Revolutionary patriot. BAC; BUIB; DAFA; DEI; DEJ; EVD; FIA; FOA; HAN; SOA; SUL

Revson, Peter Jeffrey (1939?–1974). Automobile racer. JA; OLCB

Rey, Hans Augusto (1898–1977). Author, illustrator, born Germany. SM

Reyes, Albert (1956?–). Migrant worker. WECC

Reyes, Joseph Manuel de los (1905–). Physician, born Cuba. FOW

Reymont, Wladyslaw Stanislaw (1867–1926). Polish author. MANB

Reynolds, Allie (1919–). Baseball player. BOE; GIB; GRA; ROB

Reynolds, Jim (fl. 1862). Outlaw. WIAA-1

Reynolds, John (fl. 1862). Outlaw. WIAA-1

Reynolds, Sir Joshua (1723–1792). English painter. CHC

Reynolds, Malvina (1899?–). Composer, singer. BOHC

Reynolds, Phoebe (b. 1771). Heroine. CLC

Reynolds, Quentin (1902–1965). Journalist. JAD

Rhazes (850?–923?). Arabian physician. CHD†; SHG†

Rhoades, Everett (1931–). Physician. GRAC

Rhodes, Cecil John (1853–1902). British colonial administrator. ASB-1; WOA

Rhodes, Eugene Manlove (1869–1934). Author. WAA

Rhodes, John. Automobile racer. OLB

Riabouchinska, Tatiana (1918–). Russian dancer. ATA

Ribeiro, Alfonso. Actor. BRF-1

Ribner, Shoshana (1938–). Israeli swimmer, born Austria. SLA†

Ricci, Ruggiero (1920–). Violinist. EWC

Rice, Daniel McLaren, Jr. (1823–1900). Clown. KIB; KLD

Rice, Jim (1950–). Baseball player. AAS-4; RIGA†

Rice, Sam (1892–1974). Baseball player. ALB

Richard (d. 722). Saint. QUA

Richard I (Coeur de Lion) (1157–1199). King of England. BRBF; CAAA; CHG; COA; DEC; GRAB†; JOBB; SCC; TRA

Richard II (1367–1400). King of England. BRBF; DEC; GRAB†; SCC

Richard III (1452–1485). King of England. BRBF; CAAA; DEC; GRAB†; JOBB; SCC

Richard of Chichester (1198–1253). Saint. DAD-2

Richard, Henri (1936–). Canadian hockey player. FOI; FR; OBA

Richard, Maurice (Rocket) (1921–). Canadian hockey player. AAS-35; ASBA; DAG; DAGA; FICA; FR; HEG; LIAB; OBB; ORC; RAAF; SID; SUB; WAK

Richards, Dickinson Woodruff, Jr. (1895–1973). Physiologist. RIF

Richards, Ellen Swallow (1842–1911). Chemist. SC; WABC†

Richards, Sir Gordon (1904–1986). English jockey. DAG; DAGA

Richards, Keith (1943–). English singer. BUIB-1

Richards, Laura E. (1850–1943). Poet. BEF; BEH

Richards, Linda Ann (1841–1930). Nurse. COFA; WABC†; WAJ

Richards, Robert Eugene (1926–). Track athlete.
DEF; HEG; LYD

Richardson, Henry Hobson (1838–1886). Architect. LAF

Richelieu, Armand Jean du Plessis, cardinal, duc
de (1585–1642). French statesman. CAE

Richey, Anne (d. 1922). Rustler. RAB

Richter, Charles (1900–1985). Seismologist. DU-1

Richter, Hans (1843–1916). Hungarian conductor. YOM

Richter, Sviatoslav (1914–). Russian pianist.
EWC

Richthofen, Manfred von (1892–1918). German
aviator, WW I. ARD; HAMY; RADA

Rickard, Tex (1871–1929). Boxing promoter.
DAG; DAGA

Rickenbacker, Edward Vernon (1890–1973). Aviator. ARD; DAG; LEX; YAA

Rickey, Branch (Wesley Branch) (1881–1965).
Baseball executive. DAFD; FRC-1†

Rickover, Hyman George (1900–1986). Admiral,
born Russia. COR; GRB-1; KE; NAC; WEB

Ridder, Allard de (1887–). Dutch conductor.
STM†

Ride, Sally (1951–). Astronaut. DU-1; FOJ-1

Ridgway, John. British paratrooper, rower. OLC

Ridgway, Matthew Bunker (1895–). General.
RAE†

Riding, Henry (fl. 1865). Pioneer. SCB

Riedesel, Frederika von, baroness (1746–1808).
German diarist. AND

Riegels, Roy. Football player. DAI; LYC

Riegger, Wallingford (1885–1961). Composer.
POF

Rigby, Cathy (1952–). Gymnast. HOBAA; LIE;
RYA†; RYX; ST-2

Riggin, Aileen (1906–). Diver. HOBA†; JAB

Riggins, John (1949–). Football player. AAS-10

Riggs, Bobby (Robert Larimore) (1918–). Tennis
player. FOI; FOX

Riggs, Captain R. S. Naval officer. HAQ†

Riis, Jacob August (1849–1914). Journalist, reformer, born Denmark. FLBA; LOB; MEB

Riles, Wilson (1917–). Educator. DOF-1

Riley, Bennet (1787–1851). General. SEC

Riley, Bridget (1931–). English painter. WIAA

Riley, James Whitcomb (1849–1916). Poet. ALA;
BEF; BEH; LEJ; LEOB; LEPA; MAL

Rillieux, Norbert (1806–1894). Engineer. ADA;
ADB; GRAB-03; HA; HAL; HODA; KLA; ROG

Rimanoczy, Jean de (1904–). Austrian conductor.
STM†

Rimski-Korsakov, Nikolai Andreevich (1844–
1908). Russian composer. BAE; BUC; FIE†;
KAE; POG; SAA; YOJ

Rincón de Gautier, Felisa (1897–). Puerto Rican
mayor. FOW; WO

Rindt, Jochen (1942?–1970). Austrian automobile
racer. JA

Ringgold, Faith. Painter. FAH

Ringling Brothers (John, Otto, Charles, Alfred T.
and Albert C.). Circus owners. KIB; KLD

Ringo, Jim. Football player. JOA†

Ringwall, Rudolph (1891–). Conductor. STM†

Ripken, Cal, Jr. (1960–). Baseball player. HEFB†

Ripley, Ezra (d. 1841). Clergyman. WOAA†

Ripley, George (1802–1880). Literary critic, reformer. EOB

Rita of Cascia (1381–1457). Saint. DAD-1; DAD-2;
MOC

Rittenhouse, David (1732–1796). Astronomer.
BUIB†; DOG; SIA

Ritter, Tex (Woodward Maurice) (1906–1974). Actor, singer. LA

Rivera, Diego (1886–1957). Mexican painter.
KAA; NEBA; ROGB

Rivers, Joan (c. 1935–). Comedienne. MASB

Rivers, Sam (1930–). Multi-instrumentalist. UN

Rivers, Thomas Milton (1888–1962). Bacteriologist. CHE†

Rivlin, Alice Mitchell (1930?–). Economist.
BOHG

Rixey, Eppa (1891–1963). Baseball player. ALB

Rizzuto, Philip Francis (1918–). Baseball player.
BOE; FOI; GIB; KLB; ROB

Roark, Helen Wills, see Wills, Helen.

Robbins, Frederick Chapman (1916–). Pediatrician. RIF

Robbins, Mary Louise (1912–). Microbiologist.
BOHE

Robert I, King of Scotland, see Bruce, Robert the.

Robert, Nicholas-Louis (1761–1828). French inventor. FAB

Robert-Houdin, see Houdin, Jean Eugène Robert.

Roberts, Bartholomew (1682–1722). Welsh pirate. WHA†

Roberts, Fireball (Edward Glenn) (1927?–1964).
Automobile racer. LEX; LEXA

Roberts, John, Blessed (1576–1610). DAD-3

Roberts, Kenneth Lewis (1885–1957). Author.
CON

Roberts, Kenny (1951–). Motorcyclist. OLDB

Roberts, Needham. Soldier, WWI. BRB†; STQ†

Roberts, Robin (1926–). Baseball player. RIGA†;
SHH

Robertson, Isaiah. Football player. SMJ

Robertson, James (1742–1814). Pioneer. MAO

Robertson, James P. (1909–). Conductor. STM†

Robertson, Oscar (1938–). Basketball player.
BEL; DEHA-1; ETA; FRD; HEHA; HID; HOC;
PE

Robertson, Oswald Hope (1886–1966). Physician, born England. ED

Robeson, Paul (1898–1976). Singer, actor, football player. ADA; ADB; DAFG; DOBA; DOF-1; JO; RICA; ROF

Robespierre, Maximilien François Marie Isidore de (1758–1794). French revolutionist. HAK

Robin Hood. Legendary English outlaw. STP; SUK

Robins, Margaret Dreier (1868–1945). Labor leader. BI†

Robinson, Bill "Bojangles" (1878–1949). Dancer. HUC; RIC; ROF

Robinson, Brooks Calbert (1937–). Baseball player. DAFD; FRC-1†; FRD; HIF; KLB; LEY; MUB-1; MUC; PEC; PRA; RIGA†; SMF

Robinson, Charles (1818–1894). Governor. SEC

Robinson, Dave. Football player. HAGB; JOA; KABA

Robinson, Edwin Arlington (1869–1935). Poet. BEGA; SIF; WHB

Robinson, Frank (1935–). Baseball player. BRD; DA; KADA; LIC; PEC; PRA; RIGA†; SMG

Robinson, Harry A. (1942–). Journalist. STAA

Robinson, Jackie (John Roosevelt) (1919–1972). Baseball player. ALB; ASB-1; BELB; BOE; BOF; BRD; BRG; BUD-1; BUJA; DAFB; DAFC; DAFD; DAG; DAGA; DAH; DOF-1; FLD; FRC-1†; GEB; GUC; GUDA; HOBC; HOC; HUA; JOC; KLB; LEY†; LOAA; RIGA†; ROC; SCA; SHF; SHH; SMK; STO; VAE

Robinson, James (1753–1868). Soldier. WIBA

Robinson, Jean (1947?–). Bicyclist. HOBAA†

Robinson, Jerry. Cartoonist. GOB-1

Robinson, Paul. Football player. BEKB

Robinson, Ray (1921–). Boxer. ASBA; BOF; DAG; DAGA; HOC

Robinson, Robert Guy. Marine aviator. REA

Robinson, Wilbert (1864–1934). Baseball player, manager. ALB; DAFD; FRC-01; ROAA

Robinson, William E. Beverage executive. PAA

Robinson, William Ellsworth (1861–1918). Magician. GIA

Robinson, Wirt (1864–1929). Army officer, educator. RAE

Roch (1295–1327). Saint. CHD†; DAD-3; TUA

Rochambeau, comte de (Jean-Baptiste Donatien de Vimeur) (1725–1807). French soldier. SCB-1

Rochat, André. Red Cross delegate. DED

Rock, John (1890–1984). Physician. HEFA

Rock, Lee Curry. Engineer. HOG

Rock, Saint, see Roch. Saint.

Rockefeller, John Davison (1839–1937). Industrialist. ASB-1; BOD; CUC; FAC; LEM; MAL; WED

Rockefeller, Nelson Aldrich (1908–1979). Vice president of U.S. FEA; HAOA; HOEA

Rockne, Knute (1888–1931). Football coach, born Norway. DAFB; DAFG; DAG; DAGA; DAI; HEH; LEAB; LEB; LOB; LYB; VAD

Rodale, Jerome Irving (1898–1971). Organic farmer, publisher. SQA

Rodgers, Bill (1947–). Track athlete. AAS-30; BAEC; HIA-01

Rodgers, Calbraith Perry (fl. 1911). Air pilot. HAMY

Rodgers, Richard Charles (1902–1979). Composer. BAD; BEKA; EWA; MOA

Rodin, Auguste (1840–1917). French sculptor. ASB-1; DEI; DEJ

Rodney, Caesar (1728–1784). American Revolutionary patriot. BAEA; BUIB†; COJ; FEAB; MAC; SEC

Rodnina, Irina (1949–). Russian skater. LIEA

Rodriguez, Aurelio (1947–). Mexican baseball player. LEY†

Rodriguez, Benjamin (fl. 1832). Dentist. LETA

Rodriguez, Johnny (1952–). Singer. KRI-1

Rodriguez, Juan "Chi-Chi" (1935–). Golfer. BELB; FOI; FOW; IZA; NEBB

Rodriguez, Pedro (1939?–1971). Mexican automobile racer. JA

Rodriguez de Tio, Lola (1843–1924). Puerto Rican poet. WO

Rodriguez-Trias, Helen. Pediatrician, social reformer. GLO

Rodzinski, Artur (1894–1958). Austrian conductor. STM†

Roebling, John Augustus (1806–1869). Civil engineer, born Germany. CUB

Roebling, Mary G. (1906–). Banker. LES-1

Roebling, Washington Augustus (1837–1926). Civil engineer. LEGA; LYA

Roemer, Olaus (1644–1710). Danish astronomer. SHFB

Roennau, Laurel van der Wal. Biologist. HOG†

Roentgen, Wilhelm (1845–1923). German physicist. AAS-33; ASA; CAA; DEI; DEJ; FE; PRC; SHFB; SHG; STI

Rogers, Barbara. City councilwoman. WHE†

Rogers, Kenny (1938–). Singer. BUIB-01

Rogers, Robert (1731–1795). Frontier soldier. VIA

Rogers, Roy (1912–). Actor, singer. LA

Rogers, Will (1879–1935). Humorist. BOD; COKA; KAW; LEH; PHA; WAA; WAO

Rogers, Woodes (d. 1732). English privateer. WHA

Rogovin, Saul (1923–). Baseball player. RI

Rohr, Bill (William Joseph) (1945–). Baseball player. LYD

Rojas, Cookie (Octavio Rivas) (1939–). Cuban baseball player. BELA

Rolfe, Red (Robert) (1908–). Baseball player, manager. ROB

Rolland, Romain (1866–1944). French author. DED

Roller, A. Clyde (1914–). Conductor. STM†

Rollin, Betty (1936–). Author, television correspondent. SMBB-2

Rollins, Sonny (1929–). Saxophonist. UN

Roman, Nancy Grace (1925–). Astronomer. HOG; POE

Roman Nose (c. 1868). Cheyenne warrior. HED

Romanov, House of. Russian dynasty. RIA

Romanus. Saint. DAD-2

Romberg, Sigmund (1887–1951). Composer, born Hungary. EWA; MOA

Romita, John, Sr. (1930–). Cartoonist. GOB-1

Romney, George Wilcken (1907–). Cabinet member. WEC

Romuald (c. 952–1027). Saint. DAD-2

Roncone, Edward. Conductor. STM†

Ronda, Gaspar (1929?–). Automobile racer. OLB

Rondon, Cândido Mariano da Silva (1865–1958). Brazilian marshal. WOB

Ronstadt, Linda (1946–). Singer. BUIB-2; KRI

Ronzani, Gene. Football player, coach. JOA†

Rooney, Arthur Joseph (1901–). Football executive. SUD

Roosevelt, Alice Hathaway Lee (1861–1884). First wife of Theodore Roosevelt. BAG; BAG-1; MAU

Roosevelt, Edith Kermit (1861–1948). Second wife of Theodore Roosevelt. BAG; BAG-1; BLG†; CHB; KL; MAA; MAU; PRB; ROH; ROHA

Roosevelt, Eleanor (1884–1962). Author, humanitarian, wife of Franklin Delano Roosevelt. ASB-1; BAG; BAG-1; BLG; BOC; BRBE; CHB; COG; COG-1; CUC; DABB; DAD; GIBA; KE; KEE; KL; LAI; MAA; MAU; MEB; PA; PRB; ROH; ROHA; SMC; STLA; WABC†; WAR; YOA

Roosevelt, Franklin Delano (1882–1945). President of U.S. ASB; ASB-1; BAEB; BAG; BAG-1; BEB; BEC; BLA; BUIA; CAAA; CAG; CAH; COI; COS; CUC; DEI; DEJ; DOF; DUB; DUC; DUCA; FAA; FIA; FOH; FRBA; HIH; KE; LAI; LEQ; LEQA; MAB; MABA; MEB; MIA; PED; ROH; ROHA; ROK; SUBB; TAC; WEE; WHD; YOA

Roosevelt, Franklin Delano, Jr. (1914–). Politician. LAI†

Roosevelt, James (1907–). Mutual fund executive. LAI†

Roosevelt, John A. (1916–1981). Investment executive. LAI†

Roosevelt, Nicholas J. (1767–1854). Inventor. BUE

Roosevelt, Theodore (1858–1919). President of U.S. ALE; ASB; BAEB; BAG; BAG-1; BEB; BEC; BLA; BUIA; CAG; CAH; CO-1; COI; COJA; CORA; COS; CUC; DAE; DEI; DEJ; DUB; DUC; DUCA; FEA; FEC; FOH; FRBA; HAA; HAOA; HIH; HOEA; KEA; LAI; LEQ; LEQA; MAB; MABA; MAL; MEA; MEC; MIA; OLA; PED; ROH; ROHA; ROK; ROL†; STH; SUBB; WHD; WIC

Root, Elihu (1845–1937). Cabinet member. MEC†; WIC

Roper, Margaret (1505–1544). Daughter of Sir Thomas More. NOA

Rosado del Valle, Julio (1922–). Painter. NEBB

Rose of Lima (1586–1617). Saint. DAD-1; DAD-3; QUA

Rose of Viterbo (1235–1252). Saint. DAD-3

Rose, Billy (1899–1966). Theatrical producer. MOA†

Rose, Doug. Automobile racer. OLDC

Rose, Edward (d. 1834). Pioneer. BUH; HAP; SCB

Rose, Ernestine Potowski (1810–1892). Feminist, born Poland. EIA; GUBA; JOCA; LES-2; LETA

Rose, Leonard (1918–1984). Cellist. EWC·

Rose, Mauri (1906–1981). Automobile racer. LEVA; LEX

Rose, Pete (Peter Edward) (1941–). Baseball player, manager. BELB†; BRAA; BRD; CL-06; GUG; GUH; HEFB†; KADA; PRA; RIGA†; AAS-3; AAS-35

Rosen, Al (1925–). Baseball player. BUJ; RI; SLA

Rosen, Carl George Arthur (1891–1975). Research engineer. YOD

Rosen, Goody (Goodwin) (1912–). Canadian baseball player. RI

Rosen, Sheldon (1942?–). Physician. LETC

Rosenberg, Aaron (1912–1979). Football player, motion picture producer. SLA

Rosenbloom, Maxie (1904–1976). Boxer, actor. SLA

Rosenbluth, Leonard (1933–). Basketball player. SLA†

Rosendahl, Heidemarie (1948?–). German track athlete. HOBAA†

Rosenfeld, Fanny (1903–1969). Canadian track athlete, born Russia. SLA

Rosenfeld, Morris (1862–1923). Poet, born Poland. LETA

Rosenstock, Joseph (1895–1985). Polish conductor. STM†

Rosenthal, Manuel (1904–). French conductor. STM†

Rosenwald, Julius (1862–1932). Merchant, philanthropist. ALD; CUC; LETA

Rosevear, Robert A. (1915–). Conductor. STM†

Rosewall, Ken (1934–). Australian tennis player. LAHA

Ross, Barney (1909–1967). Boxer. PIB; PIBA; SCA; SLA; VAE

Ross, Betsy (1752–1836). Legendary maker of first American flag. AND; DOD; LOA†; STJ

Ross, Diana (1944–). Singer, actress. AB; BOHC; BUIB-2

Ross, Edmund G. (1826–1907). Senator. KEC; KED

Ross, George (1730–1779). American Revolutionary patriot. BAEA; BUIB†; COJ†; FEAB

Ross, Hugh (1898–). English conductor. STM†

Ross, Sir James Clark (1800–1862). Scottish explorer. DOC†; ROL

Ross, Sir John (1777–1856). Scottish arctic explorer. ROL†

Ross, John (1790–1866). Cherokee Indian chief. HED; MAO; STAB

Ross, John Osage (b. 1814). Osage Indian. JOD

Ross, Sir Ronald (1857–1932). English physician. AAS-31; DEB; RIF; ROA

Ross, Ruth N. Journalist. STAA

Rosse, 3d earl of, see Parsons, William.

Rossetti, Christina Georgina (1830–1894). English poet. BEH; COP

Rossini, Gioacchino (1792–1868). Italian composer. BAE; KAE; SAA

Rossovich, Tim. Football player. ST

Rostropovich, Mstislav (1927–). Russian cellist. EWC

Rote, Kyle, Jr. (1950–). Soccer player. ADL; GUEC-1

Rote, Tobin. Football player. JOA†

Roth, Esther (1952–). Israeli track athlete. SLA

Roth, Joe (d. 1977). Football player. AAS-24; CL-04

Roth, Mark (1951–). Bowler. SLA

Roth, Werner (1948–). Soccer player, born Yugoslavia. GUEC-1

Rothschild, Edmond de (1845–1934). French financier. KAD

Rothschild, Mayer Amschel (1743–1812). German financier. PEB

Rottman, Leon (1934–). Romanian canoe racer. SLA†

Rouault, Georges (1871–1958). French painter. KAA

Roundfield, Dan (1953–). Basketball player. AAS-7

Roush, Edd J. (1893–1988). Baseball player. ALB; RIGA†

Rousseau, Jean Jacques (1712–1778). French philosopher. FRE

Roux, Pierre Paul Émile (1853–1933). French bacteriologist. DEB; RIE; ROA

Rowan, Andrew Summers (1857–1943). Army officer. RAE†

Rowan, Carl Thomas (1925–). Author. SQB; STAA; YOI

Rowan, Dan (1922–1987). Comedian. BUR-1

Rowlandson, Mary (c. 1635–1678). Indian captive. DI

Rowson, Susanna Haswell (1762–1824). Actress, born England. DOG

Royall, Anne Newport (1769–1854). Traveler, author. ARB

Roybal, Edward Ross (1916–). Congressman. WH-1

Rozeanu, Angelica (1921–). Romanian table tennis player. SLA

Rubens, Peter Paul (1577–1640). Flemish painter. CHC; KAA; MAI

Rubenstein, Louis (1861–1931). Canadian skater. SLA

Rubin, Barbara Jo (1949–). Jockey. HOBA†; HOBAA†

Rubin, Vera C. (1928–). Astronomer. GL

Rubinstein, Anton (1829–1894). Russian pianist, composer. CHF

Rubinstein, Artur (1889–1982). Pianist, born Poland. GRB-1; MANB; PIAA

Rubinstein, Helena (1870?–1965). Cosmetician, born Poland. LIA

Ruby, Harry (1895–1974). Songwriter. MOA

Rudel, Julius (1921–). Conductor, born Austria. STM†

Rudi, Joseph Oden (1946–). Baseball player. BELA

Rudkin, Margaret Fogharty (1897–1967). Bakery executive. LAH; LES-1; PAA

Rudnick, Dorothea (1907–). Embryologist. YOF

Rudolf, Max (1902–). Conductor, born Germany. STM†

Rudolf, Robert C. Conductor. STM†

Rudolph, Wilma G. (1940–). Track athlete. DAFB; DAJ; GEA; GED; GEDA; HIA; HOBA; HOBAA; JAB; LEYB; LYD; OCA; RYA

Ruef, Abraham (1864–1936). Political leader. COGC

Ruel, Muddy (Herold) (1896–1963). Baseball player. HIC

Ruether, Rosemary (1936–). Author, educator. GIB-1

Ruffian. Racehorse. HOBAA

Ruffin, Josephine St. Pierre (1842–1924). Civil rights leader. GRAB-01

Ruffin, Nate. Football player. BELB

Ruffing, Red (1905?–1986). Baseball player. ROB

Ruggles, David (1810–1849). Abolitionist. GRAB-05

Ruiz Belvis, Segundo (1829–1867). Puerto Rican lawyer, government worker. TU

Ruland, Jeff (1958–). Basketball player. AAS-7

Rumford, Benjamin Thompson, count (1753–1814). English physicist, born U.S. CAA; FE; HYB; RAD; SHFB; SIA; STI

Rumsey, James (1743–1792). Inventor. HYA†

Rupp, Adolph (1902–1977). Basketball coach. HEH; HID

Rush, Benjamin (1745–1813). Physician, American Revolutionary patriot. BAEA; BUIB†; COJ†; CUC; ED; FEAB; MAC

Rusk, Dean (1909–). Ex-Secretary of State. HEEA

Rusk, Howard A. (1901–). Physician. CHE; HEFA

Ruskin, John (1819–1900). English author. BEI

Russell, Andy (Charles Andrew) (1941–). Football player. BELB

Russell, Anna (1911–). English musical satirist, born Canada. MASB

Russell, Benjamin (1761–1845). Journalist. SQB†

Russell, Bertrand Arthur William Russell, 3d earl (1872–1970). English philosopher. HAJ; KE; OZA

Russell, Charles Edward (1860–1941). Author, journalist. COGB

Russell, Charles Marion (1864–1926). Painter. HEDA; HOD; WAA

Russell, Elizabeth Shull (1913–). Geneticist. YOF

Russell, Harold (1914–). Veterans' leader. LYA

Russell, Lillian (1861–1922). Actress. WABC†

Russell, Myron E. (1904–). Conductor. STM†

Russell, Theodore (1911–). Conductor. STM†

Russell, William Felton (1934–). Basketball player. ASBA; BEL; DEF; HEHA; HID; HOBC; HOC; KADA; KLBA; LEW; PE; RAAB; RICA

Russell, Sir William Howard (1820–1907). British war correspondent. FLBB

Russwurm, John B. (1799–1851). Journalist. ADB; BEJ

Rustin, Bayard (1910–1987). Civil rights leader. FAG; YOI

Ruth. Biblical character. LER

Ruth, Babe (George Herman) (1895–1948). Baseball player. ALB; ASB; ASB-1; BED; BOE; BUD-1; BUJ; COKB; DA; DAA; DAFB; DAFC; DAFD; DAG; DAGA; DAH; DEI; DEJ; EPA; FRC-1†; GEC; GIB; GR; GUC; GUDA; HEG; HIF; HOC; LAC; LEF; LEV; LIAA†; LYC; MUB-1; MUC; RAAA; RIGA†; ROB; SH; SHB; SHC; SHH; SID; SMK; WAC

Rutherford, Ernest Rutherford, 1st baron (1871–1937). New Zealand physicist. ASA; BIA; FE; MOBA; POD; PRC; RID; SHFB; SIA

Rutledge, Edward (1749–1800). American Revolutionary patriot. BAEA; BUIB†; COJ†; FEAB; MAC

Rutledge, John (1739–1800). Jurist. BUIB†; FEAA

Ryan, Frank Beall (1936?–). Football player. ANC

Ryan, Nolan (Lynn Nolan) (1947–). Baseball player. AAS-2; AAS-35; GUDA; GUED-01; GUG; RIGA†; SMH

Ryder, Albert Pinkham (1847–1917). Painter. FRA; MAG; SIE

Rydstrom, Pat. Histopathologist. HOG

Ryun, Jim (1947–). Track athlete. AAS-26; BELB; BRE; DAFB; DAJ; KADA; LEYB; ST-1

Rzewska, Josepha Rozanka (1899–). Librarian, born Poland. BAEA-1

S

Saadia ben Joseph (Saadyah Gaon) (892–942). Egyptian Hebraist. GRB-1; GUA; KAC; LERA

Saarinen, Eero (1910–1961). Architect, born Finland. FOF; LAF; LEDA

Saarinen, Eliel (1873–1950). Architect, born Finland. LAF

Saavedra Lamas, Carlos (1880–1959). Argentine statesman. MEC†; WIC

Sabas (5th century). Saint. DAD-3

Sabas, the Goth (4th century). Saint. DAD-2

Sabata, Victor de (1892–1967). Italian conductor. STM†

Sabatini, Guglielmo (1902–). Conductor, born Italy. STM†

Saberhagen, Bret (1964–). Baseball player. HEFB†

Sabin, Albert Bruce (1906–). Physician, born Russia. CHE†; COLA; RIE

Sabin, Florence Rena (1871–1953). Anatomist. BUDA; FOG; HA-1; STLA

Sabine, Sir Edward (1778–1883). English astronomer, born Ireland. FE

Sabine, Wallace Clement (1868–1919). Physicist. FE

Sable, Jean Baptiste Pointe de, *see* Pointe de Sable, Jean Baptiste.

Sacajawea (1787–1812). Shoshone Indian guide. BEC; BUI; DOD; FOR; GRAD; HEC; LEK; ROI; STJ; WAB; WABC

Sacher, Paul (1906–). Swiss conductor. YOM†

Sachs, Eddie (Edward Julius) (1927–1964). Automobile racer. LEX; OLAB

Sachs, Nelly (1891–1970). Swedish poet, born Germany. SHFE

Sackson, David (1912–). Conductor. STM†

Sackville, George Sackville Germain, 1st viscount, *see* Germain, George Sackville.

Sackville-West, Victoria (1892–1962). English author. SMA

Sadat, Anwar el- (1918–1981). Egyptian president. ASB-1; DU-1

Sadowski, Anthony (1670?–1736). Frontiersman, born Poland. PIAA

Saidenberg, Daniel (1906–). Conductor, born Canada. STM†

Sailer, Toni (1935–). Austrian skier. ALBA; DEF; GED; GEDA; LEYB†

St. Denis, Ruth (1878–1968). Dancer. FOGC†

Saint-Gaudens, Augustus (1848–1907). Sculptor, born Ireland. ASB; BEA

Saint-Germain, Comte de, pseud. (1710?–1782?). Adventurer, occulist, in Paris. COEA

St. Johns, Adela Rogers (1894–). Journalist. JAE

Saint-Saëns, Camille (1835–1921). French composer. KAE

Sainte-Marie, Buffy (1942?–). Singer, composer. BOHC

Sakharov, Andrei D. (1921–). Russian physicist. AAS-34; DU-1; MEC

Saladin (1138–1193). Sultan of Egypt and Syria. CAAA

Salanter, Israel (1810–1883). Lithuanian rabbi. GEF; GUB; KAD

Salazar, Alberto (1958–). Track athlete, born Cuba. AAS-30

Salazar, António de Oliveira (1889–1970). Portuguese chief of state. ARA

Salem, Peter (1750?–1816). American Revolutionary patriot. ADB; BRG; BUIB†; DAF-1; DOB; ROG; STQ†; WIBA

Salisbury, Joan Curlee, see Curlee-Salisbury, Joan.

Salk, Jonas Edward (1914–). Physician. ASB-1; BEK; BOB; CHE†; COLA; DU-1; FAA; FE; GRB-1; HEFA; LEG; LETA; RIE; ROA; SIC; SUF; YOA

Salomon, Haym (1740–1785). American Revolutionary patriot, born Poland. ALD; BOK; BUIB†; GRB-1; GUB; HAN†; LERA; LETA; LOB; PEB; SOA

Salomons, Sir David (1797–1873). English statesman. GEF

Salvador, Francis (1747–1776). American Revolutionary patriot. GRB-1; LETA

Sammartino, Bruno. Wrestler. BELB

Sample, James (1910–). Conductor. STM†

Sampson, Deborah, see Gannet, Deborah Sampson.

Sampter, Jessie (b. 1883?). Poet, Zionist. ALD

Samson (490–565). Saint. WIB

Samuel, Gerard (1924–). Conductor, born Germany. STM†

Samuel ha-Nagid (993–1055). Spanish rabbi, statesman. GUA

Samuel ibn Adiya (fl. 540). Arabian poet. GEF

Samuel Yarhina'ah (177–257). Babylonian rabbi. KAC

San Juan, Pedro. Spanish conductor. STM†

San Martin, Jose de (1778–1850). Argentine statesman. BAA; BACA; LAB; OLA; YOFA

Sanborn, Franklin Benjamin (1831–1917). Journalist. WOAA

Sanchez, Yolanda. Human services consultant, reformer. GLO

Sanchia (c. 1180–1229). Saint. DAD-2

Sanctorius (1561–1636). Italian physiologist. SHG

Sandberg, Ryne (1959–). Baseball player. HEFB†

Sandburg, Carl (1878–1967). Poet, biographer. BEF; BEH; BOA; HEF; KE†; SIF

Sande, Earl (1898–1968). Jockey. DAG

Sanders, Bill (William Willard) (1933?–). Cartoonist. DEDC

Sanders, Charlie (1946–). Football player. AAS-19; DEHA

Sanders, Harriet (1834–1909). Pioneer. JOB

Sanders, Marlene (1931–). Television producer. WA

Sanderson, Derek Michael (1946–). Canadian hockey player. ORB

Sandoval, Hilary (1930–). Government official. NEAA

Sandow, Eugene (1867–1925). Professional strongman, born Germany. PHA

Sands, Sam (b. 1800). Colonial boy. CAD

Sanford, Maria Louisa (1836–1920). Educator. BUDA†

Sanger, Margaret (1883–1966). Nurse, leader in birth control movement. ARAA; ARB; BRBE; GIBA; KOA; ROJ; SC; STLA; WABC

Sanguillen, Manuel DeJesus (1944–). Panamanian baseball player. TUB

Sansan. Author, born China. CAHA

Santa Anna, Antonio López de (1795–1876). Mexican general, politician. NEBA

Santander, Francisco de Paula (1792–1840). Colombian general, president. LAB

Santayana, George (1863–1952). Poet, philosopher, born Spain. LO

Santee, David (1957–). Skater. VAD-6

Santee, James. Skater. VAD-6

Santi, Raffaello, see Raphael.

Santo, Ron (1940–). Baseball player. BRE; LEY; PRA

Santos-Dumont, Alberto (1873–1932). Brazilian aeronaut. BRBA

Saperstein, Abraham M. (1903–1966). Basketball coach, owner. SLA

Sarah. Biblical character. LER

Sarasate, Pablo de (1844–1908). Spanish violin virtuoso. CHFA

Sarazen, Gene (1901–). Golfer. LABA

Sargent, John Singer (1856–1925). Painter. CUC; FRA; LEE; MAG; SIE

Sargent, Sir Malcolm (1895–1967). English conductor. STM†; YOM

Sarmiento, Domingo Faustino (1811–1888). Argentine statesman, educator. COG; KEE; LAB; WO

Sarnoff, David (1891–1971). Radio and television executive, born Russia. GRB-1; LAG; LETA

Sarton, May (1912–). Author, poet, born Belgium. OCB

Sartre, Jean Paul (1905–1980). French author, philosopher. KE†

Sasso, Sandy (1947–). Rabbi. SMBB-1

Satanta (1820–1878). Kiowa Indian chief. FRAB

Satie, Erik (1866–1925). French composer. SAA

Sato, Eisaku (1901–1975). Japanese premier. MEC; WECA

Saubert, Jean. Skier. HOBA†

Saudan, Sylvain. Swiss skier. FRCA

Sauer, George, Jr. Football player. BELB; CO

Saund, Dalip (1899–1973). Congressman, born India. LIA

Saunders, Sir Charles Edward (1867–1937). Canadian wheat expert. DEA†

Saunders, Raymond (Raymond the Great) (1877–1948). Magician. GIA

Saunders, Suzanne. Lawyer. HOD-1

Saunders, William (1836–1914). Canadian agriculturist. DEA†

Saussure, Nicolas Théodore de (1767–1845). Swiss agricultural chemist. CAB

Savage, Augusta Christine (1900–1962). Sculptor. BEBA

Savage, Swede (David Earl, Jr.) (1947–1973). Automobile racer. JA

Savio, Dominic (1842–1957). Saint. DAD-1; DAD-2

Savitt, Richard (1927–). Tennis player. SLA

Sawchuk, Terry (1929–1970). Canadian hockey player. ETB; FR; LIAB; OBA; OBB; ORA; ORC; WAK

Sawyer, Helen (1905–). Astronomer. YOF

Sax, Adolphe (Antoine Joseph) (1814–1894). Belgian musical instruments maker. LAE

Sayers, Dorothy L. (1893–1957). English author. SMA

Sayers, Gale (1943–). Football player. BEKB; BELB; COFB; DAFG; DAI; DUF; FRD; HAD; KADA; LEZB; LIB; LIBB; RAAE

Scarborough, William Saunders (1852–1926). Educator. ADA; ADB; BRB†

Scarlatti, Alessandro (1659–1725). Italian composer. BAE; SAA

Scarlatti, Domenico (1685–1757). Italian composer, harpsichordist. BEN; KAE; SAA

Scarry, Richard (1919–). Author, illustrator. SM

Schacht, Al (1892–1984). Baseball player. LIAA†; RI; SLA†

Schaefer, Germany (Herman) (1878–1919). Baseball player. LIAA†

Schalk, Ray (1892–1970). Baseball player. ALB; HIC

Schang, Walter Henry (1889–1965). Baseball player. HIC

Scharff, Mary. Basketball player. HOBAA†

Scharff-Goldhaber, Gertrude (1911–). Physicist. PAC

Schaus, Frederick (1925–). Basketball manager. LEW

Schayes, Adolph (1928–). Basketball player. BEL; HEHA; HID; PE; RAAB; SLA

Schayes, Dan (1959–). Basketball player. SLA†

Schechter, Solomon (1850–1915). Hebraist, born Romania. GRB-1; GUB; KAD; LERA; LETA; PEB

Scheckter, Jody (1950–). South African automobile racer. OLCB; SLA

Scheele, Karl Wilhelm (1742–1786). Swedish chemist. SOB

Scheer, Leo (1909–). Conductor. STM†

Schenkman, Edgar (1908–). Conductor. STM†

Scherchen, Hermann (1891–1966). German conductor. STM†; YOM

Scherman, Thomas (1917–1979). Conductor. STM†

Schick, Béla (1877–1967). Pediatrician, born Hungary. RIE

Schick, George (1908–). Conductor, born Czechoslovakia. STM†

Schiff, Jacob Henry (1847–1920). Financier, philanthropist, born Germany. LETA

Schimmel, Gertrude (1918–). Policewoman. WA

Schindler, Raymond Campbell (1882–1959). Detective. LID

Schippers, Thomas (1930–1977). Conductor. STM†

Schirra, Walter Marty, Jr. (1923–). Astronaut. LEL; NEB; THC

Schliemann, Heinrich (1822–1890). German archaeologist. ELA

Schmidt, Bernhard V. (1879–1935). Russian lens grinder. LAA

Schmidt, Joseph Paul (1932–). Football player. ANA

Schmidt, Kathy (1953–). Javelin thrower. GLB

Schmidt, Mike (1949–). Baseball player. AAS-4; RIGA†

Schmidt, Milt. Canadian hockey player. ORC

Schmidt, Oscar, Jr. Naval officer. REA

Schmorell, Alexander (d. 1943). German resistance worker. LAD

Schnabel, Artur (1882–1951). Austrian pianist, composer. CHF

Schneider, Martin (fl. 1783). Pioneer. STA

Schneiderman, Rose (1882–1972). Labor leader. BI†

Schnitzer, Eduard, *see* Emin Pasha, Mehmed.

Schoeder, Walter (1917–). Conductor. STM†

Schoenberg, Arnold, *see* Schönberg, Arnold.

Schoendienst, Red (Albert Fred) (1923–). Baseball player. BUJ; BUJA; DEG; SCA

Scholastica. Saint. DAD-2

Scholl, Hans (1918?–1943). German resistance worker. LAD

Scholl, Sophie (1921?–1943). German resistance worker. LAD

Schollander, Donald Arthur (1946–). Swimmer. ALBA; BRE; DEF; HOC; KADA; LEYB; LOAA

Scholz, Robert (1902–). Conductor, born Austria. STM†

Schomberg, Arthur Alfonso (1874–1938). Historian. ADB

Schomburg, Alex. Cartoonist. GOB-1

Schönberg, Arnold (1874–1951). Composer, born Austria. BEKA; BUC; EWAA; KAE; SAA†; YOL

Schoolcraft, Henry Rowe (1793–1864). Ehtnologist. HAO; LED

Schouten, Willem Cornelis (1567?–1625). Dutch navigator. ROL†

Schreiber, Avery (1935–). Comedian. BUR-1

Schreyvogel, Charles (1861–1912). Painter. HEDA

Schriever, Bernard A. (1910–). General, born Germany. NEB

Schroeder, Patricia Scott (1940–). Congresswoman. GRAB-1†; SWI; WHE

Schubert, Franz Peter (1797–1828). Austrian composer. BEN; BRF; BUD; DEI; DEJ; FIE; GOA; KAE; SAA; WIA; YOK

Schuetz, Heinrich, *see* Schütz, Heinrich.

Schulmeister, Karl (1770–1853). French spy. SUG

Schulte, Frederick (1881–). Conductor. STM†

Schulte, Karl. Conductor. STM†

Schultz, Dave (1949–). Canadian hockey player. THG

Schuman, William (1910–). Composer. BAD; MAF; POF

Schumann, Clara (1819–1896). German pianist. CHF

Schumann, Robert Alexander (1810–1856). German composer. BRF; BUD; FIE; KAE; SAA; YOJ

Schumann-Heink, Ernestine (1861–1936). Singer, born Austria. MAT-1

Schurz, Carl (1829–1906). Journalist, statesman, born Germany. CUB; LEB; LOB; STH

Schuster, George (b. 1874). Automobile racer. SUA

Schütz, Heinrich (1585–1672). German composer. BEM

Schuyler, Philip John (1733–1804). American Revolutionary patriot, senator. SOA

Schwann, Theodor (1810–1882). German physiologist. COLA

Schwartz, Arthur (1900–1984). Songwriter. MOA

Schwartz, Will (1923–). Conductor. STM†

Schweitzer, Albert (1875–1965). French missionary, theologian, musician. BAF; BEC; EVD; FOJ; KE; KEE; LO; MAN; MEA; MEC; WIC; YOA

Schwerner, Michael Henry (1939–1964). Civil rights worker. STJB†

Schwieger, Hans (1906–). Conductor, born Germany. STM

Scipio Africanus Major (Publius Cornelius Scipio Africanus) (234?–183 B.C.). Roman general. COM

Scobee, Dick (Francis Richard) (1939–1986). Astronaut. COE-1

Score, Herbert Jude (1933–). Baseball player. BRD; NEA; RIGA†

Scorsese, Martin (1942–). Motion picture director. SMBB-3

Scotland, Alexander (1896?–). English spy. KN

Scott, Abigail, *see* Duniway, Abigail Scott.

Scott, Austin. Journalist. STAA

Scott, Blanche Stuart. Aviator. HIFD†

Scott, Charlie. Basketball player. HIBA

Scott, David R. (1932–). Astronaut. THC

Scott, Dred (1795?–1858). Slave. KADB

Scott, George (1943–). Baseball player. KLBB; LEY

Scott, Hazel (1920–1981). Pianist. BOG

Scott, Hugh Lenox (1853–1934). General. RAE†

Scott, Irene Feagin (1912–). Judge. SWI

Scott, John (1630?–1696). English adventurer. CAF

Scott, Michael (1907–1983). South African clergyman. LEA

Scott, Nan. Microbiologist, polar researcher. LA-1

Scott, Robert Falcon (1868–1912). English explorer. COC; DOBB; DOC; HOB; KNA†; MOB; ROL

Scott, Sir Walter (1771–1832). Scottish author. COB; COO; STL

Scott, Winfield (1786–1866). General. EDA; MAL; WHD†

Scott Brown, Denise (1931–). Architect, born South Africa. GIB-1

Scriabin, Aleksandr Nikolaievich (1872–1915). Russian composer. BUC; POG

Scripps, Edward Wyllis (1854–1926). Journalist. CUC; SQB

Seabury, Samuel (1729–1796). Clergyman. BUIB†

Seagrave, Gordon Stifler (1897–1965). Medical missionary. FAA

Sears, Eleanora (1881–1968). Sportswoman. HOBA; HOBAA; RYA†

Seaver, Tom (George Thomas) (1944–). Baseball player. AAS-2; BELB†; BUJA; FRD; GUE; GUG; LEZ; MUB-1; RIGA†; SA-3; SMH

Sebastian (3d century). Saint. DAD-1; DAD-2

Sebold, William G. (1897?–). Counterspy. HAB

Secunda, Sholom (1894–). Conductor, born Russia. STM†

Seddon, Margaret Rhea (1947–). Astronaut, surgeon. FOC-1; FOJ-1; HIFD; SMBC-2

Sedgwick, Theodore (1746–1813). Jurist. BUIB†

Sedode, Julia Barbara de Lima (b. 1858). Grandmother of Annie Jiagge. CRA

Sedran, Barney (1891–1969). Basketball player. SLA

See, Orley. Conductor. STM†

Seebeck, Thomas Johann (1770–1831). German physicist. FE

Seeger, Ruth Crawford (1901–1953). Composer. SC-02

Segrè, Emilio Gino (1905–). Physicist, born Italy. LET

Seguin, Juan N. (1806–1889). Texas patriot. KUA

Seiberling, Frank A. (1859–1955). Rubber executive. HYA†

Seibert, Florence Barbara (1897–). Biochemist. GEA

Seibert, Mike. Skater. VAD-6

Seidell, Joe. Basketball coach. LEW

Seidler, Maren. Shot-putter. HOBAA†

Seixas, Gershom Mendez (1746–1816). Rabbi. LETA

Seligman, Joseph (1819–1880). Financier, born Germany. LETA

Seligson, Julius (1909–). Tennis player. SLA

Sellins, Fannie (1870–1919). Labor leader. BI†

Selmon, Lee Roy (1954–). Football player. AAS-16

Selormey, Francis (1927–). Ghanaian government official. OJA

Seltzer, Louis (1897–1980). Journalist. PAA

Semiramis. Legendary queen of Assyria. PA

Semmelweis, Ignaz Philipp (1818–1865). Hungarian obstetrician. ROA; SIC†

Semon, Waldo L. (1898–). Chemist. PAB

Sendak, Maurice (1928–). Author, illustrator. SM

Seneca, Lucius Annaeus (4 B.C.–65 A.D.). Roman statesman, philosopher. COK

Senefelder, Aloys (1771–1834). Czech inventor. FE

Senesh, Hannah (1921–1944). Israeli underground leader, born Hungary. GEF; GRB-1; LAD; STP; ROGA

Senghor, Léopold Sédar (1906–). Senegalese president. ADA; DU-1; KEF

Sennett, Mack (1880–1960). Motion picture producer. ED-1; FLBC

Sequoya (George Guess) (1770?–1843). Cherokee Indian scholar. BOK; CAGA; CUC; DEDB; HEC; HEGA; ROD; STAB; SUKA

Sereni, Enzo (1905–1944). Italian resistance worker. GRB-1; LAD

Serenus. Saint. DAD-2

Sergius of Radonezh (1314–1392). Saint. DAD-3; ONA

Serra, Junipero (1713–1784). Spanish missionary. ASB; DOCA; MAT

Servulus. Saint. DAD-3

Sessions, Roger H. (1896–1985). Composer. POF

Seton, Alexander (1520–1604). Scottish alchemist. CUA

Seton, Elizabeth Ann (1774–1821). Saint. ASB; BLF†; CUC; DAD-1; WABC†

Seton, Ernest Thompson (1860–1946). Author, naturalist, born England. CO-1

Seume, Johann. German mercenary. SOA

Seuss, Dr. (Theodore Geisel) (1904–). Author, illustrator. SM

Severin, John (1921–). Cartoonist. GOB-1

Sevier, John (1745–1815). Governor. MAO; SEC

Sévigné, Marie (de Rabutin Chantal) marquise de. French author. PA

Sevitzky, Fabien (1893–1967). Russian conductor. STM†

Sewall, Samuel (1652–1730). Jurist. BUIB†

Seward, William Henry (1801–1872). Statesman. HEEA; MAL

Sewell, Joe (1898–). Baseball player. RIGA†

Seymour, David (1911–1956). Photographer, born Poland. HOE

Seymour, Horatio (1810–1886). Politician. WHD†

Seymour, Jane (1509–1537). Consort of Henry VIII, king of England. MAOA; VAC

Shackleton, Sir Ernest Henry (1874–1922). Irish explorer. DOC; KNA; MAJ; ROL; SCBA

Shaftesbury, Anthony Ashley Cooper, 7th earl of (1801–1885). English reformer. COG; EVA

Shahn, Ben (1898–1969). Painter, born Lithuania. FRA; WIAA

Shakespeare, William (1564–1616). English playwright. COB; COP; DEI; DEJ; FRE; STK

Shalom Aleichem (Solomon Rabinowitz) (1859–1916). Author, born Russia. GRB-1

Shammai (c.50 B.C.–c.30 A.D.). Palestinian rabbi. GEF

Shamsky, Art (1941–). Baseball player. SLA†

Shanet, Howard (1918–). Conductor. STM†

Shank, Theresa (1951?–). Basketball player. ST-2

Shantz, Robert Clayton (1925–). Baseball player. BOE

Shapely, Harlow (1885–1972). Astronomer. SUE

Shapiro, Irving S. (1916–). Chemical executive. GRB-1

Sharman, William (1926–). Basketball player, coach. ARB-2; HID; LEW

Sharpless, Nansie (1932–). Biochemist. BOHA-1

Shaver, Dorothy (1897–1959). Department store executive. BOJ; CLA; FRBD; LES-1

Shaw, Anna Howard (1847–1919). Feminist, born England. LES-2; MAV

Shaw, Earl (1937–). Physicist. CAF-1

Shaw, George Bernard (1856–1950). Irish playwright, critic. ASB-1; DEI; DEJ; KE; STL

Shaw, Leslie N. (1922–). Business executive. YOI

Shaw, Robert (1916–). Conductor, chorus master. STM†

Shaw, Robert Gould (1837–1863). Soldier. BRB†

Shaw, Wilbur (1902–1954). Automobile racer. ASBA; DAG; DAGA; LEVA; LEX; YAA

Shea, Julie (1959–). Track athlete. SUDB

Shear-Yashur, Aharon. Israeli rabbi, born Germany. GRB-1

Shearer, Moira (1926–). Scottish dancer. ATA

Sheehy, Gail (1937–). Journalist, author. LETB

Shefa, Gershon (1943–). Israeli swimmer, born Palestine. SLA†

Sheftall, Benjamin (1692–1765). Philanthropist, born Germany. BUIB†

Sheftall, Mordecai (1735–1797). Businessman. BUIB†; LETA

Sheilah. Biblical character. LER

Shelby, Carroll (1923–). Automobile racer, manufacturer. LEX

Shelby, Isaac (1750–1826). Governor. BUIB†; SEC

Shelby, Joseph Orville (1830–1897). General. MAD

Shelley, Ken. Skater. VAD-6

Shelley, Percy Bysshe (1792–1822). English poet. COP

Shenaut, John. Conductor. STM†

Shepard, Alan Bartlett (1923–). Astronaut. BRBA; CAGA; COQ; FAA; LEL; LEPB; NEB; THC

Shepherd, John (1932?–). Businessman. DRA

Sheridan, Owen (1912?–). Caretaker, born Ireland. BELB

Sheridan, Philip Henry (1831–1888). General. ARE

Sherman, Allie (1923–). Football coach. HAE; SLA†

Sherman, James S. (1855–1912). Vice president of U.S. FEA; HAOA; HOEA

Sherman, Roger (1721–1793). Statesman. BAEA; BUIB†; COJ†; FEAA; FEAB; FEB; MAC

Sherman, William Tecumseh (1820–1891). General. CUC

Sherrington, Sir Charles Scott (1857–1952). English physiologist. RIF

Sherry, Larry (Lawrence) (1935–). Baseball player. GIB; RI; SLA

Shezifi, Hana (1943–). Israeli track athlete, born Iraq. SLA†

Shields, Marvin (1939?–1965). Soldier. ARBA†

Shih Huang Ti (259–210 B.C.). Emperor of China. BLW; NEC; SPA

Shippen, Margaret (1760–1804). Wife of Benedict Arnold. LOA

Shirer, William L. (1904–). Journalist, author. JAD

Shmueli, Zehava (1955–). Israeli track athlete. SLA†

Shockley, William Bradford (1910–). Physicist. AAS-33†; GRAB-3; MAPA

Shoemaker, Eugene M. (1928–). Geologist. POE

Shoemaker, Willie (1931–). Jockey. ASBA; DAG; DAGA

Shofner, Del (1934–). Football player. ANB

Sholes, Christopher Latham (1819–1890). Inventor. FE; HYA; LAE; MAL

Sholokhov, Mikhail Aleksandrovich (1905–1984). Russian novelist. POFA

Shore, Edward William (1902–1985). Hockey player, born Canada. DAG; DAGA; FICB; LIAB; OBB; ORC; SICA

Short, Barbara. Engineer. HOG†

Shorter, Frank (1947–). Track athlete. AAS-30; BAEC; HIA-01; LEYB

Shostakovich, Dmitri (1906–1975). Russian composer. KAE; POG; SAA

Shoup, George (1836–1904). Governor, senator. SEC

Shriver, Robert Sargent (1915–). First director of Peace Corps. WEB

Shula, Don (1930–). Football coach. AAS-12; HAGA

Shulamith (fl. 930 B.C.). Palestinian woman. LER

Shull, George Harrison (1874–1954). Botanist. CAB; DEA

Shuman, Ron. Automobile racer. OLDD

Shurtliff, Robert, pseud., see Gannet, Deborah Sampson.

Shuster, Joe. Cartoonist. GOB-1

Shute, Henry Augustus (1856–1943). Humorist.
BEE

Shuttlesworth, Fred (1922–). Clergyman, civil
rights worker. STF

Sibelius, Jean (1865–1957). Finnish composer.
BAE; BEKA; BUC; FIE†; KAE; SAA; YOJ

Sibley, Henry Hastings (1811–1891). Governor.
SEC

Siddons, Sarah Kemble (1755–1831). English actress. NOA; TRC

Sidney, Margaret, pseud. (1844–1924). Author.
BEI

Sidney, Sir Philip (1554–1586). English poet,
statesman. STP

Siebert, Muriel (1932–). Economist. GIB-1; GL;
GLO

Siegemundin, Justine Dittrichin (1650–1705). German midwife. MASA†

Siegl, Henry. Conductor. STM†

Siegmeister, Elie (1909–). Conductor. STM†

Siemens, Sir William (1823–1883). English inventor, born Germany. FE

Siemon, Jeffrey G. (1950–). Football player.
HAGB; SMJ

Sienkiewicz, Bill. Cartoonist. GOB-1

Sievers, Roy (1926–). Baseball player. BOE†;
BRD

Siffert, Josef (1936–). Swiss automobile racer. JA

Sigismund (1368–1437). Holy Roman Emperor.
CAAA

Sigüenza y Góngora, Carlos de (1645–1700). Mexican scholar. WOB

Sikhakane, Joyce. South African antiapartheid
worker. CRA†

Sikma, Jack (1955–). Basketball player. AAS-7

Sikorsky, Igor Ivan (1889–1972). Aeronautical engineer, born Russia. BEA; FE; LAE; LIA; LOB;
MAP

Silas, James (1949–). Basketball player. AAS-9

Silber, Jules (1876–1939). German spy. SEB

Silliman, Benjamin (1779–1864). Chemist, geologist. BUF; HYB

Sills, Beverly (1929–). Singer. DU-1; GLO; SAB;
SC-02

Silva, Manlio (1893–). Conductor, born Italy.
STM†

Silver, Abba Hillel (1893–1963). Rabbi. LETA

Silver, Horace (1928–). Composer, pianist. UN

Silver, Lou (1953–). Basketball player. SLA†

Silvera, Frank (1914–). Actor. ADA; ADB

Silverman, Jonathan. Actor. BRF-1

Silvers, Phil (1912–1985). Comedian. ALC

Simburg, Wyomia Tyus, see Tyus, Wyomia.

Simeon ben Lakish (200–275). Palestinian rabbi.
GUA

Simeon Stylites (390?–459). Saint. DAD-2; FAD

Simmons, Aloysius Harry (1903–1956). Baseball
player. ALB; DAA; RIGA†; SHH

Simmons, Ted Lyle (1949–). Baseball player.
HOCM; TUB

Simmons, William J. (1849–1890). Clergyman.
ADB; BRB†

Simms, Jacob E. Journalist. STAA

Simon. Saint, apostle. DAD-3

Simon, Neil (1927–). Playwright. GRBA

Simonson, Walt. Cartoonist. GOB-1

Simplicius. Saint, pope. DAD-2

Simpson, O. J. (Orenthal James) (1947–). Foot-
ball player, sports commentator. AAS-10;
AAS-35; DEHA-1; DEHB; DUF; GUCA; GUEB;
KADA; LEZB; LIBB; MOCA; RUA; ST

Sims, James Marion (1813–1883). Gynecologist.
POB; RIB

Sims, Tom L. Advertising executive. STAA

Sims, William Sowden (1858–1936). Admiral.
ARD; ICA; NAC

Simson, Sampson (b. 1780?). Philanthropist.
LETA

Sinclair, Sue (1954–). Aquarium animal trainer.
GUJ

Sinclair, Upton Beall (1878–1968). Author. COGB

Singer, Al (1907–1961). Boxer. SLA

Singer, Eugene José. Conductor, violinist, born
Rumania. STM†

Singer, Isaac Bashevis (1904–). Author, born Poland. GRB-1

Singer, Jacques (1912–). Conductor, born Poland.
STM†

Singleton, Benjamin "Pap" (1809–1892). Black
leader. ADA; ADB; BUH

Singstad, Ole (b. 1882). Civil engineer, born Norway. LEGA; YOD

Sinkwich, Frank. Football player. HIE

Sinnott, Michael, see Sennett, Mack.

Siple, Paul Allman (1908–1968). Explorer, geographer. YOE

Sirhan, Sirhan (1944–). Assassin, born Jordan.
RABA

Siringo, Charles A. (1855–1928). Cowboy detective. FOC; KAW; SUI

Sirpo, Boris. Conductor, born Finland. STM†

Sisler, George (1893–1973). Baseball player. ALB;
DAFC; DAFD; FRC-1†; HIF; RIGA†

Sisson, Tack "Prince" (fl. 1777). American Revolutionary patriot. WIBA†

Sisters of Charity of Providence. Missionaries.
JOB

Sita, Nana (1898–). South African pacifist. LEA

Sitting Bull (1834–1890). Sioux Indian leader.
DEDB; FRAB; HEC; HEGA; LEH; MOD;
ROD; SUKA; WAM

Sittler, Darryl (1950–). Canadian hockey player. FICA-1

Skarben, Countess Krystyna, *see* Granville, Christine.

Skelton, Red (1913–). Comedian. ALC; ED-1†

Skibine, George (1920–). Dancer, born Russia. ATA

Skinner, Burrhus Frederic (1904–). Psychologist. DU-1

Skinner, Cornelia Otis (1901–1979). Actress, author. BEE

Skoronski, Bob. Football player. JOA†

Skouras, Spyros (1893–1971). Motion picture producer, born Greece. BEA; LEN; LIA

Skowron, Bill (1930–). Baseball player. DEHA-1

Skrzypiec, Tina Marie. Boom operator. SMBC-2

Slack, Donna Lee (1961?–). Winner, Young American Medal for Bravery. ANCA

Slade, Joseph Albert. Gunfighter. JOBA

Slade, Maria Virginia (Molly). Outlaw's wife. JOB

Slater, Samuel (1768–1835). Manufacturer, born England. FAB; LEB; MAL

Slaughter, Country (Enos) (1916–). Baseball player. BUJ; DEG; GIB

Slaughter, John H. (1841–1922). Sheriff. KAW

Slavenska, Mia. Yugoslavian dancer. ATA

Slessor, Mary Mitchell (1848–1915). Scottish missionary. STP

Sloan, Alfred Pritchard, Jr. (1875–1966). Automobile executive. FAC

Sloan, Jerry (1942–). Basketball player. SA-2

Sloan, John (1871–1951). Painter. FRA; SIE

Sloan, Tod (James Forman) (1874–1933). Jockey. DAG

Slocum, Fanny (1773–1847). Indian captive. HEE

Slocum, Joshua (1844–1910). Mariner. DYA; LAA-2; SCBA

Slotin, Louis Alexander. Physicist. GEF

Smallens, Alexander (1889–1972). Conductor, born Russia. STM†

Smalley, George Washburn (1833–1916). Journalist. FLBB

Smalls, Robert (1839–1915). Naval figure, congressman. ADA; ADB; HODA; HUB; JOC; PECA; ROG; STD; STJB

Smeaton, John (1724–1792). English civil engineer. EVB

Smeeton, Beryl. English mariner. HAQ

Smeeton, Miles. English mariner. HAQ

Smetana, Bedřich (1824–1884). Czech composer. BAE; FIE†; KAE; SAA

Smethurst, Ann Orlitski. Aviator. SMBC-2

Smith (Mr.) (fl. 1928). Australian first mate of Trevessa. HAQ

Smith, Adam (1723–1790). Scottish economist. LO

Smith, Alfred Emanuel (1873–1944). Governor. WHD

Smith, Alfred J., Jr. (1949–). Painter. FAI

Smith, Amanda Berry (1837–1915). Evangelist. BLF†

Smith, Bessie (1894–1937). Singer. HUC; JOE; SUH; TEA; TEB; WAD†

Smith, Billy (1950–). Canadian hockey player. AAS-21

Smith, Charles "Bubba" (1948–). Football player. AAS-32; LIB; SMD

Smith, Elinor (1910–). Aviator. HIFD

Smith, Graham (fl. 1951). English radio astronomer. SUE

Smith, James. Indian captive. DI

Smith, James (1719–1806). American Revolutionary patriot, born Ireland. BAEA; BUIB†; COJ†; FEAB

Smith, James (1737–1813). Pioneer. STA

Smith, Jedediah Strong (1799–1831). Pioneer fur trader. BLD; BUB; BUG; FOC; HEB; HIBC; LED; WAF; WIA-1

Smith, John (1580–1631). English colonist in America. ASB; LEO; LEPF; MAT; VIA

Smith, Kate (1909–1986). Singer. GEA

Smith, Linda. Dentist. FOC-1

Smith, Logan Pearsall (1865–1946). Author. BEG

Smith, Margaret Chase (1897–). Senator. CLA; GIBA; GRAB-1; STLA; TRD; WHE

Smith, Mary Ellen, *see* Pleasant, Mary Ellen (Mammy).

Smith, Michael J. (1945–1986). Astronaut. COE-1

Smith, Ozzie (1954–). Baseball player. HEFB†

Smith, Red (Walter Wellesley) (1905–1982). Sportswriter. LEU

Smith, Robyn C. (1944?–). Jockey. ST-2

Smith, Ross. Australian aviator. HAMY†

Smith, Stacy. Skater. VAD-6

Smith, Theobald (1859–1934). Pathologist. DEB; MAL

Smith, Thomas James (1840–1870). Law officer. SUI

Smith, Vicki. Judo expert. LYE

Smith, William Eugene (1918–1978). Photographer. SUAA

Smith, William R. (1924–). Conductor. STM†

Smith, Winthrop (1893–1961). Investment executive. PAA

Smithdas, Robert (1925–). Social worker. BOHA-1

Smothers, Dick (1938–). Comedian. BUR-1

Smothers, Tom (Thomas Bolyn) (1937–). Comedian. BUR-1

Smybert, John (1688–1751). Painter, born Scotland. MAG

Smythe, John H. (1844–1908). Diplomat, lawyer. ADA; ADB

Snead, Samuel Jackson (1912–). Golfer. LABA

Snell, Matthew (1941–). Football player. LEZB†

Snell, Peter (1938–). New Zealand track athlete. DEF; LEYB†

Snider, Duke (Edwin) (1926–). Baseball player. DA; DAA; FRC-1†; GEB; GIB; RIGA†

Snively, Mike. Automobile racer. OLAB

Snowe, Olympia (1947–). Congresswoman. WHE

Snyder, Grace (1882–). Pioneer. JOB

Snyder, John. Jazz producer. UN

Sobukwe, Robert Mangaliso (1924–1978). South African political leader. LEA

Sockalexis, Louis (1873–1913). Baseball player. SMK

Socrates (470?–399 B.C.). Greek philosopher. DEI; DEJ; FRC; FRE; HAA; LO; MAJ; OZA; STP

Soddy, Frederick (1877–1956). English chemist. POD; RID

Söderblom, Nathan (1866–1931). Swedish theologian. MEC†; WIC

Sokol, Marilyn. Comedienne. MASB

Sokoloff, Nikolai (b. 1886). Conductor, born Russia. STM†; YOM

Sokolow, Nahum (1859–1936). English journalist, Zionist, born Poland. GRB-1

Solano, Francis (1549–1610). Saint. DAD-3

Solomon (d. 932 B.C.). King of Israel. CAAA; JOBB; NEC

Solomon, Harold (1952–). Tennis player. SLA

Solomon, Izler (1910–1987). Conductor. STM

Solomon ben Isaac, see Rashi.

Solomons, Adolphus Simeon (1826–1910). Publisher. LETA

Solti, Georg (1912–). Hungarian conductor. STM†; YOM†

Solzhenitsyn, Aleksandr Isaevich (1918–). Russian author. ASB-1; POFA

Somerville, Mary Fairfax (1780–1872). Scottish scientist. SC

Somohano, Arturo (1910–). Puerto Rican conductor. STM†

Sondermann, Fred S. (1923–). Educator, born Germany. CAHA

Sonni Ali, see Sunni Ali Ber.

Sophia. Consort of Ivan III, grand duke of Moscow. RIA

Sopkin, Henry (1903–). Conductor. STM

Sorantin, Eric (1905–). Conductor, born Austria. STM†

Sorge, Richard (1895–1944?). German spy for Russia. HAB

Sorrentino, Anthony (1913–). Sociologist, born Italy. BAEA-1

Soter. Saint. DAD-2

Soubirous, Bernadette, see Bernadette of Lourdes.

Soule, Aileen Riggin, see Riggin, Aileen.

Soun Diata I, see Sundiata I.

Sousa, John Philip (1854–1932). Composer. BAD; CAD; CUC; KAE; LEHB; POF

Sousa, Mathias (fl. 1642). Colonist. WIBA

Souter, Judy Cook (1944–). Bowler. HOBAA†; JABA

Southgate, Eliza (1783–1809). Student. MAV

Soutine, Chaim (1894–1943). French painter, born Lithuania. WIAA

Spaatz, Carl (1891–1974). General. SWE

Spaght, Monroe Edward (1909–). Chemist. PAB

Spahn, Warren (1921–). Baseball player. BOE; BRC; DAFC; DAFD; DAH; RIGA†; SHA; SHH; SICA

Spaight, Richard Dobbs, Sr. (1758–1802). Governor, congressman. BUIB†; FEAA

Spain, Jayne Baker (1927–). Leader in rehabilitation of disabled. LES-1†

Spalding, Albert Goodwill (1850–1915). Baseball player, sporting goods merchant. ALB; SMK

Spalding, Burleigh Folsom (1853–1934). Jurist, congressman. SEC

Spallanzani, Lazzaro (1729–1799). Italian naturalist. DEB; ROA

Sparrow, Stanwood W. (1888–1952). Automotive engineer. YOD

Spartacus (d. 71 B.C.). Roman gladiator. STP

Spassky, Boris V. (1937–). Russian chess player. LEQB

Spaulding, Asa Timothy (1902–). Insurance executive. FLD

Spaulding, Charles Clinton (1874–1952). Insurance executive. ADA; ADB; HUA; PECA; STQ†

Speaker, Tristram E. (1888–1958). Baseball player. ALB; DAFC; DAFD; DAG; DAGA; EP; FRC-1†; GUC; HIF; RIGA†; SH; WAC

Spear, Lloyd (1917–). Conductor. STM†

Speedie, Mac (1920–). Football player. ANB

Speke, John Hanning (1827–1864). English explorer. LAA-1; MOB; ROL

Spellman, Frank (1922–). Weightlifter. SLA†

Spelman, Henry (1598?–1622). Pioneer. CAF

Spemann, Hans (1869–1941). German zoologist. RIF

Spencer, Lilly Martin (1811–1902). Painter. FOGB†

Spencer, Oliver (b. 1782). Indian captive. HEE

Spender, Stephen (1909–). English poet, critic. BRBB

Spenser, Edmund (1552–1599). English poet. COP

Sperber, Paula (1951–). Bowler. HOBAA†; RYX

Spero, Donald (1938–). Boat racer. SLA†

Sperry, Elmer Ambrose (1860–1930). Engineer, inventor. YOE

Spiegler, Mordechai (1944–). Israeli soccer player, born Russia. SLA†

Spielberg, Steven (1947–). Motion picture director. SMBB-3

Spilhaus, Athelstan F. (1911–). Meteorologist, born South Africa. BRBC

Spilsbury, Sir Bernard (1877–1947). English pathologist. LID

Spinoza, Baruch or Benedict (1632–1677). Dutch philosopher. LERA; LO; OZA; PEB

Spiridion. Saint. DAD-3

Spiro, Jo Anne. Martial artist. FOC-1

Spitz, Mark (1950–). Swimmer. GEDA; GRB-1; LEYB; OCA; SLA; ST-1

Spock, Benjamin (1903–). Pediatrician. BOHA; CHE; HAJ; HOBB

Spohr, Louis (1784–1859). German violinist, composer. CHFA; YOM†

Spottiswoode, Nigel (1915–). English motion picture producer. LAE

Spottiswoode, Raymond (1913–). English motion picture producer. LAE

Sprague, Frank Julian (1857–1934). Electrical engineer. HOF

Sprecher, Jenna Garman. Marine patrol officer. SMBC-3

Springsteen, Bruce (1949–). Singer. BUIB-2

Springsteen, Jay (1957–). Motorcyclist. OLDB

Spruance, Raymond Ames (1886–1969). Admiral. ICA; NAC†

Spruill, James Polk (1931–1964). Army officer. ARBA

Spurgeon, James Robert (1870–1942). Diplomat. FLD

Spurrier, Steve (1945?). Football player. BRE

Spyri, Johanna H. (1827–1901). Swiss author. BEC

Squanto (d. 1622). Wampanoag Indian. HEC

Squire, Watson (1838–1926). Senator, governor. SEC

Stabler, Ken (1945–). Football player. AAS-20; CL-1

Stacey, May Humphreys (1837–1886). Naval officer. BUI

Stack, Walter. Track athlete. BAEC

Staël, Germaine de (Anne Louise Germaine Necker, Baronne de Staël-Hollstein) (1766–1817). French author. BOC

Staffanson, Robert L. (1921–). Conductor. STM†

Stafford, Thomas P. (1930–). Astronaut. THC

Stagg, Amos Alonzo (1862–1964). Football coach. DAFG; DAG; DAGA; DAI; HEH

Stahl, Jesse (fl. 1917). Bronc rider. STQ†

Stalin, Joseph (1879–1953). Russian chief of state. ARA; ASB-1; CAE; CL-01; COJB; DOF; KIA; TAC

Stallings, George (1867–1929). Baseball manager. PAW

Stallings, Laurence (1894–1968). Playwright. RADA

Stallworth, John (1952–). Football player. AAS-18

Stamitz, Johann Wenzel (1717–1757). Czech violinist, composer. CHFA

Stance, Emanuel (b. 1851?). Buffalo soldier. BUH

Standfield, John (fl. 1830). English trade unionist. LAD

Standfield, Thomas (fl. 1830). English trade unionist. LAD

Standish, Lora (fl. 1630). Colonial girl. BAC

Stanford, Leland (1824–1893). Railroad executive, governor. YOG

Stanger, Russell (1924–). Conductor. STM†

Stanislaus (1030–1079). Saint. DAD-2

Stanley, Francis Edgar (1849–1918). Inventor. HOF

Stanley, Freelan O. (1849–1940). Inventor. HOF

Stanley, Sir Henry Morton (1841–1904). Welsh explorer, journalist. COC; LAA-1; ROL; SQB; WIA-1

Stanley, John (1914–). Cartoonist. GOB-1

Stanley, Leonard G. (1871–). Conductor. STM†

Stanley, Wendell Meredith (1904–1971). Biochemist. BEK; SUF

Stanton, Elizabeth Cady (1815–1902). Feminist. ARAA; BUA; COG; DEDA; GIBA†; GUBA; JOCA; LES-2; MAM; MAV; NIA; PACA; WABC†

Stanton, Susan Marie. Jailer. SMBC-3

Stanup, Richard (1748–1862). Slave. WIBA

Stapleton, Maureen (1925–). Actress. DI-1†

Stapp, John Paul (1910–). Biophysicist. COQ; ED

Starbuck, Jo Jo. Ice skater. VAD-6

Stargell, Willie (Wilver Dornel) (1941–). Baseball player. AAS-4; RIGA†

Stark, Dolly. Baseball umpire. RI

Stark, Ethel. Canadian conductor. STM†

Stark, Shirley (1927–). Sculptor. FAI

Starr, Bart (1934–). Football player. ANC; DEH; DUD; DUE; HAGC; JOA; RAAD; SHEA

Starr, Belle (1848–1889). Outlaw. JOBA; RAB; SUJ

Starr, Henry (1873–1921). Outlaw. JOBA

Starr, Ringo (1940–). English singer. BUIB-1; SC-01

Stasiuk, Vic (1929–). Hockey coach. LEW

Stastny, Peter (1956–). Canadian hockey player, born Czechoslovakia. AAS-22

Staubach, Roger (1942–). Football player. AAS-20; CL-06; CL-1; DEHB; GAB; GUF; HAGC

Staupers, Mable Keaton (1890–). Nurse, civil rights leader, born West Indies. DOF-1

Stayskal, Wayne (1931–). Cartoonist. DEDC

Steenbock, Harry (1886–1967). Biochemist. DEA

Stefan, Anthony R. (1903–). Conductor, educator, born Hungary. STM†

Stefánsson, Vilhjálmur (1879–1962). Canadian explorer. BAB

Steffens, Lincoln (Joseph Lincoln) (1866–1936). Journalist. COGB; SQB; WECB

Steichen, Edward (1879–1973). Photographer. FOD; HOE

Stein, Gertrude (1874–1946). Author. KE; MUA; STLA; WABC†

Stein, Leon (1910–). Conductor. STM†

Steinbeck, John (1902–1968). Author. CON; HEF

Steinberg, William (1899–1978). Conductor, born Germany. EWD; STM

Steindel, Marx. Conductor, born Germany. STM†

Steinem, Gloria (1934–). Feminist. GIB-1; KOA; WA

Steiner, George (1918–). Conductor. STM†

Steinman, David Barnard (1886–1960). Engineer. LETA

Steinmark, Fred (1948?–1971). Football player. CL-04; LYB

Steinmetz, Charles Proteus (1865–1923). Engineer, born Germany. BEA; COKA; CUC; GRB-1; LOB; LYA

Stelmach, Nahum B. (1936–). Israeli soccer player, born Palestine. SLA†

Steloff, Frances (b. 1887). Bookseller. GIB-1; WABC†

Stender, Fay. Lawyer. LETD

Stenersen, Johanna (1959?–). Motorcyclist. BUIC

Stenerud, Jan (1943–). Football player. GUD

Stengel, Casey (Charles Dillon) (1891–1975). Baseball player, manager. AAS-1; BED; BELB; DAFC; DAFD; DAG; DAGA; FRC-01; FRC-1†; GIB†; HEH; LEW; LIAA; ROAA

Stephen (d. 36?). Saint. DAD-3; QUA

Stephen (1097?–1154). King of England. DEC; GRAB†; SCC

Stephen I of Hungary (b. 970). Saint. DAD-3

Stephen, Little, see Esteban.

Stephen Harding (d. 1134). Saint. DAD-2

Stephens, Alexander Hamilton (1812–1883). Confederate vice president. MAO

Stephenson, George (1781–1848). English inventor. EBA; EVB; FE; THA

Stephenson, Robert (1803–1859). English civil engineer. EVB

Steranko, James (1938–). Cartoonist. GOB-1

Stern, Elizabeth Gertrude (1890–1954). Author. MAV

Stern, Isaac (1920–). Violinist. EWC

Stern, Otto (1888–1969). Physicist, born Germany. LET

Sternberg, George Miller (1838–1915). Physician. ED

Steuben, Friedrich Wilhelm von (1730–1794). General, born Germany. CUB; DAFA; HAN; SCB-1; SOA

Stevens, Jennie (Little Britches) (fl. 1894). Rustler. RAB†

Stevens, John (1749–1838). Inventor. BUE; BUIB†; FAB; HYA; VIA

Stevens, Rise (1913–). Singer. SC-02†

Stevens, Robert Livingston (1787–1856). Engineer, inventor. HYA

Stevens, Thaddeus (1792–1868). Congressman, abolitionist. BEJ; BU; CAGA; STJB

Stevenson, Adlai Ewing (1835–1914). Vice president of U.S. FEA; HAOA; HOEA

Stevenson, Adlai Ewing (1900–1965). Statesman. DABB; GO; KE; WHD†

Stevenson, Robert Louis (1850–1894). Scottish author. BEH; COB; COO; DEI; DEJ; HOA; STK

Stevenson, Sybil Jordan. Telecommunications executive. HOD-1

Steward, Susan McKinney (1848–1918). Physician. LOAV

Stewart, Alexander Turney (1803–1876). Merchant, born Ireland. HOF

Stewart, Ella Phillips (1893–). Pharmacologist. LOAV

Stewart, Ellen. Theater producer, founder. GIB-1; GLO

Stewart, Isabel Maitland (1878–1963). Nurse, born Canada. YOB

Stewart, Jackie (John Young) (1939–). Scottish automobile racer. ABB; BELB; COKC; JA; OLCB; ORD

Stewart, John (1786?–1823?). Missionary. HAP

Stewart, Maria W. (1803–1879). Abolitionist. GRAB-05; WABC†

Stewart, Mary (1916–). English author. SMA

Stewart, Reginald (1902–1984). Scottish conductor. STM†

Stewart, William Morris (1827–1909). Senator. YOG

Stibitz, George Robert (1904–). Mathematician, computer pioneer. GRAB-3†

Stieber, Wilhelm (1818–1882). German spy. HAB; SUG

Stiedry, Fritz. Conductor, born Germany. STM†

Still, Art (1955–). Football player. AAS-16

Still, William (1821–1902). Underground railroad leader. ADA; ADB; GRAB-05

Still, William Grant (1895–1978). Composer. ADA; ADB; HUC; POF; RIC; RICA

Stiller, Jerry (1928–). Actor, comedian. BUR-1

Stimson, Henry Lewis (1867–1950). Statesman. HEEA

Stingley, Darryl (1951–). Football player. AAS-24

Stinson, Katherine (1893–1977). Aviator, engineer. GEDB†; HIFD

Stirling, Lord, see Alexander, William.

Stockhausen, Karlheinz (1928–). German composer, conductor. EWAA

Stocking, Clark (b. 1840). Pioneer. BUI

Stockton, Frank Richard (1834–1902). Author. BEE; BEI

Stockton, Richard (1730–1781). American Revolutionary patriot. BAEA; BUIB†; COJ†; FEAB; MAC

Stokes, Adrian (1887–1927). Irish pathologist. SHG†

Stokes, Carl B. (1927–). Mayor. BRGA; DU; FAG; GRBA; HAH; YOI

Stokes, Maurice (1933–). Basketball player. HID; HOCA

Stokowski, Leopold (1882–1977). Conductor, born England. EWD; LOB; STM; YOM

Stone, Edward Durrell (1902–1978). Architect. FOF; LEDA

Stone, George Robert (1876–1945). Baseball player. SLA

Stone, I. F. (Isidor Feinstein) (1907–). Journalist. LETB

Stone, Lucy (1818–1893). Feminist. DEDA; GUBA; LES-2; WABC

Stone, Steve (1947–). Baseball player. AAS-9; RI; SLA

Stone, Thomas (1743–1787). American Revolutionary patriot. BAEA; BUIB†; COJ†; FEAB

Stone, Thompson. Conductor. STM†

Stoneman, George (1822–1894). General. ARE

Stones, Dwight (1953?–). Track athlete. LEYB†

Storch, Marcia (1933–). Physician. LETC; WA

Storke, Harry Purnell (1905–). General. RAE

Story, Joseph (1779–1845). Supreme Court justice. FLC

Stouder, Sharon (1948–). Swimmer. HOBAA†

Stout, Penelope Thomson (1622–1732). Indian captive. CRB

Stout, William Bushnell (1880–1956). Engineer. COKA

Stowe, Harriet Beecher (1811–1896). Author. BEGA; BOA; BOC; DEI; DEJ; DOD; GIBA; JOCA; SMC; STJ; STLA; VAB; WABC†; WHB

Strachan, John R. (1916–). Government worker. YOI

Strasfogel, Ignace (1909–1982). Conductor, born Poland. STM†

Stratt, Parker (1941?–). Winner, Young American Medal for Bravery. ANCA

Stratton, Charles Sherwood (Tom Thumb) (1838–1883). Midget. KIB

Stratton, Monty (1912–1982). Baseball player. LYE

Straus, Lina. Wife of Nathan Straus. LER

Straus, Nathan (1848–1931). Merchant, philanthropist, born Germany. ALD; GRB-1; LETA; PEB

Straus, Oscar Solomon (1850–1926). Diplomat. LETA

Strauss, Johann (1825–1899). Austrian composer. KAE

Strauss, Paul. Conductor. STM†

Strauss, Richard (1864–1949). German composer. BAE; BEKA; BUC; KAE; SAA; YOM†

Stravinsky, Igor Fëdorovich (1882–1971). Composer, born Russia. ASB-1; BAE; BEKA; BUC; FIE; KAE; POG; SAA; YOL

Strawberry, Darryl (1962–). Baseball player. HEFB†

Streeter, Edward (1891–1976). Author. BEE

Stresemann, Gustav (1878–1929). German statesman. MEC†; WIC

Stresemann, Wolfgang (1904–). German conductor. STM†

Strickland, William (1914–). Conductor. STM†

Stroessner, Alfredo (1912–). President of Paraguay. BAGA

Strong, Anna Louise (1885–1970). Journalist. NIA

Strong, Caleb (1745–1819). Governor. FEAA

Strong, Ken (Elmer Kenneth) (1906–1979). Football player. DAFG; SUD

Stroyer, Jacob (b. 1846). Author. DADB

Stuart, Gilbert (1755–1828). Painter. BR; CHC; FRA; LEE; MAG; SIE

Stuart, James Ewell Brown (Jeb) (1833–1864). General. ARE; MAD

Stuart, John McDouall (1815–1866). Australian explorer, born Scotland. ROL†

Stubblefield, Philip (1913–). Conductor. STM†

Stuhldreher, Harry (1901–1965). Football player. DAG; DAGA; DAI; HIE

Stuhlinger, Ernst (1913–). Physicist, born Germany. POE

Stulberg, Julius (1913–). Conductor. STM†

Sturges, Preston (1898–1959). Motion picture director, producer. ED-1†

Sturt, Charles (1795–1869). English explorer. MOB; ROL

Sturtevant, Alfred Henry (1891–1970). Geneticist. BEK†

Stutz, Geraldine. Department store executive. GLO

Stydahar, Joseph Leo (1912–). Football player, coach. SUD

Sucre, Antonio José de (1795–1830). Venezuelan general, statesman. BAA; LAB

Sukarno, Achmed (1901–1970). Indonesian president. ARA; KEF; WEB

Sukloff, Marie. Russian terrorist. JAC

Sullivan, Anne, see Macy, Anne Sullivan.

Sullivan, Sir Arthur Seymour (1842–1900). English composer. BAE; KAE; SAA†

Sullivan, John Lawrence (1858–1918). Boxer. DAG; DAGA; RAAC

Sullivan, Kathryn (1951–). Astronaut. FOJ-1

Sullivan, Leon Howard (1922–). Clergyman, civil rights leader. DOF-1; EOA

Sullivan, Leonor K. (1904–). Congresswoman. GRAB-1†

Sullivan, Louis Henry (1856–1924). Architect. FOF; LAF; LEDA

Sultzer, Joe (1884–1981). Comedian. BUR-1

Suman, John Robert (1890–). Petroleum engineer. LEGA; YOD

Summer, Donna (1948–). Singer. BUIB-1

Summerall, Charles Pelot (1867–1955). General. RAE

Summers, Bob. Automobile racer. OLDC

Summers, John. Skater. VAD-6

Sumner, Charles (1811–1874). Senator, abolitionist. BEJ

Sun Ch'ing-ling (Sung) (1890–). Wife of Sun Yat-sen. EUA

Sun Yat-sen (1866–1925). Chinese statesman. ASB-1; CAAA; DOF; KEE; LAD; SPA

Sunday, Billy (William Ashley) (1862–1935). Evangelist. COKB; DAFD

Sundiata I. King of Mali. MIC

Sunni Ali Ber (1464–1492). Emperor of Timbuctoo. ADA; ADB; DOA; GRAB-04

Surcouf, Robert (1773–1827). French privateer. KEH

Surratt, Mary Eugenia (1820–1865). Conspirator. WABC†

Surtees, John (1934–). English automobile racer. ABB; JA; PAW

Susan (d. 238). Saint. WIB

Susanna (d. 295). Saint. QUA

Susskind, Walter (1908–). Czech conductor. STM†

Sutherland, Efua Theodora (1924–). Ghanaian author. CRA

Sutherland, Joan (1926–). Australian singer. SAB

Sutro, Adolph Heinrich Joseph (1830–1898). Mining engineer, born Germany. LETA; YOG

Sutter, Bruce (1953–). Baseball player. AAS; AAS-2

Sutter, John Augustus (1803–1880). Pioneer, born Germany. BLD; COE; DOCA

Suttner, Bertha von (1843–1914). Austrian pacifist. MEA; MEC; SHFE†; WIC

Sutton, Percy Ellis (1920–). Politician. DU

Sutton, Robert (fl. early 18th century). English apothecary. RIE†

Swain, Clara A. (1834–1910). Physician. FLA

Swalin, Benjamin (1901–). Conductor. STM

Swallow, Ellen, see Richards, Ellen Swallow.

Swan, Sir Joseph Wilson (1828–1914). English inventor. FE

Swan, Virl M. (1910–). Conductor. STM†

Swann, Lynn (1952–). Football player, sportscaster. AAS-18

Swedenborg, Emanuel (1688–1772). Swedish philosopher, scientist. COEA

Sweeney, Robert (b. 1853). Sailor, born West Indies. TA

Sweezo, William. Linotypist. GEA

Swift, Jonathan (1667–1745). English author. COO

Swigert, John L. (1931–1982). Astronaut. WIAA-5

Swinburne, Algernon Charles (1837–1909). English poet. COP

Swisshelm, Jane Grey (1815–1884). Journalist. JAE

Swithin (d. 862). Saint. WIB

Switzer, Kathy. Track athlete. BELB; HOBAA†

Swope, Gerard (1872–1957). Engineering executive, philanthropist. GRB-1

Sylvis, William H. (1828–1869). Labor leader. COH; DABA; LEHA; SEA

Symes, James Miller (1897–1976). Railroad executive. PAA

Syncletica. Saint. DAD-2

Szekely, Eva (1927–). Hungarian swimmer. SLA

Szell, George (1897–1970). Conductor, born Hungary. EWD; STM; YOM

Szent-Györgyi, Albert von (1893–1986). Biochemist, born Hungary. PAC; RIF

Szent-Györgyi, Marta von (1910–1963). Wife of Albert von Szent-Györgyi. PAC

Szold, Henrietta (1860–1945). Zionist leader. BLF; GUB; KAD; LES; LETA

Szold, Robert (1889–1977). Lawyer, philanthropist. GRB-1

T

Tabor, Baby Doe (Elizabeth Donduel) (1854–1935). Frontierswoman. RAB; WIAA-2

Tacitus, Cornelius (55?–120?). Roman historian. HIB

Taft, Alphonso (1810–1891). Jurist. LAI†

Taft, Helen Herron (1861–1943). Wife of William Howard Taft. BAG; BAG-1; BLG; CHB; KL; MAA; MAU; PRB; ROH; ROHA

Taft, Robert Alphonso (1889–1953). Senator. KEC; KED; LAI

Taft, Robert Alphonso, Jr. (1917–). Congressman. LAI†

Taft, William Howard (1857–1930). President of U.S. BAEB; BAG; BAG-1; BEB; BLA; BUIA; CAG; CAH; COI; COS; DUB; DUC; DUCA; FLC; FRBA; HIH; LAI; LEQ; LEQA; MAB; MABA; MIA; PED; ROH; ROHA; ROK†; SUBB; WHD

Taft, William Howard, III (1915–). Government official. LAI†

Taharga (fl. 688–662 B.C.). Ethiopian king. GRAB-04

Taigi, Anna Maria, Blessed (1769–1837). DAD-2

Tal, Mikhail (1936–). Latvian chess player. LEQB

Talbert, Billy (William Franklin) (1918–). Tennis player. HI

Talbert, Mary Burnett (1866–1923). Civil rights leader. DOF-1; GRAB-01

Talbot, Matthew (1856–1925). Irish religious figure. REC

Talbot, Ralph (1897–1918). Aviator. REA

Talbot, William Henry Fox (1800–1877). English inventor. FE; SHFB

Tallchief, Maria (1925–). Dancer. ATA; FOGC; GRAD

Tallchief, Marjorie (1927–). Dancer. ATA; GRAD

Tallmadge, Benjamin (1754–1835). Army officer. SEB; SOA

Tallon, Dale (Michael Dale) (1950–). Canadian hockey player. ORB

Tamerlane (1336?–1405). Mongol conqueror. BLW; CAAA

Tamm, Igor Yevgenyvich (1895–1971). Russian physicist. LET

Tammany (fl. 1685). Delaware Indian. HED

Taney, Roger Brooke (1777–1864). Supreme Court justice. FLC

Tanguay, Eva (1878–1947). Entertainer, born Canada. MASB

Tanner, Henry Ossawa (1859–1937). Painter. ADA; ADB; BEBA; BRB†; HUA; ROG

Tanner, John (1779–1846?). Indian captive. DI; HEE; RAC

Tanner, Sammy (1937?–). Motorcycle racer. OLAB

Tarbell, Ida Minerva (1857–1944). Author. COGB; DAD; WABC†; YOC

Tarcisius (fl. 258). Saint. DAD-1

Tarkenton, Francis (1940–). Football player. AAS-20; ANC; BRE; CL-1; DEH; GUEB; HAGC; RUC

Tarkington, Booth (1869–1946). Author. BEE; CON

Tarleton, Sir Banastre (1754–1833). English general. SOA

Tarrant, Caesar (d. 1796). Slave, seaman. DAF-1†; WIBA†

Tartini, Giuseppe (1692–1770). Italian composer, violinist. BEN; CHFA; SAA†

Tasman, Abel J. (1603–1659). Dutch explorer. KNB†; MOB; ROL

Tate, Allen (1899–1979). Poet. LEJ

Tati, Jacques (1908–1982). French actor, film director. ED-1†

Tatum, Art (1910–1956). Pianist. COF-1; WAD†

Tatum, Edward Lawrie (1909–1975). Biochemist. RIF

Tatum, Jack (John David) (1948–). Football player. GUCA

Taussig, Helen Brooke (1898–1986). Physician. CHE; CLA; EOA; GIB-1; RAAG

Taussig, Walter (1908–). Conductor, born Austria. STM†

Taylor, Albert (1879–1961). Physicist. COLA

Taylor, Ann (1782–1866). English poet. BEH

Taylor, Bert Leston (1866–1921). Columnist. ALA

Taylor, Bruce (1948–). Football player. GUD

Taylor, Cecil (1933–). Pianist. COF-1

Taylor, Charley (1941–). Football player. CO; DEHA-1; SMI

Taylor, Deems (1885–1966). Composer. BAD; WIA

Taylor, George (1716–1781). American Revolutionary patriot. BAEA; BUIB†; COJ†; FEAB

Taylor, Guy (1919–). Conductor. STM†

Taylor, James (1935–). Football player. BEKB; DUF; HAD; JOA

Taylor, Jane (1783–1824). English poet. BEH

Taylor, John L. Reporter. STAA

Taylor, Lawrence (1959–). Football player. AAS-15

Taylor, Lee (d. 1980). Boat racer. OLDC

Taylor, Lucy Hobbs (1833–1910). Dentist. SC†; WABC†

Taylor, Margaret Smith (1788–1852). Wife of Zachary Taylor. BAG; BAG-1; BLG†; CHA; KL; MAA; MAU; PRB; ROH; ROHA

Taylor, Maxwell Davenport (1901–1987). General. RAE; SUA

Taylor, Otis (1942–). Football player. CO; DEHA; GUF; SMI; ST

Taylor, Susie King (1848–1912). Nurse, teacher. MAV

Taylor, Valerie (1936–). Australian diver. HAKA

Taylor, Zachary (1784–1850). President of U.S. BAEB; BAG; BAG-1; BEB; BLA; BUIA; CAG; CAH; COI; COJA; COS; DUC; DUCA; FRBA;

HIH; LEQ; LEQA; MAB; MABA; MIA; PED;
ROH; ROHA; ROK†; SUBB; WHD

Tazieff, Haroun. Belgian geologist. KEH

Tchaikovsky, Peter Ilyich (1840–1893). Russian
composer. BEN; BRF; BUD; DEI; DEJ; FIE†;
GOB; KAE; POG; SAA; WIA; YOK

Tchekhov, Anton Pavlovich, *see* Chekhov, Anton
Pavlovich.

Teach, Edward, *see* Blackbeard.

Teacher, Brian (1954–). Tennis player. SLA

Teagarden, Jack (Weldon John) (1905–1964).
Trombonist. WAD†

Teague, Robert (1929–). Television reporter. FLD

Teale, Edwin Way (1899–1980). Naturalist. MIB†

Teasdale, Sara (1884–1933). Poet. BRBB

Tebbetts, Birdie (George Robert) (1914–). Baseball player, manager. HIC

Tecumseh (1768–1813). Shawnee Indian chief.
DEDB; HEC; HEGA; MAEA; MOD; ROD;
STAB; WAL

Teilhard de Chardin, Pierre (1881–1955). French
theologian, paleontologist, explorer. LO

Tekakwitha, Kateri (1656–1680). Mohawk Indian
nun. DAD-1; HED

Tekulve, Kent (1947–). Baseball player. AAS

Telemann, Georg Philipp (1681–1767). German
composer. BEM; SAA

Tell, William (fl. 1307). Swiss patriot. HEA; STP

Teller, Edward (1908–). Physicist, born Hungary.
KE†

Teltscher, Eliot (1959–). Tennis player. SLA

Temby, Stephen (1940–). Amateur radio operator. CAD

Temple, Lewis (1800–1854). Inventor. GRAB-03;
HAL

Temple, Shirley (1928–). Actress. FOR

Templeton, Alec (1910–1963). Pianist, born
Wales. GEA

Tenace, Gene (1946–). Baseball player. BELB;
SA-3

Tendler, Lew (1898–). Boxer. SLA†

Tennyson, Alfred Tennyson, 1st baron (1809–
1892). English poet. COP

Tenzing, Norgay (1914–1986). Nepalese mountaineer. KEH; MOB; PRC

Teresa, *see* Theresia, Blessed.

Teresa of Avila (1515–1582). Saint. DAD-3; QUA

Teresa of Lisieux, Saint, *see* Thérèse of Lisieux,
Saint.

Tereshkova, Valentina Vladimirova (1937–). Russian astronaut. THC

Terrell, Mary Church (1863–1954). Feminist.
ADA; ADB; LOAV; STAB-1; STB

Terry, Sonny (Saunders Teddell) (1911–1986).
Singer, harmonica player. SUH

Terry, William Harold (1898–). Baseball player,
manager. ALB; HAF; MUB-1; MUC; RIGA†

Tesla, Nikola (1857–1943). Electrical engineer,
born Croatia. BOK; FE; MAP

Tew, Thomas. Pirate. WHA†

Tewanima, Louis (d. 1969). Track athlete. HACA

Texas Rangers (Est. 1835). SUI

Thackeray, William Makepeace (1811–1863). English author. BEG; BEI; COO

Thadden-Trieglaff, Reinold von (1891–). German
church leader. BAF

Thaden, Louise (1905–). Aviator. GEDB†

Thales of Miletus (c. 636–546 B.C.). Greek philosopher, scientist. SIB†

Thant, U (1909–1974). Burmese United Nations
official. KE; WEA

Tharp, Twyla (1941–). Dancer, choreographer.
FOGC

Thatcher, Margaret (1925–). English prime minister. DU-1; GI

Thaw, William (1894–1934). Aviator, WW I.
HAMY

Thaxter, Celia (1835–1894). Poet. BEF

Thayer, Sylvanus (1785–1872). General. RAE

Thecla (30–120). Saint. DAD-1; DAD-3

Theiler, Max (1899–1972). South African virologist. AAS-31; RIF

Thelwell, Jeanne (1951–). Lawyer. SMBB

Themistocles (527?–460 B.C.). Athenian statesman, naval commander. COM; DYA; PLA

Theodora (508?–548). Consort of Justinian I, emperor of the Eastern Roman Empire. BOI

Theodore Tiro. Saint. DAD-3

Theodosius (d. 529). Saint. DAD-2

Théophane Vénard, Blessed, *see* Vénard, Jean
Théophane, Blessed.

Thérése of Lisieux (1873–1897). Saint. DAD-1;
DAD-3; MOC

Theresia, Blessed (1178–1250). DAD-2

Thiel, George (1898–). Realtor, born the Netherlands. BAEA-1

Thiel, Katie Kamp (1907–). Businesswoman,
born Germany. BAEA-1

Thieu, Nguyen-Van (1923–). President of Republic of South Vietnam. WECA

Thomas. Saint, apostle. DAD-3; QUA

Thomas à Becket (1118–1170). Saint. CHG; DAD-
3; MAJ; ONA

Thomas of Villanova (1488–1555). Saint. DAD-3;
MOC

Thomas, Andrew. Urologist. CAF-1†

Thomas, Bertram Sidney (1892–1950). British
diplomat. ROL†

Thomas, Charles A. (1900–1982). Chemical executive. PAB

Thomas, Duane (1947?–). Football player. LEZB

Thomas, George Henry (1816–1870). General. STG

Thomas, Isaiah (1749–1831). Journalist. SQB†

Thomas, James Gorman (1950–). Baseball player. AAS-4

Thomas, Jeanette. Animal behaviorist, polar researcher. LA-1

Thomas, Jesse Burgess (1777–1853). Senator. SEC

Thomas, Lowell Jackson (1892–1981). Journalist. JAD; LEN

Thomas, Martha Carey (1857–1935). Educator. BUDA†

Thomas, Norman Mattoon (1884–1968). Socialist leader. FOJ

Thomas, Pat (1954–). Football player. AAS-13

Thomas, Theodore (1835–1905). Conductor, born Germany. YOM

Thomas Aquinas (1225?–1274). Saint. DAD-2; LO; ONA; OZA

Thomas More, Saint, *see* More, Sir Thomas.

Thompson, Ben (1842?–1883?). Outlaw. JOBA

Thompson, Benjamin, *see* Rumford, Benjamin Thompson, count.

Thompson, Carolyn (1957–). State legislator. HOD-1

Thompson, Dannie. Automobile racer. OLCA

Thompson, Danny (1947–1976). Baseball player. CL-04

Thompson, David (1954–). Basketball player. AAS-5; ARB-3

Thompson, David (1770–1857). English explorer, fur trader. KNA; ROL†

Thompson, Dorothy (1894–1961). Journalist. JAE; MUA

Thompson, Era Bell (fl. 1946). Editor. DADB

Thompson, Hank (1925–). Singer. LA

Thompson, Jenn. Actress. BRF-1

Thompson, Leon E. (1928–). Conductor. STM†

Thompson, Mickey (1928–). Automobile racer. LEX; OLAB; OLB; OLCA

Thomson, Bobby (1923–). Baseball player, born Scotland. DEHA-1

Thomson, Sir Joseph John (1856–1940). English physicist. CAA; FE; MOBA; RID; SHFB; SIA

Thomson, Virgil (1896–). Composer. MAF

Thomson, William, *see* Kelvin, William Thomson, 1st baron.

Thoreau, Henry David (1817–1862). Author. ARB; BAC; BEG; BEGA; BLE; BOA; CAC; CO-1; CORA; CUC; EOB; HAJ; HIBB; HOA; MIB; RED; SQA; SUFA; WHB; WOAA

Thorne, Frank (1930–). Cartoonist. GOB-1

Thornton, Jeannye. Journalist. STAA†

Thornton, Matthew (1714–1803). American Revolutionary patriot. BAEA; BUIB†; COJ†; FEAB; MAC†

Thornton, William (1759–1828). Architect, born West Indies. BUIB†

Thorpe, Jim (1888–1953). Track athlete, football player. ASBA; BELB; DAB; DAFB; DAFG; DAG; DAGA; DAI; DAJ; DEF; DUF; FIC; HACA; HEG; HEI; HIE; HOC; LEH; LEPA; LEYB; LYB; RAAE; SID; SUD

Thothmes III, *see* Tuthmosis III.

Three Stooges, *see* Fine, Larry; Howard, Jerry; Howard, Moe; Howard, Samuel.

Thucydides (471–400? B.C.). Greek historian. HIB

Thumb, Tom, *see* Stratton, Charles Sherwood.

Thurber, James G. (1894–1961). Author, cartoonist. BEE; CUC; FLBA; GEA

Thurman, Howard (1900–1981). Protestant theologian. ADB

Thurman, Sammy Fancher. Rodeo rider. VADB

Thurston, Fuzzy (Fred). Football player. JOA

Thurston, Howard (1869–1936). Magician. GIA; KEB

Thutmose III, *see* Tuthmosis III.

Tiant, Luis (1940–). Baseball player. AAS-2

Tibbets, Paul (1915?–). Aviator. HAMY†

Tickey, Bertha Reagan (1913?–). Softball player. HOBAA†

Tickner, Charles (1953–). Skater. LIEA; VAD-6

Tiffany, Charles Lewis (1812–1902). Jeweler. LAH

Tijerina, Reies Lopez (1926–). Mexican-American leader. BENA; NEAA

Tilden, Samuel Jones (1814–1886). Governor. GO; WHD†

Tilden, William Tatem, Jr. (1893–1953). Tennis player. AAS-28; ASBA; DAG; DAGA; FOX; HEG; HI; LAHA; LEF; SID

Tilghman, William Matthew (1854–1924). Law officer. JOD; SUI

Tillery, Hubert (1920–). Conductor. STM†

Tillis, Mel (1932–). Singer, composer, comedian. HAG-1

Tilmon, James (1934–). Aviator. DRA

Timothy (d. 97? A.D.). Saint. DAD-2; QUA

Timothy, Elizabeth (d. 1757). Publisher, born the Netherlands. WABC†

Tinker, Joseph Bert (1880–1948). Baseball player. ALB; DAFD

Tinnè, Alexine (1839–1869). Dutch explorer. RIG

Tintoretto, Il (1518–1594). Italian painter. JAA

Tiradentes (1748–1792). Brazilian revolutionist. LAB

Tirpitz, Alfred von (1849–1930). German admiral. ARD

Titian (1477–1576). Italian painter. JAA; KAA; MAI

Tito, Josip Broz (1892–1980). Yugoslavian premier. ARA; COJB; DU-1; WEB

Titov, Gherman Stepanovich (1935–). Russian astronaut. NEB; THC

Tittle, Y. A. (Yelberton Abraham) (1926–). Football player. ANC; DAFG; DEH; DUD; DUE; HEI; PAW; RAAD

Titus (fl. 50). Saint. DAD-2

Tiy (fl. 1400 B.C.). Queen of Egypt. COLB

Tkaczuk, Walter Robert (1947–). Canadian hockey player. FICC; ORB

Tobias, Channing Heggie (1882–1961). Civil rights leader. DOF-1; GRAB-01

Todd, Thelma (1905–1935). Actress. MASB

Toefield, Alfred. Cyclist. BELB

Tokle, Torger (d. 1945). Skier, born Norway. DAG; DAGA

Tolan, Eddie (1909?–). Track athlete. BRB†

Tolliver, Melba. Television news reporter. STAA

Tolpuddle martyrs. LAD

Tolstoi, Lev Nikolaevich (1828–1910). Russian author. DEI; DEJ; POFA

Tolton, Augustine (1854–1897). Priest. ADA; ADB

Tomassa (1840–1888?). Indian captive. WAB

Tomlin, Lily (1939–). Actress. BOHC; MASB

Tompkins, Daniel D. (1774–1825). Vice president of U.S. FEA; HAOA; HOEA

Tonti, Henri de (1650–1704). French explorer, born Italy. MAS

Toole, Joseph (1851–1928). Governor. SEC

Toomey, Bill (William Anthony) (1939?–). Track athlete. LEYB

Toribio. Saint. DAD-2

Torno, Laurent. Conductor. STM†

Torre, Joseph Paul (1940–). Baseball player. HOCM; LEY; PEC; PRA; SHD; ZAA

Torres, John (1939?–). Sculptor. FAH

Torres, Liz. Actress. MASB

Torres, Luis de (fl. 1492). Spanish interpreter. GUB; LETA; PEB

Torres, Luis Vaez de (fl. 1606). Spanish navigator. ROL†

Torresola, Griselio (1925?–1950). Assassin. RABA

Torrey, John (1796–1873). Botanist. HYB

Torricelli, Evangelista (1608–1647). Italian mathematician, physicist. CAA; FE; SHFB

Toscanini, Arturo (1867–1957). Italian conductor. DEI; DEJ; EWB; FRB; KEE; MAS; YOH; YOM

Toth, Alex (1928–). Cartoonist. GOB-1

Toth, Andor. Conductor. STM†

Toulouse-Lautrec, Henri Marie Raymond de (1864–1901). French painter. KAA

Toumanova, Tamara (1919–). Russian dancer. ATA

Touré, Sékou (1922–1984). Guinean president. ADA; JO

Tourgee, Albion Winegar (1838–1905). Politician, author. STJC

Touro, Judah (1775–1854). Philanthropist. ALD; GUB; LERA; LETA; PEB

Toussaint, Cheryl (1953?–). Track athlete. RYX

Toussaint L'Ouverture, Pierre Dominique (1743–1803). Haitian general, liberator. ADA; ADB; BAA; BACA; KEH; MAJ; YOFA

Townes, Charles Hard (1915–). Physicist. AAS-33; COLA; DU-1; FE; MAPA; THA

Townsend, Marjorie (1930–). Electronics engineer. HOG

Townsend, Robert (b. 1753). Spy. FOA

Townsend, Sally (1760–1842). American Revolutionary patriot. CLC; STJ

Townshend, Peter (1945–). English singer. BUIB-2

Toynbee, Arnold Joseph (1889–1975). English historian. HIB†

Trafton, George (1896–1971). Football player, coach. DAFG†; SUD

Trahey, Jane (1923–). Advertising executive. LES-1

Train, George Francis (1829–1904). Financier. GUBA†; WABC†

Trajan (53–117). Emperor of Rome. CAAA; COK

Trammell, Beatrice Johnson. Nurse. BOG

Trapp, Maria Augusta (1905–1987). Austrian singer. CAHA

Travers, Pamela L. (1906–). English author, born Australia. SMB

Travis, William Barret (1809–1836). Army officer. AKC; KUA

Traynor, Pie (Harold Joseph) (1899–1972). Baseball player. ALB; DAFC; DAFD; DAH; LEY; MUB-1; MUC; RIGA†

Tremblay, Jean Claude (1939–). Canadian hockey player. LEYA

Trenck, Friedrich von der (1726–1794). German military adventurer. JAC

Tresh, Thomas Michael (1938–). Baseball player. BRD

Tressler, Donald Kiteley (1894–). Food technologist. PAB

Tretiak, Vladislav (1952–). Russian hockey player. ORA

Trevelyan, George Macaulay (1876–1962). English historian. HIB

Trevino, Lee (1939–). Golfer. AAS-27; IZA; LYB; NEAA; WH-3

Trevithick, Richard (1771–1833). English engineer, inventor. EVB

Trice, Virgil G. (1926–). Engineer. CAF-1

Trippi, Charley (1923–). Football player. DAFG; HIE; SUD

Troctula di Ruggiero (d. 1197). Italian physician. MASA; RIB; SC

Trombley, George (1884–). Conductor. STM†

Trost, Al (1949–). Soccer player. GUEC-1

Trotsky, Leon (1877–1940). Russian communist leader. COJB; NEBB-1

Trotter, James Monroe (1844–1912). Government employee. ADA; ADB

Trotter, William Monroe (1872–1934). Civil rights worker. ADB; BEJ; STJB

Trottier, Bryan (1956–). Canadian hockey player. AAS-22

Trotula, see Troctula di Ruggiero.

Trudeau, Edward Livingston (1848–1915). Physician. FAF; LYA; SHG

Trujillo, Brenda. Trucking manager. FOC-1

Trujillo Molina, Rafael Leónidas (1891–1961). Dominican chief of state. ARA; BAGA

Truman, Elizabeth V. (Bess) (1885–1982). Wife of Harry S. Truman. BAG; BAG-1; BLG; CHB; KL; MAA; MAU; PRB; ROH; ROHA

Truman, Harry S. (1884–1972). President of U.S. ALE; ASB-1; BAEB; BAG; BAG-1; BEB; BLA; BUIA; CAG; CAH; COI; COJA; COS; DEI; DEJ; DUB†; DUC; DUCA; FEA; FRBA; HADA; HAOH; HIH; HOEA; KE; LEQ; LEQA; MAB; MABA; MIA; PED; ROH; ROHA; ROK†; SUBB; WEE; WHD; YOA

Trumbull, Faith (fl. 1777). American Revolutionary patriot. CLC†

Trumbull, John (1750–1831). Jurist. BUIB†

Trumbull, John (1756–1843). Painter. BR; BUIB†; HEDA

Trumbull, Jonathan (1710–1785). Merchant, colonial leader. BUIB†; SEC

Trumpeldor, Joseph (1880–1920). Israeli settler. GRB-1; PEB; ROGA

Truog, Emil (1884–). Soil scientist. YOE

Truth, Sojourner (1797–1883). Abolitionist. ADA; ADB; BEJ; BLE; BLF†; BRB; DADA; GIBA; JO; LES-2; LOAV; WABC†; WAH

Truxtun, Thomas (1755–1822). Naval officer. BUIB†

Tschaikovsky, Peter Ilyich, see Tchaikovsky, Peter Ilyich.

Tsiolkovsky, Konstantin E. (1857–1935). Russian inventor, rocket expert. NEB; STMA; THC

Tsukahara, Mitsuo (1947–). Japanese gymnast. LIE

Tubbs, Alice Huckert (Poker Alice) (1851–1930). Gambler, born England. RAB

Tubman, Harriet (1820–1913). Abolitionist. ADA; ADB; BEJ; BRB; BRBD; BRBE; BRG; BUA; COG; DADA; DOD; GEE; GIBA; HODA; HUA; HUB; JOC; LOAV; NIA; ROG; SMC; STD; STJA; STLA; WABC†; WAH; YOC; YOI

Tubman, William V. S. (1895–1971). Liberian president. ADA

Tuchman, Barbara (1912?–). Historian. BOHG

Tucker, Richard (1913–1975). Singer. BRBB-1

Tucker, Robert Louis (1945–). Football player. GUCA

Tucker, Sophie (1884–1966). Singer, entertainer. MASB

Tucker, Tanya (1958–). Singer. KRI-1

Tull, Jethro (1674–1741). English agriculturist. CAB

Tunnell, Emlen (1926–1975). Football player, coach. DAFG; HAE; SUD

Tunney, Gene (James Joseph) (1898–1978). Boxer. DAG; DAGA; RAAC; SCA

Tupac Amaru (1544?–1571). Inca chieftain. LAB†

Tupac Amaru II (1742–1781). Peruvian revolutionist. LAB†

Tupine, Oleg (1920–). French dancer. ATA

Turgenev, Ivan Sergeevich (1818–1883). Russian author. POFA

Turing, Alan M. (1912–1954). English mathematician, computer pioneer. GRAB-3

Turkle, Brinton (1915–). Author, illustrator. SM

Turley, Bob (1930–). Baseball players. DEHA-1

Turner, Bulldog (Clyde) (1919–). Football player. DAFG; KABA; SUD

Turner, Charles Henry (1867–1923). Neurologist. BRB†; CAF-1; HAM

Turner, Clyde, see Turner, Bulldog (Clyde).

Turner, Curtis (1924–1970). Automobile racer. LEX; LEXA; YAA

Turner, Doris (1930–). Labor leader. BI†

Turner, Frederick Jackson (1861–1932). Historian. HIB

Turner, Henry McNeal (1833–1915). Bishop. ADA; ADB

Turner, Nat (1800–1831). Insurrectionist. ADA; ADB; BEJ; BRB†; GRAB-05; ROG; WIAB

Turner, Scott (1880–). Mining engineer. LEGA; YOD

Turton, Janene (1954?–). Motorcyclist. BUIC

Tuska, George. Cartoonist. GOB-1

Tutankhamen (1361–1351 B.C.). King of Egypt. COA; GRAB-04

Tuthmosis III (1504–1450 B.C.). King of Egypt. CAAA; GRAB-04

Tutu, Desmond Mpilo (1931–). South African Anglican bishop. AAS-34

Twain, Mark, pseud. (1835–1910). Author. BEC; BEE; BOA; CAC; COB; CUC; DEI; DEJ; FOH; HACB; HEF; HOA; LEGB; MAL; RAC; SMBA; STK

Tweed, William Marcy (1823–1878). Politician. COGC

Twiggs, Leo Franklin (1934–). Painter. FAI

Twyman, Jack (1934–). Basketball player. HID

Tyler, Charley (d. 1863). Pioneer. SCB

Tyler, John (1790–1862). President of U.S. ALE; BAEB; BAG; BAG-1; BEB; BLA; BUIA; CAG; CAH; COI; COS; DUC; DUCA; FEA; FRBA; HAOA; HIH; HOEA; KEC†; LEQ; LEQA; MAB; MABA; MIA; PED; ROH; ROHA; ROK†; SUBB; WHD

Tyler, Julia Gardiner (1820–1889). Second wife of John Tyler. BAG; BAG-1; BLG†; CHA; KL; MAA; MAU; PRB; ROH; ROHA†

Tyler, Letitia Christian (1790–1842). First wife of John Tyler. BAG; BAG-1; BLG†; CHA; KL; MAA; MAU; PRB; ROH; ROHA†

Tyler, Robin. Comedienne. MASB

Tyler, Royall (1757–1826). Jurist. BUIB†

Tyrrell, John F. Graphologist. LACA

Tyson, Cicely (1939?–). Actress. AB; BOHC

Tyus, Wyomia (1945–). Track athlete. HOBAA; RYA†; ST-2

Tzu Hsi (1835–1908). Empress dowager of China. BOI; FAE; LIDA; SPA

U

U Nu, *see* Nu.

U Thant, *see* Thant, U.

Ubald (1080?–1160). Saint. DAD-2

Uchida, Miki Akiyama (1903–). Businesswoman, born Japan. BAEA-1

Udo Akpabio. Nigerian tribesman. PEA

Ullman, Norm. Hockey player. ORC

Ulm, Charles. Australian aviator. HAMY

Ulmer, Fran. Mayor. WHE†

Unanue, Hipólito (1755–1833). Peruvian statesman. LAB

Underdue, James (fl. 1861). Chaplain. HODA†

Underwood, Oscar W. (1862–1929). Senator. KEC†

Undset, Sigrid (1882–1949). Norwegian author. CAHA

Unger, Garry (1947–). Canadian hockey player. FICC; LEYA; ORB

Unger, Heinz (1895–1964). Canadian conductor, born Germany. STM†

Ungerer, Tomi (1931–). French author, illustrator. SM

Unitas, Johnny (1933–). Football player. ALBA; ANC; ASBA; BUJA; DAFB; DAFG; DAGA; DAI; DEH; DEHA-1; DUD; DUE; FRD; HEI; HOC; KADA; LIBB; PAW; RAAD; SHEA; VAE

United Nations. Founded 1945. MEB

United States Bureau of Narcotics. LID

Unseld, Westley (1947?–). Basketball player. AAS-27; ARB-1; HOCA; RUB; SA-2

Unser, Al (1939?–). Automobile racer. LEVA; OLCC; ORD

Unser, Bobby (1934–). Automobile racer. LEVA; OLCC; ORD; ST-1

Unser, Del (1944–). Baseball player. AAS-25

Unteidt, Byron (1919–). Hero of school bus accident. CAD

Upshaw, Gene (1945–). Football player. AAS-11

Upton, John (fl. 1723). Pirate. WHA†

Urban V, Blessed (1310–1370). DAD-3

Urey, Harold Clayton (1893–1981). Chemist. BOB; RID

Ursula (4th century). Saint. QUA

Ussachevsky, Vladimir (1911–). Russian composer. BEKA

V

Vail, Alfred (1807–1859). Inventor. BUE

Valentine (d. 270). Saint. DAD-2; ONA

Valenzuela, Fernando (1960–). Mexican baseball player. HEFB†

Valluzzi, Bruce. Surf rider. OLD

Van Alen, Clarence R. Soldier, WW I. BRB†

Van Allen, James Alfred (1914–). Astrophysicist. HAC; NEB

Van Alstyne, Egbert (1882–1951). Songwriter. MOA

Van Breda Kolff, Bill (1922?–). Basketball coach. LEW†

Van Brocklin, Norman Mack (1926–1983). Football player, coach. ANC; DUD; DUE; RAAD

Van Buren, Hannah Hoes (1783–1819). Wife of Martin Van Buren. BAG; BAG-1; BLG†; CHA; KL; MAA; MAU; PRB; ROH; ROHA

Van Buren, Martin (1782–1862). President of U.S. BAEB; BAG; BAG-1; BEB; BLA; BUIA; CAG; CAH; COI; COS; DUC; DUCA; FEA; FRBA; HAOA; HEEA; HIH; HOEA; LEQ; LEQA; MAB; MABA; MIA; PED; ROH; ROHA; ROK†; SUBB; WHD

Van Buren, Steve (1921–). Football player. BEKB; DAFG; DUF; HAD; RAAE; SUD

Vance, Dazzy (Clarence Arthur) (1909–1961). Baseball player. ALB; FRC-1†; GEB; NEA; RIGA†

Vancouver, George (1757–1798). English explorer. KNB†; ROL

Van Damm, Sheila (1922–). English automobile racer. SLA†

Vandenberg, Roger. Army officer. RAE

Van den Burg, William (1901–). Conductor, born the Netherlands. STM†

Vanderbilt, Cornelius (1794–1877). Financier. COKB; WED

Vander Meer, John Samuel (1914–). Football player. GRA; NEA

Van der Rohe, Ludwig Mies, *see* Mies van der Rohe, Ludwig.

Van der Waals, Johannes Diederik (1837–1923). Dutch physicist. FE

Van Dyck, Sir Anthony (1599–1641). Flemish painter. CHC

Van Dyke, Fred. Surf rider. OLD

Van Eyck, Hubert, *see* Eyck, Hubert van.

Van Eyck, Jan, *see* Eyck, Jan van.

Van Fleet, James Alward (1892–). General. RAE

Van Gogh, Vincent, *see* Gogh, Vincent van.

Van Heusen, Jimmy (1913–). Songwriter. MOA

Van Horn, Edith (1920–). Labor leader. BI†

Van Iersel, Louis. Soldier, WW I, born the Netherlands. REA

Van Impe, Edward Charles (1940–). Canadian hockey player. FICB; THE

Van Lew, Elizabeth (1818–1900). Spy. FOA; SUG; WABC†

Van Lier, Norm (1946?–). Basketball player. HIBAA

Van Loon, Hendrik (1882–1944). Author, born the Netherlands. LEAB; LEB

Vann, Robert Lee (1887–1940). Journalist. ADA; ADB

Van Orsdel, William Wesley (1850–1919). Clergyman. WAA

Van Peebles, Melvin (1932–). Motion picture director. AB

Van Straten, Florence (1913–). Meteorologist. EMB†; YOF

Van Vactor, David (1906–). Conductor. STM†

Van Wolvelaere, Patty (1951?–). Track athlete. GLB

Vare, Glenna Collett, *see* Collett, Glenna.

Varèse, Edgard (1883–1965). French composer. EWAA

Vargas, Getúlio Dornelles (1883–1954). Brazilian president. BAGA; WOB

Varick, James (1750–1828). Clergyman. BUIB†

Varner, Margaret (1927–). Squash racquets player. JAB

Varthema, Ludovico de (1461?–1517?). Italian traveler. ROL

Varus. Saint. DAD-3

Vasarely, Victor (1908–). French painter, born Hungary. WIAA

Vasconcelos, José (1882–1959). Mexican educator. NEBA

Vasquez, Joseph C. (1918?–). Indian leader. GRAC

Vasquez, Pedro Ramírez. Mexican architect. NEBA

Vasquez, Tiburcio (1835–1875). Bandit. WIAA-1

Vassa, Gustavus, *see* Equiano, Olaudah.

Vataha, Randy (1948–). Football player. RUC

Vaughan, "Arky" (Joseph Floyd) (1912–1952). Baseball player. RIGA†

Vaughan Williams, Ralph (1872–1958). English composer. BUC; GOB; KAE; SAA†; YOJ

Vavilov, Nicolai Ivanovich (1887–1942). Russian botanist. WEF

Veale, Thomas (d. 1658). English pirate. WHA†

Velarde, Pablita (1918–). Painter. GRAD; WAB

Velázquez, Diego Rodríguez de Silva y (1599–1660). Spanish painter. CHC; MAI

Vénard, Jean Théophane, Blessed (1829–1861). DAD-3

Venturi, Ken (1931–). Golfer. BUJA; LABA

Venuti, Joe (1904–1978). Violinist. UN

Veracini, Francesco Maria (1685–1750). Italian violinist, composer. CHFA

Verchères, Marie Magdelaine Jarret de (1678–1747). Canadian heroine. MAJ; STP

Verdi, Giuseppe (1813–1901). Italian composer. BRF; BUD; GOB; KAE; SAA; TRC; WIA; YOJ

Vereen, Ben (1946?–). Singer, dancer. AB

Vergil, *see* Virgil.

Vermeer, Jan or Johannes (1632–1675). Dutch painter. CHC; KAA; MAI

Verne, Jules (1828–1905). French author. DEI; DEJ; STK

Verney, Edmund (1590–1642). English soldier. MAJ

Veronica (1st century). Saint. QUA

Veronica of Milan. Saint. DAD-2

Verrett, Shirley (1933?–). Singer. GRBA

Versalles, Zoilo (1940–). Cuban baseball player. IZA; PRA; SHF; VEA

Vesalius, Andreas (1514–1564). Belgian anatomist. CAA; CHD; DOE; HUD; POD; ROA; SHG; SIC

Vesco, Don (1940–). Motorcyclist. OLDB

Vesey, Denmark (1767–1822). Insurrectionist. ADA; ADB; BRB†; HODA; JO; SPB; STJA

Vespucci, Amerigo (1451–1512). Italian navigator. KNB; MOB; ROL; VIA†

Vianello, Hugo (1926–). Conductor. STM†

Vianney, Jean Baptiste Marie (1786–1859). Saint. DAD-3; MOC

Vicario, Leona (1789–1842). Mexican patriot. ROGB

Vickers, Jon (1926–). Canadian singer. BRBB-1

Victor (c. 300?). Saint. QUA

Victor, Wilma L. Educator, government official. GRAD

Victor Emanuel II (1820–1878). King of Sardinia. CAAA

Victoria (1819–1901). Queen of Great Britain and

Ireland. BOI; CAAA; CHG; COA; DEC; DEI; DEJ; FAE; GRAB; LIDA; PA; SCC; TRB; UNB

Victoria, Guadalupe, pseud. (1789–1843). Mexican soldier, political leader. NEBA

Vidocq, Eugène François (1775–1857). French police official. LACA; LID

Vieira, Antônio (1608–1697). Portuguese missionary. WOB

Vien, Joseph Marie (1716–1809). French painter. MAH†

Vieuxtemps, Henri François Joseph (1820–1881). Belgian violinist. CHFA

Vigee-Lebrun, Elisabeth (1755–1842). French painter. NE

Vigo, Francis (1747–1836). Pioneer. BUIB†

Vilas, Guillermo (1952–). Argentinian tennis player. AAS-28

Villa, Pancho (1878–1923). Mexican outlaw, revolutionist. NEBA; ROGB; WO

Villa-Lobos, Heitor (1887–1959). Brazilian composer. BACA; KAE

Villella, Edward (1936–). Dancer, choreographer. GRBA

Vincent de Paul (1581?–1660). Saint. DAD-3; MAK; QUA; STP

Vincent of Saragossa. Saint. DAD-2

Vincent Ferrer (1350–1419). Saint. DAD-2

Vinci, Leonardo da, see Leonardo da Vinci.

Vingo, Carmine. Boxer. BELB

Vinson-Owen, Maribel (1911–1961). Skater. HOBA†; HOBAA†

Violet, Arlene (1943–). State attorney general. WHE†

Viorst, Judith. Author. BOHD

Viotti, Giovanni Battista (1755–1824). Italian violinist. CHFA

Virchow, Rudolf (1821–1902). German pathologist. CHD; POB; ROA

Viren, Lasse (1949–). Finnish track athlete. SUBB-1

Virgil (70–19 B.C.). Roman poet. COK; COKB

Virgil of Salzburg (d. 784). Saint. MOC

Viscardi, Henry, Jr. (1912–). Leader in rehabilitation of disabled. LYA

Vishnetzir, Yuval (1947–). Israeli track athlete, born Palestine. SLA†

Vittorino da Feltre (Vittorino Ramboldini) (1378–1446). Italian educator. FRC

Vivaldi, Antonio (1675?–1741). Italian violinist, composer. BEM; CHFA; KAE; SAA; YOM†

Vlachos, Helen (1912?–). Greek newspaper publisher. CAHA

Vladeck, Baruch Charney (1886–1938). Journalist, born Russia. GEF

Vogel, Herb. Gymnastic coach. LEW

Vogt, William (1902–1968). Ecologist, ornithologist. SQA

Voight, Harry. Horologist. BUE

Volant, Guy (1909?–). Swiss Red Cross delegate. DED

Vollmar, Jocelyn (1925–). Dancer. ATA

Volta, Alessandro, conte (1745–1827). Italian physicist. CAA; DOE; DUA; FE; MAQ; SHFB; SIA; SOB

Voltaire (François Marie Arouet) (1694–1778). French author, philosopher. COG; DEI; DEJ; HIB; LO; OZA

Von Braun, Wernher (1912–1977). Rocket scientist, born Germany. COQ; CUB; FE; FRB; LEL; NEB; POE

Von der Ahe, Chris (19th century). Baseball team owner. DAFD

Von der Heide, Henry (1921–). Conductor. STM†

Von Humboldt, Alexander, see Humboldt, Alexander von.

Von Karajan, Herbert, see Karajan, Herbert von.

Von Kármán, Theodore, see Kármán, Theodore von.

Von Neumann, John (1903–1957). Mathematician, computer pioneer, born Hungary. GRAB-3; STN

Von Saltza, Susan Christina (1944–). Swimmer. GED; GEDA; HOBA; HOBAA; LEYB†

Von Steuben, Friedrich Wilhelm, see Steuben, Friedrich Wilhelm von.

Von Tilzer, Albert (1878–1956). Songwriter. MOA†

Von Tilzer, Harry (1872–1946). Songwriter. MOA

Von Weber, Karl Maria Friedrich Ernst, see Weber, Karl Maria Friedrich Ernst von.

Voorhees, Donald (1903–). Conductor. STM†

Vorse, Mary Heaton (1874–1966). Journalist, author. BI

Vouet, Simon (1590–1649). French painter. MAH†

Vreeland, Diana. Museum consultant, born France. GIB-1

Vrionides, Christos (1894–1961). Musicologist, born Greece. STM†

Vukovich, Bill (1919–1955). Automobile racer. LEVA; LEX; OLCA; YAA

Vukovich, Bill, Jr. (1943?–). Automobile racer. OLAB; OLCA

Vyner, Louis (1910–). Conductor. STM†

W

Waciuma, Charity. Zambian teacher, author. OJA

Waddell, Rube (George Edward) (1876–1914).

Baseball player. ALB; DAFC; DAFD; DAG; DAGA; DAH; LIAA; NEA; RIGA†

Wade, Virginia (1945–). English tennis player. AAS-9; FR-1; SUDA

Waglum, Jinnie. American Revolutionary patriot. CLC†

Wagner, "Gorgeous George" (George Raymond) (1915–1963). Wrestler. COKB

Wagner, Honus (John Peter) (1874–1955). Baseball player. ALB; BOE; DAFB; DAFC; DAFD; DAG; DAGA; DAH; EPA; FRC-1†; GUC; MUB-1; MUC; RIGA†; WAC

Wagner, Joseph Frederick (1900–). Conductor. STM†

Wagner, Richard (1813–1883). German composer. BRF; BUD; DEI; DEJ; FIE; KAE; SAA; YOK; YOM†

Wagoner, Henry O. (fl. 1860). Businessman. KADB

Wahle, Otto (1880–1965). Swimmer, born Austria. SLA

Waitz, Grete (1953–). Norwegian track athlete. AAS-30; BAEC; SUDB

Wakely, Ernie. Canadian hockey player. FICB

Waksman, Selman Abraham (1888–1973). Microbiologist, born Russia. GRB-1; LET; LETA; LIA; RIF

Walburga (710–779). Saint. DAD-2

Wald, Lillian D. (1867–1940). Social worker. ALD; BRBE†; CAGA; DOD; EIA; GEE; GIBA; GRB-1; LETA; WABC†; WRA; YOB

Waldetrudis (628–688). Saint. DAD-2

Waldo, Maxim (1907–). Conductor. STM†

Waldrop, Tony (1952?–). Track athlete. LEYB†

Walesa, Lech (1943–). Polish labor leader. AAS-34; DU-1

Walk, Neal (1948–). Basketball player. KLC; SLA†

Walker, Alice (1944–). Author. OCB†

Walker, David (1785–1830). Abolitionist. ADA; ADB; BEJ; GRAB-05; PECA; STJA

Walker, Dixie (1910–1982). Baseball player. GEB

Walker, Doak (Ewell Doak, Jr.) (1927–). Football player. BUJA; DEHB; HIE

Walker, Hal (1933?–). Television news broadcaster. STAA†

Walker, Harry William (1918–). Baseball manager. LEW

Walker, Herschel (1962–). Football player. DEHB

Walker, Jimmy (1944?–). Basketball player. SA

Walker, John (1952–). New Zealand track athlete. AAS-26

Walker, Jonathon (early 19th century). Abolitionist. ARB

Walker, Madame C. J., see Walker, Sarah Breedlove.

Walker, Maggie Lena (1867–1934). Banker. ADA; ADB; BRB; BUFA; LOAV; ROG

Walker, Margaret (1915–). Poet. ROE

Walker, Mary (1832–1919). Physician feminist. STJ

Walker, Mary Richardson (1814–1897). Missionary. JOB; ROI

Walker, Nancy (1922–). Actress. MASB

Walker, Sarah Breedlove (1867–1919). Cosmetician. ADA; ADB†; LOAV; STQ†

Walker, Thomas Calhoun (1862–1953). Author. DADB

Walker, Walton Harris (1889–1950). General. ARBA

Walker, Wayne (1936–). Football player. KABA

Walker, Wesley (1955–). Football player. AAS-18

Walker, William (1824–1860). Adventurer. WIAA-1

Wallace, Alfred Russel (1823–1913). English naturalist. ASA; BLB; MIB

Wallace, Bobby (Roderick John) (1873–1960). Baseball player. ALB

Wallace, Cookie. Boxer. BELB

Wallace, Henry A. (1888–1965). Vice president. COKA; FEA; HAOA; HOEA

Wallace, Sir William (1272?–1305). Scottish patriot. SUK

Wallach, Otto (1847–1931). German chemist. LET

Wallenda family. German-American acrobats. KIB

Wallenstein, Alfred (1898–1983). Cellist, conductor. STM

Waller, Fats (Thomas Wright) (1904–1943). Pianist. COF-1; ROF; TEA; TEB; WAD†

Walls, Everson (1959–). Football player. AAS-13

Walsh, Edward Augustine (1882–1959). Baseball player. ALB; RIGA†

Walsh, Stella (1913?–1980). Track athlete, born Poland. DAG; DAGA; HOBA; HOBAA†

Walsingham, Sir Francis (1530?–1590). English statesman. SEB

Walter of Pontoise (d. 1099). Saint. QUA

Walter, Bruno (1876–1962). German conductor. EWB; STM; YOM

Walters, Barbara (1931–). Television commentator. BOHD; GIB-1

Walton, Bill (1952–). Basketball player. AAS-5; ARB-1

Walton, George (1741–1804). American Revolutionary patriot. BAEA; BUIB†; COJ†; FEAB; MAC†

Walton, Sir William Turner (1902–1983). English composer. YOL

Waltrip, Darrell (1947–). Automobile racer. OLDD

Wanamaker, John (1838–1922). Merchant. LAH; LEM

Waner, Lloyd James (1906–1982). Baseball player. DAFD; FRC-1†

Waner, Paul (1903–1965). Baseball player. ALB; DAFD; FRC-1†; RIGA†

Wang An-shih (1021–1086). Chinese statesman. SPA

Wang Mang (33 B.C.–23 A.D.). Emperor of China. SPA

Wankel, Felix Heinrich (1902–). German engineer. FE; MAPA

Warburg, Otto Heinrich (1883–1970). German physiologist. LET

Warburg, Paul Moritz (1868–1923). Banker, born Germany. LETA

Ward, Artemas (1727–1800). General. BUIB†; SOA

Ward, John Montgomery (1860–1925). Baseball player. ALB; SMK

Ward, Lynd (1905–1985). Author, illustrator. SMAB

Ward, Macock (b. 1702). Horologist. BAC

Ward, Nancy (fl. 1785). Cherokee leader. GRAD

Ward, Rodger (1921–). Automobile racer. LEVA; LEX; LEYC; YAA

Ward, Samuel Ringgold (1817–1866). Abolitionist, clergyman. GRAB-05

Warfield, Marsha (1954–). Comedienne. MASB

Warfield, Paul (1942–). Football player. CO; DEHA; LIB; SMI; ST

Warhol, Andy (1930–1987). Painter, motion picture producer. WIAA

Waring, Julius Waties (1880–1968). Jurist. STJB

Warmerdam, Cornelius (1915–). Pole vaulter. DAFB; DAG; DAGA; DAJ; LYC

Warne, Peggy (Margaret). Nurse. CLC†

Warner, Glenn "Pop" (1871–1954). Football coach. DAFG; HEH; VAD

Warren, Earl (1891–1974). Supreme Court justice. FLC; WEB

Warren, Francis (1844–1929). Senator, governor. SEC

Warren, Gouverneur Kemble (1830–1882). General. DIA

Warren, Harry (1893–1981). Songwriter. MOA

Warren, Joseph (1741–1775). Physician, American Revolutionary patriot. DIA; SUL

Warren, Mercy Otis (1728–1814). Author. AND; WABC†

Washakie (1804?–1900). Shoshone Indian chief. HED

Washburn, Margaret Floy (1871–1939). Psychologist. EMB†

Washington, Betty. Reporter. STAA

Washington, Booker Taliaferro (1856–1915). Educator. ADA; ADB; BRB; BRBD; CUC; FIA; FOB; FOH; FRC†; HUA; JOC; LEC; LEJA; MAL; ROG; STB; STO; WAH; YOI

Washington, Gene (1947–). Football player. FRD; GUEB; GUF; ST

Washington, George (1732–1799). President of U.S. ALCA; ARAB; ASB; BAEB; BAG; BAG-1; BEB; BEC; BLA; BUIA; BUIB; CAAA; CABA; CAG; CAH; CHG; COD; COI; COJA; COS; CUC; DAC; DAE; DAF-2; DAFA; DEI; DEJ; DUB; DUC; DUCA; EVD; FEAA; FIA; FID; FOB; FOH; FRBA; HAK; HAN; HIBC; HIH; KEC†; LEAA; LEP; LEQ; LEQA; MAB; MABA; MAT; MIA; OLA; PED; ROH; ROHA; ROK; SOA; STH; SUBB; WAI; WHD

Washington, George (1817–1905). Landowner. GRAB-02; KADB; WIBA

Washington, John Alexander (d. 1943). Chaplain. FIA

Washington, Lawrence (1717–1752). Brother of George Washington. EDA

Washington, Martha Dandridge (1732–1802). Wife of George Washington. ARAB; BAG; BAG-1; BLG; CHA; KL; LEK; MAA; MAU; PRB; ROH; ROHA; STJ; WABC; WAQ

Washington, Walter (1915–). Mayor. YOI

Wassermann, Jakob (1873–1934). German author. PEB

Waterfield, Robert Staton (1920–1983). Football player; coach. DAFG; HEI; RAAD; SUD

Waters, Ethel (1900–1977). Singer. ADA; ADB; DI-1†; DOBA; HUC

Waters, Muddy (McKinley Morganfield) (1915–1983). Singer. SUH

Watkins, Sylvestre C. (1913?–). Publishing executive. BOG

Watson, Douglas. Aeronautical engineer. BOG

Watson, Ella (Cattle Kate) (1862?–1889). Rustler. RAB; WIAA-2

Watson, James Dewey (1928–). Geneticist. BEK; FE; FRE†; GRBA; RIF

Watson, Thomas J., Sr. (1874–1956). Industrialist. GRAB-3; LAG

Watson-Watt, Sir Robert Alexander (1892–1973). Scottish physicist. EVC; FE; SHFB

Watt, James (1736–1819). Scottish inventor. ASA; BIA; BOD; BUF; COL; EBA; EVB; FAB; FE; FRE; SHFB; THA

Watt, Sir Robert Alexander Watson, see Watson-Watt, Sir Robert Alexander.

Watteau, Jean Antoine (1684–1721). French painter. KAA; MAH†

Watterson, Henry (1840–1921). Journalist. SQB

Watts, André (1946–). Pianist. AB

Wauneka, Annie Dodge (1912–). Navajo Indian

public health worker. BRBE†; GRAC; GRAD; WAB

Waxman, Franz. Conductor, born Germany. STM†

Wayne, Anthony (1745–1796). General. BUIB†; MAE; RAD; SOA

Wayne, John (Marion Michael Morrison) (1907–1979). Actor. PABA

Weatherly, Joseph Herbert (1922?–1964). Automobile racer. LEX†; LEXA

Weaver, Earl (1930–). Baseball manager. FRC-01

Weaver, Robert Clifton (1907–). Sociologist. ADB; DOF-1; YOI

Webb, Aileen Osborn (1892–1979). Crafts promoter. GIB-1†

Webb, Mary (1881–1927). English author. SMA

Webb, Matthew (1848–1883). English swimmer. DAG; DAGA

Weber, Dewey (1937?–). Surf rider. OLD

Weber, Dick (1929–). Bowler. FOI; KADA

Weber, Henry (1900–). Conductor. STM†

Weber, John Roy. Conductor. STM†

Weber, Karl Maria Friedrich Ernst von (1786–1826). German composer. BRF; KAE; SAA; YOJ

Weber, Milton (1910–). Conductor, educator, born Austria. STM†

Weber, Wilhelm Eduard (1804–1891). German physicist. DUA

Webern, Anton von (1883–1945). Austrian composer. EWAA

Webster, Daniel (1782–1852). Lawyer, statesman. DEI; DEJ; HEEA; KEC; KED; LEC; STH

Webster, Mike (1952–). Football player. AAS-11

Webster, Noah (1758–1843). Lexicographer. DEI; DEJ; MAL

Webster, Timothy (1816?–1862). Spy, born England. FOA

Weddell, James (1787–1834). English navigator. ROL†

Weddle, Franklyn S. (1905–). Conductor. STM†

Wedel, Cynthia Clark (1908–1986). Religious leader. BLF†

Weicher, John (1904–). Conductor. STM†

Weill, Kurt (1900–1950). Composer, born Germany. EWA

Weinberger, Eric (1932–). Civil rights worker. COF

Weingartner, Felix von (1863–1942). Austrian conductor. YOM

Weisbogel, Albert (1844–?). Sailor. TA

Weiss, Carl Austin (1906–1935). Assassin. RABA

Weissmann, Frieder. German conductor. STM†

Weissmuller, Johnny (1904–1984). Swimmer, actor. ASBA; BELB; DAG; DAGA; DEF; GED; GEDA; HEG; HOC; HOCG; LEF; LEYB; SICA

Weisz, Richard (1879–1945). Wrestler. SLA†

Weitz, Edward (1946–). Israeli weightlifter, born Russia. SLA†

Weizmann, Chaim (1874–1952). President of Israel. DEI; DEJ; GEF; GRAB-1; GUB; KAB; KAD; LES; ROGA

Weld, Theresa (1893–). Skater. HOBAA; JAB

Weldon, Catherine. Pioneer. JOB

Weller, Thomas Huckle (1915–). Physician. RIF

Welles, Orson (1915–1985). Actor, motion picture director and producer. SMBC

Wellington, Arthur Wellesley, 1st duke of (1769–1852). British general, statesman. CHG; COD

Wellman, Walter (1858–1934). Journalist, explorer. GRB

Wells, Henry (1805–1878). Freight and banking executive. DOCA

Wells, Herbert George (1866–1946). English historian, author. ASB-1; DEI; DEJ

Wells, Horace (1815–1848). Dentist. SHG†

Wells, Ida, see Barnett, Ida Wells.

Wells, Mary Georgene (1928?–). Advertising executive. GEDB†; GRBA

Welty, Eudora (1909–). Author. MUA; OCB

Wenceslaus of Bohemia (d. 929). Saint. CAAA; DAD-3

Wennerstrom, Stig (1906–). Swedish spy. HAB

Wenrich, Percy (1887–1952). Songwriter. MOA

Werner, Bud (Wallace) (1936?–1964). Skier. FOI; HOC

Werner, Eduard (1891–). Conductor, born Austria. STM†

West, Benjamin (1730–1813). Mathematician. BUIB†

West, Benjamin (1738–1820). Painter. BR; CAD; HEDA; LEE; LEOA; SIE

West, James Edward (1876–1948). Boy Scout leader. MAL

West, Jerry (1938?–). Basketball player. BEL; BELB; ETA; FRD; HEHA; HID; KADA; PE

West, Jessamyn (1907–1984). Author. GL-1; MUA

West, Mae (1892–1980). Actress. MAOB; MASB

Westinghouse, George (1846–1914). Inventor. HYA; LAG; THA

Weston, Edward Payson (1839–1929). Track athlete. DAJ

Westphal, Paul (1950–). Basketball player. AAS-8

Wetamoo (fl. 1675). Pocasset chief. GRAD

Wettach, Adrien, see Grock, pseud.

Weyand, Ruth (1912–). Labor lawyer. BI†

Whallon, Evan. Conductor. STM†

Wharton, Edith (1862–1937). Author. BOA; CON†; STL

Wheat, Zachary Davis (1888–1972). Baseball player. ALB; GEB; RIGA†

Wheatley, Phillis (1753–1784). Poet. ADA; ADB; AND; BRB; DOB; GIBA; HUA; JOCA; LEJ; LEPA; LOAV; PECA; ROE; ROG; WIBA

Wheelan, Edgar Stow (1888–1966). Cartoonist. GOB-1

Wheeler, Candace Thurber (1827–1923). Decorative arts executive. PACB

Wheeler, Harold Alden (1903–). Radio and television engineer. YOD

Wheeler, Joseph (1836–1906). General. MAD

Wheeler, Sir Mortimer (1890–1976). English archaeologist. POC

Wheeler, William Almon (1819–1887). Vice president of U.S. FEA; HAOA; HOEA

Wheelock, Eleazar (1711–1779). Clergyman. BUIB†

Wheelwright, Esther (1696–1780). Indian captive. HEE

Whelan, Harold Paul. Conductor. STM†

Whidden, Dorothy. Artist. HOG†

Whipper, William (1805–1885). Abolitionist, businessman. ADB; GRAB-02

Whipple, George Hoyt (1878–1976). Pathologist. RIF

Whipple, Prince (1764?–1797). Soldier. DAF-1; WIBA

Whipple, William (1730–1785). American Revolutionary patriot. BAEA; BUIB†; COJ†; FEAB; MAC†

Whistler, James Abbott McNeill (1834–1903). Painter. CHC; CUC; FRA; KAA; LEE; LEOA; MAG; SIE

Whitaker, Mark (1951–). Comet finder at 16. FOR

Whitcher, Sylvanus (b. 1837?). Colonial boy. BAC

White, Andrew Dickson (1832–1918). Educator, diplomat. MAL

White, Byron Raymond (1917–). Football player, Supreme Court justice. DAFG; DAI; HIE; HOBB; HOC

White, Charles (1918–1979). Painter. ADA; ADB; FAH

White, Cheryl. Jockey. HOBAA†

White, Edward Higgins, II (1930–1967). Astronaut. COQ; LEPB†; THC

White, Ellen G. H. (1827–1915). Religious leader. WABC†

White, Elwyn Brooks (1899–1985). Author. BEG; SMB

White, Gilbert (1720–1793). English naturalist. MIB

White, Jo Jo. Basketball player. KLC

White, Margaret Bourke, *see* Bourke-White, Margaret.

White, Paul (1895–). Conductor. STM†

White, Paul Dudley (1886–1973). Cardiologist. CHE

White, Randy (1953–). Football player. AAS-16; SMJ

White, Roy (1943–). Baseball player. DEHA-1; KLBB

White, Stan. Football player. SMJ

White, Stanford (1853–1906). Architect. LAF

White, Walter F. (1893–1955). Civil rights leader. ADA; ADB; DOF-1; GRAB-01; RIC

White, William Allen (1868–1944). Journalist. COKA; FOE; SQB

White, William D. (1934–). Baseball player. GUB-1; PRA

Whitehorn, John Clare (1894–). Psychiatrist. CHE

Whiting, Richard A. (1891–1938). Songwriter. MOA

Whitman, Marcus (1802–1847). Missionary. BLC; COE; FOC; LEG; MAT

Whitman, Narcissa (1808–1847). Missionary. DAD; EVD; FOC; MAT; ROI

Whitman, Walt (1819–1892). Poet. BEF; BOA; DEI; DEJ; EOB; HACB; HEF; HIG; LEJ; SIF

Whitmire, Kathy (1946–). Mayor. WHE

Whitney, Eli (1765–1825). Inventor. BUE; CAB; CUC; DEI; DEJ; EBA; FAB; FE; HYA; LAE; MAL; RAA; THA

Whitney, Gertrude Vanderbilt (1877–1942). Sculptor, museum founder. WABC†

Whitney, Phyllis A. (1903–). Author. GL-1

Whitney, Robert (1904–). Conductor. STM

Whittaker, Joseph (b. 1684). Indian captive. CAD

Whittemore, Arthur Austin (1916–1984). Pianist. EWC

Whittier, John Greenleaf (1807–1892). Poet. BEF; BEGA; BOA; SIF

Whittle, Sir Frank (1907–). English aeronautical engineer. EVC; FE; SHFB; THA

Whitworth, Sir Joseph (1803–1887). English inventor, manufacturer. FE

Whitworth, Kathy (Kathrynne Ann) (1939–). Golfer. HOBAA†; JABA; RYX

Wick, Tempe (fl. 1781). American Revolutionary patriot. CLC

Widing, Juha Markku (1947–). Finnish hockey player. ORB

Wiener, Norbert (1894–1964). Mathematician. KE; STN

Wiesenthal, Simon (1908–). Austrian Nazi hunter, born Poland. GRB-1

Wiggan, Eleazer. Pioneer. STA

Wiggin, Kate Douglas (1856–1923). Author. BEI; COB

Wightman, Hazel Hotchkiss, *see* Hotchkiss, Hazel.

Wild Bunch. Outlaws. JOBA; SUJ

Wilder, Billy (1906–). Motion picture director, born Austria. ED-1†

Wilder, Laura Ingalls (1867–1957). Author. MUA; SMB

Wilder, Thornton Niven (1897–1975). Novelist, playwright. BEGA

Wildesen, Leslie E. (1944–). Archaeologist. WIAA-01

Wiley, Harvey Washington (1844–1930). Chemist. MAL

Wilfrid (634–709). Saint. QUA

Wilhelm, James Hoyt (1923–). Baseball player. DAFD; LEZ; SA-3; SHE

Wilhelmina (1880–1962). Queen of the Netherlands. BOI; FAE

Wilkens, Lenny. Basketball player. HIBA

Wilkes, Charles (1798–1877). Explorer. COR; DOC†; ROL

Wilkes, John (1727–1797). English political reformer. SOA

Wilkins, Alonzo. Basketball player. PIB; PIBA

Wilkins, Debbie. Motorcyclist. BUIC

Wilkins, Sir George Hubert (1888–1958). Australian explorer. GRB; ROL†

Wilkins, Maurice Hugh Frederick (1916–). British biophysicist. RIF

Wilkins, Roy (1901–1981). Civil rights leader. DOF-1; FAG; KE; YOI

Wilkinson, David (1771–1852). Inventor, manufacturer. FAB

Wilkinson, Jemima (1752–1819). Preacher. WABC†

Willard, Emma Hart (1787–1870). Educator. BUDA; COG; CUC; FLB; FRC; JOCA; LEJA; MAL; VAB; WABC†; YOC

Willard, Frances Elizabeth (1839–1898). Reformer. BRBE; GUBA; VAB; WABC

Willard, Josiah Flynt (1869–1907). Author, sociologist. COGB

Willard, Ken (1943–). Football player. BEKB; LEZB

Willard, Simon (1605–1676). Colonist. WOAA

Willett, Marinus (1740–1830). American Revolutionary officer. RAD

Willey, Gordon Randolph (1913–). Archaeologist. POC

William I, the Conqueror (1027–1087). King of England. BEO; BRBF; CAAA; CHG; COD; DEC; GRAB; JOBB; NEC; SCC; TRA

William I, the Silent (1533–1584). Prince of Orange. CAAA; HEA; MAJ; UNB

William II (1056–1100). King of England. BRBF; DEC; GRAB†; SCC

William II (1859–1941). Emperor of Germany, king of Prussia. CAAA

William III (1650–1702). King of England, Scotland, and Ireland. DEC; GRAB†; SCC; TRA

William III, prince of Orange, see William III, king of England, Scotland, and Ireland.

William IV (1765–1837). King of Great Britain and Ireland. DEC; GRAB†; SCC

William of Abbot (1127–1203). Saint. DAD-2

William of Bourges (1150–1209). Saint. DAD-2

William of Gellone (d. 812). Saint. QUA

William of Monte Vergine. Saint. DAD-2

William of Roskilde (d. 1070). Saint. MOC

William of Rubruquis (1215?–1295?). French friar. ROL†

William of York. Saint. DAD-2

Williams, Bert (1876?–1922). Actor. ADA; ADB; HUC; PHA; ROF; ROG

Williams, Betty (1943–). Irish social reformer. AAS-34; COG-1; SHFE†

Williams, Big Joe (1900–). Singer. SUH

Williams, Billy Leo (1938–). Baseball player. BELA

Williams, Buck (Charles Linwood) (1960–). Basketball player. AAS-7

Williams, Claude (1900?–). Clergyman, civil rights worker. STG

Williams, Daniel Hale (1858–1931). Surgeon. ADA; ADB; ASB; BRB†; CAF-1; DADA; HA; HAM; HODA; HUA; KLA; PECA; RICA; ROG; STO

Williams, Dick (1928–). Baseball manager. AAS-1; FRC-01

Williams, Eunice (1697–1786). Indian captive. CAF; HEE

Williams, Fannie Barrier. Reformer. DADA

Williams, George Washington (1849–1891). Black leader. ADA; ADB; BRB†

Williams, Hank (1923–1953). Singer. BUIB-01

Williams, Hank, Jr. (1949–). Singer. KRI

Williams, Harry (1879–1922). Songwriter. MOA†

Williams, Jack. Automobile racer. OLB

Williams, Joe (fl. 1912). Baseball player. SMK

Williams, John Sharp (1854–1932). Senator. MAO

Williams, Lacey Kirk. Clergyman. BRB†

Williams, Louis (1845–1886). Sailor, born Norway. TA

Williams, Mary Lou (1910–1981). Pianist, composer. GIB-1

Williams, Paul Revere (1894–1980). Architect. ADB; DOF-1; LEDA

Williams, Ralph Vaughan, see Vaughan Williams, Ralph.

Williams, Robert F. (1925–). Black leader. DADA

Williams, Robert Rampatnam (1886–1965). Chemist. YOE

Williams, Roger (1603?–1683). Clergyman, founder of Rhode Island. ARB; COG; DAC;

DEI; DEJ; FIA; FOB; LEO; LEPF; MEB; OLA; VIA†

Williams, Ted (Theodore Samuel) (1918–). Baseball player, manager. ASBA; BELB; BUD-1; BUJ; DA; DAA; DAFB; DAFC; DAFD; DAG; DAGA; DAH; DEE; DEHA-1; FIAA; FRC-1†; GEC; GR; GUC; GUDA; HIF; HOC; LEV; LIC; MUB-1; MUC; PAW; RAAA; RIGA†; SA-3; SH; SHB; SHH; SMK; VEA; WAC

Williams, William (1731–1811). American Revolutionary patriot. BAEA; BUIB†; COJ†; FEAB; MAC†

Williams, William Taylor Burwell (1869–1941). Educator. DOF-1

Williamson, Al (1931). Cartoonist. GOB-1

Williamson, Hugh (1735–1819). Surgeon, congressman. BUIB†; FEAA

Willibrord (657?–738). Saint. DAD-3

Willing, Thomas (1731–1821). Banker. BUIB†

Willis, Ann Bassett (1878–1956). Rancher. RAB

Willis, William (1893–1968?). Seaman. OLC

Willkie, Wendell Lewis (1892–1944). Lawyer. WHD

Wills, Bob (1905–1975). Band leader, fiddler. LA

Wills, Helen (1906–). Tennis player. AAS-29; ASBA; COKA; DAG; DAGA; FR-1; HI; HOBA; HOBAA; JAB; LAHA; RYA†; SICA; SUDA†

Wills, Maury (Maurice Morning) (1932–). Baseball player. DEHA-1; FOI; GEB; GUDA; KADA; PRA; ROC; SHC; VEA

Wills, William John (1834–1861). Australian explorer, born England. ROL†; WIA-1†

Willson, Meredith (1902–1984). Band leader, composer. STM†

Willstätter, Richard (1872–1942). German chemist. LET

Wilson, Alexander (1766–1813). Ornithologist, born Scotland. CO-1; CORA; HYB

Wilson, Charles T. R. (1869–1959). Scottish physicist. RID

Wilson, Edith Bolling (1872–1961). Second wife of Woodrow Wilson. BAG; BAG-1; BLG; CHB; KL; MAA; MAU; PRB; ROH; ROHA†

Wilson, Ellen Louisa (1860–1914). First wife of Woodrow Wilson. BAG; BAG-1; BLG†; CHB; KL; MAA; MAU; PRB; ROH; ROHA†

Wilson, Flip (Clerow) (1933–). Comedian. AB

Wilson, Gilbert E. (1914–). Conductor. STM†

Wilson, Harold (1916–). British ex-prime minister. WEB

Wilson, Henry (1812–1875). Vice president of U.S. FEA; HAOA; HOEA

Wilson, Jack, see Wovoka.

Wilson, James (1742–1798). American Revolutionary patriot. BAEA; BUIB†; COJ†; FEAA; FEAB; MAC

Wilson, James Finley (1881–1952). Fraternal order leader. ADA; ADB

Wilson, John (1922–). Painter, educator. FAH

Wilson, Larry (1938–). Football player. ANA; KADA

Wilson, Lewis R. "Hack" (1900–1948). Baseball player. FRC-1†

Wilson, Marie (1916–1972). Actress. MASB

Wilson, Nemiah. Football player. RUC

Wilson, Thomas (1918–). Conductor. STM†

Wilson, William (fl. 1870). Soldier. TA

Wilson, Woodrow (1856–1924). President of U.S. ARB; ASB-1; BAEB; BAG; BAG-1; BEB; BLA; BUIA; CAG; CAH; COI; COS; CUC; DEI; DEJ; DOF; DUB; DUC; DUCA; FOB; FRBA; HIH; LEQ; LEQA; MAB; MABA; MEA; MEC; MIA; PED; ROH; ROHA; ROK; SUBB; WHD; WIC

Wiltse, Lyman (1899–). Conductor. STM†

Wincenc, Joseph (1915–). Conductor. STM†

Winchester, Sarah (1839–1922). Eccentric millionairess. COKB

Windingstad, Ole (1886–1959). Norwegian conductor. STM†

Windsor, Edward, duke of, see Edward VIII, king of Great Britain and Ireland.

Windsor-Smith, Barry. Cartoonist, born England. GOB-1

Winema (fl. 1850). Modoc Indian princess. GRAD; WAB

Winfield, Dave (1951–). Baseball player. AAS-4; HEFB†

Wing, Henry (1840–1925). Journalist. FLBB

Wingate, Orde Charles (1903–1944). British general. SUA

Winifred (d. 650?). Saint. MOC

Winnemucca, Sarah (1844–1891). Paiute Indian. GRAD; TRD; WAB

Winslow, Anna Green (1760–1779). Colonial girl. CAF

Winter, Bud. Track coach. LEW

Winthrop, John (1588–1649). British colonial governor. LEO

Wirges, Gene. Newspaper editor. EOA

Wirth, Carl Anton (1912–). Conductor. STM†

Wirth, May (1896?–). Australian bareback rider. KIB

Wise, Isaac Mayer (1819–1900). Rabbi, born Czechoslovakia. GUB; KAD; LERA; LETA; PEB

Wise, Stephen Samuel (1874–1949). Rabbi, born Hungary. GEF; GRB-1; GUB; LETA

Wishnow, Emanuel (1910–). Conductor, born England. STM†

Wistar, Isaac Jones (1827–1905). Penologist. COE

Witherspoon, John (1723–1794). American Revolutionary patriot. BAEA; BUIB†; COJ†; FEAB; MAC

Witte, Luke (1950–). Basketball player. AAS-24

Wittenberg, Henri E. Journalist. STAA

Wittenberg, Henry B. (1918–). Wrestler. SLA

Wittgenstein, Paul (1887–1961). Austrian pianist. GEA

Woessner, Julius (1893–). German conductor. STM†

Wöhler, Friedrich (1800–1882). German chemist. CAA; FE

Wohlhuter, Rick (1949–). Track athlete. LEYB†

Woit, Dick. Physical therapist. BELB

Wojciechowicz, Alex (1915–). Football player. SUD

Wolcott, Oliver (1726–1797). American Revolutionary patriot. BAEA; BUIB†; COJ†; FEAB; MAC

Wolf, Hugo (1860–1903). Austrian composer. KAE; SAA

Wolf, Phil (1869–1936). Bowler, born Germany. SLA

Wolf, Warner (1937–). Sportscaster. SLA†

Wolfe, James (1727–1759). British general. MAJ

Wolfe, Thomas Clayton (1900–1938). Author. HEF

Wolfgang, Myra (1914–1976). Labor leader. BI†

Wollstonecraft, Mary, see Godwin, Mary Wollstonecraft.

Wolverton, Basil. Cartoonist. GOB-1

Wonder, Stevie (1950–). Singer, composer. BUIB-1

Wood, Ann (fl. 1855). Slave. CHFB

Wood, Gar (1880?–1971). Boat racer. DAG; DAGA

Wood, Grant (1892–1942). Painter. BOD; CUC; HEDA; LEE; LEOA; SIE

Wood, Henry (1869–1944). English conductor. YOM

Wood, Joe (b. 1889). Baseball player. NEA; RIGA†

Wood, Robert Elkington (b. 1879). Department store executive. LAH

Wood, Sally S. B. K. (1759–1855). Author. WABC†

Wood, Wally (d. 1981). Cartoonist. GOB-1

Wood, William Barry (1910–1971). Football player. HAE; JOA

Wooden, John R. (1910–). Basketball coach. LEW

Woodhull, Abraham (fl. 1775–1783). Spy. FOA†

Woodhull, Victoria (1838–1927). Feminist. GUBA; JOCA; MAT-1; WABC†

Woodmansee, John W. (1934–). Army officer. RAE

Woods, George (1943?–). Track athlete. LEYB†

Woods, Granville T. (1856–1910). Inventor. ADA;

ADB; BRB†; CAF-1; GRAB-03; HA; HAL; JO; KLA; PECA; STQ†

Woodson, Carter Goodwin (1875–1950). Historian. ADA; ADB; BRB†; DOF-1; GRAB-02; ROG; STO

Woodson, John (1586–1644). Physician. RIB†

Woodson, Sara (b. 1590). Wife of Dr. John Woodson. RIB

Woodward, Robert Upshur (1943–). Journalist. LETB

Woolf, Virginia (1882–1941). English author. BEG; SMA

Woolley, Hannah (b. 1623). English educator. BOH

Woolley, Mary Emma (1863–1947). Educator. BUDA†

Woolman, John (1720–1772). Abolitionist. VIA

Woolworth, Frank Winfield (1852–1919). Merchant. LAH

Wordsworth, William (1770–1850). English poet. COP

Workman, Fanny Bullock (1859–1925). Explorer. RIG

Worley, John C. (1919–). Conductor. STM†

Wormington, Judy (1941–). Television promotions manager. SMBB-2

Worsley, Gump (Lorne) (1929–). Canadian hockey player. FR; ORA

Worthington, Al (1929–). Baseball player, coach. DEHA-1

Worthington, Thomas (1773–1825). Senator, governor. SEC

Wottle, Dave (1950?–). Track athlete. LEYB

Wouk, Herman (1915–). Author. GRB-1

Wovoka (Jack Wilson) (1856?–1932). Paiute Indian mystic. STAB

Wrede, Mathilda (1864–1928). Finnish penal reformer. KEE

Wren, Sir Christopher (1632–1723). English architect. DEI; DEJ

Wright, Barbara P. (1920–). Physician. PAC

Wright, Frances (Fanny) (1795–1852). Feminist, abolitionist, born Scotland. GUBA†; WABC†

Wright, Frank Lloyd (1869–1959). Architect. ASB-1; CUC; FOF; HIFA; LEDA

Wright, George (1847–1937). Baseball player. ALB

Wright, Harry (William Henry) (1835–1895). Baseball manager, born England. ALB; SMK

Wright, Jane C. (1919–). Physician. HA-1; HAMA; PAC; RAAG†

Wright, Jonathan Jasper (1840–1885). Judge. ADA; ADB

Wright, Louis Tompkins (1891–1952). Physician. DOF-1; GRAB-03; HA; HAMA; PAC

Wright, Mickey (Mary Kathryn) (1935–). Golfer.
HOBA; HOBAA†

Wright, Nathan, Jr. (1923–). Black leader, theologian. HAI

Wright, Orville (1871–1948). Aviation pioneer.
ASB; ASB-1; BIA; BOD; BRBA; COL; CUC;
DEI; DEJ; DOE; EBA; EVC; EVD; FAB; FE;
FRE; HAMY; HYA†; LEL; MAT; PRC; SIA;
THA

Wright, Patience Lovell (1725–1786). Sculptor.
AND; VIA

Wright, Rebecca (fl. 1805). Pioneer. FOC

Wright, Richard (1908–1960). Author. ADA; ADB;
AKB; DABB; DADB; DOF-1; FLBA; RIC; RICA

Wright, Thelma. Canadian track athlete. GLB

Wright, Wilbur (1867–1912). Aviation pioneer.
ASB; BIA; BOD; BRBA; COL; CUC; DEI; DEJ;
DOE; EBA; EVC; EVD; FAB; FE; FRE; HAMY;
HYA†; LEL; MAT; PRC; SIA; THA

Wrightson, Berni (1948–). Cartoonist. GOB-1

Wu, Chien-Shiung (1912–). Physicist, born China.
EMB†; GIB-1; GLO; SC; YOF

Wyatt, Addie (1924–). Labor, civil rights leader.
BI; GIB-1

Wyeth, Andrew (1917–). Painter. WIAA

Wyld, James H. Rocket expert. COQ

Wylie, Elinor Morton (1885–1928). Poet, novelist.
BRBB

Wyman, Irma (1928–). Computer executive.
FRBD

Wynette, Tammy (1942–). Singer. BUIB-01

Wythe, George (1726–1806). American Revolutionary patriot. BAEA; BUIB†; COJ†; FEAA;
FEAB; MAC

X

X, Malcolm, *see* Malcolm X.

Xenakis, Yannis (1922–). Greek composer. EWAA

Xenophon (434?–355 B.C.). Greek historian. COM

Xerxes I (519?–465 B.C.). King of Persia. COA; JO

Y

Yaa Asantewa (1863–1923). Ashanti queen.
GRAB-04

Yadin, Yigael (1917–1984). Israeli archaeologist.
GRB-1; POC; ROGA

Yalow, Rosalyn Sussman (1921–). Physicist.
GIB-1; GL; GRB-1; HA-1; SHFE

Yamani, Ahmed Zaki (1930–). Saudi oil minister.
DU-1

Yancey, William Lowndes (1814–1863). Lawyer,
politician. COGA

Yang, Chen Ning (1922–). Physicist, born China.
BOB

Yarborough, Cale (1939–). Automobile racer.
LEX; LEXA

Yarborough, William (1924–). Conductor. STM†

Yarbrough, Lee Roy (1938–1984). Automobile
racer. LEX; LEXA

Yashima, Mitsu. Illustrator. SMAB

Yashima, Taro (1908–). Author, illustrator, born
Japan. SMAB

Yastrzemski, Carl Michael (1939–). Baseball
player. BRE; DEE; FRD; KADA; LIC; RIGA†

Yates, Robert (1738–1801). Jurist. FEAA

Yeager, Charles E. (1923–). Aviator. COQ

Yeats, William Butler (1865–1939). Irish poet.
BRBB

Yechiel of Paris. French rabbi. GEF

Yegorov, Boris (1937–). Russian astronaut. THC

Yehudah Halevi, *see* Judah ha-Levi.

Yehudah Hanasi, *see* Judah ha-Nasi.

Yellen, Jack (1892–). Songwriter, born Poland.
MOA

Yen, James Yang-ch'u (1894–). Chinese educator.
BAF; COG; SPA

Yeo-Thomas, Forest Frederick (1901–1964). English costume designer, spy. SEB

Yepremian, Garo Sarkis (1944–). Football player,
born Cyprus. AAS-17; GUF; RUC

Yergan, Max (1892–1975). Educator. DOF-1†

Yersin, Alexandre Émile (1863–1943). French bacteriologist. RIE†

Yette, Samuel F. (1929–). Journalist. STAA

Yevtushenko, Yevgeny Aleksandrovich (1933–).
Russian poet. POFA

Yiannopoulos, Andrew (1899?–). Theater director, born Greece. BAEA-1

Yochanan ben Zakkai, *see* Johanan ben Zakkai.

Yoffe, Avraham (1880–1960). Israeli ecologist.
GRB-1

Yoholo-Micco (1790?–1838). Creek Indian chief.
MOD

Yom Tov ben Isaac (d. 1190). English rabbi. GEF

Yonge, Charlotte Mary (1823–1901). English author. BEI

York (fl. 1804). William Clark's servant on Louisiana Expedition. BUH; HAP; KADB; SCB;
STQ†; WIBA

York, Alvin C. (1887–1964). Soldier. ARD; DIA;
ELA; FIA; REA

Youmans, Vincent (1898–1946). Composer. MOA

Young, Andrew Jackson (1932–). Mayor. DOF-1

Young, Arthur (1741–1820). English agriculturist.
CAB

Young, Brigham (1801–1877). Mormon leader. BLD; COE; FOC; HEB; LEO; LEPD

Young, Buddy (Claude) (d. 1983). Football player. FOI

Young, Candy (1962–). Track athlete. SUDB

Young, Charles (1864–1922). Army officer. ADA; ADB; BRB; DOF-1; HODA; HUB; KADB; ROG

Young, Coleman (1918–). Mayor. DOF-1

Young, Cy (Denton True) (1867–1955). Baseball player. ALB; DAFB; DAFC; DAFD; DAG; DAGA; DAH; EP; FRC-1†; RIGA†; SHA; WAG

Young, Ella Flagg (1845–1918). Educator. FLB

Young, Ewing (d. 1841). Trapper, guide. BUG

Young, Hiram (fl. 1830). Wagon maker. BUH

Young, Ida. Editor. HOG†

Young, James F. (1917–). Engineer. PAB

Young, John Watts (1930–). Astronaut. COQ; THC

Young, Lester Willis (1909–1959). Saxophonist. COF-1; JO; WAD†

Young, Robert. Australian surf rider. OLD

Young, Ross (Royce Youngs) (1897–1927). Baseball player. HAF; RIGA†

Young, Sheila (1950–). Cyclist, skater. HOBAA†; LIEA; SUBB-1

Young, Thomas (1773–1829). English physician, physicist, and Egyptologist. SHFB

Young, Whitney Moore, Jr. (1921–1971). Civil rights leader. ADB; FAG; GRAB-01; KE; WECA; YOI

Young, Wilbur (1949–). Football player. AAS-25

Younger brothers. Outlaws. JOBA; REE†

Younghusband, Sir Francis Edward (1863–1942). British explorer. ROL

Yount, Robin (1955–). Baseball player. HOCG; SMF

Youskevitch, Igor (1912–). Russian dancer. ATA

Yu-Tang, Lin, see Lin Yutang.

Z

Zaccaria, Anthony (1502–1539). Saint. DAD-3

Zachary. Saint, pope. DAD-2

Zack, Arthur (1900–). Conductor, born Russia. STM†

Zaharias, Babe (Mildred) Didrikson, see Didrikson, Babe.

Zajicek, Sarita Soto (1916–). Educator. FOW

Zakrzewska, Marie Elizabeth (1829–1902). Physician, born Germany. COFA†; FLA; LEG; RAAG†

Zale, Tony (1913–). Boxer. DEHA-1

Zalman, Shneor (1747–1812). Polish rabbi. KAD

Zane, Elizabeth (1766–1831). Heroine of Ft. Henry. AND; CAD; CLC

Zangara, Guiseppe (1900–1933). Assassin, born Italy. RABA

Zangwill, Israel (1864–1926). English author. LERA; PEB

Zapata, Emiliano (1877?–1919). Mexican revolutionist. HAK; NEBA; ROGB; WO

Zaslofsky, Max (1925–1985). Basketball player. SLA†

Zatopek, Emil (1922–). Czech track athlete. AAS-30; DAG; DAGA; HIA-01†; LEYB

Zavala, Lorenzo de (1788–1836). Mexican statesman. KUA

Zawisza, Christina (1947–). Lawyer. SMBB

Zayak, Elaine (1965–). Skater. VAD-6

Zeiss, Carl (1816–1888). German industrialist. FE

Zelle, Gertrud Margarete, see Mata Hari.

Zellner, Robert. Civil rights worker. STG

Zenger, Anna (1704–1751). Journalist. GEE; WABC†

Zenger, John Peter (1697–1746). Printer, journalist, born Germany. ARB; CUB; CUC; FIA; LOB; MEB; SQB

Zenobia (fl. 267–272). Syrian queen. FAE; PA

Zeppelin, Ferdinand Graf von (1838–1917). German inventor. FE

Zernike, Frits (b. 1888). Dutch physicist. AAS-23

Zerrahn, Carl (1826–1909). Conductor, born Germany. YOM†

Zevi, Sabbatai (1626–1676). Turkish religious figure. LERA; PEB

Ziaul-Haq, Mohammed (1924–). President of Pakistan. HAGD

Ziegfeld, Florenz (1867–1932). Theatrical producer. PHA

Zingha, Ann, see Nzinga.

Zino, Henry. Drummer. HODA

Zinsser, Hans (1878–1940). Bacteriologist. CHD

Ziolkovsky, Konstantin E., see Tsiolkovsky, Konstantin E.

Zipper, Herbert. Austrian conductor. STM†

Zita (1218–1278). Saint. MOC; ONA

Zohar, Uri (1937–). Israeli track athlete, born Palestine. SLA†

Zola, Émile (1840–1902). French author. COG

Zoritch, George (1917–). Russian dancer. ATA

Zorn, Jim (1953–). Football player. AAS-20

Zukerman, Eugenia (1944–). Flautist, television commentator. SC-02†

Zunz, Leopold (1794–1886). German Hebraist. KAD

Zworykin, Vladimir K. (1889–1982). Physicist, inventor, born Russia. YOE

Subjects

List of Subject Headings

Subject Listing of Biographees

ABOLITIONISTS

See also REFORMERS

Anderson, Osborne Perry (1830–1871). GRAB-05
Bibb, Henry (1815–1854). GRAB-05
Brown, Henry "Box" (b. 1816). BRG; JOC
Brown, John (1800–1859). BEJ; DEI; DEJ; STJA
Cary, Mary Ann Shadd (1823–1893). LOAV; WABC†
Coffin, Levi (1798–1877). COG
Concklin, Seth (fl. 1851). STJA
Cornish, Samuel E. (19th century). BEJ
Crandall, Prudence (1803–1889). BUA; CHFB; TRD; WABC†
Douglass, Frederick (1817–1895). ADA; ADB; AKB; BEJ; BRB; BRBD; BRG; DEDA; GRAB-05; HUA; HUB; JO; JOC; MAT; PECA; ROG; SPB; SQB; STD; STO; WAH; WIAB; YOI
Fairfield, John (1830?–1860). STG
Follen, Charles Theodore (1795–1840). (Born Germany). CUB
Forten, Charlotte (1838–1904). CHFB
Forten, James (1766–1842). ADA; ADB; BUIB†; DAF-1; EMA; GRAB-03; HAL†; JOC; STQ†; WIBA
Foster, Abigail Kelley (1810–1887). LES-2; WABC†
Garnet, Henry Highland (1815–1882). ADA; ADB; BEJ; BRB†; GRAB-05; ROG
Garrison, William Lloyd (1805–1879). BEJ; BOD; COG; COGA; ELA; LEC; LEZC; RED; SPB; STJA
Grimké, Angelina Emily (1805–1879). CHFB; GUBA; LES-2; STG; WABC†
Grimké, Sarah Moore (1792–1873). CHFB; GUBA; LES-2; NIA; WABC†
Hall, Prince (1735?–1807). ADA; ADB; BEJ; GRAB-05; PECA

Henson, Josiah (1789–1883). CAHA; GRAB-05
Hunnicutt, James (fl. 1865). STG
Jones, John (1816–1879). ADA; ADB; GRAB-05; KADB
Lane, Lunsford (b. 1803). DADA
Lay, Benjamin. STJA
Lovejoy, Elijah Parish (1802–1837). CHFB; COG; LEC; LEPE; MAM; MEB
Mott, Lucretia Coffin (1793–1880). COG; GIBA†; GUBA; LES-2; STJ; STLA; WABC; WAR; YOC
Parker, Theodore (1810–1860). CHFB; COG
Phillips, Wendell (1811–1884). BEJ; COG
Purvis, Robert (1810–1898). GRAB-05
Remond, Charles Lenox (1810–1873). GRAB-05
Remond, Sarah Parker (1826–1894). GRAB-05
Ruggles, David (1810–1849). GRAB-05
Stevens, Thaddeus (1792–1868). BEJ; BU; CAGA; STJB
Stewart, Maria W. (1803–1879). GRAB-05; WABC†
Still, William (1821–1902). ADA; ADB; GRAB-05
Stowe, Harriet Beecher (1811–1896). BEGA; BOA; BOC; DEI; DEJ; DOD; GIBA; JOCA; SMC; STJ; STLA; VAB; WABC†; WHB
Sumner, Charles (1811–1874). BEJ
Truth, Sojourner (1797–1883). ADA; ADB; BEJ; BLE; BLF†; BRB; DADA; GIBA; JO; LES-2; LOAV; WABC†; WAH
Tubman, Harriet (1820–1913). ADA; ADB; BEJ; BRB; BRBD; BRBE; BRG; BUA; COG; DADA; DOD; GEE; GIBA; HODA; HUA; HUB; JOC; LOAV; NIA; ROG; SMC; STD; STJA; STLA; WABC†; WAH; YOC; YOI
Wagoner, Henry O. (fl. 1860). KADB
Walker, David (1785–1830). ADA; ADB; BEJ; GRAB-05; PECA; STJA
Walker, Jonathon (early 19th century). ARB
Ward, Samuel Ringgold (1817–1866). GRAB-05
Whipper, William (1805–1885). ADB; GRAB-02

Whittier, John Greenleaf (1807–1892). BEF; BEGA; BOA; SIF

Woolman, John (1720–1772). VIA

ACTORS, ACTRESSES & ENTERTAINERS

See also CIRCUS & SHOW FIGURES; DANCERS & CHOREOGRAPHERS; MAGICIANS; MUSICIANS; MUSICIANS, JAZZ; RODEO FIGURES; SINGERS; TELEVISION & RADIO PERSONALITIES

American

Abbott, Bud (William) (1895–1974). BUR-1; ED-1†

Ace, Jane (1905–1974). MASB

Adams, Maude (1872–1953). GIBA†; VAA

Akeman, David "Stringbean" (1915–1973). HAG-1

Aldridge, Ira (1805?–1867). ADA; ADB; BRB†; HODA; HUA; PECA; ROF; ROG

Allard, Martine. BRF-1

Allen, Gracie (Grace Ethel Cecile Rosalie) (1906–1964). BUR-1; MASB

Allen, Woody (1935–). ED-1†; SMBB-3

Anderson, Mary A. (1859–1940). VAA

Arden, Eve (1912–). MASB

Autry, Gene (1907–). LA

Ball, Lucille (1911–). MASB

Ballard, Kaye (1926–). MASB

Barrymore, Ethel (1879–1959). DI-1; GIBA†; STLA

Barth, Belle (1911–1971). MASB

Bayes, Nora (1880–1928). MASB

Berg, Gertrude (1899–1966). MASB

Bernhard, Sandra (1955–). MASB

Boosler, Elayne (1953–). MASB

Booth, Edwin Thomas (1833–1893). SHFA

Booth, John Wilkes (1838–1865). RABA; SHFA

Booth, Junius Brutus (1796–1852). (Born England). SHFA

Brice, Fanny (1891–1951). DI-1†; MASB; PHA

Broderick, Matthew (1962–). BRF-1

Brooks, Mel (Melvin Kaminsky) (1926–). BUR-1; SMBB-3

Brown, Jim (James Nathaniel) (1936–). AAS-35; AKB; ALBA; BEKB; BOF; DAFB; DAFG; DAI; DUF; HAD; HEI; HIE; HOBC; HOC; KADA; RAAE; SID

Burnett, Carol (1933–). MASB

Burns, George (1896–). BUR-1

Burns, John Francis (1933–). BUR-1

Buttons, Red (1919–). ALC

Buzzi, Ruth (1937–). MASB

Callaway, Liz. BRF-1

Canova, Judy (1916–1983). MASB

Cantor, Eddie (1892–1964). ALC; LETA; PHA

Carroll, Jean (c. 1915–). MASB

Carroll, Pat (1927–). MASB

Channing, Carol (1921–). MASB

Cheech (Richard Marin) (1946–). BUR-1

Chong, Tommy (1939–). BUR-1

Clair, Dick (Richard Clair Jones) (1931?–). BUR-1

Clower, Jerry (1926–). HAG-1

Coca, Imogene (1908–). MASB

Cohan, George Michael (1878–1942). EWA; MOA

Colón, Miriam. NEBB

Connors, Chuck (1924–). HOBB

Cornell, Katharine (1898–1974). BOC; DI-1†; GIBA†

Cosby, Bill (1937–). HOBB

Costello, Lou (Louis Francis) (1908–1959). BUR-1; ED-1†

Crabtree, Lotta (1847–1924). MASB

Cushman, Charlotte Saunders (1816–1876). STJ; VAA; VAB

Daley, Cass (1915–1975). MASB

Davis, Joan (1907–1961). MASB

Davis, Sammy, Jr. (1925–). DOBA; DOF-1; ROF

Dee, Ruby (1924?–). FAG

Dern, Bruce (1936–). BELB

Diller, Phyllis (1917–). MASB

Draper, Ruth (1884–1956). MASB

Dressler, Marie (1869–1934). (Born Canada). MASB

Duncan, Rosetta (1900–1959). MASB

Duncan, Vivien (1902–). MASB

Elliott, Bob (Robert Bracket) (1923–). BUR-1

Evans, Dale (1912–). LA

Fazenda, Louise (1895–1962). MASB

Ferrer, José (1912–). FOW

Fields, Totie (1931–1978). MASB

Fields, W. C. (William Claude) (1880–1946). COKB; ED-1; KLD; MAOB; PHA

Fine, Larry (1911–1975). BUR-1; ED-1†

Fiske, Minnie Maddern (1865–1932). DI-1; GIBA†; VAA; WABC†

Forrest, Edwin (1806–1872). SHFA

Foster, Gloria (1936–). AB

Franklin, Irene (1876–1941). MASB

Friganza, Trixie (1870–1955). MASB

Garbo, Greta (1905–). (Born Sweden). ASB-1

Garland, Judy (1922–1969). FOR

Gilpin, Charles Sidney (1878–1930). ADA; ADB; DOF-1

Goldberg, Whoopi (1950–). MASB

Goulding, Ray (Raymond Walter) (1922–). BUR-1

Grant, Micki. AB

Green, Nancy (c. 1834–1923). GRAB-02

Greenwood, Charlotte (1893–1978). MASB

Gregory, Dick (1932–). DADB; EOB; RICA

Hardy, Oliver (Norvell) (1892–1957). BUR-1; ED-1; MAOB; PABA

Harris, Julie (1925–). DI-1

Harrison, Richard Berry (1864–1935). ADA; ADB; DOF-1

Hawn, Goldie (1945–). MASB

Hayes, Helen (1900–). CLA; DI-1; GIBA†

Held, Anna (1873–1918). (Born France). PHA

Herford, Beatrice (1868–1952). (Born England). MASB

Holliday, Judy (1921–1965). MASB

Hope, Bob (1903–). ALC; ED-1†

Howard, Cordelia (1848–1941). CAD

Howard, Jerry (Curly) (1911–1952). BUR-1; ED-1†

Howard, Moe (1905–1975). BUR-1; ED-1†

Howard, Samuel (Shemp) (1901–1956). BUR-1; ED-1†

Irwin, May (1862–1938). (Born Canada). MASB

Janis, Elsie (1889–1956). MASB

Jolson, Al (1886–1950). LETA

Jones, Grandpa (Louis) (1913–). HAG-1

Jones, James Earl (1931–). AB

Jordan, James Edward (1897–1988). BUR-1

Jordan, Marian Driscoll (1898–1961). BUR-1

Kahn, Madeline (1942–). MASB

Kalmar, Bert (1884–1947). MOA

Kane, Helen (1904–1966). MASB

Karloff, Boris (1887–1969). (Born England). COE-2

Keaton, Buster (1895–1977). ED-1; SMBC

Kelly, Patsy (1910–1981). MASB

Kimbrell, Marketa (1928–). (Born Czechoslovakia). WA

King, Alan (1927–). GRB-1

Kristofferson, Kris (1937–). KRI

Langdon, Harry (1884–1944). ED-1

Laurel, Stan (Arthur Stanley Jefferson) (1890–1965). (Born England). BUR-1; ED-1; MAOB; PABA

Lee, Canada (1907–1951). ADA; ADB; SCA

Lewis, Jerry (Joseph Levitch) (1926–). ALC; BUR-1; ED-1†

Lloyd, Harold (1893–1971). ED-1

Lugosi, Bela (1886–1956). (Born Hungary). COE-2

Mabley, Jackie "Moms" (1897–1975). MASB

McKinney, Nina Mae (1913–1967). LOAV

MacLaine, Shirley (1934–). FOGC; ROJ

McMahon, Jenna (Mary Virginia Skinner) (1933–). BUR-1

Macnaughton, Robert. BRF-1

Marks, Charlie (1881–1971). BUR-1

Marlowe, Julia (1866–1950). VAA; WABC†

Martin, Andrea. MASB

Martin, Dean (Dino Paul Crocetti) (1917–). BUR-1

Martin, Dick (1922–). BUR-1

Marx, Chico (Leonard) (1887–1961). BUR-1; COKB; ED-1; MAOB

Marx, Groucho (1890–1977). ALC; BUR-1; ED-1; MAOB

Marx, Gummo (Milton) (1892–1977). BUR-1; MAOB†

Marx, Harpo (Arthur) (1888–1964). BUR-1; ED-1; MAOB

Marx, Zeppo (Herbert) (1901–1979). BUR-1; ED-1; MAOB†

May, Elaine (1932–). BUR-1; MASB

Meara, Anne (1933–). BUR-1; MASB

Menken, Adah Isaacs (1835?–1868). RAB

Midler, Bette (c. 1945–). MASB

Miller, Marilyn (1898–1936). PHA

Modjeska, Helena (1840–1909). (Born Poland). MANB; PIAA

Montalban, Ricardo (1920–). (Born Mexico). FOW; NEAA

Moran, Polly (1883–1952). MASB

Moreno, Rita (1931–). DI-1†; WO

Morris, Clara (1848–1925). STJ

Murphy, Audie (1925–1971). FAA; REA

Nichols, Mike (Igor Peshowsky) (1931–). (Born Germany). BUR-1

Normand, Mabel (1892–1930). MASB

O'Neal, Ron. AB

O'Neill, James (1847–1920). (Born Ireland). SHFA

Parker, Sarah Jessica. BRE-1

Parry, Zale (1933–). HAKA

Pearl, Minnie (Sarah Ophelia Colley) (1912–). HAG-1; MASB

Picon, Molly (1898–). MASB

Pitts, Zasu (1894?–1963). MASB

Poitier, Sidney (1924–). ADB; BRG; ROF

Price, Vincent (1911–). COE-2

Quinn, Anthony (1916–). (Born Mexico). LOAA; NEAA

Radner, Gilda (1946–). MASB

Rand, Suzanne (1950–). MASB

Rasmussen, Zora. MASB

Raye, Martha (1916–). MASB

Rehan, Ada (1860–1916). (Born Ireland). VAA

Reiner, Carl (1922–). BUR-1

Ribeiro, Alfonso. BRF-1

Ritter, Tex (Woodward Maurice) (1906–1974). LA

Rivers, Joan (c. 1935–). MASB

Robeson, Paul (1898–1976). ADA; ADB; DAFG; DOBA; DOF-1; JO; RICA; ROF

Rogers, Roy (1912–). LA

Rosenbloom, Maxie (1904–1976). SLA

Rowan, Dan (1922–1987). BUR-1

Rowson, Susanna Haswell (1762–1824). (Born England). DOG

Schreiber, Avery (1935–). BUR-1
Silvera, Frank (1914–). ADA; ADB
Silverman, Jonathan. BRF-1
Silvers, Phil (1912–1985). ALC
Skinner, Cornelia Otis (1901–1979). BEE
Smothers, Dick (1938–). BUR-1
Smothers, Tom (Thomas Bolyn) (1937–). BUR-1
Sokol, Marilyn. MASB
Stiller, Jerry (1928–). BUR-1
Sultzer, Joe (1884–1981). BUR-1
Tanguay, Eva (1878–1947). (Born Canada). MASB
Temple, Shirley (1928–). FOR
Thompson, Jenn. BRF-1
Todd, Thelma (1905–1935). MASB
Tomlin, Lily (1939–). BOHC; MASB
Torres, Liz. MASB
Tucker, Sophie (1884–1966). MASB
Tyler, Robin. MASB
Tyson, Cicely (1939?–). AB; BOHC
Walker, Nancy (1922–). MASB
Warfield, Marsha (1954–). MASB
Wayne, John (Marion Michael Morrison) (1907–
    1979). PABA
Weissmuller, Johnny (1904–1984). ASBA; BELB;
    DAG; DAGA; DEF; GED; GEDA; HEG; HOC;
    HOCG; LEF; LEYB; SICA
Welles, Orson (1915–1985). SMBC
West, Mae (1892–1980). MAOB; MASB
Williams, Bert (1876?–1922). ADA; ADB; HUC;
    PHA; ROF; ROG
Wilson, Flip (Clerow) (1933–). AB
Wilson, Marie (1916–1972). MASB

Foreign
Bernhardt, Sarah (1844–1923). French. MAT-1;
    PA
Bowie, David (1947–). English. BUIB-2
Cantinflas (Mario Moreno) (1911–). Mexican.
    NEBA; WO
Caron, Leslie (1933–). French. ATA
Chaplin, Sir Charles Spencer (1889–1977). En-
    glish. ASB-1; COKB; ED-1; SMBC
Félix, Elisa Rachel (1821–1858). French. (Born
    Switzerland). LER; PEB
Fields, Gracie (1898–1979). English. MASB
Henie, Sonja (1913–1969). Norwegian. ASBA;
    DAG; DAGA; GED; GEDA; HOBAA; LEYB†;
    RYA†
Hepburn, Audrey (1929–). English. FOG
Irving, Sir Henry (1838–1905). English. TRC
Lee, Christopher (1922–). English. COE-2
Lillie, Beatrice (1898–). English. (Born Canada).
    MASB
Olivier, Laurence (1907–). English. ASB-1
Russell, Anna (1911–). English. (Born Canada).
    MASB

Siddons, Sarah Kemble (1755–1831). English.
    NOA; TRC

ADMIRALS, *see* NAVAL FIGURES

ADVENTURERS

See also EXPLORERS & DISCOVERERS; HEROES, LEG-
ENDARY & NATIONAL; MOUNTAINEERS; PIONEERS
& FRONTIER PEOPLE; SURVIVORS; TRAVELERS

Aguirre, Lope de (c. 1510–1561). Spanish. KNA
Blyth, Chay (fl. 1966). English. OLC
Bombard, Alain Louis (1924?–). French. ELA;
    HAQ
Bultema, John. WIAA-5
Casanova de Seingalt, Giovanni Giacomo (1725–
    1798). Italian. DEI; DEJ; JAC
Chichester, Sir Francis (1901–1972). English.
    OLC
Davison, Ann (fl. 1952). English. HAQ
Equiano, Olaudah (Gustavus Vassa) (1745–1801).
    English. ADA; ADB; OJA
Graham, Robin Lee (1949?–). SCBA
Long, James (1793?–1822). VIA
Losier, Roger. WIAA-5
Manry, Robert Neal (1918–1971). OLC
Morris, John. WIAA-5
Ridgway, John. OLC
Saint-Germain, Comte de, pseud. (1710?–1782?).
    COEA
Scott, John (1630?–1696). English. CAF
Smeeton, Beryl. English. HAQ
Smeeton, Miles. English. HAQ
Walker, William (1824–1860). WIAA-1

AERONAUTICAL ENGINEERS, *see* ENGINEERS, AERO-
NAUTICAL

AFRICANS

See also SPECIFIC COUNTRIES: ETHIOPIANS; GHA-
NAIANS; GUINEANS; KENYANS; LIBERIANS; MA-
LAGASIES; MOROCCANS; NIGERIANS; SENEGALESE;
SOUTH AFRICANS; TANZANIANS; UGANDANS

Abdur Rahman Sadi el Timbuctoo (1596–1660).
    Historian. ADA
Affonso I (1506–1545). King of Kongo. DOA;
    GRAB-04; MIC

Amini bin Saidi (1904?–). Tribesman. PEA
Askia Muhammad (1494–1529). Emperor of Timbuktu. ADA; ADB; BRB†; DOA; GRAB-04
Bwembya (b. 1886?). Tribesman. PEA
Cetewayo (c. 1836–1884). Zulu chief. BRB†; CAAA; MIC
Chaka (1787–1829). Zulu chief. ADA; ADB; BRB†; GRAB-04; MIC
Cinque, Joseph (1811–1852). Insurrectionist. ADA; ADB; BRB†; ROG; WOA
Coka, Gilbert (1910–). Educator. PEA
Dahia al-Kahina (fl. 667–702). Queen. GRAB-04
Gatheru, R. Mugo. College professor. OJA
Idris Alaoma (1580–1617). Sultan of Bornu. DOA; MIC
Jubo Jubogha (fl. 1880). King of Opobo. MIC
Jugurtha (fl. 188–106 B.C.). King. GRAB-04
Kayamba, Mdumi Martin (b. 1891). Teacher. PEA
Kayira, Legson Didimu. Author. OJA
Kgamanyane (fl. 1820). Chief of the Bakgatla. MIC
Khama III (d. 1980). King of the Bamangwato. MIC
Lobengula (c. 1833–1893). King of the Matabele. MIC
Mansa Musa I (1312–1337). Mali ruler. DOA; GRAB-04; PECA; POA
Massinissa (c. 238–148 B.C.). King. GRAB-04
Moshoeshoe (1790–1870). Basotho chief. GRAB-04; MIC; POA
Ndansi Kumalo (b. 1870?). Tribal chieftain. PEA
Nzinga (1582–1663). Queen. GRAB-04; JO; POA
Osei Tutu (1636–1712). King of Ashanti. GRAB-04; MIC
Quarsie, Tetteh (fl. 1879). Laborer. JO
Rashid bin Hassani (1855?). Tribesman. PEA
Sundiata I. King of Mali. MIC
Sunni Ali Ber (1464–1492). Emperor of Timbuctoo. ADA; ADB; DOA; GRAB-04
Yaa Asantewa (1863–1923). Ashanti queen. GRAB-04

AFRO-AMERICANS, see BLACKS—AMERICAN

AGRICULTURISTS

See also BOTANISTS

Bakewell, Robert (1725–1795). English. CAB
Bennett, Hugh Hammond (1881–1960). MAL
Borlaug, Norman Ernest (1914–). MEC
Boussingault, Jean Baptiste (1802–1887). French. CAB

Kim Yong-gi. Korean. RODA
Knapp, Seaman Asahel (1833–1911). MAL
Lawes, Sir John Bennett (1814–1900). English. CAB
Lubin, David (1849–1919). (Born Poland). LETA
MacKay, Angus (1840–1931). Canadian. DEA
Orr, John Boyd, 1st baron (1880–1971). Scottish. KEE; MEC; WIC
Pinckney, Eliza Lucas (1723–1793). GUBA†; SC†; WABC
Rodale, Jerome Irving (1898–1971). SQA
Truog, Emil (1884–). YOE
Tull, Jethro (1674–1741). English. CAB
Young, Arthur (1741–1820). English. CAB

AIR FORCE LEADERS

See also AIR PILOTS; AIR PIONEERS; MEDAL OF HONOR WINNERS

American
Arnold, Henry Harley (1886–1950). ARC; SWE-1
Chennault, Claire Lee (1890–1958). SWE
Davis, Benjamin O., Jr. (1912–). ADA; ADB; BOG; BRG; FLD; HUB; RIC; STO; STQ
Doolittle, James Harold (1896–). ARC; HAMY; SUA; SWE
Jabara, James A. (1923–1966). ARBA
Kelly, Colin (1915–1941). FIA
Kennedy, Joseph Patrick, Jr. (1915–1944). EDA; LAI†; SUA
King, Micki (Maxine Joyce) (1944–). BOHA; HOBAA; JABA; LEYB†; RYA†; RYX; ST-2
LeMay, Curtis Emerson (1906–). ARC; SWE
Lufberg, Raoul Gervais (d. 1918). (Born France). HAMY
Mitchell, William (1879–1936). ARD; LAC
O'Donnell, Emmett, Jr. (1906–1971). SWE
Olds, Robin (1922?–). ARBA
Rickenbacker, Edward Vernon (1890–1973). ARD; DAG; LEX; YAA
Schriever, Bernard A. (1910–). (Born Germany). NEB
Spaatz, Carl (1891–1974). SWE

Foreign
Bader, Douglas (1911–1982). English. HAMY
Barker, William George (d. 1930). Canadian. HAG
Bishop, William Avery (1894–1956). Canadian. HAG; HAMY
Collishaw, Raymond (1893–). Canadian. HAG
Gibson, Guy Penrose (1919–1944). English. HAMY

Guynemer, Georges (1894–1917). French. ARD; HAMY

McKeever, Andrew Edward (d. 1919). Canadian. HAG

Mannock, Edward (1885–1918). English. SUA

Nungesser, Charles (1892–1927). French. ARD†; SUA

Richthofen, Manfred von (1892–1918). German. ARD; HAMY; RADA

AIR PILOTS

See also AIR FORCE LEADERS; AIR PIONEERS

Allison, Bobby (Robert Arthur) (1937–). LEXA; OLCC

Ames, Julie. HIFD

Ball, Albert (1897–1917). English. HAMY

Brown, Jill Elaine. SMBC-2

Case, Sandra Williams. SMBC-2

Cobb, Geraldyn M. (1931–). GEDB; HIFD

Dengler, Dieter (1938?–). (Born Germany). ARBA

Fonck, René (1894–1953). French. HAMY

Henze, Cynthia. FOC-1

Howell, Emily (1939–). GEDB

Knight, William "Pete." ST-1

Lee, Judy Ann. SMBC-2

Lindbergh, Anne Morrow (1906–). GEDB

Mock, Jerrie (Geraldine) (1925–). GEDB

Popovich, Marina. Russian. HIFD

Post, Wiley (1900–1935). COC†; HAMY

Reitsch, Hanna (1912–1979). German. HAMY; HIFD

Smethurst, Ann Orlitski. SMBC-2

Thaw, William (1894–1934). HAMY

Tilmon, James (1934–). DRA

Vasquez, Joseph C. (1918?–). GRAC

AIR PIONEERS

See also AIR FORCE LEADERS; ENGINEERS, AERO-NAUTICAL; ROCKET & SPACE SCIENTISTS

Alcock, Sir John (1892–1919). English. COC†; HAMY

Bastie, Maryse. French. HIFD

Batten, Jean (1909–1982). New Zealand. HIFD; MO

Beachey, Lincoln (1887–1915). HAMY

Blériot, Louis (1872–1936). French. BRBA; COC†; EDA; KEH

Boucher, Helene (1908–1934). French. HIFD

Brown, Arthur Whitten (1886–1948). Scottish. COC†; HAMY

Cochran, Jacqueline (1906–1980). CLA; GEDB; HAMY; HIFD; MO; WAJ

Cockerell, Sir Christopher (1910–). English. FE; MAPA

Coleman, Bessie (1893–1926). HIFD; LOAV

Curtiss, Glenn Hammond (1878–1930). BOK; HAMY; HOF

De Seversky, Alexander P. (1894–1974). (Born Russia). GEA

Earhart, Amelia (1898–1937). BOC; BOJ; COC†; COKA; DOD; ELA; EVD; FAA; GEDB; GIBA; HAMY; HAQ; LAC; LEK; MAT-1; MO; NAB; PA; SMC; STLA; WABC†; WAE; YOC

Fairgrave, Phoebe (1903–). HIFD

Garros, Roland (d. 1918). French. HAMY

Johnson, Amy (1903–1941). English. HIFD; MO

Kingsford-Smith, Charles (1897–1935). English. HAMY

Langley, Samuel Pierpont (1834–1906). CUC; HYA†; SOB

Law, Ruth (1887–). GEDB†; HIFD

Lindbergh, Charles Augustus (1902–1974). ASB-1; BRBA; COC†; EVD; FAA; HAA; HAMY; HAQ; LAC; SQA; SUA

Love, Nancy. HIFD

Montgolfier, Jacques Étienne (1745–1799). French. BRBA; EVC; FE

Montgolfier, Joseph Michel (1740–1810). French. BRBA; EVC; FE

Nichols, Ruth (1901–1960). GEDB†; HIFD

Nobile, Umberto (b. 1885). Italian. GRB; ROL†

Piccard, Auguste (1884–1962). Swiss. BAB; COR; OLC; PRC

Quimby, Harriet (1884–1912). GEDB†; HIFD

Rodgers, Calbraith Perry (fl. 1911). HAMY

Santos-Dumont, Alberto (1873–1932). Brazilian. BRBA

Sikorsky, Igor Ivan (1889–1972). (Born Russia). BEA; FE; LAE; LIA; LOB; MAP

Skrzypiec, Tina Marie. SMBC-2

Smith, Elinor (1910–). HIFD

Stinson, Katherine (1893–1977). GEDB†; HIFD

Ulm, Charles. Australian. HAMY

Whittle, Sir Frank (1907–). English. EVC; FE; SHFB; THA

Wright, Orville (1871–1948). ASB; ASB-1; BIA; BOD; BRBA; COL; CUC; DEI; DEJ; DOE; EBA; EVC; EVD; FAB; FE; FRE; HAMY; HYA†; LEL; MAT; PRC; SIA; THA

Wright, Wilbur (1867–1912). ASB; BIA; BOD; BRBA; COL; CUC; DEI; DEJ; DOE; EBA; EVC; EVD; FAB; FE; FRE; HAMY; HYA†; LEL; MAT; PRC; SIA; THA

Yeager, Charles E. (1923–). COQ

ALCHEMISTS

Democritos, Bolos (fl. 200 B.C.). Greek. CUA; FE
Flamel, Nicholas (1330–1418). French. CUA
Go-Hung (254–334). Chinese. CUA
Jabir ibn-Hayyan (721–815). Arabian. CUA
Paracelsus (Theophrastus Bombastus von
    Hohenheim) (1493–1541). Swiss. CUA; ED-5;
    FE; POB; ROA; SHG
Seton, Alexander (1520–1604). Scottish. CUA

AMBASSADORS, *see* DIPLOMATS, U.S.; STATESMEN,
FOREIGN

AMERICAN REVOLUTIONARY FIGURES

British – Military
Burgoyne, John (1722–1792). AKA; RAD; SOA
Butler, Walter (1752–1781). SOA
Clinton, Sir Henry (1738–1795). AKA; SOA
Cornwallis, Charles Cornwallis, 1st marquis
    (1738–1805). AKA; SOA
Gage, Thomas (1721–1787). AKA; BUIB†; SOA
Howe, William Howe, 5th viscount (1729–1814).
    AKA; SOA
Tarleton, Sir Banastre (1754–1833). SOA

British – Spies
André, John (1751–1780). LOA; SOA
Bates, Ann (fl. 1778). AND

British – Statesmen
Bartlett, Josiah (1729–1795). BAEA; BUIB†;
    COJ†; FEAB; MAC
Germain, George Sackville, 1st viscount Sackville
    (1716–1785). SOA
North, Frederick, 2d earl Guilford and 8th baron
    North (1732–1792). SOA
Wilkes, John (1727–1797). SOA

Patriots – Military
Allen, Ethan (1738–1789). BUIB†; RAD; SOA
Arnold, Benedict (1741–1801). HAN; LOA; SOA
Barry, John (1745–1803). (Born Ireland). RAD
Bason, Caesar. WIBA
Bassett, Richard (1745–1815). BUIB†; FEAA
Burr, Seymour (fl. 1775). WIBA
Clark, George Rogers (1752–1818). BUIB; DAFA;
    HEB; RAD; SOA; VIA
Corbin, Margaret (1751–1800). AND; CLC; RAD

Cromwell, Oliver (1753?–1853?). ADB; DAF-1†;
    WIBA
Dabney, Austin (fl. 1779–1821). DAF-1; WIBA†
Davie, William Richardson (1756–1820). (Born
    England). FEAA
Flora, William (d. 1820). DAF-1†; WIBA
Gannet, Deborah Sampson (fl. 1776). AND; CLC;
    HODA; RAD; ROG; STQ†; WIBA
Glover, John (1732–1797). MAE; SOA
Grasse, François Joseph de (1722–1788). French.
    SOA
Greene, Nathanael (1742–1786). BUIB†; DAFA;
    MAE; SOA
Hector, Edward (d. 1834). DAF-1†; WIBA
Hopkins, Esek (1718–1802). SOA
Hull, Agrippa (1759?–1848?). DAF-1
Jeffrey, Major (fl. 1776). WIBA
Jones, John Paul (1747–1792). BUIB; COD; CUC;
    DAC; DAFA; DEI; DEJ; DYA; FIA; FID; HIBD;
    ICA; LOA; NAC; OLA; SOA
Jouett, Jack (John) (1754–1822). CAGA
Kalb, Johann (1721–1780). German. SCB-1
Knox, Henry (1750–1806). BUIB†; DAFA; MAE;
    SOA
Kosciusko, Tadeusz (1746–1817). Polish. HEA;
    LOB; MANB; PIAA; RAD; SCB-1; STP
Lafayette, Marie Joseph Paul Yves Roch Gilbert
    du Motier, marquis de (1757–1834). French.
    CUC; DEI; FRB; HAN; LAD; LOA; OLA; SCB-
    1; SOA; STP
Laurens, John (1754–1782). MAO; STG
Lee, Charles (1731–1782). BUIB†; RAD; SOA
Lee, Henry (Light-Horse Harry) (1756–1818).
    BUIB†; LOA; MAE; SOA
Lew, Brazillai (b. 1743). WIBA
McHenry, James (1753–1816). (Born Ireland).
    BUIB†; FEAA
Marion, Francis (1732–1795). ARE; HIBD; MAE;
    RAD; SOA
Martin, Joseph Plumb (b. 1760?). HIBD
Mifflin, Thomas (1744–1800). BUIB†; FEAA; SEC
Morgan, Daniel (1736–1802). BUIB†; HIBD;
    MAE; SOA
Nones, Benjamin (1757–1826). (Born France).
    GEF; LERA
Pinckney, Charles Cotesworth (1746–1825).
    BUIB†; FEAA; WHD†
Poor, Salem. DAF-1†; STQ†; WIBA
Pulaski, Casimir (1748–1779). Polish. ARE; LOB;
    MANB; PIAA; SCB-1; SOA
Putnam, Israel (1718–1790). BUIB†; FIA; OLA;
    SOA
Robinson, James (1753–1868). WIBA
Rochambeau, comte de (Jean-Baptiste Donatien
    de Vimeur) (1725–1807). French. SCB-1

Salem, Peter (1750?–1816). ADB; BRG; BUIB†; DAF-1; DOB; ROG; STQ†; WIBA

Steuben, Friedrich Wilhelm von (1730–1794). (Born Germany). CUB; DAFA; HAN; SCB-1; SOA

Ward, Artemas (1727–1800). BUIB†; SOA

Warren, Joseph (1741–1775). DIA; SUL

Washington, George (1732–1799). ALCA; ARAB; ASB; BAEB; BAG; BAG-1; BEB; BEC; BLA; BUIA; BUIB; CAAA; CABA; CAG; CAH; CHG; COD; COI; COJA; COS; CUC; DAC; DAE; DAF-2; DAFA; DEI; DEJ; DUB; DUC; DUCA; EVD; FEAA; FIA; FID; FOB; FOH; FRBA; HAK; HAN; HIBC; HIH; KEC†; LEAA; LEP; LEQ; LEQA; MAB; MABA; MAT; MIA; OLA; PED; ROH; ROHA; ROK; SOA; STH; SUBB; WAI; WHD

Wayne, Anthony (1745–1796). BUIB†; MAE; RAD; SOA

Whipple, Prince (1764?–1797). DAF-1; WIBA

Willett, Marinus (1740–1830). RAD

Patriots – Spies

Armistead, James (fl. 1781–1824). DAF-1; STQ†; WIBA

Crosby, Enoch (b. 1750). FOA

Darragh, Lydia B. (1728?–1789). AND; CLC; KN

Hale, Nathan (1755–1776). BUIB†; DEI; DEJ; EVD; FIA; FID; FOA; HAB; HIBD; KN; LEAA; LEP; LOA; SUG

Pompey. ROG; WIBA†

Tallmadge, Benjamin (1754–1835). SEB; SOA

Townsend, Robert (b. 1753). FOA

Patriots – Statesmen

Adams, John (1735–1826). ARAB; BAEA; BAEB; BAG; BAG-1; BEB; BLA; BLE; BUIA; BUIB; CAG; CAH; COI; COJ; COS; DAFA; DUB; DUC; DUCA; FEA; FEAB; FEB; FRBA; HAN; HAOA; HIH; HOEA; KEC†; LAI; LEQ; LEQA; MAB; MABA; MAC; MIA; OLA; PED; ROH; ROHA; ROK†; SUBB; WHD

Adams, Samuel (1722–1803). ARAA; ARAB; BAEA; BUIB; COJ; DAC; DIA; FEAB; HAN; HIBD; LAI; MAC; SUL

Braxton, Carter (1736–1797). BAEA; BUIB†; COJ†; FEAB

Bulloch, Archibald (1730–1777). SEC

Carroll, Charles (1737–1832). BAEA; BUIB†; COJ; FEAB†; MAC

Chase, Samuel (1741–1811). BAEA; BUIB†; COJ; FEAB; MAC

Clark, Abraham (1726–1794). BAEA; BUIB†; COJ†; FEAB; MAC†

Clymer, George (1739–1813). BAEA; BUIB†; COJ†; FEAA; FEAB

Dickinson, John (1732–1808). BUIB†; FEAA

Ellery, William (1727–1820). BAEA; BUIB†; COJ†; FEAB; MAC

Floyd, William (1734–1821). BAEA; BUIB†; COJ†; FEAB; MAC

Franklin, Benjamin (1706–1790). ALCA; ARAB; ASB; BAEA; BLE; BOD; BUE; BUIB; CAA; COJ; COR; CUC; DAC; DAFA; DEDC; DEI; DEJ; DUA; FE; FEAA; FEAB; FEB; FIA; FID; FOB; FOH; HAN; HYA; HYB; LEAA; LEC; MAC; MAQ; MAT; OLA; SHFB; SIA; SQB; STH; STI; VIA; WAI

Franks, David Salisbury (d. 1793). LETA

Gerry, Elbridge (1744–1814). BAEA; BUIB†; COJ†; FEA; FEAA; FEAB; HAOA; HOEA; MAC

Gorham, Nathaniel (1738–1796). BUIB†; FEAA

Gwinnett, Button (1735–1777). BAEA; BUIB†; COJ†; FEAB; MAC

Hall, Lyman (1724–1790). BAEA; BUIB†; COJ†; FEAB; MAC

Hancock, John (1737–1793). ARAB; BAEA; BUIB; COJ; FEAB; LOA; MAC; SOA; SUL

Harrison, Benjamin (1726–1791). BAEA; BUIB†; COJ†; LAI; MAC

Hart, John (1711?–1779). BAEA; BUIB†; COJ†; FEAB; MAC†

Henry, Patrick (1736–1799). ARAB; BUIB; CUC; DAC; DAF-2; DEI; DEJ; FIA; FID; HAK; HAN; OLA; SUL; VIA†

Hewes, Joseph (1730–1779). BAEA; BUIB†; COJ†; FEAB; MAC

Heyward, Thomas, Jr. (1746–1809). BAEA; BUIB†; COJ†; FEAB; MAC†

Hooper, William (1742–1790). BAEA; BUIB†; COJ†; FEAB; MAC†

Hopkins, Stephen (1707–1785). BAEA; BUIB†; COJ†; FEAB; MAC

Hopkinson, Francis (1737–1791). BAEA; BUIB†; COJ†; FEAB; MAC

Huntington, Samuel (1731–1796). BAEA; BUIB†; COJ; FEAB

Jefferson, Thomas (1743–1826). ALCA; ARAB; ASB; BAEA; BAEB; BAG; BAG-1; BEB; BEC; BLA; BLE; BUIA; BUIB; CAG; CAH; COG; COI; COJ; COS; CUC; DAC; DAF-2; DAFA; DEI; DEJ; DIA; DUB; DUC; DUCA; FEA; FEAB; FEB; FIA; FID; FOB; FOH; FRBA; FRE; HAN; HAOA; HEEA; HIBC†; HIH; HOEA; LEQ; LEQA; MAB; MABA; MAC; MAT; MEB; MIA; OLA; PED; ROH; ROHA; ROK; STH; SUBB; VIA; WAI; WHD

Johnson, Thomas (1732–1819). SEC

Langdon, John (1741–1819). BUIB†; FEAA; SEC

Lee, Francis L. (1734–1797). BAEA; BUIB†; COJ†; FEAB

Lee, Richard Henry (1732–1794). BAEA; BUIB†;
    COJ; FEAB; MAC
Lewis, Francis (1713–1802). BAEA; BUIB†; COJ†;
    FEAB; MAC
Livingston, Philip (1716–1778). BAEA; BUIB†;
    COJ†; FEAB; MAC
Livingston, Robert R. (1746–1813). BUE; FEB;
    HOF; VIA
Lynch, Thomas, Jr. (1749–1779). BAEA; BUIB†;
    COJ†; FEAB; MAC†
McKean, Thomas (1734–1817). BAEA; BUIB†;
    COJ†; FEAB; MAC
Mason, George (1725–1792). BUIB†; FEAA; MEB
Middleton, Arthur (1742–1787). BAEA; BUIB†;
    COJ†; FEAB; MAC
Morris, Lewis (1726–1798). BAEA; BUIB†; COJ†;
    FEAB; MAC
Morris, Robert (1734–1806). BAEA; BUIB†;
    COJ†; FEAA; FEAB; HAN; MAC
Morton, John (1724–1777). BAEA; BUIB†; COJ†;
    FEAB
Nelson, Thomas (1738–1789). BAEA; BUIB†;
    COJ†; FEAB; MAC
Otis, James (1725–1783). BUIB†; HAN
Paca, William (1740–1799). BAEA; BUIB†; COJ†;
    FEAB; MAC
Paine, Robert Treat (1731–1814). BAEA; COJ†;
    FEAB
Paine, Thomas (1737–1809). ALCA; ARAB; ARB;
    BUIB†; COG; CUC; DAFA; FIA; FLBA; HAN;
    HIBD; MAM; VIA†
Penn, John (1740–1788). BAEA; BUIB†; COJ†;
    FEAB; MAC
Read, George (1733–1798). BAEA; BUIB†; COJ†;
    FEAA; FEAB; MAC†
Revere, Paul (1735–1818). BAC; BUIB; DAFA;
    DEI; DEJ; EVD; FIA; FOA; HAN; SOA; SUL
Rodney, Caesar (1728–1784). BAEA; BUIB†; COJ;
    FEAB; MAC; SEC
Ross, George (1730–1779). BAEA; BUIB†; COJ†;
    FEAB
Rush, Benjamin (1745–1813). BAEA; BUIB†;
    COJ†; CUC; ED; FEAB; MAC
Rutledge, Edward (1749–1800). BAEA; BUIB†;
    COJ†; FEAB; MAC
Salomon, Haym (1740–1785). (Born Poland).
    ALD; BOK; BUIB†; GRB-1; GUB; HAN†;
    LERA; LETA; LOB; PEB; SOA
Salvador, Francis (1747–1776). GRB-1; LETA
Schuyler, Philip John (1733–1804). SOA
Sheftall, Mordecai (1735–1797). BUIB†; LETA
Sherman, Roger (1721–1793). BAEA; BUIB†;
    COJ†; FEAA; FEAB; FEB; MAC
Smith, James (1719–1806). (Born Ireland). BAEA;
    BUIB†; COJ†; FEAB

Stockton, Richard (1730–1781). BAEA; BUIB†;
    COJ†; FEAB; MAC
Stone, Thomas (1743–1787). BAEA; BUIB†;
    COJ†; FEAB
Taylor, George (1716–1781). BAEA; BUIB†;
    COJ†; FEAB
Thornton, Matthew (1714–1803). BAEA; BUIB†;
    COJ†; FEAB; MAC†
Walton, George (1741–1804). BAEA; BUIB†;
    COJ†; FEAB; MAC†
Whipple, William (1730–1785). BAEA; BUIB†;
    COJ†; FEAB; MAC†
Williams, William (1731–1811). BAEA; BUIB†;
    COJ†; FEAB; MAC†
Wilson, James (1742–1798). BAEA; BUIB†; COJ†;
    FEAA; FEAB; MAC
Witherspoon, John (1723–1794). BAEA; BUIB†;
    COJ†; FEAB; MAC
Wolcott, Oliver (1726–1797). BAEA; BUIB†;
    COJ†; FEAB; MAC
Wythe, George (1726–1806). BAEA; BUIB†;
    COJ†; FEAA; FEAB; MAC

Patriots – Others
Allen, Maria (fl. 1776). CAD
Attucks, Crispus (1723?–1770). ADA; ADB; BEJ;
    BRB; BRG; BUIB†; DAF-1; EMA; GRAB-02;
    HUB; JOC; LEI; PECA; ROG; STQ†; WIBA
Barker, Penelope (fl. 1774). CLC
Beman, Nathan (b. 1766). CAD
Brant, Molly (Degonwadonti) (1736–1796). AND
Champe, Elizabeth (fl. 1780). CLC
Daggett, Polly. CAD
Hart, Nancy (1735–1830). AND; CLC
Lamson, David (fl. 1775). WIBA
Langston, Dicey. CAGA
Latham, Lambert. DAF-1
Livingston, Susan (fl. 1779). TRD
Ludington, Sybil (1761–1839). CAD; CLC
McCauley, Mary (Molly Pitcher) (1754–1832).
    AND; CLC; DOD; LEAA; LEK; LOA†; PA; STJ
Manter, Parnel. CAD
Murray, Mary Lindley (fl. 1776). CLC
Pointer, Dick (d. 1827). WIBA
Redmond, Mary. CAD
Reynolds, Phoebe (b. 1771). CLC
Ross, Betsy (1752–1836). AND; DOD; LOA†; STJ
Townsend, Sally (1760–1842). CLC; STJ
Wick, Tempe (fl. 1781). CLC
Zane, Elizabeth (1766–1831). AND; CAD; CLC

ANATOMISTS

See also PHYSIOLOGISTS

Cobb, William Montague (1904–). CHE; HAMA
Fabricius ab Aquapendente, Hieronymus (1537–1619). Italian. POB
Hunter, John (1728–1793). Scottish. FE; MAR; RIB; SIC
Hunter, William (1718–1783). Scottish. MAR
Malpighi, Marcello (1628–1694). Italian. STE
Manzolini, Anne Morandi (1716–1774). Italian. RIB
Sabin, Florence Rena (1871–1953). BUDA; FOG; HA-1; STLA
Vesalius, Andreas (1514–1564). Belgian. CAA; CHD; DOE; HUD; POD; ROA; SHG; SIC

ANIMAL TRAINERS, *see* CIRCUS & SHOW FIGURES; HORSE TRAINERS

ANTHROPOLOGISTS

See also ARCHAEOLOGISTS

Bastian, Adolf (1826–1905). German. HAO
Cone, Cynthia. BOHG
Delany, Martin R. (1812–1885). ADA; ADB; BRB; GRAB-05
Goodall, Jane (1934–). English. BOHG; DU-1; SC
Heyerdahl, Thor (1914–). Norwegian. BAB; OLC; SCBA
Kingsley, Mary Henrietta (1862–1900). English. BOH; DAF; KNA; ROL†; WIA-1
Leakey, Louis S. B. (1903–1972). English. DU-1
Lévi-Strauss, Claude (1908–). French. HAO
Malinowski, Bronislaw Kasper (1884–1942). Polish. HAO
Mead, Margaret (1901–1978). BOHG; CLA; COLA; DU-1; EMB; GIB-1†; HAO; KE†; KOA; NAB; PACA; STLA
Meggers, Betty J. (1921–). PAC
Schoolcraft, Henry Rowe (1793–1864). HAO; LED

APOSTLES

Andrew (1st century). DAD-3; ONA; QUA
Bartholomew. DAD-3
James the Greater. DAD-3; QUA
James the Less. DAD-2; QUA

John, the Evangelist. DAD-2; DAD-3; ONA
Matthew. DAD-3
Matthias. DAD-2; QUA
Peter (d. 67? A.D.). DAD-1; DAD-2; DAD-3; MAJ; ONA; QUA
Philip. DAD-2
Simon. DAD-3
Thomas. DAD-3; QUA

AQUANAUTS, *see* UNDERWATER EXPLORERS

ARABIANS

Abd-er-Rahman I (731–788). Emir. CAAA
Antar (525?–615). Hero and poet. ADA; ADB
Harun al-Rashid (764?–809). Caliph. CAAA
ibn-Batuta (1304–1377). Traveler. ROL
Jabir ibn-Hayyan (721–815). Alchemist. CUA
Khwarizmi, al- (780–850). Mathematician. STN
Mohammed (570–632). Founder of Islam. BEO; CAAA; DEI; DEJ; FRE; TRC-1
Samuel ibn Adiya (fl. 540). Poet. GEF

ARCHAEOLOGISTS

See also PALEONTOLOGISTS

Anderson, Douglas Dorland (1936–). POC
Broneer, Oscar (1894–). (Born Sweden). POC
Bruhns, Karen Olsen (1941–). WIAA-01
Carter, Howard (1873–1939). English. WOA
Cesnola, Luigi Palma di (1832–1904). (Born Italy). MAS
Dunn, Mary Eubanks (1947–). WIAA-01
Evans, Clifford (1920–). PAC
Glueck, Nelson (1900–1971). GRB-1
Green, Ernestene (1939–). WIAA-01
Haury, Emil W. (1905–). POC
Irwin-Williams, Cynthia (1936–). WIAA-01
Kelley, Jane Holden (1928–). WIAA-01
Kenyon, Kathleen M. (1906–). English. RIG
Mallowan, Max E. L. (1904–1978). English. POC
Schliemann, Heinrich (1822–1890). German. ELA
Wheeler, Sir Mortimer (1890–1976). English. POC
Wildesen, Leslie E. (1944–). WIAA-01
Willey, Gordon Randolph (1913–). POC
Yadin, Yigael (1917–1984). Israeli. GRB-1; POC; ROGA

ARCHITECTS

American

Breuer, Marcel Lajos (1902–1981). (Born Hungary). LAF

Bulfinch, Charles (1763–1844). LAF; LEDA

Burnham, Daniel Hudson (1846–1912). LAF

Cerny, Robert George (1908–). LEDA

Fuller, Richard Buckminster (1895–1983). LAF

Gropius, Walter Adolf (1883–1969). (Born Germany). BEA; FOF; HIFA; LAF

Latrobe, Benjamin Henry (1764–1820). (Born England). LAF

McKim, Charles Follen (1847–1909). LAF

Mead, William Rutherford (1846–1928). LAF

Mies van der Rohe, Ludwig (1886–1969). (Born Germany). FOF; HIFA; LEDA

Neutra, Richard Joseph (1892–1970). (Born Austria). FOF; LAF

Nowicki, Matthew (1910–1950). (Born Poland). PIAA

Olmsted, Frederick Law (1822–1903). HIBB

Richardson, Henry Hobson (1838–1886). LAF

Saarinen, Eero (1910–1961). (Born Finland). FOF; LAF; LEDA

Saarinen, Eliel (1873–1950). (Born Finland). LAF

Scott Brown, Denise (1931–). (Born South Africa). GIB-1

Stone, Edward Durrell (1902–1978). FOF; LEDA

Sullivan, Louis Henry (1856–1924). FOF; LAF; LEDA

White, Stanford (1853–1906). LAF

Williams, Paul Revere (1894–1980). ADB; DOF-1; LEDA

Wright, Frank Lloyd (1869–1959). ASB-1; CUC; FOF; HIFA; LEDA

Foreign

Aleijadhino (Antônio Francisco Lisboa) (1738–1841). Brazilian. BACA

Le Corbusier (Charles-Edouard Jeanneret) (1887–1965). French. (Born Switzerland). HIFA

McHarg, Ian L. (1921–). Scottish. CORA

Mendelsohn, Eric (1887–1953). English. (Born Germany). FOF; LEDA

Michelangelo Buonarroti (1475–1564). Italian. CHC; DEI; DEJ; JAA; KAA; MAI

Nansen, Odd (1901–). Norwegian. BAF

Niemeyer, Oscar (1907–). Brazilian. BACA

Vasquez, Pedro Ramírez. Mexican. NEBA

Wren, Sir Christopher (1632–1723). English. DEI; DEJ

ARGENTINES

Belgrano, Manuel (1770–1820). General. LAB

Borges, Jorge Luis (1899–1986). Author. WO

Fangio, Juan Manuel (1912–). Automobile racer. ABB; COKC; JA; YAA

Houssay, Bernardo Alberto (1887–1971). Physiologist. RIF

Irigoyen, Hipólito (1850–1933). President. WOB

Mitre, Bartolomé (1821–1906). President. WOB

Moreno, Mariano (1778–1811). Political leader. LAB

Pérez Esquivel, Adolfo (1931–). Humanitarian. DU-1

Perón, Eva Duarte (1919–1952). Wife of Juan Domingo Perón. BAGA; LIDA; PA; WOB

Perón, Isabel (Maria Estela) (1931–). Ex-president. LIDA

Perón, Juan Domingo (1895–1974). President. ARA; BAGA; CAE; CL-01; WOB

Saavedra Lamas, Carlos (1880–1959). Statesman. MEC†; WIC

San Martin, Jose de (1778–1850). Statesman. BAA; BACA; LAB; OLA; YOFA

Sarmiento, Domingo Faustino (1811–1888). Statesman, educator. COG; KEE; LAB; WO

Vilas, Guillermo (1952–). Tennis player. AAS-28

ARMY LEADERS

See also AIR FORCE LEADERS; AMERICAN REVOLUTIONARY FIGURES—MILITARY; CHAPLAINS; CIVIL WAR FIGURES—MILITARY; HEROES, LEGENDARY & NATIONAL; MARINES, U.S.; MEDAL OF HONOR WINNERS

American

Blunt, Roger R. (1930–). RAE

Bowie, James (1799–1836). AKC; HEB; KUA; LYF; VIA

Bradley, Omar Nelson (1893–1981). ARC; RAE

Bryan, Blackshear Morrison (1900–). RAE

Carpenter, Howard (1944?–1967). ARBA

Clark, Mark Wayne (1896–1984). RAE

Clarke, Bruce Cooper (1901–). RAE

Clay, Lucius DuBignon (1897–1978). RAE

Custer, George Armstrong (1839–1876). ARE; LEP; LEPE

Daly, Moe (Maurice Francis) (d. 1944). RAE

Davis, Benjamin O. (1877–1970). ADA; ADB; FLD

Davison, Frederic Ellis (1917–). DRA

Dawkins, Peter (1938?–). RAE

Dodge, Grenville Mellen (1831–1916). MAT

Donovan, William Joseph (1883–1959). ARD; FAA

Doyle, Edward J. (d. 1942). RAE

Eaton, Ralph (1899?–). RADA

Eichelberger, Robert Lawrence (1886–1961). RAE

Eisenhower, Dwight David (1890–1969). ARC; ASB-1; BAEB; BAG; BAG-1; BEB; BLA; BUIA; CAG; CAH; COD†; COI; COJA; COS; DEI; DEJ; DUB; DUC; DUCA; FAA; FRBA; HIH; KE; LEP; LEQ; LEQA; MAB; MABA; MIA; PED; RAE; ROH; ROHA; ROK†; SCA; SUBB; SWE-1; WEE; WHD

Factor, Pompey (d. 1928). KADB

Flipper, Henry Ossian (1856–1940). HAP; HODA; KADB

Foley, Robert F. (1941–). RAE

Fraser, Harvey Reed (1916–). RAE

Goethals, George Washington (1858–1928). LEGA; RAE

Groves, Leslie Richard (1896–1970). RAE

Harmon, Ernest Nason (1894–1979). RAE

Howell, Martin Damon (1926–). RAE

Johnson, Henry (1897–1929). BRB†; HUB; STQ†

Kearny, Stephen Watts (1794–1848). BLD

Krotoshinsky, Abraham. (Born Poland). GEF; GRB-1

MacArthur, Arthur, Jr. (1845–1912). EDA

MacArthur, Douglas (1880–1964). ARC; ASB-1; COD†; CUC; DEI; DEJ; FAA; LEP; RAE; SWE-1

Marcus, Mickey (David Daniel) (1901–1948). LETA; RAE; ROGA

Marshall, George Catlett (1880–1959). ARC; COD†; HEEA; MEC†; RADA; SWE-1; WIC

Michaelis, John Hersey (1912–). ARBA

Milam, Ben (1788–1835). KUA

Murphy, Thomas R. (1943?–1966). ARBA

Navarro, José Antonio (1795–1870). KUA

Parks, David (1944–). AKB

Patton, George Smith, Jr. (1885–1945). ARC; ARE; RAE; SWE-1

Pershing, John Joseph (1860–1948). ARD; ARE; COD; DEI; DEJ; RAE

Pierce, Clinton A. (1894–). ARE

Riley, Bennet (1787–1851). SEC

Robinson, Wirt (1864–1929). RAE

Rogers, Robert (1731–1795). VIA

Scott, Winfield (1786–1866). EDA; MAL; WHD†

Shelby, Isaac (1750–1826). BUIB†; SEC

Spruill, James Polk (1931–1964). ARBA

Storke, Harry Purnell (1905–). RAE

Summerall, Charles Pelot (1867–1955). RAE

Taylor, Maxwell Davenport (1901–1987). RAE; SUA

Thayer, Sylvanus (1785–1872). RAE

Travis, William Barret (1809–1836). AKC; KUA

Vandenberg, Roger. RAE

Van Fleet, James Alward (1892–). RAE

Walker, Walton Harris (1889–1950). ARBA

Woodmansee, John W. (1934–). RAE

Young, Charles (1864–1922). ADA; ADB; BRB; DOF-1; HODA; HUB; KADB; ROG

British

Allenby, Edmund Henry Hynman, 1st viscount (1861–1936). ARD

Amherst, Jeffrey (1717–1797). SOA

Baden-Powell, Robert Stephenson Smyth, 1st baron (1857–1941). EVA; SEB

Dorchester, Sir Guy Carleton, 1st baron (1724–1808). AKA

Haig, Douglas Haig, 1st earl (1861–1928). ARD

Kitchener, Horatio Herbert, 1st earl Kitchener of Khartoum (1850–1916). ARD

Marlborough, John Churchill, 1st duke of (1650–1722). EDA

Verney, Edmund (1590–1642). MAJ

Wellington, Arthur Wellesley, 1st duke of (1769–1852). CHG; COD

Wingate, Orde Charles (1903–1944). SUA

Wolfe, James (1727–1759). MAJ

French

Dianous, Jacques (d. 1881). WOA

Dreyfus, Alfred (1859–1935). PEB

Foch, Ferdinand (1851–1929). ARD; COD

Gaulle, Charles de (1890–1970). ASB-1; CAAA; KE; WEA

Joffre, Joseph Jacques (1852–1931). ARD; RADA

Latude, Henri Maseres de (1725–1805). JAC

Pétain, Henri Philippe (1856–1951). ARD; RADA

German

Hindenburg, Paul von (1847–1934). ARD

Ludendorff, Erich Friedrich (1865–1937). ARD; RADA

Seume, Johann. SOA

Greek

Alcibiades (c. 450–404 B.C.). PLA

Themistocles (527?–460 B.C.). COM; DYA; PLA

Xenophon (434?–355 B.C.). COM

Israeli

Allon, Yigal (1918–1980). GRB-1; ROGA

Dayan, Moshe (1915–1981). Foreign minister. ROGA; GRB-1; WECA

Grossman, Noam (1927–). GEF

Netanyahu, Yonatan (1946–1976). GRB-1

Mexican

Iturbide, Augustín de (1783–1824). NEBA; YOFA

Mina, Francisco Javier (1789–1817). ROGB

Santa Anna, Antonio López de (1795–1876).
    NEBA

Mongol

Genghis Khan (1162–1227). BEO; BLW; CAAA;
    COD; KEH; NEC; UNA
Kublai Khan (1216–1294). CAAA; UNA
Tamerlane (1336?–1405). BLW; CAAA

Roman

Agricola, Gnaeus Julius (37–93). COM
Antony, Mark (83–30 B.C.). PLA
Caesar, Gaius Julius (100–44 B.C.). CAAA; COD;
    COK; COM; DEI; DEJ; KEH; PLA; UNA
Fabius (Quintus Fabius Maximus Verrucosus) (d.
    203). PLA
Horatius Cocles (6th century B.C.). COM; STP
Scipio Africanus Major (Publius Cornelius Scipio
    Africanus) (234?–183 B.C.). COM

Spanish

Díaz, Bernal (b. 1492). BACA
Franco, Francisco (1892–1975). ARA; CAE
Narváez, Pánfilo de (1480–1528). BLD†; KEG

Venezuelan

Bolívar, Simón (1783–1830). BAA; BACA; CAE;
    LAB; LAD; OLA; STP; WO; YOFA
Miranda, Francisco de (1750?–1816). BAA; LAB;
    OLA
Sucre, Antonio José de (1795–1830). BAA; LAB

Others

Alexander III, the Great (356–323 B.C.). Macedo-
    nian. CAAA; COD; DEI; DEJ; FRE; JOBB;
    KEH; KNA; MOB; NEC; PLA; UNB
Artigas, José Gervasio (1764–1850). Uruguayan.
    LAB; WOB
Attila the Hun (406?–453). BEO; BLW; CAAA;
    DEI; JOBB
Belgrano, Manuel (1770–1820). Argentine. LAB
Breckenridge, William (1906–1959). Canadian.
    (Born Scotland). RADA
Chiang Kai-shek (1886–1975). Chinese. ARA;
    ASB-1; DOF; SPA
Garibaldi, Giuseppe (1807–1882). Italian. BOD;
    MAJ
Hannibal (247–183 B.C.). Carthaginian. CAAA;
    COD; DEI; DEJ; HAA; MAJ
Hannibal, Abram (1697–1782). Russian. ADA;
    ADB
Kornilov, Lavr Georgiyevich (1870–1918). Rus-
    sian general. NEBB-1
Lawrence, Thomas Edward (1888–1935). Welsh.
    ARD

Mannerheim, Baron Carl Gustaf Emil von (1867–
    1951). Finnish. RADA
Montrose, James Graham, 5th earl and 1st mar-
    quis of (1612–1650). Scottish. MAJ; SUK
O'Higgins, Bernardo (1778–1842). Chilean. BAA;
    LAB; OLA; STP
Onoda, Hiroo (1922–). Japanese. WIAA-5
Qaddafi, Muammar el- (1942–). Libyan. HAGD
San Martin, Jose de (1778–1850). Argentine.
    BAA; BACA; LAB; OLA; YOFA

ART CRITICS, *see* CRITICS

ARTISTS, *see* CRAFTSPERSONS; ENGRAVERS & ETCHERS;
    ILLUSTRATORS; PAINTERS; SCULPTORS

ASSASSINS

Booth, John Wilkes (1838–1865). RABA; SHFA
Collazo, Oscar (1914–). RABA
Czolgosz, Leon F. (1873–1901). RABA
Guiteau, Charles Julius (1840?–1882). RABA
Oswald, Lee Harvey (1939–1963). RABA
Ray, James Earl (1928–). RABA
Sirhan, Sirhan (1944–). (Born Jordan). RABA
Torresola, Griselio (1925?–1950). RABA
Weiss, Carl Austin (1906–1935). RABA
Zangara, Guiseppe (1900–1933). (Born Italy).
    RABA

ASSYRIANS

Ashurbanipal (fl. 669–626 B.C.). King. CAAA

ASTROLOGERS

Cardano, Girolamo (1501–1576). Italian. MUB
Dee, John (1527–1608). English. COEA; CUA;
    ED-5

ASTRONAUTS

See also ROCKET & SPACE SCIENTISTS

American

Aldrin, Edwin E., Jr. (1930–). HOBB; LEPB; THC
Anders, William Alison (1933–). LEPB

Armstrong, Neil A. (1930–). DEJ; FRE; LEPB†;
  THC
Borman, Frank (1928–). LEPB; RAE; THC
Carpenter, Malcolm Scott (1925–). COR; NEB;
  THC
Cernan, Eugene A. (1934–). THC
Cleave, Mary (1947–). FOJ-1
Collins, Michael (1930–). COQ; LEPB†; THC†
Conrad, Charles, Jr. (1930–). THC
Cooper, Leroy Gordon, Jr. (1927–). THC
Dunbar, Bonnie (1949–). FOJ-1
Fisher, Anna (1949–). FOI-1; HIFD†; RAAG†
Glenn, John Herschel, Jr. (1921–). BAB; COQ;
  DIA; LEL; LEPB; NEB; THC
Gordon, Richard F., Jr. (1929–). THC
Grissom, Gus (Virgil Ivan) (1926–1967). COQ;
  LEPB†; NEB†; THC
Haise, Fred W. (1933–). WIAA-5
Jarvis, Gregory (1944–1986). COE-1
Lovell, James A., Jr. (1928–). LEPB; THC;
  WIAA-5
Lucid, Shannon (1943–). FOJ-1
McAuliffe, Christa (1948–1986). COE-1
McDivitt, James A. (1929–). THC
McNair, Ronald (1950–1986). COE-1
Onizuka, Ellison (1946–1986). COE-1
Resnik, Judith (1949–1986). COE-1; FOJ-1
Ride, Sally (1951–). DU-1; FOJ-1
Schirra, Walter Marty, Jr. (1923–). LEL; NEB;
  THC
Scobee, Dick (Francis Richard) (1939–1986).
  COE-1
Scott, David R. (1932–). THC
Seddon, Margaret Rhea (1947–). FOC-1; FOJ-1;
  HIFD; SMBC-2
Shepard, Alan Bartlett (1923–). BRBA; CAGA;
  COQ; FAA; LEL; LEPB; NEB; THC
Smith, Michael J. (1945–1986). COE-1
Stafford, Thomas P. (1930–). THC
Sullivan, Kathryn (1951–). FOJ-1
Swigert, John L. (1931–1982). WIAA-5
White, Edward Higgins, II (1930–1967). COQ;
  LEPB†; THC
Young, John Watts (1930–). COQ; THC

Russian
Belyayev, Pavel (1925–1970). THC
Bykovsky, Valeri (1934–). THC
Feoktistov, Konstantin (1926–). THC
Gagarin, Yuri Alekseyevich (1934–1968). KEH;
  MOB; NEB; PRC; THC
Komarov, Vladimir M. (1927–1967). THC
Leonov, Alexei A. (1934–). THC
Nikolayev, Andrian G. (1929–). NEB†; THC
Tereshkova, Valentina Vladimirova (1937–). THC

Titov, Gherman Stepanovich (1935–). NEB; THC
Yegorov, Boris (1937–). THC

ASTRONOMERS

American
Baade, Walter (1893–1960). (Born Germany).
  SUE
Bowditch, Nathaniel (1773–1838). MAL
Cannon, Annie Jump (1863–1941). EMB
Fleming, Williamina (1857–1911). (Born Scot-
  land). PACB
Gill, Jocelyn Ruth (1916–). POE
Hagen, John P. (1908–). YOE
Hale, George Ellery (1868–1938). LAA
Hubble, Edwin Powell (1889–1953). SUE
Langley, Samuel Pierpont (1834–1906). CUC;
  HYA†; SOB
Mitchell, Maria (1818–1889). CAD; DOD; EMB†;
  GEE; GIBA; MAV; SC; STJ; STLA; VAB;
  WABC; WAE; YOC
Reber, Grote (1911–). LAA; SUE
Rittenhouse, David (1732–1796). BUIB†; DOG;
  SIA
Rubin, Vera C. (1928–). GL
Sawyer, Helen (1905–). YOF
Shapely, Harlow (1885–1972). SUE

Danish
Brahe, Tycho (1546–1601). MOCB; PIA; SIB
Hertzsprung, Ejnar (1873–1967). SUE
Roemer, Olaus (1644–1710). SHFB

English
Adams, John Couch (1819–1892). SOB; SUE
Flamsteed, John (1646–1719). SHFB
Halley, Edmund (1656–1742). MOB; SHFB; SIA
Herschel, Caroline (1750–1848). (Born Germany).
  COLA†; NOA; PAC; SC†
Herschel, Sir William (1738–1822). (Born Ger-
  many). BOB; COLA; FE; LAA; PAC; PIA; SIA;
  SUE
Huggins, Sir William (1824–1910). SUE
Parsons, William, 3d earl of Rosse (1800–1867).
  LAA
Sabine, Sir Edward (1778–1883). (Born Ireland).
  FE
Smith, Graham (fl. 1951). SUE

Greek
Aristarchus of Samos (3d century B.C.). MOCB;
  SIB†
Eratosthenes (c. 275–195 B.C.). PIA; SHFB
Hipparchus (2d century B.C.). PIA; SIB†

Ptolemy (2d century). MOB; MOCB; PIA; SIA; SIB†

Others

Aryabhatta (c. 475–550). Indian. STN

Bessel, Friedrich Wilhelm (1784–1846). German. SUE

Copernicus, Nicolaus (1473–1543). Polish. ASA; BEP; BOB; CAA; COL; DOE; FE; MANB; MOCB; PIA; POD; SHFB; SIA; SIB; STI; SUE

Galilei, Galileo (1564–1642). Italian. ASA; BEC; BEP; BOB; CAA; COL; DEI; DEJ; DOE; EVC; FE; FRB; FRE; LAA; MAQ; MOCB; PIA; SHFB; SIA; SIB; STI; SUE; THA

Huygens, Christiaan (1629–1695). Dutch. CAA; COL; FE; SHFB; SIA

Kepler, Johannes (1571–1630). German. CAA; DOE; FE; LAA; MOCB; PIA; SHFB; SIA; SIB; STI; SUE

Lagrange, Joseph Louis (1736–1813). French. STN

Leverrier, Urbain Jean Joseph (1811–1877). French. SUE

ATHLETES, *see* INDIVIDUAL SPORTS: AUTOMOBILE RACERS; BASEBALL FIGURES; BASKETBALL FIGURES; BICYCLISTS; BOAT RACERS; BOWLERS; BOXING FIGURES; BULL FIGHTERS; FOOTBALL FIGURES; GOLFERS; GYMNASTS; HANDBALL PLAYERS; HOCKEY FIGURES; JOCKEYS; MARTIAL ARTS FIGURES; MOTORCYCLE RACERS; POLO PLAYERS; RODEO FIGURES; ROWING FIGURES; RUGBY FIGURES; SKATERS; SKIERS; SOCCER FIGURES; SOFTBALL FIGURES; SQUASH PLAYERS; SURF RIDERS; SWIMMERS & DIVERS; TABLE TENNIS PLAYERS; TENNIS PLAYERS; TRACK & FIELD ATHLETES; WATER SKIERS; WEIGHT LIFTERS; WRESTLERS

ATTORNEYS, *see* LAWYERS

AUSTRALIANS

Banfill, B. J. Nurse. WRA

Brabham, Jack (1926–). Automobile racer. ABB; JA; YAA

Bruce, Sir David (1855–1931). Bacteriologist. DEB; ROA

Burnet, Sir Macfarlane (1899–1985). Virologist. RIF

Cawley, Evonne Goolagong (1951–). Tennis player. AAS-29; FR-1; GLC; HOBAA; LAHA; MATA; SUDA

Clarke, Ron. Track athlete. DAJ

Court, Margaret (1942–). Tennis player. AAS-29; FR-1; HOBAA†; MATA; SUDA

Elliott, Herb (1938–). Track athlete. AAS-26

Farrelly, Bernard. Surf rider. OLD

Fifield, Elaine (1931–). Dancer. ATA

Florey, Sir Howard Walter (1898–1968). Pathologist. BEK†; COLA†; LAE; POB; RIF; SHG

Gould, Shane Elizabeth (1956–). Swimmer. HOBAA†; ST-1

Helpmann, Robert (1909–1986). Dancer, choreographer. ATA

Hoad, Lew (1934–). Tennis player. HI

Kenny, Elizabeth (1886–1952). Nurse. BOC; MAK; WRA

Laver, Rodney George (1938–). Tennis player. AAS-28; ASB-1; ASBA; BELB; FOX; LAHA

Mawson, Sir Douglas (1882–1958). Explorer, born England. ROL

Menzies, Sir Robert Gordon (1894–1978). Prime minister. WEB

Newton-John, Olivia (1948–). Singer, born England. KRI

Rosewall, Ken (1934–). LAHA

Smith (Mr.) (fl. 1928). First mate of Trevessa. HAQ

Sutherland, Joan (1926–). Singer. SAB

Taylor, Valerie (1936–). Diver. HAKA

Ulm, Charles. Aviator. HAMY

Wilkins, Sir George Hubert (1888–1958). Explorer. GRB; ROL†

Wirth, May (1896?–). Bareback rider. KIB

Young, Robert. Surf rider. OLD

AUSTRIANS

Auenbrugger, Leopold (1722–1809). Physician. FAF; SHG

Bárány, Robert (1876–1936). Physician. LET

Berg, Alban (1885–1935). Composer. KAE

Bruckner, Anton (1824–1896). Composer. KAE; SAA

Czerny, Karl (1791–1857). Composer, pianist. CHF

Doppler, Christian Johann (1803–1853). Physicist, mathematician. FE; HAC; SHFB

Francis Joseph I (1830–1916). Emperor. CAAA

Freud, Sigmund (1856–1939). Psychiatrist. ASB-1; CHD; FRE; KE; POD; RIB; ROA; WEF

Fried, Alfred Hermann (1864–1921). Pacifist. LET; MEC†; WIC

Haydn, Franz Joseph (1732–1809). Composer. BEN; BRF; BUD; FIE; KAE; SAA; YOK; YOM†

Karajan, Herbert von (1908–). Conductor. EWD; STM†; YOM†

Lauda, Niki (Andreas Nikilaus) (1949–). Automobile racer. AAS-9; ABB; OLCC

Mach, Ernst (1838–1916). Physicist. FE; HAC

Mahler, Gustav (1860–1911). Composer. KAE; SAA; YOM†

Maria Theresa (1717–1780). Archduchess. BOI; CAAA; FAE; LIDA; PA; TRBA

Mendel, Gregor Johann (1822–1884). Geneticist. ASA; BEK; BEP; CAA; CAB; COL; FE; HAC; SIA; STI; WEF

Mesmer, Franz Anton (1734–1815). Physician. COEA

Moser-Proell, Annemarie. Skier. WA-1

Mozart, Wolfgang Amadeus (1756–1791). Composer. BEC; BEN; BOD; BRF; BUD; DEI; DEJ; FIE; FOR; GOA; KAE; SAA; WIA; YOK; YOM†

Rindt, Jochen (1942?–1970). Automobile racer. JA

Sailer, Toni (1935–). Skier. ALBA; DEF; GED; GEDA; LEYB†

Schnabel, Artur (1882–1951). Pianist, composer. CHF

Schubert, Franz Peter (1797–1828). Composer. BEN; BRF; BUD; DEI; DEJ; FIE; GOA; KAE; SAA; WIA; YOK

Strauss, Johann (1825–1899). Composer. KAE

Suttner, Bertha von (1843–1914). Pacifist. MEA; MEC; SHFE†; WIC

Trapp, Maria Augusta (1905–1987). Singer. CAHA

Webern, Anton von (1883–1945). Composer. EWAA

Weingartner, Felix von (1863–1942). Conductor. YOM

Wiesenthal, Simon (1908–). Nazi hunter, born Poland. GRB-1

Wittgenstein, Paul (1887–1961). Pianist. GEA

Wolf, Hugo (1860–1903). Composer. KAE; SAA

AUTHORS

See also CRITICS; JOURNALISTS; LEXICOGRAPHERS; NOBEL PRIZE WINNERS—LITERATURE; PLAYWRIGHTS; POETS; PULITZER PRIZE WINNERS

Fiction – American

Alcott, Louisa May (1832–1888). ASB; BEGA; BOA; BOC; COB; DEI; DEJ; STJ; STLA; WOAA

Allen, Hervey (1889–1949). CON

Anderson, Lonzo (1905–). SMAB

Anderson, Sherwood (1876–1941). CON

Anglund, Joan Walsh (1926–). SM

Aulaire, Edgar Parin d' (1898–). (Born Switzerland). SMAB

Aulaire, Ingri d' (1904–1980). (Born Norway). SMAB

Baldwin, James (1924–1987). DADB; KE; LEGB; RICA

Baum, Lyman Frank (1856–1919). BEI

Bemelmans, Ludwig (1898–1962). (Born Austria). SM

Benét, Stephen Vincent (1898–1943). BEF; BEH; BOA; BRBB; SIF

Bishop, Claire Huchet. (Born France). SMB

Blegvad, Lenore (1926–). SMAB

Blume, Judy (1938–). GL-1

Bontemps, Arna (1902–1973). ADB; ROE

Bradbury, Ray (1920–). DU-1

Brink, Carol Ryrie (1895–1981). SMB

Bromfield, Louis (1896–1956). CON

Brown, Marcia (1918–). SM

Bryan, Dorothy (1896?–1984). SMAB

Buck, Pearl S. (1892–1973). COKA; CON; GIBA†; HEF; KOA; LEGB; MUA; OCB; SHFE

Buff, Conrad (1886–1975). (Born Switzerland). SMAB

Buff, Mary Marsh (1890–1970). SMAB

Burnett, Frances Hodgson (1849–1924). (Born England). BEI

Cable, George Washington (1844–1925). STJC

Cather, Willa (1873–1947). BOA; CON; CUC; HEF; LEK; MUA; OCB; STLA

Chase, Mary Ellen (1887–1973). CON

Chesnutt, Charles Waddell (1858–1932). ADA; ADB; BRB†; CL; DOF-1

Chute, Marchette (1909–). MUA

Coatsworth, Elizabeth (1893–). SMB

Cooper, James Fenimore (1789–1851). BOA; CAC; CUC; DEI; DEJ; HACB; HEF; LEGB

Costain, Thomas B. (1885–1965). CON

Crane, Stephen (1871–1900). CAC; HEF; JAD; STL

De Angeli, Marguerite (1889–1987). SMB

DeJong, Meindert (1910–). (Born the Netherlands). SMB

deLeeuw, Adele (1899–). SMAB

deLeeuw, Cateau (1903–). SMAB

Devlin, Harry (1918–). SMAB

Devlin, Wende (1918–). SMAB

Dodge, Mary Mapes (1831–1905). BEI; COB; STJ; YOC

Douglas, Lloyd C. (1877–1951). CON

Duvoisin, Roger (1904–1980). (Born Switzerland). SM

Edmonds, Walter Dumaux (1903–). CON

Emberley, Barbara (1932–). SMAB

Enright, Elizabeth (1909–1968). SMB

Ets, Marie Hall (1895–). SM

Faulkner, William (1897–1962). ASB-1; CAC; CON; FLBA; HEF

Feelings, Muriel (1938–). SMAB
Ferber, Edna (1887–1968). CON; LETA; ROJ
Field, Rachel (1894–1942). BEH
Fitzgerald, Francis Scott Key (1896–1940). ASB-1; CON
Freeman, Mary Eleanor Wilkins (1852–1930). BEGA
Gág, Wanda (1893–1946). SM
Guthrie, Alfred Bertram, Jr. (1901–). CON
Hader, Berta (1890?–1976). SMAB
Hader, Elmer (1889–1973). SMAB
Hawthorne, Nathaniel (1804–1864). BEGA; BOA; CAC; COB; HEF; LEGB; STK; SUFA; WHB; WOAA
Hemingway, Ernest (1899–1961). ASB-1; CAC; CON; HEF; LAC; LEGB
Henry, Marguerite (1902–). SMB
Henry, O., pseud. (1862–1910). CAC; CUC; DEI; DEJ
Hughes, Langston (1902–1967). ADA; ADB; BRBD; CAGA; DADB; DOF-1; JO; LEJ; RIC; RICA; ROE
Irving, Washington (1783–1859). BEG; BOA; CAC; COB; HACB; HEF; LEGB; MAL
James, Henry (1843–1916). ASB-1; CON†; STL
Jewett, Sarah Orne (1849–1909). BEGA
Jong, Erica (1942–). GL-1
Krumgold, Joseph (1908–1980). SMB
Lawson, Robert (1892–1957). SM
Lenski, Lois (1893–1974). SM
Lewis, Sinclair (1885–1951). BOA; CON; HEF; LEGB
Lionni, Leo (1910–). (Born the Netherlands). SM
Lofting, Hugh (1886–1947). (Born England). SMB
London, Jack (1876–1916). CAC; COB; JAD; LEGB
McCloskey, Robert (1914–). SM
McKay, Claude (1890–1948). ADA; ADB; BRB†
McNeer, May (1902–). SMAB
Marquand, John Phillips (1893–1960). BEGA; CON
Marshall, Paule (1929–). GLO
Melville, Herman (1819–1891). CAC; CUC; HACB; HEF; STL; SUFA
Mitchell, Margaret (1900–1949). CON; OCB
Momaday, N. Scott (1934–). GRAC
Morley, Christopher (1890–1957). ALA; BEF
Nabokov, Vladimir (1899–1977). (Born Russia). ASB-1
Parker, Dorothy (1893–1967). ALA; OCB
Petersham, Maud (1889–1971). SMAB
Petersham, Miska (1888–1960). (Born Hungary). SMAB
Petry, Ann (1911–). RIC; RICA
Phillips, David Graham (1867–1911). COGB
Poe, Edgar Allan (1809–1849). BEF; BEG; BOA;

CAC; COKB; HACB; HEF; HIG; LEGB; SIF; STK
Pyle, Howard (1853–1911). BEI
Rawlings, Marjorie Kinnan (1896–1953). CON
Rey, Hans Augusto (1898–1977). (Born Germany). SM
Rhodes, Eugene Manlove (1869–1934). WAA
Roberts, Kenneth Lewis (1885–1957). CON
Sarton, May (1912–). (Born Belgium). OCB
Scarry, Richard (1919–). SM
Sendak, Maurice (1928–). SM
Seuss, Dr. (Theodore Geisel) (1904–). SM
Shalom Aleichem (Solomon Rabinowitz) (1859–1916). (Born Russia). GRB-1
Sidney, Margaret, pseud. (1844–1924). BEI
Sinclair, Upton Beall (1878–1968). COGB
Singer, Isaac Bashevis (1904–). (Born Poland). GRB-1
Stein, Gertrude (1874–1946). KE; MUA; STLA; WABC†
Steinbeck, John (1902–1968). CON; HEF
Stowe, Harriet Beecher (1811–1896). BEGA; BOA; BOC; DEI; DEJ; DOD; GIBA; JOCA; SMC; STJ; STLA; VAB; WABC†; WHB
Tarkington, Booth (1869–1946). BEE; CON
Tourgee, Albion Winegar (1838–1905). STJC
Turkle, Brinton (1915–). SM
Viorst, Judith. BOHD
Ward, Lynd (1905–1985). SMAB
Welty, Eudora (1909–). MUA; OCB
West, Jessamyn (1907–1984). GL-1; MUA
Wharton, Edith (1862–1937). BOA; CON†; STL
White, Elwyn Brooks (1899–1985). BEG; SMB
Whitney, Phyllis A. (1903–). GL-1
Wiggin, Kate Douglas (1856–1923). BEI; COB
Wilder, Laura Ingalls (1867–1957). MUA; SMB
Wilder, Thornton Niven (1897–1975). BEGA
Wolfe, Thomas Clayton (1900–1938). HEF
Wouk, Herman (1915–). GRB-1
Wright, Richard (1908–1960). ADA; ADB; AKB; DABB; DADB; DOF-1; FLBA; RIC; RICA
Yashima, Taro (1908–). (Born Japan). SMAB

Fiction – English
Austen, Jane (1775–1817). BOH; COO; SMA; STK
Brontë, Anne (1820–1849). COO; SMA; STK
Brontë, Charlotte (1816–1855). COO; SMA; STK
Brontë, Emily Jane (1818–1848). COO; SMA; STK
Burney, Fanny (1752–1840). NOA; SMA
Carroll, Lewis, pseud. (1832–1898). BEH; COB; COO
Chesterton, Gilbert Keith (1874–1936). BEG
Christie, Agatha (1891–1976). SMA
Conrad, Joseph (1857–1924). (Born Poland). COO; MANB; STL

Craik, Dinah Mulock (1826–1887). BEI
Defoe, Daniel (1660–1731). COO; SEB
de la Mare, Walter John (1873–1956). BEH
Dickens, Charles (1812–1870). BOD; COB; COO;
    DEI; DEJ; HOA; STK
Disraeli, Benjamin, 1st earl of Beaconsfield
    (1804–1881). DEI; DEJ; PEB
Eliot, George, pseud. (1819–1880). COO; SMA;
    STL
Ewing, Juliana H. Gatty (1841–1885). BEI
Farjeon, Eleanor (1881–1965). BEH; SMB
Godden, Rumer (1907–). SMA; SMB
Greenaway, Kate (1846–1901). SM
Hardy, Thomas (1840–1928). COO; STL
Hudson, William Henry (1841–1922). COO
Kaye-Smith, Sheila (1887–1956). SMA
Kingsley, Charles (1819–1875). BEH; COO
Kipling, Rudyard (1865–1936). BEI; COB; COO;
    COP; STK
Lytton, Edward George Earle Lytton Bulwer, 1st
    baron (1803–1873). COO; ED-5
Milne, Alan Alexander (1882–1956). BEH; SMB
Nesbit, Edith (1858–1924). BEI
Norton, Mary (1903–). SMB
Potter, Beatrix (1866–1943). SC; SM
Ruskin, John (1819–1900). BEI
Sackville-West, Victoria (1892–1962). SMA
Sayers, Dorothy L. (1893–1957). SMA
Stewart, Mary (1916–). SMA
Swift, Jonathan (1667–1745). COO
Thackeray, William Makepeace (1811–1863).
    BEG; BEI; COO
Travers, Pamela L. (1906–). (Born Australia).
    SMB
Webb, Mary (1881–1927). SMA
Wells, Herbert George (1866–1946). ASB-1; DEI;
    DEJ
Woolf, Virginia (1882–1941). BEG; SMA
Yonge, Charlotte Mary (1823–1901). BEI
Zangwill, Israel (1864–1926). LERA; PEB

Fiction – French

Balzac, Honoré de (1799–1850). DEI; DEJ
Brunhoff, Jean de (1899–1937). SMAB
Brunhoff, Laurent de (1925–). SMAB
Dumas, Alexandre (Dumas père) (1802–1870).
    ADA; ADB; DEI; DEJ; JO
Flaubert, Gustave (1821–1880). HOA
Hugo, Victor (1802–1885). COKB; DEI; DEJ
Rolland, Romain (1866–1944). DED
Ungerer, Tomi (1931–). SM
Verne, Jules (1828–1905). DEI; DEJ; STK
Voltaire (François Marie Arouet) (1694–1778).
    COG; DEI; DEJ; HIB; LO; OZA
Zola, Émile (1840–1902). COG

Fiction – German

Hesse, Hermann (1877–1962). KE
Heyse, Paul Johann (1830–1914). LET
Wassermann, Jakob (1873–1934). PEB

Fiction – Russian

Chekhov, Anton Pavlovich (1860–1904). ASB-1;
    POFA
Dostoevski, Fëdor Mikhailovich (1821–1881).
    POFA
Ehrenburg, Ilya Grigoryevich (1891–1967). KE
Gogol, Nikolai Vasilievich (1809–1852). POFA
Gorki, Maksim (1868–1936). POFA
Mendele Mocher Sefarim (Shalom Abramovich)
    (1835–1917). Author. GRB-1
Pasternak, Boris Leonidovich (1890–1960). LET;
    POFA
Sholokhov, Mikhail Aleksandrovich (1905–1984).
    POFA
Solzhenitsyn, Aleksandr Isaevich (1918–). ASB-1;
    POFA
Tolstoi, Lev Nikolaevich (1828–1910). DEI; DEJ;
    POFA
Turgenev, Ivan Sergeevich (1818–1883). POFA

Fiction – Scottish

Barrie, Sir James M. (1860–1937). COB
Doyle, Sir Arthur Conan (1859–1930). COO
Grahame, Kenneth (1859–1932). BEI
MacDonald, George (1824–1905). BEI
Molesworth, Mary Louisa (1839–1921). BEI
Scott, Sir Walter (1771–1832). COB; COO; STL
Stevenson, Robert Louis (1850–1894). BEH;
    COB; COO; DEI; DEJ; HOA; STK

Fiction – Others

Abrahams, Peter (1919–). South African. OJA
Agnon, Shmuel Yosef (1888–1970). Israeli. GRB-
    1; ROGA
Alegria, Ciro (1909–1967). Peruvian. WO
Andersen, Hans Christian (1805–1875). Danish.
    BEI; COB; COG; DEI; DEJ; RAC
Asturias, Miguel Angel (1899–1974). Guatemalan.
    WO
Borges, Jorge Luis (1899–1986). Argentine. WO
Browne, Frances (1816–1879). Irish. BEI
Carpentier, Alejo (1904–). Cuban. WO
Cervantes Saavedra, Miguel de (1547–1616).
    Spanish. KEH; WO
Joyce, James (1882–1941). Irish. ASB-1
Lagerlof, Selma (1858–1940). Swedish. PA;
    SHFE†
Lindgren, Astrid (1907–). Swedish. SMB
Paton, Alan (1903–1988). South African. BAF;
    LEA
Peretz, Isaac Leib (1852–1915). Polish. GEF

Reymont, Wladyslaw Stanislaw (1867–1926). Polish. MANB
Spyri, Johanna H. (1827–1901). Swiss. BEC
Undset, Sigrid (1882–1949). Norwegian. CAHA

Folklore & Mythology

Asbjörnsen, Peter Christen (1812–1885). Norwegian. SMAB
Colum, Padraic (1881–1972). (Born Ireland). BEI
Grimm, Jakob (1785–1863). German. BEI; SMAB
Grimm, Wilhelm Karl (1786–1859). German. BEI; SMAB
Hamilton, Edith (1867–1963). STLA
Harris, Joel Chandler (1848–1908). COB
Lang, Andrew (1844–1912). Scottish. BEG
Moe, Jörgen Ingebretsen (1813–1882). Norwegian. SMAB

Humor

Ade, George (1866–1944). BEE
Benchley, Robert (1889–1945). BEE
Bombeck, Erma (1927–). GL-1
Buchwald, Art (1925–). LEU
Day, Clarence S., Jr. (1874–1935). BEE
Dunne, Finley Peter (1867–1936). BEE
Hale, Lucretia Peabody (1820–1900). BEE; BEI
Lardner, Ring (Ringgold Wilmer) (1885–1933). BEE
Leacock, Stephen Butler (1869–1944). Canadian. BEE
Marquis, Don (1878–1937). ALA; BEE
Rogers, Will (1879–1935). BOD; COKA; KAW; LEH; PHA; WAA; WAO
Shute, Henry Augustus (1856–1943). BEE
Skinner, Cornelia Otis (1901–1979). BEE
Stockton, Frank Richard (1834–1902). BEE; BEI
Streeter, Edward (1891–1976). BEE
Thurber, James G. (1894–1961). BEE; CUC; FLBA; GEA
Twain, Mark, pseud. (1835–1910). BEC; BEE; BOA; CAC; COB; CUC; DEI; DEJ; FOH; HACB; HEF; HOA; LEGB; MAL; RAC; SMBA; STK

Nonfiction – American

Angelou, Maya (1928–). DADB; OCB
Antin, Mary (1881–1949). (Born Russia). CAHA
Aulaire, Edgar Parin d' (1898–). (Born Switzerland). SMAB
Aulaire, Ingri d' (1904–1980). (Born Norway). SMAB
Baldwin, James (1924–1987). DADB; KE; LEGB; RICA
Beeton, Isabella Mary (1836–1865). BOH
Bok, Edward William (1863–1930). (Born the Netherlands). BOD; CAGA; CUC; FLBA; LOB

Bontemps, Arna (1902–1973). ADB; ROE
Bouton, James Alan (1939–). HOBB
Brooks, Van Wyck (1886–1963). CAC
Brothers, Joyce (1927–). BOHG
Brown, Claude (1937–). DADB
Brown, William Wells (1815–1884). CL; DADA; GRAB-05
Carson, Rachel (1907–1964). CO-1; COR; CORA; ELA; EMB; FRE; GIBA; HIBB; PACA; SC; SQA; WAP
Child, Julia (1912–). GIB-1
Chute, Marchette (1909–). MUA
Cleaver, Eldridge (1935–). DADA; HAI
Dana, Richard Henry, Jr. (1815–1882). BEGA; SUFA
deLeeuw, Cateau (1903–). SMAB
Deloria, Vine, Jr. (1934?–). GRAC
Dolan, Harry (1927–). DADA
Donnelly, Ignatius (1831–1901). LEO
Du Bois, William Edward Burghardt (1868–1963). ADA; ADB; BEJ; BRB; BRBD; DABB; DOF-1; GRAB-01; PECA; RICA; ROG; STB; STJB; STO; YOI
Emerson, Ralph Waldo (1803–1882). BEF; BEG; BEGA; BLE; BOA; CAC; CUC; DEI; DEJ; HEF; RED; SIF; SUFA; WHB; WOAA
Fenton, Carroll Lane (1900–1969). SMAB
Fenton, Mildred Adams. SMAB
Fermi, Laura (1907–1977). (Born Italy). CAHA
Friedan, Betty (1921–). GIB-1; WA
Fuller, Margaret (1810–1850). BOC; GUBA; STLA; WABC
Gregory, Dick (1932–). DADB; EOB; RICA
Haley, Alex (1921–). DOF-1; STAA
Holmes, Oliver Wendell (1809–1894). BEF; BEGA; BOA; HEF; SUFA
Huxtable, Ada Louise (1921–). GIB-1
Johnson, James Weldon (1871–1938). ADA; ADB; BRB†; DOF-1; GRAB-02; JO; RIC; RICA; ROE; ROG; STB
Karski, Jan, pseud. (Born Poland). CAHA
Kazin, Alfred (1915–). RAC
Krutch, Joseph Wood (1893–1970). CORA
Lin Yutang (1895–1976). (Born China). KE; LOB
Lindbergh, Anne Morrow (1906–). GEDB
McGinley, Phyllis (1905–1978). ALA
Nell, William Cooper (1816–1874). CHFB; GRAB-05
Richards, Laura E. (1850–1943). BEF; BEH
Rollin, Betty (1936–). SMBB-2
Roosevelt, Eleanor (1884–1962). ASB-1; BAG; BAG-1; BLG; BOC; BRBE; CHB; COG; COG-1; CUC; DABB; DAD; GIBA; KE; KEE; KL; LAI; MAA; MAU; MEB; PA; PRB; ROH; ROHA; SMC; STLA; WABC†; WAR; YOA
Rowan, Carl Thomas (1925–). SQB; STAA; YOI

Ruether, Rosemary (1936–). GIB-1
Russell, Charles Edward (1860–1941). COGB
Sandburg, Carl (1878–1967). BEF; BEH; BOA;
    HEF; KE†; SIF
Seton, Ernest Thompson (1860–1946). (Born En-
    gland). CO-1
Shalom Aleichem (Solomon Rabinowitz) (1859–
    1916). (Born Russia). GRB-1
Sheehy, Gail (1937–). LETB
Shirer, William L. (1904–). JAD
Simmons, William J. (1849–1890). ADB; BRB†
Smith, Logan Pearsall (1865–1946). BEG
Spock, Benjamin (1903–). BOHA; CHE; HAJ;
    HOBB
Steffens, Lincoln (Joseph Lincoln) (1866–1936).
    COGB; SQB; WECB
Stern, Elizabeth Gertrude (1890–1954). MAV
Stroyer, Jacob (b. 1846). DADB
Tarbell, Ida Minerva (1857–1944). COGB; DAD;
    WABC†; YOC
Thoreau, Henry David (1817–1862). ARB; BAC;
    BEG; BEGA; BLE; BOA; CAC; CO-1; CORA;
    CUC; EOB; HAJ; HIBB; HOA; MIB; RED;
    SQA; SUFA; WHB; WOAA
Trahey, Jane (1923–). LES-1
Tuchman, Barbara (1912?–). BOHG
Van Loon, Hendrik (1882–1944). (Born the Neth-
    erlands). LEAB; LEB
Warren, Mercy Otis (1728–1814). AND; WABC†
Willard, Josiah Flynt (1869–1907). COGB

Nonfiction – English

Aguilar, Grace (1816–1847). LER; PEB
Angell, Sir Norman (1874–1967). MEA; MEC;
    WIC
Astell, Mary (1668–1731). BOH
Bacon, Francis (1561–1626). BEG; LO; STI†
Belloc, Hilaire (1870–1953). BEH
Bronowski, Jacob (1908–1974). (Born Poland).
    GRB-1
Chesterton, Gilbert Keith (1874–1936). BEG
Churchill, Sir Winston Leonard Spencer (1874–
    1965). ASB-1; CHG; CUC; DEI; DEJ; DOF;
    ELA; EVA; FLBB; FRE; HIB†; JAC; JAD; KE;
    RADA; TAC; YOA
De Quincey, Thomas (1785–1859). BEG
Godwin, Mary Wollstonecraft (1759–1797). BOH;
    GUBA
Hazlitt, William (1778–1830). BEG
Hutton, William (1723–1815). RAC
Keynes, John Maynard (1883–1946). ASB-1
Lamb, Charles (1775–1834). BEG
Macaulay, Thomas Babington Macaulay, 1st
    baron (1800–1859). BEG; COP
Montagu, Lady Mary Wortley (1689–1762). BOH;
    RIE†

More, Hannah (1745–1833). NOA
More, Sir Thomas (Saint Thomas More) (1478–
    1535). DAD-3; MAJ; MOC; PEE
Orwell, George (1903–1950). ASB-1

Nonfiction – French

Chateaubriand, François René (1768–1848). RAC
Chatelet, Marquise du. Gabrielle Émilie Le
    Tonnelier du Breteuil (1706–1749). SC
Montaigne, Michel de (1533–1592). RAC
Rousseau, Jean Jacques (1712–1778). FRE
Sévigné, Marie (de Rabutin Chantal) marquise
    de. PA
Staël, Germaine de (Anne Louise Germaine
    Necker, Baronne de Staël-Hollstein) (1766–
    1817). BOC

Nonfiction – Others

Carlyle, Thomas (1795–1881). Scottish. COB
Carpentier, Alejo (1904–). Cuban. WO
Díaz, Bernal (b. 1492). Spanish. BACA
Frank, Anne (1919–1945). German. ELA; FOR;
    GRB-1
Guzmán, Martín Luis (b. 1887). Mexican. NEBA
Herzl, Theodor (1860–1904). Hungarian. GRB-1;
    GUB; KAB; KAD; LERA; LES; PEB; ROGA
Kayira, Legson Didimu. African. OJA
Modupe (1901–). Guinean. OJA
Paz, Octavio (1914–). Mexican. WO
Riedesel, Frederika von, baroness (1746–1808).
    German. AND

AUTOMOBILE RACERS

American

Allison, Bobby (Robert Arthur) (1937–). LEXA;
    OLCC
Andretti, Mario (1940–). (Born Italy). ABB; FOI;
    JA; LEX; OLAB; OLCC; ORD; YAA
Arfons, Art (1926–). LEX
Baker, Buck (Elzie Wylie) (1919–). LEX†; OLCA
Baker, Buddy (Elzie Wylie, Jr.) (1941–). OLCA
Beck, Gary. OLDA
Bettenhausen, Gary (1941?–). OLCA
Bettenhausen, Merle. OLCA
Bettenhausen, Tony (Melvin Eugene) (1916–
    1961). LEX; OLCA
Breedlove, Craig (1938–). LEX; OLAB; OLDC;
    YAA
Bryan, Jimmy (James Ernest) (1927–1960). LEX
Carter, Duane, Sr. (1913?–). OLCA
Carter, Pancho (Duane, Jr.). OLCA
Cooper, Earl (1886–1965). LEX
Dean, Al. LEW

De Palma, Ralph (1883?–1956). (Born Italy). LEX; OLAA; YAA

De Paolo, Peter (b. 1887). YAA

Donohue, Mark (1937–1975). DI-2; JA; OLCB; ORD

Flock, Tim. LEX

Follmer, George (1934–). OLCB

Foyt, Anthony Joseph (1935–). ABB; ASBA; DI-2; KADA; LEVA; LEX; LEXA; OLAA; OLCB; OLCC; ORD; YAA

Gabelich, Gary (1940–). OLDC; ST-1

Garlits, Don (1932?–). LEX; LEYC; OLB; OLCB; OLDA; ORD; ST-1; YAA

Ginther, Paul Richard (1930–). LEX

Glidden, Bob. OLDA

Golden, Bill (1933–). OLAB

Gurney, Dan (Daniel Saxon) (1931?–). JA; LEX; YAA

Guthrie, Janet (1938–). GUED-1

Hall, Jim (1935?–). JA; LEX; YAA

Heath, Allen. (Born Canada). LEX

Hill, Phil (1927–). ABB; COKC; JA; LEX; OLAB

Horn, Ted (1910–1948). LEX

Hurtubise, Jim (1931?–). LEX; OLAB; PIBA

Ivo, Tommy. OLB

Jarrett, Ned (1932–). LEX

Johncock, Gordon (1936?–). OLCB

Johnson, Junior (Robert Glenn) (1931–). LEX†; LEXA

Jones, Alan. OLDD

Jones, Parnelli (Rufus Parnell) (1933–). DI-2; LEX; ORD; YAA

Karamesines, Chris. OLB

Landy, Dick. OLB

Lorenzen, Fred (1933?–). LEX; LEXA; OLAB

McCluskey, Robert (1930?–). OLCB

McEwen, Tom. LEX†; OLB; OLDA

Malone, Art. OLB

Mays, Rex (1913?–1949). LEX

Mears, Rick. OLDD

Mears, Roger. OLDD

Meyer, Billy (1954?–). OLDD

Meyer, Louis (1904–). LEVA; LEX†

Miles, Kenneth Henry (1918–1966). (Born England). OLAB

Milton, Thomas Willard (1894?–1962). LEVA; LEX; YAA

Muldowney, Shirley. OLDA; ST-2

Mulligan, John. LEX

Nalon, Duke. YAA

Nancy, Tony. OLB

Oldfield, Barney (Berna Eli) (1878–1946). DAG; DAGA; LEX†; YAA

O'Neil, Kitty (1946–). AAS-27; HAFA

Ongais, Danny (1940–). LEX

Parsons, Johnnie (1918–). OLAA; OLCA

Parsons, Johnny (1945?–). OLCA

Pearson, David (1934–). LEX; LEXA; OLAB

Petty, Lee (1915–). LEX†; LEXA; LEYC; OLCA

Petty, Richard (1937?–). DI-2; LEX; LEXA; OLCA; OLCB; ORD; YAA

Prudhomme, Don. OLB; OLDA

Revson, Peter Jeffrey (1939?–1974). JA; OLCB

Rhodes, John. OLB

Rickenbacker, Edward Vernon (1890–1973). ARD; DAG; LEX; YAA

Roberts, Fireball (Edward Glenn) (1927?–1964). LEX; LEXA

Ronda, Gaspar (1929?–). OLB

Rose, Doug. OLDC

Rose, Mauri (1906–1981). LEVA; LEX

Sachs, Eddie (Edward Julius) (1927–1964). LEX; OLAB

Savage, Swede (David Earl, Jr.) (1947–1973). JA

Schuster, George (b. 1874). SUA

Shaw, Wilbur (1902–1954). ASBA; DAG; DAGA; LEVA; LEX; YAA

Shelby, Carroll (1923–). LEX

Shuman, Ron. OLDD

Snively, Mike. OLAB

Summers, Bob. OLDC

Thompson, Dannie. OLCA

Thompson, Mickey (1928–). LEX; OLAB; OLB; OLCA

Turner, Curtis (1924–1970). LEX; LEXA; YAA

Unser, Al (1939?–). LEVA; OLCC; ORD

Unser, Bobby (1934–). LEVA; OLCC; ORD; ST-1

Vukovich, Bill (1919–1955). LEVA; LEX; OLCA; YAA

Vukovich, Bill, Jr. (1943?–). OLAB; OLCA

Waltrip, Darrell (1947–). OLDD

Ward, Rodger (1921–). LEVA; LEX; LEYC; YAA

Weatherly, Joseph Herbert (1922?–1964). LEX†; LEXA

Williams, Jack. OLB

Yarborough, Cale (1939–). LEX; LEXA

Yarbrough, Lee Roy (1938–1984). LEX; LEXA

Foreign

Amon, Chris (1943–). New Zealand. JA

Ascari, Alberto (1919–1955). Italian. YAA

Beltoise, Jean-Pierre (1937–). French. JA

Brabham, Jack (1926–). Australian. ABB; JA; YAA

Campbell, Donald Malcolm (1921–1967). English. ALBA; ST-1

Campbell, Sir Malcolm (1885–1949). English. YAA

Caracciola, Rudolf (1901–1959). German. COKC; YAA

Clark, James (1936–1968). Scottish. ALBA; COKC; JA; ORD; YAA

Cobb, John (1899–1952). English. YAA
Dreyfus, René (1905–). French. SLA
Fangio, Juan Manuel (1912–). Argentine. ABB;
　COKC; JA; YAA
Fittipaldi, Emerson (1946–). Brazilian. ABB;
　OLCB
Hill, Graham (1929–1975). English. COKC; JA
Hulme, Dennis Clive (1936–). New Zealand. ABB;
　JA
Hunt, James (1947–). English. ABB; OLCC
Ickx, Jacky (Jacques-Bernard) (1945–). Belgian.
　JA
Lauda, Niki (Andreas Nikilaus) (1949–). Austrian.
　AAS-9; ABB; OLCC
McLaren, Bruce Leslie (1937–1970). New Zea-
　land. JA; ORD
Moss, Stirling (1929–). English. ABB; COKC; JA;
　YAA
Murphy, Jimmy (1894?–1924). Irish. LEX
Nuvolari, Tazio (1892–1953). Italian. COKC;
　SUA; YAA
Rindt, Jochen (1942?–1970). Austrian. JA
Rodriguez, Pedro (1939?–1971). Mexican. JA
Scheckter, Jody (1950–). South African. OLCB;
　SLA
Siffert, Josef (1936–). Swiss. JA
Stewart, Jackie (John Young) (1939–). Scottish.
　ABB; BELB; COKC; JA; OLCB; ORD
Surtees, John (1934–). English. ABB; JA; PAW

AUTOMOTIVE ENGINEERS, *see* ENGINEERS, AUTOMO-
TIVE

AVIATORS, *see* AIR FORCE LEADERS; AIR PILOTS; AIR
PIONEERS

AZTECS

Cuauhtémoc (1495–1525). Emperor. ROGB
Montezuma II (1480?–1520). Emperor. CAAA;
　NEC; ROGB; UNB
Quetzalcoatl. Legendary god. BACA; ROGB

BABYLONIANS

Ashi (352–427). Rabbi. GEF; GUA
Hammurabi (c. 1955–1913 B.C.). King. CAAA;
　JOBB; NEC
Hillel (fl. 30 B.C.–10 A.D.). Rabbi. GEF; GRB-1;
　GUA; KAB; KAC; LERA; LES

Rav (Abba Arika) (d. 247). Rabbi. GUA; KAC
Samuel Yarhina'ah (177–257). Rabbi. KAC

BACTERIOLOGISTS

See also MICROBIOLOGISTS; VIROLOGISTS

American
Enders, John Franklin (1897–1985). CHE†;
　COLA†; RIF; SUF
Francis, Edward (1872–1957). DEA
Noguchi, Hideyo (1876–1928). (Born Japan).
　BEA; SHG†
Reed, Walter (1851–1902). BOB; CHD; CUC;
　DEB; DOE; ED; EVD; FOH; LEC; LEPC;
　MAL; ROA; SHG; SIC
Waksman, Selman Abraham (1888–1973). (Born
　Russia). GRB-1; LET; LETA; LIA; RIF
Weller, Thomas Huckle (1915–). RIF
Zinsser, Hans (1878–1940). CHD

French
Laveran, Charles Louis (1845–1922). RIF; SHG
Nicolle, Charles Jules Henri (1866–1936).
　AAS-31; RIF
Pasteur, Louis (1822–1895). ASA; BEK; BEP;
　BUF; CAA; CAB; CHD; COL; DEB; DEI; DEJ;
　DOE; EVD; FAF; FE; FRE; HUD; POD; RIE;
　ROA; SHG; SUF
Roux, Pierre Paul Émile (1853–1933). DEB; RIE;
　ROA

German
Behring, Emil von (1854–1917). AAS-31; BEK†;
　DEB; RIE; RIF; ROA
Ehrlich, Paul (1854–1915). AAS-31; ASA; BEK;
　DEB; FE; LET; POB; RIE; RIF; ROA; SUF
Koch, Robert (1843–1910). AAS-31; BEK; COL;
　DEB; DEI; DEJ; FAF; FE; HUD; RIE; RIF;
　ROA; SUF
Löffler, Friedrich (1852–1915). DEA; RIE†; ROA

Others
Bordet, Jules (1870–1961). Belgian. RIF
Bruce, Sir David (1855–1931). Australian. DEB;
　ROA
Eijkman, Christian (1858–1930). Dutch. RIF
Fleming, Sir Alexander (1881–1955). Scottish.
　AAS-31; ASB-1; BEK; BEP; BOB; CAA; COLA;
　FE; HUD; LAE; POB; RIF; ROA; SHG; SUF
Haffkine, Waldemar Mordecai (1860–1930). Rus-
　sian. GEF; GRB-1
Kitasato, Shibasaburo (1852–1931). Japanese.
　RIE

Metchnikoff, Élie (1845–1916). Russian. COL;
DEB; LET; RIF; ROA; SOB

BALLET DANCERS, see DANCERS & CHOREOGRAPHERS

BALLOONISTS, see AIR PIONEERS

BAND LEADERS

See also CONDUCTORS

Basie, Count (William) (1904–1984). TEA; TEB;
WAD†
Cole, Nat "King" (1919–1965). ROF
Ellington, Duke (Edward Kennedy) (1899–1974).
ADA; ADB; ASB-1; COF-1; DOF-1; HODA;
HUC; MOA; RIC; RICA; ROF; TEA; TEB;
WAD
Evans, Merle (1894–1987). KIB
Figueroa, Jesús (1878–1971). NEBB
Goodman, Benny (1909–1986). COF-1; TEA; TEB;
WAD†
Henderson, Fletcher (1898–1952). COF-1; WAD†
Herman, Woody (1914–1987). TEA; TEB
Kenton, Stan (1912–1979). TEA
Wills, Bob (1905–1975). LA

BANKERS

See also BUSINESS PEOPLE; FINANCIERS

Arboleya, Carlos (1929–). (Born Cuba). FOW
Bauer, Henry (1895–). PAA
Binga, Jesse (1865–1950). ADA; ADB
Brown, Jim (James Nathaniel) (1936–). AAS-35;
AKB; ALBA; BEKB; BOF; DAFB; DAFG; DAI;
DUF; HAD; HEI; HIE; HOBC; HOC; KADA;
RAAE; SID
Clausen, Alden Winship (1923–). DU-1
Fargo, William G. (1818–1881). DOCA
Few, William (1748–1828). BUIB†; FEAA
Giannini, Amadeo Peter (1870–1949). MAS
Livingston, Homer J. (1903–1970). PAA
Overton, Anthony (1865–1946). ADA; ADB; DOF-
1; FLD
Roebling, Mary G. (1906–). LES-1
Walker, Maggie Lena (1867–1934). ADA; ADB;
BRB; BUFA; LOAV; ROG
Warburg, Paul Moritz (1868–1923). (Born Ger-
many). LETA
Wells, Henry (1805–1878). DOCA

BASEBALL FIGURES

Aaron, Hank (1934–). ASBA; BELB; BRAA;
BUD-1; DA; DAFD; DOF-1; FRC-1†; FRD;
GAB; GEC; GR; GUC; GUDA; GUE; KADA;
LEV; MUB-1; MUC; PEC; PRA; RAAA; RIGA†;
SA-3; SH; SHB; SHH
Adams, Babe (Charles Benjamin) (b. 1883). GIB
Alexander, Grover Cleveland (1887–1950). ALB;
DAFC; DAFD; DAG; DAGA; DEG†; GIB;
MUB-1; NEA; RIGA†; SHA
Allen, Richie (Richard Anthony) (1942?–). BRD;
GUE; GUG; LEY
Allison, Bob (1934–). BRD
Almon, Bill (1952–). GUB-1
Alou, Felipe (1935–). Dominican coach. DEHA-1
Alston, Walter E. (1911–1984). Manager. AAS-1;
FRC-01; FRC-1†; LEW; SMG
Anderson, Sparky (George Lee) (1934–). Manager.
SMG
Anson, Cap (Adrian Constantine) (1851–1922).
Player, manager. ALB; DAFC; DAFD; DAH;
FRC-01
Aparicio, Luis (1934–). (Born Venezuela). FRC-1†;
KLB; RIGA†; ROC
Appling, Luke. ALB; BOE; DAFC; DAFD; HIF;
RIGA†
Arnovich, Morrie (Morris) (1910–1959). RI; SLA†
Arroyo, Luis (1927–). SHE
Ashburn, Richie (1927–). BOE; BRD
Ashford, Emmett Littleton (1915?–1980). Umpire.
HOBC
Baker, Home Run (John Franklin) (1886?–1963).
ALB; DAFD; LEY; RIGA†
Bando, Salvatore Leonard (1944–). CL-06; KLBB;
LEY
Banks, Ernie (1931–). DA; DAFD; DRA; FRC-1†;
RIGA†; SHB; VEA
Barney, Rex (1924–). NEA
Barrow, Ed (1868–1953). Business manager. ALB
Bauer, Hank (Henry Albert) (1922–). Player, man-
ager. GIB
Bearden, Gene (Henry) (1920–). BUJA
Beckert, Glenn Alfred (1940–). KLB
Bell, Buddy (David Gus) (1951–). KLBB
Bench, Johnny Lee (1947–). BELB; FRD; GUDA;
GUE; GUG; HOCM; KLCA; MUB-1; RIGA†;
SHH; TUB
Bender, Chief (Charles Albert) (1883–1954). ALB;
DAFD; HACA
Berg, Moe (Morris) (1902–1972). BELB; RI; SLA†
Berra, Yogi (Lawrence Peter) (1925–). Player,
manager. BOE; DA; DAA; DAFB; DAFC;
DAFD; DAH; FRC-1†; GIB; GUDA; HIC;
HOCM; RIGA†; ROB; SHD; SHF; VEA; ZAA

Bevens, Bill (Floyd C.) (1917–). BED; BOE

Black, Joe (1924–). BOE; SHE

Blackwell, Ewell (1922–). NEA

Blomberg, Ron (1948–). SLA

Blue, Vida (1949–). AAS-2; BUJB; FRD; GUG

Bonds, Bobby Lee (1946–). KLCA

Bostock, Lyman (1950–1978). AAS-24

Boudreau, Lou (1917–). VEA

Bouton, James Alan (1939–). HOBB

Boyd, Oil Can (Dennis) (1959–). GUB-1

Boyer, Clete (Cletis LeRoy) (1937–). KLB

Boyer, Ken (1931–1982). DEG; KLB; LEY†; VEA

Brecheen, Harry (1914–). GIB

Bresnahan, Roger (1880–1944). ALB; DAFD; HAF; HIC; SHD

Brett, George Howard (1953–). AAS-3; HEFB†; KLBB; RIGA†

Brissie, Lou (Leland V.). SCA

Brock, Louis Clark (1939–). BRAA; GUDA; GUEE; RIGA†; SA-3

Brosnan, Jim (1929–). SHE

Brouthers, Dan (Dennis) (1858–1932). ALB

Brown, Bobby (Robert William) (1924–). BOE

Brown, Three-Fingered (Mordecai) (1876–1948). ALB; DAFC; DAFD; DAH; FRC-1†; RIGA†; SCA

Browning, Pete (Louis Rogers) (1861–1905). SMK

Bulkeley, Morgan (1837–1922). President of National League. ALB

Bunning, Jim (James Paul David) (1931–). LEZ; PRA

Burdette, Lew (1926–). DEHA-1; GIB

Burgess, Smoky (Forrest H.) (1927?–). DAFD; DAH

Burkett, Jesse (1870–1953). ALB

Burroughs, Jeff (1951–). BUJC

Byrd, Harry (1925–). BOE

Callison, Johnny (1939–). BUJ

Campanella, Roy (1921–). BOE; BUD-1; DADB; DAFC; DAFD; DAG; DAGA; FRC-1†; GEB; GUDA; HIC; HOCM; LYA; MUC; RIGA†; SCA; SHD; SHF; VACA; WAG; ZAA

Campaneris, Bert (Dagoberto Blanco) (1942–). Cuban. SMF

Carew, Rod (Rodney Cline) (1945–). (Born Panama). AAS-3; BRAA; GUDA; GUED-01; GUEE; IZA; MUC; RIGA†

Carey, Max (1890–). ALB; ROC

Carlton, Steven Norman (1944–). BUJB; GUG; RIGA†; SA-3; SHH

Cartwright, Alexander (1820–1892). ALB; DAFD; DAG; DAGA; SMK

Casey, Hugh (1913–1951). SHE

Cedeño, Cesar (1951–). Dominican. GUG; KLCA

Cepeda, Orlando (1937–). BRD; FOW; PRA

Chadwick, Henry (1824–1908). ALB

Chance, Dean (1941–). DEE

Chance, Frank (1877–1924). Player, manager. ALB; DAFD; FRC-01

Chase, Harold (1883–1947). SMK

Chesbro, Happy Jack (John Dwight) (1874–1931). ALB

Clarke, Fred (1872–1960). Player, manager. ALB; FRC-01

Clarkson, John (1862?–1909). ALB

Clemente, Roberto (1934–1972). BUD-1; BUJ; DAFC; DAFD; FOW; FRC-1†; FRD; GUE; IZA; KADA; NEBB; PEC; PRA; RIGA†; SHH; WH-2; WO

Cobb, Ty (Tyrus Raymond) (1886–1961). AAS-35; ALB; ASBA; BELB†; COKB; DAFB; DAFC; DAFD; DAG; DAGA; DAH; EPA; FRC-1†; GEC; GR; GUC; GUDA; HEG; HIF; HOC; MUB-1; MUC; RIGA†; ROC; SH; SHH; SID; WAC

Cochrane, Mickey (Gordon S.) (1903–1962). ALB; DAFD; GUDA; HIC; HIF; HOCM; RIGA†; SHD; SHH; VACA; WAG; ZAA

Cohen, Andy (Andrew) (1904–). RI; SLA

Colavito, Rocky (Rocco Domenico) (1933–). DA

Colbert, Nathan (1946–). KLCA

Collins, Eddie (1887–1951). ALB; DAFD; DAG; DAGA; HIF; MUB-1; RIGA†; ROC

Collins, Jimmy (1870?–1943). ALB; LEY†

Combs, Bob. Little League coach. LEW

Comiskey, Charles Albert (1859–1931). Player, manager. ALB; SMK

Connolly, Thomas Henry (1870–1961). Umpire. ALB

Cooper, Walker (1914–1958). DEG†; HIC

Courtney, Clint (1927–). BOE

Crandall, Delmar Wesley (1930–). HIC

Crawford, Wahoo Sam (Samuel Earl) (b. 1880). ALB; RIGA†

Cronin, Joe (1906–1984). Player, manager. ALB; DAFD; FRC-01; HIF; MUB-1; MUC

Cueller, Mike (Miguel) (1937–). BELA

Cummings, Candy (William Arthur) (1848–1924). ALB

Daley, Buddy Leo (1932–). GEA

Danning, Harry (1911–). RI; SLA

Dark, Alvin (1923–). Player, manager. BOE

Darling, Ron (1960–). GUB-1

Davis, Willie (1940–). LYE

Dean, Dizzy (Jay Hanna) (1911–1974). ALB; BED; BOE; BRC; BUD-1; DAFB; DAFD; DEG; FRC-1†; GIB; GRA; HOC; LIAA; NEA; RIGA†; SHH; SMK

Dean, Paul (1913–1981). GRA; NEA

Delahanty, Edward James (1867–1903). ALB; DAFD; FRC-1†

Devore, Joshua (1887–1954). BED

Dickey, Bill (William Malcolm) (1907–). ALB;

DAFD; GUDA; HIC; HIF; MUB-1; MUC; RIGA†; ROB; SHD; VACA; WAG; ZAA

Di Maggio, Joseph Paul (1914–). ALB; ALBA; ASBA; BELB; BOE; BUD-1; BUJ; DA; DAA; DAFB; DAFC; DAFD; DAG; DAGA; DAH; DEE; FIAA; GEC; GR; GUC; HIF; HOC; MUC; PAW; RIGA†; ROB; SH; SHB; SHC; SHF; SHH; VEA; WAC

Dischinger, Terry (1942?–). HOCA

Dressen, Charlie (1898–1966). Player, manager. FRC-01

Dreyfuss, Barney (1865–1932). Executive, born Germany. SLA

Drysdale, Don (Donald Scott) (1936–). GEB; GEC; LEZ; NEA; PRA; SA-3; SHA

Duffy, Hugh (1866–1954). ALB

Duren, Ryne (Rinold George) (1929–). SHE

Durocher, Leo (1906–). Manager. DEG; FRC-01; LEW; ROAA

Ehmke, Howard John (1894–1959). REB; WAG

Ennis, Del (1925–). BOE

Essegian, Chuck (Charles Abraham) (1931–). DEHA-1

Evers, John Joseph (1883–1947). ALB; DAFD

Ewing, Buck (William) (1859–1906). ALB; HAF

Faber, Red (Urban Charles) (b. 1888). ALB

Fain, Ferris (1922–). BOE

Fairly, Ron (1938–). BELA

Feller, Bob (Robert William) (1918–). ALB; BOE; BRC; DAFD; DAG; DAGA; DEE; FRC-1†; GEC; GRA; HIF; HOC; LEF; NEA; REB; SHH; WAG

Figueroa, Ed. KLBB

Fingers, Rollie (1946–). AAS; RIGA†

Fisher, Harry (1882–1967). Player, coach. SLA

Fisk, Carlton (1947–). GUG; HEFB†; HOCM; KLCA; TUB

Flick, Elmer (1876–1971). ALB

Flood, Curtis Charles (1938–). HOBC

Ford, Whitey (Edward Charles) (1928–). BOE; BRC; DAFC; GIB; FRC-1†; HIF; MUB-1; MUC; RIGA†; ROB; SHA

Foster, George (1948–). AAS-4; GUED-01

Foxx, James Emory (1907–1967). ALB; DA; DAA; DAFD; FRC-1†; LEV; RAAA; RIGA†; SHB; SHF

Freehan, Bill (1941–). BRE; ZAA

Fregosi, James Louis (1942–). LEY

Frisch, Frank (1898–1973). Player, manager. ALB; DAFD; DEG; HAF; RIGA†; SHF; VEA

Gallagher, Alan Mitchell (1945–). LEY

Galvin, James F. (1856–1902). ALB

Garvey, Steven Patrick (1948–). AAS-3; BUJC; GUED-01; RIGA†; GUEE; SMF

Gehrig, Lou (1903–1941). ALB; BEC; BOE; BUD-1; DA; DAA; DAFB; DAFC; DAFD; DAG;

DAGA; DAH; FRC-1†; GIB; GR; GUC; HIF; HOC; LIC; LYB; MUB-1; MUC; RAAA; RIGA†; ROB; SCA; SHB; SHC; SHH; WAC

Gehringer, Charles Leonard (1903–). ALB; HIF; RIGA†

Gibson, Bob (Robert) (1935–). BUJ†; DEG; FRC-1†; FRD; KADA; LEZ; MUB-1; PAW; PRA; RIGA†; SA-3; SHA

Gibson, Josh (1911–1947). AAS-24; DAFD

Gomez, Lefty (1909–). BOE; LIAA; ROB

Gordon, Sid (1918–1975). RI; SLA

Gossage, "Goose" (Richard) (1951–). AAS

Gowdy, Hank (b. 1889). Player, coach. GIB; HIC

Grabarkewitz, Bill (William Cordell) (1946–). LEY

Gray, Pete (1917–). BELB; BUJA; DAFD; PIB; PIBA

Greenberg, Hank (Henry Benjamin) (1911–1986). ALB; BOE; DAA; FRC-1†; GR; RI; RIGA†; SLA

Grich, Bobby (1949–). KLBB

Griffith, Clark (1869–1955). Manager. ALB

Grimes, Burleigh (1894–1985). Player, manager. ALB; GEB; RIGA†

Groat, Dick (1930–). DEHA-1

Grote, Jerry (Gerald Wayne) (1942–). TUB

Grove, Lefty (Robert Moses) (1900–1975). ALB; DAFD; HIF; MUB-1; NEA; RIGA†; SHF

Guidry, Ron (1950–). AAS-2; HEFB†

Gutierrez, Cesar "Coco" (1943–). SA-3

Hamilton, Billy (William Robert) (1866–1940). ALB

Harper, Tommy (1940–). LEY

Harrelson, Bud (Derrel McKinley) (1944–). KLBB

Harrelson, Ken (1941–). DEHA-1

Harris, Bucky (Stanley Raymond) (1896–1977). Manager. FRC-01

Hartnett, Gabby (Charles Leo) (1900–1972). ALB; GUDA; HIC; HOCM; RIGA†; SHD; ZAA

Hebner, Richard Joseph (1947–). LEY

Hegan, Jim (1920–1984). HIC

Heilmann, Harry (1895–1951). ALB; RIGA†

Henrich, Tommy (1916–). BOE

Herman, Babe (Floyd Caves) (1903?–1987). GEB; LIAA

Hernandez, Keith (1953–). AAS-3

Herzog, Whitey (1931–). Player, manager. FRC-01

Heyison, Marc. GUB-1

Hiller, John (1943–). AAS-27; PAW

Hodges, Gil (1924–1972). DA; DAA; GEB; KLB

Holloman, Alva (1926–). GRA

Holtzman, Ken (1945–). RI; SLA

Hornsby, Rogers (1896–1963). ALB; DAA; DAFB; DAFC; DAFD; DAG; DAGA; DAH; DEG; FIAA; FRC-1†; GR; GUC; GUDA†; MUB-1; MUC; RIGA†; SHH; WAC

Howard, Elston (1930–1980). HIC; HOCM; PRA; SHD; SHF; ZAA

Howard, Frank (Hondo) (1936–). DA

Hoy, Bill (William Ellsworth) (1865–1961). DAFD

Hubbell, Carl Owen (1903–). ALB; BRC; DAFD; DEHA-1; FRC-1†; HAF; REB; RIGA†; SHH; WAG

Hubbs, Kenneth Douglas (1941–1964). KLB

Huggins, Miller (1879–1929). Manager. ALB; FRC-01; ROAA

Hundhammer, Paul. GUB-1

Hunt, Ron (Ronald Kenneth) (1941–). SA-3

Hunter, Catfish (James Augustus) (1946–). GUB-1; KLCA; SMH

Jackson, Reggie (1946–). AAS-4; BRAA; GUG

Jackson, Travis (1903–1987). HAF

Jay, Joseph Richard (1935–). BRE

Jenkins, Ferguson Arthur (1943–). BUJB; GUB-1; GUG; KLCA; RIGA†

Jennings, Hugh Ambrose (1871–1928). Player, manager. ALB; FRC-01

Jethroe, Sam (1922–). BOE

John, Tommy (1943–). AAS-27; BRE

Johnson, Ban (Byron Bancroft) (1864–1931). President of American League. ALB

Johnson, Gus. HIBA

Johnson, Walter Perry (1887–1946). AAS-35; ALB; ASBA; BED; BRC; DAFB; DAFC; DAFD; DAG; DAGA; DAH; EPA; FRC-1†; GRA; GUC; GUDA; HIF; MUB-1; MUC; NEA; RIG†; SHA; SICA; WAG

Kaline, Albert William (1934–). BELB; BUJ; DA; HOCG; PEC; PRA; SA-3

Kauff, Benny (1891–1961). SLA

Keefe, Timothy J. (1856–1933). ALB

Keeler, Wee Willie (William Henry) (1872–1923). ALB; DAFD; DAH; FRC-1†

Kell, George Clyde (1922–). BOE; HIF

Kelly, King (Michael Joseph) (1857–1894). ALB; DAFD; SMK

Kemp, Steve (1954–). GUB-1

Keough, Matt (1955–). AAS-9

Killebrew, Harmon (1936–). DA; KADA; LEY; PEC; PRA; RAAA; RIGA†; SA-3

Kiner, Ralph M. (1922–). DA; DAA; RAAA

Kingman, Dave (1948–). AAS-4; LEY†

Kitt, Howard. BELB

Kittle, Ron (1958–). GUB-1

Klein, Chuck (1905–1958). DAA

Klem, Bill (William Joseph) (1874–1951). ALB; DAFD; DAG; DAGA; DAH; FRC-1†

Kling, Johnny (1875–1947). HIC; RI; SHD†; SLA

Konstanty, Jim (Casimer James) (1917–1976). SHE; VEA

Koosman, Jerry (1943–). KLBB

Koufax, Sandy (Sanford) (1935–). ALBA; BRC; BUD-1; DAFC; DAFD; DAH; DEHA-1; FRC-1†; GEB; GIB; GRA; GRB-1; GUC; GUDA; HOC; KADA; LYC; MUB-1; MUC; NEA; PAW; PEC; PRA; RI; RIGA†; SHA; SHC; SLA

Kuenn, Harvey (1930–1988). Baseball player, coach. BOE†; BRD

Lajoie, Napoleon (1875–1959). ALB; DAFC; DAFD; DAH; EP; RIGA†; WAC

Landis, Kenesaw Mountain (1866–1944). Commissioner. ALB

Larsen, Don (1929–). BED; GIB; GRA; SHC

Lazzeri, Tony (1904?–). ROB

LeFlore, Ron (1948–). AAS-27

Lieberman, Nancy (1958–). SLA

Lindstrom, Fred (1905–1981). HAF

Lombardi, Ernie (1908–). HIC; RIGA†; SHD†; ZAA

Lopez, Al (1908–). Player, manager. FRC-01; HIC

Lowe, Robert L. DAH

Luzinski, Greg (1950–). GUED-01

Lyle, Sparky (Albert) (1944–). AAS

Lynn, Frederic Michael (1952–). AAS-3; BUJC

Lyons, Theodore Amar (1900–1986). ALB; RIGA†

McCarthy, Joseph Vincent (1887–1978). Manager. ALB; FRC-01; HEH; VACB

McCarthy, Tommy (1864–1922). ALB

McCarver, Tim (James Timothy) (1941–). ZAA

McCovey, Willie Lee (1938–). DA; KLB; RIGA†

McDougald, Gil (1928–). BOE

McDowell, Sam (1943–). BRE; LEZ; PRA; SA-3

McGinnity, Joseph Jerome (1871–1929). ALB; DAFD; FRC-1†; HAF; RIGA†

McGraw, John Joseph (1875–1934). Manager. AAS-1; ALB; DAFC; DAFD; DAG; DAGA; DAH; FRC-01; FRC-1†; HAF; HEH; LEY†; ROAA; VACB

McGraw, Tug (Frank) (1944–). AAS

Mack, Connie (Cornelius Alexander McGillicuddy) (1862–1956). Player, manager. AAS-1; ALB; DAFD; DAG; DAGA; FRC-01; FRC-1†; GIB; HEH; ROAA; SMK; VACB

McKechnie, Bill (1886–1965). Manager. ALB; FRC-01

McLain, Dennis (1944–). KADA; LEZ; PRA; SHA

Maglie, Sal (1917–). BRC; GRA

Maloney, Jim (James William) (1940–). LEZ

Malzone, Frank (1930?–). PIB

Mantle, Mickey Charles (1931–). BOE; BUD-1; BUJA; DA; DAA; DAFB; DAFC; DAFD; DAG; DAGA; DAH; DEHA-1; FRC-1†; GEC; GR; GUC; HIF; HOC; LIC; LOAA; LYD; PAW; RAAA; RIGA†; ROB; SA-3; SH; SHB; SHF; SHH; VAE; VEA

Manush, Heinie (Henry Emmet) (1901–1971). ALB

Maranville, Rabbit (Walter James) (1892?–1954). ALB; DAFC; DAFD; LIAA

Marichal, Juan (1937–). Dominican. HAF; KADA; LEZ; PEC; PRA; RIGA†

Maris, Roger Eugene (1934–1985). ALBA; BELB; BRE; DAA; GUDA; KADA; RAAA; ROB; SHB; SHC

Marquard, Rube (Richard) (1889–1980). DAFD; DAH; FRC-1†; LOAA

Marshall, Michael Grant (1943–). AAS-2; SMH

Martin, Billy (Alfred M.) (1928–). Player, manager. AAS-1; FRC-01; GIB†; SMG

Martin, Pepper (John Leonard) (1904–). BED; BOE; DEG; GIB; ROC

Mathews, Edwin Lee (1931–). DA; DAA; DAFD; LEY†; RIGA†; SHB

Mathewson, Christy (1880–1925). ALB; BRC; DAFC; DAFD; DAG; DAGA; DAH; EPA; FRC-1†; GIB; GUC; HAF; MUB-1; MUC; NEA; RIGA†; SHA; WAG

Matlack, Jonathan T. (1950?–). KLBB

Mayberry, John Claiborn (1950–). KLCA

Mayer, Erskine (1891–1957). RI; SLA

Mays, Carl (1893–1971). DAFD

Mays, Willie Howard (1931–). ASBA; BOE; BOF; BRG; BUD-1; BUJ; DA; DAA; DAFB; DAFD; DAGA; DAH; DEE; DEHA-1; FRC-1†; FRD; GEC; GIB; GR; GUC; GUE; HAF; HOC; KADA; LEV; MUB-1; MUC; PRA; RAAA; RIC; RICA; RIGA†; ROC; SA-3; SH; SHB; SHF; SHH; SID; VEA

Mazeroski, Bill (William Stanley) (1936–). BED; GIB; PRA

Medwick, Ducky (Joe) (1911–). DEG; LIC; RIGA†

Melton, Bill (William Edwin) (1945–). BELA; LEY

Minoso, Minnie (Saturnino Orestes) (1922–). Cuban. BOE

Minton, Greg (1951–). AAS

Mize, Johnny (1913–). DA; DAA; DEG; RIGA†

Mizell, Vinegar Bend (Wilmer) (1930–). DEHA-1

Monbouquette, Bill (1936–). GRA

Morgan, Joe (1943–). AAS-23; BUJC; RIGA†; SMF

Mota, Manny (1938–). Dominican. AAS-25

Munson, Thurman Lee (1947–1979). BELA; BUJC; GUDA; GUED-01; GUEE; HOCM

Murcer, Bobby (1945–). GUG; KLCA

Murtaugh, Danny (1917–1976). Player, manager. SMG

Musial, Stanley Frank (1920–). BOE; BUD-1; BUJ; DA; DAA; DAFB; DAFC; DAFD; DAFG; DAG; DAGA; DAH; DEG; DEHA-1; FRC-1†; GR; GUC; HOC; MUB-1; MUC; PIAA; RIGA†; SH; SHB; SHF; SHH; SICA; VEA

Myer, Buddy (1904–1974). SLA; RI

Newcombe, Donald (1926–). BOE; NEA

Newsom, Bobo (Louis Norman) (1907–1962). LIAA

Nichols, Kid (Charles Augustus) (1870–1953). ALB

Niekro, Phil (1939–). AAS-2; BELA

Nuxhall, Joe (Joseph Henry) (1928–). BELB

Nye, Rich (1944–). BRE

O'Brien, Eddie (1930–). FOI

O'Brien, Johnny (1930–). FOI

Oliva, Tony (Pedro) (1940–). Cuban. PEC; PRA

Oliver, Al (1946–). AAS-3

O'Neill, Stephen Francis (1892–1962). Player, manager. HIC

O'Rourke, James Henry (1853–1919). ALB

Ott, Mel (Melvin Thomas) (1909–1958). Player, manager. ALB; BOE; DA; DAA; DAFB; DAFC; DAFD; DAH; FRC-1†; GEC; HAF; MUC; RIGA†; SH; SHB

Owen, Mickey (Arnold Malcolm) (1917–). BED; HIC

Page, Joseph Francis (1917–1980). SHE

Paige, Satchel (Leroy) (1906–1982). ASBA; BOF; BRC; BUD-1; DAFC; DAFD; DAH; FRC-1†; LIAA†; SMK

Palmer, Jim (James Alvin) (1945–). AAS-2; BUJB; MUB-1; RIGA†

Parker, Dave (1951–). AAS-3

Pasquel, Jorge (1907–1955). Mexican executive. NEBA

Patek, Fred (1944–). AAS-23

Pearson, Albie (1935–). BRD; FOI

Pelty, Barney (1880–1939). SLA

Pennock, Herbert Jefferis (1894–1948). ALB; RIGA†; ROB

Perez, Tony (Atanasio Rigal) (1942–). Cuban. BELA; LEY; WH-3

Perranoski, Ronald Peter (1937–). SHE

Perry, Gaylord Jackson (1938–). AAS-2; BUJB; PRA; SMH

Petrocelli, Rico (America P.) (1943–). LEY

Phillips, Lefty (Harold) (1919–1972). Manager. LEW

Piersall, Jim (1929–). VAE

Pike, Lipman (1845–1893). Player, manager. SLA

Plank, Eddie (1875–1926). ALB; MUB-1; RIGA†

Powell, Boog (John Wesley) (1941–). DEHA-1; KLB

Quisenberry, Dan (1953–). AAS; HEFB

Radatz, Richard Raymond (1937–). SHE

Radbourn, Old Hoss (Charles Gardner) (1853–1897). ALB

Rader, Douglas Lee (1944–). BELA; LEY†

Reese, Pee Wee (Harold Henry) (1919–). BOE; GEB; KLB

Reiser, Pete (Harold Patrick) (1920–). GEB; RIGA†; ROC; VAE

Reulbach, Edward (1882–1961). SLA

Reynolds, Allie (1919–). BOE; GIB; GRA; ROB

Rice, Jim (1950–). AAS-4; RIGA†

Rice, Sam (1892–1974). ALB

Rickey, Branch (Wesley Branch) (1881–1965). Executive. DAFD; FRC-1†

Rixey, Eppa (1891–1963). ALB

Rizzuto, Philip Francis (1918–). BOE; FOI; GIB; KLB; ROB

Roberts, Robin (1926–). RIGA†; SHH

Robinson, Brooks Calbert (1937–). DAFD; FRC-1†; FRD; HIF; KLB; LEY; MUB-1; MUC; PEC; PRA; RIGA†; SMF

Robinson, Frank (1935–). BRD; DA; KADA; LIC; PEC; PRA; RIGA†; SMG

Robinson, Jackie (John Roosevelt) (1919–1972). ALB; ASB-1; BELB; BOE; BOF; BRD; BRG; BUD-1; BUJA; DAFB; DAFC; DAFD; DAG; DAGA; DAH; DOF-1; FLD; FRC-1†; GEB; GUC; GUDA; HOBC; HOC; HUA; JOC; KLB; LEY†; LOAA; RIGA†; ROC; SCA; SHF; SHH; SMK; STO; VAE

Robinson, Wilbert (1864–1934). Player, manager. ALB; DAFD; FRC-01; ROAA

Rogovin, Saul (1923–). RI

Rohr, Bill (William Joseph) (1945–). LYD

Rojas, Cookie (Octavio Rivas) (1939–). Cuban. BELA

Rolfe, Red (Robert) (1908–). Player, manager. ROB

Rose, Pete (Peter Edward) (1941–). Player, manager. BELB†; BRAA; BRD; CL-06; GUG; GUH; HEFB†; KADA; PRA; RIGA†; AAS-3; AAS-35

Rosen, Al (1925–). BUJ; RI; SLA

Rosen, Goody (Goodwin) (1912–). Canadian. RI

Roush, Edd J. (1893–1988). ALB; RIGA†

Rudi, Joseph Oden (1946–). BELA

Ruel, Muddy (Herold) (1896–1963). HIC

Ruffing, Red (1905?–1986). ROB

Ruth, Babe (George Herman) (1895–1948). ALB; ASB; ASB-1; BED; BOE; BUD-1; BUJ; COKB; DA; DAA; DAFB; DAFC; DAFD; DAG; DAGA; DAH; DEI; DEJ; EPA; FRC-1†; GEC; GIB; GR; GUC; GUDA; HEG; HIF; HOC; LAC; LEF; LEV; LIAA†; LYC; MUB-1; MUC; RAAA; RIGA†; ROB; SH; SHB; SHC; SHH; SID; SMK; WAC

Ryan, Nolan (Lynn Nolan) (1947–). AAS-2; AAS-35; GUDA; GUED-01; GUG; RIGA†; SMH

Sanguillen, Manuel DeJesus (1944–). Panamanian. TUB

Santo, Ron (1940–). BRE; LEY; PRA

Schacht, Al (1892–1984). LIAA†; RI; SLA†

Schalk, Ray (1892–1970). ALB; HIC

Schang, Walter Henry (1889–1965). HIC

Schmidt, Mike (1949–). AAS-4; RIGA†

Schoendienst, Red (Albert Fred) (1923–). BUJ; BUJA; DEG; SCA

Score, Herbert Jude (1933–). BRD; NEA; RIGA†

Scott, George (1943–). KLBB; LEY

Seaver, Tom (George Thomas) (1944–). AAS-2; BELB†; BUJA; FRD; GUE; GUG; LEZ; MUB-1; RIGA†; SA-3; SMH

Sherry, Larry (Lawrence) (1935–). GIB; RI; SLA

Sievers, Roy (1926–). BOE†; BRD

Silas, James (1949–). AAS-9

Simmons, Aloysius Harry (1903–1956). ALB; DAA; RIGA†; SHH

Simmons, Ted Lyle (1949–). HOCM; TUB

Sisler, George (1893–1973). ALB; DAFC; DAFD; FRC-1†; HIF; RIGA†

Skowron, Bill (1930–). DEHA-1

Slaughter, Country (Enos) (1916–). BUJ; DEG; GIB

Snider, Duke (Edwin) (1926–). DA; DAA; FRC-1†; GEB; GIB; RIGA†

Sockalexis, Louis (1873–1913). SMK

Spahn, Warren (1921–). BOE; BRC; DAFC; DAFD; DAH; RIGA†; SHA; SHH; SICA

Spalding, Albert Goodwill (1850–1915). ALB; SMK

Speaker, Tristram E. (1888–1958). ALB; DAFC; DAFD; DAG; DAGA; EP; FRC-1†; GUC; HIF; RIGA†; SH; WAC

Stallings, George (1867–1929). Manager. PAW

Stargell, Willie (Wilver Dornel) (1941–). AAS-4; RIGA†

Stark, Dolly. Umpire. RI

Stengel, Casey (Charles Dillon) (1891–1975). Player, manager. AAS-1; BED; BELB; DAFC; DAFD; DAG; DAGA; FRC-01; FRC-1†; GIB†; HEH; LEW; LIAA; ROAA

Stone, George Robert (1876–1945). SLA

Stone, Steve (1947–). AAS-9; RI; SLA

Stratton, Monty (1912–1982). LYE

Sunday, Billy (William Ashley) (1862–1935). COKB; DAFD

Sutter, Bruce (1953–). AAS; AAS-2

Tebbetts, Birdie (George Robert) (1914–). Player, manager. HIC

Tekulve, Kent (1947–). AAS

Tenace, Gene (1946–). BELB; SA-3

Terry, William Harold (1898–). Player, manager. ALB; HAF; MUB-1; MUC; RIGA†

Thomas, James Gorman (1950–). AAS-4

Thompson, Danny (1947–1976). CL-04

Thomson, Bobby (1923–). (Born Scotland). DEHA-1

Tiant, Luis (1940–). AAS-2

Tinker, Joseph Bert (1880–1948). ALB; DAFD

Torre, Joseph Paul (1940–). HOCM; LEY; PEC; PRA; SHD; ZAA

Traynor, Pie (Harold Joseph) (1899–1972). ALB; DAFC; DAFD; DAH; LEY; MUB-1; MUC; RIGA†

Tresh, Thomas Michael (1938–). BRD

Turley, Bob (1930–). DEHA-1

Unser, Del (1944–). AAS-25

Vance, Dazzy (Clarence Arthur) (1909–1961). ALB; FRC-1†; GEB; NEA; RIGA†

Vander Meer, John Samuel (1914–). GRA; NEA

Versalles, Zoilo (1940–). Cuban. IZA; PRA; SHF; VEA

Von der Ahe, Chris (19th century). Club owner. DAFD

Waddell, Rube (George Edward) (1876–1914). ALB; DAFC; DAFD; DAG; DAGA; DAH; LIAA; NEA; RIGA†

Wagner, Honus (John Peter) (1874–1955). ALB; BOE; DAFB; DAFC; DAFD; DAG; DAGA; DAH; EPA; FRC-1†; GUC; MUB-1; MUC; RIGA†; WAC

Walker, Dixie (1910–1982). GEB

Walker, Harry William (1918–). Manager. LEW

Wallace, Bobby (Roderick John) (1873–1960). ALB

Walsh, Edward Augustine (1882–1959). ALB; RIGA†

Waner, Lloyd James (1906–1982). DAFD; FRC-1†

Waner, Paul (1903–1965). ALB; DAFD; FRC-1†; RIGA†

Ward, John Montgomery (1860–1925). ALB; SMK

Weaver, Earl (1930–). Manager. FRC-01

Wheat, Zachary Davis (1888–1972). ALB; GEB; RIGA†

White, Roy (1943–). DEHA-1; KLBB

White, William D. (1934–). GUB-1; PRA

Wilhelm, James Hoyt (1923–). DAFD; LEZ; SA-3; SHE

Williams, Billy Leo (1938–). BELA

Williams, Dick (1928–). Manager. AAS-1; FRC-01

Williams, Joe (fl. 1912). SMK

Williams, Ted (Theodore Samuel) (1918–). Player, manager. ASBA; BELB; BUD-1; BUJ; DA; DAA; DAFB; DAFC; DAFD; DAG; DAGA; DAH; DEE; DEHA-1; FIAA; FRC-1†; GEC; GR; GUC; GUDA; HIF; HOC; LEV; LIC; MUB-1; MUC; PAW; RAAA; RIGA†; SA-3; SH; SHB; SHH; SMK; VEA; WAC

Wills, Maury (Maurice Morning) (1932–). DEHA-1; FOI; GEB; GUDA; KADA; PRA; ROC; SHC; VEA

Winfield, Dave (1951–). AAS-4; HEFB†

Wood, Joe (b. 1889). NEA; RIGA†

Worthington, Al (1929–). Player, coach. DEHA-1

Wright, George (1847–1937). ALB

Wright, Harry (William Henry) (1835–1895). Manager, born England. ALB; SMK

Yastrzemski, Carl Michael (1939–). BRE; DEE; FRD; KADA; LIC; RIGA†

Young, Cy (Denton True) (1867–1955). ALB; DAFB; DAFC; DAFD; DAG; DAGA; DAH; EP; FRC-1†; RIGA†; SHA; WAG

Young, Ross (Royce Youngs) (1897–1927). HAF; RIGA†

Yount, Robin (1955–). HOCG; SMF

BASKETBALL FIGURES

Abdul-Jabbar, Kareem (1947–). AAS-35; ARB-1; ASBA; FRD; GAB; GUEA; KADA; KLBA; KLC; RAAB; SA; SA-1; SA-2

Archibald, Nate "Tiny" (1948–). AAS-6; ARB-4; HIBAA

Arizin, Paul (1929–). PE

Attles, Alvin (1936–). Coach. ARB-2

Auerbach, Red (Arnold) (1917–). Coach. HEH; HID; LEW†; SLA

Barry, Rick (1944–). ARB-3; DEHA-1; FRD; HOCA; RAAB; SA-1; SA-2

Baylor, Ed (Elgin) (1935?–). BEL; HEHA; HID; PE; RAAB

Bellamy, Walt (1939–). HOCA

Belmont, Joe. Coach. LEW

Bing, Dave (1943–). ARB-4; BEL; PAW

Bird, Larry (1956–). AAS-8

Birdsong, Otis (1955–). AAS-8

Blazejowski, Carol (1956–). GUED-1

Bradley, Bill (William Warren) (1943–). BOHA; BRE; HOC; PAW

Bridgeman, Junior (Ulysses) (1953–). AAS-25

Brody, Tal (1943–). Israeli. (Born U.S.). SLA

Brown, Fred (1948–). AAS-8

Brown, Roger. HIBA

Buckner, Quinn (1954–). AAS-6

Calvin, Mack (1948–). HIBAA

Chamberlain, Wilt (Wilton Norman) (1936–). AAS-35; ALBA; ASBA; BEL; BOF; DEHA-1; ETA; GUEA; HEHA; HID; HOC; KADA; KLBA; PE; RAAB

Collins, Doug (1951–). ARB-4

Costello, Larry (1932–). Player, coach. DEHA-1

Cousy, Bob (Robert) (1928–). ASBA; BEL; BUJA; DAG; DAGA; DEHA-1; FOI; HEG; HEHA; HID; HOC; PE; SID

Cowens, Dave (1948–). AAS-5; ARB-1; BELB; GUEA; KLC; RUB

Cummings, Terry (1961–). AAS-7

Cunningham, Billy (1943–). SA

Dampier, Louis (1944–). HIBAA

Daniels, Mel. HIBA
Dantley, Adrian (1956–). AAS-7
Davis, Johnny (1955–). AAS-6
DeBusschere, Dave (1940–). DEHA-1; HIBA
Erving, Julius (Dr. J.) (1950–). AAS-5; ARB-3;
    GUEA; GUH; SA-1; SA-2
Felix, Ray (1930–). HOCA
Fitch, Bill (1936?–). Coach. ARB-2
Ford, Phil (1956–). AAS-6
Frazier, Walt (1945–). ARB-4; DEHA-1; GUEA;
    SA; SA-1; SA-2
Free, "World B" (Lloyd) (1953–). AAS-8
Friedman, Max (b. 1889). SLA
Fulks, Joe (1922?–). PE
Gervin, George (1952–). AAS-8
Gilmore, Artis (1948–). AAS-5; SA-1
Goodrich, Gail (1943–). HIBAA
Gottlieb, Eddie (1898–1979). Coach, administra-
    tor, born Russia. SLA
Greer, Hal. HIBA
Grunfeld, Ernie (1955–). (Born Romania). SLA
Havlicek, John (1940–). ARB-3; CL-06; DEHA-1;
    GUEA; PAW; PE; SA; SA-2
Hawkins, Connie (1942–). AAS-24; DEHA-1; SA
Hayes, Elvin (1945–). AAS-5; PE; SA
Haywood, Spencer (1949–). LOAA; SA; SA-1
Heinsohn, Tommy (Thomas William) (1934–).
    HID; HOCA
Heyman, Art (1942–). SLA
Holman, Nat (1896–). Coach. BEL; HEHA; HID;
    SLA
Holzman, Red (William) (1920–). Coach. ARB-2;
    SLA
Hudson, Lou (1944–). SA
Issel, Dan (1948–). HIBA
Johnson, Earvin "Magic" (1959–). AAS-6
Johnson, Marques (1956–). AAS-5
Jones, Bobby (1951–). AAS-25
Jones, K. C. (1932–). Player, coach. ARB-2
Keller, Billy. HIBAA
Kerr, John (1932–). Coach. LEW
King, Bernard (1956–). AAS-8
Lanier, Bob (1948–). CL-06; KLC; RUB
Lapchick, Joseph Bohomiel (1900–1970). Coach.
    HEH; HID; LEW†
Lewis, Fritz (Fred) (1944–). HIBAA
Litwack, Harry (1907–). Coach, born Austria.
    SLA
Love, Bob. HIBA
Lovellette, Clyde (1929–). DEHA-1
Lucas, Jerry (1940–). GED; GEDA; HEHA; HID;
    HOCA; RAAB
Lucas, John (1953–). AAS-6
Lucas, Maurice (1952–). AAS-7
Luisetti, Hank (Angelo Enrico) (1916–). HID
McAdoo, Bob (1951–). AAS-5; ARB-1; RUB; SA-2

Macauley, Ed (1927?–). Coach. HID
McGinnis, George (1950–). ARB-3; SA-1
McKinney, Bones (Horace). HID
Malone, Moses (1955–). AAS-5; AAS-7; HOCG
Maravich, Pete (1947–1988). ARB-4; FRD; KADA;
    KLC; SA-1; SA-2
Martin, Slater (1925–). HEHA; HID
Meineke, Donald Edward. HOCA
Meminger, Dean (1948–). HIBAA
Mikan, George L. (1924–). ASBA; BEL; DAG;
    DAGA; HEHA; HID; HOC; LYE; PE; RAAB;
    SICA
Miron, Charles. BELB
Monroe, Earl (1946?–). HOCA; PE; SA-2
Motta, Richard (1931–). Coach. LEW
Murphy, Calvin (1948–). AAS-23; HIBAA; KLC
Naismith, James A. (1861–1939). Originator.
    DAG; DAGA
Nater, Swen (1949?–). (Born the Netherlands).
    RUB
Newlin, Mike (1949–). AAS-8
Nixon, Norm (1955–). AAS-6
Nuñez, Tommy (1938–). Referee. WH
O'Brien, Eddie (1930–). FOI
O'Brien, Johnny (1930–). FOI
Petrie, Geoff (1948–). KLC; SA-1
Pettit, Robert (1932–). BEL; HEHA; HID; HOBB;
    PE; RAAB
Podoloff, Maurice (1890–1985). Administrator.
    SLA
Porter, Kevin (1950–). AAS-6
Reed, Willis (1942–). BEL; FRD; PAW; PE; RAAB
Robertson, Oscar (1938–). BEL; DEHA-1; ETA;
    FRD; HEHA; HID; HOC; PE
Roundfield, Dan (1953–). AAS-7
Ruland, Jeff (1958–). AAS-7
Rupp, Adolph (1902–1977). Coach. HEH; HID
Russell, William Felton (1934–). ASBA; BEL;
    DEF; HEHA; HID; HOBC; HOC; KADA;
    KLBA; LEW; PE; RAAB; RICA
Saperstein, Abraham M. (1903–1966). Coach,
    owner. SLA
Schaus, Frederick (1925–). Manager. LEW
Schayes, Adolph (1928–). BEL; HEHA; HID; PE;
    RAAB; SLA
Scott, Charlie. HIBA
Sedran, Barney (1891–1969). SLA
Seidell, Joe. Coach. LEW
Shank, Theresa (1951?–). ST-2
Shantz, Robert Clayton (1925–). BOE
Sharman, William (1926–). Player, coach. ARB-2;
    HID; LEW
Sikma, Jack (1955–). AAS-7
Sloan, Jerry (1942–). SA-2
Stokes, Maurice (1933–). HID; HOCA
Thompson, David (1954–). AAS-5; ARB-3

Twyman, Jack (1934–). HID
Unseld, Westley (1947?–). AAS-27; ARB-1; HOCA;
    RUB; SA-2
Van Lier, Norm (1946?–). HIBAA
Walk, Neal (1948–). KLC; SLA†
Walker, Jimmy (1944?–). SA
Walton, Bill (1952–). AAS-5; ARB-1
West, Jerry (1938?–). BEL; BELB; ETA; FRD;
    HEHA; HID; KADA; PE
Westphal, Paul (1950–). AAS-8
White, Jo Jo. KLC
Wilkens, Lenny. HIBA
Wilkins, Alonzo. PIB; PIBA
Williams, Buck (Charles Linwood) (1960–). AAS-7
Witte, Luke (1950–). AAS-24
Wooden, John R. (1910–). Coach. LEW

BELGIANS

Albert I (1875–1934). King. CAAA
Beernaert, Auguste Marie François (1829–1912).
    Statesman. MEC†; WIC
Bordet, Jules (1870–1961). Bacteriologist. RIF
Bruegel, Pieter, the Elder (1520?–1569). Painter.
    KAA; MAI
Damien de Veuster, Joseph (Father Damien)
    (1840–1889). Missionary. EVD; HAA; HEA;
    MAJ; MAN; STP; WRA
De Smet, Pierre Jean (1801–1873). Missionary.
    ASB
Eyck, Hubert van (1366–1426). Painter. MAI
Eyck, Jan van (1370?–1440?). Painter. KAA; MAI
Hirsch, Clara de (1833–1899). Philanthropist.
    LER
Ickx, Jacky (Jacques-Bernard) (1945–). Automo-
    bile racer. JA
Lafontaine, Henri (1854–1943). Statesman.
    MEC†; WIC
Lasso, Orlando di (1532?–1594). Composer. KAE
Magritte, René (1898–1967). Painter. WIAA
Pire, Georges Henri (1910–1969). Clergyman.
    MEC; WIC
Rubens, Peter Paul (1577–1640). Painter. CHC;
    KAA; MAI
Sax, Adolphe (Antoine Joseph) (1814–1894). Musi-
    cal instruments maker. LAE
Tazieff, Haroun. Geologist. KEH
Van Dyck, Sir Anthony (1599–1641). Painter.
    CHC
Vesalius, Andreas (1514–1564). Anatomist. CAA;
    CHD; DOE; HUD; POD; ROA; SHG; SIC
Vieuxtemps, Henri François Joseph (1820–1881).
    Violinist. CHFA

BIBLICAL FIGURES—NEW TESTAMENT

See also APOSTLES; SAINTS

Gabriel, Archangel. DAD-2; QUA
Jesus Christ. DEI; DEJ; FRE; HAJ; TRC-1
Joseph. Saint. DAD-1; DAD-2; ONA; QUA
Mary, Virgin. DAD-2; QUA
Mary Magdalen. DAD-3; ONA
Michael. Archangel. DAD-1; QUA

BIBLICAL FIGURES—OLD TESTAMENT†

Abraham. Hebrew patriarch. GEF
Ahab (d. 853? B.C.). King of Israel. JOBB
David (c. 1012–972 B.C.). King of Israel. BEC;
    CAAA; GEF; JOBB; STP
Deborah. Hebrew prophet. GEF; LER
Delilah. Philistine spy. SUG
Elijah. Hebrew prophet. GEF
Esther. Hebrew queen of Persia. LER; STP
Ezra (5th century B.C.). Hebrew prophet. GEF
Hannah. Mother of Hebrew prophet Samuel.
    LER
Hannah. Mother of the 7 Hebrew martyrs. LER
Huldah (638–608 B.C.). Hebrew prophet. LER
Isaiah. Hebrew prophet. KAB
Jeremiah (650–585 B.C.). Hebrew prophet. GEF
Jochebed. Mother of Moses. LER
Judith. Hebrew heroine. LER
Leah. Wife of Jacob. LER
Miriam. Sister of Moses. LER
Moses. CAAA; DEI; DEJ; FRE; GEF; KAB
Nebuchadnezzar II (d. 562 B.C.). King of Babylon.
    JOBB
Rachel. Wife of Jacob. LER
Rebecca. Wife of Isaac. LER
Ruth. LER
Sarah. Wife of Abraham. LER
Sheilah. Jephthah's daughter. LER
Solomon (d. 932 B.C.). King of Israel. CAAA;
    JOBB; NEC

BICYCLISTS

Meiffret, Jose (1911–). French. ST-1
Peppler, Mary Jo (1945?–). HOBAA
Toefield, Alfred. BELB
Young, Sheila (1950–). HOBAA†; LIEA; SUBB-1

BILLIARDS PLAYERS

Greenleaf, Ralph (1899?–1950). DAG; DAGA
Hoppe, Willie (1887–1959). DAG; DAGA
Mizerak, Steve. BELB

BIOCHEMISTS

American
Brown, Rachel Fuller (1898–). HA-1; YOF
Cori, Carl Ferdinand (1896–1984). (Born Czecho-
slovakia). RIF
Cori, Gerty Theresa (1896–1957). (Born Czechoslo-
vakia). RIF; SC†; SHFE†; YOF
DeVries, Yuan Lin. LA-1
Doisy, Edward Adelbert (1893–1986). RIF
Emerson, Gladys Anderson (1903–). EMB†; HA-1;
YOF
Funk, Casimir (1884–1967). (Born Poland). PIAA
Kendall, Edward Calvin (1886–1972). RIF
Kornberg, Arthur (1918–). GRB-1; LET; RIF
Lipmann, Fritz Albert (1899–1986). (Born Ger-
many). LET
Ochoa, Severo (1905–). (Born Spain). RIF
Seibert, Florence Barbara (1897–). GEA
Sharpless, Nansie (1932–). BOHA-1
Stanley, Wendell Meredith (1904–1971). BEK;
SUF
Steenbock, Harry (1886–1967). DEA
Szent-Györgyi, Albert von (1893–1986). (Born
Hungary). PAC; RIF
Tatum, Edward Lawrie (1909–1975). RIF

Foreign
Chain, Ernst Boris (1906–1979). English. (Born
Germany). BEK†; COLA†; GRB-1; LAE; LET;
POB; RIF
Dam, Henrik (1895–1976). Danish. RIF
Hopkins, Sir Frederick Gowland (1861–1947). En-
glish. RIF
Krebs, Sir Hans Adolf (1900–1981). English.
(Born Germany). LET

BIOLOGISTS

See also BACTERIOLOGISTS; BIOCHEMISTS; BIO-
PHYSICISTS; GENETICISTS; MICROBIOLOGISTS; VI-
ROLOGISTS

Carrel, Alexis (1873–1944). (Born France). POB;
RIF
Commoner, Barry (1917–). SQA

Crick, Francis H. C. (1916–). English. BEK; FE;
FRE†; RIF
Ehrlich, Paul Ralph (1932–). CORA
Helmholtz, Hermann Ludwig von (1821–1894).
German. SIA
Just, Ernest Everett (1883–1941). ADA; ADB;
BRB†; CAF-1; DOF-1; GRAB-03; HA; HAM;
KLA
McWhinnie, Mary Alice (d. 1980). LA-1
Mitchell, Mildred. HOG
Ramón y Cajal, Santiago (1852–1934). Spanish.
RIF
Ray, Dixy Lee (1914–). EMB†; GRAB-1†; WIAA-
02
Rudnick, Dorothea (1907–). YOF
Rydstrom, Pat. HOG

BIOPHYSICISTS

Branson, Herman (1914–). CAF-1
Quimby, Edith Hinkley (1891–1982). EMB†; YOF
Stapp, John Paul (1910–). COQ; ED
Wilkins, Maurice Hugh Frederick (1916–). Brit-
ish. RIF

BIRD STUDY, *see* ORNITHOLOGISTS

BLACKS

American
Aaron, Hank (1934–). Baseball player. ASBA;
BELB; BRAA; BUD-1; DA; DAFD; DOF-1;
FRC-1†; FRD; GAB; GEC; GR; GUC; GUDA;
GUE; KADA; LEV; MUB-1; MUC; PEC; PRA;
RAAA; RIGA†; SA-3; SH; SHB; SHH
Abbott, Robert Sengstacke (1870–1940). Journal-
ist, founded *Chicago Defender.* ADA; ADB;
HUA; ROG; STO
Abdul-Jabbar, Kareem (1947–). Basketball
player. AAS-35; ARB-1; ASBA; FRD; GAB;
GUEA; KADA; KLBA; KLC; RAAB; SA; SA-1;
SA-2
Abernathy, Ralph David (1926–). Clergyman,
civil rights leader. YOI
Abraham (c. 1790–c. 1870). Interpreter for
Seminoles. GRAB-02; WIBA
Adams, Eugene W. (1920–). Veterinarian. HAMA
Adams, Henry (b. 1843). Pioneer. KADB
Adderley, Herb. Football player. JOA
Ailey, Alvin (1931–). Dancer, choreographer. AB;
DOF-1

Aldridge, Ira (1805?–1867). Actor. ADA; ADB; BRB†; HODA; HUA; PECA; ROF; ROG

Ali, Muhammad (Cassius Clay) (1942–). Boxer. ASB-1; ASBA; BELB; BOHA; DAGA; FOR; GED; HOBC; HOCG; KADA; LEYB†; PAW; RAAC; RICA

Allard, Martine. Actress. BRF-1

Allen, Richard (1760–1831). Bishop. A founder of African Methodist Episcopal Church. ADA; ADB; BEJ; BRB; DADA; DOG; GRAB-05; HUA; PECA; ROG; WIBA

Allen, Richie (Richard Anthony) (1942?–). Baseball player. BRD; GUE; GUG; LEY

Alligood, Douglass L. Advertising executive. STAA

Alston, Charles H. (1907–). Painter. ADB

Amevor, Charlotte (1932–). Painter. FAH

Anderson, Marian (1902–). Singer. ADA; ADB; BOC; BRG; DOBA; DOF-1; FAA; FLD; GIBA; HUA; HUC; JOC; KE; KOA; LEHB; LEI; MAM; PACA; RIC; RICA; ROF; SC-02; SMBA; STF; STLA; STO; TRD

Anderson, Osborne Perry (1830–1871). Abolitionist. GRAB-05

Andrews, Benny (1930–). Painter. FAH

Angelou, Maya (1928–). Author. DADB; OCB

Antoine, Albert C. Rocket propulsion researcher. CAF-1

Archibald, Nate "Tiny" (1948–). Basketball player. AAS-6; ARB-4; HIBAA

Armistead, James (fl. 1781–1824). American Revolutionary patriot. DAF-1; STQ†; WIBA

Armstrong, Henry (1912–). Boxer. BUJA; DAG; DAGA; FOI

Armstrong, Louis "Satchmo" (1900–1971). Trumpeter. ADA; ADB; COF-1; FLD; HUC; LEHB; RIC; RICA; ROF; TEA; TEB; WAD

Arroyo, Martina (1936?–). Singer. AB

Ashe, Arthur (1943–). Tennis player. AAS-28; FOX; GLC; GRBA; HI; HOBC; HOD-1; KADA; LAHA; LYC

Ashford, Emmett Littleton (1915?–1980). Baseball umpire. HOBC

Ashford, Evelyn (1957–). Track athlete. SUDB

Attles, Alvin (1936–). Basketball player, coach. ARB-2

Attucks, Crispus (1723?–1770). American Revolutionary patriot. ADA; ADB; BEJ; BRB; BRG; BUIB†; DAF-1; EMA; GRAB-02; HUB; JOC; LEI; PECA; ROG; STQ†; WIBA

Baker, Al "Bubba" (1956–). Football player. AAS-16

Baker, Augusta (1911–). Librarian. FLD

Baker, Josephine (1906–1975). Singer. ROF

Baldwin, James (1924–1987). Author. DADB; KE; LEGB; RICA

Baldwin, Maria L. (1856–1922). Educator. BRB

Ballard, Audreen. Journalist. STAA

Banks, Ernie (1931–). Baseball player. DA; DAFD; DRA; FRC-1†; RIGA†; SHB; VEA

Banneker, Benjamin (1731–1806). Mathematician. ADA; ADB; BEJ; BRB; BRG; DOB; EMA; GRAB-03; HA; HAM; HODA; JOC; KLA; PECA; ROG; STQ; WIAB; WIBA

Bannister, Edward M. (1833–1901). Painter, born Canada. ADA; ADB

Barnett, Claude Albert (1889–1967). Journalist. ADB

Barnett, Ida Wells (1862–1931). Journalist, reformer. ADB; BRBE†; BUFA; HUB; LOAV; PACB; PECA; ROG; STAB-1; TRD

Barney, Lemuel J. Football player. FRD; ST

Barthé, Richmond (1901–). Sculptor. ADA; ADB; BRB†; RIC; RICA

Basie, Count (William) (1904–1984). Band leader. TEA; TEB; WAD†

Bason, Caesar. American Revolutionary patriot. WIBA

Bass, Dick (Richard Lee) (1937–). Football player. BEKB; LEZB

Bassett, Ebenezer D. (1833–1908). Diplomat. ADA; ADB

Bates, Daisy Gaston (1922–). Civil rights leader. AKB; DOF-1; GRAB-01; STF

Baylor, Ed (Elgin) (1935?–). Basketball player. BEL; HEHA; HID; PE; RAAB

Beamon, Bob (1946?–). Track athlete. OCA

Beard, Andrew J. Inventor. GRAB-03; STQ†

Bearden, Romare (1914–1988). Painter. FAH

Beauchamp, Bobby. Skater. VAD-6

Beckwith, Henry. Cowboy. STQ

Beckwourth, James P. (1798–1866). Frontiersman. ADB; BUH; GRAB-02; HAP; HUB; JO; KADB; LEI; PECA; ROG; SCB; STQ; WIBA

Belafonte, Harry (1927–). Singer. LOB; ROF

Belfield, Wendell. Veterinarian. CAF-1

Bellamy, Walt (1939–). Basketball player. HOCA

Benjamin, Bennie (1907–). Songwriter. HUC

Berry, Leonidas Harris. Physician. CAF-1

Bethune, Mary McLeod (1875–1955). Educator. ADA; ADB; BRB; BUDA; CAGA; DOF-1; FLB; FLD; GEE; GIBA; JOC; KOA; LEJA; LOAV; NAB; PECA; RIC; RICA; ROG; STLA; STO; WABC†; WIAA-8; YOI

Bibb, Henry (1815–1854). Abolitionist. GRAB-05

Biggers, John (1924–). Painter. FAH

Bing, Dave (1943–). Basketball player. ARB-4; BEL; PAW

Binga, Jesse (1865–1950). Banker. ADA; ADB

Birdsong, Otis (1955–). Basketball player. AAS-8

Black, Joe (1924–). Baseball player. BOE; SHE

Blair, Matt (1950–). Football player. AAS-15

Bland, James A. (1854–1911). Composer. ADA; ADB; HUC; LEHB; MOA

Blount, Mel (1948–). Football player. AAS-13

Blount, Mildred E. Hat designer. BOG

Blue, Vida (1949–). Baseball player. AAS-2; BUJB; FRD; GUG

Blunt, Roger R. (1930–). Army officer. RAE

Bond, Julian (1940–). State legislator, civil rights leader. BRGA; DU

Bonds, Bobby Lee (1946–). Baseball player. KLCA

Bonga, George (b. 1802). Fur trader. KADB; WIBA

Bontemps, Arna (1902–1973). Author. ADB; ROE

Borgen, Chris (1933?–). Television newscaster. STAA

Bostock, Lyman (1950–1978). Baseball player. AAS-24

Boston, Ralph (1939–). Track athlete. DAJ

Bousfield, Maudelle Brown (fl. 1906). Educator. BRB

Bowser, Mary Elizabeth (fl. 1861–1865). Spy. LOAV

Boyd, Oil Can (Dennis) (1959–). Baseball player. GUB-1

Bradford, Alex (1926?–1978). Singer, composer. AB

Braithwaite, William Stanley (1878–1962). Poet, critic. BRB†; DOF-1; ROE

Branson, Herman (1914–). Biophysicist. CAF-1

Braxton, Anthony (1945–). Saxophonist. UN

Brazile, Robert (1953–). Football player. AAS-15; SMJ

Bridgeman, Junior (Ulysses) (1953–). Basketball player. AAS-25

Brimmer, Andrew J. (1926–). Economist. YOI

Brock, Louis Clark (1939–). Baseball player. BRAA; GUDA; GUEE; RIGA†; SA-3

Brockington, John (1948–). Football player. GUF; MOCA; ST

Brooke, Edward William (1919–). Senator. ADB; DOF-1; DU†; FAG; FLD; LEI; YOI

Brooks, Gwendolyn (1917–). Poet. ADA; ADB; DRA; ROE

Broonzy, Big Bill (1893–1959). Singer. SUH

Brown, Charlotte Hawkins (1883–1961). Educator. BRB

Brown, Clara (1803–1885). Businesswoman. GRAB-02; KADB

Brown, Claude (1937–). Author. DADB

Brown, Dorothy (1919–). Surgeon. LETC

Brown, Fred (1948–). Basketball player. AAS-8

Brown, H. Rap (1943–). Activist. HAI

Brown, Henry "Box" (b. 1816). Abolitionist. BRG; JOC

Brown, James (1928–). Singer. DRA

Brown, Jill Elaine. Aviator. SMBC-2

Brown, Jim (James Nathaniel) (1936–). Football player, actor. AAS-35; AKB; ALBA; BEKB; BOF; DAFB; DAFG; DAI; DUF; HAD; HEI; HIE; HOBC; HOC; KADA; RAAE; SID

Brown, Kay (1932?–). Painter. FAI

Brown, Larry (1947–). Football player. AAS-27; DUF; GUEB; GUF; LEZB; ST

Brown, Pete Earlie (1935–). Golfer. HOBC

Brown, Rabbit (Richard) (1880–1937). Singer, guitarist. SUH

Brown, Robert Stanford. Football player. ST

Brown, Roger. Basketball player. HIBA

Brown, Roger (1937–). Football player. AAS-32

Brown, Warren (1948?–). Journalist. STAA

Brown, William Wells (1815–1884). Author. CL; DADA; GRAB-05

Bruce, Blanche K. (1841–1898). Senator. ADA; ADB; BRB; BU; PECA; STD; YOI

Brunson, Dorothy (1938–). Radio and advertising executive. GLO

Buckner, Quinn (1954–). Basketball player. AAS-6

Bunche, Ralph Johnson (1904–1971). Statesman. ADA; ADB; BRG; DOF-1; FEC; FLD; HUA; JOC; KEE; LEI; MEA; MEC; RIC; RICA; STO; WIC; YOI

Burke, Yvonne Brathwaite (1932–). Congresswoman, lawyer. BOHF; FOC-1; WIAA-02

Burleigh, Henry Thacker (1866–1949). Singer. ADA; ADB; BRB†; DOF-1

Burns, Maurice (1935?–). Painter. FAI

Burr, Seymour (fl. 1775). American Revolutionary patriot. WIBA

Burroughs, Nannie Helen (1883–1961). Educator. LOAV

Bush, George W. (1791–1867). Pioneer. BUH; GRAB-02; KADB; PECA; SCB; STQ†

Byard, Carole Marie (1941–). Painter. FAI

Byrd, Manford, Jr. (1928–). School administrator. DRA

Caffie, Barbara J. (1936?–). Television newscaster. STAA

Cain, Richard H. (1825–1887). Congressman. ADA; ADB

Caldwell, Earl (1938?–). Journalist. STAA

Calvin, Mack (1948–). Basketball player. HIBAA

Camero, Manuel (b. 1751). Settler. WIBA

Campanella, Roy (1921–). Baseball player. BOE; BUD-1; DADB; DAFC; DAFD; DAG; DAGA; FRC-1†; GEB; GUDA; HIC; HOCM; LYA; MUC; RIGA†; SCA; SHD; SHF; VACA; WAG; ZAA

Campbell, Earl (1955–). Football player. AAS-10; DEHB

Campbell, Elmer Simms (1906–1971). Cartoonist. ADA; ADB; BOG

Campbell, Robin (1958?–). Track athlete. GLB

Carew, Rod (Rodney Cline) (1945–). Baseball player, born Panama. AAS-3; BRAA; GUDA; GUED-01; GUEE; IZA; MUC; RIGA†

Carlos, John (1945?–). Track athlete. BELB

Carmichael, Berthel. Mathematician. CAF-1

Carmichael, Harold (1949–). Football player. AAS-18

Carmichael, Stokely (1941–). Civil rights leader. HAI

Carr, Frederick. Football player. SMJ

Carr, Leroy (1899–1935). Singer. SUH

Carruthers, George (c. 1940–). Physicist. CAF-1

Carter, Betty (1930–). Singer. UN

Carter, Ovie (1946?–). Photographer. STAA

Carver, George Washington (1864–1943). Botanist. ADA; ADB; ASA; ASB; ASB-1; BEC; BOD; BRB†; BRBD; CAF-1; CAGA; CO-1; COKA; CORA; CUC; DOE; DOF-1; EVD; FID; FRE; GRAB-03; HA; HAM; HODA; HUA; JOC; KE; KLA; LEI; LEPC; MAN; MAT; MEB; RIC; RICA; ROG; YOE

Cary, Mary Ann Shadd (1823–1893). Abolitionist. LOAV; WABC†

Catlett, Elizabeth (1915–). Sculptor. FAH

Cayton, Horace R. (1903–1970). Sociologist. BOG; DADB

Chamberlain, Wilt (Wilton Norman) (1936–). Basketball player. AAS-35; ALBA; ASBA; BEL; BOF; DEHA-1; ETA; GUEA; HEHA; HID; HOC; KADA; KLBA; PE; RAAB

Charles, Ray (1930–). Singer, pianist. HAFA

Charlton, Cornelius (1930?–1951). Soldier. ARBA; DIA

Chavis, John (1763?–1838). Clergyman, educator. BRB; DOB

Cheatham, Doc (1905–). Trumpeter. UN

Chesnutt, Charles Waddell (1858–1932). Author. ADA; ADB; BRB†; CL; DOF-1

Chester, Raymond (1948–). Football player. AAS-19

Chisholm, Shirley (1924–). Congresswoman. BRGA; COG-1; DRA; DU; FLD; GIBA; ROJ; WHE; YOI

Christmas, Walter. Public relations director. STAA

Clark, Kenneth Bancroft (1914–). Educator. DOF-1; FAG; YOI

Clark, Ruth (1942–). Personnel service executive. GLO

Clark, Septima Poinsette (1898–1987). Educator. BUFA

Claybourne, Braxton Daniel (1877–1935). Cowboy. JO

Cleage, Albert B. (1912–). Clergyman. HAI

Cleaver, Eldridge (1935–). Activist. DADA; HAI

Cobb, William Montague (1904–). Anatomist. CHE; HAMA

Colbert, Nathan (1946–). Baseball player. KLCA

Cole, Nat "King" (1919–1965). Pianist, singer. ROF

Coleman, Bessie (1893–1926). Aviator. HIFD; LOAV

Coleman, Ornette (1930–). Saxophonist. COF-1; WAD†

Coleman, Valerie D. Television reporter. STAA

Collins, Daniel A. (1916–). Dentist. HAMA

Coltrane, John William (1926–1967). Saxophonist. COF-1; TEB; WAD†

Conaway, James Bennett. Journalist. STAA

Conyers, John, Jr. (1929–). Congressman. BRGA; DU†; YOI

Coppin, Fanny Jackson (1836–1913). Educator. BRB

Cornish, Samuel E. (19th century). Clergyman, journalist. BEJ

Cortor, Eldzier (1916–). Painter. FAH

Cosby, Bill (1937–). Actor, entertainer. HOBB

Craft, Ellen (c. 1826–1897). Runaway slave. CHFB; LOAV; STAB-1

Craft, William (fl. 1860). Runaway slave. CHFB

Cromwell, Oliver (1753?–1853?). American Revolutionary soldier. ADB; DAF-1†; WIBA

Crummell, Alexander (1819–1898). Missionary. ADA; ADB; BRB†; GRAB-05

Cuffe, Paul (1759–1817). Seaman, colonizer. ADA; ADB; BRB; DOB; GRAB-02; HUB; PECA; WIBA

Cullen, Countee (1903–1946). Poet. ADA; ADB; ROE

Cummings, Terry (1961–). Basketball player. AAS-7

Curry, George E. Journalist. STAA

Curtis, Isaac (1950–). Football player. RUA

Dabney, Austin (fl. 1779–1821). American Revolutionary soldier. DAF-1; WIBA†

Dabney, Mrs. Civil War spy. STQ

Dailey, Ulysses Grant (1885–1961). Surgeon. ADA; ADB

Daniels, Mel. Basketball player. HIBA

Dantley, Adrian (1956–). Basketball player. AAS-7

Darden, Christine (1942–). Aerospace engineer. FOC-1

Dart, Isom, pseud. (1849–1900). Outlaw. KADB

Davis, Belva. Television newscaster. STAA

Davis, Benjamin O. (1877–1970). General. ADA; ADB; FLD

Davis, Benjamin O., Jr. (1912–). General. ADA; ADB; BOG; BRG; FLD; HUB; RIC; STO; STQ

Davis, Benjamin Jefferson (1903–1964). Communist leader. DADA

Davis, Ernie (1939–1963). Football player. CL-04

Davis, Johnny (1955–). Basketball player. AAS-6

Davis, Sammy, Jr. (1925–). Entertainer. DOBA; DOF-1; ROF

Davis, Willie (1934–). Football player. ANA; JOA

Davis, Willie (1940–). Baseball player. LYE

Davison, Frederic Ellis (1917–). General. DRA

Dawson, William Levi (1898–). Composer. ADA; ADB

Dean, Fred (1952–). Football player. AAS-16

De Carava, Roy R. (1919–). Photographer. FAH

Dee, Ruby (1924?–). Actress. FAG

Delany, Martin R. (1812–1885). Ethnologist. ADA; ADB; BRB; GRAB-05

DePriest, James (1936–). Conductor. AB

De Priest, Oscar (1871–1951). Congressman. ADA; ADB; YOI

Derham, James (b. 1762). Physician. BRB†; WIBA

Derricotte, Juliette (1897–1931). Social worker. BUFA

Dett, Robert Nathaniel (1882–1943). Composer. ADA; ADB; BRB†

Dickerson, Eric (1960–). Football player. AAS-35

Dillard, Harrison (1924?–). Track athlete. DAG; DAGA; DAJ; LEYB; PAW

Dixon, Dean (1915–1976). Conductor. ADA; ADB; BOG; HUC; RIC; RICA; STM†

Dixon, Hewritt (1940–). Football player. LEZB

Dodson, Jacob (b. 1825). Explorer. BUH; SCB; STQ

Dolan, Harry (1927–). Author. DADA

Dorsett, Tony Drew (1954–). Football player. AAS-10; DEHB

Dotson, John L., Jr. Journalist. STAA

Douglas, Emory (1943–). Graphic artist. FAI

Douglass, Frederick (1817–1895). Abolitionist. ADA; ADB; AKB; BEJ; BRB; BRBD; BRG; DEDA; GRAB-05; HUA; HUB; JO; JOC; MAT; PECA; ROG; SPB; SQB; STD; STO; WAH; WIAB; YOI

Downing, George Thomas (1819–1903). Civil rights leader, restauranteur. GRAB-01

Draper, Joanna (b. 1854). Author, former slave. DADB

Draughon, Roland (1947–). Journalist. STAA

Drew, Charles Richard (1904–1950). Surgeon. ADA; ADB; DOF-1; FRE; GRAB-03; HA; HAM; HODA; KLA; PECA; RIC; RICA; ROG; STE; STO; STQ†; WEF

Drummond, William J. (1945?–). Journalist. STAA

Du Bois, William Edward Burghardt (1868–1963). Sociologist, editor, author. ADA; ADB; BEJ; BRB; BRBD; DABB; DOF-1; GRAB-01; PECA; RICA; ROG; STB; STJB; STO; YOI

Dunbar, Ernest. Journalist. STAA

Dunbar, Paul Laurence (1872–1906). Poet. ADA; ADB; BEF; BRB; HUA; LEI; ROE; ROG

Duncan, Jim (1946?–). Football player. BELB

Duncan, Marilyn I. (1945?–). Journalist. STAA

Duncanson, Robert S. (1817–1872). Painter. ADA; ADB; BEBA

Dunham, Katherine (1910–). Dancer. ADA; ADB; FOGC; RIC; RICA

Eaton, Roy (1930–). Advertising executive. STAA

Edwards, Harry (1942–). Athlete. AKB

Edwards, William J. (b. 1869). Educator. DADB

Eller, Carl (1942–). Football player. GUF; SMD

Ellington, Anna. Neurologist. BOHE

Ellington, Duke (Edward Kennedy) (1899–1974). Band leader, composer. ADA; ADB; ASB-1; COF-1; DOF-1; HODA; HUC; MOA; RIC; RICA; ROF; TEA; TEB; WAD

Elliott, Robert B. (1842–1884). Congressman. ADA; ADB; BRB; PECA

Erving, Julius (Dr. J.) (1950–). Basketball player. AAS-5; ARB-3; GUEA; GUH; SA-1; SA-2

Evers, Charles (1922–). Mayor. DU; FAG; HAH

Evers, Medgar Wiley (1925–1963). Civil rights leader. DADA†; DOF-1; FLD

Factor, Pompey (d. 1928). Soldier. KADB

Farmer, James (1920–). Civil rights leader. DRA; GRAB-01; STF

Fauset, Crystal Bird (1893–1965). State legislator. LOAV

Feelings, Muriel (1938–). Author. SMAB

Feelings, Tom (1933–). Illustrator. SMAB

Felix, Ray (1930–). Basketball player. HOCA

Ferguson, Angella D. (1925–). Pediatrician. HAMA

Fields, Mary (1832–1914). Pioneer. BUH; GRAB-02; KADB

Fisk Jubilee Singers. Choral group. HUC

Fitzgerald, Ella (1918–). Singer. ASB-1

Flanagan, Tommy (1930–). Pianist. UN

Flipper, Henry Ossian (1856–1940). Army officer. HAP; HODA; KADB

Flood, Curtis Charles (1938–). Baseball player. HOBC

Flora, William (d. 1820). Soldier. DAF-1†; WIBA

Ford, Barney (fl. 1860). Businessman. GRAB-02; KADB

Ford, Phil (1956–). Basketball player. AAS-6

Foreman, Chuck (Walter Eugene) (1950–). Football player. AAS-10; MOCA

Forman, James (1928–). Civil rights leader. HAI

Forten, Charlotte (1838–1904). Abolitionist. CHFB

Forten, James (1766–1842). Abolitionist. ADA;

ADB; BUIB†; DAF-1; EMA; GRAB-03; HAL†; JOC; STQ†; WIBA

Fortune, Amos (c. 1710–1801). Ex-slave. WIBA

Foster, George (1948–). Baseball player. AAS-4; GUED-01

Foster, Gloria (1936–). Actress. AB

Francis, Miriam B. (1930–). Artist. FAI

Franklin, Aretha (1942–). Singer. AB; BUIB-1; JOE

Franklin, John Hope (1915–). Historian, educator. ADB; FLD

Frazier, Joe (1944–). Boxer. ASBA; BELB; GEDA

Frazier, Walt (1945–). Basketball player. ARB-4; DEHA-1; GUEA; SA; SA-1; SA-2

Free, "World B" (Lloyd) (1953–). Basketball player. AAS-8

Fuller, Solomon Carter (1872–1953). Psychiatrist, pathologist. HAMA

Gannet, Deborah Sampson (fl. 1776). American Revolutionary patriot. AND; CLC; HODA; RAD; ROG; STQ†; WIBA

Garcia (fl. 1813). Runaway slave, Indian leader. KADB

Garnet, Henry Highland (1815–1882). Abolitionist. ADA; ADB; BEJ; BRB†; GRAB-05; ROG

Garrett, Michael Lockett (1944–). Football player. BEKB; LEZB

Gaston, Arthur George (1892–). Insurance executive. ADA; ADB

Gervin, George (1952–). Basketball player. AAS-8

Gibbs, Mifflin W. (1828–1903). Jurist. KADB

Gibson, Althea (1927–). Tennis player. AAS-29; BOF; BRG; FOG; FR-1; HOBA; HOBAA; HOBC; LOAA; PIB; PIBA; RICA; ROJ; RYA†; SMC; SUDA†; VAE

Gibson, Bob (Robert) (1935–). Baseball player. BUJ†; DEG; FRC-1†; FRD; KADA; LEZ; MUB-1; PAW; PRA; RIGA†; SA-3; SHA

Gibson, Josh (1911–1947). Baseball player. AAS-24; DAFD

Gibson, Kenneth Allen (1932–). Mayor. BRGA; DU; HAH

Giggans, Jim. Television newscaster. STAA

Gillespie, Dizzy (John Birks) (1917–). Trumpeter. TEA; TEB; UN; WAD†

Gillespie, Frank L. (1867–1925). Insurance executive. ADB

Gilliam, John Rally (1945–). Football player. SMI

Gilmore, Artis (1948–). Basketball player. AAS-5; SA-1

Gilpin, Charles Sidney (1878–1930). Actor. ADA; ADB; DOF-1

Goings, William (fl. 1821). Rancher. KADB

Goldberg, Whoopi (1950–). Actress. MASB

Gomez, Manuel (1949–). Artist. FAI

Goodwin, Ruby Berkley (1903–). Poet. DADB

Gordon, Dexter (1923–). Saxophonist. UN

Goreleigh, Rex (1903–). Painter. FAH

Gourdine, Meredith (1929–). Physicist. CAF-1

Grant, M. Earl (1891?–). Financier. DRA

Grant, Micki. Actress, composer, singer. AB

Gray, Ida (1867–1953). Dentist. LOAV

Gray, Leon (1951–). Football player. AAS-11

Greaves, Clifton (b. 1858?). Buffalo soldier. BUH

Green, Charlie. Track athlete. LYE

Green, Dick (fl. 1847). Pioneer. SCB

Green, Nancy (c. 1834–1923). Posed as "Aunt Jemima". GRAB-02

Green, Patricia (1952–). A.M.E. Zion minister. SMBB-1

Greene, Joe (1946–). Football player. RUA

Greenfield, Elizabeth Taylor (1809–1876). Singer. LOAV; ROF†

Greer, Hal. Basketball player. HIBA

Gregory, Dick (1932–). Entertainer. DADB; EOB; RICA

Grier, Rosie (Roosevelt) (1932–). Football player. AAS-32

Griffin, Archie (1954–). Football player. DEHB

Griffith, Emile (1938–). Boxer, trainer. DEHA-1

Griggs, Sutton E. (1873–1930). Clergyman. KADB

Grimké, Archibald Henry (1849–1930). Lawyer. DOF-1; ROG

Grimké, Francis James (1850–1937). Clergyman, civil rights leader. BRB†; GRAB-01

Haizlip, Ellis. Television producer. AB

Haley, Alex (1921–). Author. DOF-1; STAA

Hall, Horathel (1928?–). Weaver. FAI

Hall, Lloyd Augustus (1894–1971). Food chemist. CAF-1; GRAB-03; HA

Hall, Prince (1735?–1807). Abolitionist. ADA; ADB; BEJ; GRAB-05; PECA

Hamer, Fannie Lou (1917–). Civil rights leader. BRBE†; DU; FAG; GRAB-01

Hammon, Briton (fl. 1747–1759). Indian captive. HAP

Hammon, Jupiter (1720?–1800). Poet. CL; ROE

Handy, William Christopher (1873–1958). Composer. ADA; ADB; BAD; HUA; MOA; ROG; WAD

Hansberry, Lorraine (1930–1965). Playwright. FLBA

Harper, Frances Ellen Watkins (1825–1911). Poet. LOAV; ROE; ROG; WABC†

Harris, Franco (1950–). Football player. AAS-10; GUCA; GUH; LIBB

Harris, James. Football player. CL-1

Harris, Patricia R. (1924–1985). Ambassador, educator. YOI

Harris, Tonie (1947–). Martial artist. AT

Harrison, Richard Berry (1864–1935). Actor. ADA; ADB; DOF-1

Hart, Eddie (1948–). Track athlete. AAS-24

Hastie, William Henry (1904–1976). Jurist. ADA†; ADB†; DOF-1

Hatcher, Richard Gordon (1933–). Mayor. BRGA; DRA; DU†; FAG; HAH; YOI

Hawkins, Coleman (1904–). Saxophonist. COF-1; WAD†

Hawkins, Connie (1942–). Basketball player. AAS-24; DEHA-1; SA

Hayes, Bob (Robert Lee) (1942–). Football player, track athlete. ANB; CO; DAFB; DAJ; DEHA; KADA; OCA; ST-1

Hayes, Elvin (1945–). Basketball player. AAS-5; PE; SA

Hayes, Lester (1955–). Football player. AAS-13

Hayes, Roland (1887–1976). Singer. ADA; ADB; BRB†; DOF-1; HUC

Haymond, Alvin Henry (1942–). Football player. LEZB

Haynes, George Edmund (1880–1960). Sociologist. GRAB-01

Haynes, Lemuel (1753–1833). Clergyman. ADA; BRB†; BUIB†; DAF-1†; STQ†; WIBA

Haynes, Mike (1953–). Football player. AAS-13

Haywood, Spencer (1949–). Basketball player. LOAA; SA; SA-1

Healy, James Augustine (1830–1900). Bishop. ADA; ADB

Hector, Edward (d. 1834). American Revolutionary soldier. DAF-1†; WIBA

Henderson, Fletcher (1898–1952). Band leader. COF-1; WAD†

Hendrix, Jimi (1942–1970). Guitarist. BUIB-1

Henry, Algernon P. Radio engineer. BOG

Henson, Josiah (1789–1883). Abolitionist. CAHA; GRAB-05

Henson, Matthew Alexander (1866–1955). Arctic explorer. ADA; ADB; BRB; BRG; COLA†; DOC†; GRAB-02; HAM; HAQ; HODA; HUB; JOC; LEI; PECA; ROG; STQ

Hickman, Robert T. (b. 1831). Escaped slave. KADB

Hicks, Nancy. Journalist. STAA

Hill, Calvin (1947–). Football player. AAS-25; LEZB

Hines, Earl Kenneth (1905–1983). Pianist. COF-1; UN; WAD†

Hinton, Alfred (1940–). Painter. FAI

Hinton, William A. (1883–1959). Pathologist. BRB†; HAMA

Holiday, Billie (1915–1959). Singer. BRBD; COF-1; JOE; SUH; TEA; TEB; WAD†

Holland, Jerome H. (1916–). Diplomat, football player. HOBB

Hooks, Earl (1927–). Sculptor, ceramist. FAH

Hope, John (1868–1936). Educator. ADA; ADB; BRB; DOF-1

Hopkins, Lightnin' (Sam) (1912–1982). Singer. SUH

Horne, Lena (1917–). Singer. DADB; DOBA; DOF-1; HUC; LEHB; ROF

Horton, George Moses (1798?–1880). Poet. CL

Houston, Charles Hamilton (1895–1950). Lawyer. ADA†; ADB†; DOF-1

Houston, Ken (1944–). Football player. RUA

Howard, Elston (1930–1980). Baseball player. HIC; HOCM; PRA; SHD; SHF; ZAA

Hudson, Lou (1944–). Basketball player. SA

Huggins, Edith. Television newscaster. STAA

Hughes, Langston (1902–1967). Author. ADA; ADB; BRBD; CAGA; DADB; DOF-1; JO; LEJ; RIC; RICA; ROE

Hull, Agrippa (1759?–1848?). American Revolutionary soldier. DAF-1

Hunt, Alexander Henry (1866–1938). Educator. DOF-1

Hunt, Richard H. (1935–). Sculptor. ADB

Hunter, Alberta (1895–1984). Singer. GIB-1

Hunter-Gault, Charlayne (1942?–). Broadcast journalist. GLO; STAA

Ikard, Bose (b. 1847). Cowboy. BUH; HODA; KADB; SCB; STQ

Jackson, David L. (1940?–). Journalist. STAA

Jackson, Harold (1946–). Football player. RUC

Jackson, Jesse Louis (1941–). Clergyman, civil rights leader. DRA; GRAB-01

Jackson, Mahalia (1911–1972). Singer. HUC; JOE

Jackson, Michael (1958–). Singer. BUIB-2

Jackson, Nell (1929–). Track athlete, educator. BOHA

Jackson, Reggie (1946–). Baseball player. AAS-4; BRAA; GUG

Jackson, Saunders (fl. 1849). Pioneer. HODA; SCB

Jackson, Shirley. Theoretical physicist. CAF-1

Jackson, Suzanne (1944–). Painter. FOGB

Jamison, Judith (1944–). Dancer. BOHB; FOGC

Jarrett, Vernon D. (1921–). Educator. STAA

Jasper, John (1812–1901). Clergyman. ADA; ADB; BRB

Jefferson, John (1956–). Football player. AAS-18

Jefferson, Lemon (1897–1930). Singer. ADB; COF-1; SUH; WAD†

Jeffrey, Major (fl. 1776). American Revolutionary soldier. WIBA

Jeffries, Rosalind (1930?–). Painter. FAI

Jenkins, Carol (1944–). Television newscaster. STAA

Jenkins, Ferguson Arthur (1943–). Baseball player. BUJB; GUB-1; GUG; KLCA; RIGA†

Johnson, Campbell C. (1921–). Chemical engineer. CAF-1

Johnson, Charles Spurgeon (1893–1956). Sociologist. ADA; ADB

Johnson, Earvin "Magic" (1959–). Basketball player. AAS-6

Johnson, Gary "Big Hands" (1952–). Football player. AAS-16

Johnson, Gus. Basketball player. HIBA

Johnson, Henry (b. 1859). Soldier. BUH

Johnson, Henry (1897–1929). Soldier, WWI. BRB†; HUB; STQ†

Johnson, Jack (John Arthur) (1878–1946?). Boxer. BRBD; RAAC

Johnson, James Weldon (1871–1938). Author. ADA; ADB; BRB†; DOF-1; GRAB-02; JO; RIC; RICA; ROE; ROG; STB

Johnson, John, Jr. Television producer-director. STAA

Johnson, John H. (1918–). Publisher. ADA; ADB; DOF-1; DRA; PAA; STAA†

Johnson, Lonnie (1889–1970). Singer. SUH

Johnson, Malvin Gray (1896–1934). Painter. ADA; ADB

Johnson, Marques (1956–). Basketball player. AAS-5

Johnson, Mordecai Wyatt (1890–1976). Educator. ADA; ADB; BRB; DOF-1; RIC

Johnson, Pete (1954–). Football player. AAS-32

Johnson, Rafer (1934–). Track athlete. DAJ; FIB; HOBC; HOC; LEYB

Johnson, Ronald Adolphus (1947–). Football player. GUCA; LEZB; ST

Johnson, Thomas A. (1928–). Journalist. STAA

Johnson, Willie (1902–1949). Singer. SUH

Johnston, Ernest, Jr. (1939?–). Journalist. STAA

Johnston, Joshua (1770–1830). Painter. BEBA; WIBA

Jones, Absalom (b. 1747). Clergyman. BRB

Jones, Dave "Deacon" (1938–). Football player. ANA; KADA

Jones, Frederick McKinley (1892–1961). Inventor. GRAB-03; HAL

Jones, James Earl (1931–). Actor. AB

Jones, John (1816–1879). Business executive. ADA; ADB; GRAB-05; KADB

Jones, K. C. (1932–). Basketball player, coach. ARB-2

Jones, Lawrence. Painter. FAH

Joplin, Scott (1868–1917). Pianist, composer. COF-1

Jordan, Barbara C. (1936–). Congresswoman. BOHF; GRAB-1; YOI

Julian, Percy Lavon (1899–1975). Chemist. ADA; ADB; DOF-1; FLD; GRAB-03; HA; KLA; STO

Just, Ernest Everett (1883–1941). Biologist. ADA; ADB; BRB†; CAF-1; DOF-1; GRAB-03; HA; HAM; KLA

Karenga (Ronald McKinley Everett) (1941–). Black Muslim leader. HAI

Kay, Ulysses (1917–). Composer. ADB; POF

Kearse, Amalya (1937–). Jurist. GLO

Keith, Damon Jerome (1922–). Jurist. DOF-1

Kelly, Leroy (1942–). Football player. BEKB; DUF; FRD; LEZB

King, Bernard (1956–). Basketball player. AAS-8

King, Coretta Scott (1927–). Civil rights leader. FAG; GIBA

King, John B. (1908–). Educator. FLD

King, Martin Luther, Jr. (1929–1968). Clergyman, civil rights leader. AAS-34; ADA; ADB; ASB-1; BAF; BRBD; BRG; DEJ; DOF-1; DU-1; ELA; FAA; FEC; FLD; GRAB-01; HAJ; HODA; JO; JOC; KE; LEPE; MEB; MEC; RICA; STO; WEB; WIAA-8; WIC; YOA; YOI

Kirk, Roland (1936–1976). Multi-instrumentalist. UN

Kitt, Eartha (1928–). Singer. DADB; ROF

Koontz, Elizabeth (1919–). Educator, civil rights activist. GIB-1

Koontz, Roscoe L. (1922–). Health physicist. CAF-1

Kountz, Samuel. Surgeon. CAF-1

Ladd, Ernie (1938–). Football player. AAS-32

LaFontant, Jewel Stradford (1922–). Lawyer. SWI

Lamson, David (fl. 1775). American Revolutionary patriot. WIBA

Lane, Dick (1928–). Football player. ANA

Lane, Lunsford (b. 1803). Abolitionist. DADA

Lane, MacArthur (1942–). Football player. LEZB

Laney, Lucy (1854–1933). Educator. BRB; BUDA†

Langford, Anna Riggs (1917–). Lawyer. DRA; DU

Langston, John Mercer (1829–1897). Educator, diplomat. ADA; ADB; BRB

Lanier, Bob (1948–). Basketball player. CL-06; KLC; RUB

Lanier, Willie Edward (1945–). Football player. GUD; SMJ

Latham, Lambert. American Revolutionary patriot. DAF-1

Latimer, Lewis Howard (1848–1928). Inventor. GRAB-03; HA; HAL; HODA; KLA; STQ

Lawless, Theodore Kenneth (1892–1971). Dermatologist. ADA; ADB; BRB†; CAF-1; DOF-1

Lawrence, Geraldine Anderson. Border Patrol agent. SMBC-3

Lawrence, Jacob (1917–). Painter. ADA; ADB; BEBA; DOF-1; FAH; RIC; RICA

Leadbelly (Huddie Ledbetter) (1888–1949). Singer. COF-1; HUC; SUH; WAD†

Lee, Canada (1907–1951). Boxer, actor. ADA; ADB; SCA

Lee, Joseph (1849–1905?). Inventor. GRAB-03

LeFlore, Ron (1948–). Baseball player. AAS-27

Leidesdorff, William Alexander (1810–1848). Merchant. ADA; ADB; BUH; GRAB-02; KADB

Lew, Brazillai (b. 1743). American Revolutionary soldier. WIBA

Lewis, Edmonia (1845–1890). Sculptor. ADA; ADB; KADB; ROG

Lewis, Fritz (Fred) (1944–). Basketball player. HIBAA

Lewis, Furry (Walter) (1900–). Singer. SUH

Lewis, James (1832–1897?). Government official. ADA; ADB

Lewis, James E. (1923–). Sculptor. FAH

Lewis, John (1940?–). Civil rights leader. STF

Lewis, Mary Edmonia (1846–1890). Sculptor. LOAV

Light, Allen B. (fl. 1836). Pioneer. SCB; WIBA

Lipscomb, Gene "Big Daddy" (1931–). Football player. AAS-32

Little, Floyd Douglas (1942–). Football player. DUF; LEZB; RUC

Little, Larry (1945–). Football player. GUD; RUA

Locke, Alain Leroy (1886–1954). Educator. ADA; ADB

Logan, Arthur Courtney (1909–1973). Surgeon. HAMA

Logan, Greenbury (fl. 1831). Rancher. KADB

Logan, Myra Adele (1908–1977). Surgeon. HA-1; RAAG†

Logan, Rayford Whittingham (1897–1982). Historian. DOF-1

Lomax, Almena. Journalist. STAA

Long, Jefferson Franklin (1836–1900). Congressman. ADA; ADB

Long, Loretta. Actress. BOHD

Lott, Ronnie (1959–). Football player. AAS-13

Louis, Joe (1914–1981). Boxer. ASB-1; ASBA; BELB; BOF; DAG; DAGA; HEG; HOC; LEF; LYE; PAW; RAAC; RIC; RICA; SICA

Louvestre, Mary (fl. 1861). Slave. HAB

Love, Bob. Basketball player. HIBA

Love, Nat (1854–1921). Cowboy. BRBD; KADB

Lucas, John (1953–). Basketball player. AAS-6

Lucas, Maurice (1952–). Basketball player. AAS-7

LuValle, James E. Chemist. BOG

Lynch, John Roy (1847–1939). Congressman. ADA; ADB

Mabley, Jackie "Moms" (1897–1975). Comedienne. MASB

McAdoo, Bob (1951–). Basketball player. AAS-5; ARB-1; RUB; SA-2

McCabe, Edwin P. (b. 1850). Politician. KADB

McClennan, Tommy (1908–1958?). Singer. SUH

McCovey, Willie Lee (1938–). Baseball player. DA; KLB; RIGA†

McCoy, Elijah (1843–1929). Inventor. ADB; BRB†; GRAB-03; HA; HAL; KLA; STQ†

McCullough, Geraldine (1922–). Sculptor. ADB

McGee, Henry W. (1910–). Government employee. YOI

McGhee, Brownie (Walter Brown) (1915–). Singer. SUH

McGinnis, George (1950–). Basketball player. ARB-3; SA-1

McIntyre, Ken (1931–). Multi-instrumentalist. UN

McJunkin, George (1851–1922). Cowboy. KAW

McKay, Claude (1890–1948). Author, poet. ADA; ADB; BRB†

Mackey, John (1942–). Football player. AAS-19; CO; HOBC

McKinney, Nina Mae (1913–1967). Actress. LOAV

McKissick, Floyd B. (1922–). Civil rights leader. FAG; HAI; YOI

McNair, Ronald (1950–1986). Astronaut, physicist. COE-1

Mahoney, Mary Eliza (1845–1926). Nurse. LOAV

Malcolm X (1925–1965). Leader. ADB; AKB; BRBD; DABB; DADB; FAG; GRAB-01; HAI; HAK; HODA; JO; RICA

Malone, Moses (1955–). Basketball player. AAS-5; AAS-7; HOCG

Manning, Madeline (1948–). Track athlete. SUDB

Marion. Runaway. BEOA

Marrant, John (fl. 1755). Missionary. HAP; WIBA

Marshall, Jim (James Lawrence) (1937–). Football player. SMD

Marshall, Paule (1929–). Author. GLO

Marshall, Thurgood (1908–). Supreme Court justice. ADA; ADB; BRG; DOF-1; FAG; FLC; FLD; STF; WEC; YOI

Martin, Harvey (1950–). Football player. AAS-16

Mason, Biddy (1818–1891). Businesswoman. BUH; GRAB-02; KADB; STQ†

Massiah, Frederick McDonald (b. 1884). Civil engineer, born West Indies. CAF-1

Matney, William C., Jr. Television newscaster. STAA

Matson, Ollie (1930–). Football player. HAD; RAAE

Matthews, Vincent Edward (1947–). Track athlete, wood sculptor. BOHA

Matzeliger, Jan Ernst (1852–1889). Inventor. ADA; ADB; BRB†; BRG; GRAB-03; HA; HAL; KLA; PECA; ROG; STQ†

May, Emmett M. Labor organizer. BOG

Mayberry, John Claiborn (1950–). Baseball player. KLCA

Maynard, Valerie (1937–). Sculptor. FAI

Mays, Benjamin E. (1895–1984). Educator. ADB; DOF-1

Mays, Willie Howard (1931–). Baseball player. ASBA; BOE; BOF; BRG; BUD-1; BUJ; DA; DAA; DAFB; DAFD; DAGA; DAH; DEE; DEHA-1; FRC-1†; FRD; GEC; GIB; GR; GUC; GUE; HAF; HOC; KADA; LEV; MUB-1; MUC; PRA; RAAA; RIC; RICA; RIGA†; ROC; SA-3; SH; SHB; SHF; SHH; SID; VEA

Meminger, Dean (1948–). Basketball player. HIBAA

Meredith, James Howard (1933–). Civil rights leader. DADA†; FLD; STJB

Merrick, John (1859–1919). Insurance executive. ADB; BRB

Mesa, Antonio. Pioneer. SCB

Millar, Onnie (1918–). Painter, sculptor. FAI

Miller, Dorie (1919–1943). Naval hero. HODA; HUB; RIC; STQ†

Mingus, Charles (1922–1979). Bassist. UN

Mitchell, Arthur (1934–). Dancer, choreographer. AB

Mitchell, Arthur Wergs (1883–1968). Congressman. ADA; ADB

Mitchell, Bobby (1935–). Football player. ANB; DEHA-1

Mitchell, Clarence, Jr. (1911–1984). Civil rights leader. DOF-1

Mitchell, Clarence, III (1939?–). State legislator. DU

Mitchell, John R., Jr. (1863–1929). Journalist, reformer. GRAB-01

Monk, Theolonius (1920–1982). Pianist. COF-1; WAD†

Monroe, Earl (1946?–). Basketball player. HOCA; PE; SA-2

Montgomery, Wilbert (1954–). Football player. AAS-10

Moody, Anne (1940–). Civil rights worker. AKB; DADB

Moore, Carman (1936–). Music critic, composer. AB

Moore, Harry Tyson (1905–1951). Civil rights leader. DOF-1

Moore, Lenny (1933–). Football player. BEKB; HAE; RAAE

Morgan, Garrett A. (1875–1963). Manufacturer. ADA; ADB; GRAB-03; HA; HAL; KLA; STQ†

Morgan, Joe (1943–). Baseball player. AAS-23; BUJC; RIGA†; SMF

Morgan, Norma (1928–). Painter. FAH

Morisey, A. Alexander. Public relations executive. STAA

Morris, Ed (fl. 1861). Pioneer. SCB

Morris, Mercury (Eugene) (1947–). Football player. MOCA

Morton, "Jelly Roll" (Ferdinand Joseph) (1885–1941). Pianist. COF-1; HUC; WAD†

Motley, Constance Baker (1921–). Jurist. DU; FLD; GIB-1; STLA; YOI

Motley, Marion (1920–). Football player. DAFG; SUD

Moton, Robert Russa (1867–1940). Educator. BRB; DOF-1

Mulzac, Hugh Nathaniel (1886–1971). Sea captain, born West Indies. HUB; ROG; STF

Murphy, Calvin (1948–). Basketball player. AAS-23; HIBAA; KLC

Murphy, Carl James (1889–1967). Journalist, civil rights leader. DOF-1

Murphy, Isaac (1856–1896). Jockey. HOBC

Myers, Isaac (1835–1891). Labor leader. ADB; GRAB-01

Nance, Jim (1942–). Football player. LEZB; LIBA

Neals, Otto (1931?–). Sculptor. FAI

Nell, William Cooper (1816–1874). Author. CHFB; GRAB-05

Newsome, Effie Lee (b. 1885). Poet. ROE

Newsome, Ozzie (1956–). Football player. AAS-19

Newton, Huey P. (1942–). Civil rights leader. HAI

Nixon, Norm (1955–). Basketball player. AAS-6

Noble, Gil. Television newscaster. STAA

Norton, Eleanor Holmes (1937–). Lawyer. GIB-1; LETD; WA

Obey, Trudel Mimms. Painter. FAI

Odoms, Riley (1950–). Football player. AAS-19

Oliver, Joe (1885–1938). Cornetist. TEA; TEB; WAD†

Oliver, Kermit (1943–). Painter. FAI

O'Neal, John. Civil rights worker. COF

O'Neal, Regina. Television producer. FOC-1

O'Neal, Ron. Actor. AB

Osborne, Estelle Massey (1903–). Nurse. YOB

Outterbridge, John W. (1933–). Painter, sculptor. FAI

Overton, Anthony (1865–1946). Banker. ADA; ADB; DOF-1; FLD

Owens, Jesse (1913–1980). Track athlete. ASB-1; ASBA; BOF; BOHA; BRB†; DAFB; DAG; DAGA; DAJ; DEF; HEG; HIA; HOC; HODA; LEYB; LYB; OCA; RIC; RICA; SID; VAE

Pacheco, Luis (1800–1895). Guide and interpreter. HAP

Page, Alan (1945–). Football player. GUD; SMD; ST

Paige, Satchel (Leroy) (1906–1982). Baseball player. ASBA; BOF; BRC; BUD-1; DAFC; DAFD; DAH; FRC-1†; LIAA†; SMK

Palmer, L. F., Jr. (1923?–). Journalist. STAA

Parker, Charlie (1920–1955). Saxophonist. COF-1; TEB; RICA; WAD†

Parks, David (1944–). Soldier. AKB

Parks, Gordon Alexander Buchanan (1912–). Photographer. ADA; ADB; DOF-1

Parks, Rosa Lee (1913–). Civil rights leader. COG-1; DOF-1; STF

Patterson, Floyd (1935–). Boxer. DADB; DEF; DEHA-1; LEYB; OCA

Patterson, Lawrence Patrick. Editor. STAA

Paul, Thomas (1773–1831). Clergyman. ADA; ADB

Payne, Daniel Alexander (1811–1893). Bishop. ADA; ADB; BRB

Payton, Walter (1954–). Football player. AAS-10; AAS-35

Pearson, Drew (1951–). Football player. AAS-18

Pennington, James W. C. (c. 1809–1870). Civil rights leader, clergyman. GRAB-02

Peoples, Woody (1943–). Football player. AAS-9

Perkins, Don. Football player. BEKB

Perkins, Marion (1908–1961). Sculptor. ADA; ADB

Perry, Jean. Journalist. STAA

Perry, Joe (Fletcher) (1927–). Football player. HAD; RAAE

Perry, William (1962–). Football player. AAS-32

Petry, Ann (1911–). Author. RIC; RICA

Phelps, Don G. (1929?–). Radio and television commentator. STAA

Phillips, Bertrand (1938–). Painter, photographer. FAI

Phillips, Vel (1924–). Government official. YOI

Pickens, William (1881–1954). Government official. DADA; DADB

Pickett, Bill (1861–1932). Cowboy. GRAB-02; HODA; KADB; STQ†; WAA

Pinchback, Pinckney Benton Stewart (1837–1921). Political leader. ADA; ADB; BRB†; CHFB

Pippin, Horace (1888–1946). Painter. ADA; ADB; BEBA

Pittman, Dorothy Hughes (1938–). Educator. WA

Pleasant, Mary Ellen (Mammy) (1814?–1904). Businesswoman. BUH; LOAV; STQ†; WIAA-2

Plunkett, Sherman (1933–). Football player. AAS-32

Pointe de Sable, Jean Baptiste (1745–1818). Founder of Chicago, born Haiti. ADA; ADB; BUH; DOB; GRAB-02; HUB; KADB; LEI; LEPD; PECA; ROG; STQ; WIBA

Pointer, Dick (d. 1827). American Revolutionary patriot. WIBA

Poitier, Sidney (1924–). Actor. ADB; BRG; ROF

Pollard, Frederick (1894–1986). Football player. DAFB; DAFG; DAI; HOBC

Pompey. Slave, American Revolutionary patriot. ROG; WIBA†

Pompey (d. 1788). Indian captive and interpreter. HAP

Poor, Salem. American Revolutionary patriot. DAF-1†; STQ†; WIBA

Porter, Kevin (1950–). Basketball player. AAS-6

Poston, Ersa Hines (1921–). State official. YOI

Poston, Ted (1906–). Journalist. STAA

Pouissant, Renee (1944–). Television newscaster. SMBB-2

Powell, Adam Clayton, Sr. (1865–1953). Clergyman. ADA; ADB; BRB†; RIC

Powell, Adam Clayton, Jr. (1908–1972). Congressman, clergyman. DU†; HAI; YOI

Powell, Bud (Earl) (1924–1966). Pianist. COF-1; WAD†

Powell, Clilian (1894–). Physician, insurance executive. CAF-1

Powell, Marvin (1955–). Football player. AAS-11

Price, Florence Beatrice Smith (1888–1933). Composer. LOAV

Price, Leontyne (1927–). Singer. ADB; DOF-1; ROF; SAB; SC-02

Pride, Charley (1938–). Singer. BUIB-01; KRI

Prince, Lucy Terry (1731–1821). Poet. KADB

Proctor, Barbara Gardner (1932–). Advertising executive. FRBD

Prosser, Gabriel (1775–1800). Insurrectionist. BRB†; EMA; HUB; ROG

Pruitt, Greg (1951–). Football player. AAS-10; AAS-23

Purvis, Robert (1810–1898). Abolitionist. GRAB-05

Rainey, Ma (Gertrude Malissa Nix Pridgett) (1886–1939). Singer. JOE; SUH; WAD†

Randolph, Asa Philip (1889–1979). Labor leader. ADA; ADB; BRG; COH; DABA; DADA; DOF-1; FLD; GRAB-01; HUA; LEHA; RIC; RICA; SEA; STF; WIAA-8; YOI

Rapier, James T. (1839–1884). Congressman. ADA; ADB; BU

Rashad, Ahmad (Bobby Moore) (1949–). Football player, sportscaster. AAS-18

Raspberry, William J. (1935?–). Columnist. STAA

Reed, Willis (1942–). Basketball player. BEL; FRD; PAW; PE; RAAB

Reeves, Bass (1840–1910). Lawman. KADB

Remond, Charles Lenox (1810–1873). Abolitionist. GRAB-05

Remond, Sarah Parker (1826–1894). Abolitionist. GRAB-05

Revels, Hiram Rhoades (1822–1901). Senator. ADA; ADB; BRB†; BU; YOI

Ribeiro, Alfonso. Actor. BRF-1

Rice, Jim (1950–). Baseball player. AAS-4; RIGA†

Riding, Henry (fl. 1865). Pioneer. SCB

Riles, Wilson (1917–). Educator. DOF-1

Rillieux, Norbert (1806–1894). Engineer. ADA; ADB; GRAB-03; HA; HAL; HODA; KLA; ROG

Ringgold, Faith. Painter. FAH

Rivers, Sam (1930–). Multi-instrumentalist. UN

Robertson, Isaiah. Football player. SMJ

Robertson, Oscar (1938–). Basketball player. BEL; DEHA-1; ETA; FRD; HEHA; HID; HOC; PE

Robeson, Paul (1898–1976). Singer, actor, football player. ADA; ADB; DAFG; DOBA; DOF-1; JO; RICA; ROF

Robinson, Bill "Bojangles" (1878–1949). Dancer. HUC; RIC; ROF

Robinson, Dave. Football player. HAGB; JOA; KABA

Robinson, Frank (1935–). Baseball player. BRD; DA; KADA; LIC; PEC; PRA; RIGA†; SMG

Robinson, Harry A. (1942–). Journalist. STAA

Robinson, Jackie (John Roosevelt) (1919–1972). Baseball player. ALB; ASB-1; BELB; BOE; BOF; BRD; BRG; BUD-1; BUJA; DAFB; DAFC; DAFD; DAG; DAGA; DAH; DOF-1; FLD; FRC-1†; GEB; GUC; GUDA; HOBC; HOC; HUA; JOC; KLB; LEY†; LOAA; RIGA†; ROC; SCA; SHF; SHH; SMK; STO; VAE

Robinson, James (1753–1868). Soldier. WIBA

Robinson, Paul. Football player. BEKB

Robinson, Ray (1921–). Boxer. ASBA; BOF; DAG; DAGA; HOC

Rollins, Sonny (1929–). Saxophonist. UN

Rose, Edward (d. 1834). Pioneer. BUH; HAP; SCB

Ross, Diana (1944–). Singer, actress. AB; BOHC; BUIB-2

Ross, Ruth N. Journalist. STAA

Roundfield, Dan (1953–). Basketball player. AAS-7

Rowan, Carl Thomas (1925–). Author. SQB; STAA; YOI

Rudolph, Wilma G. (1940–). Track athlete. DAFB; DAJ; GEA; GED; GEDA; HIA; HOBA; HOBAA; JAB; LEYB; LYD; OCA; RYA

Ruffin, Josephine St. Pierre (1842–1924). Civil rights leader. GRAB-01

Ruffin, Nate. Football player. BELB

Ruggles, David (1810–1849). Abolitionist. GRAB-05

Russell, William Felton (1934–). Basketball player. ASBA; BEL; DEF; HEHA; HID; HOBC; HOC; KADA; KLBA; LEW; PE; RAAB; RICA

Russwurm, John B. (1799–1851). Journalist. ADB; BEJ

Rustin, Bayard (1910–1987). Civil rights leader. FAG; YOI

Salem, Peter (1750?–1816). American Revolutionary patriot. ADB; BRG; BUIB†; DAF-1; DOB; ROG; STQ†; WIBA

Sanders, Charlie (1946–). Football player. AAS-19; DEHA

Savage, Augusta Christine (1900–1962). Sculptor. BEBA

Sayers, Gale (1943–). Football player. BEKB; BELB; COFB; DAFG; DAI; DUF; FRD; HAD; KADA; LEZB; LIB; LIBB; RAAE

Scarborough, William Saunders (1852–1926). Educator. ADA; ADB; BRB†

Schomberg, Arthur Alfonso (1874–1938). Historian. ADB

Scott, Austin. Journalist. STAA

Scott, Charlie. Basketball player. HIBA

Scott, Dred (1795?–1858). Slave. KADB

Scott, George (1943–). Baseball player. KLBB; LEY

Scott, Hazel (1920–1981). Pianist. BOG

Selmon, Lee Roy (1954–). Football player. AAS-16

Shaw, Earl (1937–). Physicist. CAF-1

Shaw, Leslie N. (1922–). Business executive. YOI

Shepherd, John (1932?–). Businessman. DRA

Shuttlesworth, Fred (1922–). Clergyman, civil rights worker. STF

Silas, James (1949–). Basketball player. AAS-9

Silver, Horace (1928–). Composer, pianist. UN

Silvera, Frank (1914–). Actor. ADA; ADB

Simms, Jacob E. Journalist. STAA

Simpson, O. J. (Orenthal James) (1947–). Football player, sports commentator. AAS-10; AAS-35; DEHA-1; DEHB; DUF; GUCA; GUEB; KADA; LEZB; LIBB; MOCA; RUA; ST

Sims, Tom L. Advertising executive. STAA

Singleton, Benjamin "Pap" (1809–1892). Leader. ADA; ADB; BUH

Smalls, Robert (1839–1915). Naval figure, congressman. ADA; ADB; HODA; HUB; JOC; PECA; ROG; STD; STJB

Smith, Alfred J., Jr. (1949–). Painter. FAI

Smith, Bessie (1894–1937). Singer. HUC; JOE; SUH; TEA; TEB; WAD†

Smith, Charles "Bubba" (1948–). Football player. AAS-32; LIB; SMD

Smith, Linda. Dentist. FOC-1

Smith, Vicki. Judo expert. LYE

Smythe, John H. (1844–1908). Diplomat, lawyer. ADA; ADB

Sousa, Mathias (fl. 1642). Colonist. WIBA

Spaulding, Asa Timothy (1902–). Insurance executive. FLD

Spaulding, Charles Clinton (1874–1952). Insurance executive. ADA; ADB; HUA; PECA; STQ†

Spurgeon, James Robert (1870–1942). Diplomat. FLD

Stallworth, John (1952–). Football player. AAS-18

Stance, Emanuel (b. 1851?). Buffalo soldier. BUH

Stanup, Richard (1748–1862). Slave. WIBA

Stargell, Willie (Wilver Dornel) (1941–). Baseball player. AAS-4; RIGA†

Stark, Shirley (1927–). Sculptor. FAI

Staupers, Mable Keaton (1890–). Nurse, civil rights leader, born West Indies. DOF-1

Stevenson, Sybil Jordan. Telecommunications executive. HOD-1

Steward, Susan McKinney (1848–1918). Physician. LOAV

Stewart, Ella Phillips (1893–). Pharmacologist. LOAV

Stewart, Ellen. Theater producer, founder. GIB-1; GLO

Stewart, John (1786?–1823?). Missionary. HAP

Stewart, Maria W. (1803–1879). Abolitionist. GRAB-05; WABC†

Still, Art (1955–). Football player. AAS-16

Still, William (1821–1902). Underground railroad leader. ADA; ADB; GRAB-05

Still, William Grant (1895–1978). Composer. ADA; ADB; HUC; POF; RIC; RICA

Stingley, Darryl (1951–). Football player. AAS-24

Stokes, Carl B. (1927–). Mayor. BRGA; DU; FAG; GRBA; HAH; YOI

Stokes, Maurice (1933–). Basketball player. HID; HOCA

Strachan, John R. (1916–). Government worker. YOI

Stroyer, Jacob (b. 1846). Author. DADB

Sullivan, Leon Howard (1922–). Clergyman, civil rights leader. DOF-1; EOA

Summer, Donna (1948–). Singer. BUIB-1

Sutton, Percy Ellis (1920–). Politician. DU

Swann, Lynn (1952–). Football player, sportscaster. AAS-18

Sweeney, Robert (b. 1853). Sailor, born West Indies. TA

Talbert, Mary Burnett (1866–1923). Civil rights leader. DOF-1; GRAB-01

Tanner, Henry Ossawa (1859–1937). Painter. ADA; ADB; BEBA; BRB†; HUA; ROG

Tatum, Art (1910–1956). Pianist. COF-1; WAD†

Tatum, Jack (John David) (1948–). Football player. GUCA

Taylor, Bruce (1948–). Football player. GUD

Taylor, Cecil (1933–). Pianist. COF-1

Taylor, Charley (1941–). Football player. CO; DEHA-1; SMI

Taylor, John L. Reporter. STAA

Taylor, Lawrence (1959–). Football player. AAS-15

Taylor, Otis (1942–). Football player. CO; DEHA; GUF; SMI; ST

Taylor, Susie King (1848–1912). Nurse, teacher. MAV

Teague, Robert (1929–). Television reporter. FLD

Temple, Lewis (1800–1854). Inventor. GRAB-03; HAL

Terrell, Mary Church (1863–1954). Feminist. ADA; ADB; LOAV; STAB-1; STB

Terry, Sonny (Saunders Teddell) (1911–1986). Singer, harmonica player. SUH

Thelwell, Jeanne (1951–). Lawyer. SMBB

Thomas, Duane (1947?–). Football player. LEZB

Thomas, Pat (1954–). Football player. AAS-13

Thompson, David (1954–). Basketball player. AAS-5; ARB-3

Thompson, Era Bell (fl. 1946). Editor. DADB

Thurman, Howard (1900–1981). Protestant theologian. ADB

Tilmon, James (1934–). Aviator. DRA

Tobias, Channing Heggie (1882–1961). Civil rights leader. DOF-1; GRAB-01

Tolliver, Melba. Television news reporter. STAA

Tolton, Augustine (1854–1897). Priest. ADA; ADB

Torres, John (1939?–). Sculptor. FAH

Toussaint, Cheryl (1953?–). Track athlete. RYX

Trammell, Beatrice Johnson. Nurse. BOG

Trice, Virgil G. (1926–). Engineer. CAF-1

Trotter, James Monroe (1844–1912). Government employee. ADA; ADB

Trotter, William Monroe (1872–1934). Civil rights worker. ADB; BEJ; STJB

Truth, Sojourner (1797–1883). Abolitionist. ADA; ADB; BEJ; BLE; BLF†; BRB; DADA; GIBA; JO; LES-2; LOAV; WABC†; WAH

Tubman, Harriet (1820–1913). Abolitionist. ADA; ADB; BEJ; BRB; BRBD; BRBE; BRG; BUA; COG; DADA; DOD; GEE; GIBA; HODA; HUA; HUB; JOC; LOAV; NIA; ROG; SMC; STD; STJA; STLA; WABC†; WAH; YOC; YOI

Tunnell, Emlen (1926–1975). Football player, coach. DAFG; HAE; SUD

Turner, Henry McNeal (1833–1915). Bishop. ADA; ADB

Turner, Nat (1800–1831). Insurrectionist. ADA; ADB; BEJ; BRB†; GRAB-05; ROG; WIAB

Twiggs, Leo Franklin (1934–). Painter. FAI

Tyler, Charley (d. 1863). Pioneer. SCB

Tyson, Cicely (1939?–). Actress. AB; BOHC

Tyus, Wyomia (1945–). Track athlete. HOBAA; RYA†; ST-2

Unseld, Westley (1947?–). Basketball player. AAS-27; ARB-1; HOCA; RUB; SA-2

Upshaw, Gene (1945–). Football player. AAS-11

Van Lier, Norm (1946?–). Basketball player. HIBAA

Vann, Robert Lee (1887–1940). Journalist. ADA; ADB

Van Peebles, Melvin (1932–). Motion picture director. AB

Vereen, Ben (1946?–). Singer, dancer. AB

Verrett, Shirley (1933?–). Singer. GRBA

Vesey, Denmark (1767–1822). Insurrectionist. ADA; ADB; BRB†; HODA; JO; SPB; STJA

Wagoner, Henry O. (fl. 1860). Abolitionist. KADB

Walker, David (1785–1830). Abolitionist. ADA; ADB; BEJ; GRAB-05; PECA; STJA

Walker, Herschel (1962–). Football player. DEHB

Walker, Jimmy (1944?–). Basketball player. SA

Walker, Maggie Lena (1867–1934). Banker. ADA; ADB; BRB; BUFA; LOAV; ROG

Walker, Margaret (1915–). Poet. ROE

Walker, Sarah Breedlove (1867–1919). Cosmetician. ADA; ADB†; LOAV; STQ†

Walker, Thomas Calhoun (1862–1953). Author. DADB

Walker, Wesley (1955–). Football player. AAS-18

Waller, Fats (Thomas Wright) (1904–1943). Pianist. COF-1; ROF; TEA; TEB; WAD†

Walls, Everson (1959–). Football player. AAS-13

Ward, Samuel Ringgold (1817–1866). Abolitionist, clergyman. GRAB-05

Warfield, Marsha (1954–). Comedienne. MASB

Warfield, Paul (1942–). Football player. CO; DEHA; LIB; SMI; ST

Washington, Betty. Reporter. STAA

Washington, Booker Taliaferro (1856–1915). Educator. ADA; ADB; BRB; BRBD; CUC; FIA; FOB; FOH; FRC†; HUA; JOC; LEC; LEJA; MAL; ROG; STB; STO; WAH; YOI

Washington, Gene (1947–). Football player. FRD; GUEB; GUF; ST

Washington, George (1817–1905). Landowner. GRAB-02; KADB; WIBA

Washington, Walter (1915–). Mayor. YOI

Waters, Ethel (1900–1977). Singer. ADA; ADB; DI-1†; DOBA; HUC

Waters, Muddy (McKinley Morganfield) (1915–1983). Singer. SUH

Watkins, Sylvestre C. (1913?–). Publishing executive. BOG

Watson, Douglas. Aeronautical engineer. BOG

Watts, André (1946–). Pianist. AB

Weaver, Robert Clifton (1907–). Sociologist. ADB; DOF-1; YOI

Wheatley, Phillis (1753–1784). Poet. ADA; ADB; AND; BRB; DOB; GIBA; HUA; JOCA; LEJ; LEPA; LOAV; PECA; ROE; ROG; WIBA

Whipper, William (1805–1885). Abolitionist, businessman. ADB; GRAB-02

Whipple, Prince (1764?–1797). Soldier. DAF-1; WIBA

White, Charles (1918–1979). Painter. ADA; ADB; FAH

White, Jo Jo. Basketball player. KLC

White, Roy (1943–). Baseball player. DEHA-1; KLBB

White, Walter F. (1893–1955). Civil rights leader. ADA; ADB; DOF-1; GRAB-01; RIC

White, William D. (1934–). Baseball player. GUB-1; PRA

Wilkens, Lenny. Basketball player. HIBA

Wilkins, Alonzo. Basketball player. PIB; PIBA

Wilkins, Roy (1901–1981). Civil rights leader. DOF-1; FAG; KE; YOI

Williams, Bert (1876?–1922). Actor. ADA; ADB; HUC; PHA; ROF; ROG

Williams, Big Joe (1900–). Singer. SUH

Williams, Buck (Charles Linwood) (1960–). Basketball player. AAS-7

Williams, Daniel Hale (1858–1931). Surgeon. ADA; ADB; ASB; BRB†; CAF-1; DADA; HA; HAM; HODA; HUA; KLA; PECA; RICA; ROG; STO

Williams, Fannie Barrier. Reformer. DADA

Williams, George Washington (1849–1891). Leader. ADA; ADB; BRB†

Williams, Joe (fl. 1912). Baseball player. SMK

Williams, Mary Lou (1910–1981). Pianist, composer. GIB-1

Williams, Paul Revere (1894–1980). Architect. ADB; DOF-1; LEDA

Williams, Robert F. (1925–). Activist. DADA

Williams, William Taylor Burwell (1869–1941). Educator. DOF-1

Wills, Maury (Maurice Morning) (1932–). Baseball player. DEHA-1; FOI; GEB; GUDA; KADA; PRA; ROC; SHC; VEA

Wilson, Flip (Clerow) (1933–). Comedian. AB

Wilson, James Finley (1881–1952). Fraternal order leader. ADA; ADB

Wilson, John (1922–). Painter, educator. FAH

Wilson, Nemiah. Football player. RUC

Winfield, Dave (1951–). Baseball player. AAS-4; HEFB†

Wittenberg, Henri E. Journalist. STAA

Wonder, Stevie (1950–). Singer, composer. BUIB-1

Wood, Ann (fl. 1855). Slave. CHFB

Wood, William Barry (1910–1971). Football player. HAE; JOA

Woods, Granville T. (1856–1910). Inventor. ADA; ADB; BRB†; CAF-1; GRAB-03; HA; HAL; JO; KLA; PECA; STQ†

Woodson, Carter Goodwin (1875–1950). Historian. ADA; ADB; BRB†; DOF-1; GRAB-02; ROG; STO

Wright, Barbara P. (1920–). Physician. PAC

Wright, Jane C. (1919–). Physician. HA-1; HAMA; PAC; RAAG†

Wright, Jonathan Jasper (1840–1885). Judge.
ADA; ADB

Wright, Louis Tompkins (1891–1952). Physician.
DOF-1; GRAB-03; HA; HAMA; PAC

Wright, Nathan, Jr. (1923–). Leader, theologian.
HAI

Wright, Richard (1908–1960). Author. ADA; ADB;
AKB; DABB; DADB; DOF-1; FLBA; RIC; RICA

Wyatt, Addie (1924–). Labor, civil rights leader.
BI; GIB-1

Yette, Samuel F. (1929–). Journalist. STAA

York (fl. 1804). William Clark's servant on Louisiana Expedition. BUH; HAP; KADB; SCB;
STQ†; WIBA

Young, Andrew Jackson (1932–). Mayor. DOF-1

Young, Buddy (Claude) (d. 1983). Football player.
FOI

Young, Charles (1864–1922). Army officer. ADA;
ADB; BRB; DOF-1; HODA; HUB; KADB; ROG

Young, Coleman (1918–). Mayor. DOF-1

Young, Hiram (fl. 1830). Wagon maker. BUH

Young, Lester Willis (1909–1959). Saxophonist.
COF-1; JO; WAD†

Young, Whitney Moore, Jr. (1921–1971). Civil
rights leader. ADB; FAG; GRAB-01; KE;
WECA; YOI

Young, Wilbur (1949–). Football player. AAS-25

Zino, Henry. Drummer. HODA

Foreign

Abdur Rahman Sadi el Timbuctoo (1596–1660).
African historian. ADA

Abrahams, Peter (1919–). South African author.
OJA

Affonso I (1506–1545). King of Kongo. DOA;
GRAB-04; MIC

Akhnaton (fl. 1379–1362 B.C.). King of Egypt.
CAAA; GRAB-04; JOBB; NEC; UNA

Amin, Idi (1925?–). Ex-president of Uganda.
CL-01

Amini bin Saidi (1904?–). African tribesman.
PEA

Askia Muhammad (1494–1529). Emperor of Timbuktu. ADA; ADB; BRB†; DOA; GRAB-04

Azikiwe, Nnamdi (1904–). Governor-general of Nigeria. ADA

Balewa, Sir Abubakar Tafawa (1912–1966).
Prime minister of Nigeria. KEF

Bam, Brigalia (1933–). South African social
worker. CRA

Bayi, Filbert (1954–). Tanzanian track athlete.
AAS-26; LEYB†

Bikila, Abebe (1932–1973). Ethiopian track athlete. AAS-30; DAJ; HIA-01†; LEYB

Bridgetower, George Augustus (1780–1860). Polish violinist. ADA; ADB

Brutus, Dennis (1924–). South African poet. LEA

Bwembya (b. 1886?). African tribesman. PEA

Captein, Jacques E. J. (b. 1745). Dutch clergyman, born Africa. ADA; ADB

Cetewayo (c. 1836–1884). Zulu chief. BRB†;
CAAA; MIC

Chaka (1787–1829). Zulu chief. ADA; ADB;
BRB†; GRAB-04; MIC

Christophe, Henri (1767–1820). King of Haiti.
ADA; ADB; DAF-1†; JO; STQ†; WIBA

Cinque, Joseph (1811–1852). African insurrectionist. ADA; ADB; BRB†; ROG; WOA

Coka, Gilbert (1910–). African educator. PEA

Coleridge-Taylor, Samuel (1875–1912). English
composer. ADA; ADB; BRB†

Crowther, Samuel Ajayi (1808–1891). Nigerian
bishop. POA

Dahia al-Kahina (fl. 667–702). African queen.
GRAB-04

Dessalines, Jean Jacques (1758–1806). Emperor
of Haiti. ADA; ADB

Duvalier, François (1907–1971). President of
Haiti. ARA; BAGA

Equiano, Olaudah (Gustavus Vassa) (1745–1801).
English adventurer. ADA; ADB; OJA

Esteban or Estevanico (d. 1539). Spanish ex-
plorer. ADB; BLD†; BUH; GRAB-02; HAP;
HUB; JO†; KADB; LEI; PECA; SCB; STQ;
VIA; WIBA

Fafunwa, Babs. Nigerian educator. OJA

Garvey, Marcus A. (1887–1940). Jamaican nationalist movement leader, in U.S. ADA; ADB;
ARAA; BEJ; BRBD; GRAB-01; JO

Gatheru, R. Mugo. African college professor. OJA

Gudit (fl. 937–997). Ethiopian queen. GRAB-04

Guillen, Nicolás (1902–). Cuban poet. WO

Haile Selassie I (1891–1975). Emperor of Ethiopia. ADA; DU-1; GRAB-04

Haile Selassie, Tsahai (1919–1942). Princess of
Ethiopia. MAK

Hannibal, Abram (1697–1782). Russian general.
ADA; ADB

Hatshepsut (1578–1457 B.C.). Queen of Egypt.
BOI; COLB; GRAB-04

Idris Alaoma (1580–1617). Sultan of Bornu. DOA;
MIC

Ighodaro, Irene Elizabeth. Nigerian physician.
CRA

Jiagge, Annie. Ghanaian jurist. CRA

Jugurtha (fl. 188–106 B.C.). African king.
GRAB-04

Kayamba, Mdumi Martin (b. 1891). African
teacher. PEA

Kayira, Legson Didimu. Malawian author. OJA

Keino, Kipchoge (1940–). Kenyan track athlete.
AAS-26; LEYB†

Kenyatta, Jomo (1893?–1978). Kenyan prime minister. ADA; KEF

Kenyatta, Margaret Wambui (1928–). Kenyan mayor. CRA

Kgamanyane (fl. 1820). Bakgatla chief. MIC

Khama III (d. 1980). King of the Bamangwato. MIC

Konie, Gwendoline Chomba (1938–). Zambian U.N. delegate. CRA

Lobengula (c. 1833–1893). Matabele king. MIC

Luthuli, Albert John (1899–1967). South African political leader. ADA; FOJ; LEA; MEC; WIC

McKenley, Herb. Jamaican track athlete. HIA

Makeba, Miriam (1932–). South African singer. CRA

Makeda (fl. 960–930 B.C.). Queen of Sheba. GRAB-04

Mandela, Nelson (1918–). South African lawyer. DU-1; LEA

Mansa Musa I (1312–1337). Ruler of Mali. DOA; GRAB-04; PECA; POA

Marichal, Juan (1937–). Dominican baseball player. HAF; KADA; LEZ; PEC; PRA; RIGA†

Massinissa (c. 238–148 B.C.). African king. GRAB-04

Mboya, Thomas Joseph (1930–1969). Kenyan minister of justice. ADA; KE; POA

Menelik II (1844–1913). Emperor of Abyssinia. ADA; ADB; GRAB-03

Menes (fl. 3100–3038 B.C.). King of Egypt. GRAB-04

Mockerie, Parmenas (1900–). Kenyan teacher. PEA

Modupe (1901–). Guinean prince. OJA

Mohammed V (1910–1961). King of Morocco. KEF

Moore, Kofoworola Aina (1913–). Nigerian tribeswoman. PEA

Moshoeshoe (1790–1870). African ruler. GRAB-04; MIC; POA

Ndansi Kumalo (b. 1870?). African chieftain. PEA

Nefertiti (fl. 1372–1350 B.C.). Queen of Egypt. COLB; FAE; GRAB-04; JO†; PA

Nino, Pedro Alonso (1468?–1505). Spanish navigator. HODA

Nkrumah, Kwame (1909–1972). Ghanaian president. ADA; JO; KEF; WEA

Nosente (b. 1865?). South African tribeswoman. PEA

Nyerere, Julius Kambarage (1921–). President of Tanzanian republic. ADA; DU-1; KE; KEF

Nzinga (1582–1663). African queen. GRAB-04; JO; POA

Osei Tutu (1636–1712). King of Ashanti. GRAB-04; MIC

Piankhi (fl. 741–721 B.C.). King of Ethiopia. ADA; ADB; GRAB-04

Quarsie, Tetteh (fl. 1879). African laborer. JO

Rashid bin Hassani (1855?). African tribesman. PEA

Selormey, Francis (1927–). Ghanaian government official. OJA

Senghor, Léopold Sédar (1906–). Senegalese president. ADA; DU-1; KEF

Sobukwe, Robert Mangaliso (1924–1978). South African political leader. LEA

Sundiata I. King of Mali. MIC

Sunni Ali Ber (1464–1492). Emperor of Timbuctoo. ADA; ADB; DOA; GRAB-04

Sutherland, Efua Theodora (1924–). Ghanaian author. CRA

Taharga (fl. 688–662 B.C.). Ethiopian king. GRAB-04

Touré, Sékou (1922–1984). Guinean president. ADA; JO

Toussaint L'Ouverture, Pierre Dominique (1743–1803). Haitian general, liberator. ADA; ADB; BAA; BACA; KEH; MAJ; YOFA

Tubman, William V. S. (1895–1971). Liberian president. ADA

Tutankhamen (1361–1351 B.C.). King of Egypt. COA; GRAB-04

Tuthmosis III (1504–1450 B.C.). King of Egypt. CAAA; GRAB-04

Tutu, Desmond Mpilo (1931–). South African Anglican bishop. AAS-34

Udo Akpabio. Nigerian tribesman. PEA

Waciuma, Charity. Zambian teacher, author. OJA

Yaa Asantewa (1863–1923). Ashanti queen. GRAB-04

BLIND

See also DEAF; DISABLED

Braille, Louis (1809–1852). French, blind and teacher of blind. EVA; FE; FOR; FRB; FRE

Bridgman, Laura Dewey (1829–1889). Teacher. LYA

Charles, Ray (1930–). Singer, pianist. HAFA

Feliciano, José (1945–). Singer. FOW; LYA; WH-2

Fiorito, Eunice (1930–). Advocate for the disabled. BOHA-1

Jefferson, Lemon (1897–1930). Singer. ADB; COF-1; SUH; WAD†

Johnson, Willie (1902–1949). Singer. SUH

Julio P. (1958?–). SIAA

Keller, Helen Adams (1880–1968). BEC; BOC; CAD; DOD; EVA; EVD; FAA; FOR; FRE; GIBA; MAJ; STLA; WAJ

Kirk, Roland (1936–1976). Multi-instrumentalist. UN

Macy, Anne Sullivan (1866–1936). Teacher of Helen Keller. FAA†; LEJA; SMC; STJ; STLA

Milsap, Ronnie (1944–). Singer. KRI-1

Smithdas, Robert (1925–). Social worker. BOHA-1

Templeton, Alec (1910–1963). Pianist, born Wales. GEA

Terry, Sonny (Saunders Teddell) (1911–1986). Singer, harmonica player. SUH

Thurber, James G. (1894–1961). Author, cartoonist. BEE; CUC; FLBA; GEA

Wonder, Stevie (1950–). Singer, composer. BUIB-1

BOAT RACERS

Brockman, Shimson (1958–). Israeli. SLA

Campbell, Donald Malcolm (1921–1967). English. ALBA; ST-1

Campbell, Sir Malcolm (1885–1949). English. YAA

Friedlander, Ethan (1957–). Israeli. SLA

Mosbacher, Emil, Jr. (1922–). HOC

Taylor, Lee (d. 1980). OLDC

Wood, Gar (1880?–1971). DAG; DAGA

BOLIVIANS

Laredo, Jaime (1941–). Violinist. EWC

BOTANISTS

See also AGRICULTURISTS; GENETICISTS

American

Ballard, Ernesta Drinker (1920–). Horticulturist. GIB-1

Bartram, John (1699–1777). CO-1; JEA

Burbank, Luther (1849–1926). BOB; CO-1; CUC; DEI; DEJ; DOCA; DOE; FOH; HYB; WAP

Carleton, Mark Alfred (1866–1925). DEA

Carver, George Washington (1864–1943). ADA; ADB; ASA; ASB; ASB-1; BEC; BOD; BRB†; BRBD; CAF-1; CAGA; CO-1; COKA; CORA; CUC; DOE; DOF-1; EVD; FID; FRE; GRAB-03; HA; HAM; HODA; HUA; JOC; KE; KLA; LEI; LEPC; MAN; MAT; MEB; RIC; RICA; ROG; YOE

Colden, Cadwallader (1688–1776). (Born Ireland). PAC

Fairchild, David Grandison (1869–1954). MIB

Farquhar, Jane Colden (1724–1766). EMB†; PAC

Gray, Asa (1810–1888). HYB

Hoffer, George Nissley (1887–1963). DEA

Jones, Donald Forsha (1890–1963). CAB

Nuttall, Thomas (1786–1859). (Born England). JEA

Palmer, Edward (1831–1911). (Born England). CO-1

Perrine, Henry (1797–1840). BLC; JEA

Shull, George Harrison (1874–1954). CAB; DEA

Torrey, John (1796–1873). HYB

Foreign

Beijerinck, Martinus Willem (1851–1931). Dutch. SUF

Douglas, David (1798–1834). Scottish. JEA

Geddes, Sir Patrick (1854–1932). Scottish. COLA

Linnaeus, Carl (1707–1778). Swedish. BLB; CAB; COLA; FE; MIB; STI

Michaux, André (1746–1802). French. JEA

Michaux, François André (1770–1855). French. JEA

Vavilov, Nicolai Ivanovich (1887–1942). Russian. WEF

BOWLERS

Asher, Barry (1946–). SLA

Billick, George (1910–). ALBA

Carter, Don (1930–). DEHA-1

Day, Ned (Edward Gately) (1911?–1971). DAG; DAGA

Garms, Shirley Rudolph (1924–). JAB; LEF

Holman, Marshall (1954–). SLA

Ladewig, Marion (1914?–). HOBA; HOBAA

Lindsey, Mortimer (1888–1959). SLA

McCutcheon, Floretta Doty (1888–1967). HOBA; HOBAA; JAB

Martin, Sylvia Wene (1930–). HOBA; SLA

Roth, Mark (1951–). SLA

Souter, Judy Cook (1944–). HOBAA†; JABA

Sperber, Paula (1951–). HOBAA†; RYX

Weber, Dick (1929–). FOI; KADA

Wolf, Phil (1869–1936). (Born Germany). SLA

BOXING FIGURES

Ali, Muhammad (Cassius Clay) (1942–). ASB-1; ASBA; BELB; BOHA; DAGA; FOR; GED; HOBC; HOCG; KADA; LEYB†; PAW; RAAC; RICA

Armstrong, Henry (1912–). BUJA; DAG; DAGA; FOI
Attell, Abe (1884–1969). SLA
Berlenbach, Paul. PIB; PIBA
Cerdan, Marcel, Jr. (1916–1949). French. BELB
Corbett, Jim (James John) (1866–1933). RAAC
Dempsey, Jack (1895–1983). ASBA; BELB†; DAG; DAGA; HEG; HOC; LAC; LEF; RAAC; SID
Fields, Jackie (1908–). SLA
Fitzsimmons, Robert P. (1863–1918). English. DAG; DAGA; RAAC
Fleischer, Nat (1887–1972). Promoter, editor. SLA
Frazier, Joe (1944–). ASBA; BELB; GEDA
Graziano, Rocky (1922–). DEHA-1
Griffith, Emile (1938–). DEHA-1
Jeffries, Jim (James Jackson) (1875–1952). RAAC
Johnson, Jack (John Arthur) (1878–1946?). BRBD; RAAC
Kabakoff, Harry. Manager. LEW
Kaplan, Louis "Kid" (1902–1970). (Born Russia). SLA
Ketchel, Stanley (1886–1910). DAG; DAGA
LaMotta, Jake (1921–). BELB
Lee, Canada (1907–1951). ADA; ADB; SCA
Leonard, Benny (1896–1947). DAG; DAGA; SLA
Levinsky, Battling (Barney Lebrowitz) (1891–1949). SLA
Lewis, Ted "Kid" (1894–1970). English. SLA
Louis, Joe (1914–1981). ASB-1; ASBA; BELB; BOF; DAG; DAGA; HEG; HOC; LEF; LYE; PAW; RAAC; RIC; RICA; SICA
Marciano, Rocky (1923–1969). ASBA; HOC; RAAC
Mendoza, Daniel (1764–1836). English. SLA
Nash, Charlie. Irish. BELB
Ortega, Gaspar (1935–). Mexican. IZA
Patterson, Floyd (1935–). DADB; DEF; DEHA-1; LEYB; OCA
Pep, Willie (Guiglermo Papaleo) (1922–). DEHA-1
Rickard, Tex (1871–1929). Promoter. DAG; DAGA
Robinson, Ray (1921–). ASBA; BOF; DAG; DAGA; HOC
Rosenbloom, Maxie (1904–1976). SLA
Ross, Barney (1909–1967). PIB; PIBA; SCA; SLA; VAE
Singer, Al (1907–1961). SLA
Sullivan, John Lawrence (1858–1918). DAG; DAGA; RAAC
Tunney, Gene (James Joseph) (1898–1978). DAG; DAGA; RAAC; SCA
Vingo, Carmine. BELB
Wallace, Cookie. BELB
Zale, Tony (1913–). DEHA-1

BOY SCOUTS, see SCOUT LEADERS

BOYS, see CHILDREN

BRAZILIANS

Aleijadhino (Antônio Francisco Lisboa) (1738–1841). Architect, sculptor. BACA
Bonifácio, José (1763–1838). Statesman. LAB; WOB
Brasiliano, Roc (fl. 1660). Pirate. LACB
Dulce, Sister (Dulce Lopes Pontes) (1913–). Nun. MAK
Fittipaldi, Emerson (1946–). Automobile racer. ABB; OLCB
Nabuco, Joaquim (1849–1910). Diplomat, reformer. WOB
Niemeyer, Oscar (1907–). Architect. BACA
Pedro I (1798–1834). Emperor. LAB; YOFA
Pedro II (1825–1891). Emperor. BACA; LAB; OLA
Pelé (1940–). Soccer player. AAS-23; ASB-1; ASBA; FOR; GUEC-1
Rondon, Cândido Mariano da Silva (1865–1958). Marshal. WOB
Santos-Dumont, Alberto (1873–1932). Aeronaut. BRBA
Tiradentes (1748–1792). Revolutionist. LAB
Vargas, Getúlio Dornelles (1883–1954). President. BAGA; WOB
Villa-Lobos, Heitor (1887–1959). Composer. BACA; KAE

BRITISH, see ENGLISH; IRISH; SCOTTISH; WELSH

BUILDERS, see ARCHITECTS; ENGINEERS, CIVIL

BULL FIGHTERS

Franklin, Sidney (1903–1976). SLA
Manolete (1917–1947). Spanish. PIB

BURMESE

Nu (1907–). Statesman. KEF
Thant, U (1909–1974). Statesman. KE; WEA

BUSINESS PEOPLE

See also BANKERS; FINANCIERS; TRANSPORTATION LEADERS

American

Alligood, Douglass L. Advertising executive. STAA

Arden, Elizabeth (1884–1966). Cosmetician. LAH; LES-1

Armour, Philip Danforth (1832–1901). Meat industrialist. LAG; WED

Backer, Steve. Jazz producer. UN

Bates, Mercedes (1915–). Food industry executive. FRBD

Beech, Olive Ann (1903–). Aviation executive. LES-1; PAA

Birdseye, Clarence (1886–1956). Frozen food industrialist. LAG

Borgenicht, Louis (fl. 1889). Manufacturer. LETA

Broom, Jacob (1752–1810). FEAA

Brown, Clara (1803–1885). GRAB-02; KADB

Brown, John (1736–1803). SEC

Brunson, Dorothy (1938–). Radio and advertising executive. GLO

Carnegie, Andrew (1835–1919). Steel industrialist, born Scotland. BEA; CUC; DEI; DEJ; EVA; LAG; LEM; LOB; MAL; WED

Carr, Harold Noflet (1921–). Airline executive. PAA

Christmas, Walter. Public relations. STAA

Chrysler, Walter Percy (1875–1940). Automobile manufacturer. COKA

Clark, Ruth (1942–). Personnel service executive. GLO

Cochran, Jacqueline (1906–1980). Cosmetician. CLA; GEDB; HAMY; HIFD; MO; WAJ

Colbert, Lester (1905–). Automobile executive. PAA

Cooney, Joan Ganz (1929–). Television producer. GIB-1; LES-1

Cooper, Peter (1791–1883). Manufacturer. HOF

Cordiner, Ralph (1900–1973). Executive. PAA

Cousins, Jane "Casey" (1924–). Real estate executive. LES-1

Curtice, Harlow H. (1893–1962). Automobile executive. PAA

Day, James E. (1905–1980). Stock exchange executive. PAA

Deere, John (1804–1886). Manufacturer. HOF

Dix, Henry (1850?–1938). Manufacturer, born Russia. LETA

Downing, George Thomas (1819–1903). Restauranteur. GRAB-01

Drake, Edwin Laurentine (1819–1880). Oil pioneer. FAB

Duke, James Buchanan (1856–1925). Tobacco industrialist. WED

Du Pont, Eleuthère Irénée (1771–1834). Manufacturer, born France. LEM; LOB

Eastman, George (1854–1932). Photography industrialist. CUC; FE; LAG; LEM; MAL; RIBA

Eaton, Roy (1930–). Advertising executive. STAA

Engstrom, Elmer William (1901–1984). Electronics executive. PAB

Evans, Jane (1944–). Mail-order executive. FRBD

Ferkauf, Eugene (1921–). Merchant. GRB-1; LAH

Firestone, Harvey Samuel (1868–1938). Rubber industrialist. LAG

Fitzsimons, Thomas (1741–1811). (Born Ireland). FEAA

Ford, Barney (fl. 1860). GRAB-02; KADB

Ford, Henry (1863–1947). Industrialist. ASB-1; BOD; BUE; COKB; CUC; DEI; DEJ; EVB; FAC; FE; FOH; FRE; LAG; LEM; MAL; MAT; WED

Fuller, Alfred Carl (1885–1973). Manufacturer. LAG

Funston, George Keith (1910–). Stock exchange executive. PAA

Gamberg, Abe (1893–). (Born Russia). BAEA-1

Gary, Elbert Henry (1846–1927). Steel executive. HOF

Gaston, Arthur George (1892–). Insurance executive. ADA; ADB

Getty, J. Paul (1892–1976). Oil executive. COKB; DU-1

Gillespie, Frank L. (1867–1925). Insurance executive. ADB

Gimbel, Adam (1817–1896). Merchant, born Germany. LETA

Gomez, Benjamin (fl. 1791). Book dealer. LETA

Gregg, Maxine. Jazz agent. UN

Grossinger, Jennie (1892–1972). Hotel executive. PAA

Guggenheim, Meyer (1828–1905). Copper industrialist, born Switzerland. LETA; WED

Hall, Charles Martin (1863–1914). Aluminum executive. FAB; FE; LEN

Hall, Jim (1935?–). Automobile manufacturer. JA; LEX; YAA

Hanway, Howard. Insurance executive. PAA

Hartford, George Ludlum (1865–1957). Merchant. LAH

Hays, Moses Michael (1739–1805). Insurance. LETA

Hendricks, Harmon (fl. 1812). Copper merchant. LETA

Hicks, Beatrice Alice (1919–). Engineering executive. PAA

Hilton, Conrad Nicholson (1887–1979). Hotel executive. LAG; LEN; PAA

Holman, Eugene (1895–1962). Petroleum executive. PAA

Hughes, Howard, Jr. (1905–1976). Aviation, motion picture executive. COKB; DU-1

Johnson, Howard Deering (1897–1972). Restaurant executive. LAH

Kaman, Charles Huron (1919–). Aviation executive. PAB

Kappel, Frederick Russell (1902–). Utilities executive. PAA

Katz, Chaim Moshe. (Born Russia). GRB-1

Kettering, Charles F. (1876–1958). Automobile executive. HYA†; YOE

Kroc, Ray (1902–1984). Restaurant executive. DU-1

Kroll, Alex. Advertising executive. HOBB

Lasker, Albert (1880–1952). Advertising executive, born Germany. CUC; LETA

Leidesdorff, William Alexander (1810–1848). Merchant. ADA; ADB; BUH; GRAB-02; KADB

Levitt, William Jaird (1907–). Builder. PAA

Levy, Aaron (1742–1815). Merchant, born the Netherlands. LETA

Levy, Hayman (1721–1789). Fur trader. LETA

Lewis, Tillie (1901–1977). Food packing executive. LES-1

Liebenow, Robert C. (1922–). Association executive. PAA

Lindo, Moses (d. 1774). Merchant. LETA

Link, Edwin Albert (1904–1981). Aviation executive. BRBC; COR

Lopez, Aaron (1731–1782). Merchant. LETA

McCormick, Cyrus Hall (1809–1884). Inventor. CAB; EBA; FAB; FE; HYA; LAG; LEN; MAL; MAT; RAA; WED

Macy, Rowland Hussey (1822–1877). Merchant. LAH

Mardikian, George M. (1903–). Restaurateur, born Armenia. CAHA

Mason, Biddy (1818–1891). BUH; GRAB-02; KADB; STQ†

Merrick, John (1859–1919). Insurance executive. ADB; BRB

Morgan, Garrett A. (1875–1963). Manufacturer. ADA; ADB; GRAB-03; HA; HAL; KLA; STQ†

Morisey, A. Alexander. Public relations executive. STAA

Nitschelm, Ade. Hotel owner. PAA

Nitschelm, Terry. Hotel owner. PAA

Noble, Edward J. (1882–1958). Manufacturer. LEN

Palmer, Bruce (1908–). Insurance executive. PAA

Peabody, George (1795–1869). Merchant. LEM

Penney, James Cash (1875–1971). Merchant. LAH; LEN

Powell, Clilian (1894–). Insurance executive. CAF-1

Proctor, Barbara Gardner (1932–). Advertising executive. FRBD

Robinson, William E. Beverage executive. PAA

Rockefeller, John Davison (1839–1937). Industrialist. ASB-1; BOD; CUC; FAC; LEM; MAL; WED

Rosenwald, Julius (1862–1932). Merchant. ALD; CUC; LETA

Rubinstein, Helena (1870?–1965). Cosmetician, born Poland. LIA

Rudkin, Margaret Fogharty (1897–1967). Bakery executive. LAH; LES-1; PAA

Sarnoff, David (1891–1971). Radio and television executive, born Russia. GRB-1; LAG; LETA

Shapiro, Irving S. (1916–). Chemical executive. GRB-1

Shaver, Dorothy (1897–1959). Department store executive. BOJ; CLA; FRBD; LES-1

Shaw, Leslie N. (1922–). YOI

Sheftall, Mordecai (1735–1797). BUIB†; LETA

Shepherd, John (1932?–). Entrepreneur. DRA

Sims, Tom L. Advertising executive. STAA

Slater, Samuel (1768–1835). Manufacturer, born England. FAB; LEB; MAL

Sloan, Alfred Pritchard, Jr. (1875–1966). Automobile executive. FAC

Smith, Winthrop (1893–1961). Investment executive. PAA

Snyder, John. Jazz producer. UN

Spaght, Monroe Edward (1909–). Oil executive. PAB

Spalding, Albert Goodwill (1850–1915). Sporting goods merchant. ALB; SMK

Spaulding, Asa Timothy (1902–). Insurance executive. FLD

Spaulding, Charles Clinton (1874–1952). Insurance executive. ADA; ADB; HUA; PECA; STQ†

Sperry, Elmer Ambrose (1860–1930). Engineering executive. YOE

Steloff, Frances (b. 1887). Bookseller. GIB-1; WABC†

Stevenson, Sybil Jordan. Telecommunications executive. HOD-1

Stewart, Alexander Turney (1803–1876). Merchant, born Ireland. HOF

Straus, Nathan (1848–1931). Merchant, born Germany. ALD; GRB-1; LETA; PEB

Stutz, Geraldine. Department store executive. GLO

Swope, Gerard (1872–1957). Engineering executive. GRB-1

Thomas, Charles A. (1900–1982). Chemical executive. PAB

Tiffany, Charles Lewis (1812–1902). Jeweler. LAH

Trahey, Jane (1923–). Advertising executive. LES-1

Trujillo, Brenda. Trucking manager. FOC-1

Walker, Sarah Breedlove (1867–1919). Cosmetician. ADA; ADB†; LOAV; STQ†

Wanamaker, John (1838–1922). Merchant. LAH; LEM

Watkins, Sylvestre C. (1913?–). Publishing executive. BOG

Watson, Thomas J., Sr. (1874–1956). Industrialist. GRAB-3; LAG

Wells, Mary Georgene (1928?–). Advertising executive. GEDB†; GRBA

Westinghouse, George (1846–1914). Manufacturer. HYA; LAG; THA

Wheeler, Candace Thurber (1827–1923). Decorative arts executive. PACB

Whipper, William (1805–1885). ADB; GRAB-02

Wilkinson, David (1771–1852). Manufacturer. FAB

Wood, Robert Elkington (b. 1879). Department store executive. LAH

Woolworth, Frank Winfield (1852–1919). Merchant. LAH

Wyman, Irma (1928–). Computer executive. FRBD

Foreign

Arkwright, Sir Richard (1732–1792). English manufacturer. FAB; FE

Benz, Karl (1844–1929). German automobile manufacturer. FAB; FE

Calas, Jean (1688–1762). French merchant. COG

Darby, Abraham (c. 1678–1717). English manufacturer. FE

Eisenberg, Shaul (1921–). Israeli. (Born Germany). GRB-1

Ferguson, Harry George (1884–1960). Irish manufacturer. LAE

Hargreaves, James (c. 1722–1778). English manufacturer. FE

Morita, Akio (1921–). Japanese electronics executive. DU-1

Newcomen, Thomas (1663–1729). English manufacturer. FE

Nobel, Alfred Bernhard (1833–1896). Swedish manufacturer. EVA; HAC; LAE; MAP; MEC; RIF

Whitworth, Sir Joseph (1803–1887). English manufacturer. FE

Zeiss, Carl (1816–1888). German industrialist. FE

CABINET MEMBERS, U.S.

Acheson, Dean Gooderham (1893–1971). HEEA

Blaine, James Gillespie (1830–1893). HEEA; WHD†

Brown, Harold (1927–). Ex-Secretary of Defense. GRB-1

Calhoun, John Caldwell (1782–1850). FEA; HAOA; HOEA; KEC†; STH

Clay, Henry (1777–1852). GO; HEEA; STH; WHD

Dole, Elizabeth (1936–). Ex-Secretary of Transportation. WHE

Dulles, John Foster (1888–1959). HEEA

Gallatin, Albert (1761–1849). (Born Switzerland). DOG

Goldberg, Arthur J. (1908–). LETA; WEC

Hamilton, Alexander (1755–1804). BUIB; CUC; DEI; DEJ; FAC; FEAA; FOB; LEB; LOA; MAL; OLA; SEC; SQB†; STH

Hay, John Milton (1838–1905). HEEA

Heckler, Margaret (1931–). Ex-Secretary of Health and Human Services. WHE

Hills, Carla Anderson (1934–). Ex-Secretary of Housing and Urban Development. SWI

Hobby, Oveta Culp (1905–). Ex-Secretary of Health, Education and Welfare. STLA

Hull, Cordell (1871–1955). HEEA; MEC†; WIC

Kellogg, Frank Billings (1856–1937). HEEA; MEC†; WIC

Kissinger, Henry Alfred (1923–). Ex-Secretary of State, born Germany. MEC

Lansing, Robert (1864–1928). HEEA

McNamara, Robert Strange (1916–). Ex-Secretary of Defense. WEC

Perkins, Frances (1882–1965). BI; BOC; CLA; SMC; WABC; WHE

Peterson, Esther Eggertsen (1906–). Ex-Director of Consumer Affairs. WIAA-02

Randolph, Edmund Jennings (1753–1813). BUIB; FEAA; SEC

Romney, George Wilcken (1907–). WEC

Root, Elihu (1845–1937). MEC†; WIC

Rusk, Dean (1909–). Ex-Secretary of State. HEEA

Schurz, Carl (1829–1906). (Born Germany). CUB; LEB; LOB; STH

Seward, William Henry (1801–1872). HEEA; MAL

Stimson, Henry Lewis (1867–1950). HEEA

Straus, Oscar Solomon (1850–1926). LETA

Wallace, Henry A. (1888–1965). COKA; FEA; HAOA; HOEA

Weaver, Robert Clifton (1907–). Ex-Secretary of Housing and Urban Development. ADB; DOF-1; YOI

Webster, Daniel (1782–1852). DEI; DEJ; HEEA; KEC; KED; LEC; STH

CANADIANS

Apps, Syl (1915–). Hockey player. MANA

Apps, Syl, II (1947–). Hockey player. FICA-1

Banting, Sir Frederick Grant (1891–1941). Physician. AAS-31; BEK; DOE; HUD; POB; RIF; ROA

Barker, William George (d. 1930). Aviator, WW I. HAG

Barkley, Doug (Norman Douglas) (1937–). Hockey player, coach. FICB

Bathgate, Andy (Andrew James) (1932–). Hockey player. ORC

Beliveau, Jean (1931–). Hockey player. FICA; FR; LIAB; OBA; OBB; ORC; RAAF

Binkley, Lee. Hockey player. FICB

Bishop, William Avery (1894–1956). Aviator, WW I. HAG; HAMY

Blake, Toe (Hector) (1912–). Hockey coach. LEW; ORC

Boivin, Leo (1932–). Hockey player. OBA

Bossy, Mike (1957–). Hockey player. AAS-22; OLDE

Bower, Johnny (1924?–). Hockey player. ORA

Breckenridge, William (1906–1959). Soldier, born Scotland. RADA

Brodeur, Richard (1952–). Hockey player. AAS-21

Bucyk, John Paul (1935–). Hockey player. OBB

Cashman, Wayne (1945–). Hockey player. THG

Cheevers, Gerry (1940–). Hockey player. LEYA; ORA

Ciccarelli, Dino (1960–). Hockey player. AAS-22

Clancy, King (Francis Michael) (1903–1986). Hockey player. OBA; OBB

Clarke, Bobby (Robert Earle) (1949–). Hockey player. AAS-27; CL-06; FICA-1; GUEC; GUH; LEYA; MANA; ORB; THD

Collishaw, Raymond (1893–). Aviator, WW I. HAG

Cournoyer, Ivan Serge (1943–). Hockey player. CL-06; LEYA; THG

Dionne, Marcel (1951–). Hockey player. AAS-22; AAS-23; FICA-1; FICC; MANA; OLDE; ORB

Dryden, Ken (Kenneth Wayne) (1947?–). Hockey player. FICA-1; FICC; GUEC; LEYA; ORA; ORB; THF

Dunlop, Florence (1896–1963). Educator. FLB

Durnan, Bill (William Ronald) (1915–). Hockey player. ORA; ORC

Esposito, Phil (1942–). Hockey player. AAS-21; DEHA-1; FICA; FR; FRD; GUEC; LEYA; OBB; OLDE; ORC; RAAF; THD

Esposito, Tony (Anthony James) (1943–). Hockey player. LEYA; ORA; ORB; THF

Ferguson, John. Hockey player. FICB

Geoffrion, Bernard "Boom-Boom" (1931–). Hockey player. OBA; ORC; RAAF

Gilbert, Gilles (1949–). Hockey player. THF

Gilbert, Rod (Rodrique Gabriel) (1941–). Hockey player. DEHA-1; LEYA; OBB

Gladstone, James (b. 1887). Politician. GRAC

Gold, Arthur (1919–). Pianist. EWC

Goldsworthy, Bill (William Alfred) (1944–). Hockey player. LEYA; ORB

Gould, Glenn (1932–1982). Pianist. EWC

Grant, Danny (1946–). Hockey player. FICC

Green, Ted (Edward Joseph) (1940–). Hockey player. LOAA

Greene, Nancy (1943–). Skier. FRCA

Gretzky, Wayne (1961–). Hockey player. AAS-22; AAS-35; ASB-1; HOCG; OLDE

Guevremont, Jocelyn (1951–). Hockey player. FICC

Hall, Glenn (1931?–). Hockey player. ETB; ORA; ORC; WAK

Harper, Terry (Terrance Victor) (1940–). Hockey player. LEYA

Harvey, Douglas (1924–). Hockey player. LIAB; OBB; ORC

Henderson, Paul Garnet (1943–). Hockey player. LEYA

Henning, Doug (1947–). Magician. FOGA

Howe, Mark Steven (1955–). Hockey player. MANA

Howell, Henry Vernon (1932–). Hockey player. OBA

Hull, Bobby (Robert Marvin) (1939–). Hockey player. ASBA; DEHA-1; FICA; FR; FRD; KADA; LEYA; LIAB; LYB; OBA; OBB; ORC; RAAF; SUB; WAK

Hull, Dennis William (1944–). Hockey player. FICB; LEYA

Imlach, Punch (George) (1918–1987). Hockey coach. LEW

Johnson, E. Pauline (1862–1913). Poet. GRAD

Karsh, Yousuf (1908–). Photographer, born Armenia. FOD

Kelly, Leonard Patrick (1927–). Hockey player. FR; LIAB

Keon, David Michael (1940–). Hockey player. FICA; LEYA

La Fleur, Guy Damien (1951–). Hockey player. AAS-22; FICA-1; MANA; OLDE; ORB

La Vérendrye, Pierre Gaultier de Varennes, sieur de (1685–1749). Explorer. ARF

Leach, Reggie (1950–). Hockey player. AAS-9

Leacock, Stephen Butler (1869–1944). Author. BEE

Lee, Jason (1803–1845). Missionary. YOG

Lindsay, Ted (Robert Blake Theodore) (1925–). Hockey player. FR; LIAB; OBB; ORC; RAAF

Liut, Mike (1956–). Hockey player. AAS-21

MacKay, Angus (1840–1931). Agriculturist. DEA

McKeever, Andrew Edward (d. 1919). Aviator, WWI. HAG

McKenzie, John Albert (1937–). Hockey player. OBB

Magnuson, Keith Arien (1947–). Hockey player. FICC; ORB

Magnussen, Karen (1952–). Skater. VADA

Mahovlich, Frank (1938–). Hockey player. LEYA; OBA; OBB; ORC; RAAF

Martin, Richard Lionel (1951–). Hockey player. LEYA; MANA; ORB; THG

Meloche, Gilles. Hockey player. FICC

Moog, Andy (1960–). Hockey player. AAS-21

Morenz, Howie (1902–1937). Hockey player. FR; OBB; ORC; SUB; WAK

Murray, Anne (1945–). Singer. KRI

Neilson, Jim (James Anthony) (1940–). Hockey player. LEYA

Orr, Bobby (1948–). Hockey player. ASBA; FICA; FR; FRD; GAB; GUEC; KADA; LEYA; LIAB; OBA; OBB; ORB; ORC; RAAF; THE; WAK

Osler, Sir William (1849–1919). Physician. CHD; RIB

Palmateer, Mike (1954–). Hockey player. AAS-21

Parent, Bernard Marcel (1945–). Hockey player. LEYA; THF

Park, Brad (Douglas Bradford) (1948–). Hockey player. FICA-1; FICC; LEYA; OBB; ORB; THE

Patrick, Lester (1883–1960). Hockey player, coach. DAG; DAGA; HEH; PAW

Pearson, Lester Bowles (1897–1972). Statesman. MEA; MEC; WEC; WIC

Peeters, Pete (1957–). Hockey player. AAS-21

Perreault, Gilbert (1950–). Hockey player. AAS-22; FICC; LEYA; MANA; ORB; THD

Pilote, Pierre Paul (1931–). Hockey player. ORC

Plante, Jacques (1929–1986). Hockey player. ETB; FRD; LIAB; OBB; ORA; ORC; WAK

Polis, Greg (1950–). Hockey player. FICC

Potvin, Denis Charles (1953–). Hockey player. FICA-1; GUEC; MANA; OLDE; THE

Ratelle, Jean (1940–). Hockey player. FICB

Redmond, Mickey (Michael Edward) (1947–). Hockey player. LEYA; ORB

Resch, Glenn "Chico" (1948–). Hockey player. AAS-21

Richard, Henri (1936–). Hockey player. FOI; FR; OBA

Richard, Maurice (Rocket) (1921–). Hockey player. AAS-35; ASBA; DAG; DAGA; FICA; FR;

HEG; LIAB; OBB; ORC; RAAF; SID; SUB; WAK

Rosenfeld, Fanny (1903–1969). Track athlete, born Russia. SLA

Rubenstein, Louis (1861–1931). Skater. SLA

Sanderson, Derek Michael (1946–). Hockey player. ORB

Sawchuk, Terry (1929–1970). Hockey player. ETB; FR; LIAB; OBA; OBB; ORA; ORC; WAK

Schmidt, Milt. Hockey player. ORC

Schultz, Dave (1949–). Hockey player. THG

Sittler, Darryl (1950–). Hockey player. FICA-1

Smith, Billy (1950–). Hockey player. AAS-21

Stastny, Peter (1956–). Hockey player, born Czechoslovakia. AAS-22

Stefánsson, Vilhjálmur (1879–1962). Explorer. BAB

Tallon, Dale (Michael Dale) (1950–). Hockey player. ORB

Tkaczuk, Walter Robert (1947–). Hockey player. FICC; ORB

Tremblay, Jean Claude (1939–). Hockey player. LEYA

Trottier, Bryan (1956–). Hockey player. AAS-22

Unger, Garry (1947–). Hockey player. FICC; LEYA; ORB

Van Impe, Edward Charles (1940–). Hockey player. FICB; THE

Verchères, Marie Magdelaine Jarret de (1678–1747). Heroine. MAJ; STP

Vickers, Jon (1926–). Singer. BRBB-1

Wakely, Ernie. Hockey player. FICB

Worsley, Gump (Lorne) (1929–). Hockey player. FR; ORA

Wright, Thelma. Track athlete. GLB

CAR RACERS, *see* AUTOMOBILE RACERS

CARTHAGINIANS

Hannibal (247–183 B.C.). General. CAAA; COD; DEI; DEJ; HAA; MAJ

Hanno (fl. 450 B.C.). Navigator. DYA

CARTOGRAPHERS, *see* GEOGRAPHERS

CARTOONISTS & CARICATURISTS

Adams, Neal. GOB-1

Baker, Matt. GOB-1

Barks, Carl (1901–). GOB-1
Barry, Dan (1923–). GOB-1
Beck, Charles Clarence (1910–). GOB-1
Biro, Charles (1911–1972). GOB-1
Block, Herbert Lawrence (1909–). DEDC
Briefer, Dick. GOB-1
Buscema, John (1927–). GOB-1
Byrne, John (1950–). (Born England). GOB-1
Campbell, Elmer Simms (1906–1971). ADA; ADB;
    BOG
Capp, Al (Alfred G. Caplin) (1909–1979). GEA
Carlson, George (1887–1962). GOB-1
Chaykin, Howard. GOB-1
Colan, Gene (1926–). GOB-1
Cole, Jack (1914–1958). GOB-1
Crandall, Reed (d. 1982). GOB-1
Darcy, Tom (Thomas Francis). DEDC
Darling, Jay Norwood (1876–1962). DEDC
Davenport, Homer Calvin (1867–1912). DEDC
Davis, Jack (1926–). GOB-1
Disney, Walt (Walter Elias) (1901–1966). ASB-1;
    COKA; FLBC; LAG; LEN; LEPA; PABA; WAO
Ditko, Steve (1927–). GOB-1
Eisner, Will (1917–). GOB-1
Elias, Lee (1920–). (Born England). GOB-1
Evans, George (1920–). GOB-1
Everett, William Blake (1917–1973). GOB-1
Fine, Lou (1915–1971). GOB-1
Fitzpatrick, Daniel Robert (1891–). DEDC
Frazetta, Frank (1928–). GOB-1
Guardineer, Fred (1913–). GOB-1
Gustavson, Paul (1917–). (Born Finland). GOB-1
Kane, Bob (1916–). GOB-1
Kane, Gil (1926–). (Born Russia). GOB-1
Kelly, Walter Crawford (1913–1973). GOB-1
Keppler, Joseph (1838–1894). (Born Austria).
    DEDC
Kirby, Jack (1917–). GOB-1
Kirby, Rollin (1875–1952). DEDC
Krigstein, Bernard (1919–). GOB-1
Kubert, Joe. GOB-1
Kurtzman, Harvey (1924–). GOB-1
Maneely, Joe (1926–1958). GOB-1
Marsh, Jesse (d. 1966). GOB-1
Mauldin, Bill (William Henry) (1921–). DEDC
Mayer, Sheldon. GOB-1
Meskin, Mort (1916–). GOB-1
Miller, Frank (1957–). GOB-1
Montana, Bob (1920–1975). GOB-1
Nast, Thomas (1840–1902). (Born Germany).
    CUB; DEDC
Nordling, Klaus (1915–). (Born Finland). GOB-1
Opper, Frederick Burr (1857–1937). DEDC
Osrin, Raymond Harold (1928–). DEDC
Perez, George. GOB-1

Pini, Wendy. GOB-1
Powell, Bob (d. 1967). GOB-1
Raboy, Mac (1916–1967). GOB-1
Robinson, Jerry. GOB-1
Romita, John, Sr. (1930–). GOB-1
Sanders, Bill (William Willard) (1933?–). DEDC
Schomburg, Alex. GOB-1
Severin, John (1921–). GOB-1
Shuster, Joe. GOB-1
Sienkiewicz, Bill. GOB-1
Simonson, Walt. GOB-1
Stanley, John (1914–). GOB-1
Stayskal, Wayne (1931–). DEDC
Steranko, James (1938–). GOB-1
Thorne, Frank (1930–). GOB-1
Thurber, James G. (1894–1961). BEE; CUC;
    FLBA; GEA
Toth, Alex (1928–). GOB-1
Tuska, George. GOB-1
Wheelan, Edgar Stow (1888–1966). GOB-1
Williamson, Al (1931). GOB-1
Windsor-Smith, Barry. (Born England). GOB-1
Wolverton, Basil. GOB-1
Wood, Wally (d. 1981). GOB-1
Wrightson, Berni (1948–). GOB-1

CATTLEMEN, *see* RANCHERS & CATTLEMEN

CELLISTS, *see* MUSICIANS—CELLISTS

CHAPLAINS

Capodanno, Vincent R. (d. 1967). ARBA
Four Chaplains (d. 1943). FIA
Fox, George Lansing (1900–1943). FIA
Goode, Alexander David (1911–1943). FIA; GEF;
    GRB-1
O'Callahan, Joseph T. (1905–). BRA; REA
Poling, Clark (d. 1943). FIA
Washington, John Alexander (d. 1943). FIA

CHEFS

Child, Julia (1912–). GIB-1

CHEMISTS

See also ALCHEMISTS; BIOCHEMISTS; NOBEL PRIZE WINNERS—CHEMISTRY

American

Abel, John Jacob (1857–1938). POB
Babcock, Stephen Moulton (1843–1931). DEA
Baekeland, Leo Hendrik (1863–1944). (Born Belgium). FE; THA; YOE
Calvin, Melvin (1911–). BEK
Carothers, Wallace Hume (1896–1937). FE
Cottrell, Frederick Gardner (1877–1948). MAPA; YOE
Darken, Lawrence Stamper (1909–). PAB
Dawson, Merna. HOG
Dorset, Marion (1872–1935). DEA
Frey, Charles N. (b. 1885). PAB
Hall, Charles Martin (1863–1914). FAB; FE; LEN
Hall, Lloyd Augustus (1894–1971). CAF-1; GRAB-03; HA
Herty, Charles Holmes (1867–1938). MAL
Julian, Percy Lavon (1899–1975). ADA; ADB; DOF-1; FLD; GRAB-03; HA; KLA; STO
Langmuir, Irving (1881–1957). ASA
Libby, Willard Frank (1908–1980). AAS-33; POC
Lippert, Arnold Leroy (1910–). PAB
LuValle, James E. BOG
Mark, Herman Francis (1895–). (Born Austria). BOB
Olson, Edith. HOG
Pauling, Linus Carl (1901–). AAS-34; MEB; MEC; WIC
Richards, Ellen Swallow (1842–1911). SC; WABC†
Semon, Waldo L. (1898–). PAB
Silliman, Benjamin (1779–1864). BUF; HYB
Tressler, Donald Kiteley (1894–). PAB
Urey, Harold Clayton (1893–1981). BOB; RID
Wiley, Harvey Washington (1844–1930). MAL
Williams, Robert Rampatnam (1886–1965). YOE

English

Aston, Francis William (1877–1945). RID; SHFB†
Boyle, Robert (1627–1691). CAA; FE; MOBA; SIA
Cavendish, Henry (1731–1810). CAA; FE; SHFB
Crookes, Sir William (1832–1919). FE; SIA
Dalton, John (1766–1844). CAA; FE; MOBA; SHFB; SIA; STI
Davy, Sir Humphry (1778–1829). CAA; COL; DUA; FE; SHFB; SOB; STI; THA
Faraday, Michael (1791–1867). ASA; BEP; BIA; BOB; BOD; CAA; COLA; DEI; DEJ; DOE; DUA; FE; MAQ; SHFB; SIA; STI; THA
Gilbert, Sir Joseph Henry (1817–1901). CAB

Hodgkin, Dorothy Crowfoot (1910–). HA-1; SHFE
Perkin, Sir William Henry (1838–1907). ASA; FE; SHFB
Price, James (1752–1785). CUA
Priestley, Joseph (1733–1804). CAA; DABB; FE; SHFB; STI
Soddy, Frederick (1877–1956). POD; RID

French

Curie, Marie Sklodowska (1867–1934). (Born Poland). ASA; ASB-1; BEC; BEP; BOB; BOC; BOH; BUF; CAA; COL; DEI; DEJ; DOE; EVD; FE; FRE; HUE; KOA; MAJ; MANB; MASA; PA; PAC; POD; RID; SC; SHFB; SHFE†; SIA; STI
Curie, Pierre (1859–1906). ASA; BOB; BUF; DOE; PAC; RID; STI
Gay-Lussac, Joseph Louis (1778–1850). SHFB
Lavoisier, Antoine Laurent (1743–1794). ASA; CAA; CAB; COL; DOE; MOBA; POD; SHFB; STI
Moissan, Henri (1852–1907). LET
Pasteur, Louis (1822–1895). ASA; BEK; BEP; BUF; CAA; CAB; CHD; COL; DEB; DEI; DEJ; DOE; EVD; FAF; FE; FRE; HUD; POD; RIE; ROA; SHG; SUF

German

Baeyer, Adolf von (1835–1917). LET
Bunsen, Robert Wilhelm (1811–1899). SHFB
Domagk, Gerhard (1895–1964). AAS-31; RIF; ROA
Haber, Fritz (1868–1934). FE; LET
Hahn, Otto (1879–1968). FE
Kekule, Friedrich (1829–1896). FE
Liebig, Justus von (1803–1873). CAB
Wallach, Otto (1847–1931). LET
Willstätter, Richard (1872–1942). LET
Wöhler, Friedrich (1800–1882). CAA; FE

Scottish

Black, Joseph (1728–1799). BUF
Dewar, Sir James (1842–1923). SHFB
Ramsay, Sir William (1852–1916). COLA†; SHFB

Swedish

Arrhenius, Svante August (1859–1927). FE
Berzelius, Jöns Jakob, baron (1779–1848). MOBA; SHFB
Nobel, Alfred Bernhard (1833–1896). EVA; HAC; LAE; MAP; MEC; RIF
Scheele, Karl Wilhelm (1742–1786). SOB

Swiss

Müller, Paul Hermann (1899–1965). AAS-31†; RIF

Reichstein, Tadeus (1897–). (Born Poland). LET; RIF

Saussure, Nicolas Théodore de (1767–1845). CAB

Others

Avogadro, Amedeo (1776–1856). Italian. CAA; MOBA; SHFB

Cannizzaro, Stanislao (1826–1910). Italian. MOBA

Hevesy, George de (1885–1966). Hungarian. LET

Mendeleev, Dmitri I. (1834–1907). Russian. CAA; COLA; FE; MOBA; SHFB

CHESS PLAYERS

Alekhine, Alexander (1892–1946). Russian. LEQB

Botvinnik, Mikhail M. (1911–). Russian. LEQB

Capablanca, José R. (1888–1942). Cuban. LEQB

Fischer, Bobby (Robert James) (1943–). BELB; FOR; LEQB; RHA

Keres, Paul (1916–1975). Estonian. LEQB

Lasker, Emanuel (1868–1941). German. LEQB; RHA

Marshall, Frank James (1877–1944). LEQB

Menchik, Vera (1906–1944). Russian. LEQB

Pillsbury, Harry Nelson (1872–1906). LEQB

Reshevsky, Samuel (1911–). (Born Poland). LEQB; RHA

Spassky, Boris V. (1937–). Russian. LEQB

Tal, Mikhail (1936–). Latvian. LEQB

CHICANOS, *see* MEXICAN AMERICANS

CHILDREN

See also RUNAWAYS

Adh-Dhîb, Muhammed (1931?–). FOR

Anning, Mary (1799–1847). English. FOR

Barker, Sarah (b. 1803). CAD

Bedell, Grace (b. 1849). CAD

Bell, Caroline D. (1928–). English. CAHA

Bell, Edward A. (1930–). English. CAHA

Bergeman, Gerald (1940?–). ANCA

Browne, Michael (1967?–). ANCA

Chalmers, Willie (b. 1765). CAD

Christie, David (1960?–). ANCA

Christie, Robert (1961?–). ANCA

Colburn, Zerah (1804–1839). FOR

Conkling, Hilda (1910–1986). FOR

Cornick, Wade (1965?–). ANCA

Cotter, Jim (b. 1834). CAD

Dale, Jerome (1964?–). ANCA

Dean, Stewart (fl. 1785). CAD

Delgado, Estrella (1958?–). WECC

de Sautuola, Maria (1870–1946). Spanish. FOR

Devereux, Henry Kelsey. CAD

Francisco, Peter (1760?–1831). CAD

Frank, Anne (1919–1945). German. ELA; FOR; GRB-1

Giffen, Isaac Newton (b. 1848). CAD

Gillett, Joshua (fl. 1813). BAC

Gregory, Darryl (1962?–). ANCA

Heide, Dirk van der, pseud. (1928?–). (Born the Netherlands). CAHA

Helme, Johnny. BAC

Howard, Cordelia (1848–1941). CAD

Hutchinson, Abigail (b. 1829?). CAD

Ide, Simeon (b. 1794?). BAC

Jay, Allen (1831–1910). CAD

Jefferson, Joseph (1829–1905). CAD

Jemison, Mary (1743–1833). DI; HEE

Jupille, Jean Baptiste. French. FAF

Kieff, Elaine (1948?–). ANCA

Kilmer, Gordon (1946–). ANCA

Lee, George (b. 1774). BAC

Lefferts, Rebecca (b. 1829?). BAC

Loura, Philip (1967?–). ANCA

Maffitt, John Newland (1819–1886). CAD

Metcalf, Betsy (b. 1787). BAC

Moyer, Daniel (b. 1787). BAC

Murray, Harold (1942?–). ANCA

Oñate, Cristóbal de (fl. 1598). NAA

Peterson, Joel (1968?–). ANCA

Phipps, James (b. 1788). FAF

Pickersgill, Caroline (b. 1800). BAC; CAD

Ramírez, Armando Socarras (1963?–). Cuban. CAHA

Reynolds, Phoebe (b. 1771). CLC

Sands, Sam (b. 1800). CAD

Slack, Donna Lee (1961?–). ANCA

Southgate, Eliza (1783–1809). MAV

Stratt, Parker (1941?–). ANCA

Temple, Shirley (1928–). FOR

Unteidt, Byron (1919–). CAD

Ward, Macock (b. 1702). BAC

Whitaker, Mark (1951–). FOR

Whitcher, Sylvanus (b. 1837?). BAC

Zane, Elizabeth (1766–1831). AND; CAD; CLC

CHILEANS

Bello, Andrés (1781–1865). Statesman, born Venezuela. WOB

Medina, José Toribio (1852–1930). Scholar. WOB

Mistral, Gabriela (1889–1957). Poet, educator. BACA; SHFE†; WO

Neruda, Pablo (1904–1973). Poet, statesman. WO
O'Higgins, Bernardo (1778–1842). Soldier, statesman. BAA; LAB; OLA; STP

CHINESE

Cheng, Chi (1944–). Track athlete. AAS-24;
HOBAA; ST-1
Chiang Kai-shek (1886–1975). Nationalist leader.
ARA; ASB-1; DOF; SPA
Chiang Mei-ling (1897–). Wife of Chiang Kai-
shek. EUA; PA
Chou En-lai (1898–1976). Communist leader. SPA
Confucius (551–479 B.C.). Philosopher. DEI; DEJ;
LO; SPA
Go-Hung (254–334). Alchemist. CUA
Hsuan-Tsang (600?–664). Traveler. ROL
Hsüan Tsung (685–762). Emperor. SPA
Hung Hsiu-ch'üan (1812–1864). Revolutionist.
SPA
K'ang-hsi (1654–1722). Emperor. NEC
Lao-tzu (c. 604–531 B.C.). Philosopher. LO
Lim, Kim San (1916–). Singapore government of-
ficial. RODA
Mao Tse-tung (1893–1976). Communist leader.
ARA; ASB-1; CAAA; CAE; COJB; DOF; DU-1;
HAK; KE; SPA; WEA
Shih Huang Ti (259–210 B.C.). Emperor. BLW;
NEC; SPA
Sun Yat-sen (1866–1925). Statesman. ASB-1;
CAAA; DOF; KEE; LAD; SPA
Tzu Hsi (1835–1908). Empress. BOI; FAE; LIDA;
SPA
Wang An-shih (1021–1086). Statesman. SPA
Wang Mang (33 B.C.–23 A.D.). Emperor. SPA
Yen, James Yang-ch'u (1894–). Educator. BAF;
COG; SPA

CHOREOGRAPHERS, *see* DANCERS & CHOREOGRA-
PHERS

CHRISTIAN SCIENCE LEADERS, *see* RELIGIOUS LEAD-
ERS, PROTESTANT

CIRCUS & SHOW FIGURES

See also RODEO FIGURES

Adler, Felix (d. 1960). Clown. KIB
Bailey, Mollie Arline (1841–1918). Circus owner.
KIB

Baker, John. Manager, Buffalo Bill's Wild West
Show. JOD
Barnum, Phineas Taylor (1810–1891). Circus
showman. DEI; DEJ; KIB; KLD
Beatty, Clyde (1905–1965). Animal trainer. KIB
Codona, Alfredo (1894–1937). Italian aerialist.
SUA
Cody, William Frederick (Buffalo Bill) (1846–
1917). Wild West showman. BUI; COE; DEI;
DEJ; KEH; KIB; WAF
Concello, Antoinette. Aerialist. KIB
Concello, Arthur Vas. Aerialist. KIB
Evans, Merle (1894–1987). Circus bandmaster.
KIB
Forsyth, Jane (1929–). Animal trainer. GUJ
Griebling, Otto (1896–1972). Clown, born Ger-
many. KIB
Grock, pseud. (1880–1959). German clown. KLD
Jacobs, Lou (1903?–). Clown, born Germany. KIB
Kelly, Emmett (1898–1979). Clown. KIB
Leitzel, Lillian (1882–1931). Aerialist, born Ger-
many. KIB
Oakley, Annie (1860–1926). Markswoman. DAG;
DAGA; KIB; WAE
Rice, Daniel McLaren, Jr. (1823–1900). Clown.
KIB; KLD
Ringling Brothers (John, Otto, Charles, Alfred T.
and Albert C.). Circus owners. KIB; KLD
Sandow, Eugene (1867–1925). Strongman, born
Germany. PHA
Sinclair, Sue (1954–). Aquarium animal trainer.
GUJ
Stratton, Charles Sherwood (Tom Thumb) (1838–
1883). KIB
Wallenda family. German-American acrobats.
KIB
Wirth, May (1896?–). Australian bareback rider.
KIB

CIVIL ENGINEERS, *see* ENGINEERS, CIVIL

CIVIL RIGHTS LEADERS

Abernathy, Ralph David (1926–). YOI
Aronson, Henry M. (1935?–). COF
Bates, Daisy Gaston (1922–). AKB; DOF-1;
GRAB-01; STF
Bond, Julian (1940–). BRGA; DU
Braden, Anne (1924–). STG
Carmichael, Stokely (1941–). HAI
Conde, Carlos. NEAA
Downing, George Thomas (1819–1903). GRAB-01

Evers, Medgar Wiley (1925–1963). DADA†; DOF-1; FLD

Farmer, James (1920–). DRA; GRAB-01; STF

Forman, James (1928–). HAI

Gonzales, Rodolfo (1929–). NEAA

Grimké, Francis James (1850–1937). BRB†; GRAB-01

Hamer, Fannie Lou (1917–). BRBE†; DU; FAG; GRAB-01

Horton, Myles (1905–). STG

Jackson, Jesse Louis (1941–). DRA; GRAB-01

King, Coretta Scott (1927–). FAG; GIBA

King, Martin Luther, Jr. (1929–1968). AAS-34; ADA; ADB; ASB-1; BAF; BRBD; BRG; DEJ; DOF-1; DU-1; ELA; FAA; FEC; FLD; GRAB-01; HAJ; HODA; JO; JOC; KE; LEPE; MEB; MEC; RICA; STO; WEB; WIAA-8; WIC; YOA; YOI

Koontz, Elizabeth (1919–). GIB-1

Lewis, John (1940?–). STF

McKissick, Floyd B. (1922–). FAG; HAI; YOI

Malcolm X (1925–1965). ADB; AKB; BRBD; DABB; DADB; FAG; GRAB-01; HAI; HAK; HODA; JO; RICA

Marshall, Thurgood (1908–). ADA; ADB; BRG; DOF-1; FAG; FLC; FLD; STF; WEC; YOI

Meredith, James Howard (1933–). DADA†; FLD; STJB

Mitchell, Clarence, Jr. (1911–1984). DOF-1

Moody, Anne (1940–). AKB; DADB

Moore, Harry Tyson (1905–1951). DOF-1

Murphy, Carl James (1889–1967). DOF-1

Newton, Huey P. (1942–). HAI

Ogden, Dunbar (1903–). STG

O'Neal, John. COF

Parks, Rosa Lee (1913–). COG-1; DOF-1; STF

Pennington, James W. C. (c. 1809–1870). GRAB-02

Ruffin, Josephine St. Pierre (1842–1924). GRAB-01

Rustin, Bayard (1910–1987). FAG; YOI

Shuttlesworth, Fred (1922–). STF

Staupers, Mable Keaton (1890–). (Born West Indies). DOF-1

Sullivan, Leon Howard (1922–). DOF-1; EOA

Talbert, Mary Burnett (1866–1923). DOF-1; GRAB-01

Tobias, Channing Heggie (1882–1961). DOF-1; GRAB-01

Trotter, William Monroe (1872–1934). ADB; BEJ; STJB

Weinberger, Eric (1932–). COF

White, Walter F. (1893–1955). ADA; ADB; DOF-1; GRAB-01; RIC

Wilkins, Roy (1901–1981). DOF-1; FAG; KE; YOI

Williams, Claude (1900?–). STG

Wright, Nathan, Jr. (1923–). HAI

Wyatt, Addie (1924–). BI; GIB-1

Young, Whitney Moore, Jr. (1921–1971). ADB; FAG; GRAB-01; KE; WECA; YOI

Zellner, Robert. STG

CIVIL WAR FIGURES

Northern – Military

Anderson, Osborne Perry (1830–1871). GRAB-05

Grant, Ulysses Simpson (1822–1885). BAEB; BAG; BAG-1; BEB; BLA; BUIA; CAG; CAH; COD; COI; COJA; COS; CUC; DEI; DEJ; DUB; DUC; DUCA; FID; FRBA; HIH; LEP; LEQ; LEQA; MAB; MABA; MIA; PED; RAE; ROH; ROHA; ROK†; SUBB; WHD

Kilpatrick, Hugh Judson (1836–1881). ARE

Knefler, Frederick (fl. 1864). (Born Hungary). LETA

McClellan, George Brinton (1826–1885). GO; WHD†

Sheridan, Philip Henry (1831–1888). ARE

Sherman, William Tecumseh (1820–1891). CUC

Smalls, Robert (1839–1915). ADA; ADB; HODA; HUB; JOC; PECA; ROG; STD; STJB

Stoneman, George (1822–1894). ARE

Thomas, George Henry (1816–1870). STG

Warren, Gouverneur Kemble (1830–1882). DIA

Northern – Spies

Baker, Lafayette Curry (1826–1868). SUG

Bowser, Mary Elizabeth (fl. 1861–1865). LOAV

Cushman, Pauline (1833–1893). RAB

Dabney, Mrs. STQ

Edmonds, Sarah Emma (1841–1898). FOA; KN; SUG; WABC†

Lewis, Pryce (fl. 1861–1864). English. FOA

Louvestre, Mary (fl. 1861). HAB

Van Lew, Elizabeth (1818–1900). FOA; SUG; WABC†

Webster, Timothy (1816?–1862). (Born England). FOA

Northern – Others

Frietchie, Barbara (1766–1862). DOD

Southern – Military

Butler, Matthew Calbraith (1836–1909). MAD

de Leon, David (1813–1872). GRB-1

Forrest, Nathan Bedford (1821–1877). ARE; MAD

Hampton, Wade (1818–1902). MAD

Jackson, Thomas Jonathan (Stonewall Jackson) (1824–1863). ARE; MAO

Lee, Robert Edward (1807–1870). ASB; CHG;

COD; CUC; DEI; DEJ; FIA; FID; HAA; LEP;
MAO; MAT; RAE†
Morgan, John Hunt (1825–1864). MAD
Mosby, John Singleton (1833–1916). MAD
Shelby, Joseph Orville (1830–1897). MAD
Stuart, James Ewell Brown (Jeb) (1833–1864).
ARE; MAD
Wheeler, Joseph (1836–1906). MAD

Southern – Spies
Bowie, Walter (1837?–1864). FOA
Boyd, Belle (1844–1900). FOA; MAO; SEB; SUG;
WABC†
Davis, Sam (1842–1863). MAO
Greenhow, Rose O'Neal (1817–1864). FOA; HAB;
SUG; WABC†

Southern – Statesmen
Davis, Jefferson (1808–1889). MAO
Stephens, Alexander Hamilton (1812–1883). MAO

CLARINETISTS, *see* MUSICIANS—CLARINETISTS

CLERGYMEN, *see* CHAPLAINS; RELIGIOUS LEADERS, JEW-
ISH; RELIGIOUS LEADERS, PROTESTANT; RELIGIOUS LEAD-
ERS, ROMAN CATHOLIC

CLOWNS, *see* CIRCUS & SHOW FIGURES; RODEO FIG-
URES

COACHES, *see* INDIVIDUAL SPORTS

COLLEGE PERSONNEL, *see* EDUCATORS

COLOMBIANS

Santander, Francisco de Paula (1792–1840). General, president. LAB

COLONIAL AMERICANS

See also AMERICAN REVOLUTIONARY FIGURES;
FOUNDERS OF CITIES & COLONIES; PIONEERS &
FRONTIER PEOPLE

Bradford, William (1590–1657). DAC; DIA; MAT;
OLA; VIA
Bradstreet, Anne Dudley (1612?–1672). JOCA;
OCB; VIA; WABC†
Brent, Margaret (1600?–1671?). GUBA†; VIA;
WABC

Colden, Cadwallader (1688–1776). (Born Ireland).
PAC
Gardiner, David (b. 1636). CAF
Gardiner, Lion (1599–1663). CAF
Harriman, Mercy (b. 1758). BAC
Hunt, Nathan (fl. 1840). BAC
Hutchinson, Anne Marbury (1591–1643). BLF;
CRB; DAD; DOD; JOCA; SMC; VIA; WABC;
WAR; YOC
Jenifer, Daniel of St. Thomas (1723–1790).
BUIB†; FEAA
Milledge, John (1721–1781). CAF
Minuit, Peter (1580–1638). Dutch. LEO; VIA
Moody, Lady Deborah (1600–1669?). CRB; JOCA;
WABC†
Smith, John (1580–1631). English. ASB; LEO;
LEPF; MAT; VIA
Sousa, Mathias (fl. 1642). WIBA
Standish, Lora (fl. 1630). BAC
Stout, Penelope Thomson (1622–1732). CRB
Willard, Simon (1605–1676). WOAA
Winslow, Anna Green (1760–1779). CAF
Winthrop, John (1588–1649). LEO

COLONIZERS, *see* FOUNDERS OF CITIES & COLONIES

COLUMNISTS, *see* JOURNALISTS

COMEDIANS, *see* ACTORS, ACTRESSES & ENTERTAIN-
ERS; TELEVISION & RADIO PERSONALITIES

COMMENTATORS, *see* TELEVISION & RADIO PERSON-
ALITIES

COMMUNISTS

See also SOCIALISTS

Castro, Fidel (1926–). Cuban. ARA; BAGA; DU-1;
HAK; WEA
Chou En-lai (1898–1976). Chinese. SPA
Davis, Benjamin Jefferson (1903–1964). DADA
Flynn, Elizabeth Gurley (1890–1964). ARAA
Guevara, Ché (Ernesto) (1928–1967). Cuban. HAK
Ho Chi Minh (1890–1969). Vietnamese. ASB-1;
HAK; WECA
Khrushchev, Nikita S. (1894–1971). Russian.
ARA; COJB; DOF; KE; WEA
Kosygin, Aleksei N. (1904–1980). Russian. WEC
Lenin, Nikolai (Vladimir Illich Ulyanov) (1870–
1924). Russian. ARA; ASB-1; CAAA; COJB;
DEI; DEJ; DOF; NEBB-1
Mao Tse-tung (1893–1976). Chinese. ARA; ASB-1;

CAAA; CAE; COJB; DOF; DU-1; HAK; KE;
SPA; WEA

Stalin, Joseph (1879–1953). Russian. ARA; ASB-
1; CAE; CL-01; COJB; DOF; KIA; TAC

Tito, Josip Broz (1892–1980). Yugoslavian. ARA;
COJB; DU-1; WEB

Trotsky, Leon (1877–1940). Russian. COJB;
NEBB-1

COMPOSERS

American

Ager, Milton (1893–1979). MOA
Babbitt, Milton (1916–). EWAA
Ball, Ernest (1878–1927). MOA
Ballard, Louis W. (1931–). GRAC
Barber, Samuel (1910–1981). BAD; KAE; MAF;
POF
Benjamin, Bennie (1907–). HUC
Berlin, Irving (1888–). (Born Russia). ASB-1;
BAD; EWA; LEHB; LETA; LIA; MOA
Bernstein, Leonard (1918–). EWA; EWD; KAE;
LEHB; LETA; MAF; POF; SAA†; STM; YOM†
Billings, William (1746–1800). YOJ
Blake, Ran (1935–). UN
Bland, James A. (1854–1911). ADA; ADB; HUC;
LEHB; MOA
Bloch, Ernest (1880–1959). (Born Switzerland).
GRB-1; KAE
Bock, Jerry (1928–). EWA
Bradford, Alex (1926?–1978). AB
Braxton, Anthony (1945–). UN
Brown, Nacio Herb (1896–1964). MOA
Burke, Johnny (1908–1964). MOA
Cage, John (1912–). BEKA; EWAA
Carmichael, Hoagy (1899–1981). MOA
Carpenter, John Alden (1876–1951). BAD; BUC
Cohan, George Michael (1878–1942). EWA; MOA
Cole, Nat "King" (1919–1965). ROF
Conrad, Con (Conrad Dober) (1891–1938). MOA
Copland, Aaron (1900–). BAD; BEKA; BEN;
KAE; KE; MAF; POF; SAA†; YOL
Cowell, Henry Dixon (1897–1965). POF
Creston, Paul (1906–). POF
Dawson, William Levi (1898–). ADA; ADB
Dello Joio, Norman (1913–). MAF; POF
Dett, Robert Nathaniel (1882–1943). ADA; ADB;
BRB†
Donaldson, Walter (1893–1947). MOA
Dubin, Al (1891–1945). (Born Switzerland). MOA
Edwards, Gus (1879–1945). (Born Germany).
MOA
Ellington, Duke (Edward Kennedy) (1899–1974).
ADA; ADB; ASB-1; COF-1; DOF-1; HODA;

HUC; MOA; RIC; RICA; ROF; TEA; TEB;
WAD
Foss, Lukas (1922–). (Born Germany). MAF; POF;
STM†
Foster, Stephen Collins (1826–1864). BAD; BUD;
CUC; DEI; DEJ; KAE; MOA; POF; SMBA; WIA
Friml, Rudolf (1879–1972). (Born Czechoslova-
kia). EWA; MOA
Gershwin, George (1898–1937). ALD; BAD;
BEKA; BUC; CUC; DEI; DEJ; EWA; FIE;
KAE; LAC; LETA; MAF; MOA; POF; SAA†;
WIA; YOJ
Gottschalk, Louis Moreau (1829–1869). CHF;
LEHB
Gould, Morton (1913–). POF; STM†
Grant, Micki. AB
Griffes, Charles Tomlinson (1884–1920). BAD;
BUC; KAE; MAF; POF
Grofé, Ferde (1892–1972). POF
Handy, William Christopher (1873–1958). ADA;
ADB; BAD; HUA; MOA; ROG; WAD
Hanson, Howard (1896–1981). MAF; POF; STM†
Harris, Roy Ellsworth (1898–1979). BAD; KAE;
MAF; POF
Hefti, Neal (1922–). UN
Henderson, Ray (1896–1970). MOA
Herbert, Victor (1859–1924). (Born Ireland).
BAD; CUC; DEI; DEJ; EWA; KAE; MOA
Hernandez, Raphael (1893–). FOW
Hindemith, Paul (1895–1963). (Born Germany).
BEKA; KAE; SAA; YOL
Hovhaness, Alan (1911–). POF
Ives, Charles (1874–1954). BAD; EWAA; FIE;
KAE; MAF; POF; SAA†
Jacobs-Bond, Carrie (1862–1946). MOA; STJ
Joplin, Scott (1868–1917). COF-1
Kay, Ulysses (1917–). ADB; POF
Kern, Jerome (1885–1945). BAD; CUC; EWA;
MOA; WIA
Kreisler, Fritz (1875–1962). (Born Austria).
CHFA; RADA
Lockwood, Normand (1906–). POF
Loesser, Frank (1910–1969). EWA; MOA
Loewe, Frederick (1904–1988). (Born Austria).
EWA
MacDowell, Edward Alexander (1861–1908).
BAD; BRF; BUD; KAE; MAF; POF
McHugh, Jimmy (1894–). MOA
Mennin, Peter (1923–1983). POF
Menotti, Gian-Carlo (1911–). (Born Italy). BEKA;
KAE; LIA; MAF; POF
Monk, Theolonius (1920–1982). COF-1; WAD†
Moore, Carman (1936–). AB
Moore, Douglas Stuart (1893–1969). MAF; POF
Nelson, Willie (1933–). BUIB-01; KRI
Nevin, Ethelbert W. (1862–1901). BAD

Partch, Harry (1901–1974). EWAA
Parton, Dolly (1946–). BUIB-01; KRI-1
Piston, Walter (1894–1976). BAD; MAF; POF
Porter, Cole (1893–1964). EWA; MOA
Porter, Quincy (1897–1966). POF
Price, Florence Beatrice Smith (1888–1933). LOAV
Reynolds, Malvina (1899?–). BOHC
Riegger, Wallingford (1885–1961). POF
Rodgers, Richard Charles (1902–1979). BAD; BEKA; EWA; MOA
Romberg, Sigmund (1887–1951). (Born Hungary). EWA; MOA
Ruby, Harry (1895–1974). MOA
Sainte-Marie, Buffy (1942?–). BOHC
Schönberg, Arnold (1874–1951). (Born Austria). BEKA; BUC; EWAA; KAE; SAA†; YOL
Schuman, William (1910–). BAD; MAF; POF
Schwartz, Arthur (1900–1984). MOA
Seeger, Ruth Crawford (1901–1953). SC-02
Sessions, Roger H. (1896–1985). POF
Silver, Horace (1928–). UN
Sousa, John Philip (1854–1932). BAD; CAD; CUC; KAE; LEHB; POF
Still, William Grant (1895–1978). ADA; ADB; HUC; POF; RIC; RICA
Stravinsky, Igor Fëdorovich (1882–1971). (Born Russia). ASB-1; BAE; BEKA; BUC; FIE; KAE; POG; SAA; YOL
Taylor, Deems (1885–1966). BAD; WIA
Thomson, Virgil (1896–). MAF
Tillis, Mel (1932–). HAG-1
Van Alstyne, Egbert (1882–1951). MOA
Van Heusen, Jimmy (1913–). MOA
Von Tilzer, Harry (1872–1946). MOA
Warren, Harry (1893–1981). MOA
Weill, Kurt (1900–1950). (Born Germany). EWA
Wenrich, Percy (1887–1952). MOA
Whiting, Richard A. (1891–1938). MOA
Williams, Mary Lou (1910–1981). GIB-1
Wills, Bob (1905–1975). LA
Wonder, Stevie (1950–). BUIB-1
Yellen, Jack (1892–). (Born Poland). MOA
Youmans, Vincent (1898–1946). MOA

Austrian
Berg, Alban (1885–1935). KAE
Bruckner, Anton (1824–1896). KAE; SAA
Czerny, Karl (1791–1857). CHF
Haydn, Franz Joseph (1732–1809). BEN; BRF; BUD; FIE; KAE; SAA; YOK; YOM†
Mahler, Gustav (1860–1911). KAE; SAA; YOM†
Mozart, Wolfgang Amadeus (1756–1791). BEC; BEN; BOD; BRF; BUD; DEI; DEJ; FIE; FOR; GOA; KAE; SAA; WIA; YOK; YOM†
Schnabel, Artur (1882–1951). CHF

Schubert, Franz Peter (1797–1828). BEN; BRF; BUD; DEI; DEJ; FIE; GOA; KAE; SAA; WIA; YOK
Strauss, Johann (1825–1899). KAE
Webern, Anton von (1883–1945). EWAA
Wolf, Hugo (1860–1903). KAE; SAA

Czech
Dussek, Jan Ladislav (1760–1812). CHF
Dvořak, Antonin (1841–1904). BAE; BEN; BUC; DEI; DEJ; FIE†; KAE; SAA; YOJ
Janáček, Leoš (1854–1928). YOL
Moscheles, Ignaz (1794–1870). CHF
Smetana, Bedřich (1824–1884). BAE; FIE†; KAE; SAA

English
Arne, Thomas Augustine (1710–1778). YOJ
Britten, Benjamin (1913–1976). BEKA; KAE; YOJ
Byrd, William (1543–1623). KAE
Coleridge-Taylor, Samuel (1875–1912). ADA; ADB; BRB†
Coward, Noel (1889–1973). ASB-1
Delius, Frederick (1862–1934). BUC; KAE; SAA†
Elgar, Sir Edward William (1857–1934). BAE; BEN; BUC; GOA; KAE; SAA†; YOK
Gilbert, William Schwenk (1836–1911). ASB-1
Handel, George Frederick (1685–1759). (Born Germany). BEN; BRF; BUD; FIE; GOA; KAE; SAA; YOK; YOM†
John, Elton (1947–). BUIB-1
Lennon, John (1940–1980). BUIB-1; SC-01
McCartney, Paul (1942–). BUIB-1; SC-01
Purcell, Henry (1659–1695). BAE; BEM; KAE; SAA; YOK
Sullivan, Sir Arthur Seymour (1842–1900). BAE; KAE; SAA†
Vaughan Williams, Ralph (1872–1958). BUC; GOB; KAE; SAA†; YOJ
Walton, Sir William Turner (1902–1983). YOL

French
Berlioz, Hector (1803–1869). BRF; FIE; KAE; SAA; YOM†
Bizet, Georges (1838–1875). BAE; KAE; SAA
Boulez, Pierre (1925–). EWAA
Chausson, Ernest Amédee (1855–1899). KAE
Couperin, François (1668–1733). BEM; KAE
Debussy, Claude Achille (1862–1918). BRF; BUD; FIE; KAE; SAA
Dukas, Paul (1865–1935). KAE
Fauré, Gabriel Urbain (1845–1924). KAE
Franck, César Auguste (1822–1890). (Born Belgium). BRF; KAE

Gounod, Charles François (1818–1893). BAE; KAE

Honegger, Arthur (1892–1955). KAE

Indy, Vincent d' (1851–1931). KAE

Kreutzer, Rodolphe (1766–1831). CHFA

Leclair, Jean Marie (1697–1764). CHFA

Lully, Jean Baptiste (1632–1687). (Born Italy). BEM; CHFA; KAE; SAA; YOM†

Massenet, Jules (1842–1912). BAE; KAE

Milhaud, Darius (1892–1974). KAE

Offenbach, Jacques (1819–1880). KAE

Rameau, Jean Philippe (1683–1764). BEM; KAE

Ravel, Maurice (1875–1937). BUC; KAE; SAA; YOL

Saint-Saëns, Camille (1835–1921). KAE

Satie, Erik (1866–1925). SAA

Varèse, Edgard (1883–1965). EWAA

German

Bach, Carl Philipp Emanuel (1714–1788). KAE; SAA†; YOM†

Bach, Johann Christian (1735–1782). CHF; SAA†; YOM†

Bach, Johann Sebastian (1685–1750). BEN; BRF; BUD; DEI; DEJ; FIE; GOB; KAE; SAA; WIA; YOK; YOM†

Beethoven, Ludwig van (1770–1827). BEN; BRF; BUD; DEI; DEJ; FIE; FRE; GOB; KAE; MAJ; SAA; WIA; YOK; YOM†

Brahms, Johannes (1833–1897). BEN; BRF; BUD; DEI; DEJ; FIE; KAE; SAA; WIA; YOK

Bruch, Max (1838–1920). KAE

Cramer, Johann Baptist (1771–1858). CHF

Gluck, Christoph Willibald (1714–1787). BRF; BUD; KAE; SAA

Hummel, Johann Nepomuk (1778–1837). CHF

Humperdinck, Engelbert (1854–1921). BAE; BUC

Mendelssohn, Felix (1809–1847). BEN; BRF; BUD; DEI; DEJ; FIE; GOA; KAE; SAA; YOK; YOM†

Schumann, Robert Alexander (1810–1856). BRF; BUD; FIE; KAE; SAA; YOJ

Schütz, Heinrich (1585–1672). BEM

Spohr, Louis (1784–1859). CHFA; YOM†

Stockhausen, Karlheinz (1928–). EWAA

Strauss, Richard (1864–1949). BAE; BEKA; BUC; KAE; SAA; YOM†

Telemann, Georg Philipp (1681–1767). BEM; SAA

Wagner, Richard (1813–1883). BRF; BUD; DEI; DEJ; FIE; KAE; SAA; YOK; YOM†

Weber, Karl Maria Friedrich Ernst von (1786–1826). BRF; KAE; SAA; YOJ

Hungarian

Bartók, Béla (1881–1945). ASB-1; BEKA; BUC; FIE†; KAE; SAA; YOL

Kodály, Zoltán (1882–1967). KAE

Liszt, Franz (1811–1886). BRF; BUD; CHF; FIE; KAE; SAA; YOH

Italian

Boccherini, Luigi (1743–1805). KAE

Busoni, Ferruccio (1866–1924). CHF

Cherubini, Luigi (1760–1842). KAE

Clementi, Muzio (1752–1832). CHF

Corelli, Arcangelo (1653–1713). BEM; CHFA; KAE; YOM†

Donizetti, Gaetano (1797–1848). KAE

Frescobaldi, Girolamo (1583–1643). BEM

Gabrieli, Giovanni (c. 1555–1612). BEM

Gesualdo, Carlo (1560–1613). BEM

Leoncavallo, Ruggiero (1858–1919). KAE

Mascagni, Pietro (1863–1945). KAE

Monteverdi, Claudio (1567–1643). BEM; FIE; KAE; SAA

Palestrina, Giovanni Pierluigi da (1526?–1594). BRF; BUD; KAE; YOJ

Pergolesi, Giovanni Battista (1710–1746). KAE

Puccini, Giacomo (1858–1924). BAE; KAE; SAA

Respighi, Ottorino (1879–1936). BUC; KAE

Rossini, Gioacchino (1792–1868). BAE; KAE; SAA

Scarlatti, Alessandro (1659–1725). BAE; SAA

Scarlatti, Domenico (1685–1757). BEN; KAE; SAA

Tartini, Giuseppe (1692–1770). BEN; CHFA; SAA†

Verdi, Giuseppe (1813–1901). BRF; BUD; GOB; KAE; SAA; TRC; WIA; YOJ

Vivaldi, Antonio (1675?–1741). BEM; CHFA; KAE; SAA; YOM†

Russian

Balakireff, Mili Alekseyevich (1837–1910). POG; SAA†

Borodin, Alexander P. (1833–1887). BAE; KAE; POG; SAA

Cui, César Antonovich (1835–1918). POG; SAA†

Glazunov, Aleksandr Konstantinovich (1865–1936). POG

Glière, Reinhold Moritzovich (1875–1956). POG

Glinka, Mikhail Ivanovich (1804–1857). KAE; POG; SAA

Kabalevsky, Dmitri Borisovich (1904–). POG

Khachaturian, Aram (1903–1978). KAE; POG

Miakovsky, Nikolai Yakovlevich (1891–1950). POG

Mussorgsky, Modest Petrovich (1839–1881). BAE; BUC; FIE†; KAE; POG; SAA

Prokofiev, Sergei Sergeevich (1891–1953). BEKA; BUC; KAE; POG; SAA; YOL

Rachmaninoff, Sergei (1873–1943). BAE; BEN; KAE; POG; SAA

Rimski-Korsakov, Nikolai Andreevich (1844–1908). BAE; BUC; FIE†; KAE; POG; SAA; YOJ

Rubinstein, Anton (1829–1894). CHF

Scriabin, Aleksandr Nikolaievich (1872–1915). BUC; POG

Shostakovich, Dmitri (1906–1975). KAE; POG; SAA

Tchaikovsky, Peter Ilyich (1840–1893). BEN; BRF; BUD; DEI; DEJ; FIE†; GOB; KAE; POG; SAA; WIA; YOK

Ussachevsky, Vladimir (1911–). BEKA

Spanish

Albéniz, Isaac (1860–1909). KAE; SAA

Falla, Manuel de (1876–1946). BUC; KAE; SAA†; YOL

Granados, Enrique (1867–1916). KAE; SAA†

Others

Buxtehude, Dietrich (1637–1707). Swedish. BEM

Chávez, Carlos (1899–1978). Mexican. KAE; NEBA; ROGB; STM†; WO

Chopin, Frédéric François (1810–1849). Polish. BEN; BRF; BUD; DEI; DEJ; FIE; GOB; KAE; MANB; SAA; WIA; YOJ

Enesco, Georges (1881–1955). Romanian. KAE; YOM†

Field, John (1782–1837). Irish. CHF

Grieg, Edvard Hagerup (1843–1907). Norwegian. BRF; BUD; DEI; DEJ; FIE†; GOA; KAE; SAA

Lasso, Orlando di (1532?–1594). Belgian. KAE

Nielsen, Carl A. (1865–1931). Danish. YOL

Sibelius, Jean (1865–1957). Finnish. BAE; BEKA; BUC; FIE†; KAE; SAA; YOJ

Vieuxtemps, Henri François Joseph (1820–1881). Belgian. CHFA

Villa-Lobos, Heitor (1887–1959). Brazilian. BACA; KAE

Xenakis, Yannis (1922–). Greek. EWAA

COMPUTER PEOPLE

Babbage, Charles (1792–1871). English. COLA; FE; FRE; GRAB-3; WEF

Bardeen, John (1908–). AAS-33†; GRAB-3; MAPA

Brattain, Walter Houser (1902–1987). AAS-33†; GRAB-3; MAPA

Eckert, J. Presper (1919–). GRAB-3

Hopper, Grace Murray (1906–). GIB-1; GRAB-3

Lovelace, Lady Ada (Byron) (1815–1852). English. GRAB-3; WEF

Mauchly, John W. (1907–1980). GRAB-3

Shockley, William Bradford (1910–). AAS-33†; GRAB-3; MAPA

Turing, Alan M. (1912–1954). English. GRAB-3

Von Neumann, John (1903–1957). (Born Hungary). GRAB-3; STN

CONDUCTORS

See also BAND LEADERS

American

Abravanel, Maurice (1903–). (Born Turkey). STM

Allesandro, Victor (1915–). STM

Bergmann, Carl (1821–1876). (Born Germany). YOM

Bernstein, Leonard (1918–). EWA; EWD; KAE; LEHB; LETA; MAF; POF; SAA†; STM; YOM†

Brico, Antonia (1902–). (Born the Netherlands). SC-02; STM†

Caldwell, Sarah (1924–). GIB-1; SC-02†

Caston, Saul (1901–). STM

Damrosch, Walter (1862–1950). (Born Germany). CUC

DePriest, James (1936–). AB

Dixon, Dean (1915–1976). ADA; ADB; BOG; HUC; RIC; RICA; STM†

Dorati, Antal (1906–). (Born Hungary). STM; YOM

Freccia, Massimo (1906–). (Born Italy). STM

Golschmann, Vladimir (1893–1972). (Born France). STM

Harrison, Guy Fraser (1894–). (Born England). STM

Hendl, Walter (1917–). STM

Hilsberg, Alexander (1900–1961). (Born Russia). STM

Johnson, Thor (1913–1975). STM

Jorda, Enrique (1911–). (Born Spain). STM

Klemperer, Otto (1885–1973). (Born Germany). EWD; STM†; YOM

Koussevitzky, Serge (1874–1951). (Born Russia). EWB; YOM

Krips, Josef (1902–1974). (Born Austria). EWD; STM

Leinsdorf, Erich (1912–). (Born Austria). BEA; EWD; STM; YOM

Maazel, Lorin (1930–). EWD

Mitchell, Howard (1911–). STM

Mitropoulos, Dimitri (1896–1960). (Born Greece). EWB; STM; YOM

Monteux, Pierre (1875–1964). (Born France). EWB; STM; YOM

Ormandy, Eugene (1899–1985). (Born Hungary). EWD; STM; YOM

Queler, Eve (1936–). WA

Reiner, Fritz (1888–1963). (Born Hungary). EWB; STM

Schwieger, Hans (1906–). (Born Germany). STM

Sokoloff, Nikolai (b. 1886). (Born Russia). STM†; YOM

Solomon, Izler (1910–1987). STM

Sopkin, Henry (1903–). STM

Steinberg, William (1899–1978). (Born Germany). EWD; STM

Stokowski, Leopold (1882–1977). (Born England). EWD; LOB; STM; YOM

Swalin, Benjamin (1901–). STM

Szell, George (1897–1970). (Born Hungary). EWD; STM; YOM

Thomas, Theodore (1835–1905). (Born Germany). YOM

Wallenstein, Alfred (1898–1983). STM

Whitney, Robert (1904–). STM

Foreign

Barbirolli, John (1899–1970). English. STM†; YOM

Beecham, Sir Thomas (1879–1961). English. EWB; STM†; YOM

Beinum, Eduard van (1901–1959). Dutch. STM; YOM†

Boulez, Pierre (1925–). French. EWAA

Colonne, Edouard (1838–1910). French. YOM

Fricsay, Ferenc (1914–1963). Hungarian. STM†; YOM

Furtwaengler, Wilhelm (1886–1954). German. EWB; YOM†

Jullien, Louis Antoine (1812–1860). French. YOM

Karajan, Herbert von (1908–). Austrian. EWD; STM†; YOM†

Lamoureux, Charles (1834–1899). French. YOM

Manns, August (1825–1907). English. (Born Germany). YOM

Mehta, Zubin (1936–). Indian. EWD

Munch, Charles (1891–1968). French. EWD; STM; YOM

Nikisch, Arthur (1855–1922). Hungarian. YOM

Paray, Paul (b. 1886). French. STM

Richter, Hans (1843–1916). Hungarian. YOM

Sargent, Sir Malcolm (1895–1967). English. STM†; YOM

Scherchen, Hermann (1891–1966). German. STM†; YOM

Stockhausen, Karlheinz (1928–). German. EWAA

Toscanini, Arturo (1867–1957). Italian. DEI; DEJ; EWB; FRB; KEE; MAS; YOH; YOM

Walter, Bruno (1876–1962). German. EWB; STM; YOM

Weingartner, Felix von (1863–1942). Austrian. YOM

Wood, Henry (1869–1944). English. YOM

CONGRESSMEN, *see* LEGISLATORS, U.S.

CONSERVATIONISTS, *see* ECOLOGISTS

CONSORTS OF RULERS, *see* RULERS

CORNETISTS, *see* MUSICIANS—TRUMPETERS & CORNETISTS

COSMETICIANS, *see* BUSINESS PEOPLE

COSTUME DESIGNERS, *see* DESIGNERS

COWBOYS

See also LAW ENFORCERS; PIONEERS & FRONTIER PEOPLE; RANCHERS & CATTLEMEN; RODEO FIGURES

Beckwith, Henry. STQ

Claybourne, Braxton Daniel (1877–1935). JO

Crosby, Bob. WAA

Ikard, Bose (b. 1847). BUH; HODA; KADB; SCB; STQ

Linderman, Bill (1920–1965). KAW

Love, Nat (1854–1921). BRBD; KADB

McJunkin, George (1851–1922). KAW

Pickett, Bill (1861–1932). GRAB-02; HODA; KADB; STQ†; WAA

Rogers, Will (1879–1935). BOD; COKA; KAW; LEH; PHA; WAA; WAO

Siringo, Charles A. (1855–1928). FOC; KAW; SUI

Slaughter, John H. (1841–1922). KAW

CRAFTSPERSONS

Burningham, Charlene. Weaver. BOHB

Cellini, Benvenuto (1500–1571). Italian goldsmith. DEI; DEJ; JAC; RAC

Dat-So-La-Lee (1830–1925). Washoe Indian basket maker. WAB

Francis, Miriam B. (1930–). FAI

Gomez, Manuel (1949–). FAI

Hall, Horathel (1928?–). Weaver. FAI

Hunt, Nathan (fl. 1840). Colonial basket maker. BAC

Martinez, Maria Montoya (b. 1881). Pueblo Indian pottery maker. GRAC; GRAD; LEH; WAB

Myers, Myer (1723–1795). Silversmith. LETA

Phyfe, Duncan (1768–1854). Cabinetmaker, born Scotland. BAC

Revere, Paul (1735–1818). Silversmith. BAC;

BUIB; DAFA; DEI; DEJ; EVD; FIA; FOA;
HAN; SOA; SUL

CRIMINALS & OUTLAWS

See also ASSASSINS; PIRATES, BUCCANEERS &
PRIVATEERS; SPIES & INTELLIGENCE AGENTS; TRAI-
TORS

Alvord, Burt (d. 1923). WIAA-1
Apache Kid (fl. 1880–1890). SUJ
Bass, Sam (1851–1878). JOBA; REE; SUJ
Bell, Tom, pseud. (d. 1856). WIAA-1
Billy the Kid (1859–1881). JOBA; REE; SUJ
Black Bart (fl. 1875). JOBA; REE; SUJ; WIAA-1
Burrows, Rube (1854–1890). REE
Carlisle, Bill (b. 1890). REE
Cartouche, Dominique (Louis Dominique
    Bourguignon) (1693–1721). French. SUG
Cassidy, Butch (George Leroy Parker) (1867–
    1912). JOBA; REE; SUJ†
Chacon, Augustin (d. 1902). Mexican. JOBA
Chato, El. WIAA-1
Cherokee Bill (b. 1876). KADB; SUJ
Cook, Bill (b. 1873). SUJ
Cooper, Dan B. (fl. 1971). WIAA-1
Dalton brothers (fl. 1890). JOBA; REE; SUJ
Dart, Isom, pseud. (1849–1900). KADB
D'Autremont brothers (fl. 1904–1958). WIAA-1
Doolin, Bill (d. 1896). JOBA; SUJ
Hardin, John Welsey (1853–1895). JOBA; REE;
    SUJ
Harpe, Micajah (Big Harpe) (fl. 1790). JOBA
Harpe, Wiley (Little Harpe) (fl. 1790). JOBA
Hart, Pearl (fl. 1903). WIAA-2
Hodges, Ben (d. 1929). KADB
Holliday, Doc (John Henry) (1852–1887). JOBA
Horn, Tom (1860–1903). JOBA; KAW; SUI
James, Frank (1844–1915). JOBA; REE
James, Jesse (1847–1882). JOBA; REE; SUJ
Jennings, Al (1863–1962). JOBA
Ketchum, Thomas Edward (1865?–1901). WIAA-1
Kuhl, Benjamin (d. 1944). WIAA-1
Melendrez, Antonio (fl. 1860). Mexican. WIAA-1
Miner, Bill (1847–1913). JOBA
Murrieta, Joaquin (1832?–1853). Mexican. JOBA;
    SUJ; WIAA-1
Plummer, Henry (d. 1864). JOBA; WIAA-1
Rattlesnake Jake (d. 1884). JOBA
Reno brothers (fl. 1860). JOBA; SUJ
Reynolds, Jim (fl. 1862). WIAA-1
Reynolds, John (fl. 1862). WIAA-1
Richey, Anne (d. 1922). RAB
Slade, Joseph Albert. JOBA
Starr, Belle (1848–1889). JOBA; RAB; SUJ

Starr, Henry (1873–1921). JOBA
Thompson, Ben (1842?–1883?). JOBA
Vasquez, Tiburcio (1835–1875). WIAA-1
Villa, Pancho (1878–1923). Mexican. NEBA;
    ROGB; WO
Watson, Ella (Cattle Kate) (1862?–1889). RAB;
    WIAA-2
Wild Bunch. JOBA; SUJ
Younger brothers. JOBA; REE†

CRIMINOLOGISTS, *see* LAW ENFORCERS

CRITICS

Arnold, Matthew (1822–1888). English, literature.
    COP
Atkinson, Brooks (1894–1984). Drama. LEU
Braithwaite, William Stanley (1878–1962). Litera-
    ture. BRB†; DOF-1; ROE
Brooks, Van Wyck (1886–1963). Literature. CAC
Fletcher, John Gould (1886–1950). Literature.
    SIF
Huxtable, Ada Louise (1921–). Architecture.
    GIB-1
Johnson, Samuel (1709–1784). English, litera-
    ture. BEG; BOD
Kazin, Alfred (1915–). RAC
Moore, Carman (1936–). Music. AB
Parker, Dorothy (1893–1967). Drama. ALA; OCB
Ripley, George (1802–1880). EOB
Shaw, George Bernard (1856–1950). Irish, art,
    music, drama. ASB-1; DEI; DEJ; KE; STL
Spender, Stephen (1909–). English. BRBB
Taylor, Deems (1885–1966). Music. BAD; WIA
Thomson, Virgil (1896–). Music. MAF

CUBANS

Alonso, Alicia (1921–). Dancer. ATA; WO
Batista, Fulgencio (1901–1973). President. ARA
Campaneris, Bert (Dagoberto Blanco) (1942–).
    Baseball player. SMF
Capablanca, José R. (1888–1942). Chess player.
    LEQB
Carpentier, Alejo (1904–). Author. WO
Carvaljal, Felix (b. 1873?). Track athlete. DAJ;
    FIC
Castro, Fidel (1926–). Premier. ARA; BAGA;
    DU-1; HAK; WEA
Finlay, Carlos Juan (1833–1915). Physician.
    FOW; SHG; SIC†; WO

Guevara, Ché (Ernesto) (1928–1967). Revolutionary. HAK

Guillen, Nicolás (1902–). Poet. WO

Juantorena, Alberto (1951?–). Track athlete. SUBB-1

Martí, José Julian (1853–1895). Patriot. BAA; WO; YOFA

Minoso, Minnie (Saturnino Orestes) (1922–). Baseball player. BOE

Oliva, Tony (Pedro) (1940–). Baseball player. PEC; PRA

Perez, Tony (Atanasio Rigal) (1942–). Baseball player. BELA; LEY; WH-3

Ramírez, Armando Socarras (1963?–). Escapee. CAHA

Rojas, Cookie (Octavio Rivas) (1939–). Baseball player. BELA

Versalles, Zoilo (1940–). Baseball player. IZA; PRA; SHF; VEA

CZARS, *see* RULERS—RUSSIAN

CZECHS

Comenius, John Amos (1592–1670). Theologian, educator. FRC

Dussek, Jan Ladislav (1760–1812). Pianist, composer. CHF

Dvořak, Antonin (1841–1904). Composer. BAE; BEN; BUC; DEI; DEJ; FIE†; KAE; SAA; YOJ

Janáček, Leoš (1854–1928). Composer. YOL

Masaryk, Thomas Garrigue (1850–1937). Statesman, philosopher. LAD

Mohorovicic, Andrija (1857–1936). Geologist. HAC

Moscheles, Ignaz (1794–1870). Composer. CHF

Reich, Haviva (1914–1944). Resistance worker. LAD

Senefelder, Aloys (1771–1834). Inventor. FE

Smetana, Bedřich (1824–1884). Composer. BAE; FIE†; KAE; SAA

Stamitz, Johann Wenzel (1717–1757). Violinist, composer. CHFA

Zatopek, Emil (1922–). Track athlete. AAS-30; DAG; DAGA; HIA-01†; LEYB

DANCERS & CHOREOGRAPHERS

Adams, Diana (1927?–). ATA

Ailey, Alvin (1931–). AB; DOF-1

Alonso, Alicia (1921–). Cuban. ATA; WO

Babilee, Jean (1923–). French. ATA

Balanchine, George (1904–1983). Choreographer, born Russia. ASB-1; DU-1

Boris, Ruthanna (1918–). ATA

Caron, Leslie (1933–). French. ATA

Chauviré, Yvette (1917–). French. ATA

Chouteau, Yvonne (1929–). ATA

Danielian, Leon (1920–). ATA

Danilova, Alexandra. Russian. ATA

Dean, Laura. GLO

De Mille, Agnes (1908–). CLA; FOGC; GIB-1; STLA

Dolin, Anton (1904–1983). English. ATA

Duncan, Isadora (1878–1927). EOB; FOGC; MAT-1; STLA; WABC†

Dunham, Katherine (1910–). ADA; ADB; FOGC; RIC; RICA

Eglevsky, André (1917–1977). (Born Russia). ATA

Fifield, Elaine (1931–). Australian. ATA

Fonteyn, Margot (1919–). English. ATA

Franklin, Frederic (1914–). English. ATA

Graham, Martha (1893–). BOHB; FOGC; STLA

Gregory, Cynthia (1946–). BOHB; FOGC

Grey, Beryl (1927–). English. ATA

Helpmann, Robert (1909–1986). Australian. ATA

Hightower, Rosella (1920–). ATA

Jamison, Judith (1944–). BOHB; FOGC

Jeanmaire, Renée (1924–). French. ATA

Kaye, Nora (1920–1987). ATA

Kirkland, Gelsey (1952–). FOGC

Kriza, John (1919–). ATA

Laing, Hugh (1911–). English. ATA

LeClerq, Tanaquil (1929–). French. ATA

Lichine, David (1910–). (Born Russia). ATA

Lifar, Serge (1905–1986). (Born Russia). ATA

Limón, José (1908–1972). (Born Mexico). FOW; WO

Marchand, Colette (1925–). French. ATA

Markova, Alicia (1910–). English. ATA

Mitchell, Arthur (1934–). AB

Montez, Lola (1818?–1861). RAB; WABC†

Moylan, Mary Ellen (1926–). ATA

Novak, Nina. Polish. ATA

Pavlova, Anna (1881–1931). Russian. TRC; YOH

Petit, Roland (1924–). French. ATA

Reed, Janet (1916–). ATA

Riabouchinska, Tatiana (1918–). Russian. ATA

Robinson, Bill "Bojangles" (1878–1949). HUC; RIC; ROF

Shearer, Moira (1926–). Scottish. ATA

Skibine, George (1920–). (Born Russia). ATA

Slavenska, Mia. Yugoslavian. ATA

Tallchief, Maria (1925–). ATA; FOGC; GRAD

Tallchief, Marjorie (1927–). ATA; GRAD

Tharp, Twyla (1941–). FOGC

Toumanova, Tamara (1919–). Russian. ATA

Tupine, Oleg (1920–). French. ATA

Vereen, Ben (1946?–). AB
Villella, Edward (1936–). GRBA
Vollmar, Jocelyn (1925–). ATA
Youskevitch, Igor (1912–). Russian. ATA
Zoritch, George (1917–). Russian. ATA

DANES

Andersen, Hans Christian (1805–1875). Author. BEI; COB; COG; DEI; DEJ; RAC
Bajer, Frederik (1839–1922). Statesman. MEC†; WIC
Bering, Vitus J. (1680–1741). Explorer. KNB; ROL
Blegvad, Erik (1923–). Illustrator. SMAB
Bohr, Niels H. D. (1885–1962). Physicist. CAA; COLA; FE; LET; MOBA; RID; SIA
Brahe, Tycho (1546–1601). Astronomer. MOCB; PIA; SIB
Bruun, Anton Frederick (1901–1961). Oceanographer. BRBC
Canute II, the Great (944?–1035). King. CAAA; JOBB
Canute IV (d. 1086). King. DAD-2
Christian IV (1577–1648). King of Denmark and Norway. HEA
Dam, Henrik (1895–1976). Biochemist. RIF
Grundtvig, Nikolai F. S. (1783–1872). Educator. COG
Hertzsprung, Ejnar (1873–1967). Astronomer. SUE
Kierkegaard, Sören Aabye (1813–1855). Philosopher. LO
Kold, Christen Mikkelsen (1816–1870). Educator. COG
Krogh, August (1874–1949). Physiologist. RIF
Margaret (1353–1412). Queen. BOI
Nielsen, Carl A. (1865–1931). Composer. YOL
Oersted, Hans Christian (1777–1851). Physicist. DUA
Roemer, Olaus (1644–1710). Astronomer. SHFB

DEAF

See also BLIND; DISABLED

Berlenbach, Paul. Boxer. PIB; PIBA
Bridgman, Laura Dewey (1829–1889). Teacher. LYA
George G. (1953–). (Born Cuba). SIAA
Hoy, Bill (William Ellsworth) (1865–1961). Baseball player. DAFD
Keller, Helen Adams (1880–1968). BEC; BOC;

CAD; DOD; EVA; EVD; FAA; FOR; FRE; GIBA; MAJ; STLA; WAJ
O'Neil, Kitty (1946–). AAS-27; HAFA
Sharpless, Nansie (1932–). BOHA-1
Smithdas, Robert (1925–). BOHA-1
Sweezo, William. GEA
Tsiolkovsky, Konstantin E. (1857–1935). Russian. NEB; STMA; THC

DECLARATION OF INDEPENDENCE SIGNERS, *see* AMERICAN REVOLUTIONARY FIGURES—PATRIOTS—STATESMEN

DENTISTS

Blue Spruce, George (1931–). GRAC
Collins, Daniel A. (1916–). HAMA
Gray, Ida (1867–1953). LOAV
Morton, William (1819–1868). DOE; HUD; LEG; MAL; POD; PRC; ROA; SHG; SIC
Rodriguez, Benjamin (fl. 1832). LETA
Smith, Linda. FOC-1

DESIGNERS

Blount, Mildred E. Hats. BOG
Chanel, Coco (1883–1971). French fashion. FRBD
Erte (Romain de Tirtoff) (1892–). French costume, born Russia. ASB-1
Head, Edith (1907–1981). Costumes. FOG
Loewy, Raymond (1893–1986). Industrial, born France. BEA

DETECTIVES, *see* LAW ENFORCERS

DICTIONARY MAKERS, *see* LEXICOGRAPHERS

DIPLOMATS, U.S.

Adams, Charles Francis (1807–1886). LAI
Bancroft, George (1800–1891). HIB
Barlow, Joel (1754–1812). DOG
Bassett, Ebenezer D. (1833–1908). ADA; ADB
Galbraith, John Kenneth (1908–). KE
Gallatin, Albert (1761–1849). (Born Switzerland). DOG
Goldberg, Arthur J. (1908–). LETA; WEC
Gronouski, John Austin (1919–). PIAA

Harris, Patricia R. (1924–1985). YOI
Holland, Jerome H. (1916–). HOBB
Kellogg, Frank Billings (1856–1937). HEEA; MEC†; WIC
Lamar, Mirabeau Buonparte (1798–1859). AKC
Langston, John Mercer (1829–1897). ADA; ADB; BRB
Livingston, Robert R. (1746–1813). BUE; FEB; HOF; VIA
Luce, Clare Boothe (1903–1987). CLA; GRAB-1
Schurz, Carl (1829–1906). (Born Germany). CUB; LEB; LOB; STH
Smythe, John H. (1844–1908). ADA; ADB
Spurgeon, James Robert (1870–1942). FLD
Stevenson, Adlai Ewing (1900–1965). DABB; GO; KE; WHD†
White, Andrew Dickson (1832–1918). MAL
Young, Andrew Jackson (1932–). DOF-1

DISABLED

See also BLIND; DEAF

Armas, Jay J. (1933?–). No hands. HAFA
Bader, Douglas (1911–1982). English, both legs amputated. HAMY
Bearden, Gene (Henry) (1920–). BUJA
Campanella, Roy (1921–). Paralyzed. BOE; BUD-1; DADB; DAFC; DAFD; DAG; DAGA; FRC-1†; GEB; GUDA; HIC; HOCM; LYA; MUC; RIGA†; SCA; SHD; SHF; VACA; WAG; ZAA
Capp, Al (Alfred G. Caplin) (1909–1979). False leg. GEA
Carlson, Earl (1897–). Cerebral palsy. LEG
Clarke, Bobby (Robert Earle) (1949–). Canadian, diabetic. AAS-27; CL-06; FICA-1; GUEC; GUH; LEYA; MANA; ORB; THD
Cunningham, Glenn (1909–1988). Crippled foot. AAS-26; BUJA; DAG; DAGA; DAJ; GEA; HOC; LYA; LYC; PIB; PIBA; SCA
Daniels, Susan (1948–). Polio victim. BOHA-1
Debbie P. (1960–). Deformed leg. SIAA
DeMar, Clarence (1888?–1958). Crooked foot. DAG; DAGA; DAJ; HIA-01†; PIB
Down, Linda (1956–). Cerebral palsy. GLO
Ewry, Ray C. (b. 1873). Polio victim. DAG; DAGA; DAJ; FIC; LEYB†
Fine, Lou (1915–1971). Polio victim. GOB-1
Fry, Johnny (c. 1953–). No legs. HAFA
Funk, Casimir (1884–1967). Deformed hip, born Poland. PIAA
Gray, Pete (1917–). One armed. BELB; BUJA; DAFD; PIB; PIBA

Hawking, Stephen (1942–). English, paralyzed. BOHA-1
Heath, Allen. One armed, born Canada. LEX
J. B. (1946?–). Hemophiliac. SIAA
Johnson, Wendell (1906–). Stutterer. GEA
Kellen, James (1932–). One arm, both legs paralyzed. GEA
Kennedy, Edward M., Jr. (1961?–). One leg amputated. HAFA
Kessel, Mary Hickman. One arm paralyzed. GEA
Kierkegaard, Sören Aabye (1813–1855). Danish. LO
Lear, Edward (1812–1888). English, epileptic. BEH; SM
Lewis, Furry (Walter) (1900–). Leg. SUH
Marilyn H. (1959?–). Arthritic. SIAA
Michael (1950?–). Leukemia victim. SIAA
Miller, Kathy (1964?–). Accident victim. HAFA
Pete M. (1955–). Paralyzed. SIAA
Powell, John Wesley (1834–1902). Amputee. CORA; FOC; HIBC; LYA
Roebling, Washington Augustus (1837–1926). Caisson disease. LEGA; LYA
Roosevelt, Franklin Delano (1882–1945). Polio victim. ASB; ASB-1; BAEB; BAG; BAG-1; BEB; BEC; BLA; BUIA; CAAA; CAG; CAH; COI; COS; CUC; DEI; DEJ; DOF; DUB; DUC; DUCA; FAA; FIA; FOH; FRBA; HIH; KE; LAI; LEQ; LEQA; MAB; MABA; MEB; MIA; PED; ROH; ROHA; ROK; SUBB; TAC; WEE; WHD; YOA
Rudolph, Wilma G. (1940–). Leg. DAFB; DAJ; GEA; GED; GEDA; HIA; HOBA; HOBAA; JAB; LEYB; LYD; OCA; RYA
Russell, Harold (1914–). Both hands amputated. LYA
Santo, Ron (1940–). Diabetic. BRE; LEY; PRA
Seibert, Florence Barbara (1897–). Limp. GEA
Stallings, Laurence (1894–1968). Amputee. RADA
Steinmetz, Charles Proteus (1865–1923). (Born Germany). BEA; COKA; CUC; GRB-1; LOB; LYA
Stratton, Monty (1912–1982). False leg. LYE
Talbert, Billy (William Franklin) (1918–). Diabetic. HI
Tenace, Gene (1946–). Ulcers. BELB; SA-3
Tillis, Mel (1932–). Stutterer. HAG-1
Toulouse-Lautrec, Henri Marie Raymond de (1864–1901). French, deformed. KAA
Venturi, Ken (1931–). Finger disease. BUJA; LABA
Viscardi, Henry, Jr. (1912–). No legs. LYA
Wilkins, Alonzo. Wheelchair. PIB; PIBA
Wittgenstein, Paul (1887–1961). Austrian, one armed. GEA

DISABLED, MENTALLY

Meyers, Roger (1948–). BOHA-1
Miller, Kathy (1964?–). Accident victim. HAFA

DISCIPLES, *see* APOSTLES

DISEASE VICTIMS, *see* DISABLED

DIVERS, *see* SWIMMERS & DIVERS; UNDERWATER EXPLORERS

DOCTORS, *see* PHYSICIANS & SURGEONS; VETERINARIANS

DOMINICANS

Cedeño, Cesar (1951–). Baseball player. GUG;
    KLCA
Duarte, Juan Pablo (1813–1876). Revolutionist.
    WO
Marichal, Juan (1937–). Baseball player. HAF;
    KADA; LEZ; PEC; PRA; RIGA†
Mota, Manny (1938–). Baseball player. AAS-25
Trujillo Molina, Rafael Leónidas (1891–1961).
    Chief of state. ARA; BAGA

DRAMA CRITICS, *see* CRITICS

DRAMATISTS, *see* PLAYWRIGHTS

DRUG EXPERTS, *see* PHARMACOLOGISTS

DUTCH

Aboab, Isaac de Fonseca (1605–1693). Rabbi.
    LETA
Asser, Tobias M. C. (1838–1913). Statesman.
    LET; MEC†; WIC
Barents, Willem (d. 1597). Explorer. DOC; KNB;
    MOB; ROL†
Beijerinck, Martinus Willem (1851–1931). Botanist. SUF
Beinum, Eduard van (1901–1959). Conductor.
    STM; YOM†

Blankers-Koen, Fanny (Francina) (1918–). Track
    athlete. DAJ; HOBAA
Captein, Jacques E. J. (b. 1745). Clergyman, born
    Africa. ADA; ADB
Cruyff, Johan (1947–). Soccer player. ADL
Dubois, Eugène (1858–1940). Paleontologist. SOB
Eijkman, Christian (1858–1930). Bacteriologist.
    RIF
Einthoven, Willem (1860–1927). Physiologist.
    AAS-33; FE; RIF
Erasmus, Desiderius (1466–1536). Scholar. DEI;
    DEJ
Fokker, Anthony (1890–1939). Aviator, inventor.
    HAMY
Gogh, Vincent van (1853–1890). Painter. DEI;
    DEJ; KAA; MAH; WIAA
Hals, Frans (1580–1666). Painter. CHC; MAI
Huygens, Christiaan (1629–1695). Mathematician, physicist, astronomer. CAA; COL; FE;
    SHFB; SIA
Juliana (1909–). Queen. BOI; FAE
Leeghwater, Jan Adriaasz (1575–1650). Engineer.
    FE
Leeuwenhoek, Anton van (1632–1723). Naturalist. ASA; BEP; CAA; COL; DEB; DOE; FE;
    MIB; SHFB; SUF; THA
Lippershey, Hans (1570–1619). Spectacle maker.
    FE; LAA†
Mata Hari (Gertrud Margarete Zelle) (1876–
    1917). Dancer, spy. HAB; KN; SUG
Menasseh ben Israel (1604–1657). Rabbi. GUB;
    KAB; LERA; LES; PEB
Minuit, Peter (1580–1638). Colonial official. LEO;
    VIA
Nienhuys, Janna. Nurse. MAK
Okker, Tom (1944–). Tennis player. SLA
Rembrandt Hermanszoon van Rijn (1606–1669).
    Painter. CHC; DEI; DEJ; KAA; MAI
Spinoza, Baruch or Benedict (1632–1677). Philosopher. LERA; LO; OZA; PEB
Tasman, Abel J. (1603–1659). Explorer. KNB†;
    MOB; ROL
Tinnè, Alexine (1839–1869). Explorer. RIG
Van der Waals, Johannes Diederik (1837–1923).
    Physicist. FE
Vermeer, Jan or Johannes (1632–1675). Painter.
    CHC; KAA; MAI
Wilhelmina (1880–1962). Queen. BOI; FAE
William I, the Silent (1533–1584). Stadtholder.
    CAAA; HEA; MAJ; UNB
Zernike, Frits (b. 1888). Physicist. AAS-23

EARTH SCIENTISTS, *see* GEOLOGISTS

ECCENTRICS

Baker, Mary "Caraboo" (c. 1826). English. COKB
Brady, James Buchanan ("Diamond Jim") (1856–1917). COKB; LAH
Brown, Molly (Maggie Tobin) (1873?–1932). RAB
Caruso, Enrico (1873–1921). Italian. ASB-1; COKB; DEI; DEJ; YOH
Catherine II, the Great (1729–1796). BEO; BOI; CAAA; COKB; DAK; DEI; DEJ; FAE; LIDA; RIA; TRBA
Chaplin, Sir Charles Spencer (1889–1977). English. ASB-1; COKB; ED-1; SMBC
Christina (1626–1689). BOI; COKB; TRBA; UNA
Cobb, Ty (Tyrus Raymond) (1886–1961). AAS-35; ALB; ASBA; BELB†; COKB; DAFB; DAFC; DAFD; DAG; DAGA; DAH; EPA; FRC-1†; GEC; GR; GUC; GUDA; HEG; HIF; HOC; MUB-1; MUC; RIGA†; ROC; SH; SHH; SID; WAC
Edison, Thomas Alva (1847–1931). ASA; ASB-1; BEC; BIA; BOB; BOD; BUE; CAD; COKB; COL; CUC; DEI; DEJ; DOE; EBA; EVC; FAB; FE; FOH; FRE; HYA; LEN; LEPA; MAT; PRC; RAA; RIBA; SHFB; SIA; THA
Eugenie (1826–1910). French. COKB
Fields, W. C. (William Claude) (1880–1946). COKB; ED-1; KLD; MAOB; PHA
Ford, Henry (1863–1947). ASB-1; BOD; BUE; COKB; CUC; DEI; DEJ; EVB; FAC; FE; FOH; FRE; LAG; LEM; MAL; MAT; WED
Frederick II, the Great (1712–1786). CAAA; CAE; COA; COD; COKB; DEI; DEJ; NEC; UNA
Getty, J. Paul (1892–1976). COKB; DU-1
Green, Hetty (1835–1916). COKB
Hearst, William Randolph (1863–1951). ARAA; COKB; CUC
Hoover, J. Edgar (1895–1972). COKA; COKB; LAC; LACA; LID
Hughes, Howard, Jr. (1905–1976). COKB; DU-1
Hutton, Barbara (1912–1979). COKB
Kelly, Alvin "Shipwreck" (1885–1952). COKB
Ludwig II (1845–1886). COKB
McFadden, Bernarr (1868–1955). COKB
Nightingale, Florence (1820–1910). English. ASB-1; BOC; BOH; COKB; DEI; DEJ; EVD; FAF; FRE; HUE; MAK; MAN; MASA; PA; SC; STP; WRA
Poe, Edgar Allan (1809–1849). BEF; BEG; BOA; CAC; COKB; HACB; HEF; HIG; LEGB; SIF; STK
Randolph, John (1773–1833). COKB
Rasputin, Grigori (1872–1916). COKB
Ruth, Babe (George Herman) (1895–1948). ALB; ASB; ASB-1; BED; BOE; BUD-1; BUJ; COKB; DA; DAA; DAFB; DAFC; DAFD; DAG; DAGA; DAH; DEI; DEJ; EPA; FRC-1†; GEC; GIB; GR; GUC; GUDA; HEG; HIF; HOC; LAC; LEF; LEV; LIAA†; LYC; MUB-1; MUC; RAAA; RIGA†; ROB; SH; SHB; SHC; SHH; SID; SMK; WAC
Wagner, "Gorgeous George" (George Raymond) (1915–1963). COKB
Winchester, Sarah (1839–1922). COKB

ECOLOGISTS

See also NATURALISTS

Bradley, Guy (1870–1905). CORA
Brower, David Ross (1912–). SQA
Commoner, Barry (1917–). SQA
Krutch, Joseph Wood (1893–1970). CORA
Leopold, Aldo (1886–1948). HIBB; MIB†; SQA
Marsh, George Perkins (1801–1882). CORA; HIBB; SQA
Muir, John (1838–1914). (Born Scotland). BEA; BLB; CO-1; CORA; CUC; DOCA; HEB; HIBB; MAL; MIB; SQA; WAP
Patrick, Ruth (1907–). EMB
Pinchot, Gifford (1865–1946). CORA; HIBB; SQA
Redford, Lola (1938–). WA
Roosevelt, Theodore (1858–1919). ALE; ASB; BAEB; BAG; BAG-1; BEB; BEC; BLA; BUIA; CAG; CAH; CO-1; COI; COJA; CORA; COS; CUC; DAE; DEI; DEJ; DUB; DUC; DUCA; FEA; FEC; FOH; FRBA; HAA; HAOA; HIH; HOEA; KEA; LAI; LEQ; LEQA; MAB; MABA; MAL; MEA; MEC; MIA; OLA; PED; ROH; ROHA; ROK; ROL†; STH; SUBB; WHD; WIC
Vogt, William (1902–1968). SQA
Yoffe, Avraham (1880–1960). Israeli. GRB-1

ECONOMISTS

Balch, Emily Green (1867–1961). MEC; SHFE†; WIC
Brimmer, Andrew J. (1926–). YOI
Compton, Wilson Martindale (1890–1967). BOB
Galbraith, John Kenneth (1908–). KE
Keynes, John Maynard (1883–1946). English. ASB-1
Rivlin, Alice Mitchell (1930?–). BOHG
Siebert, Muriel (1932–). GIB-1; GL; GLO
Smith, Adam (1723–1790). Scottish. LO

EDITORS, *see* JOURNALISTS

EDUCATORS

American

Adler, Felix (1851–1933). (Born Germany). BEA
Alcott, Bronson (1799–1888). ASB; COG; DEDA; WOAA
Anguiano, Lupe (1929–). NEAA
Baldwin, Maria L. (1856–1922). BRB
Beecher, Catharine Esther (1800–1878). BUDA†; FRC; WABC
Benítez, Jaime (1908–). NEBB
Berry, Martha McChesney (1866–1942). BUDA; FLB; FOG; LEJA; MAO
Bethune, Mary McLeod (1875–1955). ADA; ADB; BRB; BUDA; CAGA; DOF-1; FLB; FLD; GEE; GIBA; JOC; KOA; LEJA; LOAV; NAB; PECA; RIC; RICA; ROG; STLA; STO; WABC†; WIAA-8; YOI
Bonnin, Gertrude Simmons (1875–1936?). GRAD
Bousfield, Maudelle Brown (fl. 1906). BRB
Brown, Charlotte Hawkins (1883–1961). BRB
Burroughs, Nannie Helen (1883–1961). LOAV
Butler, Nicholas Murray (1862–1947). MEA; MEC; WIC
Byrd, Manford, Jr. (1928–). DRA
Chavis, John (1763?–1838). BRB; DOB
Clark, Kenneth Bancroft (1914–). DOF-1; FAG; YOI
Clark, Septima Poinsette (1898–1987). BUFA
Conant, James Bryant (1893–1978). LEJA
Coppin, Fanny Jackson (1836–1913). BRB
Cordero y Molina, Rafael (1790–1868). TU
Crandall, Prudence (1803–1889). BUA; CHFB; TRD; WABC†
Demmert, Archie W. (1909–). GRAC
Dewey, John (1859–1952). CUC; FRC†; LEJA; OZA
Dickey, Sarah (1838–1904). CHFB
Dilworth, Mary Jane (1831–1877). BUI
Doherty, Robert Ernest (1885–1950). YOD
Du Bois, William Edward Burghardt (1868–1963). ADA; ADB; BEJ; BRB; BRBD; DABB; DOF-1; GRAB-01; PECA; RICA; ROG; STB; STJB; STO; YOI
Edwards, William J. (b. 1869). DADB
Egan, Sister Jogues (Joan) (1918–). (Born Ireland). SMBB-1
Evans, John (1814–1897). SEC
Fader, Daniel. EOA
Flexner, Abraham (1866–1959). LETA
Franklin, John Hope (1915–). ADB; FLD
Fraser, Harvey Reed (1916–). RAE
Gildersleeve, Virginia Crocheron (1877–1965). CLA; FLB
Ginsburg, Ruth Bader (1933–). GIB-1; SWI

Harris, Patricia R. (1924–1985). YOI
Hatathli, Ned (1923–). GRAC
Hatcher, Orie Latham (1868–1946). PACB
Hill, Patty Smith (1868–1946). BUDA
Hope, John (1868–1936). ADA; ADB; BRB; DOF-1
Horne, Esther Burnett (fl. 1955). GRAD
Hostos, Eugenio Maríe de (1839–1903). TU
Hunt, Alexander Henry (1866–1938). DOF-1
Jackson, Nell (1929–). BOHA
Jarrett, Vernon D. (1921–). STAA
Johnson, Mordecai Wyatt (1890–1976). ADA; ADB; BRB; DOF-1; RIC
King, John B. (1908–). FLD
Koontz, Elizabeth (1919–). GIB-1
Laney, Lucy (1854–1933). BRB; BUDA†
Langston, John Mercer (1829–1897). ADA; ADB; BRB
Locke, Alain Leroy (1886–1954). ADA; ADB
Lyon, Mary (1797–1849). BOC; BOJ; BUDA; COG; CUC; DAD; DOD; FLB; FRC; LEJA; STLA; VAB; WABC†
McAuliffe, Christa (1948–1986). COE-1
McGuffey, William Holmes (1800–1873). CAGA; CUC; HEB; LEJA; MAL
McIver, Charles Duncan (1860–1906). MAO
Mann, Horace (1796–1859). COG; CUC; FOH; FRC; LEC; LEJA; LEPC; MAT; RED
Mays, Benjamin E. (1895–1984). ADB; DOF-1
Meléndez, Cóncha (1904–). NEBB
Moise, Penina (1797–1880). LER; LETA
Moton, Robert Russa (1867–1940). BRB; DOF-1
Nash, Alice Morrison (1879?–1966). FLB
Nava, Julian (1927–). FOW
Nogales, Louis (1943–). NEAA
Palmer, Alice Freeman (1855–1902). BUDA†; FLB; VAB
Peabody, Elizabeth Palmer (1804–1894). BUDA†; FLB; LEK; WABC†
Persky, Daniel (1887–1962). (Born Russia). GRB-1
Pittman, Dorothy Hughes (1938–). WA
Quincy, Josiah, Jr. (1772–1864). BOK
Ramos, Elaine Abraham. GRAD
Revel, Bernard (1885–1940). (Born Russia). KAD; LETA
Riles, Wilson (1917–). DOF-1
Robinson, Wirt (1864–1929). RAE
Ruether, Rosemary (1936–). GIB-1
Scarborough, William Saunders (1852–1926). ADA; ADB; BRB†
Simmons, William J. (1849–1890). ADB; BRB†
Sondermann, Fred S. (1923–). (Born Germany). CAHA
Taylor, Susie King (1848–1912). MAV
Washington, Booker Taliaferro (1856–1915)

ADA; ADB; BRB; BRBD; CUC; FIA; FOB; FOH; FRC†; HUA; JOC; LEC; LEJA; MAL; ROG; STB; STO; WAH; YOI

White, Andrew Dickson (1832–1918). MAL

Willard, Emma Hart (1787–1870). BUDA; COG; CUC; FLB; FRC; JOCA; LEJA; MAL; VAB; WABC†; YOC

Williams, William Taylor Burwell (1869–1941). DOF-1

Young, Ella Flagg (1845–1918). FLB

Zajicek, Sarita Soto (1916–). FOW

Foreign

Alcuin (735–804). English. FRC

Buisson, Ferdinand (1841–1932). French. MEC†; WIC

Coka, Gilbert (1910–). African. PEA

Comenius, John Amos (1592–1670). Czechoslovakian. FRC

Dunlop, Florence (1896–1963). Canadian. FLB

Encarnacion, Rosario de Jesus. Philippine. RODA

Fafunwa, Babs. Nigerian. OJA

Froebel, Friedrich Wilhelm (1782–1852). German. COG; FRC

Gatheru, R. Mugo. African. OJA

Grundtvig, Nikolai F. S. (1783–1872). Danish. COG

Hussein, Taha (1889–1973). Egyptian. BAF

Kayamba, Mdumi Martin (b. 1891). African. PEA

Kold, Christen Mikkelsen (1816–1870). Danish. COG

Mistral, Gabriela (1889–1957). Chilean. BACA; SHFE†; WO

Mockerie, Parmenas (1900–). Kenyan. PEA

Montessori, Maria (1870–1952). Italian. STP

Orlean, Judah Leib. Polish. GEF

Pestalozzi, Johann Heinrich (1746–1827). Swiss. FRC

Pitman, Sir Isaac (1813–1897). English. FE

Quintilian (Marcus Fabius Quintilianus) (35?–95?). Roman. FRC

Sarmiento, Domingo Faustino (1811–1888). Argentine. COG; KEE; LAB; WO

Vasconcelos, José (1882–1959). Mexican. NEBA

Vittorino da Feltre (Vittorino Ramboldini) (1378–1446). Italian. FRC

Waciuma, Charity. Zambian. OJA

Woolley, Hannah (b. 1623). English. BOH

Yen, James Yang-ch'u (1894–). Chinese. BAF; COG; SPA

EGYPTIANS

Akhnaton (fl. 1379–1362 B.C.). King. CAAA; GRAB-04; JOBB; NEC; UNA

Ankhesnamun (fl. 1358 B.C.). Queen. COLB

Cheops (fl. 2900 B.C.). King. CAAA

Cleopatra (69–30 B.C.). Queen. BOI; CAAA; COA; DEI; DEJ; FAE; LIDA; PA; TRBA

Hatshepsut (1578–1457 B.C.). Queen. BOI; COLB; GRAB-04

Hussein, Taha (1889–1973). Author, educator. BAF

Imhotep (fl. 2980–2950 B.C.). Physician. JO

Menes (fl. 3100–3038 B.C.). King. GRAB-04

Mubarak, Mohamed Hosni (1928–). President. HAGD

Nasser, Gamal Abdel (1918–1970). President of United Arab Republic. ARA; KE; KEF; WEA

Nefertari (13th century B.C.). Queen. COLB

Nefertiti (fl. 1372–1350 B.C.). Queen. COLB; FAE; GRAB-04; JO†; PA

Ptolemy I (Ptolemy Soter) (367?–283 B.C.). King. NEC

Saadia ben Joseph (Saadyah Gaon) (892–942). Hebraist. GRB-1; GUA; KAC; LERA

Sadat, Anwar el- (1918–1981). President. ASB-1; DU-1

Tiy (fl. 1400 B.C.). Queen. COLB

Tutankhamen (1361–1351 B.C.). King. COA; GRAB-04

Tuthmosis III (1504–1450 B.C.). King. CAAA; GRAB-04

ELECTRICAL ENGINEERS, *see* ENGINEERS, ELECTRICAL

EMPERORS, *see* RULERS

ENGINEERS

See also ENGINEERS, AERONAUTICAL; ENGINEERS, AUTOMOTIVE; ENGINEERS, CIVIL; ENGINEERS, ELECTRICAL; ENGINEERS, MECHANICAL; ENGINEERS, MINING; ENGINEERS, TELEVISION & RADIO

American

Campbell, Billie L. GL

Davidson, J. Brownlee (1880–1957). LEGA; YOD

Doherty, Robert Ernest (1885–1950). YOD

Gilbreth, Lillian M. (1878–1972). BOJ; EMB; CLA; LEGA; STLA

Goethals, George Washington (1858–1928). LEGA; RAE

Johnson, Campbell C. (1921–). CAF-1

Maynard, Harold Bright (1902–). YOD

Mead, Elwood (1858–1936). LEGA

Rock, Lee Curry. HOG

Stout, William Bushnell (1880–1956). COKA

Suman, John Robert (1890–). LEGA; YOD
Townsend, Marjorie (1930–). HOG
Trice, Virgil G. (1926–). CAF-1
Young, James F. (1917–). PAB

English

Aveling, Thomas (1824–1881). LAE
Bessemer, Sir Henry (1813–1898). ASA; EBA;
    FAB; FE; LAE; THA
Brindley, James (1716–1772). EVB
Low, Archibald Montgomery (1888–1956). LAE
Parsons, Sir Charles Algernon (1854–1931). EVB;
    FE; SHFB
Trevithick, Richard (1771–1833). EVB

Others

Andriamanjato, Rahantavololona. Malagasy. CRA
Leeghwater, Jan Adriaasz (1575–1650). Dutch.
    FE
Lenoir, Etienne (1822–1900). French. FE
McAdam, John Loudon (1756–1836). Scottish.
    FAB; FE
Nasmyth, James (1808–1890). Scottish. EVB; FE

ENGINEERS, AERONAUTICAL

See also AIR PIONEERS; ROCKET & SPACE SCIEN-
TISTS

Andrée, Salomon A. (1854–1897). Swedish.
    DOC†; GRB
Cockerell, Sir Christopher (1910–). English. FE;
    MAPA
Darden, Christine (1942–). FOC-1
De Seversky, Alexander P. (1894–1974). (Born
    Russia). GEA
Gilruth, Robert Rowe (1913–). POE
Lilienthal, Otto (1848–1896). German. BRBA
Myers, Joyce Carpenter. SMBC-2
Watson, Douglas. BOG

ENGINEERS, AUTOMOTIVE

Benz, Karl (1844–1929). German. FAB; FE
Daimler, Gottlieb (1834–1900). German. EBA;
    FE; THA
Sparrow, Stanwood W. (1888–1952). YOD
Wankel, Felix Heinrich (1902–). German. FE;
    MAPA

ENGINEERS, CIVIL

Brunel, Isambard Kingdom (1806–1869). English.
    EVB; FE
Dodge, Grenville Mellen (1831–1916). MAT
Eiffel, Alexandre Gustave (1832–1923). French.
    EVB
L'Enfant, Pierre Charles (1754–1825). (Born
    France). LEO
Lesseps, Ferdinand de (1805–1894). French. EVB;
    WOA
Massiah, Frederick McDonald (b. 1884). (Born
    West Indies). CAF-1
Morgan, Arthur Ernest (1878–1975). YOD
Patterson, John (fl. 1898). English. WOA
Rennie, John (1761–1821). Scottish. EVB
Roebling, John Augustus (1806–1869). (Born Ger-
    many). CUB
Roebling, Washington Augustus (1837–1926).
    LEGA; LYA
Singstad, Ole (b. 1882). (Born Norway). LEGA;
    YOD
Smeaton, John (1724–1792). English. EVB
Steinman, David Barnard (1886–1960). LETA
Stephenson, Robert (1803–1859). English. EVB

ENGINEERS, ELECTRICAL

Armstrong, Edwin Howard (1890–1954). MAPA
Bush, Vannevar (1890–1974). LEGA; YOD
Carrier, Willis Haviland (1876–1950). FAB; YOE
Engstrom, Elmer William (1901–1984). PAB
Fleming, Sir John Ambrose (1849–1945). English.
    BUF†; SHFB
Jarvis, Gregory (1944–1986). COE-1
Kettering, Charles F. (1876–1958). HYA†; YOE
Lieu, Winston Hong (1963–). (Born Vietnam).
    HOD-1
Marconi, Guglielmo (1874–1937). Italian. AAS-33;
    BOB; COL; EBA; EVC; FAB; FE; FRE; PRC;
    SHFB; SIA; THA
Peden, Irene. LA-1
Sprague, Frank Julian (1857–1934). HOF
Steinmetz, Charles Proteus (1865–1923). (Born
    Germany). BEA; COKA; CUC; GRB-1; LOB;
    LYA
Tesla, Nikola (1857–1943). (Born Croatia). BOK;
    FE; MAP

ENGINEERS, MECHANICAL

Diesel, Rudolf C. (1858–1913). German. FAB; FE; LAE; MAP; THA

Ericsson, John (1803–1889). (Born Sweden). HYA

Flanders, Ralph Edward (1880–1970). YOD

Fulton, Robert (1765–1815). COL; CUC; DEI; DEJ; EBA; EVC; FAB; FE; HYA; LAE; LEL; MAL; THA

Glennon, Nan. HOG

Kahn, Anthony (1961–). HOD-1

Kovago, Jozsef. (Born Hungary). CAHA

Lake, Simon (1866–1945). HYA†; MAP; OLC

Rillieux, Norbert (1806–1894). ADA; ADB; GRAB-03; HA; HAL; HODA; KLA; ROG

Rosen, Carl George Arthur (1891–1975). YOD

Stevens, Robert Livingston (1787–1856). HYA

Watt, James (1736–1819). Scottish. ASA; BIA; BOD; BUF; COL; EBA; EVB; FAB; FE; FRE; SHFB; THA

ENGINEERS, MINING

Bascom, Willard (1917–). COR

Flipper, Henry Ossian (1856–1940). HAP; HODA; KADB

Hahn, Emily (1905–). ROJ

Milne, John (1850–1913). English. COLA

Sutro, Adolph Heinrich Joseph (1830–1898). (Born Germany). LETA; YOG

Turner, Scott (1880–). LEGA; YOD

ENGINEERS, TELEVISION & RADIO

Henry, Algernon P. BOG

Jansky, Karl Guthe (1905–1949). BUF†; SUE

Pierce, John Robinson (1910–). COQ

Wheeler, Harold Alden (1903–). YOD

ENGLISH

See also RULERS—ENGLISH

Abrahams, Harold (1899–1978). Track athlete. SLA

Adams, John Couch (1819–1892). Astronomer. SOB; SUE

Addison, Thomas (1793–1860). Physician. POB

Adrian, Edgar Douglas (1889–1977). Physiologist. RIF

Aguilar, Grace (1816–1847). Author. LER; PEB

Alcock, Sir John (1892–1919). Aviator. COC†; HAMY

Alcuin (735–804). Educator. FRC

Allenby, Edmund Henry Hynman, 1st viscount (1861–1936). Field marshal. ARD

Amherst, Jeffrey (1717–1797). Field marshal. SOA

Anderson, Elizabeth Garrett (1836–1917). Physician. HUE; MAJ; MASA

Angell, Sir Norman (1874–1967). Author. MEA; MEC; WIC

Anning, Mary (1799–1847). Fossil finder at 11. FOR

Arkwright, Sir Richard (1732–1792). Inventor, manufacturer. FAB; FE

Arne, Thomas Augustine (1710–1778). Composer. YOJ

Arnold, Matthew (1822–1888). Poet, critic. COP

Astell, Mary (1668–1731). Author. BOH

Aston, Francis William (1877–1945). Chemist, physicist. RID; SHFB†

Austen, Jane (1775–1817). Author. BOH; COO; SMA; STK

Aveling, Thomas (1824–1881). Inventor, engineer. LAE

Avery, John "Long Ben" (b. 1665). Pirate. LACB

Babbage, Charles (1792–1871). Mathematician. COLA; FE; FRE; GRAB-3; WEF

Bacon, Francis (1561–1626). Author, philosopher. BEG; LO; STI†

Bacon, Roger (1214?–1294). Scientist, philosopher. MAQ

Baden-Powell, Robert Stephenson Smyth, 1st baron (1857–1941). Soldier, founder of English Boy Scouts. EVA; SEB

Bader, Douglas (1911–1982). English aviator. HAMY

Baker, Lady Florence von Sass (fl. 1863–1893). Explorer, born Hungary. RIG

Baker, Mary "Caraboo" (c. 1826). Imposter. COKB

Baker, Sir Samuel White (1821–1893). Explorer. LAA-1; ROL

Bakewell, Robert (1725–1795). Agriculturist. CAB

Banks, Sir Joseph (1743–1820). Naturalist. BLB

Bannister, Roger Gilbert (1929–). Track athlete. AAS-26; ALBA; ASB-1; ASBA; DAFB; DAG; DAGA; DAJ; PRC

Barbirolli, John (1899–1970). Conductor. STM†; YOM

Barna, Gyozo Victor (1911–1972). Table tennis player, born Hungary. SLA

Barry, James, pseud. (1795–1865). Army physician. MASA

Beatty, David, 1st earl (1871–1936). Admiral. ARD

Beecham, Sir Thomas (1879–1961). Conductor. EWB; STM†; YOM

Bell, Caroline D. (1928–). Child. CAHA

Bell, Edward A. (1930–). Child. CAHA

Belloc, Hilaire (1870–1953). Author. BEH

Bessemer, Sir Henry (1813–1898). Engineer, inventor. ASA; EBA; FAB; FE; LAE; THA

Bird, Isabella Lucy (1831–1904). Traveler. JOB; RIG

Blake, William (1757–1827). Poet, illustrator, engraver. BEH; COP

Bligh, William (1754–1817). Naval officer. SCBA

Blyth, Chay (fl. 1966). Adventurer. OLC

Boleyn, Anne (1507–1536). Second wife of Henry VIII, king of England. MAOA; VAC

Bonnet, Stede (d. 1718). Pirate. WHA

Booth, Evangeline Cory (1865–1950). Salvation Army commander. STP

Booth, Hubert Cecil (1871–1955). Inventor. LAE

Booth, William (1829–1912). Religious leader, founder Salvation Army. EVA

Bowie, David (1947–). Singer, actor. BUIB-2

Boyle, Robert (1627–1691). Physicist, chemist. CAA; FE; MOBA; SIA

Bramah, Joseph (1748–1814). Inventor. FE

Bream, Julian (1933–). Classical guitarist, lutist. EWC

Brindley, James (1716–1772). Engineer. EVB

Brine, James (1812–1902). Trade unionist. LAD

Britten, Benjamin (1913–1976). Composer. BEKA; KAE; YOJ

Bronowski, Jacob (1908–1974). Mathematician, author, born Poland. GRB-1

Brontë, Anne (1820–1849). Author. COO; SMA; STK

Brontë, Charlotte (1816–1855). Author. COO; SMA; STK

Brontë, Emily Jane (1818–1848). Author. COO; SMA; STK

Brooke, Rupert (1887–1915). Poet. COP

Browning, Elizabeth Barrett (1809–1861). Poet. BOC

Browning, Robert (1812–1889). Poet. COP

Brunel, Isambard Kingdom (1806–1869). Civil engineer. EVB; FE

Burgoyne, John (1722–1792). Army officer. AKA; RAD; SOA

Burney, Fanny (1752–1840). Author. NOA; SMA

Burton, Sir Richard Francis (1821–1890). Explorer. COL; MOB; ROL

Buxton, Angela (1934–). Tennis player. SLA

Byrd, William (1543–1623). Composer, organist. KAE

Byron, George Gordon Noel, 6th baron (1788–1824). Poet. COP; DEI

Calvert, Cecilius, 2nd baron Baltimore (1605–1675). Colonizer of Maryland. LEO; MEB

Calvert, Charles, 3rd baron Baltimore (1637–1715). Colonizer of Maryland. LEO; MEB

Calvert, George, 1st baron Baltimore (1580?–1632). Proprietor in America. MEB; VIA

Campbell, Donald Malcolm (1921–1967). Automobile and speedboat racer. ALBA; ST-1

Campbell, Sir Malcolm (1885–1949). Automobile and speedboat racer. YAA

Campion, Edmund (1540–1581). Jesuit martyr. DAD-3; MAJ

Carroll, Lewis, pseud. (1832–1898). Author. BEH; COB; COO

Carter, Howard (1873–1939). Archaeologist. WOA

Cartwright, Edmund (1743–1823). Inventor. EBA

Cavell, Edith (1865–1915). Nurse. HAA; MAJ; MAK; RADA; WRA

Cavendish, Henry (1731–1810). Chemist, physicist. CAA; FE; SHFB

Caxton, William (1422?–1491). Printer. DEI; DEJ

Cecil of Chelwood, Edgar Algernon Robert Gascoyne-Cecil, 1st viscount (1864–1958). Statesman. MEC†; WIC

Chadwick, Sir James (1891–1974). Physicist. FE; RID

Chain, Ernst Boris (1906–1979). Biochemist, born Germany. BEK†; COLA†; GRB-1; LAE; LET; POB; RIF

Chamberlain, Sir Austen (1863–1937). Statesman. MEC†; WIC

Chancellor, Richard (d. 1556). Explorer. KNB; ROL†

Chaplin, Sir Charles Spencer (1889–1977). Actor. ASB-1; COKB; ED-1; SMBC

Chaucer, Geoffrey (1340?–1400). Poet. COP

Chesterton, Gilbert Keith (1874–1936). Author. BEG

Chichester, Sir Francis (1901–1972). Cartographer, yachtsman. OLC

Christie, Agatha (1891–1976). Author. SMA

Churchill, Sir Winston Leonard Spencer (1874–1965). Statesman, author. ASB-1; CHG; CUC; DEI; DEJ; DOF; ELA; EVA; FLBB; FRE; HIB†; JAC; JAD; KE; RADA; TAC; YOA

Clapton, Eric (1945–). Singer, guitarist. BUIB-1

Clinton, Sir Henry (1738–1795). General. AKA; SOA

Cobb, John (1899–1952). Automobile racer. YAA

Cockcroft, Sir John Douglas (1897–1967). Physicist. FE

Cockerell, Sir Christopher (1910–). Inventor. FE; MAPA

Coe, Sebastian (1956–). Track athlete. AAS-26

Coleridge, Samuel Taylor (1772–1834). Poet. COP; RAC

Coleridge-Taylor, Samuel (1875–1912). Composer. ADA; ADB; BRB†

Congreve, Sir William (1772–1828). Inventor. STMA

Conrad, Joseph (1857–1924). Author, born Poland. COO; MANB; STL

Cook, James (1728–1779). Explorer. COC; COL; DAF; DOBB; DOC; DYA; FAF; GRC; KEH; KNB; LAA-2; MOB; ROL; WIA-1

Cornwallis, Charles Cornwallis, 1st marquis (1738–1805). General. AKA; SOA

Coward, Noel (1889–1973). Composer, playwright. ASB-1

Cowley, Abraham (1618–1667). Poet. COP

Craik, Dinah Mulock (1826–1887). Author. BEI

Cranmer, Thomas (1489–1556). Archbishop of Canterbury. MAJ

Cremer, Sir William Randal (1838–1908). Pacifist. MEA; MEC; WIC

Crick, Francis H. C. (1916–). Biologist. BEK; FE; FRE†; RIF

Cromwell, Oliver (1599–1658). Lord Protector. CAAA; CAE; DEC; DEI; DEJ; GRAB

Crookes, Sir William (1832–1919). Physicist, chemist. FE; SIA

Crowley, Aleister (1875–1947). Magician. ED-5

Curry, John (1949–). Skater. LIEA; VAD-6

Dale, Sir Henry Hallett (1875–1968). Physiologist. RIF

Dalton, John (1766–1844). Chemist, physicist. CAA; FE; MOBA; SHFB; SIA; STI

Daltrey, Roger (1945–). Singer. BUIB-2

Dampier, William (1652–1715). Pirate, explorer. KNB; MOB

Darby, Abraham (c. 1678–1717). Manufacturer. FE

Darling, Grace Horsley (1815–1842). Heroine. MAJ; STP

Darwin, Charles Robert (1809–1882). Naturalist. ASA; BEK; BEP; BLB; CAA; CAB; COL; DEI; DEJ; DOE; FE; FRE; MIB; MOB; POD; SIA; SOB; STI

Davison, Ann (fl. 1952). Adventurer. HAQ

Davy, Sir Humphry (1778–1829). Chemist. CAA; COL; DUA; FE; SHFB; SOB; STI; THA

Dee, John (1527–1608). Mathematician, astrologer. COEA; CUA; ED-5

Defoe, Daniel (1660–1731). Author. COO; SEB

de la Mare, Walter John (1873–1956). Author. BEH

Delius, Frederick (1862–1934). Composer. BUC; KAE; SAA†

De Quincey, Thomas (1785–1859). Author. BEG

Dickens, Charles (1812–1870). Author. BOD; COB; COO; DEI; DEJ; HOA; STK

Disraeli, Benjamin, 1st earl of Beaconsfield (1804–1881). Prime minister. DEI; DEJ; PEB

Dolin, Anton (1904–1983). Dancer, choreographer. ATA

Dorchester, Sir Guy Carleton, 1st baron (1724–1808). Governor. AKA

Doughty, Charles Montagu (1843–1926). Poet, traveler. MOB; ROL†; WIA-1

Drake, Sir Francis (1540–1596). Explorer, privateer. DYA; GRAA; KEH; LAA-2; LACB; MOB; ROL

Dryden, John (1631–1700). Poet. COP

Elgar, Sir Edward William (1857–1934). Composer. BAE; BEN; BUC; GOA; KAE; SAA†; YOK

Eliot, George, pseud. (1819–1880). Author. COO; SMA; STL

Eliot, Thomas Stearns (1888–1965). Poet, born U.S. ASB-1; BRBB; COP

Entwistle, John (1944–). Musician. BUIB-2

Equiano, Olaudah (Gustavus Vassa) (1745–1801). Adventurer. ADA; ADB; OJA

Erskine, Thomas (1750–1823). Jurist. COG

Evans, Sir Edward Ratcliffe Garth Russell (1881–1957). Explorer. ROL

Ewing, Juliana H. Gatty (1841–1885). Author. BEI

Fabian, Robert (1901–1978). Detective. LID

Faraday, Michael (1791–1867). Chemist, physicist. ASA; BEP; BIA; BOB; BOD; CAA; COLA; DEI; DEJ; DOE; DUA; FE; MAQ; SHFB; SIA; STI; THA

Farjeon, Eleanor (1881–1965). Author. BEH; SMB

Fawcett, Percy Harrison (1867–1925?). Explorer. KNA; ROL†

Fenton, Roger (1819–1869). Photographer. HOE

Fields, Gracie (1898–1979). Singer, comedienne. MASB

Fitzsimmons, Robert P. (1863–1918). Boxer. DAG; DAGA; RAAC

Flamsteed, John (1646–1719). Astronomer. SHFB

Fleming, Sir John Ambrose (1849–1945). Electrical engineer. BUF†; SHFB

Flinders, Matthew (1774–1814). Explorer. KNB; ROL

Fonteyn, Margot (1919–). Dancer. ATA

Foote, Alexander (1905–). Spy. SEB

Fox, George (1624–1691). Quaker leader. FOJ

Franklin, Frederic (1914–). Dancer. ATA

Franklin, Sir John (1786–1847). Explorer. DOC; KNB; MOB; ROL

Freud, Anna (1895–1982). Psychiatrist, born Austria. CHE

Frobisher, Sir Martin (1535?–1594). Explorer. DOC; GRAA; KNB; ROL†

Fry, Elizabeth Gurney (1780–1845). Reformer. BOH; NOA; STP

Fuchs, Sir Vivian Ernest (1908–). Geologist. DOC†; KNA†; MOB; ROL

Gage, Thomas (1721–1787). General. AKA; BUIB†; SOA

Gainsborough, Thomas (1727–1788). Painter. CHC; DEI; DEJ

Germain, George Sackville, 1st viscount Sackville (1716–1785). Colonial administrator. SOA

Gibb, Barry (1946–). Singer. BUIB-1

Gibb, Maurice (1949–). Singer. BUIB-1

Gibb, Robin (1949–). Singer. BUIB-1

Gibbon, Edward (1737–1794). Historian. HIB

Gibson, Guy Penrose (1919–1944). Aviator, WWII. HAMY

Gilbert, Sir Joseph Henry (1817–1901). Agricultural chemist. CAB

Gilbert, William (1540–1603). Physician, physicist. SHFB; SIA

Gilbert, William Schwenk (1836–1911). Composer. ASB-1

Godden, Rumer (1907–). Author. SMA; SMB

Godiva, Lady (c. 1040–1080). Legendary horseback rider. COKB

Godwin, Mary Wollstonecraft (1759–1797). Author. BOH; GUBA

Goodall, Jane (1934–). Anthropologist. BOHG; DU-1; SC

Gray, Thomas (1716–1771). Poet. COP

Greenaway, Kate (1846–1901). Illustrator. SM

Grenfell, Sir Wilfred Thomason (1865–1940). Physician. MAN

Grey, Beryl (1927–). Dancer. ATA

Grogan, Ewart Scott (1874–1967). Zoologist. WOA

Haig, Douglas Haig, 1st earl (1861–1928). Soldier. ARD

Hales, Stephen (1677–1761). Physiologist. CAB

Halley, Edmund (1656–1742). Astronomer. MOB; SHFB; SIA

Hammett, James (fl. 1830). Trade unionist. LAD

Handel, George Frederick (1685–1759). Composer, born Germany. BEN; BRF; BUD; FIE; GOA; KAE; SAA; YOK; YOM†

Hardy, Thomas (1840–1928). Author. COO; STL

Hargreaves, James (c. 1722–1778). Inventor, manufacturer. FE

Harold II (1022?–1066). King. CHG; GRAB†; SCC; UNB

Harrison, George (1943–). Singer. BUIB-1; SC-01

Harrison, John (1693–1776). Horologist, inventor. FEAB; MOB

Harvey, William (1578–1657). Physician. ASA; BEP; CAA; CHD; COL; DEI; DEJ; DOE; FE; FRE; POD; ROA; SHG; SIA; SIC; STE

Hawking, Stephen (1942–). English physicist. BOHA-1

Hazlitt, William (1778–1830). Author. BEG

Hearne, Samuel (1745–1792). Explorer. ARF

Henday, Anthony (fl. 1754). Explorer. ARF

Henry, Sir Edward Richart, bart (1850–1931). Government official. LACA

Hepburn, Audrey (1929–). Actress. FOG

Herbert, Walter William (1934–). Surveyor. ROL

Hereward (fl. 1070–1071). Patriot. SUK

Herschel, Caroline (1750–1848). Astronomer, born Germany. COLA†; NOA; PAC; SC†

Herschel, Sir William (1738–1822). Astronomer, born Germany. BOB; COLA; FE; LAA; PAC; PIA; SIA; SUE

Hill, Archibald Vivian (1886–1977). Physiologist. RIF

Hill, Graham (1929–1975). Automobile racer. COKC; JA

Hill, Sir Rowland (1795–1879). Postal reformer. EVA

Hodgkin, Dorothy Crowfoot (1910–). Crystallographer. HA-1; SHFE

Hogarth, William (1697–1794). Painter. KAA

Hooke, Robert (1635–1703). Physicist. CAA

Hopkins, Sir Frederick Gowland (1861–1947). Biochemist. RIF

Hounsfield, Godfrey (1919–). Inventor. AAS-33

Howe, William Howe, 5th viscount (1729–1814). General. AKA; SOA

Hudson, Henry (1575?–1611). Explorer. COC; DEI; DEJ; DOC; GRAA; GRC; KNB; MAT; MOB; ROL

Hudson, William Henry (1841–1922). Author, naturalist. COO

Huggins, Sir William (1824–1910). Astronomer. SUE

Hunt, James (1947–). Automobile racer. ABB; OLCC

Hutton, William (1723–1815). Author. RAC

Irving, Sir Henry (1838–1905). Actor. TRC

Jagger, Mick (1944–). Singer. BUIB-1

Jellicoe, John Rushworth Jellicoe, 1st earl (1859–1935). Admiral. ARD

Jenner, Edward (1749–1823). Physician. ASA; CAA; CHD; COL; FAF†; FE; HUD; POD; RIE; ROA; SHG; SIC; SUF

Jex-Blake, Sophia (1840–1912). Physician. HUE; MASA†; SC†

John, Elton (1947–). Singer, composer. BUIB-1

Johnson, Amy (1903–1941). Aviator. HIFD; MO

Johnson, Samuel (1709–1784). Lexicographer. BEG; BOD

Johnson, Sir William (1715–1774). Colonial official. VIA

Jonson, Ben (1573?–1637). Playwright, poet. DEI; DEJ

Joule, James Prescott (1818–1889). Physicist. FE; SHFB

Kauffmann, Angelica (1741–1807). Painter, born Switzerland. BOH; NE

Kaye-Smith, Sheila (1887–1956). Author. SMA

Keats, John (1795–1821). Poet. COP

Kelsey, Henry (1670–1729). Explorer. ARF

Kelvin, William Thomson, 1st baron (1824–1907). Mathematician, physicist. BOB; DUA; FE; LAE; SIA

Kenyon, Kathleen M. (1906–). Archaeologist. RIG

Keynes, John Maynard (1883–1946). Economist. ASB-1

Kingsford-Smith, Charles (1897–1935). Aviator. HAMY

Kingsley, Charles (1819–1875). Author. BEH; COO

Kingsley, Mary Henrietta (1862–1900). Ethnologist. BOH; DAF; KNA; ROL†; WIA-1

Kipling, Rudyard (1865–1936). Author. BEI; COB; COO; COP; STK

Kitchener, Horatio Herbert, 1st earl Kitchener of Khartoum (1850–1916). Field marshall. ARD

Krebs, Sir Hans Adolf (1900–1981). Biochemist, born Germany. LET

Laing, Hugh (1911–). Dancer. ATA

Lamb, Charles (1775–1834). Author. BEG

Low, Archibald Montgomery (1888–1956). Engineer. LAE

Lawes, Sir John Bennett (1814–1900). Agriculturist. CAB

Leakey, Louis S. B. (1903–1972). Anthropologist. DU-1

Lear, Edward (1812–1888). Author, illustrator. BEH; SM

Lee, Christopher (1922–). Actor. COE-2

Lennon, John (1940–1980). Singer. BUIB-1; SC-01

Lewis, Pryce (fl. 1861–1864). Spy. FOA

Lewis, Ted "Kid" (1894–1970). Boxer. SLA

Lillie, Beatrice (1898–). Actress, born Canada. MASB

Linacre, Thomas (1460?–1524). Physician. MAR

Lister, Joseph, 1st baron Lister of Lyme Regis (1827–1912). Surgeon. ASB-1; BIA; CHD; COL; DOE; FAF; FE; HUD; POD; ROA; SHG; SIC

Lloyd George, David (1863–1945). Statesman. ASB-1

Locke, John (1632–1704). Philosopher. LO; OZA

Lovelace, Lady Ada (Byron) (1815–1852). Mathematician. GRAB-3; WEF

Loveless, George (fl. 1830). Trade unionist. LAD

Loveless, James (fl. 1830). Trade unionist. LAD

Lytton, Edward George Earle Lytton Bulwer, 1st baron (1803–1873). Author. COO; ED-5

Macaulay, Thomas Babington Macaulay, 1st baron (1800–1859). Author. BEG; COP

McCartney, Paul (1942–). Singer. BUIB-1; SC-01

McClintock, Sir Francis Leopold (1819–1907). Admiral, explorer. DOC

MacKenzie, Sir Morell (1837–1892). Laryngologist. MAR

Macmillan, Harold (1894–1986). Statesman. WEA

Mallowan, Max E. L. (1904–1978). Archaeologist. POC

Mannock, Edward (1885–1918). Aviator, WWI. SUA

Manns, August (1825–1907). Conductor, born Germany. YOM

Markova, Alicia (1910–). Dancer. ATA

Marlborough, John Churchill, 1st duke of (1650–1722). Military commander. EDA

Marlowe, Christopher (1564–1593). Playwright. TRC

Masefield, John (1878–1967). Author, poet. COP

Maskelyne, Jasper Nevil (1839–1917). Magician. KEB

Maxim, Sir Hiram Stevens (1840–1916). Inventor, born U.S. MAP

Medawar, Peter Brian (1915–1987). Zoologist. CHE†; RIF

Mendelsohn, Eric (1887–1953). Architect, born Germany. FOF; LEDA

Mendoza, Daniel (1764–1836). Boxer. SLA

Mercury, Freddie (1946–). Singer. BUIB-2

Milne, Alan Alexander (1882–1956). Author. BEH; SMB

Milne, John (1850–1913). Mining engineer. COLA

Milton, John (1608–1674). Poet. COP

Montagu, Lady Mary Wortley (1689–1762). Author. BOH; RIE†

Montefiore, Sir Moses (1784–1885). Philanthropist. GRB-1; KAB; KAD; LERA; LES; PEB

Moon, Keith (1946–1978). Singer. BUIB-2

More, Hannah (1745–1833). Author. NOA

More, Sir Thomas (Saint Thomas More) (1478–1535). Statesman, author. DAD-3; MAJ; MOC; PEE

Morgan, Sir Henry (1635?–1688). Buccaneer. LACB; PABB; SC-1

Moss, Stirling (1929–). Automobile racer. ABB; COKC; JA; YAA

Neil, Arthur Fowler. Detective. LID

Nelson, Horatio, viscount (1758–1805). Naval hero. CHG; COD; MAJ; SCBA

Nesbit, Edith (1858–1924). Author. BEI

Newcomen, Thomas (1663–1729). Inventor, manufacturer. FE

Newman, John Henry (1801–1890). Theologian. DEI; DEJ

Newton, Sir Isaac (1642–1727). Mathematician, physicist. ASA; BEP; BIA; BOB; CAA; COL; DEI; DEJ; DOE; FE; FRE; LAA; MAQ; MOCB; MUB; PIA; POD; SHFB; SIA; SIB†; STI; STN; SUE

Nightingale, Florence (1820–1910). Nurse. ASB-1; BOC; BOH; COKB; DEI; DEJ; EVD; FAF; FRE; HUE; MAK; MAN; MASA; PA; SC; STP; WRA

Noel-Baker, Philip John (1889–1982). Pacifist. MEC†; WIC

North, Frederick, 2d earl Guilford and 8th baron North (1732–1792). Statesman. SOA

Norton, Mary (1903–). Author. SMB

Noyes, Alfred (1880–1958). Poet. BEH; COP

Oastler, Richard (1789–1861). Reformer. COG

Oglethorpe, James Edward (1696–1785). Colonizer of Georgia. LEO; MAO; VIA

Olivier, Laurence (1907–). Actor. ASB-1

Orwell, George (1903–1950). Author. ASB-1

Ovett, Steve (1955–). Track athlete. AAS-26

Owen, Wilfred (1893–1918). Poet. COP

Palgrave, William Gifford (1826–1888). Jesuit missionary. ROL

Pankhurst, Emmeline Goulden (1858–1928). Feminist. BOH

Parsons, Sir Charles Algernon (1854–1931). Engineer. EVB; FE; SHFB

Parsons, William, 3d earl of Rosse (1800–1867). Astronomer. LAA

Paston, Margery (mid-15th century). Letter writer. NOA

Patterson, John (fl. 1898). Engineer. WOA

Peel, Sir Robert (1788–1850). Statesman. LACA

Perkin, Sir William Henry (1838–1907). Chemist. ASA; FE; SHFB

Perry, Fred (1909–). Tennis player. FOX

Philby, Harry St. John Bridger (1885–1960). Explorer. ROL

Pitman, Sir Isaac (1813–1897). Educator, inventor. FE

Pitt, William, 1st earl of Chatham (1708–1778). Statesman. OLA; SOA

Plimsoll, Samuel (1824–1898). Reformer. EVA

Pope, Alexander (1688–1744). Poet. COP

Potter, Beatrix (1866–1943). Author, illustrator. SC; SM

Price, James (1752–1785). Chemist. CUA

Priestley, Joseph (1733–1804). Chemist. CAA; DABB; FE; SHFB; STI

Purcell, Henry (1659–1695). Composer. BAE; BEM; KAE; SAA; YOK

Raleigh, Sir Walter (1552–1618). Statesman, explorer. DEI; DEJ; KNA†; ROL

Rawlinson, Sir Henry Creswicke (1810–1895). Orientalist. COL

Read, Mary (1680–1721). Pirate. PABB; SC-1; WHA†

Reynolds, Sir Joshua (1723–1792). Painter. CHC

Rhodes, Cecil John (1853–1902). Colonial administrator. ASB-1; WOA

Richards, Sir Gordon (1904–1986). Jockey. DAG; DAGA

Richards, Keith (1943–). Singer. BUIB-1

Riley, Bridget (1931–). Painter. WIAA

Rogers, Woodes (d. 1732). Privateer. WHA

Ross, Sir Ronald (1857–1932). Physician. AAS-31; DEB; RIF; ROA

Rossetti, Christina Georgina (1830–1894). Poet. BEH; COP

Rumford, Benjamin Thompson, count (1753–1814). Physicist, born U.S. CAA; FE; HYB; RAD; SHFB; SIA; STI

Ruskin, John (1819–1900). Author. BEI

Russell, Bertrand Arthur William Russell, 3d earl (1872–1970). Philosopher. HAJ; KE; OZA

Russell, Sir William Howard (1820–1907). War correspondent. FLBB

Sabine, Sir Edward (1778–1883). Astronomer, born Ireland. FE

Sackville-West, Victoria (1892–1962). Author. SMA

Salomons, Sir David (1797–1873). Statesman. GEF

Sargent, Sir Malcolm (1895–1967). Conductor. STM†; YOM

Sayers, Dorothy L. (1893–1957). Author. SMA

Scotland, Alexander (1896?–). Spy. KN

Scott, John (1630?–1696). Adventurer. CAF

Scott, Robert Falcon (1868–1912). Explorer. COC; DOBB; DOC; HOB; KNA†; MOB; ROL

Shaftesbury, Anthony Ashley Cooper, 7th earl of (1801–1885). Reformer. COG; EVA

Shakespeare, William (1564–1616). Playwright. COB; COP; DEI; DEJ; FRE; STK

Shelley, Percy Bysshe (1792–1822). Poet. COP

Sherrington, Sir Charles Scott (1857–1952). Physiologist. RIF

Siddons, Sarah Kemble (1755–1831). Actress. NOA; TRC

Sidney, Sir Philip (1554–1586). Poet, statesman. STP

Siemens, Sir William (1823–1883). Inventor, born Germany. FE

Smeaton, John (1724–1792). Civil engineer. EVB

Smeeton, Beryl. Mariner. HAQ

Smeeton, Miles. Mariner. HAQ

Smith, Graham (fl. 1951). Radio astronomer. SUE

Soddy, Frederick (1877–1956). Chemist. POD; RID

Speke, John Hanning (1827–1864). Explorer. LAA-1; MOB; ROL

Spender, Stephen (1909–). Poet, critic. BRBB

Spenser, Edmund (1552–1599). Poet. COP

Spilsbury, Sir Bernard (1877–1947). Pathologist. LID

Spottiswoode, Nigel (1915–). Motion picture producer. LAE

Spottiswoode, Raymond (1913–). Motion picture producer. LAE

Standfield, John (fl. 1830). Trade unionist. LAD

Standfield, Thomas (fl. 1830). Trade unionist. LAD

Starr, Ringo (1940–). Singer. BUIB-1; SC-01

Stephenson, George (1781–1848). Inventor. EBA; EVB; FE; THA

Stephenson, Robert (1803–1859). Civil engineer. EVB

Stewart, Mary (1916–). Author. SMA

Sturt, Charles (1795–1869). Explorer. MOB; ROL

Sullivan, Sir Arthur Seymour (1842–1900). Composer. BAE; KAE; SAA†

Surtees, John (1934–). Automobile racer. ABB; JA; PAW

Swan, Sir Joseph Wilson (1828–1914). Inventor. FE

Swift, Jonathan (1667–1745). Author. COO

Swinburne, Algernon Charles (1837–1909). Poet. COP

Talbot, William Henry Fox (1800–1877). Inventor. FE; SHFB

Tarleton, Sir Banastre (1754–1833). English general. SOA

Taylor, Ann (1782–1866). Poet. BEH

Taylor, Jane (1783–1824). Poet. BEH

Tennyson, Alfred Tennyson, 1st baron (1809–1892). Poet. COP

Thackeray, William Makepeace (1811–1863). Author. BEG; BEI; COO

Thatcher, Margaret (1925–). Prime minister. DU-1; GI

Thompson, David (1770–1857). Explorer, fur trader. KNA; ROL†

Thomson, Sir Joseph John (1856–1940). Physicist. CAA; FE; MOBA; RID; SHFB; SIA

Townshend, Peter (1945–). Singer. BUIB-2

Travers, Pamela L. (1906–). Author, born Australia. SMB

Trevelyan, George Macaulay (1876–1962). Historian. HIB

Trevithick, Richard (1771–1833). Engineer, inventor. EVB

Tull, Jethro (1674–1741). Agriculturist. CAB

Vancouver, George (1757–1798). Explorer. KNB†; ROL

Vaughan Williams, Ralph (1872–1958). Composer. BUC; GOB; KAE; SAA†; YOJ

Verney, Edmund (1590–1642). Soldier. MAJ

Wade, Virginia (1945–). Tennis player. AAS-9; FR-1; SUDA

Wallace, Alfred Russel (1823–1913). Naturalist. ASA; BLB; MIB

Walsingham, Sir Francis (1530?–1590). Statesman. SEB

Walton, Sir William Turner (1902–1983). Composer. YOL

Webb, Mary (1881–1927). Author. SMA

Webb, Matthew (1848–1883). Swimmer. DAG; DAGA

Wellington, Arthur Wellesley, 1st duke of (1769–1852). General, statesman. CHG; COD

Wells, Herbert George (1866–1946). Historian, author. ASB-1; DEI; DEJ

Wheeler, Sir Mortimer (1890–1976). Archaeologist. POC

White, Gilbert (1720–1793). Naturalist. MIB

Whittle, Sir Frank (1907–). Aeronautical engineer. EVC; FE; SHFB; THA

Whitworth, Sir Joseph (1803–1887). Inventor, manufacturer. FE

Wilkes, John (1727–1797). Political reformer. SOA

Wilson, Harold (1916–). Ex-prime minister. WEB

Wingate, Orde Charles (1903–1944). General. SUA

Wolfe, James (1727–1759). General. MAJ

Wood, Henry (1869–1944). Conductor. YOM

Woolf, Virginia (1882–1941). Author. BEG; SMA

Woolley, Hannah (b. 1623). Educator. BOH

Wordsworth, William (1770–1850). Poet. COP

Wren, Sir Christopher (1632–1723). Architect. DEI; DEJ

Yeo-Thomas, Forest Frederick (1901–1964). Costume designer, spy. SEB

Yom Tov ben Isaac (d. 1190). Rabbi. GEF

Yonge, Charlotte Mary (1823–1901). Author. BEI

Young, Arthur (1741–1820). Agriculturist. CAB

Young, Thomas (1773–1829). Physician, physicist, and Egyptologist. SHFB

Younghusband, Sir Francis Edward (1863–1942). Explorer. ROL

Zangwill, Israel (1864–1926). Author. LERA; PEB

ENGRAVERS & ETCHERS

See also ILLUSTRATORS; PAINTERS

Blake, William (1757–1827). English. BEH; COP

Comstock, Anna Botsford (1854–1930). EMB†;
  PAC; YOC
Dürer, Albrecht (1471–1528). German. CHC;
  KAA; MAI
Rembrandt Hermanszoon van Rijn (1606–1669).
  Dutch. CHC; DEI; DEJ; KAA; MAI
Whistler, James Abbott McNeill (1834–1903).
  CHC; CUC; FRA; KAA; LEE; LEOA; MAG; SIE

ENTOMOLOGISTS

Comstock, John Henry (1849–1931). PAC
Ehrlich, Paul Ralph (1932–). CORA
Fabre, Jean Henri (1823–1915). French. MIB

ESTONIANS

Keres, Paul (1916–1975). Chess player. LEQB

ETCHERS, *see* ENGRAVERS & ETCHERS

ETHIOPIANS

Bikila, Abebe (1932–1973). Track athlete. AAS-30;
  DAJ; HIA-01†; LEYB
Gudit (fl. 937–997). Queen. GRAB-04
Haile Selassie I (1891–1975). Emperor. ADA;
  DU-1; GRAB-04
Haile Selassie, Tsahai (1919–1942). Princess.
  MAK
Makeda (fl. 960–930 B.C.). Queen of Sheba.
  GRAB-04
Menelik II (1844–1913). Emperor of Abyssinia.
  ADA; ADB; GRAB-03
Piankhi (fl. 741–721 B.C.). King. ADA; ADB;
  GRAB-04
Taharga (fl. 688–662 B.C.). King. GRAB-04

ETHNOLOGISTS, *see* ANTHROPOLOGISTS

EXECUTIVES, *see* BUSINESS PEOPLE

EXPLORERS & DISCOVERERS

See also ADVENTURERS; ASTRONAUTS; GEOGRA-
PHERS; PIONEERS & FRONTIER PEOPLE; TRAVELERS;
UNDERWATER EXPLORERS

American
Akeley, Carl Ethan (1864–1926). BAB
Akeley, Delia J. Denning (1870?–1933?). RIG
Andrews, Roy Chapman (1884–1960). BAB
Boyd, Louise Arner (1887–1972). RIG
Byrd, Richard Evelyn (1888–1957). BAB; COC;
  COKA; CUC; DOC; ELA; FAA; FOH; GRB;
  ICA; LAC; NAC; ROL
Clark, William (1770–1838). BLC; BUB; COC;
  CUC; DOBB; FIA; FOB; FOC; GRC; HEB;
  HIBC; JEA; LED; MAO; ROL†
Colter, John (1775–1813). BUB; BUG; FOC; JAC;
  LED
Dodson, Jacob (b. 1825). BUH; SCB; STQ
Ellsworth, Lincoln (1880–1951). GRB
Frémont, John Charles (1813–1890). BUB; CUC;
  DOCA; FOC; HEB; HIBC; HOB; LED; ROL;
  WHD
Gray, Robert (1755–1806). BUB
Henson, Matthew Alexander (1866–1955). ADA;
  ADB; BRB; BRG; COLA†; DOC†; GRAB-02;
  HAM; HAQ; HODA; HUB; JOC; LEI; PECA;
  ROG; STQ
James, Edwin (1797–1861). FOC
Ledyard, John (1751–1789). BLD; BUB; FOC
Lewis, Meriwether (1774–1809). BLC; BUB; COC;
  CUC; DOBB; FIA; FOB; FOC; GRC; HEB;
  HIBC; JEA; LED; MAL; MAO; ROL
Peary, Robert Edwin (1856–1920). BAB; COC†;
  COLA; CUC; DOBB; DOC; EDA; FIA; GRC;
  HAQ; ICA; KNB†; NAC; ROL†
Pike, Zebulon Montgomery (1779–1813). BUB;
  CUC; FOC; HEB; LED; NAA; ROL†
Schoolcraft, Henry Rowe (1793–1864). HAO;
  LED
Siple, Paul Allman (1908–1968). YOE
Wellman, Walter (1858–1934). GRB
Wilkes, Charles (1798–1877). COR; DOC†; ROL
Workman, Fanny Bullock (1859–1925). RIG

Dutch
Barents, Willem (d. 1597). DOC; KNB; MOB;
  ROL†
Tasman, Abel J. (1603–1659). KNB†; MOB; ROL
Tinnè, Alexine (1839–1869). RIG

English
Baker, Lady Florence von Sass (fl. 1863–1893).
  (Born Hungary). RIG

Burton, Sir Richard Francis (1821–1890). COL; MOB; ROL

Chancellor, Richard (d. 1556). KNB; ROL†

Cook, James (1728–1779). COC; COL; DAF; DOBB; DOC; DYA; FAF; GRC; KEH; KNB; LAA-2; MOB; ROL; WIA-1

Dampier, William (1652–1715). KNB; MOB

Drake, Sir Francis (1540–1596). DYA; GRAA; KEH; LAA-2; LACB; MOB; ROL

Evans, Sir Edward Ratcliffe Garth Russell (1881–1957). ROL

Fawcett, Percy Harrison (1867–1925?). KNA; ROL†

Flinders, Matthew (1774–1814). KNB; ROL

Franklin, Sir John (1786–1847). DOC; KNB; MOB; ROL

Frobisher, Sir Martin (1535?–1594). DOC; GRAA; KNB; ROL†

Hearne, Samuel (1745–1792). ARF

Henday, Anthony (fl. 1754). ARF

Herbert, Walter William (1934–). ROL

Hudson, Henry (1575?–1611). COC; DEI; DEJ; DOC; GRAA; GRC; KNB; MAT; MOB; ROL

Kelsey, Henry (1670–1729). ARF

McClintock, Sir Francis Leopold (1819–1907). DOC

Philby, Harry St. John Bridger (1885–1960). ROL

Raleigh, Sir Walter (1552–1618). DEI; DEJ; KNA†; ROL

Scott, Robert Falcon (1868–1912). COC; DOBB; DOC; HOB; KNA†; MOB; ROL

Speke, John Hanning (1827–1864). LAA-1; MOB; ROL

Sturt, Charles (1795–1869). MOB; ROL

Thompson, David (1770–1857). KNA; ROL†

Vancouver, George (1757–1798). KNB†; ROL

Younghusband, Sir Francis Edward (1863–1942). ROL

French

Brazza, Pierre Paul François Camille Savorgnan de (1852–1905). ROL

Caillé, René Auguste (1799–1838). ROL

Cartier, Jacques (1491–1557). ABA; GRC; KEH; MOB; ROL

Champlain, Samuel de (1567–1635). ABA; COC; HIBC; KNA; ROL

Duluth, Daniel Greysolon, sieur (1636–1710). ABA

Joliet, Louis (1645–1700). ABA; GRC; HIBC; ROL†

La Pérouse, Jean François de Galaup, comte de (1741–1788). KNB†; MOB

La Salle, Robert Cavelier, sieur de (1643–1687). ABA; GRC; KNA; LED; LYF; MAT; ROL

Marquette, Jacques (1637–1675). ABA; ASB; GRC; ROL†

Radisson, Pierre Esprit (1636?–1710). ARF

Tonti, Henri de (1650–1704). (Born Italy). MAS

Italian

Cabot, John (1450–1498). GRAA; GRC; KNB; MOB; ROL

Cabot, Sebastian (1476–1557). MOB; ROL†

Columbus, Christopher (1451–1506). ASB; COC; DAF; DEI; DEJ; DOBB; DYA; EVD; GRC; KEH; KNB; MAT; MOB; OLA; PRC; ROL; VIA; WIA-1

Nobile, Umberto (b. 1885). GRB; ROL†

Vespucci, Amerigo (1451–1512). KNB; MOB; ROL; VIA†

Norwegian

Amundsen, Roald (1872–1928). BAB; COC†; COL; DOBB; DOC; GRB; GRC; KEH; KNA†; KNB†; MOB; PRC; ROL; WIA-1

Eric the Red (fl. 10th century). DYA; KEH; KNB; MOB; ROL†

Ericsson, Leif (fl. 1000). COC; HEA; MOB; ROL†; VIA†

Herjolfsson, Bjarni (fl. 985). DYA; MOB†; VIA†

Heyerdahl, Thor (1914–). BAB; OLC; SCBA

Ingolf (10th century). MOB

Nansen, Fridtjof (1861–1930). COC†; COG; DOC; HEA; KEE; KNB†; MEA; MEC; MOB; ROL; WIC

Portuguese

Covilham, Peter de (1450?–1545). KNA

Dias, Bartholomeu (1450?–1500). ROL

Gama, Vasco da (c. 1469–1524). COC; COL; DAF; GRC; KEH; MOB; ROL

Magellan, Ferdinand (1480–1521). COC; COL; DYA; EVD; GRC; HEA; KEH; KNB; LAA-2; MOB; PRC; ROL

Scottish

Livingstone, David (1813–1873). COC; COL; DAF; DOBB; HOB; KNA; LAA-1; MOB; RIB; ROL; STP; WOA

MacKenzie, Sir Alexander (1764–1820). COC; KNA; MOB; ROL

Park, Mungo (1771–1806). KNA; MOB; ROL†

Ross, Sir James Clark (1800–1862). DOC†; ROL

Spanish

Almagro, Diego de (1475?–1538). ROL

Alvarado, Pedro de (1495?–1541). ROL

Anza, Juan Bautista de (1735–1788). YOG

Balboa, Vasco Núñez de (1475–1517). COC; KNA; ROL

Cabeza de Vaca, Álvar Núñez (1490–1557).
BLD†; KEG; LYF; NAA; ROL
Coronado, Francisco Vásquez de (1510–1554).
ASB; BLD; COC; GAA; KEG; NAA; ROL
Cortes, Hernando (1485–1547). BEO; COC; GAA;
KEG; KNA; MOB; ROL
De Soto, Hernando (1500–1542). DEI; DEJ; GRC;
LED; LEPF; ROL
Escalante, Silvestre Vélez de (fl. 1768–1779). FOC
Esteban or Estevanico (d. 1539). ADB; BLD†;
BUH; GRAB-02; HAP; HUB; JO†; KADB; LEI;
PECA; SCB; STQ; VIA; WIBA
Mendana de Neyra, Álvaro de (1541–1595). KNB
Nino, Pedro Alonso (1468?–1505). HODA
Orellana, Francisco de (1500–1549). MOB; ROL
Pizarro, Francisco (1471?–1541). GAA; KEG;
KNA; MOB; ROL†; WIA-1
Ponce de León, Juan (1460–1521). COKB; KEG;
ROL†

Swedish

Andrée, Salomon A. (1854–1897). DOC†; GRB
Hedin, Sven Anders (1865–1952). BAB; HOB;
ROL†
Nordenskjöld, Nils Adolf (1832–1901). COC†;
KNB; ROL

Others

Bellingshausen, Fabian von (1778–1852). Rus-
sian. DOC†; MOB; ROL†
Bering, Vitus J. (1680–1741). Danish. KNB; ROL
Burke, Robert O'Hara (1820–1861). Irish. ROL;
WIA-1
La Vérendrye, Pierre Gaultier de Varennes, sieur
de (1685–1749). Canadian. ARF
Leichhardt, Friedrich Wilhelm (1813–1848). Ger-
man. KNA; ROL†
Mawson, Sir Douglas (1882–1958). Australian.
(Born England). ROL
Pytheas (4th century B.C.). Greek. DYA; KNB;
MOB; ROL†
Shackleton, Sir Ernest Henry (1874–1922). Irish.
DOC; KNA; MAJ; ROL; SCBA
Stanley, Sir Henry Morton (1841–1904). Welsh.
COC; LAA-1; ROL; SQB; WIA-1
Stefánsson, Vilhjálmur (1879–1962). Canadian.
BAB
Wilkins, Sir George Hubert (1888–1958). Austra-
lian. GRB; ROL†

FARMERS, *see* AGRICULTURISTS

FEMINISTS

Anthony, Mary. GUBA
Anthony, Susan Brownell (1820–1906). ASB-1;
BOC; BOJ; COG; CUC; DABB; DAD; DEDA;
DOD; ELA; GIBA†; GUBA; LEK; LES-2; NAB;
PA; SMC; STJ; STLA; TRD; VAB; WABC;
WAR
Blatch, Harriot Stanton (1856–1940). LES-2;
WABC†
Bloomer, Amelia Jenks (1818–1894). ARB; DEDA;
GUBA; LES-2
Brent, Margaret (1600?–1671?). GUBA†; VIA;
WABC
Brown, Antoinette Blackwell (1825–1921). BLF†;
BOJ; LES-2
Catt, Carrie Chapman (1859–1947). COG; FAA;
JOCA; WABC†
Davis, Pauline Wright (1813–1876). GUBA†;
LES-2
Duniway, Abigail Scott (1834–1915). GEE; ROI;
WABC
Friedan, Betty (1921–). GIB-1; WA
Fuller, Margaret (1810–1850). BOC; GUBA;
STLA; WABC
Gilman, Charlotte Perkins (1860–1935). NIA
Godwin, Mary Wollstonecraft (1759–1797). En-
glish. BOH; GUBA
Grimké, Angelina Emily (1805–1879). CHFB;
GUBA; LES-2; STG; WABC†
Grimké, Sarah Moore (1792–1873). CHFB;
GUBA; LES-2; NIA; WABC†
Hatcher, Orie Latham (1868–1946). PACB
Howe, Julia Ward (1819–1910). BOC; DAD;
DEDA; DEI; DEJ; GIBA†; WABC†
Lockwood, Belva Ann (1830–1917). BOJ; WABC
Mott, Lucretia Coffin (1793–1880). COG; GIBA†;
GUBA; LES-2; STJ; STLA; WABC; WAR; YOC
Pankhurst, Emmeline Goulden (1858–1928). En-
glish. BOH
Rankin, Jeannette (1880–1973). FOJ; GRAB-1;
WABC†; WHE
Rose, Ernestine Potowski (1810–1892). (Born Po-
land). EIA; GUBA; JOCA; LES-2; LETA
Shaw, Anna Howard (1847–1919). (Born En-
gland). LES-2; MAV
Stanton, Elizabeth Cady (1815–1902). ARAA;
BUA; COG; DEDA; GIBA†; GUBA; JOCA;
LES-2; MAM; MAV; NIA; PACA; WABC†
Steinem, Gloria (1934–). GIB-1; KOA; WA
Stone, Lucy (1818–1893). DEDA; GUBA; LES-2;
WABC
Terrell, Mary Church (1863–1954). ADA; ADB;
LOAV; STAB-1; STB
Walker, Mary (1832–1919). STJ

Woodhull, Victoria (1838–1927). GUBA; JOCA; MAT-1; WABC†

FINANCIERS

See also BANKERS; BUSINESS PEOPLE

Astor, John Jacob (1763–1848). (Born Germany). CUB; CUC; HOF; LEM; LEPC; LOB

Baruch, Bernard M. (1870–1965). GRB-1; LETA

Brady, James Buchanan ("Diamond Jim") (1856–1917). COKB; LAH

Cornell, Ezra (1807–1874). BOD

Field, Cyrus West (1819–1892). MAL

Grant, M. Earl (1891?–). DRA

Green, Hetty (1835–1916). COKB

Hart, Ephraim (1747–1825). (Born Bavaria). LETA

Hopkins, Johns (1795–1873). CUC

Morgan, John Pierpont (1837–1913). CUC; FAC; WED

Rhodes, Cecil John (1853–1902). ASB-1; WOA

Rothschild, Edmond de (1845–1934). French. KAD

Rothschild, Mayer Amschel (1743–1812). German. PEB

Schiff, Jacob Henry (1847–1920). (Born Germany). LETA

Seligman, Joseph (1819–1880). (Born Germany). LETA

Vanderbilt, Cornelius (1794–1877). COKB; WED

FINNS

Katz, Elias (1901–1947). Track athlete. SLA

Mannerheim, Baron Carl Gustaf Emil von (1867–1951). Soldier, statesman. RADA

Nurmi, Paavo (1897–1973). Track athlete. ASBA; DAFB; DAG; DAGA; DAJ; DEF; FIC; HIA; LEYB; SICA

Sibelius, Jean (1865–1957). Composer. BAE; BEKA; BUC; FIE†; KAE; SAA; YOJ

Viren, Lasse (1949–). Track athlete. SUBB-1

Widing, Juha Markku (1947–). Hockey player. ORB

Wrede, Mathilda (1864–1928). Penal reformer. KEE

FIRE FIGHTERS

Kupper, Sandy. FOC-1

FIRST LADIES

Adams, Abigail (1744–1818). ARAB; BAG; BAG-1; BLG†; CHA; DAD; HIBD; JOCA; KL; MAA; MAU; PRB; ROH; ROHA; WABC†; WAQ

Adams, Louisa Catherine (1775–1852). BAG; BAG-1; BLG†; CHA; KL; MAA; MAU; PRB; ROH; ROHA

Arthur, Ellen Lewis (1837–1880). BAG; BAG-1; BLG†; CHB; KL; MAA; MAU; PRB; ROH; ROHA

Carter, Rosalynn Smith (1927–). BAG-1; BLG; KL; MAU; SMBD

Cleveland, Frances Folsom (1864–1947). BAG; BAG-1; BLG; CHB; KL; MAA; MAU; PRB; ROH; ROHA

Coolidge, Grace Anna (1879–1957). BAG; BAG-1; BLG; CHB; KL; MAA; MAAA; MAU; PRB; ROH; ROHA

Eisenhower, Mamie Geneva (1896–1979). BAG; BAG-1; BLG; CHB; KL; MAA; MAU; PRB; ROH; ROHA

Fillmore, Abigail Powers (1798–1853). BAG; BAG-1; BLG†; CHA; KL; MAA; MAU; PRB; ROH; ROHA

Ford, Elizabeth Bloomer (1918–). BAG-1; BLG; KL; MAU; SMBD

Garfield, Lucretia Rudolph (1832–1918). BAG; BAG-1; BLG†; CHB; KL; MAA; MAU; PRB; ROH; ROHA

Grant, Julia Dent (1826–1902). BAG; BAG-1; BLG†; CHB; KL; MAA; MAU; PRB; ROH; ROHA

Harding, Florence Kling (1860–1924). BAG; BAG-1; BLG; CHB; KL; MAA; MAU; PRB; ROH; ROHA

Harrison, Anna Symmes (1775–1864). BAG; BAG-1; BLG†; CHA; KL; MAA; MAU; PRB; ROH; ROHA

Hayes, Lucy Ware (1831–1889). BAG; BAG-1; BLG†; CHB; KL; MAA; MAU; PRB; ROH; ROHA

Hoover, Lou Henry (1875–1944). BAG; BAG-1; BLG; CHB; KL; MAA; MAU; PRB; ROH; ROHA

Johnson, Claudia Alta (Lady Bird) (1912–). BAG; BAG-1; BLG; CHB; KL; MAA; MAU; ROHA; SMBD

Johnson, Eliza McCardle (1810–1876). BAG; BAG-1; BLG†; CHB; KL; MAA; MAU; PRB; ROH; ROHA

Lincoln, Mary Todd (1818–1882). BAG; BAG-1; BLG; CHA; KL; MAA; MAU; PRB; ROH; ROHA; WAQ

McKinley, Ida Saxton (1847–1907). BAG; BAG-1;

BLG†; CHB; KL; MAA; MAU; PRB; ROH; ROHA

Madison, Dolley Payne Todd (1768–1849). BAG; BAG-1; BLG; CHA; DAD; DOD; KL; LEK; MAA; MAU; PRB; ROH; ROHA; SMC; STJ; TRD; WABC; WAQ

Monroe, Elizabeth (1768–1830). BAG; BAG-1; BLG†; CHA; KL; MAA; MAU; PRB; ROH; ROHA

Nixon, Thelma (Pat) (1912–). BAG; BAG-1; BLG; CHB; KL; MAU; ROHA; SMBD

Onassis, Jacqueline Lee Bouvier Kennedy (1929–). Wife of John Fitzgerald Kennedy. BAG; BAG-1; BLG; CHB; KL; MAA; MAU; PRB; ROH; ROHA

Pierce, Jane Appleton (1806–1863). BAG; BAG-1; BLG†; CHA; KL; MAA; MAU; PRB; ROH; ROHA

Polk, Sarah Childress (1803–1891). BAG; BAG-1; BLG†; CHA; KL; MAA; MAU; PRB; ROH; ROHA

Reagan, Anne Robbins (Nancy) (1921–). BLG; KL; MAU; SMBD

Roosevelt, Edith Kermit (1861–1948). BAG; BAG-1; BLG†; CHB; KL; MAA; MAU; PRB; ROH; ROHA

Roosevelt, Eleanor (1884–1962). ASB-1; BAG; BAG-1; BLG; BOC; BRBE; CHB; COG; COG-1; CUC; DABB; DAD; GIBA; KE; KEE; KL; LAI; MAA; MAU; MEB; PA; PRB; ROH; ROHA; SMC; STLA; WABC†; WAR; YOA

Taft, Helen Herron (1861–1943). BAG; BAG-1; BLG; CHB; KL; MAA; MAU; PRB; ROH; ROHA

Taylor, Margaret Smith (1788–1852). BAG; BAG-1; BLG†; CHA; KL; MAA; MAU; PRB; ROH; ROHA

Truman, Elizabeth V. (Bess) (1885–1982). BAG; BAG-1; BLG; CHB; KL; MAA; MAU; PRB; ROH; ROHA

Tyler, Julia Gardiner (1820–1889). BAG; BAG-1; BLG†; CHA; KL; MAA; MAU; PRB; ROH; ROHA†

Tyler, Letitia Christian (1790–1842). BAG; BAG-1; BLG†; CHA; KL; MAA; MAU; PRB; ROH; ROHA†

Washington, Martha Dandridge (1732–1802). ARAB; BAG; BAG-1; BLG; CHA; KL; LEK; MAA; MAU; PRB; ROH; ROHA; STJ; WABC; WAQ

Wilson, Edith Bolling (1872–1961). BAG; BAG-1; BLG; CHB; KL; MAA; MAU; PRB; ROH; ROHA†

Wilson, Ellen Louisa (1860–1914). BAG; BAG-1; BLG†; CHB; KL; MAA; MAU; PRB; ROH; ROHA†

FISH STUDY, see ICHTHYOLOGISTS

FOLKLORISTS, see AUTHORS—FOLKLORE & MYTHOLOGY

FOOTBALL FIGURES

Abramowicz, Daniel. DEHA

Adderley, Herb. JOA

Agganis, Harry (1930–1955). CL-04; HIE

Allen, George (1922–). Coach. AAS-12; HAGA; LEW

Alworth, Lance (1940–). CO; DEHA; FRD; KADA; LIBA

Amos, John. BELB

Anderson, Donny (1943–). JOA†; LEZB

Anderson, Kenneth Allan (1943–). AAS-20; CL-1

Baker, Al "Bubba" (1956–). AAS-16

Barney, Lemuel J. FRD; ST

Bass, Dick (Richard Lee) (1937–). BEKB; LEZB

Battles, Cliff (d. 1981). Player, coach. DAFG; SUD

Baugh, Sammy (Samuel Adrian) (1914–). Player, coach. ANC; ASBA; DAB; DAFB; DAFG; DAG; DAGA; DAI; DEH; DUD; DUE; HEI; HOC; RAAD; SUC; SUD

Baughan, Maxie. KABA

Bednarik, Chuck (Charles Phillip) (1925–). ANA; DAFG; DAI; SUD

Bell, Bert (de Benneville) (1895–1959). Commissioner. DAB; SUD

Benirschke, Rolf (1955–). AAS-17

Bergey, Bill L. (1945–). RUA; SMJ

Berry, Raymond (1933–). CO; DAFG; DEHA; HAE

Bidwill, Charles E. (1895?–1947). Executive. SUD

Biletnikoff, Frederick. DEHA; SMI

Bingaman, Les (1926–). AAS-32

Blaik, Earl Henry (1892–). Coach. RAE

Blair, Matt (1950–). AAS-15

Blanchard, Doc (Felix) (1924–). DAFB; DAFG; DAI; DEHB; HIE; HOC

Blanda, George (1927–). AAS-17; DAFG; GUD; LIBA; LIBB

Bleier, Rocky (1946–). AAS-27

Blood, Johnny, sobriquet (1903–1985). DAB; DAFG; DAI; JOA†; SUD

Blount, Mel (1948–). AAS-13

Booth, Albie (1908–). FOI; HIE

Bradley, Bill. GUCA; ST

Bradshaw, Terry (1948–). AAS-20; CL-1; GUCA; RUA; ST

Brazile, Robert (1953–). AAS-15; SMJ

Brickley, Charley (1898–1949). DAFG

Brockington, John (1948–). GUF; MOCA; ST

Brodie, John (1935?–). DUD
Brown, Bill (William Dorsey). BEKB
Brown, Larry (1947–). AAS-27; DUF; GUEB;
　GUF; LEZB; ST
Brown, Paul (1908–). Coach. AAS-12; DAFG; SUD
Brown, Robert Stanford. ST
Brown, Roger (1937–). AAS-32
Bryant, Paul "Bear" (1913–1983). Player, coach.
　LEW
Buoniconti, Nick (1940–). DEHA-1
Butkus, Dick (Richard Marvin) (1942–). ANA;
　ASBA; DAFG; FRD; GUF; HAGB; KABA;
　KADA; ST
Butz, Dave (1950–). AAS-32
Caffey, Leo Roy. JOA
Cagle, Red (Christian Keener) (d. 1942). HIE
Camp, Walter Chauncey (1859–1925). Coach.
　DAFG; DAG; DAGA; DAI
Campbell, Earl (1955–). AAS-10; DEHB
Carmichael, Harold (1949–). AAS-18
Carpenter, William (1937–). DIA; RAE
Carr, Frederick. SMJ
Carr, Joseph (1880–1939). President of N.F.L.
　DAB; SUD
Casper, Dave (1951–). AAS-19
Chamberlin, Guy (1894–1967). Player, coach.
　DAFG†; SUD
Chandler, Don. JOA
Chester, Raymond (1948–). AAS-19
Clark, Dutch (Earl Harry) (1906–1978). DAB;
　DAFG; HEI; SUD
Collins, Gary. CO
Conerly, Charley (1922–). DUD; DUE
Conzelman, Jimmy (James Gleason) (1898?–).
　Coach. SUD
Cook, Greg (Gregory Lynn) (1947?–). LEZA
Cousineau, Tom (1957–). AAS-15
Cox, Fred (1938–). AAS-17
Cromwell, Nolan (1955–). AAS-13
Crowley, James (1902?–1986). DAG; DAGA; DAI;
　HIE
Csonka, Larry (1946–). AAS-10; BELB; DUF;
　GUEB; GUF; LEZB; MOCA; ST
Curtis, Isaac (1950–). RUA
Curtis, Mike (1943–). KABA; ST
Davis, Al (1929–). Coach, owner. SLA
Davis, Ernie (1939–1963). CL-04
Davis, Glenn (1924–). DAFB; DAFG; DAI; DEHB;
　HIE; HOC
Davis, Willie (1934–). ANA; JOA
Dawson, Lenny (1935–). DEH; DUD; DUE;
　LEZA; LIBA; RAAD; SHEA
Dean, Fred (1952–). AAS-16
DeLamielleure, Joe (1951–). AAS-11
Dempsey, Tom (1941–). AAS-17; AAS-27; BELB;
　LIBB

Dickerson, Eric (1960–). AAS-35
Dierdorf, Dan (1949–). AAS-11
Ditka, Michael (1939–). Player, coach. ANB; BRE
Dixon, Hewritt (1940–). LEZB
Donovan, Art (1933–). SUD
Dorsett, Tony Drew (1954–). AAS-10; DEHB
Driscoll, John Leo. Player, coach. SUD
Dudley, William (1922?–). DAFG; SUD
Duncan, Jim (1946?–). BELB
Eller, Carl (1942–). GUF; SMD
Farr, Mel (1943–). LEZB
Federspiel, Joe. SMJ
Fencik, Gary (1954–). AAS-13
Ferguson, Joe. CL-1
Fischer, Pat (1940–). RUC
Flutie, Doug (1962–). DEHB
Foreman, Chuck (Walter Eugene) (1950–).
　AAS-10; MOCA
Fortmann, Daniel John (1916–). DAFG†; SUD
Four Horsemen of Notre Dame. DAFG; DAG;
　DAGA; DAI; HIE
Fouts, Dan (1951–). AAS-20
Francis, Russ (1953–). AAS-19
Franklin, Tony (1956–). AAS-17
Friedman, Benny (1905–1982). DAFG; SLA
Fuqua, Frenchy. BELB
Gabriel, Roman (1940–). DUD; DUE; LEZA;
　SHEA
Garrett, Michael Lockett (1944–). BEKB; LEZB
Giammona, Louie (1953–). AAS-25
Gifford, Frank (1930–). HAE
Gilchrist, Cookie (Carlton C.) (1935–). LIBA
Gilliam, John Rally (1945–). SMI
Gillman, Sidney (1911–). Player, coach. SLA
Gipp, George (1895–1920). DAFB; DAFG; DAG;
　DAGA; DAI; HIE
Goldberg, Marshall (1917–). HIE; SLA
Gradishar, Randy (1952–). AAS-15; SMJ
Graham, Otto (1921–). ANC; DAFB; DAFG; DAI;
　DEH; DEHA-1; DUD; DUE; HEI; HOC; RAAD;
　SUC; SUD
Grange, Red (Harold Edward) (1903–). ASBA;
　COFB; DAB; DAFB; DAFG; DAG; DAGA; DAI;
　DUF; HAD; HEG; HEI; HIE; HOC; RAAE;
　SID; SUD
Granger, Hoyle. BEKB
Grant, Bud (Harold P.) (1927–). Coach. AAS-12;
　HAGA
Gray, Leon (1951–). AAS-11
Greene, Joe (1946–). RUA
Grier, Rosie (Roosevelt) (1932–). AAS-32
Griese, Bob (Robert Allen) (1945–). AAS-20; CL-1;
　DUE; FRD; GUF; HAGC; LEZA; ST
Griffin, Archie (1954–). DEHB
Grossman, Randy (1952–). SLA
Groza, Lou (1924–). AAS-17; DAFG; DAI; HAE

Guy, Ray (1949–). RUA

Guyon, Joe (1892–1971). DAFG; SUD

Halas, George (1895–1983). Coach. AAS-12; DAB; DAFG; DAI; SUD

Ham, Jack (1948–). AAS-15

Hannah, John (1951–). AAS-11

Harmon, Thomas D. (1919–). HIE

Harris, Franco (1950–). AAS-10; GUCA; GUH; LIBB

Harris, James. CL-1

Harris, Sigmund (1883–1964). SLA

Hart, Jim (James Warren) (1944–). CL-1; LIB

Hayes, Bob (Robert Lee) (1942–). ANB; CO; DAFB; DAJ; DEHA; KADA; OCA; ST-1

Hayes, Lester (1955–). AAS-13

Haymond, Alvin Henry (1942–). LEZB

Haynes, Abner (1937–). LIBA

Haynes, Mike (1953–). AAS-13

Healey, Ed (1895?–1978). SUD

Heffelfinger, Pudge (William Walter) (1867–1954). DAFG; DAG; DAGA; DAI

Hein, Mel (Melvin John) (1909–). DAB; DAFG; DAI; HEI; KABA; SUD

Heisman, John William (1869–1936). Coach. DAFG; VAD

Hendricks, Ted (1947–). AAS-15

Henry, Pete (Wilbur) (1897–1952). DAB; DAFG; SUD

Herber, Arnie (1910–1969). JOA†; SUD

Herrera, Efren (1951–). AAS-17

Hill, Calvin (1947–). AAS-25; LEZB

Hinkey, Frank (1871–1925). DAFG

Hinkle, Clarke (1912–). DAFG†; JOA†; SUD

Hirsch, Elroy "Crazylegs" (1924–). CO; DAFG; HAE; SUD

Holland, Jerome H. (1916–). HOBB

Hornung, Paul Vernon (1935–). BEKB; DEHB; DUF; HAD; HIE; JOA; KADA

Houston, Ken (1944–). RUA

Howley, Chuck (Charles Louis). KABA

Howton, Bill (1930–). ANB

Hubbard, Cal (Robert Calvin) (1900–1977). DAB; DAFG; DAI; HEI; SUD

Huff, Sam (Robert Lee) (1934–). ANA

Hutson, Don (Donald Montgomery) (1913–). ANB; CO; DAB; DAFB; DAFG; DAG; DAGA; DAI; HEI; JOA; SUC; SUD

Jackson, Harold (1946–). RUC

Jefferson, John (1956–). AAS-18

Jensen, Jackie (1927–1982). HIE

Jeter, Bob. JOA

Johnson, Bob (1946–). CL-06

Johnson, Charley (1938–). ANC; DEH; DEHA-1

Johnson, Gary "Big Hands" (1952–). AAS-16

Johnson, Pete (1954–). AAS-32

Johnson, Ronald Adolphus (1947–). GUCA; LEZB; ST

Jones, Bert (1951–). AAS-20; CL-1; LIBB

Jones, Dave "Deacon" (1938–). ANA; KADA

Jordan, Henry (1935–). ANA; JOA

Jordan, Lee Roy. HAGB

Jurgensen, Sonny (Christian Adolph) (1934–). DUD; DUE; LEZA; SHEA

Justice, Charlie. HIE

Kapp, Joe (1938–). LEZA; LIBB; LYD; NEAA

Kazmaier, Dick (1930–). HIE

Kelley, Larry (Lawrence Morgan) (1915–). DAFG; DAI

Kelly, Leroy (1942–). BEKB; DUF; FRD; LEZB

Kiesling, Walt (1903–1962). Player, coach. DAFG†; SUD

Kiick, Jim (1946–). LEZB

Kilmer, Billy (1939–). GUF

Kinnick, Nile (1919–1943). HIE

Klecko, Joe (1953–). AAS-16

Kramer, Jerry (1936–). DAFG; JOA; PIB; PIBA

Kramer, Ron (1935–). AAS-19; JOA†

Kroll, Alex. HOBB

Kunz, George (1947–). CL-06

Kwalick, Ted (Thaddeus John, Jr.) (1947–). GUCA

Ladd, Ernie (1938–). AAS-32

Lambeau, Curly (Earl Louis) (1898–1965). Executive. DAB; DAFG; JOA; SUD

Lambert, Jack (1952–). AAS-15; SMJ

Lamonica, Daryle Pat (1941–). LEZA

Landry, Greg (Gregory Paul) (1946–). GUCA; ST

Landry, Tom (Thomas Wade) (1924–). Coach. AAS-12; HAGA

Lane, Dick (1928–). ANA

Lane, MacArthur (1942–). LEZB

Langer, Jim (1948–). AAS-11

Lanier, Willie Edward (1945–). GUD; SMJ

Largent, Steve (1954–). AAS-18

Lavelli, Dante (1923–). ANB

Layden, Elmer (1902?–1973). DAG; DAGA; DAI; HIE

Layne, Bobby (Robert Lawrence) (1926–1986). DAFG; DEH; DUD; DUE; SUD

Leahy, Frank (1908–1973). Coach. DAFG

LeBaron, Eddie (Edward W., Jr.) (1930?–). DAFG; DAI; FOI; HAE

LeClair, Jim. SMJ

Lemm, Wally (1919–). Coach. LEW

Levy, Marv (1928–). Coach. SLA

Lilly, Robert Lewis (1939–). ANA; SMD; ST

Lipscomb, Gene "Big Daddy" (1931–). AAS-32

Little, Floyd Douglas (1942–). DUF; LEZB; RUC

Little, Larry (1945–). GUD; RUA

Lombardi, Vincent (1913–1970). Coach. AAS-12; DAFG; DAI; HEH; JOA

Lott, Ronnie (1959–). AAS-13

Lowe, Paul (1936–). LIBA

Luckman, Sidney (1916–). ANC; DAFG; DAI; DEH; DUD; DUE; HEI; HOC; RAAD; SLA; SUD

Lurtsema, Bob (1942–). AAS-25

Lyman, Roy (1898–). DAFG; SUD

McAfee, George (1918?–). DAFG†; SUD

McDonald, Tommy. CO; FOI; HAE

McElhenny, Hugh (1928–). BEKB; DUF; HAD; RAAE

McGee, William Max. JOA

McKay, John (1923?–). Coach. LEW

Mackey, John (1942–). AAS-19; CO; HOBC

McMillin, Bo (1895?–1952). HIE

Mahan, Eddie (1892?–). HIE

Manning, Archie (Elisha Archibald) (1949–). AAS-20; GUCA

Mara, Timothy James (1887–1959). Executive. DAB; SUD

Marchetti, Gino (1927–). ANA

Marcol, Chester (1949–). (Born Poland). GUCA

Marshall, George Preston (1896–). Executive. DAB; SUD

Marshall, Jim (James Lawrence) (1937–). SMD

Martin, Harvey (1950–). AAS-16

Matson, Ollie (1930–). HAD; RAAE

Maynard, Don (1937–). CO; DEHA; LIBA; LIBB

Meggyesy, Dave (1941–). LOAA

Meredith, Don (1938–). DEH

Michalske, August. Player, coach. SUD

Miller, Don (1902–1979). DAG; DAGA; DAI; HIE

Millner, Wayne (1913–). SUD

Mitchell, Bobby (1935–). ANB; DEHA-1

Mix, Ronald (1938–). SLA

Montgomery, Wilbert (1954–). AAS-10

Moore, Lenny (1933–). BEKB; HAE; RAAE

Morris, Mercury (Eugene) (1947–). MOCA

Morton, Craig (1943–). LEZA

Motley, Marion (1920–). DAFG; SUD

Nagurski, Bronko (1908–). ASBA; COFB; COKB; DAB; DAFB; DAFG; DAG; DAGA; DAI; DUF; HAD; HEI; HIE; HOC; SUD

Namath, Joe Willie (1943–). ASBA; BELB; DAFG; DEHA-1; DUD; DUE; FRD; GUEB; HAGC; KADA; LEZA; PAW; RAAD; SHEA; ST

Nance, Jim (1942–). LEZB; LIBA

Nelson, Bill (William Keith) (1941–). LEZA

Nevers, Ernie (1903–1976). DAB; DAFB; DAFG; DAI; HAD; HEI; RAAE; SUD

Newman, Harry (1909–). SLA

Newsome, Ozzie (1956–). AAS-19

Niland, John Hugh (1944–). GUF; ST

Nitschke, Ray. JOA; KABA

Nobis, Tommy (1943–). ANA; HAGB; KABA

Noll, Chuck (1932–). Coach. AAS-12

O'Dea, Pat (1873–1962). (Born Australia). DAFG; DAI

Odoms, Riley (1950–). AAS-19

Olsen, Merlin (1940–). FRD

Orr, Jimmy (1935–). ANB

Owen, Steve (1898–1964). Player, coach. SUD

Page, Alan (1945–). GUD; SMD; ST

Parker, Jim (1934–). BELB

Parks, David Wayne (1941–). ANB

Pastorini, Dan (1941–). CL-1

Payton, Walter (1954–). AAS-10; AAS-35

Pearson, Drew (1951–). AAS-18

Peoples, Woody (1943–). AAS-9

Perkins, Don. BEKB

Perry, Joe (Fletcher) (1927–). HAD; RAAE

Perry, William (1962–). AAS-32

Plunkett, Jim (1947–). AAS-9; CL-1; DEHB; GUD; NEAA; ST; WH-3

Plunkett, Sherman (1933–). AAS-32

Pollard, Frederick (1894–1986). DAFB; DAFG; DAI; HOBC

Pont, John (1928?–). Coach. LEW

Post, Dick (1945–). LEZB

Powell, Marvin (1955–). AAS-11

Prothro, Tom (James Thompson) (1920?–). Coach. LEW

Pruitt, Greg (1951–). AAS-10; AAS-23

Rashad, Ahmad (Bobby Moore) (1949–). AAS-18

Ray, Hugh (1883–1956). Executive. SUD

Reeves, Dan (1912–). Executive. SUD

Reid, Michael B. (1948–). GUCA

Rentzel, Lance (1943?–). BELB

Retzlaff, Pete (Palmer Edward) (1932–). ANB

Riegels, Roy. DAI; LYC

Riggins, John (1949–). AAS-10

Robertson, Isaiah. SMJ

Robinson, Dave. HAGB; JOA; KABA

Robinson, Paul. BEKB

Rockne, Knute (1888–1931). Coach, born Norway. DAFB; DAFG; DAG; DAGA; DAI; HEH; LEAB; LEB; LOB; LYB; VAD

Rooney, Arthur Joseph (1901–). Executive. SUD

Rosenberg, Aaron (1912–1979). SLA

Rossovich, Tim. ST

Roth, Joe (d. 1977). AAS-24; CL-04

Ruffin, Nate. BELB

Russell, Andy (Charles Andrew) (1941–). BELB

Ryan, Frank Beall (1936?–). ANC

Sanders, Charlie (1946–). AAS-19; DEHA

Sauer, George, Jr. BELB; CO

Sayers, Gale (1943–). BEKB; BELB; COFB; DAFG; DAI; DUF; FRD; HAD; KADA; LEZB; LIB; LIBB; RAAE

Schmidt, Joseph Paul (1932–). ANA

Selmon, Lee Roy (1954–). AAS-16

Sherman, Allie (1923–). Coach. HAE; SLA†

Shofner, Del (1934–). ANB
Shula, Don (1930–). Coach. AAS-12; HAGA
Siemon, Jeffrey G. (1950–). HAGB; SMJ
Simpson, O. J. (Orenthal James) (1947–). AAS-10;
    AAS-35; DEHA-1; DEHB; DUF; GUCA; GUEB;
    KADA; LEZB; LIBB; MOCA; RUA; ST
Sinkwich, Frank. HIE
Smith, Charles "Bubba" (1948–). AAS-32; LIB;
    SMD
Speedie, Mac (1920–). ANB
Spurrier, Steve (1945?). BRE
Stabler, Ken (1945–). AAS-20; CL-1
Stagg, Amos Alonzo (1862–1964). Coach. DAFG;
    DAG; DAGA; DAI; HEH
Stallworth, John (1952–). AAS-18
Starr, Bart (1934–). ANC; DEH; DUD; DUE;
    HAGC; JOA; RAAD; SHEA
Staubach, Roger (1942–). AAS-20; CL-06; CL-1;
    DEHB; GAB; GUF; HAGC
Steinmark, Fred (1948?–1971). CL-04; LYB
Stenerud, Jan (1943–). GUD
Still, Art (1955–). AAS-16
Stingley, Darryl (1951–). AAS-24
Strong, Ken (Elmer Kenneth) (1906–1979).
    DAFG; SUD
Stuhldreher, Harry (1901–1965). DAG; DAGA;
    DAI; HIE
Stydahar, Joseph Leo (1912–). Player, coach.
    SUD
Swann, Lynn (1952–). AAS-18
Tarkenton, Francis (1940–). AAS-20; ANC; BRE;
    CL-1; DEH; GUEB; HAGC; RUC
Tatum, Jack (John David) (1948–). GUCA
Taylor, Bruce (1948–). GUD
Taylor, Charley (1941–). CO; DEHA-1; SMI
Taylor, James (1935–). BEKB; DUF; HAD; JOA
Taylor, Lawrence (1959–). AAS-15
Taylor, Otis (1942–). CO; DEHA; GUF; SMI; ST
Thomas, Duane (1947?–). LEZB
Thomas, Pat (1954–). AAS-13
Thorpe, Jim (1888–1953). ASBA; BELB; DAB;
    DAFB; DAFG; DAG; DAGA; DAI; DAJ; DEF;
    DUF; FIC; HACA; HEG; HEI; HIE; HOC;
    LEH; LEPA; LEYB; LYB; RAAE; SID; SUD
Thurston, Fuzzy (Fred). JOA
Tittle, Y. A. (Yelberton Abraham) (1926–). ANC;
    DAFG; DEH; DUD; DUE; HEI; PAW; RAAD
Trafton, George (1896–1971). Player, coach.
    DAFG†; SUD
Trippi, Charley (1923–). DAFG; HIE; SUD
Tucker, Robert Louis (1945–). GUCA
Tunnell, Emlen (1926–1975). Player, coach.
    DAFG; HAE; SUD
Turner, Bulldog (Clyde) (1919–). DAFG; KABA;
    SUD
Unitas, Johnny (1933–). ALBA; ANC; ASBA;

BUJA; DAFB; DAFG; DAGA; DAI; DEH;
    DEHA-1; DUD; DUE; FRD; HEI; HOC; KADA;
    LIBB; PAW; RAAD; SHEA; VAE
Upshaw, Gene (1945–). AAS-11
Van Brocklin, Norman Mack (1926–1983). ANC;
    DUD; DUE; RAAD
Van Buren, Steve (1921–). BEKB; DAFG; DUF;
    HAD; RAAE; SUD
Vataha, Randy (1948–). RUC
Walker, Doak (Ewell Doak, Jr.) (1927–). BUJA;
    DEHB; HIE
Walker, Herschel (1962–). DEHB
Walker, Wayne (1936–). KABA
Walker, Wesley (1955–). AAS-18
Walls, Everson (1959–). AAS-13
Warfield, Paul (1942–). CO; DEHA; LIB; SMI; ST
Warner, Glenn "Pop" (1871–1954). Coach. DAFG;
    HEH; VAD
Washington, Gene (1947–). FRD; GUEB; GUF;
    ST
Waterfield, Robert Staton (1920–1983). Player,
    coach. DAFG; HEI; RAAD; SUD
Webster, Mike (1952–). AAS-11
White, Byron Raymond (1917–). DAFG; DAI;
    HIE; HOBB; HOC
White, Randy (1953–). AAS-16; SMJ
White, Stan. SMJ
Willard, Ken (1943–). BEKB; LEZB
Wilson, Larry (1938–). ANA; KADA
Wilson, Nemiah. RUC
Wojciechowicz, Alex (1915–). SUD
Wood, William Barry (1910–1971). HAE; JOA
Yepremian, Garo Sarkis (1944–). (Born Cyprus).
    AAS-17; GUF; RUC
Young, Buddy (Claude) (d. 1983). FOI
Young, Wilbur (1949–). AAS-25
Zorn, Jim (1953–). AAS-20

FOREIGN-BORN, *see* IMMIGRANTS TO U.S.

FOSSIL EXPERTS, *see* PALEONTOLOGISTS

FOUNDERS OF CITIES & COLONIES

See also COLONIAL AMERICANS; PIONEERS &
FRONTIER PEOPLE

Austin, Stephen Fuller (1793–1836). Texas. AKC;
    KUA; LYF; MAO; VIA
Bulkeley, Peter (1583–1659). Concord, Mass.
    WOAA
Calvert, Cecilius, 2nd baron Baltimore (1605–
    1675). Maryland. LEO; MEB

Calvert, Charles, 3rd baron Baltimore (1637–1715). Maryland. LEO; MEB

Calvert, George, 1st baron Baltimore (1580?–1632). Maryland. MEB; VIA

Cuffe, Paul (1759–1817). Sierra Leone. ADA; ADB; BRB; DOB; GRAB-02; HUB; PECA; WIBA

Henderson, Richard (1735–1785). Kentucky. STA

Moody, Lady Deborah (1600–1669?). First woman in America granted patent to erect a town. CRB; JOCA; WABC†

Oglethorpe, James Edward (1696–1785). Georgia. LEO; MAO; VIA

Penn, William (1644–1718). Pennsylvania. ASB; COG; DEI; DEJ; FOB; FOJ; HAJ; LAD; LEO; LEPF; LEZC; MAM; MAT; MEB; OLA; VIA

Pointe de Sable, Jean Baptiste (1745–1818). Chicago. ADA; ADB; BUH; DOB; GRAB-02; HUB; KADB; LEI; LEPD; PECA; ROG; STQ; WIBA

Willard, Simon (1605–1676). Concord, Massachusetts. WOAA

Williams, Roger (1603?–1683). Rhode Island. ARB; COG; DAC; DEI; DEJ; FIA; FOB; LEO; LEPF; MEB; OLA; VIA†

FRENCH

See also RULERS—FRENCH

Ampère, André Marie (1775–1836). Mathematician, physicist. CAA; DUA; FE; SHFB; SIA

Appert, Nicolas (c. 1750–1841). Inventor. FE

Babilee, Jean (1923–). Dancer. ATA

Balzac, Honoré de (1799–1850). Author. DEI; DEJ

Bart, Jean (1651–1702). Privateer. KEH

Bartholdi, Frédéric Auguste (1834–1904). Sculptor. DIA

Bastie, Maryse. Aviator. HIFD

Becquerel, Antoine Henri (1852–1908). Physicist. ASA; FE; MOBA; SHFB; SOB

Beltoise, Jean-Pierre (1937–). Automobile racer. JA

Bergson, Henri (1859–1941). Philosopher. LET

Berlioz, Hector (1803–1869). Composer. BRF; FIE; KAE; SAA; YOM†

Bernhardt, Sarah (1844–1923). Actress. MAT-1; PA

Bertillon, Alphonse (1853–1914). Criminologist. FE; LACA; LID

Bettignies, Louise de (1888?–1918). Spy. SEB; SUG

Bizet, Georges (1838–1875). Composer. BAE; KAE; SAA

Blériot, Louis (1872–1936). Aviator. BRBA; COC†; EDA; KEH

Blum, Léon (1872–1950). Statesman. ARAA

Bombard, Alain Louis (1924?–). Physician and adventurer. ELA; HAQ

Bonheur, Rosa (1822–1899). Painter. BOC

Boucher, Helene (1908–1934). Aviator. HIFD

Boulez, Pierre (1925–). Composer, conductor. EWAA

Bourgeois, Léon Victor Auguste (1851–1925). Statesman. MEC†; WIC

Boussingault, Jean Baptiste (1802–1887). Agricultural chemist. CAB

Braille, Louis (1809–1852). Teacher of the blind. EVA; FE; FOR; FRB; FRE

Braque, Georges (1882–1963). Painter. MAH

Brazza, Pierre Paul François Camille Savorgnan de (1852–1905). Explorer. ROL

Briand, Aristide (1862–1932). Statesman. MEC†; WIC

Broglie, Louis-Victor de (1892–1987). Physicist. FE

Brunhoff, Jean de (1899–1937). Author, illustrator. SMAB

Brunhoff, Laurent de (1925–). Author, illustrator. SMAB

Buisson, Ferdinand (1841–1932). Educator. MEC†; WIC

Caillé, René Auguste (1799–1838). Explorer. ROL

Calas, Jean (1688–1762). Merchant. COG

Carnot, Nicholas Léonard Sadi (1796–1832). Physicist. HAC; SHFB

Caron, Leslie (1933–). Dancer, actress. ATA

Cartier, Jacques (1491–1557). Explorer. ABA; GRC; KEH; MOB; ROL

Cartier-Bresson, Henri (1908–). Photographer. HOE

Cartouche, Dominique (Louis Dominique Bourguignon) (1693–1721). Criminal. SUG

Cassin, René (1887–1976). Statesman. MEC†; WIC

Cerdan, Marcel, Jr. (1916–1949). Boxer. BELB

Cézanne, Paul (1839–1906). Painter. ASB-1; KAA; MAH; WIAA

Champlain, Samuel de (1567–1635). Explorer. ABA; COC; HIBC; KNA; ROL

Chanel, Coco (1883–1971). Fashion designer. FRBD

Chateaubriand, François René (1768–1848). Author, statesman. RAC

Chatelet, Marquise du. Gabrielle Émilie Le Tonnelier du Breteuil (1706–1749). Author, physicist. SC

Chausson, Ernest Amédée (1855–1899). Composer. KAE

Chauviré, Yvette (1917–). Dancer. ATA

Clemenceau, Georges (1841–1929). Statesman. ASB-1; COKB

Cochet, Henri (1901–1987). Tennis player. FOX

Coictier, Jacques (1482–1506). Physician. MAR

Colonne, Edouard (1838–1910). Conductor. YOM

Coriolis, Gaspard Gustave de (1792–1843). Mathematician. HAC

Carot, Jean Baptiste (1796–1875). Painter. CHC; DEI; DEJ; MAH

Coulomb, Charles Augustin de (1736–1806). Physicist. SHFB

Couperin, François (1668–1733). Composer, harpsichordist. BEM; KAE

Cousteau, Jacques Yves (1910–). Underwater explorer. COR; DU-1; ELA; FE; OLC; PRC; SCBA; SQA

Crémieux, Isaac-Adolphe (1796–1880). Statesman. KAD

Curie, Marie Sklodowska (1867–1934). Chemist, physicist, born Poland. ASA; ASB-1; BEC; BEP; BOB; BOC; BOH; BUF; CAA; COL; DEI; DEJ; DOE; EVD; FE; FRE; HUE; KOA; MAJ; MANB; MASA; PA; PAC; POD; RID; SC; SHFB; SHFE†; SIA; STI

Curie, Pierre (1859–1906). Chemist. ASA; BOB; BUF; DOE; PAC; RID; STI

Cuvier, Georges (1769–1832). Zoologist. FE

Daguerre, Louis Jacques (1787–1851). Inventor. FE; FRE; THA

Daumier, Honoré (1808–1879). Painter. KAA

David, Jacques Louis (1748–1825). Painter. KAA; MAH†

Debussy, Claude Achille (1862–1918). Composer. BRF; BUD; FIE; KAE; SAA

Degas, Edgar (1834–1917). Painter. KAA; MAH

Delacroix, Eugène (1798–1863). Painter. KAA; MAH

Descartes, René (1596–1650). Philosopher, mathematician. LO; MUB; OZA; SHFB; SIA; STN

Dianous, Jacques (d. 1881). Soldier. WOA

Dreyfus, Alfred (1859–1935). Soldier. PEB

Dreyfus, René (1905–). Automobile racer. SLA

Dubuffet, Jean (1901–1985). Painter. WIAA

Dukas, Paul (1865–1935). Composer. KAE

Duluth, Daniel Greysolon, sieur (1636–1710). Explorer. ABA

Dumas, Alexandre (Dumas père) (1802–1870). Author. ADA; ADB; DEI; DEJ; JO

Eiffel, Alexandre Gustave (1832–1923). Engineer. EVB

Erte (Romain de Tirtoff) (1892–). Artist, costume designer, born Russia. ASB-1

Esnault-Pelteri, Robert (1881–1957). Engineer. STMA

Estournelles de Constant, Paul Henri Benjamin, baron d' (1852–1924). Statesman. MEC†; WIC

Eugenie (1826–1910). Wife of Napoleon III. COKB

Fabre, Jean Henri (1823–1915). Entomologist. MIB

Fauré, Gabriel Urbain (1845–1924). Composer. KAE

Felicie, Jacoba (fl. 1322). Medical practitioner. MASA†; SC

Félix, Elisa Rachel (1821–1858). Actress, born Switzerland. LER; PEB

Flamel, Nicholas (1330–1418). Alchemist. CUA

Flaubert, Gustave (1821–1880). Author. HOA

Foch, Ferdinand (1851–1929). Soldier. ARD; COD

Fonck, René (1894–1953). Aviator, WWI. HAMY

Foucault, Jean Bernard Léon (1819–1868). Physicist. CAA; FE; SHFB

Fournier, Pierre (1906–1986). Cellist. EWC

Franck, César Auguste (1822–1890). Composer, organist, born Belgium. BRF; KAE

Froissart, Jean (1337–1407). Historian. HIB

Galard, Geneviève de (1925–). Nurse. MAK

Galois, Evariste (1811–1832). Mathematician. MUB; STN

Garros, Roland (d. 1918). Aviator, WW I. HAMY

Gauguin, Paul (1848–1903). Painter. KAA; MAH; WIAA

Gaulle, Charles de (1890–1970). President. ASB-1; CAAA; KE; WEA

Gay-Lussac, Joseph Louis (1778–1850). Chemist, physicist. SHFB

Goron, Marie-François (1847–1933). Detective. LID

Gounod, Charles François (1818–1893). Composer. BAE; KAE

Grasse, François Joseph de (1722–1788). Naval officer. SOA

Guynemer, Georges (1894–1917). Aviator, WWI. ARD; HAMY

Herzog, Maurice (1919–). Mountaineer. HAQ; HOB; KEH

Hollard, Michel Louis. Spy. HAB

Honegger, Arthur (1892–1955). Composer. KAE

Houdin, Jean Eugène Robert (1805–1871). Magician. EDA; FOGA; GIA; KEB; KLD

Hugo, Victor (1802–1885). Author. COKB; DEI; DEJ

Indy, Vincent d' (1851–1931). Composer. KAE

Jacquard, Joseph-Marie (1752–1834). Inventor. FE

Jeanmaire, Renée (1924–). Dancer. ATA

Joan of Arc (1412–1431). Saint. CHG; DAD-1; DAD-2; DEI; DEJ; ELA; EVD; HAA; HEA; MAJ; MOC; ONA; PA; PEE; STP

Joffre, Joseph Jacques (1852–1931). Field marshal. ARD; RADA

Joliet, Louis (1645–1700). Explorer. ABA; GRC; HIBC; ROL†

Joliot-Curie, Frédéric (1900–1958). Physicist. FE; RID

Joliot-Curie, Irène (1897–1956). Physicist. FE; RID; SC†; SHFE†

Jouhaux, Léon (1879–1954). Labor leader, politician. MEC; WIC

Jullien, Louis Antoine (1812–1860). Conductor. YOM

Jupille, Jean Baptiste. First rabies inoculé. FAF

Killy, Jean-Claude (1943–). Skier. FRCA; LEYB†

Kreutzer, Rodolphe (1766–1831). Violinist. CHFA

Lachenal, Louis. Mountaineer. HAQ

Lacoste, René (1904?–). Tennis player. FOX

Laënnec, René Théophile (1781–1826). Physician. FAF; HUD; SHG

Lafayette, Marie Joseph Paul Yves Roch Gilbert du Motier, marquis de (1757–1834). Statesman and officer. CUC; DEI; FRB; HAN; LAD; LOA; OLA; SCB-1; SOA; STP

Lafitte, Jean (1780?–1826?). Pirate. LACB; SC-1; VIA

Lagrange, Joseph Louis (1736–1813). Mathematician, astronomer. STN

Lamarck, Jean Baptiste Pierre Antoine de (1744–1829). Naturalist. STI

Lamoureux, Charles (1834–1899). Conductor. YOM

La Pérouse, Jean François de Galaup, comte de (1741–1788). Explorer. KNB†; MOB

Larrey, Dominique Jean (1766–1842). Surgeon. MAR

La Salle, Robert Cavelier, sieur de (1643–1687). Explorer. ABA; GRC; KNA; LED; LYF; MAT; ROL

Latude, Henri Maseres de (1725–1805). Soldier. JAC

Laurencin, Marie (1885–1956). Painter. NE

Laveran, Charles Louis (1845–1922). Bacteriologist. RIF; SHG

Lavoisier, Antoine Laurent (1743–1794). Chemist. ASA; CAA; CAB; COL; DOE; MOBA; POD; SHFB; STI

Leclair, Jean Marie (1697–1764). Violinist. CHFA

LeClercq, Tanaquil (1929–). Dancer. ATA

Le Corbusier (Charles-Edouard Jeanneret) (1887–1965). Architect, born Switzerland. HIFA

Léger, Fernand (1881–1955). Painter. WIAA

Lenglen, Suzanne (1899–1938). Tennis player. DAG; DAGA; FR-1; HI; HOBAA; LAHA; SUDA†

Lenoir, Etienne (1822–1900). Engineer. FE

Lesseps, Ferdinand de (1805–1894). Engineer. EVB; WOA

Leverrier, Urbain Jean Joseph (1811–1877). Astronomer. SUE

Levi, Eliphas (Constant, Alphonse Louis) (1810–1875). Cabalist. ED-5

Lévi-Strauss, Claude (1908–). Anthropologist. HAO

Lifar, Serge (1905–1986). Dancer, choreographer, born Russia. ATA

Lippmann, Gabriel (1845–1921). Physicist. LET

L'Olonnois (1630?–1671). Pirate. LACB

Louis, Pierre Charles Alexandre (1787–1872). Physician. POB

Lucieto, Charles (fl. 1918). Spy. SEB

Lully, Jean Baptiste (1632–1687). Composer, born Italy. BEM; CHFA; KAE; SAA; YOM†

Lumière, Auguste (1862–1954). Inventor. FE

Lumière, Louis (1864–1948). Inventor. FE

Mance, Jeanne (1606–1673). Missionary nurse. MAK

Manet, Édouard (1832–1883). Painter. KAA; MAH

Marchand, Colette (1925–). Dancer. ATA

Marie Antoinette (1755–1793). Queen. COA; DAK; DEI; DEJ; FAE; UNA

Marillac, Louise de (1591–1660). Nurse. MAK

Marquette, Jacques (1637–1675). Missionary, explorer. ABA; ASB; GRC; ROL†

Massenet, Jules (1842–1912). Composer. BAE; KAE

Matisse, Henri (1869–1954). Painter. KAA; MAH; WIAA

Meiffret, Jose (1911–). Bicyclist. ST-1

Michaux, André (1746–1802). Botanist. JEA

Michaux, François André (1770–1855). Botanist. JEA

Milhaud, Darius (1892–1974). Composer. KAE

Millet, Jean François (1814–1875). Painter. CHC

Mitterand, François (1916–). President. DU-1

Moissan, Henri (1852–1907). Chemist. LET

Molière (Jean Baptiste Poquelin) (1622–1673). Playwright. TRC

Monet, Claude (1840–1926). Painter. KAA

Montaigne, Michel de (1533–1592). Essayist. RAC

Montgolfier, Jacques Étienne (1745–1799). Inventor. BRBA; EVC; FE

Montgolfier, Joseph Michel (1740–1810). Inventor. BRBA; EVC; FE

Morisot, Berthe (1841–1895). Painter. NE

Munch, Charles (1891–1968). Conductor. EWD; STM; YOM

Necker, Oliver (1440?–1484). Barber-surgeon. MAR

Nicolle, Charles Jules Henri (1866–1936). Bacteriologist. AAS-31; RIF

Niepce, Joseph-Nicephore (1765–1833). Inventor. FE

Nungesser, Charles (1892–1927). Aviator, WWI. ARD†; SUA

Offenbach, Jacques (1819–1880). Composer. KAE

Paray, Paul (b. 1886). Conductor. STM

Paré, Ambroise (1510?–1590). Surgeon. CHD; HUD; ROA; SHG; SIC

Pascal, Blaise (1623–1662). Philosopher, mathematician. GRAB-3; MUB; SOB

Passy, Frédéric (1822–1912). Economist, statesman. MEA; MEC; WIC

Pasteur, Louis (1822–1895). Chemist. ASA; BEK; BEP; BUF; CAA; CAB; CHD; COL; DEB; DEI; DEJ; DOE; EVD; FAF; FE; FRE; HUD; POD; RIE; ROA; SHG; SUF

Pétain, Henri Philippe (1856–1951). Marshall. ARD; RADA

Petit, Roland (1924–). Dancer, choreographer. ATA

Pierre, Abbé (Henri Groués) (1910–). Priest, resistance worker. BAF

Poussin, Nicolas (1594–1665). Painter. KAA; MAH†

Radisson, Pierre Esprit (1636?–1710). Explorer, trader. ARF

Rameau, Jean Philippe (1683–1764). Composer. BEM; KAE

Rashi (Solomon ben Isaac) (1040–1105). Hebraist. GEF; GRB-1; GUA; KAC; LERA; LES

Ravel, Maurice (1875–1937). Composer. BUC; KAE; SAA; YOL

Reinhardt, Django (1910–1951). Guitarist. COF-1

Renault, Louis (1843–1918). Jurist. MEC†; WIC

Renoir, Auguste (1841–1919). Painter. ASB-1; KAA; MAH

Richelieu, Armand Jean du Plessis, cardinal, duc de (1585–1642). Statesman. CAE

Robert, Nicholas-Louis (1761–1828). Inventor. FAB

Robespierre, Maximilien François Marie Isidore de (1758–1794). Revolutionist. HAK

Rochambeau, comte de (Jean-Baptiste Donatien de Vimeur) (1725–1807). Soldier. SCB-1

Rodin, Auguste (1840–1917). Sculptor. ASB-1; DEI; DEJ

Rolland, Romain (1866–1944). Author. DED

Rothschild, Edmond de (1845–1934). Financier. KAD

Rouault, Georges (1871–1958). Painter. KAA

Rousseau, Jean Jacques (1712–1778). Philosopher. FRE

Roux, Pierre Paul Émile (1853–1933). Bacteriologist. DEB; RIE; ROA

Saint-Saëns, Camille (1835–1921). Composer. KAE

Satie, Erik (1866–1925). Composer. SAA

Schulmeister, Karl (1770–1853). Spy. SUG

Schweitzer, Albert (1875–1965). Missionary, theologian, musician. BAF; BEC; EVD; FOJ; KE; KEE; LO; MAN; MEA; MEC; WIC; YOA

Sévigné, Marie (de Rabutin Chantal) marquise de. Author. PA

Soutine, Chaim (1894–1943). Painter, born Lithuania. WIAA

Staël, Germaine de (Anne Louise Germaine Necker, Baronne de Staël-Hollstein) (1766–1817). Author. BOC

Surcouf, Robert (1773–1827). Privateer. KEH

Teilhard de Chardin, Pierre (1881–1955). Theologian, paleontologist, explorer. LO

Tonti, Henri de (1650–1704). Explorer, born Italy. MAS

Toulouse-Lautrec, Henri Marie Raymond de (1864–1901). Painter. KAA

Tupine, Oleg (1920–). Dancer. ATA

Ungerer, Tomi (1931–). Author, illustrator. SM

Varèse, Edgard (1883–1965). Composer. EWAA

Vasarely, Victor (1908–). Painter, born Hungary. WIAA

Verne, Jules (1828–1905). Author. DEI; DEJ; STK

Vidocq, Eugène François (1775–1857). Police official. LACA; LID

Vigee-Lebrun, Elisabeth (1755–1842). Painter. NE

Voltaire (François Marie Arouet) (1694–1778). Author, philosopher. COG; DEI; DEJ; HIB; LO; OZA

Watteau, Jean Antoine (1684–1721). Painter. KAA; MAH†

Yechiel of Paris. Rabbi. GEF

Zola, Émile (1840–1902). Author. COG

FRONTIERSMEN, see PIONEERS & FRONTIER PEOPLE

FURNITURE MAKERS, see CRAFTSPERSONS

GENERALS, see AIR FORCE LEADERS; AMERICAN REVOLUTIONARY FIGURES—MILITARY; ARMY LEADERS

GENETICISTS

Beadle, George Wells (1903–). RIF

East, Edward Murray (1879–1938). CAB

Lederberg, Joshua (1925–). GRB-1; LET; RIF

McClintock, Barbara (1902–). SHFE

McKusick, Victor. LETC

Mendel, Gregor Johann (1822–1884). Austrian. ASA; BEK; BEP; CAA; CAB; COL; FE; HAC; SIA; STI; WEF

Morgan, Thomas Hunt (1866–1945). BEK; COLA; RIF

Muller, Hermann Joseph (1890–1967). BEK; LET; RIF

Russell, Elizabeth Shull (1913–). YOF

Watson, James Dewey (1928–). BEK; FE; FRE†; GRBA; RIF

GEOGRAPHERS

Behaim, Martin (1459?–1507). German. VIA

Cresques Lo Juheu (fl. 1375). Spanish. GEF

Eratosthenes (c. 275–195 B.C.). Greek. PIA; SHFB

Hedin, Sven Anders (1865–1952). Swedish. BAB; HOB; ROL†

Mercator, Gerardus (1512–1594). German. FE

Ptolemy (2d century). Greek. MOB; MOCB; PIA; SIA; SIB†

Pytheas (4th century B.C.). Greek. DYA; KNB; MOB; ROL†

Siple, Paul Allman (1908–1968). YOE

Thompson, David (1770–1857). English. KNA; ROL†

GEOLOGISTS

See also OCEANOGRAPHERS; PALEONTOLOGISTS

Askin, Rosemary. LA-1

Atwood, Genevieve (1946–). WIAA-02

Cashman, Katharine. LA-1

Dana, James Dwight (1813–1895). HYB

Ewing, W. Maurice (1906–1974). BRBC; COR

Fuchs, Sir Vivian Ernest (1908–). English. DOC†; KNA†; MOB; ROL

Jones, Lois. LA-1

King, Clarence (1842–1901). YOG

Lyell, Sir Charles (1797–1875). Scottish. BEP; STI

Marvin, Ursula (1921–). LA-1

Mohorovicic, Andrija (1857–1936). Czech. HAC

Powell, John Wesley (1834–1902). CORA; FOC; HIBC; LYA

Silliman, Benjamin (1779–1864). BUF; HYB

Tazieff, Haroun. Belgian. KEH

GERMANS

Adenauer, Konrad (1876–1967). Chancellor. WEA

Agricola, Georgius (1494–1555). Mineralogist. FE; SHFB

Agrippa, Cornelius Heinrich (1486?–1535). Philosopher. COEA; ED-5

Bach, Carl Philipp Emanuel (1714–1788). Composer. KAE; SAA†; YOM†

Bach, Johann Christian (1735–1782). Composer, organist. CHF; SAA†; YOM†

Bach, Johann Sebastian (1685–1750). Composer, organist. BEN; BRF; BUD; DEI; DEJ; FIE; GOB; KAE; SAA; WIA; YOK; YOM†

Baeck, Leo (1873–1956). Rabbi. GEF; GRB-1; GUB; KAB

Baeyer, Adolf von (1835–1917). Chemist. LET

Bastian, Adolf (1826–1905). Ethnologist. HAO

Beckenbauer, Franz (1945–). Soccer player. ADL

Beethoven, Ludwig van (1770–1827). Composer. BEN; BRF; BUD; DEI; DEJ; FIE; FRE; GOB; KAE; MAJ; SAA; WIA; YOK; YOM†

Behaim, Martin (1459?–1507). Geographer. VIA

Behring, Emil von (1854–1917). Bacteriologist. AAS-31; BEK†; DEB; RIE; RIF; ROA

Benz, Karl (1844–1929). Engineer, automobile manufacturer. FAB; FE

Bessel, Friedrich Wilhelm (1784–1846). Astronomer. SUE

Bismarck, Otto von (1815–1898). Statesman. CAE

Born, Max (1882–1970). Physicist. LET

Brahms, Johannes (1833–1897). Composer. BEN; BRF; BUD; DEI; DEJ; FIE; KAE; SAA; WIA; YOK

Brandt, Willy (1913–). Statesman. MEC; WECA

Bruch, Max (1838–1920). Composer. KAE

Bunsen, Robert Wilhelm (1811–1899). Chemist. SHFB

Cantor, Georg (1845–1918). Mathematician. MUB

Caracciola, Rudolf (1901–1959). Automobile racer. COKC; YAA

Cierpinski, Waldemar (1950–). Track athlete. AAS-30

Cramer, Johann Baptist (1771–1858). Pianist, composer. CHF

Daimler, Gottlieb (1834–1900). Engineer, inventor. EBA; FE; THA

Diesel, Rudolf C. (1858–1913). Inventor. FAB; FE; LAE; MAP; THA

Dietz, Johann (1665–1738). Barber-surgeon. RAC

Domagk, Gerhard (1895–1964). Chemist. AAS-31; RIF; ROA

Dürer, Albrecht (1471–1528). Painter, engraver. CHC; KAA; MAI

Ehrlich, Paul (1854–1915). Bacteriologist. AAS-31; ASA; BEK; DEB; FE; LET; POB; RIE; RIF; ROA; SUF

Ender, Kornelia (1958–). Swimmer. SUBB-1

Erhard, Ludwig (1897–1977). Chancellor. WEB

Faas, Horst (1933–). Photographer. HOE

Fahrenheit, Gabriel Daniel (1686–1736). Physicist. SHFB

Flatow, Alfred (b. 1869). Gymnast. SLA

Forssmann, Werner (1904–1979). Surgeon. RIF

Frank, Anne (1919–1945). Nazi victim, author. ELA; FOR; GRB-1

Frank, Johann Peter (1745–1821). Physician. MAR

Frankel, Zecharias (1801–1875). Rabbi. KAD

Fraunhofer, Joseph von (1787–1826). Physicist. FE; LAA; SHFB; SUE

Froebel, Friedrich Wilhelm (1782–1852). Educator. COG; FRC

Furtwaengler, Wilhelm (1886–1954). Conductor. EWB; YOM†

Gauss, Karl Friedrich (1777–1855). Mathematician. COLA; DUA; MUB; SIA; STN

Geiger, Abraham (1810–1874). Theologian. KAD

Geiger, Johannes Wilhelm (1882–1945). Physicist. HAC

Gluck, Christoph Willibald (1714–1787). Composer. BRF; BUD; KAE; SAA

Goethe, Johann Wolfgang von (1749–1832). Poet. DEI; DEJ

Graf, Willi (d. 1943). Resistance worker. LAD

Grimm, Jakob (1785–1863). Author. BEI; SMAB

Grimm, Wilhelm Karl (1786–1859). Author. BEI; SMAB

Grock, pseud. (1880–1959). Clown. KLD

Guericke, Otto von (1602–1686). Physicist. MAQ; SHFB

Gutenberg, Johann (c. 1397–1468). Printer. ASA; COL; DEI; DEJ; EBA; FE; FRE; THA

Haber, Fritz (1868–1934). Chemist. FE; LET

Hahn, Otto (1879–1968). Chemist, physicist. FE

Hegel, Georg Wilhelm Friedrich (1770–1831). Philosopher. LO; OZA

Heine, Heinrich (1797–1856). Poet. PEB

Helmholtz, Hermann Ludwig von (1821–1894). Physicist, biologist. SIA

Hertz, Gustav (1887–1975). Physicist. LET

Hertz, Heinrich Rudolf (1857–1894). Physicist. CAA; COLA; FE; SHFB; SIA; SOB

Herz, Henriette (1764–1847). Society leader. LER

Hesse, Hermann (1877–1962). Author. KE

Heyse, Paul Johann (1830–1914). Author. LET

Hindenburg, Paul von (1847–1934). President. ARD

Hirsch, Samson Raphael (1808–1888). Theologian. KAD

Hitler, Adolf (1889–1945). Chief of state. ARA; ASB-1; BLW; CAE; CL-01; DOF; KIA; TAC

Holbein, Hans (the Younger) (1497–1543). Painter. KAA

Huber, Kurt (1890?–1943). Resistance worker. LAD

Humboldt, Alexander von (1769–1859). Naturalist. BLB; HOB; KNA; MOB; ROL; WIA-1

Hummel, Johann Nepomuk (1778–1837). Composer. CHF

Humperdinck, Engelbert (1854–1921). Composer. BAE; BUC

Josselman of Rosheim (1478?–1554). Knight. GEF

Kalb, Johann (1721–1780). Soldier of fortune in the American Revolution. SCB-1

Kant, Immanuel (1724–1804). Philosopher. LO; OZA

Kekule, Friedrich (1829–1896). Chemist. FE

Kepler, Johannes (1571–1630). Astronomer. CAA; DOE; FE; LAA; MOCB; PIA; SHFB; SIA; SIB; STI; SUE

Kiesinger, Kurt Georg (1904–). Ex-chancellor. WECA

Kirchhoff, Gustav Robert (1824–1887). Physicist. FE; SHFB; SUE

Kirchner, Ernst Ludwig (1880–1938). Painter. WIAA

Koch, Robert (1843–1910). Bacteriologist. AAS-31; BEK; COL; DEB; DEI; DEJ; FAF; FE; HUD; RIE; RIF; ROA; SUF

König, Friedrich (1774–1833). Printer. FE; LAE

Kossel, Albrecht (1853–1927). Physiologist. RIF

Lasker, Emanuel (1868–1941). Chess player. LEQB; RHA

Laue, Max von (1879–1960). Physicist. FE

Leibniz, Gottfried Wilhelm freiherr von (1646–1716). Mathematician, philosopher. GRAB-3†; SHFB

Leichhardt, Friedrich Wilhelm (1813–1848). Explorer. KNA; ROL†

Liebig, Justus von (1803–1873). Chemist. CAB

Lilienthal, Otto (1848–1896). Aeronautical engineer. BRBA

Lody, Karl Hans (d. 1914). Spy. HAB

Löffler, Friedrich (1852–1915). Bacteriologist. DEA; RIE†; ROA

Luckner, Felix von (1881–1966). Naval figure. ARD

Ludendorff, Erich Friedrich (1865–1937). General. ARD; RADA

Ludwig II (1845–1886). King of Germany. COKB

Luther, Martin (1483–1546). Religious reformer. DEI; DEJ; FRC; FRE; HAA

Marx, Karl Heinrich (1818–1883). Political philosopher. COJB; FRE; HAK; LO

Mauermayer, Gisela (1914?–). Discus thrower. BELB

Meir ben Baruch of Rothenburg (1220–1293). Rabbi. GEF; GUA; KAC

Mendelssohn, Felix (1809–1847). Composer. BEN;

BRF; BUD; DEI; DEJ; FIE; GOA; KAE; SAA; YOK; YOM†

Mendelssohn, Moses (1729–1786). Philosopher. GUB; KAB; KAC; LEF; LERA; PEB

Mercator, Gerardus (1512–1594). Geographer. FE

Mommsen, Theodor (1817–1903). Historian. HIB

Mössbauer, Rudolf Ludwig (1929–). Physicist. HAC

Nietzsche, Friedrich Wilhelm (1844–1900). Philosopher. LO

Nipkow, Paul (1860–1940). Inventor. FE

Ohm, Georg Simon (1787–1854). Physicist. CAA; DUA; FE

Ossietzky, Carl von (1889–1938). Pacifist. AAS-34; MEA; MEC; WIC

Otto, Nikolaus August (1832–1891). Inventor. FAB; FE; THA

Planck, Max Karl (1858–1947). Physicist. CAA; FE; SHFB

Probst, Christoph (1919?–1943). Resistance worker. LAD

Quidde, Ludwig (1858–1941). Historian. MEC†; WIC

Ranke, Leopold von (1795–1886). Historian. HIB

Reitsch, Hanna (1912–1979). Aviator. HAMY; HIFD

Richthofen, Manfred von (1892–1918). Aviator, WW I. ARD; HAMY; RADA

Riedesel, Frederika von, baroness (1746–1808). Diarist. AND

Roentgen, Wilhelm (1845–1923). Physicist. AAS-33; ASA; CAA; DEI; DEJ; FE; PRC; SHFB; SHG; STI

Rothschild, Mayer Amschel (1743–1812). Financier. PEB

Scherchen, Hermann (1891–1966). Conductor. STM†; YOM

Schliemann, Heinrich (1822–1890). Archaeologist. ELA

Schmorell, Alexander (d. 1943). Resistance worker. LAD

Scholl, Hans (1918?–1943). Resistance worker. LAD

Scholl, Sophie (1921?–1943). Resistance worker. LAD

Schumann, Clara (1819–1896). Pianist. CHF

Schumann, Robert Alexander (1810–1856). Composer. BRF; BUD; FIE; KAE; SAA; YOJ

Schütz, Heinrich (1585–1672). Composer. BEM

Schwann, Theodor (1810–1882). Physiologist. COLA

Seebeck, Thomas Johann (1770–1831). Physicist. FE

Seume, Johann. Mercenary. SOA

Silber, Jules (1876–1939). Spy. SEB

Sorge, Richard (1895–1944?). Spy for Russia. HAB

Spemann, Hans (1869–1941). Zoologist. RIF

Spohr, Louis (1784–1859). Violinist, composer. CHFA; YOM†

Stieber, Wilhelm (1818–1882). Spy. HAB; SUG

Stockhausen, Karlheinz (1928–). Composer, conductor. EWAA

Strauss, Richard (1864–1949). Composer. BAE; BEKA; BUC; KAE; SAA; YOM†

Stresemann, Gustav (1878–1929). Statesman. MEC†; WIC

Telemann, Georg Philipp (1681–1767). Composer. BEM; SAA

Thadden-Trieglaff, Reinold von (1891–). Church leader. BAF

Tirpitz, Alfred von (1849–1930). Admiral. ARD

Trenck, Friedrich von der (1726–1794). Military adventurer. JAC

Virchow, Rudolf (1821–1902). Pathologist. CHD; POB; ROA

Wagner, Richard (1813–1883). Composer. BRF; BUD; DEI; DEJ; FIE; KAE; SAA; YOK; YOM†

Wallach, Otto (1847–1931). Chemist. LET

Walter, Bruno (1876–1962). Conductor. EWB; STM; YOM

Wankel, Felix Heinrich (1902–). Engineer. FE; MAPA

Warburg, Otto Heinrich (1883–1970). Physiologist. LET

Wassermann, Jakob (1873–1934). Author. PEB

Weber, Karl Maria Friedrich Ernst von (1786–1826). Composer. BRF; KAE; SAA; YOJ

Weber, Wilhelm Eduard (1804–1891). Physicist. DUA

Willstätter, Richard (1872–1942). Chemist. LET

Wöhler, Friedrich (1800–1882). Chemist. CAA; FE

Zeiss, Carl (1816–1888). Industrialist. FE

Zeppelin, Ferdinand Graf von (1838–1917). Inventor. FE

Zunz, Leopold (1794–1886). Hebraist. KAD

GHANAIANS

Jiagge, Annie. Jurist. CRA

Nkrumah, Kwame (1909–1972). President. ADA; JO; KEF; WEA

Selormey, Francis (1927–). Government official. OJA

Sutherland, Efua Theodora (1924–). Author. CRA

GIRL SCOUTS, *see* SCOUT LEADERS

GIRLS, *see* CHILDREN

GOLDSMITHS, *see* CRAFTSPERSONS

GOLFERS

Barron, Herman (1909–1976). SLA
Baugh, Laura Z. (1955–). HOBAA
Beard, Frank (1939–). BELB
Berg, Patty (Patricia Jane) (1918?–). HOBA;
    HOBAA
Brown, Pete Earlie (1935–). HOBC
Casper, Billy (William Earl) (1931–). KADA;
    LABA
Collett, Glenna (1903–). HOBA; HOBAA; JAB
Didrikson, Babe (Mildred) (1914–1956). ASB-1;
    ASBA; CLA; DAG; DAGA; DAJ; DEF; FRB;
    GED; GEDA; GEE; GIBA; HIA; HOBA;
    HOBAA; JAB; LEYB; LYB; PACA; PIB; PIBA;
    RYA; SCA; SID; ST-2; STLA; VAE
Hagen, Walter (1892–1969). DAG; DAGA; LABA
Hogan, Ben (1912–). ASBA; BUJA; DAG; DAGA;
    DEHA-1; FOI; HOC; LABA; PAW; PIB; PIBA;
    SCA; SICA; VAE
Jones, Bobby (Robert Tyre) (1902–1971). ALBA;
    ASBA; DAG; DAGA; HEG; HOC; LABA; LEF;
    SICA
Lopez, Nancy (1957–). GUED-1
Nicklaus, Jack (1940–). ASB-1; ASBA; HOC;
    KADA; LABA
Ouimet, Francis (1894–1967). DAG; DAGA; LABA
Palmer, Arnold (1929–). ASBA; BELB; HOC;
    KADA; LABA
Rankin, Judy (Judith Torleumke) (1945–). GUED
Rodriguez, Juan "Chi-Chi" (1935–). BELB; FOI;
    FOW; IZA; NEBB
Sarazen, Gene (1901–). LABA
Snead, Samuel Jackson (1912–). LABA
Trevino, Lee (1939–). AAS-27; IZA; LYB; NEAA;
    WH-3
Venturi, Ken (1931–). BUJA; LABA
Whitworth, Kathy (Kathrynne Ann) (1939–).
    HOBAA†; JABA; RYX
Wright, Mickey (Mary Kathryn) (1935–). HOBA;
    HOBAA†

GOVERNMENT WORKERS

Badillo, Herman (1929–). FOW; NEBB; WO
Banuelos, Romana Acosta (1925–). FOW
Benítez, Jaime (1908–). NEBB
Bruce, Louis R. (1906–). GRAC
Fairgrave, Phoebe (1903–). HIFD

Hanks, Nancy (1927–1983). GIB-1
Irey, Elmer Lincoln (1888–1948). LID
Lewis, James (1832–1897?). ADA; ADB
Lim, Kim San (1916–). RODA
McGee, Henry W. (1910–). YOI
Maymi, Carmen Rosa (1938–). NEBB; WH-2
Myerson, Bess (1924–). BOHF; GRB-1
Old Coyote, Barney (1923–). GRAC
Peterson, Helen L. (1915–). GRAC
Phillips, Vel (1924–). YOI
Pickens, William (1881–1954). DADA; DADB
Poston, Ersa Hines (1921–). YOI
Priest, Ivy Baker (1905–1975). FOG
Ramirez, Henry M. (1929–). NEAA
Rivlin, Alice Mitchell (1930?–). BOHG
Ruiz Belvis, Segundo (1829–1867). TU
Sandoval, Hilary (1930–). NEAA
Shriver, Robert Sargent (1915–). WEB
Strachan, John R. (1916–). YOI
Trotter, James Monroe (1844–1912). ADA; ADB
Victor, Wilma L. GRAD

GOVERNORS, U.S.

Alexander, Moses (1853–1932). LETA
Altgeld, John Peter (1847–1902). (Born Germany).
    KEC†; WECB
Bassett, Richard (1745–1815). BUIB†; FEAA
Call, Richard Keith (1791–1862). SEC
Castro, Raúl Héctor (1916–). (Born Mexico). WH
Chittenden, Thomas (1730–1797). SEC
Claiborne, William Charles (1775–1817). MAO;
    SEC
Clinton, DeWitt (1769–1828). MAL; WHD†
Conway, James Sevier (1798–1855). SEC
Curry, George (1863–1947). SEC
Davie, William Richardson (1756–1820). (Born
    England). FEAA
Dewey, Thomas Edmund (1902–1971). GO;
    WHD†
Dodge, Henry (1782–1867). SEC
Duval, William Pope (1784–1854). MAO
Farrington, Wallace (1871–1933). SEC
Grasso, Ella (1919–1981). BOHF; GRAB-1; WHE
Gruening, Ernest Henry (1887–1974). SEC
Haskell, Charles Nathaniel (1860–1933). SEC
Hearnes, Warren Eastman (1923–). RAE
Holmes, David (1770–1832). SEC
Hunt, George Wylie (1859–1934). SEC
Johnson, Thomas (1732–1819). SEC
King, William (1768–1852). SEC
La Follette, Robert Marion, Sr. (1855–1925).
    ARAA; LAI
Landon, Alfred Mossman (1887–1987). GO;
    WHD†

Lehman, Herbert H. (1878–1963). GRB-1; LETA
Livingston, William (1723–1790). BUIB†; FEAA; SEC
Long, Earl Kemp (1895–1960). LAI
Long, Huey Pierce (1893–1935). COGA; LAI
McNair, Alexander (1775–1826). SEC
McRae, Thomas Chipman (1851–1929). MAO
Martin, Alexander (b. 1740). FEAA
Mason, Stevens Thomson (1811–1843). SEC
Mellette, Arthur (1842–1896). SEC
Mercer, John Francis (1759–1821). FEAA
Mifflin, Thomas (1744–1800). BUIB†; FEAA; SEC
Muñoz Marín, Luis (1898–1980). NEBB; STC; TU; WO
Nye, James Warren (1814–1876). SEC
Paterson, William (1745–1806). BUIB†; FEAA
Pierpont, Francis Harrison (1814–1899). SEC
Pinckney, Charles (1757–1824). BUIB†; FEAA; SEC
Randolph, Edmund Jennings (1753–1813). BUIB; FEAA; SEC
Ray, Dixy Lee (1914–). EMB†; GRAB-1†; WIAA-02
Robinson, Charles (1818–1894). SEC
Rockefeller, Nelson Aldrich (1908–1979). FEA; HAOA; HOEA
Sevier, John (1745–1815). MAO; SEC
Shelby, Isaac (1750–1826). BUIB†; SEC
Shoup, George (1836–1904). SEC
Sibley, Henry Hastings (1811–1891). SEC
Smith, Alfred Emanuel (1873–1944). WHD
Spaight, Richard Dobbs, Sr. (1758–1802). BUIB†; FEAA
Squire, Watson (1838–1926). SEC
Stanford, Leland (1824–1893). YOG
Stevenson, Adlai Ewing (1900–1965). DABB; GO; KE; WHD†
Strong, Caleb (1745–1819). FEAA
Tilden, Samuel Jones (1814–1886). GO; WHD†
Toole, Joseph (1851–1928). SEC
Trumbull, Jonathan (1710–1785). BUIB†; SEC
Warren, Francis (1844–1929). SEC
Worthington, Thomas (1773–1825). SEC

GRAPHOLOGISTS

Tyrrell, John F. LACA

GREEKS

Agnodice (fl. 300 B.C.). Physician. SC
Alcibiades (c. 450–404 B.C.). Athenian general, statesman. PLA

Alexander III, the Great (356–323 B.C.). King of Macedon. CAAA; COD; DEI; DEJ; FRE; JOBB; KEH; KNA; MOB; NEC; PLA; UNB
Apollonius of Tyana (c. 3 B.C.–c. 100 A.D.). Magician. ED-5
Archimedes (287?–212 B.C.). Mathematician, inventor. ASA; BEP; CAA; DOE; EVC; FE; MAQ; MUB; SHFB; SIA; STN; THA
Aristarchus of Samos (3d century B.C.). Astronomer. MOCB; SIB†
Aristotle (384–322 B.C.). Philosopher. CAA; DEI; DEJ; FE; FRC; LO; OZA; PIA; SIA; SIB†
Asklepios (c. 1300 B.C.). Physician. SHG
Democritos, Bolos (fl. 200 B.C.). Alchemist. CUA; FE
Demosthenes (384–322 B.C.). Athenian statesman. PLA
Empedocles (c. 490–430 B.C.). Philosopher. FE
Eratosthenes (c. 275–195 B.C.). Astronomer, geographer. PIA; SHFB
Euclid (fl. 300 B.C.). Mathematician. CAA; MUB; SHFB; STN
Galen (130–200). Physician. CAA; CHD; POD; ROA; SHG; SIA; SIC
Herodotus (484?–425 B.C.). Historian. HIB; ROL†
Hipparchus (2d century B.C.). Astronomer. PIA; SIB†
Hippocrates (460–377 B.C.). Physician. CAA; CHD; DEI; DEJ; DOE; FE; POD; ROA; SHG; SIC
Homer (9th century B.C.?). Poet. DEI; DEJ
Hypatia (370–415). Philosopher. SC
Leonidas I (d. 480 B.C.). King of Sparta. CAAA; COM; MAJ
Leucippus (5th century B.C.). Philosopher. SHFB
Loues, Spiridon (19th century). Track athlete. HIA; HIA-01†; LEYB†
Pericles (d. 429 B.C.). Athenian statesman. CAAA; COM; HEA; PLA
Plato (427–347 B.C.). Philosopher. DEI; DEJ; FRC; LO; OZA; SIB†
Plutarch (46?–120). Biographer. HIB
Polybius (205?–125? B.C.). Historian. HIB
Ptolemy (2d century). Scientist of Alexandria. MOB; MOCB; PIA; SIA; SIB†
Pythagoras (6th century B.C.). Philosopher, mathematician. CAA; MUB; SHFB; SIB†
Pytheas (4th century B.C.). Navigator. DYA; KNB; MOB; ROL†
Socrates (470?–399 B.C.). Philosopher. DEI; DEJ; FRC; FRE; HAA; LO; MAJ; OZA; STP
Themistocles (527?–460 B.C.). Athenian statesman, naval commander. COM; DYA; PLA
Thucydides (471–400? B.C.). Historian. HIB
Vlachos, Helen (1912?–). Newspaper publisher. CAHA
Xenakis, Yannis (1922–). Composer. EWAA
Xenophon (434?–355 B.C.). Historian. COM

GUATEMALANS

Asturias, Miguel Angel (1899–1974). Author. WO

GUINEANS

Modupe (1901–). Prince. OJA
Touré, Sékou (1922–1984). President. ADA; JO

GUITARISTS, *see* MUSICIANS—GUITARISTS

GYMNASTS

Andrianov, Nikolai (1952–). Russian. LIE
Comaneci, Nadia (1961–). Romanian. FOR;
  GUED; LIE
Conner, Bart (1958–). LIE
Flatow, Alfred (b. 1869). German. SLA
Keleti, Agnes (1921–). Israeli. (Born Hungary).
  SLA
Kim, Nelli (1957–). Russian. LIE; SUBB-1
Korbut, Olga (1956–). Russian. HOBAA; LIE
Rigby, Cathy (1952–). HOBAA; LIE; RYA†; RYX;
  ST-2
Tsukahara, Mitsuo (1947–). Japanese. LIE

HAITIANS

Christophe, Henri (1767–1820). King. ADA; ADB;
  DAF-1†; JO; STQ†; WIBA
Dessalines, Jean Jacques (1758–1806). Emperor.
  ADA; ADB
Duvalier, François (1907–1971). President. ARA;
  BAGA
Toussaint L'Ouverture, Pierre Dominique (1743–
  1803). Liberator. ADA; ADB; BAA; BACA;
  KEH; MAJ; YOFA

HANDBALL PLAYERS

Hershkowitz, Victor (1918–). SLA
Jacobs, James (1931–). SLA

HANDICAPPED, PHYSICALLY, *see* DISABLED

HANDICRAFTERS, *see* CRAFTSPERSONS

HANDWRITING EXPERTS, *see* GRAPHOLOGISTS

HARPSICHORDISTS, *see* MUSICIANS—
HARPSICHORDISTS

HAT DESIGNERS, *see* DESIGNERS

HAWAIIANS

Kahanamoku, Duke Paoa (1890–1968). Swimmer.
  FIC; LEYB†; OLD
Kamehameha I, the Great (1737?–1819). King.
  NEC
Mink, Patsy Takemoto (1927–). Congresswoman.
  BOHF

HEALTH LEADERS, *see* PUBLIC HEALTH LEADERS

HEROES, LEGENDARY & NATIONAL

Alexander Nevski (1220?–1263). Russian. MAJ
Antar (525?–615). Arabian. ADA; ADB
Arthur (6th century). King of the Britons. JOBB;
  NEC; SUK
Cid Campeador, El (1040?–1099). Spanish. HEA
Joan of Arc (1412–1431). CHG; DAD-1; DAD-2;
  DEI; DEJ; ELA; EVD; HAA; HEA; MAJ; MOC;
  ONA; PA; PEE; STP
Robin Hood. English outlaw. STP; SUK
Tell, William (fl. 1307). Swiss. HEA; STP

HEROES, LESSER KNOWN

Barlass, Kate (15th century). Scottish. MAJ
Bates, Abigail (fl. 1814). CLC
Bates, Rebecca (fl. 1814). CLC
Bergeman, Gerald (1940?–). ANCA
Browne, Michael (1967?–). ANCA
Christie, David (1960?–). ANCA
Christie, Robert (1961?–). ANCA
Cornick, Wade (1965?–). ANCA
Dale, Jerome (1964?–). ANCA
Darling, Grace Horsley (1815–1842). English.
  MAJ; STP
Gregory, Darryl (1962?–). ANCA

Hendee, Hannah (fl. 1780). CLC
Kieff, Elaine (1948?–). ANCA
Kilmer, Gordon (1946–). ANCA
Lewis, Idawally (1814–1910). CAD; DOD
Loura, Philip (1967?–). ANCA
MacDonald, Flora (1721–1790). Scottish. MAJ
Murray, Harold (1942?–). ANCA
Peterson, Joel (1968?–). ANCA
Slack, Donna Lee (1961?–). ANCA
Stratt, Parker (1941?–). ANCA
Temby, Stephen (1940–). CAD
Verchères, Marie Magdelaine Jarret de (1678–
    1747). Canadian. MAJ; STP

HISPANIC-AMERICANS

See also PUERTO RICANS

Estrada, Isabel. Physician. FOC-1
Herrera, Efren (1951–). Football player. AAS-17
Rodriguez, Johnny (1952–). Singer. KRI-1
Tiant, Luis (1940–). Baseball player. AAS-2

HISTORIANS

American
Adams, Henry Brooks (1838–1918). HIB
Bancroft, George (1800–1891). HIB
Beard, Charles Austin (1874–1948). HIB
Franklin, John Hope (1915–). ADB; FLD
Logan, Rayford Whittingham (1897–1982).
    DOF-1
McMaster, John Bach (1852–1932). HIB
Parkman, Francis (1823–1893). CAC; HEB; HIB;
    SUFA
Parrington, Vernon Louis (1871–1929). HIB
Prescott, William Hickling (1796–1859). CAC;
    HIB†; SUFA
Ruether, Rosemary (1936–). GIB-1
Schomberg, Arthur Alfonso (1874–1938). ADB
Tuchman, Barbara (1912?–). BOHG
Turner, Frederick Jackson (1861–1932). HIB
Woodson, Carter Goodwin (1875–1950). ADA;
    ADB; BRB†; DOF-1; GRAB-02; ROG; STO

Foreign
Abdur Rahman Sadi el Timbuctoo (1596–1660).
    African. ADA
Carlyle, Thomas (1795–1881). Scottish. COB
Froissart, Jean (1337–1407). French. HIB
Garcilaso de la Vega (called el Inca) (1539?–
    1616). Peruvian. BACA
Gibbon, Edward (1737–1794). English. HIB

Herodotus (484?–425 B.C.). Greek. HIB; ROL†
Josephus Flavius (37–100). Palestinian. LERA;
    LES
Medina, José Toribio (1852–1930). Chilean. WOB
Mommsen, Theodor (1817–1903). German. HIB
Plutarch (46?–120). Greek. HIB
Polybius (205?–125? B.C.). Greek. HIB
Quidde, Ludwig (1858–1941). German. MEC†;
    WIC
Ranke, Leopold von (1795–1886). German. HIB
Sigüenza y Góngora, Carlos de (1645–1700). Mexi-
    can. WOB
Tacitus, Cornelius (55?–120?). Roman. HIB
Thucydides (471–400? B.C.). Greek. HIB
Trevelyan, George Macaulay (1876–1962). En-
    glish. HIB
Voltaire (François Marie Arouet) (1694–1778).
    French. COG; DEI; DEJ; HIB; LO; OZA
Wells, Herbert George (1866–1946). English.
    ASB-1; DEI; DEJ
Xenophon (434?–355 B.C.). Greek. COM

HOCKEY FIGURES

Apps, Syl (1915–). Canadian. MANA
Apps, Syl, II (1947–). Canadian. FICA-1
Barkley, Doug (Norman Douglas) (1937–). Cana-
    dian player, coach. FICB
Bathgate, Andy (Andrew James) (1932–). Cana-
    dian. ORC
Beliveau, Jean (1931–). Canadian. FICA; FR;
    LIAB; OBA; OBB; ORC; RAAF
Berenson, Gordon (1941?–). FICA
Binkley, Lee. Canadian. FICB
Blair, Wren. Coach. LEW
Blake, Toe (Hector) (1912–). Canadian coach.
    LEW; ORC
Boivin, Leo (1932–). Canadian. OBA
Bossy, Mike (1957–). Canadian. AAS-22; OLDE
Bower, Johnny (1924?–). Canadian. ORA
Brodeur, Richard (1952–). Canadian. AAS-21
Bucyk, John Paul (1935–). Canadian. OBB
Cashman, Wayne (1945–). Canadian. THG
Cheevers, Gerry (1940–). Canadian. LEYA; ORA
Ciccarelli, Dino (1960–). Canadian. AAS-22
Clancy, King (Francis Michael) (1903–1986). Ca-
    nadian. OBA; OBB
Clarke, Bobby (Robert Earle) (1949–). Canadian.
    AAS-27; CL-06; FICA-1; GUEC; GUH; LEYA;
    MANA; ORB; THD
Cournoyer, Ivan Serge (1943–). Canadian. CL-06;
    LEYA; THG
Craig, Jim (1957–). OLDE
Delvecchio, Alex (Fats) (1931–). Canadian player,
    coach. DEHA-1

Dionne, Marcel (1951–). Canadian. AAS-22; AAS-23; FICA-1; FICC; MANA; OLDE; ORB

Dryden, Ken (Kenneth Wayne) (1947?–). Canadian. FICA-1; FICC; GUEC; LEYA; ORA; ORB; THF

Durnan, Bill (William Ronald) (1915–). Canadian. ORA; ORC

Esposito, Phil (1942–). Canadian. AAS-21; DEHA-1; FICA; FR; FRD; GUEC; LEYA; OBB; OLDE; ORC; RAAF; THD

Esposito, Tony (Anthony James) (1943–). Canadian. LEYA; ORA; ORB; THF

Ferguson, John. Canadian. FICB

Fleming, Reggie (1936–). (Born Canada). FICB

Geoffrion, Bernard "Boom-Boom" (1931–). Canadian. OBA; ORC; RAAF

Giacomin, Edward (1939–). FICA

Gilbert, Gilles (1949–). Canadian. THF

Gilbert, Rod (Rodrique Gabriel) (1941–). Canadian. DEHA-1; LEYA; OBB

Goldsworthy, Bill (William Alfred) (1944–). Canadian. LEYA; ORB

Grant, Danny (1946–). Canadian. FICC

Green, Ted (Edward Joseph) (1940–). Canadian. LOAA

Gretzky, Wayne (1961–). Canadian. AAS-22; AAS-35; ASB-1; HOCG; OLDE

Guevremont, Jocelyn (1951–). Canadian. FICC

Hall, Glenn (1931?–). Canadian. ETB; ORA; ORC; WAK

Harper, Terry (Terrance Victor) (1940–). Canadian. LEYA

Harvey, Douglas (1924–). Canadian. LIAB; OBB; ORC

Henderson, Paul Garnet (1943–). Canadian. LEYA

Howe, Gordie (1928–). (Born Canada). ALBA; ASBA; BUJA; FICA; FR; FRD; HEG; LIAB; OBA; OBB; ORC; PAW; PIBA; RAAF; SICA

Howe, Mark Steven (1955–). Canadian. MANA

Howell, Henry Vernon (1932–). Canadian. OBA

Hull, Bobby (Robert Marvin) (1939–). Canadian. ASBA; DEHA-1; FICA; FR; FRD; KADA; LEYA; LIAB; LYB; OBA; OBB; ORC; RAAF; SUB; WAK

Hull, Dennis William (1944–). Canadian. FICB; LEYA

Imlach, Punch (George) (1918–1987). Canadian coach. LEW

Johnston, Eddie (1935–). Canadian player, manager. DEHA-1

Kelly, Leonard Patrick (1927–). Canadian. FR; LIAB

Keon, David Michael (1940–). Canadian. FICA; LEYA

La Fleur, Guy Damien (1951–). Canadian. AAS-22; FICA-1; MANA; OLDE; ORB

Leach, Reggie (1950–). Canadian. AAS-9

Lindsay, Ted (Robert Blake Theodore) (1925–). Canadian. FR; LIAB; OBB; ORC; RAAF

Liut, Mike (1956–). Canadian. AAS-21

McKenzie, John Albert (1937–). Canadian. OBB

Magnuson, Keith Arien (1947–). Canadian. FICC; ORB

Mahovlich, Frank (1938–). Canadian. LEYA; OBA; OBB; ORC; RAAF

Martin, Richard Lionel (1951–). Canadian. LEYA; MANA; ORB; THG

Meloche, Gilles. Canadian. FICC

Mikita, Stan (1940–). (Born Czechoslovakia). GUEC; LEYA; LIAB; OBA; OBB; ORC; RAAF; THD

Moog, Andy (1960–). Canadian. AAS-21

Morenz, Howie (1902–1937). Canadian. FR; OBB; ORC; SUB; WAK

Neilson, Jim (James Anthony) (1940–). Canadian. LEYA

Orr, Bobby (1948–). Canadian. ASBA; FICA; FR; FRD; GAB; GUEC; KADA; LEYA; LIAB; OBA; OBB; ORB; ORC; RAAF; THE; WAK

Palmateer, Mike (1954–). Canadian. AAS-21

Parent, Bernard Marcel (1945–). Canadian. LEYA; THF

Park, Brad (Douglas Bradford) (1948–). Canadian. FICA-1; FICC; LEYA; OBB; ORB; THE

Patrick, Lester (1883–1960). Canadian player, coach. DAG; DAGA; HEH; PAW

Peeters, Pete (1957–). Canadian. AAS-21

Perreault, Gilbert (1950–). Canadian. AAS-22; FICC; LEYA; MANA; ORB; THD

Pilote, Pierre Paul (1931–). Canadian. ORC

Plante, Jacques (1929–1986). Canadian. ETB; FRD; LIAB; OBB; ORA; ORC; WAK

Polis, Greg (1950–). Canadian. FICC

Potvin, Denis Charles (1953–). Canadian. FICA-1; GUEC; MANA; OLDE; THE

Ratelle, Jean (1940–). Canadian. FICB

Redmond, Mickey (Michael Edward) (1947–). LEYA; ORB

Resch, Glenn "Chico" (1948–). Canadian. AAS-21

Richard, Henri (1936–). Canadian. FOI; FR; OBA

Richard, Maurice (Rocket) (1921–). Canadian. AAS-35; ASBA; DAG; DAGA; FICA; FR; HEG; LIAB; OBB; ORC; RAAF; SID; SUB; WAK

Sanderson, Derek Michael (1946–). Canadian. ORB

Sawchuk, Terry (1929–1970). Canadian. ETB; FR; LIAB; OBA; OBB; ORA; ORC; WAK

Schmidt, Milt. Canadian. ORC

Schultz, Dave (1949–). Canadian. THG

Shore, Edward William (1902–1985). (Born Can-

ada). DAG; DAGA; FICB; LIAB; OBB; ORC;
SICA
Sittler, Darryl (1950–). Canadian. FICA-1
Smith, Billy (1950–). Canadian. AAS-21
Stasiuk, Vic (1929–). Coach. LEW
Stastny, Peter (1956–). Canadian. (Born Czecho-
slovakia). AAS-22
Tallon, Dale (Michael Dale) (1950–). Canadian.
ORB
Tkaczuk, Walter Robert (1947–). Canadian. FICC;
ORB
Tremblay, Jean Claude (1939–). Canadian. LEYA
Tretiak, Vladislav (1952–). Russian. ORA
Trottier, Bryan (1956–). Canadian. AAS-22
Ullman, Norm. ORC
Unger, Garry (1947–). Canadian. FICC; LEYA;
ORB
Van Impe, Edward Charles (1940–). Canadian.
FICB; THE
Wakely, Ernie. Canadian. FICB
Widing, Juha Markku (1947–). Finnish. ORB
Worsley, Gump (Lorne) (1929–). Canadian. FR;
ORA

HORSE TRAINERS

Bailie, Sally (1937–). (Born England). GUJ
Jacobs, Hirsch (1904–1970). SLA

HORTICULTURISTS, *see* AGRICULTURISTS; BOTANISTS

HOTEL OWNERS, *see* BUSINESS PEOPLE

HUMANITARIANS

See also ABOLITIONISTS; NOBEL PRIZE WINNERS—
PEACE; PACIFISTS; PHILANTHROPISTS; RED CROSS
WORKERS; REFORMERS; SOCIAL WORKERS

Ceresole, Pierre (1879–1945). Swiss. KEE
Howe, Samuel Gridley (1801–1876). DEDA
Mother Theresa (1910–). Indian. (Born Yugosla-
via). ASB-1; DU-1; SHFE
Nansen, Odd (1901–). Norwegian. BAF
Pérez Esquivel, Adolfo (1931–). Argentine. DU-1
Roosevelt, Eleanor (1884–1962). ASB-1; BAG;
BAG-1; BLG; BOC; BRBE; CHB; COG; COG-1;
CUC; DABB; DAD; GIBA; KE; KEE; KL; LAI;
MAA; MAU; MEB; PA; PRB; ROH; ROHA;
SMC; STLA; WABC†; WAR; YOA
Schweitzer, Albert (1875–1965). French. BAF;

BEC; EVD; FOJ; KE; KEE; LO; MAN; MEA;
MEC; WIC; YOA

HUMORISTS, *see* AUTHORS—HUMOR; CARTOONISTS &
CARICATURISTS

HUNGARIANS

Bartók, Béla (1881–1945). Composer. ASB-1;
BEKA; BUC; FIE†; KAE; SAA; YOL
Fricsay, Ferenc (1914–1963). Conductor. STM†;
YOM
Hajos-Guttman, Alfred (1878–1955). Swimmer.
SLA
Herzl, Theodor (1860–1904). Author, Zionist.
GRB-1; GUB; KAB; KAD; LERA; LES; PEB;
ROGA
Hevesy, George de (1885–1966). Chemist. LET
Joachim, Joseph (1831–1907). Violinist, com-
poser. CHFA
Kodály, Zoltán (1882–1967). Composer. KAE
Liszt, Franz (1811–1886). Composer, pianist.
BRF; BUD; CHF; FIE; KAE; SAA; YOH
Nikisch, Arthur (1855–1922). Conductor. YOM
Richter, Hans (1843–1916). Conductor. YOM
Semmelweis, Ignaz Philipp (1818–1865). Obstetri-
cian. ROA; SIC†
Szekely, Eva (1927–). Swimmer. SLA

ICHTHYOLOGISTS

Clark, Eugenie (1922–). EMB; HAKA

ILLUSTRATORS

See also CARTOONISTS & CARICATURISTS; ENGRAV-
ERS & ETCHERS; PAINTERS

Abbey, Edwin Austin (1852–1911). CHC
Adams, Adrienne (1906–). SMAB
Anglund, Joan Walsh (1926–). SM
Aulaire, Edgar Parin d' (1898–). (Born Switzer-
land). SMAB
Aulaire, Ingri d' (1904–1980). (Born Norway).
SMAB
Bemelmans, Ludwig (1898–1962). (Born Austria).
SM
Blake, William (1757–1827). English. BEH; COP
Blegvad, Erik (1923–). Danish. SMAB
Brown, Marcia (1918–). SM

Brunhoff, Jean de (1899–1937). French. SMAB
Brunhoff, Laurent de (1925–). French. SMAB
Bryan, Marguerite. SMAB
Buff, Conrad (1886–1975). (Born Switzerland). SMAB
Buff, Mary Marsh (1890–1970). SMAB
De Angeli, Marguerite (1889–1987). SMB
deLeeuw, Cateau (1903–). SMAB
Devlin, Harry (1918–). SMAB
Devlin, Wende (1918–). SMAB
Duvoisin, Roger (1904–1980). (Born Switzerland). SM
Emberley, Edward Randolph (1931–). SMAB
Ets, Marie Hall (1895–). SM
Feelings, Tom (1933–). SMAB
Fenton, Carroll Lane (1900–1969). SMAB
Gág, Wanda (1893–1946). SM
Glackens, William James (1870–1938). DEDC
Greenaway, Kate (1846–1901). English. SM
Gropper, William (1897–1977). DEDC
Hader, Berta (1890?–1976). SMAB
Hader, Elmer (1889–1973). SMAB
Lawson, Robert (1892–1957). SM
Lear, Edward (1812–1888). English. BEH; SM
Lenski, Lois (1893–1974). SM
Lionni, Leo (1910–). (Born the Netherlands). SM
McCloskey, Robert (1914–). SM
Nast, Thomas (1840–1902). (Born Germany). CUB; DEDC
Opper, Frederick Burr (1857–1937). DEDC
Petersham, Maud (1889–1971). SMAB
Petersham, Miska (1888–1960). (Born Hungary). SMAB
Potter, Beatrix (1866–1943). English. SC; SM
Pyle, Howard (1853–1911). BEI
Rey, Hans Augusto (1898–1977). (Born Germany). SM
Scarry, Richard (1919–). SM
Sendak, Maurice (1928–). SM
Seuss, Dr. (Theodore Geisel) (1904–). SM
Turkle, Brinton (1915–). SM
Ungerer, Tomi (1931–). French. SM
Ward, Lynd (1905–1985). SMAB
Yashima, Mitsu. SMAB
Yashima, Taro (1908–). (Born Japan). SMAB

IMMIGRANTS TO U.S.

Austrian

Bemelmans, Ludwig (1898–1962). Author, illustrator. SM
Brill, Abraham Arden (1874–1948). Psychiatrist. LETA

Frankfurter, Felix (1882–1965). Supreme Court justice. LIA; LOB
Goldberger, Joseph (1874–1929). Physician. ALD; DEA; GEF
Goldhaber, Maurice (1911–). Physicist. PAC
Keppler, Joseph (1838–1894). Cartoonist. DEDC
Kreisler, Fritz (1875–1962). Violinist. CHFA; RADA
Krips, Josef (1902–1974). Conductor. EWD; STM
Landsteiner, Karl (1868–1943). Pathologist. CHE†; COLA†; FE; LET; RIF; STE
Leinsdorf, Erich (1912–). Conductor. BEA; EWD STM; YOM
Litwack, Harry (1907–). Basketball coach. SLA
Loewe, Frederick (1904–1988). Composer. EWA
Mark, Herman Francis (1895–). Chemist. BOB
Neutra, Richard Joseph (1892–1970). Architect. FOF; LAF
Rabi, Isidor Isaac (1898–1988). Physicist. GRB-1; LET
Schönberg, Arnold (1874–1951). Composer. BEKA; BUC; EWAA; KAE; SAA†; YOL
Schumann-Heink, Ernestine (1861–1936). Singer. MAT-1
Wahle, Otto (1880–1965). Swimmer. SLA

Bavarian

Hart, Ephraim (1747–1825). Financier. LETA

Belgian

Baekeland, Leo Hendrik (1863–1944). Chemist, inventor. FE; THA; YOE
Sarton, May (1912–). Author, poet. OCB

Canadian

Bannister, Edward M. (1833–1901). Painter. ADA; ADB
Coughlin, Charles Edward (1891–1979). Clergyman. COGA
Dressler, Marie (1869–1934). Comedienne. MASB
Fleming, Reggie (1936–). Hockey player. FICB
Heath, Allen. Automobile racer. LEX
Howe, Gordie (1928–). Hockey player. ALBA; ASBA; BUJA; FICA; FR; FRD; HEG; LIAB; OBA; OBB; ORC; PAW; PIBA; RAAF; SICA
Irwin, May (1862–1938). Comedienne. MASB
Kelsey, Frances Oldham (1914–). Physician. EOA; TRD
Newcomb, Simon (1835–1909). Astronomer. HYB
Nutting, Mary Adelaide (1858–1948). Nursing educator. YOB
Shore, Edward William (1902–1985). Hockey player. DAG; DAGA; FICB; LIAB; OBB; ORC; SICA

Stewart, Isabel Maitland (1878–1963). Nurse. YOB

Tanguay, Eva (1878–1947). Entertainer. MASB

Chinese

Lee, Tsung-Dao (1926–). Physicist. BOB

Lin Yutang (1895–1976). Author, philologist. KE; LOB

Ng Poon Chew (1866–1931). Clergyman, editor. CUC

Sansan. Author. CAHA

Wu, Chien-Shiung (1912–). Physicist. EMB†; GIB-1; GLO; SC; YOF

Yang, Chen Ning (1922–). Physicist. BOB

Cuban

Arboleya, Carlos (1929–). Banker. FOW

Arnaz, Desi (1917–1986). Entertainer. FOW

George G. (1953–). Deaf. SIAA

Reyes, Joseph Manuel de los (1905–). Physician. FOW

Salazar, Alberto (1958–). Track athlete. AAS-30

Czech

Cecilia, Sister. Nun. CAHA

Connolly, Olga Fikotova (1933–). Track athlete. HOBA; HOBAA

Cori, Carl Ferdinand (1896–1984). Biochemist. RIF

Cori, Gerty Theresa (1896–1957). Biochemist. RIF; SC†; SHFE†; YOF

Friml, Rudolf (1879–1972). Composer. EWA; MOA

Hlavaty, Jana (1941–). Skier. WA-1

Kimbrell, Marketa (1928–). Actress. WA

Mikita, Stan (1940–). Hockey player. GUEC; LEYA; LIAB; OBA; OBB; ORC; RAAF; THD

Navratilova, Martina (1956–). Tennis player. AAS-29; ASB-1; FR-1

Pluhar, Ivan. Escapee from Soviet labor camp. JAC

Prochazka, Anne (1897–). Nurse. YOB

Wise, Isaac Mayer (1819–1900). Rabbi. GUB; KAD; LERA; LETA; PEB

Danish

Carlsen, Henrik K. (1915–). Sea captain. SUA

Madsen, Chris (1852–1944). Law officer. SUI

Riis, Jacob August (1849–1914). Journalist, reformer. FLBA; LOB; MEB

Dutch

Bok, Edward William (1863–1930). Author, editor. BOD; CAGA; CUC; FLBA; LOB

DeJong, Meindert (1910–). Author. SMB

De Kooning, Willem (1904–). Painter. WIAA

Heide, Dirk van der (1928?–). Refugee. CAHA

Levy, Aaron (1742–1815). Merchant. LETA

Levy, Asser (d. 1681?). Pioneer. LETA

Lionni, Leo (1910–). Author, illustrator. SM

Muste, Abraham Johannes (1885–1967). Clergyman, pacifist. FOJ; LEZC

Nater, Swen (1949?–). Basketball player. RUB

Thiel, George (1898–). Realtor. BAEA-1

Van Iersel, Louis. Soldier. REA

Van Loon, Hendrik (1882–1944). Author. LEAB; LEB

English

Auden, Wystan Hugh (1907–1973). Poet. BEA; BRBB; COP

Bailie, Sally (1937–). Horse trainer. GUJ

Beaton, Cecil W. (1904–1980). Photographer. FOD

Blackwell, Elizabeth (1821–1910). Physician. BOC; BUA; CHD; COG; CUC; DOD; GEE; GIBA; HUE; JOCA; LOB; MASA; RAAG†; SC†; SMC; TRD; WABC; YOC

Booth, Junius Brutus (1796–1852). Actor. SHFA

Burnett, Frances Hodgson (1849–1924). Author. BEI

Byrne, John (1950–). Cartoonist. GOB-1

Cole, Thomas (1801–1848). Painter. HEDA; LEB

Davie, William Richardson (1756–1820). Lawyer, governor. FEAA

Elias, Lee (1920–). Cartoonist. GOB-1

Gompers, Samuel (1850–1924). Labor leader. ARAA; BEA; COH; CUC; DABA; FAC; FOB; GRB-1; LEHA; LETA; LOB; MAL; MEB; SEA

Hare, James Henry (1856–1946). Photographer. HOE

Harrison, Guy Fraser (1894–). Conductor. STM

Herford, Beatrice (1868–1952). Comedienne. MASB

Hitchcock, Alfred Joseph (1899–1980). Motion picture director. ASB-1; BEA; FLBC; PABA; SMBC

Jackson, Solomon Henry (d. 1847). Publisher. LETA

Karloff, Boris (1887–1969). Actor. COE-2

Latrobe, Benjamin Henry (1764–1820). Architect. LAF

Laurel, Stan (1890–1965). Comedian. BUR-1; ED-1; MAOB; PABA

Lofting, Hugh (1886–1947). Author. SMB

McPartland, Marian (1920–). Pianist. UN

Mayo, William Worrall (1819–1911). Surgeon. BOD; CHE; HEB; LEAB; LEB

Miles, Kenneth Henry (1918–1966). Automobile racer. OLAB

Nuttall, Thomas (1786–1859). Botanist, ornithologist. JEA

Palmer, Edward (1831–1911). Botanist. CO-1
Robertson, Oswald Hope (1886–1966). Physician. ED
Rowson, Susanna Haswell (1762–1824). Actress. DOG
Seton, Ernest Thompson (1860–1946). Author, naturalist. CO-1
Shaw, Anna Howard (1847–1919). Feminist. LES-2; MAV
Slater, Samuel (1768–1835). Manufacturer. FAB; LEB; MAL
Stokowski, Leopold (1882–1977). Conductor. EWD; LOB; STM; YOM
Windsor-Smith, Barry. Cartoonist. GOB-1
Wright, Harry (1835–1895). Baseball manager. ALB; SMK

Finnish
Gustavson, Paul (1917–). Cartoonist. GOB-1
Saarinen, Eero (1910–1961). Architect. FOF; LAF; LEDA
Saarinen, Eliel (1873–1950). Architect. LAF

French
Audubon, John James (1785–1851). Ornithologist, painter. BEA; BEC; BOK; CO-1; CORA; CUC; DEI; DEJ; FOH; HEB; HYB; LEAB; LEB; LOB; MAL; MIB; SIE; WAP
Bishop, Claire Huchet. Author. SMB
Carrel, Alexis (1873–1944). Surgeon, biologist. POB; RIF
Cournand, André Frédéric (1895–1988). Physiologist. RIF
Duchamp, Marcel (1887–1968). Painter. WIAA
Du Pont, Eleuthère Irénée (1771–1834). Industrialist. LEM; LOB
Golschmann, Vladimir (1893–1972). Conductor. STM
Held, Anna (1873–1918). Comedienne. PHA
L'Enfant, Pierre Charles (1754–1825). Engineer. LEO
Loewy, Raymond (1893–1986). Industrial designer. BEA
Merton, Thomas (1915–1968). Trappist poet. EOB
Monteux, Pierre (1875–1964). Conductor. EWB; STM; YOM
Nones, Benjamin (1757–1826). American Revolutionary patriot. GEF; LERA
Vreeland, Diana. Museum consultant. GIB-1

German
Adler, Felix (1851–1933). Educator, ethical reformer. BEA
Altgeld, John Peter (1847–1902). Governor. KEC†; WECB

Astor, John Jacob (1763–1848). Pioneer fur trader, financier. CUB; CUC; HOF; LEM; LEPC; LOB
Baade, Walter (1893–1960). Astronomer. SUE
Berger, Karl (1935–). Vibraphonist. UN
Bergmann, Carl (1821–1876). Conductor. YOM
Bergmann, Gretel (1914–). Track athlete. SLA
Berliner, Emile (1851–1929). Inventor. HYA; LETA
Beshar, Christine (1929–). Lawyer. SMBB
Bierstadt, Albert (1830–1902). Painter. HEDA
Damrosch, Walter (1862–1950). Conductor. CUC
Dengler, Dieter (1938?–). Aviator. ARBA
Dreschkoff, Gisela. Physicist, polar researcher. LA-1
Dreyfuss, Barney (1865–1932). Baseball executive. SLA
Edwards, Gus (1879–1945). Songwriter. MOA
Ehricke, Krafft Arnold (1917–1984). Aeronautical engineer. NEB
Einhorn, David (1809–1879). Rabbi. GUB
Einstein, Albert (1879–1955). Theoretical physicist. ASA; ASB-1; BEA; BEP; BOB; BUF; CAA; COL; CUC; DEI; DEJ; DOE; FE; FRE; GEF; GRB-1; GUB; KE; LEL; LES; LET; LETA; MAM; MOBA; POD; RID; SHFB; SIA; YOA
Follen, Charles Theodore (1795–1840). Abolitionist. CUB
Foss, Lukas (1922–). Composer. MAF; POF; STM†
Franck, James (1882–1964). Physicist. LET
Frankl, Viktor. Concentration camp survivor. WIAA-5
Gimbel, Adam (1817–1896). Merchant. LETA
Goeppert-Mayer, Maria (1906–1972). Theoretical physicist. HA-1; SC†; SHFE
Gropius, Walter Adolf (1883–1969). Architect. BEA; FOF; HIFA; LAF
Herrmann, Alexander (1843–1896). Magician. FOGA; GIA; KEB
Hindemith, Paul (1895–1963). Composer. BEKA; KAE; SAA; YOL
Hofmann, Hans (1880–1966). Painter. BEA; WIAA
Horney, Karen (1885–1952). Psychiatrist. FLA; LEG; RAAG†
Jacobi, Abraham (1830–1919). Pediatrician. LETA
Jacobs, Lou (1903?–). Clown. KIB
Kissinger, Henry Alfred (1923–). Ex-Secretary of State. MEC
Klemperer, Otto (1885–1973). Conductor. EWD; STM†; YOM
Lasker, Albert (1880–1952). Advertising executive. CUC; LETA
Leutze, Emanuel (1816–1868). Painter. HEDA
Lipmann, Fritz Albert (1899–1986). Biochemist. LET

Loewi, Otto (1873–1961). Pharmacologist. LET; RIF

Lubitsch, Ernst (1892–1947). Motion picture director. FLBC

Mergenthaler, Ottmar (1854–1899). Inventor. BEA; CUB; FE; HYA†; LAE; LEB; MAL; THA

Meyerhof, Otto Fritz (1884–1951). Physiologist. LET; RIF

Michelson, Albert Abraham (1852–1931). Physicist. CAA; FE; GRB-1; LET; LETA; SIA; STI

Mies van der Rohe, Ludwig (1886–1969). Architect. FOF; HIFA; LEDA

Muller-Schwarze, Christine. Psychologist, polar researcher. LA-1

Nast, Thomas (1840–1902). Cartoonist. CUB; DEDC

Nichols, Mike (1931–). Comedian, motion picture and theater producer, director. BUR-1

Rey, Hans Augusto (1898–1977). Author, illustrator. SM

Roebling, John Augustus (1806–1869). Civil engineer. CUB

Sandow, Eugene (1867–1925). Professional strongman. PHA

Schiff, Jacob Henry (1847–1920). Financier, philanthropist. LETA

Schriever, Bernard A. (1910–). General. NEB

Schurz, Carl (1829–1906). Journalist, statesman. CUB; LEB; LOB; STH

Schwieger, Hans (1906–). Conductor. STM

Seligman, Joseph (1819–1880). Financier. LETA

Sondermann, Fred S. (1923–). Educator. CAHA

Steinberg, William (1899–1978). Conductor. EWD; STM

Steinmetz, Charles Proteus (1865–1923). Engineer. BEA; COKA; CUC; GRB-1; LOB; LYA

Stern, Otto (1888–1969). Physicist. LET

Steuben, Friedrich Wilhelm von (1730–1794). General. CUB; DAFA; HAN; SCB-1; SOA

Straus, Nathan (1848–1931). Merchant, philanthropist. ALD; GRB-1; LETA; PEB

Stuhlinger, Ernst (1913–). Physicist. POE

Sutro, Adolph Heinrich Joseph (1830–1898). Mining engineer. LETA; YOG

Sutter, John Augustus (1803–1880). Pioneer. BLD; COE; DOCA

Thiel, Katie Kamp (1907–). Businesswoman. BAEA-1

Thomas, Theodore (1835–1905). Conductor. YOM

Von Braun, Wernher (1912–1977). Rocket scientist. COQ; CUB; FE; FRB; LEL; NEB; POE

Warburg, Paul Moritz (1868–1923). Banker. LETA

Weill, Kurt (1900–1950). Composer. EWA

Wolf, Phil (1869–1936). Bowler. SLA

Zakrzewska, Marie Elizabeth (1829–1902). Physician. COFA†; FLA; LEG; RAAG†

Zenger, John Peter (1697–1746). Printer, journalist. ARB; CUB; CUC; FIA; LOB; MEB; SQB

Greek

Mitropoulos, Dimitri (1896–1960). Conductor. EWB; STM; YOM

Skouras, Spyros (1893–1971). Motion picture producer. BEA; LEN; LIA

Yiannopoulos, Andrew (1899?–). Theater director. BAEA-1

Hungarian

Breuer, Marcel Lajos (1902–1981). Architect. LAF

Capa, Robert (1913–1954). Photographer. HOE

Dorati, Antal (1906–). Conductor. STM; YOM

Kármán, Theodor von (1881–1963). Aeronautical engineer. COQ; NEB

Kertesz, André (1894–1985). Photographer. HOE

Knefler, Frederick (fl. 1864). General. LETA

Kocak, Matej (1882–1918). Marine. TA

Kovago, Jozsef. Mechanical engineer. CAHA

Lugosi, Bela (1886–1956). Actor. COE-2

Ormandy, Eugene (1899–1985). Conductor. EWD; STM; YOM

Petersham, Miska (1888–1960). Author, illustrator. SMAB

Pulitzer, Joseph (1847–1911). Journalist. ASB; BEA; CUC; LEM; LOB; LYA; SQB

Reiner, Fritz (1888–1963). Conductor. EWB; STM

Romberg, Sigmund (1887–1951). Composer. EWA; MOA

Schick, Béla (1877–1967). Pediatrician. RIE

Szell, George (1897–1970). Conductor. EWD; STM; YOM

Szent-Györgyi, Albert von (1893–1986). Biochemist. PAC; RIF

Von Neumann, John (1903–1957). Mathematician, computer pioneer. GRAB-3; STN

Wise, Stephen Samuel (1874–1949). Rabbi. GEF; GRB-1; GUB; LETA

Indian

Mangrulkar, Latika. Social worker. FOC-1

Saund, Dalip (1899–1973). Congressman. LIA

Irish

Anthony, Sister (1814–1897). Nun, nurse. COFA

Barry, John (1745–1803). Naval officer. RAD

Colum, Padraic (1881–1972). Author. BEI

Connor, Patrick Edward (1820–1891). Journalist. SEC

Cooper, John (1832–1891). Sailor. TA

Fitzsimons, Thomas (1741–1811). Businessman. FEAA

Goulding, Denis (1893–). No description BAEA-1

Herbert, Victor (1859–1924). Composer. BAD; CUC; DEI; DEJ; EWA; KAE; MOA

Hogan, Henry (fl. 1875). Soldier. TA

Holland, John Philip (1842–1914). Inventor. COR; HYA; THA

Jones, Mary Harris (1830–1930). Labor leader. BI; BRBE†; GEE; MAV; NIA; PACA; TRD; WABC†

King, John (1865–1938). Sailor. TA

Leonard, Patrick (fl. 1870). Soldier. TA

McHenry, James (1753–1816). American Revolutionary patriot. BUIB†; FEAA

O'Neill, James (1847–1920). Actor. SHFA

Rehan, Ada (1860–1916). Actress. VAA

Saint-Gaudens, Augustus (1848–1907). Sculptor. ASB; BEA

Sheridan, Owen (1912?–). Caretaker. BELB

Stewart, Alexander Turney (1803–1876). Merchant. HOF

Italian

Andretti, Mario (1940–). Automobile racer. ABB; FOI; JA; LEX; OLAB; OLCC; ORD; YAA

Brumidi, Constantino (1805–1880). Painter. MAS

Cabrini, Frances Xavier (1850–1917). Saint. ASB; BLF†; DAD-1; DAD-3; MAS; STLA

Capra, Frank (1897–). Motion picture director. ED-1†; FLBC; SMBC

Cesnola, Luigi Palma di (1832–1904). Archaeologist. MAS

Chinaglia, Giorgio (1947–). Soccer player. ADL

De Palma, Ralph (1883?–1956). Automobile racer. LEX; OLAA; YAA

Fermi, Enrico (1901–1954). Physicist. BEA; BIA; BOB; CAA; COLA; CUC; FE; FRE; LEL; LET; MAS; RID; SHFB; SIA; YOE

Fermi, Laura (1907–1977). Author, wife of Enrico Fermi. CAHA

Freccia, Massimo (1906–). Conductor. STM

Menotti, Gian-Carlo (1911–). Composer. BEKA; KAE; LIA; MAF; POF

Segrè, Emilio Gino (1905–). Physicist. LET

Sorrentino, Anthony (1913–). Sociologist. BAEA-1

Zangara, Guiseppe (1900–1933). Assassin. RABA

Japanese

Noguchi, Hideyo (1876–1928). Bacteriologist. BEA; SHG†

Uchida, Miki Akiyama (1903–). Businesswoman. BAEA-1

Yashima, Taro (1908–). Author, illustrator. SMAB

Lithuanian

Hillman, Sidney (1887–1946). Labor leader. COH; DABA; SEA

Hoffenstein, Samuel Goodman (1890–1947). Poet. ALA

Shahn, Ben (1898–1969). Painter. FRA; WIAA

Norwegian

Aulaire, Ingri d' (1904–1980). Author, illustrator. SMAB

Bjurstedt, Molla (1892?–1959). Tennis player. HOBAA

Rockne, Knute (1888–1931). Football coach. DAFB; DAFG; DAG; DAGA; DAI; HEH; LEAB; LEB; LOB; LYB; VAD

Singstad, Ole (b. 1882). Civil engineer. LEGA; YOD

Tokle, Torger (d. 1945). Skier. DAG; DAGA

Williams, Louis (1845–1886). Sailor. TA

Polish

Dubinsky, David (1892–1982). Labor leader. BEA; COH; DABA; LEHA; LIA; SEA

Funk, Casimir (1884–1967). Biochemist. PIAA

Karski, Jan, pseud. Author. CAHA

Krotoshinsky, Abraham. Soldier. GEF; GRB-1

Lubin, David (1849–1919). Agriculturist. LETA

Marcol, Chester (1949–). Football player. GUCA

Modjeska, Helena (1840–1909). Actress. MANB; PIAA

Nowicki, Matthew (1910–1950). Architect. PIAA

Reshevsky, Samuel (1911–). Chess player. LEQB; RHA

Rose, Ernestine Potowski (1810–1892). Feminist. EIA; GUBA; JOCA; LES-2; LETA

Rosenfeld, Morris (1862–1923). Poet. LETA

Rubinstein, Artur (1889–1982). Pianist. GRB-1; MANB; PIAA

Rubinstein, Helena (1870?–1965). Cosmetician. LIA

Rzewska, Josepha Rozanka (1899–). Librarian. BAEA-1

Sadowski, Anthony (1670?–1736). Frontiersman. PIAA

Salomon, Haym (1740–1785). American Revolutionary patriot. ALD; BOK; BUIB†; GRB-1; GUB; HAN†; LERA; LETA; LOB; PEB; SOA

Seymour, David (1911–1956). Photographer. HOE

Singer, Isaac Bashevis (1904–). Author. GRB-1

Walsh, Stella (1913?–1980). Track athlete. DAG; DAGA; HOBA; HOBAA†

Yellen, Jack (1892–). Songwriter. MOA

Romanian

Grunfeld, Ernie (1955–). Basketball player. SLA

Schechter, Solomon (1850–1915). Hebraist. GRB-1; GUB; KAD; LERA; LETA; PEB

Russian

Antin, Mary (1881–1949). Author. CAHA

Balanchine, George (1904–1983). Choreographer. ASB-1; DU-1

Berlin, Irving (1888–). Composer. ASB-1; BAD; EWA; LEHB; LETA; LIA; MOA

Brenner, Victor David (1871–1924). Sculptor. LETA

De Seversky, Alexander P. (1894–1974). Aeronautical engineer. GEA

Dix, Henry (1850?–1938). Manufacturer. LETA

Eglevsky, André (1917–1977). Dancer. ATA

Gallitzin, Demetrius Augustine (1770–1840). Missionary. ASB

Gamberg, Abe (1893–). Businessman. BAEA-1

Gordon, Morris (1895–). Tailor. BAEA-1

Gottlieb, Eddie (1898–1979). Basketball coach, administrator. SLA

Grosman, Tatyana (1904–). Lithographer. GIB-1

Hilsberg, Alexander (1900–1961). Conductor. STM

Joseph, Jacob (1848–1902). Rabbi. LETA

Kane, Gil (1926–). Cartoonist. GOB-1

Kaplan, Louis "Kid" (1902–1970). Boxer. SLA

Koussevitzky, Serge (1874–1951). Conductor. EWB; YOM

Lichine, David (1910–). Dancer, choreographer. ATA

Loeb, Sophie Irene (1876–1929). Journalist, reformer. LER

Nabokov, Vladimir (1899–1977). Author. ASB-1

Nevelson, Louise (1900–1988). Sculptor. BOHB; FOGB; GIB-1

Persky, Daniel (1887–1962). Hebraist, educator. GRB-1

Pious, Minerva (1909–1979). Comedienne. MASB

Revel, Bernard (1885–1940). Rabbi, educator. KAD; LETA

Rickover, Hyman George (1900–1986). Admiral. COR; GRB-1; KE; NAC; WEB

Sabin, Albert Bruce (1906–). Physician. CHE†; COLA; RIE

Sarnoff, David (1891–1971). Radio and television executive. GRB-1; LAG; LETA

Sikorsky, Igor Ivan (1889–1972). Aeronautical engineer. BEA; FE; LAE; LIA; LOB; MAP

Skibine, George (1920–). Dancer. ATA

Sokoloff, Nikolai (b. 1886). Conductor. STM†; YOM

Solzhenitsyn, Aleksandr Isaevich (1918–). Author. ASB-1; POFA

Stravinsky, Igor Fëdorovich (1882–1971). Composer. ASB-1; BAE; BEKA; BUC; FIE; KAE; POG; SAA; YOL

Vladeck, Baruch Charney (1886–1938). Journalist. GEF

Waksman, Selman Abraham (1888–1973). Microbiologist. GRB-1; LET; LETA; LIA; RIF

Zworykin, Vladimir K. (1889–1982). Physicist, inventor. YOE

Scottish

Bell, Alexander Graham (1847–1922). Inventor. ASB-1; BEA; COL; CUC; DEI; DEJ; DOE; EBA; EVC; FAB; FE; FRE; HYA; LEAB; LEB; MAL; MAT; SHFB; SIA; THA

Bowers, Eilley Orrum (fl. 1858). Mine owner. WIAA-2

Carnegie, Andrew (1835–1919). Industrialist. BEA; CUC; DEI; DEJ; EVA; LAG; LEM; LOB; MAL; WED

Fleming, Williamina (1857–1911). Astronomer. PACB

McArthur, Lachlan (1915–). Sales representative. BAEA-1

Muir, John (1838–1914). Naturalist. BEA; BLB; CO-1; CORA; CUC; DOCA; HEB; HIBB; MAL; MIB; SQA; WAP

Murray, Philip (1886–1952). Labor leader. BEA; COH; DABA; SEA

Phyfe, Duncan (1768–1854). Cabinetmaker. BAC

Pinkerton, Allan (1819–1884). Detective. FOA; LACA; LID; SUI

Reston, James Barrett (1909–). Journalist. LEU

Smybert, John (1688–1751). Painter. MAG

Thomson, Bobby (1923–). Baseball player. DEHA-1

Wilson, Alexander (1766–1813). Ornithologist. CO-1; CORA; HYB

South African

Scott Brown, Denise (1931–). Architect. GIB-1

Spilhaus, Athelstan F. (1911–). Meteorologist. BRBC

Spanish

Jorda, Enrique (1911–). Conductor. STM

Ochoa, Severo (1905–). Biochemist. RIF

Santayana, George (1863–1952). Poet, philosopher. LO

Swedish

Broneer, Oscar (1894–). Archaeologist. POC

Edgren, Edith Svensson (1899?–). Housekeeper. BAEA-1

Ericsson, John (1803–1889). Inventor. HYA

Garbo, Greta (1905–). Actress. ASB-1

Swiss

Agassiz, Alexander (1835–1910). Oceanographer, zoologist. COR
Agassiz, Louis (1807–1873). Naturalist. HYB; MIB
Aulaire, Edgar Parin d' (1898–). Author, illustrator. SMAB
Bloch, Ernest (1880–1959). Composer. GRB-1; KAE
Bloch, Felix (1905–1983). Physicist. LET
Buff, Conrad (1886–1975). Author, illustrator. SMAB
Dubin, Al (1891–1945). Songwriter. MOA
Duvoisin, Roger (1904–1980). Author, illustrator. SM
Gallatin, Albert (1761–1849). Statesman. DOG
Guggenheim, Meyer (1828–1905). Industrialist. LETA; WED
Kübler-Ross, Elisabeth (1926–). Psychiatrist. BOHE; GIB-1

West Indian

Mulzac, Hugh Nathaniel (1886–1971). Sea captain. HUB; ROG; STF
Staupers, Mable Keaton (1890–). Nurse, civil rights leader. DOF-1
Sweeney, Robert (b. 1853). Sailor. TA

Yugoslavian

Pupin, Michael Idvorsky (1858–1935). Physicist, inventor. BUF; LEB; LOB
Roth, Werner (1948–). Soccer player. GUEC-1

Others

Abravanel, Maurice (1903–). Turkish. Conductor. STM
Aparicio, Luis (1934–). Venezuelan. Baseball player. FRC-1†; KLB; RIGA†; ROC
Berger, Isaac (1936–). Israeli. Weightlifter. SLA
Carew, Rod (1945–). Panamanian. Baseball player. AAS-3; BRAA; GUDA; GUED-01; GUEE; BUH; DOB; GRAB-02; HUB; KADB; LEI; LEPD; PECA; PECB; ROG; STQ; WIBA
Cukela, Louis (1888–1956). Serbian. Marine officer. TA
Hart, Ephraim (1747–1825). Bavarian. Financier. LETA
Lieu, Winston Hong (1963–). Vietnamese. Electrical engineer. HOD-1
Mardikian, George M. (1903–). Armenian. Restaurateur. CAHA
O'Dea, Pat (1873–1962). Australian. Football player. DAFG; DAI
Pickering, William H. (1910–). New Zealand. Physicist. COQ
Pointe de Sable, Jean Baptiste (1745–1818). Haitian. Founder of Chicago. ADA; ADB; IZA; MUC; RIGA†
Ramcharan, Savitri (1923–). Trinidadian. Physician, researcher. RAAG
Sirhan, Sirhan (1944–). Jordanian. Assassin. RABA
Templeton, Alec (1910–1963). Welsh. Pianist. GEA
Tesla, Nikola (1857–1943). Croatian. Electrical engineer. BOK; FE; MAP
Yepremian, Garo Sarkis (1944–). Cypriot. Football player. AAS-17; GUF; RUC

INCAS

Atahualpa (1500?–1533). King. CAAA

INDIAN CAPTIVES

Boone, Jemima (b. 1762). CAD
Bradley, Isaac (b. 1680). CAD
Brayton, Matthew (1818–1862). HEE
Brown, Joseph (b. 1773). HEE
Brown, Thomas (b. 1740). HEE
Fletcher, Lizzie (b. 1863). JOD
Fletcher, Mary (b. 1851?). JOD
German sisters (Addie, Catherine, Julia, Sophia) (fl. 1870). JOB; JOD
Gyles, John (b. 1742?). CAF
Hammon, Briton (fl. 1747–1759). HAP
Ingles, Mary (fl. 1755). STA
Jemison, Mary (1743–1833). DI; HEE
Jewitt, John R. (1783–1821). DI
Jones, Horatio (1762–1836). HEE
Kelly, Fanny (1845–1904). DI; JOB
Leining, Regina (b. 1745). HEE
Oatman, Mary Ann (1842?–1853?). JOD
Oatman, Olive (1838?–1903). JOD
Parker, Cynthia Ann (1827–1864). HEE; JOB; JOD; WAB
Pompey (d. 1788). HAP
Quinton, Stockwell (fl. 1677). WIAA-5
Rowlandson, Mary (c. 1635–1678). DI
Slocum, Fanny (1773–1847). HEE
Smith, James. DI
Spencer, Oliver (b. 1782). HEE
Stout, Penelope Thomson (1622–1732). CRB
Tanner, John (1779–1846?). DI; HEE; RAC
Tomassa (1840–1888?). WAB
Wheelwright, Esther (1696–1780). HEE

Whittaker, Joseph (b. 1684). CAD
Williams, Eunice (1697–1786). CAF; HEE

INDIANS, AMERICAN, *see* NATIVE AMERICANS

INDIANS, ASIAN

Akbar the Great (1542–1605). Emperor of Hindustan. CAAA
Aryabhatta (c. 475–550). Mathematician, astronomer. STN
Asoka the Great (d. 232 B.C.). King of Magadha. CAAA; NEC
Bhave, Vinoba (1895–1982). Mystic, reformer. BAF; RODA
Buddha (Gautama Buddha) (563?–483 B.C.). Philosopher. FRE; TRC-1
Chandragupta Maurya (c. 321–c. 298 B.C.). King of Magadha. CAAA
Gandhi, Indira Nehru (1917–1984). Prime minister. ASB-1; DU-1; GI; LIDA; WECA
Gandhi, Mohandas Karamchand (1869–1948). Nationalist leader. ASB-1; BEC; DEI; DEJ; DOF; FOJ; FRE; HAA; HAJ; KE; KEE; LAD; MAN; STP; YOA
Mehta, Zubin (1936–). Conductor. EWD
Nehru, Jawaharlal (1889–1964). Prime minister. ARAA; ASB-1; KEF; WEA
Pandit, Vijaya Lakshmi (1900–). Diplomat. KE
Ramcharan, Savitri (1923–). Physician, researcher, born Trinidad. RAAG

INDONESIANS

Banda (1900–1950). Spy. SUG
Kodijat, Raden (1890–). Physician. RODA
Lubis, Mochtar (1922–). Journalist. RODA
Sukarno, Achmed (1901–1970). President. ARA; KEF; WEB

INDUSTRIAL DESIGNERS, *see* DESIGNERS

INDUSTRIALISTS, *see* BUSINESS PEOPLE

INSECT STUDY, *see* ENTOMOLOGISTS

INSTRUMENTALISTS, *see* MUSICIANS

INVALIDS, *see* DISABLED

INVENTORS

American

Armstrong, Edwin Howard (1890–1954). MAPA
Baekeland, Leo Hendrik (1863–1944). (Born Belgium). FE; THA; YOE
Beard, Andrew J. GRAB-03; STQ†
Bell, Alexander Graham (1847–1922). (Born Scotland). ASB-1; BEA; COL; CUC; DEI; DEJ; DOE; EBA; EVC; FAB; FE; FRE; HYA; LEAB; LEB; MAL; MAT; SHFB; SIA; THA
Berliner, Emile (1851–1929). (Born Germany). HYA; LETA
Birdseye, Clarence (1886–1956). LAG
Borden, Gail (1801–1874). FAB; MAL
Carlson, Chester F. (1906–1968). FE; MAPA
Carothers, Wallace Hume (1896–1937). FE
Carrier, Willis Haviland (1876–1950). FAB; YOE
Colt, Samuel (1814–1862). FRB; HEB; HOF; HYA†
Curtiss, Glenn Hammond (1878–1930). BOK; HAMY; HOF
Davenport, Thomas (1802–1851). HYA†; MAP
De Forest, Lee (1873–1961). COLA; CUC; FAB; HYA; LEL; MAP; THA
Eastman, George (1854–1932). CUC; FE; LAG; LEM; MAL; RIBA
Eckert, J. Presper (1919–). GRAB-3
Edison, Thomas Alva (1847–1931). ASA; ASB-1; BEC; BIA; BOB; BOD; BUE; CAD; COKB; COL; CUC; DEI; DEJ; DOE; EBA; EVC; FAB; FE; FOH; FRE; HYA; LEN; LEPA; MAT; PRC; RAA; RIBA; SHFB; SIA; THA
Ericsson, John (1803–1889). (Born Sweden). HYA
Evans, Oliver (1755–1819). HYA
Fairchild, Sherman Mills (1896–1971). MAPA
Fitch, John (1743–1798). BUE; BUIB†; HYA
Fulton, Robert (1765–1815). COL; CUC; DEI; DEJ; EBA; EVC; FAB; FE; HYA; LAE; LEL; MAL; THA
Goodyear, Charles (1800–1860). DOE; FAB; HOF; HYA; LAE; MAL; MAP; RAA; RIBA
Holland, John Philip (1842–1914). (Born Ireland). COR; HYA; THA
Howe, Elias (1819–1867). FE; HYA; LAE; RAA; THA
Jenkins, Charles Francis (1867–1934). HYA
Jones, Frederick McKinley (1892–1961). GRAB-03; HAL
Kelly, William (1811–1888). BUE
Land, Edwin Herbert (1909–). FE; MAPA; PAB
Latimer, Lewis Howard (1848–1928). GRAB-03; HA; HAL; HODA; KLA; STQ
Lee, Joseph (1849–1905?). GRAB-03
Link, Edwin Albert (1904–1981). BRBC; COR

McCormick, Cyrus Hall (1809–1884). CAB; EBA;
FAB; FE; HYA; LAG; LEN; MAL; MAT; RAA;
WED

McCoy, Elijah (1843–1929). ADB; BRB†; GRAB-
03; HA; HAL; KLA; STQ†

Matzeliger, Jan Ernst (1852–1889). ADA; ADB;
BRB†; BRG; GRAB-03; HA; HAL; KLA; PECA;
ROG; STQ†

Mauchly, John W. (1907–1980). GRAB-3

Maxim, Hudson (1853–1927). MAP

Mergenthaler, Ottmar (1854–1899). (Born Germany). BEA; CUB; FE; HYA†; LAE; LEB;
MAL; THA

Momsen, Charles Bowers (1896–1967). OLC

Morgan, Garrett A. (1875–1963). ADA; ADB;
GRAB-03; HA; HAL; KLA; STQ†

Morse, Samuel F. B. (1791–1872). BUE; COL;
EBA; EVC; FE; HYA; LAE; LEL; MAL; SHFB;
THA

Otis, Elisha Graves (1811–1861). HOF

Pullman, George Mortimer (1831–1897). HOF

Pupin, Michael Idvorsky (1858–1935). (Born Yugoslavia). BUF; LEB; LOB

Roosevelt, Nicholas J. (1767–1854). BUE

Shaw, Earl (1937–). CAF-1

Sholes, Christopher Latham (1819–1890). FE;
HYA; LAE; MAL

Sperry, Elmer Ambrose (1860–1930). YOE

Sprague, Frank Julian (1857–1934). HOF

Stanley, Francis Edgar (1849–1918). HOF

Stanley, Freelan O. (1849–1940). HOF

Steinmetz, Charles Proteus (1865–1923). (Born
Germany). BEA; COKA; CUC; GRB-1; LOB;
LYA

Stevens, John (1749–1838). BUE; BUIB†; FAB;
HYA; VIA

Stevens, Robert Livingston (1787–1856). HYA

Temple, Lewis (1800–1854). GRAB-03; HAL

Tesla, Nikola (1857–1943). (Born Croatia). BOK;
FE; MAP

Vail, Alfred (1807–1859). BUE

Voight, Harry. BUE

Westinghouse, George (1846–1914). HYA; LAG;
THA

Whitney, Eli (1765–1825). BUE; CAB; CUC; DEI;
DEJ; EBA; FAB; FE; HYA; LAE; MAL; RAA;
THA

Wilkinson, David (1771–1852). FAB

Woods, Granville T. (1856–1910). ADA; ADB;
BRB†; CAF-1; GRAB-03; HA; HAL; JO; KLA;
PECA; STQ†

Wright, Orville (1871–1948). ASB; ASB-1; BIA;
BOD; BRBA; COL; CUC; DEI; DEJ; DOE;
EBA; EVC; EVD; FAB; FE; FRE; HAMY;
HYA†; LEL; MAT; PRC; SIA; THA

Wright, Wilbur (1867–1912). ASB; BIA; BOD;

BRBA; COL; CUC; DEI; DEJ; DOE; EBA;
EVC; EVD; FAB; FE; FRE; HAMY; HYA†;
LEL; MAT; PRC; SIA; THA

Zworykin, Vladimir K. (1889–1982). (Born Russia). YOE

English

Arkwright, Sir Richard (1732–1792). FAB; FE

Aveling, Thomas (1824–1881). LAE

Bessemer, Sir Henry (1813–1898). ASA; EBA;
FAB; FE; LAE; THA

Booth, Hubert Cecil (1871–1955). LAE

Bramah, Joseph (1748–1814). FE

Cartwright, Edmund (1743–1823). EBA

Congreve, Sir William (1772–1828). STMA

Hargreaves, James (c. 1722–1778). FE

Harrison, John (1693–1776). FEAB; MOB

Hill, Sir Rowland (1795–1879). EVA

Hounsfield, Godfrey (1919–). AAS-33

Maxim, Sir Hiram Stevens (1840–1916). (Born
U.S.). MAP

Newcomen, Thomas (1663–1729). FE

Pitman, Sir Isaac (1813–1897). FE

Siemens, Sir William (1823–1883). (Born Germany). FE

Stephenson, George (1781–1848). EBA; EVB; FE;
THA

Swan, Sir Joseph Wilson (1828–1914). FE

Talbot, William Henry Fox (1800–1877). FE;
SHFB

Trevithick, Richard (1771–1833). EVB

Turing, Alan M. (1912–1954). GRAB-3

Whittle, Sir Frank (1907–). EVC; FE; SHFB; THA

Whitworth, Sir Joseph (1803–1887). FE

French

Appert, Nicolas (c. 1750–1841). FE

Braille, Louis (1809–1852). EVA; FE; FOR; FRB;
FRE

Daguerre, Louis Jacques (1787–1851). FE; FRE;
THA

Jacquard, Joseph-Marie (1752–1834). FE

Lenoir, Etienne (1822–1900). FE

Le Prince, Louis Aime Augustin. BUE

Lumière, Auguste (1862–1954). FE

Lumière, Louis (1864–1948). FE

Montgolfier, Jacques Étienne (1745–1799).
BRBA; EVC; FE

Montgolfier, Joseph Michel (1740–1810). BRBA;
EVC; FE

Niepce, Joseph-Nicephore (1765–1833). FE

Robert, Nicholas-Louis (1761–1828). FAB

German

Daimler, Gottlieb (1834–1900). EBA; FE; THA

Diesel, Rudolf C. (1858–1913). FAB; FE; LAE; MAP; THA

Gutenberg, Johann (c. 1397–1468). ASA; COL; DEI; DEJ; EBA; FE; FRE; THA

König, Friedrich (1774–1833). FE; LAE

Nipkow, Paul (1860–1940). FE

Otto, Nikolaus August (1832–1891). FAB; FE; THA

Zeppelin, Ferdinand Graf von (1838–1917). FE

Scottish

Baird, John Logie (1888–1946). EVC; FE; PRC; SHFB; THA

Murdock, William (1754–1839). FE; LAE

Watt, James (1736–1819). ASA; BIA; BOD; BUF; COL; EBA; EVB; FAB; FE; FRE; SHFB; THA

Others

Archimedes (287?–212 B.C.). Greek. ASA; BEP; CAA; DOE; EVC; FE; MAQ; MUB; SHFB; SIA; STN; THA

Dunlop, John Boyd (1840–1921). Irish. (Born Scotland). FE

Fokker, Anthony (1890–1939). Dutch. HAMY

Leonardo da Vinci (1452–1519). Italian. CAA; CHC; DEI; DEJ; EVC; FE; JAA; KAA; MAI; SHFB; SIA

Marconi, Guglielmo (1874–1937). Italian. AAS-33; BOB; COL; EBA; EVC; FAB; FE; FRE; PRC; SHFB; SIA; THA

Sax, Adolphe (Antoine Joseph) (1814–1894). Belgian. LAE

Schmidt, Bernhard V. (1879–1935). Russian. LAA

Senefelder, Aloys (1771–1834). Czech. FE

Tsiolkovsky, Konstantin E. (1857–1935). Russian. NEB; STMA; THC

IRANIANS

Khomeini, Ruhollah (1900?–). Religious and political leader. HAGD

IRISH

Allingham, William (1824–1889). Poet. BEH

Barnardo, Thomas John (1845–1905). Physician, social reformer. EVA

Brian Boru (926–1014). Ruler. CAAA

Browne, Frances (1816–1879). Author. BEI

Burke, Robert O'Hara (1820–1861). Explorer. ROL; WIA-1

Corrigan, Mairead (1944–). Social reformer. AAS-34; COG-1; SHFE†

Dunlop, John Boyd (1840–1921). Inventor, born Scotland. FE

Ferguson, Harry George (1884–1960). Manufacturer. LAE

Field, John (1782–1837). Pianist, composer. CHF

Galvin, Edward J. (1882–1956). Bishop. REC

Garrett, Eileen J. (1893–1970). Medium. COEA

Joyce, James (1882–1941). Author. ASB-1

McAuley, Mary Catherine, Mother (1787–1841). REC

MacBride, Sean (1904–1988). Foreign minister. MEC

Mathew, Theobald (1790–1856). Priest. REC

Montez, Lola (1818?–1861). Dancer. RAB; WABC†

Murphy, Jimmy (1894?–1924). Automobile racer. LEX

Nash, Charlie. Boxer. BELB

O'Crohan, Tomás (1856–1937). Scholar. RAC

Shackleton, Sir Ernest Henry (1874–1922). Explorer. DOC; KNA; MAJ; ROL; SCBA

Shaw, George Bernard (1856–1950). Playwright, critic. ASB-1; DEI; DEJ; KE; STL

Talbot, Matthew (1856–1925). Religious figure. REC

Williams, Betty (1943–). Social reformer. AAS-34; COG-1; SHFE†

Yeats, William Butler (1865–1939). Poet. BRBB

ISRAELIS

Agnon, Shmuel Yosef (1888–1970). Author. GRB-1; ROGA

Allon, Yigal (1918–1980). General. GRB-1; ROGA

Ashkenasi, Shmuel (1941–). Violinist. EWC

Bar-Ilan, David (1930–). Pianist. EWC

Barenboim, Daniel (1942–). Pianist. EWC

Begin, Menachem (1913–). Ex-prime minister, born Poland. ASB-1; GRB-1; HAGD

Ben-Gurion, David (1886–1973). Prime minister. GRB-1; GUB; KE; KEF; ROGA; WEA

Ben-Porat, Miriam (1918–). Supreme Court justice, born Lithuania. GRB-1

Ben-Zvi, Yitzhak (1884–1963). President, born Russia. GRB-1

Branover, Herman (1931–). Physicist, educator, born Russia. GRB-1

Brockman, Shimson (1958–). Boat racer. SLA

Brody, Tal (1943–). Basketball player, born U.S. SLA

Chizick, Sarah. Settler. LER

Cohen, Eli (1924–1965). Spy, born Egypt. GRB-1

David. Pilgrim, born Yemen. GRB-1

Dayan, Moshe (1915–1981). Foreign minister. ROGA; GRB-1; WECA

Eisenberg, Shaul (1921–). Businessman, born Germany. GRB-1

Eliav, Aryeh Lyova (1921–). Political figure, born Russia. GRB-1

Eshkol, Levi (1895–1969). Prime minister, born Russia. GRB-1

Freier, Recha (1892–). Resistance leader, born Germany. GRB-1

Friedlander, Ethan (1957–). Boat racer. SLA

Glickstein, Shlomo (1958–). Tennis player. SLA

Grossman, Noam (1927–). Soldier. GEF

Keleti, Agnes (1921–). Gymnast, born Hungary. SLA

Kluger, Ruth. Rescue worker, born Rumania. GRB-1

Kook, Abraham Isaac (1865–1935). Rabbi. GRB-1

Kuchler, Lena. Child psychologist, born Poland. GRB-1

Levin, Aryeh (b. 1885). Rabbi, born Russia. GRB-1

Lubetkin, Tzivia (1914–1978). Resistance leader, born Poland. GRB-1

Meir, Golda (1898–1978). Prime minister. GI; GRB-1; KE†; KOA; LIDA; ROGA

Navon, Yitzhak (1921–). President. GRB-1

Netanyahu, Yonatan (1946–1976). Army officer. GRB-1

Roth, Esther (1952–). Track athlete. SLA

Senesh, Hannah (1921–1944). Underground leader, born Hungary. GEF; GRB-1; LAD; STP; ROGA

Shear-Yashur, Aharon. Rabbi, born Germany. GRB-1

Trumpeldor, Joseph (1880–1920). Settler. GRB-1; PEB; ROGA

Weizmann, Chaim (1874–1952). President. DEI; DEJ; GEF; GRAB-1; GUB; KAB; KAD; LES; ROGA

Yadin, Yigael (1917–1984). Archaeologist. GRB-1; POC; ROGA

Yoffe, Avraham (1880–1960). Ecologist. GRB-1

ITALIANS

Angelico, Fra (1400–1455). Painter. MAI

Ascari, Alberto (1919–1955). Automobile racer. YAA

Avogadro, Amedeo (1776–1856). Chemist, physicist. CAA; MOBA; SHFB

Balsamo, Joseph (Cagliostro) (1743–c. 1800). Magician, charlatan. ED-5

Boccherini, Luigi (1743–1805). Composer. KAE

Boccioni, Umberto (1882–1916). Painter. WIAA

Botticelli, Sandro (1444?–1510). Painter. JAA; KAA; MAI

Bovet, Daniele (1907–). Pharmacologist, born Switzerland. RIF

Busoni, Ferruccio (1866–1924). Pianist, composer. CHF

Cabot, John (1450–1498). Explorer. GRAA; GRC; KNB; MOB; ROL

Cabot, Sebastian (1476–1557). Explorer. MOB; ROL†

Cannizzaro, Stanislao (1826–1910). Chemist. MOBA

Caravaggio, Michelangelo da (1565–1609). Painter. KAA

Cardano, Girolamo (1501–1576). Mathematician, physician, astrologer. MUB

Carpini, Giovanni de Piano (c. 1180–1252). Traveler. KNA

Caruso, Enrico (1873–1921). Singer. ASB-1; COKB; DEI; DEJ; YOH

Casanova de Seingalt, Giovanni Giacomo (1725–1798). Adventurer. DEI; DEJ; JAC

Cellini, Benvenuto (1500–1571). Goldsmith, sculptor. DEI; DEJ; JAC; RAC

Cherubini, Luigi (1760–1842). Composer. KAE

Clementi, Muzio (1752–1832). Composer, pianist. CHF

Codona, Alfredo (1894–1937). Circus aerialist. SUA

Columbus, Christopher (1451–1506). Explorer. ASB; COC; DAF; DEI; DEJ; DOBB; DYA; EVD; GRC; KEH; KNB; MAT; MOB; OLA; PRC; ROL; VIA; WIA-1

Corelli, Arcangelo (1653–1713). Composer. BEM; CHFA; KAE; YOM†

Corelli, Franco (1924?–). Singer. BRBB-1

Dante, Alighieri (1265–1321). Poet. DEI; DEJ

Donizetti, Gaetano (1797–1848). Composer. KAE

Fabricius ab Aquapendente, Hieronymus (1537–1619). Anatomist. POB

Fallaci, Oriana (1930–). Journalist. LETB

Fracastoro, Girolamo (1483–1553). Physician. POB

Francesca, Piero della (1420?–1492). Painter. JAA; MAI

Frescobaldi, Girolamo (1583–1643). Composer, organist. BEM

Gabrieli, Giovanni (c. 1555–1612). Composer. BEM

Galilei, Galileo (1564–1642). Astronomer, physicist. ASA; BEC; BEP; BOB; CAA; COL; DEI; DEJ; DOE; EVC; FE; FRB; FRE; LAA; MAQ; MOCB; PIA; SHFB; SIA; SIB; STI; SUE; THA

Galvani, Luigi (1737–1798). Physicist, physician. DUA; MAQ

Garibaldi, Giuseppe (1807–1882). Patriot. BOD; MAJ

Gesualdo, Carlo (1560–1613). Composer. BEM

Giorgione, Il (c. 1478–1510). Painter. JAA

Giotto di Bondone (c. 1266–1337). Painter. CHC; JAA; KAA; MAI

Golgi, Camillo (1844–1926). Neurologist. RIF

Grassi, Giovanni Battista (1854–1925). Zoologist. DEB; ROA

John XXIII (1881–1963). Pope. ASB-1; KE; YOA

Leonardo da Vinci (1452–1519). Artist, inventor. CAA; CHC; DEI; DEJ; EVC; FE; JAA; KAA; MAI; SHFB; SIA

Leoncavallo, Ruggiero (1858–1919). Composer. KAE

Lippi, Fra Filippo (1406?–1469). Painter. CHC

Malpighi, Marcello (1628–1694). Anatomist. STE

Manzolini, Anne Morandi (1716–1774). Anatomist. RIB

Marconi, Guglielmo (1874–1937). Inventor. AAS-33; BOB; COL; EBA; EVC; FAB; FE; FRE; PRC; SHFB; SIA; THA

Masaccio (1401–1428). Painter. JAA; KAA; MAI

Mascagni, Pietro (1863–1945). Composer. KAE

Mazzei, Philip (1730–1816). Physician. MAS

Michelangelo Buonarroti (1475–1564). Artist. CHC; DEI; DEJ; JAA; KAA; MAI

Modigliani, Amedeo (1884–1920). Painter. KAA

Moneta, Ernesto Teodoro (1833–1918). Journalist, pacifist. MEC†; WIC

Montessori, Maria (1870–1952). Physician, educator. STP

Monteverdi, Claudio (1567–1643). Composer. BEM; FIE; KAE; SAA

Mussolini, Benito (1883–1945). Chief of state. ARA; ARAA; ASB-1; CAE; DOF; KIA; TAC

Nobile, Umberto (b. 1885). Explorer. GRB; ROL†

Nuvolari, Tazio (1892–1953). Automobile racer. COKC; SUA; YAA

Paganini, Nicolò (1782–1840). Violinist. CHFA; YOH

Palestrina, Giovanni Pierluigi da (1526?–1594). Composer. BRF; BUD; KAE; YOJ

Paul VI (1897–1978). Pope. WEB

Pavarotti, Luciano (1935–). Singer. BRBB-1

Pergolesi, Giovanni Battista (1710–1746). Composer. KAE

Pius XI (1857–1939). Pope. BOD

Polo, Marco (1254–1324). Traveler. COC; COL; DAF; DEI; DEJ; DYA; FRE; GRC; KEH; KNA; MOB; ROL

Puccini, Giacomo (1858–1924). Composer. BAE; KAE; SAA

Raphael (Raffaello Santi) (1483–1520). Painter. CHC; JAA; KAA; MAI

Respighi, Ottorino (1879–1936). Composer. BUC; KAE

Rossini, Gioacchino (1792–1868). Composer. BAE; KAE; SAA

Sanctorius (1561–1636). Physiologist. SHG

Scarlatti, Alessandro (1659–1725). Composer. BAE; SAA

Scarlatti, Domenico (1685–1757). Composer, harpsichordist. BEN; KAE; SAA

Sereni, Enzo (1905–1944). Resistance worker. GRB-1; LAD

Spallanzani, Lazzaro (1729–1799). Naturalist. DEB; ROA

Tartini, Giuseppe (1692–1770). Composer, violinist. BEN; CHFA; SAA†

Tintoretto, Il (1518–1594). Painter. JAA

Titian (1477–1576). Painter. JAA; KAA; MAI

Torricelli, Evangelista (1608–1647). Mathematician, physicist. CAA; FE; SHFB

Toscanini, Arturo (1867–1957). Conductor. DEI; DEJ; EWB; FRB; KEE; MAS; YOH; YOM

Troctula di Ruggiero (d. 1197). Physician. MASA; RIB; SC

Varthema, Ludovico de (1461?–1517?). Traveler. ROL

Veracini, Francesco Maria (1685–1750). Violinist, composer. CHFA

Verdi, Giuseppe (1813–1901). Composer. BRF; BUD; GOB; KAE; SAA; TRC; WIA; YOJ

Vespucci, Amerigo (1451–1512). Navigator. KNB; MOB; ROL; VIA†

Victor Emanuel II (1820–1878). King. CAAA

Viotti, Giovanni Battista (1755–1824). Violinist. CHFA

Vittorino da Feltre (Vittorino Ramboldini) (1378–1446). Educator. FRC

Vivaldi, Antonio (1675?–1741). Violinist, composer. BEM; CHFA; KAE; SAA; YOM†

Volta, Alessandro, conte (1745–1827). Physicist. CAA; DOE; DUA; FE; MAQ; SHFB; SIA; SOB

JAMAICANS

Flood, James (fl. early 18th century). Pirate. WHA

Garvey, Marcus A. (1887–1940). Nationalist movement leader, in U.S. ADA; ADB; ARAA; BEJ; BRBD; GRAB-01; JO

McKenley, Herb. Track athlete. HIA

JAPANESE

Hanaoka, Seishu (1760–1835). Surgeon. RIB

Hirohito (1901–). Emperor. ASB-1; DU-1; WEB

Kagawa, Toyohiko (1888–1960). Evangelist. BAF; KEE

Kitasato, Shibasaburo (1852–1931). Bacteriologist. RIE

Kurosawa, Akira (1910–). Motion picture director. RODA
Morita, Akio (1921–). Electronics executive. DU-1
Mutsuhito (1852–1912). Emperor. CAAA
Onoda, Hiroo (1922–). Soldier. WIAA-5
Sato, Eisaku (1901–1975). Premier. MEC; WECA
Tsukahara, Mitsuo (1947–). Gymnast. LIE

JAZZ MUSICIANS, *see* MUSICIANS, JAZZ

JEWS

See also BIBLICAL LEADERS—OLD TESTAMENT;
CHAPLAINS; RELIGIOUS LEADERS—JEWISH

American
Ager, Milton (1893–1979). Songwriter. MOA
Alexander, Moses (1853–1932). Governor. LETA
Allen, Woody (1935–). Actor, motion picture director. ED-1†; SMBB-3
Antin, Mary (1881–1949). Author, born Russia. CAHA
Arnovich, Morrie (Morris) (1910–1959). Baseball player. RI; SLA†
Asher, Barry (1946–). Bowler. SLA
Attell, Abe (1884–1969). Boxer. SLA
Auerbach, Red (Arnold) (1917–). Baseball coach. HEH; HID; LEW†; SLA
Bar Cochba, Simon (d. 135). Insurrectionist. LERA
Barron, Herman (1909–1976). Golfer. SLA
Baruch, Bernard M. (1870–1965). Financier, statesman. GRB-1; LETA
Bayes, Nora (1880–1928). Singer, comedienne. MASB
Belasco, David (1854–1931). Playwright, theater producer. LETA
Benjamin, Judah Philip (1811–1884). Senator. LETA
Benny, Jack (1894–1974). Comedian. ALC
Berg, Gertrude (1899–1966). Actress, playwright. MASB
Berg, Moe (Morris) (1902–1972). Baseball player, spy. BELB; RI; SLA†
Berger, Isaac (Ike) (1936–). Weightlifter, born Israel. SLA
Bergmann, Gretel (Margarethe) (1914–). Track athlete, born Germany. SLA
Berle, Milton (1908–). Comedian. ALC
Berlin, Irving (1888–). Composer, born Russia. ASB-1; BAD; EWA; LEHB; LETA; LIA; MOA
Berliner, Emile (1851–1929). Inventor, born Germany. HYA; LETA

Bernstein, Carl (1944–). Journalist. LETB
Bernstein, Leonard (1918–). Composer, conductor. EWA; EWD; KAE; LEHB; LETA; MAF; POF; SAA†; STM; YOM†
Bloch, Ernest (1880–1959). Composer, born Switzerland. GRB-1; KAE
Bloch, Felix (1905–1983). Physicist, born Switzerland. LET
Blomberg, Ron (1948–). Baseball player. SLA
Boosler, Elayne (1953–). Comedienne. MASB
Borgenicht, Louis (fl. 1889). Businessman. LETA
Brandeis, Louis Dembitz (1856–1941). Supreme Court justice. ALD; EIA; FLC; GEF; GRB-1; GUB; LETA
Brenner, Victor David (1871–1924). Sculptor, born Russia. LETA
Brice, Fanny (1891–1951). Singer, comedienne. DI-1†; MASB; PHA
Brill, Abraham Arden (1874–1948). Psychiatrist, born Austria. LETA
Brooks, Mel (Melvin Kaminsky) (1926–). Actor, comedian, motion picture director. BUR-1; SMBB-3
Brown, Harold (1927–). Ex-Secretary of Defense. GRB-1
Caesar, Sid (1922–). Comedian. ALC
Calvin, Melvin (1911–). Chemist. BEK
Cantor, Eddie (1892–1964). Comedian. ALC; LETA; PHA
Capa, Robert (1913–1954). Photographer, born Hungary. HOE
Capp, Al (Alfred G. Caplin) (1909–1979). Cartoonist. GEA
Cardozo, Benjamin Nathan (1870–1938). Supreme Court justice. FLC
Carew, Rod (Rodney Cline) (1945–). Baseball player, born Panama. AAS-3; BRAA; GUDA; GUED-01; GUEE; IZA; MUC; RIGA†
Cohen, Andy (Andrew) (1904–). Baseball player. RI; SLA
Cohen, Maxwell (1908–). Lawyer. UN
Commoner, Barry (1917–). Biologist. SQA
Conrad, Con (Conrad Dober) (1891–1938). Songwriter. MOA
Copeland, Lillian (1904–1964). Track athlete. SLA
Copland, Aaron (1900–). Composer. BAD; BEKA; BEN; KAE; KE; MAF; POF; SAA†; YOL
Damrosch, Walter (1862–1950). Conductor, born Germany. CUC
Danning, Harry (1911–). Baseball player. RI; SLA
Davis, Al (1929–). Football coach, owner. SLA
Davis, Sammy, Jr. (1925–). Entertainer. DOBA; DOF-1; ROF
de Leon, David (1813–1872). Physician. GRB-1

Dix, Henry (1850?–1938). Manufacturer, born Russia. LETA

Dreyfuss, Barney (1865–1932). Baseball executive, born Germany. SLA

Dubinsky, David (1892–1982). Labor leader, born Poland. BEA; COH; DABA; LEHA; LIA; SEA

Einstein, Albert (1879–1955). Theoretical physicist, born Germany. ASA; ASB-1; BEA; BEP; BOB; BUF; CAA; COL; CUC; DEI; DEJ; DOE; FE; FRE; GEF; GRB-1; GUB; KE; LEL; LES; LET; LETA; MAM; MOBA; POD; RID; SHFB; SIA; YOA

Epstein, Charlotte (1884–1938). Swimming administrator. SLA

Erlanger, Joseph (1874–1965). Physiologist. LET; RIF

Ezekiel, Sir Moses Jacob (1844–1917). Sculptor. LETA

Ferber, Edna (1887–1968). Author. CON; LETA; ROJ

Ferkauf, Eugene (1921–). Merchant. GRB-1; LAH

Fermi, Laura (1907–1977). Author, wife of Enrico Fermi, born Italy. CAHA

Fields, Jackie (1908–). Boxer. SLA

Fischer, Bobby (Robert James) (1943–). Chess player. BELB; FOR; LEQB; RHA

Fisher, Harry (1882–1967). Basketball player, coach. SLA

Flam, Herbert (1928–). Tennis player. SLA

Fleischer, Nat (1887–1972). Boxing promoter, editor. SLA

Flexner, Abraham (1866–1959). Educator. LETA

Foss, Lukas (1922–). Composer, born Germany. MAF; POF; STM†

Franck, James (1882–1964). Physicist, born Germany. LET

Frankfurter, Felix (1882–1965). Supreme Court justice, born Austria. LIA; LOB

Frankl, Viktor. Concentration camp survivor, born Germany. WIAA-5

Franklin, Sidney (1903–1976). Bullfighter. SLA

Franks, David Salisbury (d. 1793). American Revolutionary patriot. LETA

Friedan, Betty (1921–). Author, feminist. GIB-1; WA

Friedman, Benny (1905–1982). Football player. DAFG; SLA

Friedman, Max (b. 1889). Basketball player. SLA

Funk, Casimir (1884–1967). Biochemist, born Poland. PIAA

Gamberg, Abe (1893–). Businessman, born Russia. BAEA-1

Gershwin, George (1898–1937). Composer. ALD; BAD; BEKA; BUC; CUC; DEI; DEJ; EWA; FIE; KAE; LAC; LETA; MAF; MOA; POF; SAA†; WIA; YOJ

Gillman, Sidney (1911–). Football player, coach. SLA

Gimbel, Adam (1817–1896). Merchant, born Germany. LETA

Ginsburg, Ruth Bader (1933–). Jurist. GIB-1; SWI

Glueck, Nelson (1900–1971). Archaeologist. GRB-1

Goldberg, Arthur J. (1908–). Statesman. LETA; WEC

Goldberg, Marshall (1917–). Football player. HIE; SLA

Goldberger, Joseph (1874–1929). Physician, born Austria. ALD; DEA; GEF

Goldfadden, Abraham (1840–1908). Founder of Yiddish theater. LETA

Goldhaber, Maurice (1911–). Physicist, born Austria. PAC

Goldwyn, Samuel (1882–1974). Motion picture producer. LETA

Gomez, Benjamin (fl. 1791). Book dealer. LETA

Gompers, Samuel (1850–1924). Labor leader, born England. ARAA; BEA; COH; CUC; DABA; FAC; FOB; GRB-1; LEHA; LETA; LOB; MAL; MEB; SEA

Goodman, Benny (1909–1986). Clarinetist, band leader. COF-1; TEA; TEB; WAD†

Gordon, Sid (1918–1975). Baseball player. RI; SLA

Gottfried, Brian (1952–). Tennis player. SLA

Gottlieb, Eddie (1898–1979). Basketball coach, administrator, born Russia. SLA

Gratz, Rebecca (1781–1869). Philanthropist. GRB-1; LER; LETA; PEB

Greenberg, Hank (Henry Benjamin) (1911–1986). Baseball player. ALB; BOE; DAA; FRC-1†; GR; RI; RIGA†; SLA

Grosman, Tatyana (1904–). Lithographer, born Russia. GIB-1

Grossinger, Jennie (1892–1972). Hotel executive. PAA

Grossman, Randy (1952–). Football player. SLA

Grunfeld, Ernie (1955–). Basketball player, born Romania. SLA

Guggenheim, Meyer (1828–1905). Industrialist, born Switzerland. LETA; WED

Hammerstein, Oscar, II (1895–1960). Librettist. BEKA†; MOA

Hardeen (Theo Weiss) (1876–1945). Magician. GIA

Harris, Sigmund (1883–1964). Football player. SLA

Hart, Ephraim (1747–1825). Financier, born Bavaria. LETA

Hays, Isaac (1796–1879). Ophthalmologist. LETA

Hays, Moses Michael (1739–1805). Businessman. LETA

Heldman, Julie (1945–). Tennis player. SLA

Hellman, Lillian (1905–1984). Playwright, author. DI-1; GIB-1†

Hendricks, Harmon (fl. 1812). Merchant. LETA

Hershkowitz, Victor (1918–). Handball player. SLA

Heyman, Art (1942–). Basketball player. SLA

Hillman, Sidney (1887–1946). Labor leader, born Lithuania. COH; DABA; SEA

Holliday, Judy (1921–1965). Actress. MASB

Holman, Marshall (1954–). Bowler. SLA

Holman, Nat (1896–). Basketball coach. BEL; HEHA; HID; SLA

Holtzman, Elizabeth (1941–). Congresswoman. BOHF

Holtzman, Ken (1945–). Baseball player. RI; SLA

Holzman, Red (William) (1920–). Basketball coach. ARB-2; SLA

Houdini, Harry (1874–1926). Magician. FOGA; GIA; KEB; KLD; WAO

Jackson, Solomon Henry (d. 1847). Publisher, born England. LETA

Jacobi, Abraham (1830–1919). Pediatrician, born Germany. LETA

Jacobs, Hirsch (1904–1970). Horse trainer. SLA

Jacobs, James (1931–). Handball player. SLA

Jaffee, Irving (1906–1981). Skater. SLA

Jolson, Al (1886–1950). Actor, singer. LETA

Jones, Henry (fl. 1843). Founder of B'nai B'rith. LETA

Kanokogi, Rusty (1935–). Martial artist. AT

Kaplan, Louis "Kid" (1902–1970). Boxer, born Russia. SLA

Katz, Chaim Moshe. Businessman, born Russia. GRB-1

Kauff, Benny (1891–1961). Baseball player. SLA

Kazin, Alfred (1915–). Author, critic. RAC

Kern, Jerome (1885–1945). Composer. BAD; CUC; EWA; MOA; WIA

King, Alan (1927–). Comedian. GRB-1

Kissinger, Henry Alfred (1923–). Ex-Secretary of State, born Germany. MEC

Klemperer, Otto (1885–1973). Conductor, born Germany. EWD; STM†; YOM

Kling, Johnny (1875–1947). Baseball player. HIC; RI; SHD†; SLA

Knefler, Frederick (fl. 1864). General, born Hungary. LETA

Kornberg, Arthur (1918–). Biochemist. GRB-1; LET; RIF

Koufax, Sandy (Sanford) (1935–). Baseball player. ALBA; BRC; BUD-1; DAFC; DAFD; DAH; DEHA-1; FRC-1†; GEB; GIB; GRA; GRB-1; GUC; GUDA; HOC; KADA; LYC;

MUB-1; MUC; NEA; PAW; PEC; PRA; RI; RIGA†; SHA; SHC; SLA

Koussevitzky, Serge (1874–1951). Conductor, born Russia. EWB; YOM

Krotoshinsky, Abraham. Soldier, born Poland. GEF; GRB-1

Lasker, Albert (1880–1952). Advertising executive, born Germany. CUC; LETA

Lazarus, Emma (1849–1887). Poet. DOD; GRB-1; GUB; LEK; LER; LETA; PEB

Lederberg, Joshua (1925–). Geneticist. GRB-1; LET; RIF

Lehman, Herbert H. (1878–1963). Governor. GRB-1; LETA

Leinsdorf, Erich (1912–). Conductor, born Austria. BEA; EWD; STM; YOM

Leonard, Benny (1896–1947). Boxer. DAG; DAGA; SLA

Levenson, Sam (1911–1980). Humorist. ALC

Levine, Samuel Albert (1891–1966). Cardiologist. LETA

Levinsky, Battling (Barney Lebrowitz) (1891–1949). Boxer. SLA

Levitt, William Jaird (1907–). Builder. PAA

Levy, Aaron (1742–1815). Merchant, born the Netherlands. LETA

Levy, Asser (d. 1681?). Pioneer, born the Netherlands. LETA

Levy, Hayman (1721–1789). Fur trader. LETA

Levy, Marv (1928–). Football coach. SLA

Levy, Moses (1757–1826). Jurist. LETA

Levy, Uriah Phillips (1792–1862). Naval officer. ALD; EIA; GEF; GRB-1; LERA; LETA

Lewis, Jerry (Joseph Levitch) (1926–). Comedian. ALC; BUR-1; ED-1†

Lewis, Tillie (1901–1977). Food packing executive. LES-1

Libow, Carol. Lawyer. LETD

Lieberman, Nancy (1958–). Basketball player. SLA

Lindo, Moses (d. 1774). Merchant. LETA

Lindsey, Mortimer (1888–1959). Bowler. SLA

Lipmann, Fritz Albert (1899–1986). Biochemist, born Germany. LET

Litwack, Harry (1907–). Basketball coach, born Austria. SLA

Loeb, Sophie Irene (1876–1929). Journalist, reformer, born Russia. LER

Loewi, Otto (1873–1961). Pharmacologist, born Germany. LET; RIF

Lopez, Aaron (1731–1782). Merchant. LETA

Lubin, David (1849–1919). Agriculturist, born Poland. LETA

Luckman, Sidney (1916–). Football player. ANC; DAFG; DAI; DEH; DUD; DUE; HEI; HOC; RAAD; SLA; SUD

Marcus, Mickey (David Daniel) (1901–1948).
Army officer. LETA; RAE; ROGA

Marshall, Louis (1856–1929). Lawyer. LETA

Martin, Sylvia Wene (1930–). Bowler. HOBA;
SLA

Marx, Chico (Leonard) (1887–1961). Comedian.
BUR-1; COKB; ED-1; MAOB

Marx, Groucho (1890–1977). Comedian. ALC;
BUR-1; ED-1; MAOB

Marx, Gummo (Milton) (1892–1977). Comedian.
BUR-1; MAOB†

Marx, Harpo (Arthur) (1888–1964). Comedian.
BUR-1; ED-1; MAOB

Marx, Zeppo (Herbert) (1901–1979). Comedian.
BUR-1; ED-1; MAOB†

Mattathias (d. 166 B.C.). Hebrew patriot. GEF;
GUA

May, Elaine (1932–). Actress, comedienne, motion picture director. BUR-1; MASB

Mayer, Erskine (1891–1957). Baseball player. RI;
SLA

Mazursky, Paul (1930–). Motion picture director.
SMBB-3

Menuhin, Yehudi (1916–). Violinist. COKA

Meyerhof, Otto Fritz (1884–1951). Physiologist,
born Germany. LET; RIF

Michelson, Albert Abraham (1852–1931). Physicist, born Germany. CAA; FE; GRB-1; LET;
LETA; SIA; STI

Midler, Bette (c. 1945–). Singer, actress. MASB

Miller, Walter (1890–). Jockey. SLA

Mix, Ronald (1938–). Football player. SLA

Moise, Penina (1797–1880). Educator. LER;
LETA

Muller, Hermann Joseph (1890–1967). Geneticist.
BEK; LET; RIF

Myer, Buddy (1904–1974). Baseball player. SLA;
RI

Myers, Laurence E. "Lon" (1858–1899). Track athlete. DAJ; SLA

Myers, Myer (1723–1795). Silversmith. LETA

Myerson, Bess (1924–). Municipal official. BOHF;
GRB-1

Newman, Harry (1909–). Football player. SLA

Nichols, Mike (Igor Peshowsky) (1931–). Comedian, motion picture and theater producer, director, born Germany. BUR-1

Noah, Mordecai Manuel (1785–1851). Journalist.
LERA; LETA; PEB

Nones, Benjamin (1757–1826). American Revolutionary patriot, born France. GEF; LERA

Ochs, Adolph Simon (1858–1935). Journalist.
CUC; LETA

Oppenheimer, Julius Robert (1904–1967). Physicist. ARB; ASB-1; FE; RID

Ormandy, Eugene (1899–1985). Conductor, born
Hungary. EWD; STM; YOM

Papp, Joseph (1921–). Theatrical producer, director. EOA

Peerce, Jan (1904–1984). Singer. GRB-1

Pelty, Barney (1880–1939). Baseball player. SLA

Persky, Daniel (1887–1962). Hebraist, educator,
born Russia. GRB-1

Picon, Molly (1898–). Actress. MASB

Pike, Lipman (1845–1893). Baseball player, manager. SLA

Pilpel, Harriet Fleischl (1911–). Lawyer. SWI

Pincus, Jacob (1838–1918). Jockey. SLA

Podoloff, Maurice (1890–1985). Basketball administrator. SLA

Pulitzer, Joseph (1847–1911). Journalist, born
Hungary. ASB; BEA; CUC; LEM; LOB; LYA;
SQB

Queler, Eve (1936–). Conductor. WA

Rabi, Isidor Isaac (1898–1988). Physicist, born
Austria. GRB-1; LET

Reiner, Carl (1922–). Comedian, motion picture
producer. BUR-1

Reiner, Fritz (1888–1963). Conductor, born Hungary. EWB; STM

Reshevsky, Samuel (1911–). Chess player, born
Poland. LEQB; RHA

Reulbach, Edward (1882–1961). Baseball player.
SLA

Revel, Bernard (1885–1940). Rabbi, educator,
born Russia. KAD; LETA

Rickover, Hyman George (1900–1986). Admiral,
born Russia. COR; GRB-1; KE; NAC; WEB

Rivers, Joan (c. 1935–). Comedienne. MASB

Rodgers, Richard Charles (1902–1979). Composer. BAD; BEKA; EWA; MOA

Rodriguez, Benjamin (fl. 1832). Dentist. LETA

Rogovin, Saul (1923–). Baseball player. RI

Romberg, Sigmund (1887–1951). Composer, born
Hungary. EWA; MOA

Rose, Ernestine Potowski (1810–1892). Feminist,
born Poland. EIA; GUBA; JOCA; LES-2; LETA

Rose, Mauri (1906–1981). Automobile racer.
LEVA; LEX

Rosen, Al (1925–). Baseball player. BUJ; RI; SLA

Rosenberg, Aaron (1912–1979). Football player,
motion picture producer. SLA

Rosenbloom, Maxie (1904–1976). Boxer, actor.
SLA

Rosenfeld, Morris (1862–1923). Poet, born Poland. LETA

Rosenwald, Julius (1862–1932). Merchant, philanthropist. ALD; CUC; LETA

Ross, Barney (1909–1967). Boxer. PIB; PIBA;
SCA; SLA; VAE

Roth, Mark (1951–). Bowler. SLA

Rubinstein, Artur (1889–1982). Pianist, born Poland. GRB-1; MANB; PIAA

Rubinstein, Helena (1870?–1965). Cosmetician, born Poland. LIA

Sabin, Albert Bruce (1906–). Physician, born Russia. CHE†; COLA; RIE

Salk, Jonas Edward (1914–). Physician. ASB-1; BEK; BOB; CHE†; COLA; DU-1; FAA; FE; GRB-1; HEFA; LEG; LETA; RIE; ROA; SIC; SUF; YOA

Salomon, Haym (1740–1785). American Revolutionary patriot, born Poland. ALD; BOK; BUIB†; GRB-1; GUB; HAN†; LERA; LETA; LOB; PEB; SOA

Salvador, Francis (1747–1776). American Revolutionary patriot. GRB-1; LETA

Sampter, Jessie (b. 1883?). Poet, Zionist. ALD

Saperstein, Abraham M. (1903–1966). Basketball coach, owner. SLA

Sarnoff, David (1891–1971). Radio and television executive, born Russia. GRB-1; LAG; LETA

Savitt, Richard (1927–). Tennis player. SLA

Schacht, Al (1892–1984). Baseball player. LIAA†; RI; SLA†

Schayes, Adolph (1928–). Basketball player. BEL; HEHA; HID; PE; RAAB; SLA

Schechter, Solomon (1850–1915). Hebraist, born Romania. GRB-1; GUB; KAD; LERA; LETA; PEB

Schick, Béla (1877–1967). Pediatrician, born Hungary. RIE

Schiff, Jacob Henry (1847–1920). Financier, philanthropist, born Germany. LETA

Schönberg, Arnold (1874–1951). Composer, born Austria. BEKA; BUC; EWAA; KAE; SAA†; YOL

Schreiber, Avery (1935–). Comedian. BUR-1

Schwartz, Arthur (1900–1984). Songwriter. MOA

Sedran, Barney (1891–1969). Basketball player. SLA

Segrè, Emilio Gino (1905–). Physicist, born Italy. LET

Seligman, Joseph (1819–1880). Financier, born Germany. LETA

Seligson, Julius (1909–). Tennis player. SLA

Sendak, Maurice (1928–). Author, illustrator. SM

Seymour, David (1911–1956). Photographer, born Poland. HOE

Shahn, Ben (1898–1969). Painter, born Lithuania. FRA; WIAA

Shalom Aleichem (Solomon Rabinowitz) (1859–1916). Author, born Russia. GRB-1

Shapiro, Irving S. (1916–). Chemical executive. GRB-1

Sheftall, Mordecai (1735–1797). Businessman. BUIB†; LETA

Sherry, Larry (Lawrence) (1935–). Baseball player. GIB; RI; SLA

Sills, Beverly (1929–). Singer. DU-1; GLO; SAB; SC-02

Silverman, Jonathan. Actor. BRF-1

Silvers, Phil (1912–1985). Comedian. ALC

Simon, Neil (1927–). Playwright. GRBA

Simson, Sampson (b. 1780?). Philanthropist. LETA

Singer, Al (1907–1961). Boxer. SLA

Singer, Isaac Bashevis (1904–). Author, born Poland. GRB-1

Slotin, Louis Alexander. Physicist. GEF

Solomon, Harold (1952–). Tennis player. SLA

Solomons, Adolphus Simeon (1826–1910). Publisher. LETA

Sondermann, Fred S. (1923–). Educator, born Germany. CAHA

Spielberg, Steven (1947–). Motion picture director. SMBB-3

Spitz, Mark (1950–). Swimmer. GEDA; GRB-1; LEYB; OCA; SLA; ST-1

Stark, Dolly. Baseball umpire. RI

Stein, Gertrude (1874–1946). Author. KE; MUA; STLA; WABC†

Steinberg, William (1899–1978). Conductor, born Germany. EWD; STM

Steinman, David Barnard (1886–1960). Engineer. LETA

Steinmetz, Charles Proteus (1865–1923). Engineer, born Germany. BEA; COKA; CUC; GRB-1; LOB; LYA

Stern, Elizabeth Gertrude (1890–1954). Author. MAV

Stern, Isaac (1920–). Violinist. EWC

Stern, Otto (1888–1969). Physicist, born Germany. LET

Stiller, Jerry (1928–). Actor, comedian. BUR-1

Stone, George Robert (1876–1945). Baseball player. SLA

Stone, I. F. (Isidor Feinstein) (1907–). Journalist. LETB

Stone, Steve (1947–). Baseball player. AAS-9; RI; SLA

Straus, Nathan (1848–1931). Merchant, philanthropist, born Germany. ALD; GRB-1; LETA; PEB

Straus, Oscar Solomon (1850–1926). Diplomat. LETA

Sutro, Adolph Heinrich Joseph (1830–1898). Mining engineer, born Germany. LETA; YOG

Swope, Gerard (1872–1957). Engineering executive, philanthropist. GRB-1

Szold, Henrietta (1860–1945). Zionist leader. BLF; GUB; KAD; LES; LETA

Szold, Robert (1889–1977). Lawyer, philanthropist. GRB-1

Teacher, Brian (1954–). Tennis player. SLA

Teltscher, Eliot (1959–). Tennis player. SLA

Touro, Judah (1775–1854). Philanthropist. ALD; GUB; LERA; LETA; PEB

Tucker, Richard (1913–1975). Singer. BRBB-1

Viorst, Judith. Author. BOHD

Vladeck, Baruch Charney (1886–1938). Journalist, born Russia. GEF

Wahle, Otto (1880–1965). Swimmer, born Austria. SLA

Waksman, Selman Abraham (1888–1973). Microbiologist, born Russia. GRB-1; LET; LETA; LIA; RIF

Wald, Lillian D. (1867–1940). Social worker. ALD; BRBE†; CAGA; DOD; EIA; GEE; GIBA; GRB-1; LETA; WABC†; WRA; YOB

Warburg, Paul Moritz (1868–1923). Banker, born Germany. LETA

Weill, Kurt (1900–1950). Composer, born Germany. EWA

Weinberger, Eric (1932–). Civil rights worker. COF

Wiener, Norbert (1894–1964). Mathematician. KE; STN

Wittenberg, Henry B. (1918–). Wrestler. SLA

Wolf, Phil (1869–1936). Bowler, born Germany. SLA

Wouk, Herman (1915–). Author. GRB-1

Yalow, Rosalyn Sussman (1921–). Physicist. GIB-1; GL; GRB-1; HA-1; SHFE

Yellen, Jack (1892–). Songwriter, born Poland. MOA

Foreign

Abrahams, Harold (1899–1978). English track athlete. SLA

Agnon, Shmuel Yosef (1888–1970). Israeli author. GRB-1; ROGA

Aguilar, Grace (1816–1847). English author. LER; PEB

Allon, Yigal (1918–1980). Israeli general. GRB-1; ROGA

Anilewicz, Mordecai (1919–1943). Polish resistance worker. GRB-1

Ashkenasi, Shmuel (1941–). Israeli violinist. EWC

Asser, Tobias M. C. (1838–1913). Dutch statesman. LET; MEC†; WIC

Baeyer, Adolf von (1835–1917). German chemist. LET

Bar-Ilan, David (1930–). Israeli pianist. EWC

Bárány, Robert (1876–1936). Austrian physician. LET

Barenboim, Daniel (1942–). Israeli pianist. EWC

Barna, Gyozo Victor (1911–1972). English table tennis player, born Hungary. SLA

Begin, Menachem (1913–). Israeli ex-prime minister, born Poland. ASB-1; GRB-1; HAGD

Ben-Gurion, David (1886–1973). Israeli prime minister. GRB-1; GUB; KE; KEF; ROGA; WEA

Ben-Porat, Miriam (1918–). Israeli Supreme Court justice, born Lithuania. GRB-1

Ben Yehudah, Eliezer (1858–1922). Lithuanian Hebraist. GRB-1; GUB; PEB; ROGA

Ben-Zvi, Yitzhak (1884–1963). President of Israel, born Russia. GRB-1

Benjamin of Tudela (d. 1173). Spanish traveler. LES

Bergson, Henri (1859–1941). French philosopher. LET

Bialik, Chaim Nachman (1873–1934). Russian Hebrew poet. GEF; GRB-1; GUB; KAD; PEB

Blum, Léon (1872–1950). French statesman. ARAA

Born, Max (1882–1970). German physicist. LET

Botvinnik, Mikhail M. (1911–). Russian chess player. LEQB

Branover, Herman (1931–). Israeli physicist, educator, born Russia. GRB-1

Brockman, Shimson (1958–). Israeli boat racer. SLA

Brody, Tal (1943–). Israeli basketball player, born U.S. SLA

Bronowski, Jacob (1908–1974). English mathematician, author, born Poland. GRB-1

Buxton, Angela (1934–). English tennis player. SLA

Chagall, Marc (1887–1985). Russian painter. GRB-1; WIAA

Chain, Ernst Boris (1906–1979). English biochemist, born Germany. BEK†; COLA†; GRB-1; LAE; LET; POB; RIF

Cohen, Eli (1924–1965). Israeli spy, born Egypt. GRB-1

Colonne, Edouard (1838–1910). French conductor. YOM

Crémieux, Isaac-Adolphe (1796–1880). French statesman. KAD

Cresques Lo Juheu (fl. 1375). Spanish mapmaker. GEF

David. Israeli pilgrim, born Yemen. GRB-1

Dayan, Moshe (1915–1981). Israeli foreign minister. ROGA; GRB-1; WECA

Dreyfus, Alfred (1859–1935). French soldier. PEB

Dreyfus, René (1905–). French automobile racer. SLA

Ehrenburg, Ilya Grigoryevich (1891–1967). Russian author. KE

Ehrlich, Paul (1854–1915). German bacteriologist. AAS-31; ASA; BEK; DEB; FE; LET; POB; RIE; RIF; ROA; SUF

Eisenberg, Shaul (1921–). Israeli businessman, born Germany. GRB-1

Eliav, Aryeh Lyova (1921–). Israeli political figure, born Russia. GRB-1

Eshkol, Levi (1895–1969). Israeli prime minister, born Russia. GRB-1

Félix, Elisa Rachel (1821–1858). French actress, born Switzerland. LER; PEB

Flatow, Alfred (b. 1869). German gymnast. SLA

Frank, Anne (1919–1945). German Nazi victim, author. ELA; FOR; GRB-1

Freier, Recha (1892–). Israeli resistance leader, born Germany. GRB-1

Freud, Anna (1895–1982). English psychiatrist, born Austria. CHE

Freud, Sigmund (1856–1939). Austrian psychiatrist. ASB-1; CHD; FRE; KE; POD; RIB; ROA; WEF

Fried, Alfred Hermann (1864–1921). Austrian pacifist. LET; MEC†; WIC

Friedlander, Ethan (1957–). Israeli boat racer. SLA

Glickstein, Shlomo (1958–). Israeli tennis player. SLA

Grossman, Noam (1927–). Israeli soldier. GEF

Haber, Fritz (1868–1934). German chemist. FE; LET

Haffkine, Waldemar Mordecai (1860–1930). Russian bacteriologist. GEF; GRB-1

Hajos-Guttman, Alfred (1878–1955). Hungarian swimmer. SLA

Heine, Heinrich (1797–1856). German poet. PEB

Helena. Mesopotamian queen, convert to Judaism. LER

Herschel, Caroline (1750–1848). English astronomer, born Germany. COLA†; NOA; PAC; SC†

Herschel, Sir William (1738–1822). English astronomer, born Germany. BOB; COLA; FE; LAA; PAC; PIA; SIA; SUE

Hertz, Gustav (1887–1975). German physicist. LET

Hertz, Heinrich Rudolf (1857–1894). German physicist. CAA; COLA; FE; SHFB; SIA; SOB

Herzl, Theodor (1860–1904). Hungarian author, Zionist. GRB-1; GUB; KAB; KAD; LERA; LES; PEB; ROGA

Hevesy, George de (1885–1966). Hungarian chemist. LET

Heyse, Paul Johann (1830–1914). German author. LET

Hirsch, Clara de (1833–1899). Belgian philanthropist. LER

Jabotinsky, Vladimir (1880–1940). Russian Zionist. GRB-1

Joachim, Joseph (1831–1907). Hungarian violinist, composer. CHFA

Judah ha-Levi (c. 1085–1140). Spanish Hebrew poet, rabbi, physician. GEF; GRB-1; GUA; KAC; LERA; LES

Katz, Elias (1901–1947). Finnish track athlete. SLA

Keleti, Agnes (1921–). Israeli gymnast, born Hungary. SLA

Kirszenstein-Szewinska, Irena (1946–). Polish track athlete, born Russia. SLA

Kluger, Ruth. Israeli rescue worker, born Rumania. GRB-1

Korczak, Janus (1878–1942). Polish physician. GRB-1

Krebs, Sir Hans Adolf (1900–1981). English biochemist, born Germany. LET

Kuchler, Lena. Israeli child psychologist, born Poland. GRB-1

Landowska, Wanda (1877–1959). Polish harpsichordist. FOG

Lasker, Emanuel (1868–1941). German chess player. LEQB; RHA

Lemkin, Raphael (1900–). Polish lawyer. BAF

Lenglen, Suzanne (1899–1938). French tennis player. DAG; DAGA; FR-1; HI; HOBAA; LAHA; SUDA†

Lévi-Strauss, Claude (1908–). French anthropologist. HAO

Lewis, Ted "Kid" (1894–1970). English boxer. SLA

Lippmann, Gabriel (1845–1921). French physicist. LET

Lopez, Roderigo (1525–1594). Portuguese physician. MAR

Lubetkin, Tzivia (1914–1978). Israeli resistance leader, born Poland. GRB-1

Markova, Alicia (1910–). English dancer. ATA

Meir, Golda (1898–1978). Israeli prime minister. GI; GRB-1; KE†; KOA; LIDA; ROGA

Meitner, Lise (1878–1968). Swedish physicist, born Austria. HA-1; RID†; SC†; YOF

Mendele Mocher Sefarim (Shalom Abramovich) (1835–1917). Russian author. GRB-1

Mendelsohn, Eric (1887–1953). English architect, born Germany. FOF; LEDA

Mendesia, Gracia (1510–1568). Portuguese philanthropist. LER; LES

Mendoza, Daniel (1764–1836). English boxer. SLA

Metchnikoff, Élie (1845–1916). Russian bacteriologist. COL; DEB; LET; RIF; ROA; SOB

Milhaud, Darius (1892–1974). French composer. KAE

Modigliani, Amedeo (1884–1920). Italian painter. KAA

Moissan, Henri (1852–1907). French chemist. LET

Montefiore, Sir Moses (1784–1885). English philanthropist. GRB-1; KAB; KAD; LERA; LES; PEB

Moscheles, Ignaz (1794–1870). Czech composer. CHF

Nachmanides. Spanish philosopher. LERA

Nasi, Joseph (1510–1579). Portuguese statesman. GUB; KAB; PEB

Navon, Yitzhak (1921–). President of Israel. GRB-1

Netanyahu, Yonatan (1946–1976). Israeli army officer. GRB-1

Nunoz, Maria (fl. 1590). Portuguese émigré. LER

Offenbach, Jacques (1819–1880). French composer. KAE

Okker, Tom (1944–). Dutch tennis player. SLA

Orlean, Judah Leib. Polish educator. GEF

Paray, Paul (b. 1886). French conductor. STM

Peretz, Isaac Leib (1852–1915). Polish Yiddish author. GEF

Reich, Haviva (1914–1944). Czech resistance worker. LAD

Reichstein, Tadeus (1897–). Swiss organic chemist, born Poland. LET; RIF

Rosen, Goody (Goodwin) (1912–). Canadian baseball player. RI

Rosenfeld, Fanny (1903–1969). Canadian track athlete, born Russia. SLA

Roth, Esther (1952–). Israeli track athlete. SLA

Rothschild, Edmond de (1845–1934). French financier. KAD

Rothschild, Mayer Amschel (1743–1812). German financier. PEB

Rozeanu, Angelica (1921–). Romanian table tennis player. SLA

Rubenstein, Louis (1861–1931). Canadian skater. SLA

Rubinstein, Anton (1829–1894). Russian pianist, composer. CHF

Sachs, Nelly (1891–1970). Swedish poet, born Germany. SHFE

Samuel ibn Adiya (fl. 540). Arabian poet. GEF

Scheckter, Jody (1950–). South African automobile racer. OLCB; SLA

Senesh, Hannah (1921–1944). Israeli underground leader, born Hungary. GEF; GRB-1; LAD; STP; ROGA

Sereni, Enzo (1905–1944). Italian resistance worker. GRB-1; LAD

Shulamith (fl. 930 B.C.). Palestinian woman. LER

Sokolow, Nahum (1859–1936). English journalist, Zionist, born Poland. GRB-1

Soutine, Chaim (1894–1943). French painter, born Lithuania. WIAA

Spinoza, Baruch or Benedict (1632–1677). Dutch philosopher. LERA; LO; OZA; PEB

Szekely, Eva (1927–). Hungarian swimmer. SLA

Tamm, Igor Yevgenyvich (1895–1971). Russian physicist. LET

Torres, Luis de (fl. 1492). Spanish interpreter. GUB; LETA; PEB

Trotsky, Leon (1877–1940). Russian communist leader. COJB; NEBB-1

Trumpeldor, Joseph (1880–1920). Israeli settler. GRB-1; PEB; ROGA

Wallach, Otto (1847–1931). German chemist. LET

Walter, Bruno (1876–1962). German conductor. EWB; STM; YOM

Warburg, Otto Heinrich (1883–1970). German physiologist. LET

Wassermann, Jakob (1873–1934). German author. PEB

Weizmann, Chaim (1874–1952). President of Israel. DEI; DEJ; GEF; GRAB-1; GUB; KAB; KAD; LES; ROGA

Wiesenthal, Simon (1908–). Austrian Nazi hunter, born Poland. GRB-1

Willstätter, Richard (1872–1942). German chemist. LET

Yadin, Yigael (1917–1984). Israeli archaeologist. GRB-1; POC; ROGA

Yoffe, Avraham (1880–1960). Israeli ecologist. GRB-1

Zangwill, Israel (1864–1926). English author. LERA; PEB

JOCKEYS

Arcaro, Eddie (1916–). ASBA; DAG; DAGA; LYD

Bacon, Mary (1950?–). HOBAA

Cauthen, Steve (1960–). HOCG

Farber, Bea. FOC-1

Hartack, Bill (1932–). DEHA-1

Kusner, Kathy (1940?–). GUED; HOBA; HOBAA; RYA

McCreary, Conn. BUJA

Miller, Walter (1890–). SLA

Murphy, Isaac (1856–1896). HOBC

Pincus, Jacob (1838–1918). SLA

Richards, Sir Gordon (1904–1986). English. DAG; DAGA

Sande, Earl (1898–1968). DAG

Shoemaker, Willie (1931–). ASBA; DAG; DAGA

Sloan, Tod (James Forman) (1874–1933). DAG

Smith, Robyn C. (1944?–). ST-2

JORDANIANS

Hussein Ibn Talal (1935–). King. HAGD; KEF

JOURNALISTS

Abbott, Robert Sengstacke (1870–1940). Founded *Chicago Defender*. ADA; ADB; HUA; ROG; STO

Adams, Franklin Pierce (1881–1960). Columnist. ALA

Ballard, Audreen. STAA

Barnard, Kate (1875–1930). PACB; TRD; VIA

Barnett, Claude Albert (1889–1967). ADB

Barnett, Ida Wells (1862–1931). ADB; BRBE†; BUFA; HUB; LOAV; PACB; PECA; ROG; STAB-1; TRD

Benét, William Rose (1886–1950). BEF

Berger, Meyer (1898–1959). LEU

Bernstein, Carl (1944–). LETB

Black, Winifred (1863–1936). JAE

Bok, Edward William (1863–1930). Editor, born the Netherlands. BOD; CAGA; CUC; FLBA; LOB

Broun, Heywood Campbell (1888–1939). LEU

Brown, Warren (1948?–). STAA

Buchwald, Art (1925–). LEU

Caldwell, Earl (1938?–). STAA

Cannon, Jimmy (1909–1973). BELB

Cary, Mary Ann Shadd (1823–1893). LOAV; WABC†

Cochrane, Elizabeth (1867–1922). JAE; JOCA; SQB; WAE

Conaway, James Bennett. STAA

Conde, Carlos. NEAA

Connor, Patrick Edward (1820–1891). (Born Ireland). SEC

Cornish, Samuel E. (19th century). BEJ

Craig, Daniel (1814–1895). SQB

Creelman, James (1859–1915). FLBB

Curry, George E. STAA

Daly, Thomas Augustine (1871–1948). BEH

Davis, Richard Harding (1864–1916). FLBB; JAD

Day, Dorothy (1897–1980). BLF; COG-1; NIA; ROJ

Dodge, Mary Mapes (1831–1905). BEI; COB; STJ; YOC

Door, Rheta Childe (1872–1948). JAE

Dotson, John L., Jr. STAA

Draughon, Roland (1947–). STAA

Drummond, William J. (1945?–). STAA

Du Bois, William Edward Burghardt (1868–1963). ADA; ADB; BEJ; BRB; BRBD; DABB; DOF-1; GRAB-01; PECA; RICA; ROG; STB; STJB; STO; YOI

Ducommun, Élie (1833–1906). Swiss. MEC†; WIC

Dunbar, Ernest. STAA

Duncan, Marilyn I. (1945?–). STAA

Fallaci, Oriana (1930–). Italian. LETB

Field, Eugene (1850–1895). BEE; BEF; BEH; LEJ; LEOB

Gibbons, Floyd Phillips (1887–1939). FLBB

Goddard, Mary Katherine (1736–1816). YOC

Grady, Henry Woodfin (1850–1889). SQB

Graham, Katharine Meyer (1917–). BOHD

Greeley, Horace (1811–1872). ARB; FLBA; LEC; MAL; SQB; WHD

Greeley-Smith, Nixola (1880–1919). JAE

Green, Abel (1900–1973). LEU

Hearst, William Randolph (1863–1951). ARAA; COKB; CUC

Hicks, Nancy. STAA

Higgins, Marguerite (1920–1966). ARBA; FLBB; JAD; JAE

Hunter-Gault, Charlayne (1942?–). GLO; STAA

Jackson, David L. (1940?–). STAA

Jackson, Solomon Henry (d. 1847). (Born England). LETA

Johnson, John H. (1918–). ADA; ADB; DOF-1; DRA; PAA; STAA†

Johnson, Thomas A. (1928–). STAA

Johnston, Ernest, Jr. (1939?–). STAA

Kieran, John Francis (1892–1981). FOE

Kilgallen, Dorothy (1913–1965). JAE

Kuhn, Irene Corbally (1900–). JAE

Lippmann, Walter (1889–1974). FOE

Loeb, Sophie Irene (1876–1929). (Born Russia). LER

Lomax, Almena. STAA

Lubis, Mochtar (1922–). Indonesian. RODA

McCormick, Anne O'Hare (1881–1954). CLA; WABC†

McFadden, Bernarr (1868–1955). Founded *Physical Culture*. COKB

MacGahan, Januarius Aloysius (1844–1878). FLBB

McGill, Ralph Emerson (1898–1969). FLBA

Marín Solá, Ramón (1832–1902). Puerto Rican. TU

Mencken, Henry Louis (1880–1956). BEG

Mitchell, John R., Jr. (1863–1929). GRAB-01

Moneta, Ernesto Teodoro (1833–1918). Italian. MEC†; WIC

Moyers, William D. (1934–). GRBA

Murphy, Carl James (1889–1967). DOF-1

Ng Poon Chew (1866–1931). (Born China). CUC

Noah, Mordecai Manuel (1785–1851). LERA; LETA; PEB

Ochs, Adolph Simon (1858–1935). CUC; LETA

Palmer, L. F., Jr. (1923?–). STAA
Patterson, Lawrence Patrick. STAA
Perry, Jean. STAA
Pintong, Nilawan (1916–). Thai. RODA
Porter, Sylvia (1913–). BOHG; GIB-1; LEU
Poston, Ted (1906–). STAA
Pulitzer, Joseph (1847–1911). (Born Hungary).
    ASB; BEA; CUC; LEM; LOB; LYA; SQB
Pyle, Ernest Taylor (1900–1945). FAA; FIA;
    FLBB; FOE; JAD; LEU; SQB
Raab, Selwyn (1934?–). LETB
Raspberry, William J. (1935?–). STAA
Raymond, Arthur. GRAC
Reston, James Barrett (1909–). (Born Scotland).
    LEU
Reynolds, Quentin (1902–1965). JAD
Riis, Jacob August (1849–1914). (Born Denmark).
    FLBA; LOB; MEB
Robinson, Harry A. (1942–). STAA
Rodale, Jerome Irving (1898–1971). SQA
Ross, Ruth N. STAA
Russell, Charles Edward (1860–1941). COGB
Russell, Sir William Howard (1820–1907). FLBB
Russwurm, John B. (1799–1851). ADB; BEJ
St. Johns, Adela Rogers (1894–). JAE
Sanborn, Franklin Benjamin (1831–1917). WOAA
Schurz, Carl (1829–1906). (Born Germany). CUB;
    LEB; LOB; STH
Scott, Austin. STAA
Scripps, Edward Wyllis (1854–1926). CUC; SQB
Seltzer, Louis (1897–1980). PAA
Sheehy, Gail (1937–). LETB
Simms, Jacob E. STAA
Smalley, George Washburn (1833–1916). FLBB
Smith, Red (Walter Wellesley) (1905–1982). LEU
Sokolow, Nahum (1859–1936). English Zionist,
    born Poland. GRB-1
Solomons, Adolphus Simeon (1826–1910). LETA
Stanley, Sir Henry Morton (1841–1904). Welsh.
    COC; LAA-1; ROL; SQB; WIA-1
Steffens, Lincoln (Joseph Lincoln) (1866–1936).
    COGB; SQB; WECB
Stone, I. F. (Isidor Feinstein) (1907–). LETB
Strong, Anna Louise (1885–1970). NIA
Swisshelm, Jane Grey (1815–1884). JAE
Taylor, Bert Leston (1866–1921). ALA
Taylor, John L. STAA
Thomas, Lowell Jackson (1892–1981). JAD; LEN
Thompson, Dorothy (1894–1961). JAE; MUA
Thompson, Era Bell (fl. 1946). DADB
Vann, Robert Lee (1887–1940). ADA; ADB
Vlachos, Helen (1912?–). Greek. CAHA
Vladeck, Baruch Charney (1886–1938). (Born Rus-
    sia). GEF
Vorse, Mary Heaton (1874–1966). BI
Washington, Betty. STAA

Watterson, Henry (1840–1921). SQB
White, William Allen (1868–1944). COKA; FOE;
    SQB
Wing, Henry (1840–1925). FLBB
Wirges, Gene. EOA
Wittenberg, Henri E. STAA
Woodward, Robert Upshur (1943–). LETB
Yette, Samuel F. (1929–). STAA
Zenger, Anna (1704–1751). GEE; WABC†
Zenger, John Peter (1697–1746). (Born Germany).
    ARB; CUB; CUC; FIA; LOB; MEB; SQB

JUDGES, see JURISTS

JURISTS

Allen, Florence Ellinwood (1884–1966). WHE
Bedford, Gunning (1747–1812). BUIB†; FEAA
Ben-Porat, Miriam (1918–). Israeli Supreme
    Court justice, born Lithuania. GRB-1
Blair, John (1732–1800). Supreme Court justice.
    BUIB†; FEAA
Brandeis, Louis Dembitz (1856–1941). Supreme
    Court justice. ALD; EIA; FLC; GEF; GRB-1;
    GUB; LETA
Brearly, David (1745–1790). BUIB†; FEAA
Cardozo, Benjamin Nathan (1870–1938). Su-
    preme Court justice. FLC
Chase, Salmon Portland (1808–1873). Supreme
    Court justice. FLC
Chase, Samuel (1741–1811). Supreme Court jus-
    tice. BAEA; BUIB†; COJ; FEAB; MAC
Coleman, Mary Stallings. SWI
Donlon, Mary Honor. CLA
Ellsworth, Oliver (1745–1807). Supreme Court
    justice. FEAA
Erskine, Thomas (1750–1823). English. COG
Field, Stephen Johnson (1816–1899). Supreme
    Court justice. FLC
Frankfurter, Felix (1882–1965). Supreme Court
    justice, born Austria. LIA; LOB
Gibbs, Mifflin W. (1828–1903). KADB
Ginsburg, Ruth Bader (1933–). GIB-1; SWI
Goldberg, Arthur J. (1908–). LETA; WEC
Harlan, John Marshall (1833–1911). Supreme
    Court justice. STJC
Hastie, William Henry (1904–1976). ADA†;
    ADB†; DOF-1
Holmes, Oliver Wendell, Jr. (1841–1935). Su-
    preme Court justice. COKA; CUC; FLC; MEB;
    RED
Hufstedler, Shirley (1925–). GIB-1

Hughes, Charles Evans (1862–1948). Supreme
Court justice. FLC; HEEA; KEC†; WHD†
Ingersoll, Jared (1749–1822). BUIB†; FEAA
Iredell, James (1751–1799). Supreme Court jus-
tice. SEC
Jay, John (1745–1829). Supreme Court justice.
FLC
Jiagge, Annie. Ghanaian. CRA
Johnson, Thomas (1732–1819). Supreme Court
justice. SEC
Kearse, Amalya (1937–). GLO
Keith, Damon Jerome (1922–). DOF-1
Lansing, John, Jr. (1754–1829). FEAA
Levy, Moses (1757–1826). LETA
Marshall, John (1755–1835). Supreme Court jus-
tice. BUIB; CUC; DEI; DEJ; FLC; FOB; LOA;
MAL; OLA; STH
Marshall, Thurgood (1908–). Supreme Court jus-
tice. ADA; ADB; BRG; DOF-1; FAG; FLC; FLD;
STF; WEC; YOI
Motley, Constance Baker (1921–). DU; FLD; GIB-
1; STLA; YOI
O'Connor, Sandra Day (1930–). Supreme Court
justice. DU-1; SMBB; WHE
Parsons, Theophilus (1750–1813). SEC
Paterson, William (1745–1806). Supreme Court
justice. BUIB†; FEAA
Polier, Justine Wise (1903–). GIB-1
Renault, Louis (1843–1918). French. MEC†; WIC
Rutledge, John (1739–1800). BUIB†; FEAA
Scott, Irene Feagin (1912–). SWI
Spalding, Burleigh Folsom (1853–1934). SEC
Story, Joseph (1779–1845). Supreme Court jus-
tice. FLC
Taft, William Howard (1857–1930). BAEB; BAG;
BAG-1; BEB; BLA; BUIA; CAG; CAH; COI;
COS; DUB; DUC; DUCA; FLC; FRBA; HIH;
LAI; LEQ; LEQA; MAB; MABA; MIA; PED;
ROH; ROHA; ROK†; SUBB; WHD
Taney, Roger Brooke (1777–1864). Supreme
Court justice. FLC
Waring, Julius Waties (1880–1968). STJB
Warren, Earl (1891–1974). Supreme Court jus-
tice. FLC; WEB
White, Byron Raymond (1917–). Supreme Court
justice. DAFG; DAI; HIE; HOBB; HOC
Wright, Jonathan Jasper (1840–1885). ADA; ADB
Yates, Robert (1738–1801). FEAA

KENYANS

Keino, Kipchoge (1940–). Track athlete. AAS-26;
LEYB†
Kenyatta, Jomo (1893?–1978). Prime minister.
ADA; KEF

Kenyatta, Margaret Wambui (1928–). Mayor.
CRA
Mboya, Thomas Joseph (1930–1969). Minister of
justice. ADA; KE; POA
Mockerie, Parmenas (1900–). Teacher. PEA

KINGS, *see* RULERS

KOREANS

Kim Yong-gi. Agriculturist. RODA

LABOR LEADERS

American
Bagley, Sarah G. (fl. 1835–1847). WABC
Chavez, Cesar Estrada (1927–). DU-1; FOW; HAJ;
NEAA; WO
Debs, Eugene Victor (1855–1926). ARB; SEA;
WECB
Dubinsky, David (1892–1982). (Born Poland).
BEA; COH; DABA; LEHA; LIA; SEA
Flynn, Elizabeth Gurley (1890–1964). ARAA
Gompers, Samuel (1850–1924). (Born England).
ARAA; BEA; COH; CUC; DABA; FAC; FOB;
GRB-1; LEHA; LETA; LOB; MAL; MEB; SEA
Green, William (1873–1952). COH; DABA; LEHA;
SEA
Haywood, William Dudley (1869–1928). COH;
DABA; LEHA; SEA
Hillman, Sidney (1887–1946). (Born Lithuania).
COH; DABA; SEA
Huerta, Dolores (1930–). BI; BOHF; DI; NEAA
Jones, Mary Harris (1830–1930). (Born Ireland).
BI; BRBE†; GEE; MAV; NIA; PACA; TRD;
WABC†
Lewis, John Llewellyn (1880–1969). COH; DABA;
FAC; LEHA; SEA
May, Emmett M. BOG
Meany, George (1894–1980). DABA; DU-1; LEHA;
SEA
Murray, Philip (1886–1952). (Born Scotland).
BEA; COH; DABA; SEA
Myers, Isaac (1835–1891). ADB; GRAB-01
Powderly, Terence Vincent (1849–1924). COH;
DABA; LEHA; SEA
Randolph, Asa Philip (1889–1979). ADA; ADB;
BRG; COH; DABA; DADA; DOF-1; FLD;
GRAB-01; HUA; LEHA; RIC; RICA; SEA; STF;
WIAA-8; YOI

Reuther, Walter Philip (1907–1970). COH; DABA; LEHA; SEA; WEC

Sylvis, William H. (1828–1869). COH; DABA; LEHA; SEA

Wyatt, Addie (1924–). BI; GIB-1

English

Brine, James (1812–1902). LAD
Hammett, James (fl. 1830). LAD
Loveless, George (fl. 1830). LAD
Loveless, James (fl. 1830). LAD
Standfield, John (fl. 1830). LAD
Standfield, Thomas (fl. 1830). LAD

LATIN AMERICANS, *see* INDIVIDUAL COUNTRIES

LATVIANS

Tal, Mikhail (1936–). Chess player. LEQB

LAW ENFORCERS

Armas, Jay J. (1933?–). Private investigator. HAFA

Baca, Elfego (1865–1945). Sheriff. BENA

Bertillon, Alphonse (1853–1914). French. FE; LACA; LID

Chenkin, George B. (1897?–1962). Detective. LACA

Courtright, T. I. (1848–1887). Marshal. SUI

Earp, Wyatt Berry Stapp (1848–1929). COE; SUI

Fabian, Robert (1901–1978). English. LID

Faurot, Joseph A. (1872–1942). LACA

Garrett, Patrick Floyd (1850–1908). SUI

Goron, Marie-François (1847–1933). French. LID

Guzman, Virginia Quintana (1940?–). Police-woman. SMBC-3

Henry, Sir Edward Richart, bart (1850–1931). Commissioner of Scotland Yard. LACA

Hickok, Wild Bill (James Butler) (1837–1876). Marshal. COE; SUI

Higgins, Maureen Anne. F.B.I. agent. SMBC-3

Hoover, J. Edgar (1895–1972). Director of F.B.I. COKA; COKB; LAC; LACA; LID

Kandler, Elizabeth Aytes. Superintendent of corrections. SMBC-3

Karansky, Priscilla Pepper. Mounted police officer. SMBC-3

Lawrence, Geraldine Anderson. Border Patrol agent. SMBC-3

McNamara, Rae Hassell. State director of prisons. SMBC-3

Madsen, Chris (1852–1944). (Born Denmark). SUI

Masterson, Bat (William Barclay) (1853–1921). SUI

Morris, Kathryn Harper. Airport security agent. SMBC-3

Mossman, Burton C. (1867–1956). WAA

Murray, John Wilson (b. 1840). Scottish. LID

Neil, Arthur Fowler. English. LID

Pence, Donna Marie. Narcotics agent. SMBC-3

Pinkerton, Allan (1819–1884). (Born Scotland). FOA; LACA; LID; SUI

Reeves, Bass (1840–1910). KADB

Schimmel, Gertrude (1918–). WA

Schindler, Raymond Campbell (1882–1959). LID

Siringo, Charles A. (1855–1928). FOC; KAW; SUI

Slaughter, John H. (1841–1922). KAW

Smith, Thomas James (1840–1870). SUI

Sprecher, Jenna Garman. Marine patrol officer. SMBC-3

Stanton, Susan Marie. Jailer. SMBC-3

Texas Rangers (Est. 1835). SUI

Tilghman, William Matthew (1854–1924). JOD; SUI

United States Bureau of Narcotics. LID

Vidocq, Eugène François (1775–1857). French. LACA; LID

LAWYERS

See also JURISTS

Badillo, Herman (1929–). FOW; NEBB; WO

Bellows, Carole Kamin (1935–). SWI

Benjamin, Judah Philip (1811–1884). LETA

Bennett, Robert LaFollette (1912–). GRAC

Beshar, Christine (1929–). (Born Germany). SMBB

Broege, Carl. LETD

Brown, Louise (1943–). SMBB

Burke, Yvonne Brathwaite (1932–). BOHF; FOC-1; WIAA-02

Clark, Beverly. FOC-1

Clyne, Bernie (1931?–). LETD

Cohen, Maxwell (1908–). UN

Darrow, Clarence Seward (1857–1938). LAC; WECB

Davie, William Richardson (1756–1820). (Born England). FEAA

Donovan, William Joseph (1883–1959). ARD; FAA

Ginsburg, Ruth Bader (1933–). GIB-1; SWI

Graff, Sunny. AT

Grimké, Archibald Henry (1849–1930). DOF-1; ROG

Halpern, Charlie. LETD
Hills, Carla Anderson (1934–). SWI
Houston, Charles Hamilton (1895–1950). ADA†;
 ADB†; DOF-1
Houston, Temple. SUI
Huber, Linda. LETD
Hufstedler, Shirley (1925–). GIB-1
Ingersoll, Robert Green (1833–1899). WECB
Kennedy, Robert Francis (1925–1968). LAI†;
 WEC
Kline, Tony. LETD
LaFontant, Jewel Stradford (1922–). SWI
Langford, Anna Riggs (1917–). DRA; DU
Lemkin, Raphael (1900–). Polish. BAF
Libow, Carol. LETD
Lockwood, Belva Ann (1830–1917). BOJ; WABC
Mandela, Nelson (1918–). South African. DU-1;
 LEA
Marquette, Turner (1829–1894). SEC
Marshall, Louis (1856–1929). LETA
Martin, Luther (1748–1792). FEAA
Mentschikoff, Soia (1915–). SMBB; SWI
Moore, Beverly. LETD
Murphy, Betty Southard (1929?–). SWI
Nader, Ralph (1934–). DU-1; EOA; GRBA
Norton, Eleanor Holmes (1937–). GIB-1; LETD;
 WA
Owens, Elisabeth. SWI
Pilpel, Harriet Fleischl (1911–). SWI
Pinckney, Charles Cotesworth (1746–1825).
 BUIB†; FEAA; WHD†
Raggio, Louise Ballerstedt (1919–). SWI
Ruiz Belvis, Segundo (1829–1867). Puerto Rican.
 TU
Saunders, Suzanne. HOD-1
Smythe, John H. (1844–1908). ADA; ADB
Stender, Fay. LETD
Stewart, William Morris (1827–1909). YOG
Szold, Robert (1889–1977). GRB-1
Thelwell, Jeanne (1951–). SMBB
Webster, Daniel (1782–1852). DEI; DEJ; HEEA;
 KEC; KED; LEC; STH
Willkie, Wendell Lewis (1892–1944). WHD
Yancey, William Lowndes (1814–1863). COGA
Zawisza, Christina (1947–). SMBB

LEADERS OF COUNTRIES, *see* PRESIDENTS, U.S.;
STATESMEN, FOREIGN

LEGISLATORS, U.S.

Abzug, Bella (1920–). Congresswoman. GIB-1;
 GRAB-1†

Atwood, Genevieve (1946–). State legislator.
 WIAA-02
Badillo, Herman (1929–). Congressman. FOW;
 NEBB; WO
Baldwin, Abraham (1754–1807). Senator. BUIB†;
 FEAA
Bassett, Richard (1745–1815). Senator. BUIB†;
 FEAA
Benjamin, Judah Philip (1811–1884). Senator.
 LETA
Benton, Thomas Hart (1782–1858). Senator, con-
 gressman. KEC; KED
Bibb, William Wyatt (1781–1820). Senator, con-
 gressman. SEC
Blount, William (1749–1800). Congressman, sena-
 tor. BUIB†; FEAA; MAO
Bond, Julian (1940–). State legislator. BRGA; DU
Bradley, Bill (William Warren) (1943–). Senator.
 BOHA; BRE; HOC; PAW
Brooke, Edward William (1919–). Senator. ADB;
 DOF-1; DU†; FAG; FLD; LEI; YOI
Bruce, Blanche K. (1841–1898). Senator. ADA;
 ADB; BRB; BU; PECA; STD; YOI
Bryan, William Jennings (1860–1925). Congress-
 man. GO; WHD
Burke, Yvonne Brathwaite (1932–). Congress-
 woman, lawyer. BOHF; FOC-1; WIAA-02
Butler, Pierce (1744–1822). Senator. BUIB†;
 FEAA
Cain, Richard H. (1825–1887). Congressman.
 ADA; ADB
Calhoun, John Caldwell (1782–1850). Senator,
 congressman. FEA; HAOA; HOEA; KEC†;
 STH
Carroll, Daniel (1730–1796). Congressman.
 BUIB†; FEAA
Chisholm, Shirley (1924–). Congresswoman.
 BRGA; COG-1; DRA; DU; FLD; GIBA; ROJ;
 WHE; YOI
Clay, Henry (1777–1852). Statesman. GO; HEEA;
 STH; WHD
Conyers, John, Jr. (1929–). Congressman. BRGA;
 DU†; YOI
Dayton, Jonathan (1760–1824). Senator. BUIB†;
 FEAA
De Priest, Oscar (1871–1951). Congressman. ADA;
 ADB; YOI
Dodge, Henry (1782–1867). Senator. SEC
Donnelly, Ignatius (1831–1901). Congressman.
 LEO
Elliott, Robert B. (1842–1884). Congressman.
 ADA; ADB; BRB; PECA
Ellsworth, Oliver (1745–1807). Senator. FEAA
Fauset, Crystal Bird (1893–1965). State legisla-
 tor. LOAV

Fenwick, Millicent (1910–). Congresswoman. WIAA-02

Ferraro, Geraldine (1935–). Congresswoman. GLO; WHE

Few, William (1748–1828). Senator. BUIB†; FEAA

Fulbright, James William (1905–). Senator. ARB

Gilman, Nicholas (1755–1814). Senator. BUIB†; FEAA

Gonzalez, Henry Barbosa (1916–). Congressman. NEAA; WH-1

Griffiths, Martha W. (1912–). Congresswoman. GRAB-1

Hanna, Mark (Marcus Alonzo) (1837–1904). Senator. COGC

Holtzman, Elizabeth (1941–). Congresswoman. BOHF

Houston, Samuel (1793–1863). Senator, congressman. AKC; ARE; BOK; COE; FIA; HEB; KEC; KED; KUA; LYF; MAL; MAO; MAT; SEC; WAN

Hull, Cordell (1871–1955). Congressman, senator. HEEA; MEC†; WIC

Humphrey, Hubert Horatio (1911–1978). Senator. FEA; HADA; HOEA; WEC; WHD

Johnson, William Samuel (1727–1819). Senator. BUIB†; FEAA

Jones, George Wallace (1804–1896). Senator. SEC

Jordan, Barbara C. (1936–). Congresswoman. BOHF; GRAB-1; YOI

Kassebaum, Nancy Landon (1932–). Senator. WIAA-02

Kennedy, Robert Francis (1925–1968). Senator. LAI†; WEC

King, Rufus (1755–1827). Senator, diplomat. BUIB†; FEAA; WHD†

Krupsak, Mary Anne (1932–). State official. GRAB-1

La Follette, Robert Marion, Jr. (1895–1953). Senator. LAI

La Follette, Robert Marion, Sr. (1855–1925). Senator. ARAA; LAI

Lamar, Lucius Quintus Cincinnatus (1825–1893). Senator, congressman. KEC; KED

Lansing, John, Jr. (1754–1829). State legislator. FEAA

Long, Jefferson Franklin (1836–1900). Congressman. ADA; ADB

Long, Russell B. (1918–). Senator. LAI

Lynch, John Roy (1847–1939). Congressman. ADA; ADB

McCarthy, Eugene Joseph (1916–). Senator. ✏ WECA

McCarthy, Joseph R. (1908–1957). Senator. COGA

Martin, Alexander (b. 1740). Senator. FEAA

Mercer, John Francis (1759–1821). Congressman. FEAA

Mink, Patsy Takemoto (1927–). Congresswoman. BOHF

Mitchell, Arthur Wergs (1883–1968). Congressman. ADA; ADB

Mitchell, Clarence, III (1939?–). State legislator. DU

Montoya, Joseph Manuel (1915–1978). Senator. FOW; NEAA

Morris, Gouverneur (1752–1816). Senator. BUIB†; FEAA

Murphy, John Michael (1926–). Congressman. RAE

Muskie, Edmund S. (1914–). Senator. PIAA

Norris, George William (1861–1944). Senator. HIBB; KEC; KED; SQA

Nye, James Warren (1814–1876). Governor, senator. SEC

Paterson, William (1745–1806). Senator. BUIB†; FEAA

Petigru, James Louis (1789–1863). State congressman. STH

Pinckney, Charles (1757–1824). Senator, congressman. BUIB†; FEAA; SEC

Powell, Adam Clayton, Jr. (1908–1972). Congressman. DU†; HAI; YOI

Pryor, Taylor (1931–). State legislator. BRBC

Randolph, John (1773–1833). Congressman. COKB

Rankin, Jeannette (1880–1973). Congresswoman. FOJ; GRAB-1; WABC†; WHE

Rapier, James T. (1839–1884). Congressman. ADA; ADB; BU

Raymond, Arthur. State legislator. GRAC

Reifel, Ben (1906–). Congressman. GRAC

Revels, Hiram Rhoades (1822–1901). Senator. ADA; ADB; BRB†; BU; YOI

Ross, Edmund G. (1826–1907). Senator. KEC; KED

Roybal, Edward Ross (1916–). Congressman. WH-1

Saund, Dalip (1899–1973). Congressman, born India. LIA

Schroeder, Patricia Scott (1940–). Congresswoman. GRAB-1†; SWI; WHE

Schurz, Carl (1829–1906). Senator, born Germany. CUB; LEB; LOB; STH

Schuyler, Philip John (1733–1804). Senator. SOA

Seward, William Henry (1801–1872). Senator. HEEA; MAL

Shoup, George (1836–1904). Senator. SEC

Smalls, Robert (1839–1915). Congressman. ADA; ADB; HODA; HUB; JOC; PECA; ROG; STD; STJB

Smith, Margaret Chase (1897–). Senator. CLA;
   GIBA; GRAB-1; STLA; TRD; WHE
Snowe, Olympia (1947–). Congresswoman. WHE
Spaight, Richard Dobbs, Sr. (1758–1802). Con-
   gressman. BUIB†; FEAA
Spalding, Burleigh Folsom (1853–1934). Congress-
   man. SEC
Squire, Watson (1838–1926). Senator. SEC
Stephens, Alexander Hamilton (1812–1883). Con-
   gressman. MAO
Stevens, Thaddeus (1792–1868). Congressman.
   BEJ; BU; CAGA; STJB
Stewart, William Morris (1827–1909). Senator.
   YOG
Sumner, Charles (1811–1874). Senator. BEJ
Taft, Robert Alphonso (1889–1953). Senator.
   KEC; KED; LAI
Thomas, Jesse Burgess (1777–1853). Senator.
   SEC
Thompson, Carolyn (1957–). State legislator.
   HOD-1
Tweed, William Marcy (1823–1878). Congress-
   man, senator. COGC
Warren, Francis (1844–1929). Senator. SEC
Webster, Daniel (1782–1852). Senator, congress-
   man. DEI; DEJ; HEEA; KEC; KED; LEC; STH
Williams, John Sharp (1854–1932). Senator.
   MAO
Williamson, Hugh (1735–1819). Congressman.
   BUIB†; FEAA
Worthington, Thomas (1773–1825). Senator. SEC
Yancey, William Lowndes (1814–1863). Congress-
   man. COGA

LEXICOGRAPHERS

Ben Yehudah, Eliezer (1858–1922). Lithuanian
   Hebraist. GRB-1; GUB; PEB; ROGA
Johnson, Samuel (1709–1784). English. BEG;
   BOD
Webster, Noah (1758–1843). DEI; DEJ; MAL

LIBERIANS

Brooks, Angie Elizabeth (1928–). U.N. official.
   CRA
Tubman, William V. S. (1895–1971). President.
   ADA

LIBRARIANS

Baker, Augusta (1911–). FLD

Billings, John Shaw (1838–1913). ED
Kellen, James (1932–). GEA
MacLeish, Archibald (1892–1982). BRBB
Moore, Anne Carroll (1871–1961). FOG
Rzewska, Josepha Rozanka (1899–). (Born Po-
   land). BAEA-1

LIBRETTISTS, *see* PLAYWRIGHTS

LIBYANS

Qaddafi, Muammar el- (1942–). Military leader.
   HAGD

LITERARY CRITICS, *see* CRITICS

LITHUANIANS

Ben Yehudah, Eliezer (1858–1922). Hebraist.
   GRB-1; GUB; PEB; ROGA
Elijah ben Solomon (Elijah Gaon) (1720–1797).
   Hebrew scholar. KAC; LERA; PEB
Salanter, Israel (1810–1883). Rabbi. GEF; GUB;
   KAD

MAGICIANS

Anderson, John Henry (Professor) (1814–1874).
   Scottish. FOGA; GIA
Apollonius of Tyana (c. 3 B.C.–c. 100 A.D.). Greek.
   ED-5
Balsamo, Joseph (Cagliostro) (1743–c. 1800). Ital-
   ian. ED-5
Blackstone, Harry (1885–1965). KEB
Carter, Charles J. (Carter the Great) (1874–1936).
   KEB
Crowley, Aleister (1875–1947). English. ED-5
Hardeen (Theo Weiss) (1876–1945). GIA
Henning, Doug (1947–). Canadian. FOGA
Herrmann, Alexander (Herrmann the Great)
   (1843–1896). (Born Germany). FOGA; GIA;
   KEB
Houdin, Jean Eugène Robert (1805–1871).
   French. EDA; FOGA; GIA; KEB; KLD
Houdini, Harry (1874–1926). FOGA; GIA; KEB;
   KLD; WAO
Julian (c. 331–363). Roman. ED-5
Kellar, Harry (1849–1922). GIA; KEB

Levi, Eliphas (Constant, Alphonse Louis) (1810–1875). French. ED-5
Maskelyne, Jasper Nevil (1839–1917). English. KEB
Nicola, William Mozart (The Great Nicola) (1880–1946). KEB
Robinson, William Ellsworth (1861–1918). GIA
Saunders, Raymond (Raymond the Great) (1877–1948). GIA
Thurston, Howard (1869–1936). GIA; KEB

MALAGASIES

Andriamanjato, Rahantavololona. Engineer. CRA

MALAYSIANS

Rahman, Tunku Abdul (1903–). Ex-prime minister. KEF
Razak bin Hussain, Tun Abdul (1922–). Political leader. RODA

MANUFACTURERS, *see* BUSINESS PEOPLE

MAPMAKERS, *see* GEOGRAPHERS

MARINE BIOLOGISTS, *see* OCEANOGRAPHERS

MARINE GEOLOGISTS, *see* OCEANOGRAPHERS

MARINES, U.S.

See also MEDAL OF HONOR WINNERS

Carlson, Evans Fordyce (1896–1947). ARC

MARSHALS, *see* LAW ENFORCERS

MARTIAL ARTS FIGURES

Austin, Beth. AT
Bates, Laverne (1934–). AT
Dacanay, Pattie. AT
Eads, Valerie. AT
Ellman, Annie (1950–). AT
Graff, Sunny. AT
Harris, Tonie (1947–). AT

Kanokogi, Rusty (1935–). AT
Smith, Vicki. LYE
Spiro, Jo Anne. FOC-1

MATHEMATICIANS

American

Bailie, Ann Eckels. HOG
Banneker, Benjamin (1731–1806). ADA; ADB; BEJ; BRB; BRG; DOB; EMA; GRAB-03; HA; HAM; HODA; JOC; KLA; PECA; ROG; STQ; WIAB; WIBA
Bowditch, Nathaniel (1773–1838). MAL
Carmichael, Berthel. CAF-1
Cornish, Samuel E. (19th century). BEJ
Einstein, Albert (1879–1955). (Born Germany). ASA; ASB-1; BEA; BEP; BOB; BUF; CAA; COL; CUC; DEI; DEJ; DOE; FE; FRE; GEF; GRB-1; GUB; KE; LEL; LES; LET; LETA; MAM; MOBA; POD; RID; SHFB; SIA; YOA
Mann, Helen. HOG
Von Neumann, John (1903–1957). (Born Hungary). GRAB-3; STN
Wiener, Norbert (1894–1964). KE; STN

English

Babbage, Charles (1792–1871). COLA; FE; FRE; GRAB-3; WEF
Bronowski, Jacob (1908–1974). (Born Poland). GRB-1
Dee, John (1527–1608). COEA; CUA; ED-5
Kelvin, William Thomson, 1st baron (1824–1907). BOB; DUA; FE; LAE; SIA
Lovelace, Lady Ada (Byron) (1815–1852). GRAB-3; WEF
Newton, Sir Isaac (1642–1727). ASA; BEP; BIA; BOB; CAA; COL; DEI; DEJ; DOE; FE; FRE; LAA; MAQ; MOCB; MUB; PIA; POD; SHFB; SIA; SIB†; STI; STN; SUE

French

Ampère, André Marie (1775–1836). CAA; DUA; FE; SHFB; SIA
Chatelet, Marquise du. Gabrielle Émilie Le Tonnelier du Breteuil (1706–1749). SC
Coriolis, Gaspard Gustave de (1792–1843). HAC
Descartes, René (1596–1650). LO; MUB; OZA; SHFB; SIA; STN
Galois, Evariste (1811–1832). MUB; STN
Lagrange, Joseph Louis (1736–1813). STN
Pascal, Blaise (1623–1662). GRAB-3; MUB; SOB

German

Cantor, Georg (1845–1918). MUB

Gauss, Karl Friedrich (1777–1855). COLA; DUA; MUB; SIA; STN

Leibniz, Gottfried Wilhelm freiherr von (1646–1716). GRAB-3†; SHFB

Greek

Archimedes (287?–212 B.C.). ASA; BEP; CAA; DOE; EVC; FE; MAQ; MUB; SHFB; SIA; STN; THA

Euclid (fl. 300 B.C.). CAA; MUB; SHFB; STN

Ptolemy (2d century). MOB; MOCB; PIA; SIA; SIB†

Pythagoras (6th century B.C.). CAA; MUB; SHFB; SIB†

Others

Aryabhatta (c. 475–550). Indian. STN

Cardano, Girolamo (1501–1576). Italian. MUB

Doppler, Christian Johann (1803–1853). Austrian. FE; HAC; SHFB

Euler, Leonhard (1707–1783). Swiss. MUB

Huygens, Christiaan (1629–1695). Dutch. CAA; COL; FE; SHFB; SIA

Khwarizmi, al- (780–850). Arabian. STN

Lobachevsky, Nikolai (1793–1856). Russian. MUB

Napier, John (1550–1617). Scottish. SHFB

Somerville, Mary Fairfax (1780–1872). Scottish. SC

Torricelli, Evangelista (1608–1647). Italian. CAA; FE; SHFB

MAYORS, U.S.

Byrne, Jane (1934–). WHE

Cisneros, Henry (1947–). HOD-1

Evers, Charles (1922–). DU; FAG; HAH

Gibson, Kenneth Allen (1932–). BRGA; DU; HAH

Hague, Frank (1876–1956). COGC

Hatcher, Richard Gordon (1933–). BRGA; DRA; DU†; FAG; HAH; YOI

Hayes, Janet Gray Frazee (1926–). WIAA-02

La Guardia, Fiorello Henry (1882–1947). MAS

Lindsay, John Vliet (1921–). WEC

Rincón de Gautier, Felisa (1897–). Puerto Rican. FOW; WO

Stokes, Carl B. (1927–). BRGA; DU; FAG; GRBA; HAH; YOI

Washington, Walter (1915–). YOI

Whitmire, Kathy (1946–). WHE

Young, Andrew Jackson (1932–). DOF-1

Young, Coleman (1918–). DOF-1

MECHANICAL ENGINEERS, *see* ENGINEERS, MECHANICAL

MEDAL OF HONOR WINNERS

Baldwin, Frank (1842–1923). Soldier. TA

Boyington, Pappy (Gregory) (1913–1988). Aviator. HAMY

Brown, Bobbie E. (fl. 1945). Soldier. REA

Brown, Melvin L. (d. 1950). Soldier. REA

Bush, Robert Eugene (fl. 1945). Naval medical corpsman. REA

Butler, Smedley Darlington (1881–1940). Marine officer. TA

Castle, Frederick W. (d. 1944). Aviator. REA

Charlton, Cornelius (1930?–1951). Soldier. ARBA; DIA

Cooper, John (1832–1891). Sailor, born Ireland. TA

Cromwell, John P. (1901–1943). Naval officer. REA

Cukela, Louis (1888–1956). Marine officer, born Serbia. TA

Custer, Thomas Ward (1845–1876). Soldier. TA

Daly, Daniel Joseph (1873–1937). Marine. TA

Dean, William Frishe (1899–1981). General. REA

Donovan, William Joseph (1883–1959). General. ARD; FAA

Doolittle, James Harold (1896–). General. ARC; HAMY; SUA; SWE

Elrod, Henry Talmage (1905–1941). Marine aviator. BRA; REA

Factor, Pompey (d. 1928). Soldier. KADB

Fluckey, Eugene Bennett (1913–). Naval officer. BRA

Greaves, Clifton (b. 1858?). Buffalo soldier. BUH

Hanson, Robert (1920–1944). Marine aviator. BRA

Hogan, Henry (fl. 1875). Soldier, born Ireland. TA

Izac, Edouard Victor M. (fl. 1918). Naval officer. REA

Janson, Ernest August (1878–1930). Marine. TA

Johnson, Henry (b. 1859). Soldier. BUH

Kanell, Billie Gene (d. 1951). Soldier. REA

Kelly, John Joseph (1898–1957). Marine. TA

King, John (1865–1938). Sailor, born Ireland. TA

Kocak, Matej (1882–1918). Marine, born Hungary. TA

Leonard, Patrick (fl. 1870). Soldier, born Ireland. TA

Luke, Frank, Jr. (d. 1918). Aviator, WW I. HAMY; REA

MacArthur, Arthur, Jr. (1845–1912). Army officer. EDA

McCandless, Bruce (1911–). Naval officer. BRA

McCloy, John (1876–1945). Sailor. TA

Mullen, Patrick (b. 1838). Sailor. TA

Murphy, Audie (1925–1971). Soldier, WW II.
FAA; REA
O'Callahan, Joseph T. (1905–). Chaplain. BRA;
REA
O'Hare, Edward "Butch" (1914–). Naval aviator.
REA
Paige, Mitchell (b. 1918). Marine, WW II. BRA
Preston, Arthur Murray (1914–). Naval officer.
BRA
Pruitt, John Henry (1896–1918). Marine. TA
Rickenbacker, Edward Vernon (1890–1973). Avia-
tor. ARD; DAG; LEX; YAA
Robinson, Robert Guy. Marine aviator. REA
Schmidt, Oscar, Jr. Naval officer. REA
Stance, Emanuel (b. 1851?). Buffalo soldier. BUH
Sweeney, Robert (b. 1853). Sailor, born West In-
dies. TA
Talbot, Ralph (1897–1918). Aviator. REA
Van Iersel, Louis. Soldier, WW I, born the Nether-
lands. REA
Weisbogel, Albert (1844–?). Sailor. TA
Williams, Louis (1845–1886). Sailor, born Nor-
way. TA
Wilson, William (fl. 1870). Soldier. TA
York, Alvin C. (1887–1964). Soldier. ARD; DIA;
ELA; FIA; REA

MERCHANTS, *see* BUSINESS PEOPLE

METEOROLOGISTS

Nagler, Kenneth M. (1920–). POE
Spilhaus, Athelstan F. (1911–). (Born South Af-
rica). BRBC
Van Straten, Florence (1913–). EMB†; YOF

MEXICAN AMERICANS

Anguiano, Lupe (1929–). Social worker, educator.
NEAA
Baca, Elfego (1865–1945). Lawyer, sheriff. BENA
Banuelos, Romana Acosta (1925–). Ex-treasurer
of U.S. FOW
Carr, Vikki. Singer. NEAA; WH
Castillo, Rosa. Migrant worker. WECC
Castro, Raúl Héctor (1916–). Governor, born Mex-
ico. WH
Chavez, Cesar Estrada (1927–). Labor leader.
DU-1; FOW; HAJ; NEAA; WO
Cisneros, Henry (1947–). Mayor. HOD-1

Conde, Carlos. Civil rights leader. NEAA
Delgado, Estrella (1958?–). Migrant worker.
WECC
Estrada, Miguel (1938–). Migrant worker. WECC
Fender, Freddy (1937–). Singer. KRI
Garcia, Forresto (1954?–). Migrant worker.
WECC
Garcia, Hector (1914–). Physician, born Mexico.
FOW
Gonzales, Pancho (Richard Alonzo) (1928–). Ten-
nis player. AAS-28; ASBA; BELB; DEHA-1;
FOW; FOX; HI; HOC; LAHA; LYE; NEAA
Gonzales, Rodolfo (1929–). Social welfare leader.
NEAA
Gonzalez, Henry Barbosa (1916–). Congressman.
NEAA; WH-1
Gonzalez, Natividad Martinez (1907–). House-
wife, born Mexico. BAEA-1
Gutierrez, José Angel. Political leader. NEAA
Guzman, Virginia Quintana (1940?–). Police-
woman. SMBC-3
Huerta, Dolores (1930–). Labor leader. BI;
BOHF; DI; NEAA
Kapp, Joe (1938–). Football player. LEZA; LIBB;
LYD; NEAA
Limón, José (1908–1972). Dancer, born Mexico.
FOW; WO
Lopez, Antonio (1897–). Migrant worker. WECC
Lopez, Trini (1937–). Singer. NEAA; WH-1
Montalban, Ricardo (1920–). Actor, born Mexico.
FOW; NEAA
Montoya, Joseph Manuel (1915–1978). Senator.
FOW; NEAA
Nava, Julian (1927–). Educator. FOW
Nogales, Louis (1943–). College administrator.
NEAA
Nuñez, Tommy (1938–). Basketball referee. WH
Plunkett, Jim (1947–). Football player. AAS-9;
CL-1; DEHB; GUD; NEAA; ST; WH-3
Quinn, Anthony (1916–). Actor, born Mexico.
LOAA; NEAA
Ramirez, Doria (1952?–). Migrant worker.
WECC
Ramirez, Henry M. (1929–). Government official.
NEAA
Reyes, Albert (1956?–). Migrant worker. WECC
Roybal, Edward Ross (1916–). Congressman.
WH-1
Sandoval, Hilary (1930–). Government official.
NEAA
Tijerina, Reies Lopez (1926–). Revolutionist.
BENA; NEAA
Trevino, Lee (1939–). Golfer. AAS-27; IZA; LYB;
NEAA; WH-3
Zajicek, Sarita Soto (1916–). Educator. FOW

MEXICANS

Cantinflas (Mario Moreno) (1911–). Actor. NEBA; WO
Cárdenas, Lázaro (1895–1970). Soldier, statesman. ARAA; NEBA; ROGB
Chacon, Augustin (d. 1902). Outlaw. JOBA
Chávez, Carlos (1899–1978). Composer. KAE; NEBA; ROGB; STM†; WO
Díaz, Porfirio (1830–1915). President. BAGA; NEBA; WOB
Dominguez, (Maria) Josefa Ortiz de (1768–1824). Patriot. NEBA; ROGB
Echeverría, Luís (1922–). Ex-president. NEBA
Guerrero, Vicente (1783?–1831). Statesman. ROGB
Guzmán, Martín Luis (b. 1887). Author. NEBA
Hidalgo y Costilla, Miguel (1753–1811). Revolutionist. BAA; BACA; NEBA; ROGB; WO; YOFA
Iturbide, Augustín de (1783–1824). Soldier, emperor. NEBA; YOFA
Juana Inés de la Cruz, Sister (1651–1695). Nun, poet. BACA; ROGB
Juárez, Benito Pablo (1806–1872). President. BAA; BACA; NEBA; ROGB; WO; WOB; YOFA
Ledón, Amalia. Diplomat. NEBA
Madero, Francisco Indalecio (1873–1913). Statesman. NEBA
Martinez, Antonio José (1793–1865). Priest. BENA
Melendrez, Antonio (fl. 1860). Outlaw. WIAA-1
Mina, Francisco Javier (1789–1817). Revolutionist. ROGB
Montezuma II (1480?–1520). Aztec emperor. CAAA; NEC; ROGB; UNB
Morelos y Pavon, José Mariá (1765–1815). Patriot. BAA; NEBA; ROGB; WOB; YOFA
Murrieta, Joaquin (1832?–1853). Outlaw. JOBA; SUJ; WIAA-1
Orozco, José Clemente (1883–1949). Painter. BACA; KE; ROGB; WO
Ortega, Gaspar (1935–). Boxer. IZA
Ortiz Mena, Antonio (1908–). Government official. NEBA
Pasquel, Jorge (1907–1955). Baseball executive. NEBA
Paz, Octavio (1914–). Poet, essayist. WO
Rivera, Diego (1886–1957). Painter. KAA; NEBA; ROGB
Rodriguez, Pedro (1939?–1971). Automobile racer. JA
Santa Anna, Antonio López de (1795–1876). General, politician. NEBA

Sigüenza y Góngora, Carlos de (1645–1700). Scholar. WOB
Vasconcelos, José (1882–1959). Educator. NEBA
Vasquez, Pedro Ramírez. Architect. NEBA
Vicario, Leona (1789–1842). Patriot. ROGB
Victoria, Guadalupe, pseud. (1789–1843). Statesman. NEBA
Villa, Pancho (1878–1923). Revolutionary leader. NEBA; ROGB; WO
Zapata, Emiliano (1877?–1919). Revolutionist. HAK; NEBA; ROGB; WO
Zavala, Lorenzo de (1788–1836). Statesman. KUA

MICROBIOLOGISTS

See also BACTERIOLOGISTS; VIROLOGISTS

Borlaug, Norman Ernest (1914–). MEC
Friedmann, Roseli Ocampo (1937–). LA-1
Robbins, Mary Louise (1912–). BOHE
Scott, Nan. LA-1

MIDWIVES

Bourgeois, Louyse (1563–1636). French. MASA
Hewitt, Margaret. BOHE

MIGRANT LABORERS

Castillo, Rosa. WECC
Delgado, Estrella (1958?–). WECC
Estrada, Miguel (1938–). WECC
Garcia, Forresto (1954?–). WECC
Lopez, Antonio (1897–). WECC
Ramirez, Doria (1952?–). WECC
Reyes, Albert (1956?–). WECC

MILITARY LEADERS, *see* AIR FORCE LEADERS; AMERICAN REVOLUTIONARY FIGURES—MILITARY; ARMY LEADERS; CIVIL WAR FIGURES—MILITARY; MARINES, U.S.; MEDAL OF HONOR WINNERS; NAVAL FIGURES

MINERALOGISTS

Agricola, Georgius (1494–1555). German. FE; SHFB

MINING ENGINEERS, *see* ENGINEERS, MINING

MINISTERS, *see* CHAPLAINS; MISSIONARIES; RELIGIOUS LEADERS, PROTESTANT

MISSIONARIES

See also APOSTLES; SAINTS

Captein, Jacques E. J. (b. 1745). Dutch. (Born Africa). ADA; ADB
Crowther, Samuel Ajayi (1808–1891). Nigerian. POA
Crummell, Alexander (1819–1898). ADA; ADB; BRB†; GRAB-05
Damien de Veuster, Joseph (Father Damien) (1840–1889). Belgian. EVD; HAA; HEA; MAJ; MAN; STP; WRA
De Smet, Pierre Jean (1801–1873). Belgian. ASB
Escalante, Silvestre Vélez de (fl. 1768–1779). Spanish. FOC
Gallitzin, Demetrius Augustine (1770–1840). (Born Russia). ASB
Galvin, Edward J. (1882–1956). Irish. REC
Laubach, Frank (1884–1970). COG
Lee, Jason (1803–1845). Canadian. YOG
Livingstone, David (1813–1873). Scottish. COC; COL; DAF; DOBB; HOB; KNA; LAA-1; MOB; RIB; ROL; STP; WOA
Marquette, Jacques (1637–1675). French. ABA; ASB; GRC; ROL†
Marrant, John (fl. 1755). HAP; WIBA
Mary Loyola, Sister. ROI
Palgrave, William Gifford (1826–1888). ROL
Seagrave, Gordon Stifler (1897–1965). FAA
Serra, Junipero (1713–1784). Spanish. ASB; DOCA; MAT
Sisters of Charity of Providence. JOB
Slessor, Mary Mitchell (1848–1915). Scottish. STP
Stewart, John (1786?–1823?). HAP
Vieira, Antônio (1608–1697). Portuguese. WOB
Walker, Mary Richardson (1814–1897). JOB; ROI
Whitman, Marcus (1802–1847). BLC; COE; FOC; LEG; MAT
Whitman, Narcissa (1808–1847). DAD; EVD; FOC; MAT; ROI

MORMON LEADERS, *see* RELIGIOUS LEADERS, PROTESTANT

MOROCCANS

Mohammed V (1910–1961). King. KEF

MOTION PICTURE INDUSTRY

See also ACTORS, ACTRESSES & ENTERTAINERS

Allen, Woody (1935–). ED-1†; SMBB-3
Altman, Robert (1925–). SMBB-3
Brooks, Mel (Melvin Kaminsky) (1926–). BUR-1; SMBB-3
Capra, Frank (1897–). (Born Italy). ED-1†; FLBC; SMBC
Coppola, Francis (1939–). SMBB-3
Cukor, George (1899–1983). SMBC
DeMille, Cecil Blount (1881–1959). ASB-1; FLBC
DePalma, Brian (1940–). SMBB-3
Disney, Walt (Walter Elias) (1901–1966). ASB-1; COKA; FLBC; LAG; LEN; LEPA; PABA; WAO
Flaherty, Robert Joseph (1884–1951). FLBC
Ford, John (1895–1973). FLBC; SMBC
Goldwyn, Samuel (1882–1974). LETA
Griffith, David Wark (1875–1948). FLBC; SMBC
Hawks, Howard (1896–1977). ED-1†; SMBC
Hawn, Goldie (1945–). MASB
Hitchcock, Alfred Joseph (1899–1980). (Born England). ASB-1; BEA; FLBC; PABA; SMBC
Hughes, Howard, Jr. (1905–1976). COKB; DU-1
Huston, John (1906–1987). SMBC
Keaton, Buster (1895–1977). ED-1; SMBC
Kubrick, Stanley (1928–). FLBC
Kurosawa, Akira (1910–). Japanese. RODA
Lubitsch, Ernst (1892–1947). (Born Germany). FLBC
Lucas, George (1944–). SMBB-3
May, Elaine (1932–). BUR-1; MASB
Mazursky, Paul (1930–). SMBB-3
Nichols, Mike (Igor Peshowsky) (1931–). (Born Germany). BUR-1
O'Neil, Kitty (1946–). Stuntwoman. AAS-27; HAFA
Porter, Edwin Stanton (1870–1941). FLBC
Reiner, Carl (1922–). BUR-1
Rosenberg, Aaron (1912–1979). SLA
Scorsese, Martin (1942–). SMBB-3
Sennett, Mack (1880–1960). ED-1; FLBC
Skouras, Spyros (1893–1971). (Born Greece). BEA; LEN; LIA
Spielberg, Steven (1947–). SMBB-3
Spottiswoode, Nigel (1915–). English. LAE
Spottiswoode, Raymond (1913–). English. LAE
Van Peebles, Melvin (1932–). AB

Warhol, Andy (1930–1987). WIAA
Welles, Orson (1915–1985). SMBC

MOTOR BOAT RACERS, *see* BOAT RACERS

MOTORCYCLE RACERS

Beck, Trudy (1960?–). BUIC
Cox, Diane (1958?–). BUIC
Fuller, Peggy (1955?–). BUIC
Glasgow, Nancy Payne (1955?–). BUIC
Hannah, Bob (1956?–). OLDB
Kirk, Tammy Jo (1964–). BUIC
Nixon, Gary (1941–). OLDB
Rayborn, Calvin (1940–). ST-1
Roberts, Kenny (1951–). OLDB
Springsteen, Jay (1957–). OLDB
Stenersen, Johanna (1959?–). BUIC
Tanner, Sammy (1937?–). OLAB
Turton, Janene (1954?–). BUIC
Vesco, Don (1940–). OLDB
Wilkins, Debbie. BUIC

MOUNTAINEERS

Herzog, Maurice (1919–). French. HAQ; HOB;
　KEH
Hillary, Sir Edmund (1919–). New Zealander.
　ASB-1; BAB; COLA; DU-1; KEH; MOB; PRC;
　ROL†
Lachenal, Louis. French. HAQ
Peck, Annie Smith (1850–1935). PACB
Tenzing, Norgay (1914–1986). Nepalese. KEH;
　MOB; PRC
Workman, Fanny Bullock (1859–1925). RIG

MURDERERS, *see* ASSASSINS; CRIMINALS & OUTLAWS

MUSEUM FIGURES

Miller, Dorothy Canning (1904–). Curator. GIB-1
Vreeland, Diana. Consultant, born France. GIB-1

MUSIC CRITICS, *see* CRITICS

MUSICIANS

See also BAND LEADERS; COMPOSERS; CONDUC-
TORS; MUSICIANS, JAZZ; SINGERS

Cellists
Casals, Pablo (1876–1973). Spanish. CAHA
Fournier, Pierre (1906–1986). French. EWC
Rose, Leonard (1918–1984). EWC
Rostropovich, Mstislav (1927–). Russian. EWC
Wallenstein, Alfred (1898–1983). STM

Clarinetists
Goodman, Benny (1909–1986). COF-1; TEA; TEB;
　WAD†
Herman, Woody (1914–1987). TEA; TEB

Guitarists
Bream, Julian (1933–). English. EWC
Campbell, Glen (1936–). KRI-1
Clapton, Eric (1945–). English. BUIB-1
Clark, Roy. HAG-1
Collins, Judy (1939–). BOHC; SC-02
Entwistle, John (1944–). English. BUIB-2
Feliciano, José (1945–). FOW; LYA; WH-2
Hendrix, Jimi (1942–1970). BUIB-1
Reinhardt, Django (1910–1951). French. COF-1

Harpsichordists
Couperin, François (1668–1733). French. BEM;
　KAE
Landowska, Wanda (1877–1959). Polish. FOG
Scarlatti, Domenico (1685–1757). Italian. BEN;
　KAE; SAA

Organists
Bach, Johann Christian (1735–1782). German.
　CHF; SAA†; YOM†
Bach, Johann Sebastian (1685–1750). German.
　BEN; BRF; BUD; DEI; DEJ; FIE; GOB; KAE;
　SAA; WIA; YOK; YOM†
Buxtehude, Dietrich (1637–1707). Swedish. BEM
Byrd, William (1543–1623). English. KAE
Franck, César Auguste (1822–1890). French.
　(Born Belgium). BRF; KAE
Frescobaldi, Girolamo (1583–1643). Italian. BEM
Schweitzer, Albert (1875–1965). French. BAF;
　BEC; EVD; FOJ; KE; KEE; LO; MAN; MEA;
　MEC; WIC; YOA

Pianists
Albéniz, Isaac (1860–1909). Spanish. KAE; SAA
Bar-Ilian, David (1930–). Israeli. EWC
Barenboim, Daniel (1942–). Israeli. EWC
Blake, Ran (1935–). UN

Busoni, Ferruccio (1866–1924). Italian. CHF

Carreño, Teresa (1853–1917). Venezuelan. CHF

Clementi, Muzio (1752–1832). Italian. CHF

Cliburn, Van (1934–). EWC; LEHB

Cole, Nat "King" (1919–1965). ROF

Cramer, Johann Baptist (1771–1858). German. CHF

Czerny, Karl (1791–1857). Austrian. CHF

Dussek, Jan Ladislav (1760–1812). Czech. CHF

Field, John (1782–1837). Irish. CHF

Figueroa, Carmen Sanabria de (1882–1954). NEBB

Fizdale, Robert (1920–). EWC

Fleisher, Leon (1928–). EWC

Gilels, Emil G. (1916–1985). Russian. EWC

Gold, Arthur (1919–). Canadian. EWC

Gottschalk, Louis Moreau (1829–1869). CHF; LEHB

Gould, Glenn (1932–1982). Canadian. EWC

Graffman, Gary (1918–). EWC

Hines, Earl Kenneth (1905–1983). COF-1; UN; WAD†

Istomin, Eugene (1925–). EWC

Janis, Byron (1928–). EWC

John, Elton (1947–). English. BUIB-1

Joplin, Scott (1868–1917). COF-1

Landowska, Wanda (1877–1959). Polish. FOG

Lewis, Jerry Lee (1935–). BUIB-01

Liszt, Franz (1811–1886). Hungarian. BRF; BUD; CHF; FIE; KAE; SAA; YOH

Lowe, Jack (1917–). EWC

Monk, Theolonius (1920–1982). COF-1; WAD†

Morton, "Jelly Roll" (Ferdinand Joseph) (1885–1941). COF-1; HUC; WAD†

Paderewski, Ignace Jan (1860–1941). Polish. CHF; MANB; PIAA

Powell, Bud (Earl) (1924–1966). COF-1; WAD†

Rachmaninoff, Sergei (1873–1943). Russian. BAE; BEN; KAE; POG; SAA

Revere, Paul. LEHB

Richter, Sviatoslav (1914–). Russian. EWC

Rubinstein, Anton (1829–1894). Russian. CHF

Rubinstein, Artur (1889–1982). (Born Poland). GRB-1; MANB; PIAA

Schnabel, Artur (1882–1951). Austrian. CHF

Schumann, Clara (1819–1896). German. CHF

Scott, Hazel (1920–1981). BOG

Silver, Horace (1928–). UN

Tatum, Art (1910–1956). COF-1; WAD†

Taylor, Cecil (1933–). COF-1

Templeton, Alec (1910–1963). (Born Wales). GEA

Waller, Fats (Thomas Wright) (1904–1943). COF-1; ROF; TEA; TEB; WAD†

Watts, André (1946–). AB

Whittemore, Arthur Austin (1916–1984). EWC

Williams, Mary Lou (1910–1981). GIB-1

Wittgenstein, Paul (1887–1961). Austrian. GEA

Saxophonists

Braxton, Anthony (1945–). UN

Coleman, Ornette (1930–). COF-1; WAD†

Coltrane, John William (1926–1967). COF-1; TEB; WAD†

Gordon, Dexter (1923–). UN

Hawkins, Coleman (1904–). COF-1; WAD†

Parker, Charlie (1920–1955). COF-1; TEB; RICA; WAD†

Young, Lester Willis (1909–1959). COF-1; JO; WAD†

Trumpeters & Cornetists

Armstrong, Louis "Satchmo" (1900–1971). ADA; ADB; COF-1; FLD; HUC; LEHB; RIC; RICA; ROF; TEA; TEB; WAD

Cheatham, Doc (1905–). UN

Gillespie, Dizzy (John Birks) (1917–). TEA; TEB; UN; WAD†

Oliver, Joe (1885–1938). TEA; TEB; WAD†

Vibraphonists

Berger, Karl (1935–). (Born Germany). UN

Violinists

Ashkenasi, Shmuel (1941–). Israeli. EWC

Bridgetower, George Augustus (1780–1860). Polish. ADA; ADB

Bull, Ole (1810–1880). Norwegian. BOD; CHFA

Corelli, Arcangelo (1653–1713). Italian. BEM; CHFA; KAE; YOM†

Enesco, Georges (1881–1955). Romanian. KAE; YOM†

Figueroa, José (1905–). NEBB

Jenson, Dylana (1961–). SC-02

Joachim, Joseph (1831–1907). Hungarian. CHFA

Kreisler, Fritz (1875–1962). (Born Austria). CHFA; RADA

Kreutzer, Rodolphe (1766–1831). French. CHFA

Laredo, Jaime (1941–). Bolivian. EWC

Leclair, Jean Marie (1697–1764). French. CHFA

Menuhin, Yehudi (1916–). COKA

Oistrakh, David (1908–1974). Russian. EWC

Paganini, Nicolò (1782–1840). Italian. CHFA; YOH

Ricci, Ruggiero (1920–). EWC

Sarasate, Pablo de (1844–1908). Spanish. CHFA

Spohr, Louis (1784–1859). German. CHFA; YOM†

Stamitz, Johann Wenzel (1717–1757). Czech. CHFA

Stern, Isaac (1920–). EWC

Tartini, Giuseppe (1692–1770). Italian. BEN; CHFA; SAA†

Veracini, Francesco Maria (1685–1750). Italian. CHFA

Vieuxtemps, Henri François Joseph (1820–1881). Belgian. CHFA

Viotti, Giovanni Battista (1755–1824). Italian. CHFA

Vivaldi, Antonio (1675?–1741). Italian. BEM; CHFA; KAE; SAA; YOM†

MUSICIANS, JAZZ

Armstrong, Louis "Satchmo" (1900–1971). Trumpeter. ADA; ADB; COF-1; FLD; HUC; LEHB; RIC; RICA; ROF; TEA; TEB; WAD

Basie, Count (William) (1904–1984). Band leader. TEA; TEB; WAD†

Beiderbecke, Bix (Leon Bismarck) (1903–1931). Cornetist. COF-1; TEA; TEB; WAD†

Berger, Karl (1935–). Vibraphonist, born Germany. UN

Blake, Ran (1935–). Composer, pianist. UN

Braxton, Anthony (1945–). Saxophonist. UN

Broonzy, Big Bill (1893–1959). Singer. SUH

Brown, Rabbit (Richard) (1880–1937). Singer, guitarist. SUH

Carr, Leroy (1899–1935). Singer. SUH

Carter, Betty (1930–). Singer. UN

Charles, Ray (1930–). Singer, pianist. HAFA

Cheatham, Doc (1905–). Trumpeter. UN

Cole, Nat "King" (1919–1965). Pianist, singer. ROF

Coleman, Ornette (1930–). Saxophonist. COF-1; WAD†

Coltrane, John William (1926–1967). Saxophonist. COF-1; TEB; WAD†

Ellington, Duke (Edward Kennedy) (1899–1974). Band leader, composer. ADA; ADB; ASB-1; COF-1; DOF-1; HODA; HUC; MOA; RIC; RICA; ROF; TEA; TEB; WAD

Fitzgerald, Ella (1918–). Singer. ASB-1

Flanagan, Tommy (1930–). Pianist. UN

Gillespie, Dizzy (John Birks) (1917–). Trumpeter. TEA; TEB; UN; WAD†

Goodman, Benny (1909–1986). Clarinetist, band leader. COF-1; TEA; TEB; WAD†

Gordon, Dexter (1923–). Saxophonist. UN

Hawkins, Coleman (1904–). Saxophonist. COF-1; WAD†

Henderson, Fletcher (1898–1952). Band leader. COF-1; WAD†

Herman, Woody (1914–1987). Clarinetist, band leader. TEA; TEB

Hines, Earl Kenneth (1905–1983). Pianist. COF-1; UN; WAD†

Holiday, Billie (1915–1959). Singer. BRBD; COF-1; JOE; SUH; TEA; TEB; WAD†

Hopkins, Lightnin' (Sam) (1912–1982). Singer. SUH

Hunter, Alberta (1895–1984). Singer. GIB-1

Jefferson, Lemon (1897–1930). Singer. ADB; COF-1; SUH; WAD†

Johnson, Lonnie (1889–1970). Singer. SUH

Johnson, Willie (1902–1949). Singer. SUH

Joplin, Scott (1868–1917). Pianist, composer. COF-1

Kenton, Stan (1912–1979). Band leader. TEA

Kirk, Roland (1936–1976). Multi-instrumentalist. UN

Leadbelly (Huddie Ledbetter) (1888–1949). Singer. COF-1; HUC; SUH; WAD†

Lewis, Furry (Walter) (1900–). Singer. SUH

McClennan, Tommy (1908–1958?). Singer. SUH

McGhee, Brownie (Walter Brown) (1915–). Singer. SUH

McIntyre, Ken (1931–). Multi-instrumentalist. UN

McPartland, Marian (1920–). Pianist, born England. UN

Mantilla, Ray (1934–). Percussionist. UN

Mingus, Charles (1922–1979). Bassist. UN

Monk, Theolonius (1920–1982). Pianist. COF-1; WAD†

Morton, "Jelly Roll" (Ferdinand Joseph) (1885–1941). Pianist. COF-1; HUC; WAD†

Oliver, Joe (1885–1938). Cornetist. TEA; TEB; WAD†

Parker, Charlie (1920–1955). Saxophonist. COF-1; TEB; RICA; WAD†

Powell, Bud (Earl) (1924–1966). Pianist. COF-1; WAD†

Rainey, Ma (Gertrude Malissa Nix Pridgett) (1886–1939). Singer. JOE; SUH; WAD†

Reinhardt, Django (1910–1951). French guitarist. COF-1

Rivers, Sam (1930–). Multi-instrumentalist. UN

Rollins, Sonny (1929–). Saxophonist. UN

Silver, Horace (1928–). Composer, pianist. UN

Smith, Bessie (1894–1937). Singer. HUC; JOE; SUH; TEA; TEB; WAD†

Tatum, Art (1910–1956). Pianist. COF-1; WAD†

Taylor, Cecil (1933–). Pianist. COF-1

Terry, Sonny (Saunders Teddell) (1911–1986). Singer, harmonica player. SUH

Venuti, Joe (1904–1978). Violinist. UN

Waller, Fats (Thomas Wright) (1904–1943). Pianist. COF-1; ROF; TEA; TEB; WAD†

Waters, Muddy (McKinley Morganfield) (1915–1983). Singer. SUH

Williams, Big Joe (1900–). Singer. SUH

Williams, Mary Lou (1910–1981). Pianist, composer. GIB-1
Young, Lester Willis (1909–1959). Saxophonist. COF-1; JO; WAD†
Zino, Henry. Drummer. HODA

NATIVE AMERICANS

See also INDIAN CAPTIVES

Adams, Henry (Hank) (1944–). Youth leader. GRAC
Altoha, Wallace (1870?–1937). WAA
Awendes (fl. 1823). Seneca boy. CAD
Ballard, Louis W. (1931–). Composer. GRAC
Bender, Chief (Charles Albert) (1883–1954). Baseball player. ALB; DAFD; HACA
Bennett, Robert LaFollette (1912–). Lawyer. GRAC
Big Eyes (fl. 1535). Wichita woman. WAB
Black Hawk (1767–1838). Sac and Fox chief. DEDB; HEC; MOD; STAB; WAL
Blue Spruce, George (1931–). Dentist. GRAC
Blythe, Jarrett (1886–). Cherokee leader. GRAC
Bonnin, Gertrude Simmons (1875–1936?). Sioux educator. GRAD
Bosomworth, Mary Musgrove Matthews (1700–1762?). Creek princess. GRAD
Brant, Joseph (1742–1807). Mohawk war chief. DEDB; HEC; HEGA
Brant, Molly (Degonwadonti) (1736–1796). Mohawk. AND
Bruce, Louis R. (1906–). Government official. GRAC
Captain Jack (d. 1873). Modoc subchief. HED
Clark, Beverly. Lawyer. FOC-1
Clevenger, Johanna. Psychiatrist. FOC-1
Cochise (1815?–1874). Apache chief. DEDB; HEC; MAEA
Cook, Leon F. (1939–). Chippewa social worker. GRAC
Crazy Horse (1849?–1877). Sioux chief. DEDB; HEC; HEGA; STAB; SUKA; WAM
Dat-So-La-Lee (1830–1925). Washoe basket maker. WAB
Deloria, Vine, Jr. (1934?–). Author. GRAC
Demmert, Archie W. (1909–). Educator. GRAC
Dull Knife (1828?–1879). Cheyenne war chief. MOD
Francis, Milly Hadjo (b. 1802). Creek. GRAD
Gahadiyas. Seneca boy. CAD
Gall (1840?–1894). Sioux chief. DEDB
Geronimo (c. 1829–1909). Apache war chief. DEDB; HEC; LEH; MOD; STAB†; SUKA

Gladstone, James (b. 1887). Canadian politician. GRAC
Guyon, Joe (1892–1971). Football player. DAFG; SUD
Harris, LaDonna (1931–). Comanche social welfare leader. GRAC
Hatathli, Ned (1923–). Navajo educator. GRAC
Hiawatha (fl. 1550). Onondaga chief. ROD
Hightower, Rosella (1920–). Dancer. ATA
Horne, Esther Burnett (fl. 1955). Educator. GRAD
Houser, Allan (1914–). Painter, sculptor. GRAC
Howe, Oscar (1915–). Painter. LEH; LEOA
Indian Emily (d. 1873). Apache girl. WAB
Johnson, E. Pauline (1862–1913). Canadian poet. GRAD
Jones, Harold S. (1909–). Clergyman. GRAC
Joseph (Chief Joseph) (1840?–1904). Nez Percé leader. DEDB; ELA; FRAB; HED; HEGA; MOD; STAB; SUKA; WAM
Juana Maria. Princess. WIAA-2
Kahn, Anthony (1961–). Mechanical engineer. HOD-1
Keeler, William Wayne (1908–). Cherokee chief. GRAC
Keokuk (fl. 1790–1848). Sac chief. DEDB
Lawson, Roberta Campbell (1878–1940). Community leader. GRAD
Little Crow (1803?–1863). Sioux leader. HED
Little Turtle (1752–1812). Miami chief. HED
MacDonald, Peter (1928–). Navajo leader. GRAC
Maquinna (fl. 1800). Nootka chief. ROD
Martinez, Maria Montoya (b. 1881). Pueblo pottery maker. GRAC; GRAD; LEH; WAB
Massasoit (d. 1661). Wampanoag chief. WAL
Mills, Billy (1938–). Track athlete. DEF; GRAC; HIA; LEYB; LYC; OCA
Mo-Keen (1849–1934). Medicine man. JOD
Momaday, N. Scott (1934–). Author. GRAC
Mountain Wolf Woman (1884–1960). Winnebago. MAV
Neosho (b. 1846). Creek patriot. WAB
Old Coyote, Barney (1923–). Educator and government official. GRAC
Osceola (c. 1800–1838). Seminole leader. DEDB; HEC; HEGA; JO†; LEH; MAEA; MOD; STAB; WAL
Parker, Ely (1828–1905). Iroquois sachem. HED
Parker, Quanah (1845?–1911). Comanche chief. FRAB; HED; MOD; WAM
Pasquala (1809?–1824). Tulare girl. HED
Peterson, Helen L. (1915–). Government official. GRAC
Philip (King Philip) (1637–1676). Wampanoag chief. DEDB; HED; HEGA; ROD; STAB†; VIA
Picotte, Susan LaFlesche (1865–1915). Physician. GRAD; RAAG†

Pocahontas (1595?–1617). Princess. CAD; DOD; GRAD; HEC; LEH; LEPF; PA; STJ; VIA; WAB; WABC

Pontiac (1720?–1769). Ottawa chief. DEDB; HEC; HEGA; LEH; ROD; STAB

Popé (d. 1690). Pueblo medicine man. HED; ROD; STAB†

Powhatan (1550–1618). ROD

Ramos, Elaine Abraham. Educator. GRAD

Raymond, Arthur. State legislator and journalist. GRAC

Red Cloud (1822–1909). FRAB; HED; MOD

Red Jacket (1758?–1830). Seneca chief. MOD

Reifel, Ben (1906–). Congressman. GRAC

Rhoades, Everett (1931–). Physician. GRAC

Roman Nose (c. 1868). Cheyenne warrior. HED

Ross, John (1790–1866). Cherokee chief. HED; MAO; STAB

Ross, John Osage (b. 1814). JOD

Sacajawea (1787–1812). Shoshone guide. BEC; BUI; DOD; FOR; GRAD; HEC; LEK; ROI; STJ; WAB; WABC

Sainte-Marie, Buffy (1942?–). Singer, composer. BOHC

Satanta (1820–1878). Kiowa chief. FRAB

Sequoya (George Guess) (1770?–1843). Cherokee scholar. BOK; CAGA; CUC; DEDB; HEC; HEGA; ROD; STAB; SUKA

Sitting Bull (1834–1890). DEDB; FRAB; HEC; HEGA; LEH; MOD; ROD; SUKA; WAM

Sockalexis, Louis (1873–1913). Baseball player. SMK

Squanto (d. 1622). Wampanoag. HEC

Tallchief, Maria (1925–). Dancer. ATA; FOGC; GRAD

Tallchief, Marjorie (1927–). Dancer. ATA; GRAD

Tammany (fl. 1685). Delaware. HED

Tecumseh (1768–1813). Shawnee chief. DEDB; HEC; HEGA; MAEA; MOD; ROD; STAB; WAL

Tekakwitha, Kateri (1656–1680). Mohawk nun. DAD-1; HED

Tewanima, Louis (d. 1969). Track athlete. HACA

Thorpe, Jim (1888–1953). Track athlete, football player. ASBA; BELB; DAB; DAFB; DAFG; DAG; DAGA; DAI; DAJ; DEF; DUF; FIC; HACA; HEG; HEI; HIE; HOC; LEH; LEPA; LEYB; LYB; RAAE; SID; SUD

Vasquez, Joseph C. (1918?–). Aviator. GRAC

Velarde, Pablita (1918–). Painter. GRAD; WAB

Victor, Wilma L. Educator, government official. GRAD

Ward, Nancy (fl. 1785). Cherokee leader. GRAD

Washakie (1804?–1900). Shoshone chief. HED

Wauneka, Annie Dodge (1912–). Navajo public health worker. BRBE†; GRAC; GRAD; WAB

Wetamoo (fl. 1675). Pocasset chief. GRAD

Winema (fl. 1850). Modoc princess. GRAD; WAB

Winnemucca, Sarah (1844–1891). Paiute. GRAD; TRD; WAB

Wovoka (Jack Wilson) (1856?–1932). Paiute mystic. STAB

Yoholo-Micco (1790?–1838). Creek chief. MOD

NATURALISTS

See also BOTANISTS; ECOLOGISTS; ENTOMOLOGISTS; ICHTHYOLOGISTS; ORNITHOLOGISTS; ZOOLOGISTS

American

Agassiz, Louis (1807–1873). (Born Switzerland). HYB; MIB

Akeley, Carl Ethan (1864–1926). BAB

Andrews, Roy Chapman (1884–1960). BAB

Barbour, Thomas (1884–1946). MIB

Bartram, William (1739–1823). BLB; CO-1; JEA

Beebe, William (1877–1962). BAB; COKA; COLA; COR; MIB†

Burroughs, John (1837–1921). CO-1; CORA; MIB

Carson, Rachel (1907–1964). CO-1; COR; CORA; ELA; EMB; FRE; GIBA; HIBB; PACA; SC; SQA; WAP

Comstock, Anna Botsford (1854–1930). EMB†; PAC; YOC

Leopold, Aldo (1886–1948). HIBB; MIB†; SQA

Muir, John (1838–1914). (Born Scotland). BEA; BLB; CO-1; CORA; CUC; DOCA; HEB; HIBB; MAL; MIB; SQA; WAP

Seton, Ernest Thompson (1860–1946). (Born England). CO-1

Thoreau, Henry David (1817–1862). ARB; BAC; BEG; BEGA; BLE; BOA; CAC; CO-1; CORA; CUC; EOB; HAJ; HIBB; HOA; MIB; RED; SQA; SUFA; WHB; WOAA

Foreign

Banks, Sir Joseph (1743–1820). English. BLB

Darwin, Charles Robert (1809–1882). English. ASA; BEK; BEP; BLB; CAA; CAB; COL; DEI; DEJ; DOE; FE; FRE; MIB; MOB; POD; SIA; SOB; STI

Hudson, William Henry (1841–1922). English. COO

Humboldt, Alexander von (1769–1859). German. BLB; HOB; KNA; MOB; ROL; WIA-1

Lamarck, Jean Baptiste Pierre Antoine de (1744–1829). French. STI

Leeuwenhoek, Anton van (1632–1723). Dutch. ASA; BEP; CAA; COL; DEB; DOE; FE; MIB; SHFB; SUF; THA

Spallanzani, Lazzaro (1729–1799). Italian. DEB; ROA

Wallace, Alfred Russel (1823–1913). English. ASA; BLB; MIB

White, Gilbert (1720–1793). English. MIB

NAVAL FIGURES

See also AMERICAN REVOLUTIONARY FIGURES— MILITARY; CIVIL WAR FIGURES—MILITARY; EXPLORERS & DISCOVERERS; MEDAL OF HONOR WINNERS

American

Anderson, William Robert (1921–). COR; SCBA

Barney, Joshua (1759–1818). BUIB†; MAE

Barry, John (1745–1803). (Born Ireland). RAD

Buchanan, Franklin (1800–1874). ICA

Byrd, Richard Evelyn (1888–1957). BAB; COC; COKA; CUC; DOC; ELA; FAA; FOH; GRB; ICA; LAC; NAC; ROL

Carlsen, Henrik K. (1915–). (Born Denmark). SUA

Cushing, William Barker (1842–1874). ICA

Dana, Richard Henry, Jr. (1815–1882). BEGA; SUFA

Decatur, Stephen (1779–1820). COD; CUC; ICA; NAC

Dewey, George (1837–1917). COD; CUC; ICA; NAC

Ellsberg, Edward (1891–). OLC

Farragut, David Glasgow (1801–1870). BOD; CUC; FIA; FID; ICA; NAC

Halsey, William Frederick (1882–1959). ARC; ICA; NAC

Jones, John Paul (1747–1792). BUIB; COD; CUC; DAC; DAFA; DEI; DEJ; DYA; FIA; FID; HIBD; ICA; LOA; NAC; OLA; SOA

King, Ernest Joseph (1878–1956). ARC; COD†; NAC

Lawrence, James (1781–1813). ICA; LEAA; LEP; NAC

Levy, Uriah Phillips (1792–1862). ALD; EIA; GEF; GRB-1; LERA; LETA

Macdonough, Thomas (1783–1825). ICA

Maury, Matthew Fontaine (1806–1873). COLA; COR; MAL; STI

Miller, Dorie (1919–1943). HODA; HUB; RIC; STQ†

Miller, Hugh Barr. HAQ

Mitscher, Marc A. (1887–1947). NAC

Momsen, Charles Bowers (1896–1967). OLC

Mulzac, Hugh Nathaniel (1886–1971). (Born West Indies). HUB; ROG; STF

Nimitz, Chester William (1885–1966). ARC; ICA; NAC

Peary, Robert Edwin (1856–1920). BAB; COC†; COLA; CUC; DOBB; DOC; EDA; FIA; GRC; HAQ; ICA; KNB†; NAC; ROL†

Perry, Matthew Calbraith (1794–1858). COD; ICA; MOB

Perry, Oliver Hazard (1785–1819). ICA; LEP; NAC

Philip, John Woodward (1840–1900). FID

Porter, David (1780–1843). ICA

Porter, David Dixon (1813–1891). ICA; NAC

Rickover, Hyman George (1900–1986). (Born Russia). COR; GRB-1; KE; NAC; WEB

Sims, William Sowden (1858–1936). ARD; ICA; NAC

Slocum, Joshua (1844–1910). DYA; LAA-2; SCBA

Spruance, Raymond Ames (1886–1969). ICA; NAC†

Stacey, May Humphreys (1837–1886). BUI

Wilkes, Charles (1798–1877). COR; DOC†; ROL

Willis, William (1893–1968?). OLC

British

Beatty, David, 1st earl (1871–1936). ARD

Bligh, William (1754–1817). SCBA

Drake, Sir Francis (1540–1596). DYA; GRAA; KEH; LAA-2; LACB; MOB; ROL

Jellicoe, John Rushworth Jellicoe, 1st earl (1859–1935). ARD

Nelson, Horatio, viscount (1758–1805). CHG; COD; MAJ; SCBA

Others

Bart, Jean (1651–1702). French. KEH

Grasse, François Joseph de (1722–1788). French. SOA

Hanno (fl. 450 B.C.). Carthaginian. DYA

Luckner, Felix von (1881–1966). German. ARD

Smith (Mr.) (fl. 1928). Australian. HAQ

Tirpitz, Alfred von (1849–1930). German. ARD

NAVIGATORS, *see* EXPLORERS & DISCOVERERS; GEOGRAPHERS; NAVAL FIGURES

NEPALESE

Tenzing, Norgay (1914–1986). Mountaineer. KEH; MOB; PRC

NEW ZEALANDERS

Amon, Chris (1943–). Automobile racer. JA

Batten, Jean (1909–1982). Aviator. HIFD; MO

Hillary, Sir Edmund (1919–). Mountaineer. ASB-1; BAB; COLA; DU-1; KEH; MOB; PRC; ROL†

Hulme, Dennis Clive (1936–). Automobile racer. ABB; JA

McLaren, Bruce Leslie (1937–1970). Automobile racer. JA; ORD

Rutherford, Ernest Rutherford, 1st baron (1871–1937). Physicist. ASA; BIA; FE; MOBA; POD; PRC; RID; SHFB; SIA

Snell, Peter (1938–). Track athlete. DEF; LEYB†

Walker, John (1952–). Track athlete. AAS-26

Wilkins, Maurice Hugh Frederick (1916–). Biophysicist. RIF

NEWSCASTERS, *see* TELEVISION & RADIO PERSONALITIES

NEWSPAPER WORKERS, *see* JOURNALISTS

NICARAGUANS

Dario, Rubén (Felix Rubén Garcia Sarmiento) (1867–1916). Poet. WO

NIGERIANS

Azikiwe, Nnamdi (1904–). Governor-general. ADA

Balewa, Sir Abubakar Tafawa (1912–1966). Prime minister. KEF

Crowther, Samuel Ajayi (1808–1891). Bishop. POA

Fafunwa, Babs. Educator. OJA

Ighodaro, Irene Elizabeth. Physician. CRA

Moore, Kofoworola Aina (1913–). Tribeswoman. PEA

Udo Akpabio. Tribesman. PEA

NOBEL PRIZE WINNERS

Chemistry – American

Calvin, Melvin (1911–). BEK

Langmuir, Irving (1881–1957). ASA

Libby, Willard Frank (1908–1980). AAS-33; POC

Pauling, Linus Carl (1901–). AAS-34; MEB; MEC; WIC

Stanley, Wendell Meredith (1904–1971). BEK; SUF

Urey, Harold Clayton (1893–1981). BOB; RID

Chemistry – English

Aston, Francis William (1877–1945). RID; SHFB†

Hodgkin, Dorothy Crowfoot (1910–). HA-1; SHFE

Soddy, Frederick (1877–1956). POD; RID

Chemistry – French

Curie, Marie Sklodowska (1867–1934). (Born Poland). ASA; ASB-1; BEC; BEP; BOB; BOC; BOH; BUF; CAA; COL; DEI; DEJ; DOE; EVD; FE; FRE; HUE; KOA; MAJ; MANB; MASA; PA; PAC; POD; RID; SC; SHFB; SHFE†; SIA; STI

Joliot-Curie, Frédéric (1900–1958). FE; RID

Joliot-Curie, Irène (1897–1956). FE; RID; SC†; SHFE†

Moissan, Henri (1852–1907). LET

Chemistry – German

Baeyer, Adolf von (1835–1917). LET

Haber, Fritz (1868–1934). FE; LET

Wallach, Otto (1847–1931). LET

Willstätter, Richard (1872–1942). LET

Chemistry – Others

Hevesy, George de (1885–1966). Hungarian. LET

Ramsay, Sir William (1852–1916). Scottish. COLA†; SHFB

Rutherford, Ernest Rutherford, 1st baron (1871–1937). New Zealand. ASA; BIA; FE; MOBA; POD; PRC; RID; SHFB; SIA

Literature

Agnon, Shmuel Yosef (1888–1970). Israeli. GRB-1; ROGA

Asturias, Miguel Angel (1899–1974). Guatemalan. WO

Bergson, Henri (1859–1941). French. LET

Buck, Pearl S. (1892–1973). COKA; CON; GIBA†; HEF; KOA; LEGB; MUA; OCB; SHFE

Churchill, Sir Winston Leonard Spencer (1874–1965). English. ASB-1; CHG; CUC; DEI; DEJ; DOF; ELA; EVA; FLBB; FRE; HIB†; JAC; JAD; KE; RADA; TAC; YOA

Eliot, Thomas Stearns (1888–1965). English. (Born U.S.). ASB-1; BRBB; COP

Faulkner, William (1897–1962). ASB-1; CAC; CON; FLBA; HEF

Hemingway, Ernest (1899–1961). ASB-1; CAC; CON; HEF; LAC; LEGB

Hesse, Hermann (1877–1962). German. KE

Heyse, Paul Johann (1830–1914). German. LET

Kipling, Rudyard (1865–1936). English. BEI; COB; COO; COP; STK

Lagerlof, Selma (1858–1940). Swedish. PA; SHFE†

Lewis, Sinclair (1885–1951). BOA; CON; HEF; LEGB

Mommsen, Theodor (1817–1903). German. HIB

Neruda, Pablo (1904–1973). Chilean. WO

O'Neill, Eugene Gladstone (1888–1953). ASB-1; BOA; DEI; DEJ; SHFA

Pasternak, Boris Leonidovich (1890–1960). Russian. LET; POFA

Reymont, Wladyslaw Stanislaw (1867–1926). Polish. MANB

Rolland, Romain (1866–1944). French. DED

Russell, Bertrand Arthur William Russell, 3d earl (1872–1970). English. HAJ; KE; OZA

Sachs, Nelly (1891–1970). Swedish. (Born Germany). SHFE

Shaw, George Bernard (1856–1950). Irish. ASB-1; DEI; DEJ; KE; STL

Sholokhov, Mikhail Aleksandrovich (1905–1984). Russian. POFA

Singer, Isaac Bashevis (1904–). (Born Poland). GRB-1

Steinbeck, John (1902–1968). CON; HEF

Undset, Sigrid (1882–1949). Norwegian. CAHA

Yeats, William Butler (1865–1939). Irish. BRBB

Medicine & Physiology – American

Beadle, George Wells (1903–). RIF

Carrel, Alexis (1873–1944). (Born France). POB; RIF

Cori, Carl Ferdinand (1896–1984). (Born Czechoslovakia). RIF

Cori, Gerty Theresa (1896–1957). (Born Czechoslovakia). RIF; SC†; SHFE†; YOF

Cournand, André Frédéric (1895–1988). (Born France). RIF

Doisy, Edward Adelbert (1893–1986). RIF

Enders, John Franklin (1897–1985). CHE†; COLA†; RIF; SUF

Erlanger, Joseph (1874–1965). LET; RIF

Gasser, Herbert Spencer (1888–1963). RIF

Hench, Philip Showalter (1896–1965). RIF

Kendall, Edward Calvin (1886–1972). RIF

Kornberg, Arthur (1918–). GRB-1; LET; RIF

Landsteiner, Karl (1868–1943). (Born Austria). CHE†; COLA†; FE; LET; RIF; STE

Lederberg, Joshua (1925–). GRB-1; LET; RIF

Lipmann, Fritz Albert (1899–1986). (Born Germany). LET

Loewi, Otto (1873–1961). (Born Germany). LET; RIF

McClintock, Barbara (1902–). SHFE

Meyerhof, Otto Fritz (1884–1951). (Born Germany). LET; RIF

Minot, George Richards (1885–1950). RIF

Morgan, Thomas Hunt (1866–1945). BEK; COLA; RIF

Muller, Hermann Joseph (1890–1967). BEK; LET; RIF

Murphy, William Parry (1892–). RIF

Ochoa, Severo (1905–). (Born Spain). RIF

Richards, Dickinson Woodruff, Jr. (1895–1973). RIF

Robbins, Frederick Chapman (1916–). RIF

Szent-Györgyi, Albert von (1893–1986). (Born Hungary). PAC; RIF

Tatum, Edward Lawrie (1909–1975). RIF

Waksman, Selman Abraham (1888–1973). (Born Russia). GRB-1; LET; LETA; LIA; RIF

Watson, James Dewey (1928–). BEK; FE; FRE†; GRBA; RIF

Weller, Thomas Huckle (1915–). RIF

Whipple, George Hoyt (1878–1976). RIF

Yalow, Rosalyn Sussman (1921–). GIB-1; GL; GRB-1; HA-1; SHFE

Medicine & Physiology – Dutch

Eijkman, Christian (1858–1930). RIF

Einthoven, Willem (1860–1927). AAS-33; FE; RIF

Zernike, Frits (b. 1888). AAS-23

Medicine & Physiology – English

Adrian, Edgar Douglas (1889–1977). RIF

Chain, Ernst Boris (1906–1979). (Born Germany). BEK†; COLA†; GRB-1; LAE; LET; POB; RIF

Crick, Francis H. C. (1916–). BEK; FE; FRE†; RIF

Dale, Sir Henry Hallett (1875–1968). RIF

Hill, Archibald Vivian (1886–1977). RIF

Hopkins, Sir Frederick Gowland (1861–1947). RIF

Hounsfield, Godfrey (1919–). AAS-33

Krebs, Sir Hans Adolf (1900–1981). (Born Germany). LET

Medawar, Peter Brian (1915–1987). CHE†; RIF

Ross, Sir Ronald (1857–1932). AAS-31; DEB; RIF; ROA

Sherrington, Sir Charles Scott (1857–1952). RIF

Wilkins, Maurice Hugh Frederick (1916–). RIF

Medicine & Physiology – German

Behring, Emil von (1854–1917). AAS-31; BEK†; DEB; RIE; RIF; ROA

Domagk, Gerhard (1895–1964). AAS-31; RIF; ROA

Ehrlich, Paul (1854–1915). AAS-31; ASA; BEK; DEB; FE; LET; POB; RIE; RIF; ROA; SUF

Forssmann, Werner (1904–1979). RIF

Koch, Robert (1843–1910). AAS-31; BEK; COL; DEB; DEI; DEJ; FAF; FE; HUD; RIE; RIF; ROA; SUF

Kossel, Albrecht (1853–1927). RIF

Spemann, Hans (1869–1941). RIF
Warburg, Otto Heinrich (1883–1970). LET

Medicine & Physiology – Swiss
Kocher, Emil Theodor (1841–1917). POB; RIF
Müller, Paul Hermann (1899–1965). AAS-31†; RIF
Reichstein, Tadeus (1897–). (Born Poland). LET; RIF

Medicine & Physiology – Others
Bárány, Robert (1876–1936). Austrian. LET
Bordet, Jules (1870–1961). Belgian. RIF
Bovet, Daniele (1907–). Italian. (Born Switzerland). RIF
Burnet, Sir Macfarlane (1899–1985). Australian. RIF
Dam, Henrik (1895–1976). Danish. RIF
Fleming, Sir Alexander (1881–1955). Scottish. AAS-31; ASB-1; BEK; BEP; BOB; CAA; COLA; FE; HUD; LAE; POB; RIF; ROA; SHG; SUF
Florey, Sir Howard Walter (1898–1968). Australian. BEK†; COLA†; LAE; POB; RIF; SHG
Golgi, Camillo (1844–1926). Italian. RIF
Houssay, Bernardo Alberto (1887–1971). Argentine. RIF
Krogh, August (1874–1949). Danish. RIF
Laveran, Charles Louis (1845–1922). French. RIF; SHG
Macleod, John James R. (1876–1935). Scottish. BEK†; RIF
Metchnikoff, Élie (1845–1916). Russian. COL; DEB; LET; RIF; ROA; SOB
Nicolle, Charles Jules Henri (1866–1936). French. AAS-31; RIF
Pavlov, Ivan Petrovich (1849–1936). Russian. ASB-1; CAA; FE; RIF; SIA
Ramón y Cajal, Santiago (1852–1934). Spanish. RIF
Theiler, Max (1899–1972). South African. AAS-31; RIF

Peace – American
See also PACIFISTS
Addams, Jane (1860–1935). AAS-34; BOC; BRBE; CAGA; COG; COKA; CUC; DEDA; DOD; FEC; FOH; FOJ; GIBA; LEZC; MAN; MASA; MAT; MEA; MEC; NAB; PA; PACA; SHFE†; STJ; STLA; WABC†; WECB; WIC
American Friends Service Committee. MEA; MEC
Balch, Emily Green (1867–1961). MEC; SHFE†; WIC
Borlaug, Norman Ernest (1914–). MEC
Bunche, Ralph Johnson (1904–1971). ADA; ADB; BRG; DOF-1; FEC; FLD; HUA; JOC; KEE; LEI; MEA; MEC; RIC; RICA; STO; WIC; YOI

Butler, Nicholas Murray (1862–1947). MEA; MEC; WIC
Dawes, Charles Gates (1865–1951). FEA; HAOA; HOEA; MEC†; WIC
Hull, Cordell (1871–1955). HEEA; MEC†; WIC
Kellogg, Frank Billings (1856–1937). HEEA; MEC†; WIC
King, Martin Luther, Jr. (1929–1968). AAS-34; ADA; ADB; ASB-1; BAF; BRBD; BRG; DEJ; DOF-1; DU-1; ELA; FAA; FEC; FLD; GRAB-01; HAJ; HODA; JO; JOC; KE; LEPE; MEB; MEC; RICA; STO; WEB; WIAA-8; WIC; YOA; YOI
Marshall, George Catlett (1880–1959). ARC; COD†; HEEA; MEC†; RADA; SWE-1; WIC
Mott, John Raleigh (1865–1955). MEC†; WIC
Pauling, Linus Carl (1901–). AAS-34; MEB; MEC; WIC
Roosevelt, Theodore (1858–1919). ALE; ASB; BAEB; BAG; BAG-1; BEB; BEC; BLA; BUIA; CAG; CAH; CO-1; COI; COJA; CORA; COS; CUC; DAE; DEI; DEJ; DUB; DUC; DUCA; FEA; FEC; FOH; FRBA; HAA; HAOA; HIH; HOEA; KEA; LAI; LEQ; LEQA; MAB; MABA; MAL; MEA; MEC; MIA; OLA; PED; ROH; ROHA; ROK; ROL†; STH; SUBB; WHD; WIC
Root, Elihu (1845–1937). MEC†; WIC
Wilson, Woodrow (1856–1924). ARB; ASB-1; BAEB; BAG; BAG-1; BEB; BLA; BUIA; CAG; CAH; COI; COS; CUC; DEI; DEJ; DOF; DUB; DUC; DUCA; FOB; FRBA; HIH; LEQ; LEQA; MAB; MABA; MEA; MEC; MIA; PED; ROH; ROHA; ROK; SUBB; WHD; WIC

Peace – Belgian
Beernaert, Auguste Marie François (1829–1912). MEC†; WIC
Lafontaine, Henri (1854–1943). MEC†; WIC
Pire, Georges Henri (1910–1969). MEC; WIC

Peace – English
Angell, Sir Norman (1874–1967). MEA; MEC; WIC
British Friends Service Council. MEA
Cecil of Chelwood, Edgar Algernon Robert Gascoyne-Cecil, 1st viscount (1864–1958). MEC†; WIC
Chamberlain, Sir Austen (1863–1937). MEC†; WIC
Cremer, Sir William Randal (1838–1908). MEA; MEC; WIC
Henderson, Arthur (1863–1935). MEC†; WIC
Noel-Baker, Philip John (1889–1982). MEC†; WIC

Peace – French
Bourgeois, Léon Victor Auguste (1851–1925). MEC†; WIC

Briand, Aristide (1862–1932). MEC†; WIC
Buisson, Ferdinand (1841–1932). MEC†; WIC
Cassin, René (1887–1976). MEC†; WIC
Estournelles de Constant, Paul Henri Benjamin, baron d' (1852–1924). MEC†; WIC
Jouhaux, Léon (1879–1954). MEC; WIC
Passy, Frédéric (1822–1912). MEA; MEC; WIC
Renault, Louis (1843–1918). MEC†; WIC
Schweitzer, Albert (1875–1965). BAF; BEC; EVD; FOJ; KE; KEE; LO; MAN; MEA; MEC; WIC; YOA

Peace – German
Brandt, Willy (1913–). MEC; WECA
Ossietzky, Carl von (1889–1938). AAS-34; MEA; MEC; WIC
Quidde, Ludwig (1858–1941). MEC†; WIC
Stresemann, Gustav (1878–1929). MEC†; WIC

Peace – Irish
Corrigan, Mairead (1944–). AAS-34; COG-1; SHFE†
MacBride, Sean (1904–1988). MEC
Williams, Betty (1943–). AAS-34; COG-1; SHFE†

Peace – Swedish
Arnoldson, Klas Pontus (1844–1916). MEC; WIC
Branting, Karl Hjalmar (1860–1925). MEC†; WIC
Hammarskjöld, Dag (1905–1961). FOJ; KE; MEC; WIC; YOA
Myrdal, Alva (1902–1986). DU-1; SHFE
Söderblom, Nathan (1866–1931). MEC†; WIC

Peace – Swiss
Ducommun, Élie (1833–1906). MEC†; WIC
Dunant, Jean Henri (1828–1910). DED; EVA; MEA; MEC; WIC; WRA
Gobat, Charles Albert (1843–1914). MEC†; WIC
International Red Cross of Geneva. MEA

Peace – Others
Asser, Tobias M. C. (1838–1913). Dutch. LET; MEC†; WIC
Bajer, Frederik (1839–1922). Danish. MEC†; WIC
Begin, Menachem (1913–). Israeli. (Born Poland). ASB-1; GRB-1; HAGD
Fried, Alfred Hermann (1864–1921). Austrian. LET; MEC†; WIC
Lange, Christian Louis (1869–1938). Norwegian. MEC†; WIC
Luthuli, Albert John (1899–1967). South African. ADA; FOJ; LEA; MEC; WIC
Moneta, Ernesto Teodoro (1833–1918). Italian. MEC†; WIC
Mother Theresa (1910–). Indian. (Born Yugoslavia). ASB-1; DU-1; SHFE

Nansen, Fridtjof (1861–1930). Norwegian. COC†; COG; DOC; HEA; KEE; KNB†; MEA; MEC; MOB; ROL; WIC
Orr, John Boyd, 1st baron (1880–1971). Scottish. KEE; MEC; WIC
Pearson, Lester Bowles (1897–1972). Canadian. MEA; MEC; WEC; WIC
Pérez Esquivel, Adolfo (1931–). Argentine. DU-1
Saavedra Lamas, Carlos (1880–1959). Argentine. MEC†; WIC
Sadat, Anwar el- (1918–1981). Egyptian. ASB-1; DU-1
Sakharov, Andrei D. (1921–). Russian. AAS-34; DU-1; MEC
Sato, Eisaku (1901–1975). Japanese. MEC; WECA
Suttner, Bertha von (1843–1914). Austrian. MEA; MEC; SHFE†; WIC
Tutu, Desmond Mpilo (1931–). South African. AAS-34
Walesa, Lech (1943–). Polish. AAS-34; DU-1

Physics – American
Bardeen, John (1908–). AAS-33†; GRAB-3; MAPA
Bloch, Felix (1905–1983). (Born Switzerland). LET
Brattain, Walter Houser (1902–1987). AAS-33†; GRAB-3; MAPA
Compton, Arthur Holly (1892–1962). BAF; BOB; RID
Einstein, Albert (1879–1955). (Born Germany). ASA; ASB-1; BEA; BEP; BOB; BUF; CAA; COL; CUC; DEI; DEJ; DOE; FE; FRE; GEF; GRB-1; GUB; KE; LEL; LES; LET; LETA; MAM; MOBA; POD; RID; SHFB; SIA; YOA
Fermi, Enrico (1901–1954). (Born Italy). BEA; BIA; BOB; CAA; COLA; CUC; FE; FRE; LEL; LET; MAS; RID; SHFB; SIA; YOE
Franck, James (1882–1964). (Born Germany). LET
Goeppert-Mayer, Maria (1906–1972). (Born Germany). HA-1; SC†; SHFE
Lawrence, Ernest Orlando (1901–1958). ASA; CUC; RID; SIA
Lee, Tsung-Dao (1926–). (Born China). BOB
Michelson, Albert Abraham (1852–1931). (Born Germany). CAA; FE; GRB-1; LET; LETA; SIA; STI
Millikan, Robert Andrews (1868–1953). CUC
Rabi, Isidor Isaac (1898–1988). (Born Austria). GRB-1; LET
Segrè, Emilio Gino (1905–). (Born Italy). LET
Shockley, William Bradford (1910–). AAS-33†; GRAB-3; MAPA
Stern, Otto (1888–1969). (Born Germany). LET

Townes, Charles Hard (1915–). AAS-33; COLA; DU-1; FE; MAPA; THA
Yang, Chen Ning (1922–). (Born China). BOB

Physics – English
Chadwick, Sir James (1891–1974). FE; RID
Cockcroft, Sir John Douglas (1897–1967). FE
Thomson, Sir Joseph John (1856–1940). CAA; FE; MOBA; RID; SHFB; SIA

Physics – French
Becquerel, Antoine Henri (1852–1908). ASA; FE; MOBA; SHFB; SOB
Curie, Marie Sklodowska (1867–1934). (Born Poland). ASA; ASB-1; BEC; BEP; BOB; BOC; BOH; BUF; CAA; COL; DEI; DEJ; DOE; EVD; FE; FRE; HUE; KOA; MAJ; MANB; MASA; PA; PAC; POD; RID; SC; SHFB; SHFE†; SIA; STI
Curie, Pierre (1859–1906). ASA; BOB; BUF; DOE; PAC; RID; STI
Lippmann, Gabriel (1845–1921). LET

Physics – German
Born, Max (1882–1970). LET
Hertz, Gustav (1887–1975). LET
Laue, Max von (1879–1960). FE
Mössbauer, Rudolf Ludwig (1929–). HAC
Planck, Max Karl (1858–1947). CAA; FE; SHFB
Roentgen, Wilhelm (1845–1923). AAS-33; ASA; CAA; DEI; DEJ; FE; PRC; SHFB; SHG; STI

Physics – Others
Bohr, Niels H. D. (1885–1962). Danish. CAA; COLA; FE; LET; MOBA; RID; SIA
Marconi, Guglielmo (1874–1937). Italian. AAS-33; BOB; COL; EBA; EVC; FAB; FE; FRE; PRC; SHFB; SIA; THA
Tamm, Igor Yevgenyvich (1895–1971). Russian. LET
Van der Waals, Johannes Diederik (1837–1923). Dutch. FE
Wilson, Charles T. R. (1869–1959). Scottish. RID

NOBLES, *see* RULERS

NORWEGIANS

Amundsen, Roald (1872–1928). Polar explorer. BAB; COC†; COL; DOBB; DOC; GRB; GRC; KEH; KNA†; KNB†; MOB; PRC; ROL; WIA-1
Asbjörnsen, Peter Christen (1812–1885). Folklorist. SMAB

Bjerknes, Vilhelm (1862–1951). Physicist. FE
Bull, Ole (1810–1880). Violinist. BOD; CHFA
Eric the Red (fl. 10th century). Navigator. DYA; KEH; KNB; MOB; ROL†
Ericsson, Leif (fl. 1000). Explorer. COC; HEA; MOB; ROL†; VIA†
Grieg, Edvard Hagerup (1843–1907). Composer. BRF; BUD; DEI; DEJ; FIE†; GOA; KAE; SAA
Harold I, the Fairhaired (850?–933). King of Norway. JOBB
Henie, Sonja (1913–1969). Skater, actress. ASBA; DAG; DAGA; GED; GEDA; HOBAA; LEYB†; RYA†
Herjolfsson, Bjarni (fl. 985). Explorer. DYA; MOB†; VIA†
Heyerdahl, Thor (1914–). Anthropologist. BAB; OLC; SCBA
Ingolf (10th century). Explorer. MOB
Lange, Christian Louis (1869–1938). Pacifist, statesman. MEC†; WIC
Moe, Jörgen Ingebretsen (1813–1882). Folklorist. SMAB
Munch, Edward (1863–1944). Painter. WIAA
Nansen, Fridtjof (1861–1930). Explorer, statesman. COC†; COG; DOC; HEA; KEE; KNB†; MEA; MEC; MOB; ROL; WIC
Nansen, Odd (1901–). Architect, humanitarian. BAF
Undset, Sigrid (1882–1949). Author. CAHA
Waitz, Grete (1953–). Track athlete. AAS-30; BAEC; SUDB

NOVELISTS, *see* AUTHORS—FICTION

NURSES

American
Anthony, Sister (Mary Ellen O'Connell) (1814–1897). (Born Ireland). COFA
Barton, Clara (1821–1912). BEC; BOC; CUC; DED; DEI; DEJ; DOD; FOH; GIBA; JOCA; LEK; LEPC; MAK; MAT; PA; SMC; STJ; STLA; WABC†
Bickerdyke, Mary Ann Ball (1817–1901). MAK; WABC†; WRA
Blake, Florence G. (1907–). YOB
Breckinridge, Mary (1877–1965). COFA; MAK; WRA
Dalstrom, Ingeborg. WRA
Day, Enid. WRA
Edmonds, Sarah Emma (1841–1898). FOA; KN; SUG; WABC†
Floyd, Theodora A. (1896–). YOB

Goodrich, Annie Warburton (1866–1954). YOB
Gowan, M. Olivia, Sister (1888–). YOB
Jaissle, Louise. WRA
Kempner, Mary Jean. WRA
Lally, Grace. WRA
Leone, Lucile Petry (1902–). YOB
McKinney, Sally Zumaris (1915–). COFA
Mahoney, Mary Eliza (1845–1926). LOAV
Nutting, Mary Adelaide (1858–1948). (Born Canada). YOB
O'Hara, Dee. COFA; HOG†
Osborne, Estelle Massey (1903–). YOB
Prochazka, Anne (1897–). (Born Czechoslovakia). YOB
Richards, Linda Ann (1841–1930). COFA; WABC†; WAJ
Sanger, Margaret (1883–1966). ARAA; ARB; BRBE; GIBA; KOA; ROJ; SC; STLA; WABC
Staupers, Mable Keaton (1890–). (Born West Indies). DOF-1
Stewart, Isabel Maitland (1878–1963). (Born Canada). YOB
Taylor, Susie King (1848–1912). MAV
Trammell, Beatrice Johnson. BOG
Wald, Lillian D. (1867–1940). ALD; BRBE†; CAGA; DOD; EIA; GEE; GIBA; GRB-1; LETA; WABC†; WRA; YOB

Foreign

Banfill, B. J. Australian. WRA
Cavell, Edith (1865–1915). English. HAA; MAJ; MAK; RADA; WRA
Felicie, Jacoba (fl. 1322). French. MASA†; SC
Galard, Geneviève de (1925–). French. MAK
Haile Selassie, Tsahai (1919–1942). MAK
Ileana. Romanian. WRA
Kenny, Elizabeth (1886–1952). Australian. BOC; MAK; WRA
Mance, Jeanne (1606–1673). French. MAK
Marillac, Louise de (1591–1660). French. MAK
Nienhuys, Janna. Dutch. MAK
Nightingale, Florence (1820–1910). English. ASB-1; BOC; BOH; COKB; DEI; DEJ; EVD; FAF; FRE; HUE; MAK; MAN; MASA; PA; SC; STP; WRA

NUTRITIONISTS

Emerson, Gladys Anderson (1903–). EMB†; HA-1; YOF
Finkelstein, Beatrice. HOG
Frey, Charles N. (b. 1885). PAB
Richards, Ellen Swallow (1842–1911). SC; WABC†

OCEANOGRAPHERS

See also UNDERWATER EXPLORERS

Agassiz, Alexander (1835–1910). (Born Switzerland). COR
Bruun, Anton Frederick (1901–1961). Danish. BRBC
Clark, Eugenie (1922–). EMB; HAKA
Cromwell, Townsend (1922–1958). BRBC
Dill, Robert F. (1927–). OLC
Ewing, W. Maurice (1906–1974). BRBC; COR
Grigg, Rick (1938?–). OLD
Iselin, Columbus O'Donnell (1904–1971). BRBC
Maury, Matthew Fontaine (1806–1873). COLA; COR; MAL; STI
Mead, Sylvia Earle (1935–). GL; HA-1; HAKA
Piccard, Jacques (1922–). Swiss. BAB; COLA; COR; OLC
Pryor, Taylor (1931–). BRBC
Rechnitzer, Andreas B. OLC
Revelle, Roger (1909–). BRBC; COR

OLYMPIC ATHLETES, *see* INDIVIDUAL SPORTS

ORGANISTS, *see* MUSICIANS—ORGANISTS

ORNITHOLOGISTS

Audubon, John James (1785–1851). (Born Haiti). BEA; BEC; BOK; CO-1; CORA; CUC; DEI; DEJ; FOH; HEB; HYB; LEAB; LEB; LOB; MAL; MIB; SIE; WAP
Beebe, William (1877–1962). BAB; COKA; COLA; COR; MIB†
Chapman, Frank Michler (1864–1945). MIB
Nuttall, Thomas (1786–1859). (Born England). JEA
Vogt, William (1902–1968). SQA
Wilson, Alexander (1766–1813). (Born Scotland). CO-1; CORA; HYB

OUTLAWS, *see* CRIMINALS & OUTLAWS

PACIFISTS

See also NOBEL PRIZE WINNERS—PEACE

Arnoldson, Klas Pontus (1844–1916). Swedish.
 MEC; WIC
Berrigan, Daniel (1921–). LEZC
Berrigan, Philip (1923–). LEZC
Cremer, Sir William Randal (1838–1908). English. MEA; MEC; WIC
Fox, George (1624–1691). English. FOJ
Fried, Alfred Hermann (1864–1921). Austrian.
 LET; MEC†; WIC
Holmes, John Haynes (1879–1964). LEZC
Lange, Christian Louis (1869–1938). Norwegian.
 MEC†; WIC
Moneta, Ernesto Teodoro (1833–1918). Italian.
 MEC†; WIC
Muste, Abraham Johannes (1885–1967). (Born the Netherlands). FOJ; LEZC
Noel-Baker, Philip John (1889–1982). English.
 MEC†; WIC
Ossietzky, Carl von (1889–1938). German.
 AAS-34; MEA; MEC; WIC
Quidde, Ludwig (1858–1941). German. MEC†;
 WIC
Sita, Nana (1898–). South African. LEA
Spock, Benjamin (1903–). BOHA; CHE; HAJ;
 HOBB
Suttner, Bertha von (1843–1914). Austrian. MEA;
 MEC; SHFE†; WIC

PAINTERS

See also ENGRAVERS & ETCHERS; ILLUSTRATORS

American
Abbey, Edwin Austin (1852–1911). CHC
Allston, Washington (1779–1843). FRA
Alston, Charles H. (1907–). ADB
Amevor, Charlotte (1932–). FAH
Andrews, Benny (1930–). FAH
Audubon, John James (1785–1851). (Born Haiti).
 BEA; BEC; BOK; CO-1; CORA; CUC; DEI;
 DEJ; FOH; HEB; HYB; LEAB; LEB; LOB;
 MAL; MIB; SIE; WAP
Bannister, Edward M. (1833–1901). (Born Canada). ADA; ADB
Bearden, Romare (1914–1988). FAH
Beaux, Cecilia (1863–1942). NE
Bellows, George Wesley (1882–1925). MAG; SIE
Bierstadt, Albert (1830–1902). (Born Germany).
 HEDA
Biggers, John (1924–). FAH

Bingham, George Caleb (1811–1879). FRA;
 HEDA; LEE; SIE
Brown, Kay (1932?–). FAI
Brumidi, Constantino (1805–1880). (Born Italy).
 MAS
Burns, Maurice (1935?–). FAI
Burton, Marie. BOHB
Byard, Carole Marie (1941–). FAI
Cassatt, Mary (1845–1926). CUC; FOGB; FRA;
 LEE; MAG; NE; STJ; STLA; WABC†
Catlin, George (1796–1872). FOC; HEB; HEDA;
 HOD
Cole, Thomas (1801–1848). (Born England).
 HEDA; LEB
Copley, John Singleton (1738–1815). BR; MAG;
 SIE
Cortor, Eldzier (1916–). FAH
Davies, Arthur B. (1862–1928). LEE; SIE
Davis, Stuart (1894–). FRA
De Kooning, Willem (1904–). (Born the Netherlands). WIAA
Douglas, Emory (1943–). FAI
Duchamp, Marcel (1887–1968). (Born France).
 WIAA
Duncanson, Robert S. (1817–1872). ADA; ADB;
 BEBA
Eakins, Thomas (1844–1916). FRA; MAG; SIE
Frankenthaler, Helen (1928–). FOGB
Glackens, William James (1870–1938). DEDC
Goreleigh, Rex (1903–). FAH
Gropper, William (1897–1977). DEDC
Henri, Robert (1865–1929). MAG
Hinton, Alfred (1940–). FAI
Hofmann, Hans (1880–1966). (Born Germany).
 BEA; WIAA
Homer, Winslow (1836–1910). CHC; DEI; DEJ;
 FRA; HEDA; KAA; LEE; LEOA; MAG; SIE;
 SMBA
Houser, Allan (1914–). GRAC
Howe, Oscar (1915–). LEH; LEOA
Inness, George (1825–1894). FRA; HEDA; MAG;
 SIE
Jackson, Suzanne (1944–). FOGB
Jeffries, Rosalind (1930?–). FAI
Johnson, Malvin Gray (1896–1934). ADA; ADB
Johnston, Joshua (1770–1830). BEBA; WIBA
Jones, Lawrence. FAH
Lawrence, Jacob (1917–). ADA; ADB; BEBA;
 DOF-1; FAH; RIC; RICA
Leutze, Emanuel (1816–1868). (Born Germany).
 HEDA
Lichtenstein, Roy (1923–). WIAA
Man Ray (1890–1976). ASB-1
Marin, John (1870–1953). FRA
Millar, Onnie (1918–). FAI
Miller, Alfred Jacob (1810–1874). HEDA; HOD

Morgan, Norma (1928–). FAH

Moses, Anna Mary Robertson (Grandma Moses) (1860–1961). CUC; FOGB; PA

Obey, Trudel Mimms. FAI

O'Keeffe, Georgia (1887–1986). CLA; FOGB; GIBA; NE

Oliver, Kermit (1943–). FAI

Outterbridge, John W. (1933–). FAI

Peale, Charles Willson (1741–1827). BR; LEE; SIE

Phillips, Bertrand (1938–). FAI

Pippin, Horace (1888–1946). ADA; ADB; BEBA

Pollock, Jackson (1912–1956). FRA; WIAA

Prendergast, Maurice Brazil (1861–1924). MAG

Remington, Frederic (1861–1909). HEDA; HOD; KAW

Ringgold, Faith. FAH

Rosado del Valle, Julio (1922–). NEBB

Russell, Charles Marion (1864–1926). HEDA; HOD; WAA

Ryder, Albert Pinkham (1847–1917). FRA; MAG; SIE

Sargent, John Singer (1856–1925). CUC; FRA; LEE; MAG; SIE

Schreyvogel, Charles (1861–1912). HEDA

Shahn, Ben (1898–1969). (Born Lithuania). FRA; WIAA

Sloan, John (1871–1951). FRA; SIE

Smith, Alfred J., Jr. (1949–). FAI

Smybert, John (1688–1751). (Born Scotland). MAG

Stuart, Gilbert (1755–1828). BR; CHC; FRA; LEE; MAG; SIE

Tanner, Henry Ossawa (1859–1937). ADA; ADB; BEBA; BRB†; HUA; ROG

Trumbull, John (1756–1843). BR; BUIB†; HEDA

Twiggs, Leo Franklin (1934–). FAI

Velarde, Pablita (1918–). GRAD; WAB

Warhol, Andy (1930–1987). WIAA

West, Benjamin (1738–1820). BR; CAD; HEDA; LEE; LEOA; SIE

Whistler, James Abbott McNeill (1834–1903). CHC; CUC; FRA; KAA; LEE; LEOA; MAG; SIE

White, Charles (1918–1979). ADA; ADB; FAH

Wilson, John (1922–). FAH

Wood, Grant (1892–1942). BOD; CUC; HEDA; LEE; LEOA; SIE

Wyeth, Andrew (1917–). WIAA

Dutch

Gogh, Vincent van (1853–1890). DEI; DEJ; KAA; MAH; WIAA

Hals, Frans (1580–1666). CHC; MAI

Rembrandt Hermanszoon van Rijn (1606–1669). CHC; DEI; DEJ; KAA; MAI

Vermeer, Jan or Johannes (1632–1675). CHC; KAA; MAI

English

Gainsborough, Thomas (1727–1788). CHC; DEI; DEJ

Hogarth, William (1697–1794). KAA

Kauffmann, Angelica (1741–1807). (Born Switzerland). BOH; NE

Reynolds, Sir Joshua (1723–1792). CHC

Riley, Bridget (1931–). WIAA

Flemish

Bruegel, Pieter, the Elder (1520?–1569). KAA; MAI

Eyck, Hubert van (1366–1426). MAI

Eyck, Jan van (1370?–1440?). KAA; MAI

Rubens, Peter Paul (1577–1640). CHC; KAA; MAI

Van Dyck, Sir Anthony (1599–1641). CHC

French

Bonheur, Rosa (1822–1899). BOC

Braque, Georges (1882–1963). MAH

Cézanne, Paul (1839–1906). ASB-1; KAA; MAH; WIAA

Carot, Jean Baptiste (1796–1875). CHC; DEI; DEJ; MAH

Daumier, Honoré (1808–1879). KAA

David, Jacques Louis (1748–1825). KAA; MAH†

Degas, Edgar (1834–1917). KAA; MAH

Delacroix, Eugène (1798–1863). KAA; MAH

Dubuffet, Jean (1901–1985). WIAA

Gauguin, Paul (1848–1903). KAA; MAH; WIAA

Laurencin, Marie (1885–1956). NE

Léger, Fernand (1881–1955). WIAA

Manet, Édouard (1832–1883). KAA; MAH

Matisse, Henri (1869–1954). KAA; MAH; WIAA

Millet, Jean François (1814–1875). CHC

Monet, Claude (1840–1926). KAA

Morisot, Berthe (1841–1895). NE

Poussin, Nicolas (1594–1665). KAA; MAH†

Renoir, Auguste (1841–1919). ASB-1; KAA; MAH

Rouault, Georges (1871–1958). KAA

Soutine, Chaim (1894–1943). (Born Lithuania). WIAA

Toulouse-Lautrec, Henri Marie Raymond de (1864–1901). Painter. KAA

Vasarely, Victor (1908–). (Born Hungary). WIAA

Vigee-Lebrun, Elisabeth (1755–1842). NE

Watteau, Jean Antoine (1684–1721). KAA; MAH†

German

Dürer, Albrecht (1471–1528). CHC; KAA; MAI

Holbein, Hans (the Younger) (1497–1543). KAA

Kirchner, Ernst Ludwig (1880–1938). WIAA

Italian

Angelico, Fra (1400–1455). MAI
Boccioni, Umberto (1882–1916). WIAA
Botticelli, Sandro (1444?–1510). JAA; KAA; MAI
Caravaggio, Michelangelo da (1565–1609). KAA
Francesca, Piero della (1420?–1492). JAA; MAI
Giorgione, Il (c. 1478–1510). JAA
Giotto di Bondone (c. 1266–1337). CHC; JAA;
    KAA; MAI
Leonardo da Vinci (1452–1519). CAA; CHC; DEI;
    DEJ; EVC; FE; JAA; KAA; MAI; SHFB; SIA
Lippi, Fra Filippo (1406?–1469). CHC
Masaccio (1401–1428). JAA; KAA; MAI
Michelangelo Buonarroti (1475–1564). CHC; DEI;
    DEJ; JAA; KAA; MAI
Modigliani, Amedeo (1884–1920). KAA
Raphael (Raffaello Santi) (1483–1520). CHC;
    JAA; KAA; MAI
Tintoretto, Il (1518–1594). JAA
Titian (1477–1576). JAA; KAA; MAI

Spanish

Dali, Salvador (1904–). WIAA
Goya y Lucientes, Francisco José de (1746–1828).
    KAA; MAI
Greco, El (1548?–1614?). (Born Greece). CHC;
    KAA; MAI
Picasso, Pablo (1881–1973). ASB-1; DABB; DEI;
    DEJ; DU-1; FOR; FRE; KAA; KE†; MAH;
    WIAA; WO
Velázquez, Diego Rodríguez de Silva y (1599–
    1660). CHC; MAI

Others

Bodmer, Karl (1809–1893). Swiss. HEDA; HOD
Chagall, Marc (1887–1985). Russian. GRB-1;
    WIAA
Kandinsky, Wassily (1866–1944). Russian. KAA
Klee, Paul (1879–1940). Swiss. KAA; WIAA
Magritte, René (1898–1967). Belgian. WIAA
Munch, Edward (1863–1944). Norwegian. WIAA
Orozco, José Clemente (1883–1949). Mexican.
    BACA; KE; ROGB; WO
Rivera, Diego (1886–1957). Mexican. KAA;
    NEBA; ROGB

PAKISTANIS

Ayub Khan, Mohammad (1907–1974). Ex-
    president. WEC
Jinnah, Mohammed Ali (1876–1948). Governor-
    general. KEF
Ziaul-Haq, Mohammed (1924–). President. HAGD

PALEONTOLOGISTS

See also ARCHAEOLOGISTS

Cope, Edward Drinker (1840–1897). HYB
Dubois, Eugène (1858–1940). Dutch. SOB
Gejvall, Nils-Gustaf (1915–). Swedish. POC
Leidy, Joseph (1823–1891). HYB
Marsh, Othniel Charles (1831–1899). HYB
Teilhard de Chardin, Pierre (1881–1955). French.
    LO

PALESTINIANS

Arafat, Yasir (1929–). Guerrilla leader, born
    Egypt. HAGD

PALESTINIANS, ANCIENT

Akiba ben Joseph (c. 50–132). Rabbi. GEF;
    GRB-1; GUA; KAB; KAC; LERA
Gamaliel (d. 50?). Rabbi. GUA
Johanan ben Zakkai (d. 80 A.D.?). Rabbi. GEF;
    GUA; LERA; LES
Josephus Flavius (37–100). General, historian.
    LERA; LES
Joshua ben Chananiah (c. 35–130). Rabbi. GUA
Joshua ben Levi (3d century). Rabbi. GUA
Judah ben Babba (fl. 135). Rabbi. GEF
Judah ha-Nasi (Judah the Prince) (135–220).
    Rabbi. GUA; KAC; LERA
Meir (2d century). Rabbi. GUA
Simeon ben Lakish (200–275). Rabbi. GUA

PANAMANIANS

Sanguillen, Manuel DeJesus (1944–). Baseball
    player. TUB

PARAGUAYANS

Francia, José Gaspar Rodríguez (1766–1840).
    Chief of state. WOB
Stroessner, Alfredo (1912–). President. BAGA

PATHOLOGISTS

Florey, Sir Howard Walter (1898–1968). Australian. BEK†; COLA†; LAE; POB; RIF; SHG
Fuller, Solomon Carter (1872–1953). HAMA
Landsteiner, Karl (1868–1943). (Born Austria). CHE†; COLA†; FE; LET; RIF; STE
Mohler, John Robbins (1875–1952). DEA
Smith, Theobald (1859–1934). DEB; MAL
Spilsbury, Sir Bernard (1877–1947). English. LID
Virchow, Rudolf (1821–1902). German. CHD; POB; ROA
Whipple, George Hoyt (1878–1976). RIF

PATRIOTS, see AMERICAN REVOLUTIONARY FIGURES—PATRIOTS; HEROES, LEGENDARY & NATIONAL; RESISTANCE LEADERS

PERSIANS, ANCIENT

Cyrus (600?–529 B.C.). King. CAAA; COA
Darius (558?–486? B.C.). King. CAAA; COA
Xerxes I (519?–465 B.C.). King. COA; JO

PERUVIANS

Alegria, Ciro (1909–1967). Author. WO
Atahualpa (1500?–1533). Incan king. CAAA
Garcilaso de la Vega (called el Inca) (1539?–1616). Historian. BACA
González Prada, Manuel (1848–1918). Reformer. WOB
Perez de Cuéllar, Javier (1920–). Statesman. DU-1
Unanue, Hipólito (1755–1833). Statesman. LAB

PHARMACOLOGISTS

Abel, John Jacob (1857–1938). POB
Bovet, Daniele (1907–). Italian. (Born Switzerland). RIF
Loewi, Otto (1873–1961). (Born Germany). LET; RIF
Stewart, Ella Phillips (1893–). LOAV

PHILANTHROPISTS

See also HUMANITARIANS

Armour, Philip Danforth (1832–1901). LAG; WED
Carnegie, Andrew (1835–1919). (Born Scotland). BEA; CUC; DEI; DEJ; EVA; LAG; LEM; LOB; MAL; WED
Cooper, Peter (1791–1883). HOF
Cornell, Ezra (1807–1874). BOD
Cuffe, Paul (1759–1817). ADA; ADB; BRB; DOB; GRAB-02; HUB; PECA; WIBA
Duke, James Buchanan (1856–1925). WED
Eastman, George (1854–1932). CUC; FE; LAG; LEM; MAL; RIBA
Gratz, Rebecca (1781–1869). GRB-1; LER; LETA; PEB
Hearst, Phoebe Apperson (1842–1919). CUC
Hirsch, Clara de (1833–1899). Belgian. LER
Hopkins, Johns (1795–1873). CUC
Lasker, Albert (1880–1952). (Born Germany). CUC; LETA
Lathrop, Rose Hawthorne (Mother Mary Alphonsa) (1851–1926). MAK; WRA; YOC
Montefiore, Sir Moses (1784–1885). English. GRB-1; KAB; KAD; LERA; LES; PEB
Morgan, John Pierpont (1837–1913). CUC; FAC; WED
Nobel, Alfred Bernhard (1833–1896). Swedish. EVA; HAC; LAE; MAP; MEC; RIF
Owen, Robert (1771–1858). Welsh. DEDA; EVA
Peabody, George (1795–1869). LEM
Pulitzer, Joseph (1847–1911). (Born Hungary). ASB; BEA; CUC; LEM; LOB; LYA; SQB
Rhodes, Cecil John (1853–1902). ASB-1; WOA
Rockefeller, John Davison (1839–1937). ASB-1; BOD; CUC; FAC; LEM; MAL; WED
Rosenwald, Julius (1862–1932). ALD; CUC; LETA
Rothschild, Edmond de (1845–1934). French. KAD
Schiff, Jacob Henry (1847–1920). (Born Germany). LETA
Simson, Sampson (b. 1780?). LETA
Stanford, Leland (1824–1893). YOG
Straus, Nathan (1848–1931). (Born Germany). ALD; GRB-1; LETA; PEB
Swope, Gerard (1872–1957). GRB-1
Szold, Robert (1889–1977). GRB-1
Touro, Judah (1775–1854). ALD; GUB; LERA; LETA; PEB

PHILIPPINE

Encarnacion, Rosario de Jesus. Teacher, civic
leader. RODA
Encarnacion, Silvino (1913–). Civic leader. RODA
Magsaysay, Ramón (1907–1957). President. KEF;
RODA

PHILOSOPHERS

See also RELIGIOUS LEADERS—JEWISH; RELIGIOUS
LEADERS—PROTESTANT; RELIGIOUS LEADERS—
ROMAN CATHOLIC

American
Dewey, John (1859–1952). CUC; FRC†; LEJA;
OZA
Emerson, Ralph Waldo (1803–1882). BEF; BEG;
BEGA; BLE; BOA; CAC; CUC; DEI; DEJ; HEF;
RED; SIF; SUFA; WHB; WOAA
James, William (1842–1910). LO
Langer, Susanne Katherine (1895–1985). STLA
Santayana, George (1863–1952). (Born Spain).
LO

English
Bacon, Francis (1561–1626). BEG; LO; STI†
Bacon, Roger (1214?–1294). MAQ
Locke, John (1632–1704). LO; OZA
Russell, Bertrand Arthur William Russell, 3d earl
(1872–1970). HAJ; KE; OZA

French
Bergson, Henri (1859–1941). LET
Descartes, René (1596–1650). LO; MUB; OZA;
SHFB; SIA; STN
Pascal, Blaise (1623–1662). GRAB-3; MUB; SOB
Rousseau, Jean Jacques (1712–1778). FRE
Voltaire (François Marie Arouet) (1694–1778).
COG; DEI; DEJ; HIB; LO; OZA

German
Agrippa, Cornelius Heinrich (1486?–1535). COEA;
ED-5
Hegel, Georg Wilhelm Friedrich (1770–1831). LO;
OZA
Kant, Immanuel (1724–1804). LO; OZA
Leibniz, Gottfried Wilhelm freiherr von (1646–
1716). GRAB-3†; SHFB
Marx, Karl Heinrich (1818–1883). COJB; FRE;
HAK; LO
Mendelssohn, Moses (1729–1786). GUB; KAB;
KAC; LEF; LERA; PEB
Nietzsche, Friedrich Wilhelm (1844–1900). LO

Greek
Aristotle (384–322 B.C.). CAA; DEI; DEJ; FE;
FRC; LO; OZA; PIA; SIA; SIB†
Empedocles (c. 490–430 B.C.). FE
Hypatia (370–415). SC
Leucippus (5th century B.C.). SHFB
Plato (427–347 B.C.). DEI; DEJ; FRC; LO; OZA;
SIB†
Pythagoras (6th century B.C.). CAA; MUB; SHFB;
SIB†
Socrates (470?–399 B.C.). DEI; DEJ; FRC; FRE;
HAA; LO; MAJ; OZA; STP

Others
Buddha (Gautama Buddha) (563?–483 B.C.). In-
dian. FRE; TRC-1
Confucius (551–479 B.C.). Chinese. DEI; DEJ; LO;
SPA
Erasmus, Desiderius (1466–1536). Dutch. DEI;
DEJ
Kierkegaard, Sören Aabye (1813–1855). Danish.
LO
Kropotkin, Pëtr Alekseevich (1842–1921). Rus-
sian. RAC
Lao-tzu (c. 604–531 B.C.). Chinese. LO
Maimonides (Moses ben Maimon) (1135–1204).
Spanish. GEF; GRB-1; GUA; KAB; KAC;
LERA; LES; MAR
Nachmanides. Spanish. LERA
Seneca, Lucius Annaeus (4 B.C.–65 A.D.). Roman.
COK
Spinoza, Baruch or Benedict (1632–1677). Dutch.
LERA; LO; OZA; PEB
Swedenborg, Emanuel (1688–1772). Swedish.
COEA

PHOTOGRAPHERS

Abbott, Berenice (1898–). SUAA
Adams, Ansel E. (1902–1984). FOD
Beaton, Cecil W. (1904–1980). (Born England).
FOD
Bourke-White, Margaret (1904–1971). FAA; FOE;
GEE; GIBA; HOE; ROJ; SQB; SUAA
Brady, Matthew B. (1823–1896). HOE; SUAA
Capa, Robert (1913–1954). (Born Hungary). HOE
Carter, Ovie (1946?–). STAA
Cartier-Bresson, Henri (1908–). French. HOE
Curtis, Edward Sheriff (1868–1952). SUAA
Daguerre, Louis Jacques (1787–1851). French.
FE; FRE; THA
De Carava, Roy R. (1919–). FAH
Duncan, David Douglas (1916–). FOD; HOE
Evans, Walker (1903–1975). SUAA
Faas, Horst (1933–). German. HOE

Fenton, Roger (1819–1869). English. HOE
Hare, James Henry (1856–1946). (Born England). HOE
Hine, Lewis (1874–1940). SUAA
Jackson, William Henry (1843–1942). SUAA
Johnson, Martin Elmer (1884–1937). COKA
Johnson, Osa Helen (1894–1953). COKA
Karsh, Yousuf (1908–). Canadian. (Born Armenia). FOD
Kertesz, André (1894–1985). (Born Hungary). HOE
Lange, Dorothea (1895–1965). STLA; SUAA
Leibovitz, Annie (1949–). BOHD
Man Ray (1890–1976). ASB-1
Morgan, Barbara (1900–). BOHB
Mydans, Carl (1907–). HOE
Parks, Gordon Alexander Buchanan (1912–). ADA; ADB; DOF-1
Phillips, Bertrand (1938–). FAI
Seymour, David (1911–1956). (Born Poland). HOE
Smith, William Eugene (1918–1978). SUAA
Steichen, Edward (1879–1973). FOD; HOE

PHYSICAL THERAPISTS

Woit, Dick. BELB

PHYSICALLY HANDICAPPED, *see* DISABLED

PHYSICIANS & SURGEONS

See also ANATOMISTS; BACTERIOLOGISTS; DENTISTS; GENETICISTS; MICROBIOLOGISTS; NOBEL PRIZE WINNERS—MEDICINE & PHYSIOLOGY; PATHOLOGISTS; PHYSIOLOGISTS; PSYCHIATRISTS & PSYCHOLOGISTS; VETERINARIANS; VIROLOGISTS

American
Adelman, Susan. Surgeon. FOC-1
Albright, Tenley (1935–). BOHA; HOBA; HOBAA; HOBB; LEYB†; PIBA
Apgar, Virginia (1909–1974). RAAG
Armstrong, Harry George (1899–). ED
Ashford, Bailey Kelly (1873–1934). ED
Baker, Sara Josephine (1873–1945). PACB
Bard, Samuel (1742–1821). MAR
Barringer, Emily Dunning (1876–1961). FLA; MASA
Bartlett, Josiah (1729–1795). BAEA; BUIB†; COJ†; FEAB; MAC

Baumgartner, Leona (1902–). FLA
Beaumont, William (1785–1853). Surgeon. BLC; ED
Berry, Charles A. (1923–). POE
Berry, Leonidas Harris. CAF-1
Billings, John Shaw (1838–1913). ED
Blackwell, Elizabeth (1821–1910). (Born England). BOC; BUA; CHD; COG; CUC; DOD; GEE; GIBA; HUE; JOCA; LOB; MASA; RAAG†; SC†; SMC; TRD; WABC; YOC
Blalock, Alfred (1899–1964). Surgeon. CHE
Bond, George F. (1915–). BRBC; COR
Brown, Dorothy (1919–). Surgeon. LETC
Calderone, Mary Steichen (1904–). BOHE; GIB-1
Carlson, Earl (1897–). LEG
Carrel, Alexis (1873–1944). Surgeon, born France. POB; RIF
Clarke, Nancy Talbot (1825–1901). MASA
Coe, Urling C. (fl. 1905). WAA
Cooper, Irving Spencer (1922–1985). Surgeon. HEFA
Crumbine, Samuel Jay (1862–1954). BLC; LEG
Cushing, Harvey Williams (1869–1939). Surgeon. CHD; CHE†; SIC
Dailey, Ulysses Grant (1885–1961). Surgeon. ADA; ADB
de Leon, David (1813–1872). GRB-1
Derham, James (b. 1762). BRB†; WIBA
Dick, George Frederick (1881–1967). RIE
Dick, Gladys H. (1881–1963). RIE
Dooley, Thomas Anthony (1927–1961). ASB
Drew, Charles Richard (1904–1950). Surgeon. ADA; ADB; DOF-1; FRE; GRAB-03; HA; HAM; HODA; KLA; PECA; RIC; RICA; ROG; STE; STO; STQ†; WEF
Eliot, Martha May (1891–1978). CHE
Ellington, Anna. BOHE
Esposito, Vince. LETC
Estrada, Isabel. FOC-1
Evans, John (1814–1897). SEC
Ferguson, Angella D. (1925–). HAMA
Fisher, Anna (1949–). FOI-1; HIFD†; RAAG†
Fowler, Lydia Folger (1822–1879). MASA
Garcia, Hector (1914–). (Born Mexico). FOW
Goldberger, Joseph (1874–1929). (Born Austria). ALD; DEA; GEF
Gorgas, William Crawford (1854–1920). COL
Grant, David N. W. (1891–1964). Surgeon. ED
Griffin, John (d. 1898). Surgeon. BLC
Guion, Connie Meyers (1882–1971). FLA
Halsted, William Stewart (1852–1922). Surgeon. CHE†; LEG; SIC
Hamilton, Alice (1869–1970). BOJ; BRBE; CHD; FLA; HA-1; MASA; PACA; RAAG†; SC†
Hays, Isaac (1796–1879). LETA
Hench, Philip Showalter (1896–1965). RIF

Hinton, William A. (1883–1959). BRB†; HAMA

Hofmann, Adele (1926–). RAAG

Jacobi, Abraham (1830–1919). (Born Germany). LETA

Jacobi, Mary Putnam (1842–1906). FLA; HUE; MASA; RAAG†; WABC†

Jonasson, Olga (1934–). Transplant surgeon. RAAG

Jordan, Sara (1884–1959). FLA

Kelsey, Frances Oldham (1914–). (Born Canada). EOA; TRD

Kountz, Samuel. Surgeon. CAF-1

Kübler-Ross, Elisabeth (1926–). (Born Switzerland). BOHE; GIB-1

Lawless, Theodore Kenneth (1892–1971). ADA; ADB; BRB†; CAF-1; DOF-1

Levine, Samuel Albert (1891–1966). LETA

Lillehei, Clarence Walton (1918–). Surgeon. HEFA; LEG; SIC

Logan, Arthur Courtney (1909–1973). Surgeon. HAMA

Logan, Myra Adele (1908–1977). Surgeon. HA-1; RAAG†

Long, Crawford Williamson (1815–1878). Surgeon. BLC; LEG†; SHG; SIC†

Lovelace, William Randolph, II. Surgeon. ED

McClurg, James (1746–1823). FEAA

McDowell, Ephraim (1771–1830). Surgeon. BLC; LEG; RIB; SHG; SIC

Marsh, John (1799–1856). COE

Mayo, Charles Horace (1865–1939). Surgeon. BOD; CHE; COKA; CUC

Mayo, William James (1861–1939). Surgeon. BOD; CHE; COKA; CUC

Mayo, William Worrall (1819–1911). Surgeon, born England. BOD; CHE; HEB; LEAB; LEB

Minot, George Richards (1885–1950). RIF

Murphy, John Benjamin (1857–1916). Surgeon. RIB

Murphy, William Parry (1892–). RIF

Nichol, Kathryn (1937–). BOHE

Owens-Adair, Bethenia (1840–1926). ARB; BLC; JOB

Pearce, Louise (1885–1959). FLA

Perrine, Henry (1797–1840). BLC; JEA

Picotte, Susan LaFlesche (1865–1915). GRAD; RAAG†

Powell, Clilian (1894–). CAF-1

Ramcharan, Savitri (1923–). (Born Trinidad). RAAG

Ramey, Estelle (1917–). BOHE

Reed, Walter (1851–1902). BOB; CHD; CUC; DEB; DOE; ED; EVD; FOH; LEC; LEPC; MAL; ROA; SHG; SIC

Reyes, Joseph Manuel de los (1905–). (Born Cuba). FOW

Rhoades, Everett (1931–). GRAC

Robbins, Frederick Chapman (1916–). RIF

Robertson, Oswald Hope (1886–1966). (Born England). ED

Rock, John (1890–1984). HEFA

Rodriguez-Trias, Helen. GLO

Rosen, Sheldon (1942?–). LETC

Rush, Benjamin (1745–1813). BAEA; BUIB†; COJ†; CUC; ED; FEAB; MAC

Rusk, Howard A. (1901–). CHE; HEFA

Sabin, Albert Bruce (1906–). (Born Russia). CHE†; COLA; RIE

Salk, Jonas Edward (1914–). ASB-1; BEK; BOB; CHE†; COLA; DU-1; FAA; FE; GRB-1; HEFA; LEG; LETA; RIE; ROA; SIC; SUF; YOA

Schick, Béla (1877–1967). (Born Hungary). RIE

Seagrave, Gordon Stifler (1897–1965). FAA

Seddon, Margaret Rhea (1947–). Surgeon. FOC-1; FOJ-1; HIFD; SMBC-2

Sims, James Marion (1813–1883). POB; RIB

Spock, Benjamin (1903–). BOHA; CHE; HAJ; HOBB

Sternberg, George Miller (1838–1915). ED

Steward, Susan McKinney (1848–1918). LOAV

Storch, Marcia (1933–). LETC; WA

Swain, Clara A. (1834–1910). FLA

Taussig, Helen Brooke (1898–1986). CHE; CLA; EOA; GIB-1; RAAG

Trudeau, Edward Livingston (1848–1915). FAF; LYA; SHG

Turner, Charles Henry (1867–1923). BRB†; CAF-1; HAM

Walker, Mary (1832–1919). STJ

Weller, Thomas Huckle (1915–). RIF

White, Paul Dudley (1886–1973). CHE

Williams, Daniel Hale (1858–1931). Surgeon. ADA; ADB; ASB; BRB†; CAF-1; DADA; HA; HAM; HODA; HUA; KLA; PECA; RICA; ROG; STO

Williamson, Hugh (1735–1819). Surgeon. BUIB†; FEAA

Wright, Barbara P. (1920–). PAC

Wright, Jane C. (1919–). HA-1; HAMA; PAC; RAAG†

Wright, Louis Tompkins (1891–1952). DOF-1; GRAB-03; HA; HAMA; PAC

Zakrzewska, Marie Elizabeth (1829–1902). (Born Germany). COFA†; FLA; LEG; RAAG†

Austrian

Auenbrugger, Leopold (1722–1809). FAF; SHG

Bárány, Robert (1876–1936). LET

Mesmer, Franz Anton (1734–1815). COEA

English

Addison, Thomas (1793–1860). POB

Anderson, Elizabeth Garrett (1836–1917). HUE;
MAJ; MASA
Barry, James, pseud. (1795–1865). MASA
Gilbert, William (1540–1603). SHFB; SIA
Grenfell, Sir Wilfred Thomason (1865–1940).
MAN
Harvey, William (1578–1657). ASA; BEP; CAA;
CHD; COL; DEI; DEJ; DOE; FE; FRE; POD;
ROA; SHG; SIA; SIC; STE
Jenner, Edward (1749–1823). ASA; CAA; CHD;
COL; FAF†; FE; HUD; POD; RIE; ROA; SHG;
SIC; SUF
Jex-Blake, Sophia (1840–1912). HUE; MASA†;
SC†
Linacre, Thomas (1460?–1524). MAR
Lister, Joseph, 1st baron Lister of Lyme Regis
(1827–1912). Surgeon. ASB-1; BIA; CHD;
COL; DOE; FAF; FE; HUD; POD; ROA; SHG;
SIC
MacKenzie, Sir Morell (1837–1892). MAR
Ross, Sir Ronald (1857–1932). AAS-31; DEB;
RIF; ROA
Young, Thomas (1773–1829). SHFB

French
Bombard, Alain Louis (1924?–). ELA; HAQ
Coictier, Jacques (1482–1506). MAR
Laënnec, René Théophile (1781–1826). FAF;
HUD; SHG
Larrey, Dominique Jean (1766–1842). Surgeon.
MAR
Laveran, Charles Louis (1845–1922). RIF; SHG
Louis, Pierre Charles Alexandre (1787–1872).
POB
Nicolle, Charles Jules Henri (1866–1936).
AAS-31; RIF
Paré, Ambroise (1510?–1590). Surgeon. CHD;
HUD; ROA; SHG; SIC
Roux, Pierre Paul Émile (1853–1933). DEB; RIE;
ROA
Schweitzer, Albert (1875–1965). BAF; BEC; EVD;
FOJ; KE; KEE; LO; MAN; MEA; MEC; WIC;
YOA

German
Behring, Emil von (1854–1917). AAS-31; BEK†;
DEB; RIE; RIF; ROA
Forssmann, Werner (1904–1979). Surgeon. RIF
Frank, Johann Peter (1745–1821). MAR

Greek
Agnodice (fl. 300 B.C.). SC
Asklepios (c. 1300 B.C.). SHG
Galen (130–200). CAA; CHD; POD; ROA; SHG;
SIA; SIC

Hippocrates (460–377 B.C.). CAA; CHD; DEI;
DEJ; DOE; FE; POD; ROA; SHG; SIC

Italian
Cardano, Girolamo (1501–1576). MUB
Fracastoro, Girolamo (1483–1553). POB
Galvani, Luigi (1737–1798). DUA; MAQ
Golgi, Camillo (1844–1926). RIF
Mazzei, Philip (1730–1816). MAS
Troctula di Ruggiero (d. 1197). MASA; RIB; SC

Scottish
Bell, Sir Charles (1774–1842). Surgeon. RIB
Ferrier, David (1843–1928). POB
Hunter, John (1728–1793). Surgeon. FE; MAR;
RIB; SIC

Others
Aspasia (fl. 2d century). Roman. SC
Banting, Sir Frederick Grant (1891–1941). Cana-
dian. AAS-31; BEK; DOE; HUD; POB; RIF;
ROA
Barnard, Christiaan N. (1922–). South African.
DEJ; DU-1; FE
Barnardo, Thomas John (1845–1905). Irish. EVA
Betances y Alarcón, Ramón Emeterio (1827–
1898). Puerto Rican. TU; WO
Bruce, Sir David (1855–1931). Australian. DEB;
ROA
Burnet, Sir Macfarlane (1899–1985). Australian.
RIF
Finlay, Carlos Juan (1833–1915). Cuban. FOW;
SHG; SIC†; WO
Hanaoka, Seishu (1760–1835). Japanese surgeon.
RIB
Ighodaro, Irene Elizabeth. Nigerian. CRA
Imhotep (fl. 2980–2950 B.C.). Egyptian. JO
Judah ha-Levi (c. 1085–1140). Spanish. GEF;
GRB-1; GUA; KAC; LERA; LES
Kocher, Emil Theodor (1841–1917). Swiss sur-
geon. POB; RIF
Kodijat, Raden (1890–). Indonesian. RODA
Korczak, Janus (1878–1942). Polish. GRB-1
Lopez, Roderigo (1525–1594). Portuguese. MAR
Maimonides (Moses ben Maimon) (1135–1204).
Spanish. GEF; GRB-1; GUA; KAB; KAC;
LERA; LES; MAR
Osler, Sir William (1849–1919). Canadian. CHD;
RIB
Paracelsus (Theophrastus Bombastus von
Hohenheim) (1493–1541). Swiss. CUA; ED-5;
FE; POB; ROA; SHG
Semmelweis, Ignaz Philipp (1818–1865). Hungar-
ian. ROA; SIC†

PHYSICISTS

See also BIOPHYSICISTS

American

Ancker-Johnson, Betsy (1927–). GL; LES-1†
Bache, Alexander Dallas (1806–1867). SIA
Bardeen, John (1908–). AAS-33†; GRAB-3; MAPA
Bloch, Felix (1905–1983). (Born Switzerland). LET
Brattain, Walter Houser (1902–1987). AAS-33†; GRAB-3; MAPA
Brown, Harold (1927–). GRB-1
Carruthers, George (c. 1940–). CAF-1
Compton, Arthur Holly (1892–1962). BAF; BOB; RID
Compton, Karl Taylor (1887–1954). BOB
Dreschkoff, Gisela. (Born Germany). LA-1
Einstein, Albert (1879–1955). (Born Germany). ASA; ASB-1; BEA; BEP; BOB; BUF; CAA; COL; CUC; DEI; DEJ; DOE; FE; FRE; GEF; GRB-1; GUB; KE; LEL; LES; LET; LETA; MAM; MOBA; POD; RID; SHFB; SIA; YOA
Fermi, Enrico (1901–1954). (Born Italy). BEA; BIA; BOB; CAA; COLA; CUC; FE; FRE; LEL; LET; MAS; RID; SHFB; SIA; YOE
Franck, James (1882–1964). (Born Germany). LET
Gibbs, Josiah Willard (1839–1903). SIA
Goeppert-Mayer, Maria (1906–1972). (Born Germany). HA-1; SC†; SHFE
Goldhaber, Maurice (1911–). (Born Austria). PAC
Gourdine, Meredith (1929–). CAF-1
Hafstad, Lawrence Randolph (1904–). PAB
Henry, Joseph (1797–1878). ASA; BUE; BUF; CAA; DUA; FE; HYB; SHFB; SIA; SOB
Jackson, Shirley. CAF-1
Koontz, Roscoe L. (1922–). CAF-1
Lawrence, Ernest Orlando (1901–1958). ASA; CUC; RID; SIA
Lee, Tsung-Dao (1926–). (Born China). BOB
McNair, Ronald (1950–1986). COE-1
Michelson, Albert Abraham (1852–1931). (Born Germany). CAA; FE; GRB-1; LET; LETA; SIA; STI
Millikan, Robert Andrews (1868–1953). CUC
Norwood, Virginia. HOG
Oppenheimer, Julius Robert (1904–1967). ARB; ASB-1; FE; RID
Pupin, Michael Idvorsky (1858–1935). (Born Yugoslavia). BUF; LEB; LOB
Rabi, Isidor Isaac (1898–1988). (Born Austria). GRB-1; LET
Richter, Charles (1900–1985). DU-1
Sabine, Wallace Clement (1868–1919). FE

Scharff-Goldhaber, Gertrude (1911–). PAC
Segrè, Emilio Gino (1905–). (Born Italy). LET
Shaw, Earl (1937–). CAF-1
Shockley, William Bradford (1910–). AAS-33†; GRAB-3; MAPA
Slotin, Louis Alexander. GEF
Stern, Otto (1888–1969). (Born Germany). LET
Taylor, Albert (1879–1961). COLA
Townes, Charles Hard (1915–). AAS-33; COLA; DU-1; FE; MAPA; THA
Wu, Chien-Shiung (1912–). (Born China). EMB†; GIB-1; GLO; SC; YOF
Yalow, Rosalyn Sussman (1921–). GIB-1; GL; GRB-1; HA-1; SHFE
Yang, Chen Ning (1922–). (Born China). BOB
Zworykin, Vladimir K. (1889–1982). (Born Russia). YOE

Dutch

Huygens, Christiaan (1629–1695). CAA; COL; FE; SHFB; SIA
Van der Waals, Johannes Diederik (1837–1923). FE
Zernike, Frits (b. 1888). AAS-23

English

Aston, Francis William (1877–1945). RID; SHFB†
Boyle, Robert (1627–1691). CAA; FE; MOBA; SIA
Cavendish, Henry (1731–1810). CAA; FE; SHFB
Chadwick, Sir James (1891–1974). FE; RID
Cockcroft, Sir John Douglas (1897–1967). FE
Crookes, Sir William (1832–1919). FE; SIA
Dalton, John (1766–1844). CAA; FE; MOBA; SHFB; SIA; STI
Faraday, Michael (1791–1867). ASA; BEP; BIA; BOB; BOD; CAA; COLA; DEI; DEJ; DOE; DUA; FE; MAQ; SHFB; SIA; STI; THA
Gilbert, William (1540–1603). SHFB; SIA
Hawking, Stephen (1942–). BOHA-1
Hooke, Robert (1635–1703). CAA
Joule, James Prescott (1818–1889). FE; SHFB
Kelvin, William Thomson, 1st baron (1824–1907). BOB; DUA; FE; LAE; SIA
Newton, Sir Isaac (1642–1727). ASA; BEP; BIA; BOB; CAA; COL; DEI; DEJ; DOE; FE; FRE; LAA; MAQ; MOCB; MUB; PIA; POD; SHFB; SIA; SIB†; STI; STN; SUE
Rumford, Benjamin Thompson, count (1753–1814). (Born U.S.). CAA; FE; HYB; RAD; SHFB; SIA; STI
Thomson, Sir Joseph John (1856–1940). CAA; FE; MOBA; RID; SHFB; SIA
Young, Thomas (1773–1829). SHFB

French

Ampère, André Marie (1775–1836). CAA; DUA; FE; SHFB; SIA

Becquerel, Antoine Henri (1852–1908). ASA; FE; MOBA; SHFB; SOB

Broglie, Louis-Victor de (1892–1987). FE

Carnot, Nicholas Léonard Sadi (1796–1832). HAC; SHFB

Coulomb, Charles Augustin de (1736–1806). SHFB

Curie, Marie Sklodowska (1867–1934). (Born Poland). ASA; ASB-1; BEC; BEP; BOB; BOC; BOH; BUF; CAA; COL; DEI; DEJ; DOE; EVD; FE; FRE; HUE; KOA; MAJ; MANB; MASA; PA; PAC; POD; RID; SC; SHFB; SHFE†; SIA; STI

Foucault, Jean Bernard Léon (1819–1868). CAA; FE; SHFB

Gay-Lussac, Joseph Louis (1778–1850). SHFB

Joliot-Curie, Frédéric (1900–1958). FE; RID

Joliot-Curie, Irène (1897–1956). FE; RID; SC†; SHFE†

Lippmann, Gabriel (1845–1921). LET

German

Born, Max (1882–1970). LET

Fahrenheit, Gabriel Daniel (1686–1736). SHFB

Fraunhofer, Joseph von (1787–1826). FE; LAA; SHFB; SUE

Geiger, Johannes Wilhelm (1882–1945). HAC

Guericke, Otto von (1602–1686). MAQ; SHFB

Hahn, Otto (1879–1968). FE

Helmholtz, Hermann Ludwig von (1821–1894). SIA

Hertz, Gustav (1887–1975). LET

Hertz, Heinrich Rudolf (1857–1894). CAA; COLA; FE; SHFB; SIA; SOB

Kirchhoff, Gustav Robert (1824–1887). FE; SHFB; SUE

Laue, Max von (1879–1960). FE

Mössbauer, Rudolf Ludwig (1929–). HAC

Ohm, Georg Simon (1787–1854). CAA; DUA; FE

Planck, Max Karl (1858–1947). CAA; FE; SHFB

Roentgen, Wilhelm (1845–1923). AAS-33; ASA; CAA; DEI; DEJ; FE; PRC; SHFB; SHG; STI

Seebeck, Thomas Johann (1770–1831). FE

Weber, Wilhelm Eduard (1804–1891). DUA

Italian

Avogadro, Amedeo (1776–1856). CAA; MOBA; SHFB

Galilei, Galileo (1564–1642). ASA; BEC; BEP; BOB; CAA; COL; DEI; DEJ; DOE; EVC; FE; FRB; FRE; LAA; MAQ; MOCB; PIA; SHFB; SIA; SIB; STI; SUE; THA

Galvani, Luigi (1737–1798). DUA; MAQ

Torricelli, Evangelista (1608–1647). CAA; FE; SHFB

Volta, Alessandro, conte (1745–1827). CAA; DOE; DUA; FE; MAQ; SHFB; SIA; SOB

Scottish

Dewar, Sir James (1842–1923). SHFB

Maxwell, James Clerk (1831–1879). CAA; DUA; FE; SHFB; SIA

Watson-Watt, Sir Robert Alexander (1892–1973). EVC; FE; SHFB

Wilson, Charles T. R. (1869–1959). RID

Others

Bjerknes, Vilhelm (1862–1951). Norwegian. FE

Bohr, Niels H. D. (1885–1962). Danish. CAA; COLA; FE; LET; MOBA; RID; SIA

Branover, Herman (1931–). Israeli. (Born Russia). GRB-1

Doppler, Christian Johann (1803–1853). Austrian. FE; HAC; SHFB

Euler, Leonhard (1707–1783). Swiss. MUB

Mach, Ernst (1838–1916). Austrian. FE; HAC

Meitner, Lise (1878–1968). Swedish. (Born Austria). HA-1; RID†; SC†; YOF

Oersted, Hans Christian (1777–1851). Danish. DUA

Piccard, Auguste (1884–1962). Swiss. BAB; COR; OLC; PRC

Rutherford, Ernest Rutherford, 1st baron (1871–1937). New Zealand. ASA; BIA; FE; MOBA; POD; PRC; RID; SHFB; SIA

Sakharov, Andrei D. (1921–). Russian. AAS-34; DU-1; MEC

Tamm, Igor Yevgenyvich (1895–1971). Russian. LET

PHYSIOLOGISTS

See also ANATOMISTS

American

Anderson, Evelyn M. (1899–). HOG

Cournand, André Frédéric (1895–1988). (Born France). RIF

Erlanger, Joseph (1874–1965). LET; RIF

Gasser, Herbert Spencer (1888–1963). RIF

Jackson, Margaret. HOG

Meyerhof, Otto Fritz (1884–1951). (Born Germany). LET; RIF

Ramey, Estelle (1917–). BOHE

Richards, Dickinson Woodruff, Jr. (1895–1973). RIF

Foreign

Adrian, Edgar Douglas (1889–1977). English. RIF

Dale, Sir Henry Hallett (1875–1968). English. RIF

Einthoven, Willem (1860–1927). Dutch. AAS-33; FE; RIF

Hales, Stephen (1677–1761). English. CAB

Hill, Archibald Vivian (1886–1977). English. RIF

Houssay, Bernardo Alberto (1887–1971). Argentine. RIF

Kossel, Albrecht (1853–1927). German. RIF

Krogh, August (1874–1949). Danish. RIF

Macleod, John James R. (1876–1935). Scottish. BEK†; RIF

Pavlov, Ivan Petrovich (1849–1936). Russian. ASB-1; CAA; FE; RIF; SIA

Sanctorius (1561–1636). Italian. SHG

Schwann, Theodor (1810–1882). German. COLA

Sherrington, Sir Charles Scott (1857–1952). English. RIF

Warburg, Otto Heinrich (1883–1970). German. LET

PIANISTS, *see* MUSICIANS—PIANISTS

PILGRIM FATHERS, *see* COLONIAL AMERICANS

PILOTS, *see* AIR FORCE LEADERS; AIR PILOTS; AIR PIONEERS

PIONEERS & FRONTIER PEOPLE

See also COLONIAL AMERICANS; INDIAN CAPTIVES

Adair, James (1709?–1783). Trader. STA

Adams, Henry (b. 1843). KADB

Adams, John Capen (also known as James Capen Adams) (1812?–1860). COE

Astor, John Jacob (1763–1848). (Born Germany). CUB; CUC; HOF; LEM; LEPC; LOB

Austin, Moses (1761–1821). AKC; LYF; VIA

Austin, Stephen Fuller (1793–1836). AKC; KUA; LYF; MAO; VIA

Bailey, Ann "Mad Ann" (1742–1825). CLC; DOD; STJ

Barcelo, Gertrudis (La Doña Tules) (d. 1852). RAB; WIAA-2

Bean, "Judge" Roy (1825–1904). SUI

Beckwourth, James P. (1798–1866). ADB; BUH; GRAB-02; HAP; HUB; JO; KADB; LEI; PECA; ROG; SCB; STQ; WIBA

Bent, William (1809–1869). FOC

Bonga, George (b. 1802). KADB; WIBA

Boone, Daniel (1734–1820). BUB; COE; CUC; DEI; DEJ; EVD; FIA; FOC; HEB; LED; LEPD; MAO; MAT; VIA; WAN

Bowers, Eilley Orrum (fl. 1858). (Born Scotland). WIAA-2

Bowie, James (1799–1836). AKC; HEB; KUA; LYF; VIA

Bridger, James (1804–1881). BUG; BUI; COE; FOC; HEB; LED; LEPD; WAF

Buckner, Aylett C. (fl. 1822). VIA

Bulette, Julia (1832?–1867). RAB†; WIAA-2

Burdan, Molly (1853–1888). RAB

Bush, George W. (1791–1867). BUH; GRAB-02; KADB; PECA; SCB; STQ†

Byers, William Newton (1831–1903). YOG

Calamity Jane (1852?–1903). RAB; SUI

Carson, Kit (Christopher) (1809–1868). Scout. BUG; BUI; CAD; COE; DEI; DEJ; FIA; FOC; NAA; WAF

Chapman, John (Johnny Appleseed) (1774–1847). BAC; BEC; CAGA; CO-1; HEB; LEC; LEPD; SQA

Charboneau, Baptiste (1805–1885). Fur trader. JOD

Chouteau, René Auguste (1749–1829). Fur trader. BUI

Cody, William Frederick (Buffalo Bill) (1846–1917). Scout. BUI; COE; DEI; DEJ; KEH; KIB; WAF

Colter, John (1775–1813). Fur trapper. BUB; BUG; FOC; JAC; LED

Cooper, Arvazine Angeline (1845–1929). MAV

Crawford, Jane Todd (1763–1842). RIB

Crockett, Davy (1786–1836). AKC; COE; FOC; KUA; LYF; MAO; WAN

Croghan, George (d. 1782). Trader. VIA

Downie, William (fl. 1850). FOC

Fargo, William G. (1818–1881). Freight and banking executive. DOCA

Fields, Mary (1832–1914). BUH; GRAB-02; KADB

Fitzpatrick, Thomas (1799–1854). BUG

Green, Dick (fl. 1847). SCB

Gregg, Josiah (1806–1850). HEB; NAA

Hickok, Wild Bill (James Butler) (1837–1876). Scout. COE; SUI

Jackson, Saunders (fl. 1849). HODA; SCB

Kenton, Simon (1755–1836). COE

King, John I. (b. 1848). JOD

Lane, Lydia (fl. 1863). NAA

Levy, Asser (d. 1681?). (Born the Netherlands). LETA

Lewis, Margaret. STJ

Light, Allen B. (fl. 1836). SCB; WIBA

Lisa, Manuel (1772–1820). BUG

Long, Jane W. (1798–1880). MAO

Majors, Alexander. EDA

Meek, Joseph L. (1810–1875). Fur trapper. BUG; FOC; SEC

Meeker, Ezra (1830–1928). HEB

Mercer, Asa Shinn (1829–1917). JOB

Mesa, Antonio. SCB

Morris, Ed (fl. 1861). SCB

Oatman, Lorenzo (1837–1900?). BUI

Orchard, Sadie (1863?–1943). RAB

Pacheco, Luis (1800–1895). HAP

Pancoast, Charles Edward (1818–1906). COE

Parker, Isaac Charles (1838–1896). SUI

Pearson, Flora (1851–1925). BUI

Peg-Leg Annie (1860?–1933). RAB

Phillips, John (1832?–1883). SUA

Reed, Virginia (b. 1833). FOC

Riding, Henry (fl. 1865). SCB

Robertson, James (1742–1814). MAO

Rogers, Robert (1731–1795). VIA

Rose, Edward (d. 1834). BUH; HAP; SCB

Sadowski, Anthony (1670?–1736). (Born Poland). PIAA

Sanders, Harriet (1834–1909). JOB

Schneider, Martin (fl. 1783). STA

Smith, James (1737–1813). STA

Smith, Jedediah Strong (1799–1831). BLD; BUB; BUG; FOC; HEB; HIBC; LED; WAF; WIA-1

Snyder, Grace (1882–). JOB

Spelman, Henry (1598?–1622). CAF

Stocking, Clark (b. 1840). BUI

Sutter, John Augustus (1803–1880). (Born Germany). BLD; COE; DOCA

Tabor, Baby Doe (Elizabeth Donduel) (1854–1935). RAB; WIAA-2

Tubbs, Alice Huckert (Poker Alice) (1851–1930). (Born England). RAB

Tyler, Charley (d. 1863). SCB

Weldon, Catherine. JOB

Wells, Henry (1805–1878). Freight and banking executive. DOCA

Whitman, Marcus (1802–1847). BLC; COE; FOC; LEG; MAT

Whitman, Narcissa (1808–1847). DAD; EVD; FOC; MAT; ROI

Wiggan, Eleazer. STA

Wistar, Isaac Jones (1827–1905). COE

Wright, Rebecca (fl. 1805). FOC

Young, Brigham (1801–1877). BLD; COE; FOC; HEB; LEO; LEPD

Young, Ewing (d. 1841). BUG

Young, Hiram (fl. 1830). BUH

PIRATES, BUCCANEERS & PRIVATEERS

Avery, John "Long Ben" (b. 1665). English. LACB

Bart, Jean (1651–1702). French. KEH

Bartolomey the Portuguese. LACB

Blackbeard (d. 1718). English. LACB; PABB; SC-1; WHA

Bonnet, Stede (d. 1718). English. WHA

Bonny, Anne (1700–1720). English. PABB; SC-1; WHA†

Brasiliano, Roc (fl. 1660). Brazilian. LACB

Dampier, William (1652–1715). English. KNB; MOB

Flood, James (fl. early 18th century). Jamaican. WHA

Kidd, William (Captain) (1645?–1701). Scottish. LACB; PABB; SC-1

Lafitte, Jean (1780?–1826?). French. LACB; SC-1; VIA

L'Olonnois (1630?–1671). French. LACB

Morgan, Sir Henry (1635?–1688). LACB; PABB; SC-1

Read, Mary (1680–1721). English. PABB; SC-1; WHA†

Rogers, Woodes (d. 1732). English. WHA

Surcouf, Robert (1773–1827). French. KEH

PLANT EXPERTS, *see* AGRICULTURISTS; BOTANISTS

PLAYWRIGHTS

Ade, George (1866–1944). BEE

Baldwin, James (1924–1987). DADB; KE; LEGB; RICA

Barrie, Sir James M. (1860–1937). Scottish. COB

Belasco, David (1854–1931). LETA

Berg, Gertrude (1899–1966). MASB

Chekhov, Anton Pavlovich (1860–1904). Russian. ASB-1; POFA

Cohan, George Michael (1878–1942). EWA; MOA

Coward, Noel (1889–1973). English. ASB-1

Hammerstein, Oscar, II (1895–1960). BEKA†; MOA

Hansberry, Lorraine (1930–1965). FLBA

Harbach, Otto (1873–1963). MOA

Hellman, Lillian (1905–1984). DI-1; GIB-1†

Jonson, Ben (1573?–1637). English. DEI; DEJ

Lope de Vega, Félix (1562–1635). Spanish. WO

Luce, Clare Boothe (1903–1987). CLA; GRAB-1

Marlowe, Christopher (1564–1593). English. TRC

Molière (Jean Baptiste Poquelin) (1622–1673). French. TRC

O'Neill, Eugene Gladstone (1888–1953). ASB-1; BOA; DEI; DEJ; SHFA

Shakespeare, William (1564–1616). English. COB; COP; DEI; DEJ; FRE; STK

Shalom Aleichem (Solomon Rabinowitz) (1859–1916). (Born Russia). GRB-1

Shaw, George Bernard (1856–1950). ASB-1; DEI; DEJ; KE; STL

Simon, Neil (1927–). GRBA

Stallings, Laurence (1894–1968). RADA

Wilder, Thornton Niven (1897–1975). BEGA

POETS

American

Adams, Franklin Pierce (1881–1960). ALA

Armour, Richard Willard (1906–). ALA

Auden, Wystan Hugh (1907–1973). (Born England). BEA; BRBB; COP

Barlow, Joel (1754–1812). DOG

Bates, Katherine Lee (1859–1929). CAGA

Benét, Rosemary Carr (1898–1962). BEH

Benét, Stephen Vincent (1898–1943). BEF; BEH; BOA; BRBB; SIF

Benét, William Rose (1886–1950). BEF

Bradstreet, Anne Dudley (1612?–1672). JOCA; OCB; VIA; WABC†

Braithwaite, William Stanley (1878–1962). BRB†; DOF-1; ROE

Brooks, Gwendolyn (1917–). ADA; ADB; DRA; ROE

Bryant, William Cullen (1794–1878). BEF; BEGA; BOA; HACB; SIF

Colum, Padraic (1881–1972). (Born Ireland). BEI

Conkling, Hilda (1910–1986). FOR

Cullen, Countee (1903–1946). ADA; ADB; ROE

Daly, Thomas Augustine (1871–1948). BEH

Davies, Mary Carolyn. BEF

Dickinson, Emily (1830–1886). BEF; BEGA; EOB; HIG; LEK; MUA; OCB; SIF; STLA; WABC†; WHB

Dunbar, Paul Laurence (1872–1906). ADA; ADB; BEF; BRB; HUA; LEI; ROE; ROG

Emerson, Ralph Waldo (1803–1882). BEF; BEG; BEGA; BLE; BOA; CAC; CUC; DEI; DEJ; HEF; RED; SIF; SUFA; WHB; WOAA

Field, Eugene (1850–1895). BEE; BEF; BEH; LEJ; LEOB

Field, Rachel (1894–1942). BEH

Fishback, Margaret (1904–1985). ALA

Fletcher, John Gould (1886–1950). SIF

Frost, Robert (1874–1963). ASB-1; BEF; BEGA; BEH; HEF; KE; LEJ; LEOB; SIF; WHB

Goodwin, Ruby Berkley (1903–). DADB

Guitarman, Arthur (1871–1943). ALA

Hammon, Jupiter (1720?–1800). CL; ROE

Harper, Frances Ellen Watkins (1825–1911). LOAV; ROE; ROG; WABC†

Herford, Oliver (1863–1935). ALA

Hoffenstein, Samuel Goodman (1890–1947). (Born Lithuania). ALA

Holmes, Oliver Wendell (1809–1894). BEF; BEGA; BOA; HEF; SUFA

Horton, George Moses (1798?–1880). CL

Hughes, Langston (1902–1967). ADA; ADB; BRBD; CAGA; DADB; DOF-1; JO; LEJ; RIC; RICA; ROE

Johnson, James Weldon (1871–1938). ADA; ADB; BRB†; DOF-1; GRAB-02; JO; RIC; RICA; ROE; ROG; STB

Jong, Erica (1942–). GL-1

Lanier, Sidney (1842–1881). SIF

Lazarus, Emma (1849–1887). DOD; GRB-1; GUB; LEK; LER; LETA; PEB

Lindsay, Vachel (1879–1931). BEF; BEH; BRBB; HEF; LEJ; SIF

Longfellow, Henry Wadsworth (1807–1882). BEF; BEGA; BEH; BOA; COB; DEI; DEJ; HEF; HIG; LEJ; LEOB; MAL; SIF; SMBA; SUFA

Lowell, Amy (1874–1925). BEGA; MUA; SIF

Lowell, James Russell (1819–1891). BEF; BEGA; SUFA

McGinley, Phyllis (1905–1978). ALA

McKay, Claude (1890–1948). ADA; ADB; BRB†

MacLeish, Archibald (1892–1982). BRBB

Markham, Edwin (1852–1940). MAM

Masters, Edgar Lee (1869–1950). SIF

Meléndez, Cóncha (1904–). Puerto Rican. NEBB

Merton, Thomas (Father M. Louis) (1915–1968). (Born France). EOB

Millay, Edna St. Vincent (1892–1950). BEGA; FRB; GIBA†; LEJ; LEOB; MUA; OCB; SIF; STLA; WHB

Monroe, Harriet (1861–1936). STLA

Moore, Clement Clarke (1779–1863). BEF; BEH

Morley, Christopher (1890–1957). ALA; BEF

Nash, Ogden (1902–1971). ALA; BEE

Newsome, Effie Lee (b. 1885). ROE

Poe, Edgar Allan (1809–1849). BEF; BEG; BOA; CAC; COKB; HACB; HEF; HIG; LEGB; SIF; STK

Pound, Ezra (1885–1972). ASB-1

Prince, Lucy Terry (1731–1821). KADB

Richards, Laura E. (1850–1943). BEF; BEH

Riley, James Whitcomb (1849–1916). ALA; BEF; BEH; LEJ; LEOB; LEPA; MAL

Robinson, Edwin Arlington (1869–1935). BEGA; SIF; WHB

Rosenfeld, Morris (1862–1923). (Born Poland). LETA

Sampter, Jessie (b. 1883?). ALD

Sandburg, Carl (1878–1967). BEF; BEH; BOA; HEF; KE†; SIF

Santayana, George (1863–1952). (Born Spain).
LO

Sarton, May (1912–). (Born Belgium). OCB

Tate, Allen (1899–1979). LEJ

Teasdale, Sara (1884–1933). BRBB

Thaxter, Celia (1835–1894). BEF

Walker, Margaret (1915–). ROE

Wheatley, Phillis (1753–1784). ADA; ADB; AND;
BRB; DOB; GIBA; HUA; JOCA; LEJ; LEPA;
LOAV; PECA; ROE; ROG; WIBA

Whitman, Walt (1819–1892). BEF; BOA; DEI;
DEJ; EOB; HACB; HEF; HIG; LEJ; SIF

Whittier, John Greenleaf (1807–1892). BEF;
BEGA; BOA; SIF

Wylie, Elinor Morton (1885–1928). BRBB

English

Arnold, Matthew (1822–1888). COP

Belloc, Hilaire (1870–1953). BEH

Blake, William (1757–1827). BEH; COP

Brooke, Rupert (1887–1915). COP

Browning, Elizabeth Barrett (1809–1861). BOC

Browning, Robert (1812–1889). COP

Byron, George Gordon Noel, 6th baron (1788–
1824). COP; DEI

Chaucer, Geoffrey (1340?–1400). COP

Coleridge, Samuel Taylor (1772–1834). COP; RAC

Cowley, Abraham (1618–1667). COP

de la Mare, Walter John (1873–1956). BEH

Doughty, Charles Montagu (1843–1926). MOB;
ROL†; WIA-1

Dryden, John (1631–1700). COP

Eliot, Thomas Stearns (1888–1965). (Born U.S.).
ASB-1; BRBB; COP

Farjeon, Eleanor (1881–1965). BEH; SMB

Gray, Thomas (1716–1771). COP

Greenaway, Kate (1846–1901). SM

Jonson, Ben (1573?–1637). DEI; DEJ

Keats, John (1795–1821). COP

Kipling, Rudyard (1865–1936). BEI; COB; COO;
COP; STK

Lear, Edward (1812–1888). BEH; SM

Macaulay, Thomas Babington Macaulay, 1st
baron (1800–1859). BEG; COP

Masefield, John (1878–1967). COP

Milne, Alan Alexander (1882–1956). BEH; SMB

Milton, John (1608–1674). COP

Noyes, Alfred (1880–1958). BEH; COP

Owen, Wilfred (1893–1918). COP

Pope, Alexander (1688–1744). COP

Rossetti, Christina Georgina (1830–1894). BEH;
COP

Shelley, Percy Bysshe (1792–1822). COP

Sidney, Sir Philip (1554–1586). STP

Spender, Stephen (1909–). BRBB

Spenser, Edmund (1552–1599). COP

Swinburne, Algernon Charles (1837–1909). COP

Taylor, Ann (1782–1866). BEH

Taylor, Jane (1783–1824). BEH

Tennyson, Alfred Tennyson, 1st baron (1809–
1892). COP

Wordsworth, William (1770–1850). COP

Puerto Rican

Burgos, Julia de (1914–1953). WO

Diego, José de (1866–1918). STC; TU

Palés Matos, Luis (1898–1959). NEBB

Rodriguez de Tio, Lola (1843–1924). WO

Roman

Horace (65–8 B.C.). COK

Lucretius (Titus Lucretius Carus) (96?–55 B.C.).
LO

Virgil (70–19 B.C.). COK; COKB

Russian

Bialik, Chaim Nachman (1873–1934). GEF; GRB-
1; GUB; KAD; PEB

Pushkin, Aleksandr Sergeevich (1799–1837). ADA;
ADB; JO; POFA

Yevtushenko, Yevgeny Aleksandrovich (1933–).
POFA

Others

Allingham, William (1824–1889). Irish. BEH

Borges, Jorge Luis (1899–1986). Argentine. WO

Brutus, Dennis (1924–). South African. LEA

Burns, Robert (1759–1796). Scottish. COB

Dante, Alighieri (1265–1321). Italian. DEI; DEJ

Dario, Rubén (Felix Rubén Garcia Sarmiento)
(1867–1916). Nicaraguan. WO

Goethe, Johann Wolfgang von (1749–1832). German. DEI; DEJ

Guillen, Nicolás (1902–). Cuban. WO

Heine, Heinrich (1797–1856). German. PEB

Homer (9th century B.C.?). Greek. DEI; DEJ

Johnson, E. Pauline (1862–1913). Canadian.
GRAD

Juana Inés de la Cruz, Sister (1651–1695). Mexican. BACA; ROGB

Judah ha-Levi (c. 1085–1140). Spanish. GEF;
GRB-1; GUA; KAC; LERA; LES

Mickiewicz, Adam (1798–1855). Polish. MANB

Mistral, Gabriela (1889–1957). Chilean. BACA;
SHFE†; WO

Neruda, Pablo (1904–1973). Chilean. WO

Paz, Octavio (1914–). Mexican. WO

Sachs, Nelly (1891–1970). Swedish. (Born Germany). SHFE

Samuel ibn Adiya (fl. 540). Arabian. GEF

Stevenson, Robert Louis (1850–1894). Scottish.
BEH; COB; COO; DEI; DEJ; HOA; STK

Sutherland, Efua Theodora (1924–). Ghanaian. CRA
Yeats, William Butler (1865–1939). Irish. BRBB

Walesa, Lech (1943–). Labor leader. AAS-34; DU-1
Zalman, Shneor (1747–1812). Rabbi. KAD

POLE VAULTERS, see TRACK & FIELD ATHLETES

POLICE OFFICIALS, see LAW ENFORCERS

POLES

Aaron of Tulchin. Rabbi. GEF
Anilewicz, Mordecai (1919–1943). Resistance worker. GRB-1
Bridgetower, George Augustus (1780–1860). Violinist. ADA; ADB
Chopin, Frédéric François (1810–1849). Composer. BEN; BRF; BUD; DEI; DEJ; FIE; GOB; KAE; MANB; SAA; WIA; YOJ
Copernicus, Nicolaus (1473–1543). Astronomer. ASA; BEP; BOB; CAA; COL; DOE; FE; MANB; MOCB; PIA; POD; SHFB; SIA; SIB; STI; SUE
Granville, Christine (d. 1952). Spy. SEB
Isaac, Levi (1740–1809). Rabbi. KAD
Israel ben Eliezer (Baal Shem Tov) (1700–1760). Hasidic leader. GEF; GUB; KAC; LERA; LES; PEB
Jadwiga (1373–1399). Queen. MANB
John III Sobieski (1624–1696). King. MAJ
John Paul II (1920–). Pope. DU-1; MANB
Kagan, Israel Meir (1838–1933). Rabbi. KAD
Kirszenstein-Szewinska, Irena (1946–). Track athlete, born Russia. SLA
Korczak, Janus (1878–1942). Physician. GRB-1
Kosciusko, Tadeusz (1746–1817). General in American Revolution. HEA; LOB; MANB; PIAA; RAD; SCB-1; STP
Landowska, Wanda (1877–1959). Harpsichordist. FOG
Lemkin, Raphael (1900–). Lawyer. BAF
Malinowski, Bronislaw Kasper (1884–1942). Anthropologist. HAO
Mickiewicz, Adam (1798–1855). Poet. MANB
Novak, Nina. Dancer. ATA
Orlean, Judah Leib. Educator. GEF
Paderewski, Ignace Jan (1860–1941). Pianist, statesman. CHF; MANB; PIAA
Peretz, Isaac Leib (1852–1915). Yiddish author. GEF
Pilsudski, Józef (1867–1935). General, statesman. CAAA
Pulaski, Casimir (1748–1779). Nobleman in American Revolution. ARE; LOB; MANB; PIAA; SCB-1; SOA
Reymont, Wladyslaw Stanislaw (1867–1926). Author. MANB

POLITICAL FIGURES

See also GOVERNORS, U.S.; LEGISLATORS, U.S.; MAYORS, U.S.; PRESIDENTS, U.S.; STATESMEN, FOREIGN; VICE PRESIDENTS, U.S.

Baldorioty de Castro, Román (1822–1889). Puerto Rican. TU
Barbosa, José Celso (1857–1921). Puerto Rican. STC; TU
Eliav, Aryeh Lyova (1921–). Israeli. (Born Russia). GRB-1
Gutierrez, José Angel. Mexican-American. NEAA
Krupsak, Mary Anne (1932–). GRAB-1
McCabe, Edwin P. (b. 1850). KADB
Moreno, Mariano (1778–1811). Argentine. LAB
Muñoz Rivera, Luis (1859–1916). Puerto Rican. NEBB; STC; TU
Pinchback, Pinckney Benton Stewart (1837–1921). ADA; ADB; BRB†; CHFB
Robespierre, Maximilien François Marie Isidore de (1758–1794). French. HAK
Ruef, Abraham (1864–1936). COGC
Sutton, Percy Ellis (1920–). DU

POLO PLAYERS

Hitchcock, Thomas, Jr. (1900–1944). DAG; DAGA
Sears, Eleanora (1881–1968). HOBA; HOBAA; RYA†

POPES, see RELIGIOUS LEADERS—ROMAN CATHOLIC; SAINTS

PORTUGUESE

Abravanel, Isaac (1437–1508). Statesman, Jewish theologian. GUA; KAB; KAC; LERA; LES
Covilham, Peter de (1450?–1545). Explorer. KNA
Dias, Bartholomeu (1450?–1500). Navigator. ROL
Gama, Vasco da (c. 1469–1524). Explorer. COC; COL; DAF; GRC; KEH; MOB; ROL

Henry (Henry the Navigator) (1394–1460). Prince of Portugal. GRC; KNB; MOB

Lopez, Roderigo (1525–1594). Physician. MAR

Magellan, Ferdinand (1480–1521). Explorer. COC; COL; DYA; EVD; GRC; HEA; KEH; KNB; LAA-2; MOB; PRC; ROL

Mendesia, Gracia (1510–1568). Philanthropist. LER; LES

Nasi, Joseph (1510–1579). Statesman. GUB; KAB; PEB

Salazar, António de Oliveira (1889–1970). Chief of state. ARA

Vieira, Antônio (1608–1697). Missionary. WOB

POTTERY MAKERS, *see* CRAFTSPERSONS

PREMIERS, *see* STATESMEN, FOREIGN

PRESIDENTS' WIVES, *see* FIRST LADIES

PRESIDENTS, FOREIGN, *see* STATESMEN, FOREIGN

PRESIDENTS, U.S.

Adams, John (1735–1826). ARAB; BAEA; BAEB; BAG; BAG-1; BEB; BLA; BLE; BUIA; BUIB; CAG; CAH; COI; COJ; COS; DAFA; DUB; DUC; DUCA; FEA; FEAB; FEB; FRBA; HAN; HAOA; HIH; HOEA; KEC†; LAI; LEQ; LEQA; MAB; MABA; MAC; MIA; OLA; PED; ROH; ROHA; ROK†; SUBB; WHD

Adams, John Quincy (1767–1848). BAEB; BAG; BAG-1; BEB; BLA; BUIA; CAG; CAH; COG; COI; COS; DAE; DUB; DUC; DUCA; FOR; FRBA; HEEA; HIH; KEC; KED; LAI; LEQ; LEQA; MAB; MABA; MAL; MIA; PED; RED; ROH; ROHA; ROK†; SUBB; WHD

Arthur, Chester Alan (1830–1886). ALE; BAEB; BAG; BAG-1; BEB; BLA; BUIA; CAG; CAH; COI; COS; DAE; DUC; DUCA; FEA; FRBA; HAOA; HIH; HOEA; KEA; LEQ; LEQA; MAB; MABA; MIA; PED; ROH; ROHA; ROK†; SUBB; WHD

Buchanan, James (1791–1868). BAEB; BAG; BAG-1; BEB; BLA; BUIA; CAG; CAH; COI; COS; DUC; DUCA; FRBA; HEEA; HIH; LEQ; LEQA; MAB; MABA; MIA; PED; ROH; ROHA; ROK†; SUBB; WHD

Carter, Jimmy (James Earl) (1924–). BAG-1; BEB; BLA; COI; COS; DUCA; FRBA; LEQA; SUBB; WHD

Cleveland, Grover (1837–1908). BAEB; BAG; BAG-1; BEB; BLA; BUIA; CAG; CAH; COI; COS; DUB; DUC; DUCA; FRBA; HIH; LEQ; LEQA; MAB; MABA; MIA; PED; ROH; ROHA; ROK†; SUBB; WHD

Coolidge, Calvin (1872–1933). ALE; BAEB; BAG; BAG-1; BEB; BLA; BOD; BUIA; CAG; CAH; COI; COS; DUB; DUC; DUCA; FEA; FRBA; HAOA; HIH; HOEA; LEQ; LEQA; MAB; MABA; MIA; PED; ROH; ROHA; ROK†; SUBB; WHD

Eisenhower, Dwight David (1890–1969). ARC; ASB-1; BAEB; BAG; BAG-1; BEB; BLA; BUIA; CAG; CAH; COD†; COI; COJA; COS; DEI; DEJ; DUB; DUC; DUCA; FAA; FRBA; HIH; KE; LEP; LEQ; LEQA; MAB; MABA; MIA; PED; RAE; ROH; ROHA; ROK†; SCA; SUBB; SWE-1; WEE; WHD

Fillmore, Millard (1800–1874). ALE; BAEB; BAG; BAG-1; BEB; BLA; BUIA; CAG; CAH; COI; COS; DUC; DUCA; FEA; FRBA; HAOA; HIH; HOEA; LEQ; LEQA; MAB; MABA; MIA; PED; ROH; ROHA; ROK†; SUBB; WHD

Ford, Gerald R. (1913–). BAG-1; BEB; BEB-1; BLA; BUIA; COI; COS; DUCA; FEA; FRBA; HAOA; HOEA; LEQA; SUBB; WHD

Garfield, James Abram (1831–1881). BAEB; BAG; BAG-1; BEB; BLA; BUIA; CAG; CAH; COI; COJA; COS; DUC; DUCA; FRBA; HIH; KEA; LEQ; LEQA; MAB; MABA; MIA; PED; ROH; ROHA; ROK†; SUBB; WHD

Grant, Ulysses Simpson (1822–1885). BAEB; BAG; BAG-1; BEB; BLA; BUIA; CAG; CAH; COD; COI; COJA; COS; CUC; DEI; DEJ; DUB; DUC; DUCA; FID; FRBA; HIH; LEP; LEQ; LEQA; MAB; MABA; MIA; PED; RAE; ROH; ROHA; ROK†; SUBB; WHD

Harding, Warren Gamaliel (1865–1923). BAEB; BAG; BAG-1; BEB; BLA; BUIA; CAG; CAH; COI; COS; DUB; DUC; DUCA; FRBA; HIH; LEQ; LEQA; MAB; MABA; MIA; PED; ROH; ROHA; ROK†; SUBB; WHD

Harrison, Benjamin (1833–1901). BAEB; BAG; BAG-1; BEB; BLA; BUIA; CAG; CAH; COI; COJA; COS; DUC; DUCA; FRBA; HIH; LAI; LEQ; LEQA; MAB; MABA; MIA; PED; ROH; ROHA; ROK†; SUBB; WHD

Harrison, William Henry (1773–1841). BAEB; BAG; BAG-1; BEB; BLA; BUIA; CAG; CAH; COI; COJA; COS; DUC; DUCA; FRBA; HIH; LAI; LEQ; LEQA; MAB; MABA; MIA; PED; ROH; ROHA; ROK†; SEC; SUBB; WHD

Hayes, Rutherford Birchard (1822–1893). BAEB; BAG; BAG-1; BEB; BLA; BUIA; CAG; CAH; COI; COJA; COS; DUC; DUCA; FRBA; HIH; LEQ; LEQA; MAB; MABA; MIA; PED; ROH; ROHA; ROK†; SUBB; WHD

Hoover, Herbert Clark (1874–1964). BAEB; BAG;

BAG-1; BEB; BLA; BUIA; CAG; CAH; COI;
COS; CUC; DUB; DUC; DUCA; FRBA; HIH;
LEN; LEQ; LEQA; MAB; MABA; MAL; MIA;
PED; ROH; ROHA; ROK†; SUBB; WHD

Jackson, Andrew (1767–1845). ARE; BAEB; BAG;
BAG-1; BEB; BLA; BUIA; CAG; CAH; COD;
COI; COJA; COS; DAC; DEI; DEJ; DUB; DUC;
DUCA; FRBA; HIH; LEP; LEQ; LEQA; LOA;
MAB; MABA; MAO; MIA; OLA; PED; ROH;
ROHA; ROK; STH; SUBB; WAN; WHD

Jefferson, Thomas (1743–1826). ALCA; ARAB;
ASB; BAEA; BAEB; BAG; BAG-1; BEB; BEC;
BLA; BLE; BUIA; BUIB; CAG; CAH; COG;
COI; COJ; COS; CUC; DAC; DAF-2; DAFA;
DEI; DEJ; DIA; DUB; DUC; DUCA; FEA;
FEAB; FEB; FIA; FID; FOB; FOH; FRBA;
FRE; HAN; HAOA; HEEA; HIBC†; HIH;
HOEA; LEQ; LEQA; MAB; MABA; MAC; MAT;
MEB; MIA; OLA; PED; ROH; ROHA; ROK;
STH; SUBB; VIA; WAI; WHD

Johnson, Andrew (1808–1875). ALE; BAEB; BAG;
BAG-1; BEB; BLA; BUIA; CAG; CAH; COI;
COS; DAE; DUC; DUCA; FEA; FRBA; HAOA;
HIH; HOEA; KEA; KEC†; LEQ; LEQA; MAB;
MABA; MIA; PED; ROH; ROHA; ROK†;
SUBB; WHD

Johnson, Lyndon Baines (1908–1973). ALE;
BAEB; BAG; BAG-1; BEB; BLA; BUIA; CAG;
CAH; COI; COS; DUB; DUC; DUCA; FEA;
FRBA; HAOA; HIH; HOEA; KEA; LEQ;
LEQA; MAB; MABA; MIA; PED; ROHA;
ROK†; SUBB; WEB; WEE; WHD

Kennedy, John Fitzgerald (1917–1963). ASB;
BAEB; BAG; BAG-1; BEB; BEC; BLA; BUIA;
CAAA; CAG; CAH; COI; COJA; COS; CUC;
DEI; DEJ; DIA; DUB; DUC; DUCA; FAA; FIA;
FRBA; HIH; KE; KEA; LAI; LEPE; LEQ;
LEQA; MAB; MABA; MIA; PED; ROH; ROHA;
ROK; SCA; SCBA; SUBB; WEA; WEE; WHD;
YOA

Lincoln, Abraham (1809–1865). ASB; BAEB;
BAG; BAG-1; BEB; BEC; BLA; BOD; BUIA;
CAAA; CAG; CAH; CHG; COG; COI; COS;
CUC; DAC; DAE; DEI; DEJ; DIA; DUB; DUC;
DUCA; EVD; FIA; FOB; FOH; FRBA; HIH;
KEA; LEPE; LEQ; LEQA; MAB; MABA; MAT;
MIA; OLA; PED; ROH; ROHA; ROK; STH;
STJA; SUBB; WHD

McKinley, William (1843–1901). BAEB; BAG;
BAG-1; BEB; BLA; BUIA; CAG; CAH; COI;
COJA; COS; DUC; DUCA; FRBA; HIH; KEA;
LEQ; LEQA; MAB; MABA; MIA; PED; ROH;
ROHA; ROK†; SUBB; WHD

Madison, James (1751–1836). BAEB; BAG;
BAG-1; BEB; BLA; BUIA; BUIB; CAG; CAH;
COI; COS; DUB†; DUC; DUCA; FEAA; FRBA;

HEEA; HIH; LEQ; LEQA; LOA; MAB; MABA;
MEB; MIA; PED; ROH; ROHA; ROK†; STH;
SUBB; WHD

Monroe, James (1758–1831). BAEB; BAG; BAG-1;
BEB; BLA; BUIA; CAG; CAH; COI; COJA;
COS; DEI; DEJ; DUB†; DUC; DUCA; FRBA;
HEEA; HIH; LEQ; LEQA; LOA; MAB; MABA;
MIA; PED; ROH; ROHA; ROK†; STH; SUBB;
WHD

Nixon, Richard Milhous (1913–). BAEB; BAG;
BAG-1; BEB; BLA; BUIA; CAG; COI; COJA;
COS; DUC; DUCA; FEA; FRBA; HAOA; HIH;
HOEA; LEQ; LEQA; MABA; ROHA; ROK†;
SUBB; WECA; WHD

Pierce, Franklin (1804–1869). BAEB; BAG;
BAG-1; BEB; BLA; BUIA; CAG; CAH; COI;
COS; DUC; DUCA; FRBA; HIH; LEQ; LEQA;
MAB; MABA; MIA; PED; ROH; ROHA; ROK†;
SUBB; WHD

Polk, James Knox (1795–1849). BAEB; BAG;
BAG-1; BEB; BLA; BUIA; CAG; CAH; COI;
COS; DUC; DUCA; FRBA; HIH; LEQ; LEQA;
MAB; MABA; MAL; MIA; PED; ROH; ROHA;
ROK†; SUBB; WHD

Reagan, Ronald Wilson (1911–). BEB; BLA; COI;
COS; FRBA; SUBB; WHD

Roosevelt, Franklin Delano (1882–1945). ASB;
ASB-1; BAEB; BAG; BAG-1; BEB; BEC; BLA;
BUIA; CAAA; CAG; CAH; COI; COS; CUC;
DEI; DEJ; DOF; DUB; DUC; DUCA; FAA; FIA;
FOH; FRBA; HIH; KE; LAI; LEQ; LEQA;
MAB; MABA; MEB; MIA; PED; ROH; ROHA;
ROK; SUBB; TAC; WEE; WHD; YOA

Roosevelt, Theodore (1858–1919). ALE; ASB;
BAEB; BAG; BAG-1; BEB; BEC; BLA; BUIA;
CAG; CAH; CO-1; COI; COJA; CORA; COS;
CUC; DAE; DEI; DEJ; DUB; DUC; DUCA;
FEA; FEC; FOH; FRBA; HAA; HAOA; HIH;
HOEA; KEA; LAI; LEQ; LEQA; MAB; MABA;
MAL; MEA; MEC; MIA; OLA; PED; ROH;
ROHA; ROK; ROL†; STH; SUBB; WHD; WIC

Taft, William Howard (1857–1930). BAEB; BAG;
BAG-1; BEB; BLA; BUIA; CAG; CAH; COI;
COS; DUB; DUC; DUCA; FLC; FRBA; HIH;
LAI; LEQ; LEQA; MAB; MABA; MIA; PED;
ROH; ROHA; ROK†; SUBB; WHD

Taylor, Zachary (1784–1850). BAEB; BAG;
BAG-1; BEB; BLA; BUIA; CAG; CAH; COI;
COJA; COS; DUC; DUCA; FRBA; HIH; LEQ;
LEQA; MAB; MABA; MIA; PED; ROH; ROHA;
ROK†; SUBB; WHD

Truman, Harry S. (1884–1972). ALE; ASB-1;
BAEB; BAG; BAG-1; BEB; BLA; BUIA; CAG;
CAH; COI; COJA; COS; DEI; DEJ; DUB†;
DUC; DUCA; FEA; FRBA; HADA; HAOH;
HIH; HOEA; KE; LEQ; LEQA; MAB; MABA;

MIA; PED; ROH; ROHA; ROK†; SUBB; WEE;
WHD; YOA

Tyler, John (1790–1862). ALE; BAEB; BAG;
BAG-1; BEB; BLA; BUIA; CAG; CAH; COI;
COS; DUC; DUCA; FEA; FRBA; HAOA; HIH;
HOEA; KEC†; LEQ; LEQA; MAB; MABA;
MIA; PED; ROH; ROHA; ROK†; SUBB; WHD

Van Buren, Martin (1782–1862). BAEB; BAG;
BAG-1; BEB; BLA; BUIA; CAG; CAH; COI;
COS; DUC; DUCA; FEA; FRBA; HAOA; HEEA;
HIH; HOEA; LEQ; LEQA; MAB; MABA; MIA;
PED; ROH; ROHA; ROK†; SUBB; WHD

Washington, George (1732–1799). ALCA; ARAB;
ASB; BAEB; BAG; BAG-1; BEB; BEC; BLA;
BUIA; BUIB; CAAA; CABA; CAG; CAH; CHG;
COD; COI; COJA; COS; CUC; DAC; DAE;
DAF-2; DAFA; DEI; DEJ; DUB; DUC; DUCA;
EVD; FEAA; FIA; FID; FOB; FOH; FRBA;
HAK; HAN; HIBC; HIH; KEC†; LEAA; LEP;
LEQ; LEQA; MAB; MABA; MAT; MIA; OLA;
PED; ROH; ROHA; ROK; SOA; STH; SUBB;
WAI; WHD

Wilson, Woodrow (1856–1924). ARB; ASB-1;
BAEB; BAG; BAG-1; BEB; BLA; BUIA; CAG;
CAH; COI; COS; CUC; DEI; DEJ; DOF; DUB;
DUC; DUCA; FOB; FRBA; HIH; LEQ; LEQA;
MAB; MABA; MEA; MEC; MIA; PED; ROH;
ROHA; ROK; SUBB; WHD; WIC

PRIESTS, *see* RELIGIOUS LEADERS—ROMAN CATHOLIC

PRIME MINISTERS, *see* STATESMEN, FOREIGN

PRINTERS

See also JOURNALISTS

Caxton, William (1422?–1491). English. DEI; DEJ

Franklin, Benjamin (1706–1790). ALCA; ARAB;
ASB; BAEA; BLE; BOD; BUE; BUIB; CAA;
COJ; COR; CUC; DAC; DAFA; DEDC; DEI;
DEJ; DUA; FE; FEAA; FEAB; FEB; FIA; FID;
FOB; FOH; HAN; HYA; HYB; LEAA; LEC;
MAC; MAQ; MAT; OLA; SHFB; SIA; SQB;
STH; STI; VIA; WAI

Grosman, Tatyana (1904–). Lithographer, born
Russia. GIB-1

Gutenberg, Johann (c. 1397–1468). German. ASA;
COL; DEI; DEJ; EBA; FE; FRE; THA

König, Friedrich (1774–1833). German. FE; LAE

Zenger, John Peter (1697–1746). (Born Germany).
ARB; CUB; CUC; FIA; LOB; MEB; SQB

PRIZE FIGHTERS, *see* BOXING FIGURES

PRIZE WINNERS, *see* NAMES OF AWARDS, E.G., MEDAL
OF HONOR, NOBEL, PULITZER

PROPHETS, BIBLICAL, *see* BIBLICAL FIGURES—OLD TES-
TAMENT; RELIGIOUS FIGURES

PSYCHIATRISTS & PSYCHOLOGISTS

Brill, Abraham Arden (1874–1948). (Born Austria). LETA

Brothers, Joyce (1927–). BOHG

Clevenger, Johanna. FOC-1

Daniels, Susan (1948–). BOHA-1

Densen-Gerber, Judianne (1934–). GIB-1

Freud, Anna (1895–1982). English. (Born Austria). CHE

Freud, Sigmund (1856–1939). Austrian. ASB-1;
CHD; FRE; KE; POD; RIB; ROA; WEF

Fuller, Solomon Carter (1872–1953). HAMA

Guild, Elizabeth. HOG

Hollingworth, Leta Stetter (1886–1939). HA-1;
PACB

Horney, Karen (1885–1952). (Born Germany).
FLA; LEG; RAAG†

James, William (1842–1910). LO

Jung, Carl Gustav (1875–1961). Swiss. KE

Kline, Nathan Schellenberg (1916–). HEFA

Kübler-Ross, Elisabeth (1926–). (Born Switzerland). BOHE; GIB-1

Kuchler, Lena. Israeli. (Born Poland). GRB-1

Menninger, Karl Augustus (1893–1966). CHE

Menninger, William Claire (1899–1966). CHE

Muller-Schwarze, Christine. (Born Germany).
LA-1

Oliver, Donna. LA-1

Skinner, Burrhus Frederic (1904–). DU-1

Whitehorn, John Clare (1894–). CHE

PUBLIC HEALTH LEADERS

See also NURSES; PHYSICIANS & SURGEONS; SO-
CIAL WORKERS

Baker, Sara Josephine (1873–1945). PACB

Breckinridge, Mary (1877–1965). COFA; MAK;
WRA

Calderone, Mary Steichen (1904–). BOHE; GIB-1

Eliot, Martha May (1891–1978). CHE

Floyd, Theodora A. (1896–). YOB

Goldberger, Joseph (1874–1929). (Born Austria).
ALD; DEA; GEF

Wald, Lillian D. (1867–1940). ALD; BRBE†; CAGA; DOD; EIA; GEE; GIBA; GRB-1; LETA; WABC†; WRA; YOB

Wauneka, Annie Dodge (1912–). BRBE†; GRAC; GRAD; WAB

PUERTO RICANS

Arroyo, Luis (1927–). Baseball player. SHE

Badillo, Herman (1929–). Lawyer, government official. FOW; NEBB; WO

Baldorioty de Castro, Román (1822–1889). Political leader. TU

Barbosa, José Celso (1857–1921). Political leader. STC; TU

Benítez, Jaime (1908–). Government official, educator. NEBB

Betances y Alarcón, Ramón Emeterio (1827–1898). Physician. TU; WO

Burgos, Julia de (1914–1953). Poet. WO

Cepeda, Orlando (1937–). Baseball player. BRD; FOW; PRA

Clemente, Roberto (1934–1972). Baseball player. BUD-1; BUJ; DAFC; DAFD; FOW; FRC-1†; FRD; GUE; IZA; KADA; NEBB; PEC; PRA; RIGA†; SHH; WH-2; WO

Collazo, Oscar (1914–). Revolutionist. RABA

Colón, Miriam. Actress. NEBB

Cordero y Molina, Rafael (1790–1868). Educator. TU

Díaz, Justino (1940–). Singer. NEBB

Diego, José de (1866–1918). Poet. STC; TU

Feliciano, José (1945–). Singer. FOW; LYA; WH-2

Ferrer, José (1912–). Actor, director. FOW

Figueroa, Carmen Sanabria de (1882–1954). Pianist. NEBB

Figueroa, Ed. Baseball player. KLBB

Figueroa, Jesús (1878–1971). Band leader. NEBB

Figueroa, José (1905–). Violinist. NEBB

Hernandez, Raphael (1893–). Composer. FOW

Hostos, Eugenio Maríe de (1839–1903). Educator. TU

Marín Solá, Ramón (1832–1902). Publisher. TU

Maymi, Carmen Rosa (1938–). Government official. NEBB; WH-2

Meléndez, Cóncha (1904–). Poet, educator. NEBB

Moreno, Rita (1931–). Actress. DI-1†; WO

Moscoso, Teodoro (1910–). Diplomat. NEBB

Muñoz Marín, Luis (1898–1980). Ex-governor of Puerto Rico. NEBB; STC; TU; WO

Muñoz Rivera, Luis (1859–1916). Political leader. NEBB; STC; TU

Palés Matos, Luis (1898–1959). Poet. NEBB

Power Giralt, Ramón (1775–1813). Patriot. TU

Rincón de Gautier, Felisa (1897–). Mayor. FOW; WO

Rodriguez, Juan "Chi-Chi" (1935–). Golfer. BELB; FOI; FOW; IZA; NEBB

Rodriguez de Tio, Lola (1843–1924). Poet. WO

Rodriguez-Trias, Helen. Pediatrician, social reformer. GLO

Rosado del Valle, Julio (1922–). Painter. NEBB

Ruiz Belvis, Segundo (1829–1867). Lawyer, government worker. TU

Sanchez, Yolanda. Human services consultant, reformer. GLO

Torres, Liz. Actress. MASB

Torresola, Griselio (1925?–1950). Assassin. RABA

PULITZER PRIZE WINNERS

Biography or Autobiography

Adams, Henry Brooks (1838–1918). HIB

Bok, Edward William (1863–1930). (Born the Netherlands). BOD; CAGA; CUC; FLBA; LOB

Cushing, Harvey Williams (1869–1939). CHD; CHE†; SIC

James, Henry (1843–1916). ASB-1; CON†; STL

Lindbergh, Charles Augustus (1902–1974). ASB-1; BRBA; COC†; EVD; FAA; HAA; HAMY; HAQ; LAC; SQA; SUA

Pupin, Michael Idvorsky (1858–1935). (Born Yugoslavia). BUF; LEB; LOB

Richards, Laura E. (1850–1943). BEF; BEH

Russell, Charles Edward (1860–1941). COGB

White, William Allen (1868–1944). COKA; FOE; SQB

Drama

Bock, Jerry (1928–). EWA

Hammerstein, Oscar, II (1895–1960). BEKA†; MOA

Loesser, Frank (1910–1969). EWA; MOA

MacLeish, Archibald (1892–1982). BRBB

O'Neill, Eugene Gladstone (1888–1953). ASB-1; BOA; DEI; DEJ; SHFA

Rodgers, Richard Charles (1902–1979). BAD; BEKA; EWA; MOA

Wilder, Thornton Niven (1897–1975). BEGA

Fiction

Bromfield, Louis (1896–1956). CON

Buck, Pearl S. (1892–1973). COKA; CON; GIBA†; HEF; KOA; LEGB; MUA; OCB; SHFE

Cather, Willa (1873–1947). BOA; CON; CUC; HEF; LEK; MUA; OCB; STLA

Faulkner, William (1897–1962). ASB-1; CAC; CON; FLBA; HEF

Ferber, Edna (1887–1968). CON; LETA; ROJ
Guthrie, Alfred Bertram, Jr. (1901–). CON
Hemingway, Ernest (1899–1961). ASB-1; CAC; CON; HEF; LAC; LEGB
Lewis, Sinclair (1885–1951). BOA; CON; HEF; LEGB
Marquand, John Phillips (1893–1960). BEGA; CON
Mitchell, Margaret (1900–1949). CON; OCB
Momaday, N. Scott (1934–). GRAC
Rawlings, Marjorie Kinnan (1896–1953). CON
Sinclair, Upton Beall (1878–1968). COGB
Steinbeck, John (1902–1968). CON; HEF
Tarkington, Booth (1869–1946). BEE; CON
Welty, Eudora (1909–). MUA; OCB
Wharton, Edith (1862–1937). BOA; CON†; STI
Wilder, Thornton Niven (1897–1975). BEGA
Wouk, Herman (1915–). GRB-1

History

Acheson, Dean Gooderham (1893–1971). HEEA
Brooks, Van Wyck (1886–1963). CAC
Parrington, Vernon Louis (1871–1929). HIB
Pershing, John Joseph (1860–1948). ARD; ARE; COD; DEI; DEJ; RAE
Sandburg, Carl (1878–1967). BEF; BEH; BOA; HEF; KE†; SIF
Sims, William Sowden (1858–1936). ARD; ICA; NAC
Turner, Frederick Jackson (1861–1932). HIB

Journalism

Atkinson, Brooks (1894–1984). LEU
Berger, Meyer (1898–1959). LEU
Block, Herbert Lawrence (1909–). DEDC
Buchwald, Art (1925–). LEU
Darcy, Tom (Thomas Francis). DEDC
Darling, Jay Norwood (1876–1962). DEDC
Faas, Horst (1933–). German. HOE
Fitzpatrick, Daniel Robert (1891–). DEDC
Higgins, Marguerite (1920–1966). ARBA; FLBB; JAD; JAE
Kirby, Rollin (1875–1952). DEDC
Lippmann, Walter (1889–1974). FOE
McCormick, Anne O'Hare (1881–1954). CLA; WABC†
McGill, Ralph Emerson (1898–1969). FLBA
Mauldin, Bill (William Henry) (1921–). DEDC
Pyle, Ernest Taylor (1900–1945). FAA; FIA; FLBB; FOE; JAD; LEU; SQB
Reston, James Barrett (1909–). (Born Scotland). LEU
Smith, Red (Walter Wellesley) (1905–1982). LEU
White, William Allen (1868–1944). COKA; FOE; SQB

Music

Barber, Samuel (1910–1981). BAD; KAE; MAF; POF
Copland, Aaron (1900–). BAD; BEKA; BEN; KAE; KE; MAF; POF; SAA†; YOL
Dello Joio, Norman (1913–). MAF; POF
Hanson, Howard (1896–1981). MAF; POF; STM†
Ives, Charles (1874–1954). BAD; EWAA; FIE; KAE; MAF; POF; SAA†
Joplin, Scott (1868–1917). COF-1
Menotti, Gian-Carlo (1911–). (Born Italy). BEKA; KAE; LIA; MAF; POF
Moore, Douglas Stuart (1893–1969). MAF; POF
Piston, Walter (1894–1976). BAD; MAF; POF
Porter, Quincy (1897–1966). POF
Schuman, William (1910–). BAD; MAF; POF
Sessions, Roger H. (1896–1985). POF
Thomson, Virgil (1896–). MAF

Nonfiction

Tuchman, Barbara (1912?–). BOHG

Poetry

Auden, Wystan Hugh (1907–1973). (Born England). BEA; BRBB; COP
Benét, Stephen Vincent (1898–1943). BEF; BEH; BOA; BRBB; SIF
Benét, William Rose (1886–1950). BEF
Brooks, Gwendolyn (1917–). ADA; ADB; DRA; ROE
Fletcher, John Gould (1886–1950). SIF
Frost, Robert (1874–1963). ASB-1; BEF; BEGA; BEH; HEF; KE; LEJ; LEOB; SIF; WHB
Lowell, Amy (1874–1925). BEGA; MUA; SIF
McGinley, Phyllis (1905–1978). ALA
Millay, Edna St. Vincent (1892–1950). BEGA; FRB; GIBA†; LEJ; LEOB; MUA; OCB; SIF; STLA; WHB
Robinson, Edwin Arlington (1869–1935). BEGA; SIF; WHB
Sandburg, Carl (1878–1967). BEF; BEH; BOA; HEF; KE†; SIF
Teasdale, Sara (1884–1933). BRBB

Special Citation

Haley, Alex (1921–). DOF-1; STAA
Hammerstein, Oscar, II (1895–1960). BEKA†; MOA
Roberts, Kenneth Lewis (1885–1957). CON
Rodgers, Richard Charles (1902–1979). BAD; BEKA; EWA; MOA
Schuman, William (1910–). BAD; MAF; POF
Seuss, Dr. (Theodore Geisel) (1904–). SM
White, Elwyn Brooks (1899–1985). BEG; SMB

QUAKERS, *see* RELIGIOUS LEADERS—PROTESTANT

QUEENS, *see* RULERS

RABBIS, *see* CHAPLAINS; RELIGIOUS LEADERS—JEWISH

RACERS, *see* AUTOMOBILE RACERS; BICYCLISTS; BOAT RACERS; MOTORCYCLE RACERS

RADIO & TELEVISION ENGINEERS, *see* ENGINEERS, TELEVISION & RADIO

RADIO PERSONALITIES, *see* TELEVISION & RADIO PERSONALITIES

RAILROAD LEADERS, *see* TRANSPORTATION LEADERS

RANCHERS & CATTLEMEN

See also COWBOYS; PIONEERS AND FRONTIER PEOPLE

Alderson, Nannie (1860–1947). JOB
Altoha, Wallace (1870?–1937). WAA
Chisum, John Simpson (1824–1884). NAA; WAA
Goings, William (fl. 1821). KADB
Goodnight, Charles (1836–1929). BLD; WAA
Hagerman, James J. (fl. 1870). NAA
King, Richard (1824–1885). KAW; WAA
Logan, Greenbury (fl. 1831). KADB
Mossman, Burton C. (1867–1956). WAA
Willis, Ann Bassett (1878–1956). RAB

REBELS, *see* RESISTANCE LEADERS

RED CROSS WORKERS

Barton, Clara (1821–1912). Founder of American Red Cross. BEC; BOC; CUC; DED; DEI; DEJ; DOD; FOH; GIBA; JOCA; LEK; LEPC; MAK; MAT; PA; SMC; STJ; STLA; WABC†
Beckh, Herbert. DED
Courvoisier, Jean. Swiss. DED
David, François-Eugène. Swiss. DED
Dunant, Jean Henri (1828–1910). Swiss founder of Red Cross. DED; EVA; MEA; MEC; WIC; WRA
Junod, Marcel (1904?–1961). Swiss. DED
Olivet, Georges (1927?–1960). DED
Rochat, André. DED
Rolland, Romain (1866–1944). French. DED

Solomons, Adolphus Simeon (1826–1910). LETA
Volant, Guy (1909?–). Swiss. DED

REFORMERS

See also ABOLITIONISTS; FEMINISTS; HUMANITARIANS; MISSIONARIES; PACIFISTS; SOCIAL WORKERS

Baker, Sara Josephine (1873–1945). PACB
Barnard, Kate (1875–1930). PACB; TRD; VIA
Barnardo, Thomas John (1845–1905). Irish. EVA
Barnett, Ida Wells (1862–1931). ADB; BRBE†; BUFA; HUB; LOAV; PACB; PECA; ROG; STAB-1; TRD
Bhave, Vinoba (1895–1982). Indian. BAF; RODA
Bloomer, Amelia Jenks (1818–1894). ARB; DEDA; GUBA; LES-2
Comstock, Anthony (1844–1915). DEDA
Corrigan, Mairead (1944–). Irish. AAS-34; COG-1; SHFE†
Dix, Dorothea Lynde (1802–1887). BRBE†; BUA; DAD; DEDA; DOD; FID; MASA; STLA; WABC†; WAJ; YOC
Dow, Neal (1804–1897). DEDA
Fry, Elizabeth Gurney (1780–1845). English. BOH; NOA; STP
González Prada, Manuel (1848–1918). Peruvian. WOB
Hatcher, Orie Latham (1868–1946). PACB
Kagawa, Toyohiko (1888–1960). Japanese. BAF; KEE
Kuhn, Margaret (1905–). COG-1; GIB-1
Loeb, Sophie Irene (1876–1929). (Born Russia). LER
McDowell, Mary E. (1854–1936). PACB; WABC†
Mitchell, John R., Jr. (1863–1929). GRAB-01
Nabuco, Joaquim (1849–1910). Brazilian. WOB
Nader, Ralph (1934–). DU-1; EOA; GRBA
Noyes, John Humphrey (1811–1886). DEDA
Oastler, Richard (1789–1861). English. COG
Plimsoll, Samuel (1824–1898). English. EVA
Riis, Jacob August (1849–1914). (Born Denmark). FLBA; LOB; MEB
Ripley, George (1802–1880). EOB
Rodriguez-Trias, Helen. GLO
Sanger, Margaret (1883–1966). ARAA; ARB; BRBE; GIBA; KOA; ROJ; SC; STLA; WABC
Shaftesbury, Anthony Ashley Cooper, 7th earl of (1801–1885). English. COG; EVA
Willard, Frances Elizabeth (1839–1898). BRBE; GUBA; VAB; WABC
Williams, Betty (1943–). Irish. AAS-34; COG-1; SHFE†
Williams, Fannie Barrier. DADA
Wrede, Mathilda (1864–1928). Finnish. KEE

RELATIVES OF FAMOUS MEN & WOMEN

See also FIRST LADIES

Baeta, Henrietta Louise (1881–1971). Mother of Annie Jiagge. CRA

Bell, Marion Shaw (1786–1876). Wife of Dr. Charles Bell. RIB

Beruria (2d century). Wife of Rabbi Meir of Palestine. LER

Chiang Mei-ling (1897–). Wife of Chiang Kai-shek. EUA; PA

Cobb, James. Son of Ty Cobb. BELB

Custer, Elizabeth Bacon (1842–1933). Wife of General Custer. JOB

Eppes, Maria Jefferson (1778–1804). Daughter of Thomas Jefferson. PRB

Eugenie (1826–1910). Wife of Napoleon III. COKB

Freud, Martha Bernays (1861–1951). RIB

Godolphin, Margaret (1652–1678). Wife of Sidney Godolphin. NOA

Grey, Lady Katherine (1540–1568). Sister of Lady Jane Grey. NOA

Grey, Lady Mary (1545–1578). Sister of Lady Jane Grey. NOA

Harrison, Caroline (1832–1892). First wife of President Benjamin Harrison. BAG; BAG-1; BLG†; CHB; KL; MAA; MAU; PRB; ROH; ROHA

Hunter, Anne Home (1742–1821). Wife of John Hunter. RIB

Ima Shalom. Member of Hillel family. LER

Jackson, Rachel (1767–1828). Wife of Andrew Jackson. BAG; BAG-1; BLG†; CHA; KL; MAA; MAU; PRB; ROH; ROHA

Jefferson, Martha Wayles Skelton (1748–1782). Wife of Thomas Jefferson. BAG; BAG-1; BLG†; CHA; KL; MAA; MAU; ROH; ROHA

Kennedy, Edward M., Jr. (1961?–). Son of Senator Edward M. Kennedy. HAFA

Kung, Ai-ling Sung (1888–1973). Wife of H. H. Kung. EUA

Lane, Harriet (1830–1903). Niece of President Buchanan. BLG†; CHA; KL; MAA†; PRB; ROH; ROHA; STJ

Livingstone, Mary Moffatt (1821–1862). Wife of David Livingstone. RIB

Lombardi, Vincent, II (1942–). Son of Vincent Lombardi. BELB

McDowell, Sarah Shelby (1785–1840). Wife of Dr. Ephraim McDowell. RIB

Mantle, Elvin C. Father of Mickey Mantle, baseball player. EDA

Mariamne (d. 29 B.C.). Wife of Herod the Great. LER

Montefiore, Judith (1784–1862). Wife of Sir Moses Montefiore. LER

Murphy, Jeannette Plamondon (1867–1921). Wife of Dr. John Benjamin Murphy. RIB

Osler, Grace Revere (1854–1928). Wife of Sir William Osler. RIB

Pepys, Elizabeth (1640–1669). Wife of Samuel Pepys. NOA

Perón, Eva Duarte (1919–1952). Wife of Juan Domingo Perón. BAGA; LIDA; PA; WOB

Plummer, Electa (b. 1842). Wife of Henry Plummer. JOB

Rachel (fl. 100). Wife of Akiba ben Joseph, Palestinian rabbi. LER

Randolph, Martha Jefferson (1772–1836). Daughter of Thomas Jefferson. PRB

Roosevelt, Alice Hathaway Lee (1861–1884). First wife of Theodore Roosevelt. BAG; BAG-1; MAU

Roper, Margaret (1505–1544). Daughter of Sir Thomas More. NOA

Sedode, Julia Barbara de Lima (b. 1858). Grandmother of Annie Jiagge. CRA

Shippen, Margaret (1760–1804). Wife of Benedict Arnold. LOA

Straus, Lina. Wife of Nathan Straus. LER

Sun Ch'ing-ling (Sung) (1890–). Wife of Sun Yat-sen. EUA

Szent-Györgyi, Marta von (1910–1963). Wife of Albert von Szent-Györgyi. PAC

Van Buren, Hannah Hoes (1783–1819). Wife of Martin Van Buren. BAG; BAG-1; BLG†; CHA; KL; MAA; MAU; PRB; ROH; ROHA

Washington, Lawrence (1717–1752). Brother of George Washington. EDA

Woodson, Sara (b. 1590). Wife of Dr. John Woodson. RIB

RELIGIOUS LEADERS

See also APOSTLES; BIBLICAL FIGURES—NEW TESTAMENT; BIBLICAL FIGURES—OLD TESTAMENT; CHAPLAINS; MISSIONARIES; SAINTS

Jewish

Aaron of Tulchin. Polish rabbi. GEF

Aboab, Isaac de Fonseca (1605–1693). Dutch rabbi. LETA

Abravanel, Isaac (1437–1508). Portuguese theologian. GUA; KAB; KAC; LERA; LES

Akiba ben Joseph (c. 50–132). Palestinian rabbi. GEF; GRB-1; GUA; KAB; KAC; LERA

Ashi (352–427). Babylonian rabbi. GEF; GUA

Baeck, Leo (1873–1956). German rabbi. GEF; GRB-1; GUB; KAB

Caro, Joseph (1488–1575). Spanish Talmudist. KAC

Einhorn, David (1809–1879). Rabbi, born Germany. GUB

Elijah ben Solomon (Elijah Gaon) (1720–1797). Lithuanian Hebrew scholar. KAC; LERA; PEB

Frankel, Zecharias (1801–1875). German rabbi. KAD

Gamaliel (d. 50?). Palestinian rabbi. GUA

Geiger, Abraham (1810–1874). German theologian. KAD

Gratz, Rebecca (1781–1869). Sunday schools organizer. GRB-1; LER; LETA; PEB

Hillel (fl. 30 B.C.–10 A.D.). Babylonian rabbi. GEF; GRB-1; GUA; KAB; KAC; LERA; LES

Hirsch, Samson Raphael (1808–1888). German theologian. KAD

Isaac, Levi (1740–1809). Polish rabbi. KAD

Israel ben Eliezer (Baal Shem Tov) (1700–1760). Polish Hasidic leader. GEF; GUB; KAC; LERA; LES; PEB

Johanan ben Zakkai (d. 80 A.D.?). Palestinian rabbi. GEF; GUA; LERA; LES

Joseph, Jacob (1848–1902). Rabbi, born Russia. LETA

Joshua ben Chananiah (c. 35–130). Palestinian rabbi. GUA

Joshua ben Levi (3d century). Palestinian rabbi. GUA

Josselman of Rosheim (1478?–1554). German knight. GEF

Judah ben Babba (fl. 135). Palestinian rabbi. GEF

Judah ha-Levi (c. 1085–1140). Spanish rabbi. GEF; GRB-1; GUA; KAC; LERA; LES

Judah ha-Nasi (Judah the Prince) (135–220). Palestinian rabbi. GUA; KAC; LERA

Kagan, Israel Meir (1838–1933). Polish rabbi. KAD

Kook, Abraham Isaac (1865–1935). Israeli rabbi. GRB-1

Levi, Yitzhok (fl. 1789). Ukrainian rabbi. GEF

Levin, Aryeh (b. 1885). Israeli rabbi, born Russia. GRB-1

Maccabaeus, Judah (d. 160 B.C.). Palestinian military leader. GUA; KAB

Maccabees (2d–1st century B.C.). Palestinian patriots. LES; STP

Magnes, Judah Leon (1877–1948). Rabbi. GUB

Maimonides (Moses ben Maimon) (1135–1204). Spanish philosopher. GEF; GRB-1; GUA; KAB; KAC; LERA; LES; MAR

Mattathias (d. 166 B.C.). Founder of Maccabees. GEF; GUA

Meir (2d century). Palestinian rabbi. GUA

Meir ben Baruch of Rothenburg (1220–1293). German rabbi. GEF; GUA; KAC

Menasseh ben Israel (1604–1657). Dutch rabbi. GUB; KAB; LERA; LES; PEB

Mendelssohn, Moses (1729–1786). German philosopher. GUB; KAB; KAC; LEF; LERA; PEB

Moise, Penina (1797–1880). Educator. LER; LETA

Monis, Judah (1683–1764). Rabbi, born Italy. LETA

Montefiore, Sir Moses (1784–1885). English philanthropist. GRB-1; KAB; KAD; LERA; LES; PEB

Moses ben Enoch (d. 965). Spanish rabbi. GUA; LERA

Nehemiah (5th century B.C.). GEF

Philo Judaeus (c. 20 B.C.–50 A.D.). Alexandrian philosopher. GEF; LERA

Rashi (Solomon ben Isaac) (1040–1105). French Hebraist. GEF; GRB-1; GUA; KAC; LERA; LES

Rav (Abba Arika) (d. 247). Babylonian rabbi. GUA; KAC

Revel, Bernard (1885–1940). Rabbi, educator, born Russia. KAD; LETA

Saadia ben Joseph (Saadyah Gaon) (892–942). Egyptian Hebraist. GRB-1; GUA; KAC; LERA

Salanter, Israel (1810–1883). Lithuanian rabbi. GEF; GUB; KAD

Samuel ha-Nagid (993–1055). Spanish rabbi. GUA

Samuel Yarhina'ah (177–257). Babylonian rabbi. KAC

Sasso, Sandy (1947–). Rabbi. SMBB-1

Schechter, Solomon (1850–1915). Hebraist, born Romania. GRB-1; GUB; KAD; LERA; LETA; PEB

Seixas, Gershom Mendez (1746–1816). Rabbi. LETA

Shammai (c.50 B.C.–c.30 A.D.). Palestinian rabbi. GEF

Shear-Yashur, Aharon. Israeli rabbi, born Germany. GRB-1

Silver, Abba Hillel (1893–1963). Rabbi, Zionist. LETA

Simeon ben Lakish (200–275). Palestinian rabbi. GUA

Wise, Isaac Mayer (1819–1900). Rabbi, president Hebrew Union College, born Czechoslovakia. GUB; KAD; LERA; LETA; PEB

Wise, Stephen Samuel (1874–1949). Rabbi, born Hungary. GEF; GRB-1; GUB; LETA

Yechiel of Paris. French rabbi. GEF

Yom Tov ben Isaac (d. 1190). English rabbi. GEF

Zalman, Shneor (1747–1812). Polish rabbi. KAD

Zevi, Sabbatai (1626–1676). Turkish. LERA; PEB

Zunz, Leopold (1794–1886). German Hebraist.
KAD

Protestant

Abernathy, Ralph David (1926–). YOI

Allen, Richard (1760–1831). Bishop. A founder of African Methodist Episcopal Church. ADA; ADB; BEJ; BRB; DADA; DOG; GRAB-05; HUA; PECA; ROG; WIBA

Asbury, Francis (1745–1816). Bishop, born England. BUIB†; CAGA

Beecher, Lyman (1775–1863). COGA

Booth, Evangeline Cory (1865–1950). English Salvation Army commander. STP

Booth, William (1829–1912). English founder of Salvation Army. EVA

Brown, Antoinette Blackwell (1825–1921). BLF†; BOJ; LES-2

Bulkeley, Peter (1583–1659). WOAA

Chavis, John (1763?–1838). BRB; DOB

Cleage, Albert B. (1912–). HAI

Comenius, John Amos (1592–1670). Czechoslovakian theologian. FRC

Cranmer, Thomas (1489–1556). Archbishop of Canterbury. MAJ

Douglas, Lloyd C. (1877–1951). CON

Dyer, Mary (1591?–1660). CRB; WABC†

Eddy, Mary Baker (1821–1910). BLF; BUA; KOA; STLA; WABC†

Fox, George (1624–1691). English. FOJ

Fry, Elizabeth Gurney (1780–1845). English. BOH; NOA; STP

Garnet, Henry Highland (1815–1882). ADA; ADB; BEJ; BRB†; GRAB-05; ROG

Green, Patricia (1952–). A.M.E. Zion minister. SMBB-1

Griggs, Sutton E. (1873–1930). KADB

Grimké, Francis James (1850–1937). BRB†; GRAB-01

Grundtvig, Nikolai F. S. (1783–1872). Danish. COG

Hawkes, Daphne (1938–). Episcopal priest. SMBB-1

Haynes, Lemuel (1753–1833). ADA; BRB†; BUIB†; DAF-1†; STQ†; WIBA

Holmes, John Haynes (1879–1964). LEZC

Hutchinson, Anne Marbury (1591–1643). BLF; CRB; DAD; DOD; JOCA; SMC; VIA; WABC; WAR; YOC

Jackson, Jesse Louis (1941–). DRA; GRAB-01

Jasper, John (1812–1901). ADA; ADB; BRB

Jones, Absalom (b. 1747). BRB

Jones, Harold S. (1909–). GRAC

King, Martin Luther, Jr. (1929–1968). AAS-34; ADA; ADB; ASB-1; BAF; BRBD; BRG; DEJ; DOF-1; DU-1; ELA; FAA; FEC; FLD; GRAB-01; HAJ; HODA; JO; JOC; KE; LEPE; MEB; MEC; RICA; STO; WEB; WIAA-8; WIC; YOA; YOI

Lee, Ann (1736–1784). AND; BLF; WABC

Luther, Martin (1483–1546). German. DEI; DEJ; FRC; FRE; HAA

McPherson, Aimee Semple (1890–1944). WIAA-2

Moody, Dwight Lyman (1837–1899). LEC

Mott, Lucretia Coffin (1793–1880). COG; GIBA†; GUBA; LES-2; STJ; STLA; WABC; WAR; YOC

Muste, Abraham Johannes (1885–1967). (Born the Netherlands). FOJ; LEZC

Naudé, C. F. Beyers (1915–). South African. LEA

Ogden, Dunbar (1903–). STG

Parker, Theodore (1810–1860). CHFB; COG

Parris, Samuel (1653–1720). COGA

Paul, Thomas (1773–1831). ADA; ADB

Payne, Daniel Alexander (1811–1893). ADA; ADB; BRB

Penn, William (1644–1718). ASB; COG; DEI; DEJ; FOB; FOJ; HAJ; LAD; LEO; LEPF; LEZC; MAM; MAT; MEB; OLA; VIA

Pennington, James W. C. (c. 1809–1870). GRAB-02

Piccard, Jeannette R. (1895–1981). Episcopal priest. BLF†; SMBB-1

Powell, Adam Clayton, Sr. (1865–1953). ADA; ADB; BRB†; RIC

Powell, Adam Clayton, Jr. (1908–1972). DU†; HAI; YOI

Schweitzer, Albert (1875–1965). French. BAF; BEC; EVD; FOJ; KE; KEE; LO; MAN; MEA; MEC; WIC; YOA

Scott, Michael (1907–1983). South African. LEA

Shuttlesworth, Fred (1922–). STF

Söderblom, Nathan (1866–1931). Swedish. MEC†; WIC

Sullivan, Leon Howard (1922–). DOF-1; EOA

Sunday, Billy (William Ashley) (1862–1935). COKB; DAFD

Thadden-Trieglaff, Reinold von (1891–). German. BAF

Thurman, Howard (1900–1981). ADB

Tobias, Channing Heggie (1882–1961). DOF-1; GRAB-01

Turner, Henry McNeal (1833–1915). ADA; ADB

Tutu, Desmond Mpilo (1931–). South African Anglican bishop. AAS-34

Van Orsdel, William Wesley (1850–1919). WAA

Ward, Samuel Ringgold (1817–1866). GRAB-05

Williams, Claude (1900?–). STG

Williams, Roger (1603?–1683). ARB; COG; DAC; DEI; DEJ; FIA; FOB; LEO; LEPF; MEB; OLA; VIA†

Young, Brigham (1801–1877). BLD; COE; FOC; HEB; LEO; LEPD

Roman Catholic

Abad Queipo, Manuel (1751–1825). Spanish bishop. WOB

Amadeus IX, Blessed (1435–1472). DAD-2

Anthony, Sister (Mary Ellen O'Connell) (1814–1897). (Born Ireland). COFA

Berrigan, Daniel (1921–). LEZC

Berrigan, Philip (1923–). LEZC

Billiart, Marie Rose, Blessed (1751–1816). DAD-2

Campion, Edmund (1540–1581). English Jesuit martyr. DAD-3; MAJ

Cecilia, Sister. Nun, born Czechoslovakia. CAHA

Celestine V (1215–1296). Pope. DAD-2

Cerioli, Constanza, Blessed (1816–1865). DAD-3

Charles of Blois, Blessed (1319–1364). DAD-3

Contardo Ferrini, Blessed. DAD-3

Coughlin, Charles Edward (1891–1979). (Born Canada). COGA

Delanoue, Jeanne, Blessed (1666–1736). DAD-3

Duchesne, Rose Philippine, Blessed (1769–1852). DAD-3

Dulce, Sister (Dulce Lopes Pontes) (1913–). Brazilian. MAK

Egan, Sister Jogues (Joan) (1918–). Nun, educator, born Ireland. SMBB-1

Erasmus, Desiderius (1466–1536). Dutch. DEI; DEJ

Everard Hanse, Blessed. DAD-3

Felton, John, Blessed (d. 1570). DAD-3

Fontaine, Madeleine, Blessed. DAD-2

Franco, Lippi, Blessed (1211–1291). DAD-3

Gowan, M. Olivia, Sister (1888–). YOB

Gwyn, Richard, Blessed (d. 1584). DAD-3

Healy, James Augustine (1830–1900). ADA; ADB

Herst, Richard, Blessed. DAD-3'

John XXIII (1881–1963). Pope. ASB-1; KE; YOA

John Paul II (1920–). Pope. DU-1; MANB

Juana Inés de la Cruz, Sister (1651–1695). Mexican. BACA; ROGB

Lathrop, Rose Hawthorne (Mother Mary Alphonsa) (1851–1926). MAK; WRA; YOC

Louis of Thuringia, Blessed. DAD-3

Lucera, Francis Anthony, Blessed. DAD-3

McAuley, Mary Catherine, Mother (1787–1841). Irish. REC

Madeline of Canossa, Blessed. DAD-3

Martinez, Antonio José (1793–1865). Mexican. BENA

Mary of the Incarnation, Blessed. DAD-2

Mathew, Theobald (1790–1856). Irish. REC

Merton, Thomas (Father M. Louis) (1915–1968). Trappist monk, born France. EOB

Mother Theresa (1910–). Indian. (Born Yugoslavia). ASB-1; DU-1; SHFE

Nestorius (d. 451?). SHG

Newman, John Henry (1801–1890). English. DEI; DEJ

Osanna of Mantua, Blessed. DAD-2

Pallotta, Maria Assunta, Blessed (1878–1905). DAD-3

Paul VI (1897–1978). Pope. WEB

Pierre, Abbé (Henri Grouès) (1910–). French. BAF

Pire, Georges Henri (1910–1969). Belgian. MEC; WIC

Pius XI (1857–1939). BOD

Plunkett, Oliver, Blessed (1629–1681). DAD-3; REC

Richelieu, Armand Jean du Plessis, cardinal, duc de (1585–1642). French. CAE

Roberts, John, Blessed (1576–1610). DAD-3

Taigi, Anna Maria, Blessed (1769–1837). DAD-2

Tekakwitha, Kateri (1656–1680). DAD-1; HED

Theresia, Blessed (1178–1250). DAD-2

Tolton, Augustine (1854–1897). ADA; ADB

Urban V, Blessed (1310–1370). DAD-3

Vénard, Jean Théophane, Blessed (1829–1861). DAD-3

Others

Buddha (Gautama Buddha) (563?–483 B.C.). Indian. FRE; TRC-1

Confucius (551–479 B.C.). Chinese. DEI; DEJ; LO; SPA

Khomeini, Ruhollah (1900?–). Iranian. HAGD

Mohammed (570–632). Founder of Islam. BEO; CAAA; DEI; DEJ; FRE; TRC-1

REPORTERS, *see* JOURNALISTS

RESISTANCE LEADERS

Anilewicz, Mordecai (1919–1943). Polish. GRB-1

Arafat, Yasir (1929–). Palestinian. (Born Egypt). HAGD

Cinque, Joseph (1811–1852). African insurrectionist. ADA; ADB; BRB†; ROG; WOA

Duarte, Juan Pablo (1813–1876). Dominican. WO

Freier, Recha (1892–). Israeli. (Born Germany). GRB-1

Garcia (fl. 1813). KADB

Glendower, Owen (1359?–1416). Welsh. SUK

Graf, Willi (d. 1943). German. LAD

Hereward (fl. 1070–1071). English. SUK

Hidalgo y Costilla, Miguel (1753–1811). Mexican. BAA; BACA; NEBA; ROGB; WO; YOFA

Huber, Kurt (1890?–1943). German. LAD

Hung Hsiu-ch'üan (1812–1864). Chinese. SPA

Kluger, Ruth. Israeli. (Born Rumania). GRB-1

Llewelyn ab Gruffydd (d. 1282). SUK

Lubetkin, Tzivia (1914–1978). Israeli. (Born Poland). GRB-1

Maccabaeus, Judah (d. 160 B.C.). GUA; KAB

Maccabees (2d–1st century B.C.). LES; STP

Mandela, Nelson (1918–). South African. DU-1; LEA

Martí, José Julian (1853–1895). Cuban. BAA; WO; YOFA

Mattathias (d. 166 B.C.). Hebrew patriot. GEF; GUA

Pierre, Abbé (Henri Groués) (1910–). French. BAF

Probst, Christoph (1919?–1943). German. LAD

Prosser, Gabriel (1775–1800). BRB†; EMA; HUB; ROG

Reich, Haviva (1914–1944). Czech. LAD

Schmorell, Alexander (d. 1943). German. LAD

Scholl, Hans (1918?–1943). German. LAD

Scholl, Sophie (1921?–1943). German. LAD

Senesh, Hannah (1921–1944). Israeli. (Born Hungary). GEF; GRB-1; LAD; STP; ROGA

Sereni, Enzo (1905–1944). Italian. GRB-1; LAD

Spartacus (d. 71 B.C.). Roman. STP

Sukloff, Marie. Russian. JAC

Turner, Nat (1800–1831). ADA; ADB; BEJ; BRB†; GRAB-05; ROG; WIAB

Vesey, Denmark (1767–1822). ADA; ADB; BRB†; HODA; JO; SPB; STJA

Walesa, Lech (1943–). Polish. AAS-34; DU-1

Wallace, Sir William (1272?–1305). Scottish. SUK

REVIEWERS, *see* CRITICS

ROCKET & SPACE SCIENTISTS

See also ASTRONAUTS

Antoine, Albert C. CAF-1

Congreve, Sir William (1772–1828). English. STMA

Drake, Frank Donald (1930–). COQ

Ehricke, Krafft Arnold (1917–1984). (Born Germany). NEB

Esnault-Pelteri, Robert (1881–1957). French. STMA

Faget, Maxime A. POE

Friedman, Herbert (1916–). LAA

Goddard, Robert Hutchings (1882–1945). ASA; BOK; COLA; COQ; FAA; FE; LEGA; NAA; NEB; RIBA; SIA; STMA; THA; THC; YOE

Johnston, Richard S. (1926–). POE

Kármán, Theodor von (1881–1963). (Born Hungary). COQ; NEB

Kraft, Christopher Columbus, Jr. (1924–). COQ; POE

Newell, Homer Edward (1915–). POE

North, Warren J. POE

Oberth, Hermann Julius (1894–). Romanian. NEB; STMA; THC

Parks, Robert J. (1922–). COQ

Pickering, William H. (1910–). (Born New Zealand). COQ

Pressly, Eleanor C. (1918–). HOG

Roman, Nancy Grace (1925–). HOG; POE

Shoemaker, Eugene M. (1928–). POE

Stuhlinger, Ernst (1913–). (Born Germany). POE

Tsiolkovsky, Konstantin E. (1857–1935). Russian. NEB; STMA; THC

Van Allen, James Alfred (1914–). HAC; NEB

Von Braun, Wernher (1912–1977). (Born Germany). COQ; CUB; FE; FRB; LEL; NEB; POE

Wyld, James H. COQ

RODEO FIGURES

Brorsen, Metha (1964?–). VADB

Bussey, Sheila (1950?–). VADB

Fuchs, Becky (1955?–). VADB

Johnson, Dammy Williams. VADB

Johnson, Trudy (1965?–). VADB

Linderman, Bill (1920–1965). KAW

Pirtle, Sue. VADB

Prudom, Benjie Bell Elizabeth. Clown. VADB

Thurman, Sammy Fancher. VADB

ROMANIANS

Comaneci, Nadia (1961–). Gymnast. FOR; GUED; LIE

Enesco, Georges (1881–1955). Composer, violinist. KAE; YOM†

Ileana. Princess, nurse. WRA

Nastase, Ilie (1946–). Tennis player. FOX

Oberth, Hermann Julius (1894–). Physicist. NEB; STMA; THC

Rozeanu, Angelica (1921–). Table tennis player. SLA

ROMANS, ANCIENT

Agricola, Gnaeus Julius (37–93). General. COM

Antony, Mark (83–30 B.C.). Soldier, politician. PLA

Aspasia (fl. 2d century). Physician. SC

Augustus (63 B.C.–14 A.D.). Emperor. CAAA; COK; NEC

Caesar, Gaius Julius (100–44 B.C.). General, statesman. CAAA; COD; COK; COM; DEI; DEJ; KEH; PLA; UNA

Cato, Marcus Porcius (234–149 B.C.). Statesman. PLA

Cicero, Marcus Tullius (106–43 B.C.). Statesman. COK; PLA

Constantine I, the Great (280–337). Emperor. CAAA; COK; NEC

Diocletian (245–313). Emperor. COK

Fabius (Quintus Fabius Maximus Verrucosus) (d. 203). Soldier, statesman. PLA

Galla Placidia (388–450). Empress. TRBA

Hadrian (76–138). Emperor. CAAA; COA; COK

Horace (65–8 B.C.). Poet. COK

Horatius Cocles (6th century B.C.). Soldier. COM; STP

Julian (c. 331–363). Emperor. ED-5

Justinian I, the Great (483–565). Emperor. BEO; CAAA

Lucretius (Titus Lucretius Carus) (96?–55 B.C.). Philosophical poet. LO

Marcus Aurelius (121–180). Emperor. CAAA; COA; COK

Nero (37–68). BLW; COK; DEI; DEJ; JOBB

Quintilian (Marcus Fabius Quintilianus) (35?–95?). Rhetorician. FRC

Scipio Africanus Major (Publius Cornelius Scipio Africanus) (234?–183 B.C.). General. COM

Seneca, Lucius Annaeus (4 B.C.–65 A.D.). Statesman, philosopher. COK

Spartacus (d. 71 B.C.). Gladiator. STP

Tacitus, Cornelius (55?–120?). Historian. HIB

Theodora (508?–548). Consort of Justinian I. BOI

Trajan (53–117). Emperor. CAAA; COK

Virgil (70–19 B.C.). Poet. COK; COKB

ROWING FIGURES

Callow, Russell S. (1890–1961). Coach. HEH
Connibear, Hiram (d. 1917). Coach. DAG; DAGA
Kelly, John B. (1889–1960). DAG; DAGA

RUGBY FIGURES

Canessa, Roberto (1953?–). Uruguayan. WIAA-5
Parrado, Nando (1950?–). Uruguayan. WIAA-5

RULERS

African

Affonso I (1506–1545). DOA; GRAB-04; MIC

Askia Muhammad (1494–1529). ADA; ADB; BRB†; DOA; GRAB-04

Cetewayo (c. 1836–1884). BRB†; CAAA; MIC

Chaka (1787–1829). ADA; ADB; BRB†; GRAB-04; MIC

Dahia al-Kahina (fl. 667–702). GRAB-04

Idris Alaoma (1580–1617). DOA; MIC

Jubo Jubogha (fl. 1880). MIC

Jugurtha (fl. 188–106 B.C.). GRAB-04

Kgamanyane (fl. 1820). MIC

Khama III (d. 1980). MIC

Lobengula (c. 1833–1893). MIC

Mansa Musa I (1312–1337). DOA; GRAB-04; PECA; POA

Massinissa (c. 238–148 B.C.). GRAB-04

Moshoeshoe (1790–1870). GRAB-04; MIC; POA

Nzinga (1582–1663). GRAB-04; JO; POA

Osei Tutu (1636–1712). GRAB-04; MIC

Sundiata I. MIC

Sunni Ali Ber (1464–1492). ADA; ADB; DOA; GRAB-04

Yaa Asantewa (1863–1923). GRAB-04

Assyrian

Ashurbanipal (fl. 669–626 B.C.). CAAA

Austrian

Francis Joseph I (1830–1916). CAAA

Maria Theresa (1717–1780). BOI; CAAA; FAE; LIDA; PA; TRBA

Aztec

Cuauhtémoc (1495–1525). ROGB

Montezuma II (1480?–1520). CAAA; NEC; ROGB; UNB

Babylonian

Hammurabi (c. 1955–1913 B.C.). CAAA; JOBB; NEC

Nebuchadnezzar II (d. 562 B.C.). JOBB

Belgian

Albert I (1875–1934). CAAA

Brazilian

Pedro I (1798–1834). LAB; YOFA

Pedro II (1825–1891). BACA; LAB; OLA

Chinese

Hsüan Tsung (685–762). SPA

K'ang-hsi (1654–1722). NEC

Shih Huang Ti (259–210 b.c.). BLW; NEC; SPA
Tzu Hsi (1835–1908). BOI; FAE; LIDA; SPA
Wang Mang (33 b.c.–23 a.d.). SPA

Danish

Canute II, the Great (944?–1035). CAAA; JOBB
Christian IV (1577–1648). HEA
Margaret (1353–1412). BOI

Dutch

Juliana (1909–). BOI; FAE
Wilhelmina (1880–1962). BOI; FAE
William I, the Silent (1533–1584). CAAA; HEA;
    MAJ; UNB

Egyptian

Akhnaton (fl. 1379–1362 b.c.). CAAA; GRAB-04;
    JOBB; NEC; UNA
Ankhesnamun (fl. 1358 b.c.). COLB
Cheops (fl. 2900 b.c.). CAAA
Cleopatra (69–30 b.c.). BOI; CAAA; COA; DEI;
    DEJ; FAE; LIDA; PA; TRBA
Hatshepsut (1578–1457 b.c.). BOI; COLB; GRAB-
    04
Menes (fl. 3100–3038 b.c.). GRAB-04
Nefertari (13th century b.c.). COLB
Nefertiti (fl. 1372–1350 b.c.). COLB; FAE; GRAB-
    04; JO†; PA
Ptolemy I (Ptolemy Soter) (367?–283 b.c.). NEC
Tiy (fl. 1400 b.c.). COLB
Tutankhamen (1361–1351 b.c.). COA; GRAB-04
Tuthmosis III (1504–1450 b.c.). CAAA; GRAB-04

English

Alfred the Great (849–899). CAAA; CHG; COA;
    DEC; DEI; DEJ; HEA; JOBB; MAJ; NEC;
    SUK; TRA; UNB
Anne (1665–1714). DEC; GRAB†; LIDA; SCC;
    TRB
Anne (1950–). HOBAA
Anne of Cleves (1515–1557). MAOA; VAC
Arthur (6th century). JOBB; NEC; SUK
Boleyn, Anne (1507–1536). MAOA; VAC
Boudicca (d. 62 a.d.). BOI; CAAA; TRBA
Caractacus (fl. 50 a.d.). MAJ; SUK
Catherine of Aragon (1485–1536). Consort of
    Henry VIII, king of England. MAOA; VAC
Charles I (1600–1649). CAAA; DEC; GRAB; SCC;
    TRA
Charles II (1630–1685). CAAA; DEC; GRAB; JAC;
    SCC; TRA; UNA
Edward I (1239–1307). BRBF; CAAA; DEC;
    GRAB; SCC
Edward II (1284–1327). BRBF; DEC; GRAB†;
    SCC

Edward III (1312–1377). BRBF; CAAA; DEC;
    GRAB; SCC
Edward IV (1442–1483). BRBF; DEC; GRAB;
    SCC
Edward V (1470–1483). BRBF; DEC; GRAB†;
    SCC
Edward VI (1537–1553). DEC; GRAB†; SCC
Edward VII (1841–1910). CAAA; DEC; GRAB†;
    SCC
Edward VIII (1894–1972). DEC; GRAB†; SCC
Edward the Confessor (1002?–1066). DAD-3;
    GRAB†; QUA; SCC
Eleanor of Aquitaine (1122?–1204). Consort of
    Henry II, king of England. BOI; DAK
Elizabeth I (1533–1603). BOI; CAAA; CHG; COA;
    DAK; DEC; DEI; DEJ; FAE; FRE; GRAB;
    HAA; LIDA; PA; SCC; TRB; UNB
Elizabeth II (1926–). BOI; DEC; DU-1; FAE;
    GRAB; LIDA; SCC; TRB; WEB
George I (1660–1727). DEC; GRAB; SCC
George II (1683–1760). DEC; GRAB; SCC
George III (1738–1820). DEC; GRAB; SCC; SOA
George IV (1762–1830). DEC; GRAB; SCC
George V (1865–1936). CAAA; DEC; GRAB; SCC
George VI (1895–1952). CAAA; DEC; GRAB;
    NEC; SCC; TRA
Grey, Lady Jane (1537–1554). DEC; SCC†
Harold II (1022?–1066). CHG; GRAB†; SCC; UNB
Henry I (1068–1135). BRBF; DEC; GRAB†; SCC
Henry II (1133–1189). BRBF; CAAA; CHG; DEC;
    GRAB; SCC
Henry III (1207–1272). BRBF; DEC; GRAB; SCC
Henry IV (1367–1413). BRBF; DEC; GRAB†; SCC
Henry V (1387–1422). BRBF; CAAA; CHG; DEC;
    GRAB†; SCC
Henry VI (1421–1471). BRBF; DEC; GRAB; SCC
Henry VII (1457–1509). CAAA; DEC; GRAB; SCC
Henry VIII (1491–1547). CAAA; CHG; DEC; DEI;
    DEJ; GRAB; JOBB; NEC; SCC
Howard, Catherine (1520?–1542). Consort of
    Henry VIII, king of England. MAOA; VAC
James I (1566–1625). DEC; GRAB; SCC
James II (1633–1701). DEC; GRAB†; SCC
John (1167?–1216). BRBF; DEC; GRAB†; SCC
Mary I (1516–1558). BOI; DEC; GRAB†; LIDA;
    SCC; TRB
Mary II (1662–1694). DEC†; GRAB†; LIDA†;
    SCC; TRB
Maud (1102–1167). BRBF; TRB
Parr, Catherine (1512–1548). Consort of Henry
    VIII, king of England. MAOA; VAC
Philip (1921–). Consort of Elizabeth II, queen of
    Great Britain. DEC; SQA
Richard I (Coeur de Lion) (1157–1199). BRBF;
    CAAA; CHG; COA; DEC; GRAB†; JOBB; SCC;
    TRA

Richard II (1367–1400). BRBF; DEC; GRAB†; SCC

Richard III (1452–1485). BRBF; CAAA; DEC; GRAB†; JOBB; SCC

Seymour, Jane (1509–1537). Consort of Henry VIII, king of England. MAOA; VAC

Stephen (1097?–1154). DEC; GRAB†; SCC

Victoria (1819–1901). BOI; CAAA; CHG; COA; DEC; DEI; DEJ; FAE; GRAB; LIDA; PA; SCC; TRB; UNB

William I, the Conqueror (1027–1087). BEO; BRBF; CAAA; CHG; COD; DEC; GRAB; JOBB; NEC; SCC; TRA

William II (1056–1100). BRBF; DEC; GRAB†; SCC

William III (1650–1702). DEC; GRAB†; SCC; TRA

William IV (1765–1837). DEC; GRAB†; SCC

Ethiopian

Gudit (fl. 937–997). GRAB-04

Haile Selassie I (1891–1975). ADA; DU-1; GRAB-04

Makeda (fl. 960–930 B.C.). GRAB-04

Menelik II (1844–1913). ADA; ADB; GRAB-03

Piankhi (fl. 741–721 B.C.). ADA; ADB; GRAB-04

Taharga (fl. 688–662 B.C.). GRAB-04

French

Catherine de Medici (1519–1589). BOI; CAAA; FAE; LIDA

Charlemagne (742–814). BEO; CAAA; COA; DEI; DEJ; HEA; JOBB; NEC; UNA

Henry IV, of Navarre (1553–1610). CAAA; JOBB

Josephine (1763–1814). FAE

Louis IX (1214–1270). CAAA; DAD-3; NEC; ONA; QUA

Louis XI (1423–1483). CAAA

Louis XIV (1638–1715). CAAA; COA; JOBB; NEC; UNB

Louis XVI (1754–1793). CAAA

Marie Antoinette (1755–1793). COA; DAK; DEI; DEJ; FAE; UNA

Napoleon I (Napoleon Bonaparte) (1769–1821). BEO; CAAA; CAE; COD; DEI; DEJ; FRE; NEC; UNB

Napoleon III (Louis Napoleon) (1808–1873). JAC

German

Frederick II, the Great (1712–1786). CAAA; CAE; COA; COD; COKB; DEI; DEJ; NEC; UNA

Frederick William I (1688–1740). COA

Ludwig II (1845–1886). COKB

William II (1859–1941). CAAA

Greek

Leonidas I (d. 480 B.C.). CAAA; COM; MAJ

Haitian

Christophe, Henri (1767–1820). ADA; ADB; DAF-1†; JO; STQ†; WIBA

Dessalines, Jean Jacques (1758–1806). ADA; ADB

Hawaiian

Kamehameha I, the Great (1737?–1819). NEC

Holy Roman Empire

Charles V (1500–1558). CAAA; COA

Frederick I, called Frederick Barbarossa (1123?–1190). CAAA

Frederick II (1194–1250). BEO; CAAA

Otto I, the Great (912–973). CAAA

Sigismund (1368–1437). CAAA

Incan

Atahualpa (1500?–1533). CAAA

Indian

Akbar the Great (1542–1605). CAAA

Asoka the Great (d. 232 B.C.). CAAA; NEC

Chandragupta Maurya (c. 321–c. 298 B.C.). CAAA

Irish

Brian Boru (926–1014). CAAA

Israeli

Ahab (d. 853? B.C.). JOBB

David (c. 1012–972 B.C.). BEC; CAAA; GEF; JOBB; STP

Solomon (d. 932 B.C.). CAAA; JOBB; NEC

Italian

Victor Emanuel II (1820–1878). CAAA

Japanese

Hirohito (1901–). ASB-1; DU-1; WEB

Mutsuhito (1852–1912). CAAA

Jordanian

Hussein Ibn Talal (1935–). HAGD; KEF

Judean

Herod the Great (73?–4 B.C.). CAAA; LERA

Lydian

Croesus (d. 547 B.C.). COA; JOBB

Macedonian

Alexander III, the Great (356–323 B.C.). CAAA; COD; DEI; DEJ; FRE; JOBB; KEH; KNA; MOB; NEC; PLA; UNB

Mongol
Genghis Khan (1162–1227). BEO; BLW; CAAA;
   COD; KEH; NEC; UNA
Kublai Khan (1216–1294). CAAA; UNA
Tamerlane (1336?–1405). BLW; CAAA

Moroccan
Mohammed V (1910–1961). KEF

Muslim
Abd-er-Rahman I (731–788). CAAA
Harun al-Rashid (764?–809). CAAA
Saladin (1138–1193). CAAA

Norwegian
Harold I, the Fairhaired (850?–933). JOBB

Ottoman Empire
Bayezid I (1347–1403). BEO
Mohammed II (The Conqueror) (1430–1481).
   BEO; BLW; CAAA
Murad I (1319–1389). BEO
Murad II (1403?–1451). BEO
Orkhan (1288?–1362). BEO

Parthian
Mithridates VI (c. 131–63 B.C.). JOBB; SUG

Persian
Cyrus (600?–529 B.C.). CAAA; COA
Darius (558?–486? B.C.). CAAA; COA
Xerxes I (519?–465 B.C.). COA; JO

Polish
Jadwiga (1373–1399). MANB
John III Sobieski (1624–1696). MAJ

Roman
Antony, Mark (83–30 B.C.). PLA
Augustus (63 B.C.–14 A.D.). CAAA; COK; NEC
Constantine I, the Great (280–337). CAAA; COK;
   NEC
Diocletian (245–313). COK
Galla Placidia (388–450). TRBA
Hadrian (76–138). CAAA; COA; COK
Julian (c. 331–363). ED-5
Justinian I, the Great (483–565). BEO; CAAA
Marcus Aurelius (121–180). CAAA; COA; COK
Nero (37–68). BLW; COK; DEI; DEJ; JOBB
Theodora (508?–548). Consort of Justinian I. BOI
Trajan (53–117). CAAA; COK

Russian
Alexander I (1777–1825). RIA
Alexander II (1818–1881). RIA

Alexander III (1845–1894). RIA
Basil III Ivanovich (1479–1533). RIA
Catherine II, the Great (1729–1796). BEO; BOI;
   CAAA; COKB; DAK; DEI; DEJ; FAE; LIDA;
   RIA; TRBA
Elizabeth Petrovna (1709–1762). LIDA; RIA
Ivan III, the Great (1440–1505). CAAA; RIA
Ivan IV, the Terrible (1530–1584). BLW; JOBB;
   RIA
Nicholas I (1796–1855). RIA
Nicholas II (1868–1918). RIA
Paul I (1754–1801). RIA
Peter I, the Great (1672–1725). CAAA; COA;
   COKB; HEA; NEC; RIA; UNB
Sophia. Consort of Ivan III, grand duke of Moscow. RIA

Saudi
Fahd ibn Abdul Aziz al Saud (1922–). HAGD

Scottish
Bruce, Robert the (1274–1329). CAAA; HEA;
   MAJ; SUK
Mary, Queen of Scots (1542–1587). BOI; DEI;
   DEJ; FAE; UNA

Spanish
Ferdinand V (1452–1516). CAAA; NEC
Isabella I (1451–1504). BOI; CAAA; DAK; FAE;
   LIDA; PA; TRBA
Philip II (1527–1598). CAAA

Swedish
Charles XII (1682–1718). CAAA
Christina (1626–1689). BOI; COKB; TRBA; UNA
Eric IX (Eric the Saint) (d. 1160). QUA
Gustavus II (Gustavas Adolphus) (1594–1632).
   CAAA; HEA

Syrian
Zenobia (fl. 267–272). FAE; PA

Thai
Rama V (1853–1910). CAAA

RUNAWAYS

Angelo. BEOA
Annie. BEOA
Jeff. BEOA
Larry. BEOA
Marion. BEOA

Michael. BEOA
Ralph. BEOA

RUNNERS, see TRACK & FIELD ATHLETES

RUSSIANS

See also RULERS—RUSSIAN

Abel, Rudolf Ivanovich (1902–1971). Spy. HAB; KN

Alekhine, Alexander (1892–1946). Chess player. LEQB

Alexander Nevski (1220?–1263). Saint and hero. MAJ

Andrianov, Nikolai (1952–). Gymnast. LIE

Balakireff, Mili Alekseyevich (1837–1910). Composer. POG; SAA†

Bellingshausen, Fabian von (1778–1852). Explorer. DOC†; MOB; ROL†

Belyayev, Pavel (1925–1970). Astronaut. THC

Bialik, Chaim Nachman (1873–1934). Hebrew poet. GEF; GRB-1; GUB; KAD; PEB

Blavatsky, Elena Petrovna (1831–1891). Theosophist. COEA; MAT-1

Borodin, Alexander P. (1833–1887). Composer. BAE; KAE; POG; SAA

Botvinnik, Mikhail M. (1911–). Chess player. LEQB

Brezhnev, Leonid Ilyich (1906–1982). Communist leader. WEC

Brumel, Valeri (1942–). Track athlete. DAFB; DAJ; GED

Bykovsky, Valeri (1934–). Astronaut. THC

Chagall, Marc (1887–1985). Painter. GRB-1; WIAA

Chekhov, Anton Pavlovich (1860–1904). Author. ASB-1; POFA

Cui, César Antonovich (1835–1918). Composer. POG; SAA†

Danilova, Alexandra. Dancer. ATA

Dostoevski, Fëdor Mikhailovich (1821–1881). Novelist. POFA

Ehrenburg, Ilya Grigoryevich (1891–1967). Author. KE

Feoktistov, Konstantin (1926–). Astronaut. THC

Gagarin, Yuri Alekseyevich (1934–1968). Astronaut. KEH; MOB; NEB; PRC; THC

Gilels, Emil G. (1916–1985). Pianist. EWC

Glazunov, Aleksandr Konstantinovich (1865–1936). Composer. POG

Glière, Reinhold Moritzovich (1875–1956). Composer. POG

Glinka, Mikhail Ivanovich (1804–1857). Composer. KAE; POG; SAA

Gogol, Nikolai Vasilievich (1809–1852). Author. POFA

Gorki, Maksim (1868–1936). Author. POFA

Gouzenko, Igor S. (1915–). Ex-government official. CAHA

Gromyko, Andrei (1909–). Communist leader. DU-1

Haffkine, Waldemar Mordecai (1860–1930). Bacteriologist. GEF; GRB-1

Hannibal, Abram (1697–1782). General. ADA; ADB

Jabotinsky, Vladimir (1880–1940). Zionist. GRB-1

Kabalevsky, Dmitri Borisovich (1904–). Composer. POG

Kandinsky, Wassily (1866–1944). Painter. KAA

Kerensky, Alexander Feodorovitch (1881–1970). Political leader. NEBB-1

Khachaturian, Aram (1903–1978). Composer. KAE; POG

Khrushchev, Nikita S. (1894–1971). Communist leader. ARA; COJB; DOF; KE; WEA

Kim, Nelli (1957–). Gymnast. LIE; SUBB-1

Komarov, Vladimir M. (1927–1967). Astronaut. THC

Korbut, Olga (1956–). Gymnast. HOBAA; LIE

Kornilov, Lavr Georgiyevich (1870–1918). General. NEBB-1

Kosygin, Aleksei N. (1904–1980). Communist leader. WEC

Kropotkin, Pëtr Alekseevich (1842–1921). Philosopher. RAC

Lenin, Nikolai (Vladimir Illich Ulyanov) (1870–1924). Communist leader. ARA; ASB-1; CAAA; COJB; DEI; DEJ; DOF; NEBB-1

Leonov, Alexei A. (1934–). Astronaut. THC

Levi, Yitzhok (fl. 1789). Rabbi. GEF

Lobachevsky, Nikolai (1793–1856). Mathematician. MUB

Lonsdale, Gordon Arnold (1924?–1970). Spy. SEB

Menchik, Vera (1906–1944). Chess player. LEQB

Mendele Mocher Sefarim (Shalom Abramovich) (1835–1917). Author. GRB-1

Mendeleev, Dmitri I. (1834–1907). Chemist. CAA; COLA; FE; MOBA; SHFB

Metchnikoff, Élie (1845–1916). Bacteriologist. COL; DEB; LET; RIF; ROA; SOB

Miakovsky, Nikolai Yakovlevich (1891–1950). Composer. POG

Mussorgsky, Modest Petrovich (1839–1881). Composer. BAE; BUC; FIE†; KAE; POG; SAA

Nikolayev, Andrian G. (1929–). Astronaut. NEB†; THC

Oistrakh, David (1908–1974). Violinist. EWC

Pasternak, Boris Leonidovich (1890–1960). Author. LET; POFA

Pavlov, Ivan Petrovich (1849–1936). Physiologist. ASB-1; CAA; FE; RIF; SIA

Pavlova, Anna (1881–1931). Dancer. TRC; YOH

Popovich, Marina. Test pilot. HIFD

Prokofiev, Sergei Sergeevich (1891–1953). Composer. BEKA; BUC; KAE; POG; SAA; YOL

Pushkin, Aleksandr Sergeevich (1799–1837). Poet. ADA; ADB; JO; POFA

Rachmaninoff, Sergei (1873–1943). Composer, pianist. BAE; BEN; KAE; POG; SAA

Riabouchinska, Tatiana (1918–). Dancer. ATA

Richter, Sviatoslav (1914–). Pianist. EWC

Rimski-Korsakov, Nikolai Andreevich (1844–1908). Composer. BAE; BUC; FIE†; KAE; POG; SAA; YOJ

Rodnina, Irina (1949–). Skater. LIEA

Rostropovich, Mstislav (1927–). Cellist. EWC

Rubinstein, Anton (1829–1894). Pianist, composer. CHF

Sakharov, Andrei D. (1921–). Physicist. AAS-34; DU-1; MEC

Schmidt, Bernhard V. (1879–1935). Lens grinder. LAA

Scriabin, Aleksandr Nikolaievich (1872–1915). Composer. BUC; POG

Sholokhov, Mikhail Aleksandrovich (1905–1984). Novelist. POFA

Shostakovich, Dmitri (1906–1975). Composer. KAE; POG; SAA

Spassky, Boris V. (1937–). Chess player. LEQB

Stalin, Joseph (1879–1953). Chief of state. ARA; ASB-1; CAE; CL-01; COJB; DOF; KIA; TAC

Sukloff, Marie. Terrorist. JAC

Tamm, Igor Yevgenyvich (1895–1971). Physicist. LET

Tchaikovsky, Peter Ilyich (1840–1893). Composer. BEN; BRF; BUD; DEI; DEJ; FIE†; GOB; KAE; POG; SAA; WIA; YOK

Tereshkova, Valentina Vladimirova (1937–). Astronaut. THC

Titov, Gherman Stepanovich (1935–). Astronaut. NEB; THC

Tolstoi, Lev Nikolaevich (1828–1910). Author. DEI; DEJ; POFA

Toumanova, Tamara (1919–). Dancer. ATA

Tretiak, Vladislav (1952–). Hockey player. ORA

Trotsky, Leon (1877–1940). Communist leader. COJB; NEBB-1

Tsiolkovsky, Konstantin E. (1857–1935). Inventor, rocket expert. NEB; STMA; THC

Turgenev, Ivan Sergeevich (1818–1883). Author. POFA

Ussachevsky, Vladimir (1911–). Composer. BEKA

Vavilov, Nicolai Ivanovich (1887–1942). Botanist. WEF

Yegorov, Boris (1937–). Astronaut. THC

Yevtushenko, Yevgeny Aleksandrovich (1933–). Poet. POFA

Youskevitch, Igor (1912–). Dancer. ATA

Zoritch, George (1917–). Dancer. ATA

SAILBOAT RACERS, *see* BOAT RACERS

SAILORS, *see* NAVAL FIGURES

SAINTS

Abraham. DAD-2

Adelaide of Turin (c. 1020–1091). DAD-3

Aelred (1110–1167). DAD-2

Agatha (d. 250?). DAD-2; QUA

Agnes (291–304). DAD-1; DAD-2; ONA; QUA; WIB

Agnes of Montepulciano (c. 1268–1317). DAD-2

Aidan (d. 651). DAD-3

Alban (3d or 4th century). DAD-2; ONA

Albert (d. 997). WIB

Albert the Great (1206–1280). CUA; DAD-3; MOC; ONA; QUA

Alexander. DAD-3

Alexander the Coalman (d. 275). DAD-3

Alexis. DAD-3

Alice de Bourgotte (d. 1466). QUA

Allucio. DAD-3

Aloysius Gonzaga (1568–1591). DAD-1; DAD-2; MOC

Alphege of Canterbury (954–1012). DAD-2

Alphonsus Liguori (1696–1787). DAD-3

Alphonsus Rodriguez (1531–1617). DAD-3; MOC

Ambrose (340–397). DAD-3; ONA

Andrew (1st century). DAD-3; ONA; QUA

Angela dei Merici (1474?–1540). DAD-2; QUA

Anne. Mother of Virgin Mary. DAD-1; DAD-3; ONA; QUA; WIB

Anselm of Canterbury (1033–1109). DAD-2

Anthony of Egypt (250–356). DAD-2

Anthony of Padua (1195–1231). DAD-1; DAD-2; MOC; ONA; QUA

Antonino. DAD-2

Antony (251–356). ONA

Anysia. DAD-3

Apollo (c. 316–395). ONA

Apollonia of Alexandria. DAD-2

Archibald (d. 675). WIB

Athanasia. DAD-3

Athanasius (4th century). DAD-2

Audrey (c. 630–679). DAD-2

Augustine (354–430). DAD-3; LO; MOC; ONA; QUA

Augustine of Canterbury (d. 604). DAD-2

Avellino, Andrew (1521–1608). DAD-3

Bademus. DAD-2

Barbara (d. 235?). QUA

Barbatus (d. 682). DAD-2

Barnabas (1st century). DAD-2

Bartholomea (1807–1833). DAD-1

Bartholomew. DAD-3

Bartholomew (d. 1193). TUA

Basil the Great (329–379). DAD-2

Bathildis (d. 680). DAD-2

Bede the Venerable (672–735). DAD-2

Bellarmine, Robert (1542–1621). DAD-2; QUA

Benedict (480–543). CHD†; DAD-1; DAD-2; ONA

Benedict the Moor (1526–1589). DAD-1; DAD-2

Bénézet (1165–1184). ONA

Bernadette of Lourdes (1844–1879). DAD-1; DAD-2

Bernard of Clairvaux (1090–1153). DAD-3; QUA

Bernard of Menthon (996?–1081?). MOC; ONA

Bernardine of Siena (1380–1444). DAD-1; DAD-2

Bertha (d. 725). DAD-3; QUA

Bertrand, Louis (1526–1581). DAD-3

Bibiana. DAD-3

Bichier Des Agnes, Jeanne Elisabeth. DAD-3

Blaise (d. 316). DAD-2; PEE; WIB

Bobola, Andrew (1591–1657). DAD-2

Bonaventure (1217–1274). DAD-3

Boniface (672–754). DAD-2

Boniface of Tarsus. DAD-2

Borgia, Francis (1510–1572). DAD-3

Boris. DAD-3

Borromeo, Charles (1538–1584). DAD-3; QUA

Bosco, John (1815–1888). DAD-1; DAD-2

Botvid (d. 1120). DAD-3

Brendan of Clonfert (484–577). REC

Bridget of Sweden (1303–1373). DAD-3; ONA; QUA

Brigid of Kildare (453–523). DAD-1; DAD-2; FAD; MAK†; ONA; REC; TUA

Bruno (b. 1101). DAD-3

Cabrini, Frances Xavier (1850–1917). (Born Italy). ASB; BLF†; DAD-1; DAD-3; MAS; STLA

Caius. DAD-2

Cajetan (1480–1547). DAD-3

Callistus I (fl. 217). Pope. DAD-3

Camillus de Lellis (1550–1614). DAD-1; DAD-3

Canisius, Peter (1521–1597). DAD-2

Canute IV (d. 1086). DAD-2

Caracciolo, Francis (1563–1608). DAD-2

Casimir (1458–1484). DAD-2; ONA

Catherine of Alexandria (4th century). DAD-3; PEE; QUA

Catherine of Genoa (1447–1510). MOC

Catherine of Ricci (1522–1590). DAD-2

Catherine of Siena (1347–1380). DAD-1; DAD-2; ONA; TUA

Catherine of Sweden (1331–1381). DAD-2

Cecilia. DAD-1; DAD-3

Celestine V (1215–1296). DAD-2

Chanel, Peter (1803–1841). DAD-2

Chantal, Jane Frances de (1572–1641). DAD-1; DAD-3

Christina. QUA

Christopher (3d century). FAD; ONA; PEE

Ciaran (516–549). TUA

Clare (1193?–1253). DAD-1; DAD-3; MAK†; ONA; QUA

Claver, Peter (1580–1654). DAD-3

Cleopatra. DAD-3

Clotilda (470–545). DAD-2

Colman of Kilmacduagh (d. 632). ONA

Columban (543?–615). DAD-1; DAD-3; REC

Columcille (521–597). CHD†; DAD-2; REC

Conrad of Piacenza (d. 1351). MOC

Cosmas (3d century). CHD†; DAD-3

Cottolengo, Joseph Benedict. DAD-1

Cunegundes. DAD-2

Cuthbert (635?–687). CHD†; DAD-2

Cyprian. DAD-3

Cyril (827–869). DAD-3

Cyril of Jerusalem (d. 387). DAD-2

Damien. DAD-3

David (500?–589). ONA

David I of Scotland (b. 1080). DAD-2

Dismas (1st century). MOC

Dominic (1170–1221). DAD-3; ONA

Dominic of Silos (d. 1076). DAD-3

Dorothea (d. 303). DAD-2; FAD; ONA; QUA

Dositheus. DAD-2

Dympna (7th century). DAD-1

Edith of Wilton. DAD-3

Edmund the Martyr (841–869). DAD-3; MOC

Edmund Rich (1170?–1240). QUA

Edward the Confessor (1002?–1066). DAD-3; GRAB†; QUA; SCC

Elizabeth of Hungary (1207–1231). DAD-1; DAD-3; HEA; MAK†; MOC; ONA; QUA; TUA

Elizabeth of Portugal (1271–1336). DAD-3; MOC

Emiliani, Jerome (1486–1537). DAD-3

Emily de Rodat. DAD-3

Ephrem (306–373). DAD-2

Eric IX (Eric the Saint) (d. 1160). QUA

Eucherius of Orléans (7th century). DAD-2

Eudes, John (1601–1680). DAD-3

Eudocia. DAD-2

Eulogius (580–607). DAD-3

Eulogius of Spain (810–859). DAD-2

Euphrasia (380–410). DAD-2

Evaristus (fl. 97–105). DAD-3

Falconieri, Juliana (1270–1341). DAD-2

Faustinus. DAD-2

Felicitas. DAD-2

Felicity. DAD-3

Felix. DAD-3

Felix of Cantalice (1515–1587). DAD-2

Fidelis of Sigmaringen (1578–1622). DAD-2

Finnian (b. 549). DAD-3

Flannan. DAD-3

Flora of Beaulieu. DAD-3

Foillan. DAD-3

Fourier, Peter (1565–1640). DAD-3

Frances of Rome (1384–1440). DAD-1

Francis de Posadas. DAD-3

Francis de Sales (1567–1622). DAD-2

Francis of Assisi (1182–1226). BEC; DAD-1; DAD-3; FAD; HEA; MOC; ONA; PEE; QUA; TUA

Francis of Paola (1416–1507). DAD-2

Francis Xavier (1506–1552). DAD-1; DAD-3; KNA

Frederick (d. 838). QUA

Fulgentius. DAD-2

Gabriel of Our Lady of Sorrows. DAD-2

Gall (d. 646). MOC

Gemma (1878–1903). DAD-1

Genesius. MOC; PEE

Geneviève (420?–500?). DAD-2; MOC; ONA

George (d. 303?). DAD-2; ONA; PEE; QUA

Gerard Sagredo (980–1046). QUA

Germaine. DAD-1; DAD-2

Germanus of Auxerre. DAD-3

Gertrude the Great (1256–1302). DAD-1; DAD-3; QUA

Giles (7th century). DAD-3; FAD

Gillian (d. 1340). WIB

Gleb. DAD-3

Godric (1065?–1170). MOC

Goretti, Mary (1890–1902). DAD-1; DAD-3

Gregory I, the Great (c. 540–604). DAD-2

Gregory VII (b. 1020). DAD-2

Gregory of Nazianzus (330–390). DAD-2

Hallvard (d. 1043). MOC

Hedwig (1174–1243). ONA

Helena (c. 248–328). DAD-1; DAD-3; ONA; QUA

Heliodorus. DAD-3

Henry (973–1024). DAD-3; QUA

Herbert (970–1021). QUA

Herman Joseph. DAD-2

Hermenegild (d. 585). DAD-2

Hilarion (4th century). DAD-3

Hilary of Poitiers (315–367). DAD-2

Hildegard of Bingen (1098–1179). DAD-3; MAK†; MASA; SC

Honoratus (d. 430). DAD-2

Hubert (7th century). FAD; QUA

Hugh of Grenoble (1053–1131). DAD-2; QUA

Hugh of Lincoln (1135–1200). ONA

Hunna (d. 679). MOC

Hyacintha (d. 1640). MOC

Ignatius of Laconi (1701–1781). DAD-2

Ignatius of Loyola (1491–1556). DAD-3; FRC; MOC

Irenaeus (140–202). DAD-2

Irene (d. 653). QUA

Isabel (1225–1270). WIB

Isidore (1070–1130). MOC; ONA

James the Greater. DAD-3; QUA

James the Less. DAD-2; QUA

James Intercisus. DAD-3

Jerome (342–420). DAD-3; TUA

Joan (1st century). QUA

Joan of Arc (1412–1431). CHG; DAD-1; DAD-2; DEI; DEJ; ELA; EVD; HAA; HEA; MAJ; MOC; ONA; PA; PEE; STP

Joan of Valois (1464–1505). DAD-2; MOC

Jogues, Isaac (1607–1646). DAD-1

John the Baptist. DAD-2; QUA

John of the Cross (1542–1591). DAD-3

John the Dwarf (5th century). MOC; ONA

John, the Evangelist. DAD-2; DAD-3; ONA

John of God (1495–1550). DAD-2

John of Matha (1160–1213). DAD-2

John of Sahagun. DAD-2

John Baptiste de la Salle. DAD-1; DAD-2

John Berchmans (1599–1621). DAD-1; DAD-3; MOC

John Cantius (1390–1473). DAD-3

John Capistrano (1386–1456). DAD-2

John Chrysostom (349–407). DAD-2

John Climacus (579–649). DAD-2

John Damascene (645–750). DAD-2

John Gualbert (d. 1073). DAD-3; MOC

John Joseph of the Cross (1654–1734). DAD-2

Jonas. DAD-2

Joseph. DAD-1; DAD-2; ONA; QUA

Joseph of Arimathea. ONA

Joseph of Cupertino (1603–1663). DAD-3

Joseph Calasanctius. DAD-3

Jovita. DAD-2

Jude. DAD-3

Julia. DAD-2

Julian. DAD-2; QUA

Julitta (d. 305?). MOC

Justin (100–165). DAD-2; ONA

Kenneth (515–599). DAD-3; MOC

Kevin. DAD-1

Kostka, Stanislaus (1550–1568). DAD-1; DAD-3

Labouré, Catherine (1806–1876). DAD-3

Labre, Benedict (1748–1783). DAD-2; MOC

Laurence O'Toole (1128–1180). DAD-3; REC

Lawrence (d. 258). DAD-3; QUA

Lawrence of Brindisi (1559–1619). DAD-3

Lawrence Justinian (1381–1456). DAD-3
Leger. DAD-3
Leo I, the Great (390–461). DAD-2; QUA
Leonard (1677–1751). WIB
Louis IX (1214–1270). CAAA; DAD-3; NEC; ONA; QUA
Lucian (d. 312). DAD-2
Lucy (d. 304). DAD-1; DAD-3; QUA; WIB
Ludger (742–809). DAD-2
Luke. DAD-3; QUA
Lupicinus. DAD-2
Lydwina. DAD-2
Majella, Gerard (1726–1755). DAD-2; DAD-3
Malachy (1094?–1148). DAD-3; REC
Marcian (4th century). DAD-3
Margaret (255–275). QUA
Margaret of Cortona (1247–1297). DAD-2; MOC
Margaret of Scotland (1045–1093). DAD-1; DAD-2; ONA; TUA
Margaret Mary. DAD-1; DAD-3
Mark the Evangelist. DAD-2
Martha. DAD-3; QUA
Martin of Tours (316?–397). DAD-1; DAD-3; FAD; ONA; QUA
Mary the Martyr. DAD-3
Mary, Virgin. DAD-2; QUA
Mary Magdalen. DAD-3; ONA
Mary Magdelen dei Pazzi. DAD-2
Mary Magdelen Postel (1756–1846). MOC
Matilda (895–968). DAD-2; QUA
Matthew. DAD-3
Matthias. DAD-2; QUA
Melania (383–439). DAD-3
Methodius (826–885). DAD-3
Michael. MOC
Monica (332–387). DAD-1; DAD-2; MOC; QUA
More, Sir Thomas (Saint Thomas More) (1478–1535). DAD-3; MAJ; MOC; PEE
Moses the Black (330–405). ONA
Narcissus. DAD-3
Neri, Philip (1515–1595). DAD-1; DAD-2; MOC; QUA
Nicholas (d. 343). DAD-3; FAD; ONA; PEE; QUA
Nilus the Elder (d. 430). DAD-3
Nino. DAD-3
Norbert (d. 1134). DAD-2
Notburga (1265–1313). DAD-3; MOC
Odo of Cluny (d. 942). DAD-3
Olga (d. 969). WIB
Olympias (d. 408). DAD-3
Onesimus (d. 90?). DAD-2; MOC
Pacificus of San Severino (1653–1721). DAD-3
Pamphilus (d. 310). DAD-2
Pantaleon. DAD-3
Paschal Baylon (1540–1592). DAD-2; MOC
Patricia (d. 665?). ONA

Patrick (389?–461). DAD-1; DAD-2; FAD; HEA; MOC; ONA; QUA; REC; TUA
Paul (d. 67? A.D.). DAD-1; DAD-2; ONA; QUA
Paul, the Egyptian Hermit. DAD-2
Pelagius. DAD-2
Penelope (d. 67? A.D.). WIB
Peregrine (13th century). DAD-1
Perpetua (d. 202). DAD-2
Peter (d. 67? A.D.). DAD-1; DAD-2; DAD-3; MAJ; ONA; QUA
Peter of Tarentaise (1102–1174). DAD-2
Peter of Verona. DAD-2
Peter Chrysologus (400–450). DAD-3
Peter Nolasco (c. 1182–1249?). DAD-2
Petroc (6th century). MOC
Philip. DAD-2
Philip of Thrace. DAD-3
Philip of Zell. DAD-2
Philip Benizi (1223–1285). DAD-3
Pius V (1504–1572). DAD-2
Pius X (1835–1914). DAD-3
Polycarp (2d century). DAD-2
Porphyry (d. 420). DAD-2
Porres, Martin de (1579–1639). ADA; ADB; DAD-1; DAD-3; PEE
Pothinus. DAD-2
Praxedes. DAD-3
Radegund. DAD-3
Raphael. DAD-3
Raymond of Pennafort. DAD-2
Raymond Nonnatus (1200–1240). MOC
Regis, John Francis (1597–1640). DAD-2
Remigius (c. 437–c. 533). DAD-3
Richard (d. 722). QUA
Richard of Chichester (1198–1253). DAD-2
Rita of Cascia (1381–1457). DAD-1; DAD-2; MOC
Roch (1295–1327). CHD†; DAD-3; TUA
Romanus. DAD-2
Romuald (c. 952–1027). DAD-2
Rose of Lima (1586–1617). DAD-1; DAD-3; QUA
Rose of Viterbo (1235–1252). DAD-3
Sabas (5th century). DAD-3
Sabas, the Goth (4th century). DAD-2
Samson (490–565). WIB
Sanchia (c. 1180–1229). DAD-2
Savio, Dominic (1842–1957). DAD-1; DAD-2
Scholastica. DAD-2
Sebastian (3d century). DAD-1; DAD-2
Serenus. DAD-2
Sergius of Radonezh (1314–1392). DAD-3; ONA
Servulus. DAD-3
Seton, Elizabeth Ann (1774–1821). ASB; BLF†; CUC; DAD-1; WABC†
Simeon Stylites (390?–459). DAD-2; FAD
Simon. DAD-3
Simplicius. Pope. DAD-2

Solano, Francis (1549–1610). DAD-3
Soter. DAD-2
Spiridion. DAD-3
Stanislaus (1030–1079). DAD-2
Stephen (d. 36?). DAD-3; QUA
Stephen I of Hungary (b. 970). DAD-3
Stephen Harding (d. 1134). DAD-2
Susan (d. 238). WIB
Susanna (d. 295). QUA
Swithin (d. 862). WIB
Syncletica. DAD-2
Tarcisius (fl. 258). DAD-1
Teresa of Avila (1515–1582). DAD-3; QUA
Thecla (30–120). DAD-1; DAD-3
Theodore Tiro. DAD-3
Theodosius (d. 529). DAD-2
Thèrése of Lisieux (1873–1897). DAD-1; DAD-3;
    MOC
Thomas. DAD-3; QUA
Thomas à Becket (1118–1170). CHG; DAD-3;
    MAJ; ONA
Thomas of Villanova (1488–1555). DAD-3; MOC
Thomas Aquinas (1225?–1274). DAD-2; LO; ONA;
    OZA
Timothy (d. 97? A.D.). DAD-2; QUA
Titus (fl. 50). DAD-2
Toribio. DAD-2
Ubald (1080?–1160). DAD-2
Ursula (4th century). QUA
Valentine (d. 270). DAD-2; ONA
Varus. DAD-3
Veronica (1st century). QUA
Veronica of Milan. DAD-2
Vianney, Jean Baptiste Marie (1786–1859).
    DAD-3; MOC
Victor (c. 300?). QUA
Vincent de Paul (1581?–1660). DAD-3; MAK;
    QUA; STP
Vincent of Saragossa. DAD-2
Vincent Ferrer (1350–1419). DAD-2
Virgil of Salzburg (d. 784). MOC
Walburga (710–779). DAD-2
Waldetrudis (628–688). DAD-2
Walter of Pontoise (d. 1099). QUA
Wenceslaus of Bohemia (d. 929). CAAA; DAD-3
Wilfrid (634–709). QUA
William of Abbot (1127–1203). DAD-2
William of Bourges (1150–1209). DAD-2
William of Gellone (d. 812). QUA
William of Monte Vergine. DAD-2
William of Roskilde (d. 1070). MOC
William of York. DAD-2
Willibrord (657?–738). DAD-3
Winifred (d. 650?). MOC
Zaccaria, Anthony (1502–1539). DAD-3

Zachary. Pope. DAD-2
Zita (1218–1278). MOC; ONA

SAUDIS

Fahd ibn Abdul Aziz al Saud (1922–). King.
    HAGD
Yamani, Ahmed Zaki (1930–). Oil minister. DU-1

SCIENTISTS

See also AGRICULTURISTS; ANATOMISTS; ANTHRO-
POLOGISTS; ARCHAEOLOGISTS; ASTRONOMERS;
BACTERIOLOGISTS; BIOCHEMISTS; BIOLOGISTS;
BIOPHYSICISTS; BOTANISTS; CHEMISTS; ECOLO-
GISTS; ENGINEERS; ENTOMOLOGISTS; GENETI-
CISTS; GEOGRAPHERS; GEOLOGISTS; ICHTHYOLO-
GISTS; INVENTORS; MATHEMATICIANS; METEO-
ROLOGISTS; MICROBIOLOGISTS; MINERALOGISTS;
NATURALISTS; NUTRITIONISTS; OCEANOGRAPHERS;
ORNITHOLOGISTS; PALEONTOLOGISTS; PATHOLO-
GISTS; PHARMACOLOGISTS; PHYSICIANS & SUR-
GEONS; PHYSICISTS; PHYSIOLOGISTS; ROCKET &
SPACE SCIENTISTS; VETERINARIANS; VIROLOGISTS;
ZOOLOGISTS

Bacon, Roger (1214?–1294). English. MAQ
Bronowski, Jacob (1908–1974). English. (Born Po-
    land). GRB-1
Flume, Jimmie. HOG
Franklin, Benjamin (1706–1790). ALCA; ARAB;
    ASB; BAEA; BLE; BOD; BUE; BUIB; CAA;
    COJ; COR; CUC; DAC; DAFA; DEDC; DEI;
    DEJ; DUA; FE; FEAA; FEAB; FEB; FIA; FID;
    FOB; FOH; HAN; HYA; HYB; LEAA; LEC;
    MAC; MAQ; MAT; OLA; SHFB; SIA; SQB;
    STH; STI; VIA; WAI
Lippershey, Hans (1570–1619). Dutch. FE; LAA†
Thomas, Jeanette. LA-1

SCIENTOLOGISTS

Hubbard, L. Ron (1911–1986). COEA

SCOTS

Anderson, John Henry (Professor) (1814–1874).
    Magician. FOGA; GIA
Baird, John Logie (1888–1946). Inventor. EVC;
    FE; PRC; SHFB; THA

Barlass, Kate (15th century). Heroine. MAJ
Barrie, Sir James M. (1860–1937). Author, play-
wright. COB
Bell, Sir Charles (1774–1842). Surgeon. RIB
Black, Joseph (1728–1799). Chemist. BUF
Brown, Arthur Whitten (1886–1948). Aviator.
COC†; HAMY
Bruce, Robert the (1274–1329). King. CAAA;
HEA; MAJ; SUK
Burns, Robert (1759–1796). Poet. COB
Carlyle, Thomas (1795–1881). Author, historian.
COB
Clark, James (1936–1968). Automobile racer.
ALBA; COKC; JA; ORD; YAA
Dewar, Sir James (1842–1923). Chemist, physi-
cist. SHFB
Douglas, David (1798–1834). Botanist. JEA
Doyle, Sir Arthur Conan (1859–1930). Author.
COO
Ferrier, David (1843–1928). Neurologist. POB
Fleming, Sir Alexander (1881–1955). Bacteriolo-
gist. AAS-31; ASB-1; BEK; BEP; BOB; CAA;
COLA; FE; HUD; LAE; POB; RIF; ROA; SHG;
SUF
Geddes, Sir Patrick (1854–1932). Botanist. COLA
Grahame, Kenneth (1859–1932). Author. BEI
Henderson, Arthur (1863–1935). Statesmen.
MEC†; WIC
Home, Daniel Dunglas (1833–1886). Spiritualist.
COEA
Hunter, John (1728–1793). Surgeon, anatomist.
FE; MAR; RIB; SIC
Hunter, William (1718–1783). Anatomist. MAR
Kidd, William (Captain) (1645?–1701). Pirate.
LACB; PABB; SC-1
Lang, Andrew (1844–1912). Author. BEG
Livingstone, David (1813–1873). Missionary, ex-
plorer. COC; COL; DAF; DOBB; HOB; KNA;
LAA-1; MOB; RIB; ROL; STP; WOA
Lyell, Sir Charles (1797–1875). Geologist. BEP;
STI
McAdam, John Loudon (1756–1836). Engineer.
FAB; FE
MacDonald, Flora (1721–1790). Heroine. MAJ
MacDonald, George (1824–1905). Author. BEI
McHarg, Ian L. (1921–). Architect. CORA
MacKenzie, Sir Alexander (1764–1820). Explorer.
COC; KNA; MOB; ROL
Macleod, John James R. (1876–1935). Physiolo-
gist. BEK†; RIF
Mary, Queen of Scots (1542–1587). BOI; DEI;
DEJ; FAE; UNA
Maxwell, James Clerk (1831–1879). Physicist.
CAA; DUA; FE; SHFB; SIA

Molesworth, Mary Louisa (1839–1921). Author.
BEI
Montrose, James Graham, 5th earl and 1st mar-
quis of (1612–1650). Soldier. MAJ; SUK
Murdock, William (1754–1839). Inventor. FE;
LAE
Murray, John Wilson (b. 1840). Detective. LID
Napier, John (1550–1617). Mathematician. SHFB
Nasmyth, James (1808–1890). Engineer. EVB; FE
Orr, John Boyd, 1st baron (1880–1971). Agricul-
turist. KEE; MEC; WIC
Park, Mungo (1771–1806). Explorer. KNA; MOB;
ROL†
Ramsay, Sir William (1852–1916). Chemist.
COLA†; SHFB
Rennie, John (1761–1821). Engineer. EVB
Ross, Sir James Clark (1800–1862). Explorer.
DOC†; ROL
Scott, Sir Walter (1771–1832). Author. COB;
COO; STL
Seton, Alexander (1520–1604). Alchemist. CUA
Shearer, Moira (1926–). Dancer. ATA
Slessor, Mary Mitchell (1848–1915). Missionary.
STP
Smith, Adam (1723–1790). Economist. LO
Somerville, Mary Fairfax (1780–1872). Scientist.
SC
Stevenson, Robert Louis (1850–1894). Author.
BEH; COB; COO; DEI; DEJ; HOA; STK
Stewart, Jackie (John Young) (1939–). Automo-
bile racer. ABB; BELB; COKC; JA; OLCB;
ORD
Wallace, Sir William (1272?–1305). Patriot. SUK
Watson-Watt, Sir Robert Alexander (1892–1973).
Physicist. EVC; FE; SHFB
Watt, James (1736–1819). Inventor. ASA; BIA;
BOD; BUF; COL; EBA; EVB; FAB; FE; FRE;
SHFB; THA
Wilson, Charles T. R. (1869–1959). Physicist. RID

SCOUT LEADERS

Baden-Powell, Robert Stephenson Smyth, 1st
baron (1857–1941). English founder of English
Boy Scouts. EVA; SEB
Low, Juliette (1860–1927). Founder of American
Girl Scouts. DOD; PACA
West, James Edward (1876–1948). American Boy
Scouts executive. MAL

SCOUTS, *see* PIONEERS & FRONTIER PEOPLE

SCULPTORS

Aleijadhino (Antônio Francisco Lisboa) (1738–1841). Brazilian. BACA

Barthé, Richmond (1901–). ADA; ADB; BRB†; RIC; RICA

Bartholdi, Frédéric Auguste (1834–1904). French. DIA

Brenner, Victor David (1871–1924). (Born Russia). LETA

Catlett, Elizabeth (1915–). FAH

Cellini, Benvenuto (1500–1571). Italian. DEI; DEJ; JAC; RAC

Chatham, Alice King. HOG

Erte (Romain de Tirtoff) (1892–). French. (Born Russia). ASB-1

Ezekiel, Sir Moses Jacob (1844–1917). LETA

Hoffman, Malvina (1887–1966). CLA; COKA; STLA; WABC†

Hooks, Earl (1927–). FAH

Houser, Allan (1914–). GRAC

Hunt, Richard H. (1935–). ADB

Leonardo da Vinci (1452–1519). Italian. CAA; CHC; DEI; DEJ; EVC; FE; JAA; KAA; MAI; SHFB; SIA

Lewis, Edmonia (1845–1890). ADA; ADB; KADB; ROG

Lewis, James E. (1923–). FAH

Lewis, Mary Edmonia (1846–1890). LOAV

McCullough, Geraldine (1922–). ADB

Maynard, Valerie (1937–). FAI

Michelangelo Buonarroti (1475–1564). Italian. CHC; DEI; DEJ; JAA; KAA; MAI

Millar, Onnie (1918–). FAI

Neals, Otto (1931?–). FAI

Nevelson, Louise (1900–1988). (Born Russia). BOHB; FOGB; GIB-1

Outterbridge, John W. (1933–). FAI

Perkins, Marion (1908–1961). ADA; ADB

Remington, Frederic (1861–1909). HEDA; HOD; KAW

Rodin, Auguste (1840–1917). French. ASB-1; DEI; DEJ

Saint-Gaudens, Augustus (1848–1907). (Born Ireland). ASB; BEA

Savage, Augusta Christine (1900–1962). BEBA

Stark, Shirley (1927–). FAI

Torres, John (1939?–). FAH

Wright, Patience Lovell (1725–1786). AND; VIA

SEAMEN, see NAVAL FIGURES

SECRET AGENTS, see AMERICAN REVOLUTIONARY

FIGURES—SPIES; CIVIL WAR FIGURES—SPIES; SPIES AND INTELLIGENCE AGENTS

SENATORS, see LEGISLATORS, U.S.

SENEGALESE

Senghor, Léopold Sédar (1906–). President. ADA; DU-1; KEF

SHERIFFS, see LAW ENFORCERS

SHOWMEN, see CIRCUS & SHOW FIGURES; RODEO FIGURES

SILVERSMITHS, see CRAFTSPERSONS

SINGERS

American

Anderson, Marian (1902–). ADA; ADB; BOC; BRG; DOBA; DOF-1; FAA; FLD; GIBA; HUA; HUC; JOC; KE; KOA; LEHB; LEI; MAM; PACA; RIC; RICA; ROF; SC-02; SMBA; STF; STLA; STO; TRD

Arroyo, Martina (1936?–). AB

Autry, Gene (1907–). LA

Baker, Josephine (1906–1975). ROF

Bayes, Nora (1880–1928). MASB

Belafonte, Harry (1927–). LOB; ROF

Bradford, Alex (1926?–1978). AB

Broonzy, Big Bill (1893–1959). SUH

Brown, James (1928–). DRA

Brown, Rabbit (Richard) (1880–1937). SUH

Burleigh, Henry Thacker (1866–1949). ADA; ADB; BRB†; DOF-1

Callaway, Liz. BRF-1

Campbell, Glen (1936–). KRI-1

Canova, Judy (1916–1983). MASB

Carmichael, Hoagy (1899–1981). MOA

Carr, Leroy (1899–1935). SUH

Carr, Vikki. NEAA; WH

Carter, Alvin Pleasant (1891–1960). KR

Carter, Betty (1930–). UN

Carter, Maybelle (1909–1978). KR

Carter, Sara (1899–). KR

Cash, Johnny (1932–). BUIB-01

Charles, Ray (1930–). HAFA

Clark, Roy. HAG-1

Cole, Nat "King" (1919–1965). ROF

Collins, Judy (1939–). BOHC; SC-02
Davis, Mac (1942–). KRI
Denver, John (1943–). KRI-1
Díaz, Justino (1940–). NEBB
Evans, Dale (1912–). LA
Farrell, Eileen (1920–). SAB
Feliciano, José (1945–). FOW; LYA; WH-2
Fender, Freddy (1937–). KRI
Fisk Jubilee Singers. HUC
Fitzgerald, Ella (1918–). ASB-1
Franklin, Aretha (1942–). AB; BUIB-1; JOE
Franklin, Irene (1876–1941). MASB
Garland, Judy (1922–1969). FOR
Gayle, Crystal (1951–). KRI
Grant, Micki. AB
Greenfield, Elizabeth Taylor (1809–1876). LOAV;
    ROF†
Hall, Tom T. (1936–). KRI-1
Harris, Emmylou (1947–). KRI-1
Hayes, Roland (1887–1976). ADA; ADB; BRB†;
    DOF-1; HUC
Hendrix, Jimi (1942–1970). BUIB-1
Holiday, Billie (1915–1959). BRBD; COF-1; JOE;
    SUH; TEA; TEB; WAD†
Hopkins, Lightnin' (Sam) (1912–1982). SUH
Horne, Lena (1917–). DADB; DOBA; DOF-1;
    HUC; LEHB; ROF
Horne, Marilyn (1934–). SAB
Hunter, Alberta (1895–1984). GIB-1
Jackson, Mahalia (1911–1972). HUC; JOE
Jackson, Michael (1958–). BUIB-2
Jefferson, Lemon (1897–1930). ADB; COF-1;
    SUH; WAD†
Jennings, Waylon (1937–). KRI-1
Johnson, Lonnie (1889–1970). SUH
Johnson, Willie (1902–1949). SUH
Jolson, Al (1886–1950). LETA
Joplin, Janis (1943–1970). BUIB-1
Kahn, Madeline (1942–). MASB
Kane, Helen (1904–1966). MASB
Kitt, Eartha (1928–). DADB; ROF
Kristofferson, Kris (1937–). KRI
Leadbelly (Huddie Ledbetter) (1888–1949).
    COF-1; HUC; SUH; WAD†
Lewis, Furry (Walter) (1900–). SUH
Lewis, Jerry Lee (1935–). BUIB-01
Lopez, Trini (1937–). NEAA; WH-1
Lynn, Judy (1936–). LA
Lynn, Loretta (1935–). BUIB-01
McClennan, Tommy (1908–1958?). SUH
McClintock, Harry (1882–1957). LA
McGhee, Brownie (Walter Brown) (1915–). SUH
Martin, Dean (Dino Paul Crocetti) (1917–).
    BUR-1
Midler, Bette (c. 1945–). MASB
Milsap, Ronnie (1944–). KRI-1

Montana, Patsy (1914–). LA
Morrison, Jim (1943–1971). BUIB-2
Nelson, Willie (1933–). BUIB-01; KRI
Parton, Dolly (1946–). BUIB-01; KRI-1
Peerce, Jan (1904–1984). GRB-1
Ponselle, Rosa (1897–1981). STLA
Presley, Elvis (1935–1977). BUIB-1
Price, Leontyne (1927–). ADB; DOF-1; ROF; SAB;
    SC-02
Pride, Charley (1938–). BUIB-01; KRI
Rainey, Ma (Gertrude Malissa Nix Pridgett)
    (1886–1939). JOE; SUH; WAD†
Raye, Martha (1916–). MASB
Reeves, Goebel (1899–1959). LA
Revere, Paul. LEHB
Reynolds, Malvina (1899?–). BOHC
Ritter, Tex (Woodward Maurice) (1906–1974). LA
Robeson, Paul (1898–1976). ADA; ADB; DAFG;
    DOBA; DOF-1; JO; RICA; ROF
Rodriguez, Johnny (1952–). KRI-1
Rogers, Kenny (1938–). BUIB-01
Rogers, Roy (1912–). LA
Ronstadt, Linda (1946–). BUIB-2; KRI
Ross, Diana (1944–). AB; BOHC; BUIB-2
Sainte-Marie, Buffy (1942?–). BOHC
Schumann-Heink, Ernestine (1861–1936). (Born
    Austria). MAT-1
Sills, Beverly (1929–). DU-1; GLO; SAB; SC-02
Smith, Bessie (1894–1937). HUC; JOE; SUH;
    TEA; TEB; WAD†
Smith, Kate (1909–1986). GEA
Springsteen, Bruce (1949–). BUIB-2
Summer, Donna (1948–). BUIB-1
Terry, Sonny (Saunders Teddell) (1911–1986).
    SUH
Thompson, Hank (1925–). LA
Tillis, Mel (1932–). HAG-1
Tucker, Richard (1913–1975). BRBB-1
Tucker, Tanya (1958–). KRI-1
Vereen, Ben (1946?–). AB
Verrett, Shirley (1933?–). GRBA
Waters, Ethel (1900–1977). ADA; ADB; DI-1†;
    DOBA; HUC
Waters, Muddy (McKinley Morganfield) (1915–
    1983). SUH
Williams, Big Joe (1900–). SUH
Williams, Hank (1923–1953). BUIB-01
Williams, Hank, Jr. (1949–). KRI
Wonder, Stevie (1950–). BUIB-1
Wynette, Tammy (1942–). BUIB-01

Foreign
Bowie, David (1947–). English. BUIB-2
Caruso, Enrico (1873–1921). Italian. ASB-1;
    COKB; DEI; DEJ; YOH
Clapton, Eric (1945–). English. BUIB-1

Corelli, Franco (1924?–). Italian. BRBB-1
Daltrey, Roger (1945–). English. BUIB-2
Domingo, Placido (1941–). Spanish. BRBB-1
Gibb, Barry (1946–). English. BUIB-1
Gibb, Maurice (1949–). English. BUIB-1
Gibb, Robin (1949–). English. BUIB-1
Harrison, George (1943–). English. BUIB-1;
  SC-01
Jagger, Mick (1944–). English. BUIB-1
John, Elton (1947–). English. BUIB-1
Lennon, John (1940–1980). English. BUIB-1;
  SC-01
Lind, Jenny (1820–1887). Swedish. BOC; TRC
McCartney, Paul (1942–). English. BUIB-1; SC-01
Makeba, Miriam (1932–). South African. CRA
Mercury, Freddie (1946–). English. BUIB-2
Moon, Keith (1946–1978). English. BUIB-2
Murray, Anne (1945–). Canadian. KRI
Newton-John, Olivia (1948–). Australian. (Born
  England). KRI
Nilsson, Birgit (1918–). Swedish. SAB
Pavarotti, Luciano (1935–). Italian. BRBB-1
Richards, Keith (1943–). English. BUIB-1
Starr, Ringo (1940–). English. BUIB-1; SC-01
Sutherland, Joan (1926–). Australian. SAB
Townshend, Peter (1945–). English. BUIB-2
Trapp, Maria Augusta (1905–1987). Austrian.
  CAHA
Vickers, Jon (1926–). Canadian. BRBB-1

SKATERS

Albright, Tenley (1935–). BOHA; HOBA; HOBAA;
  HOBB; LEYB†; PIBA
Allen, Lisa-Marie (1960–). VAD-6
Babilonia, Tai (1960–). VAD-6
Beauchamp, Bobby. VAD-6
Blumberg, Judy. VAD-6
Button, Dick (1929–). DAG; DAGA; HEG; HOC;
  LEYB; LIEA
Cramer, Scott. VAD-6
Curry, John (1949–). English. LIEA; VAD-6
deLeeuw, Diane (1956–). (Born the Netherlands).
  VAD-6; VADA
Fleming, Peggy (1948–). GRBA; HOBA; HOBAA;
  LEYB; LIEA; LYC; RYA; VADA
Fratianne, Linda (1960–). VAD-6
Gardner, Randy (1958–). VAD-6
Hamill, Dorothy (1956–). GUED; HOBAA; LIEA;
  VADA
Hamilton, Scott (1958–). VAD-6
Heiden, Beth (1959–). HOCG
Heiden, Eric (1958–). HOCG; LIEA
Heiss, Carol (1940–). DEF; DEHA-1; HOBA;
  HOBAA; JAB; LEF; PIBA

Henie, Sonja (1913–1969). Norwegian. ASBA;
  DAG; DAGA; GED; GEDA; HOBAA; LEYB†;
  RYA†
Henning, Anne (1956?–). HOBAA†; LEYB†; ST-2
Jaffee, Irving (1906–1981). SLA
Lynn, Janet (1953–). HOBAA; JABA; RYX;
  VAD-6; VADA
Magnussen, Karen (1952–). Canadian. VADA
Rodnina, Irina (1949–). Russian. LIEA
Rubenstein, Louis (1861–1931). Canadian. SLA
Santee, David (1957–). VAD-6
Santee, James. VAD-6
Seibert, Mike. VAD-6
Shelley, Ken. VAD-6
Smith, Stacy. VAD-6
Starbuck, Jo Jo. VAD-6
Summers, John. VAD-6
Tickner, Charles (1953–). LIEA; VAD-6
Weld, Theresa (1893–). HOBAA; JAB
Young, Sheila (1950–). HOBAA†; LIEA; SUBB-1
Zayak, Elaine (1965–). VAD-6

SKIERS

See also WATER SKIERS

Chaffee, Suzy (1947–). FRCA; HOBAA
Cochran, Barbara Ann (1951–). FRCA; HOBAA†;
  LEYB†; RYX; ST-2; WA-1
Cochran, Linda (1954–). HOBAA†; RYX
Cochran, Marilyn (1950–). HOBAA†; RYX
Fraser, Gretchen Kunigk (1919–). HOBA;
  HOBAA; JAB; LEYB
Greene, Nancy (1943–). Canadian. FRCA
Hlavaty, Jana (1941–). (Born Czechoslovakia).
  WA-1
Killy, Jean-Claude (1943–). French. FRCA;
  LEYB†
Koch, Bill (1955?–). FRCA
Lawrence, Andrea Mead (1932–). HOBA; HOBAA;
  LEYB
McKinney, Steve. FRCA
Moser-Proell, Annemarie. Austrian. WA-1
Nelson, Cindy (1955–). GUED; JABA; WA-1
Pitou, Penny. HOBA
Sailer, Toni (1935–). Austrian. ALBA; DEF; GED;
  GEDA; LEYB†
Saudan, Sylvain. Swiss. FRCA
Tokle, Torger (d. 1945). (Born Norway). DAG;
  DAGA
Werner, Bud (Wallace) (1936?–1964). FOI; HO

SKIERS, WATER, *see* WATER SKIERS

SOCCER FIGURES

Beckenbauer, Franz (1945–). German. ADL
Chinaglia, Giorgio (1947–). (Born Italy). ADL
Cruyff, Johan (1947–). Dutch. ADL
McAlister, Jim (1957–). ADL; GUEC-1
Messing, Shep (1949–). ADL; GUEC-1
Pelé (1940–). Brazilian. AAS-23; ASB-1; ASBA;
    FOR; GUEC-1
Rote, Kyle, Jr. (1950–). ADL; GUEC-1
Roth, Werner (1948–). (Born Yugoslavia).
    GUEC-1
Trost, Al (1949–). GUEC-1

SOCIAL WORKERS

See also PUBLIC HEALTH LEADERS; REFORMERS

Addams, Jane (1860–1935). AAS-34; BOC; BRBE;
    CAGA; COG; COKA; CUC; DEDA; DOD; FEC;
    FOH; FOJ; GIBA; LEZC; MAN; MASA; MAT;
    MEA; MEC; NAB; PA; PACA; SHFE†; STJ;
    STLA; WABC†; WECB; WIC
Anguiano, Lupe (1929–). NEAA
Bam, Brigalia (1933–). South African. CRA
Brace, Charles Loring (1826–1890). COG
Cook, Leon F. (1939–). GRAC
Derricotte, Juliette (1897–1931). BUFA
Fiorito, Eunice (1930–). BOHA-1
Kelley, Florence (1859–1932). BRBE; WABC†
Kessel, Mary Hickman. GEA
Lathrop, Julia Clifford (1858–1932). BRBE†;
    MEB
Lenroot, Katharine F. (1891–). CLA
McDowell, Mary E. (1854–1936). PACB; WABC†
Mangrulkar, Latika. (Born India). FOC-1
Mott, John Raleigh (1865–1955). MEC†; WIC
Perkins, Frances (1882–1965). BI; BOC; CLA;
    SMC; WABC; WHE
Sanchez, Yolanda. GLO
Smithdas, Robert (1925–). BOHA-1
Stern, Elizabeth Gertrude (1890–1954). MAV
Viscardi, Henry, Jr. (1912–). LYA
Wald, Lillian D. (1867–1940). ALD; BRBE†;
    CAGA; DOD; EIA; GEE; GIBA; GRB-1; LETA;
    WABC†; WRA; YOB

SOCIALISTS

See also COMMUNISTS

Debs, Eugene Victor (1855–1926). ARB; SEA;
    WECB

Marx, Karl Heinrich (1818–1883). German.
    COJB; FRE; HAK; LO
Thomas, Norman Mattoon (1884–1968). FOJ

SOCIOLOGISTS

Balch, Emily Green (1867–1961). MEC; SHFE†;
    WIC
Cayton, Horace R. (1903–1970). BOG; DADB
Du Bois, William Edward Burghardt (1868–
    1963). ADA; ADB; BEJ; BRB; BRBD; DABB;
    DOF-1; GRAB-01; PECA; RICA; ROG; STB;
    STJB; STO; YOI
Haynes, George Edmund (1880–1960). GRAB-01
Johnson, Charles Spurgeon (1893–1956). ADA;
    ADB
Myrdal, Alva (1902–1986). Swedish. DU-1; SHFE
Sorrentino, Anthony (1913–). (Born Italy).
    BAEA-1
Weaver, Robert Clifton (1907–). ADB; DOF-1;
    YOI
Willard, Josiah Flynt (1869–1907). COGB

SOFTBALL FIGURES

Joyce, Joan (1940–). GUED-1; HOBAA

SOUTH AFRICANS

Abrahams, Peter (1919–). Author. OJA
Bam, Brigalia (1933–). Social worker. CRA
Barnard, Christiaan N. (1922–). Surgeon. DEJ;
    DU-1; FE
Brutus, Dennis (1924–). Poet. LEA
Kruger, Stephanus Johannes Paulus (1825–1904).
    Statesman. WOA
Luthuli, Albert John (1899–1967). Political
    leader. ADA; FOJ; LEA; MEC; WIC
Makeba, Miriam (1932–). Singer. CRA
Mandela, Nelson (1918–). Lawyer. DU-1; LEA
Naudé, C. F. Beyers (1915–). Clergyman. LEA
Nosente (b. 1865?). Tribeswoman. PEA
Paton, Alan (1903–1988). Author. BAF; LEA
Scheckter, Jody (1950–). Automobile racer.
    OLCB; SLA
Scott, Michael (1907–1983). Clergyman. LEA
Sita, Nana (1898–). Pacifist. LEA
Sobukwe, Robert Mangaliso (1924–1978). Politi-
    cal leader. LEA
Theiler, Max (1899–1972). Virologist. AAS-31;
    RIF

SOUTH AMERICANS, *see* INDIVIDUAL COUNTRIES

SPACE EXPLORERS, *see* ASTRONAUTS; ROCKET & SPACE SCIENTISTS

SPANISH

Abad Queipo, Manuel (1751–1825). Bishop. WOB

Aguirre, Lope de (c. 1510–1561). Adventurer. KNA

Albéniz, Isaac (1860–1909). Composer, pianist. KAE; SAA

Almagro, Diego de (1475?–1538). Soldier. ROL

Alvarado, Pedro de (1495?–1541). Soldier. ROL

Anza, Juan Bautista de (1735–1788). Explorer. YOG

Balboa, Vasco Núñez de (1475–1517). Explorer. COC; KNA; ROL

Benjamin of Tudela (d. 1173). Traveler. LES

Cabeza de Vaca, Álvar Núñez (1490–1557). Explorer. BLD†; KEG; LYF; NAA; ROL

Caro, Joseph (1488–1575). Talmudist. KAC

Casals, Pablo (1876–1973). Cellist. CAHA

Cervantes Saavedra, Miguel de (1547–1616). Author. KEH; WO

Cid Campeador, El (1040?–1099). Soldier, hero. HEA

Coronado, Francisco Vásquez de (1510–1554). Explorer. ASB; BLD; COC; GAA; KEG; NAA; ROL

Cortes, Hernando (1485–1547). Explorer. BEO; COC; GAA; KEG; KNA; MOB; ROL

Cresques Lo Juheu (fl. 1375). Mapmaker. GEF

Dali, Salvador (1904–). Painter. WIAA

de Sautuola, Maria (1870–1946). Discoverer of prehistoric cave paintings at 8. FOR

De Soto, Hernando (1500–1542). Explorer. DEI; DEJ; GRC; LED; LEPF; ROL

Díaz, Bernal (b. 1492). Soldier, author. BACA

Domingo, Placido (1941–). Singer. BRBB-1

Escalante, Silvestre Vélez de (fl. 1768–1779). Explorer, missionary. FOC

Esteban or Estevanico (d. 1539). Explorer. ADB; BLD†; BUH; GRAB-02; HAP; HUB; JO†; KADB; LEI; PECA; SCB; STQ; VIA; WIBA

Falla, Manuel de (1876–1946). Composer. BUC; KAE; SAA†; YOL

Ferdinand V (1452–1516). King. CAAA; NEC

Franco, Francisco (1892–1975). Chief of state. ARA; CAE

Goya y Lucientes, Francisco José de (1746–1828). Painter. KAA; MAI

Granados, Enrique (1867–1916). Composer. KAE; SAA†

Greco, El (1548?–1614?). Painter, born Greece. CHC; KAA; MAI

ibn-Ezra, Abraham (1089–1164). Traveler. LERA

Isabella I (1451–1504). Queen. BOI; CAAA; DAK; FAE; LIDA; PA; TRBA

Judah ha-Levi (c. 1085–1140). Hebrew poet, rabbi, physician. GEF; GRB-1; GUA; KAC; LERA; LES

Lope de Vega, Félix (1562–1635). Playwright. WO

Maimonides (Moses ben Maimon) (1135–1204). Hebrew philosopher. GEF; GRB-1; GUA; KAB; KAC; LERA; LES; MAR

Manolete (1917–1947). Bullfighter. PIB

Mendana de Neyra, Álvaro de (1541–1595). Explorer. KNB

Mendoza, Antonio de (1490–1552). Colonial governor. WOB

Moses ben Enoch (d. 965). Rabbi. GUA; LERA

Nachmanides. Philosopher. LERA

Narváez, Pánfilo de (1480–1528). Soldier. BLD†; KEG

Orellana, Francisco de (1500–1549). Explorer. MOB; ROL

Philip II (1527–1598). King. CAAA

Picasso, Pablo (1881–1973). Painter. ASB-1; DABB; DEI; DEJ; DU-1; FOR; FRE; KAA; KE†; MAH; WIAA; WO

Pizarro, Francisco (1471?–1541). Conqueror. GAA; KEG; KNA; MOB; ROL†; WIA-1

Ponce de León, Juan (1460–1521). Explorer. COKB; KEG; ROL†

Ramón y Cajal, Santiago (1852–1934). Histologist. RIF

Samuel ha-Nagid (993–1055). Rabbi, statesman. GUA

Sarasate, Pablo de (1844–1908). Violin virtuoso. CHFA

Serra, Junipero (1713–1784). Missionary. ASB; DOCA; MAT

Torres, Luis de (fl. 1492). Interpreter. GUB; LETA; PEB

Velázquez, Diego Rodríguez de Silva y (1599–1660). Painter. CHC; MAI

SPIES & INTELLIGENCE AGENTS

See also AMERICAN REVOLUTIONARY FIGURES—SPIES; CIVIL WAR FIGURES—SPIES; TRAITORS

Abel, Rudolf Ivanovich (1902–1971). Russian. HAB; KN

Banda (1900–1950). Indonesian. SUG

Bazna, Elyesa (1904–). Turkish. HAB

Berg, Moe (Morris) (1902–1972). BELB; RI; SLA†

Bettignies, Louise de (1888?–1918). French. SEB; SUG

Cohen, Eli (1924–1965). Israeli. (Born Egypt). GRB-1

Dickinson, Velvalee. KN

Donovan, William Joseph (1883–1959). ARD; FAA

Foote, Alexander (1905–). English. SEB

Granville, Christine (d. 1952). Polish. SEB

Hollard, Michel Louis. French. HAB

Lody, Karl Hans (d. 1914). German. HAB

Lonsdale, Gordon Arnold (1924?–1970). Russian. SEB

Lucieto, Charles (fl. 1918). French. SEB

Mata Hari (Gertrud Margarete Zelle) (1876–1917). Dutch. HAB; KN; SUG

Ortiz, Peter J. KN

Powers, Francis Gary (1929–1977). KN

Schulmeister, Karl (1770–1853). French. SUG

Scotland, Alexander (1896?–). English. KN

Sebold, William G. (1897?–). HAB

Silber, Jules (1876–1939). German. SEB

Sorge, Richard (1895–1944?). German. HAB

Stieber, Wilhelm (1818–1882). German. HAB; SUG

Walsingham, Sir Francis (1530?–1590). English. SEB

Wennerstrom, Stig (1906–). Swedish. HAB

Yeo-Thomas, Forest Frederick (1901–1964). English. SEB

SPIRITUALISTS

Blavatsky, Elena Petrovna (1831–1891). Russian. COEA; MAT-1

Garrett, Eileen J. (1893–1970). Irish. COEA

Home, Daniel Dunglas (1833–1886). Scottish. COEA

SPORTS FIGURES, see INDIVIDUAL SPORTS CATEGORIES AS NOTED UNDER "ATHLETES"

SPORTSCASTERS, see TELEVISION & RADIO PERSONALITIES

SQUASH PLAYERS

Sears, Eleanora (1881–1968). HOBA; HOBAA; RYA†

Varner, Margaret (1927–). JAB

SRI LANKANS

Bandaranaike, Sirimavo (1916–). Ex-prime minister. GI

STATESMEN, FOREIGN

Argentine

Irigoyen, Hipólito (1850–1933). President. WOB

Mitre, Bartolomé (1821–1906). President. WOB

Perón, Isabel (Maria Estela) (1931–). Ex-president. LIDA

Perón, Juan Domingo (1895–1974). President. ARA; BAGA; CAE; CL-01; WOB

Saavedra Lamas, Carlos (1880–1959). Diplomat. MEC†; WIC

San Martin, Jose de (1778–1850). BAA; BACA; LAB; OLA; YOFA

Sarmiento, Domingo Faustino (1811–1888). COG; KEE; LAB; WO

Australian

Menzies, Sir Robert Gordon (1894–1978). Prime minister. WEB

Belgian

Beernaert, Auguste Marie François (1829–1912). Minister. MEC†; WIC

Lafontaine, Henri (1854–1943). Senator. MEC†; WIC

Brazilian

Bonifácio, José (1763–1838). LAB; WOB

Nabuco, Joaquim (1849–1910). WOB

Vargas, Getúlio Dornelles (1883–1954). President. BAGA; WOB

Burmese

Nu (1907–). Prime minister. KEF

Thant, U (1909–1974). Diplomat. KE; WEA

Canadian

Pearson, Lester Bowles (1897–1972). MEA; MEC; WEC; WIC

Chilean

Bello, Andrés (1781–1865). (Born Venezuela). WOB

Neruda, Pablo (1904–1973). Diplomat. WO

O'Higgins, Bernardo (1778–1842). BAA; LAB; OLA; STP

Chinese

Chiang Kai-shek (1886–1975). Nationalist leader. ARA; ASB-1; DOF; SPA

Chou En-lai (1898–1976). Communist leader. SPA

Mao Tse-tung (1893–1976). Communist leader. ARA; ASB-1; CAAA; CAE; COJB; DOF; DU-1; HAK; KE; SPA; WEA

Sun Yat-sen (1866–1925). ASB-1; CAAA; DOF; KEE; LAD; SPA

Wang An-shih (1021–1086). SPA

Colombian

Santander, Francisco de Paula (1792–1840). President. LAB

Cuban

Batista, Fulgencio (1901–1973). President. ARA

Castro, Fidel (1926–). Premier. ARA; BAGA; DU-1; HAK; WEA

Czech

Masaryk, Thomas Garrigue (1850–1937). LAD

Danish

Bajer, Frederik (1839–1922). MEC†; WIC

Dominican

Trujillo Molina, Rafael Leónidas (1891–1961). Chief of state. ARA; BAGA

Dutch

Asser, Tobias M. C. (1838–1913). LET; MEC†; WIC

Egyptian

Mubarak, Mohamed Hosni (1928–). President. HAGD

Nasser, Gamal Abdel (1918–1970). President. ARA; KE; KEF; WEA

Sadat, Anwar el- (1918–1981). President. ASB-1; DU-1

English

Cecil of Chelwood, Edgar Algernon Robert Gascoyne-Cecil, 1st viscount (1864–1958). MEC†; WIC

Chamberlain, Sir Austen (1863–1937). Cabinet member. MEC†; WIC

Churchill, Sir Winston Leonard Spencer (1874–1965). Prime minister. ASB-1; CHG; CUC; DEI; DEJ; DOF; ELA; EVA; FLBB; FRE; HIB†; JAC; JAD; KE; RADA; TAC; YOA

Cromwell, Oliver (1599–1658). Lord Protector. CAAA; CAE; DEC; DEI; DEJ; GRAB

Disraeli, Benjamin, 1st earl of Beaconsfield (1804–1881). Prime minister. DEI; DEJ; PEB

Henderson, Arthur (1863–1935). Cabinet member. MEC†; WIC

Lloyd George, David (1863–1945). ASB-1

Macmillan, Harold (1894–1986). Prime minister. WEA

More, Sir Thomas (Saint Thomas More) (1478–1535). DAD-3; MAJ; MOC; PEE

Peel, Sir Robert (1788–1850). LACA

Pitt, William, 1st earl of Chatham (1708–1778). OLA; SOA

Rhodes, Cecil John (1853–1902). ASB-1; WOA

Salomons, Sir David (1797–1873). Mayor of London. GEF

Sidney, Sir Philip (1554–1586). STP

Thatcher, Margaret (1925–). Prime minister. DU-1; GI

Walsingham, Sir Francis (1530?–1590). SEB

Wellington, Arthur Wellesley, 1st duke of (1769–1852). CHG; COD

Wilson, Harold (1916–). Ex-prime minister. WEB

Finnish

Mannerheim, Baron Carl Gustaf Emil von (1867–1951). RADA

French

Blum, Léon (1872–1950). Premier. ARAA

Bourgeois, Léon Victor Auguste (1851–1925). Premier. MEC†; WIC

Briand, Aristide (1862–1932). Prime minister. MEC†; WIC

Cassin, René (1887–1976). MEC†; WIC

Chateaubriand, François René (1768–1848). Minister, diplomat. RAC

Clemenceau, Georges (1841–1929). Premier. ASB-1; COKB

Crémieux, Isaac-Adolphe (1796–1880). KAD

Estournelles de Constant, Paul Henri Benjamin, baron d' (1852–1924). Diplomat. MEC†; WIC

Gaulle, Charles de (1890–1970). President. ASB-1; CAAA; KE; WEA

Mitterand, François (1916–). President. DU-1

Passy, Frédéric (1822–1912). MEA; MEC; WIC

Richelieu, Armand Jean du Plessis, cardinal, duc de (1585–1642). CAE

German

Adenauer, Konrad (1876–1967). Chancellor. WEA

Bismarck, Otto von (1815–1898). CAE

Brandt, Willy (1913–). Ex-chancellor. MEC; WECA

Erhard, Ludwig (1897–1977). Chancellor. WEB

Hindenburg, Paul von (1847–1934). President. ARD

Hitler, Adolf (1889–1945). Chief of state. ARA; ASB-1; BLW; CAE; CL-01; DOF; KIA; TAC

Kiesinger, Kurt Georg (1904–). Ex-chancellor.
WECA

Stresemann, Gustav (1878–1929). Chancellor,
minister. MEC†; WIC

Ghanaian

Nkrumah, Kwame (1909–1972). President. ADA;
JO; KEF; WEA

Greek

Demosthenes (384–322 B.C.). PLA

Pericles (d. 429 B.C.). CAAA; COM; HEA; PLA

Themistocles (527?–460 B.C.). COM; DYA; PLA

Guinean

Touré, Sékou (1922–1984). President. ADA; JO

Haitian

Duvalier, François (1907–1971). President. ARA;
BAGA

Toussaint L'Ouverture, Pierre Dominique (1743–
1803). ADA; ADB; BAA; BACA; KEH; MAJ;
YOFA

Indian

Gandhi, Indira Nehru (1917–1984). Prime minister. ASB-1; DU-1; GI; LIDA; WECA

Gandhi, Mohandas Karamchand (1869–1948).
ASB-1; BEC; DEI; DEJ; DOF; FOJ; FRE; HAA;
HAJ; KE; KEE; LAD; MAN; STP; YOA

Nehru, Jawaharlal (1889–1964). Prime minister.
ARAA; ASB-1; KEF; WEA

Pandit, Vijaya Lakshmi (1900–). Diplomat. KE

Indonesian

Sukarno, Achmed (1901–1970). President. ARA;
KEF; WEB

Irish

MacBride, Sean (1904–1988). Foreign minister.
MEC

Israeli

Begin, Menachem (1913–). Ex-prime minister,
born Poland. ASB-1; GRB-1; HAGD

Ben-Gurion, David (1886–1973). Prime minister.
GRB-1; GUB; KE; KEF; ROGA; WEA

Ben-Zvi, Yitzhak (1884–1963). President, born
Russia. GRB-1

Dayan, Moshe (1915–1981). Foreign minister.
ROGA; GRB-1; WECA

Eshkol, Levi (1895–1969). Prime minister, born
Russia. GRB-1

Meir, Golda (1898–1978). Prime minister. GI;
GRB-1; KE†; KOA; LIDA; ROGA

Navon, Yitzhak (1921–). President. GRB-1

Weizmann, Chaim (1874–1952). President. DEI;
DEJ; GEF; GRAB-1; GUB; KAB; KAD; LES;
ROGA

Italian

Mussolini, Benito (1883–1945). Chief of state.
ARA; ARAA; ASB-1; CAE; DOF; KIA; TAC

Japanese

Sato, Eisaku (1901–1975). Premier. MEC; WECA

Kenyan

Kenyatta, Jomo (1893?–1978). Prime minister.
ADA; KEF

Mboya, Thomas Joseph (1930–1969). Minister of
justice. ADA; KE; POA

Liberian

Tubman, William V. S. (1895–1971). President.
ADA

Malaysian

Rahman, Tunku Abdul (1903–). Ex-prime minister. KEF

Razak bin Hussain, Tun Abdul (1922–). Minister.
RODA

Mexican

Cárdenas, Lázaro (1895–1970). President. ARAA;
NEBA; ROGB

Díaz, Porfirio (1830–1915). President. BAGA;
NEBA; WOB

Echeverría, Luís (1922–). Ex-president. NEBA

Guerrero, Vicente (1783?–1831). President. ROGB

Juárez, Benito Pablo (1806–1872). President.
BAA; BACA; NEBA; ROGB; WO; WOB; YOFA

Madero, Francisco Indalecio (1873–1913). President. NEBA

Morelos y Pavon, José Mariá (1765–1815). BAA;
NEBA; ROGB; WOB; YOFA

Ortiz Mena, Antonio (1908–). NEBA

Santa Anna, Antonio López de (1795–1876).
NEBA

Victoria, Guadalupe, pseud. (1789–1843). President. NEBA

Zavala, Lorenzo de (1788–1836). Governor. KUA

Nigerian

Azikiwe, Nnamdi (1904–). Governor-general. ADA

Balewa, Sir Abubakar Tafawa (1912–1966).
Prime minister. KEF

Norwegian

Lange, Christian Louis (1869–1938). MEC†; WIC

Nansen, Fridtjof (1861–1930). COC†; COG; DOC;

HEA; KEE; KNB†; MEA; MEC; MOB; ROL; WIC

Pakistani
Ayub Khan, Mohammad (1907–1974). Ex-president. WEC
Jinnah, Mohammed Ali (1876–1948). KEF
Ziaul-Haq, Mohammed (1924–). President. HAGD

Paraguayan
Francia, José Gaspar Rodríguez (1766–1840). Chief of state. WOB
Stroessner, Alfredo (1912–). President. BAGA

Peruvian
Perez de Cuéllar, Javier (1920–). Diplomat. DU-1
Unanue, Hipólito (1755–1833). LAB

Philippine
Magsaysay, Ramón (1907–1957). President. KEF; RODA

Polish
Paderewski, Ignace Jan (1860–1941). CHF; MANB; PIAA
Pilsudski, Józef (1867–1935). CAAA

Portuguese
Abravanel, Isaac (1437–1508). GUA; KAB; KAC; LERA; LES
Nasi, Joseph (1510–1579). GUB; KAB; PEB
Salazar, António de Oliveira (1889–1970). Chief of state. ARA

Roman
Caesar, Gaius Julius (100–44 B.C.). CAAA; COD; COK; COM; DEI; DEJ; KEH; PLA; UNA
Cato, Marcus Porcius (234–149 B.C.). PLA
Cicero, Marcus Tullius (106–43 B.C.). COK; PLA
Seneca, Lucius Annaeus (4 B.C.–65 A.D.). COK

Russian
Brezhnev, Leonid Ilyich (1906–1982). Communist leader. WEC
Gromyko, Andrei (1909–). Communist leader. DU-1
Kerensky, Alexander Feodorovitch (1881–1970). Political leader. NEBB-1
Khrushchev, Nikita S. (1894–1971). Communist leader. ARA; COJB; DOF; KE; WEA
Kosygin, Aleksei N. (1904–1980). Communist leader. WEC
Lenin, Nikolai (Vladimir Illich Ulyanov) (1870–1924). Communist leader. ARA; ASB-1; CAAA; COJB; DEI; DEJ; DOF; NEBB-1

Stalin, Joseph (1879–1953). Chief of state. ARA; ASB-1; CAE; CL-01; COJB; DOF; KIA; TAC

Saudi
Yamani, Ahmed Zaki (1930–). Oil minister. DU-1

Senegalese
Senghor, Léopold Sédar (1906–). President. ADA; DU-1; KEF

South African
Kruger, Stephanus Johannes Paulus (1825–1904). WOA
Luthuli, Albert John (1899–1967). ADA; FOJ; LEA; MEC; WIC
Sobukwe, Robert Mangaliso (1924–1978). Founder of Pan-Africanist Congress. LEA

Spanish
Franco, Francisco (1892–1975). Chief of state. ARA; CAE
Mendoza, Antonio de (1490–1552). WOB
Samuel ha-Nagid (993–1055). GUA

Sri Lankan
Bandaranaike, Sirimavo (1916–). Ex-prime minister. GI

Swedish
Branting, Karl Hjalmar (1860–1925). Prime minister. MEC†; WIC
Hammarskjöld, Dag (1905–1961). FOJ; KE; MEC; WIC; YOA

Swiss
Gobat, Charles Albert (1843–1914). MEC†; WIC

Syrian
Assad, Hafez el- (1928?–). President. HAGD

Tanzanian
Nyerere, Julius Kambarage (1921–). President. ADA; DU-1; KE; KEF

Tunisian
Bourguiba, Habib ben Ali (1904–). President. KEF

Turkish
Ataturk, Mustafa Kemal (1881–1938). President. ARA; CAAA; HAK

Ugandan
Amin, Idi (1925?–). Ex-president. CL-01

Uruguayan

Batlle y Ordóñez, José (1865–1929). President.
WOB

Venezuelan

Bolívar, Simón (1783–1830). BAA; BACA; CAE;
LAB; LAD; OLA; STP; WO; YOFA
Guzmán Blanco, Antonio (1829–1899). President.
WOB
Páez, José Antonio (1790–1873). President. LAB
Sucre, Antonio José de (1795–1830). First presi-
dent of Bolivia. BAA; LAB

Vietnamese

Ho Chi Minh (1890–1969). ASB-1; HAK; WECA
Ky, Nguyen Cao (1930–). WECA
Thieu, Nguyen-Van (1923–). WECA

Yugoslavian

Tito, Josip Broz (1892–1980). Premier. ARA;
COJB; DU-1; WEB

STATESMEN, U.S., *see* CABINET MEMBERS, U.S.; DIPLO-
MATS, U.S.; GOVERNORS, U.S.; LEGISLATORS, U.S.; MAY-
ORS, U.S.; PRESIDENTS, U.S.; VICE PRESIDENTS, U.S.

SUFFRAGISTS, *see* FEMINISTS

SULTANS, *see* RULERS

SUPREME COURT JUSTICES, *see* JURISTS

SURF RIDERS

Bigler, Steve. OLD
Carroll, Charles Curtis "Corky" (1947?–). OLD
Codgen, Claude. OLD
Doyle, Mike. OLD
Farrelly, Bernard. Australian. OLD
Frye, Harry Richard. OLD
Grigg, Rick (1938?–). OLD
Hemmings, Fred, Jr. OLD
James, Don. OLD
Kahanamoku, Duke Paoa (1890–1968). FIC;
LEYB†; OLD
Miller, Russell C. OLD
Munoz, Michael French (1937–). OLD
Noll, Greg (1937–). OLD
Nuuhiwa, David (1951?–). OLD
Peterson, Preston. OLD
Propper, Gary. OLD
Valluzzi, Bruce. OLD
Van Dyke, Fred. OLD

Weber, Dewey (1937?–). OLD
Young, Robert. Australian. OLD

SURGEONS, *see* PHYSICIANS & SURGEONS

SURVIVORS

Canessa, Roberto (1953?–). Uruguayan air crash
victim. WIAA-5
Milley, Levi (fl. 1958). WIAA-5
Onoda, Hiroo (1922–). Japanese. WIAA-5
Parrado, Nando (1950?–). Uruguayan. WIAA-5

SWEDES

Andrée, Salomon A. (1854–1897). Polar explorer.
DOC†; GRB
Arnoldson, Klas Pontus (1844–1916). Pacifist.
MEC; WIC
Arrhenius, Svante August (1859–1927). Chemist.
FE
Berzelius, Jöns Jakob, baron (1779–1848). Chem-
ist. MOBA; SHFB
Borg, Björn (1956–). Tennis player. AAS-28; FOX;
GLC
Branting, Karl Hjalmar (1860–1925). Statesman.
MEC†; WIC
Buxtehude, Dietrich (1637–1707). Composer, or-
ganist. BEM
Charles XII (1682–1718). King. CAAA
Christina (1626–1689). Queen. BOI; COKB;
TRBA; UNA
Eric IX (Eric the Saint) (d. 1160). King. QUA
Gejvall, Nils-Gustaf (1915–). Osteologist. POC
Gustavus II (Gustavas Adolphus) (1594–1632).
King. CAAA; HEA
Hammarskjöld, Dag (1905–1961). Statesman.
FOJ; KE; MEC; WIC; YOA
Hedin, Sven Anders (1865–1952). Geographer, ex-
plorer. BAB; HOB; ROL†
Lagerlof, Selma (1858–1940). Author. PA; SHFE†
Lind, Jenny (1820–1887). Singer. BOC; TRC
Lindgren, Astrid (1907–). Author. SMB
Linnaeus, Carl (1707–1778). Botanist. BLB; CAB;
COLA; FE; MIB; STI
Meitner, Lise (1878–1968). Physicist, born Aus-
tria. HA-1; RID†; SC†; YOF
Myrdal, Alva (1902–1986). Sociologist. DU-1;
SHFE
Nilsson, Birgit (1918–). Singer. SAB
Nobel, Alfred Bernhard (1833–1896). Manufac-

turer, philanthropist. EVA; HAC; LAE; MAP; MEC; RIF

Nordenskjöld, Nils Adolf (1832–1901). Geologist, explorer. COC†; KNB; ROL

Sachs, Nelly (1891–1970). Poet, born Germany. SHFE

Scheele, Karl Wilhelm (1742–1786). Chemist. SOB

Söderblom, Nathan (1866–1931). Theologian. MEC†; WIC

Swedenborg, Emanuel (1688–1772). Philosopher, scientist. COEA

Wennerstrom, Stig (1906–). Spy. HAB

SWIMMERS & DIVERS

Babashoff, Shirley (1957–). GLA; JABA

Bartz, Jennifer (1955–). RYX

Belote, Melissa (1956–). RYA; ST-2

Berg, Sharon (1955–). RYX

Buzonas, Gail Johnson. GLA

Chadwick, Florence May (1918–). DAG; DAGA; HOBA; HOBAA

Chavoor, Sherm. Coach. LEW

Curtis, Ann (1926–). HOBA†; HOBAA; JAB

De Varona, Donna (1947–). BOHA

Ederle, Gertrude C. (1906–). BUJA; DAG; DAGA; HOBA; HOBAA; RYA†

Ender, Kornelia (1958–). German. SUBB-1

Epstein, Charlotte (1884–1938). Administrator. SLA

Garner, "Kati" (Nancy) (1953–). HAKA

Genesko, Lynn (1955–). RYX

Gould, Shane Elizabeth (1956–). Australian. HOBAA†; ST-1

Hajos-Guttman, Alfred (1878–1955). Hungarian. SLA

Heddy, Kathy (1959?–). GLA

Kahanamoku, Duke Paoa (1890–1968). FIC; LEYB†; OLD

King, Micki (Maxine Joyce) (1944–). BOHA; HOBAA; JABA; LEYB†; RYA†; RYX; ST-2

Kiphuth, Robert John Herman (1890–1967). Coach. HEH

Lee, Sammy (1920–). FOI; PIBA

Loock, Christine. GLA

McCormick, Patricia Keller (1930–). HOBA; HOBAA

MacInnis, Nina (1954–). RYX

Meyer, Deborah (1952–). HOBAA†; LEYB

Nyad, Diana (1950–). GLA; GUED-1; HOBAA†

Parry, Zale (1933–). HAKA

Riggin, Aileen (1906–). HOBA†; JAB

Schollander, Donald Arthur (1946–). ALBA; BRE; DEF; HOC; KADA; LEYB; LOAA

Spitz, Mark (1950–). GEDA; GRB-1; LEYB; OCA; SLA; ST-1

Szekely, Eva (1927–). Hungarian. SLA

Von Saltza, Susan Christina (1944–). GED; GEDA; HOBA; HOBAA; LEYB†

Wahle, Otto (1880–1965). (Born Austria). SLA

Webb, Matthew (1848–1883). English. DAG; DAGA

Weissmuller, Johnny (1904–1984). ASBA; BELB; DAG; DAGA; DEF; GED; GEDA; HEG; HOC; HOCG; LEF; LEYB; SICA

SWISS

Bodmer, Karl (1809–1893). Painter. HEDA; HOD

Ceresole, Pierre (1879–1945). Humanitarian. KEE

Courvoisier, Jean. Red Cross delegate. DED

David, François-Eugène. Journalist, Red Cross delegate. DED

Ducommun, Élie (1833–1906). Journalist. MEC†; WIC

Dunant, Jean Henri (1828–1910). Founder of Red Cross. DED; EVA; MEA; MEC; WIC; WRA

Euler, Leonhard (1707–1783). Mathematician, physicist. MUB

Gobat, Charles Albert (1843–1914). Statesman. MEC†; WIC

Jung, Carl Gustav (1875–1961). Psychologist, psychiatrist. KE

Junod, Marcel (1904?–1961). Physician, Red Cross delegate. DED

Keller, Hannes (1934–). Sea diver. OLC

Klee, Paul (1879–1940). Painter. KAA; WIAA

Kocher, Emil Theodor (1841–1917). Surgeon. POB; RIF

Müller, Paul Hermann (1899–1965). Chemist. AAS-31†; RIF

Paracelsus (Theophrastus Bombastus von Hohenheim) (1493–1541). Physician, alchemist. CUA; ED-5; FE; POB; ROA; SHG

Pestalozzi, Johann Heinrich (1746–1827). Educational reformer. FRC

Piccard, Auguste (1884–1962). Physicist. BAB; COR; OLC; PRC

Piccard, Jacques (1922–). Oceanographer. BAB; COLA; COR; OLC

Reichstein, Tadeus (1897–). Organic chemist, born Poland. LET; RIF

Saudan, Sylvain. Skier. FRCA

Saussure, Nicolas Théodore de (1767–1845). Agricultural chemist. CAB

Siffert, Josef (1936–). Automobile racer. JA

Spyri, Johanna H. (1827–1901). Author. BEC

Tell, William (fl. 1307). Patriot. HEA; STP

Volant, Guy (1909?–). Red Cross delegate. DED

SYRIANS

Assad, Hafez el- (1928?–). President. HAGD

SYRIANS, ANCIENT

Zenobia (fl. 267–272). Queen. FAE; PA

TABLE TENNIS PLAYERS

Barna, Gyozo Victor (1911–1972). English. (Born
   Hungary). SLA
Rozeanu, Angelica (1921–). Romanian. SLA

TANZANIANS

Bayi, Filbert (1954–). Track athlete. AAS-26;
   LEYB†
Nyerere, Julius Kambarage (1921–). President.
   ADA; DU-1; KE; KEF

TEACHERS, *see* EDUCATORS

TEACHERS OF BLIND, *see* BLIND

TELEVISION & RADIO ENGINEERS, *see* ENGINEERS,
TELEVISION & RADIO

TELEVISION & RADIO PERSONALITIES

See also ACTORS, ACTRESSES & ENTERTAINERS

Aaron, Chloe (1938–). Programming executive.
   SMBB-2
Ace, Jane (1905–1974). Comedienne. MASB
Akeman, David "Stringbean" (1915–1973). Come-
   dian. HAG-1
Allen, Fred (1894–1956). Comedian. ALC
Allen, Gracie (Grace Ethel Cecile Rosalie) (1906–
   1964). Comedienne. BUR-1; MASB
Arden, Eve (1912–). Actress. MASB
Arnaz, Desi (1917–1986). Entertainer, born Cuba.
   FOW
Austin, Andy (Ann Collier) (1935–). Artist.
   SMBB-2
Autry, Gene (1907–). Actor, singer. LA
Ball, Lucille (1911–). Comedienne. MASB

Ballard, Kaye (1926–). Comedienne, singer.
   MASB
Benny, Jack (1894–1974). Comedian. ALC
Berg, Gertrude (1899–1966). Actress, playwright.
   MASB
Berle, Milton (1908–). Comedian. ALC
Borgen, Chris (1933?–). Newscaster. STAA
Bouton, James Alan (1939–). Sportscaster. HOBB
Bradshaw, Terry (1948–). Sportscaster. AAS-20;
   CL-1; GUCA; RUA; ST
Brice, Fanny (1891–1951). Singer, comedienne.
   DI-1†; MASB; PHA
Brothers, Joyce (1927–). Psychologist. BOHG
Burnett, Carol (1933–). Actress. MASB
Burns, George (1896–). Comedian. BUR-1
Burns, John Francis (1933–). Comedian, televi-
   sion writer, producer. BUR-1
Burns, Kenneth Charles "Jethro." Comedian,
   singer. HAG-1
Buzzi, Ruth (1937–). Comedienne. MASB
Caesar, Sid (1922–). Comedian. ALC
Caffie, Barbara J. (1936?–). Newscaster. STAA
Campbell, Archie (1914–1987). Comedian. HAG-1
Canova, Judy (1916–1983). Singer, comedienne.
   MASB
Cantor, Eddie (1892–1964). Comedian. ALC;
   LETA; PHA
Carroll, Pat (1927–). Actress. MASB
Chevalier, Ann. Camera photographer. BOHD
Child, Julia (1912–). Chef. GIB-1
Clair, Dick (Richard Clair Jones) (1931?–). Come-
   dian, television writer. BUR-1
Clark, Roy. Singer, guitarist. HAG-1
Coca, Imogene (1908–). Comedienne. MASB
Coleman, Valerie D. Reporter. STAA
Cooney, Joan Ganz (1929–). Television producer.
   GIB-1; LES-1
Correll, Charles J. (1890–1972). Comedian.
   BUR-1
Cox, Wally (1924–1973). Comedian. ALC
Cronkite, Walter (1916–). Commentator. JAD
Culver, Carmen (1939–). Screenwriter. SMBB-2
Daley, Cass (1915–1975). Comedienne. MASB
Davis, Belva. Newscaster. STAA
Davis, Joan (1907–1961). Actress. MASB
Dean, Dizzy (Jay Hanna) (1911–1974).
   Sportscaster. ALB; BED; BOE; BRC; BUD-1;
   DAFB; DAFD; DEG; FRC-1†; GIB; GRA; HOC;
   LIAA; NEA; RIGA†; SHH; SMK
De Varona, Donna (1947–). Broadcaster. BOHA
Elliott, Bob (Robert Bracket) (1923–). Comedian.
   BUR-1
Embery, Joan (1949–). Zoo promoter. GUJ
Evans, Dale (1912–). Actress, singer. LA
Fields, Gracie (1898–1979). English singer, come-
   dienne. MASB

Ford, Whitey "Duke of Paducah" (1901–). Comedian. HAG-1

Frederick, Pauline (1908–). CLA

Gifford, Frank (1930–). Sportscaster. HAE

Giggans, Jim. News reporter. STAA

Gleason, Jackie (1916–1987). Comedian. ALC

Gobel, George (1919–). Comedian. ALC; HAG-1

Godfrey, Arthur (1903–1983). Entertainer. ALC

Goldman, Connie. Broadcaster. BOHD

Gosden, Freeman (1899–1982). Comedian. BUR-1

Goulding, Ray (Raymond Walter) (1922–). Comedian. BUR-1

Graziano, Rocky (1922–). Actor. DEHA-1

Haizlip, Ellis. Television producer. AB

Hall, Karen. Producer. HOD-1

Harmon, Thomas D. (1919–). Sportscaster. HIE

Harper, Valerie (1940–). Actress. BOHC

Harrelson, Ken (1941–). Sportscaster. DEHA-1

Hartack, Bill (1932–). Sportscaster. DEHA-1

Haynes, Henry Doyle "Homer" (1918?–1970). Comedian, singer. HAG-1

Hill, Pamela (1938–). Producer. SMBB-2

Huggins, Edith. Newscaster. STAA

Hunter-Gault, Charlayne (1942?–). Newscaster. GLO; STAA

Jarvis, Lucy (1919–). Television producer. GIB-1

Jenkins, Carol (1944–). Newscaster. STAA

Johnson, John, Jr. Producer-director. STAA

Jones, Grandpa (Louis) (1913–). Comedian. HAG-1

Kiner, Ralph M. (1922–). Sportscaster. DA; DAA; RAAA

Korris, Risa (1946–). Camera woman. SMBB-2

Levenson, Sam (1911–1980). Comedian. ALC

Long, Loretta. Actress. BOHD

McMahon, Jenna (Mary Virginia Skinner) (1933–). Comedienne, television writer. BUR-1

Macon, Uncle Dave (David Harrison) (1870–1952). Comedian. HAG-1

Martin, Andrea. Comedienne. MASB

Martin, Dean (Dino Paul Crocetti) (1917–). Comedian, singer. BUR-1

Martin, Dick (1922–). Comedian. BUR-1

Marx, Groucho (1890–1977). ALC; BUR-1; ED-1; MAOB

Matney, William C., Jr. Newscaster. STAA

Meara, Anne (1933–). Actress, comedienne. BUR-1; MASB

Montana, Patsy (1914–). Singer. LA

Moyers, William D. (1934–). Commentator. GRBA

Murrow, Edward Roscoe (1908–1965). Commentator. FAA; FOE; LETB; SQB

Noble, Gil. Newscaster. STAA

Olsen, Merlin (1940–). FRD

O'Neal, Regina. Television producer. FOC-1

Palmer, Arnold (1929–). ASBA; BELB; HOC; KADA; LABA

Pearl, Minnie (Sarah Ophelia Colley) (1912–). Comedienne. HAG-1; MASB

Phelps, Don G. (1929?–). Commentator. STAA

Pious, Minerva (1909–1979). Comedienne, born Russia. MASB

Pouissant, Renee (1944–). Newscaster. SMBB-2

Price, Vincent (1911–). Actor. COE-2

Rashad, Ahmad (Bobby Moore) (1949–). Sportscaster. AAS-18

Raye, Martha (1916–). Singer, comedienne. MASB

Ribeiro, Alfonso. BRF-1

Ritter, Tex (Woodward Maurice) (1906–1974). Actor, singer. LA

Rivers, Joan (c. 1935–). Comedienne. MASB

Rogers, Roy (1912–). Actor, singer. LA

Rollin, Betty (1936–). Television correspondent. SMBB-2

Rowan, Carl Thomas (1925–). Commentator. SQB; STAA; YOI

Rowan, Dan (1922–1987). Comedian. BUR-1

Sanders, Marlene (1931–). Television producer. WA

Sarnoff, David (1891–1971). Executive, born Russia. GRB-1; LAG; LETA

Schreiber, Avery (1935–). Comedian. BUR-1

Simpson, O. J. (Orenthal James) (1947–). Sports commentator. AAS-10; AAS-35; DEHA-1; DEHB; DUF; GUCA; GUEB; KADA; LEZB; LIBB; MOCA; RUA; ST

Skelton, Red (1913–). Comedian. ALC; ED-1†

Smothers, Dick (1938–). Comedian. BUR-1

Smothers, Tom (Thomas Bolyn) (1937–). Comedian. BUR-1

Starbuck, Jo Jo. Commentator. VAD-6

Swann, Lynn (1952–). Sportscaster. AAS-18

Teague, Robert (1929–). Newscaster. FLD

Thomas, Lowell Jackson (1892–1981). Commentator. JAD; LEN

Tillis, Mel (1932–). Singer, composer, comedian. HAG-1

Tolliver, Melba. News reporter. STAA

Walker, Nancy (1922–). Actress. MASB

Walters, Barbara (1931–). Commentator. BOHD; GIB-1

Wills, Bob (1905–1975). Band leader, fiddler. LA

Wilson, Marie (1916–1972). Actress. MASB

Wormington, Judy (1941–). Promotions manager. SMBB-2

TENNIS PLAYERS

Ashe, Arthur (1943–). AAS-28; FOX; GLC; GRBA; HI; HOBC; HOD-1; KADA; LAHA; LYC

Austin, Tracy (1962–). AAS-23; AAS-29; FOR; GUED-1; HOCG

Bjurstedt, Molla (1892?–1959). (Born Norway). HOBAA

Borg, Björn (1956–). Swedish. AAS-28; FOX; GLC

Budge, Don (John Donald) (1915–). DAG; DAGA; FOX; HI; LAHA

Buxton, Angela (1934–). English. SLA

Casals, Rosemary (1948–). MATA; SUDA

Cawley, Evonne Goolagong (1951–). Australian. AAS-29; FR-1; GLC; HOBAA; LAHA; MATA; SUDA

Cochet, Henri (1901–1987). French. FOX

Connolly, Maureen (1934–1969). ALBA; DAG; DAGA; FR-1; HI; HOBA; HOBAA†; SUDA†

Connors, Jimmy (James Scott) (1952–). AAS-28; FOX; GLC; LAHA

Court, Margaret (1942–). Australian. AAS-29; FR-1; HOBAA†; MATA; SUDA

Evert, Chris (Christine Marie) (1954–). AAS-29; BELB; FR-1; GLC; GUED; GUH; HOBAA; LAHA; MATA; SUDA

Flam, Herbert (1928–). SLA

Gibson, Althea (1927–). AAS-29; BOF; BRG; FOG; FR-1; HOBA; HOBAA; HOBC; LOAA; PIB; PIBA; RICA; ROJ; RYA†; SMC; SUDA†; VAE

Glickstein, Shlomo (1958–). Israeli. SLA

Gonzales, Pancho (Richard Alonzo) (1928–). AAS-28; ASBA; BELB; DEHA-1; FOW; FOX; HI; HOC; LAHA; LYE; NEAA

Gottfried, Brian (1952–). SLA

Heldman, Julie (1945–). SLA

Hoad, Lew (1934–). Australian. HI

Hotchkiss, Hazel (1886–1974). HOBAA; SUDA†

Jacobs, Helen (1908–). FR-1; SUDA†

King, Billie Jean (1943–). AAS-29; FR-1; GIB-1; GLC; HI; HOBA; HOBAA; JABA; KOA; LAHA; MATA; RYA; RYX; ST-2; SUDA

Kramer, Jack (John Albert) (1921–). FOX; HI; HOC

Lacoste, René (1904?–). French. FOX

Laver, Rodney George (1938–). Australian. AAS-28; ASB-1; ASBA; BELB; FOX; LAHA

Lenglen, Suzanne (1899–1938). French. DAG; DAGA; FR-1; HI; HOBAA; LAHA; SUDA†

McEnroe, John (1959–). AAS-28; HOCG

Marble, Alice (1913–). FR-1; JAB; SUDA†

Nastase, Ilie (1946–). Romanian. FOX

Navratilova, Martina (1956–). (Born Czechoslovakia). AAS-29; ASB-1; FR-1

Okker, Tom (1944–). Dutch. SLA

Perry, Fred (1909–). English. FOX

Riggs, Bobby (Robert Larimore) (1918–). FOI; FOX

Rosewall, Ken (1934–). Australian. LAHA

Savitt, Richard (1927–). SLA

Sears, Eleanora (1881–1968). HOBA; HOBAA; RYA†

Seligson, Julius (1909–). SLA

Solomon, Harold (1952–). SLA

Talbert, Billy (William Franklin) (1918–). HI

Teacher, Brian (1954–). SLA

Teltscher, Eliot (1959–). SLA

Tilden, William Tatem, Jr. (1893–1953). AAS-28; ASBA; DAG; DAGA; FOX; HEG; HI; LAHA; LEF; SID

Vilas, Guillermo (1952–). Argentinian. AAS-28

Wade, Virginia (1945–). English. AAS-9; FR-1; SUDA

Wills, Helen (1906–). AAS-29; ASBA; COKA; DAG; DAGA; FR-1; HI; HOBA; HOBAA; JAB; LAHA; RYA†; SICA; SUDA†

THAI

Pintong, Nilawan (1916–). Editor and publisher. RODA

Rama V (1853–1910). King. CAAA

THEATER PRODUCERS & DIRECTORS

See also ACTORS, ACTRESSES & ENTERTAINERS; DANCERS & CHOREOGRAPHERS; MAGICIANS; PLAYWRIGHTS; SINGERS

Belasco, David (1854–1931). LETA

Goldfadden, Abraham (1840–1908). LETA

Papp, Joseph (1921–). EOA

Stewart, Ellen. GIB-1; GLO

Yiannopoulos, Andrew (1899?–). (Born Greece). BAEA-1

Ziegfeld, Florenz (1867–1932). PHA

THEOLOGIANS, *see* RELIGIOUS LEADERS—JEWISH; RELIGIOUS LEADERS—PROTESTANT; RELIGIOUS LEADERS—ROMAN CATHOLIC; SAINTS

TRACK & FIELD ATHLETES

American

Ashford, Evelyn (1957–). SUDB

Barron, Gayle (1945–). HIA-01

Beamon, Bob (1946?–). OCA

Bergmann, Gretel (Margarethe) (1914–). (Born Germany). SLA

Bjorklund, Garry (1951–). HIA-01

Boston, Ralph (1939–). DAJ

Campbell, Robin (1958?–). GLB

Carlos, John (1945?–). BELB

Connolly, Harold (1931–). HIA

Connolly, James B. (1868–1957). DAG; DAGA; DAJ; DEF

Connolly, Olga Fikotova (1933–). (Born Czechoslovakia). HOBA; HOBAA

Copeland, Lillian (1904–1964). SLA

Cromwell, Dean Bartlett (1879–1962). Track coach. HEH

Cunningham, Glenn (1909–1988). AAS-26; BUJA; DAG; DAGA; DAJ; GEA; HOC; LYA; LYC; PIB; PIBA; SCA

Cushman, Cliff. LYD

Davis, Walt (1930?–). DAG; DAGA

Decker, Mary (1958–). AAS-26; HOBAA†; LEYB†; ST-2; SUDB

DeMar, Clarence (1888?–1958). DAG; DAGA; DAJ; HIA-01†; PIB

Dern, Bruce (1936–). BELB

Didrikson, Babe (Mildred) (1914–1956). ASB-1; ASBA; CLA; DAG; DAGA; DAJ; DEF; FRB; GED; GEDA; GEE; GIBA; HIA; HOBA; HOBAA; JAB; LEYB; LYB; PACA; PIB; PIBA; RYA; SCA; SID; ST-2; STLA; VAE

Dillard, Harrison (1924?–). DAG; DAGA; DAJ; LEYB; PAW

Edwards, Harry (1942–). AKB

Ewry, Ray C. (b. 1873). DAG; DAGA; DAJ; FIC; LEYB†

Frederick, Jane (1952–). GLB

Garrett, Robert. DEF; FIC

Green, Charlie. LYE

Hart, Eddie (1948–). AAS-24

Hayes, Bob (Robert Lee) (1942–). ANB; CO; DAFB; DAJ; DEHA; KADA; OCA; ST-1

Hayes, Johnny (1886?–1965). DAJ; DEF

Huntley, Joni. GLB

Jackson, Nell (1929–). BOHA

Jenner, Bruce (1949–). SUBB-1

Johnson, Rafer (1934–). DAJ; FIB; HOBC; HOC; LEYB

Kraenzlein, Alvin (1876–1928). DAJ; LEYB†

Larrieu, Francie (1952–). HOBAA; JABA; LEYB†

Lindgren, Gerry (1946?–). FOI

Longacre, Jay. BAEC

Manning, Madeline (1948–). SUDB

Mathias, Bob (Robert Bruce) (1930–). BOHA; DAFB; DAG; DAGA; DAJ; DEF; FIB; GED; GEDA; HEG; HIA; HOBB; HOC; HOCG; LEF; LEYB; OCA; SICA

Matson, Randy (1945–). DAFB; DAJ; HOC

Matthews, Vincent Edward (1947–). BOHA

Meredith, James E. (1893?–1957). HIA

Miller, Kathy (1964?–). HAFA

Mills, Billy (1938–). DEF; GRAC; HIA; LEYB; LYC; OCA

Morcom, Richard "Boo". BELB

Myers, Laurence E. "Lon" (1858–1899). DAJ; SLA

Nelson, Van. LYE

O'Brien, Parry (1932–). DAG; DAGA; GED; GEDA

Oerter, Al (1936–). DAJ; LEYB†; OCA

Owens, Jesse (1913–1980). ASB-1; ASBA; BOF; BOHA; BRB†; DAFB; DAG; DAGA; DAJ; DEF; HEG; HIA; HOC; HODA; LEYB; LYB; OCA; RIC; RICA; SID; VAE

Paddock, Charles (1900–1943). DAG; DAGA; DAJ

Pennel, John (1940–). DAJ

Reel, Vince (1914–). LEW

Richards, Robert Eugene (1926–). DEF; HEG; LYD

Rodgers, Bill (1947–). AAS-30; BAEC; HIA-01

Rudolph, Wilma G. (1940–). DAFB; DAJ; GEA; GED; GEDA; HIA; HOBA; HOBAA; JAB; LEYB; LYD; OCA; RYA

Ryun, Jim (1947–). AAS-26; BELB; BRE; DAFB; DAJ; KADA; LEYB; ST-1

Salazar, Alberto (1958–). (Born Cuba). AAS-30

Schmidt, Kathy (1953–). GLB

Shea, Julie (1959–). SUDB

Shorter, Frank (1947–). AAS-30; BAEC; HIA-01; LEYB

Stack, Walter. BAEC

Switzer, Kathy. BELB; HOBAA†

Tewanima, Louis (d. 1969). HACA

Thorpe, Jim (1888–1953). ASBA; BELB; DAB; DAFB; DAFG; DAG; DAGA; DAI; DAJ; DEF; DUF; FIC; HACA; HEG; HEI; HIE; HOC; LEH; LEPA; LEYB; LYB; RAAE; SID; SUD

Toomey, Bill (William Anthony) (1939?–). LEYB

Toussaint, Cheryl (1953?–). RYX

Tyus, Wyomia (1945–). HOBAA; RYA†; ST-2

Van Wolvelaere, Patty (1951?–). GLB

Vogel, Herb. Coach. LEW

Walsh, Stella (1913?–1980). (Born Poland). DAG; DAGA; HOBA; HOBAA†

Warmerdam, Cornelius (1915–). DAFB; DAG; DAGA; DAJ; LYC

Weston, Edward Payson (1839–1929). DAJ

Winter, Bud. Coach. LEW

Wottle, Dave (1950?–). LEYB

Young, Candy (1962–). SUDB

Foreign

Abrahams, Harold (1899–1978). English. SLA

Bannister, Roger Gilbert (1929–). English. AAS-26; ALBA; ASB-1; ASBA; DAFB; DAG; DAGA; DAJ; PRC

Bayi, Filbert (1954–). Tanzanian. AAS-26; LEYB†

Bikila, Abebe (1932–1973). Ethiopian. AAS-30; DAJ; HIA-01†; LEYB

Blankers-Koen, Fanny (Francina) (1918–). Dutch. DAJ; HOBAA

Brumel, Valeri (1942–). Russian. DAFB; DAJ; GED

Carvaljal, Felix (b. 1873?). Cuban. DAJ; FIC

Cheng, Chi (1944–). Chinese. AAS-24; HOBAA; ST-1

Cierpinski, Waldemar (1950–). German. AAS-30

Clarke, Ron. Australian. DAJ

Coe, Sebastian (1956–). English. AAS-26

Elliott, Herb (1938–). Australian. AAS-26

Juantorena, Alberto (1951?–). Cuban. SUBB-1

Katz, Elias (1901–1947). Finnish. SLA

Keino, Kipchoge (1940–). Kenyan. AAS-26; LEYB†

Kirszenstein-Szewinska, Irena (1946–). Polish. (Born Russia). SLA

Loues, Spiridon (19th century). Greek. HIA; HIA-01†; LEYB†

McKenley, Herb. Jamaican. HIA

Mauermayer, Gisela (1914?–). German. BELB

Nurmi, Paavo (1897–1973). Finnish. ASBA; DAFB; DAG; DAGA; DAJ; DEF; FIC; HIA; LEYB; SICA

Ovett, Steve (1955–). English. AAS-26

Rosenfeld, Fanny (1903–1969). Canadian. (Born Russia). SLA

Roth, Esther (1952–). Israeli. SLA

Snell, Peter (1938–). New Zealand. DEF; LEYB†

Viren, Lasse (1949–). Finnish. SUBB-1

Waitz, Grete (1953–). Norwegian. AAS-30; BAEC; SUDB

Walker, John (1952–). New Zealand. AAS-26

Wright, Thelma. Canadian. GLB

Zatopek, Emil (1922–). Czech. AAS-30; DAG; DAGA; HIA-01†; LEYB

TRADE UNIONISTS, *see* LABOR LEADERS

TRAITORS

See also AMERICAN REVOLUTIONARY FIGURES—SPIES; CIVIL WAR FIGURES—SPIES; SPIES & INTELLIGENCE AGENTS

Arnold, Benedict (1741–1801). HAN; LOA; SOA

Josephus Flavius (37–100). Palestinian. LERA; LES

Lee, Charles (1731–1782). BUIB†; RAD; SOA

TRANSPORTATION LEADERS

Dodge, Grenville Mellen (1831–1916). Railroad developer. MAT

Genet, Arthur Samuel (1909–). Bus lines executive. PAA

Harriman, Edward Henry (1848–1909). Railroad executive. CUC

Hill, James Jerome (1838–1916). Railroad builder. LEM; WED

Law, George (1806–1881). HOF

Stanford, Leland (1824–1893). Railroad executive. YOG

Symes, James Miller (1897–1976). Railroad executive. PAA

Vanderbilt, Cornelius (1794–1877). COKB; WED

TRAPPERS, *see* PIONEERS & FRONTIER PEOPLE

TRAVELERS

See also EXPLORERS & DISCOVERERS

Baker, Sir Samuel White (1821–1893). English. LAA-1; ROL

Benjamin of Tudela (d. 1173). Spanish. LES

Bird, Isabella Lucy (1831–1904). English. JOB; RIG

Carpini, Giovanni de Piano (c. 1180–1252). Italian. KNA

Doughty, Charles Montagu (1843–1926). English. MOB; ROL†; WIA-1

Hahn, Emily (1905–). ROJ

Hsuan-Tsang (600?–664). Chinese. ROL

ibn-Batuta (1304–1377). ROL

ibn-Ezra, Abraham (1089–1164). Spanish. LERA

Palgrave, William Gifford (1826–1888). ROL

Peck, Annie Smith (1850–1935). PACB

Polo, Marco (1254–1324). Italian. COC; COL; DAF; DEI; DEJ; DYA; FRE; GRC; KEH; KNA; MOB; ROL

Royall, Anne Newport (1769–1854). ARB

Thomas, Lowell Jackson (1892–1981). JAD; LEN

Varthema, Ludovico de (1461?–1517?). Italian. ROL

TRUMPETERS, *see* MUSICIANS—TRUMPETERS & CORNET-ISTS

TSARS, *see* RULERS—RUSSIAN

TUNISIANS

Bourguiba, Habib ben Ali (1904–). President. KEF

TURKS

Ataturk, Mustafa Kemal (1881–1938). President. ARA; CAAA; HAK
Bayezid I (1347–1403). Sultan of Ottoman Empire. BEO
Bazna, Elyesa (1904–). Spy. HAB
Croesus (d. 547 B.C.). King of Lydia. COA; JOBB
Mohammed II (The Conqueror) (1430–1481). Sultan. BEO; BLW; CAAA
Murad I (1319–1389). Sultan. BEO
Murad II (1403?–1451). Sultan. BEO
Orkhan (1288?–1362). Sultan. BEO
Zevi, Sabbatai (1626–1676). Religious figure. LERA; PEB

UGANDANS

Amin, Idi (1925?–). Ex-president. CL-01

UNDERGROUND LEADERS, *see* RESISTANCE LEADERS

UNDERWATER EXPLORERS

See also OCEANOGRAPHERS

Bascom, Willard (1917–). COR
Bass, George F. (1932–). POC
Beebe, William (1877–1962). BAB; COKA; COLA; COR; MIB†
Carpenter, Malcolm Scott (1925–). COR; NEB; THC
Cousteau, Jacques Yves (1910–). French. COR; DU-1; ELA; FE; OLC; PRC; SCBA; SQA
Keller, Hannes (1934–). Swiss. OLC

Piccard, Auguste (1884–1962). Swiss. BAB; COR; OLC; PRC
Taylor, Valerie (1936–). Australian. HAKA

UNION LEADERS, *see* LABOR LEADERS

UNITED NATIONS OFFICIALS

Brooks, Angie Elizabeth (1928–). Liberian. CRA
Bunche, Ralph Johnson (1904–1971). ADA; ADB; BRG; DOF-1; FEC; FLD; HUA; JOC; KEE; LEI; MEA; MEC; RIC; RICA; STO; WIC; YOI
Hammarskjöld, Dag (1905–1961). Swedish. FOJ; KE; MEC; WIC; YOA
Konie, Gwendoline Chomba (1938–). Zambian. CRA
Ledón, Amalia. Mexican. NEBA
Orr, John Boyd, 1st baron (1880–1971). Scottish. KEE; MEC; WIC
Stevenson, Adlai Ewing (1900–1965). DABB; GO; KE; WHD†
Thant, U (1909–1974). Burmese. KE; WEA

UNITED STATES HISTORY, *see* AMERICAN REVOLUTIONARY FIGURES; CIVIL WAR FIGURES

URUGUAYANS

Artigas, José Gervasio (1764–1850). General. LAB; WOB
Batlle y Ordóñez, José (1865–1929). President. WOB
Canessa, Roberto (1953?–). Rugby player. WIAA-5
Parrado, Nando (1950?–). Rugby player. WIAA-5

VENEZUELANS

Bolívar, Simón (1783–1830). Statesman. BAA; BACA; CAE; LAB; LAD; OLA; STP; WO; YOFA
Carreño, Teresa (1853–1917). Pianist. CHF
Guzmán Blanco, Antonio (1829–1899). President. WOB
Miranda, Francisco de (1750?–1816). Patriot. BAA; LAB; OLA
Páez, José Antonio (1790–1873). President. LAB
Sucre, Antonio José de (1795–1830). General, statesman. BAA; LAB

VETERINARIANS

Adams, Eugene W. (1920–). HAMA
Belfield, Wendell. CAF-1
McGinnis, Terri (1947–). GUJ

VICE PRESIDENTS, U.S.

Agnew, Spiro Theodore (1918–). FEA; HAOA;
HOEA
Barkley, Alben William (1877–1956). FEA;
HAOA; HOEA
Breckinridge, John Cabell (1821–1875). FEA;
HAOA; HOEA
Burr, Aaron (1756–1836). BUIB; FEA; GO;
HAOA; HOEA
Bush, George (1924–). HAOA; HOEA
Calhoun, John Caldwell (1782–1850). FEA;
HAOA; HOEA; KEC†; STH
Clinton, George (1739–1812). BUIB†; FEA;
HAOA; HOEA
Colfax, Schuyler (1823–1885). FEA; HAOA;
HOEA
Curtis, Charles (1860–1936). FEA; HAOA; HOEA;
LEH
Dallas, George Mifflin (1792–1864). FEA; HAOA;
HOEA
Dawes, Charles Gates (1865–1951). FEA; HAOA;
HOEA; MEC†; WIC
Fairbanks, Charles Warren (1852–1918). FEA;
HAOA; HOEA
Garner, John Nance (1868–1967). FEA; HAOA;
HOEA
Gerry, Elbridge (1744–1814). BAEA; BUIB†;
COJ†; FEA; FEAA; FEAB; HAOA; HOEA; MAC
Hamlin, Hannibal (1809–1891). FEA; HAOA;
HOEA
Hendricks, Thomas Andrews (1819–1885). FEA;
HAOA; HOEA
Hobart, Garret A. (1844–1899). FEA; HAOA;
HOEA
Humphrey, Hubert Horatio (1911–1978). FEA;
HADA; HOEA; WEC; WHD
Johnson, Richard Mentor (1780–1850). FEA;
HAOA; HOEA
King, William Rufus Devane (1786–1853). FEA;
HAOA; HOEA
Marshall, Thomas Riley (1854–1925). FEA;
HAOA; HOEA
Mondale, Walter F. (1928–). FEA; HAOA; HOEA
Morton, Levi Parsons (1824–1920). FEA; HAOA;
HOEA
Rockefeller, Nelson Aldrich (1908–1979). FEA;
HAOA; HOEA

Sherman, James S. (1855–1912). FEA; HAOA;
HOEA
Stevenson, Adlai Ewing (1835–1914). FEA;
HAOA; HOEA
Tompkins, Daniel D. (1774–1825). FEA; HAOA;
HOEA
Wallace, Henry A. (1888–1965). COKA; FEA;
HAOA; HOEA
Wheeler, William Almon (1819–1887). FEA;
HAOA; HOEA
Wilson, Henry (1812–1875). FEA; HAOA; HOEA

VIETNAMESE

Ho Chi Minh (1890–1969). ASB-1; HAK; WECA
Ky, Nguyen Cao (1930–). WECA
Thieu, Nguyen-Van (1923–). WECA

VIKINGS, *see* NORWEGIANS

VIOLINISTS, *see* MUSICIANS—VIOLINISTS

VIROLOGISTS

See also BACTERIOLOGISTS; MICROBIOLOGISTS

Burnet, Sir Macfarlane (1899–1985). Australian.
RIF
Cox, Herald Rea (1907–). PAB
Goodpasture, Ernest William (1886–1960). SUF
Sabin, Albert Bruce (1906–). (Born Russia).
CHE†; COLA; RIE
Salk, Jonas Edward (1914–). ASB-1; BEK; BOB;
CHE†; COLA; DU-1; FAA; FE; GRB-1; HEFA;
LEG; LETA; RIE; ROA; SIC; SUF; YOA
Theiler, Max (1899–1972). South African. AAS-31;
RIF

VOCALISTS, *see* SINGERS

WATER SKIERS

McCormick, Ricky. LYD

WEATHER SCIENTISTS, *see* METEOROLOGISTS

WEAVERS, *see* CRAFTSPERSONS

WEIGHT LIFTERS

Anderson, Paul (1932–). OCA
Berger, Isaac (Ike) (1936–). (Born Israel). SLA

WELSH

Glendower, Owen (1359?–1416). Rebel. SUK
Lawrence, Thomas Edward (1888–1935). Soldier. ARD
Llewelyn ab Gruffydd (d. 1282). Prince of North Wales. SUK
Owen, Robert (1771–1858). Philanthropist. DEDA; EVA
Stanley, Sir Henry Morton (1841–1904). Explorer, journalist. COC; LAA-1; ROL; SQB; WIA-1

WIVES OF FAMOUS MEN, *see* FIRST LADIES; RELATIVES OF FAMOUS MEN & WOMEN

WOMEN

See also RELATIVES OF FAMOUS MEN & WOMEN

African
Dahia al-Kahina (fl. 667–702). Queen. GRAB-04
Nzinga (1582–1663). Queen. GRAB-04; JO; POA
Yaa Asantewa (1863–1923). Ashanti queen. GRAB-04

American
Aaron, Chloe (1938–). Television programming executive. SMBB-2
Abbott, Berenice (1898–). Photographer. SUAA
Abzug, Bella (1920–). Congresswoman. GIB-1; GRAB-1†
Ace, Jane (1905–1974). Comedienne. MASB
Adams, Adrienne (1906–). Illustrator. SMAB
Adams, Diana (1927?–). Dancer. ATA
Adams, Maude (1872–1953). Actress. GIBA†; VAA
Addams, Jane (1860–1935). Social worker. AAS-34; BOC; BRBE; CAGA; COG; COKA; CUC; DEDA; DOD; FEC; FOH; FOJ; GIBA; LEZC; MAN; MASA; MAT; MEA; MEC; NAB; PA; PACA; SHFE†; STJ; STLA; WABC†; WECB; WIC
Adelman, Susan. Surgeon. FOC-1
Akeley, Delia J. Denning (1870?–1933?). Explorer. RIG

Albright, Tenley (1935–). Skater, physician. BOHA; HOBA; HOBAA; HOBB; LEYB†; PIBA
Alcott, Louisa May (1832–1888). Author. ASB; BEGA; BOA; BOC; COB; DEI; DEJ; STJ; STLA; WOAA
Alderson, Nannie (1860–1947). Ranch owner. JOB
Allard, Martine. Actress. BRF-1
Allen, Florence Ellinwood (1884–1966). Jurist. WHE
Allen, Gracie (Grace Ethel Cecile Rosalie) (1906–1964). Comedienne. BUR-1; MASB
Allen, Lisa-Marie (1960–). Skater. VAD-6
Ames, Julie. Aviator. HIFD
Amevor, Charlotte (1932–). Painter. FAH
Ancker-Johnson, Betsy (1927–). Physicist, automotive executive. GL; LES-1†
Anderson, Evelyn M. (1899–). Physiologist. HOG
Anderson, Marian (1902–). Singer. ADA; ADB; BOC; BRG; DOBA; DOF-1; FAA; FLD; GIBA; HUA; HUC; JOC; KE; KOA; LEHB; LEI; MAM; PACA; RIC; RICA; ROF; SC-02; SMBA; STF; STLA; STO; TRD
Anderson, Mary A. (1859–1940). Actress. VAA
Angelou, Maya (1928–). Author. DADB; OCB
Anglund, Joan Walsh (1926–). Author, illustrator. SM
Anguiano, Lupe (1929–). Social worker, educator. NEAA
Anthony, Mary. Feminist. GUBA
Anthony, Sister (Mary Ellen O'Connell) (1814–1897). Nun, nurse, born Ireland. COFA
Anthony, Susan Brownell (1820–1906). Feminist. ASB-1; BOC; BOJ; COG; CUC; DABB; DAD; DEDA; DOD; ELA; GIBA†; GUBA; LEK; LES-2; NAB; PA; SMC; STJ; STLA; TRD; VAB; WABC; WAR
Antin, Mary (1881–1949). Author, born Russia. CAHA
Apgar, Virginia (1909–1974). Physician. RAAG
Applebee, Constance (b. 1874). Field hockey coach, born England. HOBAA
Arden, Elizabeth (1884–1966). Cosmetician. LAH; LES-1
Arden, Eve (1912–). Actress. MASB
Arroyo, Martina (1936?–). Singer. AB
Ashford, Evelyn (1957–). Track athlete. SUDB
Askin, Rosemary. Geologist, polar researcher. LA-1
Atwood, Genevieve (1946–). State legislator, state geologist. WIAA-02
Aulaire, Ingri d' (1904–1980). Author, illustrator, born Norway. SMAB
Auld, Sophia (fl. 1825). Teacher of Frederick Douglass. STG

Austin, Andy (Ann Collier) (1935–). Television artist. SMBB-2

Austin, Beth. Martial artist. AT

Austin, Tracy (1962–). Tennis player. AAS-23; AAS-29; FOR; GUED-1; HOCG

Babashoff, Shirley (1957–). Swimmer. GLA; JABA

Babilonia, Tai (1960–). Skater. VAD-6

Bacon, Mary (1950?–). Jockey. HOBAA

Bagley, Sarah G. (fl. 1835–1847). Union leader. WABC

Bailey, Ann "Mad Ann" (1742–1825). Frontier heroine. CLC; DOD; STJ

Bailey, Mollie Arline (1841–1918). Circus owner. KIB

Bailie, Ann Eckels. Mathematician. HOG

Bailie, Sally (1937–). Horse trainer, born England. GUJ

Baker, Augusta (1911–). Librarian. FLD

Baker, Josephine (1906–1975). Singer. ROF

Baker, Sara Josephine (1873–1945). Physician, reformer. PACB

Balch, Emily Green (1867–1961). Economist, sociologist. MEC; SHFE†; WIC

Baldwin, Maria L. (1856–1922). Educator. BRB

Ball, Lucille (1911–). Comedienne. MASB

Ballard, Audreen. Journalist. STAA

Ballard, Ernesta Drinker (1920–). GIB-1

Ballard, Kaye (1926–). Comedienne, singer. MASB

Barber, Linda Elaine. FAA inspector. SMBC-2

Barcelo, Gertrudis (La Doña Tules) (d. 1852). Frontierswoman. RAB; WIAA-2

Barker, Penelope (fl. 1774). American Revolutionary patriot. CLC

Barnard, Kate (1875–1930). Journalist, social reformer. PACB; TRD; VIA

Barnett, Ida Wells (1862–1931). Journalist, reformer. ADB; BRBE†; BUFA; HUB; LOAV; PACB; PECA; ROG; STAB-1; TRD

Barringer, Emily Dunning (1876–1961). Physician. FLA; MASA

Barron, Gayle (1945–). Track athlete. HIA-01

Barrymore, Ethel (1879–1959). Actress. DI-1; GIBA†; STLA

Barth, Belle (1911–1971). Comedienne. MASB

Barton, Clara (1821–1912). Nurse, founder of American Red Cross. BEC; BOC; CUC; DED; DEI; DEJ; DOD; FOH; GIBA; JOCA; LEK; LEPC; MAK; MAT; PA; SMC; STJ; STLA; WABC†

Bartz, Jennifer (1955–). Swimmer. RYX

Bates, Abigail (fl. 1814). Heroine, War of 1812. CLC

Bates, Daisy Gaston (1922–). Civil rights leader. AKB; DOF-1; GRAB-01; STF

Bates, Katherine Lee (1859–1929). Poet. CAGA

Bates, Laverne (1934–). Martial artist. AT

Bates, Mercedes (1915–). Food industry executive. FRBD

Bates, Rebecca (fl. 1814). Heroine, War of 1812. CLC

Baugh, Laura Z. (1955–). Golfer. HOBAA

Baumgartner, Leona (1902–). Physician. FLA

Bayes, Nora (1880–1928). Singer, comedienne. MASB

Beaux, Cecilia (1863–1942). Painter. NE

Beck, Trudy (1960?–). Motorcyclist. BUIC

Beech, Olive Ann (1903–). Aviation executive. LES-1; PAA

Beecher, Catharine Esther (1800–1878). Educator. BUDA†; FRC; WABC

Beeton, Isabella Mary (1836–1865). Author. BOH

Bellows, Carole Kamin (1935–). Lawyer. SWI

Belote, Melissa (1956–). Swimmer. RYA; ST-2

Benét, Rosemary Carr (1898–1962). Poet. BEH

Berg, Gertrude (1899–1966). Actress, playwright. MASB

Berg, Patty (Patricia Jane) (1918?–). Golfer. HOBA; HOBAA

Berg, Sharon (1955–). Swimmer. RYX

Bergmann, Gretel (Margarethe) (1914–). Track athlete, born Germany. SLA

Bernhard, Sandra (1955–). Actress. MASB

Berry, Martha McChesney (1866–1942). Educator. BUDA; FLB; FOG; LEJA; MAO

Beshar, Christine (1929–). Lawyer, born Germany. SMBB

Bethune, Mary McLeod (1875–1955). Educator. ADA; ADB; BRB; BUDA; CAGA; DOF-1; FLB; FLD; GEE; GIBA; JOC; KOA; LEJA; LOAV; NAB; PECA; RIC; RICA; ROG; STLA; STO; WABC†; WIAA-8; YOI

Bickerdyke, Mary Ann Ball (1817–1901). Nurse. MAK; WABC†; WRA

Big Eyes (fl. 1535). Wichita Indian. WAB

Bishop, Claire Huchet. Author, born France. SMB

Bjurstedt, Molla (1892?–1959). Tennis player, born Norway. HOBAA

Black, Winifred (1863–1936). Journalist. JAE

Blackwell, Elizabeth (1821–1910). Physician, born England. BOC; BUA; CHD; COG; CUC; DOD; GEE; GIBA; HUE; JOCA; LOB; MASA; RAAG†; SC†; SMC; TRD; WABC; YOC

Blake, Florence G. (1907–). Nurse. YOB

Blatch, Harriot Stanton (1856–1940). Feminist. LES-2; WABC†

Blazejowski, Carol (1956–). Basketball player. GUED-1

Blegvad, Lenore (1926–). Author. SMAB

Bloomer, Amelia Jenks (1818–1894). Social reformer. ARB; DEDA; GUBA; LES-2

Blount, Mildred E. Hat designer. BOG

Blumberg, Judy. Skater. VAD-6

Blume, Judy (1938–). Author. GL-1

Bombeck, Erma (1927–). Author. GL-1

Bonnin, Gertrude Simmons (1875–1936?). Sioux Indian educator. GRAD

Boosler, Elayne (1953–). Comedienne. MASB

Boris, Ruthanna (1918–). Dancer, choreographer. ATA

Bosomworth, Mary Musgrove Matthews (1700–1762?). Creek Indian princess. GRAD

Bourke-White, Margaret (1904–1971). Photographer. FAA; FOE; GEE; GIBA; HOE; ROJ; SQB; SUAA

Bousfield, Maudelle Brown (fl. 1906). Educator. BRB

Bowers, Eilley Orrum (fl. 1858). Mine owner, born Scotland. WIAA-2

Bowser, Mary Elizabeth (fl. 1861–1865). Spy. LOAV

Boyd, Belle (1844–1900). Spy. FOA; MAO; SEB; SUG; WABC†

Boyd, Louise Arner (1887–1972). Arctic explorer. RIG

Braden, Anne (1924–). Civil rights worker. STG

Bradstreet, Anne Dudley (1612?–1672). Poet. JOCA; OCB; VIA; WABC†

Brant, Molly (Degonwadonti) (1736–1796). American Revolutionary patriot. AND

Breckinridge, Mary (1877–1965). Nurse. COFA; MAK; WRA

Brent, Margaret (1600?–1671?). Colonial feminist. GUBA†; VIA; WABC

Brice, Fanny (1891–1951). Singer, comedienne. DI-1†; MASB; PHA

Brico, Antonia (1902–). Conductor, born the Netherlands. SC-02; STM†

Bridgman, Laura Dewey (1829–1889). Blind, deaf teacher of the deaf and blind. LYA

Brink, Carol Ryrie (1895–1981). Author. SMB

Brooks, Gwendolyn (1917–). Poet. ADA; ADB; DRA; ROE

Brorsen, Metha (1964?–). Rodeo rider. VADB

Brothers, Joyce (1927–). Psychologist, TV personality. BOHG

Brown, Antoinette Blackwell (1825–1921). Ordained minister. BLF†; BOJ; LES-2

Brown, Charlotte Hawkins (1883–1961). Educator. BRB

Brown, Clara (1803–1885). Businesswoman. GRAB-02; KADB

Brown, Dorothy (1919–). Surgeon. LETC

Brown, Jill Elaine. Aviator. SMBC-2

Brown, Kay (1932?–). Painter. FAI

Brown, Louise (1943–). Lawyer. SMBB

Brown, Marcia (1918–). Author, illustrator. SM

Brown, Molly (Maggie Tobin) (1873?–1932). Eccentric. RAB

Brown, Rachel Fuller (1898–). Biochemist. HA-1; YOF

Bruhns, Karen Olsen (1941–). Archaeologist. WIAA-01

Brunson, Dorothy (1938–). Radio and advertising executive. GLO

Bryan, Dorothy (1896?–1984). Author. SMAB

Bryan, Marguerite. Illustrator. SMAB

Buck, Pearl S. (1892–1973). Author. COKA; CON; GIBA†; HEF; KOA; LEGB; MUA; OCB; SHFE

Buff, Mary Marsh (1890–1970). Author, illustrator. SMAB

Bulette, Julia (1832?–1867). Frontierswoman. RAB†; WIAA-2

Burdan, Molly (1853–1888). Frontierswoman. RAB

Burke, Yvonne Brathwaite (1932–). Congresswoman, lawyer. BOHF; FOC-1; WIAA-02

Burnett, Carol (1933–). Actress. MASB

Burnett, Frances Hodgson (1849–1924). Author, born England. BEI

Burningham, Charlene. Weaver, sculptor. BOHB

Burroughs, Nannie Helen (1883–1961). Educator. LOAV

Burton, Marie. Painter. BOHB

Bussey, Sheila (1950?–). Rodeo rider. VADB

Buzonas, Gail Johnson. Swimmer. GLA

Buzzi, Ruth (1937–). Comedienne. MASB

Byard, Carole Marie (1941–). Painter. FAI

Byrne, Jane (1934–). Mayor. WHE

Caffie, Barbara J. (1936?–). Television newscaster. STAA

Calamity Jane (1852?–1903). Frontier character, markswoman. RAB; SUI

Calderone, Mary Steichen (1904–). Physician, public health educator. BOHE; GIB-1

Caldwell, Sarah (1924–). Conductor. GIB-1; SC-02†

Callaway, Liz. Actress, singer. BRF-1

Campbell, Billie L. Structural engineer. GL

Campbell, Robin (1958?–). Track athlete. GLB

Candelaria, Andrea Castanon (1785–1899). Texas patriot. KUA

Cannon, Annie Jump (1863–1941). Astronomer. EMB

Canova, Judy (1916–1983). Singer, comedienne. MASB

Carmichael, Berthel. Mathematician. CAF-1

Carr, Vikki. Singer. NEAA; WH

Carroll, Jean (c. 1915–). Comedienne. MASB

Carroll, Pat (1927–). Actress. MASB

Carson, Rachel (1907–1964). Author, marine biologist. CO-1; COR; CORA; ELA; EMB; FRE; GIBA; HIBB; PACA; SC; SQA; WAP

Carter, Betty (1930–). Singer. UN

Carter, Maybelle (1909–1978). Singer. KR

Carter, Sara (1899–). Singer. KR

Cary, Mary Ann Shadd (1823–1893). Abolitionist. LOAV; WABC†

Casals, Rosemary (1948–). Tennis player. MATA; SUDA

Case, Sandra Williams. Aviator. SMBC-2

Cashman, Katharine. Geologist, polar researcher. LA-1

Cassatt, Mary (1845–1926). Painter. CUC; FOGB; FRA; LEE; MAG; NE; STJ; STLA; WABC†

Castillo, Rosa. Migrant worker. WECC

Cather, Willa (1873–1947). Author. BOA; CON; CUC; HEF; LEK; MUA; OCB; STLA

Catlett, Elizabeth (1915–). Sculptor. FAH

Catt, Carrie Chapman (1859–1947). Feminist. COG; FAA; JOCA; WABC†

Cecilia, Sister. Nun, born Czechoslovakia. CAHA

Chadwick, Florence May (1918–). Swimmer. DAG; DAGA; HOBA; HOBAA

Chaffee, Suzy (1947–). Skier. FRCA; HOBAA

Champe, Elizabeth (fl. 1780). American Revolutionary patriot. CLC

Channing, Carol (1921–). Actress. MASB

Chase, Mary Ellen (1887–1973). Author. CON

Chatham, Alice King. Sculptor. HOG

Chevalier, Ann. Television photographer. BOHD

Child, Julia (1912–). Chef. GIB-1

Chisholm, Shirley (1924–). Congresswoman. BRGA; COG-1; DRA; DU; FLD; GIBA; ROJ; WHE; YOI

Chouteau, Yvonne (1929–). Dancer. ATA

Chute, Marchette (1909–). Author. MUA

Clark, Beverly. Lawyer. FOC-1

Clark, Eugenie (1922–). Ichthyologist, oceanographer. EMB; HAKA

Clark, Ruth (1942–). Personnel service executive. GLO

Clark, Septima Poinsette (1898–1987). Educator. BUFA

Clarke, Nancy Talbot (1825–1901). Physician. MASA

Cleave, Mary (1947–). Astronaut. FOJ-1

Clevenger, Johanna. Psychiatrist. FOC-1

Coatsworth, Elizabeth (1893–). Author. SMB

Cobb, Geraldyn M. (1931–). Aviator. GEDB; HIFD

Coca, Imogene (1908–). Comedienne. MASB

Cochran, Barbara Ann (1951–). Skier. FRCA; HOBAA†; LEYB†; RYX; ST-2; WA-1

Cochran, Jacqueline (1906–1980). Cosmetician, aviator. CLA; GEDB; HAMY; HIFD; MO; WAJ

Cochran, Linda (1954–). Skier. HOBAA†; RYX

Cochran, Marilyn (1950–). Skier. HOBAA†; RYX

Cochrane, Elizabeth (1867–1922). Journalist. JAE; JOCA; SQB; WAE

Coleman, Bessie (1893–1926). Aviator. HIFD; LOAV

Coleman, Mary Stallings. Judge. SWI

Coleman, Valerie D. Television reporter. STAA

Collett, Glenna (1903–). Golfer. HOBA; HOBAA; JAB

Collins, Judy (1939–). Singer, guitarist. BOHC; SC-02

Colón, Miriam. Actress. NEBB

Comstock, Anna Botsford (1854–1930). Naturalist, wood engraver. EMB†; PAC; YOC

Concello, Antoinette. Aerialist. KIB

Cone, Cynthia. Anthropologist. BOHG

Connolly, Maureen (1934–1969). Tennis player. ALBA; DAG; DAGA; FR-1; HI; HOBA; HOBAA†; SUDA†

Connolly, Olga Fikotova (1933–). Track athlete, born Czechoslovakia. HOBA; HOBAA

Cooney, Joan Ganz (1929–). Television producer. GIB-1; LES-1

Cooper, Arvazine Angeline (1845–1929). Pioneer. MAV

Copeland, Lillian (1904–1964). Track athlete. SLA

Coppin, Fanny Jackson (1836–1913). Educator. BRB

Corbin, Margaret (1751–1800). American Revolutionary patriot. AND; CLC; RAD

Cori, Gerty Theresa (1896–1957). Biochemist, born Czechoslovakia. RIF; SC†; SHFE†; YOF

Cornell, Katharine (1898–1974). Actress. BOC; DI-1†; GIBA†

Cousins, Jane "Casey" (1924–). Real estate executive. LES-1

Cox, Diane (1958?–). Motorcyclist. BUIC

Crabtree, Lotta (1847–1924). Comedienne. MASB

Craft, Ellen (c. 1826–1897). Runaway slave. CHFB; LOAV; STAB-1

Crandall, Prudence (1803–1889). Educator, abolitionist. BUA; CHFB; TRD; WABC†

Crane, Jocelyn (1909–). Zoologist. YOF

Crawford, Jane Todd (1763–1842). Pioneer. RIB

Culver, Carmen (1939–). Television screenwriter. SMBB-2

Curtis, Ann (1926–). Swimmer. HOBA†; HOBAA; JAB

Cushman, Charlotte Saunders (1816–1876). Actress. STJ; VAA; VAB

Cushman, Pauline (1833–1893). Civil War spy. RAB

Dacanay, Pattie. Martial artist. AT

Daley, Cass (1915–1975). Comedienne. MASB

Dalstrom, Ingeborg. Student nurse. WRA

Daniels, Susan (1948–). Psychologist. BOHA-1

Darden, Christine (1942–). Aerospace engineer. FOC-1

Darragh, Lydia B. (1728?–1789). Spy. AND; CLC; KN

Dat-So-La-Lee (1830–1925). Washoe Indian basket maker. WAB

Davies, Mary Carolyn. Poet. BEF

Davis, Belva. Television newscaster. STAA

Davis, Joan (1907–1961). Actress. MASB

Davis, Pauline Wright (1813–1876). Feminist. GUBA†; LES-2

Dawson, Merna. Chemist. HOG

Day, Dorothy (1897–1980). Journalist. BLF; COG-1; NIA; ROJ

Day, Enid. Nurse's aide. WRA

Dean, Laura. Dancer, choreographer. GLO

De Angeli, Marguerite (1889–1987). Author, illustrator. SMB

Decker, Mary (1958–). Track athlete. AAS-26; HOBAA†; LEYB†; ST-2; SUDB

Dee, Ruby (1924?–). Actress. FAG

deLeeuw, Adele (1899–). Author. SMAB

deLeeuw, Cateau (1903–). Author, illustrator. SMAB

deLeeuw, Diane (1956–). Skater, born the Netherlands. VAD-6; VADA

De Mille, Agnes (1908–). Dancer, choreographer. CLA; FOGC; GIB-1; STLA

Densen-Gerber, Judianne (1934–). Psychiatrist. GIB-1

Derricotte, Juliette (1897–1931). Social worker. BUFA

De Varona, Donna (1947–). Swimmer, TV broadcaster. BOHA

Devlin, Wende (1918–). Author, illustrator. SMAB

DeVries, Yuan Lin. Biochemist, polar researcher. LA-1

Dick, Gladys H. (1881–1963). Physician. RIE

Dickey, Sarah (1838–1904). Educator. CHFB

Dickinson, Emily (1830–1886). Poet. BEF; BEGA; EOB; HIG; LEK; MUA; OCB; SIF; STLA; WABC†; WHB

Dickinson, Velvalee. Spy. KN

Didrikson, Babe (Mildred) (1914–1956). Track athlete, golfer. ASB-1; ASBA; CLA; DAG; DAGA; DAJ; DEF; FRB; GED; GEDA; GEE; GIBA; HIA; HOBA; HOBAA; JAB; LEYB; LYB; PACA; PIB; PIBA; RYA; SCA; SID; ST-2; STLA; VAE

Diller, Phyllis (1917–). Comedienne. MASB

Dilworth, Mary Jane (1831–1877). Educator. BUI

Dix, Dorothea Lynde (1802–1887). Reformer. BRBE†; BUA; DAD; DEDA; DOD; FID; MASA; STLA; WABC†; WAJ; YOC

Dodge, Mary Mapes (1831–1905). Author, editor. BEI; COB; STJ; YOC

Dole, Elizabeth (1936–). Ex-Secretary of Transportation. WHE

Donlon, Mary Honor. Jurist. CLA

Door, Rheta Childe (1872–1948). Journalist. JAE

Down, Linda (1956–). University counselor. GLO

Draper, Joanna (b. 1854). Author, former slave. DADB

Draper, Ruth (1884–1956). Actress, comedienne. MASB

Dreschkoff, Gisela. Physicist, polar researcher, born Germany. LA-1

Dressler, Marie (1869–1934). Comedienne, born Canada. MASB

Dunbar, Bonnie (1949–). Astronaut. FOJ-1

Duncan, Isadora (1878–1927). Dancer. EOB; FOGC; MAT-1; STLA; WABC†

Duncan, Marilyn I. (1945?–). Journalist. STAA

Duncan, Rosetta (1900–1959). Comedienne. MASB

Duncan, Vivien (1902–). Comedienne. MASB

Dunham, Katherine (1910–). Dancer. ADA; ADB; FOGC; RIC; RICA

Duniway, Abigail Scott (1834–1915). Feminist. GEE; ROI; WABC

Dunn, Mary Eubanks (1947–). Archaeologist. WIAA-01

Dyer, Mary (1591?–1660). Quaker martyr. CRB; WABC†

Eads, Valerie. Martial artist. AT

Earhart, Amelia (1898–1937). Aviator. BOC; BOJ; COC†; COKA; DOD; ELA; EVD; FAA; GEDB; GIBA; HAMY; HAQ; LAC; LEK; MAT-1; MO; NAB; PA; SMC; STLA; WABC†; WAE; YOC

Eddy, Mary Baker (1821–1910). Christian Science leader. BLF; BUA; KOA; STLA; WABC†

Ederle, Gertrude C. (1906–). Swimmer. BUJA; DAG; DAGA; HOBA; HOBAA; RYA†

Edgren, Edith Svensson (1899?–). Housekeeper, born Sweden. BAEA-1

Edmonds, Sarah Emma (1841–1898). Nurse, spy. FOA; KN; SUG; WABC†

Egan, Sister Jogues (Joan) (1918–). Nun, educator, born Ireland. SMBB-1

Eliot, Martha May (1891–1978). Physician. CHE

Ellington, Anna. Neurologist. BOHE

Ellman, Annie (1950–). Martial artist. AT

Emberley, Barbara (1932–). Author. SMAB

Embery, Joan (1949–). Zoo promoter. GUJ

Emerson, Gladys Anderson (1903–). Biochemist. EMB†; HA-1; YOF

Enright, Elizabeth (1909–1968). Author. SMB

Epstein, Charlotte (1884–1938). Swimming administrator. SLA

Estrada, Isabel. Physician. FOC-1

Ets, Marie Hall (1895–). Author, illustrator. SM

Evans, Dale (1912–). Actress, singer. LA

Evans, Jane (1944–). Mail-order executive. FRBD

Evert, Chris (Christine Marie) (1954–). Tennis player. AAS-29; BELB; FR-1; GLC; GUED; GUH; HOBAA; LAHA; MATA; SUDA

Fairgrave, Phoebe (1903–). Aviator, government official. HIFD

Farber, Bea. Harness racing driver. FOC-1

Farquhar, Jane Colden (1724–1766). Botanist. EMB†; PAC

Farrell, Eileen (1920–). Singer. SAB

Fauset, Crystal Bird (1893–1965). State legislator. LOAV

Fazenda, Louise (1895–1962). Comedienne. MASB

Feelings, Muriel (1938–). Author. SMAB

Fenton, Mildred Adams. Author. SMAB

Fenwick, Millicent (1910–). Congresswoman. WIAA-02

Ferber, Edna (1887–1968). Author. CON; LETA; ROJ

Ferguson, Angella D. (1925–). Pediatrician. HAMA

Fermi, Laura (1907–1977). Author, wife of Enrico Fermi, born Italy. CAHA

Ferraro, Geraldine (1935–). Congresswoman. GLO; WHE

Field, Rachel (1894–1942). Author. BEH

Fields, Mary (1832–1914). Pioneer. BUH; GRAB-02; KADB

Fields, Totie (1931–1978). Comedienne. MASB

Finkelstein, Beatrice. Nutritionist. HOG

Fiorito, Eunice (1930–). Advocate for the disabled. BOHA-1

Fishback, Margaret (1904–1985). Poet. ALA

Fisher, Anna (1949–). Astronaut, physician. FOI-1; HIFD†; RAAG†

Fiske, Minnie Maddern (1865–1932). Actress. DI-1; GIBA†; VAA; WABC†

Fitzgerald, Ella (1918–). Singer. ASB-1

Fleming, Peggy (1948–). Skater. GRBA; HOBA; HOBAA; LEYB; LIEA; LYC; RYA; VADA

Fleming, Williamina (1857–1911). Astronomer, born Scotland. PACB

Floyd, Theodora A. (1896–). Nurse. YOB

Flume, Jimmie. Scientist. HOG

Flynn, Elizabeth Gurley (1890–1964). Communist leader. ARAA

Forsyth, Jane (1929–). Animal trainer. GUJ

Forten, Charlotte (1838–1904). Abolitionist. CHFB

Foster, Abigail Kelley (1810–1887). Abolitionist. LES-2; WABC†

Foster, Gloria (1936–). Actress. AB

Fowler, Lydia Folger (1822–1879). Physician. MASA

Francis, Milly Hadjo (b. 1802). Creek Indian. GRAD

Frankenthaler, Helen (1928–). Painter. FOGB

Franklin, Aretha (1942–). Singer. AB; BUIB-1; JOE

Franklin, Irene (1876–1941). Singer, comedienne. MASB

Fraser, Gretchen Kunigk (1919–). Skier. HOBA; HOBAA; JAB; LEYB

Fratianne, Linda (1960–). Skater. VAD-6

Frederick, Jane (1952–). Track athlete. GLB

Frederick, Pauline (1908–). Radio commentator. CLA

Freeman, Mary Eleanor Wilkins (1852–1930). Author. BEGA

Friedan, Betty (1921–). Author, feminist. GIB-1; WA

Friedmann, Roseli Ocampo (1937–). Microbiologist, polar researcher. LA-1

Frietchie, Barbara (1766–1862). Civil War heroine. DOD

Friganza, Trixie (1870–1955). Comedienne. MASB

Fuchs, Becky (1955?–). Rodeo rider. VADB

Fuller, Margaret (1810–1850). Author, feminist. BOC; GUBA; STLA; WABC

Fuller, Peggy (1955?–). Motorcyclist. BUIC

Gág, Wanda (1893–1946). Author, illustrator. SM

Gannet, Deborah Sampson (fl. 1776). American Revolutionary patriot. AND; CLC; HODA; RAD; ROG; STQ†; WIBA

Garbo, Greta (1905–). Actress, born Sweden. ASB-1

Garland, Judy (1922–1969). Actress, singer. FOR

Garms, Shirley Rudolph (1924–). Bowler. JAB; LEF

Garner, "Kati" (Nancy) (1953–). Diver. HAKA

Gayle, Crystal (1951–). Singer. KRI

Genesko, Lynn (1955–). Swimmer. RYX

Gibson, Althea (1927–). Tennis player. AAS-29; BOF; BRG; FOG; FR-1; HOBA; HOBAA; HOBC; LOAA; PIB; PIBA; RICA; ROJ; RYA†; SMC; SUDA†; VAE

Gilbreth, Lillian M. (1878–1972). Engineer. BOJ; EMB; CLA; LEGA; STLA

Gildersleeve, Virginia Crocheron (1877–1965). Educator. CLA; FLB

Gill, Jocelyn Ruth (1916–). Astronomer. POE

Gilman, Charlotte Perkins (1860–1935). Feminist. NIA

Ginsburg, Ruth Bader (1933–). Jurist. GIB-1; SWI

Glasgow, Nancy Payne (1955?–). Motorcyclist. BUIC

Glennon, Nan. Mechanical engineer. HOG

Goddard, Mary Katherine (1736–1816). Journalist. YOC

Goeppert-Mayer, Maria (1906–1972). Theoretical physicist, born Germany. HA-1; SC†; SHFE

Goldberg, Whoopi (1950–). Actress. MASB

Goldman, Connie. Broadcaster. BOHD

Gonzalez, Natividad Martinez (1907–). Housewife, born Mexico. BAEA-1

Goodrich, Annie Warburton (1866–1954). Nurse. YOB

Goodwin, Ruby Berkley (1903–). Poet. DADB

Gowan, M. Olivia, Sister (1888–). Nurse. YOB

Graff, Sunny. Lawyer, martial artist. AT

Graham, Katharine Meyer (1917–). Publisher. BOHD

Graham, Martha (1893–). Dancer. BOHB; FOGC; STLA

Grant, Micki. Actress, composer, singer. AB

Grasso, Ella (1919–1981). Governor. BOHF; GRAB-1; WHE

Gratz, Rebecca (1781–1869). Philanthropist. GRB-1; LER; LETA; PEB

Gray, Ida (1867–1953). Dentist. LOAV

Greeley-Smith, Nixola (1880–1919). Journalist. JAE

Green, Ernestene (1939–). Archaeologist. WIAA-01

Green, Hetty (1835–1916). Financier. COKB

Green, Nancy (c. 1834–1923). Posed as "Aunt Jemima". GRAB-02

Green, Patricia (1952–). A.M.E. Zion minister. SMBB-1

Greenfield, Elizabeth Taylor (1809–1876). Singer. LOAV; ROF†

Greenhow, Rose O'Neal (1817–1864). Spy. FOA; HAB; SUG; WABC†

Greenwood, Charlotte (1893–1978). Actress. MASB

Gregg, Maxine. Jazz agent. UN

Gregory, Cynthia (1946–). Dancer. BOHB; FOGC

Griffiths, Martha W. (1912–). Congresswoman. GRAB-1

Grimké, Angelina Emily (1805–1879). Abolitionist, feminist. CHFB; GUBA; LES-2; STG; WABC†

Grimké, Sarah Moore (1792–1873). Abolitionist, feminist. CHFB; GUBA; LES-2; NIA; WABC†

Grosman, Tatyana (1904–). Lithographer, born Russia. GIB-1

Grossinger, Jennie (1892–1972). Hotel executive. PAA

Guild, Elizabeth. Psychologist. HOG

Guion, Connie Meyers (1882–1971). Physician. FLA

Guthrie, Janet (1938–). Automobile racer. GUED-1

Guzman, Virginia Quintana (1940?–). Policewoman. SMBC-3

Hader, Berta (1890?–1976). Author, illustrator. SMAB

Hahn, Emily (1905–). Mining engineer, traveler. ROJ

Hale, Lucretia Peabody (1820–1900). Author. BEE; BEI

Hall, Horathel (1928?–). Weaver. FAI

Hall, Karen. Television producer. HOD-1

Hamer, Fannie Lou (1917–). Civil rights leader. BRBE†; DU; FAG; GRAB-01

Hamill, Dorothy (1956–). Skater. GUED; HOBAA; LIEA; VADA

Hamilton, Alice (1869–1970). Physician. BOJ; BRBE; CHD; FLA; HA-1; MASA; PACA; RAAG†; SC†

Hamilton, Edith (1867–1963). Author. STLA

Hanks, Nancy (1927–1983). Chair of National Endowment for the Arts. GIB-1

Hansberry, Lorraine (1930–1965). Playwright. FLBA

Harper, Frances Ellen Watkins (1825–1911). Poet. LOAV; ROE; ROG; WABC†

Harper, Valerie (1940–). Television actress. BOHC

Harris, Emmylou (1947–). Singer. KRI-1

Harris, Julie (1925–). Actress. DI-1

Harris, LaDonna (1931–). Comanche Indian leader. GRAC

Harris, Patricia R. (1924–1985). Ambassador, educator. YOI

Harris, Tonie (1947–). Martial artist. AT

Hart, Nancy (1735–1830). American Revolutionary patriot. AND; CLC

Hart, Pearl (fl. 1903). Criminal. WIAA-2

Hatcher, Orie Latham (1868–1946). Educator, reformer. PACB

Hawkes, Daphne (1938–). Episcopal priest. SMBB-1

Hawn, Goldie (1945–). Actress, motion picture producer. MASB

Hayes, Helen (1900–). Actress. CLA; DI-1; GIBA†

Hayes, Janet Gray Frazee (1926–). Ex-mayor. WIAA-02

Head, Edith (1907–1981). Costume designer. FOG

Hearst, Phoebe Apperson (1842–1919). Philanthropist. CUC

Heckler, Margaret (1931–). Ex-Secretary of Health and Human Services. WHE

Heddy, Kathy (1959?–). Swimmer. GLA

Heiden, Beth (1959–). Skater. HOCG

Heiss, Carol (1940–). Skater. DEF; DEHA-1; HOBA; HOBAA; JAB; LEF; PIBA

Held, Anna (1873–1918). Comedienne, born France. PHA

Heldman, Julie (1945–). Tennis player. SLA

Hellman, Lillian (1905–1984). Playwright, author. DI-1; GIB-1†

Hendee, Hannah (fl. 1780). American Revolutionary heroine. CLC

Henning, Anne (1956?–). Skater. HOBAA†; LEYB†; ST-2

Henry, Marguerite (1902–). Author. SMB

Henze, Cynthia. Aviator. FOC-1

Herford, Beatrice (1868–1952). Comedienne, born England. MASB

Hewitt, Margaret. Nurse-midwife. BOHE

Hicks, Beatrice Alice (1919–). Engineering executive. PAA

Hicks, Nancy. Journalist. STAA

Higgins, Marguerite (1920–1966). Journalist. ARBA; FLBB; JAD; JAE

Higgins, Maureen Anne. F.B.I. agent. SMBC-3

Hightower, Rosella (1920–). Dancer. ATA

Hill, Pamela (1938–). Television producer. SMBB-2

Hill, Patty Smith (1868–1946). Educator. BUDA

Hills, Carla Anderson (1934–). Lawyer, ex-cabinet member. SWI

Hlavaty, Jana (1941–). Skier, born Czechoslovakia. WA-1

Hobby, Oveta Culp (1905–). Ex-cabinet member. STLA

Hoffman, Malvina (1887–1966). Sculptor. CLA; COKA; STLA; WABC†

Hofmann, Adele (1926–). Physician. RAAG

Holiday, Billie (1915–1959). Singer. BRBD; COF-1; JOE; SUH; TEA; TEB; WAD†

Holliday, Judy (1921–1965). Actress. MASB

Hollingworth, Leta Stetter (1886–1939). Psychologist. HA-1; PACB

Holtzman, Elizabeth (1941–). Congresswoman. BOHF

Hopper, Grace Murray (1906–). Computer pioneer. GIB-1; GRAB-3

Horne, Esther Burnett (fl. 1955). Educator. GRAD

Horne, Lena (1917–). Singer. DADB; DOBA; DOF-1; HUC; LEHB; ROF

Horne, Marilyn (1934–). Singer. SAB

Horney, Karen (1885–1952). Psychiatrist, born Germany. FLA; LEG; RAAG†

Hotchkiss, Hazel (1886–1974). Tennis player. HOBAA; SUDA†

Howard, Cordelia (1848–1941). Actress. CAD

Howe, Julia Ward (1819–1910). Feminist. BOC; DAD; DEDA; DEI; DEJ; GIBA†; WABC†

Howell, Emily (1939–). Aviator. GEDB

Huber, Linda. Lawyer. LETD

Huerta, Dolores (1930–). Labor leader. BI; BOHF; DI; NEAA

Hufstedler, Shirley (1925–). Lawyer, jurist. GIB-1

Huggins, Edith. Television newscaster. STAA

Hunter, Alberta (1895–1984). Singer. GIB-1

Hunter-Gault, Charlayne (1942?–). Broadcast journalist. GLO; STAA

Huntley, Joni. Track athlete. GLB

Hutchinson, Anne Marbury (1591–1643). Religious liberal colonist. BLF; CRB; DAD; DOD; JOCA; SMC; VIA; WABC; WAR; YOC

Hutton, Barbara (1912–1979). Millionaire heiress. COKB

Huxtable, Ada Louise (1921–). Architecture critic, author. GIB-1

Indian Emily (d. 1873). Apache Indian girl. WAB

Irwin, May (1862–1938). Comedienne, born Canada. MASB

Irwin-Williams, Cynthia (1936–). Archaeologist. WIAA-01

Jackson, Mahalia (1911–1972). Singer. HUC; JOE

Jackson, Margaret. Physiologist. HOG

Jackson, Nell (1929–). Track athlete, educator. BOHA

Jackson, Shirley. Theoretical physicist. CAF-1

Jackson, Suzanne (1944–). Painter. FOGB

Jacobi, Mary Putnam (1842–1906). Physician. FLA; HUE; MASA; RAAG†; WABC†

Jacobs, Helen (1908–). Tennis player. FR-1; SUDA†

Jacobs-Bond, Carrie (1862–1946). Songwriter. MOA; STJ

Jaissle, Louise. Nurse. WRA

Jamison, Judith (1944–). Dancer. BOHB; FOGC

Janis, Elsie (1889–1956). Mimic. MASB

Jarvis, Lucy (1919–). Television producer. GIB-1

Jeffries, Rosalind (1930?–). Painter. FAI

Jenkins, Carol (1944–). Television newscaster. STAA

Jenson, Dylana (1961–). Violinist. SC-02

Jewett, Sarah Orne (1849–1909). Author. BEGA

Johnson, Dammy Williams. Rodeo rider. VADB

Johnson, Osa Helen (1894–1953). Photographer. COKA

Johnson, Trudy (1965?–). Rodeo rider. VADB

Jonasson, Olga (1934–). Transplant surgeon. RAAG

Jones, Lois. Geologist, polar researcher. LA-1

Jones, Mary Harris (1830–1930). Labor leader, born Ireland. BI; BRBE†; GEE; MAV; NIA; PACA; TRD; WABC†

Jong, Erica (1942–). Author, poet. GL-1

Joplin, Janis (1943–1970). Singer. BUIB-1

Jordan, Barbara C. (1936–). Congresswoman. BOHF; GRAB-1; YOI

Jordan, Marian Driscoll (1898–1961). Comedienne. BUR-1

Jordan, Sara (1884–1959). Physician. FLA

Joyce, Joan (1940–). Softball player. GUED-1; HOBAA

Juana Maria. Indian princess. WIAA-2

Kahn, Madeline (1942–). Actress, singer. MASB

Kandler, Elizabeth Aytes. Superintendent of corrections. SMBC-3

Kane, Helen (1904–1966). Singer, comedienne. MASB

Kanokogi, Rusty (1935–). Martial artist. AT

Karansky, Priscilla Pepper. Mounted police officer. SMBC-3

Kassebaum, Nancy Landon (1932–). Senator. WIAA-02

Kaye, Nora (1920–1987). Dancer. ATA

Kearse, Amalya (1937–). Jurist. GLO

Keller, Helen Adams (1880–1968). Author. BEC; BOC; CAD; DOD; EVA; EVD; FAA; FOR; FRE; GIBA; MAJ; STLA; WAJ

Kelley, Florence (1859–1932). Social worker. BRBE; WABC†

Kelley, Jane Holden (1928–). Archaeologist. WIAA-01

Kelly, Patsy (1910–1981). Actress. MASB

Kelsey, Frances Oldham (1914–). Physician, born Canada. EOA; TRD

Kempner, Mary Jean. Navy nurse, WW II. WRA

Kilgallen, Dorothy (1913–1965). Journalist. JAE

Kimbrell, Marketa (1928–). Actress, born Czechoslovakia. WA

King, Billie Jean (1943–). Tennis player. AAS-29; FR-1; GIB-1; GLC; HI; HOBA; HOBAA; JABA; KOA; LAHA; MATA; RYA; RYX; ST-2; SUDA

King, Coretta Scott (1927–). Civil rights leader. FAG; GIBA

King, Micki (Maxine Joyce) (1944–). Diver. BOHA; HOBAA; JABA; LEYB†; RYA†; RYX; ST-2

Kirk, Tammy Jo (1964–). Motorcyclist. BUIC

Kirkland, Gelsey (1952–). Dancer. FOGC

Kitt, Eartha (1928–). Singer. DADB; ROF

Koontz, Elizabeth (1919–). Educator, civil rights activist. GIB-1

Korris, Risa (1946–). Television camera woman. SMBB-2

Kraus, Mary Ellen. Air traffic controller. SMBC-2

Krupsak, Mary Anne (1932–). State official. GRAB-1

Kübler-Ross, Elisabeth (1926–). Psychiatrist, born Switzerland. BOHE; GIB-1

Kuhn, Irene Corbally (1900–). Journalist. JAE

Kuhn, Margaret (1905–). Social reformer. COG-1; GIB-1

Kupper, Sandy. Fire fighter. FOC-1

Kusner, Kathy (1940?–). Jockey. GUED; HOBA; HOBAA; RYA

Ladewig, Marion (1914?–). Bowler. HOBA; HOBAA

LaFontant, Jewel Stradford (1922–). Lawyer. SWI

Lally, Grace. Nurse. WRA

Lane, Lydia (fl. 1863). Pioneer. NAA

Laney, Lucy (1854–1933). Educator. BRB; BUDA†

Lange, Dorothea (1895–1965). Photographer. STLA; SUAA

Langer, Susanne Katherine (1895–1985). Philosopher. STLA

Langford, Anna Riggs (1917–). Lawyer. DRA; DU

Langston, Dicey. American Revolutionary patriot. CAGA

Larrieu, Francie (1952–). Track athlete. HOBAA; JABA; LEYB†

Lathrop, Julia Clifford (1858–1932). Social worker. BRBE†; MEB

Lathrop, Rose Hawthorne (Mother Mary Alphonsa) (1851–1926). Philanthropist, nun. MAK; WRA; YOC

Law, Ruth (1887–). Aviator. GEDB†; HIFD

Lawrence, Andrea Mead (1932–). Skier. HOBA; HOBAA; LEYB

Lawrence, Geraldine Anderson. Border Patrol agent. SMBC-3

Lawson, Roberta Campbell (1878–1940). Community leader. GRAD

Lazarus, Emma (1849–1887). Poet. DOD; GRB-1; GUB; LEK; LER; LETA; PEB

Lee, Ann (1736–1784). Religious mystic. AND; BLF; WABC

Lee, Judy Ann. Aviator. SMBC-2

Leibovitz, Annie (1949–). Photojournalist. BOHD

Lenroot, Katharine F. (1891–). Social worker. CLA

Lenski, Lois (1893–1974). Author, illustrator. SM

Leone, Lucile Petry (1902–). Nurse. YOB

Lewis, Edmonia (1845–1890). Sculptor. ADA; ADB; KADB; ROG

Lewis, Idawally (1814–1910). Lighthouse keeper. CAD; DOD

Lewis, Margaret. Pioneer. STJ

Lewis, Mary Edmonia (1846–1890). Sculptor. LOAV

Lewis, Tillie (1901–1977). Food packing executive. LES-1

Libow, Carol. Lawyer. LETD

Lieberman, Nancy (1958–). Basketball player. SLA

Lindbergh, Anne Morrow (1906–). Aviator, author. GEDB

Livingston, Susan (fl. 1779). American Revolutionary patriot. TRD

Lockwood, Belva Ann (1830–1917). Lawyer, feminist. BOJ; WABC

Loeb, Sophie Irene (1876–1929). Journalist, reformer, born Russia. LER

Logan, Myra Adele (1908–1977). Surgeon. HA-1; RAAG†

Lomax, Almena. Journalist. STAA

Long, Jane W. (1798–1880). Pioneer. MAO

Long, Loretta. Actress. BOHD

Loock, Christine. Diver. GLA

Lopez, Nancy (1957–). Golfer. GUED-1

Loughborough, Mary Ann Webster (1836–1887). Diarist. MAV

Louvestre, Mary (fl. 1861). Slave. HAB

Love, Nancy. Aviator. HIFD

Low, Juliette (1860–1927). Founder of Girl Scouts. DOD; PACA

Lowell, Amy (1874–1925). Poet. BEGA; MUA; SIF

Luce, Clare Boothe (1903–1987). Playwright, ambassadoor. CLA; GRAB-1

Lucid, Shannon (1943–). Astronaut. FOJ-1

Ludington, Sybil (1761–1839). American Revolutionary patriot. CAD; CLC

Lynn, Janet (1953–). Skater. HOBAA; JABA; RYX; VAD-6; VADA

Lynn, Judy (1936–). Singer. LA

Lynn, Loretta (1935–). Singer. BUIB-01

Lyon, Mary (1797–1849). Educator. BOC; BOJ; BUDA; COG; CUC; DAD; DOD; FLB; FRC; LEJA; STLA; VAB; WABC†

Mabley, Jackie "Moms" (1897–1975). Comedienne. MASB

McAuliffe, Christa (1948–1986). Astronaut, teacher. COE-1

McCauley, Mary (Molly Pitcher) (1754–1832). American Revolutionary patriot. AND; CLC; DOD; LEAA; LEK; LOA†; PA; STJ

McClintock, Barbara (1902–). Geneticist. SHFE

McCormick, Anne O'Hare (1881–1954). Journalist. CLA; WABC†

McCormick, Patricia Keller (1930–). Diver. HOBA; HOBAA

McCullough, Geraldine (1922–). Sculptor. ADB

McCutcheon, Floretta Doty (1888–1967). Bowler. HOBA; HOBAA; JAB

McDowell, Mary E. (1854–1936). Social reformer. PACB; WABC†

McGinley, Phyllis (1905–1978). Author, poet. ALA

McGinnis, Terri (1947–). Veterinarian. GUJ

MacInnis, Nina (1954–). Swimmer. RYX

McKinney, Nina Mae (1913–1967). Actress. LOAV

McKinney, Sally Zumaris (1915–). Nurse. COFA

MacLaine, Shirley (1934–). Actress. FOGC; ROJ

McMahon, Jenna (Mary Virginia Skinner) (1933–). Comedienne, television writer. BUR-1

McNamara, Rae Hassell. State director of prisons. SMBC-3

McNeer, May (1902–). Author. SMAB

McPartland, Marian (1920–). Pianist, born England. UN

McPherson, Aimee Semple (1890–1944). Evangelist. WIAA-2

McWhinnie, Mary Alice (d. 1980). Biologist, polar researcher. LA-1

Macy, Anne Sullivan (1866–1936). Teacher of Helen Keller. FAA†; LEJA; SMC; STJ; STLA

Mahoney, Mary Eliza (1845–1926). Nurse. LOAV

Mangrulkar, Latika. Social worker, born India. FOC-1

Mann, Helen. Mathematician. HOG

Manning, Madeline (1948–). Track athlete. SUDB

Marble, Alice (1913–). Tennis player. FR-1; JAB; SUDA†

Marlowe, Julia (1866–1950). Actress. VAA; WABC†

Marshall, Paule (1929–). Author. GLO

Martin, Andrea. Comedienne. MASB

Martin, Sylvia Wene (1930–). Bowler. HOBA; SLA

Martinez, Maria Montoya (b. 1881). Pueblo Indian pottery maker. GRAC; GRAD; LEH; WAB

Marvin, Ursula (1921–). Geologist, polar researcher. LA-1

Mary Loyola, Sister. Missionary. ROI

Mason, Biddy (1818–1891). Businesswoman. BUH; GRAB-02; KADB; STQ†

May, Elaine (1932–). Actress, comedienne, motion picture director. BUR-1; MASB

Maymi, Carmen Rosa (1938–). Government official. NEBB; WH-2

Mead, Margaret (1901–1978). Anthropologist. BOHG; CLA; COLA; DU-1; EMB; GIB-1†; HAO; KE†; KOA; NAB; PACA; STLA

Mead, Sylvia Earle (1935–). Aquanaut, oceanographer. GL; HA-1; HAKA

Meara, Anne (1933–). Actress, comedienne. BUR-1; MASB

Meggers, Betty J. (1921–). Anthropologist. PAC

Meléndez, Cóncha (1904–). Puerto Rican poet, educator. NEBB

Menken, Adah Isaacs (1835?–1868). Actress. RAB

Mentschikoff, Soia (1915–). Lawyer. SMBB; SWI

Meyer, Deborah (1952–). Swimmer. HOBAA†; LEYB

Midler, Bette (c. 1945–). Singer, actress. MASB

Millay, Edna St. Vincent (1892–1950). Poet. BEGA; FRB; GIBA†; LEJ; LEOB; MUA; OCB; SIF; STLA; WHB

Miller, Dorothy Canning (1904–). Museum curator. GIB-1

Miller, Kathy (1964?–). Track athlete. HAFA

Miller, Marilyn (1898–1936). PHA

Mink, Patsy Takemoto (1927–). Congresswoman. BOHF

Mitchell, Margaret (1900–1949). Author. CON; OCB

Mitchell, Maria (1818–1889). Astronomer. CAD; DOD; EMB†; GEE; GIBA; MAV; SC; STJ; STLA; VAB; WABC; WAE; YOC

Mitchell, Mildred. Bionicist. HOG

Mock, Jerrie (Geraldine) (1925–). Aviator. GEDB

Modjeska, Helena (1840–1909). Actress, born Poland. MANB; PIAA

Moise, Penina (1797–1880). Hebrew religious educator. LER; LETA

Monroe, Harriet (1861–1936). Poet. STLA

Montana, Patsy (1914–). Singer. LA

Moody, Anne (1940–). Civil rights worker. AKB; DADB

Moody, Lady Deborah (1600–1669?). First woman landowner in America. CRB; JOCA; WABC†

Moore, Anne Carroll (1871–1961). Librarian. FOG

Moore, Beverly. Lawyer. LETD

Moran, Polly (1883–1952). Comedienne. MASB

Moreno, Rita (1931–). Actress. DI-1†; WO

Morgan, Barbara (1900–). Photographer. BOHB

Morgan, Norma (1928–). Painter. FAH

Morris, Clara (1848–1925). Actress. STJ

Morris, Kathryn Harper. Airport security agent. SMBC-3

Moses, Anna Mary Robertson (Grandma Moses) (1860–1961). Painter. CUC; FOGB; PA

Motley, Constance Baker (1921–). Jurist. DU; FLD; GIB-1; STLA; YOI

Mott, Lucretia Coffin (1793–1880). Feminist, abolitionist. COG; GIBA†; GUBA; LES-2; STJ; STLA; WABC; WAR; YOC

Mountain Wolf Woman (1884–1960). Winnebago Indian. MAV

Moylan, Mary Ellen (1926–). Dancer. ATA

Muldowney, Shirley. Automobile racer. OLDA; ST-2

Muller-Schwarze, Christine. Psychologist, polar researcher, born Germany. LA-1

Murphy, Betty Southard (1929?–). Lawyer. SWI

Murray, Mary Lindley (fl. 1776). American Revolutionary patriot. CLC

Myers, Joyce Carpenter. Aeronautical engineer. SMBC-2

Myerson, Bess (1924–). Municipal official. BOHF; GRB-1

Nash, Alice Morrison (1879?–1966). Educator. FLB

Navratilova, Martina (1956–). Tennis player, born Czechoslovakia. AAS-29; ASB-1; FR-1

Nelson, Cindy (1955–). Skier. GUED; JABA; WA-1

Neosho (b. 1846). Creek Indian patriot. WAB

Nevelson, Louise (1900–1988). Sculptor, born Russia. BOHB; FOGB; GIB-1

Newsome, Effie Lee (b. 1885). Poet. ROE

Nichol, Kathryn (1937–). Pediatrician. BOHE

Nichols, Ruth (1901–1960). Aviator. GEDB†; HIFD

Nitschelm, Terry. Hotel owner. PAA

Normand, Mabel (1892–1930). Actress. MASB

Norton, Eleanor Holmes (1937–). Lawyer. GIB-1; LETD; WA

Norwood, Virginia. Physicist. HOG

Nutting, Mary Adelaide (1858–1948). Nursing educator, born Canada. YOB

Nyad, Diana (1950–). Swimmer. GLA; GUED-1; HOBAA†

Oakley, Annie (1860–1926). Markswoman. DAG; DAGA; KIB; WAE

O'Connor, Sandra Day (1930–). Supreme Court justice. DU-1; SMBB; WHE

O'Hara, Dee. Nurse. COFA; HOG†

O'Keeffe, Georgia (1887–1986). Painter. CLA; FOGB; GIBA; NE

Oliver, Donna. Psychologist, polar researcher. LA-1

Olson, Edith. Chemist. HOG

O'Neal, Regina. Television producer. FOC-1

Orchard, Sadie (1863?–1943). Frontierswoman. RAB

Osborne, Estelle Massey (1903–). Nurse. YOB

Owens, Elisabeth. Lawyer. SWI

Owens-Adair, Bethenia (1840–1926). Physician. ARB; BLC; JOB

Palmer, Alice Freeman (1855–1902). Educator. BUDA†; FLB; VAB

Parker, Dorothy (1893–1967). Author. ALA; OCB

Parker, Sarah Jessica. Actress. BRE-1

Parks, Rosa Lee (1913–). Civil rights leader. COG-1; DOF-1; STF

Parry, Zale (1933–). Underwater diving actress. HAKA

Parton, Dolly (1946–). Singer. BUIB-01; KRI-1

Patrick, Ruth (1907–). Ecologist. EMB

Peabody, Elizabeth Palmer (1804–1894). Educator. BUDA†; FLB; LEK; WABC†

Pearce, Louise (1885–1959). Physician. FLA

Pearl, Minnie (Sarah Ophelia Colley) (1912–). Comedienne. HAG-1; MASB

Pearson, Flora (1851–1925). Pioneer. BUI

Peck, Annie Smith (1850–1935). Mountaineer. PACB

Peden, Irene. Electrical engineer, polar researcher. LA-1

Peg-Leg Annie (1860?–1933). Frontierswoman. RAB

Pence, Donna Marie. Narcotics agent. SMBC-3

Peppler, Mary Jo (1945?–). Bicyclist. HOBAA

Perkins, Frances (1882–1965). Social worker, cabinet member. BI; BOC; CLA; SMC; WABC; WHE

Perry, Jean. Journalist. STAA

Petersham, Maud (1889–1971). Author, illustrator. SMAB

Peterson, Esther Eggertsen (1906–). Ex-Director of Consumer Affairs. WIAA-02

Peterson, Helen L. (1915–). Indian leader, government official. GRAC

Petry, Ann (1911–). Author. RIC; RICA

Phillips, Vel (1924–). Government official. YOI

Piccard, Jeannette R. (1895–1981). Episcopal priest. BLF†; SMBB-1

Pickersgill, Mary (fl. 1814). Flagmaker. CLC

Picon, Molly (1898–). Actress. MASB

Picotte, Susan LaFlesche (1865–1915). Physician. GRAD; RAAG†

Pilpel, Harriet Fleischl (1911–). Lawyer. SWI

Pinckney, Eliza Lucas (1723–1793). Agronomist. GUBA†; SC†; WABC

Pini, Wendy. Cartoonist. GOB-1

Pious, Minerva (1909–1979). Comedienne, born Russia. MASB

Pirtle, Sue. Rodeo rider. VADB

Pitou, Penny. Skier. HOBA

Pittman, Dorothy Hughes (1938–). Educator. WA

Pitts, Zasu (1894?–1963). Actress. MASB

Pleasant, Mary Ellen (Mammy) (1814?–1904). Businesswoman. BUH; LOAV; STQ†; WIAA-2

Pocahontas (1595?–1617). Indian princess. CAD; DOD; GRAD; HEC; LEH; LEPF; PA; STJ; VIA; WAB; WABC

Polier, Justine Wise (1903–). Jurist. GIB-1

Ponselle, Rosa (1897–1981). Singer. STLA

Porter, Sylvia (1913–). Columnist. BOHG; GIB-1; LEU

Poston, Ersa Hines (1921–). State official. YOI

Pouissant, Renee (1944–). Television newscaster. SMBB-2

Pressly, Eleanor C. (1918–). Aeronautical engineer. HOG

Price, Florence Beatrice Smith (1888–1933). Composer. LOAV

Price, Leontyne (1927–). Singer. ADB; DOF-1; ROF; SAB; SC-02

Priest, Ivy Baker (1905–1975). Federal government official. FOG

Prince, Lucy Terry (1731–1821). Poet. KADB

Prochazka, Anne (1897–). Nurse, born Czechoslovakia. YOB

Proctor, Barbara Gardner (1932–). Advertising executive. FRBD

Prudom, Benjie Bell Elizabeth. Rodeo clown. VADB

Queler, Eve (1936–). Conductor. WA

Quimby, Edith Hinkley (1891–1982). Biophysicist. EMB†; YOF

Quimby, Harriet (1884–1912). Aviator. GEDB†; HIFD

Rader, Peta (1952–). GUJ

Radner, Gilda (1946–). Actress. MASB

Raggio, Louise Ballerstedt (1919–). Lawyer. SWI

Rainey, Ma (Gertrude Malissa Nix Pridgett) (1886–1939). Singer. JOE; SUH; WAD†

Ramcharan, Savitri (1923–). Physician, researcher, born Trinidad. RAAG

Ramey, Estelle (1917–). Endocrinologist, physiologist. BOHE

Ramos, Elaine Abraham. Educator. GRAD

Rand, Suzanne (1950–). Comedienne. MASB

Rankin, Jeannette (1880–1973). Congresswoman. FOJ; GRAB-1; WABC†; WHE

Rankin, Judy (Judith Torleumke) (1945–). Golfer. GUED

Rasmussen, Zora. Comedienne. MASB

Rawlings, Marjorie Kinnan (1896–1953). Author. CON

Ray, Dixy Lee (1914–). Ex-governor, marine biologist. EMB†; GRAB-1†; WIAA-02

Raye, Martha (1916–). Singer, comedienne. MASB

Redford, Lola (1938–). Ecologist. WA

Reed, Janet (1916–). Dancer, ballet mistress. ATA

Reed, Virginia (b. 1833). Pioneer with Donner party. FOC

Rehan, Ada (1860–1916). Actress, born Ireland. VAA

Remond, Sarah Parker (1826–1894). Abolitionist. GRAB-05

Resnik, Judith (1949–1986). Astronaut. COE-1; FOJ-1

Reynolds, Malvina (1899?–). Composer, singer. BOHC

Richards, Ellen Swallow (1842–1911). Chemist. SC; WABC†

Richards, Laura E. (1850–1943). Poet. BEF; BEH

Richards, Linda Ann (1841–1930). Nurse. COFA; WABC†; WAJ

Richey, Anne (d. 1922). Rustler. RAB

Ride, Sally (1951–). Astronaut. DU-1; FOJ-1

Rigby, Cathy (1952–). Gymnast. HOBAA; LIE; RYA†; RYX; ST-2

Riggin, Aileen (1906–). Diver. HOBA†; JAB

Ringgold, Faith. Painter. FAH

Rivers, Joan (c. 1935–). Comedienne. MASB

Rivlin, Alice Mitchell (1930?–). Economist. BOHG

Robbins, Mary Louise (1912–). Microbiologist. BOHE

Rock, Lee Curry. Engineer. HOG

Rodriguez-Trias, Helen. Pediatrician, social reformer. GLO

Roebling, Mary G. (1906–). Banker. LES-1

Rollin, Betty (1936–). Author, television correspondent. SMBB-2

Roman, Nancy Grace (1925–). Astronomer. HOG; POE

Ronstadt, Linda (1946–). Singer. BUIB-2; KRI

Roosevelt, Eleanor (1884–1962). Author, humanitarian, wife of Franklin Delano Roosevelt. ASB-1; BAG; BAG-1; BLG; BOC; BRBE; COG; COG-1; CUC; DABB; DAD; GIBA; KE; KEE; KL; LAI; MAA; MAU; MEB; PA; PRB; ROH; ROHA; SMC; STLA; WABC†; WAR; YOA

Rose, Ernestine Potowski (1810–1892). Feminist, born Poland. EIA; GUBA; JOCA; LES-2; LETA

Ross, Betsy (1752–1836). Legendary maker of first American flag. AND; DOD; LOA†; STJ

Ross, Diana (1944–). Singer, actress. AB; BOHC; BUIB-2

Ross, Ruth N. Journalist. STAA

Rowlandson, Mary (c. 1635–1678). Indian captive. DI

Rowson, Susanna Haswell (1762–1824). Actress, born England. DOG

Royall, Anne Newport (1769–1854). Traveler, author. ARB

Rubin, Vera C. (1928–). Astronomer. GL

Rubinstein, Helena (1870?–1965). Cosmetician, born Poland. LIA

Rudkin, Margaret Fogharty (1897–1967). Bakery executive. LAH; LES-1; PAA

Rudnick, Dorothea (1907–). Embryologist. YOF

Rudolph, Wilma G. (1940–). Track athlete. DAFB; DAJ; GEA; GED; GEDA; HIA; HOBA; HOBAA; JAB; LEYB; LYD; OCA; RYA

Ruether, Rosemary (1936–). Author, educator. GIB-1

Ruffin, Josephine St. Pierre (1842–1924). Civil rights leader. GRAB-01

Russell, Elizabeth Shull (1913–). Geneticist. YOF

Rydstrom, Pat. Histopathologist. HOG

Rzewska, Josepha Rozanka (1899–). Librarian, born Poland. BAEA-1

Sabin, Florence Rena (1871–1953). Anatomist. BUDA; FOG; HA-1; STLA

Sacajawea (1787–1812). Shoshone Indian guide. BEC; BUI; DOD; FOR; GRAD; HEC; LEK; ROI; STJ; WAB; WABC

St. Johns, Adela Rogers (1894–). Journalist. JAE

Sainte-Marie, Buffy (1942?–). Singer, composer. BOHC

Sampter, Jessie (b. 1883?). Poet, Zionist. ALD

Sanchez, Yolanda. Human services consultant, reformer. GLO

Sanders, Harriet (1834–1909). Pioneer. JOB

Sanders, Marlene (1931–). Television producer. WA

Sanger, Margaret (1883–1966). Nurse, leader in birth control movement. ARAA; ARB; BRBE; GIBA; KOA; ROJ; SC; STLA; WABC

Sansan. Author, born China. CAHA

Sarton, May (1912–). Author, poet, born Belgium. OCB

Sasso, Sandy (1947–). Rabbi. SMBB-1

Saunders, Suzanne. Lawyer. HOD-1

Savage, Augusta Christine (1900–1962). Sculptor. BEBA

Sawyer, Helen (1905–). Astronomer. YOF

Scharff-Goldhaber, Gertrude (1911–). Physicist. PAC

Schimmel, Gertrude (1918–). Policewoman. WA

Schmidt, Kathy (1953–). Javelin thrower. GLB

Schroeder, Patricia Scott (1940–). Congresswoman. GRAB-1†; SWI; WHE

Schumann-Heink, Ernestine (1861–1936). Singer, born Austria. MAT-1

Scott, Hazel (1920–1981). Pianist. BOG

Scott, Irene Feagin (1912–). Judge. SWI

Scott, Nan. Microbiologist, polar researcher. LA-1

Scott Brown, Denise (1931–). Architect, born South Africa. GIB-1

Sears, Eleanora (1881–1968). Sportswoman. HOBA; HOBAA; RYA†

Seddon, Margaret Rhea (1947–). Astronaut, surgeon. FOC-1; FOJ-1; HIFD; SMBC-2

Seeger, Ruth Crawford (1901–1953). Composer. SC-02

Seibert, Florence Barbara (1897–). Biochemist. GEA

Seton, Elizabeth Ann (1774–1821). Saint. ASB; BLF†; CUC; DAD-1; WABC†

Shank, Theresa (1951?–). Basketball player. ST-2

Sharpless, Nansie (1932–). Biochemist. BOHA-1

Shaver, Dorothy (1897–1959). Department store executive. BOJ; CLA; FRBD; LES-1

Shaw, Anna Howard (1847–1919). Feminist, born England. LES-2; MAV

Shea, Julie (1959–). Track athlete. SUDB

Sheehy, Gail (1937–). Journalist, author. LETB

Sidney, Margaret, pseud. (1844–1924). Author. BEI

Siebert, Muriel (1932–). Economist. GIB-1; GL; GLO

Sills, Beverly (1929–). Singer. DU-1; GLO; SAB; SC-02

Sinclair, Sue (1954–). Aquarium animal trainer. GUJ

Skinner, Cornelia Otis (1901–1979). Actress, author. BEE

Skrzypiec, Tina Marie. Boom operator. SMBC-2

Slade, Maria Virginia (Molly). Outlaw's wife. JOB

Slocum, Fanny (1773–1847). Indian captive. HEE

Smethurst, Ann Orlitski. Aviator. SMBC-2

Smith, Bessie (1894–1937). Singer. HUC; JOE; SUH; TEA; TEB; WAD†

Smith, Elinor (1910–). Aviator. HIFD

Smith, Kate (1909–1986). Singer. GEA

Smith, Linda. Dentist. FOC-1

Smith, Margaret Chase (1897–). Senator. CLA; GIBA; GRAB-1; STLA; TRD; WHE

Smith, Robyn C. (1944?–). Jockey. ST-2

Smith, Stacy. Skater. VAD-6

Smith, Vicki. Judo expert. LYE

Snowe, Olympia (1947–). Congresswoman. WHE

Snyder, Grace (1882–). Pioneer. JOB

Sokol, Marilyn. Comedienne. MASB

Souter, Judy Cook (1944–). Bowler. HOBAA†; JABA

Sperber, Paula (1951–). Bowler. HOBAA†; RYX

Spiro, Jo Anne. Martial artist. FOC-1

Sprecher, Jenna Garman. Marine patrol officer. SMBC-3

Stanton, Elizabeth Cady (1815–1902). Feminist. ARAA; BUA; COG; DEDA; GIBA†; GUBA; JOCA; LES-2; MAM; MAV; NIA; PACA; WABC†

Stanton, Susan Marie. Jailer. SMBC-3

Starbuck, Jo Jo. Ice skater. VAD-6

Stark, Shirley (1927–). Sculptor. FAI

Starr, Belle (1848–1889). Outlaw. JOBA; RAB; SUJ

Staupers, Mable Keaton (1890–). Nurse, civil rights leader, born West Indies. DOF-1

Stein, Gertrude (1874–1946). Author. KE; MUA; STLA; WABC†

Steinem, Gloria (1934–). Feminist. GIB-1; KOA; WA

Steloff, Frances (b. 1887). Bookseller. GIB-1; WABC†

Stender, Fay. Lawyer. LETD

Stenersen, Johanna (1959?–). Motorcyclist. BUIC

Stern, Elizabeth Gertrude (1890–1954). Author. MAV

Stevenson, Sybil Jordan. Telecommunications executive. HOD-1

Steward, Susan McKinney (1848–1918). Physician. LOAV

Stewart, Ella Phillips (1893–). Pharmacologist. LOAV

Stewart, Ellen. Theater producer, founder. GIB-1; GLO

Stewart, Isabel Maitland (1878–1963). Nurse, born Canada. YOB

Stewart, Maria W. (1803–1879). Abolitionist. GRAB-05; WABC†

Stinson, Katherine (1893–1977). Aviator, engineer. GEDB†; HIFD

Stone, Lucy (1818–1893). Feminist. DEDA; GUBA; LES-2; WABC

Storch, Marcia (1933–). Physician. LETC; WA

Stout, Penelope Thomson (1622–1732). CRB

Stowe, Harriet Beecher (1811–1896). Author. BEGA; BOA; BOC; DEI; DEJ; DOD; GIBA; JOCA; SMC; STJ; STLA; VAB; WABC†; WHB

Strong, Anna Louise (1885–1970). Journalist. NIA

Stutz, Geraldine. Department store executive. GLO

Sullivan, Kathryn (1951–). Astronaut. FOJ-1

Summer, Donna (1948–). Singer. BUIB-1

Swain, Clara A. (1834–1910). Physician. FLA

Swisshelm, Jane Grey (1815–1884). Journalist. JAE

Switzer, Kathy. Track athlete. BELB; HOBAA†

Szold, Henrietta (1860–1945). Zionist leader. BLF; GUB; KAD; LES; LETA

Tabor, Baby Doe (Elizabeth Donduel) (1854–1935). Frontierswoman. RAB; WIAA-2

Talbert, Mary Burnett (1866–1923). Civil rights leader. DOF-1; GRAB-01

Tallchief, Maria (1925–). Dancer. ATA; FOGC; GRAD

Tallchief, Marjorie (1927–). Dancer. ATA; GRAD

Tanguay, Eva (1878–1947). Entertainer, born Canada. MASB

Tarbell, Ida Minerva (1857–1944). Author. COGB; DAD; WABC†; YOC

Taussig, Helen Brooke (1898–1986). Physician. CHE; CLA; EOA; GIB-1; RAAG

Taylor, Susie King (1848–1912). Nurse, teacher. MAV

Teasdale, Sara (1884–1933). Poet. BRBB

Tekakwitha, Kateri (1656–1680). Mohawk Indian nun. DAD-1; HED

Terrell, Mary Church (1863–1954). Feminist. ADA; ADB; LOAV; STAB-1; STB

Tharp, Twyla (1941–). Dancer, choreographer. FOGC

Thaxter, Celia (1835–1894). Poet. BEF

Thelwell, Jeanne (1951–). Lawyer. SMBB

Thomas, Jeanette. Animal behaviorist, polar researcher. LA-1

Thompson, Carolyn (1957–). State legislator. HOD-1

Thompson, Dorothy (1894–1961). Journalist. JAE; MUA

Thompson, Era Bell (fl. 1946). Editor. DADB

Thompson, Jenn. Actress. BRF-1

Thurman, Sammy Fancher. Rodeo rider. VADB

Todd, Thelma (1905–1935). Actress. MASB

Tolliver, Melba. Television news reporter. STAA

Tomlin, Lily (1939–). Actress. BOHC; MASB

Torres, Liz. Actress. MASB

Toussaint, Cheryl (1953?–). Track athlete. RYX

Townsend, Marjorie (1930–). Electronics engineer. HOG

Townsend, Sally (1760–1842). American Revolutionary patriot. CLC; STJ

Trahey, Jane (1923–). Advertising executive. LES-1

Trammell, Beatrice Johnson. Nurse. BOG

Trujillo, Brenda. Trucking manager. FOC-1

Truth, Sojourner (1797–1883). Abolitionist. ADA; ADB; BEJ; BLE; BLF†; BRB; DADA; GIBA; JO; LES-2; LOAV; WABC†; WAH

Tubbs, Alice Huckert (Poker Alice) (1851–1930). Gambler, born England. RAB

Tubman, Harriet (1820–1913). Abolitionist. ADA; ADB; BEJ; BRB; BRBD; BRBE; BRG; BUA; COG; DADA; DOD; GEE; GIBA; HODA; HUA; HUB; JOC; LOAV; NIA; ROG; SMC; STD; STJA; STLA; WABC†; WAH; YOC; YOI

Tuchman, Barbara (1912?–). Historian. BOHG

Tucker, Sophie (1884–1966). Singer, entertainer. MASB

Tucker, Tanya (1958–). Singer. KRI-1

Turton, Janene (1954?–). Motorcyclist. BUIC

Tyler, Robin. Comedienne. MASB

Tyson, Cicely (1939?–). Actress. AB; BOHC

Tyus, Wyomia (1945–). Track athlete. HOBAA; RYA†; ST-2

Uchida, Miki Akiyama (1903–). Businesswoman, born Japan. BAEA-1

Van Lew, Elizabeth (1818–1900). Spy. FOA; SUG; WABC†

Van Straten, Florence (1913–). Meteorologist. EMB†; YOF

Van Wolvelaere, Patty (1951?–). Track athlete. GLB

Varner, Margaret (1927–). Squash racquets player. JAB

Velarde, Pablita (1918–). Painter. GRAD; WAB

Verrett, Shirley (1933?–). Singer. GRBA

Victor, Wilma L. Educator, government official. GRAD

Viorst, Judith. Author. BOHD

Vollmar, Jocelyn (1925–). Dancer. ATA

Von Saltza, Susan Christina (1944–). Swimmer. GED; GEDA; HOBA; HOBAA; LEYB†

Vorse, Mary Heaton (1874–1966). Journalist, author. BI

Vreeland, Diana. Museum consultant, born France. GIB-1

Wald, Lillian D. (1867–1940). Social worker. ALD; BRBE†; CAGA; DOD; EIA; GEE; GIBA; GRB-1; LETA; WABC†; WRA; YOB

Walker, Maggie Lena (1867–1934). Banker. ADA; ADB; BRB; BUFA; LOAV; ROG

Walker, Margaret (1915–). Poet. ROE

Walker, Mary (1832–1919). Physician feminist. STJ

Walker, Mary Richardson (1814–1897). Missionary. JOB; ROI

Walker, Nancy (1922–). Actress. MASB

Walker, Sarah Breedlove (1867–1919). Cosmetician. ADA; ADB†; LOAV; STQ†

Walsh, Stella (1913?–1980). Track athlete, born Poland. DAG; DAGA; HOBA; HOBAA†

Walters, Barbara (1931–). Television commentator. BOHD; GIB-1

Ward, Nancy (fl. 1785). Cherokee leader. GRAD

Warfield, Marsha (1954–). Comedienne. MASB

Warren, Mercy Otis (1728–1814). Author. AND; WABC†

Washington, Betty. Reporter. STAA

Waters, Ethel (1900–1977). Singer. ADA; ADB; DI-1†; DOBA; HUC

Watson, Ella (Cattle Kate) (1862?–1889). Rustler. RAB; WIAA-2

Wauneka, Annie Dodge (1912–). Navajo Indian public health worker. BRBE†; GRAC; GRAD; WAB

Weld, Theresa (1893–). Skater. HOBAA; JAB

Weldon, Catherine. Pioneer. JOB

Wells, Mary Georgene (1928?–). Advertising executive. GEDB†; GRBA

Welty, Eudora (1909–). Author. MUA; OCB

West, Jessamyn (1907–1984). Author. GL-1; MUA

West, Mae (1892–1980). Actress. MAOB; MASB

Wetamoo (fl. 1675). Pocasset chief. GRAD

Wharton, Edith (1862–1937). Author. BOA; CON†; STL

Wheatley, Phillis (1753–1784). Poet. ADA; ADB; AND; BRB; DOB; GIBA; HUA; JOCA; LEJ; LEPA; LOAV; PECA; ROE; ROG; WIBA

Wheeler, Candace Thurber (1827–1923). Decorative arts executive. PACB

Whitman, Narcissa (1808–1847). Missionary. DAD; EVD; FOC; MAT; ROI

Whitmire, Kathy (1946–). Mayor. WHE

Whitney, Phyllis A. (1903–). Author. GL-1

Whitworth, Kathy (Kathrynne Ann) (1939–). Golfer. HOBAA†; JABA; RYX

Wick, Tempe (fl. 1781). American Revolutionary patriot. CLC

Wiggin, Kate Douglas (1856–1923). Author. BEI; COB

Wilder, Laura Ingalls (1867–1957). Author. MUA; SMB

Wildesen, Leslie E. (1944–). Archaeologist. WIAA-01

Wilkins, Debbie. Motorcyclist. BUIC

Willard, Emma Hart (1787–1870). Educator.
BUDA; COG; CUC; FLB; FRC; JOCA; LEJA;
MAL; VAB; WABC†; YOC

Willard, Frances Elizabeth (1839–1898). Reformer. BRBE; GUBA; VAB; WABC

Williams, Fannie Barrier. Reformer. DADA

Williams, Mary Lou (1910–1981). Pianist, composer. GIB-1

Willis, Ann Bassett (1878–1956). Rancher. RAB

Wills, Helen (1906–). Tennis player. AAS-29;
ASBA; COKA; DAG; DAGA; FR-1; HI; HOBA;
HOBAA; JAB; LAHA; RYA†; SICA; SUDA†

Wilson, Marie (1916–1972). Actress. MASB

Winema (fl. 1850). Modoc Indian princess.
GRAD; WAB

Winnemucca, Sarah (1844–1891). Paiute Indian.
GRAD; TRD; WAB

Wood, Ann (fl. 1855). Slave. CHFB

Woodhull, Victoria (1838–1927). Feminist.
GUBA; JOCA; MAT-1; WABC†

Workman, Fanny Bullock (1859–1925). Explorer.
RIG

Wormington, Judy (1941–). Television promotions manager. SMBB-2

Wright, Barbara P. (1920–). Physician. PAC

Wright, Jane C. (1919–). Physician. HA-1; HAMA;
PAC; RAAG†

Wright, Mickey (Mary Kathryn) (1935–). Golfer.
HOBA; HOBAA†

Wright, Patience Lovell (1725–1786). Sculptor.
AND; VIA

Wright, Rebecca (fl. 1805). Pioneer. FOC

Wu, Chien-Shiung (1912–). Physicist, born China.
EMB†; GIB-1; GLO; SC; YOF

Wyatt, Addie (1924–). Labor, civil rights leader.
BI; GIB-1

Wylie, Elinor Morton (1885–1928). Poet, novelist.
BRBB

Wyman, Irma (1928–). Computer executive.
FRBD

Wynette, Tammy (1942–). Singer. BUIB-01

Yalow, Rosalyn Sussman (1921–). Physicist.
GIB-1; GL; GRB-1; HA-1; SHFE

Yashima, Mitsu. Illustrator. SMAB

Young, Candy (1962–). Track athlete. SUDB

Young, Ella Flagg (1845–1918). Educator. FLB

Young, Sheila (1950–). Cyclist, skater. HOBAA†;
LIEA; SUBB-1

Zajicek, Sarita Soto (1916–). Educator. FOW

Zakrzewska, Marie Elizabeth (1829–1902). Physician, born Germany. COFA†; FLA; LEG;
RAAG†

Zawisza, Christina (1947–). Lawyer. SMBB

Zayak, Elaine (1965–). Skater. VAD-6

Zenger, Anna (1704–1751). Journalist. GEE;
WABC†

Australian

Cawley, Evonne Goolagong (1951–). Tennis
player. AAS-29; FR-1; GLC; HOBAA; LAHA;
MATA; SUDA

Court, Margaret (1942–). Tennis player. AAS-29;
FR-1; HOBAA†; MATA; SUDA

Fifield, Elaine (1931–). Dancer. ATA

Gould, Shane Elizabeth (1956–). Swimmer.
HOBAA†; ST-1

Kenny, Elizabeth (1886–1952). Nurse. BOC;
MAK; WRA

Newton-John, Olivia (1948–). Singer, born England. KRI

Sutherland, Joan (1926–). Singer. SAB

Taylor, Valerie (1936–). Diver. HAKA

Wirth, May (1896?–). Bareback rider. KIB

Austrian

Maria Theresa (1717–1780). Archduchess. BOI;
CAAA; FAE; LIDA; PA; TRBA

Moser-Proell, Annemarie. Skier. WA-1

Suttner, Bertha von (1843–1914). Pacifist. MEA;
MEC; SHFE†; WIC

Trapp, Maria Augusta (1905–1987). Singer. CAHA

Canadian

Dunlop, Florence (1896–1963). Educator. FLB

Greene, Nancy (1943–). Skier. FRCA

Johnson, E. Pauline (1862–1913). Poet. GRAD

Murray, Anne (1945–). Singer. KRI

Rosenfeld, Fanny (1903–1969). Track athlete,
born Russia. SLA

Wright, Thelma. Track athlete. GLB

Chinese

Cheng, Chi (1944–). Track athlete. AAS-24;
HOBAA; ST-1

Chiang Mei-ling (1897–). Wife of Chiang Kai-shek. EUA; PA

Tzu Hsi (1835–1908). Empress. BOI; FAE; LIDA;
SPA

Dutch

Blankers-Koen, Fanny (Francina) (1918–). Track
athlete. DAJ; HOBAA

Juliana (1909–). Queen. BOI; FAE

Mata Hari (Gertrud Margarete Zelle) (1876–
1917). Dancer, spy. HAB; KN; SUG

Nienhuys, Janna. Nurse. MAK

Tinnè, Alexine (1839–1869). Explorer. RIG

Wilhelmina (1880–1962). Queen. BOI; FAE

Egyptian

Ankhesnamun (fl. 1358 B.C.). Queen. COLB

Cleopatra (69–30 B.C.). Queen. BOI; CAAA; COA;
DEI; DEJ; FAE; LIDA; PA; TRBA

Hatshepsut (1578–1457 B.C.). Queen. BOI; COLB; GRAB-04

Nefertari (13th century B.C.). Queen. COLB

Nefertiti (fl. 1372–1350 B.C.). Queen. COLB; FAE; GRAB-04; JO†; PA

Tiy (fl. 1400 B.C.). Queen. COLB

English

Aguilar, Grace (1816–1847). Author. LER; PEB

Anderson, Elizabeth Garrett (1836–1917). Physician. HUE; MAJ; MASA

Anne (1665–1714). Queen of Great Britain and Ireland. DEC; GRAB†; LIDA; SCC; TRB

Anne (1950–). Princess of Great Britain. HOBAA

Anne of Cleves (1515–1557). Consort of Henry VIII, king of England. MAOA; VAC

Anning, Mary (1799–1847). Fossil finder at 11. FOR

Astell, Mary (1668–1731). Author. BOH

Austen, Jane (1775–1817). Author. BOH; COO; SMA; STK

Baker, Lady Florence von Sass (fl. 1863–1893). Explorer, born Hungary. RIG

Baker, Mary "Caraboo" (c. 1826). Imposter. COKB

Barry, James, pseud. (1795–1865). Army physician. MASA

Bird, Isabella Lucy (1831–1904). Traveler. JOB; RIG

Boleyn, Anne (1507–1536). Second wife of Henry VIII, king of England. MAOA; VAC

Bonny, Anne (1700–1720). Pirate. PABB; SC-1; WHA†

Booth, Evangeline Cory (1865–1950). Salvation Army commander. STP

Boudicca (d. 62 A.D.). Queen of the Iceni. BOI; CAAA; TRBA

Brontë, Anne (1820–1849). Author. COO; SMA; STK

Brontë, Charlotte (1816–1855). Author. COO; SMA; STK

Brontë, Emily Jane (1818–1848). Author. COO; SMA; STK

Browning, Elizabeth Barrett (1809–1861). Poet. BOC

Burney, Fanny (1752–1840). Author. NOA; SMA

Buxton, Angela (1934–). Tennis player. SLA

Catherine of Aragon (1485–1536). Consort of Henry VIII, king of England. MAOA; VAC

Cavell, Edith (1865–1915). Nurse. HAA; MAJ; MAK; RADA; WRA

Christie, Agatha (1891–1976). Author. SMA

Craik, Dinah Mulock (1826–1887). Author. BEI

Darling, Grace Horsley (1815–1842). Heroine. MAJ; STP

Davison, Ann (fl. 1952). Adventurer. HAQ

Eleanor of Aquitaine (1122?–1204). Consort of Henry II, king of England. BOI; DAK

Eliot, George, pseud. (1819–1880). Author. COO; SMA; STL

Elizabeth I (1533–1603). Queen of England and Ireland. BOI; CAAA; CHG; COA; DAK; DEC; DEI; DEJ; FAE; FRE; GRAB; HAA; LIDA; PA; SCC; TRB; UNB

Elizabeth II (1926–). Queen of Great Britain and Northern Ireland. BOI; DEC; DU-1; FAE; GRAB; LIDA; SCC; TRB; WEB

Ewing, Juliana H. Gatty (1841–1885). Author. BEI

Farjeon, Eleanor (1881–1965). Author. BEH; SMB

Fields, Gracie (1898–1979). Singer, comedienne. MASB

Fonteyn, Margot (1919–). Dancer. ATA

Freud, Anna (1895–1982). Psychiatrist, born Austria. CHE

Fry, Elizabeth Gurney (1780–1845). Reformer. BOH; NOA; STP

Godden, Rumer (1907–). Author. SMA; SMB

Godiva, Lady (c. 1040–1080). Legendary horseback rider. COKB

Godwin, Mary Wollstonecraft (1759–1797). Author. BOH; GUBA

Goodall, Jane (1934–). Anthropologist. BOHG; DU-1; SC

Greenaway, Kate (1846–1901). Illustrator. SM

Grey, Beryl (1927–). Dancer. ATA

Grey, Lady Jane (1537–1554). Candidate for the throne of England. DEC; SCC†

Hepburn, Audrey (1929–). Actress. FOG

Herschel, Caroline (1750–1848). Astronomer, born Germany. COLA†; NOA; PAC; SC†

Hodgkin, Dorothy Crowfoot (1910–). Crystallographer. HA-1; SHFE

Howard, Catherine (1520?–1542). Consort of Henry VIII, king of England. MAOA; VAC

Jex-Blake, Sophia (1840–1912). Physician. HUE; MASA†; SC†

Johnson, Amy (1903–1941). Aviator. HIFD; MO

Kauffmann, Angelica (1741–1807). Painter, born Switzerland. BOH; NE

Kaye-Smith, Sheila (1887–1956). Author. SMA

Kenyon, Kathleen M. (1906–). Archaeologist. RIG

Kingsley, Mary Henrietta (1862–1900). Ethnologist. BOH; DAF; KNA; ROL†; WIA-1

Lillie, Beatrice (1898–). Actress, born Canada. MASB

Lovelace, Lady Ada (Byron) (1815–1852). Mathematician. GRAB-3; WEF

Markova, Alicia (1910–). Dancer. ATA

Mary I (1516–1558). Queen. BOI; DEC; GRAB†; LIDA; SCC; TRB

Mary II (1662–1694). Queen. DEC†; GRAB†; LIDA†; SCC; TRB

Maud (1102–1167). Queen. BRBF; TRB

Montagu, Lady Mary Wortley (1689–1762). Author. BOH; RIE†

More, Hannah (1745–1833). Author. NOA

Nesbit, Edith (1858–1924). Author. BEI

Nightingale, Florence (1820–1910). Nurse. ASB-1; BOC; BOH; COKB; DEI; DEJ; EVD; FAF; FRE; HUE; MAK; MAN; MASA; PA; SC; STP; WRA

Norton, Mary (1903–). Author. SMB

Pankhurst, Emmeline Goulden (1858–1928). Feminist. BOH

Parr, Catherine (1512–1548). Consort of Henry VIII, king of England. MAOA; VAC

Paston, Margery (mid-15th century). Letter writer. NOA

Potter, Beatrix (1866–1943). Author, illustrator. SC; SM

Read, Mary (1680–1721). Pirate. PABB; SC-1; WHA†

Riley, Bridget (1931–). Painter. WIAA

Rossetti, Christina Georgina (1830–1894). Poet. BEH; COP

Russell, Anna (1911–). Musical satirist, born Canada. MASB

Sackville-West, Victoria (1892–1962). Author. SMA

Sayers, Dorothy L. (1893–1957). Author. SMA

Seymour, Jane (1509–1537). Consort of Henry VIII, king of England. MAOA; VAC

Siddons, Sarah Kemble (1755–1831). Actress. NOA; TRC

Smeeton, Beryl. Mariner. HAQ

Stewart, Mary (1916–). Author. SMA

Taylor, Ann (1782–1866). Poet. BEH

Taylor, Jane (1783–1824). Poet. BEH

Thatcher, Margaret (1925–). Prime minister. DU-1; GI

Travers, Pamela L. (1906–). Author, born Australia. SMB

Victoria (1819–1901). Queen. BOI; CAAA; CHG; COA; DEC; DEI; DEJ; FAE; GRAB; LIDA; PA; SCC; TRB; UNB

Wade, Virginia (1945–). Tennis player. AAS-9; FR-1; SUDA

Webb, Mary (1881–1927). Author. SMA

Woolf, Virginia (1882–1941). Author. BEG; SMA

Woolley, Hannah (b. 1623). Educator. BOH

Yonge, Charlotte Mary (1823–1901). Author. BEI

Ethiopian

Gudit (fl. 937–997). Queen. GRAB-04

Haile Selassie, Tsahai (1919–1942). MAK

Makeda (fl. 960–930 b.c.). Queen of Sheba. GRAB-04

French

Bastie, Maryse. Aviator. HIFD

Bernhardt, Sarah (1844–1923). Actress. MAT-1; PA

Bettignies, Louise de (1888?–1918). Spy. SEB; SUG

Bonheur, Rosa (1822–1899). Painter. BOC

Boucher, Helene (1908–1934). Aviator. HIFD

Bourgeois, Louyse (1563–1636). Midwife. MASA

Caron, Leslie (1933–). Dancer, actress. ATA

Catherine de Medici (1519–1589). Queen of France. BOI; CAAA; FAE; LIDA

Chanel, Coco (1883–1971). Fashion designer. FRBD

Chatelet, Marquise du. Gabrielle Émilie Le Tonnelier du Breteuil (1706–1749). Author, physicist. SC

Chauviré, Yvette (1917–). Dancer. ATA

Curie, Marie Sklodowska (1867–1934). Chemist, physicist, born Poland. ASA; ASB-1; BEC; BEP; BOB; BOC; BOH; BUF; CAA; COL; DEI; DEJ; DOE; EVD; FE; FRE; HUE; KOA; MAJ; MANB; MASA; PA; PAC; POD; RID; SC; SHFB; SHFE†; SIA; STI

Eugenie (1826–1910). Wife of Napoleon III. COKB

Felicie, Jacoba (fl. 1322). Medical practitioner. MASA†; SC

Félix, Elisa Rachel (1821–1858). Actress, born Switzerland. LER; PEB

Galard, Geneviève de (1925–). Nurse. MAK

Jeanmaire, Renée (1924–). Dancer. ATA

Joliot-Curie, Irène (1897–1956). Physicist. FE; RID; SC†; SHFE†

Josephine (1763–1814). Empress. FAE

Laurencin, Marie (1885–1956). Painter. NE

LeClerq, Tanaquil (1929–). Dancer. ATA

Lenglen, Suzanne (1899–1938). Tennis player. DAG; DAGA; FR-1; HI; HOBAA; LAHA; SUDA†

Mance, Jeanne (1606–1673). Missionary nurse. MAK

Marchand, Colette (1925–). Dancer. ATA

Marie Antoinette (1755–1793). Queen. COA; DAK; DEI; DEJ; FAE; UNA

Marillac, Louise de (1591–1660). Nurse. MAK

Morisot, Berthe (1841–1895). Painter. NE

Sévigné, Marie (de Rabutin Chantal) marquise de. Author. PA

Staël, Germaine de (Anne Louise Germaine Necker, Baronne de Staël-Hollstein) (1766–1817). Author. BOC

Vigee-Lebrun, Elisabeth (1755–1842). Painter. NE

German
Ender, Kornelia (1958–). Swimmer. SUBB-1
Herz, Henriette (1764–1847). Society leader. LER
Mauermayer, Gisela (1914?–). Discus thrower. BELB
Reitsch, Hanna (1912–1979). Aviator. HAMY; HIFD
Scholl, Sophie (1921?–1943). Resistance worker. LAD
Schumann, Clara (1819–1896). Pianist. CHF

Greek
Agnodice (fl. 300 B.C.). Physician. SC
Hypatia (370–415). Philosopher. SC
Vlachos, Helen (1912?–). Newspaper publisher. CAHA

Indian
Gandhi, Indira Nehru (1917–1984). Prime minister. ASB-1; DU-1; GI; LIDA; WECA
Mother Theresa (1910–). Humanitarian, born Yugoslavia. ASB-1; DU-1; SHFE
Pandit, Vijaya Lakshmi (1900–). Diplomat. KE

Irish
Browne, Frances (1816–1879). Author. BEI
Corrigan, Mairead (1944–). Social reformer. AAS-34; COG-1; SHFE†
McAuley, Mary Catherine, Mother (1787–1841). REC
Montez, Lola (1818?–1861). Dancer. RAB; WABC†
Williams, Betty (1943–). Social reformer. AAS-34; COG-1; SHFE†

Israeli
Ben-Porat, Miriam (1918–). Supreme Court justice, born Lithuania. GRB-1
Chizick, Sarah. Settler. LER
Freier, Recha (1892–). Resistance leader, born Germany. GRB-1
Keleti, Agnes (1921–). Gymnast, born Hungary. SLA
Kluger, Ruth. Rescue worker, born Rumania. GRB-1
Kuchler, Lena. Child psychologist, born Poland. GRB-1
Lubetkin, Tzivia (1914–1978). Resistance leader, born Poland. GRB-1
Meir, Golda (1898–1978). Prime minister. GI; GRB-1; KE†; KOA; LIDA; ROGA
Roth, Esther (1952–). Track athlete. SLA
Senesh, Hannah (1921–1944). Underground leader, born Hungary. GEF; GRB-1; LAD; STP; ROGA

Italian
Fallaci, Oriana (1930–). Journalist. LETB
Manzolini, Anne Morandi (1716–1774). Anatomist. RIB
Montessori, Maria (1870–1952). Physician, educator. STP
Troctula di Ruggiero (d. 1197). Physician. MASA; RIB; SC

Mexican
Dominguez, (Maria) Josefa Ortiz de (1768–1824). Patriot. NEBA; ROGB
Ledón, Amalia. Diplomat. NEBA
Vicario, Leona (1789–1842). Patriot. ROGB

Norwegian
Henie, Sonja (1913–1969). Skater, actress. ASBA; DAG; DAGA; GED; GEDA; HOBAA; LEYB†; RYA†
Undset, Sigrid (1882–1949). Author. CAHA
Waitz, Grete (1953–). Track athlete. AAS-30; BAEC; SUDB

Polish
Granville, Christine (d. 1952). Spy. SEB
Jadwiga (1373–1399). Queen. MANB
Kirszenstein-Szewinska, Irena (1946–). Track athlete, born Russia. SLA
Landowska, Wanda (1877–1959). Harpsichordist. FOG
Novak, Nina. Dancer. ATA

Puerto Rican
Burgos, Julia de (1914–1953). Poet. WO
Rincón de Gautier, Felisa (1897–). Mayor. FOW; WO
Rodriguez de Tio, Lola (1843–1924). Poet. WO

Roman
Aspasia (fl. 2d century). Physician. SC
Galla Placidia (388–450). Empress of the West. TRBA
Theodora (508?–548). Consort of Justinian I. BOI

Romanian
Comaneci, Nadia (1961–). Gymnast. FOR; GUED; LIE
Ileana. Princess, nurse. WRA
Rozeanu, Angelica (1921–). Table tennis player. SLA

Russian

Blavatsky, Elena Petrovna (1831–1891). Theosophist. COEA; MAT-1

Catherine II, the Great (1729–1796). Empress of
Russia. BEO; BOI; CAAA; COKB; DAK; DEI;
DEJ; FAE; LIDA; RIA; TRBA

Danilova, Alexandra. Dancer. ATA

Elizabeth Petrovna (1709–1762). Empress. LIDA;
RIA

Kim, Nelli (1957–). Gymnast. LIE; SUBB-1

Korbut, Olga (1956–). Gymnast. HOBAA; LIE

Menchik, Vera (1906–1944). Chess player. LEQB

Pavlova, Anna (1881–1931). Dancer. TRC; YOH

Popovich, Marina. Test pilot. HIFD

Riabouchinska, Tatiana (1918–). Dancer. ATA

Rodnina, Irina (1949–). Skater. LIEA

Sophia. Consort of Ivan III, grand duke of Moscow. RIA

Sukloff, Marie. Terrorist. JAC

Tereshkova, Valentina Vladimirova (1937–). Astronaut. THC

Toumanova, Tamara (1919–). Dancer. ATA

Scottish

Barlass, Kate (15th century). Heroine. MAJ

MacDonald, Flora (1721–1790). Heroine. MAJ

Mary, Queen of Scots (1542–1587). BOI; DEI;
DEJ; FAE; UNA

Molesworth, Mary Louisa (1839–1921). Author.
BEI

Shearer, Moira (1926–). Dancer. ATA

Slessor, Mary Mitchell (1848–1915). Missionary.
STP

Somerville, Mary Fairfax (1780–1872). Scientist.
SC

South African

Bam, Brigalia (1933–). Social worker. CRA

Makeba, Miriam (1932–). Singer. CRA

Nosente (b. 1865?). Tribeswoman. PEA

Swedish

Christina (1626–1689). Queen. BOI; COKB;
TRBA; UNA

Lagerlof, Selma (1858–1940). Author. PA; SHFE†

Lind, Jenny (1820–1887). Singer. BOC; TRC

Lindgren, Astrid (1907–). Author. SMB

Meitner, Lise (1878–1968). Physicist, born Austria. HA-1; RID†; SC†; YOF

Myrdal, Alva (1902–1986). Sociologist. DU-1;
SHFE

Nilsson, Birgit (1918–). Singer. SAB

Sachs, Nelly (1891–1970). Poet, born Germany.
SHFE

Others

Alonso, Alicia (1921–). Cuban dancer. ATA; WO

Andriamanjato, Rahantavololona. Malagasy engineer. CRA

Ariadne (2500 B.C.). Cretian legendary princess.
PA

Banda (1900–1950). Indonesian spy. SUG

Bandaranaike, Sirimavo (1916–). Sri Lankan ex-
prime minister. GI

Batten, Jean (1909–1982). New Zealand aviator.
HIFD; MO

Brooks, Angie Elizabeth (1928–). Liberian U.N.
official. CRA

Carreño, Teresa (1853–1917). Venezuelan pianist.
CHF

Dulce, Sister (Dulce Lopes Pontes) (1913–). Brazilian nun. MAK

Encarnacion, Rosario de Jesus. Philippine
teacher, civic leader. RODA

Helena. Mesopotamian queen, convert to Judaism. LER

Hirsch, Clara de (1833–1899). Belgian philanthropist. LER

Ighodaro, Irene Elizabeth. Nigerian physician.
CRA

Isabella I (1451–1504). Spanish queen. BOI;
CAAA; DAK; FAE; LIDA; PA; TRBA

Jiagge, Annie. Ghanaian jurist. CRA

Kenyatta, Margaret Wambui (1928–). Kenyan
mayor. CRA

Konie, Gwendoline Chomba (1938–). Zambian
U.N. delegate. CRA

Margaret (1353–1412). Danish queen. BOI

Mendesia, Gracia (1510–1568). Portuguese philanthropist. LER; LES

Mistral, Gabriela (1889–1957). Chilean poet, educator. BACA; SHFE†; WO

Moore, Kofoworola Aina (1913–). Nigerian
tribeswoman. PEA

Nunoz, Maria (fl. 1590). Portuguese émigré. LER

Perón, Isabel (Maria Estela) (1931–). Argentine
ex-president. LIDA

Pintong, Nilawan (1916–). Thai editor and publisher. RODA

Reich, Haviva (1914–1944). Czech resistance
worker. LAD

Semiramis. Assyrian legendary queen. PA

Slavenska, Mia. Yugoslavian dancer. ATA

Spyri, Johanna H. (1827–1901). Swiss author.
BEC

Sutherland, Efua Theodora (1924–). Ghanaian author. CRA

Szekely, Eva (1927–). Hungarian swimmer. SLA

Waciuma, Charity. Zambian teacher, author. OJA

Wrede, Mathilda (1864–1928). Finnish penal reformer. KEE

Zenobia (fl. 267–272). Syrian queen. FAE; PA

WOMEN'S RIGHTS WORKERS, *see* FEMINISTS

WRESTLERS

Gable, Dan (1949?–). BELB; LEYB†
Gotch, Frank (b. 1878). DAG; DAGA
McCann, Terry. FOI
Sammartino, Bruno. BELB
Wagner, "Gorgeous George" (George Raymond) (1915–1963). COKB
Wittenberg, Henry B. (1918–). SLA

WRITERS, *see* AUTHORS

YUGOSLAVS

Slavenska, Mia. Dancer. ATA
Tito, Josip Broz (1892–1980). Premier. ARA; COJB; DU-1; WEB

ZAMBIANS

Konie, Gwendoline Chomba (1938–). U.N. delegate. CRA
Waciuma, Charity. Teacher, author. OJA

ZIONISTS

Ben Yehudah, Eliezer (1858–1922). Lithuanian. GRB-1; GUB; PEB; ROGA
Ben-Zvi, Yitzhak (1884–1963). (Born Russia). GRB-1
Bialik, Chaim Nachman (1873–1934). Russian. GEF; GRB-1; GUB; KAD; PEB

Brandeis, Louis Dembitz (1856–1941). ALD; EIA; FLC; GEF; GRB-1; GUB; LETA
Herzl, Theodor (1860–1904). Hungarian. GRB-1; GUB; KAB; KAD; LERA; LES; PEB; ROGA
Jabotinsky, Vladimir (1880–1940). Russian. GRB-1
Sampter, Jessie (b. 1883?). ALD
Silver, Abba Hillel (1893–1963). LETA
Sokolow, Nahum (1859–1936). English. (Born Poland). GRB-1
Szold, Henrietta (1860–1945). BLF; GUB; KAD; LES; LETA
Trumpeldor, Joseph (1880–1920). Israeli. GRB-1; PEB; ROGA
Weizmann, Chaim (1874–1952). DEI; DEJ; GEF; GRAB-1; GUB; KAB; KAD; LES; ROGA

ZOO PEOPLE

Embery, Joan (1949–). GUJ
Rader, Peta (1952–). GUJ

ZOOLOGISTS

See also ENTOMOLOGISTS; GENETICISTS; ICHTHYOLOGISTS; NATURALISTS; ORNITHOLOGISTS

Agassiz, Alexander (1835–1910). (Born Switzerland). COR
Crane, Jocelyn (1909–). YOF
Cuvier, Georges (1769–1832). French. FE
Grassi, Giovanni Battista (1854–1925). Italian. DEB; ROA
Grogan, Ewart Scott (1874–1967). English. WOA
Jordan, David Starr (1851–1931). HYB
Medawar, Peter Brian (1915–1987). CHE†; RIF
Morgan, Thomas Hunt (1866–1945). BEK; COLA; RIF
Nansen, Fridtjof (1861–1930). Norwegian. COC†; COG; DOC; HEA; KEE; KNB†; MEA; MEC; MOB; ROL; WIC
Spemann, Hans (1869–1941). German. RIF

Book Titles

Indexed Books by Title

ABC's of African History. Christine C. Johnson. Vantage, 1971 (o.p.) (JO)
Beckwourth, James P.; Christophe, Henri; Claybourne, Braxton Daniel; Douglass, Frederick; Dumas, Alexandre (Dumas père); Esteban or Estevanico†; Garvey, Marcus A.; Hughes, Langston; Imhotep; Johnson, James Weldon; King, Martin Luther, Jr.; Malcolm X; Nefertiti†; Nkrumah, Kwame; Nzinga; Osceola†; Pushkin, Aleksandr Sergeevich; Quarsie, Tetteh; Robeson, Paul; Touré, Sékou; Truth, Sojourner; Vesey, Denmark; Woods, Granville T.; Xerxes I; Young, Lester Willis.

ABC's of Black History. Deloris L. Holt. Ritchie, 1971 (o.p.) (HODA)
Aldridge, Ira; Banneker, Benjamin; Carver, George Washington; Drew, Charles Richard; Ellington, Duke; Flipper, Henry Ossian; Gannet, Deborah Sampson; Henson, Matthew Alexander; Ikard, Bose; Jackson, Saunders; King, Martin Luther, Jr.; Latimer, Lewis Howard; Malcolm X; Miller, Dorie; Nino, Pedro Alonso; Owens, Jesse; Pickett, Bill; Quarles, Benjamin†; Rillieux, Norbert; Smalls, Robert; Tubman, Harriet; Underdue, James†; Vesey, Denmark; Williams, Daniel Hale; Young, Charles; Zino, Henry.

Aces, Heroes, and Daredevils of the Air. LeRoy Hayman. Messner, 1981 (o.p.) (HAMY)
Alcock, Sir John; Bader, Douglas; Ball, Albert; Beachey, Lincoln; Bishop, William Avery; Boyington, Pappy (Gregory); Brown, Arthur Whitten; Cochran, Jacqueline; Curtiss, Glenn Hammond; Doolittle, James Harold; Earhart, Amelia; Fokker, Anthony; Fonck, René; Garros, Roland; Gibson, Guy Penrose; Guynemer, Georges; Kingsford-Smith, Charles; Lindbergh, Charles Augustus; Lufberg, Raoul Gervais; Luke, Frank, Jr.; Post, Wiley; Reitsch, Hanna; Richthofen, Manfred von; Rodgers, Calbraith Perry; Smith, Ross†; Thaw, William; Tibbets, Paul†; Ulm, Charles; Wright, Orville; Wright, Wilbur.

Adventurers in Buckskin. Bennett Wayne. Garrard, 1973 (WAF)
Bridger, James; Carson, Kit; Cody, William Frederick; Smith, Jedediah Strong.

Adventures in Courage: The Skymasters. Dennis Brennan. Reilly & Lee, 1968 (o.p.) (BRBA)
Blériot, Louis; Lilienthal, Otto; Lindbergh, Charles Augustus; Montgolfier, Jacques Étienne; Montgolfier, Joseph Michel; Santos-Dumont, Alberto; Shepard, Alan Bartlett; Wright, Orville; Wright, Wilbur.

AFL Dream Backfield. Howard Liss. Cowles Bk. Co., 1969 (o.p.) (LIBA)
Alworth, Lance; Blanda, George; Dawson, Lenny; Gilchrist, Cookie; Haynes, Abner; Lowe, Paul; Maynard, Don; Nance, Jim.

African Heroes. Naomi Mitchison. FS&G, 1968 (o.p.) (MIC)
Affonso I; Cetewayo; Chaka; Idris Alaoma; Jubo Jubogha; Kgamanyane; Khama III; Lobengula; Moshoeshoe; Osei Tutu; Sundiata I.

Afro-Americans '76: Black Americans in the Founding of Our Nation. Eugene Winslow. Afro-Am, 1975 (WIBA)
Abraham; Allen, Richard; Armistead, James; Attucks, Crispus; Banneker, Benjamin; Bason, Caesar; Beckwourth, James P.; Bonga, George; Burr, Seymour; Camero, Manuel; Charlton,

Samuel†; Christophe, Henri; Cromwell, Oliver; Cuffe, Paul; Dabney, Austin†; Derham, James; Esteban or Estevanico; Flora, William; Forten, James; Fortune, Amos; Gannet, Deborah Sampson; Haynes, Lemuel; Hector, Edward; Jeffrey, Major; Johnston, Joshua; Lamson, David; Lew, Brazillai; Light, Allen B.; Marrant, John; Matthews, Saul†; Pointe de Sable, Jean Baptiste; Pointer, Dick; Pompey†; Poor, Salem; Ranger, Joseph†; Robinson, James; Salem, Peter; Sisson, Tack "Prince"†; Sousa, Mathias; Stanup, Richard; Tarrant, Caesar†; Washington, George; Wheatley, Phillis; Whipple, Prince; York.

After Olympic Glory: The Lives of Ten Outstanding Medalists. Larry Borstein. Warne, 1978 (o.p.) (BOHA)
Albright, Tenley; Ali, Muhammad; Bradley, Bill; De Varona, Donna; Jackson, Nell; King, Micki; Mathias, Bob; Matthews, Vincent Edward; Owens, Jesse; Spock, Benjamin.

Against All Odds. John Jacobs. Macmillan, 1967 (o.p.) (JAC)
Casanova de Seingalt, Giovanni Giacomo; Cellini, Benvenuto; Charles II; Churchill, Sir Winston Leonard Spencer; Colter, John; Latude, Henri Maseres de; Napoleon III; Pluhar, Ivan; Sukloff, Marie; Trenck, Friedrich von der.

Against Odds. Basil Heatter. FS&G, 1970 (o.p.) (HAQ)
Bombard, Alain Louis; Davison, Ann; Earhart, Amelia; Henson, Matthew Alexander; Herzog, Maurice; Lachenal, Louis; Lindbergh, Charles Augustus; McMorris, C. H.†; Miller, Hugh Barr; Peary, Robert Edwin; Riggs, Captain R. S.†; Smeeton, Beryl; Smeeton, Miles; Smith (Mr.).

Ahead of Their Time. Boys Life Editors. Putnam, 1968 (o.p.) (BOK)
Audubon, John James; Curtiss, Glenn Hammond; Goddard, Robert Hutchings; Houston, Samuel; Quincy, Josiah, Jr.; Salomon, Haym; Sequoya; Tesla, Nikola.

Album of the Presidents. Jeanne A. Rowe. Watts, 1969 (o.p.) (ROK)
Adams, John†; Adams, John Quincy†; Arthur, Chester Alan†; Buchanan, James†; Cleveland, Grover†; Coolidge, Calvin†; Eisenhower, Dwight David†; Fillmore, Millard†; Garfield, James Abram†; Grant, Ulysses Simpson†; Harding, Warren Gamaliel†; Harrison, Benjamin†; Harrison, William Henry†; Hayes, Rutherford Birchard†; Hoover, Herbert Clark†; Jackson, Andrew; Jefferson, Thomas; Johnson, Andrew†; Johnson, Lyndon Baines†; Kennedy, John Fitzgerald; Lincoln, Abraham; McKinley, William†; Madison, James†; Monroe, James†; Nixon, Richard Milhous†; Pierce, Franklin†; Polk, James Knox†; Roosevelt, Franklin Delano; Roosevelt, Theodore; Taft, William Howard†; Taylor, Zachary†; Truman, Harry S.†; Tyler, John†; Van Buren, Martin†; Washington, George; Wilson, Woodrow.

Alchemists: Fathers of Practical Chemistry. Richard Cummings. McKay, 1966 (o.p.) (CUA)
Albert the Great; Dee, John; Democritos, Bolos; Flamel, Nicholas; Go-Hung; Jabir ibn-Hayyan; Paracelsus; Price, James; Seton, Alexander.

All Kinds of Kings: From Hammurabi to Louis XIV. Johanna Johnston & Murry Karmiller. Norton, 1970 (o.p.) (JOBB)
Ahab; Akhnaton; Alexander III, the Great; Alfred the Great; Arthur; Attila the Hun; Canute II, the Great; Charlemagne; Croesus; David; Hammurabi; Harold I, the Fairhaired; Henry IV, of Navarre; Henry VIII; Ivan IV, the Terrible; Louis XIV; Midas; Minos; Mithridates VI; Nebuchadnezzar II; Nero; Richard I; Richard III; Solomon; William I, the Conqueror.

All-Stars of the NFL. Bob Rubin. Random, 1976 (o.p.) (RUA)
Bergey, Bill L.; Bradshaw, Terry; Curtis, Isaac; Greene, Joe; Guy, Ray; Houston, Ken; Little, Larry; Simpson, O. J.

All Stars of the Outfield. Milton J. Shapiro. Messner, 1970 (o.p.) (SH)
Aaron, Hank; Cobb, Ty; Di Maggio, Joseph Paul; Mantle, Mickey Charles; Mays, Willie Howard; Musial, Stanley Frank; Ott, Mel; Ruth, Babe; Speaker, Tristram E.; Williams, Ted.

All the Home Run Kings. Arthur Daley. Putnam, 1972 (o.p.) (DA)
Aaron, Hank; Banks, Ernie; Berra, Yogi; Colavito, Rocky; Di Maggio, Joseph Paul; Foxx, James Emory; Gehrig, Lou; Hodges, Gil; Howard, Frank; Kaline, Albert William; Killebrew, Harmon; Kiner, Ralph M.; McCovey, Willie Lee; Mantle, Mickey Charles; Mathews, Edwin Lee; Mays, Willie Howard; Mize, Johnny; Musial, Stanley Frank; Ott, Mel; Robinson, Frank; Ruth, Babe; Snider, Duke; Williams, Ted.

America and Its Presidents. Earl Schenck Miers. G&D, 1966 (o.p.) (MIA)
Adams, John; Adams, John Quincy; Arthur, Chester Alan; Buchanan, James; Cleveland, Grover; Coolidge, Calvin; Eisenhower, Dwight David; Fillmore, Millard; Garfield, James Abram; Grant, Ulysses Simpson; Harding, Warren Gamaliel; Harrison, Benjamin; Harrison, William Henry; Hayes, Rutherford Birchard; Hoover, Herbert Clark; Jackson, Andrew; Jefferson, Thomas; Johnson, Andrew; Johnson, Lyndon Baines; Kennedy, John Fitzgerald; Lincoln, Abraham; McKinley, William; Madison, James; Monroe, James; Pierce, Franklin; Polk, James Knox; Roosevelt, Franklin Delano; Roosevelt, Theodore; Taft, William Howard; Taylor, Zachary; Truman, Harry S.; Tyler, John; Van Buren, Martin; Washington, George; Wilson, Woodrow.

America Becomes Free. L. Edmond Leipold. T. S. Denison, 1972 (o.p.) (LEAA)
Franklin, Benjamin; Hale, Nathan; Lawrence, James; McCauley, Mary; Washington, George.

American Assassins. Jo Anne Ray. Lerner, 1974 (RABA)
Booth, John Wilkes; Butler, Norman†; Collazo, Oscar; Czolgosz, Leon F.; Guiteau, Charles Julius; Hayer, Talmadge†; Johnson, Thomas†; Oswald, Lee Harvey; Ray, James Earl; Sirhan, Sirhan; Torresola, Griselio; Weiss, Carl Austin; Zangara, Guiseppe.

American Composers. Elsa Z. Posell. HM, 1963 (o.p.) (POF)
Barber, Samuel; Bernstein, Leonard; Copland, Aaron; Cowell, Henry Dixon; Creston, Paul; Dello Joio, Norman; Foss, Lukas; Foster, Stephen Collins; Gershwin, George; Gould, Morton; Griffes, Charles Tomlinson; Grofé, Ferde; Hanson, Howard; Harris, Roy Ellsworth; Hovhaness, Alan; Ives, Charles; Kay, Ulysses; Lockwood, Normand; MacDowell, Edward Alexander; Mennin, Peter; Menotti, Gian-Carlo; Moore, Douglas Stuart; Piston, Walter; Porter, Quincy; Riegger, Wallingford; Schuman, William; Sessions, Roger H.; Sousa, John Philip; Still, William Grant.

American Composers of Our Time. Joseph Machlis. T Y Crowell, 1963 (o.p.) (MAF)
Barber, Samuel; Bernstein, Leonard; Copland, Aaron; Dello Joio, Norman; Foss, Lukas; Gershwin, George; Griffes, Charles Tomlinson; Hanson, Howard; Harris, Roy Ellsworth; Ives, Charles; MacDowell, Edward Alexander; Menotti, Gian-Carlo; Moore, Douglas Stuart; Piston, Walter; Schuman, William; Thomson, Virgil.

American Filmmakers Today. Dian G. Smith. Messner, 1983 (o.p.) (SMBB-3)
Allen, Woody; Altman, Robert; Brooks, Mel; Coppola, Francis; DePalma, Brian; Lucas, George; Mazursky, Paul; Scorsese, Martin; Spielberg, Steven.

American Heroes of Asian Wars. Army Times Editors. Dodd, 1968 (o.p.) (ARBA)
Capodanno, Vincent R.; Carpenter, Howard; Charlton, Cornelius; Dengler, Dieter; Higgins, Marguerite; Jabara, James A.; Michaelis, John Hersey; Murphy, Thomas R.; Olds, Robin; Shields, Marvin†; Spruill, James Polk; Walker, Walton Harris.

American Heroes of the Twentieth Century. Harold Faber & Doris Faber. Random, 1967 (o.p.) (FAA)
Anderson, Marian; Bourke-White, Margaret; Byrd, Richard Evelyn; Catt, Carrie Chapman; Donovan, William Joseph; Earhart, Amelia; Eisenhower, Dwight David; Goddard, Robert Hutchings; Keller, Helen Adams; Kennedy, John Fitzgerald; King, Martin Luther, Jr.; Lindbergh, Charles Augustus; MacArthur, Douglas; Macy, Anne Sullivan†; Murphy, Audie; Murrow, Edward Roscoe; Pyle, Ernest Taylor; Roosevelt, Franklin Delano; Salk, Jonas Edward; Seagrave, Gordon Stifler; Shepard, Alan Bartlett.

American Indian Women. Marion E. Gridley. Hawthorn, 1974 (o.p.) (GRAD)
Bonnin, Gertrude Simmons; Bosomworth, Mary Musgrove Matthews; Dorion, Marie†; Francis, Milly Hadjo; Hill, L. Rosa Minoka†; Horne, Esther Burnett; Johnson, E. Pauline; Lawson, Roberta Campbell; Martinez, Maria Montoya; Picotte, Susan LaFlesche; Pocahontas; Ramos, Elaine Abraham; Sacajawea; Tallchief, Maria; Tallchief, Marjorie; Velarde, Pablita; Victor, Wilma L.; Ward, Nancy; Wauneka, Annie Dodge; Wetamoo; Winema; Winnemucca, Sarah.

American Inventors. Clarence J. Hylander. Macmillan, 1934 (o.p.) (HYA)
Bell, Alexander Graham; Berliner, Emile; Browning, John Moses†; Bushnell, David†; Colt,

Samuel†; Corliss, George Henry†; Davenport, Thomas†; De Forest, Lee; Edison, Thomas Alva; Ericsson, John; Evans, Oliver; Farmer, Moses G.†; Field, Stephen D.†; Fitch, John; Franklin, Benjamin; Fulton, Robert; Gatling, Richard Jordan†; Goodyear, Charles; Gray, Elisha†; Hoe, Richard March†; Holland, John Philip; Hotchkiss, Benjamin B.†; Howe, Elias; Jenkins, Charles Francis; Kettering, Charles F.†; Lake, Simon†; Langley, Samuel Pierpont†; McCormick, Cyrus Hall; Mergenthaler, Ottmar†; Morse, Samuel F. B.; Rumsey, James†; Seiberling, Frank A.†; Sholes, Christopher Latham; Stevens, John; Stevens, Robert Livingston; Westinghouse, George; Whitney, Eli; Wright, Orville†; Wright, Wilbur†.

American Olympic Stars. Dick O'Connor. Putnam, 1976 (o.p.) (OCA)
    Anderson, Paul; Beamon, Bob; Hayes, Bob; Mathias, Bob; Mills, Billy; Oerter, Al; Owens, Jesse; Patterson, Floyd; Rudolph, Wilma G.; Spitz, Mark.

American Political Bosses and Machines. Fred J. Cook. Watts, 1973 (o.p.) (COGC)
    Hague, Frank; Hanna, Mark; Ruef, Abraham; Tweed, William Marcy.

American Presidents: Biographies of the Chief Executives from Washington through Reagan. David C. Whitney. Doubleday, 1985 (WHD)
    See listing under *America and Its Presidents* by Earl S. Miers. Add: Carter, Jimmy; Ford, Gerald R.; Nixon, Richard M.; Reagan, Ronald.

American Race Car Drivers. Mark Dillon. Lerner, 1974 (DI-2)
    Donohue, Mark; Foyt, Anthony Joseph; Jones, Parnelli; Petty, Richard.

American Scientists: Pioneer Teachers and Specialists. Clarence J. Hylander. Abridged ed., Macmillan, 1963 (o.p.) (HYB)
    Agassiz, Louis; Audubon, John James; Burbank, Luther; Cope, Edward Drinker; Dana, James Dwight; Franklin, Benjamin; Gray, Asa; Henry, Joseph; Jordan, David Starr; Leidy, Joseph; Marsh, Othniel Charles; Newcomb, Simon; Rumford, Benjamin Thompson, count; Silliman, Benjamin; Torrey, John; Wilson, Alexander.

American Sea Heroes. Joseph Icenhower. Hammond, 1970 (o.p.) (ICA)
    Buchanan, Franklin; Byrd, Richard Evelyn; Cushing, William Barker; Decatur, Stephen; Dewey, George; Farragut, David Glasgow; Halsey, William Frederick; Jones, John Paul; Lawrence, James; Macdonough, Thomas; Nimitz, Chester William; Peary, Robert Edwin; Perry, Matthew Calbraith; Perry, Oliver Hazard; Porter, David; Porter, David Dixon; Sims, William Sowden; Spruance, Raymond Ames.

American Sports Heroes of Today. Fred Katz. Random, 1970 (o.p.) (KADA)
    Aaron, Hank; Abdul-Jabbar, Kareem; Ali, Muhammad; Alworth, Lance; Ashe, Arthur; Brown, Jim; Butkus, Dick; Casper, Billy; Chamberlain, Wilt; Clemente, Roberto; Foyt, Anthony Joseph; Gibson, Bob; Hayes, Bob; Hornung, Paul Vernon; Hull, Bobby; Jones, Dave "Deacon"; Killebrew, Harmon; Koufax, Sandy; McLain, Dennis; Maravich, Pete; Marichal, Juan; Maris, Roger Eugene; Mays, Willie Howard; Namath, Joe Willie; Nicklaus, Jack; Orr, Bobby; Palmer, Arnold; Robinson, Frank; Rose, Pete; Russell, William Felton; Ryun, Jim; Sayers, Gale; Schollander, Donald Arthur; Simpson, O. J.; Unitas, Johnny; Weber, Dick; West, Jerry; Wills, Maury; Wilson, Larry; Yastrzemski, Carl Michael.

American Women in Sports. Phyllis Hollander. G&D, 1972 (o.p.) (HOBA)
    Albright, Tenley; Berg, Patty; Chadwick, Florence May; Collett, Glenna; Connolly, Maureen; Connolly, Olga Fikotova; Crump, Diane†; Curtis, Ann†; Didrikson, Babe; Ederle, Gertrude C.; Fleming, Peggy; Fraser, Gretchen Kunigk; Gibson, Althea; Heiss, Carol; King, Billie Jean; Kusner, Kathy; Ladewig, Marion; Lawrence, Andrea Mead; McCormick, Patricia Keller; McCutcheon, Floretta Doty; Mann, Carol†; Martin, Sylvia Wene; Owen, Laurence†; Pitou, Penny; Riggin, Aileen†; Rubin, Barbara Jo†; Rudolph, Wilma G.; Saubert, Jean†; Sears, Eleanora; Vinson-Owen, Maribel†; Von Saltza, Susan Christina; Walsh, Stella; Wills, Helen; Wright, Mickey.

American Women of Nursing. Edna Yost. Lippincott, 1965 (o.p.) (YOB)
    Blake, Florence G.; Floyd, Theodora A.; Goodrich, Annie Warburton; Gowan, M. Olivia, Sister; Leone, Lucile Petry; Nutting, Mary Adelaide; Osborne, Estelle Massey; Prochazka, Anne; Stewart, Isabel Maitland; Wald, Lillian D.

American Women of the Space Age. Mary Finch Hoyt. Atheneum, 1966 (o.p.) (HOG)
Anderson, Evelyn M.; Bailie, Ann Eckels; Beasely, Juliet†; Chambers, Annette†; Chartz, Marcelline†; Chatham, Alice King; Dawson, Merna; Finkelstein, Beatrice; Flume, Jimmie; Glennon, Nan; Gosney, Mary Louise†; Guild, Elizabeth; Hedgepeth, Mary†; Jackson, Margaret; Mann, Helen; Mitchell, Mildred; Morris, Dorothy†; Norwood, Virginia; O'Hara, Dee†; Olson, Edith; Pinkston, Carmonelle†; Pressly, Eleanor C.; Rock, Lee Curry; Roennau, Laurel van der Wal†; Roman, Nancy Grace; Rydstrom, Pat; Short, Barbara†; Townsend, Marjorie; Whidden, Dorothy†; Young, Ida†.

Americans at Work. Adrian A. Paradis. McKay, 1958 (o.p.) (PAA)
Bauer, Henry; Beech, Olive Ann; Carr, Harold Noflet; Colbert, Lester; Cordiner, Ralph; Curtice, Harlow H.; Day, James E.; Funston, George Keith; Genet, Arthur Samuel; Grossinger, Jennie; Hanway, Howard; Hicks, Beatrice Alice; Hilton, Conrad Nicholson; Holman, Eugene; Johnson, John H.; Kappel, Frederick Russell; Levitt, William Jaird; Liebenow, Robert C.; Livingston, Homer J.; Nitschelm, Ade; Nitschelm, Terry; Palmer, Bruce; Robinson, William E.; Rudkin, Margaret Fogharty; Seltzer, Louis; Smith, Winthrop; Symes, James Miller.

Americans Born Abroad. L. Edmond Leipold. T. S. Denison, 1973 (o.p.) (LEAB)
Audubon, John James; Bell, Alexander Graham; Mayo, William Worrall; Rockne, Knute; Van Loon, Hendrik.

America's Explorers of Space. Donald W. Cox. Hammond, 1967 (o.p.) (COQ)
Collins, Michael; Drake, Frank Donald; Glenn, John Herschel, Jr.; Goddard, Robert Hutchings; Grissom, Gus; Kármán, Theodor von; Kraft, Christopher Columbus, Jr.; Parks, Robert J.; Pickering, William H.; Pierce, John Robinson; Shepard, Alan Bartlett; Stapp, John Paul; Von Braun, Wernher; White, Edward Higgins, II; Wyld, James H.; Yeager, Charles E.; Young, John Watts.

America's First Ladies 1789 to 1865. Lillie Chaffin & Miriam Butwin. Lerner, 1969 (CHA)
Adams, Abigail; Adams, Louisa Catherine; Fillmore, Abigail Powers; Harrison, Anna Symmes; Jackson, Rachel; Jefferson, Martha Wayles Skelton; Lane, Harriet; Lincoln, Mary Todd; Madison, Dolley Payne Todd; Monroe, Elizabeth; Pierce, Jane Appleton; Polk, Sarah Childress; Taylor, Margaret Smith; Tyler, Julia Gardiner; Tyler, Letitia Christian; Van Buren, Hannah Hoes; Washington, Martha Dandridge.

America's First Ladies 1865 to Present Day. Lillie Chaffin & Miriam Butwin. Lerner, 1969 (CHB)
Arthur, Ellen Lewis; Cleveland, Frances Folsom; Coolidge, Grace Anna; Eisenhower, Mamie Geneva; Garfield, Lucretia Rudolph; Grant, Julia Dent; Harding, Florence Kling; Harrison, Caroline; Hayes, Lucy Ware; Hoover, Lou Henry; Johnson, Claudia Alta; Johnson, Eliza McCardle; McKinley, Ida Saxton; Nixon, Thelma; Onassis, Jacqueline Lee Bouvier Kennedy; Roosevelt, Edith Kermit; Roosevelt, Eleanor; Taft, Helen Herron; Truman, Elizabeth V.; Wilson, Edith Bolling; Wilson, Ellen Louisa.

America's Triumph: Stories of American Jewish Heroes. Dorothy Alofsin. Arno, 1949 (ALD)
Brandeis, Louis Dembitz; Gershwin, George; Goldberger, Joseph; Levy, Uriah Phillips; Rosenwald, Julius; Salomon, Haym; Sampter, Jessie; Straus, Nathan; Touro, Judah; Wald, Lillian D.

America's Vice-Presidents: Our First Forty-three Vice-Presidents and How They Got to Be Number Two. Diana Dixon Healy. Atheneum, 1984 (o.p.) (HAOA)
Adams, John; Agnew, Spiro Theodore; Arthur, Chester Alan; Barkley, Alben William; Breckinridge, John Cabell; Burr, Aaron; Bush, George; Calhoun, John Caldwell; Clinton, George; Colfax, Schuyler; Coolidge, Calvin; Curtis, Charles; Dallas, George Mifflin; Dawes, Charles Gates; Fairbanks, Charles Warren; Fillmore, Millard; Ford, Gerald R.; Garner, John Nance; Gerry, Elbridge; Hamlin, Hannibal; Hendricks, Thomas Andrews; Hobart, Garret A.; Jefferson, Thomas; Johnson, Andrew; Johnson, Lyndon Baines; Johnson, Richard Mentor; King, William Rufus Devane; Marshall, Thomas Riley; Mondale, Walter F.; Morton, Levi Parsons; Nixon, Richard Milhous; Rockefeller, Nelson Aldrich; Roosevelt, Theodore; Sher-

man, James S.; Stevenson, Adlai Ewing; Tompkins, Daniel D.; Tyler, John; Van Buren, Martin; Wallace, Henry A.; Wheeler, William Almon; Wilson, Henry.

And Long Remember: Some Great Americans Who Have Helped Me. Dorothy C. Fisher. McGraw, 1959 (o.p.) (FID)
Carver, George Washington; Dix, Dorothea Lynde; Farragut, David Glasgow; Franklin, Benjamin; Grant, Ulysses Simpson; Hale, Nathan; Henry, Patrick; Jefferson, Thomas; Jones, John Paul; Lee, Robert Edward; Philip, John Woodward; Washington, George.

Armed with Courage. May McNeer & Lynd Ward. Abingdon, 1957 (o.p.) (MAN)
Addams, Jane; Carver, George Washington; Damien de Veuster, Joseph; Gandhi, Mohandas Karamchand; Grenfell, Sir Wilfred Thomason; Nightingale, Florence; Schweitzer, Albert.

Army Leaders of World War II. James B. Sweeney. Watts, 1984 (SWE-1)
Arnold, Henry Harley; Eisenhower, Dwight David; MacArthur, Douglas; Marshall, George Catlett; Patton, George Smith, Jr.

Arrow Book of Presidents. Sturges P. Cary. Scholastic, 1969 (o.p.) (CAG)
See listing under *America and Its Presidents* by Earl S. Miers. Add: Nixon, Richard M.

Art in the New Land: Stories of Some American Artists and Their Work. Charlie May Simon. Dutton, 1945 (o.p.) (SIE)
Audubon, John James; Bellows, George Wesley; Bingham, George Caleb; Copley, John Singleton; Davies, Arthur B.; Eakins, Thomas; Homer, Winslow; Inness, George; Peale, Charles Willson; Ryder, Albert Pinkham; Sargent, John Singer; Sloan, John; Stuart, Gilbert; West, Benjamin; Whistler, James Abbott McNeill; Wood, Grant.

Atlas of the Presidents. Donald E. Cooke. Hammond, rev. ed., 1985 (COI)
See listing under *America and Its Presidents* by Earl S. Miers. Add: Carter, Jimmy; Ford, Gerald R.; Nixon, Richard M.; Reagan, Ronald.

Atomic Pioneers: From Irish Castle to Manhattan Project. William Moore. Putnam, 1970 (o.p.) (MOBA)
Avogadro, Amedeo; Becquerel, Antoine Henri; Berzelius, Jöns Jakob, baron; Bohr, Niels H. D.; Boyle, Robert; Cannizzaro, Stanislao; Dalton, John; Einstein, Albert; Lavoisier, Antoine Laurent; Mendeleev, Dmitri I.; Rutherford, Ernest Rutherford, 1st baron; Thomson, Sir Joseph John.

Auto Racing's Young Lions. Ross Olney. Putnam, 1977 (o.p.) (OLCA)
Baker, Buck; Baker, Buddy; Bettenhausen, Gary; Bettenhausen, Merle; Bettenhausen, Tony; Bettenhausen, Tony Lee†; Carter, Duane, Sr.; Carter, Pancho; Parsons, Johnnie; Parsons, Johnny; Petty, Lee; Petty, Richard; Thompson, Dannie; Thompson, Mickey; Vukovich, Bill; Vukovich, Bill, Jr.

Banners of Courage: The Lives of Fourteen Heroic Men and Women. Robert Elliot. Platt, 1972 (o.p.) (ELA)
Anthony, Susan Brownell; Bombard, Alain Louis; Byrd, Richard Evelyn; Carson, Rachel; Churchill, Sir Winston Leonard Spencer; Cousteau, Jacques Yves; Earhart, Amelia; Frank, Anne; Garrison, William Lloyd; Joan of Arc, Saint; Joseph (Chief); King, Martin Luther, Jr.; Schliemann, Heinrich; York, Alvin C.

Baseball All-Star Game Thrills. Hal Butler. Messner, 1968 (o.p.) (BUJ)
Callison, Johnny; Clemente, Roberto; Di Maggio, Joseph Paul; Gibson, Bob†; Kaline, Albert William; Mays, Willie Howard; Musial, Stanley Frank; Rosen, Al; Ruth, Babe; Schoendienst, Red; Slaughter, Country; Williams, Ted.

Baseball Rookies Who Made Good. M. G. Bonner. Knopf, 1954 (o.p.) (BOE)
Appling, Luke; Ashburn, Richie; Berra, Yogi; Bevens, Bill; Black, Joe; Brown, Bobby; Byrd, Harry; Campanella, Roy; Courtney, Clint; Dark, Alvin; Dean, Dizzy; Di Maggio, Joseph Paul; Dropo, Walt†; Ennis, Del; Fain, Ferris; Feller, Bob; Ford, Whitey; Gehrig, Lou; Gilliam, Junior†; Gomez, Lefty; Greenberg, Hank; Henrich, Tommy; Jethroe, Sam; Kell, George Clyde; Kuenn, Harvey†; McDougald, Gil; Mantle, Mickey Charles; Martin, Pepper; Mays, Willie Howard; Minoso, Minnie; Musial, Stanley Frank; Newcombe, Donald; Ott, Mel; Reese,

Pee Wee; Reynolds, Allie; Rizzuto, Philip Francis; Robinson, Jackie; Ruth, Babe; Shantz, Robert Clayton; Sievers, Roy†; Spahn, Warren; Wagner, Honus.

Baseball Superstars. Mike Herbert. Childrens, 1986 (HEFB)
Baines, Harold†; Blyleven, Bert†; Boggs, Wade†; Brett, George Howard†; Carter, Gary†; Fisk, Carlton†; Gooden, Dwight†; Guerrero, Pedro†; Guidry, Ron†; Gwynn, Tony†; Henderson, Rickey†; Herr, Tom†; McGee, Willie†; Mattingly, Don†; Murphy, Dale†; Murray, Eddie†; Quisenberry, Dan; Ripken, Cal, Jr.†; Rose, Pete†; Saberhagen, Bret†; Sandberg, Ryne†; Smith, Ozzie†; Strawberry, Darryl†; Valenzuela, Fernando†; Winfield, Dave†.

Baseball's Ace Relief Pitchers. Nathan Aaseng. Lerner, 1984 (AAS)
Fingers, Rollie; Gossage, "Goose"; Lyle, Sparky; McGraw, Tug; Minton, Greg; Quisenberry, Dan; Sutter, Bruce; Tekulve, Kent.

Baseball's All-Stars. J. Lowell Pratt, ed. Doubleday, 1967 (o.p.) (PRA)
Aaron, Hank; Bunning, Jim; Cepeda, Orlando; Clemente, Roberto; Drysdale, Don; Gibson, Bob; Howard, Elston; Kaline, Albert William; Killebrew, Harmon; Koufax, Sandy; McDowell, Sam; McLain, Dennis; Marichal, Juan; Mays, Willie Howard; Mazeroski, Bill; Oliva, Tony; Perry, Gaylord Jackson; Robinson, Brooks Calbert; Robinson, Frank; Rose, Pete; Santo, Ron; Torre, Joseph Paul; Versalles, Zoilo; White, William D.; Wills, Maury.

Baseball's All-Time All-Stars. Jim Murphy. Clarion, 1984 (MUB-1)
Aaron, Hank; Alexander, Grover Cleveland; Bench, Johnny Lee; Cobb, Ty; Collins, Eddie; Cronin, Joe; Dickey, Bill; Ford, Whitey; Gehrig, Lou; Gibson, Bob; Grove, Lefty; Hornsby, Rogers; Johnson, Walter Perry; Koufax, Sandy; Mathewson, Christy; Mays, Willie Howard; Musial, Stanley Frank; Palmer, Jim; Plank, Eddie; Robinson, Brooks Calbert; Ruth, Babe; Seaver, Tom; Terry, William Harold; Traynor, Pie; Wagner, Honus; Williams, Ted.

Baseball's Brilliant Managers. Nathan Aaseng. Lerner, 1982 (AAS-1)
Alston, Walter E.; McGraw, John Joseph; Mack, Connie; Martin, Billy; Stengel, Casey; Williams, Dick.

Baseball's Champion Pitchers: The Cy Young Award Winners. Hal Butler. Messner, 1974 (o.p.) (BUJB)
Blue, Vida; Carlton, Steven Norman; Jenkins, Ferguson Arthur; Palmer, Jim; Perry, Gaylord Jackson.

Baseball's Finest Pitchers. Nathan Aaseng. Lerner, 1980 (AAS-2)
Blue, Vida; Guidry, Ron; Marshall, Michael Grant; Niekro, Phil; Palmer, Jim; Perry, Gaylord Jackson; Ryan, Nolan; Seaver, Tom; Sutter, Bruce; Tiant, Luis.

Baseball's Greatest Catchers. Al Hirshberg. Putnam, 1966 (o.p.) (HIC)
Berra, Yogi; Bresnahan, Roger; Campanella, Roy; Cochrane, Mickey; Cooper, Walker; Crandall, Delmar Wesley; Dickey, Bill; Gowdy, Hank; Hartnett, Gabby; Hegan, Jim; Howard, Elston; Kling, Johnny; Lombardi, Ernie; Lopez, Al; O'Neill, Stephen Francis; Owen, Mickey; Ruel, Muddy; Schalk, Ray; Schang, Walter Henry; Tebbetts, Birdie.

Baseball's Greatest Managers. Harvey Frommer. Watts, 1985 (FRC-01)
Alston, Walter E.; Anson, Cap; Chance, Frank; Clarke, Fred; Cronin, Joe; Dressen, Charlie; Durocher, Leo; Harris, Bucky; Herzog, Whitey; Huggins, Miller; Jennings, Hugh Ambrose; Lopez, Al; McCarthy, Joseph Vincent; McGraw, John Joseph; Mack, Connie; McKechnie, Bill; Martin, Billy; Robinson, Wilbert; Stengel, Casey; Weaver, Earl; Williams, Dick.

Baseball's Greatest Pitchers. Milton J. Shapiro. Messner, 1969 (o.p.) (SHA)
Alexander, Grover Cleveland; Drysdale, Don; Ford, Whitey; Gibson, Bob; Johnson, Walter Perry; Koufax, Sandy; McLain, Dennis; Mathewson, Christy; Spahn, Warren; Young, Cy.

Baseball's Greatest Sluggers. Bill Libby. Random, 1973 (LEV)
Aaron, Hank; Foxx, James Emory; Mays, Willie Howard; Ruth, Babe; Williams, Ted.

Baseball's Hall of Fame. Harvey Frommer. Watts, 1985 (FRC-1)
Aaron, Hank†; Alston, Walter E.†; Aparicio, Luis†; Banks, Ernie†; Berra, Yogi†; Bottomley, Jim†; Brown, Three-Fingered†; Campanella, Roy†; Clemente, Roberto†; Cobb, Ty†; Dean, Dizzy†; Delahanty, Edward James†; Feller, Bob†; Ford, Whitey†; Foxx, James Emory†;

Gehrig, Lou†; Gibson, Bob†; Greenberg, Hank†; Hornsby, Rogers†; Hubbell, Carl Owen†; Irvin, Monte†; Johnson, Walter Perry†; Keeler, Wee Willie†; Klem, Bill†; Koufax, Sandy†; McGinnity, Joseph Jerome†; McGraw, John Joseph†; Mack, Connie†; Mantle, Mickey Charles†; Marquard, Rube†; Mathewson, Christy†; Mays, Willie Howard†; Musial, Stanley Frank†; Ott, Mel†; Paige, Satchel†; Rickey, Branch†; Robinson, Brooks Calbert†; Robinson, Jackie†; Ruth, Babe†; Sisler, George†; Snider, Duke†; Speaker, Tristram E.†; Stengel, Casey†; Vance, Dazzy†; Wagner, Honus†; Waner, Lloyd James†; Waner, Paul†; Williams, Ted†; Wilson, Lewis R. "Hack"†; Young, Cy†.

Baseball's Home-Run Hitters. Richard Rainbolt. Lerner, 1975 (RAAA)
Aaron, Hank; Foxx, James Emory; Gehrig, Lou; Killebrew, Harmon; Kiner, Ralph M.; Mantle, Mickey Charles; Maris, Roger Eugene; Mays, Willie Howard; Ruth, Babe; Williams, Ted.

Baseball's Hottest Hitters. Nathan Aaseng. Lerner, 1983 (AAS-3)
Brett, George Howard; Carew, Rod; Garvey, Steven Patrick; Hernandez, Keith; Lynn, Frederic Michael; Oliver, Al; Parker, Dave; Rose, Pete.

Baseball's Most Colorful Managers. Ray Robinson. Putnam, 1969 (o.p.) (ROAA)
Durocher, Leo; Huggins, Miller; McGraw, John Joseph; Mack, Connie; Robinson, Wilbert; Stengel, Casey.

Baseball's Most Valuable Players. Hal Butler. Messner, 1977 (o.p.) (BUJC)
Burroughs, Jeff; Garvey, Steven Patrick; Lynn, Frederic Michael; Morgan, Joe; Munson, Thurman Lee.

Baseball's Most Valuable Players. George Vecsey. Random, 1966 (o.p.) (VEA)
Banks, Ernie; Berra, Yogi; Boudreau, Lou; Boyer, Ken; Di Maggio, Joseph Paul; Frisch, Frank; Konstanty, Jim; Mantle, Mickey Charles; Mays, Willie Howard; Musial, Stanley Frank; Versalles, Zoilo; Williams, Ted; Wills, Maury.

Baseball's Power Hitters. Nathan Aaseng. Lerner, 1983 (AAS-4)
Foster, George; Jackson, Reggie; Kingman, Dave; Rice, Jim; Schmidt, Mike; Stargell, Willie; Thomas, James Gorman; Winfield, Dave.

Baseball's Youngest Big Leaguers. John Devaney. HR&W, 1969 (o.p.) (DEE)
Chance, Dean; Di Maggio, Joseph Paul; Feller, Bob; Mays, Willie Howard; Williams, Ted; Yastrzemski, Carl Michael.

Baseball's Zaniest Stars. Howard Liss. Random, 1971 (o.p.) (LIAA)
Dean, Dizzy; Gaedel, Eddie†; Gomez, Lefty; Herman, Babe; Hogan, Shanty†; Maranville, Rabbit; Mueller, Heinie†; Newsom, Bobo; Paige, Satchel†; Ruth, Babe†; Schacht, Al†; Schaefer, Germany†; Stengel, Casey; Waddell, Rube.

Basepaths: From the Minor Leagues to the Majors and Beyond. Marc Gunther. Scribner, 1984 (GUB-1)
Almon, Bill; Boyd, Oil Can; Darling, Ron; Heyison, Marc; Hundhammer, Paul; Hunter, Catfish; Jenkins, Ferguson Arthur; Kemp, Steve; Kittle, Ron; White, William D.

Basketball Superstars: Three Great Pros. Les Etter. Garrard, 1974 (ETA)
Chamberlain, Wilt; Robertson, Oscar; West, Jerry.

Basketball's Big Men. Richard Rainbolt. Lerner, 1975 (RAAB)
Abdul-Jabbar, Kareem; Barry, Rick; Baylor, Ed; Chamberlain, Wilt; Lucas, Jerry; Mikan, George L.; Pettit, Robert; Reed, Willis; Russell, William Felton; Schayes, Adolph.

Basketball's Greatest Stars. Al Hirshberg. Putnam, 1963 (o.p.) (HID)
Auerbach, Red; Baylor, Ed; Chamberlain, Wilt; Cousy, Bob; Heinsohn, Tommy; Holman, Nat; Lapchick, Joseph Bohomiel; Lucas, Jerry; Luisetti, Hank; Macauley, Ed; McKinney, Bones; Martin, Slater; Mikan, George L.; Pettit, Robert; Robertson, Oscar; Rupp, Adolph; Russell, William Felton; Schayes, Adolph; Sharman, William; Stokes, Maurice; Twyman, Jack; West, Jerry.

Basketball's High Flyers. Nathan Aaseng. Lerner, 1980 (AAS-5)
Cowens, Dave; Erving, Julius; Gilmore, Artis; Hayes, Elvin; Johnson, Marques; McAdoo, Bob; Malone, Moses; Thompson, David; Walton, Bill.

Basketball's Playmakers. Nathan Aaseng. Lerner, 1983 (AAS-6)
Archibald, Nate "Tiny"; Buckner, Quinn; Davis, Johnny; Ford, Phil; Johnson, Earvin "Magic"; Lucas, John; Nixon, Norm; Porter, Kevin.

Basketball's Power Players. Nathan Aaseng. Lerner, 1985 (AAS-7)
Cummings, Terry; Dantley, Adrian; Lucas, Maurice; Malone, Moses; Roundfield, Dan; Ruland, Jeff; Sikma, Jack; Williams, Buck.

Basketball's Sharpshooters. Nathan Aaseng. Lerner, 1983 (AAS-8)
Bird, Larry; Birdsong, Otis; Brown, Fred; Free, "World B"; Gervin, George; King, Bernard; Newlin, Mike; Westphal, Paul.

Beginnings. Gwendolyn Reed, comp. Atheneum, 1971 (o.p.) (RAC)
Andersen, Hans Christian; Cellini, Benvenuto; Chateaubriand, François René; Coleridge, Samuel Taylor; Dietz, Johann; Hutton, William; Kazin, Alfred; Kropotkin, Pëtr Alekseevich; Montaigne, Michel de; O'Crohan, Tomás; Tanner, John; Twain, Mark, pseud.

Behind the Plate: Three Great Catchers. Guernsey Van Riper, Jr. Garrard, 1973 (o.p.) (VACA)
Campanella, Roy; Cochrane, Mickey; Dickey, Bill.

Behind the Wheel: Great Road Racing Drivers. Robert B. Jackson. Walck, 1971 (o.p.) (JA)
Amon, Chris; Andretti, Mario; Beltoise, Jean-Pierre; Brabham, Jack; Clark, James; Donohue, Mark; Fangio, Juan Manuel; Gurney, Dan; Hall, Jim; Hill, Graham; Hill, Phil; Hulme, Dennis Clive; Ickx, Jacky; McLaren, Bruce Leslie; Moss, Stirling; Revson, Peter Jeffrey; Rindt, Jochen; Rodriguez, Pedro; Savage, Swede; Siffert, Josef; Stewart, Jackie; Surtees, John.

Benefactors of the World. I. O. Evans. Warne, 1968 (o.p.) (EVA)
Baden-Powell, Robert Stephenson Smyth, 1st baron; Barnardo, Thomas John; Booth, William; Braille, Louis; Carnegie, Andrew; Churchill, Sir Winston Leonard Spencer; Dunant, Jean Henri; Hill, Sir Rowland; Keller, Helen Adams; Nobel, Alfred Bernhard; Owen, Robert; Plimsoll, Samuel; Shaftesbury, Anthony Ashley Cooper, 7th earl of.

Best Book of Heroes and Heroines. Pauline Rush Evans, ed. Doubleday, 1964 (o.p.) (EVD)
Boone, Daniel; Carver, George Washington; Columbus, Christopher; Curie, Marie Sklodowska; Damien de Veuster, Joseph; Earhart, Amelia; Hale, Nathan; Joan of Arc; Keller, Helen Adams; Lincoln, Abraham; Lindbergh, Charles Augustus; Magellan, Ferdinand; Nightingale, Florence; Pasteur, Louis; Reed, Walter; Revere, Paul; Schweitzer, Albert; Washington, George; Whitman, Narcissa; Wright, Orville; Wright, Wilbur.

Best in Baseball. Robert H. Shoemaker. T Y Crowell, 3d rev. ed., 1974 (o.p.) (SHH)
Aaron, Hank; Bench, Johnny Lee; Carlton, Steven Norman; Clemente, Roberto; Cobb, Ty; Cochrane, Mickey; Dean, Dizzy; Di Maggio, Joseph Paul; Feller, Bob; Gehrig, Lou; Hornsby, Rogers; Hubbell, Carl Owen; Mantle, Mickey Charles; Mays, Willie Howard; Musial, Stanley Frank; Roberts, Robin; Robinson, Jackie; Ruth, Babe; Simmons, Aloysius Harry; Spahn, Warren; Williams, Ted.

Beyond the Dream: Occasional Heroes of Sports. Ira Berkow. Atheneum, 1975 (o.p.) (BELB)
Aaron, Hank; Ali, Muhammad; Amos, John; Beard, Frank; Bench, Johnny Lee; Berg, Moe; Cannon, Jimmy; Carlos, John; Cerdan, Marcel, Jr.; Citation; Cobb, James; Cobb, Ty†; Cowens, Dave; Csonka, Larry; Dempsey, Jack†; Dempsey, Tom; Dern, Bruce; Di Maggio, Joseph Paul; Duncan, Jim; Evert, Chris; Fischer, Bobby; Frazier, Joe; Fuqua, Frenchy; Gable, Dan; Gonzales, Pancho; Gray, Pete; Hoist the Flag; Kaline, Albert William; Kitt, Howard; LaMotta, Jake; Laver, Rodney George; Lombardi, Vincent, II; Louis, Joe; Marceau, Marcel†; Maris, Roger Eugene; Mauermayer, Gisela; Miron, Charles; Mizerak, Steve; Moore, Marianne Craig†; Morcom, Richard "Boo"; Namath, Joe Willie; Nash, Charlie; Nuxhall, Joe; Palmer, Arnold; Parker, Jim; Rentzel, Lance; Robinson, Jackie; Rodriguez, Juan "Chi-Chi"; Rose, Pete†; Ruffin, Nate; Russell, Andy; Ryun, Jim; Sammartino, Bruno; Sauer, George, Jr.; Sayers, Gale; Seaver, Tom†; Sheridan, Owen; Stengel, Casey; Stewart, Jackie; Switzer,

Kathy; Tenace, Gene; Thorpe, Jim; Toefield, Alfred; Vingo, Carmine; Wallace, Cookie; Weissmuller, Johnny; West, Jerry; Williams, Ted; Woit, Dick.

Big League Pitchers and Catchers. Bennett Wayne. Garrard, 1974 (WAG)
Campanella, Roy; Cochrane, Mickey; Dickey, Bill; Ehmke, Howard John; Feller, Bob; Hubbell, Carl Owen; Johnson, Walter Perry; Mathewson, Christy; Young, Cy.

Big Star Fallin' Mama: Five Women in Black Music. Hettie Jones. Viking, 1974 (o.p.) (JOE)
Franklin, Aretha; Holiday, Billie; Jackson, Mahalia; Rainey, Ma; Smith, Bessie.

Bitter Choice: Eight South Africans' Resistance to Tyranny. Colin Legum & Margaret Legum. World Pub., 1968 (o.p.) (LEA)
Brutus, Dennis; Luthuli, Albert John; Mandela, Nelson; Naudé, C. F. Beyers; Paton, Alan; Scott, Michael; Sita, Nana; Sobukwe, Robert Mangaliso.

Black American Leaders. Margaret B. Young. Watts, 1969 (o.p.) (YOI)
Abernathy, Ralph David; Bethune, Mary McLeod; Brimmer, Andrew J.; Brooke, Edward William; Bruce, Blanche K.; Bunche, Ralph Johnson; Chisholm, Shirley; Clark, Kenneth Bancroft; Conyers, John, Jr.; De Priest, Oscar; Douglass, Frederick; Du Bois, William Edward Burghardt; Harris, Patricia R.; Hatcher, Richard Gordon; Jordan, Barbara C.; King, Martin Luther, Jr.; McGee, Henry W.; McKissick, Floyd B.; Marshall, Thurgood; Motley, Constance Baker; Phillips, Vel; Poston, Ersa Hines; Powell, Adam Clayton, Jr.; Randolph, Asa Philip; Revels, Hiram Rhoades; Rowan, Carl Thomas; Rustin, Bayard; Shaw, Leslie N.; Stokes, Carl B.; Strachan, John R.; Tubman, Harriet; Washington, Booker Taliaferro; Washington, Walter; Weaver, Robert Clifton; Wilkins, Roy; Young, Whitney Moore, Jr.

Black Artists of the New Generation. Elton C. Fax. Dodd, 1977 (o.p.) (FAI)
Brown, Kay; Burns, Maurice; Byard, Carole Marie; Chandler, Dana C.; Douglas, Emory; Francis, Miriam B.; Gomez, Manuel; Hall, Horathel; Hinton, Alfred; Jeffries, Rosalind; Maynard, Valerie; Millar, Onnie; Neals, Otto; Obey, Trudel Mimms; Oliver, Kermit; Outterbridge, John W.; Phillips, Bertrand; Smith, Alfred J., Jr.; Stark, Shirley; Twiggs, Leo Franklin.

Black Courage. A. E. Schraff. Macrae, 1969 (o.p.) (SCB)
Beckwourth, James P.; Bush, George W.; Dodson, Jacob; Esteban or Estevanico; Green, Dick; Ikard, Bose; Jackson, Saunders; Light, Allen B.; Mesa, Antonio; Morris, Ed; Riding, Henry; Rose, Edward; Tyler, Charley; York.

Black Crusaders for Freedom. Bennett Wayne. Garrard, 1974 (WAH)
Douglass, Frederick; Truth, Sojourner; Tubman, Harriet; Washington, Booker Taliaferro.

Black Defiance: Black Profiles in Courage. Jay David, ed. Morrow, 1972 (o.p.) (DADA)
Allen, Richard; Brown, William Wells; Cleaver, Eldridge; Davis, Benjamin Jefferson; Dolan, Harry; Evers, Medgar Wiley†; Lane, Lunsford; Meredith, James Howard†; Pickens, William; Randolph, Asa Philip; Truth, Sojourner; Tubman, Harriet; Williams, Daniel Hale; Williams, Fannie Barrier; Williams, Robert F.

Black Foremothers: Three Lives. Dorothy Sterling. Feminist Pr., 1979 (STAB-1)
Barnett, Ida Wells; Craft, Ellen; Terrell, Mary Church.

Black Frontiersmen: Adventures of Negroes among American Indians, 1528–1918. J. Norman Heard. Har-Row, 1969 (HAP)
Beckwourth, James P.; Esteban or Estevanico; Flipper, Henry Ossian; Hammon, Briton; Johnson, Britton†; Marrant, John; Pacheco, Luis; Pompey; Rose, Edward; Stewart, John; York.

Black Heroes of the American Revolution. Burke Davis. HarBraceJ, 1976 (DAF-1)
Antigua†; Armistead, James; Attucks, Crispus; Besse, Martial†; Christophe, Henri†; Cromwell, Oliver†; Dabney, Austin; Flora, William†; Forten, James; Haynes, Lemuel†; Hector, Edward†; Hull, Agrippa; Latchom, George†; Latham, Lambert; Lee, William†; Matthews, Saul†; Poor, Salem†; Quaco†; Ranger, Joseph†; Salem, Peter; Tarrant, Caesar†; Whipple, Prince.

Black People Who Made the Old West. William Loren Katz. T Y Crowell, 1977 (KADB)
Adams, Henry; Beckwourth, James P.; Bonga, George; Brown, Clara; Bush, George W.; Cherokee Bill; Dart, Isom; Esteban or Estevanico; Factor, Pompey; Fields, Mary; Flipper, Henry Ossian; Ford, Barney; Garcia; Gibbs, Mifflin W.; Goings, William; Griggs, Sutton E.; Hickman, Robert T.; Hodges, Ben; Ikard, Bose; Jones, John; Leidesdorff, William Alexander; Lewis, Edmonia; Logan, Greenbury; Love, Nat; McCabe, Edwin P.; Mason, Biddy; Pickett, Bill; Pointe de Sable, Jean Baptiste; Prince, Lucy Terry; Reeves, Bass; Scott, Dred; Wagoner, Henry O.; Washington, George; York; Young, Charles.

Black Pioneers of Science and Invention. Louis Haber. HarBraceJ, 1970 (HA)
Banneker, Benjamin; Carver, George Washington; Drew, Charles Richard; Hall, Lloyd Augustus; Julian, Percy Lavon; Just, Ernest Everett; Latimer, Lewis Howard; McCoy, Elijah; Matzeliger, Jan Ernst; Morgan, Garrett A.; Rillieux, Norbert; Williams, Daniel Hale; Woods, Granville T.; Wright, Louis Tompkins.

Black Politicians. Richard Bruner. McKay, 1971 (o.p.) (BRGA)
Bond, Julian; Chisholm, Shirley; Conyers, John, Jr.; Gibson, Kenneth Allen; Hatcher, Richard Gordon; Stokes, Carl B.

Black Roots: An Anthology. Jay David & Catherine J. Greene, eds. Lothrop, 1971 (o.p.) (DADB)
Angelou, Maya; Baldwin, James; Brown, Claude; Campanella, Roy; Cayton, Horace R.; Draper, Joanna; Edwards, William J.; Goodwin, Ruby Berkley; Gregory, Dick; Horne, Lena; Hughes, Langston; Kitt, Eartha; Malcolm X; Moody, Anne; Patterson, Floyd; Pickens, William; Stroyer, Jacob; Thompson, Era Bell; Walker, Thomas Calhoun; Wright, Richard.

Black Stars. Stanlee Brimberg. Dodd, 1974 (o.p.) (BRBD)
Carver, George Washington; Douglass, Frederick; Du Bois, William Edward Burghardt; Garvey, Marcus A.; Holiday, Billie; Hughes, Langston; Johnson, Jack; King, Martin Luther, Jr.; Love, Nat; Malcolm X; Tubman, Harriet; Washington, Booker Taliaferro.

Black Winners: A History of Spingarn Medalists, 1915–1983. Melvin I. Douglass. Gaus, 1984, pap. (DOF-1)
Aaron, Hank; Ailey, Alvin; Anderson, Marian; Bates, Daisy Gaston; Bethune, Mary McLeod; Braithwaite, William Stanley; Brooke, Edward William; Bunche, Ralph Johnson; Burleigh, Henry Thacker; Carver, George Washington; Chesnutt, Charles Waddell; Clark, Kenneth Bancroft; Davis, Sammy, Jr.; Drew, Charles Richard; Du Bois, William Edward Burghardt; Ellington, Duke; Evers, Medgar Wiley; Gilpin, Charles Sidney; Grimké, Archibald Henry; Haley, Alex; Harrison, Richard Berry; Hastie, William Henry; Hayes, Roland; Hope, John; Horne, Lena; Houston, Charles Hamilton; Hughes, Langston; Hunt, Alexander Henry; Johnson, James Weldon; Johnson, John H.; Johnson, Mordecai Wyatt; Julian, Percy Lavon; Just, Ernest Everett; Keith, Damon Jerome; King, Martin Luther, Jr.; Lawless, Theodore Kenneth; Lawrence, Jacob; Logan, Rayford Whittingham; Marshall, Thurgood; Mays, Benjamin E.; Mitchell, Clarence, Jr.; Moore, Harry Tyson; Moton, Robert Russa; Murphy, Carl James; Overton, Anthony; Parks, Gordon Alexander Buchanan; Parks, Rosa Lee; Price, Leontyne; Randolph, Asa Philip; Riles, Wilson; Robeson, Paul; Robinson, Jackie; Staupers, Mable Keaton; Sullivan, Leon Howard; Talbert, Mary Burnett; Tobias, Channing Heggie; Weaver, Robert Clifton; White, Walter F.; Wilkins, Roy; Williams, Paul Revere; Williams, William Taylor Burwell; Woodson, Carter Goodwin; Wright, Louis Tompkins; Wright, Richard; Yergan, Max†; Young, Andrew Jackson; Young, Charles; Young, Coleman.

Black Women of Valor. Olive W. Burt. Messner, 1974 (o.p.) (BUFA)
Barnett, Ida Wells; Clark, Septima Poinsette; Derricotte, Juliette; Walker, Maggie Lena.

Blacks in Communications: Journalism, Public Relations and Advertising. M. L. Stein. Messner, 1972 (o.p.) (STAA)
Alligood, Douglass L.; Ballard, Audreen; Bennett, Lerone, Jr.†; Borgen, Chris; Brown, Warren; Caffie, Barbara J.; Caldwell, Earl; Campbell, Barbara†; Carter, Ovie; Christmas, Walter; Coleman, Valerie D.; Conaway, James Bennett; Curry, George E.; Davis, Belva; Dotson, John L., Jr.; Draughon, Roland; Drummond, William J.; Dunbar, Ernest; Duncan, Marilyn I.;

Eaton, Roy; Giggans, Jim; Haley, Alex; Hicks, Nancy; Hilliard, William Arthur†; Holsen-dolph, Ernest†; Huggins, Edith; Hunter-Gault, Charlayne; Jackson, David L.; Jarrett, Vernon D.; Jenkins, Carol; Johnson, John, Jr.; Johnson, John H.†; Johnson, Thomas A.; Johnston, Ernest, Jr.; Lomax, Almena; Matney, William C., Jr.; Morisey, A. Alexander; Noble, Gil; Palmer, L. F., Jr.; Parker, Angela Claire†; Patterson, Lawrence Patrick; Perry, Jean; Phelps, Don G.; Poston, Ted; Raspberry, William J.; Robinson, Harry A.; Ross, Ruth N.; Rowan, Carl Thomas; Scott, Austin; Simms, Jacob E.; Sims, Tom L.; Taylor, John L.; Thornton, Jeannye†; Tolliver, Melba; Walker, Hal†; Washington, Betty; Wittenberg, Henri E.; Yette, Samuel F.

Blacks in Science: Astrophysicist to Zoologist. Hattie Carwell. Exposition, 1977 (o.p.) (CAF-1)
Antoine, Albert C.; Belfield, Wendell; Berry, Leonidas Harris; Branson, Herman; Carmichael, Berthel; Carruthers, George; Carver, George Washington; Gourdine, Meredith; Hall, Lloyd Augustus; Harris, James†; Jackson, Shirley; Johnson, Campbell C.; Just, Ernest Everett; Koontz, Roscoe L.; Kountz, Samuel; Lawless, Theodore Kenneth; McClendon, Dorothy†; Massiah, Frederick McDonald; Powell, Clilian; Rabb, Maurice†; Shaw, Earl; Thomas, An-drew†; Trice, Virgil G.; Turner, Charles Henry; Williams, Daniel Hale; Woods, Granville T.

Blood Brothers: Four Men of Science. Emma Gelders Sterne. Knopf, 1959 (o.p.) (STE)
Drew, Charles Richard; Harvey, William; Landsteiner, Karl; Malpighi, Marcello.

Bold Leaders of the American Revolution. Red Reeder. Little, 1973 (o.p.) (RAD)
Allen, Ethan; Barry, John; Burgoyne, John; Clark, George Rogers; Corbin, Margaret; Gannet, Deborah Sampson; Kosciusko, Tadeusz; Lee, Charles; Marion, Francis; Rumford, Benjamin Thompson, count; Wayne, Anthony; Willett, Marinus.

Bold Leaders of World War I. Red Reeder. Little, 1974 (o.p.) (RADA)
Breckenridge, William; Cavell, Edith; Churchill, Sir Winston Leonard Spencer; Eaton, Ralph; Joffre, Joseph Jacques; Kreisler, Fritz; Ludendorff, Erich Friedrich; Mannerheim, Baron Carl Gustaf Emil von; Marshall, George Catlett; Pétain, Henri Philippe; Richthofen, Manfred von; Stallings, Laurence.

Book of Baseball Greats. S. H. Burchard. HarBraceJ, 1983 (o.p.) (BUD-1)
Aaron, Hank; Campanella, Roy; Clemente, Roberto; Dean, Dizzy; Di Maggio, Joseph Paul; Gehrig, Lou; Koufax, Sandy; Mantle, Mickey Charles; Mays, Willie Howard; Musial, Stanley Frank; Paige, Satchel; Robinson, Jackie; Ruth, Babe; Williams, Ted.

Book of Famous Queens. Lydia Farmer. T Y Crowell, 1964 (o.p.) (FAE)
Catherine II, the Great; Catherine de Medici; Cleopatra; Elizabeth I; Elizabeth II; Isabella I; Josephine; Juliana; Maria Theresa; Marie Antoinette; Mary, Queen of Scots; Nefertiti; Tzu Hsi; Victoria; Wilhelmina; Zenobia.

Book of Heroes: Great Europeans Who Live in the Hearts of Their People. Dorothy Heiderstadt. Bobbs, 1954 (o.p.) (HEA)
Alfred the Great; Bruce, Robert the; Charlemagne; Christian IV; Cid Campeador, El; Damien de Veuster, Joseph; Elizabeth of Hungary; Ericsson, Leif; Francis of Assisi, Saint; Gustavus II; Joan of Arc, Saint; Kosciusko, Tadeusz; Magellan, Ferdinand; Nansen, Fridtjof; Patrick, Saint; Pericles; Peter I, the Great; Tell, William; William I, the Silent.

Boxing's Heavyweight Champions. Richard Rainbolt. Lerner, 1975 (RAAC)
Ali, Muhammad; Corbett, Jim; Dempsey, Jack; Fitzsimmons, Robert P.; Jeffries, Jim; Johnson, Jack; Louis, Joe; Marciano, Rocky; Sullivan, John Lawrence; Tunney, Gene.

Boyhoods of Great Composers, Book 1. Catherine Gough. Walck, 1960 (o.p.) (GOA)
Elgar, Sir Edward William; Grieg, Edvard Hagerup; Handel, George Frederick; Men-delssohn, Felix; Mozart, Wolfgang Amadeus; Schubert, Franz Peter.

Boyhoods of Great Composers, Book 2. Catherine Gough. Walck, 1963 (o.p.) (GOB)
Bach, Johann Sebastian; Beethoven, Ludwig van; Chopin, Frédéric François; Tchaikovsky, Peter Ilyich; Vaughan Williams, Ralph; Verdi, Giuseppe.

Boys from Liverpool. Nicholas Schaffner. Methuen, 1980 (SC-01)
Harrison, George; Lennon, John; McCartney, Paul; Starr, Ringo.

Brave and the Free. Sister Mary Francis Assisi. Ginn, 1967 (o.p.) (ASB)
Alcott, Bronson; Alcott, Louisa May; Cabrini, Frances Xavier, Saint; Carver, George Washington; Columbus, Christopher; Coronado, Francisco Vásquez de; De Smet, Pierre Jean; Dooley, Thomas Anthony; Franklin, Benjamin; Gallitzin, Demetrius Augustine; Jefferson, Thomas; Kennedy, John Fitzgerald; Lee, Robert Edward; Lincoln, Abraham; Marquette, Jacques; Penn, William; Pulitzer, Joseph; Roosevelt, Franklin Delano; Roosevelt, Theodore; Ruth, Babe; Saint-Gaudens, Augustus; Serra, Junipero; Seton, Elizabeth Ann, Saint; Smith, John; Washington, George; Williams, Daniel Hale; Wright, Orville; Wright, Wilbur.

Brave Men: Twelve Portraits of Courage. Mark Sufrin. Platt, 1967 (o.p.) (SUA)
Carlsen, Henrik K.; Codona, Alfredo; Doolittle, James Harold; Kennedy, Joseph Patrick, Jr.; Lindbergh, Charles Augustus; Mannock, Edward; Nungesser, Charles; Nuvolari, Tazio; Phillips, John; Schuster, George; Taylor, Maxwell Davenport; Wingate, Orde Charles.

Breaking In: Nine First Person Accounts about Becoming an Athlete. Lawrence T. Lorimer, comp. Random, 1974 (o.p.) (LOAA)
Gibson, Althea; Green, Ted; Haywood, Spencer; Mantle, Mickey Charles; Marquard, Rube; Meggyesy, Dave; Quinn, Anthony; Robinson, Jackie; Schollander, Donald Arthur.

Breakthrough: Women in Archaeology. Barbara Williams. Walker, 1981 (WIAA-01)
Bruhns, Karen Olsen; Dunn, Mary Eubanks; Green, Ernestene; Irwin-Williams, Cynthia; Kelley, Jane Holden; Wildesen, Leslie E.

Breakthrough: Women in Aviation. Elizabeth Simpson Smith. Walker, 1981 (o.p.) (SMBC-2)
Barber, Linda Elaine; Brown, Jill Elaine; Case, Sandra Williams; Kraus, Mary Ellen; Lee, Judy Ann; Myers, Joyce Carpenter; Seddon, Margaret Rhea; Skrzypiec, Tina Marie; Smethurst, Ann Orlitski.

Breakthrough: Women in Law. Betsy Covington Smith. Walker, 1984 (SMBB)
Beshar, Christine; Brown, Louise; Mentschikoff, Soia; O'Connor, Sandra Day; Thelwell, Jeanne; Zawisza, Christina.

Breakthrough: Women in Law Enforcement. Elizabeth Simpson Smith. Walker, 1982 (o.p.) (SMBC-3)
Guzman, Virginia Quintana; Higgins, Maureen Anne; Kandler, Elizabeth Aytes; Karansky, Priscilla Pepper; Lawrence, Geraldine Anderson; McNamara, Rae Hassell; Morris, Kathryn Harper; Pence, Donna Marie; Sprecher, Jenna Garman; Stanton, Susan Marie.

Breakthrough: Women in Politics. Barbara Williams. Walker, 1979 (WIAA-02)
Atwood, Genevieve; Burke, Yvonne Brathwaite; Fenwick, Millicent; Hayes, Janet Gray Frazee; Kassebaum, Nancy Landon; Peterson, Esther Eggertsen; Ray, Dixy Lee.

Breakthrough: Women in Religion. Betsy Covington Smith. Walker, 1978 (o.p.) (SMBB-1)
Egan, Sister Jogues; Green, Patricia; Hawkes, Daphne; Piccard, Jeannette R.; Sasso, Sandy.

Breakthrough: Women in Science. Diana C. Gleasner. Walker, 1983 (GL)
Ancker-Johnson, Betsy; Campbell, Billie L.; Mead, Sylvia Earle; Rubin, Vera C.; Siebert, Muriel; Yalow, Rosalyn Sussman.

Breakthrough: Women in Television. Betsy Covington Smith. Walker, 1981 (SMBB-2)
Aaron, Chloe; Austin, Andy; Culver, Carmen; Hill, Pamela; Korris, Risa; Pouissant, Renee; Rollin, Betty; Wormington, Judy.

Breakthrough: Women in Writing. Diana C. Gleasner. Walker, 1980 (GL-1)
Blume, Judy; Bombeck, Erma; Jong, Erica; West, Jessamyn; Whitney, Phyllis A.

Breakthroughs in Science. Isaac Asimov. HM, 1959 (o.p.) (ASA)
Archimedes; Becquerel, Antoine Henri; Bessemer, Sir Henry; Carver, George Washington; Copernicus, Nicolaus; Curie, Marie Sklodowska; Curie, Pierre; Darwin, Charles Robert; Edison, Thomas Alva; Ehrlich, Paul; Einstein, Albert; Faraday, Michael; Galilei, Galileo;

Goddard, Robert Hutchings; Gutenberg, Johann; Harvey, William; Henry, Joseph; Jenner, Edward; Langmuir, Irving; Lavoisier, Antoine Laurent; Lawrence, Ernest Orlando; Leeuwenhoek, Anton van; Mendel, Gregor Johann; Newton, Sir Isaac; Pasteur, Louis; Perkin, Sir William Henry; Roentgen, Wilhelm; Rutherford, Ernest Rutherford, 1st baron; Wallace, Alfred Russel; Watt, James.

Brotherhood of Pirates. Judith Schoder. Messner, 1979 (o.p.) (SC-1)
Blackbeard; Bonny, Anne; Kidd, William (Captain); Lafitte, Jean; Morgan, Sir Henry; Read, Mary.

Bull on Ice!!! Robert McAdam. Bowmar, 1971 (o.p.) (LYB)
Didrikson, Babe; Gehrig, Lou; Hull, Bobby; Owens, Jesse; Rockne, Knute; Steinmark, Fred; Thorpe, Jim; Trevino, Lee.

By-lines: Profiles in Investigative Journalism. Elizabeth Levy. Four Winds, 1975 (o.p.) (LETB)
Bernstein, Carl; Fallaci, Oriana; Murrow, Edward Roscoe; Raab, Selwyn; Sheehy, Gail; Stone, I. F.; Woodward, Robert Upshur.

Captains. Jack Clary. Atheneum, 1978 (o.p.) (CL-06)
Bando, Salvatore Leonard; Clarke, Bobby; Cournoyer, Ivan Serge; Havlicek, John; Johnson, Bob; Kunz, George; Lanier, Bob; Rose, Pete; Staubach, Roger.

Captains of Industry, by the editors of American Heritage. Bernard A. Weisberger. Har-Row, 1966 (o.p.) (WED)
Armour, Philip Danforth; Carnegie, Andrew; Duke, James Buchanan; Ford, Henry; Guggenheim, Meyer; Hill, James Jerome; McCormick, Cyrus Hall; Morgan, John Pierpont; Rockefeller, John Davison; Vanderbilt, Cornelius.

Carter Family: Country Music's First Family. Robert K. Krishef & Stacy Harris. Lerner, 1978 (KR)
Carter, Alvin Pleasant; Carter, Maybelle; Carter, Sara.

Catchers (Stars of the NL & AL). Anthony Tuttle. Creative Ed, 1976 (o.p.) (TUB)
Bench, Johnny Lee; Fisk, Carlton; Grote, Jerry; Sanguillen, Manuel DeJesus; Simmons, Ted Lyle.

Cavalcade of Young Americans. Carl Carmer, ed. Lothrop, 1958 (o.p.) (CAD)
Allen, Maria; Awendes; Barker, Sarah; Bedell, Grace; Beman, Nathan; Boone, Jemima; Bradley, Isaac; Carson, Kit; Chalmers, Willie; Cotter, Jim; Daggett, Polly; Dean, Stewart; Devereux, Henry Kelsey; Edison, Thomas Alva; Francisco, Peter; Gahadiyas; Giffen, Isaac Newton; Howard, Cordelia; Hutchinson, Abigail; Jay, Allen; Jefferson, Joseph; Keller, Helen Adams; Lewis, Idawally; Ludington, Sybil; Maffitt, John Newland; Manter, Parnel; Mitchell, Maria; Pickersgill, Caroline; Pocahontas; Redmond, Mary; Sands, Sam; Sousa, John Philip; Temby, Stephen; Unteidt, Byron; West, Benjamin; Whittaker, Joseph; Zane, Elizabeth.

Centers (Stars of the NBA). Robert Armstrong. Creative Ed, 1977 (o.p.) (ARB-1)
Abdul-Jabbar, Kareem; Cowens, Dave; McAdoo, Bob; Unseld, Westley; Walton, Bill.

Challenged by Handicap: Adventures in Courage. Richard B. Lyttle. Reilly & Lee, 1971 (o.p.) (LYA)
Bridgman, Laura Dewey; Campanella, Roy; Cunningham, Glenn; Feliciano, José; Powell, John Wesley; Pulitzer, Joseph; Roebling, Washington Augustus; Russell, Harold; Steinmetz, Charles Proteus; Trudeau, Edward Livingston; Viscardi, Henry, Jr.

Champions. Bernard Garfinkel. Platt, 1972 (o.p.) (FRD)
Aaron, Hank; Abdul-Jabbar, Kareem; Alworth, Lance; Barney, Lemuel J.; Barry, Rick; Bench, Johnny Lee; Blue, Vida; Butkus, Dick; Clemente, Roberto; Esposito, Phil; Gibson, Bob; Griese, Bob; Howe, Gordie; Hull, Bobby; Kelly, Leroy; Maravich, Pete; Mays, Willie Howard; Namath, Joe Willie; Olsen, Merlin; Orr, Bobby; Plante, Jacques; Reed, Willis; Robertson, Oscar; Robinson, Brooks Calbert; Sayers, Gale; Seaver, Tom; Unitas, Johnny; Washington, Gene; West, Jerry; Yastrzemski, Carl Michael.

Champions at Bat: Three Power Hitters. Ann Finlayson. Garrard, 1970 (FIAA)
  Di Maggio, Joseph Paul; Hornsby, Rogers; Williams, Ted.

Champions at Speed. Richard Corson. Dodd, 1979 (o.p.) (COKC)
  Caracciola, Rudolf; Clark, James; Fangio, Juan Manuel; Hill, Graham; Hill, Phil; Moss, Stirling; Nuvolari, Tazio; Stewart, Jackie.

Champions of Labor. David F. Selvin. Abelard, 1967 (o.p.) (SEA)
  Debs, Eugene Victor; Dubinsky, David; Gompers, Samuel; Green, William; Haywood, William Dudley; Hillman, Sidney; Lewis, John Llewellyn; Meany, George; Murray, Philip; Powderly, Terence Vincent; Randolph, Asa Philip; Reuther, Walter Philip; Sylvis, William H.

Champions of Peace. Edith Patterson Meyer. Little, 1959 (o.p.) (MEA)
  Addams, Jane; American Friends Service Committee; Angell, Sir Norman; British Friends Service Council; Bunche, Ralph Johnson; Butler, Nicholas Murray; Cremer, Sir William Randal; Dunant, Jean Henri; International Red Cross of Geneva; Nansen, Fridtjof; Ossietzky, Carl von; Passy, Frédéric; Pearson, Lester Bowles; Roosevelt, Theodore; Schweitzer, Albert; Suttner, Bertha von; Wilson, Woodrow.

Champions of Sports: Adventures in Courage. George Vass. Reilly & Lee, 1970 (o.p.) (VAE)
  Didrikson, Babe; Gibson, Althea; Hogan, Ben; Mantle, Mickey Charles; Owens, Jesse; Piersall, Jim; Reiser, Pete; Robinson, Jackie; Ross, Barney; Unitas, Johnny.

Champions of the Bat: Baseball's Greatest Sluggers. Milton J. Shapiro. Messner, 1967 (o.p.) (SHB)
  Aaron, Hank; Banks, Ernie; Di Maggio, Joseph Paul; Foxx, James Emory; Gehrig, Lou; Mantle, Mickey Charles; Maris, Roger Eugene; Mathews, Edwin Lee; Mays, Willie Howard; Musial, Stanley Frank; Ott, Mel; Ruth, Babe; Williams, Ted.

Champions of the Four Freedoms. Edith Patterson Meyer. Little, 1966 (o.p.) (MEB)
  American Library Association; Calvert, Cecilius, 2nd baron Baltimore; Calvert, Charles, 3rd baron Baltimore; Calvert, George, 1st baron Baltimore; Carver, George Washington; Gompers, Samuel; Holmes, Oliver Wendell, Jr.; Jefferson, Thomas; King, Martin Luther, Jr.; Lathrop, Julia Clifford; Lovejoy, Elijah Parish; Madison, James; Mason, George; National Conference of Christians and Jews; Pauling, Linus Carl; Peace Corps; Penn, William; Riis, Jacob August; Roosevelt, Eleanor; Roosevelt, Franklin Delano; United Nations; Williams, Roger; Zenger, John Peter.

Champions of the Indianapolis 500: The Men Who Have Won More Than Once. Bill Libby. Dodd, 1976 (o.p.) (LEVA)
  Foyt, Anthony Joseph; Meyer, Louis; Milton, Thomas Willard; Rose, Mauri; Shaw, Wilbur; Unser, Al; Unser, Bobby; Vukovich, Bill; Ward, Rodger.

Champions of the Tennis Court. Hal Higdon. P-H, 1971 (o.p.) (HI)
  Ashe, Arthur; Budge, Don; Connolly, Maureen; Gonzales, Pancho; Hoad, Lew; King, Billie Jean; Kramer, Jack; Lenglen, Suzanne; Talbert, Billy; Tilden, William Tatem, Jr.; Wills, Helen.

Changing of the Guard: The New Breed of Black Politicians. Alfred Duckett. Coward, 1972 (o.p.) (DU)
  Bond, Julian; Brooke, Edward William†; Chisholm, Shirley; Conyers, John, Jr.†; Crockett, George†; Dawson, William L.†; Diggs, Charles Cole†; Evers, Charles; Evers, Myrlie†; Gibson, Kenneth Allen; Hamer, Fannie Lou; Hatcher, Richard Gordon†; Langford, Anna Riggs; Mitchell, Clarence, III; Motley, Constance Baker; Powell, Adam Clayton, Jr.†; Stokes, Carl B.; Sutton, Percy Ellis.

Changing Vice-Presidency. Roy Hoopes. T Y Crowell, 1981 (HOEA)
  See listing under *America's Vice-Presidents* by Diana Dixon Healy.

Chief Cloud of Dust. Robert McAdam. Bowmar, 1972 (o.p.) (LYC)
  Ashe, Arthur; Cunningham, Glenn; Fleming, Peggy; Koufax, Sandy; Mills, Billy; Riegels, Roy; Ruth, Babe; Warmerdam, Cornelius.

Children in Medicine. Muriel Farr. P-H, 1964 (o.p.) (FAF)
Auenbrugger, Leopold; Cook, James; Jenner, Edward†; Jupille, Jean Baptiste; Koch, Robert; Laënnec, René Théophile; Lister, Joseph, 1st baron Lister of Lyme Regis; Nightingale, Florence; Pasteur, Louis; Phipps, James; Trudeau, Edward Livingston.

Children of the Handcrafts. Carolyn Sherwin Bailey. Viking, 1935 (o.p.) (BAC)
Chapman, John; Gillett, Joshua; Harriman, Mercy; Helme, Johnny; Hunt, Nathan; Ide, Simeon; Lee, George; Lefferts, Rebecca; Metcalf, Betsy; Moyer, Daniel; Phyfe, Duncan; Pickersgill, Caroline; Revere, Paul; Standish, Lora; Thoreau, Henry David; Ward, Macock; Whitcher, Sylvanus.

China's Leaders in Ideas and Action. Cornelia Spencer. Macrae, 1966 (o.p.) (SPA)
Chiang Kai-shek; Chou En-lai; Confucius; Hsüan Tsung; Hung Hsiu-ch'üan; Mao Tse-tung; Shih Huang Ti; Sun Yat-sen; Tzu Hsi; Wang An-shih; Wang Mang; Yen, James Yang-ch'u.

Circus Heroes and Heroines. Rhina Kirk. Hammond, 1972 (o.p.) (KIB)
Adler, Felix; Bailey, Mollie Arline; Barnum, Phineas Taylor; Beatty, Clyde; Cody, William Frederick; Concello, Antoinette; Concello, Arthur Vas; Evans, Merle; Griebling, Otto; Jacobs, Lou; Kelly, Emmett; Leitzel, Lillian; Oakley, Annie; Rice, Daniel McLaren, Jr.; Ringling Brothers (John, Otto, Charles, Alfred T. and Albert C.); Stratton, Charles Sherwood; Wallenda family; Wirth, May.

Citizens Born Abroad. L. Edmond Leipold. T. S. Denison, 1967 (o.p.) (LEB)
Audubon, John James; Bell, Alexander Graham; Cole, Thomas; Hamilton, Alexander; Mayo, William Worrall; Mergenthaler, Ottmar; Pupin, Michael Idvorsky; Rockne, Knute; Schurz, Carl; Slater, Samuel; Van Loon, Hendrik.

Coaches. Bill Libby. Regnery, 1972 (o.p.) (LEW)
Allen, George; Alston, Walter E.; Auerbach, Red†; Belmont, Joe; Blair, Wren; Blake, Toe; Brawner, Clint†; Bryant, Paul "Bear"; Chavoor, Sherm; Combs, Bob; Dean, Al; Durocher, Leo; Holovak, Mike†; Imlach, Punch; Kabakoff, Harry; Kerr, John; Lapchick, Joseph Bohomiel†; Lemm, Wally; McKay, John; Melnick, Bob†; Motta, Richard; Mullaney, Joe†; Phillips, Lefty; Pont, John; Prothro, Tom; Reel, Vince; Russell, William Felton; Schaus, Frederick; Seidell, Joe; Sharman, William; Stasiuk, Vic; Stengel, Casey; Van Breda Kolff, Bill†; Vogel, Herb; Walker, Harry William; Winter, Bud; Wooden, John R.

Coaches (Stars of the NBA). Robert Armstrong. Creative Ed, 1977 (o.p.) (ARB-2)
Attles, Alvin; Fitch, Bill; Holzman, Red; Jones, K. C.; Sharman, William.

Coaches (Stars of the NFL). Sam Hasegawa. Creative Ed, 1975 (o.p.) (HAGA)
Allen, George; Grant, Bud; Landry, Tom; Shula, Don.

Comeback: Six Remarkable People Who Triumphed over Disability. Frank Bowe. Har-Row, 1981 (BOHA-1)
Daniels, Susan; Fiorito, Eunice; Hawking, Stephen; Meyers, Roger; Sharpless, Nansie; Smithdas, Robert.

Comeback Stars of Pro Sports. Nathan Aaseng. Lerner, 1983 (AAS-9)
Keough, Matt; Lauda, Niki; Leach, Reggie; Peoples, Woody; Plunkett, Jim; Silas, James; Stone, Steve; Wade, Virginia.

Comedians of Country Music. Stacy Harris. Lerner, 1978 (HAG-1)
Akeman, David "Stringbean"; Burns, Kenneth Charles "Jethro"; Campbell, Archie; Clark, Roy; Clower, Jerry; Ford, Whitey "Duke of Paducah"; Gobel, George; Haynes, Henry Doyle "Homer"; Jones, Grandpa; Macon, Uncle Dave; Pearl, Minnie; Tillis, Mel.

Composers for the American Musical Theatre. David Ewen. Dodd, 1968 (o.p.) (EWA)
Berlin, Irving; Bernstein, Leonard; Bock, Jerry; Cohan, George Michael; Friml, Rudolf; Gershwin, George; Herbert, Victor; Kern, Jerome; Loesser, Frank; Loewe, Frederick; Porter, Cole; Rodgers, Richard Charles; Romberg, Sigmund; Weill, Kurt.

Composers of Tomorrow's Music. David Ewen. Greenwood repr. of 1971 ed., 1980 (EWAA)
Babbitt, Milton; Boulez, Pierre; Cage, John; Ives, Charles; Partch, Harry; Schönberg, Arnold; Stockhausen, Karlheinz; Varèse, Edgard; Webern, Anton von; Xenakis, Yannis.

Computer Pioneers. Laura Greene. Watts, 1985 (GRAB-3)
Atanasoff, John Vincent†; Babbage, Charles; Backus, John W.†; Bardeen, John; Brattain, Walter Houser; Burroughs, William S.†; Eckert, J. Presper; Felt, Dorr E.†; Grant, George Barnard†; Hollerith, Herman†; Hopper, Grace Murray; Leibniz, Gottfried Wilhelm freiherr von†; Lovelace, Lady Ada; Mauchly, John W.; Morland, Samuel†; Pascal, Blaise; Shockley, William Bradford; Stibitz, George Robert†; Turing, Alan M.; Von Neumann, John; Watson, Thomas J., Sr.

Conquistadors. Elizabeth Poe Kerby. Putnam, 1969 (o.p.) (KEG)
Cabeza de Vaca, Álvar Núñez; Coronado, Francisco Vásquez de; Cortes, Hernando; Narváez, Pánfilo de; Pizarro, Francisco; Ponce de León, Juan.

Contemporary American Indian Leaders. Marion E. Gridley. Dodd, 1972 (o.p.) (GRAC)
Adams, Henry; Ballard, Louis W.; Bennett, Robert LaFollette; Blue Spruce, George; Blythe, Jarrett; Bruce, Louis R.; Cook, Leon F.; Deloria, Vine, Jr.; Demmert, Archie W.; Gladstone, James; Harris, LaDonna; Hatathli, Ned; Houser, Allan; Jones, Harold S.; Keeler, William Wayne; MacDonald, Peter; Martinez, Maria Montoya; Mills, Billy; Momaday, N. Scott; Old Coyote, Barney; Peterson, Helen L.; Raymond, Arthur; Reifel, Ben; Rhoades, Everett; Vasquez, Joseph C.; Wauneka, Annie Dodge.

Contemporary Black Leaders. Elton C. Fax. Dodd, 1970 (o.p.) (FAG)
Brooke, Edward William; Clark, Kenneth Bancroft; Dee, Ruby; Evers, Charles; Hamer, Fannie Lou; Hatcher, Richard Gordon; King, Coretta Scott; McKissick, Floyd B.; Malcolm X; Marshall, Thurgood; Rustin, Bayard; Stokes, Carl B.; Wilkins, Roy; Young, Whitney Moore, Jr.

Contributions of Women: Art. Carol Fowler. Dillon, 1976 (FOGB)
Cassatt, Mary; Chicago, Judy†; Dickinson, Eleanor Creekmore†; Escobar, Marisol†; Frankenthaler, Helen; Guggenheim, Peggy†; Hartigan, Grace†; Jackson, Suzanne; Krasner, Lee†; Mitchell, Joan†; Moses, Anna Mary Robertson; Neel, Alice†; Nevelson, Louise; O'Keeffe, Georgia; Spencer, Lilly Martin†.

Contributions of Women: Aviation. Ann Genett. Dillon, 1975 (GEDB)
Cobb, Geraldyn M.; Cochran, Jacqueline; Earhart, Amelia; Gaffaney, Mary†; Gilbert, Edwina†; Howell, Emily; Law, Ruth†; Lindbergh, Anne Morrow; Marshall, Ellen Church†; Mock, Jerrie; Nichols, Ruth†; Omlie, Phoebe Fairgrave†; Quimby, Harriet†; Stinson, Katherine†; Thaden, Louise†; Wells, Mary Georgene†.

Contributions of Women: Business. Nancy Smiler Levinson. Dillon, 1981 (LES-1)
Ancker-Johnson, Betsy†; Arden, Elizabeth; Beech, Olive Ann; Chapin, Jane†; Cooney, Joan Ganz; Cousins, Jane "Casey"; Esty, Jane†; Harper, Beverly†; Hume, Jo Ann†; Lansing, Sherry†; Lewis, Tillie; Roebling, Mary G.; Rudkin, Margaret Fogharty; Shaver, Dorothy; Spain, Jayne Baker†; Trahey, Jane.

Contributions of Women: Dance. Carol Fowler. Dillon, 1979 (FOGC)
Chase, Lucia†; Corkle, Francesca†; De Mille, Agnes; Duncan, Isadora; Dunham, Katherine; Graham, Martha; Gregory, Cynthia; Jamison, Judith; Kirkland, Gelsey; MacLaine, Shirley; Prowse, Juliet†; St. Denis, Ruth†; Tallchief, Maria; Tharp, Twyla.

Contributions of Women: Education. Mary W. Burgess. Dillon, 1975 (o.p.) (BUDA)
Beecher, Catharine Esther†; Berry, Martha McChesney; Bethune, Mary McLeod; Blow, Susan Elizabeth†; Fuller, Sarah†; Hill, Patty Smith; Laney, Lucy†; Lyon, Mary; Palmer, Alice Freeman†; Peabody, Elizabeth Palmer†; Sabin, Florence Rena; Sanford, Maria Louisa†; Thomas, Martha Carey†; Willard, Emma Hart; Woolley, Mary Emma†.

Contributions of Women: Labor. Marcia McKenna Biddle. Dillon, 1979 (BI)
Clauss, Carin†; Haley, Margaret†; Huerta, Dolores; Jones, Mary Harris; Nestor, Agnes†; Perkins, Frances; Robins, Margaret Dreier†; Schneiderman, Rose†; Sellins, Fannie†; Turner, Doris†; Van Horn, Edith†; Vorse, Mary Heaton; Weyand, Ruth†; Wolfgang, Myra†; Wyatt, Addie.

Contributions of Women: Literature. Karen O'Connor. Dillon, 1984 (OCB)
Angelou, Maya; Bradstreet, Anne Dudley; Buck, Pearl S.; Cather, Willa; Dickinson, Emily;

McCarthy, Mary†; McCullers, Carson†; Millay, Edna St. Vincent; Mitchell, Margaret; O'Connor, Flannery†; Parker, Dorothy; Porter, Katherine Anne†; Sarton, May; Walker, Alice†; Welty, Eudora.

Contributions of Women: Medicine. Demerris C. Ranahan. Dillon, 1981 (RAAG)
Apgar, Virginia; Blackwell, Elizabeth†; Fisher, Anna†; Hamilton, Alice†; Hofmann, Adele; Horney, Karen†; Jacobi, Mary Putnam†; Jonasson, Olga; Logan, Myra Adele†; Picotte, Susan LaFlesche†; Ramcharan, Savitri; Taussig, Helen Brooke; Wright, Jane C.†; Zakrzewska, Marie Elizabeth†.

Contributions of Women: Music. Catherine Scheader. Dillon, 1985 (SC-02)
Anderson, Marian; Beach, Mrs. H. H. A.†; Bley, Carla†; Brico, Antonia; Caldwell, Sarah†; Collins, Judy; Fine, Vivian†; Fox, Carol†; Jenson, Dylana; Powell, Maude†; Price, Leontyne; Seeger, Ruth Crawford; Sills, Beverly; Stevens, Risé†; Zukerman, Eugenia†.

Contributions of Women: Politics and Government. Louise G. Greenbaum. Dillon, 1977 (o.p.) (GRAB-1)
Abzug, Bella†; Cockerell, Lila†; Costanza, Margaret†; Douglas, Helen Gahagan†; Grasso, Ella; Griffiths, Martha W.; Jordan, Barbara C.; Krupsak, Mary Anne; Luce, Clare Boothe; Rankin, Jeannette; Ray, Dixy Lee†; Reed, Betty Lou†; Schroeder, Patricia Scott†; Smith, Margaret Chase; Sullivan, Leonor K.†; Weizmann, Chaim.

Contributions of Women: Religion. Naomi Bloom. Dillon, 1978 (o.p.) (BLF)
Brown, Antoinette Blackwell†; Cabrini, Frances Xavier†; Day, Dorothy; Eddy, Mary Baker; Harkness, Georgia†; Hutchinson, Anne Marbury; Lee, Ann; Piccard, Jeannette R.†; Preisand, Sally†; Seton, Elizabeth Ann†; Smith, Amanda Berry†; Szold, Henrietta; Truth, Sojourner†; Wedel, Cynthia Clark†.

Contributions of Women: Science. Diane Emberlin. Dillon, 1977 (o.p.) (EMB)
Britton, Elizabeth Gertrude†; Cannon, Annie Jump; Carson, Rachel; Clark, Eugenie; Comstock, Anna Botsford†; Emerson, Gladys Anderson†; Farquhar, Jane Colden†; Gilbreth, Lillian M.; Mead, Margaret; Mitchell, Maria†; Patrick, Ruth; Quimby, Edith Hinkley†; Ray, Dixy Lee†; Van Straten, Florence†; Washburn, Margaret Floy†; Wu, Chien-Shiung†.

Contributions of Women: Social Reform. Ruth F. Brin. Dillon, 1977 (o.p.) (BRBE)
Addams, Jane; Barnett, Ida Wells†; Curlee-Salisbury, Joan†; Dix, Dorothea Lynde†; Hall, Helen†; Hamer, Fannie Lou†; Hamilton, Alice; Jones, Mary Harris†; Kelley, Florence; Lathrop, Julia Clifford†; Roosevelt, Eleanor; Sanger, Margaret; Tubman, Harriet; Wald, Lillian D.†; Wauneka, Annie Dodge†; Willard, Frances Elizabeth.

Contributions of Women: Sports. Joan Ryan. Dillon, 1975 (RYA)
Belote, Melissa; Didrikson, Babe; Ederle, Gertrude C.†; Fleming, Peggy; Gibson, Althea†; Henie, Sonja†; King, Billie Jean; King, Micki†; Kusner, Kathy; Rigby, Cathy†; Rudolph, Wilma G.; Sears, Eleanora†; Tyus, Wyomia†; Wills, Helen†.

Contributions of Women: Theater. Ann Dillon & Cynthia Bix. Dillon, 1978 (DI-1)
Bancroft, Anne†; Barrymore, Ethel; Brice, Fanny†; Cornell, Katharine†; Dewhurst, Colleen†; Fiske, Minnie Maddern; Gordon, Ruth†; Harris, Julie; Hayes, Helen; Hellman, Lillian; Martin, Mary†; Merman, Ethel†; Moreno, Rita†; Stapleton, Maureen†; Waters, Ethel†.

Courage Makes the Champion. Gene Schoor. Van Nos Reinhold, 1967 (o.p.) (SCA)
Brissie, Lou; Brown, Three-Fingered; Campanella, Roy; Cunningham, Glenn; Didrikson, Babe; Eisenhower, Dwight David; Gehrig, Lou; Hogan, Ben; Kennedy, John Fitzgerald; Lee, Canada; Robinson, Jackie; Ross, Barney; Schoendienst, Red; Tunney, Gene.

Cowboys and Cattlemen. Lela Waltrip & Rufus Waltrip. McKay, 1967 (o.p.) (WAA)
Altoha, Wallace; Chisum, John Simpson; Coe, Urling C.; Crosby, Bob; Goodnight, Charles; King, Richard; Mossman, Burton C.; Pickett, Bill; Rhodes, Eugene Manlove; Rogers, Will; Russell, Charles Marion; Van Orsdel, William Wesley.

Crusaders for a Cause. L. Edmond Leipold. T. S. Denison, 1967 (o.p.) (LEC)
Chapman, John; Franklin, Benjamin; Garrison, William Lloyd; Greeley, Horace; Lovejoy,

Elijah Parish; Mann, Horace; Moody, Dwight Lyman; Reed, Walter; Washington, Booker Taliaferro; Webster, Daniel.

Crusaders for Freedom. Henry Steele Commager. Doubleday, 1962 (o.p.) (COG)
Adams, John Quincy; Addams, Jane; Alcott, Bronson; Andersen, Hans Christian; Anthony, Susan Brownell; Blackwell, Elizabeth; Brace, Charles Loring; Calas, Jean; Catt, Carrie Chapman; Coffin, Levi; Erskine, Thomas; Froebel, Friedrich Wilhelm; Garrison, William Lloyd; Grundtvig, Nikolai F. S.; Jefferson, Thomas; Kold, Christen Mikkelsen; Laubach, Frank; Lincoln, Abraham; Lovejoy, Elijah Parish; Lyon, Mary; Mann, Horace; Mott, Lucretia Coffin; Nansen, Fridtjof; Oastler, Richard; Paine, Thomas; Parker, Theodore; Penn, William; Phillips, Wendell; Roosevelt, Eleanor; Sarmiento, Domingo Faustino; Shaftesbury, Anthony Ashley Cooper, 7th earl of; Stanton, Elizabeth Cady; Tubman, Harriet; Voltaire; Willard, Emma Hart; Williams, Roger; Yen, James Yang-ch'u; Zola, Émile.

Czars and Czarinas of Russia. Tamara Talbot Rice. Lothrop, 1968 (o.p.) (RIA)
Alexander I; Alexander II; Alexander III; Basil III Ivanovich; Catherine II, the Great; Elizabeth Petrovna; Godunov, Boris Fëdorovich†; Ivan III, the Great; Ivan IV, the Terrible; Nicholas I; Nicholas II; Paul I; Peter I, the Great; Romanov, House of; Sophia.

Dancers of the Ballet: Biographies. Margaret F. Atkinson & May Hillman. Knopf, 1955 (o.p.) (ATA)
Adams, Diana; Alonso, Alicia; Babilee, Jean; Boris, Ruthanna; Caron, Leslie; Chauviré, Yvette; Chouteau, Yvonne; Danielian, Leon; Danilova, Alexandra; Dolin, Anton; Eglevsky, André; Fifield, Elaine; Fonteyn, Margot; Franklin, Frederic; Grey, Beryl; Helpmann, Robert; Hightower, Rosella; Jeanmaire, Renée; Kaye, Nora; Kriza, John; Laing, Hugh; LeClerq, Tanaquil; Lichine, David; Lifar, Serge; Marchand, Colette; Markova, Alicia; Moylan, Mary Ellen; Novak, Nina; Petit, Roland; Reed, Janet; Riabouchinska, Tatiana; Shearer, Moira; Skibine, George; Slavenska, Mia; Tallchief, Maria; Tallchief, Marjorie; Toumanova, Tamara; Tupine, Oleg; Vollmar, Jocelyn; Youskevitch, Igor; Zoritch, George.

Daring Sea Captains. Marcia Scott. Lerner, 1973 (o.p.) (SCBA)
Anderson, William Robert; Bligh, William; Cousteau, Jacques Yves; Graham, Robin Lee; Heyerdahl, Thor; Kennedy, John Fitzgerald; Nelson, Horatio, viscount; Shackleton, Sir Ernest Henry; Slocum, Joshua.

Day They Made the Record Book. Milton J. Shapiro. Messner, 1968 (o.p.) (SHC)
Di Maggio, Joseph Paul; Gehrig, Lou; Koufax, Sandy; Larsen, Don; Maris, Roger Eugene; Ruth, Babe; Wills, Maury.

Decathlon Men: Greatest Athletes in the World. Ann Finlayson. Garrard, 1966 (o.p.) (FIB)
Johnson, Rafer; Mathias, Bob.

Defenders: Osceola, Tecumseh, Cochise. Ann McGovern. Scholastic, 1987, pap. (MAEA)
Cochise; Osceola; Tecumseh.

Defensive Linemen (Stars of the NFL). Jay H. Smith. Creative Ed, 1975 (o.p.) (SMD)
Eller, Carl; Lilly, Robert Lewis; Marshall, Jim; Page, Alan; Smith, Charles "Bubba".

Demagogues. Fred J. Cook. Macmillan, 1972 (o.p.) (COGA)
Beecher, Lyman; Coughlin, Charles Edward; Garrison, William Lloyd; Long, Huey Pierce; McCarthy, Joseph R.; Parris, Samuel; Yancey, William Lowndes.

Dictators. Jules Archer. Hawthorn, 1967 (o.p.) (ARA)
Ataturk, Mustafa Kemal; Batista, Fulgencio; Castro, Fidel; Chiang Kai-shek; Duvalier, François; Franco, Francisco; Hitler, Adolf; Khrushchev, Nikita S.; Lenin, Nikolai; Mao Tse-tung; Mussolini, Benito; Nasser, Gamal Abdel; Perón, Juan Domingo; Salazar, António de Oliveira; Stalin, Joseph; Sukarno, Achmed; Tito, Josip Broz; Trujillo Molina, Rafael Leónidas.

Dictators of Latin America. Patricia Baum. Putnam, 1972 (o.p.) (BAGA)
Castro, Fidel; Díaz, Porfirio; Duvalier, François; Perón, Eva Duarte; Perón, Juan Domingo; Stroessner, Alfredo; Trujillo Molina, Rafael Leónidas; Vargas, Getúlio Dornelles.

Different Drummers. Antoinette May. Les Femmes, 1976, pap. (o.p.) (MAT-1)
Bernhardt, Sarah; Blavatsky, Elena Petrovna; Duncan, Isadora; Earhart, Amelia; Schumann-Heink, Ernestine; Woodhull, Victoria.

Disease Fighters: The Nobel Prize in Medicine. Nathan Aaseng. Lerner, 1987 (AAS-31)
Banting, Sir Frederick Grant; Behring, Emil von; Domagk, Gerhard; Ehrlich, Paul; Fleming, Sir Alexander; Koch, Robert; Müller, Paul Hermann†; Nicolle, Charles Jules Henri; Ross, Sir Ronald; Theiler, Max.

Divas. Winthrop Sargeant. Coward, 1973 (o.p.) (SAB)
Farrell, Eileen; Horne, Marilyn; Nilsson, Birgit; Price, Leontyne; Sills, Beverly; Sutherland, Joan.

Doctors for the People: Profiles of Six Who Serve. Elizabeth Levy. Knopf, 1977 (o.p.) (LETC)
Brown, Dorothy; Door, The; Esposito, Vince; McKusick, Victor; Rosen, Sheldon; Storch, Marcia.

Doctors in Petticoats. Alice Fleming. Lippincott, 1964 (o.p.) (FLA)
Barringer, Emily Dunning; Baumgartner, Leona; Guion, Connie Meyers; Hamilton, Alice; Horney, Karen; Jacobi, Mary Putnam; Jordan, Sara; Pearce, Louise; Swain, Clara A.; Zakrzewska, Marie Elizabeth.

Doctors to the Great. Elaine Mardus & Miriam Lang. Dial, 1962 (o.p.) (MAR)
Bard, Samuel; Coictier, Jacques; Frank, Johann Peter; Hunter, John; Hunter, William; Larrey, Dominique Jean; Linacre, Thomas; Lopez, Roderigo; MacKenzie, Sir Morell; Maimonides; Necker, Oliver.

Doctors Who Saved Lives. Lynne Poole & Gray Poole. Dodd, 1966 (o.p.) (POB)
Abel, John Jacob; Addison, Thomas; Banting, Sir Frederick Grant; Carrel, Alexis; Chain, Ernst Boris; Ehrlich, Paul; Fabricius ab Aquapendente, Hieronymus; Ferrier, David; Fleming, Sir Alexander; Florey, Sir Howard Walter; Fracastoro, Girolamo; Kocher, Emil Theodor; Louis, Pierre Charles Alexandre; Paracelsus; Sims, James Marion; Virchow, Rudolf.

Doers and Dreamers: Social Reformers of the Nineteenth Century. Lynne Deur. Lerner, 1972 (DEDA)
Addams, Jane; Alcott, Bronson; Anthony, Susan Brownell; Bloomer, Amelia Jenks; Comstock, Anthony; Dix, Dorothea Lynde; Douglass, Frederick; Dow, Neal; Howe, Julia Ward; Howe, Samuel Gridley; Noyes, John Humphrey; Owen, Robert; Stanton, Elizabeth Cady; Stone, Lucy.

Double Winners of the Medal of Honor. Raymond J. Tassin. Daring, 1986 (TA)
Baldwin, Frank; Butler, Smedley Darlington; Cooper, John; Cukela, Louis; Custer, Thomas Ward; Daly, Daniel Joseph; Hogan, Henry; Janson, Ernest August; Kelly, John Joseph; King, John; Kocak, Matej; Leonard, Patrick; McCloy, John; Mullen, Patrick; Pruitt, John Henry; Sweeney, Robert; Weisbogel, Albert; Williams, Louis; Wilson, William.

Dreamers and Doers. Norman Richards. Atheneum, 1984 (RIBA)
Eastman, George; Edison, Thomas Alva; Goddard, Robert Hutchings; Goodyear, Charles.

Dreams into Deeds: Nine Women Who Dared. Linda Peavy & Ursula Smith. Scribner, 1985 (PACA)
Addams, Jane; Anderson, Marian; Carson, Rachel; Didrikson, Babe; Hamilton, Alice; Jones, Mary Harris; Low, Juliette; Mead, Margaret; Stanton, Elizabeth Cady.

Ebony Book of Black Achievement. Margaret Peters. Johnson Chi, rev. ed., 1974 (o.p.) (PECA)
Aldridge, Ira; Allen, Richard; Attucks, Crispus; Banneker, Benjamin; Barnett, Ida Wells; Beckwourth, James P.; Bethune, Mary McLeod; Bruce, Blanche K.; Bush, George W.; Cuffe, Paul; Douglass, Frederick; Drew, Charles Richard; Du Bois, William Edward Burghardt; Elliott, Robert B.; Esteban or Estevanico; Hall, Primus†; Hall, Prince; Henson, Matthew Alexander; Mansa Musa I; Matzeliger, Jan Ernst; Pointe de Sable, Jean Baptiste; Smalls, Robert; Spaulding, Charles Clinton; Walker, David; Wheatley, Phillis; Williams, Daniel Hale; Woods, Granville T.

Eight Black American Inventors. Robert C. Hayden. A-W, 1972 (o.p.) (HAL)
Anderson, Jo†; Blair, Henry†; Forten, James†; Jones, Frederick McKinley; Latimer, Lewis Howard; McCoy, Elijah; Matzeliger, Jan Ernst; Morgan, Garrett A.; Rillieux, Norbert; Temple, Lewis; Woods, Granville T.

Eleven Who Dared. Hermann Hagedorn. Scholastic, 1967 (o.p.) (HAA)
Cavell, Edith; Damien de Veuster, Joseph; Elizabeth I; Gandhi, Mohandas Karamchand; Hannibal; Joan of Arc; Lee, Robert Edward; Lindbergh, Charles Augustus; Luther, Martin; Roosevelt, Theodore; Socrates.

Engineers of the World. I. O. Evans. Warne, 1963 (o.p.) (EVB)
Brindley, James; Brunel, Isambard Kingdom; Eiffel, Alexandre Gustave; Ford, Henry; Lesseps, Ferdinand de; Nasmyth, James; Parsons, Sir Charles Algernon; Rennie, John; Smeaton, John; Stephenson, George; Stephenson, Robert; Trevithick, Richard; Watt, James.

English Explorers of North America. Neil Grant. Messner, 1970 (o.p.) (GRAA)
Cabot, John; Drake, Sir Francis; Frobisher, Sir Martin; Hudson, Henry.

Explorers: Adventures in Courage. Edward F. Dolan, Jr. Reilly & Lee, 1970 (o.p.) (DOBB)
Amundsen, Roald; Clark, William; Columbus, Christopher; Cook, James; Lewis, Meriwether; Livingstone, David; Peary, Robert Edwin; Scott, Robert Falcon.

Explorers of Man: Five Pioneers in Anthropology. H. R. Hays. Macmillan, 1971 (o.p.) (HAO)
Bastian, Adolf; Lévi-Strauss, Claude; Malinowski, Bronislaw Kasper; Mead, Margaret; Schoolcraft, Henry Rowe.

Explorers of Our Land. L. Edmond Leipold. T. S. Denison, 1967 (o.p.) (LED)
Boone, Daniel; Bridger, James; Clark, William; Colter, John; De Soto, Hernando; Frémont, John Charles; La Salle, Robert Cavelier, sieur de; Lewis, Meriwether; Pike, Zebulon Montgomery; Schoolcraft, Henry Rowe; Smith, Jedediah Strong.

Explorers of the Arctic and Antarctic. Edward F. Dolan, Jr. Macmillan, 1968 (o.p.) (DOC)
Amundsen, Roald; Andrée, Salomon A.†; Barents, Willem; Bartlett, Robert Abram†; Bellingshausen, Fabian von†; Byrd, Richard Evelyn; Cook, James; De Long, George Washington†; Franklin, Sir John; Frobisher, Sir Martin; Fuchs, Sir Vivian Ernest†; Henson, Matthew Alexander†; Hudson, Henry; McClintock, Sir Francis Leopold; Nansen, Fridtjof; Peary, Robert Edwin; Ross, Sir James Clark†; Scott, Robert Falcon; Shackleton, Sir Ernest Henry; Wilkes, Charles†.

Explorers of the Deep: Pioneers of Oceanography. Donald W. Cox. Hammond, 1968 (o.p.) (COR)
Agassiz, Alexander; Anderson, William Robert; Bascom, Willard; Beebe, William; Bond, George F.; Carpenter, Malcolm Scott; Carson, Rachel; Cousteau, Jacques Yves; Ewing, W. Maurice; Franklin, Benjamin; Holland, John Philip; Link, Edwin Albert; Maury, Matthew Fontaine; Piccard, Auguste; Piccard, Jacques; Revelle, Roger; Rickover, Hyman George; Wilkes, Charles.

Exploring the World. Stella Davies. Roy, 1965 (o.p.) (DAF)
Columbus, Christopher; Cook, James; Gama, Vasco da; Kingsley, Mary Henrietta; Livingstone, David; Polo, Marco.

Exploring the World. Patrick Moore. Watts, 1966 (o.p.) (MOB)
Alexander III, the Great; Amundsen, Roald; Barents, Willem; Bellingshausen, Fabian von; Burton, Sir Richard Francis; Cabot, John; Cabot, Sebastian; Cartier, Jacques; Columbus, Christopher; Cook, James; Cortes, Hernando; Dampier, William; Darwin, Charles Robert; Doughty, Charles Montagu; Drake, Sir Francis; Eric the Red; Ericsson, Leif; Franklin, Sir John; Fuchs, Sir Vivian Ernest; Gagarin, Yuri Alekseyevich; Gama, Vasco da; Halley, Edmund; Harrison, John; Henry the Navigator; Herjolfsson, Bjarni†; Hillary, Sir Edmund; Hudson, Henry; Humboldt, Alexander von; Ingolf; La Pérouse, Jean François de Galaup, comte de; Livingstone, David; MacKenzie, Sir Alexander; Magellan, Ferdinand; Nansen, Fridtjof; Orellana, Francisco de; Park, Mungo; Perry, Matthew Calbraith; Pizarro, Francisco; Polo, Marco; Ptolemy; Pytheas; Scott, Robert Falcon; Speke, John Hanning; Sturt, Charles; Tasman, Abel J.; Tenzing, Norgay; Vespucci, Amerigo.

Faces of Freedom. Myron Emanuel. Scholastic, 1971 (o.p.) (EMA)
  Attucks, Crispus; Banneker, Benjamin; Forten, James; Prosser, Gabriel.

Famous American Architects. Sigmund A. Lavine. Dodd, 1967 (o.p.) (LAF)
  Breuer, Marcel Lajos; Bulfinch, Charles; Burnham, Daniel Hudson; Fuller, Richard Buckminster; Gropius, Walter Adolf; Latrobe, Benjamin Henry; McKim, Charles Follen; Mead, William Rutherford; Neutra, Richard Joseph; Richardson, Henry Hobson; Saarinen, Eero; Saarinen, Eliel; Sullivan, Louis Henry; White, Stanford.

Famous American Architects. L. Edmond Leipold. T. S. Denison, 1972 (o.p.) (LEDA)
  Bulfinch, Charles; Cerny, Robert George; Mendelsohn, Eric; Mies van der Rohe, Ludwig; Saarinen, Eero; Stone, Edward Durrell; Sullivan, Louis Henry; Williams, Paul Revere; Wright, Frank Lloyd.

Famous American Artists. L. Edmond Leipold. T. S. Denison, 1969 (o.p.) (LEE)
  Bingham, George Caleb; Cassatt, Mary; Davies, Arthur B.; Homer, Winslow; Peale, Charles Willson; Sargent, John Singer; Stuart, Gilbert; West, Benjamin; Whistler, James Abbott McNeill; Wood, Grant.

Famous American Athletes. William Heuman. Dodd, 1963 (o.p.) (HEG)
  Button, Dick; Cobb, Ty; Cousy, Bob; Dempsey, Jack; Grange, Red; Howe, Gordie; Jones, Bobby; Louis, Joe; Mathias, Bob; Owens, Jesse; Richard, Maurice; Richards, Robert Eugene; Ruth, Babe; Thorpe, Jim; Tilden, William Tatem, Jr.; Weissmuller, Johnny.

Famous American Athletes. L. Edmond Leipold. T. S. Denison, 1969 (o.p.) (LEF)
  Dempsey, Jack; Feller, Bob; Garms, Shirley Rudolph; Heiss, Carol; Jones, Bobby; Louis, Joe; Mathias, Bob; Mendelssohn, Moses; Ruth, Babe; Tilden, William Tatem, Jr.; Weissmuller, Johnny.

Famous American Authors. Sarah K. Bolton. T Y Crowell, 1954 (o.p.) (BOA)
  Alcott, Louisa May; Benét, Stephen Vincent; Bryant, William Cullen; Cather, Willa; Cooper, James Fenimore; Emerson, Ralph Waldo; Hawthorne, Nathaniel; Holmes, Oliver Wendell; Irving, Washington; Lewis, Sinclair; Longfellow, Henry Wadsworth; O'Neill, Eugene Gladstone; Poe, Edgar Allan; Sandburg, Carl; Stowe, Harriet Beecher; Thoreau, Henry David; Twain, Mark, pseud.; Wharton, Edith; Whitman, Walt; Whittier, John Greenleaf.

Famous American Cowboys. Bern Keating. Rand, 1977 (o.p.) (KAW)
  Horn, Tom; King, Richard; Linderman, Bill; McJunkin, George; Remington, Frederic; Rogers, Will; Siringo, Charles A.; Slaughter, John H.

Famous American Doctors. L. Edmond Leipold. T. S. Denison, 1969 (o.p.) (LEG)
  Carlson, Earl; Crumbine, Samuel Jay; Halsted, William Stewart; Horney, Karen; Jackson, Charles Thomas†; Lillehei, Clarence Walton; Long, Crawford Williamson†; McDowell, Ephraim; Morton, William; Salk, Jonas Edward; Whitman, Marcus; Zakrzewska, Marie Elizabeth.

Famous American Engineers. L. Edmond Leipold. T. S. Denison, 1972 (o.p.) (LEGA)
  Bush, Vannevar; Davidson, J. Brownlee; Gilbreth, Lillian M.; Goddard, Robert Hutchings; Goethals, George Washington; Mead, Elwood; Roebling, Washington Augustus; Singstad, Ole; Suman, John Robert; Turner, Scott.

Famous American Fiction Writers. L. Edmond Leipold. T. S. Denison, 1972 (o.p.) (LEGB)
  Baldwin, James; Buck, Pearl S.; Cooper, James Fenimore; Hawthorne, Nathaniel; Hemingway, Ernest; Irving, Washington; Lewis, Sinclair; London, Jack; Poe, Edgar Allan; Twain, Mark, pseud.

Famous American Humorists. Laura Benét. Dodd, 1959 (o.p.) (BEE)
  Ade, George; Benchley, Robert; Day, Clarence S., Jr.; Dunne, Finley Peter; Field, Eugene; Hale, Lucretia Peabody; Lardner, Ring; Leacock, Stephen Butler; Marquis, Don; Nash, Ogden; Shute, Henry Augustus; Skinner, Cornelia Otis; Stockton, Frank Richard; Streeter, Edward; Tarkington, Booth; Thurber, James G.; Twain, Mark, pseud.

Famous American Humorous Poets. Everett S. Allen. Dodd, 1968 (o.p.) (ALA)
  Adams, Franklin Pierce; Armour, Richard Willard; Fishback, Margaret; Guitarman, Arthur;

Herford, Oliver; Hoffenstein, Samuel Goodman; McGinley, Phyllis; Marquis, Don; Morley, Christopher; Nash, Ogden; Parker, Dorothy; Riley, James Whitcomb; Taylor, Bert Leston.

Famous American Indians. William Heuman. Dodd, 1972 (o.p.) (HEGA)
Brant, Joseph; Crazy Horse; Joseph; Osceola; Philip; Pontiac; Sequoya; Sitting Bull; Tecumseh.

Famous American Indians. L. Edmond Leipold. T. S. Denison, 1967 (o.p.) (LEH)
Curtis, Charles; Geronimo; Howe, Oscar; Martinez, Maria Montoya; Osceola; Pocahontas; Pontiac; Rogers, Will; Sitting Bull; Thorpe, Jim.

Famous American Labor Leaders. L. Edmond Leipold. T. S. Denison, 1972 (o.p.) (LEHA)
Dubinsky, David; Gompers, Samuel; Green, William; Haywood, William Dudley; Lewis, John Llewellyn; Meany, George; Powderly, Terence Vincent; Randolph, Asa Philip; Reuther, Walter Philip; Sylvis, William H.

Famous American Men of Letters. Robert Cantwell. Dodd, 1956 (o.p.) (CAC)
Brooks, Van Wyck; Caldwell, Erskine†; Cooper, James Fenimore; Crane, Stephen; Dos Passos, John Roderigo†; Dreiser, Theodore†; Emerson, Ralph Waldo; Farrell, James Thomas†; Faulkner, William; Garland, Hamlin†; Hawthorne, Nathaniel; Hemingway, Ernest; Henry, O., pseud.; Howells, William Dean†; Irving, Washington; London, Jack; Melville, Herman; Parkman, Francis; Poe, Edgar Allan; Prescott, William Hickling; Thoreau, Henry David; Twain, Mark, pseud.

Famous American Military Leaders of World War II. Army Times Editors. Dodd, 1962 (o.p.) (ARC)
Arnold, Henry Harley; Bradley, Omar Nelson; Carlson, Evans Fordyce; Doolittle, James Harold; Eisenhower, Dwight David; Halsey, William Frederick; King, Ernest Joseph; LeMay, Curtis Emerson; MacArthur, Douglas; Marshall, George Catlett; Nimitz, Chester William; Patton, George Smith, Jr.

Famous American Musicians. L. Edmond Leipold. T. S. Denison, 1972 (o.p.) (LEHB)
Anderson, Marian; Armstrong, Louis "Satchmo"; Berlin, Irving; Bernstein, Leonard; Bland, James A.; Cliburn, Van; Gottschalk, Louis Moreau; Horne, Lena; Revere, Paul; Sousa, John Philip.

Famous American Negro Poets. Charlemae Rollins. Dodd, 1965 (o.p.) (ROE)
Bontemps, Arna; Braithwaite, William Stanley; Brooks, Gwendolyn; Cullen, Countee; Dunbar, Paul Laurence; Hammon, Jupiter; Harper, Frances Ellen Watkins; Hughes, Langston; Johnson, James Weldon; Newsome, Effie Lee; Walker, Margaret; Wheatley, Phillis.

Famous American Negroes. Langston Hughes. Dodd, 1954 (o.p.) (HUA)
Abbott, Robert Sengstacke; Aldridge, Ira; Allen, Richard; Anderson, Marian; Bunche, Ralph Johnson; Carver, George Washington; Douglass, Frederick; Dunbar, Paul Laurence; Handy, William Christopher; Randolph, Asa Philip; Robinson, Jackie; Spaulding, Charles Clinton; Tanner, Henry Ossawa; Tubman, Harriet; Washington, Booker Taliaferro; Wheatley, Phillis; Williams, Daniel Hale.

Famous American Negroes. L. Edmond Leipold. T. S. Denison, 1967 (o.p.) (LEI)
Anderson, Marian; Attucks, Crispus; Beckwourth, James P.; Brooke, Edward William; Bunche, Ralph Johnson; Carver, George Washington; Dunbar, Paul Laurence; Esteban or Estevanico; Henson, Matthew Alexander; Pointe de Sable, Jean Baptiste.

Famous American Painters. Roland J. McKinney. Dodd, 1955 (o.p.) (MAG)
Bellows, George Wesley; Cassatt, Mary; Copley, John Singleton; Eakins, Thomas; Henri, Robert; Homer, Winslow; Inness, George; Prendergast, Maurice Brazil; Ryder, Albert Pinkham; Sargent, John Singer; Smybert, John; Stuart, Gilbert; Whistler, James Abbott McNeill.

Famous American Pioneering Women. Edna Yost. Dodd, 1961 (o.p.) (YOC)
Blackwell, Elizabeth; Comstock, Anna Botsford; Dix, Dorothea Lynde; Dodge, Mary Mapes; Earhart, Amelia; Goddard, Mary Katherine; Hutchinson, Anne Marbury; Lathrop, Rose Hawthorne; Mitchell, Maria; Mott, Lucretia Coffin; Tarbell, Ida Minerva; Tubman, Harriet; Willard, Emma Hart.

Famous American Poets. Laura Benét. Dodd, 1950 (o.p.) (BEF)
 Benét, Stephen Vincent; Benét, William Rose; Bryant, William Cullen; Davies, Mary Carolyn; Dickinson, Emily; Dunbar, Paul Laurence; Emerson, Ralph Waldo; Field, Eugene; Frost, Robert; Holmes, Oliver Wendell; Lindsay, Vachel; Longfellow, Henry Wadsworth; Lowell, James Russell; Moore, Clement Clarke; Morley, Christopher; Poe, Edgar Allan; Richards, Laura E.; Riley, James Whitcomb; Sandburg, Carl; Thaxter, Celia; Whitman, Walt; Whittier, John Greenleaf.

Famous American Poets. L. Edmond Leipold. T. S. Denison, 1969 (o.p.) (LEJ)
 Field, Eugene; Frost, Robert; Hughes, Langston; Lindsay, Vachel; Longfellow, Henry Wadsworth; Millay, Edna St. Vincent; Riley, James Whitcomb; Tate, Allen; Wheatley, Phillis; Whitman, Walt.

Famous American Political Families. Don Lawson. Abelard, 1965 (o.p.) (LAI)
 Adams, Charles Francis; Adams, John; Adams, John Quincy; Adams, Samuel; Harrison, Benjamin (1726–1791); Harrison, Benjamin (1833–1901); Harrison, William Henry; Kennedy, Edward Moore†; Kennedy, John Fitzgerald; Kennedy, Joseph Patrick, Sr.†; Kennedy, Joseph Patrick, Jr.†; Kennedy, Robert Francis†; La Follette, Philip Fox†; La Follette, Robert Marion, Jr.; La Follette, Robert Marion, Sr.; Long, Earl Kemp; Long, Huey Pierce; Long, Russell B.; Roosevelt, Eleanor; Roosevelt, Franklin Delano; Roosevelt, Franklin Delano, Jr.†; Roosevelt, James†; Roosevelt, John A.†; Roosevelt, Theodore; Taft, Alphonso†; Taft, Robert Alphonso; Taft, Robert Alphonso, Jr.†; Taft, William Howard; Taft, William Howard, III†.

Famous American Revolutionary War Heroes. S. Carl Hirsch. Rand, 1974 (o.p.) (HIBD)
 Adams, Abigail; Adams, Samuel; Hale, Nathan; Jones, John Paul; Marion, Francis; Martin, Joseph Plumb; Morgan, Daniel; Paine, Thomas.

Famous American Spies. Rae Foley. Dodd, 1962 (o.p.) (FOA)
 Bowie, Walter; Boyd, Belle; Crosby, Enoch; Edmonds, Sarah Emma; Greenhow, Rose O'Neal; Hale, Nathan; Lewis, Pryce; Pinkerton, Allan; Revere, Paul; Townsend, Robert; Van Lew, Elizabeth; Webster, Timothy; Woodhull, Abraham†.

Famous American Statesmen. William O. Stevens. Dodd, 1953 (o.p.) (STH)
 Calhoun, John Caldwell; Clay, Henry; Franklin, Benjamin; Hamilton, Alexander; Jackson, Andrew; Jefferson, Thomas; Lincoln, Abraham; Madison, James; Marshall, John; Monroe, James; Petigru, James Louis; Roosevelt, Theodore; Schurz, Carl; Washington, George; Webster, Daniel.

Famous American Teachers. L. Edmond Leipold. T. S. Denison, 1972 (o.p.) (LEJA)
 Berry, Martha McChesney; Bethune, Mary McLeod; Conant, James Bryant; Dewey, John; Lyon, Mary; McGuffey, William Holmes; Macy, Anne Sullivan; Mann, Horace; Washington, Booker Taliaferro; Willard, Emma Hart.

Famous American Women. L. Edmond Leipold. T. S. Denison, 1967 (o.p.) (LEK)
 Anthony, Susan Brownell; Barton, Clara; Cather, Willa; Dickinson, Emily; Earhart, Amelia; Lazarus, Emma; McCauley, Mary; Madison, Dolley Payne Todd; Peabody, Elizabeth Palmer; Sacajawea; Washington, Martha Dandridge.

Famous American Women. Hope Stoddard. T Y Crowell, 1970 (o.p.) (STLA)
 Addams, Jane; Alcott, Louisa May; Anderson, Marian; Anthony, Susan Brownell; Barrymore, Ethel; Barton, Clara; Bethune, Mary McLeod; Cabrini, Frances Xavier, Saint; Cassatt, Mary; Cather, Willa; De Mille, Agnes; Dickinson, Emily; Didrikson, Babe; Dix, Dorothea Lynde; Duncan, Isadora; Earhart, Amelia; Eddy, Mary Baker; Fuller, Margaret; Gilbreth, Lillian M.; Graham, Martha; Hamilton, Edith; Hobby, Oveta Culp; Hoffman, Malvina; Keller, Helen Adams; Lange, Dorothea; Langer, Susanne Katherine; Lyon, Mary; Macy, Anne Sullivan; Mead, Margaret; Millay, Edna St. Vincent; Mitchell, Maria; Monroe, Harriet; Motley, Constance Baker; Mott, Lucretia Coffin; Ponselle, Rosa; Roosevelt, Eleanor; Sabin, Florence Rena; Sanger, Margaret; Smith, Margaret Chase; Stein, Gertrude; Stowe, Harriet Beecher; Tubman, Harriet.

Famous American Women Athletes. Helen Hull Jacobs. Dodd, 1964 (o.p.) (JAB)
 Collett, Glenna; Curtis, Ann; Didrikson, Babe; Fraser, Gretchen Kunigk; Garms, Shirley

Rudolph; Heiss, Carol; McCutcheon, Floretta Doty; Marble, Alice; Riggin, Aileen; Rudolph, Wilma G.; Varner, Margaret; Weld, Theresa; Wills, Helen.

Famous Astronomers. James S. Pickering. Dodd, 1968 (o.p.) (PIA)
Aristotle; Brahe, Tycho; Copernicus, Nicolaus; Eratosthenes; Galilei, Galileo; Herschel, Sir William; Hipparchus; Kepler, Johannes; Newton, Sir Isaac; Ptolemy.

Famous Author-Illustrators for Young People. Norah Smaridge. Dodd, 1973 (o.p.) (SM)
Anglund, Joan Walsh; Bemelmans, Ludwig; Brown, Marcia; Duvoisin, Roger; Ets, Marie Hall; Gág, Wanda; Greenaway, Kate; Lawson, Robert; Lear, Edward; Lenski, Lois; Lionni, Leo; McCloskey, Robert; Potter, Beatrix; Rey, Hans Augusto; Scarry, Richard; Sendak, Maurice; Seuss, Dr.; Turkle, Brinton; Ungerer, Tomi.

Famous Authors for Young People. Ramon P. Coffman & Nathan Goodman. Dodd, 1943 (o.p.) (COB)
Alcott, Louisa May; Andersen, Hans Christian; Barrie, Sir James M.; Burns, Robert; Carlyle, Thomas; Carroll, Lewis; Dickens, Charles; Dodge, Mary Mapes; Harris, Joel Chandler; Hawthorne, Nathaniel; Irving, Washington; Kipling, Rudyard; London, Jack; Longfellow, Henry Wadsworth; Scott, Sir Walter; Shakespeare, William; Stevenson, Robert Louis; Twain, Mark, pseud.; Wiggin, Kate Douglas.

Famous Aviators of World War II. James B. Sweeney. Watts, 1987 (SWE)
Chennault, Claire Lee; Doolittle, James Harold; LeMay, Curtis Emerson; O'Donnell, Emmett, Jr.; Spaatz, Carl.

Famous Baseball Stars. Bill Gutman. Dodd, 1973 (o.p.) (GUC)
Aaron, Hank; Cobb, Ty; Di Maggio, Joseph Paul; Gehrig, Lou; Hornsby, Rogers; Johnson, Walter Perry; Koufax, Sandy; Mantle, Mickey Charles; Mathewson, Christy; Mays, Willie Howard; Musial, Stanley Frank; Robinson, Jackie; Ruth, Babe; Speaker, Tristram E.; Wagner, Honus; Williams, Ted.

Famous Black Entertainers of Today. Raoul Abdul. Dodd, 1974 (o.p.) (AB)
Ailey, Alvin; Arroyo, Martina; Bradford, Alex; DePriest, James; Foster, Gloria; Franklin, Aretha; Grant, Micki; Haizlip, Ellis; Jones, James Earl; Mitchell, Arthur; Moore, Carman; O'Neal, Ron; Ross, Diana; Tyson, Cicely; Van Peebles, Melvin; Vereen, Ben; Watts, André; Wilson, Flip.

Famous British Novelists. John Cournos & Sybil Norton. Dodd, 1952 (o.p.) (COO)
Austen, Jane; Blackmore, Richard Doddridge†; Brontë, Anne; Brontë, Charlotte; Brontë, Emily Jane; Carroll, Lewis; Conrad, Joseph; Defoe, Daniel; Dickens, Charles; Doyle, Sir Arthur Conan; Eliot, George, pseud.; Hardy, Thomas; Hudson, William Henry; Kingsley, Charles; Kipling, Rudyard; Lytton, Edward George Earle Lytton Bulwer, 1st baron; Scott, Sir Walter; Stevenson, Robert Louis; Swift, Jonathan; Thackeray, William Makepeace.

Famous British Poets. John Cournos & Sybil Norton. Dodd, 1952 (COP)
Arnold, Matthew; Auden, Wystan Hugh; Blake, William; Brooke, Rupert; Browning, Robert; Byron, George Gordon Noel, 6th baron; Chaucer, Geoffrey; Coleridge, Samuel Taylor; Cowley, Abraham; Dryden, John; Eliot, Thomas Stearns; Gray, Thomas; Keats, John; Kipling, Rudyard; Macaulay, Thomas Babington Macaulay, 1st baron; Masefield, John; Milton, John; Noyes, Alfred; Owen, Wilfred; Pope, Alexander; Rossetti, Christina Georgina; Shakespeare, William; Shelley, Percy Bysshe; Spenser, Edmund; Swinburne, Algernon Charles; Tennyson, Alfred Tennyson, 1st baron; Wordsworth, William.

Famous British Women Novelists. Norah Smaridge. Dodd, 1967 (o.p.) (SMA)
Austen, Jane; Brontë, Anne; Brontë, Charlotte; Brontë, Emily Jane; Burney, Fanny; Christie, Agatha; Eliot, George, pseud.; Godden, Rumer; Kaye-Smith, Sheila; Sackville-West, Victoria; Sayers, Dorothy L.; Stewart, Mary; Webb, Mary; Woolf, Virginia.

Famous Builders of California. Edward F. Dolan, Jr. Dodd, 1987 (DOCA)
Burbank, Luther; Fargo, William G.; Frémont, John Charles; Muir, John; Serra, Junipero; Sutter, John Augustus; Wells, Henry.

Famous Chess Players. Peter Morris Lerner. Lerner, 1973 (o.p.) (LEQB)
   Alekhine, Alexander; Botvinnik, Mikhail M.; Capablanca, José R.; Fischer, Bobby; Keres, Paul; Lasker, Emanuel; Marshall, Frank James; Menchik, Vera; Pillsbury, Harry Nelson; Reshevsky, Samuel; Spassky, Boris V.; Tal, Mikhail.

Famous Coaches. William Heuman. Dodd, 1968 (o.p.) (HEH)
   Auerbach, Red; Callow, Russell S.; Cromwell, Dean Bartlett; Kiphuth, Robert John Herman; Lapchick, Joseph Bohomiel; Lombardi, Vincent; McCarthy, Joseph Vincent; McGraw, John Joseph; Mack, Connie; Patrick, Lester; Rockne, Knute; Rupp, Adolph; Stagg, Amos Alonzo; Stengel, Casey; Warner, Glenn "Pop."

Famous Composers for Young People. Gladys Burch & John Wolcott. Dodd, 1939 (o.p.) (BUD)
   Bach, Johann Sebastian; Beethoven, Ludwig van; Brahms, Johannes; Chopin, Frédéric François; Debussy, Claude Achille; Foster, Stephen Collins; Gluck, Christoph Willibald; Grieg, Edvard Hagerup; Handel, George Frederick; Haydn, Franz Joseph; Liszt, Franz; MacDowell, Edward Alexander; Mendelssohn, Felix; Mozart, Wolfgang Amadeus; Palestrina, Giovanni Pierluigi da; Schubert, Franz Peter; Schumann, Robert Alexander; Tchaikovsky, Peter Ilyich; Verdi, Giuseppe; Wagner, Richard.

Famous Conductors. David Ewen. Dodd, 1966 (o.p.) (EWB)
   Beecham, Sir Thomas; Furtwaengler, Wilhelm; Koussevitzky, Serge; Mitropoulos, Dimitri; Monteux, Pierre; Reiner, Fritz; Toscanini, Arturo; Walter, Bruno.

Famous Crimefighters. Robert D. Larranaga. Lerner, 1970 (o.p.) (LACA)
   Bertillon, Alphonse; Chenkin, George B.; Faurot, Joseph A.; Henry, Sir Edward Richart, bart; Hoover, J. Edgar; Peel, Sir Robert; Pinkerton, Allan; Tyrrell, John F.; Vidocq, Eugène François.

Famous English and American Essayists. Laura Benét. Dodd, 1966 (o.p.) (BEG)
   Bacon, Francis; Chesterton, Gilbert Keith; De Quincey, Thomas; Emerson, Ralph Waldo; Hazlitt, William; Irving, Washington; Johnson, Samuel; Lamb, Charles; Lang, Andrew; Macaulay, Thomas Babington Macaulay, 1st baron; Mencken, Henry Louis; Poe, Edgar Allan; Smith, Logan Pearsall; Thackeray, William Makepeace; Thoreau, Henry David; White, Elwyn Brooks; Woolf, Virginia.

Famous Explorers: Brief Biographies. Theodore Rowland-Entwistle & Jean Cook. David & Charles, 1974 (o.p.) (ROL)
   Almagro, Diego de; Alvarado, Pedro de; Amundsen, Roald; Baffin, William†; Baker, Sir Samuel White; Balboa, Vasco Núñez de; Barents, Willem†; Bass, George†; Bellingshausen, Fabian von†; Bering, Vitus J.; Biscoe, John†; Brazza, Pierre Paul François Camille Savorgnan de; Burke, Robert O'Hara; Burton, Sir Richard Francis; Byrd, Richard Evelyn; Cabeza de Vaca, Álvar Núñez; Cabot, John; Cabot, Sebastian†; Cabral, Pedro Álvares†; Caillé, René Auguste; Cano, Juan Sebastian del†; Cartier, Jacques; Champlain, Samuel de; Chancellor, Richard†; Chang Ch'ien†; Clapperton, Hugh†; Clark, William†; Columbus, Christopher; Cook, James; Coronado, Francisco Vásquez de; Cortes, Hernando; Davis, John†; Denham, Dixon†; De Soto, Hernando; Dias, Bartholomeu; Doughty, Charles Montagu†; Drake, Sir Francis; Dumont d'Urville, Jules Sébastian César†; Emin Pasha, Mehmed†; Eric the Red†; Ericsson, Leif†; Evans, Sir Edward Ratcliffe Garth Russell; Eyre, Edward John†; Fawcett, Percy Harrison†; Flinders, Matthew; Franklin, Sir John; Frémont, John Charles; Frobisher, Sir Martin†; Fuchs, Sir Vivian Ernest; Gama, Vasco da; Gilbert, Sir Humphrey†; Grant, James Augustus†; Hedin, Sven Anders†; Herbert, Walter William; Herodotus†; Hillary, Sir Edmund†; Hsuan-Tsang; Hudson, Henry; Humboldt, Alexander von; ibn-Batuta; ibn-Jubayr†; Jansz, Willem†; Jimenez de Quesada, Gonzalo†; John of Pian del Carpine†; Joliet, Louis†; Kingsley, Mary Henrietta†; Lander, Richard Lemon†; La Salle, Robert Cavelier, sieur de; Leichhardt, Friedrich Wilhelm†; Lewis, Meriwether; Livingstone, David; MacKenzie, Sir Alexander; MacMillan, Donald Baxter†; Magellan, Ferdinand; Marquette, Jacques†; Mawson, Sir Douglas; Mitchell, Sir Thomas Livingstone†; Muqaddasi-al, Muhammad ibn-Ahmad†; Nachtigal, Gustav†; Nansen, Fridtjof; Niebuhr, Carsten†; Nobile, Umberto†; Nordenskjöld, Nils Adolf; Orellana, Francisco de; Páez Xaramillo, Pedro†; Palgrave,

William Gifford; Park, Mungo†; Parry, Sir William Edward†; Peary, Robert Edwin†; Philby, Harry St. John Bridger; Pike, Zebulon Montgomery†; Pizarro, Francisco†; Pizarro, Gonzalo†; Polo, Marco; Ponce de León, Juan†; Przhevalski, Nikolai M.†; Pytheas†; Raleigh, Sir Walter; Roosevelt, Theodore†; Ross, Sir James Clark; Ross, Sir John†; Schouten, Willem Cornelis†; Scott, Robert Falcon; Shackleton, Sir Ernest Henry; Speke, John Hanning; Stanley, Sir Henry Morton; Stuart, John McDouall†; Sturt, Charles; Tasman, Abel J.; Thomas, Bertram Sidney†; Thompson, David†; Torres, Luis Vaez de†; Vancouver, George; Varthema, Ludovico de; Vespucci, Amerigo; Weddell, James†; Wilkes, Charles; Wilkins, Sir George Hubert†; William of Rubruquis†; Wills, William John†; Younghusband, Sir Francis Edward.

Famous Explorers for Young People. Ramon P. Coffman & Nathan Goodman. Dodd, 1945 (o.p.) (COC)
Alcock, Sir John†; Amundsen, Roald†; Balboa, Vasco Núñez de; Blériot, Louis†; Brown, Arthur Whitten†; Byrd, Richard Evelyn; Champlain, Samuel de; Clark, William; Columbus, Christopher; Cook, James; Coronado, Francisco Vásquez de; Cortes, Hernando; Earhart, Amelia†; Ericsson, Leif; Gama, Vasco da; Hudson, Henry; Lewis, Meriwether; Lindbergh, Charles Augustus†; Livingstone, David; MacKenzie, Sir Alexander; Magellan, Ferdinand; Nansen, Fridtjof†; Nordenskjöld, Nils Adolf†; Payer, Julius von†; Peary, Robert Edwin†; Polo, Marco; Post, Wiley†; Scott, Robert Falcon; Stanley, Sir Henry Morton.

Famous Fighters of World War I. Army Times Editors. Dodd, 1964 (o.p.) (ARD)
Allenby, Edmund Henry Hynman, 1st viscount; Beatty, David, 1st earl; Donovan, William Joseph; Foch, Ferdinand; Guynemer, Georges; Haig, Douglas Haig, 1st earl; Hindenburg, Paul von; Jellicoe, John Rushworth Jellicoe, 1st earl; Joffre, Joseph Jacques; Kitchener, Horatio Herbert, 1st earl Kitchener of Khartoum; Lawrence, Thomas Edward; Luckner, Felix von; Ludendorff, Erich Friedrich; Mitchell, William; Nungesser, Charles†; Pershing, John Joseph; Pétain, Henri Philippe; Richthofen, Manfred von; Rickenbacker, Edward Vernon; Sims, William Sowden; Tirpitz, Alfred von; York, Alvin C.

Famous French Painters. Roland J. McKinney. Dodd, 1960 (o.p.) (MAH)
Boucher, François†; Braque, Georges; Cézanne, Paul; Chardin, Jean Baptiste Siméon†; Clouet, François†; Clouet, Jean†; Corot, Jean Baptiste; David, Jacques Louis†; Degas, Edgar; Delacroix, Eugène; Fouquet, Jean†; Fragonard, Jean-Honoré†; Gauguin, Paul; Gogh, Vincent van; Gros, Antoine Jean†; Ingres, Jean Auguste Dominique†; La Tour, Georges de†; Le Brun, Charles†; Le Nain, Louis†; Le Sueur, Eustache†; Lorrain, Claude†; Manet, Édouard; Matisse, Henri; Picasso, Pablo; Poussin, Nicolas†; Renoir, Auguste; Vien, Joseph Marie†; Vouet, Simon†; Watteau, Jean Antoine†.

Famous Generals and Admirals for Young People. Ramon P. Coffman & Nathan Goodman. Dodd, 1945 (o.p.) (COD)
Alexander III, the Great; Alexander, Harold Rupert Leofric George, 1st earl†; Caesar, Gaius Julius; Decatur, Stephen; Dewey, George; Eisenhower, Dwight David†; Foch, Ferdinand; Frederick II, the Great; Genghis Khan; Grant, Ulysses Simpson; Hannibal; Jackson, Andrew; Jones, John Paul; King, Ernest Joseph†; Lee, Robert Edward; MacArthur, Douglas†; Marshall, George Catlett†; Montgomery, Bernard Law, 1st viscount Montgomery of Alamein†; Napoleon I; Nelson, Horatio, viscount; Perry, Matthew Calbraith; Pershing, John Joseph; Washington, George; Wellington, Arthur Wellesley, 1st duke of; William I, the Conqueror.

Famous Girls of the Past. Dora Northcroft. Verry, 1966 (o.p.) (NOA)
Burney, Fanny; Fry, Elizabeth Gurney; Godolphin, Margaret; Grey, Lady Katherine; Grey, Lady Mary; Herschel, Caroline; More, Hannah; Paston, Margery; Pepys, Elizabeth; Roper, Margaret; Siddons, Sarah Kemble.

Famous Historians. Frank Ernest Hill. Dodd, 1966 (o.p.) (HIB)
Adams, Henry Brooks; Bancroft, George; Beard, Charles Austin; Churchill, Sir Winston Leonard Spencer†; Froissart, Jean; Gibbon, Edward; Herodotus; Hume, David†; McMaster, John Bach; Mommsen, Theodor; Morison, Samuel Eliot†; Motley, John Lothrop†; Nevins, Allan†; Parkman, Francis; Parrington, Vernon Louis; Plutarch; Polybius; Prescott, William

Hickling†; Ranke, Leopold von; Tacitus, Cornelius; Thucydides; Toynbee, Arnold Joseph†; Trevelyan, George Macaulay; Turner, Frederick Jackson; Voltaire.

Famous Hockey Players. Trent Frayne. Dodd, 1973 (o.p.) (FR)
Beliveau, Jean; Esposito, Phil; Howe, Gordie; Hull, Bobby; Kelly, Leonard Patrick; Lindsay, Ted; Morenz, Howie; Orr, Bobby; Richard, Henri; Richard, Maurice; Sawchuk, Terry; Worsley, Gump.

Famous Indian Chiefs. John W. Moyer. Hubbard Pr., 1957 (o.p.) (MOD)
Black Hawk; Dull Knife; Geronimo; Joseph; Osceola; Parker, Quanah; Red Cloud; Red Jacket; Sitting Bull; Tecumseh; Yoholo-Micco.

Famous Industrialists. Sigmund A. Lavine. Dodd, 1961 (o.p.) (LAG)
Armour, Philip Danforth; Birdseye, Clarence; Carnegie, Andrew; Disney, Walt; Eastman, George; Firestone, Harvey Samuel; Ford, Henry; Fuller, Alfred Carl; Hilton, Conrad Nicholson; McCormick, Cyrus Hall; Sarnoff, David; Watson, Thomas J., Sr.; Westinghouse, George.

Famous Instrumentalists. David Ewen. Dodd, 1965 (o.p.) (EWC)
Ashkenasi, Shmuel; Bar-Ilian, David; Barenboim, Daniel; Bream, Julian; Cliburn, Van; Fizdale, Robert; Fleisher, Leon; Fournier, Pierre; Gilels, Emil G.; Gold, Arthur; Gould, Glenn; Graffman, Gary; Istomin, Eugene; Janis, Byron; Laredo, Jaime; Lowe, Jack; Oistrakh, David; Ricci, Ruggiero; Richter, Sviatoslav; Rose, Leonard; Rostropovich, Mstislav; Stern, Isaac; Whittemore, Arthur Austin.

Famous Inventors for Young People. Irmengarde Eberle. Dodd, 1941 (o.p.) (EBA)
Bell, Alexander Graham; Bessemer, Sir Henry; Cartwright, Edmund; Daimler, Gottlieb; Edison, Thomas Alva; Fulton, Robert; Gutenberg, Johann; McCormick, Cyrus Hall; Marconi, Guglielmo; Morse, Samuel F. B.; Stephenson, George; Watt, James; Whitney, Eli; Wright, Orville; Wright, Wilbur.

Famous Justices of the Supreme Court. James J. Flynn. Dodd, 1968 (o.p.) (FLC)
Brandeis, Louis Dembitz; Cardozo, Benjamin Nathan; Chase, Salmon Portland; Field, Stephen Johnson; Holmes, Oliver Wendell, Jr.; Hughes, Charles Evans; Jay, John; Marshall, John; Marshall, Thurgood; Story, Joseph; Taft, William Howard; Taney, Roger Brooke; Warren, Earl.

Famous Kings and Queens for Young People. Ramon P. Coffman. Dodd, 1974 (o.p.) (COA)
Alfred the Great; Charlemagne; Charles V; Cleopatra; Croesus; Cyrus; Darius; Elizabeth I; Frederick II, the Great; Frederick William I; Hadrian; Louis XIV; Marcus Aurelius; Marie Antoinette; Peter I, the Great; Richard I; Tutankhamen; Victoria; Xerxes I.

Famous Labor Leaders. Patricia Daniels. Dodd, 1970 (DABA)
Dubinsky, David; Gompers, Samuel; Green, William; Haywood, William Dudley; Hillman, Sidney; Lewis, John Llewellyn; Meany, George; Murray, Philip; Powderly, Terence Vincent; Randolph, Asa Philip; Reuther, Walter Philip; Sylvis, William H.

Famous Latin-American Liberators. Bernadine Bailey. Dodd, 1960 (o.p.) (BAA)
Bolívar, Simón; Hidalgo y Costilla, Miguel; Juárez, Benito Pablo; Martí, José Julian; Miranda, Francisco de; Morelos y Pavon, José Mariá; O'Higgins, Bernardo; San Martin, Jose de; Sucre, Antonio José de; Toussaint L'Ouverture, Pierre Dominique.

Famous Literary Teams for Young People. Norah Smaridge. Dodd, 1977 (o.p.) (SMAB)
Adams, Adrienne; Anderson, Lonzo; Asbjörnsen, Peter Christen; Aulaire, Edgar Parin d'; Aulaire, Ingri d'; Blegvad, Erik; Blegvad, Lenore; Brunhoff, Jean de; Brunhoff, Laurent de; Bryan, Dorothy; Bryan, Marguerite; Buff, Conrad; Buff, Mary Marsh; deLeeuw, Adele; deLeeuw, Cateau; Devlin, Harry; Devlin, Wende; Emberley, Barbara; Emberley, Edward Randolph; Feelings, Muriel; Feelings, Tom; Fenton, Carroll Lane; Fenton, Mildred Adams; Grimm, Jakob; Grimm, Wilhelm Karl; Hader, Berta; Hader, Elmer; McNeer, May; Moe, Jörgen Ingebretsen; Petersham, Maud; Petersham, Miska; Ward, Lynd; Yashima, Mitsu; Yashima, Taro.

Famous Makers of America. Rae Foley. Dodd, 1963 (o.p.) (FOB)
Clark, William; Franklin, Benjamin; Gompers, Samuel; Hamilton, Alexander; Jefferson, Thomas; Lewis, Meriwether; Lincoln, Abraham; Marshall, John; Penn, William; Washington, Booker Taliaferro; Washington, George; Williams, Roger; Wilson, Woodrow.

Famous Mathematicians. Frances Benson Stonaker. Lippincott, 1966 (o.p.) (STN)
Archimedes; Aryabhatta; Descartes, René; Euclid; Galois, Evariste; Gauss, Karl Friedrich; Khwarizmi, al-; Lagrange, Joseph Louis; Newton, Sir Isaac; Von Neumann, John; Wiener, Norbert.

Famous Men of Medicine. Caroline A. Chandler. Dodd, 1950 (o.p.) (CHD)
Avicenna†; Benedict, Saint†; Blackwell, Elizabeth; Columcille, Saint†; Cosmas, Saint†; Cushing, Harvey Williams; Cuthbert, Saint†; Damian, Saint†; Freud, Sigmund; Galen; Hamilton, Alice; Harvey, William; Hippocrates; Jenner, Edward; Lister, Joseph, 1st baron Lister of Lyme Regis; Osler, Sir William; Paré, Ambroise; Pasteur, Louis; Reed, Walter; Rhazes†; Roch, Saint†; Vesalius, Andreas; Virchow, Rudolf; Zinsser, Hans.

Famous Men of Modern Biology. Melvin Berger. T Y Crowell, 1968 (BEK)
Banting, Sir Frederick Grant; Behring, Emil von†; Best, Charles H.†; Bridges, Calvin Blackman†; Calvin, Melvin; Chain, Ernst Boris†; Crick, Francis H. C.; Darwin, Charles Robert; Ehrlich, Paul; Fleming, Sir Alexander; Florey, Sir Howard Walter†; Francis, Thomas, Jr.†; Hata, Sahachiro†; Koch, Robert; Lysenko, Trofim Denisovich†; Macleod, John James R.†; Mendel, Gregor Johann; Morgan, Thomas Hunt; Muller, Hermann Joseph; Pasteur, Louis; Salk, Jonas Edward; Stanley, Wendell Meredith; Sturtevant, Alfred Henry†; Watson, James Dewey.

Famous Men of Science. Sarah K. Bolton. T Y Crowell, 1960 (o.p.) (BOB)
Burbank, Luther; Compton, Arthur Holly; Compton, Karl Taylor; Compton, Wilson Martindale; Copernicus, Nicolaus; Curie, Marie Sklodowska; Curie, Pierre; Edison, Thomas Alva; Einstein, Albert; Faraday, Michael; Fermi, Enrico; Fleming, Sir Alexander; Galilei, Galileo; Herschel, Sir William; Kelvin, William Thomson, 1st baron; Lee, Tsung-Dao; Marconi, Guglielmo; Mark, Herman Francis; Newton, Sir Isaac; Reed, Walter; Salk, Jonas Edward; Urey, Harold Clayton; Yang, Chen Ning.

Famous Merchants. Sigmund A. Lavine. Dodd, 1965 (o.p.) (LAH)
Arden, Elizabeth; Brady, James Buchanan ("Diamond Jim"); Ferkauf, Eugene; Hartford, George Ludlum; Johnson, Howard Deering; Macy, Rowland Hussey; Penney, James Cash; Rudkin, Margaret Fogharty; Tiffany, Charles Lewis; Wanamaker, John; Wood, Robert Elkington; Woolworth, Frank Winfield.

Famous Mexican-Americans. Clarke Newlon. Dodd, 1972 (o.p.) (NEAA)
Anguiano, Lupe; Carr, Vikki; Chavez, Cesar Estrada; Conde, Carlos; Gonzales, Pancho; Gonzales, Rodolfo; Gonzalez, Henry Barbosa; Gutierrez, José Angel; Huerta, Dolores; Kapp, Joe; Lopez, Trini; Montalban, Ricardo; Montoya, Joseph Manuel; Nogales, Louis; Plunkett, Jim; Quinn, Anthony; Ramirez, Henry M.; Sandoval, Hilary; Tijerina, Reies Lopez; Trevino, Lee.

Famous Modern American Novelists. John Cournos. Dodd, 1952 (o.p.) (CON)
Allen, Hervey; Anderson, Sherwood; Bromfield, Louis; Buck, Pearl S.; Cather, Willa; Chase, Mary Ellen; Costain, Thomas B.; Douglas, Lloyd C.; Dreiser, Theodore†; Edmonds, Walter Dumaux; Faulkner, William; Ferber, Edna; Fitzgerald, Francis Scott Key; Glasgow, Ellen†; Guthrie, Alfred Bertram, Jr.; Hemingway, Ernest; James, Henry†; Lewis, Sinclair; Marquand, John Phillips; Mitchell, Margaret; Rawlings, Marjorie Kinnan; Roberts, Kenneth Lewis; Steinbeck, John; Tarkington, Booth; Wharton, Edith†.

Famous Modern American Women Athletes. Helen Hull Jacobs. Dodd, 1975 (o.p.) (JABA)
Babashoff, Shirley; King, Billie Jean; King, Micki; Larrieu, Francie; Lynn, Janet; Nelson, Cindy; Souter, Judy Cook; Whitworth, Kathy.

Famous Modern American Women Writers. Jane Muir. Dodd, 1959 (o.p.) (MUA)
Buck, Pearl S.; Cather, Willa; Chute, Marchette; Dickinson, Emily; Lowell, Amy; Millay,

Edna St. Vincent; Stein, Gertrude; Thompson, Dorothy; Welty, Eudora; West, Jessamyn; Wilder, Laura Ingalls.

Famous Modern Artists: From Cézanne to Pop Art. Charlotte Willard. Platt, 1971 (o.p.) (WIAA)
Boccioni, Umberto; Cézanne, Paul; Chagall, Marc; Dali, Salvador; De Kooning, Willem; Dubuffet, Jean; Duchamp, Marcel; Gauguin, Paul; Gogh, Vincent van; Hofmann, Hans; Kirchner, Ernst Ludwig; Klee, Paul; Léger, Fernand; Lichtenstein, Roy; Magritte, René; Matisse, Henri; Munch, Edward; Picasso, Pablo; Pollock, Jackson; Riley, Bridget; Shahn, Ben; Soutine, Chaim; Vasarely, Victor; Warhol, Andy; Wyeth, Andrew.

Famous Modern Conductors. David Ewen. Dodd, 1967 (o.p.) (EWD)
Bernstein, Leonard; Karajan, Herbert von; Klemperer, Otto; Krips, Josef; Leinsdorf, Erich; Maazel, Lorin; Mehta, Zubin; Munch, Charles; Ormandy, Eugene; Steinberg, William; Stokowski, Leopold; Szell, George.

Famous Modern Explorers. Bernadine Bailey. Dodd, 1963 (o.p.) (BAB)
Akeley, Carl Ethan; Amundsen, Roald; Andrews, Roy Chapman; Beebe, William; Byrd, Richard Evelyn; Glenn, John Herschel, Jr.; Hedin, Sven Anders; Heyerdahl, Thor; Hillary, Sir Edmund; Peary, Robert Edwin; Piccard, Auguste; Piccard, Jacques; Stefánsson, Vilhjálmur.

Famous Modern Men of Medicine. Caroline A. Chandler. Dodd, 1965 (o.p.) (CHE)
Armstrong, Charles†; Blalock, Alfred; Bodian, David†; Cobb, William Montague; Cushing, Harvey Williams†; DeBakey, Michael Ellis†; Deutsch, Albert†; Eliot, Martha May; Enders, John Franklin†; Francis, Thomas, Jr.†; Freud, Anna; Halsted, William Stewart†; Heine, Jacob von†; Horstmann, Dorothy Millicent†; Howe, Howard A.†; Kolff, Willem†; Landsteiner, Karl†; Mayo, Charles Horace; Mayo, William James; Mayo, William Worrall; Medawar, Peter Brian†; Medin, Oskar†; Melnick, Joseph Louis†; Menninger, Karl Augustus; Menninger, William Claire; Morgan, Isabel†; O'Connor, Basil†; Paul, John R.†; Rivers, Thomas Milton†; Rusk, Howard A.; Sabin, Albert Bruce†; Salk, Jonas Edward†; Spock, Benjamin; Taussig, Helen Brooke; White, Paul Dudley; Whitehorn, John Clare.

Famous Modern Newspaper Writers. Mildred Lewis & Milton Lewis. Dodd, 1962 (o.p.) (LEU)
Atkinson, Brooks; Berger, Meyer; Broun, Heywood Campbell; Buchwald, Art; Green, Abel; Porter, Sylvia; Pyle, Ernest Taylor; Reston, James Barrett; Smith, Red.

Famous Modern Storytellers for Young People. Norah Smaridge. Dodd, 1969 (o.p.) (SMB)
Bishop, Claire Huchet; Brink, Carol Ryrie; Coatsworth, Elizabeth; De Angeli, Marguerite; DeJong, Meindert; Enright, Elizabeth; Farjeon, Eleanor; Godden, Rumer; Henry, Marguerite; Krumgold, Joseph; Lindgren, Astrid; Lofting, Hugh; Milne, Alan Alexander; Norton, Mary; Travers, Pamela L.; White, Elwyn Brooks; Wilder, Laura Ingalls.

Famous Naturalists. Lorus J. Milne & Margery J. Milne. Dodd, 1952 (o.p.) (MIB)
Agassiz, Louis; Allen, Arthur A.†; Audubon, John James; Barbour, Thomas; Beebe, William†; Burroughs, John; Chapman, Frank Michler; Cottam, Clarence†; Darwin, Charles Robert; Ditmars, Raymond Lee†; Fabre, Jean Henri; Fairchild, David Grandison; Leeuwenhoek, Anton van; Leopold, Aldo†; Linnaeus, Carl; Muir, John; Murphy, Robert Cushman†; Peattie, Donald Culross†; Teale, Edwin Way†; Thoreau, Henry David; Wallace, Alfred Russel; White, Gilbert.

Famous Negro Athletes. Arna Bontemps. Dodd, 1964 (o.p.) (BOF)
Brown, Jim; Chamberlain, Wilt; Gibson, Althea; Louis, Joe; Mays, Willie Howard; Owens, Jesse; Paige, Satchel; Robinson, Jackie; Robinson, Ray.

Famous Negro Entertainers of Stage, Screen and TV. Charlemae Rollins. Dodd, 1967 (o.p.) (ROF)
Aldridge, Ira; Anderson, Marian; Armstrong, Louis "Satchmo"; Baker, Josephine; Belafonte, Harry; Bethune, Thomas Green†; Cole, Nat "King"; Davis, Sammy, Jr.; Ellington, Duke; Greenfield, Elizabeth Taylor†; Horne, Lena; Jones, Sisseretta†; Kitt, Eartha; Poitier, Sidney; Price, Leontyne; Robeson, Paul; Robinson, Bill "Bojangles"; Waller, Fats; Williams, Bert.

Famous Negro Heroes of America. Langston Hughes. Dodd, 1958 (o.p.) (HUB)
Attucks, Crispus; Barnett, Ida Wells; Beckwourth, James P.; Cuffe, Paul; Davis, Benjamin O., Jr.; Douglass, Frederick; Esteban or Estevanico; Henson, Matthew Alexander; Johnson, Henry; Miller, Dorie; Mulzac, Hugh Nathaniel; Pointe de Sable, Jean Baptiste; Prosser, Gabriel; Smalls, Robert; Tubman, Harriet; Young, Charles.

Famous Negro Music Makers. Langston Hughes. Dodd, 1955 (o.p.) (HUC)
Anderson, Marian; Armstrong, Louis "Satchmo"; Benjamin, Bennie; Bland, James A.; Dixon, Dean; Ellington, Duke; Fisk Jubilee Singers; Hayes, Roland; Horne, Lena; Jackson, Mahalia; Leadbelly; Morton, "Jelly Roll"; Robinson, Bill "Bojangles"; Smith, Bessie; Still, William Grant; Waters, Ethel; Williams, Bert.

Famous New England Authors. Laura Benét. Dodd, 1970 (o.p.) (BEGA)
Alcott, Louisa May; Bryant, William Cullen; Dana, Richard Henry, Jr.; Dickinson, Emily; Emerson, Ralph Waldo; Freeman, Mary Eleanor Wilkins; Frost, Robert; Hawthorne, Nathaniel; Holmes, Oliver Wendell; Jewett, Sarah Orne; Longfellow, Henry Wadsworth; Lowell, Amy; Lowell, James Russell; Marquand, John Phillips; Millay, Edna St. Vincent; Robinson, Edwin Arlington; Stowe, Harriet Beecher; Thoreau, Henry David; Whittier, John Greenleaf; Wilder, Thornton Niven.

Famous Old Masters of Painting. Roland J. McKinney. Dodd, 1951 (o.p.) (MAI)
Angelico, Fra; Botticelli, Sandro; Bruegel, Pieter, the Elder; Dürer, Albrecht; Eyck, Hubert van; Eyck, Jan van; Francesca, Piero della; Giotto di Bondone; Goya y Lucientes, Francisco José de; Greco, El; Hals, Frans; Leonardo da Vinci; Masaccio; Michelangelo Buonarroti; Raphael; Rembrandt Hermanszoon van Rijn; Rubens, Peter Paul; Titian; Velázquez, Diego Rodríguez de Silva y; Vermeer, Jan or Johannes.

Famous Photographers. Aylesa Forsee. Macrae, 1968 (o.p.) (FOD)
Adams, Ansel E.; Beaton, Cecil W.; Duncan, David Douglas; Karsh, Yousuf; Steichen, Edward.

Famous Physicists. A. L. Mann & A. C. Vivian. John Day, 1963 (o.p.) (MAQ)
Archimedes; Bacon, Roger; Faraday, Michael; Franklin, Benjamin; Galilei, Galileo; Galvani, Luigi; Guericke, Otto von; Newton, Sir Isaac; Volta, Alessandro, conte.

Famous Pioneers. Franklin Folsom. Harvey, 1963 (o.p.) (FOC)
Bent, William; Boone, Daniel; Bridger, James; Carson, Kit; Catlin, George; Clark, William; Colter, John; Crockett, Davy; Downie, William; Escalante, Silvestre Vélez de; Frémont, John Charles; James, Edwin; Ledyard, John; Lewis, Meriwether; Meek, Joseph L.; Pike, Zebulon Montgomery; Powell, John Wesley; Reed, Virginia; Siringo, Charles A.; Smith, Jedediah Strong; Whitman, Marcus; Whitman, Narcissa; Wright, Rebecca; Young, Brigham.

Famous Pioneers for Young People. Ramon P. Coffman & Nathan Goodman. Dodd, 1945 (o.p.) (COE)
Adams, John Capen; Boone, Daniel; Bridger, James; Carson, Kit; Cody, William Frederick; Crockett, Davy; Earp, Wyatt Berry Stapp; Hickok, Wild Bill; Houston, Samuel; Kenton, Simon; Marsh, John; Pancoast, Charles Edward; Sutter, John Augustus; Whitman, Marcus; Wistar, Isaac Jones; Young, Brigham.

Famous Pioneers in Space. Clarke Newlon. Dodd, 1963 (o.p.) (NEB)
Carpenter, Malcolm Scott; Ehricke, Krafft Arnold; Gagarin, Yuri Alekseyevich; Glenn, John Herschel, Jr.; Goddard, Robert Hutchings; Grissom, Gus†; Kármán, Theodor von; Nikolayev, Andrian G.†; Oberth, Hermann Julius; Popovich, Pavel Romanovich†; Schirra, Walter Marty, Jr.; Schriever, Bernard A.; Shepard, Alan Bartlett; Titov, Gherman Stepanovich; Tsiolkovsky, Konstantin E.; Van Allen, James Alfred; Von Braun, Wernher.

Famous Pirates of the New World. A. B. C. Whipple. Random, 1958 (o.p.) (WHA)
Bellamy, Charles†; Blackbeard; Bonnet, Stede; Bonny, Anne†; Bull, Dixey†; Cobham, Captain†; Daniel, Captain†; Every, Henry†; Flood, James; Fly, William†; Gibbs, Charles†; Greaves, Red Legs†; Kennedy, Captain†; Le Grand, Pierre†; Mission, Captain†; Rackam,

Jack†; Read, Mary†; Roberts, Bartholomew†; Rogers, Woodes; Tew, Thomas†; Upton, John†; Veale, Thomas†.

Famous Poets for Young People. Laura Benét. Dodd, 1964 (o.p.) (BEH)
Allingham, William; Belloc, Hilaire; Benét, Rosemary Carr; Benét, Stephen Vincent; Blake, William; Carroll, Lewis; Daly, Thomas Augustine; de la Mare, Walter John; Farjeon, Eleanor; Field, Eugene; Field, Rachel; Frost, Robert; Kingsley, Charles; Lear, Edward; Lindsay, Vachel; Longfellow, Henry Wadsworth; Milne, Alan Alexander; Moore, Clement Clarke; Noyes, Alfred; Richards, Laura E.; Riley, James Whitcomb; Rossetti, Christina Georgina; Sandburg, Carl; Stevenson, Robert Louis; Taylor, Ann; Taylor, Jane.

Famous Pro Basketball Stars. William Heuman. Dodd, 1970 (o.p.) (HEHA)
Baylor, Ed; Chamberlain, Wilt; Cousy, Bob; Holman, Nat; Lucas, Jerry; Martin, Slater; Mikan, George L.; Pettit, Robert; Robertson, Oscar; Russell, William Felton; Schayes, Adolph; West, Jerry.

Famous Pro Football Stars. William Heuman. Dodd, 1967 (o.p.) (HEI)
Baugh, Sammy; Brown, Jim; Clark, Dutch; Graham, Otto; Grange, Red; Hein, Mel; Hubbard, Cal; Hutson, Don; Luckman, Sidney; Nagurski, Bronko; Nevers, Ernie; Thorpe, Jim; Tittle, Y. A.; Unitas, Johnny; Waterfield, Robert Staton.

Famous Puerto Ricans. Clarke Newlon. Dodd, 1975 (o.p.) (NEBB)
Badillo, Herman; Benítez, Jaime; Clemente, Roberto; Colón, Miriam; Díaz, Justino; Figueroa, Carmen Sanabria de; Figueroa, Jesús; Figueroa, José; Figueroa Family; Maymi, Carmen Rosa; Meléndez, Cóncha; Moscoso, Teodoro; Muñoz Marín, Luis; Muñoz Rivera, Luis; Palés Matos, Luis; Rodriguez, Juan "Chi-Chi"; Rosado del Valle, Julio.

Famous Scientists. William O. Stevens. Dodd, 1952 (o.p.) (STI)
Bacon, Francis†; Copernicus, Nicolaus; Curie, Marie Sklodowska; Curie, Pierre; Dalton, John; Darwin, Charles Robert; Davy, Sir Humphry; Faraday, Michael; Franklin, Benjamin; Galilei, Galileo; Kepler, Johannes; Lamarck, Jean Baptiste Pierre Antoine de; Lavoisier, Antoine Laurent; Linnaeus, Carl; Lyell, Sir Charles; Maury, Matthew Fontaine; Mendel, Gregor Johann; Michelson, Albert Abraham; Newton, Sir Isaac; Priestley, Joseph; Roentgen, Wilhelm; Rumford, Benjamin Thompson, count.

Famous Scientists and Astronauts. L. Edmond Leipold. T. S. Denison, 1967 (o.p.) (LEL)
De Forest, Lee; Einstein, Albert; Fermi, Enrico; Fulton, Robert; Glenn, John Herschel, Jr.; Morse, Samuel F. B.; Schirra, Walter Marty, Jr.; Shepard, Alan Bartlett; Von Braun, Wernher; Wright, Orville; Wright, Wilbur.

Famous Signers of the Declaration. Dorothy Horton McGee. Dodd, 1955 (o.p.) (MAC)
Adams, John; Adams, Samuel; Bartlett, Josiah; Carroll, Charles; Chase, Samuel; Clark, Abraham†; Ellery, William; Floyd, William; Franklin, Benjamin; Gerry, Elbridge; Gwinnett, Button; Hall, Lyman; Hancock, John; Harrison, Benjamin; Hart, John†; Hewes, Joseph; Heyward, Thomas, Jr.†; Hooper, William†; Hopkins, Stephen; Hopkinson, Francis; Jefferson, Thomas; Lee, Richard Henry; Lewis, Francis; Livingston, Philip; Lynch, Thomas, Jr.†; McKean, Thomas; Middleton, Arthur; Morris, Lewis; Morris, Robert; Nelson, Thomas; Paca, William; Penn, John; Read, George†; Rodney, Caesar; Rush, Benjamin; Rutledge, Edward; Sherman, Roger; Stockton, Richard; Thornton, Matthew†; Walton, George†; Whipple, William†; Williams, William†; Wilson, James; Witherspoon, John; Wolcott, Oliver; Wythe, George.

Famous Spies. Frank Surge. Lerner, 1969 (o.p.) (SUG)
Baker, Lafayette Curry; Banda; Bettignies, Louise de; Boyd, Belle; Cartouche, Dominique; Delilah; Edmonds, Sarah Emma; Greenhow, Rose O'Neal; Hale, Nathan; Mata Hari; Mithridates VI; Schulmeister, Karl; Stieber, Wilhelm; Van Lew, Elizabeth.

Famous Storytellers for Young People. Laura Benét. Dodd, 1968 (o.p.) (BEI)
Andersen, Hans Christian; Baum, Lyman Frank; Browne, Frances; Burnett, Frances Hodgson; Colum, Padraic; Craik, Dinah Mulock; Dodge, Mary Mapes; Ewing, Juliana H. Gatty; Grahame, Kenneth; Grimm, Jakob; Grimm, Wilhelm Karl; Hale, Lucretia Peabody; Kipling, Rudyard; MacDonald, George; Molesworth, Mary Louisa; Nesbit, Edith; Pyle, Howard;

Ruskin, John; Sidney, Margaret, pseud.; Stockton, Frank Richard; Thackeray, William Makepeace; Wiggin, Kate Douglas; Yonge, Charlotte Mary.

Famous Tennis Players. Trent Frayne. Dodd, 1977 (o.p.) (FOX)
Ashe, Arthur; Borg, Björn; Borotra, Jean†; Brugnon, Jacques†; Budge, Don; Cochet, Henri; Connors, Jimmy; Gonzales, Pancho; Kramer, Jack; Lacoste, René; Laver, Rodney George; Nastase, Ilie; Perry, Fred; Riggs, Bobby; Tilden, William Tatem, Jr.

Famous Twentieth-Century Leaders. Frank Donovan. Dodd, 1964 (o.p.) (DOF)
Chiang Kai-shek; Churchill, Sir Winston Leonard Spencer; Gandhi, Mohandas Karamchand; Hitler, Adolf; Khrushchev, Nikita S.; Lenin, Nikolai; Mao Tse-tung; Mussolini, Benito; Roosevelt, Franklin Delano; Stalin, Joseph; Sun Yat-sen; Wilson, Woodrow.

Famous Women of America. William O. Stevens. Dodd, 1950 (o.p.) (STJ)
Addams, Jane; Alcott, Louisa May; Anthony, Susan Brownell; Bailey, Ann "Mad Ann"; Barton, Clara; Cassatt, Mary; Cushman, Charlotte Saunders; Dodge, Mary Mapes; Jacobs-Bond, Carrie; Lane, Harriet; Lewis, Margaret; McCauley, Mary; Macy, Anne Sullivan; Madison, Dolley Payne Todd; Mitchell, Maria; Morris, Clara; Mott, Lucretia Coffin; Pocahontas; Ross, Betsy; Sacajawea; Stowe, Harriet Beecher; Townsend, Sally; Walker, Mary; Washington, Martha Dandridge.

Famous Women Tennis Players. Trent Frayne. Dodd, 1979 (o.p.) (FR-1)
Cawley, Evonne Goolagong; Connolly, Maureen; Court, Margaret; Evert, Chris; Gibson, Althea; Jacobs, Helen; King, Billie Jean; Lenglen, Suzanne; Marble, Alice; Navratilova, Martina; Wade, Virginia; Wills, Helen.

Famous Young Rebels. Jules Archer. Messner, 1973 (ARAA)
Adams, Samuel; Blum, Léon; Cárdenas, Lázaro; Flynn, Elizabeth Gurley; Garvey, Marcus A.; Gompers, Samuel; Hearst, William Randolph; La Follette, Robert Marion, Sr.; Mussolini, Benito; Nehru, Jawaharlal; Sanger, Margaret; Stanton, Elizabeth Cady.

Fathers of America's Freedom: The Story of the Signers of the Declaration of Independence. Donald E. Cooke. Hammond, 1969 (o.p.) (COJ)
Adams, John; Adams, Samuel; Bartlett, Josiah†; Braxton, Carter†; Carroll, Charles; Chase, Samuel; Clark, Abraham†; Clymer, George†; Ellery, William†; Floyd, William†; Franklin, Benjamin; Gerry, Elbridge†; Gwinnett, Button†; Hall, Lyman†; Hancock, John; Harrison, Benjamin†; Hart, John†; Hewes, Joseph†; Heyward, Thomas, Jr.†; Hooper, William†; Hopkins, Stephen†; Hopkinson, Francis†; Huntington, Samuel; Jefferson, Thomas; Lee, Francis L.†; Lee, Richard Henry; Lewis, Francis†; Livingston, Philip†; Lynch, Thomas, Jr.†; McKean, Thomas†; Middleton, Arthur†; Morris, Lewis†; Morris, Robert†; Morton, John†; Nelson, Thomas†; Paca, William†; Paine, Robert Treat†; Penn, John†; Read, George†; Rodney, Caesar; Ross, George†; Rush, Benjamin†; Rutledge, Edward†; Sherman, Roger†; Smith, James†; Stockton, Richard†; Stone, Thomas†; Taylor, George†; Thornton, Matthew†; Walton, George†; Whipple, William†; Williams, William†; Wilson, James†; Witherspoon, John†; Wolcott, Oliver†; Wythe, George†.

Fathers of Industries. Leonard M. Fanning. Lippincott, 1962 (o.p.) (FAB)
Arkwright, Sir Richard; Bell, Alexander Graham; Benz, Karl; Bessemer, Sir Henry; Borden, Gail; Carrier, Willis Haviland; De Forest, Lee; Diesel, Rudolf C.; Drake, Edwin Laurentine; Edison, Thomas Alva; Fulton, Robert; Goodyear, Charles; Hall, Charles Martin; McAdam, John Loudon; McCormick, Cyrus Hall; Marconi, Guglielmo; Otto, Nikolaus August; Robert, Nicholas-Louis; Slater, Samuel; Stevens, John; Watt, James; Whitney, Eli; Wilkinson, David; Wright, Orville; Wright, Wilbur.

Fifteen Famous Latin Americans. Helen Bailey & Maria C. Grijalva. P-H, 1971 (o.p.) (BACA)
Aleijadhino; Bolívar, Simón; Díaz, Bernal; Garcilaso de la Vega; Hidalgo y Costilla, Miguel; Juana Inés de la Cruz, Sister; Juárez, Benito Pablo; Mistral, Gabriela; Niemeyer, Oscar; Orozco, José Clemente; Pedro II; Quetzalcoatl; San Martin, Jose de; Toussaint L'Ouverture, Pierre Dominigue; Villa-Lobos, Heitor.

Fifty Useful Americans. Wheeler McMillen. Putnam, 1965 (o.p.) (MAL)
Adams, John Quincy; Audubon, John James; Bell, Alexander Graham; Bennett, Hugh Ham-

mond; Borden, Gail; Bowditch, Nathaniel; Carnegie, Andrew; Clinton, DeWitt; Eastman, George; Field, Cyrus West; Ford, Henry; Fulton, Robert; Gompers, Samuel; Goodyear, Charles; Greeley, Horace; Hamilton, Alexander; Herty, Charles Holmes; Hoover, Herbert Clark; Houston, Samuel; Irving, Washington; Knapp, Seaman Asahel; Lewis, Meriwether; Longfellow, Henry Wadsworth; McCormick, Cyrus Hall; McGuffey, William Holmes; Marshall, John; Maury, Matthew Fontaine; Mergenthaler, Ottmar; Morse, Samuel F. B.; Morton, William; Muir, John; Polk, James Knox; Reed, Walter; Riley, James Whitcomb; Rockefeller, John Davison; Roosevelt, Theodore; Scott, Winfield; Seward, William Henry; Sholes, Christopher Latham; Slater, Samuel; Smith, Theobald; Twain, Mark, pseud.; Washington, Booker Taliaferro; Webster, Noah; West, James Edward; White, Andrew Dickson; Whitney, Eli; Wiley, Harvey Washington; Willard, Emma Hart.

Fifty Voices of the Twentieth Century. Emery Kelen, ed. Lothrop, 1970 (o.p.) (KE)
Anderson, Marian; Baldwin, James; Ben-Gurion, David; Carver, George Washington; Churchill, Sir Winston Leonard Spencer; Copland, Aaron; Ehrenburg, Ilya Grigoryevich; Einstein, Albert; Eisenhower, Dwight David; Freud, Sigmund; Frost, Robert; Galbraith, John Kenneth; Gandhi, Mohandas Karamchand; Gaulle, Charles de; Hammarskjöld, Dag; Hesse, Hermann; John XXIII, Pope; Jung, Carl Gustav; Kennedy, John Fitzgerald; Khrushchev, Nikita S.; King, Martin Luther, Jr.; Lin Yutang; McLuhan, (Herbert) Marshall†; Mao Tsetung; Mboya, Thomas Joseph; Mead, Margaret†; Meir, Golda†; Moore, Marianne Craig†; Nasser, Gamal Abdel; Niebuhr, Reinhold†; Nyerere, Julius Kambarage; Orozco, José Clemente; Pandit, Vijaya Lakshmi; Picasso, Pablo†; Rickover, Hyman George; Roosevelt, Eleanor; Roosevelt, Franklin Delano; Russell, Bertrand Arthur William Russell, 3d earl; Sandburg, Carl†; Sartre, Jean Paul†; Schweitzer, Albert; Shaw, George Bernard; Stein, Gertrude; Stevenson, Adlai Ewing; Teller, Edward†; Thant, U; Truman, Harry S.; Wiener, Norbert; Wilkins, Roy; Young, Whitney Moore, Jr.

Fifty-seven Saints for Boys and Girls. Daughters of St. Paul, 1975 (DAD-1)
Agnes; Aloysius Gonzaga; Anne; Anthony of Padua; Bartholomea; Benedict; Benedict the Moor; Bernadette of Lourdes; Bernardine of Siena; Bosco, John; Brigid of Kildare; Cabrini, Frances Xavier; Camillus de Lellis; Catherine of Siena; Cecilia; Chantal, Jane Frances de; Clare; Columban; Cottolengo, Joseph Benedict; Dympna; Elizabeth of Hungary; Frances of Rome; Francis of Assisi; Francis Xavier; Gemma; Germaine; Gertrude the Great; Goretti, Mary; Helena; Joan of Arc; Jogues, Isaac; John Baptiste de la Salle; John Berchmans; Joseph; Kevin; Kostka, Stanislaus; Lucy; Margaret of Scotland; Margaret Mary; Martin of Tours; Michael; Monica; Neri, Philip; Patrick; Paul; Peregrine; Peter; Porres, Martin de; Rita of Cascia; Rose of Lima; Savio, Dominic; Sebastian; Seton, Elizabeth Ann; Tarcisius; Tekakwitha, Kateri; Thecla; Thérèse of Lisieux.

Fight Against Time: Five Athletes—A Legacy of Courage. Steven Clark. Atheneum, 1979 (o.p.) (CL-04)
Agganis, Harry; Davis, Ernie; Roth, Joe; Steinmark, Fred; Thompson, Danny.

Fighting Congressmen. Henrietta Buckmaster. Scholastic, 1971 (o.p.) (BU)
Bruce, Blanche K.; Rapier, James T.; Revels, Hiram Rhoades; Stevens, Thaddeus.

Fireballers: Baseball's Fastest Pitchers. Jack Newcombe. Putnam, 1964 (o.p.) (NEA)
Alexander, Grover Cleveland; Barney, Rex; Blackwell, Ewell; Dean, Dizzy; Dean, Paul; Drysdale, Don; Feller, Bob; Grove, Lefty; Johnson, Walter Perry; Koufax, Sandy; Mathewson, Christy; Newcombe, Donald; Score, Herbert Jude; Vance, Dazzy; Vander Meer, John Samuel; Waddell, Rube; Wood, Joe.

First Book of Kings. Douglas Newton. Watts, 1961 (o.p.) (NEC)
Akhnaton; Akihito, Togusama†; Alexander III, the Great; Alfred the Great; Arthur; Asoka the Great; Augustus; Carl-Gustav†; Charlemagne; Charles†; Constantine†; Constantine I, the Great; Ferdinand V; Frederick II, the Great; Genghis Khan; George VI; Hammurabi; Henri†; Henry VIII; Kamehameha I, the Great; K'ang-hsi; Louis IX; Louis XIV; Montezuma II; Napoleon I; Peter I, the Great; Ptolemy I; Shih Huang Ti; Solomon; William I, the Conqueror.

First Ladies. Margaret Brown Klapthor. White House Historical Assn., 1981 (KL)
See listing under *America's First Ladies,* vols. 1 and 2, by Chaffin & Butwin. Add: Reagan, Anne Robbins.

First Ladies. Kathleen Prindiville. Macmillan, rev. ed., 1964 (o.p.) (PRB)
See listing under *America's First Ladies,* vols. 1 and 2, by Chaffin & Butwin. Add: Eppes, Maria Jefferson; Randolph, Martha Jefferson. Delete: Jefferson, Martha; Johnson, Claudia Alta; Nixon, Thelma (Pat).

First Ladies: A First Book. Rhoda Blumberg. Watts, updated ed., 1981 (o.p.) (BLG)
Adams, Abigail†; Adams, Louisa Catherine†; Arthur, Ellen Lewis†; Carter, Rosalynn Smith; Cleveland, Frances Folsom; Coolidge, Grace Anna; Eisenhower, Mamie Geneva; Fillmore, Abigail Powers†; Ford, Elizabeth Bloomer; Garfield, Lucretia Rudolph†; Grant, Julia Dent†; Harding, Florence Kling; Harrison, Anna Symmes†; Harrison, Caroline†; Hayes, Lucy Ware†; Hoover, Lou Henry; Jackson, Rachel†; Jefferson, Martha Wayles Skelton†; Johnson, Claudia Alta; Johnson, Eliza McCardle†; Lane, Harriet†; Lincoln, Mary Todd; McKinley, Ida Saxton†; Madison, Dolley Payne Todd; Monroe, Elizabeth†; Nixon, Thelma; Onassis, Jacqueline Lee Bouvier Kennedy; Pierce, Jane Appleton†; Polk, Sarah Childress†; Reagan, Anne Robbins; Roosevelt, Edith Kermit†; Roosevelt, Eleanor; Taft, Helen Herron; Taylor, Margaret Smith†; Truman, Elizabeth V.; Tyler, Julia Gardiner†; Tyler, Letitia Christian†; Van Buren, Hannah Hoes†; Washington, Martha Dandridge; Wilson, Edith Bolling; Wilson, Ellen Louisa†.

First Women Who Spoke Out. Nancy Smiler Levinson. Dillon, 1983 (LES-2)
Anthony, Susan Brownell; Blatch, Harriot Stanton; Bloomer, Amelia Jenks; Brown, Antoinette Blackwell; Chapman, Maria Weston†; Child, Lydia Maria†; Davis, Pauline Wright; Foster, Abigail Kelley; Grimké, Angelina Emily; Grimké, Sarah Moore; Mott, Lucretia Coffin; Rose, Ernestine Potowski; Shaw, Anna Howard; Stanton, Elizabeth Cady; Stone, Lucy; Truth, Sojourner.

Five Artists of the Old West. Clide Hollman. Hastings, 1965 (o.p.) (HOD)
Bodmer, Karl; Catlin, George; Miller, Alfred Jacob; Remington, Frederic; Russell, Charles Marion.

Five Early American Painters. Donald Braider. Hawthorn, 1969 (o.p.) (BR)
Copley, John Singleton; Peale, Charles Willson; Stuart, Gilbert; Trumbull, John; West, Benjamin.

Five First Ladies. Elizabeth Simpson Smith. Walker, 1986 (SMBD)
Carter, Rosalynn Smith; Ford, Elizabeth Bloomer; Johnson, Claudia Alta; Nixon, Thelma (Pat); Reagan, Anne Robbins.

Five Queens of Ancient Egypt. Leonard Cottrell. Bobbs, 1969 (o.p.) (COLB)
Ankhesnamun; Hatshepsut; Nefertari; Nefertiti; Tiy.

Five Roads to the White House. Ann E. Weiss. Messner, 1970 (o.p.) (WEE)
Eisenhower, Dwight David; Johnson, Lyndon Baines; Kennedy, John Fitzgerald; Roosevelt, Franklin Delano; Truman, Harry S.

Focus on America: Profiles of Nine Photographers. Mark Sufrin. Scribner, 1987 (SUAA)
Abbott, Berenice; Bourke-White, Margaret; Brady, Matthew B.; Curtis, Edward Sheriff; Evans, Walker; Hine, Lewis; Jackson, William Henry; Lange, Dorothea; Smith, William Eugene.

Football Running Backs: Three Ground Gainers. David R. Collins. Garrard, 1976 (COFB)
Grange, Red; Nagurski, Bronko; Sayers, Gale.

Football Superstars of the '70's. Bill Gutman. Messner, 1977 (o.p.) (GUCA)
Bradley, Bill; Bradshaw, Terry; Harris, Franco; Johnson, Ronald Adolphus; Kwalick, Ted; Landry, Greg; Manning, Archie; Marcol, Chester; Reid, Michael B.; Simpson, O. J.; Tatum, Jack; Tucker, Robert Louis.

Football's Breakaway Backs. Nathan Aaseng. Lerner, 1983 (AAS-10)
   Campbell, Earl; Csonka, Larry; Dorsett, Tony Drew; Foreman, Chuck; Harris, Franco; Montgomery, Wilbert; Payton, Walter; Pruitt, Greg; Riggins, John; Simpson, O. J.

Football's Clever Quarterbacks. Richard Rainbolt. Lerner, 1975 (RAAD)
   Baugh, Sammy; Dawson, Lenny; Graham, Otto; Luckman, Sidney; Namath, Joe Willie;
   Starr, Bart; Tittle, Y. A.; Unitas, Johnny; Van Brocklin, Norman Mack; Waterfield, Robert
   Staton.

Football's Crushing Blockers. Nathan Aaseng. Lerner, 1982 (AAS-11)
   DeLamielleure, Joe; Dierdorf, Dan; Gray, Leon; Hannah, John; Langer, Jim; Powell, Marvin;
   Upshaw, Gene; Webster, Mike.

Football's Cunning Coaches. Nathan Aaseng. Lerner, 1981 (AAS-12)
   Allen, George; Brown, Paul; Grant, Bud; Halas, George; Landry, Tom; Lombardi, Vincent;
   Noll, Chuck; Shula, Don.

Football's Daring Defensive Backs. Nathan Aaseng. Lerner, 1984 (AAS-13)
   Blount, Mel; Cromwell, Nolan; Fencik, Gary; Hayes, Lester; Haynes, Mike; Lott, Ronnie;
   Thomas, Pat; Walls, Everson.

Football's Hard-Hitting Linebackers. Nathan Aaseng. Lerner, 1984 (AAS-15)
   Blair, Matt; Brazile, Robert; Cousineau, Tom; Gradishar, Randy; Ham, Jack; Hendricks,
   Ted; Lambert, Jack; Taylor, Lawrence.

Football's Incredible Bulks. Nathan Aaseng. Lerner, 1987 (AAS-32)
   Bingaman, Les; Brown, Roger; Butz, Dave; Grier, Rosie; Johnson, Pete; Ladd, Ernie;
   Lipscomb, Gene "Big Daddy"; Perry, William; Plunkett, Sherman; Smith, Charles "Bubba".

Football's Punishing Pass Rushers. Nathan Aaseng. Lerner, 1984 (AAS-16)
   Baker, Al "Bubba"; Dean, Fred; Johnson, Gary "Big Hands"; Klecko, Joe; Martin, Harvey;
   Selmon, Lee Roy; Still, Art; White, Randy.

Football's Rugged Running Backs. Richard Rainbolt. Lerner, 1975 (RAAE)
   Brown, Jim; Grange, Red; McElhenny, Hugh; Matson, Ollie; Moore, Lenny; Nevers, Ernie;
   Perry, Joe; Sayers, Gale; Thorpe, Jim; Van Buren, Steve.

Football's Steadiest Kickers. Nathan Aaseng. Lerner, 1981 (AAS-17)
   Benirschke, Rolf; Blanda, George; Cox, Fred; Dempsey, Tom; Franklin, Tony; Groza, Lou;
   Herrera, Efren; Yepremian, Garo Sarkis.

Football's Sure-Handed Receivers. Nathan Aaseng. Lerner, 1980 (AAS-18)
   Carmichael, Harold; Jefferson, John; Largent, Steve; Pearson, Drew; Rashad, Ahmad;
   Stallworth, John; Swann, Lynn; Walker, Wesley.

Football's Toughest Tight Ends. Nathan Aaseng. Lerner, 1981 (AAS-19)
   Casper, Dave; Chester, Raymond; Francis, Russ; Kramer, Ron; Mackey, John; Newsome,
   Ozzie; Odoms, Riley; Sanders, Charlie.

Football's Winning Quarterbacks. Nathan Aaseng. Lerner, 1980 (AAS-20)
   Anderson, Kenneth Allan; Bradshaw, Terry; Fouts, Dan; Griese, Bob; Jones, Bert; Manning,
   Archie; Stabler, Ken; Staubach, Roger; Tarkenton, Francis; Zorn, Jim.

Footprints. Mildred Miles Main & Samuel H. Thompson. Steck-V, 1957 (o.p.) (MAO)
   Austin, Stephen Fuller; Berry, Martha McChesney; Blount, William; Boone, Daniel; Boyd,
   Belle; Claiborne, William Charles; Clark, William; Crockett, Davy; Davis, Jefferson; Davis,
   Sam; Duval, William Pope; Houston, Samuel; Jackson, Andrew; Jackson, Thomas Jonathan;
   Laurens, John; Lee, Robert Edward; Lewis, Meriwether; Long, Jane W.; McIver, Charles
   Duncan; McRae, Thomas Chipman; Oglethorpe, James Edward; Robertson, James; Ross,
   John; Sevier, John; Stephens, Alexander Hamilton; Williams, John Sharp.

For Patriot Dream. Laura E. Cathon & Thusnelda Schmidt. Abingdon, 1970 (o.p.) (CAGA)
   Addams, Jane; Asbury, Francis; Bates, Katherine Lee; Bethune, Mary McLeod; Bok, Edward
   William; Carver, George Washington; Chapman, John; Hughes, Langston; Jouett, Jack;

Langston, Dicey; McGuffey, William Holmes; Sequoya; Shepard, Alan Bartlett; Stevens, Thaddeus; Wald, Lillian D.

Forty for Sixty. Robert McAdam. Bowmar, 1971 (o.p.) (LYD)
Arcaro, Eddie; Cushman, Cliff; Kapp, Joe; McCormick, Ricky; Mantle, Mickey Charles; Richards, Robert Eugene; Rohr, Bill; Rudolph, Wilma G.

Forwards (Stars of the NBA). Robert Armstrong. Creative Ed, 1977 (o.p.) (ARB-3)
Barry, Rick; Erving, Julius; Havlicek, John; McGinnis, George; Thompson, David.

Founders of Fortunes, Book 1. L. Edmond Leipold. T. S. Denison, 1967 (o.p.) (LEM)
Astor, John Jacob; Carnegie, Andrew; Du Pont, Eleuthère Irénée; Eastman, George; Ford, Henry; Hill, James Jerome; Peabody, George; Pulitzer, Joseph; Rockefeller, John Davison; Wanamaker, John.

Founders of Fortunes, Book 2. L. Edmond Leipold. T. S. Denison, 1967 (o.p.) (LEN)
Disney, Walt; Edison, Thomas Alva; Hall, Charles Martin; Hilton, Conrad Nicholson; Hoover, Herbert Clark; McCormick, Cyrus Hall; Noble, Edward J.; Penney, James Cash; Skouras, Spyros; Thomas, Lowell Jackson.

Founders of Our Cities. L. Edmond Leipold. T. S. Denison, 1967 (o.p.) (LEO)
Calvert, Cecilius, 2nd baron Baltimore; Calvert, Charles, 3rd baron Baltimore; Donnelly, Ignatius; L'Enfant, Pierre Charles; Minuit, Peter; Oglethorpe, James Edward; Penn, William; Smith, John; Williams, Roger; Winthrop, John; Young, Brigham.

Founding Fathers. Bennett Wayne, ed. Garrard, 1975 (WAI)
Franklin, Benjamin; Jefferson, Thomas; Washington, George.

Four American Poets: Why They Wrote. Rhoda Hoff. Walck, 1969 (o.p.) (HIG)
Dickinson, Emily; Longfellow, Henry Wadsworth; Poe, Edgar Allan; Whitman, Walt.

Four Men Who Changed the Universe. Robert Silverberg. Putnam, 1968 (o.p.) (SIB)
Anaximander†; Apollonius of Perga†; Aristarchus of Samos†; Aristotle†; Brahe, Tycho; Copernicus, Nicolaus; Eudoxus†; Galilei, Galileo; Heracleides†; Hipparchus†; Kepler, Johannes; Newton, Sir Isaac†; Philolaus†; Plato†; Ptolemy†; Pythagoras†; Thales of Miletus†.

Four Stars from the World of Sports. Clare Gault & Frank Gault. Walker, 1973 (o.p.) (GAB)
Aaron, Hank; Abdul-Jabbar, Kareem; Orr, Bobby; Staubach, Roger.

Four Took Freedom. Philip Sterling & Radford Logan. Doubleday, 1967 (STD)
Bruce, Blanche K.; Douglass, Frederick; Smalls, Robert; Tubman, Harriet.

Four Women in a Violent Time. Deborah Crawford. Crown, 1970 (o.p.) (CRB)
Dyer, Mary; Hutchinson, Anne Marbury; Moody, Lady Deborah; Stout, Penelope Thomson.

Four Women of Courage. Bennett Wayne, ed. Garrard, 1975 (WAJ)
Cochran, Jacqueline; Dix, Dorothea Lynde; Keller, Helen Adams; Richards, Linda Ann.

Framers of the Constitution (Original title: *Signers of the Constitution*). Robert G. Ferris & James H. Charleton. National Archives, 1986 (FEAA)
Baldwin, Abraham; Bassett, Richard; Bedford, Gunning; Blair, John; Blount, William; Brearly, David; Broom, Jacob; Butler, Pierce; Carroll, Daniel; Clymer, George; Davie, William Richardson; Dayton, Jonathan; Dickinson, John; Ellsworth, Oliver; Few, William; Fitzsimons, Thomas; Franklin, Benjamin; Gerry, Elbridge; Gilman, Nicholas; Gorham, Nathaniel; Hamilton, Alexander; Houston, William C.†; Houstoun, William†; Ingersoll, Jared; Jenifer, Daniel of St. Thomas; Johnson, William Samuel; King, Rufus; Langdon, John; Lansing, John, Jr.; Livingston, William; McClurg, James; McHenry, James; Madison, James; Martin, Alexander; Martin, Luther; Mason, George; Mercer, John Francis; Mifflin, Thomas; Morris, Gouverneur; Morris, Robert; Paterson, William; Pierce, William Leigh†; Pinckney, Charles; Pinckney, Charles Cotesworth; Randolph, Edmund Jennings; Read, George; Rutledge, John; Sherman, Roger; Spaight, Richard Dobbs, Sr.; Strong, Caleb; Washington, George; Williamson, Hugh; Wilson, James; Wythe, George; Yates, Robert.

Free People: The Story of the Declaration of Independence and the Men Who Wrote It.
Roberta Strauss Feuerlicht. Messner, 1969 (o.p.) (FEB)
Adams, John; Franklin, Benjamin; Jefferson, Thomas; Livingston, Robert R.; Sherman, Roger.

Freedom Builders: Great Teachers from Socrates to John Dewey. Rose Friedman. Little, 1968 (o.p.) (FRC)
Alcuin; Aristotle; Barnard, Henry†; Beecher, Catharine Esther; Comenius, John Amos; Dewey, John†; Froebel, Friedrich Wilhelm; Ignatius of Loyola, Saint; Luther, Martin; Lyon, Mary; Mann, Horace; Parker, Francis Wayland†; Pestalozzi, Johann Heinrich; Plato; Quintilian; Socrates; Vittorino da Feltre; Washington, Booker Taliaferro†; Willard, Emma Hart.

French Explorers of North America. David J. Abodaher. Messner, 1970 (o.p.) (ABA)
Cartier, Jacques; Champlain, Samuel de; Duluth, Daniel Greysolon, sieur; Joliet, Louis; La Salle, Robert Cavelier, sieur de; Marquette, Jacques.

Frontier Doctors. Wyatt Blassingame & Richard Glendinning. Watts, 1963 (o.p.) (BLC)
Beaumont, William; Clark, William; Crumbine, Samuel Jay; Griffin, John; Lewis, Meriwether; Long, Crawford Williamson; McDowell, Ephraim; Owens-Adair, Bethenia; Perrine, Henry; Whitman, Marcus.

Frontier Leaders and Pioneers. Dorothy Heiderstadt. McKay, 1962 (o.p.) (HEB)
Audubon, John James; Boone, Daniel; Bowie, James; Bridger, James; Catlin, George; Chapman, John; Clark, George Rogers; Clark, William; Colt, Samuel; Frémont, John Charles; Gregg, Josiah; Houston, Samuel; Lewis, Meriwether; McGuffey, William Holmes; Mayo, William Worrall; Meeker, Ezra; Muir, John; Parkman, Francis; Pike, Zebulon Montgomery; Smith, Jedediah Strong; Young, Brigham.

Funny Men. Steve Allen. S&S, 1956 (o.p.) (ALC)
Allen, Fred; Benny, Jack; Berle, Milton; Buttons, Red; Caesar, Sid; Cantor, Eddie; Cox, Wally; Gleason, Jackie; Gobel, George; Godfrey, Arthur; Hope, Bob; Levenson, Sam; Lewis, Jerry; Marx, Groucho; Silvers, Phil; Skelton, Red.

Funny Men of the Movies. Edward Edelson. Doubleday, 1976 (o.p.) (ED-1)
Abbott, Bud†; Allen, Woody†; Capra, Frank†; Chaplin, Sir Charles Spencer; Costello, Lou†; Errol, Leon†; Fields, W. C.; Fine, Larry†; Guinness, Sir Alec†; Hardy, Oliver; Hawks, Howard†; Hope, Bob†; Howard, Jerry†; Howard, Moe†; Howard, Samuel†; Kaye, Danny†; Keaton, Buster; Kennedy, Edgar†; Langdon, Harry; Laurel, Stan; Lewis, Jerry†; Lloyd, Harold; McCarey, Leo†; Marx, Chico; Marx, Groucho; Marx, Harpo; Marx, Zeppo; Our Gang†; Sennett, Mack; Skelton, Red†; Sturges, Preston†; Tati, Jacques†; Three Stooges, *see* Fine, Larry; Howard, Jerry; Howard, Moe; Howard, Samuel†; Wilder, Billy†.

Gallant Men: Stories of American Adventure. Everett McKinley Dirksen & H. Paul Jeffers. McGraw, 1967 (o.p.) (DIA)
Adams, Samuel; Bartholdi, Frédéric Auguste; Bradford, William; Carpenter, William; Charlton, Cornelius; Glenn, John Herschel, Jr.; Jefferson, Thomas; Kennedy, John Fitzgerald; Laboulaye, Édouard René Lefebvre de†; Lincoln, Abraham; Warren, Gouverneur Kemble; Warren, Joseph; York, Alvin C.

Gallant Women. Margaret Chase Smith & H. Paul Jeffers. McGraw, 1968 (o.p.) (SMC)
Anthony, Susan Brownell; Barton, Clara; Blackwell, Elizabeth; Earhart, Amelia; Gibson, Althea; Hutchinson, Anne Marbury; Macy, Anne Sullivan; Madison, Dolley Payne Todd; Perkins, Frances; Roosevelt, Eleanor; Stowe, Harriet Beecher; Tubman, Harriet.

Gallery of Great Americans. Andrew Curtin. Watts, 1965 (o.p.) (CUC)
Addams, Jane; Anthony, Susan Brownell; Astor, John Jacob; Audubon, John James; Barton, Clara; Bell, Alexander Graham; Blackwell, Elizabeth; Bok, Edward William; Boone, Daniel; Burbank, Luther; Byrd, Richard Evelyn; Carnegie, Andrew; Carver, George Washington; Cassatt, Mary; Cather, Willa; Churchill, Sir Winston Leonard Spencer; Clark, William; Cooper, James Fenimore; Damrosch, Walter; Decatur, Stephen; De Forest, Lee; Dewey, George; Dewey, John; Eastman, George; Edison, Thomas Alva; Einstein, Albert; Emerson, Ralph Waldo; Farragut, David Glasgow; Fermi, Enrico; Ford, Henry; Foster, Stephen Col-

lins; Franklin, Benjamin; Frémont, John Charles; Fulton, Robert; Gershwin, George; Gompers, Samuel; Grant, Ulysses Simpson; Hamilton, Alexander; Harriman, Edward Henry; Hearst, Phoebe Apperson; Hearst, William Randolph; Henry, O., pseud.; Henry, Patrick; Herbert, Victor; Holmes, Oliver Wendell, Jr.; Hoover, Herbert Clark; Hopkins, Johns; Jefferson, Thomas; Jones, John Paul; Kennedy, John Fitzgerald; Kern, Jerome; Lafayette, Marie Joseph Paul Yves Roch Gilbert du Motier, marquis de; Langley, Samuel Pierpont; Lasker, Albert; Lawrence, Ernest Orlando; Lee, Robert Edward; Lewis, Meriwether; Lincoln, Abraham; Lyon, Mary; MacArthur, Douglas; McGuffey, William Holmes; Mann, Horace; Marshall, John; Mayo, Charles Horace; Mayo, William James; Melville, Herman; Millikan, Robert Andrews; Morgan, John Pierpont; Moses, Anna Mary Robertson; Muir, John; Ng Poon Chew; Ochs, Adolph Simon; Paine, Thomas; Peary, Robert Edwin; Pike, Zebulon Montgomery; Pulitzer, Joseph; Reed, Walter; Rockefeller, John Davison; Roosevelt, Eleanor; Roosevelt, Franklin Delano; Roosevelt, Theodore; Rosenwald, Julius; Rush, Benjamin; Sargent, John Singer; Scripps, Edward Wyllis; Sequoya; Seton, Elizabeth Ann, Saint; Sherman, William Tecumseh; Sousa, John Philip; Steinmetz, Charles Proteus; Thoreau, Henry David; Thurber, James G.; Twain, Mark, pseud.; Washington, Booker Taliaferro; Washington, George; Whistler, James Abbott McNeill; Whitney, Eli; Willard, Emma Hart; Wilson, Woodrow; Wood, Grant; Wright, Frank Lloyd; Wright, Orville; Wright, Wilbur; Zenger, John Peter.

Gamebreakers of the N.F.L. Bill Gutman. Random, 1973 (o.p.) (GUD)
Blanda, George; Lanier, Willie Edward; Little, Larry; Page, Alan; Plunkett, Jim; Stenerud, Jan; Taylor, Bruce.

Generous Strangers: Six Heroes of the American Revolution. Pearle Henriksen Schultz. Vanguard, 1976 (SCB-1)
Kalb, Johann; Kosciusko, Tadeusz; Lafayette, Marie Joseph Paul Yves Roch Gilbert du Motier, marquis de; Pulaski, Casimir; Rochambeau, comte de; Steuben, Friedrich Wilhelm von.

Giants for Justice. Beth P. Wilson. HarBraceJ, 1978 (WIAA-8)
Bethune, Mary McLeod; King, Martin Luther, Jr.; Randolph, Asa Philip.

Giants of Electricity. Percy Dunsheath. T Y Crowell, 1967 (o.p.) (DUA)
Ampère, André Marie; Davy, Sir Humphry; Faraday, Michael; Franklin, Benjamin; Galvani, Luigi; Gauss, Karl Friedrich; Henry, Joseph; Kelvin, William Thomson, 1st baron; Maxwell, James Clerk; Oersted, Hans Christian; Ohm, Georg Simon; Volta, Alessandro, conte; Weber, Wilhelm Eduard.

Giants of Invention. Edgar Tharp. G&D, 1971 (o.p.) (THA)
Archimedes; Baekeland, Leo Hendrik; Baird, John Logie; Bell, Alexander Graham; Bessemer, Sir Henry; Daguerre, Louis Jacques; Daimler, Gottlieb; Davy, Sir Humphry; De Forest, Lee; Diesel, Rudolf C.; Edison, Thomas Alva; Faraday, Michael; Fulton, Robert; Galilei, Galileo; Goddard, Robert Hutchings; Gutenberg, Johann; Holland, John Philip; Howe, Elias; Leeuwenhoek, Anton van; Marconi, Guglielmo; Mergenthaler, Ottmar; Morse, Samuel F. B.; Otto, Nikolaus August; Stephenson, George; Townes, Charles Hard; Watt, James; Westinghouse, George; Whitney, Eli; Whittle, Sir Frank; Wright, Orville; Wright, Wilbur.

Giants of Jazz. Studs Terkel. T Y Crowell, 1957 (o.p.) (TEA)
Armstrong, Louis "Satchmo"; Basie, Count; Beiderbecke, Bix; Ellington, Duke; Gillespie, Dizzy; Goodman, Benny; Herman, Woody; Holiday, Billie; Kenton, Stan; Oliver, Joe; Smith, Bessie; Waller, Fats.

Giants of Jazz. Studs Terkel. T Y Crowell, rev. ed., 1975 (TEB)
Armstrong, Louis "Satchmo"; Basie, Count; Beiderbecke, Bix; Coltrane, John William; Ellington, Duke; Gillespie, Dizzy; Goodman, Benny; Herman, Woody; Holiday, Billie; Oliver, Joe; Parker, Charlie; Smith, Bessie; Waller, Fats.

Giants of Medicine. Irving Robbin. G&D, 1962 (o.p.) (ROA)
Banting, Sir Frederick Grant; Behring, Emil von; Bruce, Sir David; Domagk, Gerhard;

Ehrlich, Paul; Fleming, Sir Alexander; Freud, Sigmund; Galen; Grassi, Giovanni Battista; Harvey, William; Hippocrates; Jenner, Edward; Koch, Robert; Lister, Joseph, 1st baron Lister of Lyme Regis; Löffler, Friedrich; Metchnikoff, Élie; Morton, William; Paracelsus; Paré, Ambroise; Pasteur, Louis; Reed, Walter; Ross, Sir Ronald; Roux, Pierre Paul Émile; Salk, Jonas Edward; Semmelweis, Ignaz Philipp; Spallanzani, Lazzaro; Vesalius, Andreas; Virchow, Rudolf.

Giants of Science. Philip Cane. G&D, 1959 (o.p.) (CAA)
Ampère, André Marie; Archimedes; Aristotle; Avogadro, Amedeo; Bohr, Niels H. D.; Boyle, Robert; Cavendish, Henry; Copernicus, Nicolaus; Curie, Marie Sklodowska; Dalton, John; Darwin, Charles Robert; Davy, Sir Humphry; Einstein, Albert; Euclid; Faraday, Michael; Fermi, Enrico; Fleming, Sir Alexander; Foucault, Jean Bernard Léon; Franklin, Benjamin; Galen; Galilei, Galileo; Harvey, William; Henry, Joseph; Hertz, Heinrich Rudolf; Hippocrates; Hooke, Robert; Huygens, Christiaan; Jenner, Edward; Kepler, Johannes; Lavoisier, Antoine Laurent; Leeuwenhoek, Anton van; Leonardo da Vinci; Maxwell, James Clerk; Mendel, Gregor Johann; Mendeleev, Dmitri I.; Michelson, Albert Abraham; Newton, Sir Isaac; Ohm, Georg Simon; Pasteur, Louis; Pavlov, Ivan Petrovich; Planck, Max Karl; Priestley, Joseph; Pythagoras; Roentgen, Wilhelm; Rumford, Benjamin Thompson, count; Thomson, Sir Joseph John; Torricelli, Evangelista; Vesalius, Andreas; Volta, Alessandro, conte; Wöhler, Friedrich.

Giants of Space. Edgar Tharp. G&D, rev. ed., 1970 (o.p.) (THC)
Aldrin, Edwin E., Jr.; Armstrong, Neil A.; Belyayev, Pavel; Borman, Frank; Bykovsky, Valeri; Carpenter, Malcolm Scott; Cernan, Eugene A.; Collins, Michael†; Conrad, Charles, Jr.; Cooper, Leroy Gordon, Jr.; Feoktistov, Konstantin; Gagarin, Yuri Alekseyevich; Glenn, John Herschel, Jr.; Goddard, Robert Hutchings; Gordon, Richard F., Jr.; Grissom, Gus; Komarov, Vladimir M.; Leonov, Alexei A.; Lovell, James A., Jr.; McDivitt, James A.; Nikolayev, Andrian G.; Oberth, Hermann Julius; Popovich, Pavel Romanovich†; Schirra, Walter Marty, Jr.; Scott, David R.; Shepard, Alan Bartlett; Stafford, Thomas P.; Tereshkova, Valentina Vladimirova; Titov, Gherman Stepanovich; Tsiolkovsky, Konstantin E.; White, Edward Higgins, II; Yegorov, Boris; Young, John Watts.

Giants of the Keyboard. Victor Chapin. Lippincott, 1967 (CHF)
Bach, Johann Christian; Busoni, Ferruccio; Carreño, Teresa; Clementi, Muzio; Cramer, Johann Baptist; Czerny, Karl; Dussek, Jan Ladislav; Field, John; Gottschalk, Louis Moreau; Hummel, Johann Nepomuk; Liszt, Franz; Moscheles, Ignaz; Paderewski, Ignace Jan; Rubinstein, Anton; Schnabel, Artur; Schumann, Clara.

Giants on the Earth: Stories of Great Jewish Men and Women from the Time of Discovery of America to the Present. Deborah Pessin. Behrman, 1940 (o.p.) (PEB)
Aguilar, Grace; Ben Yehudah, Eliezer; Bialik, Chaim Nachman; Disraeli, Benjamin, 1st earl of Beaconsfield; Dreyfus, Alfred; Elijah ben Solomon; Félix, Elisa Rachel; Gratz, Rebecca; Heine, Heinrich; Herzl, Theodor; Israel ben Eliezer (Baal Shem Tov); Lazarus, Emma; Menasseh ben Israel; Mendelssohn, Moses; Montefiore, Sir Moses; Nasi, Joseph; Noah, Mordecai Manuel; Rothschild, Mayer Amschel; Salomon, Haym; Schechter, Solomon; Spinoza, Baruch or Benedict; Straus, Nathan; Torres, Luis de; Touro, Judah; Trumpeldor, Joseph; Wassermann, Jakob; Wise, Isaac Mayer; Zangwill, Israel; Zevi, Sabbatai.

Girls Can Be Anything They Want. Patricia Foote. Messner, 1980 (FOC-1)
Adelman, Susan; Burke, Yvonne Brathwaite; Clark, Beverly; Clevenger, Johanna; Darden, Christine; Estrada, Isabel; Farber, Bea; Henze, Cynthia; Kupper, Sandy; Mangrulkar, Latika; O'Neal, Regina; Seddon, Margaret Rhea; Smith, Linda; Spiro, Jo Anne; Trujillo, Brenda.

Give Me Freedom. May McNeer. Abingdon, 1964 (o.p.) (MAM)
Anderson, Marian; Einstein, Albert; Lovejoy, Elijah Parish; Markham, Edwin; Paine, Thomas; Penn, William; Stanton, Elizabeth Cady.

Glorious Triumphs: Athletes Who Conquered Adversity. Vernon Pizer. Dodd, 1968 (o.p.) (PIB)
Berlenbach, Paul; Cunningham, Glenn; DeMar, Clarence; Didrikson, Babe; Gibson, Althea;

Gray, Pete; Hogan, Ben; Kramer, Jerry; Malzone, Frank; Manolete; Ross, Barney; Wilkins, Alonzo.

Glorious Triumphs: Athletes Who Conquered Adversity. Vernon Pizer. Dodd, rev. ed., 1980 (PIBA)

Albright, Tenley; Berlenbach, Paul; Cunningham, Glenn; Didrikson, Babe; Gibson, Althea; Gray, Pete; Heiss, Carol; Hogan, Ben; Howe, Gordie; Hurtubise, Jim; Kramer, Jerry; Lee, Sammy; Ross, Barney; Wilkins, Alonzo.

Glory Runners. Al Hirshberg. Putnam, 1968 (o.p.) (HIE)

Agganis, Harry; Blanchard, Doc; Booth, Albie; Brown, Jim; Cagle, Red; Crowley, James; Davis, Glenn; Four Horsemen of Notre Dame; Gipp, George; Goldberg, Marshall; Grange, Red; Harmon, Thomas D.; Hornung, Paul Vernon; Jensen, Jackie; Justice, Charlie; Kazmaier, Dick; Kinnick, Nile; Layden, Elmer; McMillin, Bo; Mahan, Eddie; Miller, Don; Nagurski, Bronko; Sinkwich, Frank; Stuhldreher, Harry; Thorpe, Jim; Trippi, Charley; Walker, Doak; White, Byron Raymond.

Go Indians! Stories of the Great Indian Athletes of the Carlisle School. Moss Hall. Ritchie, 1971 (o.p.) (HACA)

Bender, Chief; Tewanima, Louis; Thorpe, Jim.

Good Stories for Great Birthdays. Frances Jenkins Olcott. HM, 1922 (o.p.) (OLA)

Adams, John; Bolívar, Simón; Bradford, William; Columbus, Christopher; Franklin, Benjamin; Hamilton, Alexander; Henry, Patrick; Jackson, Andrew; Jefferson, Thomas; Jones, John Paul; Lafayette, Marie Joseph Paul Yves Roch Gilbert du Motier, marquis de; Lincoln, Abraham; Marshall, John; Miranda, Francisco de; O'Higgins, Bernardo; Pedro II; Penn, William; Pitt, William, 1st earl of Chatham; Putnam, Israel; Roosevelt, Theodore; San Martin, Jose de; Washington, George; Williams, Roger.

Great Adventurers. Colman Kerr. Follett, 1967 (o.p.) (KEH)

Alexander III, the Great; Amundsen, Roald; Bart, Jean; Blériot, Louis; Caesar, Gaius Julius; Cartier, Jacques; Cervantes Saavedra, Miguel de; Cody, William Frederick; Columbus, Christopher; Cook, James; Drake, Sir Francis; Eric the Red; Gagarin, Yuri Alekseyevich; Gama, Vasco da; Genghis Khan; Herzog, Maurice; Hillary, Sir Edmund; Magellan, Ferdinand; Polo, Marco; Surcouf, Robert; Tazieff, Haroun; Tenzing, Norgay; Toussaint L'Ouverture, Pierre Dominigue.

Great Adventures in Nursing. Helen Wright & Samuel Rapport, eds. Har-Row, 1960 (o.p.) (WRA)

Banfill, B. J.; Bickerdyke, Mary Ann Ball; Breckinridge, Mary; Cavell, Edith; Dalstrom, Ingeborg; Damien de Veuster, Joseph; Day, Enid; Dunant, Jean Henri; Ileana; Jaissle, Louise; Kempner, Mary Jean; Kenny, Elizabeth; Lally, Grace; Lathrop, Rose Hawthorne; Nightingale, Florence; Wald, Lillian D.

Great American Artists. L. Edmond Leipold. T. S. Denison, 1973 (o.p.) (LEOA)

Homer, Winslow; Howe, Oscar; West, Benjamin; Whistler, James Abbott McNeill; Wood, Grant.

Great American Athletes of the Twentieth Century. Zander Hollander, comp. Random, 1966 (o.p.) (HOC)

Baugh, Sammy; Blanchard, Doc; Bradley, Bill; Brown, Jim; Button, Dick; Chamberlain, Wilt; Cobb, Ty; Cousy, Bob; Cunningham, Glenn; Davis, Glenn; Dean, Dizzy; Dempsey, Jack; Di Maggio, Joseph Paul; Feller, Bob; Gehrig, Lou; Gonzales, Pancho; Graham, Otto; Grange, Red; Hogan, Ben; Johnson, Rafer; Jones, Bobby; Koufax, Sandy; Kramer, Jack; Louis, Joe; Luckman, Sidney; Mantle, Mickey Charles; Marciano, Rocky; Mathias, Bob; Matson, Randy; Mays, Willie Howard; Mikan, George L.; Mosbacher, Emil, Jr.; Musial, Stanley Frank; Nagurski, Bronko; Nicklaus, Jack; Owens, Jesse; Palmer, Arnold; Robertson, Oscar; Robinson, Jackie; Robinson, Ray; Russell, William Felton; Ruth, Babe; Schollander, Donald Arthur; Thorpe, Jim; Unitas, Johnny; Weissmuller, Johnny; Werner, Bud; White, Byron Raymond; Williams, Ted.

Great American Cavalrymen. Army Times Editors. Dodd, 1964 (o.p.) (ARE)
Custer, George Armstrong; Forrest, Nathan Bedford; Houston, Samuel; Jackson, Andrew; Jackson, Thomas Jonathan; Kilpatrick, Hugh Judson; Marion, Francis; Patton, George Smith, Jr.; Pershing, John Joseph; Pierce, Clinton A.; Pulaski, Casimir; Sheridan, Philip Henry; Stoneman, George; Stuart, James Ewell Brown.

Great American Film Directors. Dian G. Smith. Messner, 1987 (SMBC)
Capra, Frank; Chaplin, Sir Charles Spencer; Cukor, George; Ford, John; Griffith, David Wark; Hawks, Howard; Hitchcock, Alfred Joseph; Huston, John; Keaton, Buster; Welles, Orson.

Great American Heroes. Jean Fiedler. Hart, 1966 (o.p.) (FIA)
Boone, Daniel; Carson, Kit; Clark, William; Farragut, David Glasgow; Four Chaplains; Fox, George Lansing; Franklin, Benjamin; Goode, Alexander David; Hale, Nathan; Henry, Patrick; Houston, Samuel; Jefferson, Thomas; Jones, John Paul; Kelly, Colin; Kennedy, John Fitzgerald; Lee, Robert Edward; Lewis, Meriwether; Lincoln, Abraham; Paine, Thomas; Peary, Robert Edwin; Poling, Clark; Putnam, Israel; Pyle, Ernest Taylor; Revere, Paul; Roosevelt, Franklin Delano; Washington, Booker Taliaferro; Washington, George; Washington, John Alexander; Williams, Roger; York, Alvin C.; Zenger, John Peter.

Great American Heroines. Arnold Dolin. Hart, 1960 (o.p.) (DOD)
Addams, Jane; Anthony, Susan Brownell; Bailey, Ann "Mad Ann"; Barton, Clara; Blackwell, Elizabeth; Dix, Dorothea Lynde; Earhart, Amelia; Frietchie, Barbara; Hutchinson, Anne Marbury; Keller, Helen Adams; Lazarus, Emma; Lewis, Idawally; Low, Juliette; Lyon, Mary; McCauley, Mary; Madison, Dolley Payne Todd; Mitchell, Maria; Pocahontas; Ross, Betsy; Sacajawea; Stowe, Harriet Beecher; Tubman, Harriet; Wald, Lillian D.

Great American Naturalists. Ruth Allison Coates. Lerner, 1974 (o.p.) (CO-1)
Audubon, John James; Bartram, John; Bartram, William; Burbank, Luther; Burroughs, John; Carson, Rachel; Carver, George Washington; Chapman, John; Muir, John; Palmer, Edward; Roosevelt, Theodore; Seton, Ernest Thompson; Thoreau, Henry David; Wilson, Alexander.

Great American Naval Heroes. Navy Times Editors. Dodd, 1965 (o.p.) (NAC)
Byrd, Richard Evelyn; Decatur, Stephen; Dewey, George; Farragut, David Glasgow; Halsey, William Frederick; Jones, John Paul; King, Ernest Joseph; Lawrence, James; Mitscher, Marc A.; Nimitz, Chester William; Peary, Robert Edwin; Perry, Oliver Hazard; Porter, David Dixon; Rickover, Hyman George; Sims, William Sowden; Spruance, Raymond Ames†.

Great American Negroes. Ben Richardson. T Y Crowell, 1956 (o.p.) (RIC)
Anderson, Marian; Armstrong, Louis "Satchmo"; Barthé, Richmond; Bethune, Mary McLeod; Bunche, Ralph Johnson; Carver, George Washington; Davis, Benjamin O., Jr.; Dixon, Dean; Drew, Charles Richard; Dunham, Katherine; Ellington, Duke; Hughes, Langston; Johnson, James Weldon; Johnson, Mordecai Wyatt; Lawrence, Jacob; Louis, Joe; Mays, Willie Howard; Miller, Dorie; Owens, Jesse; Petry, Ann; Powell, Adam Clayton, Sr.; Randolph, Asa Philip; Robinson, Bill "Bojangles"; Still, William Grant; White, Walter F.; Wright, Richard.

Great American Nurses. David Collins. Messner, 1971 (o.p.) (COFA)
Anthony, Sister; Breckinridge, Mary; Dimock, Susan†; McKinney, Sally Zumaris; O'Hara, Dee; Richards, Linda Ann; Zakrzewska, Marie Elizabeth†.

Great American Poets. L. Edmond Leipold. T. S. Denison, 1973 (o.p.) (LEOB)
Field, Eugene; Frost, Robert; Longfellow, Henry Wadsworth; Millay, Edna St. Vincent; Riley, James Whitcomb.

Great American Race Drivers. Bill Libby. Regnery, 1970 (o.p.) (LEX)
Andretti, Mario; Arfons, Art; Baker, Buck†; Bettenhausen, Tony; Breedlove, Craig; Bryan, Jimmy; Cooper, Earl; De Palma, Ralph; Flock, Tim; Foyt, Anthony Joseph; Garlits, Don; Ginther, Paul Richard; Gregory, Masten†; Gurney, Dan; Hall, Jim; Harroun, Ray†; Heath, Allen; Hill, Phil; Horn, Ted; Hurtubise, Jim; Jarrett, Ned; Johnson, Junior†; Jones, Parnelli; Lockhart, Frank†; Lorenzen, Fred; McEwen, Tom†; Mays, Rex; Meyer, Louis†; Milton,

Thomas Willard; Mulford, Ralph†; Mulligan, John; Murphy, Jimmy; Oldfield, Barney†; Ongais, Danny; Pearson, David; Petty, Lee†; Petty, Richard; Rickenbacker, Edward Vernon; Roberts, Fireball; Rose, Mauri; Sachs, Eddie; Shaw, Wilbur; Shelby, Carroll; Thompson, Mickey; Turner, Curtis; Vukovich, Bill; Ward, Rodger; Weatherly, Joseph Herbert†; Yarborough, Cale; Yarbrough, Lee Roy.

Great Americans. Mary Jane Fowler & Margaret Fisher. Fideler, 1968 (o.p.) (FOH)
Addams, Jane; Audubon, John James; Barton, Clara; Burbank, Luther; Byrd, Richard Evelyn; Edison, Thomas Alva; Ford, Henry; Franklin, Benjamin; Jefferson, Thomas; Lincoln, Abraham; Mann, Horace; Reed, Walter; Roosevelt, Franklin Delano; Roosevelt, Theodore; Twain, Mark, pseud.; Washington, Booker Taliaferro; Washington, George.

Great Artists of America. Lillian Freedgood. T Y Crowell, 1963 (o.p.) (FRA)
Allston, Washington; Bingham, George Caleb; Cassatt, Mary; Davis, Stuart; Eakins, Thomas; Homer, Winslow; Inness, George; Marin, John; Pollock, Jackson; Ryder, Albert Pinkham; Sargent, John Singer; Shahn, Ben; Sloan, John; Stuart, Gilbert; Whistler, James Abbott McNeill.

Great Auto Racing Champions. Ross Olney. Garrard, 1973 (OLAA)
De Palma, Ralph; Foyt, Anthony Joseph; Parsons, Johnnie.

Great Baseball Pitchers. Jim Brosnan. Random, 1965 (o.p.) (BRC)
Dean, Dizzy; Feller, Bob; Ford, Whitey; Hubbell, Carl Owen; Johnson, Walter Perry; Koufax, Sandy; Maglie, Sal; Mathewson, Christy; Paige, Satchel; Spahn, Warren.

Great Baseball Stories Today and Yesterday. Bill Gutman. Messner, 1978 (o.p.) (GUDA)
Aaron, Hank; Bench, Johnny Lee; Berra, Yogi; Brock, Louis Clark; Campanella, Roy; Carew, Rod; Cobb, Ty; Cochrane, Mickey; Dickey, Bill; Hartnett, Gabby; Hornsby, Rogers†; Johnson, Walter Perry; Koufax, Sandy; Maris, Roger Eugene; Munson, Thurman Lee; Robinson, Jackie; Ruth, Babe; Ryan, Nolan; Williams, Ted; Wills, Maury.

Great Black Americans (Formerly titled *Great American Negroes*). Ben Richardson & William A. Fahey. T Y Crowell, 2d rev. ed., 1976 (RICA)
Ali, Muhammad; Anderson, Marian; Armstrong, Louis "Satchmo"; Baldwin, James; Barthé, Richmond; Bethune, Mary McLeod; Bunche, Ralph Johnson; Carver, George Washington; Dixon, Dean; Drew, Charles Richard; Du Bois, William Edward Burghardt; Dunham, Katherine; Ellington, Duke; Gibson, Althea; Gregory, Dick; Hughes, Langston; Johnson, James Weldon; King, Martin Luther, Jr.; Lawrence, Jacob; Louis, Joe; Malcolm X; Mays, Willie Howard; Owens, Jesse; Parker, Charlie; Petry, Ann; Randolph, Asa Philip; Robeson, Paul; Russell, William Felton; Still, William Grant; Williams, Daniel Hale; Wright, Richard.

Great Catchers of the Major Leagues. Jack Zanger. Random, 1970 (ZAA)
Berra, Yogi; Campanella, Roy; Cochrane, Mickey; Dickey, Bill; Freehan, Bill; Hartnett, Gabby; Howard, Elston; Lombardi, Ernie; McCarver, Tim; Torre, Joseph Paul.

Great Centers (Stars of the NHL). Ian Thorne. Creative Ed, 1976 (o.p.) (THD)
Clarke, Bobby; Esposito, Phil; Mikita, Stan; Perreault, Gilbert.

Great Centers of Pro Basketball. Bob Rubin. Random, 1975 (RUB)
Cowens, Dave; Lanier, Bob; McAdoo, Bob; Nater, Swen; Unseld, Westley.

Great Comebacks in Sports. Phil Pepe. Hawthorn, 1975 (o.p.) (PAW)
Ali, Muhammad; Bing, Dave; Bradley, Bill; Buckpasser; Dillard, Harrison; Di Maggio, Joseph Paul; Gibson, Bob; Havlicek, John; Hiller, John; Hogan, Ben; Howe, Gordie; Koufax, Sandy; Louis, Joe; Mantle, Mickey Charles; Namath, Joe Willie; Patrick, Lester; Reed, Willis; Stallings, George; Surtees, John; Tittle, Y. A.; Unitas, Johnny; Williams, Ted.

Great Comic Book Artists. Ron Goulart. St. Martin, 1986, pap. (GOB-1)
Adams, Neal; Baker, Matt; Barks, Carl; Barry, Dan; Beck, Charles Clarence; Biro, Charles; Briefer, Dick; Buscema, John; Byrne, John; Carlson, George; Chaykin, Howard; Colan, Gene; Cole, Jack; Crandall, Reed; Davis, Jack; Ditko, Steve; Eisner, Will; Elias, Lee; Evans, George; Everett, William Blake; Fine, Lou; Frazetta, Frank; Guardineer, Fred; Gustavson, Paul; Kane, Bob; Kane, Gil; Kelly, Walter Crawford; Kirby, Jack; Krigstein, Bernard; Kubert, Joe;

Kurtzman, Harvey; Maneely, Joe; Marsh, Jesse; Mayer, Sheldon; Meskin, Mort; Miller, Frank; Montana, Bob; Nordling, Klaus; Perez, George; Pini, Wendy; Powell, Bob; Raboy, Mac; Robinson, Jerry; Romita, John, Sr.; Schomburg, Alex; Severin, John; Shuster, Joe; Sienkiewicz, Bill; Simonson, Walt; Stanley, John; Steranko, James; Thorne, Frank; Toth, Alex; Tuska, George; Wheelan, Edgar Stow; Williamson, Al; Windsor-Smith, Barry; Wolverton, Basil; Wood, Wally; Wrightson, Berni.

Great Defensemen (Stars of the NHL). Ian Thorne. Creative Ed, 1976 (o.p.) (THE)
Orr, Bobby; Park, Brad; Potvin, Denis Charles; Van Impe, Edward Charles.

Great Defensive Players of the N.F.L. Dave Anderson. Random, 1967 (o.p.) (ANA)
Bednarik, Chuck; Butkus, Dick; Davis, Willie; Huff, Sam; Jones, Dave "Deacon"; Jordan, Henry; Lane, Dick; Lilly, Robert Lewis; Marchetti, Gino; Nobis, Tommy; Schmidt, Joseph Paul; Wilson, Larry.

Great Detectives: Famous Real-Life Sleuths and Their Most Baffling Cases. Robert Liston. Platt, 1966 (o.p.) (LID)
Bertillon, Alphonse; Fabian, Robert; Goron, Marie-François; Hoover, J. Edgar; Irey, Elmer Lincoln; Murray, John Wilson; Neil, Arthur Fowler; Pinkerton, Allan; Schindler, Raymond Campbell; Spilsbury, Sir Bernard; United States Bureau of Narcotics; Vidocq, Eugène François.

Great Dissenters: Guardians of Their Country's Laws and Liberties. Fred Reinfeld. T Y Crowell, 1959 (o.p.) (RED)
Adams, John Quincy; Emerson, Ralph Waldo; Garrison, William Lloyd; Holmes, Oliver Wendell, Jr.; Mann, Horace; Thoreau, Henry David.

Great Doctors. Robert Silverberg. Putnam, 1964 (o.p.) (SIC)
Cushing, Harvey Williams; Finlay, Carlos Juan†; Galen; Halsted, William Stewart; Harvey, William; Hippocrates; Hunter, John; Jenner, Edward; Lillehei, Clarence Walton; Lister, Joseph, 1st baron Lister of Lyme Regis; Long, Crawford Williamson†; McDowell, Ephraim; Morton, William; Paré, Ambroise; Reed, Walter; Salk, Jonas Edward; Semmelweis, Ignaz Philipp†; Vesalius, Andreas.

Great Experimenters. William Bixby. McKay, 1964 (o.p.) (BIA)
Edison, Thomas Alva; Faraday, Michael; Fermi, Enrico; Lister, Joseph, 1st baron Lister of Lyme Regis; Newton, Sir Isaac; Rutherford, Ernest Rutherford, 1st baron; Watt, James; Wright, Orville; Wright, Wilbur.

Great Explorers. Joyce Grosseck & Elizabeth Attwood. Fideler, 1967 (o.p.) (GRC)
Amundsen, Roald; Cabot, John; Cartier, Jacques; Clark, William; Columbus, Christopher; Cook, James; De Soto, Hernando; Gama, Vasco da; Henry the Navigator; Hudson, Henry; Joliet, Louis; La Salle, Robert Cavelier, sieur de; Lewis, Meriwether; Magellan, Ferdinand; Marquette, Jacques; Peary, Robert Edwin; Polo, Marco.

Great Goalies (Stars of the NHL). Ian Thorne. Creative Ed, 1976 (o.p.) (THF)
Dryden, Ken; Esposito, Tony; Gilbert, Gilles; Parent, Bernard Marcel.

Great Goalies of Pro Hockey. Frank Orr. Random, 1973 (ORA)
Bower, Johnny; Cheevers, Gerry; Dryden, Ken; Durnan, Bill; Esposito, Tony; Hall, Glenn; Plante, Jacques; Sawchuk, Terry; Tretiak, Vladislav; Worsley, Gump.

Great Golfers. Rex Lardner. Putnam, 1970 (o.p.) (LABA)
Casper, Billy; Hagen, Walter; Hogan, Ben; Jones, Bobby; Nicklaus, Jack; Ouimet, Francis; Palmer, Arnold; Sarazen, Gene; Snead, Samuel Jackson; Venturi, Ken.

Great Hitters of the Major Leagues. Frank Graham, Jr. Random, 1969 (o.p.) (GR)
Aaron, Hank; Cobb, Ty; Di Maggio, Joseph Paul; Gehrig, Lou; Greenberg, Hank; Hornsby, Rogers; Mantle, Mickey Charles; Mays, Willie Howard; Musial, Stanley Frank; Ruth, Babe; Williams, Ted.

Great Indian Chiefs. Albert Roland. Macmillan, 1966 (o.p.) (ROD)
Hiawatha; Maquinna; Philip; Pontiac; Popé; Powhatan; Sequoya; Sitting Bull; Tecumseh.

Great Infielders of the Major Leagues. Dave Klein. Random, 1972 (o.p.) (KLB)
Aparicio, Luis; Beckert, Glenn Alfred; Boyer, Clete; Boyer, Ken; Hodges, Gil; Hubbs, Kenneth Douglas; McCovey, Willie Lee; Powell, Boog; Reese, Pee Wee; Rizzuto, Philip Francis; Robinson, Brooks Calbert; Robinson, Jackie.

Great Jazz Artists. James Lincoln Collier. Four Winds, 1977 (o.p.) (COF-1)
Armstrong, Louis "Satchmo"; Beiderbecke, Bix; Coleman, Ornette; Coltrane, John William; Ellington, Duke; Goodman, Benny; Hawkins, Coleman; Henderson, Fletcher; Hines, Earl Kenneth; Holiday, Billie; Jefferson, Lemon; Joplin, Scott; Leadbelly; Monk, Theolonius; Morton, "Jelly Roll"; Parker, Charlie; Powell, Bud; Reinhardt, Django; Tatum, Art; Taylor, Cecil; Waller, Fats; Young, Lester Willis.

Great Jewish Chess Champions. Harold U. Ribalow & Meir Z. Ribalow. Hippocrene, 1986 (RHA)
Fischer, Bobby; Lasker, Emanuel; Reshevsky, Samuel.

Great Jewish Women. Elma Ehrlich Levinger. Behrman, 1940 (o.p.) (LER)
Aguilar, Grace; Beruria; Chizick, Sarah; Deborah; Esther; Félix, Elisa Rachel; Gratz, Rebecca; Hannah, mother of the Seven Martyrs; Hannah, mother of Samuel; Helena; Herz, Henriette; Hirsch, Clara de; Huldah; Ima Shalom; Jochebed; Judith; Lazarus, Emma; Leah; Loeb, Sophie Irene; Mariamne; Mendesia, Gracia; Miriam; Moise, Penina; Montefiore, Judith; Nunoz, Maria; Rachel; Rachel; Rebecca; Ruth; Sarah; Sheilah; Shulamith; Straus, Lina.

Great Jews in Sports. Robert Slater. Jonathan David, 1983 (SLA)
Abrahams, Harold; Albert, Marv†; Alexander, Joe†; Allen, Mel†; Arnovich, Morrie†; Asher, Barry; Attell, Abe; Auerbach, Red; Bacher, Aron "Ali"†; Barna, Gyozo Victor; Barron, Herman; Berg, Moe†; Berger, Isaac; Bergmann, Gretel; Bergmann, Richard†; Berkowitz, Mickey†; Blomberg, Ron; Blum, Walter†; Bregman, James Steven†; Brews, Sidney†; Brockman, Shimson; Brody, Gyorgy†; Brody, Tal; Brown, Larry†; Buxton, Angela; Carmel, Zephania†; Chodorov, Ya'acov†; Cohen, Andy; Cohen, Robert†; Cohen-Mintz, Tanhum†; Copeland, Lillian; Cosell, Howard†; Danilowitz, Abraham Phineas†; Danning, Harry; Darmon, Pierre†; Davidman, Elazar†; Davis, Al; Dreyfus, René; Dreyfuss, Barney; Epstein, Charlotte; Epstein, Michael†; Fields, Jackie; Fisher, Harry; Flam, Herbert; Flatow, Alfred; Fleischer, Nat; Franklin, Sidney; Friedlander, Ethan; Friedman, Benny; Friedman, Max; Fuchs, Jeno†; Gillman, Sidney; Glaser, Pamela†; Glickman, Marty†; Glickstein, Shlomo; Goldberg, Marshall; Gomelsky, Alexander "Sascha"†; Gordon, Sid; Gottfried, Brian; Gottlieb, Eddie; Greenberg, Hank; Grossman, Randy; Grunfeld, Ernie; Gubner, Gary Jay†; Gurevitsch, Boris†; Guttmann, Bela†; Gyarmati, Andrea†; Hajos-Guttman, Alfred; Harris, Sigmund; Heldman, Julie; Herscovici, Henry†; Hershkowitz, Victor; Heyman, Art; Holman, Marshall; Holman, Nat; Holtzman, Ken; Holzman, Red; Jacobs, Hirsch; Jacobs, James; Jaffee, Irving; Kaplan, Louis "Kid"; Katz, Elias; Kauff, Benny; Kaufman, Micha†; Keleti, Agnes; Kirszenstein-Szewinska, Irena; Klein, Ralph†; Kling, Johnny; Kloss, Ilana†; Koufax, Sandy; Kramer, Barry†; Kramer, Joel†; Kronberger, Lily†; Kushnir, David†; Ladany, Shaul†; Laskau, Henry Helmut†; Lazarove, Lydia†; Leand, Andrea†; Leibowitz, Barry†; Leonard, Benny; Levinsky, Battling; Levy, Marv; Lewis, Ted "Kid"; Lieberman, Nancy; Lindsey, Mortimer; Litwack, Harry; Luckman, Sidney; McCoy, Al†; Mandy, Gyula†; Marcus, Debra Turner†; Martin, Sylvia Wene; Mayer, Erskine; Meisl, Hugo†; Melamed, Avraham†; Melnik, Faina†; Melnik, Yona†; Mendoza, Daniel; Meron, Rami†; Midler, Mark†; Miller, Walter; Mix, Ronald; Myer, Buddy; Myers, Laurence E. "Lon"; Newman, Harry; Oberlander, Fred†; Okker, Tom; Pantillat, Yair†; Peled, Paulina Peisachov†; Pelty, Barney; Perry, Aulcie†; Pike, Lipman; Pincus, Jacob; Podoloff, Maurice; Prinstein, Myer†; Reulbach, Edward; Ribner, Shoshana†; Rosen, Al; Rosenberg, Aaron; Rosenbloom, Maxie; Rosenbluth, Leonard†; Rosenfeld, Fanny; Ross, Barney; Roth, Esther; Roth, Mark; Rottman, Leon†; Rozeanu, Angelica; Rubenstein, Louis; Saperstein, Abraham M.; Savitt, Richard; Schacht, Al†; Schayes, Adolph; Schayes, Dan†; Scheckter, Jody; Sedran, Barney; Seligson, Julius; Shamsky, Art†; Shefa, Gershon†; Sherman, Allie†; Sherry, Larry; Shezifi, Hana†; Shmueli, Zehava†; Silver, Lou†; Singer, Al; Solomon, Harold; Spellman, Frank†; Spero, Donald†;

Spiegler, Mordechai†; Spitz, Mark; Stelmach, Nahum B.†; Stone, George Robert; Stone, Steve; Szekely, Eva; Teacher, Brian; Teltscher, Eliot; Tendler, Lew†; Van Damm, Sheila†; Vishnetzir, Yuval†; Wahle, Otto; Walk, Neal†; Weisz, Richard†; Weitz, Edward†; Wittenberg, Henry B.; Wolf, Phil; Wolf, Warner†; Zaslofsky, Max†; Zohar, Uri†.

Great Jews Since Bible Times. Elma Ehrlich Levinger. Behrman, 1926 (LERA)
Abravanel, Isaac; Akiba ben Joseph; Bar Cochba, Simon; Elijah ben Solomon; Herod the Great; Herzl, Theodor; Hillel; ibn-Ezra, Abraham; Israel ben Eliezer (Baal Shem Tov); Johanan ben Zakkai; Josephus Flavius; Judah ha-Levi; Judah ha-Nasi; Levy, Uriah Phillips; Maimonides; Menasseh ben Israel; Mendelssohn, Moses; Montefiore, Sir Moses; Moses ben Enoch; Nachmanides; Noah, Mordecai Manuel; Nones, Benjamin; Philo Judaeus; Rashi; Saadia ben Joseph; Salomon, Haym; Schechter, Solomon; Spinoza, Baruch or Benedict; Touro, Judah; Wise, Isaac Mayer; Zangwill, Israel; Zevi, Sabbatai.

Great Latin Sports Figures: The Proud People. Jerry Izenberg. Doubleday, 1976 (o.p.) (IZA)
Cañonero; Carew, Rod; Clemente, Roberto; Ortega, Gaspar; Rodriguez, Juan "Chi-Chi"; Trevino, Lee; Versalles, Zoilo.

Great Leaders of Greece and Rome. Leonard Cottrell. P-H, 1966 (o.p.) (COM)
Agricola, Gnaeus Julius; Caesar, Gaius Julius; Horatius Cocles; Leonidas I; Pericles; Scipio Africanus Major; Themistocles; Xenophon.

Great Linebackers of the N.F.L. Richard Kaplan. Random, 1970 (o.p.) (KABA)
Baughan, Maxie; Butkus, Dick; Curtis, Mike; Hein, Mel; Howley, Chuck; Nitschke, Ray; Nobis, Tommy; Robinson, Dave; Turner, Bulldog; Walker, Wayne.

Great Men of Medicine. Ruth Fox Hume. Random, 1961 (o.p.) (HUD)
Banting, Sir Frederick Grant; Fleming, Sir Alexander; Jenner, Edward; Koch, Robert; Laënnec, René Théophile; Lister, Joseph, 1st baron Lister of Lyme Regis; Morton, William; Paré, Ambroise; Pasteur, Louis; Vesalius, Andreas.

Great Men of Modern Agriculture. Grant G. Cannon. Macmillan, 1963 (o.p.) (CAB)
Bakewell, Robert; Boussingault, Jean Baptiste; Darwin, Charles Robert; East, Edward Murray; Gilbert, Sir Joseph Henry; Hales, Stephen; Jones, Donald Forsha; Lavoisier, Antoine Laurent; Lawes, Sir John Bennett; Liebig, Justus von; Linnaeus, Carl; McCormick, Cyrus Hall; Mendel, Gregor Johann; Pasteur, Louis; Saussure, Nicolas Théodore de; Shull, George Harrison; Tull, Jethro; Whitney, Eli; Young, Arthur.

Great Men of Science. Arnold Dolin. Hart, 1960 (o.p.) (DOE)
Archimedes; Banting, Sir Frederick Grant; Bell, Alexander Graham; Burbank, Luther; Carver, George Washington; Copernicus, Nicolaus; Curie, Marie Sklodowska; Curie, Pierre; Darwin, Charles Robert; Edison, Thomas Alva; Einstein, Albert; Faraday, Michael; Galilei, Galileo; Goodyear, Charles; Harvey, William; Hippocrates; Kepler, Johannes; Lavoisier, Antoine Laurent; Leeuwenhoek, Anton van; Lister, Joseph, 1st baron Lister of Lyme Regis; Morton, William; Newton, Sir Isaac; Pasteur, Louis; Reed, Walter; Vesalius, Andreas; Volta, Alessandro, conte; Wright, Orville; Wright, Wilbur.

Great Negroes, Past and Present. Russell L. Adams. Afro-Am, 1964 (o.p.) (ADA)
Abbott, Robert Sengstacke; Abdur Rahman Sadi el Timbuctoo; Aldridge, Ira; Allen, Richard; Anderson, Marian; Antar; Armstrong, Louis "Satchmo"; Askia Muhammad; Attucks, Crispus; Azikiwe, Nnamdi; Banneker, Benjamin; Bannister, Edward M.; Barthé, Richmond; Bassett, Ebenezer D.; Bethune, Mary McLeod; Binga, Jesse; Bland, James A.; Bridgetower, George Augustus; Brooks, Gwendolyn; Bruce, Blanche K.; Bunche, Ralph Johnson; Burleigh, Henry Thacker; Cain, Richard H.; Campbell, Elmer Simms; Captein, Jacques E. J.; Carver, George Washington; Chaka; Chesnutt, Charles Waddell; Christophe, Henri; Cinque, Joseph; Coleridge-Taylor, Samuel; Crummell, Alexander; Cuffe, Paul; Cullen, Countee; Dailey, Ulysses Grant; Davis, Benjamin O.; Davis, Benjamin O., Jr.; Dawson, William Levi; Delany, Martin R.; De Priest, Oscar; Dessalines, Jean Jacques; Dett, Robert Nathaniel; Dixon, Dean; Douglass, Frederick; Drew, Charles Richard; Du Bois, William Edward Burghardt; Dumas, Alexandre (Dumas père); Dunbar, Paul Laurence; Duncanson, Robert S.; Dunham, Katherine; Ellington, Duke; Elliott, Robert B.; Equiano, Olaudah; Forten, James; Garnet, Henry

Highland; Garvey, Marcus A.; Gaston, Arthur George; Gilpin, Charles Sidney; Haile Selassie I; Hall, Prince; Handy, William Christopher; Hannibal, Abram; Harrison, Richard Berry; Hastie, William Henry†; Hayes, Roland; Haynes, Lemuel; Healy, James Augustine; Henson, Matthew Alexander; Hope, John; Houston, Charles Hamilton†; Hughes, Langston; Jasper, John; Johnson, Charles Spurgeon; Johnson, James Weldon; Johnson, John H.; Johnson, Malvin Gray; Johnson, Mordecai Wyatt; Jones, John; Julian, Percy Lavon; Just, Ernest Everett; Kenyatta, Jomo; King, Martin Luther, Jr.; Langston, John Mercer; Lawless, Theodore Kenneth; Lawrence, Jacob; Lee, Canada; Leidesdorff, William Alexander; Lewis, Edmonia; Lewis, James; Locke, Alain Leroy; Long, Jefferson Franklin; Luthuli, Albert John; Lynch, John Roy; McKay, Claude; Marshall, Thurgood; Matzeliger, Jan Ernst; Mboya, Thomas Joseph; Menelik II; Mitchell, Arthur Wergs; Morgan, Garrett A.; Nkrumah, Kwame; Nyerere, Julius Kambarage; Overton, Anthony; Parks, Gordon Alexander Buchanan; Paul, Thomas; Payne, Daniel Alexander; Perkins, Marion; Piankhi; Pinchback, Pinckney Benton Stewart; Pippin, Horace; Pointe de Sable, Jean Baptiste; Porres, Martin de, Saint; Powell, Adam Clayton, Sr.; Pushkin, Aleksandr Sergeevich; Randolph, Asa Philip; Rapier, James T.; Revels, Hiram Rhoades; Rillieux, Norbert; Robeson, Paul; Scarborough, William Saunders; Senghor, Léopold Sédar; Silvera, Frank; Singleton, Benjamin "Pap"; Smalls, Robert; Smythe, John H.; Spaulding, Charles Clinton; Still, William; Still, William Grant; Sunni Ali Ber; Tanner, Henry Ossawa; Terrell, Mary Church; Tolton, Augustine; Touré, Sékou; Toussaint L'Ouverture, Pierre Dominigue; Trotter, James Monroe; Truth, Sojourner; Tubman, Harriet; Tubman, William V. S.; Turner, Henry McNeal; Turner, Nat; Vann, Robert Lee; Vesey, Denmark; Walker, David; Walker, Maggie Lena; Walker, Sarah Breedlove; Washington, Booker Taliaferro; Waters, Ethel; Wheatley, Phillis; White, Charles; White, Walter F.; Williams, Bert; Williams, Daniel Hale; Williams, George Washington; Wilson, James Finley; Woods, Granville T.; Woodson, Carter Goodwin; Wright, Jonathan Jasper; Wright, Richard; Young, Charles.

Great Negroes, Past and Present. Russell L. Adams. Afro-Am, 3d rev. ed., 1984 (ADB)
Delete from the 1964 edition, preceding: Abdur Rahman Sadi el Timbuctoo; Azikiwe, Nnamdi; Haile Selassie I; Haynes, Lemuel; Kenyatta, Jomo; Luthuli, Albert John; Mboya, Thomas Joseph; Nkrumah, Kwame; Nyerere, Julius Kambarage; Senghor, Léopold Sédar; Touré, Sékou; Tubman, William V. S. Add: Alston, Charles H.; Barnett, Claude Albert; Barnett, Ida Wells; Beckwourth, James P.; Bontemps, Arna; Brooke, Edward William; Cromwell, Oliver; Esteban or Estevanico; Franklin, John Hope; Gillespie, Frank L.; Hunt, Richard H.; Jefferson, Lemon; Kay, Ulysses; McCoy, Elijah; McCullough, Geraldine; Malcolm X; Mays, Benjamin E.; Merrick, John; Myers, Isaac; Poitier, Sidney; Price, Leontyne; Russwurm, John B.; Salem, Peter; Schomberg, Arthur; Simmons, William J.; Thurman, Howard; Trotter, William Monroe; Weaver, Robert Clifton; Whipper, William; Williams, Paul Revere; Young, Whitney M., Jr.

Great No-Hit Games of the Major Leagues. Frank Graham, Jr. Random, 1968 (o.p.) (GRA)
Dean, Dizzy; Dean, Paul; Feller, Bob; Holloman, Alva; Johnson, Walter Perry; Koufax, Sandy; Larsen, Don; Maglie, Sal; Monbouquette, Bill; Reynolds, Allie; Vander Meer, John Samuel.

Great Olympic Champions. John Devaney. Putnam, 1967 (o.p.) (DEF)
Connolly, James B.; Didrikson, Babe; Garrett, Robert; Hayes, Johnny; Heiss, Carol; Mathias, Bob; Mills, Billy; Nurmi, Paavo; Owens, Jesse; Patterson, Floyd; Richards, Robert Eugene; Russell, William Felton; Sailer, Toni; Schollander, Donald Arthur; Snell, Peter; Thorpe, Jim; Weissmuller, Johnny.

Great Pass Catchers in Pro Football. Howard Coan. Messner, 1971 (o.p.) (CO)
Alworth, Lance; Berry, Raymond; Collins, Gary; Hayes, Bob; Hirsch, Elroy "Crazylegs"; Hutson, Don; McDonald, Tommy; Mackey, John; Maynard, Don; Sauer, George, Jr.; Taylor, Charley; Taylor, Otis; Warfield, Paul.

Great Pass Receivers of the N.F.L. Dave Anderson. Random, 1966 (o.p.) (ANB)
Ditka, Michael; Hayes, Bob; Howton, Bill; Hutson, Don; Lavelli, Dante; Mitchell, Bobby; Orr, Jimmy; Parks, David Wayne; Retzlaff, Pete; Shofner, Del; Speedie, Mac.

Great Performers. Patricia Young. Walck, 1967 (o.p.) (YOH)
   Caruso, Enrico; Liszt, Franz; Paganini, Nicolò; Pavlova, Anna; Toscanini, Arturo.

Great Pro Quarterbacks. Lud Duroska, ed. G&D, 1972 (o.p.) (DUD)
   Baugh, Sammy; Brodie, John; Conerly, Charley; Dawson, Lenny; Gabriel, Roman; Graham, Otto; Jurgensen, Sonny; Layne, Bobby; Luckman, Sidney; Namath, Joe Willie; Starr, Bart; Tittle, Y. A.; Unitas, Johnny; Van Brocklin, Norman Mack.

Great Pro Quarterbacks. Lud Duroska, ed. G&D, rev. ed., 1974 (o.p.) (DUE)
   Baugh, Sammy; Conerly, Charley; Dawson, Lenny; Gabriel, Roman; Graham, Otto; Griese, Bob; Jurgensen, Sonny; Layne, Bobby; Luckman, Sidney; Namath, Joe Willie; Starr, Bart; Tittle, Y. A.; Unitas, Johnny; Van Brocklin, Norman Mack.

Great Pro Running Backs. Lud Duroska, ed. G&D, 1973 (o.p.) (DUF)
   Brown, Jim; Brown, Larry; Csonka, Larry; Grange, Red; Hornung, Paul Vernon; Kelly, Leroy; Little, Floyd Douglas; McElhenny, Hugh; Nagurski, Bronko; Sayers, Gale; Simpson, O. J.; Taylor, James; Thorpe, Jim; Van Buren, Steve.

Great Quarterbacks of the N.F.L. Dave Anderson. Random, 1965 (o.p.) (ANC)
   Baugh, Sammy; Graham, Otto; Johnson, Charley; Luckman, Sidney; Ryan, Frank Beall; Starr, Bart; Tarkenton, Francis; Tittle, Y. A.; Unitas, Johnny; Van Brocklin, Norman Mack.

Great Rookies of Pro Basketball. Zander Hollander, comp. Random, 1969 (o.p.) (HOCA)
   Barry, Rick; Bellamy, Walt; Dischinger, Terry; Felix, Ray; Heinsohn, Tommy; Lucas, Jerry; Meineke, Donald Edward; Monroe, Earl; Stokes, Maurice; Unseld, Westley.

Great Rookies of the Major Leagues. Jim Brosnan. Random, 1966 (o.p.) (BRD)
   Allen, Richie; Allison, Bob; Ashburn, Richie; Cepeda, Orlando; Kuenn, Harvey; Pearson, Albie; Robinson, Frank; Robinson, Jackie; Rose, Pete; Score, Herbert Jude; Sievers, Roy; Tresh, Thomas Michael.

Great Rulers of the African Past. Lavinia Dobler & William A. Brown. Doubleday, 1965 (o.p.) (DOA)
   Affonso I; Askia Muhammad; Idris Alaoma; Mansa Musa I; Sunni Ali Ber.

Great Running Backs in Pro Football. Phil Berger. Messner, 1970 (o.p.) (BEKB)
   Bass, Dick; Brown, Bill; Brown, Jim; Garrett, Michael Lockett; Granger, Hoyle; Hornung, Paul Vernon; Kelly, Leroy; McElhenny, Hugh; Moore, Lenny; Perkins, Don; Robinson, Paul; Sayers, Gale; Taylor, James; Van Buren, Steve; Willard, Ken.

Great Running Backs of the N.F.L. Jack Hand. Random, 1966 (o.p.) (HAD)
   Brown, Jim; Grange, Red; Hornung, Paul Vernon; McElhenny, Hugh; Matson, Ollie; Nagurski, Bronko; Nevers, Ernie; Perry, Joe; Sayers, Gale; Taylor, James; Van Buren, Steve.

Great War Correspondents. John Jakes. Putnam, 1967 (o.p.) (JAD)
   Churchill, Sir Winston Leonard Spencer; Crane, Stephen; Cronkite, Walter; Davis, Richard Harding; Higgins, Marguerite; London, Jack; Pyle, Ernest Taylor; Reynolds, Quentin; Shirer, William L.; Thomas, Lowell Jackson.

Great Wingmen (Stars of the NHL). Ian Thorne. Creative Ed, 1976 (o.p.) (THG)
   Cashman, Wayne; Cournoyer, Ivan Serge; Martin, Richard Lionel; Schultz, Dave.

Great Women of Medicine. Ruth Fox Hume. Random, 1964 (o.p.) (HUE)
   Anderson, Elizabeth Garrett; Blackwell, Elizabeth; Curie, Marie Sklodowska; Jacobi, Mary Putnam; Jex-Blake, Sophia; Nightingale, Florence.

Great Women Reporters. John Jakes. Putnam, 1969 (o.p.) (JAE)
   Black, Winifred; Cochrane, Elizabeth; Door, Rheta Childe; Greeley-Smith, Nixola; Higgins, Marguerite; Kilgallen, Dorothy; Kuhn, Irene Corbally; St. Johns, Adela Rogers; Swisshelm, Jane Grey; Thompson, Dorothy.

Great Women Teachers. Alice Fleming. Lippincott, 1965 (o.p.) (FLB)
   Berry, Martha McChesney; Bethune, Mary McLeod; Dunlop, Florence; Gildersleeve, Virginia Crocheron; Lyon, Mary; Nash, Alice Morrison; Palmer, Alice Freeman; Peabody, Elizabeth Palmer; Willard, Emma Hart; Young, Ella Flagg.

Guards (Stars of the NBA). Robert Armstrong. Creative Ed, 1977 (o.p.) (ARB-4)
Archibald, Nate "Tiny"; Bing, Dave; Collins, Doug; Frazier, Walt; Maravich, Pete.

Hall of Fame Baseball. Mac Davis. Collins-World, 1975 (o.p.) (DAFC)
Alexander, Grover Cleveland; Anson, Cap; Appling, Luke; Berra, Yogi; Brown, Three-Fingered; Campanella, Roy; Clemente, Roberto; Cobb, Ty; Di Maggio, Joseph Paul; Ford, Whitey; Gehrig, Lou; Hornsby, Rogers; Johnson, Walter Perry; Koufax, Sandy; Lajoie, Napoleon; McGraw, John Joseph; Mantle, Mickey Charles; Maranville, Rabbit; Mathewson, Christy; Musial, Stanley Frank; Ott, Mel; Paige, Satchel; Robinson, Jackie; Ruth, Babe; Sisler, George; Spahn, Warren; Speaker, Tristram E.; Stengel, Casey; Traynor, Pie; Waddell, Rube; Wagner, Honus; Williams, Ted; Young, Cy.

Headliners: Famous American Journalists. Aylesa Forsee. Macrae, 1967 (o.p.) (FOE)
Bourke-White, Margaret; Kieran, John Francis; Lippmann, Walter; Murrow, Edward Roscoe; Pyle, Ernest Taylor; White, William Allen.

Healers in Uniform. Edward Edelson. Doubleday, 1971 (o.p.) (ED)
Armstrong, Harry George; Ashford, Bailey Kelly; Beaumont, William; Billings, John Shaw; Grant, David N. W.; Lovelace, William Randolph, II; Reed, Walter; Robertson, Oswald Hope; Rush, Benjamin; Stapp, John Paul; Sternberg, George Miller.

Hear the Distant Applause! Six Great Ladies of the American Theatre. Marguerite Vance. Dutton, 1963 (o.p.) (VAA)
Adams, Maude; Anderson, Mary A.; Cushman, Charlotte Saunders; Fiske, Minnie Maddern; Marlowe, Julia; Rehan, Ada.

Heroes and Heroines of Many Lands. Jay Strong. Hart, 1965 (o.p.) (STP)
Bolívar, Simón; Booth, Evangeline Cory; Damien de Veuster, Joseph; Darling, Grace Horsley; David; Esther; Fry, Elizabeth Gurney; Gandhi, Mohandas Karamchand; Horatius Cocles; Joan of Arc; Kosciusko, Tadeusz; Lafayette, Marie Joseph Paul Yves Roch Gilbert du Motier, marquis de; Livingstone, David; Maccabees; Montessori, Maria; Nightingale, Florence; O'Higgins, Bernardo; Robin Hood; Senesh, Hannah; Sidney, Sir Philip; Slessor, Mary Mitchell; Socrates; Spartacus; Tell, William; Verchères, Marie Magdelaine Jarret de; Vincent de Paul.

Heroes and History. Rosemary Sutcliff. Putnam, 1965 (o.p.) (SUK)
Alfred the Great; Arthur; Bruce, Robert the; Caractacus; Glendower, Owen; Hereward; Llewelyn ab Gruffydd; Montrose, James Graham, 5th earl and 1st marquis of; Robin Hood; Wallace, Sir William.

Heroes and Leaders of West Point. Red Reeder. Nelson, 1970 (o.p.) (RAE)
Blaik, Earl Henry; Blunt, Roger R.; Borman, Frank; Bradley, Omar Nelson; Bryan, Blackshear Morrison; Carpenter, William; Clark, Mark Wayne; Clarke, Bruce Cooper; Clay, Lucius DuBignon; Daly, Moe; Dawkins, Peter; Doyle, Edward J.; Eichelberger, Robert Lawrence; Eisenhower, Dwight David; Foley, Robert F.; Fraser, Harvey Reed; Goethals, George Washington; Grant, Ulysses Simpson; Groves, Leslie Richard; Harmon, Ernest Nason; Hearnes, Warren Eastman; Howell, Martin Damon; Lee, Robert Edward†; MacArthur, Douglas; Marcus, Mickey; Murphy, John Michael; Patton, George Smith, Jr.; Pershing, John Joseph; Ridgway, Matthew Bunker†; Robinson, Wirt; Rowan, Andrew Summers†; Scott, Hugh Lenox†; Storke, Harry Purnell; Summerall, Charles Pelot; Taylor, Maxwell Davenport; Thayer, Sylvanus; Vandenberg, Roger; Van Fleet, James Alward; Woodmansee, John W.

Heroes behind the Mask: America's Greatest Catchers. Milton J. Shapiro. Messner, 1968 (o.p.) (SHD)
Berra, Yogi; Bresnahan, Roger; Campanella, Roy; Cochrane, Mickey; Dickey, Bill; Hartnett, Gabby; Howard, Elston; Kling, Johnny†; Lombardi, Ernie†; Torre, Joseph Paul.

Heroes for Our Time. Will Yolen & Kenneth S. Giniger, eds. Stackpole, 1968 (o.p.) (YOA)
Churchill, Sir Winston Leonard Spencer; Einstein, Albert; Gandhi, Mohandas Karamchand; Hammarskjöld, Dag; John XXIII; Kennedy, John Fitzgerald; King, Martin Luther, Jr.; Roose-

velt, Eleanor; Roosevelt, Franklin Delano; Salk, Jonas Edward; Schweitzer, Albert; Truman, Harry S.

Heroes in Time of War. L. Edmond Leipold. T. S. Denison, 1967 (o.p.) (LEP)
Custer, George Armstrong; Eisenhower, Dwight David; Grant, Ulysses Simpson; Hale, Nathan; Jackson, Andrew; Lawrence, James; Lee, Robert Edward; MacArthur, Douglas; Perry, Oliver Hazard; Washington, George.

Heroes of a Different Kind. L. Edmond Leipold. T. S. Denison, 1973 (o.p.) (LEPA)
Disney, Walt; Edison, Thomas Alva; Riley, James Whitcomb; Thorpe, Jim; Wheatley, Phillis.

Heroes of Civilization. Joseph Cottler & Haym Jaffe. Little, rev. ed., 1969 (o.p.) (COL)
Amundsen, Roald; Bell, Alexander Graham; Burton, Sir Richard Francis; Cook, James; Copernicus, Nicolaus; Curie, Marie Sklodowska; Darwin, Charles Robert; Davy, Sir Humphry; Edison, Thomas Alva; Einstein, Albert; Fulton, Robert; Galilei, Galileo; Gama, Vasco da; Gorgas, William Crawford; Gutenberg, Johann; Harvey, William; Huygens, Christiaan; Jenner, Edward; Koch, Robert; Lavoisier, Antoine Laurent; Leeuwenhoek, Anton van; Lister, Joseph, 1st baron Lister of Lyme Regis; Livingstone, David; Magellan, Ferdinand; Marconi, Guglielmo; Mendel, Gregor Johann; Metchnikoff, Élie; Morse, Samuel F. B.; Newton, Sir Isaac; Pasteur, Louis; Polo, Marco; Rawlinson, Sir Henry Creswicke; Watt, James; Wright, Orville; Wright, Wilbur.

Heroes of Conservation. C. B. Squire. Fleet, 1973 (SQA)
Brower, David Ross; Carson, Rachel; Chapman, John; Commoner, Barry; Cousteau, Jacques Yves; Hayes, Denis Allen†; Leopold, Aldo; Lindbergh, Charles Augustus; Marsh, George Perkins; Muir, John; Norris, George William; Philip; Pinchot, Gifford; Rodale, Jerome Irving; Thoreau, Henry David; Vogt, William.

Heroes of History: A Selection of Churchill's Favorite Historical Characters. Winston Churchill. Dodd, 1968 (o.p.) (CHG)
Alfred the Great; Churchill, Sir Winston Leonard Spencer; Elizabeth I; Harold II; Henry II; Henry V; Henry VIII; Joan of Arc; Lee, Robert Edward; Lincoln, Abraham; Nelson, Horatio, viscount; Richard I; Thomas à Becket; Victoria; Washington, George; Wellington, Arthur Wellesley, 1st duke of; William I, the Conqueror.

Heroes of Israel. Morris Rosenblum. Fleet, 1972 (ROGA)
Agnon, Shmuel Yosef; Allon, Yigal; Ben-Gurion, David; Ben Yehudah, Eliezer; Dayan, Moshe; Herzl, Theodor; Marcus, Mickey; Meir, Golda; Senesh, Hannah; Trumpeldor, Joseph; Weizmann, Chaim; Yadin, Yigael.

Heroes of Jewish Thought. Deborah Karp. Ktav, 1965, pap. (KAC)
Abravanel, Isaac; Akiba ben Joseph; Caro, Joseph; Elijah ben Solomon; Hillel; Israel ben Eliezer (Baal Shem Tov); Judah ha-Levi; Judah ha-Nasi; Maimonides; Meir ben Baruch of Rothenburg; Mendelssohn, Moses; Rashi; Rav; Saadia ben Joseph; Samuel Yarhina'ah.

Heroes of Journalism. Elizabeth D. Squire. Fleet, 1974, pap. (SQB)
Bourke-White, Margaret; Cochrane, Elizabeth; Corbett, William†; Craig, Daniel; Douglass, Frederick; Duane, William†; Edes, Benjamin†; Franklin, Benjamin; Gill, John†; Grady, Henry Woodfin; Greeley, Horace; Hamilton, Alexander†; Jones, George†; Murrow, Edward Roscoe; Pulitzer, Joseph; Pyle, Ernest Taylor; Rowan, Carl Thomas; Russell, Benjamin†; Scripps, Edward Wyllis; Stanley, Sir Henry Morton; Steffens, Lincoln; Thomas, Isaiah†; Watterson, Henry; White, William Allen; Zenger, John Peter.

Heroes of Mexico. Morris Rosenblum. Fleet, 1969 (ROGB)
Cárdenas, Lázaro; Chávez, Carlos; Cuauhtémoc; Dominguez, (Maria) Josefa Ortiz de; Guerrero, Vicente; Hidalgo y Costilla, Miguel; Juana Inés de la Cruz, Sister; Juárez, Benito Pablo; Mina, Francisco Javier; Montezuma II; Morelos y Pavon, José Mariá; Orozco, José Clemente; Quetzalcoatl; Rivera, Diego; Vicario, Leona; Villa, Pancho; Zapata, Emiliano.

Heroes of Modern Jewish Thought. Deborah Karp. Ktav, 1966, pap. (KAD)
Bialik, Chaim Nachman; Crémieux, Isaac-Adolphe; Frankel, Zecharias; Geiger, Abraham;

Herzl, Theodor; Hirsch, Samson Raphael; Isaac, Levi; Kagan, Israel Meir; Montefiore, Sir Moses; Revel, Bernard; Rothschild, Edmond de; Salanter, Israel; Schechter, Solomon; Szold, Henrietta; Weizmann, Chaim; Wise, Isaac Mayer; Zalman, Shneor; Zunz, Leopold.

Heroes of Music. Renee Fisher. Fleet, 1974 (o.p.) (FIE)
Bach, Johann Sebastian; Bartók, Béla†; Beethoven, Ludwig van; Berlioz, Hector; Brahms, Johannes; Chopin, Frédéric François; Debussy, Claude Achille; Dvořak, Antonin†; Gershwin, George; Grieg, Edvard Hagerup†; Handel, George Frederick; Haydn, Franz Joseph; Ives, Charles; Liszt, Franz; Mendelssohn, Felix; Monteverdi, Claudio; Mozart, Wolfgang Amadeus; Mussorgsky, Modest Petrovich†; Rimski-Korsakov, Nikolai Andreevich†; Schubert, Franz Peter; Schumann, Robert Alexander; Sibelius, Jean†; Smetana, Bedřich†; Stravinsky, Igor Fëdorovich; Tchaikovsky, Peter Ilyich†; Wagner, Richard.

Heroes of Pro Basketball. Phil Berger. Random, 1968 (o.p.) (BEL)
Baylor, Ed; Bing, Dave; Chamberlain, Wilt; Cousy, Bob; Holman, Nat; Mikan, George L.; Pettit, Robert; Reed, Willis; Robertson, Oscar; Russell, William Felton; Schayes, Adolph; West, Jerry.

Heroes of Pro Hockey. Stan Fischler. Random, 1971 (o.p.) (FICA)
Beliveau, Jean; Berenson, Gordon; Esposito, Phil; Giacomin, Edward; Howe, Gordie; Hull, Bobby; Keon, David Michael; Orr, Bobby; Richard, Maurice.

Heroes of Puerto Rico. Jay Nelson Tuck & Norma C. Vergara. Fleet, 1971 (TU)
Baldorioty de Castro, Román; Barbosa, José Celso; Betances y Alarcón, Ramón Emeterio; Cordero y Molina, Rafael; Diego, José de; Hostos, Eugenio Maríe de; Marín Solá, Ramón; Muñoz Marín, Luis; Muñoz Rivera, Luis; Power Giralt, Ramón; Ruiz Belvis, Segundo.

Heroes of Science. Walter Shepherd. Fleet, 1964, 1970 (o.p.) (SHFB)
Agricola, Georgius; Ampère, André Marie; Archimedes; Aston, Francis William†; Avogadro, Amedeo; Baird, John Logie; Becquerel, Antoine Henri; Bell, Alexander Graham; Berzelius, Jöns Jakob, baron; Bunsen, Robert Wilhelm; Carnot, Nicholas Léonard Sadi; Cavendish, Henry; Copernicus, Nicolaus; Coulomb, Charles Augustin de; Curie, Marie Sklodowska; Dalton, John; Davy, Sir Humphry; Descartes, René; Dewar, Sir James; Doppler, Christian Johann; Edison, Thomas Alva; Einstein, Albert; Eratosthenes; Euclid; Fahrenheit, Gabriel Daniel; Faraday, Michael; Fermi, Enrico; Flamsteed, John; Fleming, Sir John Ambrose; Foucault, Jean Bernard Léon; Franklin, Benjamin; Fraunhofer, Joseph von; Galilei, Galileo; Gay-Lussac, Joseph Louis; Gilbert, William; Guericke, Otto von; Halley, Edmund; Henry, Joseph; Hertz, Heinrich Rudolf; Huygens, Christiaan; Joule, James Prescott; Kepler, Johannes; Kirchhoff, Gustav Robert; Lavoisier, Antoine Laurent; Leeuwenhoek, Anton van; Leibniz, Gottfried Wilhelm freiherr von; Leonardo da Vinci; Leucippus; Marconi, Guglielmo; Maxwell, James Clerk; Mendeleev, Dmitri I.; Morse, Samuel F. B.; Napier, John; Newton, Sir Isaac; Parsons, Sir Charles Algernon; Perkin, Sir William Henry; Planck, Max Karl; Priestley, Joseph; Pythagoras; Ramsay, Sir William; Roemer, Olaus; Roentgen, Wilhelm; Rumford, Benjamin Thompson, count; Rutherford, Ernest Rutherford, 1st baron; Talbot, William Henry Fox; Thomson, Sir Joseph John; Torricelli, Evangelista; Volta, Alessandro, conte; Watson-Watt, Sir Robert Alexander; Watt, James; Whittle, Sir Frank; Young, Thomas.

Heroes of Soccer. Larry Adler. Messner, 1980 (ADL)
Beckenbauer, Franz; Chinaglia, Giorgio; Cruyff, Johan; McAlister, Jim; Messing, Shep; Rote, Kyle, Jr.

Heroes of Stock Car Racing. Bill Libby. Random, 1975 (o.p.) (LEXA)
Allison, Bobby; Foyt, Anthony Joseph; Johnson, Junior; Lorenzen, Fred; Pearson, David; Petty, Lee; Petty, Richard; Roberts, Fireball; Turner, Curtis; Weatherly, Joseph Herbert; Yarborough, Cale; Yarbrough, Lee Roy.

Heroes of Texas. Edward Allen. Messner, 1970 (o.p.) (AKC)
Austin, Moses; Austin, Stephen Fuller; Bowie, James; Crockett, Davy; Houston, Samuel; Lamar, Mirabeau Buonparte; Travis, William Barret.

Heroes of the American Indians. Sol Stember. Fleet, 1971 (o.p.) (STAB)
Black Hawk; Crazy Horse; Geronimo†; Joseph; Osceola; Philip†; Pontiac; Popé†; Ross, John; Sequoya; Tecumseh; Wovoka.

Heroes of the American Revolution. Burke Davis. Random, 1971 (o.p.) (DAFA)
Adams, John; Clark, George Rogers; Franklin, Benjamin; Greene, Nathanael; Jefferson, Thomas; Jones, John Paul; Knox, Henry; Paine, Thomas; Revere, Paul; Steuben, Friedrich Wilhelm von; Washington, George.

Heroes of the Bullpen: Baseball's Greatest Relief Pitchers. Milton J. Shapiro. Messner, 1967 (o.p.) (SHE)
Arroyo, Luis; Black, Joe; Brosnan, Jim; Casey, Hugh; Duren, Ryne; Konstanty, Jim; Page, Joseph Francis; Perranoski, Ronald Peter; Radatz, Richard Raymond; Wilhelm, James Hoyt.

Heroes of the Challenger. Daniel Cohen & Susan Cohen. Archway, 1986, pap. (COE-1)
Jarvis, Gregory; McAuliffe, Christa; McNair, Ronald; Onizuka, Ellison; Resnik, Judith; Scobee, Dick; Smith, Michael J.

Heroes of the Home Run. Bennett Wayne, ed. Garrard, 1973 (WAC)
Cobb, Ty; Di Maggio, Joseph Paul; Gehrig, Lou; Hornsby, Rogers; Lajoie, Napoleon; Ruth, Babe; Speaker, Tristram E.; Wagner, Honus; Williams, Ted.

Heroes of the Hot Corner: Great Third Basemen of the Major Leagues. Bill Libby. Watts, 1972 (o.p.) (LEY)
Allen, Richie; Bailey, Bob†; Baker, Home Run; Bando, Salvatore Leonard; Boyer, Ken†; Collins, Jimmy†; Fregosi, James Louis; Gallagher, Alan Mitchell; Grabarkewitz, Bill; Harper, Tommy; Hebner, Richard Joseph; Killebrew, Harmon; Kingman, Dave†; McGraw, John Joseph†; Mathews, Edwin Lee†; Melton, Bill; Nettles, Graig†; Perez, Tony; Petrocelli, Rico; Rader, Douglas Lee†; Robinson, Brooks Calbert; Robinson, Jackie†; Rodriguez, Aurelio†; Santo, Ron; Scott, George; Torre, Joseph Paul; Traynor, Pie.

Heroes of the International Red Cross. Richard Deming. Hawthorn, 1969 (o.p.) (DED)
Barton, Clara; Beckh, Herbert; Courvoisier, Jean; David, François-Eugène; Dunant, Jean Henri; Junod, Marcel; Olivet, Georges; Rochat, André; Rolland, Romain; Volant, Guy.

Heroes of the Major Leagues. Alexander Peters. Random, 1967 (o.p.) (PEC)
Aaron, Hank; Clemente, Roberto; Kaline, Albert William; Killebrew, Harmon; Koufax, Sandy; Marichal, Juan; Oliva, Tony; Robinson, Brooks Calbert; Robinson, Frank; Torre, Joseph Paul.

Heroes of the N.F.L. Jack Hand. Random, 1965 (o.p.) (HAE)
Berry, Raymond; Gifford, Frank; Groza, Lou; Hirsch, Elroy "Crazylegs"; LeBaron, Eddie; McDonald, Tommy; Moore, Lenny; Sherman, Allie; Tunnell, Emlen; Wood, William Barry.

Heroes of the Olympics. Hal Higdon. P-H, 1965 (o.p.) (HIA)
Connolly, Harold; Didrikson, Babe; Loues, Spiridon; McKenley, Herb; Mathias, Bob; Meredith, James E.; Mills, Billy; Nurmi, Paavo; Owens, Jesse; Rudolph, Wilma G.

Heroes of the Polar Skies. John Grierson. Meredith, 1967 (o.p.) (GRB)
Amundsen, Roald; Andrée, Salomon A.; Byrd, Richard Evelyn; Ellsworth, Lincoln; Nobile, Umberto; Wellman, Walter; Wilkins, Sir George Hubert.

Heroes of Today—The Astronauts. L. Edmond Leipold. T. S. Denison, 1973 (o.p.) (LEPB)
Aldrin, Edwin E., Jr.; Anders, William Alison; Armstrong, Neil A.†; Borman, Frank; Chaffee, Roger Bruce†; Collins, Michael†; Glenn, John Herschel, Jr.; Grissom, Gus†; Lovell, James A., Jr.; Shepard, Alan Bartlett; White, Edward Higgins, II†.

Heroic Nurses. Robin McKown. Putnam, 1966 (o.p.) (MAK)
Barton, Clara; Bickerdyke, Mary Ann Ball; Breckinridge, Mary; Brigid of Kildare, Saint†; Cavell, Edith; Clare, Saint†; Dulce, Sister; Elizabeth of Hungary, Saint†; Fabiola†; Galard, Geneviève de; Haile Selassie, Tsahai; Hildegard of Bingen, Saint†; Huber, Alice†; Kenny, Elizabeth; Lathrop, Rose Hawthorne; Mance, Jeanne; Marillac, Louise de; Nienhuys, Janna; Nightingale, Florence; Radegonda†; Vincent de Paul, Saint.

Heroines of America. Henry Gilfond. Fleet, 1970 (GIBA)
Adams, Maude†; Addams, Jane; Anderson, Marian; Anthony, Susan Brownell†; Barrymore, Ethel†; Barton, Clara; Bethune, Mary McLeod; Blackwell, Elizabeth; Bourke-White, Margaret; Buck, Pearl S.†; Carson, Rachel; Chisholm, Shirley; Cornell, Katharine†; Didrikson, Babe; Earhart, Amelia; Fiske, Minnie Maddern†; Hayes, Helen†; Howe, Julia Ward†; Keller, Helen Adams; King, Coretta Scott; Millay, Edna St. Vincent†; Mitchell, Maria; Mott, Lucretia Coffin†; O'Keeffe, Georgia; Roosevelt, Eleanor; Sanger, Margaret; Smith, Margaret Chase; Stanton, Elizabeth Cady†; Stowe, Harriet Beecher; Truth, Sojourner; Tubman, Harriet; Wald, Lillian D.; Wheatley, Phillis.

Heroines of '76. Elizabeth Anticaglia. Walker, 1975 (o.p.) (AND)
Bates, Ann; Brant, Molly; Corbin, Margaret; Darragh, Lydia B.; Gannet, Deborah Sampson; Hart, Nancy; Lee, Ann; McCauley, Mary; Riedesel, Frederika von, baroness; Ross, Betsy; Warren, Mercy Otis; Wheatley, Phillis; Wright, Patience Lovell; Zane, Elizabeth.

Heroines of the Early West. Nancy Ross. Random, 1960 (o.p.) (ROI)
Duniway, Abigail Scott; Mary Loyola, Sister; Sacajawea; Walker, Mary Richardson; Whitman, Narcissa.

Hidden Contributors: Black Scientists and Inventors in America. Aaron E. Klein. Doubleday, 1971 (o.p.) (KLA)
Banneker, Benjamin; Carver, George Washington; Drew, Charles Richard; Julian, Percy Lavon; Just, Ernest Everett; Latimer, Lewis Howard; McCoy, Elijah; Matzeliger, Jan Ernst; Morgan, Garrett A.; Rillieux, Norbert; Williams, Daniel Hale; Woods, Granville T.

Hispanic Heroes of the U.S.A. Book 1. Warren H. Wheelock & J. O. Maynes, Jr. EMC, 1976 (WH)
Carr, Vikki; Castro, Raúl Héctor; Nuñez, Tommy.

Hispanic Heroes of the U.S.A. Book 2. Warren H. Wheelock & J. O. Maynes, Jr. EMC, 1976 (WH-1)
Gonzalez, Henry Barbosa; Lopez, Trini; Roybal, Edward Ross.

Hispanic Heroes of the U.S.A. Book 3. Warren H. Wheelock & J. O. Maynes, Jr. EMC, 1976 (WH-2)
Clemente, Roberto; Feliciano, José; Maymi, Carmen Rosa.

Hispanic Heroes of the U.S.A. Book 4. Warren H. Wheelock & J. O. Maynes, Jr. EMC, 1976 (WH-3)
Perez, Tony; Plunkett, Jim; Trevino, Lee.

Hispanic Personalities: Celebrities of the Spanish-Speaking World. Gary Wohl & Carmen Cadilla Ruibal. Regents, 1978 (WO)
Alegria, Ciro; Alonso, Alicia; Asturias, Miguel Angel; Badillo, Herman; Betances y Alarcón, Ramón Emeterio; Bolívar, Simón; Borges, Jorge Luis; Burgos, Julia de; Cantinflas; Carpentier, Alejo; Cervantes Saavedra, Miguel de; Chávez, Carlos; Chavez, Cesar Estrada; Clemente, Roberto; Dario, Rubén; Duarte, Juan Pablo; Finlay, Carlos Juan; Guillen, Nicolás; Hidalgo y Costilla, Miguel; Juárez, Benito Pablo; Limón, José; Lope de Vega, Félix; Martí, José Julian; Mistral, Gabriela; Moreno, Rita; Muñoz Marín, Luis; Neruda, Pablo; Orozco, José Clemente; Paz, Octavio; Picasso, Pablo; Rincón de Gautier, Felisa; Rodriguez de Tio, Lola; Sarmiento, Domingo Faustino; Villa, Pancho; Zapata, Emiliano.

Hispano American Contributors to American Life. John M. Franco, et al. Benefic Pr., 1973 (o.p.) (FOW)
Arboleya, Carlos; Arnaz, Desi; Badillo, Herman; Banuelos, Romana Acosta; Cepeda, Orlando; Chavez, Cesar Estrada; Clemente, Roberto; Feliciano, José; Ferrer, José; Finlay, Carlos Juan; Garcia, Hector; Gonzales, Pancho; Hernandez, Raphael; Limón, José; Montalban, Ricardo; Montoya, Joseph Manuel; Nava, Julian; Reyes, Joseph Manuel de los; Rincón de Gautier, Felisa; Rodriguez, Juan "Chi-Chi"; Zajicek, Sarita Soto.

History's One Hundred Greatest Composers. Helen L. Kaufmann. G&D, 1957 (o.p.) (KAE)
Albéniz, Isaac; Bach, Carl Philipp Emanuel; Bach, Johann Sebastian; Barber, Samuel; Bartók, Béla; Beethoven, Ludwig van; Berg, Alban; Berlioz, Hector; Bernstein, Leonard; Bizet,

Georges; Bloch, Ernest; Boccherini, Luigi; Borodin, Alexander P.; Brahms, Johannes; Britten, Benjamin; Bruch, Max; Bruckner, Anton; Byrd, William; Chausson, Ernest Amédee; Chávez, Carlos; Cherubini, Luigi; Chopin, Frédéric François; Copland, Aaron; Corelli, Arcangelo; Couperin, François; Debussy, Claude Achille; Delius, Frederick; Donizetti, Gaetano; Dukas, Paul; Dvořak, Antonin; Elgar, Sir Edward William; Enesco, Georges; Falla, Manuel de; Fauré, Gabriel Urbain; Foster, Stephen Collins; Franck, César Auguste; Gershwin, George; Glinka, Mikhail Ivanovich; Gluck, Christoph Willibald; Gounod, Charles François; Granados, Enrique; Grieg, Edvard Hagerup; Griffes, Charles Tomlinson; Handel, George Frederick; Harris, Roy Ellsworth; Haydn, Franz Joseph; Herbert, Victor; Hindemith, Paul; Honegger, Arthur; Indy, Vincent d'; Ives, Charles; Khachaturian, Aram; Kodály, Zoltán; Lasso, Orlando di; Leoncavallo, Ruggiero; Liszt, Franz; Lully, Jean Baptiste; MacDowell, Edward Alexander; Mahler, Gustav; Mascagni, Pietro; Massenet, Jules; Mendelssohn, Felix; Menotti, Gian-Carlo; Milhaud, Darius; Monteverdi, Claudio; Mozart, Wolfgang Amadeus; Mussorgsky, Modest Petrovich; Offenbach, Jacques; Palestrina, Giovanni Pierluigi da; Pergolesi, Giovanni Battista; Prokofiev, Sergei Sergeevich; Puccini, Giacomo; Purcell, Henry; Rachmaninoff, Sergei; Rameau, Jean Philippe; Ravel, Maurice; Respighi, Ottorino; Rimski-Korsakov, Nikolai Andreevich; Rossini, Gioacchino; Saint-Saëns, Camille; Scarlatti, Domenico; Schönberg, Arnold; Schubert, Franz Peter; Schumann, Robert Alexander; Shostakovich, Dmitri; Sibelius, Jean; Smetana, Bedřich; Sousa, John Philip; Strauss, Johann; Strauss, Richard; Stravinsky, Igor Fëdorovich; Sullivan, Sir Arthur Seymour; Tchaikovsky, Peter Ilyich; Vaughan Williams, Ralph; Verdi, Giuseppe; Villa-Lobos, Heitor; Vivaldi, Antonio; Wagner, Richard; Weber, Karl Maria Friedrich Ernst von; Wolf, Hugo.

Hitters (Stars of the NL & AL). Thomas Braun. Creative Ed, 1976 (o.p.) (BRAA)
Aaron, Hank; Brock, Louis Clark; Carew, Rod; Jackson, Reggie; Rose, Pete.

Hockey Heroes: The Game's Great Players. George Sullivan. Garrard, 1969 (o.p.) (SUB)
Hull, Bobby; Morenz, Howie; Richard, Maurice.

Hockey Hotshots. Bennett Wayne, ed. Garrard, 1977 (WAK)
Hall, Glenn; Hull, Bobby; Morenz, Howie; Orr, Bobby; Plante, Jacques; Richard, Maurice; Sawchuk, Terry.

Hockey Stars of the 70s. Frank Orr. Putnam, 1973 (o.p.) (ORB)
Clarke, Bobby; Dionne, Marcel; Dryden, Ken; Esposito, Tony; Goldsworthy, Bill; La Fleur, Guy Damien; Magnuson, Keith Arien; Martin, Richard Lionel; Orr, Bobby; Park, Brad; Perreault, Gilbert; Redmond, Mickey; Sanderson, Derek Michael; Tallon, Dale; Tkaczuk, Walter Robert; Unger, Garry; Widing, Juha Markku.

Hockey: The New Champions. Dave Fisher. Platt, 1973 (o.p.) (FICC)
Dionne, Marcel; Dryden, Ken; Grant, Danny; Guevremont, Jocelyn; Magnuson, Keith Arien; Meloche, Gilles; Park, Brad; Perreault, Gilbert; Polis, Greg; Tkaczuk, Walter Robert; Unger, Garry.

Hockey's Fearless Goalies. Nathan Aaseng. Lerner, 1984 (AAS-21)
Brodeur, Richard; Esposito, Phil; Liut, Mike; Moog, Andy; Palmateer, Mike; Peeters, Pete; Resch, Glenn "Chico"; Smith, Billy.

Hockey's Greatest All-Stars. Howard Liss. Hawthorn, 1972 (o.p.) (LIAB)
Beliveau, Jean; Harvey, Douglas; Howe, Gordie; Hull, Bobby; Kelly, Leonard Patrick; Lindsay, Ted; Mikita, Stan; Orr, Bobby; Plante, Jacques; Richard, Maurice; Sawchuk, Terry; Shore, Edward William.

Hockey's Greatest Stars. Frank Orr. Putnam, 1970 (o.p.) (ORC)
Bathgate, Andy; Beliveau, Jean; Blake, Toe; Durnan, Bill; Esposito, Phil; Geoffrion, Bernard "Boom-Boom"; Hall, Glenn; Harvey, Douglas; Howe, Gordie; Hull, Bobby; Lindsay, Ted; Mahovlich, Frank; Mikita, Stan; Morenz, Howie; Orr, Bobby; Pilote, Pierre Paul; Plante, Jacques; Richard, Maurice; Sawchuk, Terry; Schmidt, Milt; Shore, Edward William; Ullman, Norm.

Hockey's Masked Men. Les Etter. Garrard, 1976 (ETB)
Hall, Glenn; Plante, Jacques; Sawchuk, Terry.

Hockey's Super Scorers. Nathan Aaseng. Lerner, 1984 (AAS-22)
Bossy, Mike; Ciccarelli, Dino; Dionne, Marcel; Gretzky, Wayne; La Fleur, Guy Damien; Perreault, Gilbert; Stastny, Peter; Trottier, Bryan.

Hockey's Top Scorers. Richard Rainbolt. Lerner, 1975 (RAAF)
Beliveau, Jean; Esposito, Phil; Geoffrion, Bernard "Boom-Boom"; Howe, Gordie; Hull, Bobby; Lindsay, Ted; Mahovlich, Frank; Mikita, Stan; Orr, Bobby; Richard, Maurice.

Hot Shots of Pro Basketball. Lou Sabin. Random, 1974 (o.p.) (SA-1)
Abdul-Jabbar, Kareem; Barry, Rick; Erving, Julius; Frazier, Walt; Gilmore, Artis; Haywood, Spencer; McGinnis, George; Maravich, Pete; Petrie, Geoff.

Hot Shots of Pro Hockey. Walt MacPeek. Random, 1975 (o.p.) (MANA)
Apps, Syl; Clarke, Bobby; Dionne, Marcel; Howe, Mark Steven; La Fleur, Guy Damien; Martin, Richard Lionel; Perreault, Gilbert; Potvin, Denis Charles.

Houdini and Other Masters of Magic. Jan Fortman. Raintree, 1977 (FOGA)
Anderson, John Henry; Henning, Doug; Herrmann, Alexander; Houdin, Jean Eugène Robert; Houdini, Harry.

How and Why Wonder Book of Famous Scientists. Jean Bethell. G&D, 1964 (o.p.) (BEP)
Archimedes; Copernicus, Nicolaus; Curie, Marie Sklodowska; Darwin, Charles Robert; Einstein, Albert; Faraday, Michael; Fleming, Sir Alexander; Galilei, Galileo; Harvey, William; Leeuwenhoek, Anton van; Lyell, Sir Charles; Mendel, Gregor Johann; Newton, Sir Isaac; Pasteur, Louis.

Hunger Fighters. Paul De Kruif. HarBraceJ, 1928 (o.p.) (DEA)
Babcock, Stephen Moulton; Carleton, Mark Alfred; Dorset, Marion; Francis, Edward; Goldberger, Joseph; Hoffer, George Nissley; Löffler, Friedrich; MacKay, Angus; Mohler, John Robbins; Reid, James L.†; Saunders, Sir Charles Edward†; Saunders, William†; Shull, George Harrison; Steenbock, Harry.

Hypatia's Sisters: Biographies of Women Scientists, Past and Present. Susan Schacher, ed. Feminists Northwest, 1976 (o.p.) (SC)
Agnesi, Maria Gaetana†; Agnodice; Aspasia; Blackwell, Elizabeth†; Brahe, Sophia†; Carson, Rachel; Cavendish, Margaret†; Chatelet, Marquise du. Gabrielle Émilie Le Tonnelier du Breteuil; Cori, Gerty Theresa†; Cunitz, Maria†; Curie, Marie Sklodowska; De Beausoliel, Martine†; Donne, Maria Dalle†; Felicie, Jacoba; Giliani, Alessandra†; Goeppert-Mayer, Maria†; Goodall, Jane; Greene, Catherine†; Hamilton, Alice†; Herschel, Caroline†; Hildegard of Bingen; Hypatia; Jex-Blake, Sophia†; Joliot-Curie, Irène†; Kies, Mary†; Kirsh, Maria†; Maltby, Margaret†; Masters, Sibella†; Meitner, Lise†; Mitchell, Maria; Nightingale, Florence; Noether, Emmy Amalie†; Pinckney, Eliza Lucas†; Potter, Beatrix; Richards, Ellen Swallow; Sanger, Margaret; Somerville, Mary Fairfax; Taylor, Lucy Hobbs†; Troctula di Ruggiero; Wu, Chien-Shiung.

I Have a Dream. Emma Gelders Sterne. Knopf, 1965 (o.p.) (STF)
Anderson, Marian; Bates, Daisy Gaston; Farmer, James; Lewis, John; Marshall, Thurgood; Mulzac, Hugh Nathaniel; Parks, Rosa Lee; Randolph, Asa Philip; Shuttlesworth, Fred.

Idea Men. Edwin P. Hoyt. Duell, 1966 (o.p.) (HOF)
Astor, John Jacob; Colt, Samuel; Cooper, Peter; Curtiss, Glenn Hammond; Deere, John; Gary, Elbert Henry; Goodyear, Charles; Hilton, Henry†; Law, George; Livingston, Robert R.; Olds, Ransom E.†; Otis, Elisha Graves; Pullman, George Mortimer; Sprague, Frank Julian; Stanley, Francis Edgar; Stanley, Freelan O.; Stewart, Alexander Turney.

Ifrikiya: True Stories of Africa and Africans. Louis Wolfe. Putnam, 1964 (o.p.) (WOA)
Ashmun, Jehudi; Carter, Howard; Cinque, Joseph; Dianous, Jacques; Grogan, Ewart Scott; Kruger, Stephanus Johannes Paulus; Lesseps, Ferdinand de; Livingstone, David; Patterson, John; Rhodes, Cecil John.

Illustrated Minute Biographies. William A. DeWitt. G&D, 1964 (o.p.) (DEI)
Alcott, Louisa May; Alexander III, the Great; Alfred the Great; Andersen, Hans Christian;

Aristotle; Attila the Hun; Audubon, John James; Bach, Johann Sebastian; Balzac, Honoré de; Barnum, Phineas Taylor; Barton, Clara; Beethoven, Ludwig van; Bell, Alexander Graham; Boone, Daniel; Brahms, Johannes; Brown, John; Burbank, Luther; Byron, George Gordon Noel, 6th baron; Caesar, Gaius Julius; Carnegie, Andrew; Carson, Kit; Caruso, Enrico; Casanova de Seingalt, Giovanni Giacomo; Catherine II, the Great; Caxton, William; Cellini, Benvenuto; Charlemagne; Chopin, Frédéric François; Churchill, Sir Winston Leonard Spencer; Cleopatra; Cody, William Frederick; Columbus, Christopher; Confucius; Cooper, James Fenimore; Carot, Jean Baptiste; Cromwell, Oliver; Curie, Marie Sklodowska; Dante, Alighieri; Darwin, Charles Robert; De Soto, Hernando; Dickens, Charles; Disraeli, Benjamin, 1st earl of Beaconsfield; Dumas, Alexandre (Dumas père); Dvořak, Antonin; Edison, Thomas Alva; Einstein, Albert; Eisenhower, Dwight David; Elizabeth I; Emerson, Ralph Waldo; Erasmus, Desiderius; Faraday, Michael; Ford, Henry; Foster, Stephen Collins; Franklin, Benjamin; Frederick II, the Great; Fulton, Robert; Gainsborough, Thomas; Galilei, Galileo; Gandhi, Mohandas Karamchand; Gershwin, George; Goethe, Johann Wolfgang von; Gogh, Vincent van; Grant, Ulysses Simpson; Grieg, Edvard Hagerup; Gutenberg, Johann; Hale, Nathan; Hamilton, Alexander; Hannibal; Harvey, William; Henry VIII; Henry, O., pseud.; Henry, Patrick; Herbert, Victor; Hippocrates; Homer; Homer, Winslow; Howe, Julia Ward; Hudson, Henry; Hugo, Victor; Jackson, Andrew; Jefferson, Thomas; Jesus Christ; Joan of Arc, Saint; Jones, John Paul; Jonson, Ben; Kennedy, John Fitzgerald; Koch, Robert; Lafayette, Marie Joseph Paul Yves Roch Gilbert du Motier, marquis de; Lee, Robert Edward; Lenin, Nikolai; Leonardo da Vinci; Lincoln, Abraham; Longfellow, Henry Wadsworth; Luther, Martin; MacArthur, Douglas; Marie Antoinette; Marshall, John; Mary, Queen of Scots; Mendelssohn, Felix; Michelangelo Buonarroti; Mohammed; Monroe, James; Moses; Mozart, Wolfgang Amadeus; Napoleon I; Nero; Newman, John Henry; Newton, Sir Isaac; Nightingale, Florence; O'Neill, Eugene Gladstone; Pasteur, Louis; Penn, William; Pershing, John Joseph; Picasso, Pablo; Plato; Polo, Marco; Raleigh, Sir Walter; Rembrandt Hermanszoon van Rijn; Revere, Paul; Rodin, Auguste; Roentgen, Wilhelm; Roosevelt, Franklin Delano; Roosevelt, Theodore; Ruth, Babe; Schubert, Franz Peter; Shakespeare, William; Shaw, George Bernard; Socrates; Stevenson, Robert Louis; Stowe, Harriet Beecher; Tchaikovsky, Peter Ilyich; Tolstoi, Lev Nikolaevich; Toscanini, Arturo; Truman, Harry S.; Twain, Mark, pseud.; Verne, Jules; Victoria; Voltaire; Wagner, Richard; Washington, George; Webster, Daniel; Webster, Noah; Weizmann, Chaim; Wells, Herbert George; Whitman, Walt; Whitney, Eli; Williams, Roger; Wilson, Woodrow; Wren, Sir Christopher; Wright, Orville; Wright, Wilbur.

Illustrated Minute Biographies. William A. DeWitt. G&D, rev. ed., 1970 (o.p.) (DEJ)
See listing under 1964 edition. Delete: Atilla the Hun; Byron, George Gordon Noel, 6th Baron; Lafayette, Marie Joseph ... Marquis de. Add: Armstrong, Neil A.; Barnard, Christiaan N.; King, Martin Luther, Jr.

In Profile: Explorers on the Nile. Andrew Langley. Silver Burdett, 1981 (LAA-1)
Baker, Sir Samuel White; Livingstone, David; Speke, John Hanning; Stanley, Sir Henry Morton.

In Profile: Founders of America. Patrick Allitt. Silver Burdett, 1983 (ALCA)
Franklin, Benjamin; Jefferson, Thomas; Paine, Thomas; Washington, George.

In Profile: Founders of Religions. Tony D. Triggs. Silver Burdett, 1981 (o.p.) (TRC-1)
Buddha; Jesus Christ; Mohammed.

In Profile: Leaders of the Russian Revolution. Fred Newman. Silver Burdett, 1981 (o.p.) (NEBB-1)
Kerensky, Alexander Feodorovitch; Kornilov, Lavr Georgiyevich; Lenin, Nikolai; Trotsky, Leon.

In Profile: Pirates and Privateers. Jeremy Pascall. Silver Burdett, 1981 (o.p.) (PABB)
Blackbeard; Bonny, Anne; Kidd, William (Captain); Morgan, Sir Henry; Read, Mary.

In Profile: The Cinema Greats. Jeremy Pascall. Silver Burdett, 1983 (PABA)
Disney, Walt; Hardy, Oliver; Hitchcock, Alfred Joseph; Laurel, Stan; Wayne, John.

In Profile: The First Men around the World. Andrew Langley. Silver Burdett, 1983 (o.p.) (LAA-2)
Cook, James; Drake, Sir Francis; Magellan, Ferdinand; Slocum, Joshua.

In Profile: Tyrants of the Twentieth Century. Philip Clark. Silver Burdett, 1981 (CL-01)
Amin, Idi; Hitler, Adolf; Perón, Juan Domingo; Stalin, Joseph.

In Profile: Women of the Air. David Mondey. Silver Burdett, 1981 (o.p.) (MO)
Batten, Jean; Cochran, Jacqueline; Earhart, Amelia; Johnson, Amy.

In Profile: Women Prime Ministers. Richard Gibbs. Silver Burdett, 1981 (o.p.) (GI)
Bandaranaike, Sirimavo; Gandhi, Indira Nehru; Meir, Golda; Thatcher, Margaret.

In Search of Peace: The Story of Four Americans Who Won the Nobel Peace Prize. Roberta Strauss Feuerlicht. Messner, 1970 (o.p.) (FEC)
Addams, Jane; Bunche, Ralph Johnson; King, Martin Luther, Jr.; Roosevelt, Theodore.

In Search of Peace: The Winners of the Nobel Peace Prize, 1901–1975. Edith Patterson Meyer. Abingdon, 1978 (o.p.) (MEC)
Addams, Jane; American Friends Service Committee; Angell, Sir Norman; Arnoldson, Klas Pontus; Asser, Tobias M. C.†; Bajer, Frederik†; Balch, Emily Green; Beernaert, Auguste Marie François†; Borlaug, Norman Ernest; Bourgeois, Léon Victor Auguste†; Brandt, Willy; Branting, Karl Hjalmar†; Briand, Aristide†; Buisson, Ferdinand†; Bunche, Ralph Johnson; Butler, Nicholas Murray; Cassin, René†; Cecil of Chelwood, Edgar Algernon Robert Gascoyne-Cecil, 1st viscount†; Chamberlain, Sir Austen†; Cremer, Sir William Randal; Dawes, Charles Gates†; Ducommun, Élie†; Dunant, Jean Henri; Estournelles de Constant, Paul Henri Benjamin, baron d'†; Fried, Alfred Hermann†; Gobat, Charles Albert†; Hammarskjöld, Dag; Henderson, Arthur†; Hull, Cordell†; Jouhaux, Léon; Kellogg, Frank Billings†; King, Martin Luther, Jr.; Kissinger, Henry Alfred; Lafontaine, Henri†; Lange, Christian Louis†; Le-duc-Tho†; Luthuli, Albert John; MacBride, Sean; Marshall, George Catlett†; Moneta, Ernesto Teodoro†; Mott, John Raleigh†; Nansen, Fridtjof; Nobel, Alfred Bernhard; Noel-Baker, Philip John†; Orr, John Boyd, 1st baron; Ossietzky, Carl von; Passy, Frédéric; Pauling, Linus Carl; Pearson, Lester Bowles; Pire, Georges Henri; Quidde, Ludwig†; Renault, Louis†; Roosevelt, Theodore; Root, Elihu†; Saavedra Lamas, Carlos†; Sakharov, Andrei D.; Sato, Eisaku; Schweitzer, Albert; Söderblom, Nathan†; Stresemann, Gustav†; Suttner, Bertha von; Wilson, Woodrow.

Indian Chiefs. Lynne Deur. Lerner, 1972 (DEDB)
Black Hawk; Brant, Joseph; Cochise; Crazy Horse; Gall; Geronimo; Joseph; Keokuk; Osceola; Philip; Pontiac; Sequoya; Sitting Bull; Tecumseh.

Indian Chiefs. Russell Freedman. Holiday, 1987 (FRAB)
Joseph; Parker, Quanah; Red Cloud; Satanta; Sitting Bull.

Indian Chiefs of the West. Felix Sutton. Messner, 1970 (o.p.) (SUKA)
Crazy Horse; Geronimo; Joseph; Sequoya; Sitting Bull.

Indian Friends and Foes. Dorothy Heiderstadt. McKay, 1958 (o.p.) (HEC)
Black Hawk; Brant, Joseph; Cochise; Crazy Horse; Geronimo; Osceola; Pocahontas; Pontiac; Sacajawea; Sequoya; Sitting Bull; Squanto; Tecumseh.

Indian Patriots of the Eastern Woodlands. Bennett Wayne, ed. Garrard, 1976 (WAL)
Black Hawk; Massasoit; Osceola; Tecumseh.

Indian Patriots of the Great West. Bennett Wayne, ed. Garrard, 1974 (WAM)
Crazy Horse; Joseph; Parker, Quanah; Sitting Bull.

Indian Women: Thirteen Who Played a Part in the History of America from Earliest Days to Now. Lela Waltrip & Rufus Waltrip. McKay, 1964 (o.p.) (WAB)
Big Eyes; Dat-So-La-Lee; Indian Emily; Martinez, Maria Montoya; Neosho; Parker, Cynthia Ann; Pocahontas; Sacajawea; Tomassa; Velarde, Pablita; Wauneka, Annie Dodge; Winema; Winnemucca, Sarah.

Individuals All. Perle Epstein. Macmillan, 1972 (o.p.) (EOB)
Dickinson, Emily; Duncan, Isadora; Gregory, Dick; Merton, Thomas; Ripley, George; Thoreau, Henry David; Whitman, Walt.

Infielders (Stars of the NL & AL). Jay H. Smith. Creative Ed, 1976 (o.p.) (SMF)
Campaneris, Bert; Garvey, Steven Patrick; Morgan, Joe; Robinson, Brooks Calbert; Yount, Robin.

Inventors behind the Inventor. Roger Burlingame. HarBraceJ, 1947 (o.p.) (BUE)
Edison, Thomas Alva; Fitch, John; Ford, Henry; Franklin, Benjamin; Henry, Joseph; Kelly, William; Le Prince, Louis Aime Augustin; Livingston, Robert R.; Morse, Samuel F. B.; Roosevelt, Nicholas J.; Stevens, John; Vail, Alfred; Voight, Harry; Whitney, Eli.

Inventors in Industry. Ruby L. Radford. Messner, 1969 (o.p.) (RAA)
Edison, Thomas Alva; Goodyear, Charles; Howe, Elias; McCormick, Cyrus Hall; Whitney, Eli.

Inventors of the World. I. O. Evans. Warne, 1962 (o.p.) (EVC)
Archimedes; Baird, John Logie; Bell, Alexander Graham; Edison, Thomas Alva; Fulton, Robert; Galilei, Galileo; Leonardo da Vinci; Marconi, Guglielmo; Montgolfier, Jacques Étienne; Montgolfier, Joseph Michel; Morse, Samuel F. B.; Watson-Watt, Sir Robert Alexander; Whittle, Sir Frank; Wright, Orville; Wright, Wilbur.

Inventors: Nobel Prizes in Chemistry, Physics, and Medicine. Nathan Aaseng. Lerner, 1987 (AAS-33)
Bardeen, John†; Brattain, Walter Houser†; Einthoven, Willem; Hounsfield, Godfrey; Libby, Willard Frank; Marconi, Guglielmo; Roentgen, Wilhelm; Shockley, William Bradford†; Townes, Charles Hard.

Irish Saints. Robert T. Reilly. FS&G, 1964 (o.p.) (REC)
Brendan of Clonfert; Brigid of Kildare; Columban; Columcille; Galvin, Edward J.; Laurence O'Toole; McAuley, Mary Catherine, Mother; Malachy; Mathew, Theobald; Patrick; Plunkett, Oliver, Blessed; Talbot, Matthew.

It's the Final Score That Counts. Phyllis Hollander & Zander Hollander. G&D, 1973 (o.p.) (HOBB)
Albright, Tenley; Aldrin, Edwin E., Jr.; Bouton, James Alan; Connors, Chuck; Cosby, Bill; Holland, Jerome H.; Kroll, Alex; Mathias, Bob; Pettit, Robert; Spock, Benjamin; White, Byron Raymond.

Jazz Lives: Portraits in Words and Pictures. Michael Ullman. New Republic, 1980 (o.p.) (UN)
Backer, Steve; Berger, Karl; Blake, Ran; Braxton, Anthony; Carter, Betty; Cheatham, Doc; Cohen, Maxwell; Flanagan, Tommy; Gillespie, Dizzy; Gordon, Dexter; Gregg, Maxine; Hefti, Neal; Hines, Earl Kenneth; Kirk, Roland; McIntyre, Ken; McPartland, Marian; Mantilla, Ray; Mingus, Charles; Rivers, Sam; Rollins, Sonny; Silver, Horace; Snyder, John; Venuti, Joe.

Jewish Baseball Stars. Harold U. Ribalow & Meir Z. Ribalow. Hippocrene, 1984 (RI)
Arnovich, Morrie; Berg, Moe; Cohen, Andy; Danning, Harry; Gordon, Sid; Greenberg, Hank; Holtzman, Ken; Kling, Johnny; Koufax, Sandy; Mayer, Erskine; Myer, Buddy; Rogovin, Saul; Rosen, Al; Rosen, Goody; Schacht, Al; Sherry, Larry; Stark, Dolly; Stone, Steve.

Jews in American Life. Tina Levitan. Hebrew Pub., 1969 (LETA)
Aboab, Isaac de Fonseca; Alexander, Moses; Barsimson, Jacob†; Baruch, Bernard M.; Belasco, David; Benjamin, Judah Philip; Berlin, Irving; Berliner, Emile; Bernstein, Leonard; Borgenicht, Louis; Brandeis, Louis Dembitz; Brenner, Victor David; Brill, Abraham Arden; Cantor, Eddie; Dix, Henry; Einstein, Albert; Ezekiel, Sir Moses Jacob; Ferber, Edna; Fischel, Arnold†; Flexner, Abraham; Franks, David Salisbury; Gershwin, George; Gimbel, Adam; Goldberg, Arthur J.; Goldfadden, Abraham; Goldwyn, Samuel; Gomez, Benjamin; Gompers, Samuel; Gratz, Rebecca; Guggenheim, Meyer; Hart, Ephraim; Hays, Isaac; Hays, Moses Michael; Hendricks, Harmon; Jackson, Solomon Henry; Jacobi, Abraham; Jolson, Al; Jones, Henry; Joseph, Jacob; Knefler, Frederick; Lasker, Albert; Lazarus, Emma; Lehman, Herbert H.; Levine, Samuel Albert; Levy, Aaron; Levy, Asser; Levy, Hayman; Levy, Moses; Levy,

Uriah Phillips; Lindo, Moses; Lopez, Aaron; Lubin, David; Marcus, Mickey; Marshall, Louis; Michelson, Albert Abraham; Moise, Penina; Monis, Judah; Myers, Myer; Noah, Mordecai Manuel; Ochs, Adolph Simon; Revel, Bernard; Rodriguez, Benjamin; Rose, Ernestine Potowski; Rosenfeld, Morris; Rosenwald, Julius; Salk, Jonas Edward; Salomon, Haym; Salvador, Francis; Sarnoff, David; Schechter, Solomon; Schiff, Jacob Henry; Seixas, Gershom Mendez; Seligman, Joseph; Sheftall, Mordecai; Silver, Abba Hillel; Simson, Sampson; Solomons, Adolphus Simeon; Steinman, David Barnard; Straus, Nathan; Straus, Oscar Solomon; Sutro, Adolph Heinrich Joseph; Szold, Henrietta; Torres, Luis de; Touro, Judah; Waksman, Selman Abraham; Wald, Lillian D.; Warburg, Paul Moritz; Wise, Isaac Mayer; Wise, Stephen Samuel.

Kids on the Run. James R. Berry. Four Winds, 1978 (o.p.) (BEOA)
Angelo; Annie; Jeff; Larry; Marion; Michael; Ralph.

Kings and Queens of England. M. C. Scott-Moncrieff. Macmillan, 1966 (o.p.) (SCC)
Anne; Charles I; Charles II; Edward I; Edward II; Edward III; Edward IV; Edward V; Edward VI; Edward VII; Edward VIII; Edward the Confessor; Elizabeth I; Elizabeth II; George I; George II; George III; George IV; George V; George VI; Grey, Lady Jane†; Harold II; Henry I; Henry II; Henry III; Henry IV; Henry V; Henry VI; Henry VII; Henry VIII; James I; James II; John; Mary I; Mary II; Richard I; Richard II; Richard III; Stephen; Victoria; William I, the Conqueror; William II; William III; William IV.

Kings and Queens of England and Great Britain. Eric R. Delderfield. Taplinger, 1966 (o.p.) (DEC)
See listing under *Kings and Queens of England* by M. C. Scott-Moncrieff. Delete: Edward the Confessor. Add: Alfred the Great; Cromwell, Oliver; Philip.

Kings and Queens of England and the United Kingdom. Neil Grant. Watts, 1971 (o.p.) (GRAB)
Anne†; Charles I; Charles II; Cromwell, Oliver; Cromwell, Richard†; Edward I; Edward II†; Edward III; Edward IV; Edward V†; Edward VI†; Edward VII†; Edward VIII†; Edward the Confessor†; Elizabeth I; Elizabeth II; George I; George II; George III; George IV; George V; George VI; Harold II†; Henry I†; Henry II; Henry III; Henry IV†; Henry V†; Henry VI; Henry VII; Henry VIII; James I; James II†; John†; Mary I†; Mary II†; Richard I†; Richard II†; Richard III†; Stephen†; Victoria; William I, the Conqueror; William II†; William III†; William IV†.

Kings and Queens: The Plantagenets of England. Janice Brooks. Nelson, 1975 (o.p.) (BRBF)
Edward I; Edward II; Edward III; Edward IV; Edward V; Henry I; Henry II; Henry III; Henry IV; Henry V; Henry VI; John; Maud; Richard I; Richard II; Richard III; William I, the Conqueror; William II.

Kings of Black Magic. I. G. Edmonds. HR&W, 1981 (o.p.) (ED-5)
Agrippa, Cornelius Heinrich; Apollonius of Tyana; Balsamo, Joseph; Crowley, Aleister; Dee, John; Faust, Johann†; Julian; Levi, Eliphas; Lytton, Edward George Earle Lytton Bulwer, 1st baron; Paracelsus.

Kings of Motor Speed. Ross Olney. Putnam, 1970 (o.p.) (OLAB)
Andretti, Mario; Breedlove, Craig; Golden, Bill; Hill, Phil; Hurtubise, Jim; Lorenzen, Fred; Miles, Kenneth Henry; Pearson, David; Sachs, Eddie; Snively, Mike; Tanner, Sammy; Thompson, Mickey; Vukovich, Bill, Jr.

Kings of the Diamond: The Immortals in Baseball's Hall of Fame. Lee Allen & Tom Meany. Putnam, 1965 (o.p.) (ALB)
Alexander, Grover Cleveland; Anson, Cap; Appling, Luke; Baker, Home Run; Barrow, Ed; Bender, Chief; Bresnahan, Roger; Brouthers, Dan; Brown, Three-Fingered; Bulkeley, Morgan; Burkett, Jesse; Carey, Max; Cartwright, Alexander; Chadwick, Henry; Chance, Frank; Chesbro, Happy Jack; Clarke, Fred; Clarkson, John; Cobb, Ty; Cochrane, Mickey; Collins, Eddie; Collins, Jimmy; Comiskey, Charles Albert; Connolly, Thomas Henry; Crawford, Wahoo Sam; Cronin, Joe; Cummings, Candy; Dean, Dizzy; Delahanty, Edward James; Dickey, Bill; Di Maggio, Joseph Paul; Duffy, Hugh; Evers, John Joseph; Ewing, Buck; Faber,

Red; Feller, Bob; Flick, Elmer; Foxx, James Emory; Frisch, Frank; Galvin, James F.; Gehrig, Lou; Gehringer, Charles Leonard; Greenberg, Hank; Griffith, Clark; Grimes, Burleigh; Grove, Lefty; Hamilton, Billy; Hartnett, Gabby; Heilmann, Harry; Hornsby, Rogers; Hubbell, Carl Owen; Huggins, Miller; Jennings, Hugh Ambrose; Johnson, Ban; Johnson, Walter Perry; Keefe, Timothy J.; Keeler, Wee Willie; Kelly, King; Klem, Bill; Lajoie, Napoleon; Landis, Kenesaw Mountain; Lyons, Theodore Amar; McCarthy, Joseph Vincent; McCarthy, Tommy; McGinnity, Joseph Jerome; McGraw, John Joseph; Mack, Connie; McKechnie, Bill; Manush, Heinie; Maranville, Rabbit; Mathewson, Christy; Nichols, Kid; O'Rourke, James Henry; Ott, Mel; Pennock, Herbert Jefferis; Plank, Eddie; Radbourn, Old Hoss; Rice, Sam; Rixey, Eppa; Robinson, Jackie; Robinson, Wilbert; Roush, Edd J.; Ruth, Babe; Schalk, Ray; Simmons, Aloysius Harry; Sisler, George; Spalding, Albert Goodwill; Speaker, Tristram E.; Terry, William Harold; Tinker, Joseph Bert; Traynor, Pie; Vance, Dazzy; Waddell, Rube; Wagner, Honus; Wallace, Bobby; Walsh, Edward Augustine; Waner, Paul; Ward, John Montgomery; Wheat, Zachary Davis; Wright, George; Wright, Harry; Young, Cy.

Kings of the Drag Strip. Ross Olney. Putnam, 1968 (o.p.) (OLB)
Garlits, Don; Ivo, Tommy; Karamesines, Chris; Landy, Dick; McEwen, Tom; Malone, Art; Nancy, Tony; Prudhomme, Don; Rhodes, John; Ronda, Gaspar; Thompson, Mickey; Williams, Jack.

Kings of the Home Run. Arthur Daley. Putnam, 1962 (o.p.) (DAA)
Berra, Yogi; Di Maggio, Joseph Paul; Foxx, James Emory; Gehrig, Lou; Greenberg, Hank; Hodges, Gil; Hornsby, Rogers; Kiner, Ralph M.; Klein, Chuck; Mantle, Mickey Charles; Maris, Roger Eugene; Mathews, Edwin Lee; Mays, Willie Howard; Mize, Johnny; Musial, Stanley Frank; Ott, Mel; Ruth, Babe; Simmons, Aloysius Harry; Snider, Duke; Williams, Ted.

Kings of the Rink. Stan Fischler. Dodd, 1978 (o.p.) (FICA-1)
Apps, Syl, II; Clarke, Bobby; Dionne, Marcel; Dryden, Ken; La Fleur, Guy Damien; Park, Brad; Potvin, Denis Charles; Sittler, Darryl.

Kings of the Surf. Ross Olney & Richard W. Graham. Putnam, 1969 (o.p.) (OLD)
Bigler, Steve; Carroll, Charles Curtis "Corky"; Codgen, Claude; Doyle, Mike; Farrelly, Bernard; Frye, Harry Richard; Grigg, Rick; Hemmings, Fred, Jr.; James, Don; Kahanamoku, Duke Paoa; Miller, Russell C.; Munoz, Michael French; Noll, Greg; Nuuhiwa, David; Peterson, Preston; Propper, Gary; Valluzzi, Bruce; Van Dyke, Fred; Weber, Dewey; Young, Robert.

Knights of the Air: Canadian Aces of World War I. John Norman Harris. St. Martin, 1958 (o.p.) (HAG)
Barker, William George; Bishop, William Avery; Collishaw, Raymond; McKeever, Andrew Edward.

Know Your Presidents and Their Wives. George E. Ross. Rand, 1960 (o.p.) (ROH)
See listing under *America and Its Presidents* by Earl S. Miers. Delete: Johnson, Lyndon. *See also* listing under *America's First Ladies*, vols. 1 and 2 by Chaffin & Butwin. Delete: Johnson, Claudia Alta. Add: Fillmore, Caroline†; Harrison, Mary†.

Know Your Presidents and Their Wives. George E. Ross. Rand, rev. ed., 1969 (o.p.) (ROHA)
See listing under *America and Its Presidents* by Earl S. Miers. Add: Nixon, Richard M. *See also* listing under *America's First Ladies*, vols. 1 and 2, by Chaffin & Butwin. Add: Nixon, Thelma (Pat); add † after the following names: Tyler, Julia; Tyler, Letitia; Wilson, Edith; Wilson, Ellen.

Ladies of Seneca Falls: The Birth of the Women's Rights Movement. Miriam Gurko. Schocken, 1976, pap. (GUBA)
Anthony, Mary; Anthony, Susan Brownell; Bloomer, Amelia Jenks; Brent, Margaret†; Davis, Pauline Wright†; Fuller, Margaret; Godwin, Mary Wollstonecraft; Grimké, Angelina Emily; Grimké, Sarah Moore; Mott, Lucretia Coffin; Pinckney, Eliza Lucas†; Rose, Ernestine Potowski; Stanton, Elizabeth Cady; Stone, Lucy; Train, George Francis†; Willard, Frances Elizabeth; Woodhull, Victoria; Wright, Frances†.

Lamp Lighters: Women in the Hall of Fame. Marguerite Vance. Dutton, 1960 (o.p.) (VAB)
Anthony, Susan Brownell; Cushman, Charlotte Saunders; Lyon, Mary; Mitchell, Maria; Palmer, Alice Freeman; Stowe, Harriet Beecher; Willard, Emma Hart; Willard, Frances Elizabeth.

Lamps to Light the Way: Our Presidents. Barbara Barclay. Bowmar, 1970 (o.p.) (BAEB)
See listing under *America and Its Presidents* by Earl S. Miers. Add: Nixon, Richard M.

Laureates: Jewish Winners of the Nobel Prize. Tina Levitan. Twayne, 1960 (o.p.) (LET)
Asser, Tobias M. C.; Baeyer, Adolf von; Bárány, Robert; Bergson, Henri; Bloch, Felix; Bohr, Niels H. D.; Born, Max; Chain, Ernst Boris; Ehrlich, Paul; Einstein, Albert; Erlanger, Joseph; Fermi, Enrico; Franck, James; Fried, Alfred Hermann; Haber, Fritz; Hertz, Gustav; Hevesy, George de; Heyse, Paul Johann; Kornberg, Arthur; Krebs, Sir Hans Adolf; Landsteiner, Karl; Lederberg, Joshua; Lipmann, Fritz Albert; Lippmann, Gabriel; Loewi, Otto; Metchnikoff, Élie; Meyerhof, Otto Fritz; Michelson, Albert Abraham; Moissan, Henri; Muller, Hermann Joseph; Pasternak, Boris Leonidovich; Rabi, Isidor Isaac; Reichstein, Tadeus; Segrè, Emilio Gino; Stern, Otto; Tamm, Igor Yevgenyvich; Waksman, Selman Abraham; Wallach, Otto; Warburg, Otto Heinrich; Willstätter, Richard.

Lawyers for the People: A New Breed of Defenders and Their Work. Elizabeth Levy. Knopf, 1974 (o.p.) (LETD)
Broege, Carl; Clyne, Bernie; Halpern, Charlie; Huber, Linda; Kline, Tony; Libow, Carol; Moore, Beverly; Norton, Eleanor Holmes; Stender, Fay.

Lays of the New Land: Stories of Some American Poets and Their Work. Charlie May Simon. Dutton, 1943 (o.p.) (SIF)
Benét, Stephen Vincent; Bryant, William Cullen; Dickinson, Emily; Emerson, Ralph Waldo; Fletcher, John Gould; Frost, Robert; Lanier, Sidney; Lindsay, Vachel; Longfellow, Henry Wadsworth; Lowell, Amy; Masters, Edgar Lee; Millay, Edna St. Vincent; Poe, Edgar Allan; Robinson, Edwin Arlington; Sandburg, Carl; Whitman, Walt; Whittier, John Greenleaf.

Leaders of Labor. Roy Cook. Lippincott, 1966 (o.p.) (COH)
Dubinsky, David; Gompers, Samuel; Green, William; Haywood, William Dudley; Hillman, Sidney; Lewis, John Llewellyn; Murray, Philip; Powderly, Terence Vincent; Randolph, Asa Philip; Reuther, Walter Philip; Sylvis, William H.

Leaders of New Nations. Leonard S. Kenworthy & Erma Ferrari. Doubleday, 1968 (o.p.) (KEF)
Balewa, Sir Abubakar Tafawa; Ben-Gurion, David; Bourguiba, Habib ben Ali; Hussein Ibn Talal; Jinnah, Mohammed Ali; Kenyatta, Jomo; Magsaysay, Ramón; Mohammed V; Nasser, Gamal Abdel; Nehru, Jawaharlal; Nkrumah, Kwame; Nu; Nyerere, Julius Kambarage; Rahman, Tunku Abdul; Senghor, Léopold Sédar; Sukarno, Achmed.

Leaders of Our People, Book 1. Joseph H. Gumbiner. UAHC, 1963 (o.p.) (GUA)
Abravanel, Isaac; Akiba ben Joseph; Ashi; Gamaliel; Hillel; Johanan ben Zakkai; Joshua ben Chananiah; Joshua ben Levi; Judah ha-Levi; Judah ha-Nasi; Maccabaeus, Judah; Maimonides; Mattathias; Meir; Meir ben Baruch of Rothenburg; Moses ben Enoch; Rashi; Rav; Saadia ben Joseph; Samuel ha-Nagid; Simeon ben Lakish.

Leaders of Our People, Book 2. Joseph H. Gumbiner. UAHC, 1965 (o.p.) (GUB)
Baeck, Leo; Ben-Gurion, David; Ben Yehudah, Eliezer; Bialik, Chaim Nachman; Brandeis, Louis Dembitz; Einhorn, David; Einstein, Albert; Herzl, Theodor; Israel ben Eliezer (Baal Shem Tov); Lazarus, Emma; Magnes, Judah Leon; Menasseh ben Israel; Mendelssohn, Moses; Nasi, Joseph; Salanter, Israel; Salomon, Haym; Schechter, Solomon; Szold, Henrietta; Torres, Luis de; Touro, Judah; Weizmann, Chaim; Wise, Isaac Mayer; Wise, Stephen Samuel.

Leaders of Our Time, Series 1. Robert N. Webb. Watts, 1964 (o.p.) (WEA)
Adenauer, Konrad; Ben-Gurion, David; Castro, Fidel; Gaulle, Charles de; Kennedy, John Fitzgerald; Khrushchev, Nikita S.; Macmillan, Harold; Mao Tse-tung; Nasser, Gamal Abdel; Nehru, Jawaharlal; Nkrumah, Kwame; Thant, U.

Leaders of Our Time, Series 2. Robert N. Webb. Watts, 1965 (o.p.) (WEB)
Elizabeth II; Erhard, Ludwig; Hirohito; Johnson, Lyndon Baines; King, Martin Luther, Jr.; Menzies, Sir Robert Gordon; Paul VI; Rickover, Hyman George; Shriver, Robert Sargent; Sukarno, Achmed; Tito, Josip Broz; Warren, Earl; Wilson, Harold.

Leaders of Our Time, Series 3. Robert N. Webb. Watts, 1966 (o.p.) (WEC)
Ayub Khan, Mohammad; Brezhnev, Leonid Ilyich; Goldberg, Arthur J.; Humphrey, Hubert Horatio; Kennedy, Robert Francis; Kosygin, Aleksei N.; Lindsay, John Vliet; McNamara, Robert Strange; Marshall, Thurgood; Pearson, Lester Bowles; Reuther, Walter Philip; Romney, George Wilcken.

Leaders of Our Time, Series 4. Robert N. Webb. Watts, 1969 (o.p.) (WECA)
Brandt, Willy; Dayan, Moshe; Gandhi, Indira Nehru; Ho Chi Minh; Kiesinger, Kurt Georg; Ky, Nguyen Cao; McCarthy, Eugene Joseph; Nixon, Richard Milhous; Sato, Eisaku; Thieu, Nguyen-Van; Young, Whitney Moore, Jr.

Leaders of the American Revolution. LeRoy Hayman. Scholastic, 1970 (o.p.) (HAN)
Adams, John; Adams, Samuel; Arnold, Benedict; Franklin, Benjamin; Henry, Patrick; Jefferson, Thomas; Lafayette, Marie Joseph Paul Yves Roch Gilbert du Motier, marquis de; Morris, Robert; Otis, James; Paine, Thomas; Revere, Paul; Salomon, Haym†; Steuben, Friedrich Wilhelm von; Washington, George.

Leaders of the Middle East. James Haskins. Enslow, 1985 (HAGD)
Arafat, Yasir; Assad, Hafez el-; Begin, Menachem; Fahd ibn Abdul Aziz al Saud; Hussein Ibn Talal; Khomeini, Ruhollah; Mubarak, Mohamed Hosni; Qaddafi, Muammar el-; Ziaul-Haq, Mohammed.

Leaders of the People. Josephine Kamm. Abelard, 1959 (o.p.) (KAB)
Abravanel, Isaac; Akiba ben Joseph; Baeck, Leo; Herzl, Theodor; Hillel; Isaiah; Maccabaeus, Judah; Maimonides; Menasseh ben Israel; Mendelssohn, Moses; Montefiore, Sir Moses; Moses; Nasi, Joseph; Weizmann, Chaim.

Legendary Outlaws of the West. Brad Williams. McKay, 1976 (o.p.) (WIAA-1)
Alvord, Burt; Bell, Tom; Black Bart; Chato, El; Cooper, Dan B.; D'Autremont Brothers; Ketchum, Thomas Edward; Kuhl, Benjamin; Melendrez, Antonio; Murrieta, Joaquin; Plummer, Henry; Reynolds, Jim; Reynolds, John; Vasquez, Tiburcio; Walker, William.

Legendary Women of the West. Brad Williams. McKay, 1978 (o.p.) (WIAA-2)
Barcelo, Gertrudis; Bowers, Eilley Orrum; Bulette, Julia; Hart, Pearl; Juana Maria; McPherson, Aimee Semple; Pleasant, Mary Ellen; Tabor, Baby Doe; Watson, Ella.

Legends of the Saints. Ann Petry. T Y Crowell, 1970 (o.p.) (PEE)
Blaise; Catherine of Alexandria; Christopher; Francis of Assisi; Genesius; George; Joan of Arc; More, Sir Thomas; Nicholas; Porres, Martin de.

Legends of the Saints. E. Lucia Turnbull. Lippincott, 1959 (o.p.) (TUA)
Bartholomew; Brigid of Kildare; Catherine of Siena; Ciaran; Elizabeth of Hungary; Francis of Assisi; Jerome; Margaret of Scotland; Patrick; Roch.

Liberators and Heroes of South America. Marion Lansing. Ayer repr. of 1940 facsimile ed. (LAB)
Artigas, José Gervasio; Belgrano, Manuel; Bolívar, Simón; Bonifácio, José; Manco Capac†; Miranda, Francisco de; Moreno, Mariano; O'Higgins, Bernardo; Páez, José Antonio; Pedro I; Pedro II; San Martin, Jose de; Santander, Francisco de Paula; Sarmiento, Domingo Faustino; Sucre, Antonio José de; Tiradentes; Tupac Amaru†; Tupac Amaru II†; Unanue, Hipólito.

Liberators of Latin America. Bob Young & Jan Young. Lothrop, 1970 (o.p.) (YOFA)
Bolívar, Simón; Hidalgo y Costilla, Miguel; Iturbide, Augustín de; Juárez, Benito Pablo; Martí, José Julian; Morelos y Pavon, José Mariá; Pedro I; San Martin, Jose de; Toussaint L'Ouverture, Pierre Dominigue.

Life Givers. David Hendin. Morrow, 1976 (o.p.) (HEFA)
Cooper, Irving Spencer; Kline, Nathan Schellenberg; Lillehei, Clarence Walton; Rock, John; Rusk, Howard A.; Salk, Jonas Edward.

Lift Every Voice: The Lives of B. T. Washington, W. E. B. DuBois, M. C. Terrell and James W. Johnson. Dorothy Sterling & Benjamin Quarles. Doubleday, 1965 (o.p.) (STB)
Du Bois, William Edward Burghardt; Johnson, James Weldon; Terrell, Mary Church; Washington, Booker Taliaferro.

Linebackers (Stars of the NFL). Sam Hasegawa. Creative Ed, 1975 (o.p.) (HAGB)
Butkus, Dick; Jordan, Lee Roy; Nobis, Tommy; Robinson, Dave; Siemon, Jeffrey G.

Little Giants of Pro Sports. Nathan Aaseng. Lerner, 1980 (AAS-23)
Austin, Tracy; Dionne, Marcel; Morgan, Joe; Murphy, Calvin; Patek, Fred; Pelé; Pruitt, Greg; Zernike, Frits.

Little League to Big League. Jim Brosnan. Random, 1968 (o.p.) (BRE)
Bradley, Bill; Ditka, Michael; Freehan, Bill; Jay, Joseph Richard; John, Tommy; McDowell, Sam; Maris, Roger Eugene; Nye, Rich; Ryun, Jim; Santo, Ron; Schollander, Donald Arthur; Spurrier, Steve; Tarkenton, Francis; Yastrzemski, Carl Michael.

Little Men in Sports. Larry Fox. G&D, 1968 (o.p.) (FOI)
Andretti, Mario; Armstrong, Henry; Booth, Albie; Cousy, Bob; Hogan, Ben; LeBaron, Eddie; Lee, Sammy; Lindgren, Gerry; McCann, Terry; McDonald, Tommy; O'Brien, Eddie; O'Brien, Johnny; Pearson, Albie; Richard, Henri; Riggs, Bobby; Rizzuto, Philip Francis; Rodriguez, Juan "Chi-Chi"; Weber, Dick; Werner, Bud; Wills, Maury; Young, Buddy.

Little Men of the NFL. Bob Rubin. Random, 1974 (RUC)
Fischer, Pat; Jackson, Harold; Little, Floyd Douglas; Tarkenton, Francis; Vataha, Randy; Wilson, Nemiah; Yepremian, Garo Sarkis.

Lives of Famous Romans. Olivia Coolidge. HM, 1965 (o.p.) (COK)
Augustus; Caesar, Gaius Julius; Cicero, Marcus Tullius; Constantine I, the Great; Diocletian; Hadrian; Horace; Marcus Aurelius; Nero; Seneca, Lucius Annaeus; Trajan; Virgil.

Lives of Girls Who Became Famous. Sarah K. Bolton. T Y Crowell, 1949 (o.p.) (BOC)
Addams, Jane; Alcott, Louisa May; Anderson, Marian; Anthony, Susan Brownell; Barton, Clara; Blackwell, Elizabeth; Bonheur, Rosa; Browning, Elizabeth Barrett; Cornell, Katharine; Curie, Marie Sklodowska; Earhart, Amelia; Fuller, Margaret; Howe, Julia Ward; Keller, Helen Adams; Kenny, Elizabeth; Lind, Jenny; Lyon, Mary; Nightingale, Florence; Perkins, Frances; Roosevelt, Eleanor; Staël, Germaine de; Stowe, Harriet Beecher.

Lives of Poor Boys Who Became Famous. Sarah K. Bolton. T Y Crowell, rev. ed., 1962 (o.p.) (BOD)
Bok, Edward William; Bull, Ole; Carver, George Washington; Coolidge, Calvin; Cornell, Ezra; Dickens, Charles; Edison, Thomas Alva; Faraday, Michael; Farragut, David Glasgow; Ford, Henry; Franklin, Benjamin; Garibaldi, Giuseppe; Garrison, William Lloyd; Johnson, Samuel; Lincoln, Abraham; Mayo, Charles Horace; Mayo, William James; Mayo, William Worrall; Mozart, Wolfgang Amadeus; Pius XI; Rockefeller, John Davison; Rogers, Will; Watt, James; Wood, Grant; Wright, Orville; Wright, Wilbur.

Lock, Stock, and Barrel. Donald J. Sobol. Westminster, 1965 (o.p.) (SOA)
Allen, Ethan; Amherst, Jeffrey; André, John; Arnold, Benedict; Burgoyne, John; Butler, Walter; Clark, George Rogers; Clinton, Sir Henry; Cornwallis, Charles Cornwallis, 1st marquis; Gage, Thomas; George III; Germain, George Sackville, 1st viscount Sackville; Glover, John; Grasse, François Joseph de; Greene, Nathanael; Hancock, John; Hopkins, Esek; Howe, William Howe, 5th viscount; Jones, John Paul; Knox, Henry; Lafayette, Marie Joseph Paul Yves Roch Gilbert du Motier, marquis de; Lee, Charles; Lee, Henry; Marion, Francis; Morgan, Daniel; North, Frederick, 2d earl Guilford and 8th baron North; Pitt, William, 1st earl of Chatham; Pulaski, Casimir; Putnam, Israel; Revere, Paul; Salomon, Haym; Schuyler, Philip

John; Seume, Johann; Steuben, Friedrich Wilhelm von; Tallmadge, Benjamin; Tarleton, Sir Banastre; Ward, Artemas; Washington, George; Wayne, Anthony; Wilkes, John.

Look-It-Up Book of Presidents. Wyatt Blassingame. Random, rev. ed., 1984 (BLA)
See listing under *America and Its Presidents* by Earl S. Miers. Add: Carter, Jimmy; Ford, Gerald R.; Nixon, Richard M.; Reagan, Ronald.

Madcap Men and Wacky Women from History. Kahane Corn & Jacki Moline. Messner, 1987 (COKB)
Baker, Mary "Caraboo"; Brady, James Buchanan ("Diamond Jim"); Caruso, Enrico; Catherine II, the Great; Chaplin, Sir Charles Spencer; Christina; Clemenceau, Georges; Cobb, Ty; Edison, Thomas Alva; Eugenie; Fields, W. C.; Ford, Henry; Frederick II, the Great; Getty, J. Paul; Godiva, Lady; Green, Hetty; Hearst, William Randolph; Hoover, J. Edgar; Hughes, Howard, Jr.; Hugo, Victor; Hutton, Barbara; Kelly, Alvin "Shipwreck"; Ludwig II; McFadden, Bernarr; Marx, Chico; Nagurski, Bronko; Nightingale, Florence; Peter I, the Great; Poe, Edgar Allan; Ponce de León, Juan; Randolph, John; Rasputin, Grigori; Ruth, Babe; Sunday, Billy; Vanderbilt, Cornelius; Virgil; Wagner, "Gorgeous George"; Winchester, Sarah.

Main Men of the Seventies: The Linebackers. Rick Smith. National Football League, 1976 (o.p.) (SMJ)
Bergey, Bill L.; Brazile, Robert; Carr, Frederick; Federspiel, Joe; Gradishar, Randy; Lambert, Jack; Lanier, Willie Edward; LeClair, Jim; Robertson, Isaiah; Siemon, Jeffrey G.; White, Randy; White, Stan.

Main Men of the Seventies: The Quarterbacks. Jack Clary. National Football League, 1975 (o.p.) (CL-1)
Anderson, Kenneth Allan; Bradshaw, Terry; Ferguson, Joe; Griese, Bob; Harris, James; Hart, Jim; Jones, Bert; Pastorini, Dan; Plunkett, Jim; Stabler, Ken; Staubach, Roger; Tarkenton, Francis.

Makers of a Better America. L. Edmond Leipold. T. S. Denison, 1972 (o.p.) (LEPC)
Astor, John Jacob; Barton, Clara; Carver, George Washington; Mann, Horace; Reed, Walter.

Makers of Latin America. Donald E. Worcester. Dutton, 1966 (o.p.) (WOB)
Abad Queipo, Manuel; Artigas, José Gervasio; Batlle y Ordóñez, José; Bello, Andrés; Bonifácio, José; Díaz, Porfirio; Francia, José Gaspar Rodríguez; González Prada, Manuel; Guzmán Blanco, Antonio; Irigoyen, Hipólito; Juárez, Benito Pablo; Medina, José Toribio; Mendoza, Antonio de; Mitre, Bartolomé; Morelos y Pavon, José Mariá; Nabuco, Joaquim; Perón, Eva Duarte; Perón, Juan Domingo; Rondon, Cândido Mariano da Silva; Sigüenza y Góngora, Carlos de; Vargas, Getúlio Dornelles; Vieira, Antônio.

Makers of the Red Revolution. Olivia Coolidge. HM, 1963 (o.p.) (COJB)
Khrushchev, Nikita S.; Lenin, Nikolai; Mao Tse-tung; Marx, Karl Heinrich; Stalin, Joseph; Tito, Josip Broz; Trotsky, Leon.

Making of a Rookie. Howard Liss. Random, 1968 (LIB)
Hart, Jim; Sayers, Gale; Smith, Charles "Bubba"; Warfield, Paul.

Managers (Stars of the NL & AL). Jay H. Smith. Creative Ed, 1976 (o.p.) (SMG)
Alston, Walter E.; Anderson, Sparky; Martin, Billy; Murtaugh, Danny; Robinson, Frank.

Mapmakers of America: From the Age of Discovery to the Space Era. S. Carl Hirsch. Viking, 1970 (o.p.) (HIBC)
Champlain, Samuel de; Clark, William; Dixon, Jeremiah†; Frémont, John Charles; Jefferson, Thomas†; Joliet, Louis; Lewis, Meriwether; Mason, Charles†; Nicollet, Joseph Nicolas†; Powell, John Wesley; Smith, Jedediah Strong; Washington, George.

Marathon Runners. Thomas Barrett & Robert Morrissey, Jr. Messner, 1981 (BAEC)
Longacre, Jay; Rodgers, Bill; Shorter, Frank; Stack, Walter; Waitz, Grete.

Marathoners. Hal Higdon. Putnam, 1980 (o.p.) (HIA-01)
Barron, Gayle; Bikila, Abebe†; Bjorklund, Garry; DeMar, Clarence†; Kelley, John A.†;

Kelley, John J.†; Kolehmainen, Hannes†; Longboat, Tom†; Loues, Spiridon†; Pheidippides†; Rodgers, Bill; Shorter, Frank; Zatopek, Emil†.

Martyred Presidents and Their Successors. Frank K. Kelly. Putnam, 1967 (o.p.) (KEA)
Arthur, Chester Alan; Garfield, James Abram; Johnson, Andrew; Johnson, Lyndon Baines; Kennedy, John Fitzgerald; Lincoln, Abraham; McKinley, William; Roosevelt, Theodore.

Masked Marvels. Phyllis Hollander & Zander Hollander. Random, 1982 (o.p.) (HOCM)
Bench, Johnny Lee; Berra, Yogi; Campanella, Roy; Cochrane, Mickey; Fisk, Carlton; Hartnett, Gabby; Howard, Elston; Munson, Thurman Lee; Simmons, Ted Lyle; Torre, Joseph Paul.

Master Magicians: Their Lives and Most Famous Tricks. Walter Gibson. Doubleday, 1966 (o.p.) (GIA)
Anderson, John Henry; Hardeen; Herrmann, Alexander; Houdin, Jean Eugène Robert; Houdini, Harry; Kellar, Harry; Robinson, William Ellsworth; Saunders, Raymond; Thurston, Howard.

Master Painters of the Renaissance. David Jacobs. Viking, 1968 (o.p.) (JAA)
Botticelli, Sandro; Francesca, Piero della; Giorgione, Il; Giotto di Bondone; Leonardo da Vinci; Masaccio; Michelangelo Buonarroti; Raphael; Tintoretto, Il; Titian.

Master Spy. Dan Halacy. McGraw, 1968 (o.p.) (HAB)
Abel, Rudolf Ivanovich; Bazna, Elyesa; Greenhow, Rose O'Neal; Hale, Nathan; Hollard, Michel Louis; Lody, Karl Hans; Louvestre, Mary; Mata Hari; Sebold, William G.; Sorge, Richard; Stieber, Wilhelm; Wennerstrom, Stig.

Masters of Art. David Kales & Emily Kales. G&D, 1967 (o.p.) (KAA)
Botticelli, Sandro; Bruegel, Pieter, the Elder; Caravaggio, Michelangelo da; Cézanne, Paul; Daumier, Honoré; David, Jacques Louis; Degas, Edgar; Delacroix, Eugène; Dürer, Albrecht; Eyck, Jan van; Gauguin, Paul; Giotto di Bondone; Gogh, Vincent van; Goya y Lucientes, Francisco José de; Greco, El; Hogarth, William; Holbein, Hans (the Younger); Homer, Winslow; Kandinsky, Wassily; Klee, Paul; Leonardo da Vinci; Manet, Édouard; Masaccio; Matisse, Henri; Michelangelo Buonarroti; Modigliani, Amedeo; Monet, Claude; Picasso, Pablo; Poussin, Nicolas; Raphael; Rembrandt Hermanszoon van Rijn; Renoir, Auguste; Rivera, Diego; Rouault, Georges; Rubens, Peter Paul; Titian; Toulouse-Lautrec, Henri Marie Raymond de; Vermeer, Jan or Johannes; Watteau, Jean Antoine; Whistler, James Abbott McNeill.

Masters of Horror. Daniel Cohen. Clarion, 1984 (COE-2)
Karloff, Boris; Lee, Christopher; Lugosi, Bela; Price, Vincent.

Masters of Magic. Lace Kendall. Macrae, 1966 (o.p.) (KEB)
Blackstone, Harry; Carter, Charles J.; Herrmann, Alexander; Houdin, Jean Eugène Robert; Houdini, Harry; Kellar, Harry; Maskelyne, Jasper Nevil; Nicola, William Mozart; Thurston, Howard.

Masters of Modern Architecture. Edwin Hoag & Joy Hoag. Bobbs, 1977 (o.p.) (HIFA)
Gropius, Walter Adolf; Le Corbusier; Mies van der Rohe, Ludwig; Wright, Frank Lloyd.

Masters of Modern Music. Melvin Berger. Lothrop, 1970 (o.p.) (BEKA)
Bartók, Béla; Britten, Benjamin; Cage, John; Copland, Aaron; Gershwin, George; Hammerstein, Oscar, II†; Hindemith, Paul; Menotti, Gian-Carlo; Prokofiev, Sergei Sergeevich; Rodgers, Richard Charles; Schönberg, Arnold; Sibelius, Jean; Strauss, Richard; Stravinsky, Igor Fëdorovich; Ussachevsky, Vladimir.

Masters of Music: Their Works, Their Lives, Their Times. Dorothy Samachson & Joseph Samachson. Doubleday, 1967 (o.p.) (SAA)
Albéniz, Isaac; Bach, Carl Philipp Emanuel†; Bach, Johann Christian†; Bach, Johann Sebastian; Bach, Wilhelm Friedemann†; Balakireff, Mili Alekseyevich†; Bartók, Béla; Beethoven, Ludwig van; Berlioz, Hector; Bernstein, Leonard†; Bizet, Georges; Borodin, Alexander P.; Brahms, Johannes; Bruckner, Anton; Chopin, Frédéric François; Copland, Aaron†; Cui, César Antonovich†; Debussy, Claude Achille; Delius, Frederick†; Dvořak, Antonin; Elgar, Sir Ed-

ward William†; Falla, Manuel de†; Gershwin, George†; Glinka, Mikhail Ivanovich; Gluck, Christoph Willibald; Granados, Enrique†; Grieg, Edvard Hagerup; Handel, George Frederick; Haydn, Franz Joseph; Hindemith, Paul; Ives, Charles†; Liszt, Franz; Lully, Jean Baptiste; Mahler, Gustav; Mendelssohn, Felix; Monteverdi, Claudio; Mozart, Wolfgang Amadeus; Mussorgsky, Modest Petrovich; Prokofiev, Sergei Sergeevich; Puccini, Giacomo; Purcell, Henry; Rachmaninoff, Sergei; Ravel, Maurice; Rimski-Korsakov, Nikolai Andreevich; Rossini, Gioacchino; Satie, Erik; Scarlatti, Alessandro; Scarlatti, Domenico; Schönberg, Arnold†; Schubert, Franz Peter; Schumann, Robert Alexander; Shostakovich, Dmitri; Sibelius, Jean; Smetana, Bedřich; Strauss, Richard; Stravinsky, Igor Fëdorovich; Sullivan, Sir Arthur Seymour†; Tartini, Giuseppe†; Tchaikovsky, Peter Ilyich; Telemann, Georg Philipp; Vaughan Williams, Ralph†; Verdi, Giuseppe; Vivaldi, Antonio; Wagner, Richard; Weber, Karl Maria Friedrich Ernst von; Wolf, Hugo.

Masters of the Occult. Daniel Cohen. Dodd, 1971 (o.p.) (COEA)
Agrippa, Cornelius Heinrich; Blavatsky, Elena Petrovna; Dee, John; Garrett, Eileen J.; Home, Daniel Dunglas; Hubbard, L. Ron; Mesmer, Franz Anton; Saint-Germain, Comte de, pseud.; Swedenborg, Emanuel.

Medal of Honor Heroes. Red Reeder. Random, 1965 (o.p.) (REA)
Brown, Bobbie E.; Brown, Melvin L.; Bush, Robert Eugene; Castle, Frederick W.; Cromwell, John P.; Dean, William Frishe; Elrod, Henry Talmage; Izac, Edouard Victor M.; Kanell, Billie Gene; Luke, Frank, Jr.; Murphy, Audie; O'Callahan, Joseph T.; O'Hare, Edward "Butch"; Robinson, Robert Guy; Schmidt, Oscar, Jr.; Talbot, Ralph; Van Iersel, Louis; York, Alvin C.

Meet the Men Who Sailed the Seas. John Dyment. Random, 1966 (o.p.) (DYA)
Columbus, Christopher; Cook, James; Drake, Sir Francis; Eric the Red; Hanno; Herjolfsson, Bjarni; Jones, John Paul; Magellan, Ferdinand; Polo, Marco; Pytheas; Slocum, Joshua; Themistocles.

Meet the Presidents. Frances Cavanah. Macrae, rev. ed., 1965 (o.p.) (CAH)
See listing under *America and Its Presidents* by Earl S. Miers.

Men Against the Sea. Ross Olney. G&D, 1969 (o.p.) (OLC)
Blyth, Chay; Chichester, Sir Francis; Cousteau, Jacques Yves; Dill, Robert F.; Ellsberg, Edward; Heyerdahl, Thor; Keller, Hannes; Lake, Simon; Manry, Robert Neal; Momsen, Charles Bowers; Piccard, Auguste; Piccard, Jacques; Rechnitzer, Andreas B.; Ridgway, John; Willis, William.

Men and Women behind the Atom. Sarah R. Riedman. Abelard, 1958 (o.p.) (RID)
Aston, Francis William; Bohr, Niels H. D.; Chadwick, Sir James; Compton, Arthur Holly; Curie, Marie Sklodowska; Curie, Pierre; Einstein, Albert; Fermi, Enrico; Joliot-Curie, Frédéric; Joliot-Curie, Irène; Lawrence, Ernest Orlando; Meitner, Lise†; Oppenheimer, Julius Robert; Rutherford, Ernest Rutherford, 1st baron; Soddy, Frederick; Thomson, Sir Joseph John; Urey, Harold Clayton; Wilson, Charles T. R.

Men in the Sea. Peter Briggs. S&S, 1968 (o.p.) (BRBC)
Bond, George F.; Bruun, Anton Frederick; Cromwell, Townsend; Ewing, W. Maurice; Iselin, Columbus O'Donnell; Link, Edwin Albert; Pryor, Taylor; Revelle, Roger; Spilhaus, Athelstan F.

Men of Ideas. John J. Loeper. Atheneum, 1970 (o.p.) (LO)
Aristotle; Augustine; Bacon, Francis; Confucius; Descartes, René; Hegel, Georg Wilhelm Friedrich; James, William; Kant, Immanuel; Kierkegaard, Sören Aabye; Lao-tzu; Locke, John; Lucretius; Marx, Karl Heinrich; Nietzsche, Friedrich Wilhelm; Plato; Santayana, George; Schweitzer, Albert; Smith, Adam; Socrates; Spinoza, Baruch or Benedict; Teilhard de Chardin, Pierre; Thomas Aquinas; Voltaire.

Men of Medicine. Katherine B. Shippen. Viking, 1957 (o.p.) (SHG)
Asklepios; Auenbrugger, Leopold; Avicenna†; Finlay, Carlos Juan; Fleming, Sir Alexander; Florey, Sir Howard Walter; Galen; Harvey, William; Hippocrates; Hunayn†; Jackson, Charles Thomas†; Jenner, Edward; Laënnec, René Théophile; Laveran, Charles Louis;

Lister, Joseph, 1st baron Lister of Lyme Regis; Long, Crawford Williamson; McDowell, Ephraim; Morton, William; Nestorius; Noguchi, Hideyo†; Paracelsus; Paré, Ambroise; Pasteur, Louis; Reed, Walter; Rhazes†; Roentgen, Wilhelm; Sanctorius; Stokes, Adrian†; Trudeau, Edward Livingston; Vesalius, Andreas; Wells, Horace†.

Men of Modern Architecture: Giants in Glass, Steel and Stone. Aylesa Forsee. Macrae, 1966 (o.p.) (FOF)
Gropius, Walter Adolf; Mendelsohn, Eric; Mies van der Rohe, Ludwig; Neutra, Richard Joseph; Saarinen, Eero; Stone, Edward Durrell; Sullivan, Louis Henry; Wright, Frank Lloyd.

Men of Power: A Book of Dictators. Albert Carr. Viking, rev. ed., 1956 (o.p.) (CAE)
Bismarck, Otto von; Bolívar, Simón; Cromwell, Oliver; Franco, Francisco; Frederick II, the Great; Hitler, Adolf; Mao Tse-tung; Mussolini, Benito; Napoleon I; Perón, Juan Domingo; Richelieu, Armand Jean du Plessis, cardinal, duc de; Stalin, Joseph.

Men of the Wild Frontier. Bennett Wayne, ed. Garrard, 1974 (WAN)
Boone, Daniel; Crockett, Davy; Houston, Samuel; Jackson, Andrew.

Men Who Changed the Map, vol. 1, A.D. 400–1914. Erick Berry & Herbert Best. Funk & W, 1967 (o.p.) (BEO)
Attila the Hun; Bayezid I; Catherine II, the Great; Charlemagne; Cortes, Hernando; Frederick II; Genghis Khan; Justinian I, the Great; Mohammed; Mohammed I†; Mohammed II (The Conqueror); Murad I; Murad II; Napoleon I; Orkhan; Osman I†; William I, the Conqueror.

Men Who Dig Up History. Lynne Poole & Gray Poole. Dodd, 1968 (o.p.) (POC)
Anderson, Douglas Dorland; Bass, George F.; Broneer, Oscar; Gejvall, Nils-Gustaf; Haury, Emil W.; Libby, Willard Frank; Mallowan, Max E. L.; Wheeler, Sir Mortimer; Willey, Gordon Randolph; Yadin, Yigael.

Men Who Fought for Freedom. Egon Larsen. Roy, 1958 (o.p.) (LAD)
Bolívar, Simón; Brine, James; Gandhi, Mohandas Karamchand; Graf, Willi; Hammett, James; Huber, Kurt; Lafayette, Marie Joseph Paul Yves Roch Gilbert du Motier, marquis de; Loveless, George; Loveless, James; Masaryk, Thomas Garrigue; Penn, William; Probst, Christoph; Reich, Haviva; Schmorell, Alexander; Scholl, Hans; Scholl, Sophie; Senesh, Hannah; Sereni, Enzo; Standfield, John; Standfield, Thomas; Sun Yat-sen; Tolpuddle martyrs.

Men Who Made Mexico. Clarke Newlon. Dodd, 1973 (o.p.) (NEBA)
Cantinflas; Cárdenas, Lázaro; Chávez, Carlos; Díaz, Porfirio; Dominguez, (Maria) Josefa Ortiz de; Echeverría, Luís; Guzmán, Martín Luis; Hidalgo y Costilla, Miguel; Iturbide, Augustín de; Juárez, Benito Pablo; Ledón, Amalia; Madero, Francisco Indalecio; Morelos y Pavon, José Mariá; Obregón, Álvaro†; Ortiz Mena, Antonio; Pasquel, Jorge; Rivera, Diego; Santa Anna, Antonio López de; Vasconcelos, José; Vasquez, Pedro Ramírez; Victoria, Guadalupe, pseud.; Villa, Pancho; Zapata, Emiliano.

Men Who Opened the West. Wyatt Blassingame & Richard Glendinning. Putnam, 1966 (o.p.) (BLD)
Cabeza de Vaca, Álvar Núñez†; Coronado, Francisco Vásquez de; Crocker, Charles†; Esteban or Estevanico†; Goodnight, Charles; Judah, Theodore Dehone†; Kearny, Stephen Watts; Ledyard, John; Loving, Oliver†; Marcos, Father†; Narváez, Pánfilo de†; Smith, Jedediah Strong; Sutter, John Augustus; Young, Brigham.

Men Who Shaped the Future: Stories of Invention and Discovery. Egon Larsen. Roy, 1954 (o.p.) (LAE)
Aveling, Thomas; Bessemer, Sir Henry; Booth, Hubert Cecil; Chain, Ernst Boris; Diesel, Rudolf C.; Ferguson, Harry George; Fleming, Sir Alexander; Florey, Sir Howard Walter; Fulton, Robert; Goodyear, Charles; Howe, Elias; Kelvin, William Thomson, 1st baron; König, Friedrich; Low, Archibald Montgomery; Mergenthaler, Ottmar; Morse, Samuel F. B.; Murdock, William; Nobel, Alfred Bernhard; Sax, Adolphe; Sholes, Christopher Latham; Sikorsky, Igor Ivan; Spottiswoode, Nigel; Spottiswoode, Raymond; Whitney, Eli.

Microbe Hunters. Paul De Kruif. HarBraceJ, 1926 (o.p.) (DEB)
Behring, Emil von; Bruce, Sir David; Ehrlich, Paul; Grassi, Giovanni Battista; Koch, Robert;

Leeuwenhoek, Anton van; Metchnikoff, Élie; Pasteur, Louis; Reed, Walter; Ross, Sir Ronald; Roux, Pierre Paul Émile; Smith, Theobald; Spallanzani, Lazzaro.

Mighty Macs: Three Famous Baseball Managers. Guernsey Van Riper, Jr. Garrard, 1972 (o.p.) (VACB)
McCarthy, Joseph Vincent; McGraw, John Joseph; Mack, Connie.

Mirror for Greatness: Six Americans. Bruce Bliven. McGraw, 1975 (o.p.) (BLE)
Adams, John; Emerson, Ralph Waldo; Franklin, Benjamin; Jefferson, Thomas; Thoreau, Henry David; Truth, Sojourner.

Modern American Career Women. Eleanor Clymer & Lillian Erlich. Dodd, 1959 (o.p.) (CLA)
Cochran, Jacqueline; De Mille, Agnes; Didrikson, Babe; Donlon, Mary Honor; Frederick, Pauline; Gilbreth, Lillian M.; Gildersleeve, Virginia Crocheron; Hayes, Helen; Hoffman, Malvina; Lenroot, Katharine F.; Luce, Clare Boothe; McCormick, Anne O'Hare; Mead, Margaret; O'Keeffe, Georgia; Perkins, Frances; Shaver, Dorothy; Smith, Margaret Chase; Taussig, Helen Brooke.

Modern American Engineers. Edna Yost. Lippincott, 1958 (o.p.) (YOD)
Bush, Vannevar; Davidson, J. Brownlee; Doherty, Robert Ernest; Flanders, Ralph Edward; Maynard, Harold Bright; Morgan, Arthur Ernest; Rosen, Carl George Arthur; Singstad, Ole; Sparrow, Stanwood W.; Suman, John Robert; Turner, Scott; Wheeler, Harold Alden.

Modern Americans in Science and Technology. Edna Yost. Dodd, 1962 (o.p.) (YOE)
Baekeland, Leo Hendrik; Carrier, Willis Haviland; Carver, George Washington; Cottrell, Frederick Gardner; Fermi, Enrico; Goddard, Robert Hutchings; Hagen, John P.; Kettering, Charles F.; Siple, Paul Allman; Sperry, Elmer Ambrose; Truog, Emil; Williams, Robert Rampatnam; Zworykin, Vladimir K.

Modern Auto Racing Superstars. Ross Olney. Dodd, 1978 (o.p.) (OLCC)
Allison, Bobby; Andretti, Mario; Foyt, Anthony Joseph; Hunt, James; Lauda, Niki; Unser, Al; Unser, Bobby.

Modern Baseball Superstars. Bill Gutman. Dodd, 1973 (o.p.) (GUE)
Aaron, Hank; Allen, Richie; Bench, Johnny Lee; Clemente, Roberto; Mays, Willie Howard; Seaver, Tom.

Modern Basketball Superstars. Bill Gutman. Dodd, 1975 (o.p.) (GUEA)
Abdul-Jabbar, Kareem; Chamberlain, Wilt; Cowens, Dave; Erving, Julius; Frazier, Walt; Havlicek, John.

Modern Composers for Young People. Gladys Burch. Dodd, 1941 (o.p.) (BUC)
Bartók, Béla; Carpenter, John Alden; Delius, Frederick; Dvořak, Antonin; Elgar, Sir Edward William; Falla, Manuel de; Gershwin, George; Griffes, Charles Tomlinson; Humperdinck, Engelbert; Mussorgsky, Modest Petrovich; Prokofiev, Sergei Sergeevich; Ravel, Maurice; Respighi, Ottorino; Rimski-Korsakov, Nikolai Andreevich; Schönberg, Arnold; Scriabin, Aleksandr Nikolaievich; Sibelius, Jean; Strauss, Richard; Stravinsky, Igor Fëdorovich; Vaughan Williams, Ralph.

Modern Drag Racing Superstars. Ross R. Olney. Dodd, 1981 (OLDA)
Beck, Gary; Garlits, Don; Glidden, Bob; McEwen, Tom; Muldowney, Shirley; Prudhomme, Don.

Modern Football Superstars. Bill Gutman. Dodd, 1974 (o.p.) (GUEB)
Brown, Larry; Csonka, Larry; Namath, Joe Willie; Simpson, O. J.; Tarkenton, Francis; Washington, Gene.

Modern Hockey Superstars. Bill Gutman. Dodd, 1976 (o.p.) (GUEC)
Clarke, Bobby; Dryden, Ken; Esposito, Phil; Mikita, Stan; Orr, Bobby; Potvin, Denis Charles.

Modern Motorcycle Superstars. Ross R. Olney. Dodd, 1980 (OLDB)
Hannah, Bob; Nixon, Gary; Roberts, Kenny; Springsteen, Jay; Vesco, Don.

Modern Olympic Superstars. George Sullivan. Dodd, 1979 (SUBB-1)
Ender, Kornelia; Jenner, Bruce; Juantorena, Alberto; Kim, Nelli; Viren, Lasse; Young, Sheila.

Modern Soccer Superstars. Bill Gutman. Dodd, 1979 (GUEC-1)
McAlister, Jim; Messing, Shep; Pelé; Rote, Kyle, Jr.; Roth, Werner; Trost, Al.

Modern Speed Record Superstars. Ross R. Olney. Dodd, 1982 (OLDC)
Breedlove, Craig; Gabelich, Gary; Joersz, Eldon†; Rose, Doug; Summers, Bob; Taylor, Lee.

Modern Women Superstars. Bill Gutman. Dodd, 1977 (GUED)
Comaneci, Nadia; Evert, Chris; Hamill, Dorothy; Kusner, Kathy; Nelson, Cindy; Rankin, Judy.

More Heroes of Civilization. Joseph Cottler & Haym Jaffe. Little, 1969 (o.p.) (COLA)
Babbage, Charles; Beebe, William; Bohr, Niels H. D.; Chain, Ernst Boris†; De Forest, Lee; Enders, John Franklin†; Faraday, Michael; Fermi, Enrico; Fleming, Sir Alexander; Florey, Sir Howard Walter†; Gauss, Karl Friedrich; Geddes, Sir Patrick; Goddard, Robert Hutchings; Henson, Matthew Alexander†; Herschel, Caroline†; Herschel, Sir William; Hertz, Heinrich Rudolf; Hillary, Sir Edmund; Landsteiner, Karl†; Linnaeus, Carl; Maury, Matthew Fontaine; Mead, Margaret; Mendeleev, Dmitri I.; Milne, John; Morgan, Thomas Hunt; Peary, Robert Edwin; Piccard, Jacques; Ramsay, Sir William†; Sabin, Albert Bruce; Salk, Jonas Edward; Schwann, Theodor; Taylor, Albert; Townes, Charles Hard.

More Indian Friends and Foes. Dorothy Heiderstadt. McKay, 1963 (o.p.) (HED)
Captain Jack; Joseph; Little Crow; Little Turtle; Parker, Ely; Parker, Quanah; Pasquala; Philip; Popé; Red Cloud; Roman Nose; Ross, John; Tammany; Tekakwitha, Kateri; Washakie.

More Modern Baseball Superstars. Bill Gutman. Dodd, 1978 (o.p.) (GUED-01)
Carew, Rod; Foster, George; Garvey, Steven Patrick; Luzinski, Greg; Munson, Thurman Lee; Ryan, Nolan.

More Modern Women Superstars. Bill Gutman. Dodd, 1979 (GUED-1)
Austin, Tracy; Blazejowski, Carol; Guthrie, Janet; Joyce, Joan; Lopez, Nancy; Nyad, Diana.

More Music Makers. Percy M. Young. Roy, 1962 (o.p.) (YOJ)
Arne, Thomas Augustine; Billings, William; Britten, Benjamin; Chopin, Frédéric François; Dvořak, Antonin; Gershwin, George; Palestrina, Giovanni Pierluigi da; Rimski-Korsakov, Nikolai Andreevich; Schumann, Robert Alexander; Sibelius, Jean; Vaughan Williams, Ralph; Verdi, Giuseppe; Weber, Karl Maria Friedrich Ernst von.

More New Breed Stars. Robert K. Krishef. Lerner, 1980 (KRI)
Davis, Mac; Fender, Freddy; Gayle, Crystal; Kristofferson, Kris; Murray, Anne; Nelson, Willie; Newton-John, Olivia; Pride, Charley; Ronstadt, Linda; Williams, Hank, Jr.

More Sports Titans of the Twentieth Century. Al Silverman. Putnam, 1969 (o.p.) (SICA)
Hogan, Ben; Howe, Gordie; Johnson, Walter Perry; Jones, Bobby; Louis, Joe; Mathias, Bob; Mikan, George L.; Musial, Stanley Frank; Nurmi, Paavo; Shore, Edward William; Spahn, Warren; Weissmuller, Johnny; Wills, Helen.

More Stories of Baseball Champions. Sam Epstein & Beryl Epstein. Garrard, 1973 (o.p.) (EP)
Lajoie, Napoleon; Speaker, Tristram E.; Young, Cy.

Mountain Men of the Early West. Olive W. Burt. Hawthorn, 1967 (o.p.) (BUG)
Bridger, James; Carson, Kit; Colter, John; Fitzpatrick, Thomas; Lisa, Manuel; Meek, Joseph L.; Smith, Jedediah Strong; Young, Ewing.

Moviemakers. Alice Fleming. St. Martin, 1973 (o.p.) (FLBC)
Capra, Frank; DeMille, Cecil Blount; Disney, Walt; Flaherty, Robert Joseph; Ford, John; Griffith, David Wark; Hitchcock, Alfred Joseph; Kubrick, Stanley; Lubitsch, Ernst; Porter, Edwin Stanton; Sennett, Mack.

Mr. President: A Book of U.S. Presidents. George Sullivan. Dodd, 1984 (SUBB)
See listing under *America and Its Presidents* by Earl S. Miers. Add: Carter, Jimmy; Ford, Gerald R.; Nixon, Richard M.; Reagan, Ronald.

Ms. Africa: Profiles of Modern African Women. Louise Crane. Lippincott, 1973 (o.p.) (CRA)
Andriamanjato, Rahantavololona; Baeta, Henrietta Louise; Bam, Brigalia; Brooks, Angie Elizabeth; Ighodaro, Irene Elizabeth; Jiagge, Annie; Kenyatta, Margaret Wambui; Konie, Gwendoline Chomba; Makeba, Miriam; Mandela, Winnie†; Sedode, Julia Barbara de Lima; Sikhakane, Joyce†; Sutherland, Efua Theodora.

Muckrakers: Crusading Journalists Who Changed America. Fred J. Cook. Doubleday, 1972 (o.p.) (COGB)
Phillips, David Graham; Russell, Charles Edward; Sinclair, Upton Beall; Steffens, Lincoln; Tarbell, Ida Minerva; Willard, Josiah Flynt.

Munson*Garvey*Brock*Carew. Bill Gutman. G&D, 1976 (o.p.) (GUEE)
Brock, Louis Clark; Carew, Rod; Garvey, Steven Patrick; Munson, Thurman Lee.

Music Makers. Percy M. Young. Roy, 1968 (o.p.) (YOK)
Bach, Johann Sebastian; Beethoven, Ludwig van; Brahms, Johannes; Elgar, Sir Edward William; Handel, George Frederick; Haydn, Franz Joseph; Mendelssohn, Felix; Mozart, Wolfgang Amadeus; Purcell, Henry; Schubert, Franz Peter; Tchaikovsky, Peter Ilyich; Wagner, Richard.

Music Makers of Today. Percy M. Young. Roy, 1958 (o.p.) (YOL)
Bartók, Béla; Copland, Aaron; Falla, Manuel de; Hindemith, Paul; Janáček, Leoš; Nielsen, Carl A.; Prokofiev, Sergei Sergeevich; Ravel, Maurice; Schönberg, Arnold; Stravinsky, Igor Fëdorovich; Walton, Sir William Turner.

Naturalists-Explorers. Wyatt Blassingame. Watts, 1964 (o.p.) (BLB)
Banks, Sir Joseph; Bartram, William; Darwin, Charles Robert; Humboldt, Alexander von; Linnaeus, Carl; Muir, John; Wallace, Alfred Russel.

Negro Builders and Heroes. Benjamin Brawley. Univ. of North Carolina Pr., 1937 (BRB)
Aldridge, Ira†; Alexander, Archie A.†; Allen, Macon B.†; Allen, Richard; Askia Muhammad†; Attucks, Crispus; Baker, John†; Baldwin, Maria L.; Banneker, Benjamin; Barthé, Richmond†; Bethune, Mary McLeod; Bousfield, Maudelle Brown; Bowen, J. W. E.†; Braithwaite, William Stanley†; Brawley, Edward M.†; Brown, Charlotte Hawkins; Bruce, Blanche K.; Burleigh, Henry Thacker†; Campbell, Robert L.†; Cardozo, Francis Louis†; Carver, George Washington†; Cary, Lott†; Cetewayo†; Chaka†; Chavis, John; Chesnutt, Charles Waddell†; Cinque, Joseph†; Coleridge-Taylor, Samuel†; Coppin, Fanny Jackson; Crummell, Alexander†; Cuffe, Paul; DeBerry, William Nelson†; Delany, Martin R.; Derham, James†; Dett, Robert Nathaniel†; Douglass, Frederick; Du Bois, William Edward Burghardt; Dunbar, Paul Laurence; Elliott, Robert B.; Fuller, Samuel Carter†; Garnet, Henry Highland†; Grimké, Francis James†; Hayes, Roland†; Haynes, Lemuel†; Henson, Matthew Alexander; Hinton, William A.†; Holly, James Theodore†; Holsey, Lucius Henry†; Hood, James Walker†; Hope, John; Jasper, John; Johnson, Henry†; Johnson, James Weldon†; Johnson, Mordecai Wyatt; Jones, Absalom; Just, Ernest Everett†; Laney, Lucy; Langston, John Mercer; Lawless, Theodore Kenneth†; McCoy, Elijah†; McKay, Claude†; Maloney, Arnold H.†; Matzeliger, Jan Ernst†; Merrick, John; Merrimon, Clifton†; Morris, Elias C.†; Moton, Robert Russa; Owens, Jesse†; Parsons, James A.†; Payne, Daniel Alexander; Pinchback, Pinckney Benton Stewart†; Poindexter, Hildrus A.†; Powell, Adam Clayton, Sr.†; Price, Joseph C.†; Prosser, Gabriel†; Revels, Hiram Rhoades†; Roberts, Needham†; Scarborough, William Saunders†; Shaw, Robert Gould†; Simmons, William J.†; Tanner, Henry Ossawa†; Tolan, Eddie†; Truth, Sojourner; Tubman, Harriet; Turner, Charles Henry†; Turner, Nat†; Van Alen, Clarence R.†; Vesey, Denmark†; Walker, Maggie Lena; Washington, Booker Taliaferro; Wheatley, Phillis; Williams, Daniel Hale†; Williams, George Washington†; Williams, Lacey Kirk†; Woods, Granville T.†; Woodson, Carter Goodwin†; Young, Charles.

Negroes in the Early West. Olive W. Burt. Messner, 1969 (o.p.) (BUH)
Beckwourth, James P.; Bush, George W.; Dodson, Jacob; Esteban or Estevanico; Fields,

Mary; Greaves, Clifton; Ikard, Bose; Johnson, Henry; Leidesdorff, William Alexander; Mason, Biddy; Pleasant, Mary Ellen; Pointe de Sable, Jean Baptiste; Rose, Edward; Singleton, Benjamin "Pap"; Stance, Emanuel; York; Young, Hiram.

Negroes of Achievement in Modern America. James J. Flynn. Dodd, 1970 (o.p.) (FLD)
Anderson, Marian; Armstrong, Louis "Satchmo"; Baker, Augusta; Bethune, Mary McLeod; Brooke, Edward William; Bunche, Ralph Johnson; Chisholm, Shirley; Davis, Benjamin O.; Davis, Benjamin O., Jr.; Evers, Medgar Wiley; Franklin, John Hope; Julian, Percy Lavon; King, John B.; King, Martin Luther, Jr.; Marshall, Thurgood; Meredith, James Howard; Motley, Constance Baker; Overton, Anthony; Randolph, Asa Philip; Robinson, Jackie; Spaulding, Asa Timothy; Spurgeon, James Robert; Teague, Robert.

Negroes Who Helped Build America. Madeline R. Stratton. Ginn, 1965 (o.p.) (STO)
Abbott, Robert Sengstacke; Anderson, Marian; Bethune, Mary McLeod; Bunche, Ralph Johnson; Davis, Benjamin O., Jr.; Douglass, Frederick; Drew, Charles Richard; Du Bois, William Edward Burghardt; Julian, Percy Lavon; King, Martin Luther, Jr.; Robinson, Jackie; Washington, Booker Taliaferro; Williams, Daniel Hale; Woodson, Carter Goodwin.

New Breed. Robert K. Krishef. Lerner, 1978 (KRI-1)
Campbell, Glen; Denver, John; Hall, Tom T.; Harris, Emmylou; Jennings, Waylon; Milsap, Ronnie; Parton, Dolly; Rodriguez, Johnny; Tucker, Tanya.

New Breed Heroes in Pro Baseball. Bill Gutman. Messner, 1974 (o.p.) (GUG)
Allen, Richie; Bench, Johnny Lee; Blue, Vida; Carlton, Steven Norman; Cedeño, Cesar; Fisk, Carlton; Jackson, Reggie; Jenkins, Ferguson Arthur; Murcer, Bobby; Rose, Pete; Ryan, Nolan; Seaver, Tom.

New Breed Heroes of Pro Football. Bill Gutman. Messner, 1973 (o.p.) (GUF)
Brockington, John; Brown, Larry; Butkus, Dick; Csonka, Larry; Eller, Carl; Griese, Bob; Kilmer, Billy; Niland, John Hugh; Staubach, Roger; Taylor, Otis; Washington, Gene; Yepremian, Garo Sarkis.

New England Men of Letters. Wilson Sullivan. Macmillan, 1972 (o.p.) (SUFA)
Dana, Richard Henry, Jr.; Emerson, Ralph Waldo; Hawthorne, Nathaniel; Holmes, Oliver Wendell; Longfellow, Henry Wadsworth; Lowell, James Russell; Melville, Herman; Parkman, Francis; Prescott, William Hickling; Thoreau, Henry David.

New Explorers: Women in Antarctica. Barbara Land. Dodd, 1981 (LA-1)
Askin, Rosemary; Cashman, Katharine; DeVries, Yuan Lin; Dreschkoff, Gisela; Friedmann, Roseli Ocampo; Jones, Lois; McWhinnie, Mary Alice; Marvin, Ursula; Muller-Schwarze, Christine; Oliver, Donna; Peden, Irene; Scott, Nan; Thomas, Jeanette.

New Trail Blazers of Technology. Harland Manchester. Scribner, 1976 (o.p.) (MAPA)
Armstrong, Edwin Howard; Bardeen, John; Brattain, Walter Houser; Carlson, Chester F.; Cockerell, Sir Christopher; Cottrell, Frederick Gardner; Fairchild, Sherman Mills; Land, Edwin Herbert; Shockley, William Bradford; Townes, Charles Hard; Wankel, Felix Heinrich.

New Women in Art and Dance. Kathleen Bowman. Creative Ed, 1976 (BOHB)
Burningham, Charlene; Burton, Marie; Graham, Martha; Gregory, Cynthia; Jamison, Judith; Morgan, Barbara; Nevelson, Louise.

New Women in Entertainment. Kathleen Bowman. Creative Ed, 1976 (BOHC)
Collins, Judy; Harper, Valerie; Reynolds, Malvina; Ross, Diana; Sainte-Marie, Buffy; Tomlin, Lily; Tyson, Cicely.

New Women in Media. Kathleen Bowman. Creative Ed, 1976 (BOHD)
Chevalier, Ann; Goldman, Connie; Graham, Katharine Meyer; Leibovitz, Annie; Long, Loretta; Viorst, Judith; Walters, Barbara.

New Women in Medicine. Kathleen Bowman. Creative Ed, 1976 (o.p.) (BOHE)
Calderone, Mary Steichen; Ellington, Anna; Hewitt, Margaret; Kübler-Ross, Elisabeth; Nichol, Kathryn; Ramey, Estelle; Robbins, Mary Louise.

New Women in Politics. Kathleen Bowman. Creative Ed, 1976 (BOHF)
Burke, Yvonne Brathwaite; Grasso, Ella; Holtzman, Elizabeth; Huerta, Dolores; Jordan, Barbara C.; Mink, Patsy Takemoto; Myerson, Bess.

New Women in Social Sciences. Kathleen Bowman. Creative Ed, 1976 (BOHG)
Brothers, Joyce; Cone, Cynthia; Goodall, Jane; Mead, Margaret; Porter, Sylvia; Rivlin, Alice Mitchell; Tuchman, Barbara.

Nine Black American Doctors. Robert C. Hayden & Jacqueline Harris. A-W, 1976 (o.p.) (HAMA)
Adams, Eugene W.; Cobb, William Montague; Collins, Daniel A.; Ferguson, Angella D.; Fuller, Solomon Carter; Hinton, William A.; Logan, Arthur Courtney; Wright, Jane C.; Wright, Louis Tompkins.

Nine Who Chose America. Life International. Dutton, 1959 (o.p.) (LIA)
Berlin, Irving; Dubinsky, David; Frankfurter, Felix; Menotti, Gian-Carlo; Rubinstein, Helena; Saund, Dalip; Sikorsky, Igor Ivan; Skouras, Spyros; Waksman, Selman Abraham.

Of Men and Numbers: The Story of the Great Mathematicians. Jane Muir. Dodd, 1961 (o.p.) (MUB)
Archimedes; Cantor, Georg; Cardano, Girolamo; Descartes, René; Euclid; Euler, Leonhard; Galois, Evariste; Gauss, Karl Friedrich; Lobachevsky, Nikolai; Newton, Sir Isaac; Pascal, Blaise; Pythagoras.

On Lutes, Recorders and Harpsichords: Men and Music of the Baroque. Freda P. Berkowitz. Atheneum, 1967 (o.p.) (BEM)
Buxtehude, Dietrich; Corelli, Arcangelo; Couperin, François; Frescobaldi, Girolamo; Gabrieli, Giovanni; Gesualdo, Carlo; Lully, Jean Baptiste; Monteverdi, Claudio; Purcell, Henry; Rameau, Jean Philippe; Schütz, Heinrich; Telemann, Georg Philipp; Vivaldi, Antonio.

On the Mound: Three Great Pitchers. Red Reeder. Garrard, 1966 (o.p.) (REB)
Ehmke, Howard John; Feller, Bob; Hubbell, Carl Owen.

On the Path of Venus. Lloyd Motz. Pantheon, 1976 (MOCB)
Aristarchus of Samos; Brahe, Tycho; Copernicus, Nicolaus; Galilei, Galileo; Kepler, Johannes; Newton, Sir Isaac; Ptolemy.

On the Way Up: What It's Like in the Minor Leagues. Dave Klein. Messner, 1977 (o.p.) (KLBB)
Bando, Salvatore Leonard; Bell, Buddy; Brett, George Howard; Figueroa, Ed; Grich, Bobby; Harrelson, Bud; Koosman, Jerry; Matlack, Jonathan T.; Scott, George; White, Roy.

One Hundred Great Kings, Queens and Rulers of the World. John Canning, ed. Taplinger, 1978, pap. (CAAA)
Abd-er-Rahman I; Akbar the Great; Akhnaton; Albert I; Alexander III, the Great; Alfred the Great; Ashurbanipal; Asoka the Great; Atahualpa; Ataturk, Mustafa Kemal; Attila the Hun; Augustus; Boudicca; Brian Boru; Bruce, Robert the; Caesar, Gaius Julius; Canute II, the Great; Catherine II, the Great; Catherine de Medici; Cetewayo; Chandragupta Maurya; Charlemagne; Charles I; Charles II; Charles V; Charles XII; Cheops; Cleopatra; Constantine I, the Great; Cromwell, Oliver; Cyrus; Darius; David; Edward I; Edward III; Edward VII; Elizabeth I; Ferdinand V; Francis Joseph I; Frederick I, called Frederick Barbarossa; Frederick II, the Great; Frederick II; Gaulle, Charles de; Genghis Khan; George V; George VI; Gustavus II; Hadrian; Hammurabi; Hannibal; Harun al-Rashid; Henry II; Henry IV, of Navarre; Henry V; Henry VII; Henry VIII; Herod the Great; Isabella I; Ivan III, the Great; Justinian I, the Great; Kennedy, John Fitzgerald; Kublai Khan; Lenin, Nikolai; Leonidas I; Lincoln, Abraham; Louis IX; Louis XI; Louis XIV; Louis XVI; Mao Tse-tung; Marcus Aurelius; Maria Theresa; Mohammed; Mohammed II (The Conqueror); Montezuma II; Moses; Mutsuhito; Napoleon I; Otto I, the Great; Pericles; Peter I, the Great; Philip II; Pilsudski, Józef; Rama V; Richard I; Richard III; Roosevelt, Franklin Delano; Saladin; Sigismund; Solomon; Sun Yat-sen; Tamerlane; Trajan; Tuthmosis III; Victor Emanuel II; Victoria; Washington, George; Wenceslaus of Bohemia; William I, the Conqueror; William I, the Silent; William II.

One Hundred Greatest Baseball Heroes. Mac Davis. G&D, 1974 (o.p.) (DAFD)

Aaron, Hank; Alexander, Grover Cleveland; Anson, Cap; Appling, Luke; Baker, Home Run; Banks, Ernie; Bender, Chief; Berra, Yogi; Bresnahan, Roger; Brown, Three-Fingered; Burgess, Smoky; Campanella, Roy; Cartwright, Alexander; Chance, Frank; Clemente, Roberto; Cobb, Ty; Cochrane, Mickey; Collins, Eddie; Cronin, Joe; Dean, Dizzy; Delahanty, Edward James; Dickey, Bill; Di Maggio, Joseph Paul; Evers, John Joseph; Feller, Bob; Foxx, James Emory; Frisch, Frank; Gehrig, Lou; Gibson, Josh; Gray, Pete; Grove, Lefty; Hornsby, Rogers; Hoy, Bill; Hubbell, Carl Owen; Johnson, Walter Perry; Keeler, Wee Willie; Kelly, King; Klem, Bill; Koufax, Sandy; Lajoie, Napoleon; McGinnity, Joseph Jerome; McGraw, John Joseph; Mack, Connie; Mantle, Mickey Charles; Maranville, Rabbit; Marquard, Rube; Mathews, Edwin Lee; Mathewson, Christy; Mays, Carl; Mays, Willie Howard; Musial, Stanley Frank; Ott, Mel; Paige, Satchel; Rickey, Branch; Robinson, Brooks Calbert; Robinson, Jackie; Robinson, Wilbert; Ruth, Babe; Sisler, George; Spahn, Warren; Speaker, Tristram E.; Stengel, Casey; Sunday, Billy; Tinker, Joseph Bert; Traynor, Pie; Von der Ahe, Chris; Waddell, Rube; Wagner, Honus; Waner, Lloyd James; Waner, Paul; Wilhelm, James Hoyt; Williams, Ted; Young, Cy.

One Hundred Greatest Baseball Players of All Time. Lawrence Ritter & Donald Honig. Crown, rev. ed., 1986 (RIGA)

Aaron, Hank†; Alexander, Grover Cleveland†; Aparicio, Luis†; Appling, Luke†; Baker, Home Run†; Banks, Ernie†; Bench, Johnny Lee†; Berra, Yogi†; Brett, George Howard†; Brock, Louis Clark†; Brown, Three-Fingered†; Campanella, Roy†; Carew, Rod†; Carlton, Steven Norman†; Clemente, Roberto†; Cobb, Ty†; Cochrane, Mickey†; Collins, Eddie†; Crawford, Wahoo Sam†; Cuyler, Hazen Shirley "Kiki"†; Dean, Dizzy†; Dickey, Bill†; Di Maggio, Joseph Paul†; Ferrell, Wes†; Fingers, Rollie†; Ford, Whitey†; Foxx, James Emory†; Frisch, Frank†; Garvey, Steven Patrick†; Gehrig, Lou†; Gehringer, Charles Leonard†; Gibson, Bob†; Goslin, "Goose"†; Greenberg, Hank†; Grimes, Burleigh†; Grove, Lefty†; Hafey, Charles "Chick"†; Hartnett, Gabby†; Heilmann, Harry†; Hornsby, Rogers†; Hubbell, Carl Owen†; Jackson, Joe "Shoeless"†; Jenkins, Ferguson Arthur†; Joss, Addie†; Killebrew, Harmon†; Koufax, Sandy†; Lajoie, Napoleon†; Lombardi, Ernie†; Lyons, Theodore Amar†; McCovey, Willie Lee†; McGinnity, Joseph Jerome†; Mantle, Mickey Charles†; Marichal, Juan†; Mathews, Edwin Lee†; Mathewson, Christy†; Mays, Willie Howard†; Medwick, Ducky†; Mize, Johnny†; Morgan, Joe†; Musial, Stanley Frank†; Ott, Mel†; Palmer, Jim†; Pennock, Herbert Jefferis†; Plank, Eddie†; Reiser, Pete†; Rice, Jim†; Roberts, Robin†; Robinson, Brooks Calbert†; Robinson, Frank†; Robinson, Jackie†; Rose, Pete†; Roush, Edd J.†; Ruth, Babe†; Ryan, Nolan†; Schmidt, Mike†; Score, Herbert Jude†; Seaver, Tom†; Sewell, Joe†; Simmons, Aloysius Harry†; Sisler, George†; Snider, Duke†; Spahn, Warren†; Speaker, Tristram E.†; Stargell, Willie†; Terry, William Harold†; Traynor, Pie†; Vance, Dazzy†; Vaughan, "Arky"†; Waddell, Rube†; Wagner, Honus†; Walsh, Edward Augustine†; Waner, Paul†; Wheat, Zachary Davis†; Williams, Ted†; Wood, Joe†; Yastrzemski, Carl Michael†; Young, Cy†; Young, Ross†.

One Hundred Greatest Football Heroes. Mac Davis. G&D, 1973 (o.p.) (DAFG)

Battles, Cliff; Baugh, Sammy; Bednarik, Chuck; Berry, Raymond; Blanchard, Doc; Blanda, George; Blood, Johnny, sobriquet; Brickley, Charley; Brown, Jim; Brown, Paul; Butkus, Dick; Camp, Walter Chauncey; Chamberlin, Guy†; Clark, Dutch; Davis, Glenn; Dudley, William; Fortmann, Daniel John†; Four Horsemen of Notre Dame; Friedman, Benny; Gipp, George; Graham, Otto; Grange, Red; Groza, Lou; Guyon, Joe; Halas, George; Heffelfinger, Pudge; Hein, Mel; Heisman, John William; Henry, Pete; Heston, William†; Hinkey, Frank; Hinkle, Clarke†; Hirsch, Elroy "Crazylegs"; Hubbard, Cal; Hutson, Don; Kelley, Larry; Kiesling, Walt†; Kramer, Jerry; Lambeau, Curly; Layne, Bobby; Leahy, Frank; LeBaron, Eddie; Lombardi, Vincent; Luckman, Sidney; Lyman, Roy; McAfee, George†; Motley, Marion; Musial, Stanley Frank; Nagurski, Bronko; Namath, Joe Willie; Nevers, Ernie; O'Dea, Pat; Pollard, Frederick; Robeson, Paul; Rockne, Knute; Sayers, Gale; Stagg, Amos Alonzo; Strong, Ken; Thorpe, Jim; Tittle, Y. A.; Trafton, George†; Trippi, Charley; Tunnell, Emlen; Turner, Bulldog; Unitas, Johnny; Van Buren, Steve; Warner, Glenn "Pop"; Waterfield, Robert Staton; White, Byron Raymond.

One Hundred Greatest Sports Heroes. Mac Davis. G&D, 1954 (o.p.) (DAG)

Alexander, Grover Cleveland; Arcaro, Eddie; Armstrong, Henry; Bannister, Roger Gilbert; Baugh, Sammy; Budge, Don; Button, Dick; Camp, Walter Chauncey; Campanella, Roy; Cartwright, Alexander; Chadwick, Florence May; Cobb, Ty; Collins, Eddie; Connibear, Hiram; Connolly, James B.; Connolly, Maureen; Cousy, Bob; Crowley, James; Cunningham, Glenn; Davis, Walt; Day, Ned; DeMar, Clarence; Dempsey, Jack; Didrikson, Babe; Dillard, Harrison; Di Maggio, Joseph Paul; Ederle, Gertrude C.; Ewry, Ray C.; Feller, Bob; Fitzsimmons, Robert P.; Four Horsemen of Notre Dame; Gehrig, Lou; Gipp, George; Gotch, Frank; Grange, Red; Greenleaf, Ralph; Hagen, Walter; Heffelfinger, Pudge; Henie, Sonja; Hitchcock, Thomas, Jr.; Hogan, Ben; Hoppe, Willie; Hornsby, Rogers; Hutson, Don; Johnson, Walter Perry; Jones, Bobby; Kelly, John B.; Ketchel, Stanley; Klem, Bill; Layden, Elmer; Lenglen, Suzanne; Leonard, Benny; Louis, Joe; McGraw, John Joseph; Mack, Connie; Mantle, Mickey Charles; Mathewson, Christy; Mathias, Bob; Mikan, George L.; Miller, Don; Musial, Stanley Frank; Nagurski, Bronko; Naismith, James A.; Nurmi, Paavo; Oakley, Annie; O'Brien, Parry; Oldfield, Barney; Ouimet, Francis; Owens, Jesse; Paddock, Charles; Patrick, Lester; Richard, Maurice; Richards, Sir Gordon; Rickard, Tex; Rickenbacker, Edward Vernon; Robinson, Jackie; Robinson, Ray; Rockne, Knute; Ruth, Babe; Sande, Earl; Shaw, Wilbur; Shoemaker, Willie; Shore, Edward William; Sloan, Tod; Speaker, Tristram E.; Stagg, Amos Alonzo; Stengel, Casey; Stuhldreher, Harry; Sullivan, John Lawrence; Thorpe, Jim; Tilden, William Tatem, Jr.; Tokle, Torger; Tunney, Gene; Waddell, Rube; Wagner, Honus; Walsh, Stella; Warmerdam, Cornelius; Webb, Matthew; Weissmuller, Johnny; Williams, Ted; Wills, Helen; Wood, Gar; Young, Cy; Zatopek, Emil.

One Hundred Greatest Sports Heroes. Mac Davis. G&D, 1972 (o.p.) (DAGA)

See listing under 1954 edition, above. Delete: Rickenbacker, Eddie; Sande, Earl; Sloan, Todd. Add: Ali, Muhammad; Mays, Willie; Unitas, Johnny.

One Hundred Greatest Women in Sports. Phyllis Hollander. G&D, 1976 (o.p.) (HOBAA)

Adam, Marianne†; Albright, Tenley; Anderton, Carol†; Anne (Princess); Applebee, Constance; Bacon, Mary; Baugh, Laura Z.; Berg, Patty; Berman, Sara Mae†; Bingay, Roberta Gibb†; Bjurstedt, Molla; Blankers-Koen, Fanny; Brown, Earlene†; Cawley, Evonne Goolagong; Chadwick, Florence May; Chaffee, Suzy; Chait, Donna†; Cheng, Chi; Chizhova, Nadyezhda†; Cochran, Barbara Ann†; Cochran, Linda†; Cochran, Marilyn†; Collett, Glenna; Connolly, Maureen†; Connolly, Olga Fikotova; Costello, Patty†; Court, Margaret†; Cox, Lynne†; Crawford, Marianne†; Crump, Diane†; Curtis, Ann; Davis, Muriel†; Decker, Mary†; Didrikson, Babe; Early, Peggy Ann†; Ederle, Gertrude C.; Evert, Chris; Fibingerova, Helena†; Fish, Jennifer†; Fleming, Peggy; Fothergill, Dorothy†; Fraser, Dawn†; Fraser, Gretchen Kunigk; Gibson, Althea; Goodwill, Linda†; Gould, Shane Elizabeth†; Hamill, Dorothy; Heiss, Carol; Henie, Sonja; Henning, Anne†; Holm, Eleanor†; Holum, Dianne†; Hotchkiss, Hazel; Joyce, Joan; King, Billie Jean; King, Micki; Korbut, Olga; Kuscsik, Nina†; Kusner, Kathy; Ladewig, Marion; Larrieu, Francie; Lawrence, Andrea Mead; Lenglen, Suzanne; Logan, Karen†; Long, Denise†; Lynn, Janet; McCormick, Patricia Keller; McCutcheon, Floretta Doty; Madison, Helene†; Mann, Carol†; Mason, Debby†; Metheny, Linda†; Meyer, Deborah†; Meyers, Mary†; Novara, Sue†; Nyad, Diana†; Ostermeyer, Micheline†; Owen, Laurence†; Palmer, Sandra†; Peppler, Mary Jo; Press, Tamara†; Rawls, Betsy†; Rawls, Katherine†; Rigby, Cathy; Robinson, Jean†; Rosendahl, Heidemarie†; Rubin, Barbara Jo†; Rudolph, Wilma G.; Ruffian; Scharff, Mary†; Sears, Eleanora; Seidler, Maren†; Souter, Judy Cook†; Sperber, Paula†; Stouder, Sharon†; Switzer, Kathy†; Tickey, Bertha Reagan†; Tyus, Wyomia; Vinson-Owen, Maribel†; Von Saltza, Susan Christina; Walsh, Stella†; Weld, Theresa; White, Cheryl†; Whitworth, Kathy†; Wills, Helen; Wright, Mickey†; Young, Sheila†.

Our Blood and Tears: Black Freedom Fighters. Ruth Wilson. Putnam, 1972 (o.p.) (WIAB)

Banneker, Benjamin; Douglass, Frederick; Turner, Nat.

Our Country Grows Up. L. Edmond Leipold. T. S. Denison, 1972 (o.p.) (LEPD)

Boone, Daniel; Bridger, James; Chapman, John; Pointe de Sable, Jean Baptiste; Young, Brigham.

Our First Ladies: From Martha Washington to Pat Ryan Nixon. Jane McConnell & Burt McConnell. T Y Crowell, 1969 (o.p.) (MAA)
See listing under *America's First Ladies*, vols. 1 and 2, by Chaffin & Butwin.

Our Foreign-Born Citizens. Annie E. S. Beard. T Y Crowell, 6th rev. ed., 1968 (BEA)
Adler, Felix; Auden, Wystan Hugh; Audubon, John James; Bell, Alexander Graham; Carnegie, Andrew; Dubinsky, David; Einstein, Albert; Fermi, Enrico; Gompers, Samuel; Gropius, Walter Adolf; Hitchcock, Alfred Joseph; Hofmann, Hans; Leinsdorf, Erich; Loewy, Raymond; Mergenthaler, Ottmar; Muir, John; Murray, Philip; Noguchi, Hideyo; Pulitzer, Joseph; Saint-Gaudens, Augustus; Sikorsky, Igor Ivan; Skouras, Spyros; Steinmetz, Charles Proteus.

Our Heroes' Heroes. I. G. Edmonds. Criterion Bks., 1966 (o.p.) (EDA)
Blériot, Louis; Houdin, Jean Eugène Robert; Kennedy, Joseph Patrick, Jr.; MacArthur, Arthur, Jr.; Majors, Alexander; Mantle, Elvin C.; Marlborough, John Churchill, 1st duke of; Peary, Robert Edwin; Scott, Winfield; Washington, Lawrence.

Our Nation's Builders. Iris Vinton. Merrill, 1968 (o.p.) (VIA)
Austin, Moses; Austin, Stephen Fuller; Barnard, Kate; Behaim, Martin; Boone, Daniel; Bowie, James; Bradford, William; Bradstreet, Anne Dudley; Brent, Margaret; Buckner, Aylett C.; Calvert, George, 1st baron Baltimore; Clark, George Rogers; Columbus, Christopher; Croghan, George; Ericsson, Leif†; Esteban or Estevanico; Fink, Mike†; Franklin, Benjamin; Henry, Patrick†; Herjolfsson, Bjarni†; Hutchinson, Anne Marbury; Jefferson, Thomas; Johnson, Sir William; Lafitte, Jean; Livingston, Robert R.; Long, James; Minuit, Peter; Oglethorpe, James Edward; Paine, Thomas†; Penn, William; Philip; Pocahontas; Rogers, Robert; Smith, John; Stevens, John; Vespucci, Amerigo†; Williams, Roger†; Woolman, John; Wright, Patience Lovell.

Pacemakers in Baseball. Mac Davis. World Pub., 1968 (o.p.) (DAH)
Anson, Cap; Berra, Yogi; Brown, Three-Fingered; Burgess, Smoky; Cobb, Ty; Di Maggio, Joseph Paul; Gehrig, Lou; Hornsby, Rogers; Johnson, Walter Perry; Keeler, Wee Willie; Klem, Bill; Koufax, Sandy; Lajoie, Napoleon; Lowe, Robert L.; McGraw, John Joseph; Mantle, Mickey Charles; Marquard, Rube; Mathewson, Christy; Mays, Willie Howard; Musial, Stanley Frank; Ott, Mel; Paige, Satchel; Robinson, Jackie; Ruth, Babe; Spahn, Warren; Traynor, Pie; Waddell, Rube; Wagner, Honus; Williams, Ted; Young, Cy.

Pacemakers in Football. Mac Davis. World Pub., 1968 (o.p.) (DAI)
Baugh, Sammy; Bednarik, Chuck; Blanchard, Doc; Blood, Johnny, sobriquet; Brown, Jim; Camp, Walter Chauncey; Crowley, James; Davis, Glenn; Four Horsemen of Notre Dame; Gipp, George; Graham, Otto; Grange, Red; Groza, Lou; Halas, George; Heffelfinger, Pudge; Hein, Mel; Hubbard, Cal; Hutson, Don; Kelley, Larry; Layden, Elmer; LeBaron, Eddie; Lombardi, Vincent; Luckman, Sidney; Miller, Don; Nagurski, Bronko; Nevers, Ernie; O'Dea, Pat; Pollard, Frederick; Riegels, Roy; Rockne, Knute; Sayers, Gale; Stagg, Amos Alonzo; Stuhldreher, Harry; Thorpe, Jim; Unitas, Johnny; White, Byron Raymond.

Pacemakers in Track and Field. Mac Davis. World Pub., 1968 (o.p.) (DAJ)
Bannister, Roger Gilbert; Bikila, Abebe; Blankers-Koen, Fanny; Boston, Ralph; Brumel, Valeri; Carvaljal, Felix; Clarke, Ron; Connolly, James B.; Cunningham, Glenn; DeMar, Clarence; Didrikson, Babe; Dillard, Harrison; Ewry, Ray C.; Hayes, Bob; Hayes, Johnny; Johnson, Rafer; Kraenzlein, Alvin; Mathias, Bob; Matson, Randy; Myers, Laurence E. "Lon"; Nurmi, Paavo; Oerter, Al; Owens, Jesse; Paddock, Charles; Pennel, John; Rudolph, Wilma G.; Ryun, Jim; Thorpe, Jim; Warmerdam, Cornelius; Weston, Edward Payson.

Pacifists: Adventures in Courage. Mary Fox. Reilly & Lee, 1971 (o.p.) (FOJ)
Addams, Jane; Fox, George; Gandhi, Mohandas Karamchand; Hammarskjöld, Dag; Luthuli, Albert John; Muste, Abraham Johannes; Penn, William; Rankin, Jeannette; Schweitzer, Albert; Thomas, Norman Mattoon.

Pacifists: Soldiers without Guns. Mark Lieberman. Praeger, 1972 (o.p.) (LEZC)
Addams, Jane; Berrigan, Daniel; Berrigan, Philip; Garrison, William Lloyd; Holmes, John Haynes; Muste, Abraham Johannes; Penn, William.

Painters of America. Dorothy Heiderstadt. McKay, 1970 (o.p.) (HEDA)
Bierstadt, Albert; Bingham, George Caleb; Bodmer, Karl; Catlin, George; Cole, Thomas; Homer, Winslow; Inness, George; Leutze, Emanuel; Miller, Alfred Jacob; Remington, Frederic; Russell, Charles Marion; Schreyvogel, Charles; Trumbull, John; West, Benjamin; Wood, Grant.

Particular Passions: Talks with Women Who Have Shaped Our Times. Lynn Gilbert & Gaylen Moore. Crown, 1981 (GIB-1)
Abzug, Bella; Allen, Dede†; Ballard, Ernesta Drinker; Calderone, Mary Steichen; Caldwell, Sarah; Child, Julia; Cooney, Joan Ganz; De Mille, Agnes; Densen-Gerber, Judianne; Friedan, Betty; Ginsburg, Ruth Bader; Grosman, Tatyana; Hanks, Nancy; Height, Dorothy†; Hellman, Lillian†; Hopper, Grace Murray; Hufstedler, Shirley; Hunter, Alberta; Huxtable, Ada Louise; Jarvis, Lucy; King, Billie Jean; Koontz, Elizabeth; Kübler-Ross, Elisabeth; Kuhn, Margaret; Mead, Margaret†; Miller, Dorothy Canning; Motley, Constance Baker; Nevelson, Louise; Norton, Eleanor Holmes; Payne-Gaposhkin, Cecelia Helena†; Polier, Justine Wise; Porter, Sylvia; Ruether, Rosemary; Scott Brown, Denise; Siebert, Muriel; Steinem, Gloria; Steloff, Frances; Stewart, Ellen; Taussig, Helen Brooke; Vreeland, Diana; Walters, Barbara; Webb, Aileen Osborn†; Williams, Mary Lou; Wu, Chien-Shiung; Wyatt, Addie; Yalow, Rosalyn Sussman.

Partners in Science. Alma Smith Payne. World Pub., 1968 (o.p.) (PAC)
Colden, Cadwallader; Comstock, Anna Botsford; Comstock, John Henry; Curie, Marie Sklodowska; Curie, Pierre; Evans, Clifford; Farquhar, Jane Colden; Goldhaber, Maurice; Herschel, Caroline; Herschel, Sir William; Meggers, Betty J.; Scharff-Goldhaber, Gertrude; Szent-Györgyi, Albert von; Szent-Györgyi, Marta von; Wright, Barbara P.; Wright, Jane C.; Wright, Louis Tompkins.

Pass to Win: Pro Football Greats. George Sullivan. Garrard, 1968 (o.p.) (SUC)
Baugh, Sammy; Graham, Otto; Hutson, Don.

Paths of Diplomacy: America's Secretaries of State. Deane Heller & David Heller. Lippincott, 1967 (o.p.) (HEEA)
Acheson, Dean Gooderham; Adams, John Quincy; Blaine, James Gillespie; Buchanan, James; Clay, Henry; Dulles, John Foster; Hay, John Milton; Hughes, Charles Evans; Hull, Cordell; Jefferson, Thomas; Kellogg, Frank Billings; Lansing, Robert; Madison, James; Marshall, George Catlett; Monroe, James; Rusk, Dean; Seward, William Henry; Stimson, Henry Lewis; Van Buren, Martin; Webster, Daniel.

Patriots in Petticoats. Patricia Edwards Clyne. Dodd, 1976 (CLC)
Arnett, Hannah†; Bailey, Ann "Mad Ann"; Barker, Penelope; Bates, Abigail; Bates, Rebecca; Champe, Elizabeth; Clay, Ann†; Cooper, Polly†; Corbin, Margaret; Darragh, Lydia B.; Emmons, Lucretia†; Gannet, Deborah Sampson; Hart, Nancy; Hendee, Hannah; Johnson, Jemima†; Kate, Mammy†; Lane, Anna Maria†; Ludington, Sybil; McCauley, Mary; Murray, Mary Lindley; Nonhelema†; Pickersgill, Mary; Reynolds, Phoebe; Townsend, Sally; Trumbull, Faith†; Waglum, Jinnie†; Warne, Peggy†; Wick, Tempe; Zane, Elizabeth.

Peace Seekers: The Nobel Peace Prize. Nathan Aaseng. Lerner, 1987 (AAS-34)
Addams, Jane; Corrigan, Mairead; King, Martin Luther, Jr.; Ossietzky, Carl von; Pauling, Linus Carl; Sakharov, Andrei D.; Tutu, Desmond Mpilo; Walesa, Lech; Williams, Betty.

People: A History of Our Time. Associated Press Editors. Gallery, 1986 (ASB-1)
Ali, Muhammad; Anthony, Susan Brownell; Balanchine, George; Bannister, Roger Gilbert; Bartók, Béla; Begin, Menachem; Bell, Alexander Graham; Berlin, Irving; Caruso, Enrico; Carver, George Washington; Cézanne, Paul; Chaplin, Sir Charles Spencer; Chekhov, Anton Pavlovich; Chiang Kai-shek; Churchill, Sir Winston Leonard Spencer; Clemenceau, Georges; Coward, Noel; Curie, Marie Sklodowska; DeMille, Cecil Blount; Didrikson, Babe; Disney, Walt; Edison, Thomas Alva; Einstein, Albert; Eisenhower, Dwight David; Eliot, Thomas Stearns; Ellington, Duke; Erte; Faulkner, William; Fitzgerald, Ella; Fitzgerald, Francis Scott Key; Fleming, Sir Alexander; Ford, Henry; Freud, Sigmund; Frost, Robert; Gandhi, Indira Nehru; Gandhi, Mohandas Karamchand; Garbo, Greta; Gaulle, Charles de; Gilbert, William Schwenk; Gretzky, Wayne; Hemingway, Ernest; Hillary, Sir Edmund; Hirohito; Hitchcock,

Alfred Joseph; Hitler, Adolf; Ho Chi Minh; James, Henry; John XXIII; Joyce, James; Keynes, John Maynard; King, Martin Luther, Jr.; Laver, Rodney George; Lenin, Nikolai; Lindbergh, Charles Augustus; Lister, Joseph, 1st baron Lister of Lyme Regis; Lloyd George, David; Louis, Joe; MacArthur, Douglas; Man Ray; Mao Tse-tung; Mother Theresa; Mussolini, Benito; Nabokov, Vladimir; Navratilova, Martina; Nehru, Jawaharlal; Nicklaus, Jack; Nightingale, Florence; Olivier, Laurence; O'Neill, Eugene Gladstone; Oppenheimer, Julius Robert; Orwell, George; Owens, Jesse; Pavlov, Ivan Petrovich; Pelé; Picasso, Pablo; Pound, Ezra; Renoir, Auguste; Rhodes, Cecil John; Robinson, Jackie; Rockefeller, John Davison; Rodin, Auguste; Roosevelt, Eleanor; Roosevelt, Franklin Delano; Ruth, Babe; Sadat, Anwar el-; Salk, Jonas Edward; Shaw, George Bernard; Solzhenitsyn, Aleksandr Isaevich; Stalin, Joseph; Stravinsky, Igor Fëdorovich; Sun Yat-sen; Truman, Harry S.; Wells, Herbert George; Wilson, Woodrow; Wright, Frank Lloyd; Wright, Orville.

People and Great Deeds. Yvonne Beckwith, ed. Standard Ed., 1966 (o.p.) (BEC)
Audubon, John James; Barton, Clara; Carver, George Washington; Chapman, John; Curie, Marie Sklodowska; David; Edison, Thomas Alva; Francis of Assisi; Galilei, Galileo; Gandhi, Mohandas Karamchand; Gehrig, Lou; Jefferson, Thomas; Keller, Helen Adams; Kennedy, John Fitzgerald; Lincoln, Abraham; Mozart, Wolfgang Amadeus; Roosevelt, Franklin Delano; Roosevelt, Theodore; Sacajawea; Schweitzer, Albert; Spyri, Johanna H.; Twain, Mark, pseud.; Washington, George.

People of Concord. James Playsted Wood. Seabury, 1970 (o.p.) (WOAA)
Alcott, Bronson; Alcott, Louisa May; Bulkeley, Peter; Emerson, Ralph Waldo; Emerson, William†; Emerson, William, Jr.†; French, Daniel Chester†; Hawthorne, Nathaniel; Ripley, Ezra†; Sanborn, Franklin Benjamin; Thoreau, Henry David; Willard, Simon.

Pictorial History of American Presidents. John Durant & Alice Durant. A S Barnes, 6th rev. ed., 1973 (o.p.) (DUC)
See listing under *America and Its Presidents* by Earl S. Miers. Add: Nixon, Richard M.

Pictorial History of American Presidents. John Durant & Alice Durant. A S Barnes, 1978 (o.p.) (DUCA)
See listing under *America and Its Presidents* by Earl S. Miers. Add: Carter, Jimmy; Ford, Gerald R.; Nixon, Richard M.

Pictorial History of Women in America. Ruth Warren. Crown, 1975 (o.p.) (WABC)
Adams, Abigail†; Addams, Jane†; Anthony, Susan Brownell; Bache, Sarah (Sally) Franklin†; Bagley, Sarah G.; Barton, Clara†; Beach, Sylvia†; Beecher, Catharine Esther; Bethune, Mary McLeod†; Bickerdyke, Mary Ann Ball†; Blackwell, Elizabeth; Blatch, Harriot Stanton†; Boyd, Belle†; Bradstreet, Anne Dudley†; Brent, Margaret; Cary, Mary Ann Shadd†; Cassatt, Mary†; Catt, Carrie Chapman†; Chestnut, Mary Boykin Miller†; Crandall, Prudence†; Crocker, Hannah Mather†; Dickinson, Emily†; Dix, Dorothea Lynde†; Dodge, Grace†; Drew, Louisa Lane†; Duncan, Isadora†; Duniway, Abigail Scott; Dyer, Mary†; Earhart, Amelia†; Eddy, Mary Baker†; Edmonds, Sarah Emma†; Farrar, Geraldine†; Fiske, Minnie Maddern†; Fletcher, Alice Cunningham†; Foster, Abigail Kelley†; Franklin, Ann Smith†; Fremstad, Anna Olivia†; Fuller, Loie†; Fuller, Margaret; Garden, Mary†; Gay, Mary Ann Harris†; Goldman, Emma†; Green, Anna Catherine†; Greenhow, Rose O'Neal†; Grimké, Angelina Emily†; Grimké, Sarah Moore†; Haddon, Elizabeth†; Harper, Frances Ellen Watkins†; Hoffman, Malvina†; Howe, Julia Ward†; Hutchinson, Anne Marbury; Jacobi, Mary Putnam†; Jones, Mary Harris†; Kelley, Florence†; La Conte, Emma†; Larcom, Lucy†; Lease, Mary†; Lee, Ann; Lockwood, Belva Ann; Lowell, Josephine Shaw†; Lyon, Mary†; McCormick, Anne O'Hare†; McDowell, Mary E.†; Madison, Dolley Payne Todd; Marlowe, Julia†; Mecom, Jane Franklin†; Mitchell, Maria; Montez, Lola†; Moody, Lady Deborah†; Morris, Esther McQuigg Slack†; Mott, Lucretia Coffin; Murray, Judith Sargent†; Nichols, Mary Grove†; Peabody, Elizabeth Palmer†; Perkins, Frances; Pinckney, Eliza Lucas; Pocahontas; Poole, Elizabeth†; Quinton, Amelia Stone†; Rankin, Jeannette†; Read, Deborah†; Richards, Ellen Swallow†; Richards, Linda Ann†; Roosevelt, Eleanor†; Russell, Lillian†; Sacajawea; Sanger, Margaret; Seton, Elizabeth Ann†; Stanton, Elizabeth Cady†; Stein, Gertrude†; Steloff, Frances†; Stewart, Maria W.†; Stone, Lucy; Stowe, Harriet Beecher†; Surratt, Mary Eugenia†; Tarbell, Ida

Minerva†; Taylor, Lucy Hobbs†; Timothy, Elizabeth†; Train, George Francis†; Truth, Sojourner†; Tubman, Harriet†; Van Lew, Elizabeth†; Wald, Lillian D.†; Warren, Mercy Otis†; Washington, Martha Dandridge; White, Ellen G. H.†; Whitney, Gertrude Vanderbilt†; Wilkinson, Jemima†; Willard, Emma Hart†; Willard, Frances Elizabeth; Wood, Sally S. B. K.†; Woodhull, Victoria†; Wright, Frances†; Zenger, Anna†.

Picture Book of American Authors. Frances Helmstadter. Sterling, 1962 (o.p.) (HEF)
Buck, Pearl S.; Cather, Willa; Cooper, James Fenimore; Crane, Stephen; Emerson, Ralph Waldo; Faulkner, William; Frost, Robert; Hawthorne, Nathaniel; Hemingway, Ernest; Holmes, Oliver Wendell; Irving, Washington; Lewis, Sinclair; Lindsay, Vachel; Longfellow, Henry Wadsworth; Melville, Herman; Poe, Edgar Allan; Sandburg, Carl; Steinbeck, John; Twain, Mark, pseud.; Whitman, Walt; Wolfe, Thomas Clayton.

Picture Book of Famous Immigrants. Evelyn Lowenstein, et al. Sterling, 1962 (o.p.) (LOB)
Astor, John Jacob; Audubon, John James; Belafonte, Harry; Blackwell, Elizabeth; Bok, Edward William; Carnegie, Andrew; Du Pont, Eleuthère Irénée; Frankfurter, Felix; Gompers, Samuel; Kosciusko, Tadeusz; Lin Yutang; Pulaski, Casimir; Pulitzer, Joseph; Pupin, Michael Idvorsky; Riis, Jacob August; Rockne, Knute; Salomon, Haym; Schurz, Carl; Sikorsky, Igor Ivan; Steinmetz, Charles Proteus; Stokowski, Leopold; Zenger, John Peter.

Piece of the Power: Four Black Mayors. James Haskins. Dial, 1972 (o.p.) (HAH)
Evers, Charles; Gibson, Kenneth Allen; Hatcher, Richard Gordon; Stokes, Carl B.

Pioneer Astronauts. Navin Sullivan. Atheneum, 1964 (o.p.) (SUE)
Adams, John Couch; Baade, Walter; Bessel, Friedrich Wilhelm; Copernicus, Nicolaus; Fraunhofer, Joseph von; Galilei, Galileo; Herschel, Sir William; Hertzsprung, Ejnar; Hubble, Edwin Powell; Huggins, Sir William; Jansky, Karl Guthe; Kepler, Johannes; Kirchhoff, Gustav Robert; Leverrier, Urbain Jean Joseph; Newton, Sir Isaac; Reber, Grote; Shapely, Harlow; Smith, Graham.

Pioneer Germ Fighters. Navin Sullivan. Atheneum, 1962 (o.p.) (SUF)
Beijerinck, Martinus Willem; Ehrlich, Paul; Enders, John Franklin; Fleming, Sir Alexander; Goodpasture, Ernest William; Jenner, Edward; Koch, Robert; Leeuwenhoek, Anton van; Pasteur, Louis; Salk, Jonas Edward; Stanley, Wendell Meredith.

Pioneers and Patriots: The Lives of Six Negroes of the Revolutionary Era. Lavinia Dobler & Edgar A. Toppin. Doubleday, 1965 (o.p.) (DOB)
Banneker, Benjamin; Chavis, John; Cuffe, Paul; Pointe de Sable, Jean Baptiste; Salem, Peter; Wheatley, Phillis.

Pioneers in Freedom: Adventures in Courage. Janet Stevenson. Reilly & Lee, 1969 (o.p.) (STJA)
Brown, John; Concklin, Seth; Garrison, William Lloyd; Lay, Benjamin; Lincoln, Abraham; Tubman, Harriet; Vesey, Denmark; Walker, David.

Pioneers in Petticoats. See *Women Who Led the Way: Eight Pioneers for Equal Rights.*

Pioneers in Print. Alice Fleming. Reilly & Lee, 1971 (o.p.) (FLBA)
Bok, Edward William; Faulkner, William; Greeley, Horace; Hansberry, Lorraine; McGill, Ralph Emerson; Paine, Thomas; Riis, Jacob August; Thurber, James G.; Wright, Richard.

Pioneers in Protest. Lerone Bennett, Jr. Johnson Chi, 1968 (o.p.) (BEJ)
Allen, Richard; Attucks, Crispus; Banneker, Benjamin; Brown, John; Cornish, Samuel E.; Douglass, Frederick; Du Bois, William Edward Burghardt; Garnet, Henry Highland; Garrison, William Lloyd; Garvey, Marcus A.; Hall, Prince; Phillips, Wendell; Russwurm, John B.; Stevens, Thaddeus; Sumner, Charles; Trotter, William Monroe; Truth, Sojourner; Tubman, Harriet; Turner, Nat; Walker, David.

Pioneers in Science. Frank Siedel & James M. Siedel. HM, 1968 (o.p.) (SIA)
Ampère, André Marie; Archimedes; Aristotle; Bache, Alexander Dallas; Bell, Alexander Graham; Bohr, Niels H. D.; Boyle, Robert; Copernicus, Nicolaus; Crookes, Sir William; Curie, Marie Sklodowska; Dalton, John; Darwin, Charles Robert; Descartes, René; Edison, Thomas Alva; Einstein, Albert; Faraday, Michael; Fermi, Enrico; Franklin, Benjamin; Galen; Galilei,

Galileo; Gauss, Karl Friedrich; Gibbs, Josiah Willard; Gilbert, William; Goddard, Robert Hutchings; Halley, Edmund; Harvey, William; Helmholtz, Hermann Ludwig von; Henry, Joseph; Herschel, Sir William; Hertz, Heinrich Rudolf; Huygens, Christiaan; Kelvin, William Thomson, 1st baron; Kepler, Johannes; Lawrence, Ernest Orlando; Leonardo da Vinci; Marconi, Guglielmo; Maxwell, James Clerk; Mendel, Gregor Johann; Michelson, Albert Abraham; Newton, Sir Isaac; Pavlov, Ivan Petrovich; Ptolemy; Rittenhouse, David; Rumford, Benjamin Thompson, count; Rutherford, Ernest Rutherford, 1st baron; Thomson, Sir Joseph John; Volta, Alessandro, conte; Wright, Orville; Wright, Wilbur.

Pioneers of Baseball. Robert Smith. Little, 1978 (o.p.) (SMK)
Browning, Pete; Cartwright, Alexander; Chase, Harold; Comiskey, Charles Albert; Dean, Dizzy; Kelly, King; Mack, Connie; Paige, Satchel; Robinson, Jackie; Ruth, Babe; Sockalexis, Louis; Spalding, Albert Goodwill; Ward, John Montgomery; Williams, Joe; Williams, Ted; Wright, Harry.

Pioneers of Ecology. Donald W. Cox. Hammond, 1971 (o.p.) (CORA)
Audubon, John James; Bradley, Guy; Burroughs, John; Carson, Rachel; Carver, George Washington; Ehrlich, Paul Ralph; Krutch, Joseph Wood; McHarg, Ian L.; Marsh, George Perkins; Muir, John; Pinchot, Gifford; Powell, John Wesley; Roosevelt, Theodore; Thoreau, Henry David; Wilson, Alexander.

Pioneers of Rocketry. Michael Stoiko. Amereon reprint, pap. (STMA)
Congreve, Sir William; Esnault-Pelteri, Robert; Goddard, Robert Hutchings; Oberth, Hermann Julius; Tsiolkovsky, Konstantin E.

Pirates and Buccaneers. Robert D. Larranaga. Lerner, 1970 (LACB)
Avery, John "Long Ben"; Bartolomey the Portuguese; Blackbeard; Brasiliano, Roc; Drake, Sir Francis; Kidd, William (Captain); Lafitte, Jean; L'Olonnois; Morgan, Sir Henry.

Pitchers (Stars of the NL & AL). Jay H. Smith. Creative Ed, 1976 (o.p.) (SMH)
Hunter, Catfish; Marshall, Michael Grant; Perry, Gaylord Jackson; Ryan, Nolan; Seaver, Tom.

Poets of Our Time. Rica Brenner. HarBraceJ, 1941 (o.p.) (BRBB)
Auden, Wystan Hugh; Benét, Stephen Vincent; Eliot, Thomas Stearns; Lindsay, Vachel; MacLeish, Archibald; Spender, Stephen; Teasdale, Sara; Wylie, Elinor Morton; Yeats, William Butler.

Polish Greats. Arnold Madison. McKay, 1980 (o.p.) (MANB)
Chopin, Frédéric François; Conrad, Joseph; Copernicus, Nicolaus; Curie, Marie Sklodowska; Jadwiga; John Paul II; Kosciusko, Tadeusz; Mickiewicz, Adam; Modjeska, Helena; Paderewski, Ignace Jan; Pulaski, Casimir; Reymont, Wladyslaw Stanislaw; Rubinstein, Artur.

Political Cartoonists. Lynne Deur. Lerner, 1972 (o.p.) (DEDC)
Block, Herbert Lawrence; Darcy, Tom; Darling, Jay Norwood; Davenport, Homer Calvin; Fitzpatrick, Daniel Robert; Franklin, Benjamin; Glackens, William James; Gropper, William; Keppler, Joseph; Kirby, Rollin; Mauldin, Bill; Nast, Thomas; Opper, Frederick Burr; Osrin, Raymond Harold; Sanders, Bill; Stayskal, Wayne.

Portraits of Nobel Laureates in Medicine and Physiology. Sarah R. Riedman & Elton T. Gustafson. Abelard, 1963 (o.p.) (RIF)
Adrian, Edgar Douglas; Banting, Sir Frederick Grant; Beadle, George Wells; Behring, Emil von; Best, Charles H.†; Bordet, Jules; Bovet, Daniele; Burnet, Sir Macfarlane; Carrel, Alexis; Chain, Ernst Boris; Cori, Carl Ferdinand; Cori, Gerty Theresa; Cournand, André Frédéric; Crick, Francis H. C.; Dale, Sir Henry Hallett; Dam, Henrik; Doisy, Edward Adelbert; Domagk, Gerhard; Eccles, Sir John Carew†; Ehrlich, Paul; Eijkman, Christian; Einthoven, Willem; Enders, John Franklin; Erlanger, Joseph; Fleming, Sir Alexander; Florey, Sir Howard Walter; Forssmann, Werner; Gasser, Herbert Spencer; Golgi, Camillo; Hench, Philip Showalter; Hill, Archibald Vivian; Hodgkin, Alan Lloyd†; Hopkins, Sir Frederick Gowland; Houssay, Bernardo Alberto; Huxley, Andrew Fielding†; Kendall, Edward Calvin; Koch, Robert; Kocher, Emil Theodor; Kornberg, Arthur; Kossel, Albrecht; Krogh, August;

Landsteiner, Karl; Laveran, Charles Louis; Lederberg, Joshua; Loewi, Otto; Macleod, John James R.; Medawar, Peter Brian; Metchnikoff, Élie; Meyerhof, Otto Fritz; Minot, George Richards; Morgan, Thomas Hunt; Muller, Hermann Joseph; Müller, Paul Hermann; Murphy, William Parry; Nicolle, Charles Jules Henri; Nobel, Alfred Bernhard; Ochoa, Severo; Pavlov, Ivan Petrovich; Ramón y Cajal, Santiago; Reichstein, Tadeus; Richards, Dickinson Woodruff, Jr.; Robbins, Frederick Chapman; Ross, Sir Ronald; Sherrington, Sir Charles Scott; Spemann, Hans; Szent-Györgyi, Albert von; Tatum, Edward Lawrie; Theiler, Max; Waksman, Selman Abraham; Watson, James Dewey; Weller, Thomas Huckle; Whipple, George Hoyt; Wilkins, Maurice Hugh Frederick.

Portraits of Nobel Laureates in Peace. John Wintterle & Richard S. Cramer. Abelard, 1971 (o.p.) (WIC)
Addams, Jane; Angell, Sir Norman; Arnoldson, Klas Pontus; Asser, Tobias M. C.; Bajer, Frederik; Balch, Emily Green; Beernaert, Auguste Marie François; Bourgeois, Léon Victor Auguste; Branting, Karl Hjalmar; Briand, Aristide; Buisson, Ferdinand; Bunche, Ralph Johnson; Butler, Nicholas Murray; Cassin, René; Cecil of Chelwood, Edgar Algernon Robert Gascoyne-Cecil, 1st viscount; Chamberlain, Sir Austen; Cremer, Sir William Randal; Dawes, Charles Gates; Ducommun, Élie; Dunant, Jean Henri; Estournelles de Constant, Paul Henri Benjamin, baron d'; Fried, Alfred Hermann; Gobat, Charles Albert; Hammarskjöld, Dag; Henderson, Arthur; Hull, Cordell; Jouhaux, Léon; Kellogg, Frank Billings; King, Martin Luther, Jr.; Lafontaine, Henri; Lange, Christian Louis; Luthuli, Albert John; Marshall, George Catlett; Moneta, Ernesto Teodoro; Mott, John Raleigh; Nansen, Fridtjof; Noel-Baker, Philip John; Orr, John Boyd, 1st baron; Ossietzky, Carl von; Passy, Frédéric; Pauling, Linus Carl; Pearson, Lester Bowles; Pire, Georges Henri; Quidde, Ludwig; Renault, Louis; Roosevelt, Theodore; Root, Elihu; Saavedra Lamas, Carlos; Schweitzer, Albert; Söderblom, Nathan; Stresemann, Gustav; Suttner, Bertha von; Wilson, Woodrow.

Possible Dream: Ten Who Dared. Marthe Gross. Chilton, 1970 (o.p.) (GRBA)
Ashe, Arthur; Fleming, Peggy; Moyers, William D.; Nader, Ralph; Simon, Neil; Stokes, Carl B.; Verrett, Shirley; Villella, Edward; Watson, James Dewey; Wells, Mary Georgene.

President Kennedy Selects Six Brave Presidents. Bill Davidson. Har-Row, 1962 (o.p.) (DAE)
Adams, John Quincy; Arthur, Chester Alan; Johnson, Andrew; Lincoln, Abraham; Roosevelt, Theodore; Washington, George.

Presidential Losers. David J. Goldman. Lerner, 1970 (GO)
Bryan, William Jennings; Burr, Aaron; Clay, Henry; Dewey, Thomas Edmund; Landon, Alfred Mossman; McClellan, George Brinton; Stevenson, Adlai Ewing; Tilden, Samuel Jones.

Presidents. Harold Coy. Watts, rev. ed., 1981 (COS)
See listing under *America and Its Presidents* by Earl S. Miers. Add: Carter, Jimmy; Ford, Gerald R.; Nixon, Richard M.; Reagan, Ronald.

Presidents in American History. Charles A. Beard & William Beard. Messner, rev. ed., 1985 (BEB)
See listing under *America and Its Presidents* by Earl S. Miers. Add: Carter, Jimmy; Ford, Gerald R.; Nixon, Richard M.; Reagan, Ronald.

Presidents in Uniform. Donald E. Cooke. Hastings, 1969 (o.p.) (COJA)
Eisenhower, Dwight David; Garfield, James Abram; Grant, Ulysses Simpson; Harrison, Benjamin; Harrison, William Henry; Hayes, Rutherford Birchard; Jackson, Andrew; Kennedy, John Fitzgerald; McKinley, William; Monroe, James; Nixon, Richard Milhous; Roosevelt, Theodore; Taylor, Zachary; Truman, Harry S.; Washington, George.

Presidents of the United States. Morris Buske, ed. Childrens, 1975 (o.p.) (BUIA)
See listing under *America and Its Presidents* by Earl S. Miers. Add: Ford, Gerald R.; Nixon, Richard M.

Presidents of the United States. Cornel Lengyel. Western Pub., rev. ed., 1969 (o.p.) (LEQ)
See listing under *America and Its Presidents* by Earl S. Miers. Add: Nixon, Richard M.

Presidents of the United States. Cornel Lengyel. Western Pub., rev. ed., 1977 (o.p.) (LEQA)
See listing under *America and Its Presidents* by Earl S. Miers. Add: Carter, Jimmy; Ford, Gerald R.; Nixon, Richard M.

Presidents of the United States. Jane McConnell & Burt McConnell. T Y Crowell, 1965 (o.p.) (MAB)
See listing under *America and Its Presidents* by Earl S. Miers.

Presidents of the United States. Jane McConnell & Burt McConnell. T Y Crowell, rev. ed., 1970 (o.p.) (MABA)
See listing under *America and Its Presidents* by Earl S. Miers. Add: Nixon, Richard M.

Presidents of the United States of America. Frank Freidel. White House Historical Assn., 1985 (FRBA)
See listing under *America and Its Presidents* by Earl S. Miers. Add: Carter, Jimmy; Ford, Gerald R.; Nixon, Richard M.; Reagan, Ronald.

Pride of Our People: The Stories of One Hundred Outstanding Jewish Men and Women. David C. Gross. Doubleday, 1979 (o.p.) (GRB-1)
Agnon, Shmuel Yosef; Akiba ben Joseph; Allon, Yigal; Anilewicz, Mordecai; Baeck, Leo; Baruch, Bernard M.; Begin, Menachem; Ben-Gurion, David; Ben-Porat, Miriam; Ben Yehudah, Eliezer; Ben-Zvi, Yitzhak; Bialik, Chaim Nachman; Bloch, Ernest; Brandeis, Louis Dembitz; Branover, Herman; Bronowski, Jacob; Brown, Harold; Chagall, Marc; Chain, Ernst Boris; Cohen, Eli; David; Dayan, Moshe; de Leon, David; Einstein, Albert; Eisenberg, Shaul; Eliav, Aryeh Lyova; Eshkol, Levi; Ferkauf, Eugene; Frank, Anne; Freier, Recha; Glueck, Nelson; Gompers, Samuel; Goode, Alexander David; Gratz, Rebecca; Haffkine, Waldemar Mordecai; Herzl, Theodor; Hillel; Jabotinsky, Vladimir; Judah ha-Levi; Katz, Chaim Moshe; King, Alan; Kluger, Ruth; Kook, Abraham Isaac; Korczak, Janus; Kornberg, Arthur; Koufax, Sandy; Krotoshinsky, Abraham; Kuchler, Lena; Lazarus, Emma; Lederberg, Joshua; Lehman, Herbert H.; Levin, Aryeh; Levy, Uriah Phillips; Lubetkin, Tzivia; Maimonides; Meir, Golda; Mendele Mocher Sefarim; Michelson, Albert Abraham; Montefiore, Sir Moses; Myerson, Bess; Navon, Yitzhak; Netanyahu, Yonatan; Peerce, Jan; Persky, Daniel; Rabi, Isidor Isaac; Rashi; Rickover, Hyman George; Rubinstein, Artur; Saadia ben Joseph; Salk, Jonas Edward; Salomon, Haym; Salvador, Francis; Sarnoff, David; Schechter, Solomon; Senesh, Hannah; Sereni, Enzo; Shalom Aleichem; Shapiro, Irving S.; Shear-Yashur, Aharon; Singer, Isaac Bashevis; Sokolow, Nahum; Spitz, Mark; Steinmetz, Charles Proteus; Straus, Nathan; Swope, Gerard; Szold, Robert; Trumpeldor, Joseph; Waksman, Selman Abraham; Wald, Lillian D.; Wiesenthal, Simon; Wise, Stephen Samuel; Wouk, Herman; Yadin, Yigael; Yalow, Rosalyn Sussman; Yoffe, Avraham.

Pro Basketball's Big Men. Dave Klein. Random, 1973 (o.p.) (KLBA)
Abdul-Jabbar, Kareem; Chamberlain, Wilt; Russell, William Felton.

Pro Basketball's Greatest: Selected All-Star Offensive and Defensive Teams. Lou Sabin. Putnam, 1976 (o.p.) (SA-2)
Abdul-Jabbar, Kareem; Barry, Rick; Erving, Julius; Frazier, Walt; Havlicek, John; McAdoo, Bob; Maravich, Pete; Monroe, Earl; Sloan, Jerry; Unseld, Westley.

Pro Basketball's Little Men. Raymond Hill. Random, 1974 (o.p.) (HIBAA)
Archibald, Nate "Tiny"; Calvin, Mack; Dampier, Louis; Goodrich, Gail; Keller, Billy; Lewis, Fritz; Meminger, Dean; Murphy, Calvin; Van Lier, Norm.

Pro Football Heroes of Today. Berry Stainback. Random, 1973 (o.p.) (ST)
Barney, Lemuel J.; Bradley, Bill; Bradshaw, Terry; Brockington, John; Brown, Larry; Brown, Robert Stanford; Butkus, Dick; Csonka, Larry; Curtis, Mike; Griese, Bob; Johnson, Ronald Adolphus; Landry, Greg; Lilly, Robert Lewis; Namath, Joe Willie; Niland, John Hugh; Page, Alan; Plunkett, Jim; Rossovich, Tim; Simpson, O. J.; Taylor, Otis; Warfield, Paul; Washington, Gene.

Pro Football's All-Time Greats: The Immortals in Pro Football's Hall of Fame. George Sullivan. Putnam, 1968 (o.p.) (SUD)
Battles, Cliff; Baugh, Sammy; Bednarik, Chuck; Bell, Bert; Bidwill, Charles E.; Blood,

Johnny, sobriquet; Brown, Paul; Carr, Joseph; Chamberlin, Guy; Clark, Dutch; Conzelman, Jimmy; Donovan, Art; Driscoll, John Leo; Dudley, William; Fortmann, Daniel John; Graham, Otto; Grange, Red; Guyon, Joe; Halas, George; Healey, Ed; Hein, Mel; Henry, Pete; Herber, Arnie; Hinkle, Clarke; Hirsch, Elroy "Crazylegs"; Hubbard, Cal; Hutson, Don; Kiesling, Walt; Lambeau, Curly; Layne, Bobby; Luckman, Sidney; Lyman, Roy; McAfee, George; Mara, Timothy James; Marshall, George Preston; Michalske, August; Millner, Wayne; Motley, Marion; Nagurski, Bronko; Nevers, Ernie; Owen, Steve; Ray, Hugh; Reeves, Dan; Rooney, Arthur Joseph; Strong, Ken; Stydahar, Joseph Leo; Thorpe, Jim; Trafton, George; Trippi, Charley; Tunnell, Emlen; Turner, Bulldog; Van Buren, Steve; Waterfield, Robert Staton; Wojciechowicz, Alex.

Pro Football's Hall of Fame. Arthur Daley. G&D, 1963 (o.p.) (DAB)
Baugh, Sammy; Bell, Bert; Blood, Johnny, sobriquet; Carr, Joseph; Clark, Dutch; Grange, Red; Halas, George; Hein, Mel; Henry, Pete; Hubbard, Cal; Hutson, Don; Lambeau, Curly; Mara, Timothy James; Marshall, George Preston; Nagurski, Bronko; Nevers, Ernie; Thorpe, Jim.

Pro Hockey Heroes of Today. Bill Libby. Random, 1974 (o.p.) (LEYA)
Cheevers, Gerry; Clarke, Bobby; Cournoyer, Ivan Serge; Dryden, Ken; Esposito, Phil; Esposito, Tony; Gilbert, Rod; Goldsworthy, Bill; Harper, Terry; Henderson, Paul Garnet; Hull, Bobby; Hull, Dennis William; Keon, David Michael; Mahovlich, Frank; Martin, Richard Lionel; Mikita, Stan; Neilson, Jim; Orr, Bobby; Parent, Bernard Marcel; Park, Brad; Perreault, Gilbert; Redmond, Mickey; Tremblay, Jean Claude; Unger, Garry.

Pro Quarterbacks. John Devaney. Putnam, 1966 (o.p.) (DEH)
Baugh, Sammy; Dawson, Lenny; Graham, Otto; Johnson, Charley; Layne, Bobby; Luckman, Sidney; Meredith, Don; Starr, Bart; Tarkenton, Francis; Tittle, Y. A.; Unitas, Johnny.

Pro Quarterbacks. Milton J. Shapiro. Messner, 1971 (o.p.) (SHEA)
Dawson, Lenny; Gabriel, Roman; Jurgensen, Sonny; Namath, Joe Willie; Starr, Bart; Unitas, Johnny.

Problem Solvers. Adrian A. Paradis. Putnam, 1964 (o.p.) (PAB)
Cox, Herald Rea; Darken, Lawrence Stamper; Engstrom, Elmer William; Frey, Charles N.; Hafstad, Lawrence Randolph; Kaman, Charles Huron; Land, Edwin Herbert; Lippert, Arnold Leroy; Semon, Waldo L.; Spaght, Monroe Edward; Thomas, Charles A.; Tressler, Donald Kiteley; Young, James F.

Profiles and Portraits of American Presidents. Margaret Bassett. McKay, 1976 (o.p.) (BAG-1)
See listing under *America and Its Presidents* by Earl S. Miers. Add: Carter, Jimmy; Ford, Gerald R.; Nixon, Richard M. *See also* listing under *America's First Ladies*, vols. 1 and 2, by Chaffin & Butwin. Add: Carter, Rosalynn; Ford, Betty.

Profiles and Portraits of American Presidents and Their Wives. Margaret Bassett. Wheelwright, 1969 (o.p.) (BAG)
See listing under *America and Its Presidents* by Earl S. Miers. Add: Nixon, Richard M. *See also* listing under *America's First Ladies*, vols. 1 and 2, by Chaffin & Butwin.

Profiles from the New Asia. Albert Roland. Macmillan, 1970 (o.p.) (RODA)
Bhave, Vinoba; Encarnacion, Rosario de Jesus; Encarnacion, Silvino; Kim Yong-gi; Kodijat, Raden; Kurosawa, Akira; Lim, Kim San; Lubis, Mochtar; Magsaysay, Ramón; Pintong, Nilawan; Razak bin Hussain, Tun Abdul.

Profiles in Achievement. Charles M. Holloway. College Board, 1987 (HOD-1)
Ashe, Arthur; Cisneros, Henry; Hall, Karen; Kahn, Anthony; Lieu, Winston Hong; Saunders, Suzanne; Stevenson, Sybil Jordan; Thompson, Carolyn.

Profiles in Black and White: Stories of Men and Women Who Fought Against Slavery. Elizabeth F. Chittenden. Scribner, 1973 (o.p.) (CHFB)
Craft, Ellen; Craft, William; Crandall, Prudence; Dickey, Sarah; Forten, Charlotte; Grimké, Angelina Emily; Grimké, Sarah Moore; Lovejoy, Elijah Parish; Nell, William Cooper; Parker, Theodore; Pinchback, Pinckney Benton Stewart; Wood, Ann.

Profiles in Black Power. James Haskins. Doubleday, 1972 (o.p.) (HAI)
Brown, H. Rap; Carmichael, Stokely; Cleage, Albert B.; Cleaver, Eldridge; Forman, James; Karenga; McKissick, Floyd B.; Malcolm X; Newton, Huey P.; Powell, Adam Clayton, Jr.; Wright, Nathan, Jr.

Profiles in Courage. John F. Kennedy. Har-Row, 1983 commemorative ed., pap. (KEC)
Adams, John†; Adams, John Quincy; Altgeld, John Peter†; Benton, Thomas Hart; Beveridge, Albert Jeremiah†; Calhoun, John Caldwell†; Houston, Samuel; Hughes, Charles Evans†; Johnson, Andrew†; Lamar, Lucius Quintus Cincinnatus; Marshall, Humphrey†; Norris, George William; Ross, Edmund G.; Taft, Robert Alphonso; Tyler, John†; Underwood, Oscar W.†; Washington, George†; Webster, Daniel.

Profiles in Courage. John F. Kennedy. Har-Row, 1964 young readers memorial ed., abridged. (o.p.) (KED)
Adams, John Quincy; Benton, Thomas Hart; Houston, Samuel; Lamar, Lucius Quintus Cincinnatus; Norris, George William; Ross, Edmund G.; Taft, Robert Alphonso; Webster, Daniel.

Proudly We Hail. Vashti Brown & Jack Brown. HM, 1968 (o.p.) (BRG)
Anderson, Marian; Attucks, Crispus; Banneker, Benjamin; Brown, Henry "Box"; Bunche, Ralph Johnson; Davis, Benjamin O., Jr.; Douglass, Frederick; Gibson, Althea; Henson, Matthew Alexander; King, Martin Luther, Jr.; Marshall, Thurgood; Matzeliger, Jan Ernst; Mays, Willie Howard; Poitier, Sidney; Randolph, Asa Philip; Robinson, Jackie; Salem, Peter; Tubman, Harriet.

Quarterbacks (Stars of the NFL). Sam Hasegawa. Creative Ed, 1975 (o.p.) (HAGC)
Griese, Bob; Namath, Joe Willie; Starr, Bart; Staubach, Roger; Tarkenton, Francis.

Queens of the Court. George Sullivan. Dodd; 1974 (o.p.) (SUDA)
Casals, Rosemary; Cawley, Evonne Goolagong; Connolly, Maureen†; Court, Margaret; Evert, Chris; Gibson, Althea†; Hotchkiss, Hazel†; Jacobs, Helen†; King, Billie Jean; Lenglen, Suzanne†; Marble, Alice†; Moran, Gussie†; Outerbridge, Mary Ewing†; Wade, Virginia; Wills, Helen†.

Quiet Rebels: Four Puerto Rican Leaders. Philip Sterling & Maria Brau. Doubleday, 1968 (STC)
Barbosa, José Celso; Diego, José de; Muñoz Marín, Luis; Muñoz Rivera, Luis.

Racers and Drivers: The Fastest Men and Cars from Barney Oldfield to Craig Breedlove. Brock Yates. Bobbs, 1968 (o.p.) (YAA)
Andretti, Mario; Ascari, Alberto; Brabham, Jack; Breedlove, Craig; Campbell, Sir Malcolm; Caracciola, Rudolf; Clark, James; Cobb, John; De Palma, Ralph; De Paolo, Peter; Fangio, Juan Manuel; Foyt, Anthony Joseph; Garlits, Don; Gurney, Dan; Hall, Jim; Jones, Parnelli; Milton, Thomas Willard; Moss, Stirling; Nalon, Duke; Nuvolari, Tazio; Oldfield, Barney; Petty, Richard; Rickenbacker, Edward Vernon; Shaw, Wilbur; Turner, Curtis; Vukovich, Bill; Ward, Rodger.

Rebels and Reformers: Biographies of Four Jewish Americans. Alberta Eiseman. Doubleday, 1976 (o.p.) (EIA)
Brandeis, Louis Dembitz; Levy, Uriah Phillips; Rose, Ernestine Potowski; Wald, Lillian D.

Receivers (Stars of the NFL). Jay H. Smith. Creative Ed, 1975 (o.p.) (SMI)
Biletnikoff, Frederick; Gilliam, John Rally; Taylor, Charley; Taylor, Otis; Warfield, Paul.

Record Breakers. Maury Allen. P-H, 1968 (o.p.) (ALBA)
Bannister, Roger Gilbert; Billick, George; Brown, Jim; Campbell, Donald Malcolm; Chamberlain, Wilt; Clark, James; Connolly, Maureen; Di Maggio, Joseph Paul; Howe, Gordie; Jones, Bobby; Koufax, Sandy; Maris, Roger Eugene; Sailer, Toni; Schollander, Donald Arthur; Unitas, Johnny.

Record Breakers of Pro Sports. Nathan Aaseng. Lerner, 1987 (AAS-35)
Abdul-Jabbar, Kareem; Brown, Jim; Chamberlain, Wilt; Cobb, Ty; Dickerson, Eric; Gretzky,

Wayne; Johnson, Walter Perry; Payton, Walter; Richard, Maurice; Rose, Pete; Ryan, Nolan; Simpson, O. J.

Record-Breakers of the Major Leagues. Lou Sabin. Random, 1974 (o.p.) (SA-3)
Aaron, Hank; Brock, Louis Clark; Carlton, Steven Norman; Drysdale, Don; Gibson, Bob; Gutierrez, Cesar "Coco"; Hunt, Ron; Kaline, Albert William; Killebrew, Harmon; McDowell, Sam; Mantle, Mickey Charles; Mays, Willie Howard; Seaver, Tom; Tenace, Gene; Wilhelm, James Hoyt; Williams, Ted.

Record Breakers of the N.F.L. Howard Liss. Random, 1975 (o.p.) (LIBB)
Blanda, George; Dempsey, Tom; Harris, Franco; Jones, Bert; Kapp, Joe; Maynard, Don; Sayers, Gale; Simpson, O. J.; Unitas, Johnny.

Remarkable Children: Twenty Who Made History. Dennis Brindell Fradin. Little, 1987 (FOR)
Adams, John Quincy; Adh-Dhîb, Muhammed; Ali, Muhammad; Anning, Mary; Austin, Tracy; Braille, Louis; Colburn, Zerah; Comaneci, Nadia; Conkling, Hilda; de Sautuola, Maria; Fischer, Bobby; Frank, Anne; Garland, Judy; Keller, Helen Adams; Mozart, Wolfgang Amadeus; Pelé; Picasso, Pablo; Sacajawea; Temple, Shirley; Whitaker, Mark.

Reporters at War. Alice Fleming. Regnery, 1970 (o.p.) (FLBB)
Churchill, Sir Winston Leonard Spencer; Creelman, James; Davis, Richard Harding; Gibbons, Floyd Phillips; Higgins, Marguerite; MacGahan, Januarius Aloysius; Pyle, Ernest Taylor; Russell, Sir William Howard; Smalley, George Washburn; Wing, Henry.

Rescue! True Stories of the Winners of the Young American Medal for Bravery. Norman D. Anderson & Walter R. Brown. Walker, 1983 (o.p.) (ANCA)
Bergeman, Gerald; Browne, Michael; Christie, David; Christie, Robert; Cornick, Wade; Dale, Jerome; Gregory, Darryl; Kieff, Elaine; Kilmer, Gordon; Loura, Philip; Murray, Harold; Peterson, Joel; Slack, Donna Lee; Stratt, Parker.

Resistance: Profiles in Nonviolence. James Haskins. Doubleday, 1970 (o.p.) (HAJ)
Chavez, Cesar Estrada; Gandhi, Mohandas Karamchand; Jesus Christ; King, Martin Luther, Jr.; Penn, William; Russell, Bertrand Arthur William Russell, 3d earl; Spock, Benjamin; Thoreau, Henry David.

Revolutionaries: Agents of Change. James Haskins. Lippincott, 1971 (o.p.) (HAK)
Ataturk, Mustafa Kemal; Castro, Fidel; Guevara, Ché; Henry, Patrick; Ho Chi Minh; Malcolm X; Mao Tse-tung; Marx, Karl Heinrich; Robespierre, Maximilien François Marie Isidore de; Washington, George; Zapata, Emiliano.

Rookie: The World of the N.B.A. Dave Klein. Regnery, 1971 (o.p.) (KLC)
Abdul-Jabbar, Kareem; Cowens, Dave; Lanier, Bob; Maravich, Pete; Murphy, Calvin; Petrie, Geoff; Walk, Neal; White, Jo Jo.

Royal Adventurers. Robert J. Unstead. Follett, 1963 (o.p.) (UNA)
Akhnaton; Caesar, Gaius Julius; Charlemagne; Charles II; Christina; Frederick II, the Great; Genghis Khan; Kublai Khan; Marie Antoinette; Mary, Queen of Scots.

Royal Opposition: The Story of the British Generals in the American Revolution. Clifford Alderman. Macmillan, 1970 (o.p.) (AKA)
Burgoyne, John; Clinton, Sir Henry; Cornwallis, Charles Cornwallis, 1st marquis; Dorchester, Sir Guy Carleton, 1st baron; Gage, Thomas; Howe, William Howe, 5th viscount.

Rulers in Petticoats. Mildred Boyd. Criterion Bks., 1966 (o.p.) (BOI)
Boudicca; Catherine II, the Great; Catherine de Medici; Christina; Cleopatra; Eleanor of Aquitaine; Elizabeth I; Elizabeth II; Hatshepsut; Isabella I; Juliana; Margaret; Maria Theresa; Mary I; Mary, Queen of Scots; Theodora; Tzu Hsi; Victoria; Wilhelmina.

Running Backs (Stars of the NFL). Charles Morse & Ann Morse. Creative Ed, 1975 (o.p.) (MOCA)
Brockington, John; Csonka, Larry; Foreman, Chuck; Morris, Mercury; Simpson, O. J.

Russian Authors. Elsa Z. Posell. HM, 1970 (o.p.) (POFA)

Chekhov, Anton Pavlovich; Dostoevski, Fëdor Mikhailovich; Gogol, Nikolai Vasilievich; Gorki, Maksim; Karamzin, Nikolai Mikhailovich†; Krylor, Ivan Andreevich†; Lermontov, Mikhail Yurievich†; Lomonosov, Mikhail Vasilievich†; Pasternak, Boris Leonidovich; Pushkin, Aleksandr Sergeevich; Sholokhov, Mikhail Aleksandrovich; Solzhenitsyn, Aleksandr Isaevich; Tolstoi, Lev Nikolaevich; Turgenev, Ivan Sergeevich; Yevtushenko, Yevgeny Aleksandrovich.

Russian Composers. Elsa Z. Posell. HM, 1967 (POG)

Balakireff, Mili Alekseyevich; Borodin, Alexander P.; Cui, César Antonovich; Glazunov, Aleksandr Konstantinovich; Glière, Reinhold Moritzovich; Glinka, Mikhail Ivanovich; Kabalevsky, Dmitri Borisovich; Khachaturian, Aram; Miakovsky, Nikolai Yakovlevich; Mussorgsky, Modest Petrovich; Prokofiev, Sergei Sergeevich; Rachmaninoff, Sergei; Rimski-Korsakov, Nikolai Andreevich; Scriabin, Aleksandr Nikolaievich; Shostakovich, Dmitri; Stravinsky, Igor Fëdorovich; Tchaikovsky, Peter Ilyich.

Saints: Adventures in Courage. Mary O'Neill. Doubleday, 1963 (o.p.) (ONA)

Agnes; Alban; Albert the Great; Ambrose; Andrew; Anne; Anthony of Padua; Antony; Apollo; Augustine; Benedict; Bénézet; Bernard of Menthon; Bridget of Sweden; Brigid of Kildare; Casimir; Catherine of Siena; Christopher; Clare; Colman of Kilmacduagh; David; Dominic; Dorothea; Elizabeth of Hungary; Francis of Assisi; Geneviève; George; Hedwig; Helena; Hugh of Lincoln; Isidore; Joan of Arc; John the Dwarf; John, the Evangelist; Joseph; Joseph of Arimathea; Justin; Louis IX; Margaret of Scotland; Martin of Tours; Mary Magdalen; Moses the Black; Nicholas; Patricia; Patrick; Paul; Peter; Sergius of Radonezh; Thomas à Becket; Thomas Aquinas; Valentine; Zita.

Saints and Your Name. Joseph Quadflieg. Pantheon, 1957 (o.p.) (QUA)

Agatha; Agnes; Albert the Great; Alice de Bourgotte; Andrew; Angela dei Merici; Anne; Anthony of Padua; Augustine; Barbara; Bellarmine, Robert; Bernard of Clairvaux; Bertha; Borromeo, Charles; Bridget of Sweden; Catherine of Alexandria; Christina; Clare; Dorothea; Edmund Rich; Edward the Confessor; Elizabeth of Hungary; Eric IX; Francis of Assisi; Frederick; Gabriel, Archangel; George; Gerard Sagredo; Gertrude the Great; Helena; Henry; Herbert; Hubert; Hugh of Grenoble; Irene; James the Greater; James the Less; Joan; John the Baptist; Joseph; Julian; Lawrence; Leo I, the Great; Louis IX; Lucy; Luke; Margaret; Martha; Martin of Tours; Mary, Virgin; Matilda; Matthias; Michael; Monica; Neri, Philip; Nicholas; Patrick; Paul; Peter; Richard; Rose of Lima; Stephen; Susanna; Teresa of Avila; Thomas; Timothy; Ursula; Veronica; Victor; Vincent de Paul; Walter of Pontoise; Wilfrid; William of Gellone.

Saints for the Small. Frank Morriss. Bruce Wis, 1964 (o.p.) (MOC)

Albert the Great; Aloysius Gonzaga; Alphonsus Rodriguez; Anthony of Padua; Augustine; Bernard of Menthon; Catherine of Genoa; Conrad of Piacenza; Dismas; Edmund the Martyr; Elizabeth of Hungary; Elizabeth of Portugal; Francis of Assisi; Gall; Genesius; Geneviève; Godric; Hallvard; Hunna; Hyacintha; Ignatius of Loyola; Isidore; Joan of Arc; Joan of Valois; John the Dwarf; John Berchmans; John Gualbert; Julitta; Kenneth; Labre, Benedict; Margaret of Cortona; Mary Magdelen Postel; Michael; Monica; More, Sir Thomas; Neri, Philip; Notburga; Onesimus; Paschal Baylon; Patrick; Petroc; Raymond Nonnatus; Rita of Cascia; Thérése of Lisieux; Thomas of Villanova; Vianney, Jean Baptiste Marie; Virgil of Salzburg; William of Roskilde; Winifred; Zita.

Saints for Young People for Every Day of the Year, vol. I. Daughters of St. Paul, 1963 (DAD-2)

Abraham; Achilleus†; Aelred; Agatha; Agnes; Agnes of Montepulciano; Alban; Aloysius Gonzaga; Alphege of Canterbury; Amadeus IX, Blessed; Angela dei Merici; Anselm of Canterbury; Anthony of Egypt; Anthony of Padua; Antonino; Apollonia of Alexandria; Athanasius; Audrey; Augustine of Canterbury; Bademus; Barachisius†; Barbatus; Barnabas; Basil the Great; Basilissa†; Bathildis; Bede the Venerable; Bellarmine, Robert; Benedict; Benedict the Moor; Bernadette of Lourdes; Bernardine of Siena; Billiart, Marie Rose, Blessed; Blaise; Bobola, Andrew; Boniface; Boniface of Tarsus; Bosco, John; Brigid of Kildare; Caius;

Canisius, Peter; Canute IV; Caracciolo, Francis; Casimir; Catherine of Ricci; Catherine of Siena; Catherine of Sweden; Celestine V.; Chanel, Peter; Clotilda; Columcille; Cunegundes; Cuthbert; Cyril of Jerusalem; David I of Scotland; Domitilla†; Dorothea; Dositheus; Ephrem; Eucherius of Orléans; Eudocia; Eulogius of Spain; Euphrasia; Falconieri, Juliana; Faustinus; Felicitas; Felix of Cantalice; Fidelis of Sigmaringen; Fontaine, Madeleine, Blessed; Francis de Sales; Francis of Paola; Fulgentius; Gabriel of Our Lady of Sorrows; Gabriel, Archangel; Geneviève; George; Germaine; Gregory I, the Great; Gregory VII; Gregory of Nazianzus; Herman Joseph; Hermenegild; Hilary of Poitiers; Honoratus; Hugh of Grenoble; Ignatius of Laconi; Irenaeus; James the Less; Joan of Arc; Joan of Valois; John the Baptist; John, the Evangelist; John of God; John of Matha; John of Sahagun; John Baptiste de la Salle; John Capistrano; John Chrysostom; John Climacus; John Damascene; John Joseph of the Cross; Jonas; Joseph; Jovita; Julia; Julian; Justin; Labre, Benedict; Leo I, the Great; Lucian; Ludger; Lupicinus; Lydwina; Majella, Gerard; Margaret of Cortona; Margaret of Scotland; Mark the Evangelist; Mary of the Incarnation, Blessed; Mary, Virgin; Mary Magdelen dei Pazzi; Matilda; Matthias; Monica; Nereus†; Neri, Philip; Norbert; Onesimus; Osanna of Mantua, Blessed; Pamphilus; Pancras†; Paschal Baylon; Patrick; Paul; Paul, the Egyptian Hermit; Pelagius; Perpetua; Peter; Peter of Tarentaise; Peter of Verona; Peter Nolasco; Philip; Philip of Zell; Pius V; Polycarp; Porphyry; Pothinus; Raymond of Pennafort; Regis, John Francis; Richard of Chichester; Rita of Cascia; Romanus; Romuald; Sabas, the Goth; Sanchia; Savio, Dominic; Scholastica; Sebastian; Serenus; Simeon Stylites; Simplicius; Soter; Stanislaus; Stephen Harding; Syncletica; Taigi, Anna Maria, Blessed; Theodosius; Theresia, Blessed; Thomas Aquinas; Timothy; Titus; Toribio; Ubald; Valentine; Veronica of Milan; Vincent of Saragossa; Vincent Ferrer; Walburga; Waldetrudis; William of Abbot; William of Bourges; William of Monte Vergine; William of York; Zachary.

Saints for Young People for Every Day of the Year, vol. II. Daughters of St. Paul, 1964 (DAD-3)

Adelaide of Turin; Aidan; Albert the Great; Alexander; Alexander the Coalman; Alexis; Allucio; Alphonsus Liguori; Alphonsus Rodriguez; Ambrose; Andrew; Anne; Anysia; Athanasia; Augustine; Avellino, Andrew; Bartholomew; Bernard of Clairvaux; Bertha; Bertrand, Louis; Bibiana; Bichier Des Agnes, Jeanne Elisabeth; Bonaventure; Borgia, Francis; Boris; Borromeo, Charles; Botvid; Bridget of Sweden; Bruno; Cabrini, Frances Xavier; Cajetan; Callistus I; Camillus de Lellis; Campion, Edmund; Catherine of Alexandria; Cecilia; Cerioli, Constanza, Blessed; Chantal, Jane Frances de; Charles of Blois, Blessed; Clare; Claver, Peter; Cleopatra; Columban; Contardo Ferrini, Blessed; Cosmas; Cyprian; Cyril; Damien; Delanoue, Jeanne, Blessed; Dominic; Dominic of Silos; Duchesne, Rose Philippine, Blessed; Edith of Wilton; Edmund the Martyr; Edward the Confessor; Elizabeth of Hungary; Elizabeth of Portugal; Emiliani, Jerome; Emily de Rodat; Eudes, John; Eulogius; Evaristus; Everard Hanse, Blessed; Felicity; Felix; Felton, John, Blessed; Finnian; Flannan; Flora of Beaulieu; Foillan; Fourier, Peter; Francis de Posadas; Francis of Assisi; Francis Xavier; Franco, Lippi, Blessed; Germanus of Auxerre; Gertrude the Great; Giles; Gleb; Goretti, Mary; Gwyn, Richard, Blessed; Helena; Heliodorus; Henry; Herst, Richard, Blessed; Hilarion; Hildegard of Bingen; Ignatius of Loyola; James the Greater; James Intercisus; Jerome; John of the Cross; John, the Evangelist; John Berchmans; John Cantius; John Gualbert; Joseph of Cupertino; Joseph Calasanctius; Jude; Kenneth; Kostka, Stanislaus; Labouré, Catherine; Laurence O'Toole; Lawrence; Lawrence of Brindisi; Lawrence Justinian; Leger; Louis IX; Louis of Thuringia, Blessed; Lucera, Francis Anthony, Blessed; Lucy; Luke; Madeline of Canossa, Blessed; Majella, Gerard; Malachy; Marcian; Margaret Mary; Martha; Martin of Tours; Mary the Martyr; Mary Magdalen; Matthew; Melania; Methodius; More, Sir Thomas; Narcissus; Nicholas; Nilus the Elder; Nino; Notburga; Odo of Cluny; Olympias; Pacificus of San Severino; Pallotta, Maria Assunta, Blessed; Pantaleon; Peter; Peter Chrysologus; Philip of Thrace; Philip Benizi; Pius X; Plunkett, Oliver, Blessed; Porres, Martin de; Praxedes; Radegund; Raphael; Remigius; Roberts, John, Blessed; Roch; Rose of Lima; Rose of Viterbo; Sabas; Sergius of Radonezh; Servulus; Simon; Solano, Francis; Spiridion; Stephen; Stephen I of Hungary; Teresa of Avila; Thecla; Theodore Tiro; Thèrèse of Lisieux; Thomas; Thomas à Becket; Thomas of Villanova; Urban V, Blessed; Varus; Vénard,

Jean Théophane, Blessed; Vianney, Jean Baptiste Marie; Vincent de Paul; Wenceslaus of Bohemia; Willibrord; Zaccaria, Anthony.

Saints Upon a Time. Joan Windham. Sheed, 1956 (o.p.) (WIB)
Agnes; Albert; Anne; Archibald; Blaise; Gillian; Isabel; Leonard; Lucy; Olga; Penelope; Samson; Susan; Swithin.

Salute to Black Civil Rights Leaders. Richard L. Green. Empak, 1987, pap. (GRAB-01)
Bates, Daisy Gaston; Downing, George Thomas; Du Bois, William Edward Burghardt; Farmer, James; Garvey, Marcus A.; Grimké, Francis James; Hamer, Fannie Lou; Haynes, George Edmund; Jackson, Jesse Louis; King, Martin Luther, Jr.; Malcolm X; Mitchell, John R., Jr.; Myers, Isaac; Randolph, Asa Philip; Ruffin, Josephine St. Pierre; Talbert, Mary Burnett; Tobias, Channing Heggie; White, Walter F.; Young, Whitney Moore, Jr.

Salute to Black Pioneers. Richard L. Green. Empak, 1986, pap. (GRAB-02)
Abraham; Attucks, Crispus; Beckwourth, James P.; Brown, Clara; Bush, George W.; Cuffe, Paul; Esteban or Estevanico; Fields, Mary; Ford, Barney; Green, Nancy; Henson, Matthew Alexander; Johnson, James Weldon; Leidesdorff, William Alexander; Mason, Biddy; Pennington, James W. C.; Pickett, Bill; Pointe de Sable, Jean Baptiste; Washington, George; Whipper, William; Woodson, Carter Goodwin.

Salute to Black Scientists and Inventors. Richard L. Green. Empak, 1985, pap. (GRAB-03)
Banneker, Benjamin; Beard, Andrew J.; Carver, George Washington; Drew, Charles Richard; Forten, James; Hall, Lloyd Augustus; Jones, Frederick McKinley; Julian, Percy Lavon; Just, Ernest Everett; Latimer, Lewis Howard; Lee, Joseph; McCoy, Elijah; Matzeliger, Jan Ernst; Menelik II; Morgan, Garrett A.; Rillieux, Norbert; Temple, Lewis; Woods, Granville T.; Wright, Louis Tompkins.

Salute to Historic African Kings and Queens. Richard L. Green, ed. Empak, 1988, pap. (GRAB-04)
Affonso I; Akhnaton; Askia Muhammad; Chaka; Dahia al-Kahina; Gudit; Haile Selassie I; Hatshepsut; Jugurtha; Makeda; Mansa Musa I; Massinissa; Menes; Moshoeshoe; Nefertiti; Nzinga; Osei Tutu; Piankhi; Sunni Ali Ber; Taharga; Tutankhamen; Tuthmosis III; Yaa Asantewa.

Salute to Historic Black Abolitionists. Richard L. Green. Empak, 1988, pap. (GRAB-05)
Allen, Richard; Anderson, Osborne Perry; Bibb, Henry; Brown, William Wells; Crummell, Alexander; Delany, Martin R.; Douglass, Frederick; Garnet, Henry Highland; Hall, Prince; Henson, Josiah; Jones, John; Nell, William Cooper; Purvis, Robert; Remond, Charles Lenox; Remond, Sarah Parker; Ruggles, David; Stewart, Maria W.; Still, William; Turner, Nat; Walker, David; Ward, Samuel Ringgold.

Salute to Historic Black Women. Dorothy M. Love, ed. Empak, 1984, pap. (LOAV)
Barnett, Ida Wells; Bethune, Mary McLeod; Bowser, Mary Elizabeth; Burroughs, Nannie Helen; Cary, Mary Ann Shadd; Coleman, Bessie; Craft, Ellen; Fauset, Crystal Bird; Gray, Ida; Greenfield, Elizabeth Taylor; Harper, Frances Ellen Watkins; Lewis, Mary Edmonia; McKinney, Nina Mae; Mahoney, Mary Eliza; Pleasant, Mary Ellen; Price, Florence Beatrice Smith; Steward, Susan McKinney; Stewart, Ella Phillips; Terrell, Mary Church; Truth, Sojourner; Tubman, Harriet; Walker, Maggie Lena; Walker, Sarah Breedlove; Wheatley, Phillis.

Scientist Versus Society. Vivian Werner. Hawthorn, 1975 (o.p.) (WEF)
Babbage, Charles; Drew, Charles Richard; Freud, Sigmund; Lovelace, Lady Ada; Mendel, Gregor Johann; Vavilov, Nicolai Ivanovich.

Scientists and Inventors. Anthony Feldman. Facts on File, 1979 (FE)
Agricola, Georgius; Ampère, André Marie; Appert, Nicolas; Archimedes; Aristotle; Arkwright, Sir Richard; Arrhenius, Svante August; Babbage, Charles; Baekeland, Leo Hendrik; Baird, John Logie; Barnard, Christiaan N.; Becquerel, Antoine Henri; Bell, Alexander Graham; Benz, Karl; Bertillon, Alphonse; Bessemer, Sir Henry; Bjerknes, Vilhelm; Bohr, Niels H. D.; Boyle, Robert; Braille, Louis; Bramah, Joseph; Broglie, Louis-Victor de; Brunel, Isambard Kingdom; Carlson, Chester F.; Carothers, Wallace Hume; Cavendish, Henry;

Seven Founders of American Literature. Carla Hancock. Blair, 1976 (o.p.) (HACB)
  Bryant, William Cullen; Cooper, James Fenimore; Irving, Washington; Melville, Herman; Poe, Edgar Allan; Twain, Mark, pseud.; Whitman, Walt.

Seven Heroes: Medal of Honor Stories of the War in the Pacific. Saul Braun. Putnam, 1965 (o.p.) (BRA)
  Elrod, Henry Talmage; Fluckey, Eugene Bennett; Hanson, Robert; McCandless, Bruce; O'Callahan, Joseph T.; Paige, Mitchell; Preston, Arthur Murray.

Seven Kings of England. Geoffrey Trease. Vanguard, 1955 (TRA)
  Alfred the Great; Charles I; Charles II; George VI; Richard I; William I, the Conqueror; William III.

Seven Queens of England. Geoffrey Trease. Vanguard, 1953 (TRB)
  Anne; Elizabeth I; Elizabeth II; Mary I; Mary II; Maud; Victoria.

Seven Sovereign Queens. Geoffrey Trease. Vanguard, 1968 (o.p.) (TRBA)
  Boudicca; Catherine II, the Great; Christina; Cleopatra; Galla Placidia; Isabella I; Maria Theresa.

Seven Stages. Geoffrey Trease. Vanguard, 1964 (TRC)
  Irving, Sir Henry; Lind, Jenny; Marlowe, Christopher; Molière; Pavlova, Anna; Siddons, Sarah Kemble; Verdi, Giuseppe.

Seven Women Explorers. Mignon Rittenhouse. Lippincott, 1964 (o.p.) (RIG)
  Akeley, Delia J. Denning; Baker, Lady Florence von Sass; Bird, Isabella Lucy; Boyd, Louise Arner; Johnson, Walter Perry†; Kenyon, Kathleen M.; Tinnè, Alexine; Workman, Fanny Bullock.

Seven Women: Great Painters. Winthrop Neilson & Frances Neilson. Chilton, 1969 (o.p.) (NE)
  Beaux, Cecilia; Cassatt, Mary; Kauffmann, Angelica; Laurencin, Marie; Morisot, Berthe; O'Keeffe, Georgia; Vigee-Lebrun, Elisabeth.

Seven Women: Portraits from the American Radical Tradition. Judith Nies. Penguin, 1978, pap. (NIA)
  Day, Dorothy; Gilman, Charlotte Perkins; Grimké, Sarah Moore; Jones, Mary Harris; Stanton, Elizabeth Cady; Strong, Anna Louise; Tubman, Harriet.

Seventeen Black Artists. Elton C. Fax. Dodd, 1971 (o.p.) (FAH)
  Amevor, Charlotte; Andrews, Benny; Bearden, Romare; Biggers, John; Catlett, Elizabeth; Cortor, Eldzier; De Carava, Roy R.; Goreleigh, Rex; Hooks, Earl; Jones, Lawrence; Lawrence, Jacob; Lewis, James E.; Morgan, Norma; Ringgold, Faith; Torres, John; White, Charles; Wilson, John.

Shapers of Africa. Florence T. Polatnick & Alberta L. Saleton. Messner, 1969 (o.p.) (POA)
  Crowther, Samuel Ajayi; Mansa Musa I; Mboya, Thomas Joseph; Moshoeshoe; Nzinga.

Shots without Guns: The Story of Vaccination. Sarah R. Riedman. Rand, 1960 (o.p.) (RIE)
  Behring, Emil von; Dick, George Frederick; Dick, Gladys H.; Ehrlich, Paul; Jenner, Edward; Kitasato, Shibasaburo; Koch, Robert; Löffler, Friedrich†; Montagu, Lady Mary Wortley†; Pasteur, Louis; Roux, Pierre Paul Émile; Sabin, Albert Bruce; Salk, Jonas Edward; Schick, Béla; Sutton, Robert†; Yersin, Alexandre Émile†.

Signers of the Declaration. Katherine L. Bakeless & John Bakeless. HM, 1969 (o.p.) (BAEA)
  See listing under *Fathers of America's Freedom* by Donald E. Cooke. Delete † after all names.

Signers of the Declaration of Independence. Robert G. Ferris & Richard E. Morris. Interpretive Pub., 1982 (o.p.) (FEAB)
  Adams, John; Adams, Samuel; Bartlett, Josiah; Braxton, Carter; Carroll, Charles†; Chase, Samuel; Clark, Abraham; Clymer, George; Ellery, William; Floyd, William; Franklin, Benjamin; Gerry, Elbridge; Gwinnett, Button; Hall, Lyman; Hancock, John; Harrison, John; Hart, John; Hewes, Joseph; Heyward, Thomas, Jr.; Hooper, William; Hopkins, Stephen; Hopkinson, Francis; Huntington, Samuel; Jefferson, Thomas; Lee, Francis L.; Lee, Richard Henry;

Lewis, Francis; Livingston, Philip; Lynch, Thomas, Jr.; McKean, Thomas; Middleton, Arthur; Morris, Lewis; Morris, Robert; Morton, John; Nelson, Thomas; Paca, William; Paine, Robert Treat; Penn, John; Read, George; Rodney, Caesar; Ross, George; Rush, Benjamin; Rutledge, Edward; Sherman, Roger; Smith, James; Stockton, Richard; Stone, Thomas; Taylor, George; Thornton, Matthew; Walton, George; Whipple, William; Williams, William; Wilson, James; Witherspoon, John; Wolcott, Oliver; Wythe, George.

Significant American Colonial Leaders. Morris Buske, ed. Childrens, 1975 (o.p.) (BUIB)

Adams, John; Adams, Samuel; Alexander, William†; Allen, Ethan†; Asbury, Francis†; Attucks, Crispus†; Baldwin, Abraham†; Barney, Joshua†; Bartlett, Josiah†; Bassett, Richard†; Bedford, Gunning†; Blair, John†; Blount, William†; Braxton, Carter†; Brearly, David†; Burr, Aaron; Butler, Pierce†; Carroll, Charles†; Carroll, Daniel†; Carroll, John†; Chase, Samuel†; Clark, Abraham†; Clark, George Rogers; Clinton, George†; Clymer, George†; Dayton, Jonathan†; Dean, Silas†; Dearborn, Henry†; Derby, Elias H.†; Derby, Richard W.†; Dickinson, John†; Duer, William†; Ellery, William†; Eustis, William†; Few, William†; Fitch, John†; Floyd, William†; Forten, James†; Franklin, Benjamin; Freneau, Philip Morin†; Gage, Thomas†; Gates, Horatio†; Gerry, Elbridge†; Gilman, Nicholas†; Gorham, Nathaniel†; Greene, Nathanael†; Gwinnett, Button†; Hale, Nathan†; Hall, Lyman†; Hamilton, Alexander; Hancock, John; Harrison, Benjamin†; Hart, John†; Haynes, Lemuel†; Henry, Patrick; Hewes, Joseph†; Heyward, Thomas, Jr.†; Hicks, Elias†; Hillegas, Michael†; Hooper, William†; Hopkins, Stephen†; Hopkinson, Francis†; Huntington, Samuel†; Hutchinson, Thomas†; Ingersoll, Jared†; Jefferson, Thomas; Jenifer, Daniel of St. Thomas†; Johnson, Samuel†; Johnson, William Samuel†; Jones, John Paul; King, Rufus†; Knox, Henry†; Langdon, John†; Laurens, Henry†; Lee, Arthur†; Lee, Charles†; Lee, Francis L.†; Lee, Henry†; Lee, Richard Henry†; Lewis, Francis†; Livingston, Philip†; Livingston, William†; Lynch, Thomas, Jr.†; McHenry, James†; McKean, Thomas†; Madison, James; Marshall, John; Mason, George†; Mather, Cotton†; Mather, Increase†; Middleton, Arthur†; Mifflin, Thomas†; Montgomery, Richard†; Morgan, Daniel†; Morgan, John†; Morris, Gouverneur†; Morris, Lewis†; Morris, Robert†; Morton, John†; Nelson, Thomas†; Osgood, Samuel†; Otis, James†; Paca, William†; Paine, Thomas†; Paterson, William†; Penn, John†; Phillips, John†; Phillips, Samuel†; Pickering, Timothy†; Pierpont, James†; Pinckney, Charles†; Pinckney, Charles Cotesworth†; Pinckney, Thomas†; Putnam, Israel†; Putnam, Rufus†; Randolph, Edmund Jennings; Randolph, Peyton†; Read, George†; Revere, Paul; Rittenhouse, David†; Rodney, Caesar†; Ross, George†; Rush, Benjamin†; Rutledge, Edward†; Rutledge, John†; Salem, Peter†; Salomon, Haym†; Seabury, Samuel†; Sedgwick, Theodore†; Sewall, Samuel†; Sheftall, Benjamin†; Sheftall, Mordecai†; Shelby, Isaac†; Sherman, Roger†; Smith, James†; Spaight, Richard Dobbs, Sr.†; Stevens, John†; Stockton, Richard†; Stone, Thomas†; Taylor, George†; Thornton, Matthew†; Thornton, William†; Trumbull, John (1750–1831)†; Trumbull, John (1756–1843)†; Trumbull, Jonathan†; Truxtun, Thomas†; Tyler, Royall†; Varick, James†; Vigo, Francis†; Walton, George†; Ward, Artemas†; Washington, George; Wayne, Anthony†; West, Benjamin†; Wheelock, Eleazar†; Whipple, William†; Williams, William†; Williamson, Hugh†; Willing, Thomas†; Wilson, James†; Witherspoon, John†; Wolcott, Oliver†; Wythe, George†.

Singers of the Blues. Frank Surge. Lerner, 1969 (o.p.) (SUH)

Broonzy, Big Bill; Brown, Rabbit; Carr, Leroy; Holiday, Billie; Hopkins, Lightnin'; Jefferson, Lemon; Johnson, Lonnie; Johnson, Willie; Leadbelly; Lewis, Furry; McClennan, Tommy; McGhee, Brownie; Rainey, Ma; Smith, Bessie; Terry, Sonny; Waters, Muddy; Williams, Big Joe.

Six Black Masters of American Art. Romare Bearden & Harry Henderson. Doubleday, 1972 (o.p.) (BEBA)

Duncanson, Robert S.; Johnston, Joshua; Lawrence, Jacob; Pippin, Horace; Savage, Augusta Christine; Tanner, Henry Ossawa.

Six Queens: The Wives of Henry VIII. Marguerite Vance. Dutton, 1965 (o.p.) (VAC)

Anne of Cleves; Boleyn, Anne; Catherine of Aragon; Howard, Catherine; Parr, Catherine; Seymour, Jane.

Six Wives of Henry VIII. Gladys Malvern. Vanguard, 1972 (o.p.) (MAOA)
Anne of Cleves; Boleyn, Anne; Catherine of Aragon; Howard, Catherine; Parr, Catherine; Seymour, Jane.

Skystars: The History of Women in Aviation. Ann Hodgman & Rudy Djabbaroff. Atheneum, 1981 (HIFD)
Ames, Julie; Bacon, Gertrude†; Bastie, Maryse; Batten, Jean; Blanchard, Sophie†; Bolland, Adrienne†; Boucher, Helene; Bradley, Lucretia†; Broadwick, Tiny†; Cobb, Geraldyn M.; Cochran, Jacqueline; Coleman, Bessie; Fairgrave, Phoebe; Fisher, Anna†; Johnson, Amy; Law, Ruth; Love, Nancy; Moisant, Mathilde†; Nichols, Ruth; Popovich, Marina; Quimby, Harriet; Raiche, Bessica†; Reitsch, Hanna; Scott, Blanche Stuart†; Seddon, Margaret Rhea; Smith, Elinor; Stinson, Katherine.

Small Hands, Big Hands: Seven Profiles of Chicano Migrant Workers and Their Families. Sandra Weiner. Pantheon, 1970 (o.p.) (WECC)
Castillo, Rosa; Delgado, Estrella; Estrada, Miguel; Garcia, Forresto; Lopez, Antonio; Ramirez, Doria; Reyes, Albert.

Soldiers in the Civil Rights War: Adventures in Courage. Janet Stevenson. Reilly & Lee, 1971 (o.p.) (STJB)
Chaney, James Earl†; Du Bois, William Edward Burghardt; Goodman, Andrew†; Meredith, James Howard; Schwerner, Michael Henry†; Smalls, Robert; Stevens, Thaddeus; Trotter, William Monroe; Waring, Julius Waties.

Some Dissenting Voices: The Story of Six American Dissenters. Arthur Weinberg & Lila Weinberg. World Pub., 1970 (o.p.) (WECB)
Addams, Jane; Altgeld, John Peter; Darrow, Clarence Seward; Debs, Eugene Victor; Ingersoll, Robert Green; Steffens, Lincoln.

Some Kings and Queens. Robert J. Unstead. Follett, 1962 (o.p.) (UNB)
Alexander III, the Great; Alfred the Great; Elizabeth I; Harold II; Louis XIV; Montezuma II; Napoleon I; Peter I, the Great; Victoria; William I, the Silent.

Some of My Favorite Spies. Ronald Seth. Chilton, 1968 (o.p.) (SEB)
Baden-Powell, Robert Stephenson Smyth, 1st baron; Bettignies, Louise de; Boyd, Belle; Defoe, Daniel; Foote, Alexander; Granville, Christine; Lonsdale, Gordon Arnold; Lucieto, Charles; Silber, Jules; Tallmadge, Benjamin; Walsingham, Sir Francis; Yeo-Thomas, Forest Frederick.

Some Went West. Dorothy M. Johnson. Dodd, 1965 (o.p.) (JOB)
Alderson, Nannie; Bird, Isabella Lucy; Custer, Elizabeth Bacon; German sisters (Addie, Catherine, Julia, Sophia); Kelly, Fanny; Mercer, Asa Shinn; Owens-Adair, Bethenia; Parker, Cynthia Ann; Plummer, Electa; Sanders, Harriet; Sisters of Charity of Providence; Slade, Maria Virginia; Snyder, Grace; Walker, Mary Richardson; Weldon, Catherine.

Sons of Liberty. Felix Sutton. Messner, 1969 (o.p.) (SUL)
Adams, Samuel; Hancock, John; Henry, Patrick; Revere, Paul; Warren, Joseph.

Soong Sisters. Roby Eunson. Watts, 1975 (o.p.) (EUA)
Chiang Mei-ling; Kung, Ai-ling Sung; Sun Ch'ing-ling.

Special Bravery. Johanna Johnston. Dodd, 1967 (o.p.) (JOC)
Anderson, Marian; Attucks, Crispus; Banneker, Benjamin; Bethune, Mary McLeod; Brown, Henry "Box"; Bunche, Ralph Johnson; Carver, George Washington; Douglass, Frederick; Forten, James; Henson, Matthew Alexander; King, Martin Luther, Jr.; Robinson, Jackie; Smalls, Robert; Tubman, Harriet; Washington, Booker Taliaferro.

Spectaculars. Gene Klinger. Reilly & Lee, 1971 (o.p.) (KLD)
Barnum, Phineas Taylor; Fields, W. C.; Grock, pseud.; Houdin, Jean Eugène Robert; Houdini, Harry; Rice, Daniel McLaren, Jr.; Ringling Brothers (John, Otto, Charles, Alfred T. and Albert C.).

Speed Kings of the Base Paths: Baseball's Greatest Runners. Ray Robinson. Putnam, 1964 (o.p.) (ROC)
Aparicio, Luis; Carey, Max; Cobb, Ty; Collins, Eddie; Martin, Pepper; Mays, Willie Howard; Reiser, Pete; Robinson, Jackie; Wills, Maury.

Speed Kings: World's Fastest Humans. Irwin Stambler. Doubleday, 1973 (o.p.) (ST-1)
Campbell, Donald Malcolm; Cheng, Chi; Gabelich, Gary; Garlits, Don; Gould, Shane Elizabeth; Hayes, Bob; Knight, William "Pete"; Meiffret, Jose; Rayborn, Calvin; Ryun, Jim; Spitz, Mark; Unser, Bobby.

Speedmakers: Great Race Drivers. David J. Abodaher. Messner, 1979 (o.p.) (ABB)
Andretti, Mario; Brabham, Jack; Fangio, Juan Manuel; Fittipaldi, Emerson; Foyt, Anthony Joseph; Hill, Phil; Hulme, Dennis Clive; Hunt, James; Lauda, Niki; Moss, Stirling; Stewart, Jackie; Surtees, John.

Sport Magazine's All-Time Stars. Tom Murray, ed. Atheneum, 1977 (o.p.) (MUC)
Aaron, Hank; Campanella, Roy; Carew, Rod; Cobb, Ty; Cronin, Joe; Dickey, Bill; Di Maggio, Joseph Paul; Ford, Whitey; Gehrig, Lou; Hornsby, Rogers; Johnson, Walter Perry; Koufax, Sandy; Mathewson, Christy; Mays, Willie Howard; Musial, Stanley Frank; Ott, Mel; Robinson, Brooks Calbert; Ruth, Babe; Terry, William Harold; Traynor, Pie; Wagner, Honus; Williams, Ted.

Sports Heroes Who Wouldn't Quit. Hal Butler. Messner, 1973 (o.p.) (BUJA)
Armstrong, Henry; Bearden, Gene; Cousy, Bob; Cunningham, Glenn; Ederle, Gertrude C.; Gray, Pete; Hogan, Ben; Howe, Gordie; McCreary, Conn; Mantle, Mickey Charles; Robinson, Jackie; Schoendienst, Red; Seaver, Tom; Unitas, Johnny; Venturi, Ken; Walker, Doak.

Sports Immortals. Associated Press Sports Staff. P-H, 1972 (o.p.) (ASBA)
Aaron, Hank; Abdul-Jabbar, Kareem; Ali, Muhammad; Arcaro, Eddie; Bannister, Roger Gilbert; Baugh, Sammy; Butkus, Dick; Chamberlain, Wilt; Cobb, Ty; Cousy, Bob; Dempsey, Jack; Didrikson, Babe; Di Maggio, Joseph Paul; Foyt, Anthony Joseph; Frazier, Joe; Gonzales, Pancho; Grange, Red; Henie, Sonja; Hogan, Ben; Howe, Gordie; Hull, Bobby; Johnson, Walter Perry; Jones, Bobby; Laver, Rodney George; Louis, Joe; Marciano, Rocky; Mays, Willie Howard; Mikan, George L.; Nagurski, Bronko; Namath, Joe Willie; Nicklaus, Jack; Nurmi, Paavo; Orr, Bobby; Owens, Jesse; Paige, Satchel; Palmer, Arnold; Pelé; Richard, Maurice; Robinson, Ray; Russell, William Felton; Shaw, Wilbur; Shoemaker, Willie; Thorpe, Jim; Tilden, William Tatem, Jr.; Unitas, Johnny; Weissmuller, Johnny; Williams, Ted; Wills, Helen.

Sports of Our Presidents. John Durant. Hastings, 1964 (o.p.) (DUB)
Adams, John; Adams, John Quincy; Cleveland, Grover; Coolidge, Calvin; Eisenhower, Dwight David; Grant, Ulysses Simpson; Harding, Warren Gamaliel; Hoover, Herbert Clark; Jackson, Andrew; Jefferson, Thomas; Johnson, Lyndon Baines; Kennedy, John Fitzgerald; Lincoln, Abraham; Madison, James†; Monroe, James†; Roosevelt, Franklin Delano; Roosevelt, Theodore; Taft, William Howard; Truman, Harry S.†; Washington, George; Wilson, Woodrow.

Sports Titans of the Twentieth Century. Al Silverman. Putnam, 1968 (o.p.) (SID)
Brown, Jim; Cobb, Ty; Cousy, Bob; Dempsey, Jack; Didrikson, Babe; Grange, Red; Mays, Willie Howard; Owens, Jesse; Richard, Maurice; Ruth, Babe; Thorpe, Jim; Tilden, William Tatem, Jr.

Spy Who Never Was and Other True Spy Stories. David C. Knight. Doubleday, 1978 (o.p.) (KN)
Abel, Rudolf Ivanovich; Darragh, Lydia B.; Dickinson, Velvalee; Edmonds, Sarah Emma; Hale, Nathan; Mata Hari; Ortiz, Peter J.; Powers, Francis Gary; Scotland, Alexander.

Stalwart Men of Early Texas. Edith McCall. Childrens, 1970 (o.p.) (LYF)
Austin, Moses; Austin, Stephen Fuller; Bowie, James; Cabeza de Vaca, Álvar Núñez; Crockett, Davy; Houston, Samuel; La Salle, Robert Cavelier, sieur de.

Star Pass Receivers of the N.F.L. John Devaney. Random, 1972 (o.p.) (DEHA)
Abramowicz, Daniel; Alworth, Lance; Berry, Raymond; Biletnikoff, Frederick; Hayes, Bob; Maynard, Don; Sanders, Charlie; Taylor, Otis; Warfield, Paul.

Star Pitchers of the Major Leagues. Bill Libby. Random, 1971 (o.p.) (LEZ)
Bunning, Jim; Drysdale, Don; Gibson, Bob; McDowell, Sam; McLain, Dennis; Maloney, Jim; Marichal, Juan; Seaver, Tom; Wilhelm, James Hoyt.

Star Quarterbacks of the N.F.L. Bill Libby. Random, 1970 (o.p.) (LEZA)
Cook, Greg; Dawson, Lenny; Gabriel, Roman; Griese, Bob; Jurgensen, Sonny; Kapp, Joe; Lamonica, Daryle Pat; Morton, Craig; Namath, Joe Willie; Nelson, Bill.

Star Running Backs of the N.F.L. Bill Libby. Random, 1971 (LEZB)
Anderson, Donny; Bass, Dick; Brown, Larry; Csonka, Larry; Dixon, Hewritt; Farr, Mel; Garrett, Michael Lockett; Haymond, Alvin Henry; Hill, Calvin; Johnson, Ronald Adolphus; Kelly, Leroy; Kiick, Jim; Lane, MacArthur; Little, Floyd Douglas; Nance, Jim; Post, Dick; Sayers, Gale; Simpson, O. J.; Snell, Matthew†; Thomas, Duane; Willard, Ken.

Stars of Pro Basketball. Lou Sabin & Dave Sendler. Random, 1970 (SA)
Abdul-Jabbar, Kareem; Cunningham, Billy; Frazier, Walt; Havlicek, John; Hawkins, Connie; Hayes, Elvin; Haywood, Spencer; Hudson, Lou; Walker, Jimmy.

Stars of the Major Leagues. Dave Klein. Random, 1974 (KLCA)
Bench, Johnny Lee; Bonds, Bobby Lee; Cedeño, Cesar; Colbert, Nathan; Fisk, Carlton; Hunter, Catfish; Jenkins, Ferguson Arthur; Mayberry, John Claiborn; Murcer, Bobby.

Stars of the Modern Olympics. Ann Finlayson. Garrard, 1967 (o.p.) (FIC)
Carvaljal, Felix; Ewry, Ray C.; Garrett, Robert; Kahanamoku, Duke Paoa; Nurmi, Paavo; Thorpe, Jim.

Stars of the Olympics. Bill Libby. Hawthorn, 1975 (o.p.) (LEYB)
Albright, Tenley†; Ali, Muhammad†; Bayi, Filbert†; Bikila, Abebe; Bragg, Don†; Button, Dick; Cochran, Barbara Ann†; Crabbe, Buster†; Crockett, Ivory†; Decker, Mary†; DeMont, Rick†; Didrikson, Babe; Dillard, Harrison; Ewry, Ray C.†; Feuerbach, Allan†; Fleming, Peggy; Fraser, Gretchen Kunigk; Gable, Dan†; Henie, Sonja†; Henning, Anne†; Holm, Eleanor†; Holum, Dianne†; Johnson, Rafer; Kahanamoku, Duke Paoa†; Keino, Kipchoge†; Killy, Jean-Claude†; King, Micki†; Kinmont, Jill†; Kraenzlein, Alvin†; Kubica, Terry†; Larrieu, Francie†; Lawrence, Andrea Mead; Leonard, "Sugar" Ray Charles†; Liquori, Marty†; Loues, Spiridon†; Mathias, Bob; Meyer, Deborah; Mills, Billy; Mimoun, Alain†; Nurmi, Paavo; Oerter, Al†; Owens, Jesse; Patterson, Floyd; Pietri, Dorando†; Prefontaine, Steve R.†; Puttemans, Emiel†; Rudolph, Wilma G.; Ryun, Jim; Sailer, Toni†; Schollander, Donald Arthur; Shorter, Frank; Snell, Peter†; Spitz, Mark; Stones, Dwight†; Thorpe, Jim; Toomey, Bill; Von Saltza, Susan Christina†; Waldrop, Tony†; Weissmuller, Johnny; Wohlhuter, Rick†; Woods, George†; Wottle, Dave; Zatopek, Emil.

Stars of the Series: A Complete History of the World Series. Joseph Gies & Robert H. Shoemaker. T Y Crowell, 1964 (o.p.) (GIB)
Adams, Babe; Alexander, Grover Cleveland; Bauer, Hank; Berra, Yogi; Brecheen, Harry; Burdette, Lew; Dean, Dizzy; Ford, Whitey; Gehrig, Lou; Gowdy, Hank; Koufax, Sandy; Larsen, Don; Mack, Connie; Martin, Billy†; Martin, Pepper; Mathewson, Christy; Mays, Willie Howard; Mazeroski, Bill; Reynolds, Allie; Rizzuto, Philip Francis; Ruth, Babe; Sherry, Larry; Slaughter, Country; Snider, Duke; Stengel, Casey†.

Stars of the Ziegfeld Follies. Julien Phillips. Lerner, 1972 (o.p.) (PHA)
Brice, Fanny; Cantor, Eddie; Fields, W. C.; Held, Anna; Miller, Marilyn; Rogers, Will; Sandow, Eugene; Williams, Bert; Ziegfeld, Florenz.

Stars on Ice. Elizabeth Van Steenwyk. Dodd, 1980 (VAD-6)
Allen, Lisa-Marie; Babilonia, Tai; Beauchamp, Bobby; Blumberg, Judy; Chin, Tiffany†; Cramer, Scott; Curry, John; deLeeuw, Diane; Fratianne, Linda; Gardner, Randy; Hamilton, Scott; Lynn, Janet; Santee, David; Santee, James; Seibert, Mike; Shelley, Ken; Smith, Stacy; Starbuck, Jo Jo; Summers, John; Tickner, Charles; Zayak, Elaine.

State Makers. Bill Severn & Sue Severn. Putnam, 1963 (o.p.) (SEC)
Bibb, William Wyatt; Brown, John; Bulloch, Archibald; Call, Richard Keith; Chittenden, Thomas; Claiborne, William Charles; Connor, Patrick Edward; Conway, James Sevier; Curry, George; Dodge, Henry; Evans, John; Farrington, Wallace; Gruening, Ernest Henry; Hamilton, Alexander; Harrison, William Henry; Haskell, Charles Nathaniel; Holmes, David; Houston, Samuel; Hunt, George Wylie; Iredell, James; Johnson, Thomas; Jones, George Wallace; King, William; Langdon, John; Livingston, William; McNair, Alexander; Marquette, Turner; Mason, Stevens Thomson; Meek, Joseph L.; Mellette, Arthur; Mifflin, Thomas; Nye, James Warren; Parsons, Theophilus; Pierpont, Francis Harrison; Pinckney, Charles; Randolph, Edmund Jennings; Riley, Bennet; Robinson, Charles; Rodney, Caesar; Sevier, John; Shelby, Isaac; Shoup, George; Sibley, Henry Hastings; Spalding, Burleigh Folsom; Squire, Watson; Thomas, Jesse Burgess; Toole, Joseph; Trumbull, Jonathan; Warren, Francis; Worthington, Thomas.

Stolen by the Indians. Dorothy Heiderstadt. McKay, 1968 (o.p.) (HEE)
Brayton, Matthew; Brown, Joseph; Brown, Thomas; Jemison, Mary; Jones, Horatio; Leining, Regina; Parker, Cynthia Ann; Slocum, Fanny; Spencer, Oliver; Tanner, John; Wheelwright, Esther; Williams, Eunice.

Stories of Champions. Sam Epstein & Beryl Epstein. Garrard, 1965 (o.p.) (EPA)
Cobb, Ty; Johnson, Walter Perry; Mathewson, Christy; Ruth, Babe; Wagner, Honus.

Stories of Courage. Cleodie Mackinnon. Watts, 1966 (o.p.) (MAJ)
Alexander Nevski; Alfred the Great; Anderson, Elizabeth Garrett; Barlass, Kate; Beethoven, Ludwig van; Bruce, Robert the; Campion, Edmund; Caractacus; Cavell, Edith; Cranmer, Thomas; Curie, Marie Sklodowska; Damien de Veuster, Joseph; Darling, Grace Horsley; Garibaldi, Giuseppe; Hannibal; Joan of Arc; John III Sobieski; Keller, Helen Adams; Leonidas I; MacDonald, Flora; Montrose, James Graham, 5th earl and 1st marquis of; More, Sir Thomas; Nelson, Horatio, viscount; Peter; Shackleton, Sir Ernest Henry; Socrates; Thomas à Becket; Toussaint L'Ouverture, Pierre Dominigue; Verchères, Marie Magdelaine Jarret de; Verney, Edmund; William I, the Silent; Wolfe, James.

Stories of Famous Explorers by Land. Frank Knight. Westminster, 1965 (o.p.) (KNA)
Aguirre, Lope de; Alexander III, the Great; Amundsen, Roald†; Balboa, Vasco Núñez de; Carpini, Giovanni de Piano; Champlain, Samuel de; Cortes, Hernando; Covilham, Peter de; Fawcett, Percy Harrison; Francis Xavier; Fuchs, Sir Vivian Ernest†; Humboldt, Alexander von; Kingsley, Mary Henrietta; La Salle, Robert Cavelier, sieur de; Leichhardt, Friedrich Wilhelm; Livingstone, David; MacKenzie, Sir Alexander; Park, Mungo; Pizarro, Francisco; Polo, Marco; Raleigh, Sir Walter†; Scott, Robert Falcon†; Shackleton, Sir Ernest Henry; Thompson, David.

Stories of Famous Explorers by Sea. Frank Knight. Westminster, 1964 (o.p.) (KNB)
Amundsen, Roald†; Barents, Willem; Bass, George†; Bering, Vitus J.; Cabot, John; Chancellor, Richard; Columbus, Christopher; Cook, James; Dampier, William; Eric the Red; Flinders, Matthew; Franklin, Sir John; Frobisher, Sir Martin; Henry the Navigator; Hudson, Henry; La Pérouse, Jean François de Galaup, comte de†; Magellan, Ferdinand; Mendana de Neyra, Álvaro de; Nansen, Fridtjof†; Nordenskjöld, Nils Adolf; Parry, Sir William Edward†; Peary, Robert Edwin†; Pytheas; Tasman, Abel J.†; Vancouver, George†; Vespucci, Amerigo.

Story behind Popular Songs. Elizabeth Rider Montgomery. Dodd, 1958 (o.p.) (MOA)
Ager, Milton; Ball, Ernest; Berlin, Irving; Bland, James A.; Brown, Nacio Herb; Burke, Johnny; Caesar, Irving†; Carmichael, Hoagy; Cobb, Will†; Cohan, George Michael; Conrad, Con; Dietz, Howard†; Dillon, Will†; Dixon, Mort†; Donaldson, Walter; Dubin, Al; Edwards, Gus; Egan, Raymond B.†; Ellington, Duke; Fields, Dorothy†; Foster, Stephen Collins; Friml, Rudolf; Gershwin, George; Gershwin, Ira†; Hammerstein, Oscar, II; Handy, William Christopher; Harbach, Otto; Henderson, Ray; Herbert, Victor; Jacobs-Bond, Carrie; Kalmar, Bert; Kern, Jerome; Loesser, Frank; McHugh, Jimmy; Murphy, Stanley†; Porter, Cole; Rodgers, Richard Charles; Romberg, Sigmund; Rose, Billy†; Ruby, Harry; Schwartz, Arthur; Van Alstyne, Egbert; Van Heusen, Jimmy; Von Tilzer, Albert†; Von Tilzer, Harry; Warren, Harry; Wenrich, Percy; Whiting, Richard A.; Williams, Harry†; Yellen, Jack; Youmans, Vincent.

Story-Lives of American Composers. Katherine L. Bakeless. Lippincott, rev. ed., 1962 (o.p.) (BAD)
Barber, Samuel; Berlin, Irving; Carpenter, John Alden; Copland, Aaron; Foster, Stephen Collins; Gershwin, George; Griffes, Charles Tomlinson; Handy, William Christopher; Harris, Roy Ellsworth; Herbert, Victor; Ives, Charles; Kern, Jerome; MacDowell, Edward Alexander; Nevin, Ethelbert W.; Piston, Walter; Rodgers, Richard Charles; Schuman, William; Sousa, John Philip; Taylor, Deems.

Story-Lives of Great Composers. Katherine L. Bakeless. Lippincott, rev. ed., 1962 (BAE)
Bizet, Georges; Borodin, Alexander P.; Dvořak, Antonin; Elgar, Sir Edward William; Gounod, Charles François; Humperdinck, Engelbert; Massenet, Jules; Mussorgsky, Modest Petrovich; Puccini, Giacomo; Purcell, Henry; Rachmaninoff, Sergei; Rimski-Korsakov, Nikolai Andreevich; Rossini, Gioacchino; Scarlatti, Alessandro; Sibelius, Jean; Smetana, Bedřich; Strauss, Richard; Stravinsky, Igor Fëdorovich; Sullivan, Sir Arthur Seymour.

Story-Lives of Master Artists. Anna C. Chandler. Lippincott, rev. ed., 1953 (o.p.) (CHC)
Abbey, Edwin Austin; Carot, Jean Baptiste; Dürer, Albrecht; Gainsborough, Thomas; Giotto di Bondone; Greco, El; Hals, Frans; Homer, Winslow; Leonardo da Vinci; Lippi, Fra Pilippo; Michelangelo Buonarroti; Millet, Jean François; Raphael; Rembrandt Hermanszoon van Rijn; Reynolds, Sir Joshua; Rubens, Peter Paul; Stuart, Gilbert; Van Dyck, Sir Anthony; Velázquez, Diego Rodríguez de Silva y; Vermeer, Jan or Johannes; Whistler, James Abbott McNeill.

Story-Lives of Master Musicians. Harriette Brower. Ayer repr. of 1922 facsimile ed. (BRF)
Bach, Johann Sebastian; Beethoven, Ludwig van; Berlioz, Hector; Brahms, Johannes; Chopin, Frédéric François; Debussy, Claude Achille; Franck, César Auguste; Gluck, Christoph Willibald; Grieg, Edvard Hagerup; Handel, George Frederick; Haydn, Franz Joseph; Liszt, Franz; MacDowell, Edward Alexander; Mendelssohn, Felix; Mozart, Wolfgang Amadeus; Palestrina, Giovanni Pierluigi da; Schubert, Franz Peter; Schumann, Robert Alexander; Tchaikovsky, Peter Ilyich; Verdi, Giuseppe; Wagner, Richard; Weber, Karl Maria Friedrich Ernst von.

Story of the Presidents of the United States. Maud Petersham & Miska Petersham. Macmillan, rev. ed., 1966 (o.p.) (PED)
See listing under *America and Its Presidents* by Earl S. Miers.

Super Champions of Auto Racing. Ross R. Olney. Clarion, 1984 (OLDD)
Jones, Alan; Mears, Rick; Mears, Roger; Meyer, Billy; Shuman, Ron; Waltrip, Darrell.

Super Champions of Ice Hockey. Ross R. Olney. Clarion, 1982 (OLDE)
Bossy, Mike; Craig, Jim; Dionne, Marcel; Esposito, Phil; Gretzky, Wayne; La Fleur, Guy Damien; Potvin, Denis Charles.

Super Showmen. Bennett Wayne, ed. Garrard, 1974 (WAO)
Disney, Walt; Houdini, Harry; Rogers, Will.

Superdrivers: Three Auto Racing Champions. Bill Libby. Garrard, 1977 (LEYC)
Garlits, Don; Petty, Lee; Ward, Rodger.

Superstars of Auto Racing. Ross Olney. Putnam, 1975 (o.p.) (OLCB)
Donohue, Mark; Fittipaldi, Emerson; Follmer, George; Foyt, Anthony Joseph; Garlits, Don; Johncock, Gordon; McCluskey, Robert; Petty, Richard; Revson, Peter Jeffrey; Scheckter, Jody; Stewart, Jackie.

Superstars of Country Music. Gene Busnar. Messner, 1984 (BUIB-01)
Cash, Johnny; Lewis, Jerry Lee; Lynn, Loretta; Nelson, Willie; Parton, Dolly; Pride, Charley; Rogers, Kenny; Williams, Hank; Wynette, Tammy.

Superstars of Rock: Their Lives and Music. Gene Busnar. Messner, 1980 (BUIB-1)
Clapton, Eric; Franklin, Aretha; Gibb, Barry; Gibb, Maurice; Gibb, Robin; Harrison, George; Hendrix, Jimi; Jagger, Mick; John, Elton; Joplin, Janis; Lennon, John; McCartney, Paul; Presley, Elvis; Richards, Keith; Starr, Ringo; Summer, Donna; Wonder, Stevie.

Superstars of Rock Two. Gene Busnar. Messner, 1984 (BUIB-2)
Bowie, David; Daltrey, Roger; Entwistle, John; Jackson, Michael; Mercury, Freddie; Moon, Keith; Morrison, Jim; Ronstadt, Linda; Ross, Diana; Springsteen, Bruce; Townshend, Peter.

Superstars of the Sports World. Bill Gutman. Messner, 1978 (o.p.) (GUH)
Clarke, Bobby; Erving, Julius; Evert, Chris; Harris, Franco; Rose, Pete.

Superstars of Women's Track. George Sullivan. Dodd, 1981 (SUDB)
Ashford, Evelyn; Decker, Mary; Manning, Madeline; Shea, Julie; Waitz, Grete; Young, Candy.

Superstars Stopped Short. Nathan Aaseng. Lerner, 1982 (AAS-24)
Bostock, Lyman; Cheng, Chi; Gibson, Josh; Hart, Eddie; Hawkins, Connie; Roth, Joe; Stingley, Darryl; Witte, Luke.

Superstars: Hockey's Greatest Players. Andy O'Brien. McGraw, 1973 (o.p.) (OBB)
Beliveau, Jean; Bucyk, John Paul; Clancy, King; Esposito, Phil; Gilbert, Rod; Harvey, Douglas; Howe, Gordie; Hull, Bobby; Lindsay, Ted; McKenzie, John Albert; Mahovlich, Frank; Mikita, Stan; Morenz, Howie; Orr, Bobby; Park, Brad; Plante, Jacques; Richard, Maurice; Sawchuk, Terry; Shore, Edward William.

Supersubs of Pro Sports. Nathan Aaseng. Lerner, 1983 (AAS-25)
Bridgeman, Junior; Giammona, Louie; Hill, Calvin; Jones, Bobby; Lurtsema, Bob; Mota, Manny; Unser, Del; Young, Wilbur.

Swords, Stars and Bars. Lee McGiffin. Dutton, 1958 (o.p.) (MAD)
Butler, Matthew Calbraith; Forrest, Nathan Bedford; Hampton, Wade; Morgan, John Hunt; Mosby, John Singleton; Shelby, Joseph Orville; Stuart, James Ewell Brown; Wheeler, Joseph.

Symphony Conductors of the U.S.A. Hope Stoddard. T Y Crowell, 1957 (o.p.) (STM)
Abravanel, Maurice; Allesandro, Victor; Beinum, Eduard van; Bernstein, Leonard; Dorati, Antal; Freccia, Massimo; Golschmann, Vladimir; Harrison, Guy Fraser; Hendl, Walter; Hilsberg, Alexander; Johnson, Thor; Jorda, Enrique; Krips, Josef; Leinsdorf, Erich; Mitchell, Howard; Mitropoulos, Dimitri; Monteux, Pierre; Munch, Charles; Ormandy, Eugene; Paray, Paul; Reiner, Fritz; Schwieger, Hans; Solomon, Izler; Sopkin, Henry; Steinberg, William; Stokowski, Leopold; Swalin, Benjamin; Szell, George; Wallenstein, Alfred; Walter, Bruno; Whitney, Robert.

Taken by the Indians: True Tales of Captivity. Alice Dickinson. Watts, 1976 (o.p.) (DI)
Huerta, Dolores; Jemison, Mary; Jewitt, John R.; Kelly, Fanny; Rowlandson, Mary; Smith, James; Tanner, John.

Tales of the Elders: A Memory Book of Men and Women Who Came to America as Immigrants, 1900–1930. Carol Ann Bales. Follett, 1977 (o.p.) (BAEA-1)
Edgren, Edith Svensson; Gamberg, Abe; Gonzalez, Natividad Martinez; Gordon, Morris; Goulding, Denis; McArthur, Lachlan; Rzewska, Josepha Rozanka; Sorrentino, Anthony; Thiel, George; Thiel, Katie Kamp; Uchida, Miki Akiyama; Yiannopoulos, Andrew.

Talking Clowns: From Laurel and Hardy to the Marx Brothers. Frank Manchel. Watts, 1976 (o.p.) (MAOB)
Fields, W. C.; Hardy, Oliver; Laurel, Stan; Marx, Chico; Marx, Groucho; Marx, Gummo†; Marx, Harpo; Marx, Zeppo†; West, Mae.

Teenagers Who Made History. Russell Freedman. Holiday, 1961 (o.p.) (FRB)
Braille, Louis; Colt, Samuel; Didrikson, Babe; Galilei, Galileo; Lafayette, Marie Joseph Paul Yves Roch Gilbert du Motier, marquis de; Millay, Edna St. Vincent; Toscanini, Arturo; Von Braun, Wernher.

Telescope Makers: From Galileo to the Space Age. Barbara Land. T Y Crowell, 1968 (o.p.) (LAA)
Fraunhofer, Joseph von; Friedman, Herbert; Galilei, Galileo; Hale, George Ellery; Herschel,

Sir William; Kepler, Johannes; Lippershey, Hans†; Newton, Sir Isaac; Parsons, William, 3d
earl of Rosse; Reber, Grote; Schmidt, Bernhard V.

Ten Africans. Margery Perham, ed. Northwestern Univ. Pr., 2d ed., 1964 (o.p.) (PEA)
Amini bin Saidi; Bwembya; Coka, Gilbert; Kayamba, Mdumi Martin; Mockerie, Parmenas;
Moore, Kofoworola Aina; Ndansi Kumalo; Nosente; Rashid bin Hassani; Udo Akpabio.

Ten Brave Men. Sonia Daugherty. Lippincott, 1951 (o.p.) (DAC)
Adams, Samuel; Bradford, William; Franklin, Benjamin; Henry, Patrick; Jackson, Andrew;
Jefferson, Thomas; Jones, John Paul; Lincoln, Abraham; Washington, George; Williams,
Roger.

Ten Brave Women. Sonia Daugherty. Lippincott, 1953 (o.p.) (DAD)
Adams, Abigail; Anthony, Susan Brownell; Dix, Dorothea Lynde; Howe, Julia Ward; Hutchin-
son, Anne Marbury; Lyon, Mary; Madison, Dolley Payne Todd; Roosevelt, Eleanor; Tarbell,
Ida Minerva; Whitman, Narcissa.

Ten Famous Lives. Plutarch. Revised by Arthur Hugh Clough. Further revised for young
readers by Charles A. Robinson, Jr. Dutton, 1962 (o.p.) (PLA)
Alcibiades; Alexander III, the Great; Antony, Mark; Caesar, Gaius Julius; Cato, Marcus
Porcius; Cicero, Marcus Tullius; Demosthenes; Fabius; Pericles; Themistocles.

Ten Heroes of the Twenties. Rex Lardner. Putnam, 1966 (o.p.) (LAC)
Byrd, Richard Evelyn; Darrow, Clarence Seward; Dempsey, Jack; Earhart, Amelia; Gersh-
win, George; Hemingway, Ernest; Hoover, J. Edgar; Lindbergh, Charles Augustus; Mitchell,
William; Ruth, Babe.

Ten Saints. Eleanor Farjeon. Walck, 1936 (o.p.) (FAD)
Brigid of Kildare; Christopher; Dorothea; Francis of Assisi; Giles; Hubert; Martin of Tours;
Nicholas; Patrick; Simeon Stylites.

Ten Tall Texans. Daniel James Kubiak. Naylor, rev. ed., 1970 (o.p.) (KUA)
Austin, Stephen Fuller; Bowie, James; Candelaria, Andrea Castanon; Crockett, Davy; Hous-
ton, Samuel; Milam, Ben; Navarro, José Antonio; Seguin, Juan N.; Travis, William Barret;
Zavala, Lorenzo de.

Ten Who Dared. Desmond Wilcox. Little, 1977 (o.p.) (WIA-1)
Amundsen, Roald; Burke, Robert O'Hara; Columbus, Christopher; Cook, James; Doughty,
Charles Montagu; Humboldt, Alexander von; Kingsley, Mary Henrietta; Pizarro, Francisco;
Smith, Jedediah Strong; Stanley, Sir Henry Morton; Wills, William John†.

Tennis: Great Stars, Great Moments. Andrew Lawrence. Putnam, 1976 (o.p.) (LAHA)
Ashe, Arthur; Budge, Don; Cawley, Evonne Goolagong; Connors, Jimmy; Evert, Chris;
Gonzales, Pancho; King, Billie Jean; Laver, Rodney George; Lenglen, Suzanne; Rosewall,
Ken; Tilden, William Tatem, Jr.; Wills, Helen.

Tenors. Herbert H. Breslin, ed. Macmillan, 1974 (o.p.) (BRBB-1)
Corelli, Franco; Domingo, Placido; Pavarotti, Luciano; Tucker, Richard; Vickers, Jon.

Their Eyes Are on the Stars: Four Black Writers. Margaret G. Clark. Garrard, 1973 (CL)
Brown, William Wells; Chesnutt, Charles Waddell; Hammon, Jupiter; Horton, George
Moses.

*These Are My People: A Treasury of Biographies of Heroes of the Jewish Spirit from
Abraham to Leo Black.* Harry Gersh. Behrman, 1959 (o.p.) (GEF)
Aaron of Tulchin; Abraham; Akiba ben Joseph; Ashi; Baeck, Leo; Bialik, Chaim Nachman;
Brandeis, Louis Dembitz; Cresques Lo Juheu; David; Deborah; Einstein, Albert; Elijah;
Ezra; Goldberger, Joseph; Goode, Alexander David; Grossman, Noam; Haffkine, Waldemar
Mordecai; Hillel; Israel ben Eliezer (Baal Shem Tov); Jeremiah; Johanan ben Zakkai;
Josselman of Rosheim; Judah ben Babba; Judah ha-Levi; Krotoshinsky, Abraham; Levi,
Yitzhok; Levy, Uriah Phillips; Maimonides; Mattathias; Meir ben Baruch of Rothenburg;
Moses; Nehemiah; Nones, Benjamin; Orlean, Judah Leib; Peretz, Isaac Leib; Philo Judaeus;
Rashi; Salanter, Israel; Salomons, Sir David; Samuel ibn Adiya; Senesh, Hannah; Shammai;

Slotin, Louis Alexander; Vladeck, Baruch Charney; Weizmann, Chaim; Wise, Stephen Samuel; Yechiel of Paris; Yom Tov ben Isaac.

They Came from Germany: The Stories of Famous German-Americans. Dieter Cunz. Dodd, 1966 (o.p.) (CUB)
Astor, John Jacob; Follen, Charles Theodore; Mergenthaler, Ottmar; Nast, Thomas; Roebling, John Augustus; Schurz, Carl; Steuben, Friedrich Wilhelm von; Von Braun, Wernher; Zenger, John Peter.

They Came from Italy: The Stories of Famous Italian-Americans. Barbara Marinacci. Dodd, 1967 (o.p.) (MAS)
Brumidi, Constantino; Cabrini, Frances Xavier; Cesnola, Luigi Palma di; Fermi, Enrico; Giannini, Amadeo Peter; La Guardia, Fiorello Henry; Mazzei, Philip; Tonti, Henri de; Toscanini, Arturo.

They Came from Poland: The Stories of Famous Polish-Americans. Laura Pilarski. Dodd, 1969 (o.p.) (PIAA)
Funk, Casimir; Gronouski, John Austin; Kosciusko, Tadeusz; Modjeska, Helena; Musial, Stanley Frank; Muskie, Edmund S.; Nowicki, Matthew; Paderewski, Ignace Jan; Pulaski, Casimir; Rubinstein, Artur; Sadowski, Anthony.

They Changed the World: The Lives of Forty-four Great Men and Women. Bernard Garfinkel. Platt, 1973 (o.p.) (FRE)
Alexander III, the Great; Armstrong, Neil A.; Babbage, Charles; Beethoven, Ludwig van; Bell, Alexander Graham; Braille, Louis; Buddha; Carson, Rachel; Carver, George Washington; Churchill, Sir Winston Leonard Spencer; Crick, Francis H. C.†; Curie, Marie Sklodowska; Daguerre, Louis Jacques; Darwin, Charles Robert; Drew, Charles Richard; Edison, Thomas Alva; Einstein, Albert; Elizabeth I; Fermi, Enrico; Ford, Henry; Freud, Sigmund; Galilei, Galileo; Gandhi, Mohandas Karamchand; Gutenberg, Johann; Harvey, William; Jefferson, Thomas; Jesus Christ; Keller, Helen Adams; Luther, Martin; Marconi, Guglielmo; Marx, Karl Heinrich; Mohammed; Moses; Napoleon I; Newton, Sir Isaac; Nightingale, Florence; Pasteur, Louis; Picasso, Pablo; Polo, Marco; Rousseau, Jean Jacques; Shakespeare, William; Socrates; Watson, James Dewey†; Watt, James; Wright, Orville; Wright, Wilbur.

They Dared to Lead: America's Black Athletes. Phyllis Hollander & Zander Hollander. G&D, 1972 (o.p.) (HOBC)
Ali, Muhammad; Ashe, Arthur; Ashford, Emmett Littleton; Brown, Jim; Brown, Pete Earlie; Flood, Curtis Charles; Gibson, Althea; Johnson, Rafer; Mackey, John; Murphy, Isaac; Pollard, Frederick; Robinson, Jackie; Russell, William Felton.

They Explored! Rhoda Hoff & Helmut De Terra. Walck, 1959 (o.p.) (HOB)
Frémont, John Charles; Hedin, Sven Anders; Herzog, Maurice; Humboldt, Alexander von; Livingstone, David; Scott, Robert Falcon.

They Fought for Freedom and Other Stories: Heroes of Jewish History. Elma Ehrlich Levinger. UAHC, 1953 (o.p.) (LES)
Abravanel, Isaac; Benjamin of Tudela; Einstein, Albert; Herzl, Theodor; Hillel; Israel ben Eliezer (Baal Shem Tov); Johanan ben Zakkai; Josephus Flavius; Judah ha-Levi; Maccabees; Maimonides; Menasseh ben Israel; Mendesia, Gracia; Montefiore, Sir Moses; Rashi; Szold, Henrietta; Weizmann, Chaim.

They Gave Their Lives. L. Edmond Leipold. T. S. Denison, 1972 (o.p.) (LEPE)
Custer, George Armstrong; Kennedy, John Fitzgerald; King, Martin Luther, Jr.; Lincoln, Abraham; Lovejoy, Elijah Parish.

They Gave Their Names to Science. Daniel S. Halacy, Jr. Putnam, 1967 (o.p.) (HAC)
Buys-Ballot, Christoph Hendrik†; Carnot, Nicholas Léonard Sadi; Coriolis, Gaspard Gustave de; Doppler, Christian Johann; Geiger, Johannes Wilhelm; Mach, Ernst; Mendel, Gregor Johann; Mohorovicic, Andrija; Mössbauer, Rudolf Ludwig; Nobel, Alfred Bernhard; Van Allen, James Alfred.

They Grew Up to Be President. Rhoda Hoff. Doubleday, 1971 (o.p.) (HIH)
  See listing under *America and Its Presidents* by Earl S. Miers. Add: Nixon, Richard M.

They Led the Way. Johanna Johnston. Scholastic, 1987, pap. (JOCA)
  Adams, Abigail; Barton, Clara; Blackwell, Elizabeth; Bradstreet, Anne Dudley; Catt, Carrie Chapman; Cochrane, Elizabeth; Hutchinson, Anne Marbury; Moody, Lady Deborah; Rose, Ernestine Potowski; Stanton, Elizabeth Cady; Stowe, Harriet Beecher; Wheatley, Phillis; Willard, Emma Hart; Woodhull, Victoria.

They Loved the Land. Bennett Wayne, ed. Garrard, 1974 (WAP)
  Audubon, John James; Burbank, Luther; Carson, Rachel; Muir, John.

They Made a Revolution: 1776. Jules Archer. St. Martin, 1973 (o.p.) (ARAB)
  Adams, Abigail; Adams, John; Adams, Samuel; Franklin, Benjamin; Hancock, John; Henry, Patrick; Jefferson, Thomas; Paine, Thomas; Washington, George; Washington, Martha Dandridge.

They Showed the Way: Forty American Negro Leaders. Charlemae Rollins. T Y Crowell, 1964 (ROG)
  Abbott, Robert Sengstacke; Aldridge, Ira; Allen, Richard; Attucks, Crispus; Banneker, Benjamin; Barnett, Ida Wells; Beckwourth, James P.; Bethune, Mary McLeod; Carver, George Washington; Cinque, Joseph; Douglass, Frederick; Drew, Charles Richard; Du Bois, William Edward Burghardt; Dunbar, Paul Laurence; Gannet, Deborah Sampson; Garnet, Henry Highland; Grimké, Archibald Henry; Handy, William Christopher; Harper, Frances Ellen Watkins; Henson, Matthew Alexander; Johnson, James Weldon; Lewis, Edmonia; Matzeliger, Jan Ernst; Mulzac, Hugh Nathaniel; Pointe de Sable, Jean Baptiste; Pompey; Prosser, Gabriel; Rillieux, Norbert; Salem, Peter; Smalls, Robert; Tanner, Henry Ossawa; Tubman, Harriet; Turner, Nat; Walker, Maggie Lena; Washington, Booker Taliaferro; Wheatley, Phillis; Williams, Bert; Williams, Daniel Hale; Woodson, Carter Goodwin; Young, Charles.

They Stand Invincible: Men Who Are Reshaping Our World. Robert M. Bartlett. T Y Crowell, 1959 (o.p.) (BAF)
  Bhave, Vinoba; Compton, Arthur Holly; Hussein, Taha; Kagawa, Toyohiko; King, Martin Luther, Jr.; Lemkin, Raphael; Nansen, Odd; Paton, Alan; Pierre, Abbé; Schweitzer, Albert; Thadden-Trieglaff, Reinold von; Yen, James Yang-ch'u.

They Took Their Stand. Emma Gelders Sterne. Macmillan, 1968 (o.p.) (STG)
  Auld, Sophia; Braden, Anne; Fairfield, John; Grimké, Angelina Emily; Horton, Myles; Hunnicutt, James; Laurens, John; Ogden, Dunbar; Thomas, George Henry; Williams, Claude; Zellner, Robert.

They Triumphed over Their Handicaps. Joan Harries. Watts, 1981 (o.p.) (HAFA)
  Armas, Jay J.; Charles, Ray; Fry, Johnny; Kennedy, Edward M., Jr.; Miller, Kathy; O'Neil, Kitty.

They Were the First. Patrick Pringle. Roy, 1965 (o.p.) (PRC)
  Amundsen, Roald; Baird, John Logie; Bannister, Roger Gilbert; Columbus, Christopher; Cousteau, Jacques Yves; Edison, Thomas Alva; Gagarin, Yuri Alekseyevich; Hillary, Sir Edmund; Magellan, Ferdinand; Marconi, Guglielmo; Morton, William; Piccard, Auguste; Roentgen, Wilhelm; Rutherford, Ernest Rutherford, 1st baron; Tenzing, Norgay; Wright, Orville; Wright, Wilbur.

They Wouldn't Quit: Stories of Handicapped People. Ravina Gelfand & Letha Patterson. Lerner, 1962 (o.p.) (GEA)
  Capp, Al; Cunningham, Glenn; Daley, Buddy Leo; De Seversky, Alexander P.; Johnson, Wendell; Kellen, James; Kessel, Mary Hickman; Rudolph, Wilma G.; Seibert, Florence Barbara; Smith, Kate; Sweezo, William; Templeton, Alec; Thurber, James G.; Wittgenstein, Paul.

Three Against Slavery. Philip Spencer. Scholastic, 1972 (o.p.) (SPB)
  Douglass, Frederick; Garrison, William Lloyd; Vesey, Denmark.

Three Conquistadors: Cortes, Coronado, Pizarro. Shannon Garst. Messner, 1947 (o.p.) (GAA)
Coronado, Francisco Vásquez de; Cortes, Hernando; Pizarro, Francisco.

Three Dictators: Mussolini, Hitler, Stalin. Stephen King-Hall. Transatlantic, 1964 (o.p.)
(KIA)
Hitler, Adolf; Mussolini, Benito; Stalin, Joseph.

Three for Revolution. Burke Davis. HarBraceJ, 1975 (o.p.) (DAF-2)
Henry, Patrick; Jefferson, Thomas; Washington, George.

Three Jazz Greats. Bennett Wayne, ed. Garrard, 1973 (o.p.) (WAD)
Armstrong, Louis "Satchmo"; Basie, Count†; Bechet, Sidney†; Beiderbecke, Bix†; Christian,
Charles†; Coleman, Ornette†; Coltrane, John William†; Davis, Miles Dewey, Jr.†; Ellington,
Duke; Gillespie, Dizzy†; Goodman, Benny†; Handy, William Christopher; Hawkins, Cole-
man†; Henderson, Fletcher†; Hines, Earl Kenneth†; Holiday, Billie†; Jefferson, Lemon†;
Leadbelly†; Modern Jazz Quartet†; Monk, Theolonius†; Morton, "Jelly Roll"†; Oliver, Joe†;
Parker, Charlie†; Powell, Bud†; Rainey, Ma†; Smith, Bessie†; Tatum, Art†; Teagarden,
Jack†; Waller, Fats†; Young, Lester Willis†.

Three Who Dared. Tom Cohen. Doubleday, 1969 (o.p.) (COF)
Aronson, Henry M.; O'Neal, John; Weinberger, Eric.

Titans of Business. Leonard M. Fanning. Lippincott, 1964 (o.p.) (FAC)
Ford, Henry; Gompers, Samuel; Hamilton, Alexander; Lewis, John Llewellyn; Morgan, John
Pierpont; Rockefeller, John Davison; Sloan, Alfred Pritchard, Jr.

Titans of the American Stage: Edwin Forrest, the Booths, the O'Neills. Dale Shaw. West-
minster, 1971 (o.p.) (SHFA)
Booth, Edwin Thomas; Booth, John Wilkes; Booth, Junius Brutus; Forrest, Edwin; O'Neill,
Eugene Gladstone; O'Neill, James.

Track's Magnificent Milers. Nathan Aaseng. Lerner, 1981 (AAS-26)
Bannister, Roger Gilbert; Bayi, Filbert; Coe, Sebastian; Cunningham, Glenn; Decker, Mary;
Elliott, Herb; Keino, Kipchoge; Ovett, Steve; Ryun, Jim; Walker, John.

Trail Blazers of American History. Miriam E. Mason & William H. Cartwright. Ginn, 1966
(o.p.) (MAT)
Addams, Jane; Barton, Clara; Bell, Alexander Graham; Boone, Daniel; Bradford, William;
Carver, George Washington; Columbus, Christopher; Dodge, Grenville Mellen; Douglass,
Frederick; Edison, Thomas Alva; Ford, Henry; Franklin, Benjamin; Houston, Samuel; Hud-
son, Henry; Jefferson, Thomas; La Salle, Robert Cavelier, sieur de; Lee, Robert Edward;
Lincoln, Abraham; McCormick, Cyrus Hall; Mann, Horace; Penn, William; Serra, Junipero;
Smith, John; Washington, George; Whitman, Marcus; Whitman, Narcissa; Wright, Orville;
Wright, Wilbur.

Trail Blazers of Technology. Harland Manchester. Scribner, 1962 (o.p.) (MAP)
Davenport, Thomas; De Forest, Lee; Diesel, Rudolf C.; Goodyear, Charles; Lake, Simon;
Maxim, Hiram Percy†; Maxim, Sir Hiram Stevens; Maxim, Hudson; Nobel, Alfred Bernhard;
Sikorsky, Igor Ivan; Tesla, Nikola.

Trailblazers in American Arts. Norah Smaridge. Messner, 1971 (o.p.) (SMBA)
Anderson, Marian; Foster, Stephen Collins; Homer, Winslow; Longfellow, Henry Wadsworth; Twain, Mark, pseud.

Triple Crown Winners. Howard Liss. Messner, 1969 (o.p.) (LIC)
Gehrig, Lou; Mantle, Mickey Charles; Medwick, Ducky; Robinson, Frank; Williams, Ted;
Yastrzemski, Carl Michael.

True Escape and Survival Stories. Gurney Williams, III. Watts, 1977 (o.p.) (WIAA-5)
Bultema, John; Canessa, Roberto; Frankl, Viktor; Haise, Fred W.; Losier, Roger; Lovell,
James A., Jr.; Milley, Levi; Morris, John; Onoda, Hiroo; Parrado, Nando; Quinton, Stockwell;
Swigert, John L.

Truth Is My Country: Portraits of Eight New England Authors. Hilda White. Doubleday, 1971 (o.p.) (WHB)
Dickinson, Emily; Emerson, Ralph Waldo; Frost, Robert; Hawthorne, Nathaniel; Millay, Edna St. Vincent; Robinson, Edwin Arlington; Stowe, Harriet Beecher; Thoreau, Henry David.

Twelve at War: Great Photographers under Fire. Robert E. Hood. Putnam, 1967 (o.p.) (HOE)
Bourke-White, Margaret; Brady, Matthew B.; Capa, Robert; Cartier-Bresson, Henri; Duncan, David Douglas; Faas, Horst; Fenton, Roger; Hare, James Henry; Kertesz, André; Mydans, Carl; Seymour, David; Steichen, Edward.

Twelve Citizens of the World. Leonard S. Kenworthy. Doubleday, 1953 (o.p.) (KEE)
Bunche, Ralph Johnson; Ceresole, Pierre; Gandhi, Mohandas Karamchand; Kagawa, Toyohiko; Nansen, Fridtjof; Orr, John Boyd, 1st baron; Roosevelt, Eleanor; Sarmiento, Domingo Faustino; Schweitzer, Albert; Sun Yat-sen; Toscanini, Arturo; Wrede, Mathilda.

Twelve Great Philosophers. Howard Ozmon. Oddo, 1968 (o.p.) (OZA)
Aristotle; Descartes, René; Dewey, John; Hegel, Georg Wilhelm Friedrich; Kant, Immanuel; Locke, John; Plato; Russell, Bertrand Arthur William Russell, 3d earl; Socrates; Spinoza, Baruch or Benedict; Thomas Aquinas; Voltaire.

Twelve Pioneers of Science. Harry Sootin. Vanguard, 1960 (SOB)
Adams, John Couch; Becquerel, Antoine Henri; Darwin, Charles Robert; Davy, Sir Humphry; Dubois, Eugène; Henry, Joseph; Hertz, Heinrich Rudolf; Langley, Samuel Pierpont; Metchnikoff, Élie; Pascal, Blaise; Scheele, Karl Wilhelm; Volta, Alessandro, conte.

Twentieth Century Women of Achievement. Samuel Kostman. Rosen, 1976 (o.p.) (KOA)
Anderson, Marian; Bethune, Mary McLeod; Buck, Pearl S.; Curie, Marie Sklodowska; Eddy, Mary Baker; King, Billie Jean; Mead, Margaret; Meir, Golda; Sanger, Margaret; Steinem, Gloria.

Twenty Modern Americans. Alice C. Cooper & Charles A. Palmer, eds. HarBraceJ, 1942 (o.p.) (COKA)
Addams, Jane; Beebe, William; Buck, Pearl S.; Byrd, Richard Evelyn; Carver, George Washington; Chrysler, Walter Percy; Disney, Walt; Earhart, Amelia; Hoffman, Malvina; Holmes, Oliver Wendell, Jr.; Hoover, J. Edgar; Johnson, Martin Elmer; Johnson, Osa Helen; Mayo, Charles Horace; Mayo, William James; Menuhin, Yehudi; Rogers, Will; Steinmetz, Charles Proteus; Stout, William Bushnell; Wallace, Henry A.; White, William Allen; Wills, Helen.

Two for the Show: Great Comedy Teams. Lonnie Burr. Messner, 1979 (o.p.) (BUR-1)
Abbott, Bud; Allen, Gracie; Brooks, Mel; Burns, George; Burns, John Francis; Cheech; Chong, Tommy; Clair, Dick; Correll, Charles J.; Costello, Lou; Elliott, Bob; Fine, Larry; Gosden, Freeman; Goulding, Ray; Hardy, Oliver; Howard, Jerry; Howard, Moe; Howard, Samuel; Jordan, James Edward; Jordan, Marian Driscoll; Laurel, Stan; Lewis, Jerry; McMahon, Jenna; Marks, Charlie; Martin, Dean; Martin, Dick; Marx, Chico; Marx, Groucho; Marx, Gummo; Marx, Harpo; Marx, Zeppo; May, Elaine; Meara, Anne; Nichols, Mike; Reiner, Carl; Rowan, Dan; Schreiber, Avery; Smothers, Dick; Smothers, Tom; Stiller, Jerry; Sultzer, Joe.

Tyrants and Conquerors. Fon W. Boardman, Jr. Walck, 1977 (o.p.) (BLW)
Attila the Hun; Genghis Khan; Hitler, Adolf; Ivan IV, the Terrible; Mohammed II (The Conqueror); Nero; Shih Huang Ti; Tamerlane.

Under the New Roof: Five Patriots of the Young Republic. Esther M. Douty. Rand, 1965 (o.p.) (DOG)
Allen, Richard; Barlow, Joel; Gallatin, Albert; Rittenhouse, David; Rowson, Susanna Haswell.

Under the Wide Sky: Tales of New Mexico and the Spanish Southwest. Thelma Campbell Nason. Follett, 1965 (o.p.) (NAA)
Cabeza de Vaca, Álvar Núñez; Carson, Kit; Chisum, John Simpson; Coronado, Francisco Vásquez de; Goddard, Robert Hutchings; Gregg, Josiah; Hagerman, James J.; Lane, Lydia; Oñate, Cristóbal de; Pike, Zebulon Montgomery.

Unfinished Symphony. Freda P. Berkowitz. Atheneum, 1963 (o.p.) (BEN)
Bach, Johann Sebastian; Beethoven, Ludwig van; Brahms, Johannes; Chopin, Frédéric François; Copland, Aaron; Dvořak, Antonin; Elgar, Sir Edward William; Handel, George Frederick; Haydn, Franz Joseph; Mendelssohn, Felix; Mozart, Wolfgang Amadeus; Rachmaninoff, Sergei; Scarlatti, Domenico; Schubert, Franz Peter; Tartini, Giuseppe; Tchaikovsky, Peter Ilyich.

Unpopular Ones. Jules Archer. Macmillan, 1968 (o.p.) (ARB)
Bloomer, Amelia Jenks; Debs, Eugene Victor; Fulbright, James William; Greeley, Horace; Oppenheimer, Julius Robert; Owens-Adair, Bethenia; Paine, Thomas; Palmer, Joseph; Royall, Anne Newport; Sanger, Margaret; Thoreau, Henry David; Walker, Jonathon; Williams, Roger; Wilson, Woodrow; Zenger, John Peter.

Unsung Black Americans and Their Notable Achievements. Edith Stull. G&D, 1971 (o.p.) (STQ)
Armistead, James†; Attucks, Crispus†; Banneker, Benjamin; Beard, Andrew J.†; Beckwith, Henry; Beckwourth, James P.; Bush, George W.†; Carney, William H.†; Christophe, Henri†; Dabney, Mrs.; Davis, Benjamin O., Jr.; Dodson, Jacob; Drew, Charles Richard†; Esteban or Estevanico; Forten, James†; Freeman, Jordian†; Gannet, Deborah Sampson†; Haynes, Lemuel†; Henry, "Big Mouth"†; Henson, Matthew Alexander; Ikard, Bose; Johnson, Henry†; Latimer, Lewis Howard; McCoy, Elijah†; Mason, Biddy†; Matthews, Saul†; Matzeliger, Jan Ernst†; Miller, Dorie†; Morgan, Garrett A.†; Pickett, Bill†; Pleasant, Mary Ellen†; Pointe de Sable, Jean Baptiste; Poor, Salem†; Roberts, Needham†; Salem, Peter†; Spaulding, Charles Clinton†; Stahl, Jesse†; Walker, Sarah Breedlove†; Woods, Granville T.†; York†.

Unsung Heroes of Pro Basketball. Raymond Hill. Random, 1973 (o.p.) (HIBA)
Brown, Roger; Daniels, Mel; DeBusschere, Dave; Greer, Hal; Issel, Dan; Johnson, Gus; Love, Bob; Scott, Charlie; Wilkens, Lenny.

Unsung Heroes of the Major Leagues. Art Berke. Random, 1976 (o.p.) (BELA)
Cueller, Mike; Fairly, Ron; Melton, Bill; Munson, Thurman Lee; Niekro, Phil; Perez, Tony; Rader, Douglas Lee; Rojas, Cookie; Rudi, Joseph Oden; Williams, Billy Leo.

Up from the Ghetto. Philip T. Drotning & Wesley South. Regnery, 1970 (o.p.) (DRA)
Banks, Ernie; Brooks, Gwendolyn; Brown, James; Byrd, Manford, Jr.; Chisholm, Shirley; Davison, Frederic Ellis; Farmer, James; Grant, M. Earl; Hatcher, Richard Gordon; Jackson, Jesse Louis; Johnson, John H.; Langford, Anna Riggs; Shepherd, John; Tilmon, James.

Up from the Minor Leagues of Hockey. Stan Fischler & Shirley Fischler. Regnery, 1971 (o.p.) (FICB)
Barkley, Doug; Binkley, Lee; Ferguson, John; Fleming, Reggie; Hull, Dennis William; Ratelle, Jean; Shore, Edward William; Van Impe, Edward Charles; Wakely, Ernie.

Valiant Women. Dixie Ann Pace. Vantage, 1972 (o.p.) (PA)
Addams, Jane; Anthony, Susan Brownell; Ariadne; Barton, Clara; Bernhardt, Sarah; Chiang Mei-ling; Cleopatra; Curie, Marie Sklodowska; Earhart, Amelia; Elizabeth I; Isabella I; Joan of Arc; Lagerlof, Selma; McCauley, Mary; Maria Theresa; Moses, Anna Mary Robertson; Nefertiti; Nightingale, Florence; Perón, Eva Duarte; Pocahontas; Roosevelt, Eleanor; Semiramis; Sévigné, Marie (de Rabutin Chantal) marquise de; Victoria; Zenobia.

Vice-Presidents of Destiny. Joseph A. Alvarez. Putnam, 1969 (o.p.) (ALE)
Arthur, Chester Alan; Coolidge, Calvin; Fillmore, Millard; Johnson, Andrew; Johnson, Lyndon Baines; Roosevelt, Theodore; Truman, Harry S.; Tyler, John.

Vice-Presidents of the United States. John D. Feerick & Emalie P. Feerick. Watts, rev. ed., 1981 (o.p.) (FEA)
See listing under *America's Vice-Presidents* by Diana Dixon Healy. Delete: Bush, George.

Violin and Its Masters. Victor Chapin. Lippincott, 1969 (o.p.) (CHFA)
Bull, Ole; Corelli, Arcangelo; Joachim, Joseph; Kreisler, Fritz; Kreutzer, Rodolphe; Leclair, Jean Marie; Lully, Jean Baptiste; Paganini, Nicolò; Sarasate, Pablo de; Spohr, Louis; Stamitz, Johann Wenzel; Tartini, Giuseppe; Veracini, Francesco Maria; Vieuxtemps, Henri François Joseph; Viotti, Giovanni Battista; Vivaldi, Antonio.

Viva Gonzales!!! Robert McAdam. Bowmar, 1971 (o.p.) (LYE)
>   Davis, Willie; Gonzales, Pancho; Green, Charlie; Louis, Joe; Mikan, George L.; Nelson, Van; Smith, Vicki; Stratton, Monty.

Voices from the Southwest. Jacqueline Bernard. Scholastic, 1972 (o.p.) (BENA)
>   Baca, Elfego; Martinez, Antonio José; Tijerina, Reies Lopez.

Voices of Joy, Voices of Freedom. Arnold Dobrin. Coward, 1972 (o.p.) (DOBA)
>   Anderson, Marian; Davis, Sammy, Jr.; Horne, Lena; Robeson, Paul; Waters, Ethel.

War Lords. A. J. P. Taylor. Penguin, pap., 1979 (TAC)
>   Churchill, Sir Winston Leonard Spencer; Hitler, Adolf; Mussolini, Benito; Roosevelt, Franklin Delano; Stalin, Joseph.

We Have Tomorrow. Arna Bontemps. HM, 1945 (o.p.) (BOG)
>   Blount, Mildred E.; Campbell, Elmer Simms; Cayton, Horace R.; Davis, Benjamin O., Jr.; Dixon, Dean; Henry, Algernon P.; LuValle, James E.; May, Emmett M.; Scott, Hazel; Trammell, Beatrice Johnson; Watkins, Sylvestre C.; Watson, Douglas.

We Wanted to Be Free: The Refugees' Own Stories. Frances Cavanah, ed. Macrae, 1971 (o.p.) (CAHA)
>   Antin, Mary; Bell, Caroline D.; Bell, Edward A.; Casals, Pablo; Cecilia, Sister; Fermi, Laura; Gouzenko, Igor S.; Heide, Dirk van der; Henson, Josiah; Karski, Jan, pseud.; Kovago, Jozsef; Mardikian, George M.; Ramírez, Armando Socarras; Sansan; Sondermann, Fred S.; Trapp, Maria Augusta; Undset, Sigrid; Vlachos, Helen.

Western Badmen. Dorothy M. Johnson. Dodd, 1970 (o.p.) (JOBA)
>   Bass, Sam; Billy the Kid; Black Bart; Cassidy, Butch; Chacon, Augustin; Dalton Brothers; Doolin, Bill; Hardin, John Welsey; Harpe, Micajah; Harpe, Wiley; Holliday, Doc; Horn, Tom; James, Frank; James, Jesse; Jennings, Al; Miner, Bill; Murrieta, Joaquin; Plummer, Henry; Rattlesnake Jake; Reno brothers; Slade, Joseph Albert; Starr, Belle; Starr, Henry; Thompson, Ben; Wild Bunch; Younger brothers.

Western Lawmen. Frank Surge. Lerner, 1969 (SUI)
>   Bean, "Judge" Roy; Calamity Jane; Courtright, T. I.; Earp, Wyatt Berry Stapp; Garrett, Patrick Floyd; Hickok, Wild Bill; Horn, Tom; Houston, Temple; Madsen, Chris; Masterson, Bat; Parker, Isaac Charles; Pinkerton, Allan; Siringo, Charles A.; Smith, Thomas James; Texas Rangers; Tilghman, William Matthew.

Western Outlaws. Vincent Paul Rennert. Macmillan, 1968 (o.p.) (REE)
>   Bass, Sam; Billy the Kid; Black Bart; Burrows, Rube; Carlisle, Bill; Cassidy, Butch; Dalton Brothers; Hardin, John Welsey; James, Frank; James, Jesse; Younger brothers†.

Western Outlaws. Frank Surge. Lerner, 1969 (o.p.) (SUJ)
>   Apache Kid; Bass, Sam; Billy the Kid; Black Bart; Cassidy, Butch†; Cherokee Bill; Cook, Bill; Dalton Brothers; Doolin, Bill; Hardin, John Welsey; James, Jesse; Murrieta, Joaquin; Reno brothers; Starr, Belle; Wild Bunch.

Western Stars of Country Music. Bonnie Lake & Robert K. Krishef. Lerner, 1978 (o.p.) (LA)
>   Autry, Gene; Evans, Dale; Lynn, Judy; McClintock, Harry; Montana, Patsy; Reeves, Goebel; Ritter, Tex; Rogers, Roy; Thompson, Hank; Wills, Bob.

Westward Adventure: The True Story of Six Pioneers. William O. Steele. HarBraceJ, 1962 (o.p.) (STA)
>   Adair, James; Henderson, Richard; Ingles, Mary; Schneider, Martin; Smith, James; Wiggan, Eleazer.

Westward—With American Explorers. Walter Buehr. Putnam, 1963 (o.p.) (BUB)
>   Boone, Daniel; Clark, William; Colter, John; Frémont, John Charles; Gray, Robert; Ledyard, John; Lewis, Meriwether; Pike, Zebulon Montgomery; Smith, Jedediah Strong.

When Our Country Was Very Young. L. Edmond Leipold. T. S. Denison, 1972 (o.p.) (LEPF)
>   De Soto, Hernando; Penn, William; Pocahontas; Smith, John; Williams, Roger.

Winners: Eight Special Young People. Dorothy Schainman Siegel. Messner, 1978 (SIAA)
Celeste N.; Debbie P.; George G.; J. B.; Julio P.; Marilyn H.; Michael; Pete M.

Winners in Gymnastics. Frank Litsky. Avon, 1984, pap. (LIE)
Andrianov, Nikolai; Comaneci, Nadia; Conner, Bart; Kim, Nelli; Korbut, Olga; Rigby, Cathy; Tsukahara, Mitsuo.

Winners Never Quit. Nathan Aaseng. Lerner, 1980 (AAS-27)
Bleier, Rocky; Brown, Larry; Clarke, Bobby; Dempsey, Tom; Hiller, John; John, Tommy; LeFlore, Ron; O'Neil, Kitty; Trevino, Lee; Unseld, Westley.

Winners of the Heisman Trophy. John Devaney. Walker, 1986 (DEHB)
Blanchard, Doc; Campbell, Earl; Davis, Glenn; Dorsett, Tony Drew; Flutie, Doug; Griffin, Archie; Hornung, Paul Vernon; Plunkett, Jim; Simpson, O. J.; Staubach, Roger; Walker, Doak; Walker, Herschel.

Winners on the Ice. Frank Litsky. Watts, 1979 (o.p.) (LIEA)
Button, Dick; Curry, John; Fleming, Peggy; Hamill, Dorothy; Heiden, Eric; Rodnina, Irina; Tickner, Charles; Young, Sheila.

Winners on the Ski Slopes. JohnDFry. Watts, 1979 (o.p.) (FRCA)
Chaffee, Suzy; Cochran, Barbara Ann; Greene, Nancy; Killy, Jean-Claude; Koch, Bill; Mc-Kinney, Steve; Saudan, Sylvain.

Winners on the Tennis Court. William G. Glickman. Avon, 1984, pap. (GLC)
Ashe, Arthur; Borg, Björn; Cawley, Evonne Goolagong; Connors, Jimmy; Evert, Chris; King, Billie Jean.

Winners under 21: America's Spectacular Young Sports Champions. Phyllis Hollander & Zander Hollander. Random, 1982, pap. (o.p.) (HOCG)
Ali, Muhammad; Austin, Tracy; Cauthen, Steve; Gretzky, Wayne; Heiden, Beth; Heiden, Eric; Kaline, Albert William; McEnroe, John; Malone, Moses; Mathias, Bob; Weissmuller, Johnny; Yount, Robin.

Winners: Women and the Nobel Prize. Barbara Shiels. Dillon, 1985 (SHFE)
Addams, Jane†; Balch, Emily Green†; Buck, Pearl S.; Cori, Gerty Theresa†; Corrigan, Mairead†; Curie, Marie Sklodowska†; Deledda, Grazia†; Goeppert-Mayer, Maria; Hodgkin, Dorothy Crowfoot; Joliot-Curie, Irène†; Lagerlof, Selma†; McClintock, Barbara; Mistral, Gabriela†; Mother Theresa; Myrdal, Alva; Sachs, Nelly; Suttner, Bertha von†; Williams, Betty†; Yalow, Rosalyn Sussman.

Winning Men of Tennis. Nathan Aaseng. Lerner, 1981 (AAS-28)
Ashe, Arthur; Borg, Björn; Connors, Jimmy; Gonzales, Pancho; Laver, Rodney George; McEnroe, John; Tilden, William Tatem, Jr.; Vilas, Guillermo.

Winning Women of Tennis. Nathan Aaseng. Lerner, 1981 (AAS-29)
Austin, Tracy; Cawley, Evonne Goolagong; Court, Margaret; Evert, Chris; Gibson, Althea; King, Billie Jean; Navratilova, Martina; Wills, Helen.

Wives of the Presidents. Arden D. Melick. Hammond, rev. ed., 1985 (MAU)
See listing under *America's First Ladies*, vols. 1 and 2, by Chaffin & Butwin. Delete: Lane, Harriet. Add: Carter, Rosalynn; Ford, Betty; Reagan, Nancy; Roosevelt, Alice H.

Women Astronauts: Aboard the Shuttle. Mary Virginia Fox. Messner, 1984 (FOJ-1)
Cleave, Mary; Dunbar, Bonnie; Lucid, Shannon; Resnik, Judith; Ride, Sally; Seddon, Margaret Rhea; Sullivan, Kathryn.

Women behind Men of Medicine. Josephine Rich. Messner, 1967 (o.p.) (RIB)
Bell, Sir Charles; Bell, Marion Shaw; Crawford, Jane Todd; Freud, Martha Bernays; Freud, Sigmund; Hanaoka, Seishu; Hunter, Anne Home; Hunter, John; Livingstone, David; Livingstone, Mary Moffatt; McDowell, Ephraim; McDowell, Sarah Shelby; Manzolini, Anne Morandi; Manzolini, Giovanni†; Murphy, Jeannette Plamondon; Murphy, John Benjamin; Osler, Grace Revere; Osler, Sir William; Otsugu†; Sims, James Marion; Troctula di Ruggiero; Woodson, John†; Woodson, Sara.

Women for Human Rights. Marcia Maher Conta. Raintree, 1979 (COG-1)
Chisholm, Shirley; Corrigan, Mairead; Day, Dorothy; Kuhn, Margaret; Parks, Rosa Lee; Roosevelt, Eleanor; Williams, Betty.

Women in Business. Laura French & Diana Stewart. Raintree, 1979 (FRBD)
Bates, Mercedes; Chanel, Coco; Evans, Jane; Proctor, Barbara Gardner; Shaver, Dorothy; Wyman, Irma.

Women in Comedy. Linda Martin & Kerry Segrave. Citadel, 1986 (MASB)
Ace, Jane; Allen, Gracie; Arden, Eve; Ball, Lucille; Ballard, Kaye; Barth, Belle; Bayes, Nora; Berg, Gertrude; Bernhard, Sandra; Boosler, Elayne; Brice, Fanny; Burnett, Carol; Buzzi, Ruth; Canova, Judy; Carroll, Jean; Carroll, Pat; Channing, Carol; Coca, Imogene; Crabtree, Lotta; Daley, Cass; Davis, Joan; Diller, Phyllis; Draper, Ruth; Dressler, Marie; Duncan, Rosetta; Duncan, Vivien; Fazenda, Louise; Fields, Gracie; Fields, Totie; Franklin, Irene; Friganza, Trixie; Goldberg, Whoopi; Greenwood, Charlotte; Hawn, Goldie; Herford, Beatrice; Holliday, Judy; Irwin, May; Janis, Elsie; Kahn, Madeline; Kane, Helen; Kelly, Patsy; Lillie, Beatrice; Mabley, Jackie "Moms"; Martin, Andrea; May, Elaine; Meara, Anne; Midler, Bette; Moran, Polly; Normand, Mabel; Pearl, Minnie; Picon, Molly; Pious, Minerva; Pitts, Zasu; Radner, Gilda; Rand, Suzanne; Rasmussen, Zora; Raye, Martha; Rivers, Joan; Russell, Anna; Sokol, Marilyn; Tanguay, Eva; Todd, Thelma; Tomlin, Lily; Torres, Liz; Tucker, Sophie; Tyler, Robin; Walker, Nancy; Warfield, Marsha; West, Mae; Wilson, Marie.

Women in Politics. Sharon Whitney & Tom Raynor. Watts, 1986 (WHE)
Allen, Florence Ellinwood; Busch, Mary†; Byrne, Jane; Chisholm, Shirley; Collins, Joanne†; Collins, Martha Layne†; Dole, Elizabeth; Ferraro, Geraldine; Gold, Shirley†; Grasso, Ella; Heckler, Margaret; Katz, Vera†; Kunin, Madeline†; O'Connor, Sandra Day; Perkins, Frances; Rankin, Jeannette; Rogers, Barbara†; Schroeder, Patricia Scott; Smith, Margaret Chase; Snowe, Olympia; Ulmer, Fran†; Violet, Arlene†; Whitmire, Kathy.

Women in Sports. Irwin Stambler. Doubleday, 1975 (o.p.) (ST-2)
Belote, Melissa; Cochran, Barbara Ann; Decker, Mary; Didrikson, Babe; Henning, Anne; King, Billie Jean; King, Micki; Muldowney, Shirley; Rigby, Cathy; Shank, Theresa; Smith, Robyn C.; Tyus, Wyomia.

Women in Sports: Figure Skating. Elizabeth Van Steenwyk. Harvey, 1976 (o.p.) (VADA)
deLeeuw, Diane; Fleming, Peggy; Hamill, Dorothy; Lynn, Janet; Magnussen, Karen.

Women in Sports: Motorcycling. Grace Butcher. Harvey, 1976 (o.p.) (BUIC)
Beck, Trudy; Cox, Diane; Fuller, Peggy; Glasgow, Nancy Payne; Kirk, Tammy Jo; Stenersen, Johanna; Turton, Janene; Wilkins, Debbie.

Women in Sports: Rodeo. Elizabeth Van Steenwyk. Harvey, 1978 (o.p.) (VADB)
Brorsen, Metha; Bussey, Sheila; Fuchs, Becky; Johnson, Dammy Williams; Johnson, Trudy; Pirtle, Sue; Prudom, Benjie Bell Elizabeth; Thurman, Sammy Fancher.

Women in Sports: Scuba Diving. Hillary Hauser. Harvey, 1976 (o.p.) (HAKA)
Clark, Eugenie; Garner, "Kati"; Mead, Sylvia Earle; Parry, Zale; Taylor, Valerie.

Women in Sports: Skiing. Claire Walter. Harvey, 1977 (o.p.) (WA-1)
Cochran, Barbara Ann; Hlavaty, Jana; Moser-Proell, Annemarie; Nelson, Cindy.

Women in Sports: Swimming. Diana C. Gleasner. Harvey, 1975 (o.p.) (GLA)
Babashoff, Shirley; Buzonas, Gail Johnson; Heddy, Kathy; Loock, Christine; Nyad, Diana.

Women in Sports: Tennis. Marion Meade. Harvey, 1975 (o.p.) (MATA)
Casals, Rosemary; Cawley, Evonne Goolagong; Court, Margaret; Evert, Chris; King, Billie Jean.

Women in Sports: Track and Field. Diana C. Gleasner. Harvey, 1977 (o.p.) (GLB)
Campbell, Robin; Frederick, Jane; Huntley, Joni; Schmidt, Kathy; Van Wolvelaere, Patty; Wright, Thelma.

Women in the Martial Arts: A New Spirit Rising. Linda Atkinson. Dodd, 1983 (AT)
Austin, Beth; Bates, Laverne; Dacanay, Pattie; Eads, Valerie; Ellman, Annie; Graff, Sunny; Harris, Tonie; Kanokogi, Rusty.

Women in the White House: Four First Ladies. Bennett Wayne, ed. Garrard, 1976 (WAQ)
Adams, Abigail; Lincoln, Mary Todd; Madison, Dolley Payne Todd; Washington, Martha Dandridge.

Women in White. Geoffrey Marks & William K. Beatty. Scribner, 1972 (o.p.) (MASA)
Addams, Jane; Anderson, Elizabeth Garrett; Barringer, Emily Dunning; Barry, James, pseud.; Blackwell, Elizabeth; Bourgeois, Louyse; Cellier, Elizabeth†; Clarke, Nancy Talbot; Curie, Marie Sklodowska; Dix, Dorothea Lynde; Du Coudray, Angélique Marguérite le Boursier†; Felicie, Jacoba†; Fowler, Lydia Folger; Gillain, Marie Anne Victoire†; Hamilton, Alice; Hildegard of Bingen; Hunt, Harriot Kenzia†; Jacobi, Mary Putnam; Jex-Blake, Sophia†; Lachapelle, Marie-Louise†; Murrell, Christine†; Nightingale, Florence; Siegemundin, Justine Dittrichin†; Troctula di Ruggiero.

Women Lawyers at Work. Elinor Porter Swiger. Messner, 1978 (o.p.) (SWI)
Bellows, Carole Kamin; Coleman, Mary Stallings; Ginsburg, Ruth Bader; Hills, Carla Anderson; LaFontant, Jewel Stradford; Mentschikoff, Soia; Murphy, Betty Southard; Owens, Elisabeth; Pilpel, Harriet Fleischl; Raggio, Louise Ballerstedt; Schroeder, Patricia Scott; Scott, Irene Feagin.

Women Making History: Conversations with Fifteen New Yorkers. Maxine Gold, ed. NYC Commission on the Status of Women, 1985 (GLO)
Brunson, Dorothy; Clark, Ruth; Dean, Laura; Down, Linda; Ferraro, Geraldine; Hunter-Gault, Charlayne; Kearse, Amalya; Marshall, Paule; Rodriguez-Trias, Helen; Sanchez, Yolanda; Siebert, Muriel; Sills, Beverly; Stewart, Ellen; Stutz, Geraldine; Wu, Chien-Shiung.

Women of Courage. Dorothy Nathan. Random, 1964 (o.p.) (NAB)
Addams, Jane; Anthony, Susan Brownell; Bethune, Mary McLeod; Earhart, Amelia; Mead, Margaret.

Women of Courage. Margaret Truman. Morrow, 1976 (o.p.) (TRD)
Anderson, Marian; Anthony, Susan Brownell; Barnard, Kate; Barnett, Ida Wells; Blackwell, Elizabeth; Crandall, Prudence; Jones, Mary Harris; Kelsey, Frances Oldham; Livingston, Susan; Madison, Dolley Payne Todd; Smith, Margaret Chase; Winnemucca, Sarah.

Women of Modern Science. Edna Yost. Greenwood repr. of 1959 ed., 1984 (YOF)
Brown, Rachel Fuller; Cori, Gerty Theresa; Crane, Jocelyn; Emerson, Gladys Anderson; Meitner, Lise; Quimby, Edith Hinkley; Rudnick, Dorothea; Russell, Elizabeth Shull; Sawyer, Helen; Van Straten, Florence; Wu, Chien-Shiung.

Women Pioneers of Science. Louis Haber. HarBraceJ, 1979 (HA-1)
Brown, Rachel Fuller; Emerson, Gladys Anderson; Goeppert-Mayer, Maria; Hamilton, Alice; Hodgkin, Dorothy Crowfoot; Hollingworth, Leta Stetter; Logan, Myra Adele; Mead, Sylvia Earle; Meitner, Lise; Sabin, Florence Rena; Wright, Jane C.; Yalow, Rosalyn Sussman.

Women Themselves. See new title *They Led the Way.*

Women Today: Ten Profiles. Greta Walker. Hawthorn, 1975 (o.p.) (WA)
Friedan, Betty; Kimbrell, Marketa; Norton, Eleanor Holmes; Pittman, Dorothy Hughes; Queler, Eve; Redford, Lola; Sanders, Marlene; Schimmel, Gertrude; Steinem, Gloria; Storch, Marcia.

Women Who Changed History: Five Famous Queens of Europe. Mary L. Davis. Lerner, 1975 (o.p.) (DAK)
Catherine II, the Great; Eleanor of Aquitaine; Elizabeth I; Isabella I; Marie Antoinette.

Women Who Changed Things: Nine Lives That Made a Difference. Linda Peavy & Ursula Smith. Scribner, 1983 (PACB)
Baker, Sara Josephine; Barnard, Kate; Barnett, Ida Wells; Fleming, Williamina; Hatcher,

Orie Latham; Hollingworth, Leta Stetter; McDowell, Mary E.; Peck, Annie Smith; Wheeler, Candace Thurber.

Women Who Dared to Be Different. Bennett Wayne, ed. Garrard, 1973 (WAE)
Cochrane, Elizabeth; Earhart, Amelia; Mitchell, Maria; Oakley, Annie.

Women Who Led the Way: Eight Pioneers for Equal Rights (Original title: *Pioneers in Petticoats*). David K. Boynick. T Y Crowell, 1959 (BOJ)
Anthony, Susan Brownell; Brown, Antoinette Blackwell; Earhart, Amelia; Gilbreth, Lillian M.; Hamilton, Alice; Lockwood, Belva Ann; Lyon, Mary; Shaver, Dorothy.

Women Who Made America Great. Harry Gersh. Lippincott, 1962 (o.p.) (GEE)
Bethune, Mary McLeod; Blackwell, Elizabeth; Bourke-White, Margaret; Didrikson, Babe; Duniway, Abigail Scott; Jones, Mary Harris; Mitchell, Maria; Tubman, Harriet; Wald, Lillian D.; Zenger, Anna.

Women Who Made History. Mary C. Borer. Warne, 1963 (o.p.) (BOH)
Astell, Mary; Austen, Jane; Beeton, Isabella Mary; Curie, Marie Sklodowska; Fry, Elizabeth Gurney; Godwin, Mary Wollstonecraft; Kauffmann, Angelica; Kingsley, Mary Henrietta; Montagu, Lady Mary Wortley; Nightingale, Florence; Pankhurst, Emmeline Goulden; Woolley, Hannah.

Women Who Reached for Tomorrow. Aylesa Forsee. Macrae, 1960 (o.p.) (FOG)
Berry, Martha McChesney; Gibson, Althea; Head, Edith; Hepburn, Audrey; Landowska, Wanda; Moore, Anne Carroll; Priest, Ivy Baker; Sabin, Florence Rena.

Women Who Ruled: Cleopatra to Elizabeth II. Robert Liston. Messner, 1978 (o.p.) (LIDA)
Anne; Catherine II, the Great; Catherine de Medici; Cleopatra; Elizabeth I; Elizabeth II; Elizabeth Petrovna; Gandhi, Indira Nehru; Isabella I; Maria Theresa; Mary I; Mary II†; Meir, Golda; Perón, Eva Duarte; Perón, Isabel; Tzu Hsi; Victoria.

Women Who Shaped History. Henrietta Buckmaster. Macmillan, 1966 (o.p.) (BUA)
Blackwell, Elizabeth; Crandall, Prudence; Dix, Dorothea Lynde; Eddy, Mary Baker; Stanton, Elizabeth Cady; Tubman, Harriet.

Women Who Win. Francene Sabin. Dell, 1977, pap. (RYX)
Bartz, Jennifer; Berg, Sharon; Cochran, Barbara Ann; Cochran, Linda; Cochran, Marilyn; Genesko, Lynn; King, Billie Jean; King, Micki; Lynn, Janet; MacInnis, Nina; Rigby, Cathy; Sperber, Paula; Toussaint, Cheryl; Whitworth, Kathy.

Women Who Work with Animals. Bill Gutman. Dodd, 1982 (GUJ)
Bailie, Sally; Embery, Joan; Forsyth, Jane; McGinnis, Terri; Rader, Peta; Sinclair, Sue.

Women with a Cause. Bennett Wayne, ed. Garrard, 1975 (WAR)
Anthony, Susan Brownell; Hutchinson, Anne Marbury; Mott, Lucretia Coffin; Roosevelt, Eleanor.

World Class Marathoners. Nathan Aaseng. Lerner, 1982 (AAS-30)
Bikila, Abebe; Cierpinski, Waldemar; Rodgers, Bill; Salazar, Alberto; Shorter, Frank; Waitz, Grete; Zatopek, Emil.

World Conductors. Percy M. Young. Abelard, 1965 (o.p.) (YOM)
Ancerl, Karel†; Bach, Carl Philipp Emanuel†; Bach, Johann Christian†; Bach, Johann Sebastian†; Barbirolli, John; Beecham, Sir Thomas; Beethoven, Ludwig van†; Beinum, Eduard van†; Bergmann, Carl; Berlioz, Hector†; Bernstein, Leonard†; Boult, Adrian†; Carewe, John†; Celibidache, Sergio†; Colonne, Edouard; Corelli, Arcangelo†; Craft, Robert†; Dorati, Antal; Enesco, Georges†; Fricsay, Ferenc; Furtwaengler, Wilhelm†; Handel, George Frederick†; Haydn, Franz Joseph†; Jullien, Louis Antoine; Karajan, Herbert von†; Klemperer, Otto; Koussevitzky, Serge; Kubelik, Rafael†; Lamoureux, Charles; Leinsdorf, Erich; Lully, Jean Baptiste†; Mahler, Gustav†; Manns, August; Mendelssohn, Felix†; Mitropoulos, Dimitri; Monteux, Pierre; Mozart, Wolfgang Amadeus†; Munch, Charles; Nikisch, Arthur; Ormandy, Eugene; Richter, Hans; Sacher, Paul†; Sargent, Sir Malcolm; Scherchen, Hermann; Sokoloff, Nikolai; Solti, Georg†; Spohr, Louis†; Stokowski, Leopold; Strauss, Rich-

ard†; Szell, George; Thomas, Theodore; Toscanini, Arturo; Vivaldi, Antonio†; Wagner, Rich-ard†; Walter, Bruno; Weingartner, Felix von; Wood, Henry; Zerrahn, Carl†.

World Series Thrills: Ten Top Thrills from 1912 to 1960. Joseph N. Bell. Messner, 1962 (o.p.) (BED)
Bevens, Bill; Dean, Dizzy; Devore, Joshua; Johnson, Walter Perry; Larsen, Don; Martin, Pepper; Mazeroski, Bill; Owen, Mickey; Ruth, Babe; Stengel, Casey.

World's Great Race Drivers. Frank Orr. Random, 1972 (o.p.) (ORD)
Andretti, Mario; Clark, James; Donohue, Mark; Foyt, Anthony Joseph; Garlits, Don; Jones, Parnelli; McLaren, Bruce Leslie; Petty, Richard; Stewart, Jackie; Unser, Al; Unser, Bobby.

Yankee Doodle Dandies: Eight Generals of the American Revolution. Lee McGiffin. Dutton, 1967 (o.p.) (MAE)
Barney, Joshua; Glover, John; Greene, Nathanael; Knox, Henry; Lee, Henry; Marion, Fran-cis; Morgan, Daniel; Wayne, Anthony.

Yea Coach! Three Great Football Coaches. Guernsey Van Riper, Jr. Garrard, 1966 (o.p.) (VAD)
Heisman, John William; Rockne, Knute; Warner, Glenn "Pop."

Year They Won the Most Valuable Player Award. Milton J. Shapiro. Messner, 1966 (o.p.) (SHF)
Berra, Yogi; Campanella, Roy; Di Maggio, Joseph Paul; Foxx, James Emory; Frisch, Frank; Grove, Lefty; Howard, Elston; Mantle, Mickey Charles; Mays, Willie Howard; Musial, Stan-ley Frank; Robinson, Jackie; Versalles, Zoilo.

Young and Black in America. Rae Pace Alexander, comp. Random, 1970 (o.p.) (AKB)
Bates, Daisy Gaston; Brown, Jim; Douglass, Frederick; Edwards, Harry; Malcolm X; Moody, Anne; Parks, David; Wright, Richard.

Young and Black in Africa. A. Okion Ojigbo, comp. Random, 1971 (o.p.) (OJA)
Abrahams, Peter; Equiano, Olaudah; Fafunwa, Babs; Gatheru, R. Mugo; Kayira, Legson Didimu; Modupe; Selormey, Francis; Waciuma, Charity.

Young and Female: Turning Points in the Lives of Eight American Women. Pat Ross, comp. Random, 1972 (ROJ)
Bourke-White, Margaret; Chisholm, Shirley; Day, Dorothy; Ferber, Edna; Gibson, Althea; Hahn, Emily; MacLaine, Shirley; Sanger, Margaret.

Young Baseball Champions. Steve Gelman. G&D, 1966 (o.p.) (GEC)
Aaron, Hank; Cobb, Ty; Di Maggio, Joseph Paul; Drysdale, Don; Feller, Bob; Mantle, Mickey Charles; Mays, Willie Howard; Ott, Mel; Ruth, Babe; Williams, Ted.

Young Colonials. Robert Carse. Norton, 1963 (o.p.) (CAF)
Gardiner, David; Gardiner, Lion; Gyles, John; Milledge, John; Scott, John; Spelman, Henry; Williams, Eunice; Winslow, Anna Green.

Young Explorers of the Northwest. Pauline Arnold. Criterion Bks., 1967 (o.p.) (ARF)
Hearne, Samuel; Henday, Anthony; Kelsey, Henry; La Vérendrye, Pierre Gaultier de Varennes, sieur de; Radisson, Pierre Esprit.

Young Hockey Champions. Andy O'Brien. Norton, 1969 (o.p.) (OBA)
Beliveau, Jean; Boivin, Leo; Clancy, King; Geoffrion, Bernard "Boom-Boom"; Howe, Gordie; Howell, Henry Vernon; Hull, Bobby; Lumley, Harry†; Mahovlich, Frank; Mikita, Stan; Orr, Bobby; Richard, Henri; Sawchuk, Terry.

Young Music Makers: Boyhoods of Famous Composers. Ireene Wicker. Bobbs, 1961 (o.p.) (WIA)
Bach, Johann Sebastian; Beethoven, Ludwig van; Brahms, Johannes; Chopin, Frédéric Fran-çois; Foster, Stephen Collins; Gershwin, George; Kern, Jerome; Mozart, Wolfgang Amadeus; Schubert, Franz Peter; Taylor, Deems; Tchaikovsky, Peter Ilyich; Verdi, Giuseppe.

Young Olympic Champions. Steve Gelman. Norton, 1964 (o.p.) (GED)
Ali, Muhammad; Brumel, Valeri; Didrikson, Babe; Henie, Sonja; Lucas, Jerry; Mathias, Bob;

Publishers

Key to Publishers

A S Barnes
Imprint of Oak Tree Publications, Inc.
9601 Aero Dr.
San Diego, CA 92123

A-W
Addison Wesley Publishing Co.
Rte. 128
Reading, MA 01867

Abelard
Imprint of Harper & Row, Publishers Inc.

Abingdon
Abingdon Press
Div. of United Methodist Pub-
lishing House
201 Eighth Ave. S.
Nashville, TN 37202

Afro-Am
Afro-Am, Inc.
819 S. Wabash Ave.
Rm. 610
Chicago, IL 60605

Amereon
Amereon, Ltd.
Box 1200
Mattituck, NY 11952

Archway
Imprint of Simon & Schuster

Arno
Imprint of Ayer

Atheneum
Atheneum Publishers
115 Fifth Ave.
New York, NY 10003

Avon
Avon Books
105 Madison Ave.
New York, NY 10016

Ayer
Ayer Co. Publishers
Box 958
382 Main St.
Salem, NH 03079

Beacon
Beacon Press
25 Beacon St.
Boston, MA 02108

Behrman
Behrman House, Inc.
235 Watchung Ave.
West Orange, NJ 07052

Blair
John F. Blair, Publisher
1406 Plaza Dr.
Winston-Salem, NC 27103

Bobbs
Bobbs-Merrill Co.
Subs. of Macmillan Publishing
Co., Inc.
866 Third Ave.
New York, NY 10022

Childrens
Childrens Press
1224 W. Van Buren St.
Chicago, IL 60607

Chilton
Subs. of ABC Publishing
Chilton Way
Radnor, PA 19089

Citadel
Imprint of Lyle Stuart, Inc.
120 Enterprise Ave.
Secaucus, NJ 07094

Clarion
Imprint of Houghton Mif-
flin Co.

College Board
College Entrance Examination
Board
45 Columbus Ave.
New York, NY 10023

Coward
Imprint of Putnam Publishing
Group

Creative Ed
Creative Education, Inc.
Box 227
123 Broad St.
Mankato, MN 56001

Criterion Bks.
Imprint of Harper & Row, Publishers Inc.

Crown
Crown Publishers, Inc.
225 Park Ave. S.
New York, NY 10003

Daring
Daring Books
2020 Ninth St. SW
Canton, OH 44706

David & Charles
Box 57
North Pomfret, VT 05033

Dell
Dell Publishing Co.
One Dag Hammarskjold Plaza
New York, NY 10017

Dghtrs St. Paul
Daughters of St. Paul
50 St. Paul's Ave.
Boston, MA 02130

Dial
Dial Books for Young Readers
Div. of E. P. Dutton
Two Park Ave.
New York, NY 10016

Dodd
Dodd, Mead & Co.
71 Fifth Ave.
New York, NY 10003

Doubleday
Doubleday & Co.
666 Fifth Ave.
New York, NY 10103

Dutton
E. P. Dutton
Two Park Ave.
New York, NY 10016

EMC
EMC Publishing Corp.
300 York Ave.
St. Paul, MN 55101

Empak
Empak Publishing
520 N. Michigan Ave.
Chicago, IL 60611

Enslow
Enslow Publishing, Inc.
Box 777
Bloy St. & Ramsey Ave.
Hillside, NJ 07205

Exposition
Exposition Press of Florida,
   Inc.
1701 Blount Rd.
Suite C
Pompano Beach, FL 33069

Facts on File
Facts on File, Inc.
460 Park Ave. S.
New York, NY 10016

Feminist Pr.
The Feminist Press at the City
   University of New York
311 E. 94 St.
New York, NY 10128

Fideler
Fideler Co.
3167 Kalamazoo Ave. SE
Grand Rapids, MI 49503

Fleet
Fleet Press Corp.
150 Fifth Ave.
New York, NY 10010

Follett
Follett Corp.
1000 W. Washington Blvd.
Chicago, IL 60607

Four Winds
Imprint of Macmillan Publishing Co., Inc.

FS&G
Farrar, Straus & Giroux
19 Union Square W.
New York, NY 10003

Funk & W
Funk & Wagnalls
Imprint of Harper & Row, Pub-
   lishers Inc.

G&D
Grosset & Dunlap, Inc.
Imprint of Putnam Publishing
   Group

Gallery
Imprint of W.H. Smith Publishers, Inc.
112 Madison Ave.
New York, NY 10016

Garrard
Garrard Publishing Co.
29 Goldsborough St.
Easton, MD 21601

Gaus
Theo Gaus, Ltd.
Box 1168
Brooklyn, NY 11202

Ginn
Ginn Press
Div. of Simon & Schuster
191 Spring St.
Lexington, MA 02173

Greenwood
Greenwood Press, Inc.
Box 5007
88 Post Rd. W.
Westport, CT 06881

Hammond
Hammond, Inc.
515 Valley St.
Maplewood, NJ 07040

Har-Row
Harper & Row, Publishers Inc.
10 E. 53 St.
New York, NY 10022

HarBraceJ
Harcourt Brace Jovanovich,
   Inc.
1250 Sixth Ave.
San Diego, CA 92101

Hastings
Hastings House, Publishers
9 E. 40 St.
New York, NY 10016

Hawthorn
Imprint of E.P. Dutton

Hebrew Pub.
Hebrew Publishing Co.
Box 020875
100 Water St.
Brooklyn, NY 11202

Hippocrene
Hippocrene Books, Inc.
171 Madison Ave.
New York, NY 10016

HM
Houghton Mifflin Co.
One Beacon St.
Boston, MA 02108

Holiday
Holiday House, Inc.
18 E. 53 St.
New York, NY 10022

Holt
Henry Holt & Co.
113 W. 18 St.
New York, NY 10011

HR&W
Holt, Rinehart & Winston
111 Fifth Ave.
New York, NY 10003

Interpretive Pub.
Interpretive Publications, Inc.
Box 1383
Flagstaff, AZ 86002

John Day
Imprint of Harper & Row, Publishers Inc.

Johnson Chi
Johnson Publishing Co., Inc.
820 S. Michigan
Chicago, IL 60605

Jonathan David
Jonathan David Publishers, Inc.
68-22 Eliot Ave.
Middle Village, NY 11379

Knopf
Alfred A. Knopf, Inc.
Subs. of Random House, Inc.
201 E. 50 St.
New York, NY 10022

Ktav
Ktav Publishing House, Inc.
Box 6249
Hoboken, NJ 07030

Lerner
Lerner Publications Co.
241 First Ave.
Minneapolis, MN 55401

Lippincott
J. B. Lippincott Co.
Subs. of Harper & Row, Publishers Inc.
E. Washington Sq.
Philadelphia, PA 19105

Little
Little, Brown & Co.
34 Beacon St.
Boston, MA 02108

Lothrop
Lothrop, Lee & Shepard Books
Div. of William Morrow & Co., Inc.
105 Madison Ave.
New York, NY 10016

McGraw
McGraw-Hill Book Co.
Div. of McGraw-Hill, Inc.
1221 Ave. of the Americas
New York, NY 10020

McKay
David McKay Co., Inc.
Subs. of Random House, Inc.
201 E. 50 St.
New York, NY 10022

Macmillan
Macmillan Publishing Co., Inc.
866 Third Ave.
New York, NY 10022

Macrae
Imprint of Franklin Watts, Inc.

Merrill
Merrill Publishing Co.
Div. of Bell and Howell
1300 Alum Creek Dr.
Columbus, OH 43216

Messner
Julian Messner, Inc.
Imprint of Simon & Schuster, Inc.

Methuen
Methuen, Inc.
29 W. 35 St.
New York, NY 10001

Morrow
William Morrow & Co.
105 Madison Ave.
New York, NY 10016

National Archives
National Archives & Records Administration
Publishing Div.
Seventh St. & Pennsylvania Ave.
Washington, DC 20408

National Football League
National Football League Properties, Inc.
410 Park Ave.
14th fl.
New York, NY 10022

Nelson
Thomas Nelson, Inc.
Nelson Place at Elm Hill Pike
Nashville, TN 37214

New Republic
The New Republic, Inc.
1220 19 St. NW
Suite 200
Washington, DC 20036

Northwestern Univ. Pr.
Northwestern University Press
Box 1093
1735 Benson Ave.
Evanston, IL 60201

Norton
W. W. Norton & Co., Inc.
500 Fifth Ave.
New York, NY 10110

NYC Commission on the Status of Women
New York City Commission on the Status of Women
52 Chambers St.
Suite 207
New York, NY 10007

Oddo
Oddo Publishing, Inc.
Box 68
Storybook Acres
Fayetteville, GA 30214

P-H
Prentice-Hall
Div. of Simon & Schuster
Rte. 9W
Englewood Cliffs, NJ 07632

Pantheon
Pantheon Books, Inc.
Div. of Random House
201 E. 50 St.
New York, NY 10022

Penguin
Imprint of Viking Penguin, Inc.

Platt
Platt & Munk Publishers
Div. of Grosset & Dunlap
200 Madison Ave.
New York, NY 10010

Praeger
Praeger Publishers
Div. of Greenwood Press, Inc.
One Madison Ave.
New York, NY 10010

Putnam
Putnam Publishing Group
200 Madison Ave.
New York, NY 10016

Raintree
Raintree Publishers, Inc.
Subs. of Somerset House Corp.
310 Wisconsin Ave.
Milwaukee, WI 53203

Rand
Rand McNally & Co.
Box 7600
Chicago, IL 60680

Random
Random House, Inc.
201 E. 50 St.
New York, NY 10022

Regents
Imprint of Simon & Schuster Higher Education Group
Prentice-Hall Bldg.
Sylvan Ave.
Englewood Cliffs, NJ 07632

Regnery
Regnery Gateway, Inc.
1130 17 St. NW
Washington, DC 20036

Ritchie
George F. Ritchie
1840 Clay St.
No. 203
San Francisco, CA 94109

Rosen
Rosen Publishing Group
29 E. 21 St.
New York, NY 10010

Roy
Roy Publishers, Inc.
30 E. 74 St.
New York, NY 10021

S&S
Simon & Schuster, Inc.
1230 Ave. of the Americas
New York, NY 10020

St. Martin
St. Martin's Press
175 Fifth Ave.
New York, NY 10010

Schocken
Schocken Books, Inc.
62 Cooper Square
New York, NY 10003

Scholastic
Scholastic, Inc.
730 Broadway
New York, NY 10003

Scribner
Subs. of Macmillan Publishing
   Co., Inc.
866 Third Ave.
New York, NY 10022

Seabury
Seabury Press, Inc.
Imprint of Harper Religious
   Books
Div. of Harper & Row
Icehouse 1-401
151 Union St.
San Francisco, CA 94111

Sheed
Sheed and Ward
Div. of National Catholic Re-
   porter Publishing Co., Inc.
Box 414292
Kansas City, MO 64141

Silver Burdett
Silver Burdett & Ginn
Subs. of Simon & Schuster,
   Inc.
250 James St.
Morristown, NJ 07960

Stackpole
Stackpole Books
Box 1831
Cameron & Kelker Sts.
Harrisburg, PA 17105

Standard Ed.
Standard Education Corp.
200 W. Monroe
Chicago, IL 60606

Steck-V
Steck-Vaughn Co.
Subs. of National Education
   Corp.
Box 26015
Austin, TX 78755

Sterling Publishing Co.
Two Park Ave.
New York, NY 10016

T S Denison
T. S. Denison & Co., Inc.
9601 Newton Ave. S.
Minneapolis, MN 55431

T Y Crowell
T. Y. Crowell Co.
Imprint of Harper & Row, Pub-
   lishers Inc.

Taplinger
Taplinger Publishing Co.
132 W. 22 St.
New York, NY 10011

Transatlantic
Transatlantic Arts, Inc.
Box 6086
Albuquerque, NM 87197

Twayne
Div. of G. K. Hall & Co.
70 Lincoln St.
Boston, MA 02111

UAHC
Union of American Hebrew
   Congregations Press
838 Fifth Ave.
New York, NY 10021

Univ. of North Carolina Pr.
University of North Carolina
   Press
Box 2288
Chapel Hill, NC 27514

Van Nos Reinhold
Van Nostrand Reinhold Co.,
   Inc.
115 Fifth Ave.
New York, NY 10003

Vanguard
Vanguard Press
424 Madison Ave.
New York, NY 10017

Vantage
Vantage Press, Inc.
516 W. 34 St.
New York, NY 10001

Verry
Lawrence Verry, Inc.
Box 215
Mystic, CT 06355

Viking
Viking Penguin, Inc.
40 W. 23 St.
New York, NY 10010

Walck
Henry Z. Walck, Inc.
Div. of David McKay Co., Inc.
201 E. 50 St.
New York, NY 10022

Walker
Walker & Co.
720 Fifth Ave.
New York, NY 10019

Warne
Frederick Warne & Co., Inc.
Div. of Viking Penguin, Inc.
40 W. 23 St.
New York, NY 10010

Watts
Franklin Watts, Inc.
387 Park Ave. S.
New York, NY 10016

Western Pub.
Western Publishing Co., Inc.
Subs. of Western Publishing
   Group
850 Third Ave.
New York, NY 10022

Westminster
Westminster Press
925 Chestnut St.
Philadelphia, PA 19107

White House Historical Assn.
740 Jackson Pl.
Washington, DC 20503